PEARSON

Chemistry

FOUNDATION EDITION

Antony C. Wilbraham • Dennis D. Staley • Michael S. Matta • Edward L. Waterman

PEARSON

Boston, Massachusetts • Chandler, Arizona • Glenview, Illinois • Upper Saddle River, New Jersey

Print Components

Student Edition

Teacher's Edition

Reading and Study Workbook

Reading and Study Workbook, Teacher's Edition

Chemistry Skills and Math Workbook

Chemistry Skills and Math Workbook, Teacher's Edition

Technology Components

Student Edition eText with audio

Teacher's Edition eText

Support:
- Math Diagnostic and Remediation
- Online Problem Sets
- Vocabulary Flashcards
- Concept Maps

Tutorials:
- Chemistry Tutorials
- Math Tutorials

Animations:
- Concepts in Action Animations
- Kinetic Art Animations
- Directed Virtual ChemLabs

Videos:
- Untamed Science® Videos

Editable Resources:
- Lab Manual
- Small-Scale Lab Manual
- Probeware Lab Manual
- Lab Practicals
- Reading and Study Workbook
- Chemistry Skills and Math Workbook
- Assessment Workbook
- PowerPoint® Presentations

CD-ROM and DVD-ROM

Exam*View*® CD-ROM

Classroom Resource DVD-ROM

Virtual ChemLab CD-ROM

PEARSON

4000000000173

ISBN-13: 978-0-13-252918-1
ISBN-10: 0-13-252918-1

5 6 7 8 9 10 V011 17 16 15 14

About the Authors

Dennis Staley earned a Master of Science in chemistry at Southern Illinois University–Edwardsville. As an instructor in the Department of Chemistry and the Office of Science and Math Education at Southern Illinois University–Edwardsville, he taught high school and college-level chemistry and also led teacher workshops. Mr. Staley has been writing high school and college-level chemistry textbooks for over 30 years. He currently enjoys gardening, bicycling, sharing hands-on science with kids, and traveling to visit his grandchildren.

Antony Wilbraham spent the majority of his career at Southern Illinois University–Edwardsville, where he currently holds the position of Emeritus Professor of Chemistry. He is a member of several professional societies. For more than 30 years, he has been writing high school and college-level chemistry textbooks, and he has published extensively in scientific journals. Professor Wilbraham enjoys traveling, woodworking, gardening, and making toys for his granddaughters.

Michael Matta earned a Bachelor of Science in chemistry at the University of Dayton and a Doctor of Philosophy in chemistry at Indiana University. He spent most of his career at Southern Illinois University–Edwardsville, where he was most recently an Emeritus Professor. Dr. Matta developed and wrote high school and college-level chemistry textbooks and related ancillaries for over 30 years and published extensively in scientific journals. He was a member of several professional societies. In his spare time, he enjoyed woodworking, watercolor painting, and playing with his six grandchildren.

Dr. Matta unexpectedly passed away in 2011. He will be greatly missed by his many friends throughout the chemistry community. His coauthors remain inspired by his dedication to education and to his commitment to engaging students in the wonders of chemistry.

Edward Waterman taught chemistry and advanced placement chemistry from 1976 to 2007 at Rocky Mountain High School in Fort Collins, Colorado. He now conducts workshops for teachers on inquiry, differentiation, small-scale chemistry, AP chemistry, and virtual chemistry laboratory. He also presents photo-essay lectures about the natural history of molecules, engaging the general public in the appreciation for and the understanding of chemistry. Mr. Waterman holds a Bachelor of Science in chemistry from Montana State University and a Master of Science in chemistry from Colorado State University. In his free time, he enjoys exploring wild places in the Rocky Mountains and on the Colorado Plateau by hiking, kayaking, and cross-country skiing.

Consultants/Reviewers

Grant Wiggins, Ed.D., is a co-author with Jay McTighe of *Understanding by Design, 2nd Edition* (ASCD 2005). His approach to instructional design provides teachers with a disciplined way of thinking about curriculum design, assessment, and instruction that moves teaching from covering content to ensuring understanding.

BIGIDEA Big Ideas are one of the core components of the Understanding by Design® methodology in the **Foundation Edition of Pearson Chemistry.** These Big Ideas, such as The Mole and Quantifying Matter, establish a conceptual framework for the program. Look for opportunities throughout each chapter to link back to the Big Ideas.

Content Reviewers

Matthew Asplund, Ph.D.
Department of Chemistry and Biochemistry
Brigham Young University
Provo, Utah

Regina M. Barrier, M.A.
Western Outreach Coordinator
The Science House
North Carolina State University
Lenoir, North Carolina

J. Phillip Bowen, Ph.D.
Department of Chemistry and Biochemistry
University of North Carolina
Greensboro, North Carolina

C. Alton Hassell, Ph.D.
Director, Undergraduate Programs
Department of Chemistry and Biochemistry
Baylor University
Waco, Texas

Tiffany R. Hayden, Ph.D.
Department of Chemistry
Erskine College
Due West, South Carolina

David J. Merkler, Ph.D.
Department of Chemistry
University of South Florida
Tampa, Florida

Eric T. Sevy, Ph.D.
Department of Chemistry and Biochemistry
Brigham Young University
Provo, Utah

William H. Steinecker, Ph.D.
Research Scholar
Miami University
Oxford, Ohio

Teacher Reviewers

Jeff Bilyeu
West Linn High School
West Linn, Oregon

Mary Chuboff, M.Ed.
Athens Academy
Athens, Georgia

Kenneth A. Greathouse, M.Ed.
Parkway Central High School
Chesterfield, Missouri

Lynn Hogue, M.S.
Associate Director, Center for Chemistry Education
Miami University
Middletown, Ohio

George "Rod" Larsen, M.S.M.
Science Department Chair
West Orange High School
Winter Garden, Florida

Nancy Monson, M.Ed.
West Linn High School
West Linn, Oregon

Michelle Tindall
Birmingham Groves High School
Beverly Hills, Michigan

Safety Consultant

Kenneth R. Roy, Ph.D.
Director of Science and Safety
Glastonbury Public Schools
Glastonbury, Connecticut

PEARSON Chemistry

FOUNDATION EDITION

Build a Solid Foundation

The *Foundation Edition of Pearson Chemistry* is a new program that delivers the same trusted content as *Pearson Chemistry* but is made more accessible by incorporating strategies such as:

- Enhanced math and problem-solving support
- Embedded reading support
- Engaging visuals that reinforce instruction
- Workbook support to help ensure content mastery
- Inquiry activities that promote scientific thinking
- Targeted digital instruction

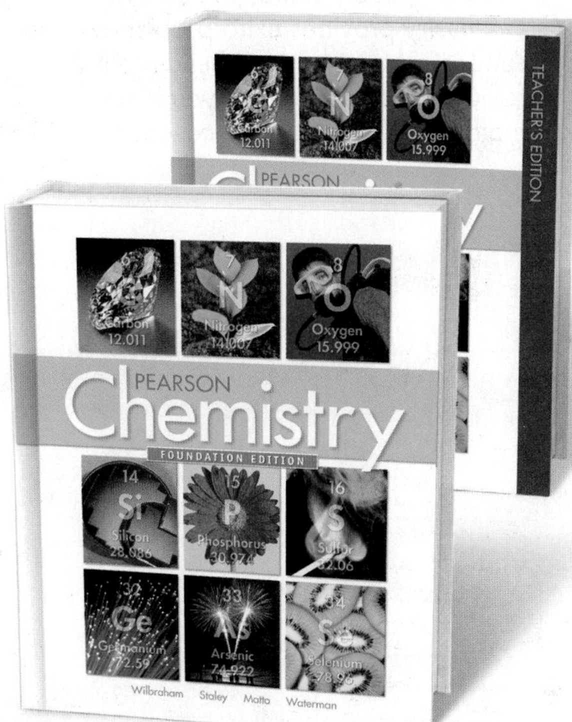

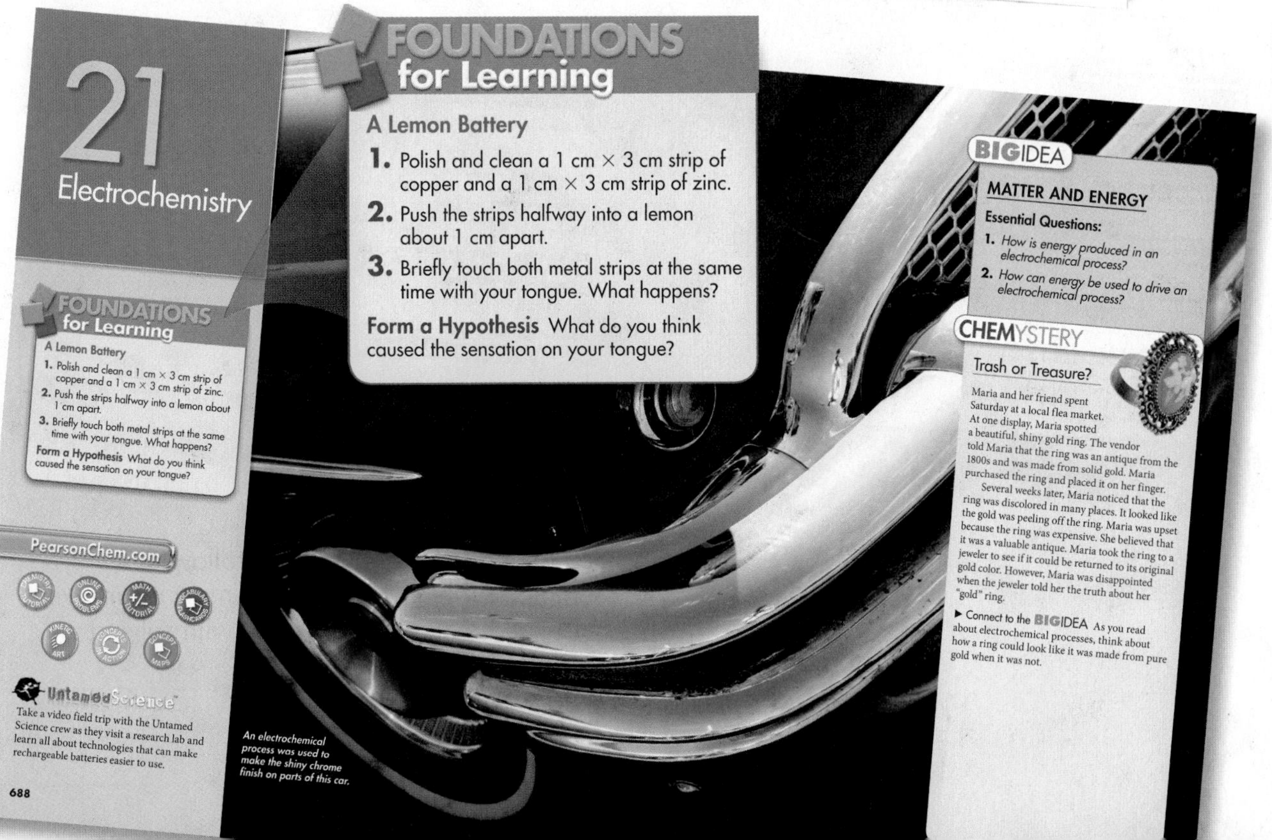

21

Electrochemistry

FOUNDATIONS for Learning

A Lemon Battery

1. Polish and clean a 1 cm × 3 cm strip of copper and a 1 cm × 3 cm strip of zinc.
2. Push the strips halfway into a lemon about 1 cm apart.
3. Briefly touch both metal strips at the same time with your tongue. What happens?

Form a Hypothesis What do you think caused the sensation on your tongue?

FOUNDATIONS for Learning

A Lemon Battery

1. Polish and clean a 1 cm × 3 cm strip of copper and a 1 cm × 3 cm strip of zinc.
2. Push the strips halfway into a lemon about 1 cm apart.
3. Briefly touch both metal strips at the same time with your tongue. What happens?

Form a Hypothesis What do you think caused the sensation on your tongue?

PearsonChem.com

Chemistry Tutorial · Online Problems · Math Tutorial · Vocabulary Flashcards · Kinetic Art · Concepts in Action · Concept Maps

UntamedScience

Take a video field trip with the Untamed Science crew as they visit a research lab and learn all about technologies that can make rechargeable batteries easier to use.

688

An electrochemical process was used to make the shiny chrome finish on parts of this car.

BIGIDEA

MATTER AND ENERGY

Essential Questions:

1. *How is energy produced in an electrochemical process?*
2. *How can energy be used to drive an electrochemical process?*

CHEMYSTERY

Trash or Treasure?

Maria and her friend spent Saturday at a local flea market. At one display, Maria spotted a beautiful, shiny gold ring. The vendor told Maria that the ring was an antique from the 1800s and was made from solid gold. Maria purchased the ring and placed it on her finger.

Several weeks later, Maria noticed that the ring was discolored in many places. It looked like the gold was peeling off the ring. Maria was upset because the ring was expensive. She believed that it was a valuable antique. Maria took the ring to a jeweler to see if it could be returned to its original gold color. However, Maria was disappointed when the jeweler told her the truth about her "gold" ring.

▶ Connect to the **BIGIDEA** As you read about electrochemical processes, think about how a ring could look like it was made from pure gold when it was not.

MATH SUPPORT

The *Foundation Edition of Pearson Chemistry* offers extra math and problem-solving support to help you successfully solve chemistry problems.

Build Math Skills ▶

The *Foundation Edition of Pearson Chemistry* provides extra problem-solving support. The embedded Build Math Skills features offer tips to help you learn the math skills you need to succeed.

BUILD Math Skills

Tips on Conversions Some stoichiometric calculations include many terms. Simplify the terms before you perform the calculations. Remove any units that cancel out. You may also notice other numbers that cancel out, such as 22.4, as shown below.

$$34\,\cancel{L\,O_2} \times \frac{1\,\cancel{mol\,O_2}}{\cancel{22.4}\,\cancel{L\,O_2}} \times \frac{2\,\cancel{mol\,NO_2}}{1\,\cancel{mol\,O_2}} \times \frac{\cancel{22.4}\,L\,NO_2}{1\,\cancel{mol\,NO_2}}$$

Go to your Chemistry Skills and Math Workbook for more practice.

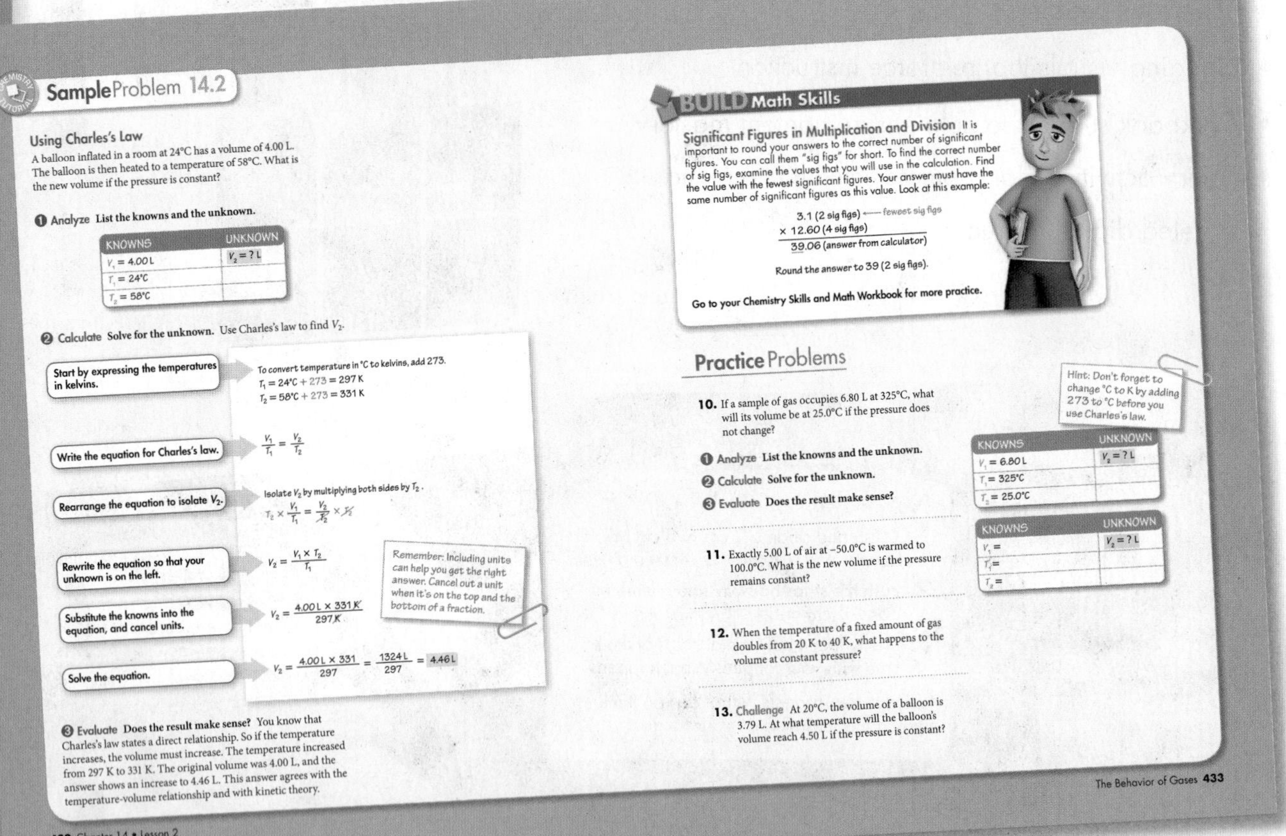

SampleProblem 14.2

Using Charles's Law

A balloon inflated in a room at 24°C has a volume of 4.00 L. The balloon is then heated to a temperature of 58°C. What is the new volume if the pressure is constant?

1 Analyze List the knowns and the unknown.

KNOWNS	UNKNOWN
V_1 = 4.00 L	V_2 = ? L
T_1 = 24°C	
T_2 = 58°C	

2 Calculate Solve for the unknown. Use Charles's law to find V_2.

Start by expressing the temperatures in kelvins. To convert temperature in °C to kelvins, add 273.
$T_1 = 24°C + 273 = 297\ K$
$T_2 = 58°C + 273 = 331\ K$

Write the equation for Charles's law. $\frac{V_1}{T_1} = \frac{V_2}{T_2}$

Rearrange the equation to isolate V_2. Isolate V_2 by multiplying both sides by T_2.
$T_2 \times \frac{V_1}{T_1} = \frac{V_2}{\cancel{T_2}} \times \cancel{T_2}$

Rewrite the equation so that your unknown is on the left. $V_2 = \frac{V_1 \times T_2}{T_1}$

Substitute the knowns into the equation, and cancel units. $V_2 = \frac{4.00\ L \times 331\ \cancel{K}}{297\ \cancel{K}}$

Remember: Including units can help you get the right answer. Cancel out a unit when it's on the top and the bottom of a fraction.

Solve the equation. $V_2 = \frac{4.00\ L \times 331}{297} = \frac{1324\ L}{297} = 4.46\ L$

3 Evaluate Does the result make sense? You know that Charles's law states a direct relationship. So if the temperature increases, the volume must increase. The temperature increased from 297 K to 331 K. The original volume was 4.00 L, and the answer shows an increase to 4.46 L. This answer agrees with the temperature-volume relationship and with kinetic theory.

432 Chapter 14 • Lesson 2

BUILD Math Skills

Significant Figures in Multiplication and Division It is important to round your answers to the correct number of significant figures. You can call them "sig figs" for short. To find the correct number of sig figs, examine the values that you will use in the calculation. Find the value with the fewest significant figures. Your answer must have the same number of significant figures as this value. Look at this example:

3.1 (2 sig figs) ← fewest sig figs
× 12.60 (4 sig figs)
39.06 (answer from calculator)

Round the answer to 39 (2 sig figs).

Go to your Chemistry Skills and Math Workbook for more practice.

Practice Problems

Hint: Don't forget to change °C to K by adding 273 to °C before you use Charles's law.

10. If a sample of gas occupies 6.80 L at 325°C, what will its volume be at 25.0°C if the pressure does not change?

1 Analyze List the knowns and the unknown.
2 Calculate Solve for the unknown.
3 Evaluate Does the result make sense?

KNOWNS	UNKNOWN
V_1 = 6.80 L	V_2 = ? L
T_1 = 325°C	
T_2 = 25.0°C	

11. Exactly 5.00 L of air at −50.0°C is warmed to 100.0°C. What is the new volume if the pressure remains constant?

KNOWNS	UNKNOWN
V_1 =	V_2 = ? L
T_1 =	
T_2 =	

12. When the temperature of a fixed amount of gas doubles from 20 K to 40 K, what happens to the volume at constant pressure?

13. Challenge At 20°C, the volume of a balloon is 3.79 L. At what temperature will the balloon's volume reach 4.50 L if the pressure is constant?

The Behavior of Gases 433

Practice Problems ▲

Scaffolded Practice Problems follow each Sample Problem. This scaffolding structure will help you become comfortable with solving chemistry problems.

READING SUPPORT

The *Foundation Edition of Pearson Chemistry* provides enhanced reading support to make the content more accessible. You will find embedded reading strategies throughout each chapter to help you along the way.

10.3 Percent Composition and Chemical Formulas

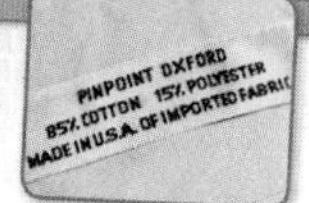

Key Questions

How do you calculate the percent composition of a compound?

How can you calculate the empirical formula of a compound?

How does the molecular formula of a compound compare with the empirical formula?

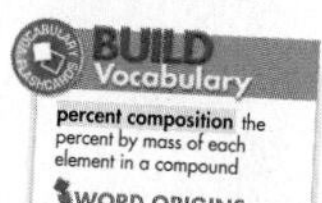

BUILD Vocabulary

percent composition the percent by mass of each element in a compound

WORD ORIGINS

The word *percent* comes from the Latin phrase meaning "by the hundred." One percent is one part of 100 equal parts.

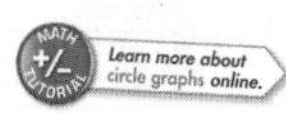

Learn more about circle graphs **online.**

CHEMISTRY & YOU

Q: What does the percent composition of a compound tell you? A tag sewn into the seam of a shirt usually tells you what fibers were used to make the cloth. It also tells you the percentage of each type of fiber. It helps to know the percentages of the fibers in the shirt because they affect how warm the shirt is, whether it will need to be ironed, and how it should be cleaned. Similarly, in chemistry, it is important to know the percentages of the elements in a compound.

Percent Composition of a Compound

In lawn care, the relative amount of each nutrient in fertilizer is important. In spring, you may use a fertilizer with a higher percent of nitrogen to "green" the grass. In fall, you may use a fertilizer with a higher percent of potassium to strengthen the roots. Knowing the relative amounts of the components of a mixture or compound is useful.

Relative amounts of elements in a compound are expressed as percent composition. **Percent composition** is the percent by mass of each element in a compound. The figures below show the percent composition of two different compounds containing potassium, chromium, and oxygen. No matter how much of a particular compound is present, the percent by mass of each element in the compound is always the same.

Percent Composition

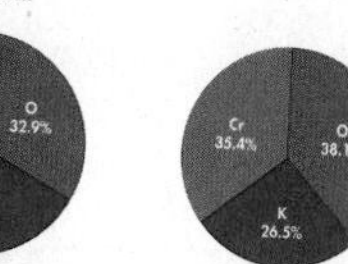

Potassium chromate (K_2CrO_4) is composed of 40.3% potassium, 26.8% chromium, and 32.9% oxygen. The sum of the percentages is 100%.

Potassium dichromate ($K_2Cr_2O_7$) is composed of 26.5% potassium, 35.4% chromium, and 38.1% oxygen. The sum of the percentages is 100%.

296 Chapter 10 • Lesson 3

Percent Composition From Mass Data If you know the relative mass of each element in a compound, you can calculate the percent composition of the compound. The percent by mass of an element in a compound is the number of grams of the element divided by the mass in grams of the compound multiplied by 100%:

$$\% \text{ by mass of element} = \frac{\text{mass of element}}{\text{mass of compound}} \times 100\%$$

Percent Composition From the Chemical Formula You can also calculate the percent composition of a compound using its chemical formula. The subscripts in the chemical formula are used to calculate the mass of each element in a mole of that compound. Using the individual masses of the elements and the molar mass, you can calculate the percent by mass of each element:

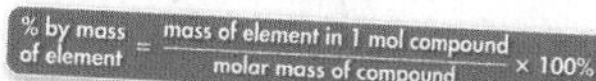

$$\% \text{ by mass of element} = \frac{\text{mass of element in 1 mol compound}}{\text{molar mass of compound}} \times 100\%$$

Percent Composition as a Conversion Factor You can use percent composition to calculate the number of grams of any element in a specific mass of a compound. To do this, multiply the mass of the compound by a conversion factor based on the percent composition of the element in the compound.

Here is an example: Propane is a fuel used in gas grills. It comes from petroleum refining or natural-gas processing. Propane has a percent composition of 81.8% carbon and 18.2% hydrogen. That means that in a 100 g sample of propane, you would have 81.8 g of carbon and 18.2 g of hydrogen. You can use the following conversion factors to solve for the mass of carbon or hydrogen contained in a specific amount of propane:

$$\frac{81.8 \text{ g C}}{100 \text{ g } C_3H_8} \text{ and } \frac{18.2 \text{ g H}}{100 \text{ g } C_3H_8}$$

If you wanted to find the mass of carbon in a sample of propane, you would use the first conversion factor. If you wanted to find the mass of hydrogen in a sample of propane, you would use the second conversion factor.

Key Question How do you calculate percent composition of a compound? **The percent by mass of an element in a compound is the number of grams of the element divided by the mass in grams of the compound multiplied by 100%.**

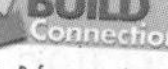

BUILD Connections

Before you take off in a large airliner, the flight attendant shows how to use the oxygen mask. The mask will drop in front of you if the plane's cabin loses too much air pressure. On some airplanes, this oxygen is produced by a chemical reaction. Chemists use the percent composition of the compounds to determine how much of each chemical is necessary to produce the correct amount of oxygen.

Learn more about percent composition **online.**

Chemical Quantities 297

BUILD Vocabulary

heat (*q*) energy that transfers from one object to another because of a temperature difference between the objects

endothermic process a process in which heat is absorbed from the surroundings

exothermic process a process in which heat is released into the surroundings

PREFIXES

The prefix *endo-* means inside, and the prefix *exo-* means outside. The prefixes tell you the direction that heat flows.

Build Vocabulary ▲

Build Vocabulary features provide support for learning essential academic and scientific vocabulary.

Build Understanding ▶

Build Understanding features provide suggestions on how to use graphic organizers and other learning strategies.

BUILD Understanding

Compare/Contrast Table
Addition and subtraction have different rules for determining the number of significant figures than multiplication and division have. Use a compare/contrast table to identify the differences and similarities between the two sets of rules.

BUILD Connections

Electron configurations are often written in shorthand. Do you ever use a shorthand way to communicate? How about when you send a text message? You may use numbers and symbols in place of words. Your friends still know what you mean because they understand the shorthand being used.

◀ Build Connections

You can use Build Connections features to make meaningful connections between science content and real-world situations.

SKILLS SUPPORT

Chemistry is not a "one-size-fits-all" subject. To fit your unique learning style, two different workbooks are available. Each workbook offers different learning-support activities to ensure success in your chemistry class.

Reading and Study Workbook

The *Reading and Study Workbook* offers learning-support activities such as:

- Reading strategies to help you prepare for what you will read in the chapter
- Review Vocabulary exercises to help you work with the chapter's key vocabulary
- Self-Check Activities to help you assess your knowledge of the chapter's key concepts
- Build Math Skills features with stepped-out tutorials on the math you need to solve various chemistry problems

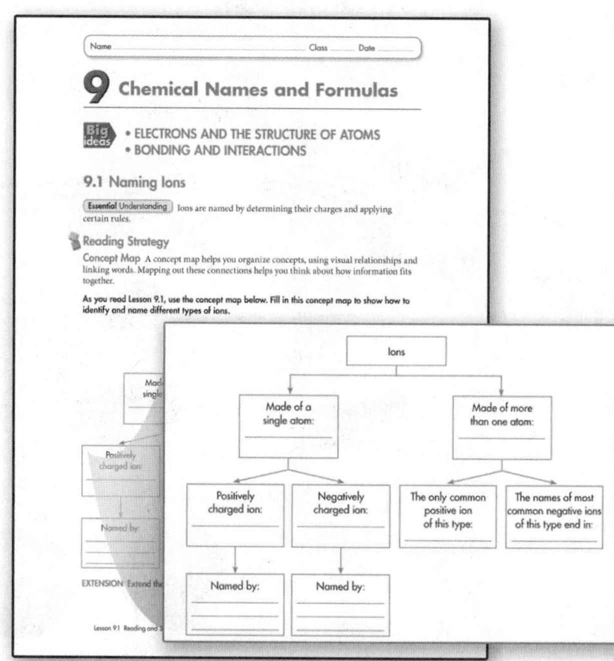
Name ______ Class ____ Date ____

9 Chemical Names and Formulas

Big ideas
- ELECTRONS AND THE STRUCTURE OF ATOMS
- BONDING AND INTERACTIONS

9.1 Naming Ions

Essential Understanding Ions are named by determining their charges and applying certain rules.

Reading Strategy

Concept Map A concept map helps you organize concepts, using visual relationships and linking words. Mapping out these connections helps you think about how information fits together.

As you read Lesson 9.1, use the concept map below. Fill in this concept map to show how to identify and name different types of ions.

Chemistry Skills and Math Workbook

The *Chemistry Skills and Math Workbook* offers the following learning-support activities:

- Standardized Test Prep tutorials with stepped-out guidance and helpful solving strategies to help you prepare for end-of-course testing
- More Practice features that offer step-by-step guided practice followed by On Your Own problems to help you master important problem-solving skills
- Interpret Graphs features to help you learn to navigate and make sense of graphs
- Interpret Data features to help you learn to successfully analyze information in data tables

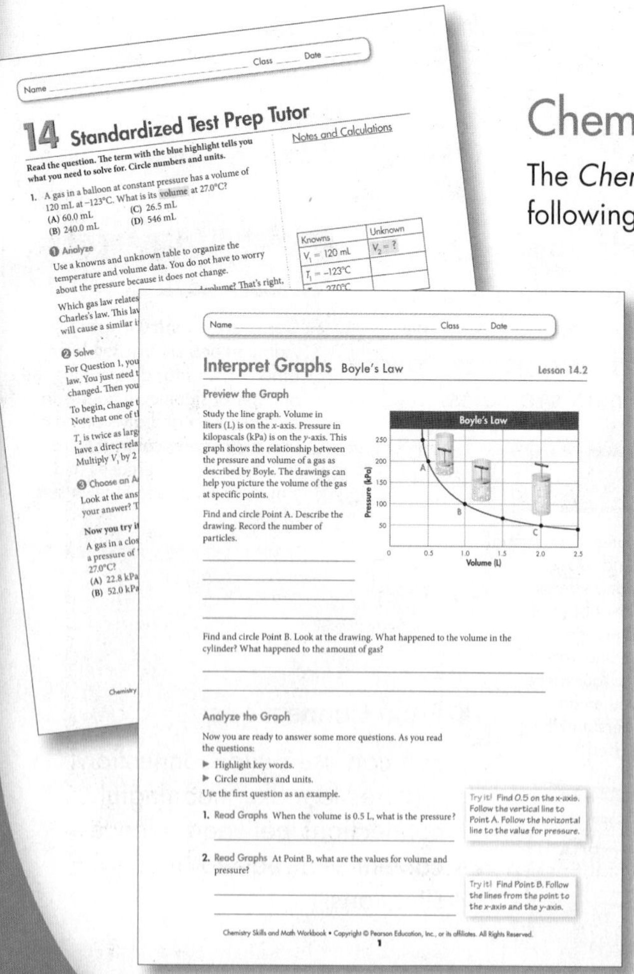
Name ______ Class ____ Date ____

14 Standardized Test Prep Tutor

Notes and Calculations

Read the question. The term with the blue highlight tells you what you need to solve for. Circle numbers and units.

1. A gas in a balloon at constant pressure has a volume of 120 mL at −123°C. What is its volume at 27.0°C?
(A) 60.0 mL (C) 26.5 mL
(B) 240.0 mL (D) 546 mL

❶ Analyze

Use a knowns and unknown table to organize the temperature and volume data. You do not have to worry about the pressure because it does not change.

Knowns	Unknown
V_1 = 120 mL	V_2 = ?
T_1 = −123°C	

Name ______ Class ____ Date ____

Interpret Graphs Boyle's Law — Lesson 14.2

Preview the Graph

Study the line graph. Volume in liters (L) is on the *x*-axis. Pressure in kilopascals (kPa) is on the *y*-axis. This graph shows the relationship between the pressure and volume of a gas as described by Boyle. The drawings can help you picture the volume of the gas at specific points.

Find and circle Point A. Describe the drawing. Record the number of particles.

Find and circle Point B. Look at the drawing. What happened to the volume in the cylinder? What happened to the amount of gas?

Analyze the Graph

Now you are ready to answer some more questions. As you read the questions:
- ▸ Highlight key words.
- ▸ Circle numbers and units.

Use the first question as an example.

1. Read Graphs When the volume is 0.5 L, what is the pressure?

Try it! Find 0.5 on the *x*-axis. Follow the vertical line to Point A. Follow the horizontal line to the value for pressure.

2. Read Graphs At Point B, what are the values for volume and pressure?

Try it! Find Point B. Follow the lines from the point to the *x*-axis and the *y*-axis.

Chemistry Skills and Math Workbook • Copyright © Pearson Education, Inc., or its affiliates. All Rights Reserved.
1

ONLINE SUPPORT—PEARSONCHEM.COM

PearsonChem.com is an engaging online environment that brings chemistry concepts to life. You and your teacher will have access to engaging Foundation Edition-specific content and activities to help support your learning style.

What's Online for Students:

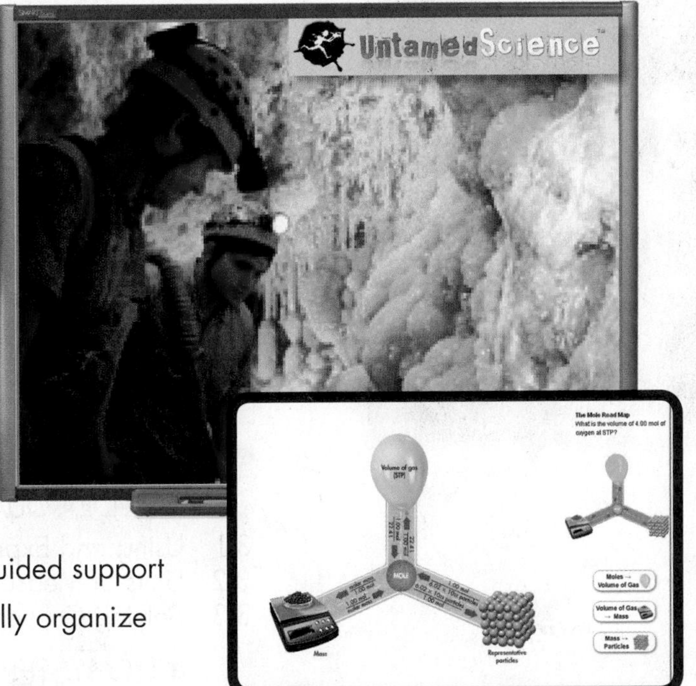

- eText with audio
- Point-of-use periodic table
- Engaging *Untamed Science* videos
- Interactive simulations and animations
- Chemistry and Math Tutorials with audio
- Online Problem Sets

Foundation-Specific Digital Support:

- Scaffolded Chemistry Tutorials with extra guided support
- Interactive Concept Maps to help you visually organize important chapter concepts
- Vocabulary Flashcards with audio to help you master chapter vocabulary (also available in Spanish)

What's Online for Teachers:

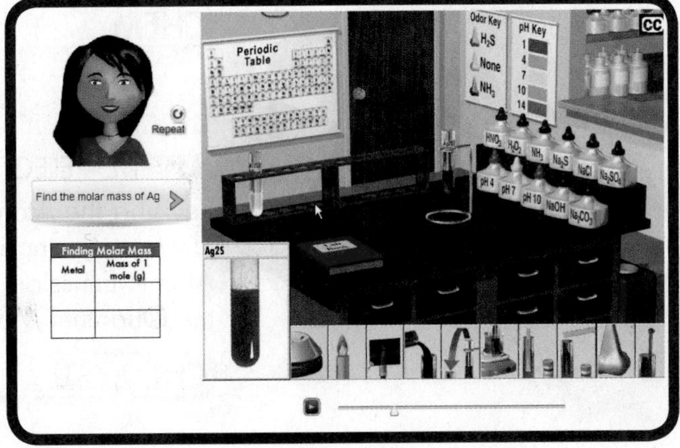

- Teacher's Edition of the eText
- Assignable Directed Virtual Labs
- Online lesson planning
- Online assessments with remediation
- Editable Resources:
  - PowerPoint presentations
  - Labs
  - Worksheets
  - Assessments

Contents

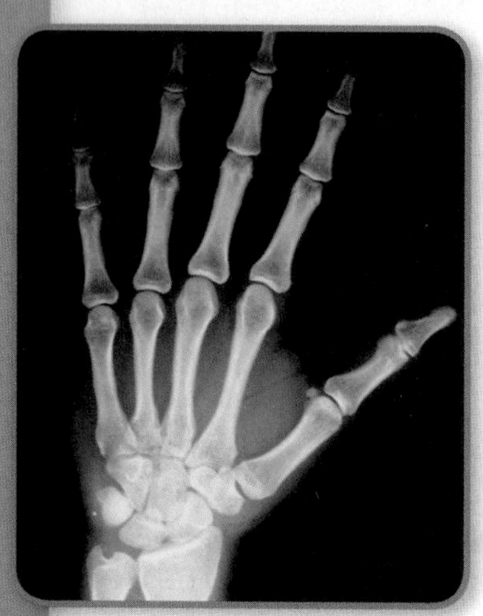

CHEMYSTERY

Enhance your understanding by exploring a chemical mystery that connects to each chapter's Big Idea. For example, you'll learn how less expensive jewelry can appear to be made of pure gold.

PearsonChem.com

What's Online

Your chemistry book comes alive online at **PearsonChem.com.** Anytime you spot one of these icons on a page, you can visit **PearsonChem.com** for an online activity, tutorial, or practice problem that helps reinforce the concepts introduced in the book.

CHEMISTRY & YOU

Feature Pages

Learn how chemistry applies to real-world events and topics. Some features include fun experiments that you can do on your own or with classmates.

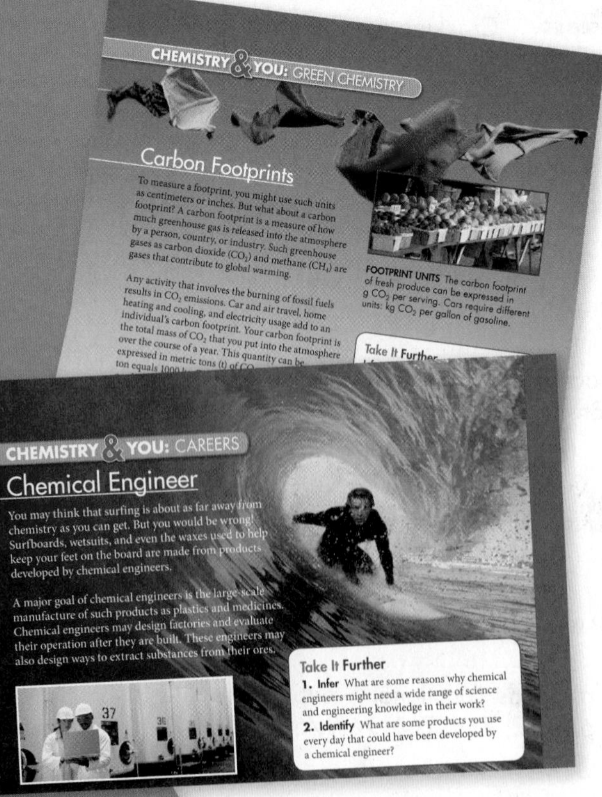

CHEMISTRY & YOU: GREEN CHEMISTRY

Carbon Footprints

To measure a footprint, you might use such units as centimeters or inches. But what about a carbon footprint? A carbon footprint is a measure of how much greenhouse gas is released into the atmosphere by a person, country, or industry. Such greenhouse gases as carbon dioxide (CO_2) and methane (CH_4) are gases that contribute to global warming.

Any activity that involves the burning of fossil fuels results in CO_2 emissions. Car and air travel, home heating and cooling, and electricity usage add to an individual's carbon footprint. Your carbon footprint is the total mass of CO_2 that you put into the atmosphere over the course of a year. This quantity can be expressed in metric tons (t) of

FOOTPRINT UNITS The carbon footprint of fresh produce can be expressed in g CO_2 per serving. Cars require different units: kg CO_2 per gallon of gasoline.

Take It Further

CHEMISTRY & YOU: CAREERS

Chemical Engineer

You may think that surfing is about as far away from chemistry as you can get. But you would be wrong! Surfboards, wetsuits, and even the waxes used to help keep your feet on the board are made from products developed by chemical engineers.

A major goal of chemical engineers is the large-scale manufacture of such products as plastics and medicines. Chemical engineers may design factories and evaluate their operation after they are built. These engineers may also design ways to extract substances from their ores.

Take It Further

1. **Infer** What are some reasons why chemical engineers might need a wide range of science and engineering knowledge in their work?
2. **Identify** What are some products you use every day that could have been developed by a chemical engineer?

FOUNDATIONS for Learning

These short activities, which use common, easy-to-find materials, are a great way to kick off each chapter.

Quick Lab

Apply chemistry concepts and skills with these quick, effective hands-on opportunities.

Probe or sensor versions available in the Probeware Lab Manual.

Sample Problems

Take advantage of these stepped-out problems to guide your solving process.

1

Introduction to Chemistry

FOUNDATIONS for Learning

Stirring Up Chemistry

1. Work with a partner. You will need food coloring, a cup of water, and a spoon.
2. Stir a few drops of food coloring into the water.
3. Observe what happens to the water and the food coloring over time.

Infer What do you think this activity has to do with chemistry?

PearsonChem.com

Take a video field trip with the Untamed Science crew to find out what makes chemists excited about their work.

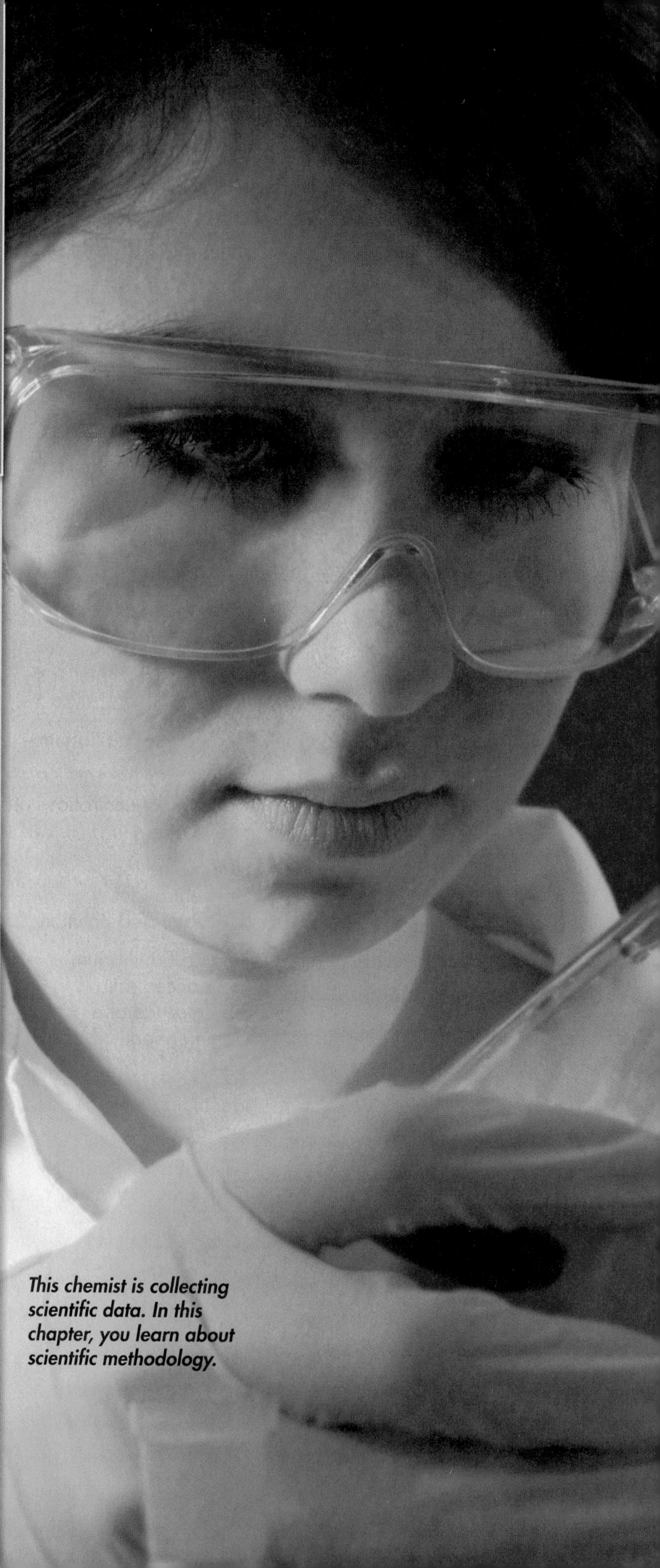

This chemist is collecting scientific data. In this chapter, you learn about scientific methodology.

BIG IDEA

CHEMISTRY AS THE CENTRAL SCIENCE

Essential Questions:

1. *Why is it important to study chemistry?*
2. *How do chemists solve problems?*

CHEMYSTERY

Is Bio Better?

You and your friends are getting ready for a picnic. You are shopping for cups, spoons, forks, and knives. At the store, you notice that there are many different kinds of spoons, forks, and knives. They are made out of different materials. Some of them are labeled "bioplastic." The labels say that the products are "Eco-Friendly," "Compostable," and "Made From Renewable Resources."

You are confused! What do these words mean? Is bioplastic better for the environment than plastic? You decide to find out more about bioplastic before you buy anything. What do you want to know about bioplastic that will help you make a good decision?

▶ Connect to the **BIG**IDEA Read about the skills and methods that are used in chemistry. Think about how they can apply to your everyday decision making.

1.1 The Scope of Chemistry

CHEMISTRY & YOU

Q: Why would chemists find this creature interesting? This is a fugu, also known as a puffer fish. People enjoy eating fugu, but it could kill them. Fugu contain a powerful poison that can kill an adult human being a few hours after eating the fish. Chefs who prepare fugu must receive training to ensure that the fish they prepare is safe to eat. However, the fugu's poison can be put to good use. Scientists discovered that they can use a form of the poison to treat pain in cancer patients.

Key Questions

Why is the scope of chemistry so vast?

What are five traditional areas of study in chemistry?

What are the central themes of chemistry?

BUILD Vocabulary

matter anything that has mass and takes up space

chemistry the study of what matter is made of and how matter changes

MULTIPLE MEANINGS
Matter not only refers to a substance, but it can also mean "something important."

What Is Chemistry?

Look around you. This book you are reading, the chair you sit in, and the computer you use are all made of matter. Matter is a word for materials, or "stuff." **Matter** is anything that has mass and takes up space. The trees, the water, and the buildings you see on the following page are all examples of matter. You cannot see all matter though. The air you breathe is matter, even though you cannot see it.

How can some creatures survive deep in the ocean where there is no light? Why do some foods taste sweet and some taste bitter? Chemistry answers these questions and the many other questions you may have about the world. **Chemistry** is the study of what matter is made of and how matter changes. All living and nonliving things are composed of matter. Therefore, chemistry affects all parts of life as well as most things that happen in nature. Chemistry is sometimes called the central science. An understanding of chemistry will help you understand many other areas of science.

Key Question Why is the scope of chemistry so vast? **Chemistry affects all parts of life as well as most things in nature. All living and nonliving things are composed of matter.**

Learn more about chemistry in your world online.

Areas of Study

The field of chemistry is very large. A chemist usually works in one of five areas of study. These five areas of study are organic chemistry, inorganic chemistry, biochemistry, analytical chemistry, and physical chemistry.

Organic chemistry is the study of all matter that contains carbon. Most of the chemicals in living things have carbon in them. The study of matter that, in general, does not contain carbon is called **inorganic chemistry**. Many inorganic chemicals are found in nonliving things, such as rocks.

Biochemistry is the study of processes that take place in living things. One of these processes is the digestion of food. **Analytical chemistry** is the study of what matter is made of. The part of chemistry that deals with changes in matter is called **physical chemistry**. Some changes in matter happen slowly, and other changes in matter happen quickly. When matter changes, there is also a transfer of energy.

These five areas of chemistry overlap each other. A chemist may work in more than one area of chemistry at once. The photograph below shows examples of the different types of research done by chemists.

Key Question What are five traditional areas of study in chemistry? **Five traditional areas of study are organic chemistry, inorganic chemistry, biochemistry, analytical chemistry, and physical chemistry.**

organic chemistry the study of all matter that contains carbon

inorganic chemistry the study of matter that, in general, does not contain carbon

biochemistry the study of processes that take place in living things

analytical chemistry the study of what matter is made of

physical chemistry the part of chemistry that deals with changes in matter

PREFIXES

The prefix *bio-* tells you that the word is about life. *Biochemistry* is a word that means the chemistry of living things.

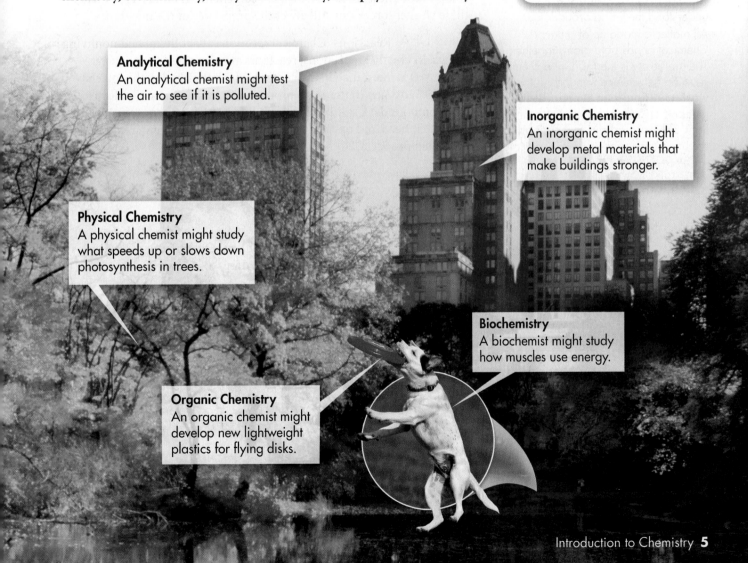

Analytical Chemistry
An analytical chemist might test the air to see if it is polluted.

Inorganic Chemistry
An inorganic chemist might develop metal materials that make buildings stronger.

Physical Chemistry
A physical chemist might study what speeds up or slows down photosynthesis in trees.

Biochemistry
A biochemist might study how muscles use energy.

Organic Chemistry
An organic chemist might develop new lightweight plastics for flying disks.

Big Ideas in Chemistry

This book contains many ideas in the science of chemistry. One of the goals of your course in chemistry is to help you understand these ideas. You can use the ideas to explain situations in real life, such as the one shown in the photograph below. Most of the topics in chemistry are connected by just a few "big ideas."

BIGIDEA **Chemistry as the Central Science** Chemistry overlaps with all the other branches of science. Scientists, including physicists, biologists, astronomers, geologists, and environmental scientists, use chemistry in their work.

BIGIDEA **Electrons and the Structure of Atoms** Carbon, oxygen, and copper are examples of elements. Elements are made of particles called atoms. Every atom contains a nucleus and one or more electrons. The electrons in the atoms of an element play a large role in determining the properties of that element.

BIGIDEA **Bonding and Interactions** Chemical compounds contain two or more elements. Strong forces hold these elements together. These forces are called chemical bonds. There are different types of chemical bonds. The type of bond affects the properties of a compound. There are also other types of forces between the particles of an element or compound. These forces are weaker than chemical bonds. However, these weaker forces can still affect the properties of the material.

BIGIDEA **Reactions** Chemical reactions affect living and nonliving things. In chemical reactions, reactants are converted to products. When you strike a match, the compounds in the head of the match react with oxygen in the air to produce a flame. This reaction forms new compounds. Light and heat are also formed. The compounds in the match head and oxygen are called reactants. The new compounds are called products.

Big Ideas
The big ideas in chemistry can help you understand the world around you. All matter is made up of atoms. Chemical bonds hold atoms together. The fire below is the result of a chemical reaction between compounds in the wood and oxygen in the air. The fire gives off energy in the form of heat and light. The gas particles in the air around the fire move faster as the air heats up.

BIGIDEA **Kinetic Theory** The particles in matter are always moving. A temperature change causes these particles to move more quickly or more slowly. Temperature and pressure determine whether a substance will be a solid, liquid, or gas.

BIGIDEA **The Mole and Quantifying Matter** The word quantifying is another word for "measure." In chemistry, it is very important to know the exact amount of material you are using. If you are going to carry out a chemical reaction, you want to use just the right amount of materials. You do not want to waste any materials. Chemists measure the amount of material with a unit called the mole.

BIGIDEA **Matter and Energy** Every process in chemistry uses energy or makes energy. This energy is often in the form of heat. You can measure the heat change that occurs in chemical reactions. You can also predict whether a reaction will occur by calculating how the energy will change.

BIGIDEA **Carbon Chemistry** There are about ten million compounds that contain carbon. Scientists make new compounds every day. They make many of these compounds from petroleum. Plastic and synthetic fibers are only two examples. Carbon compounds are the basis of life in all living things.

Key Question What are the central themes of chemistry? **Some big ideas in chemistry include chemistry as the central science; electrons and the structure of atoms; bonding and interactions; reactions; kinetic theory; the mole and quantifying matter; matter and energy; and carbon chemistry.**

1.1 LessonCheck

Key Concept Check

1. **Explain** Why does chemistry affect every part of your life and most natural events?
2. **List** Name the five traditional areas of chemistry.
3. **Review** What are the "big ideas" of chemistry?

Vocabulary Check *Choose a highlighted word from the lesson to complete the sentence correctly.*

4. The study of what matter is made of and how matter changes is called __________.
5. Someone who studies __________ might determine the energy transfer when water boils.

Think Critically

6. **Infer** A geologist is trying to identify the minerals in a rock. Why would she ask an analytical chemist to help her?

CHEMISTRY & YOU

7. Why would you study a puffer fish if you were a biochemist? Why would you study a puffer fish if you were an organic chemist? (Hint: See page 5.)

BIGIDEA
CHEMISTRY AS THE CENTRAL SCIENCE

8. Why would a student who wants to be a medical doctor need to study chemistry?

1.2 Chemistry and You

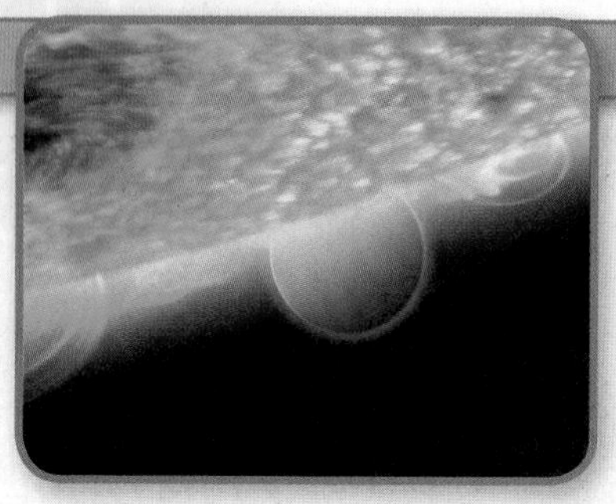

CHEMISTRY & YOU

Q: How can you use chemistry to study other worlds? The Hubble Space Telescope shows us objects far away in space. Scientists who know chemistry have used the telescope to discover water and carbon on a distant planet. Life on Earth depends on water and carbon. However, the planet scientists observed is much too hot to support life. Maybe the Hubble Space Telescope or other telescopes may someday be used to find evidence of life on other planets.

Key Questions

What are three general reasons to study chemistry?

How does chemistry affect technology and our society?

Why Study Chemistry?

You can use chemistry to answer many questions about the world around you. Should you use hot water or cold water to remove a grass stain? How could you prepare for a career in nursing, firefighting, or journalism? What would you ask your local government about moving a landfill into your town? Studying chemistry will help you understand the natural world, prepare you for a career, and make you an informed citizen.

Explaining the Natural World Chemistry can help you understand how things work. Cooking involves chemistry. Take a look at the photo on the left. Chemistry explains why cut apples turn brown if you leave them in the air. Why are boiled eggs firm and raw eggs runny? Why does water expand as it freezes? Why does yeast make bread dough rise? Chemistry can answer these questions—and many more.

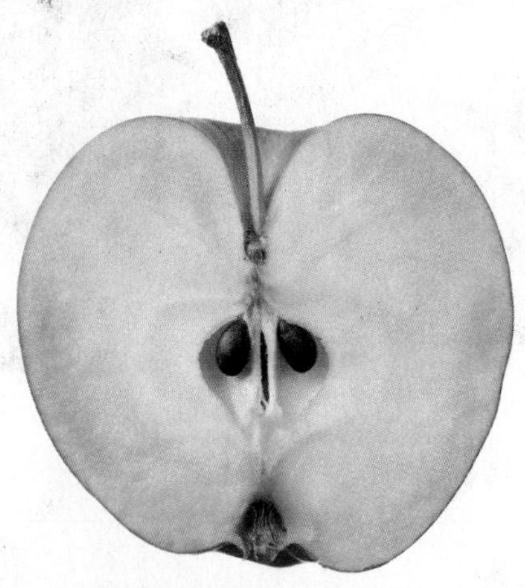

Chemistry and Food
When a cut apple sits out in air, a chemical reaction takes place. The reaction causes the color to change to brown.

Preparing for a Career Many interesting careers involve chemistry. Some of the choices may surprise you. A reporter may be asked to interview a chemist to gather background for a story. Firefighters must know which chemicals to use to fight different types of fires. People who take care of sports playing fields have to know the science of soil. Think about the career you would like to have someday. How might knowing chemistry help you?

Being an Informed Citizen Why is it valuable to explore space? How much money should people spend on research? You will make choices on questions like these and many more. You may vote directly on some science issues on a ballot. You might elect officials who have certain ideas about science research. You may speak at a meeting, write a letter to the editor, or sign a petition. When it comes to scientific research, there is no single correct answer. Knowing about science helps you form opinions and take action.

Key Question What are three general reasons to study chemistry? **Chemistry helps explain the natural world, prepare people for careers, and produce informed citizens.**

Chemistry, Technology, and Society

Do you want to do something more quickly or with less work? Technology can help you! **Technology** is the means by which a society provides its members with things they want and need. Research in chemistry that is being done today is leading to technologies that can help the environment, conserve and produce energy, improve our lives, and help us learn more about the universe.

Materials and the Environment Chemists use what they know about matter to make new and better materials. We use things that are made from plastic every day. However, making plastic and throwing it away are not good for the environment. New kinds of plastics called bioplastics may lessen our impact on the environment. Look at the figure below to see how bioplastics can be made from corn.

Energy Chemistry can help solve two important problems with energy. How can people conserve energy? How can they produce more of it? Chemists have made batteries for hybrid cars. Hybrid cars use less gasoline than other cars. Chemists have also found ways to collect energy from the sun. This energy can be converted into electricity.

technology the means by which a society provides its members with things they want and need

RELATED WORD FORMS

The adjective *high-tech* relates to new electronic devices and technologies.

Bioplastic
Polylactic acid (PLA) is a bioplastic. PLA is made from corn. It can be used to make many items that are typically made from crude oil.

Farmers grow and harvest corn. The corn is then ground up. A sugar called glucose is taken out of the ground corn.

Lactic acid is also found in your muscle tissue when you exercise.

Bacteria are added to the glucose to turn it into **lactic acid.**

Units of lactic acid are called **molecules.** Lactic acid molecules are connected to each other to make long chains called **polymers.**

Plastics are made out of **polymers.** Polymers are long chains of molecules that are chemically bonded to one another.

The polymer is called polylactic acid (PLA). The PLA is made into small pellets. The pellets can be spun into fibers or melted to take almost any shape.

compostable

Space Exploration
Chemists study matter from other bodies in the solar system. This drawing shows a robotic vehicle called *Opportunity*. The vehicle collects matter from the surface of Mars.

Medicine and Biotechnology Chemists create medicines, materials, and technologies that doctors use to treat patients. Chemists have created drugs that can treat many medical conditions. Chemists have also developed materials that can replace damaged body parts.

Genes are segments of DNA. Genes store the information that controls changes that take place in cells. Scientists can alter DNA to help people with various medical problems.

The Universe Scientists study objects across the universe. Scientists can study what stars are made out of by analyzing the light that comes from them. Planets do not give off light. This means that scientists have to use other ways to gather data from planets. The vehicle shown above collected rocks and soil from Mars. Instruments on the vehicle determined what the rocks and soil are made of. The information that the vehicle collected on the spot where it landed indicated that the spot was once covered with water.

Key Question How does chemistry affect technology and our society? **Modern research in chemistry leads to technologies that help the environment, conserve and produce energy, improve our lives, and help us learn more about the universe.**

1.2 LessonCheck

Key Concept Check

9. **List** What are three reasons for studying chemistry?

10. **Review** How has modern research in chemistry had an effect on our society?

Think Critically

11. **Form an Opinion** Would you use bioplastic products? Why or why not?

CHEMISTRY & YOU

12. How can you use chemistry to find evidence of life on other planets?

BIGIDEA
CHEMISTRY AS THE CENTRAL SCIENCE

13. A friend tells you that she does not think it is important to learn chemistry. How would you reply?

1.3 Thinking Like a Scientist

CHEMISTRY & YOU

Q: How can you test a hypothesis? In 1928, a scientist named Alexander Fleming was studying bacteria. The bacteria did not grow when it was near a certain kind of mold. Other scientists noticed the same thing, but Fleming was the first one who understood why it was important. He formed an explanation that the mold had a chemical that stopped the bacteria from growing. That chemical was penicillin. Penicillin can kill many kinds of harmful bacteria.

Key Questions

- ***How did Lavoisier change chemistry?***
- ***What steps are at the core of scientific methodology?***
- ***Why is it important to communicate and to work together in science?***

BUILD Understanding

Flowchart As you read about the scientific method, create a flowchart. Describe the steps and show how they relate to each other.

An Experimental Approach to Science

The word *chemistry* comes from the word *alchemy.* Alchemists studied matter. They began their studies in China and India as early as 400 B.C. In the eighth century, Arabs brought alchemy to Spain. From there, it quickly spread to other parts of Europe.

Alchemy Alchemists wanted a way to change metals, such as lead, into gold. They did not succeed in changing metals. However, their work helped in the development and growth of the science of chemistry.

Alchemists developed tools and techniques for working with chemicals. For example, alchemists developed processes for separating mixtures into their components. Alchemists designed equipment that they used to conduct their work. Modern versions of this equipment are still used today. Examples include beakers, flasks, funnels, and the mortar and pestle. A photo of a mortar and pestle is below.

Alchemists observed changes in matter, but they were not able to explain what caused those changes. Many years later, chemists were able to explain what caused these changes.

Mortar and Pestle
A bowl-shaped mortar and club-shaped pestle can be used to grind or crush such materials as herbs and spices. This mortar and pestle are made of a hard material called porcelain.

Antoine-Laurent Lavoisier
This portrait shows Antoine-Laurent Lavoisier and his wife Marie-Anne in 1788.

From Alchemy to Science In Europe in the 1500s, there was a shift from alchemy to science. In the 1600s, King Charles II supported science in Britain. Some scientists there formed a group called the Royal Society of London for the Promotion of Natural Knowledge. The scientists in the group discussed science topics and did experiments. The society wanted scientists to base their ideas about science on experiments and things that they could observe.

Antoine-Laurent Lavoisier In France, Antoine-Laurent Lavoisier did work in the late 1700s that changed chemistry forever. At the time, chemistry was a science based on observation. Lavoisier changed chemistry to the science of measurement. He designed a balance that could measure mass to the nearest 0.0005 gram. The balance helped scientists make careful measurements.

Lavoisier settled a debate about how materials burn. At the time, scientists thought that materials burn because they contain a substance that goes into the air as a material burns. However, scientists were ignoring something important. Metals can gain mass as they burn. Lavoisier showed that materials need oxygen to burn.

Lavoisier's wife Marie-Anne helped with his scientific work. She drew diagrams of his experiments. She also translated scientific papers from English to French.

Key Question How did Lavoisier change chemistry? **Lavoisier helped change chemistry from a science of observation to the science of measurement that it is today.**

BUILD Vocabulary

scientific methodology a general style of investigation with a logical approach to the solution of a scientific problem

observation the use of your senses to obtain information

ACADEMIC WORDS

A method is an organized plan that controls the way something is done.

Scientific Methodology

Scientists have a powerful tool that they use to get reliable results. The scientist in the photograph below is using scientific methodology. **Scientific methodology** is a general style of investigation with a logical approach to the solution of a scientific problem. Scientific methodology involves making observations, proposing and testing hypotheses, and developing theories.

Making Observations You can use the scientific methodology to solve many kinds of problems. Suppose you try to turn on a flashlight and you notice that it does not light. When you use your senses to obtain information, you make an **observation.** An observation can lead to a question: What is wrong with the flashlight?

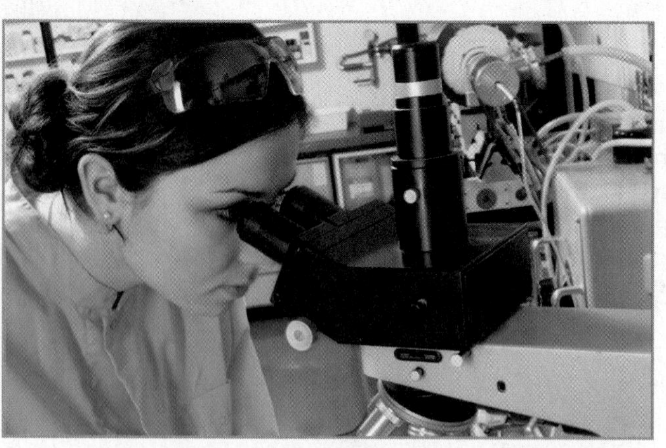

Observing With a Microscope
Observation is an important step in scientific methodology.

Testing Hypotheses If you guess that the batteries in the flashlight are dead, you make a hypothesis. A **hypothesis** is a proposed explanation for an observation. You can test your hypothesis by putting new batteries in the flashlight.

Replacing the batteries is an experiment. An **experiment** is a procedure you use to test a hypothesis. What if the flashlight lights? Then, you will know that your hypothesis was true. What if the flashlight does not work with new batteries? Then, you must come up with a new hypothesis. What else could make a flashlight not light? A new hypothesis might be that the lightbulb is burnt out. You could test the hypothesis with a new experiment. A new experiment would be to replace the bulb.

When you design experiments, some things change. The things that change are called variables. The variable you change during an experiment is the **independent variable.** The independent variable is sometimes called the manipulated variable. The variable you observe is the **dependent variable.** The dependent variable is sometimes called the responding variable. It is important during an experiment to keep all the other factors the same. Then, if anything changes, you can relate any change in the dependent variable to changes in the independent variable.

Scientists share the results of their experiments. An experiment must produce the same result no matter how many times it is repeated and who does the experiment. Then, the experimental results can be accepted. This is why scientists explain their procedures along with their results. That way, other scientists can test the experiments.

Some experiments are difficult or impossible to do. For example, atoms are so small that scientists cannot see them with their eyes. In these situations, scientists use models to understand problems. A **model** represents an object or event. A computer model of DNA is shown below. Chemists may also use models to study chemical reactions and processes.

BUILD Vocabulary

hypothesis a proposed explanation for an observation

experiment a procedure used to test a hypothesis

independent variable the variable changed during an experiment

dependent variable the variable observed during an experiment

model a representation of an object or event

PREFIXES

The words *independent* and *dependent* are alike except for the prefix *in-*. Adding the prefix *in-* changes the meaning to "not." Independent means "not dependent."

Computer Models
Scientists often use computers to model complex molecules, such as DNA.

VOCABULARY FLASHCARDS
BUILD
Vocabulary

theory a well-tested explanation for a set of observations

scientific law a brief summary of the results of many observations and experiments

MULTIPLE MEANINGS

In science, the word *law* is a summary of many observations and experiments. In everyday speech, we think of laws as rules that people should obey.

Developing Theories The figure below shows one way the steps in scientific methodology can fit together. A hypothesis needs repeated experiments before it is accepted. If scientists accept the hypothesis, it may become a theory. A **theory** is a well-tested explanation for a set of observations. Some of the theories in chemistry help you form pictures in your mind of objects or processes that you cannot see. Other theories allow you to predict how matter will change.

Scientists say that a theory can never be proved. This does not mean that the theory is unreliable. Rather, it means that the theory may need to be changed at some point in the future to explain new observations or the results of new experiments.

Scientific Laws The figure below also shows that experiments can lead to laws as well as theories. A **scientific law** is a brief summary of the results of many observations and experiments. In Chapter 14, you will study laws that describe how gases behave. One law describes the relationship between the pressure of a gas in a container and its temperature. If all the other variables do not change, the pressure of the gas increases as the temperature increases.

The scientific law described above does not try to explain why this happens. That explanation requires a theory. Scientific laws describe what happens in nature. Theories try to explain why these things happen the way they do.

Key Question What steps are at the core of scientific methodology? **Scientific methodology involves making observations, proposing and testing hypotheses, and developing theories.**

Scientific Methodology
The steps do not always happen in this order.

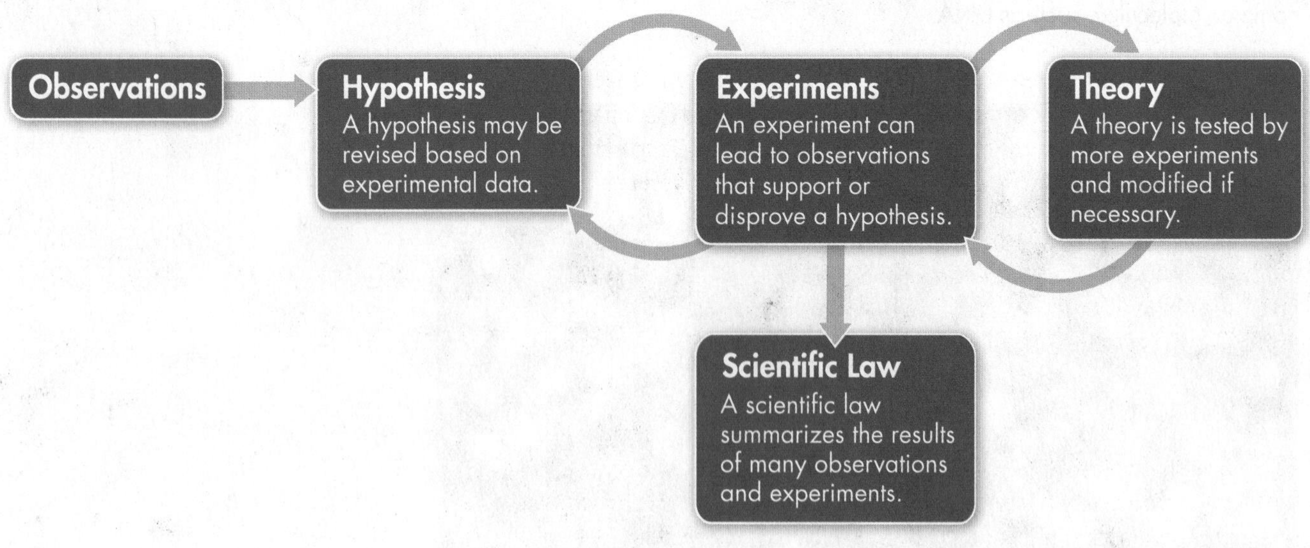
Observations
Hypothesis
A hypothesis may be revised based on experimental data.
Experiments
An experiment can lead to observations that support or disprove a hypothesis.
Theory
A theory is tested by more experiments and modified if necessary.
Scientific Law
A scientific law summarizes the results of many observations and experiments.

Quick Lab

Bubbles!

Purpose To test the hypothesis that bubble making can be affected by adding sugar or salt to a bubble-blowing mixture

Materials

- three plastic drinking cups
- measuring cup and spoons
- liquid dish detergent
- water
- table sugar
- table salt
- drinking straw

Procedure

1. Label three drinking cups 1, 2, and 3. Measure and add one teaspoon of liquid dish detergent to each cup.

2. Use the measuring cup to add two-thirds cup of water to each drinking cup. Then, swirl the cups to form a clear mixture. **CAUTION** *Wipe up any spills immediately so no one will slip and fall.*

3. Add a half teaspoon of table sugar to cup 2 and a half teaspoon of table salt to cup 3. Swirl each cup for 1 minute.

4. Dip the drinking straw into cup 1, remove it, and then blow gently into the straw to make the largest bubble you can. Practice making bubbles until you feel you have reasonable control over your bubble production.

5. Repeat Step 4 with the mixtures in cups 2 and 3.

Analyze and Conclude

1. Observe Did you observe any differences in your ability to produce bubbles when using the mixtures in cup 1 and cup 2?

2. Observe Did you observe any differences in your ability to produce bubbles when using the mixtures in cup 1 and cup 3?

3. Draw Conclusions What can you conclude about the effects of table sugar and table salt on your ability to produce bubbles?

4. Design an Experiment Propose another hypothesis related to bubble making. Design an experiment to test your hypothesis.

Collaboration and Communication

Look carefully at the teams in the photograph to the right. For a team to do well, all the team members need to work together. Team members also need to communicate with each other during a game. Scientists also work together and communicate with one another. When they do this, a successful outcome is more likely.

Collaboration Scientists collaborate, or work together, for different reasons. Some problems in science are so complicated that no single person could solve the problem alone. Each scientist in a group can bring different knowledge and different skills to solve a problem. Just talking with a scientist who has a different background can be helpful.

There are other reasons to work together. A company might give money to a university to solve a problem. The scientists at the university get the equipment and money to do the research. The scientists can give ideas to the company for new products and services.

Teamwork
For a volleyball team to win, the players must work together.

Working Together
Working in pairs or in a group can be challenging, but it can also be rewarding.

Working together is not always easy. Sometimes, people disagree about how to use resources or who does the work. People in a group may disagree about when and how to share their results. You may work in pairs in the laboratory, as the photo on the left shows. You may also work in teams. Working together can be challenging. You may also find great success working with others.

Communication In the past, scientists wrote letters to share their ideas. They formed groups to talk about their results. These groups started publishing journals. Scientists read the journals to see what other scientists discovered.

Scientists today sometimes communicate face-to-face. They also exchange ideas with other scientists by e-mail and by phone. Scientists still publish their results in journals. Journals are the most reliable places to read information about new findings in science. Experts review journal articles before they are published. Reviewers might find mistakes in the author's experiments. They may also not agree with the author's conclusions. The review process is good for science because work that is not reliable is usually not published.

The Internet is a major source of information. However, anyone can also post information on the Internet. Be sure to think about the source of the information you read on the Internet. It may not be reliable.

Key Question Why is it important to communicate and to work together in science? **When scientists communicate and work together, a successful outcome is more likely.**

1.3 LessonCheck

Key Concept Check

14. **Review** How did Lavoisier change the science of chemistry?

15. **List** What does scientific methodology involve?

16. **Explain** Why is it important for scientists to work together and communicate?

Vocabulary Check *Choose a highlighted word from the lesson to complete the sentence correctly.*

17. Scientists use the ________ to solve scientific problems.

18. A proposed explanation for observations is a(n) ________.

Think Critically

19. **Describe** What process takes place before an article is published in a scientific journal?

20. **Compare** What is the difference between a theory and a hypothesis?

CHEMISTRY & YOU

21. What was Alexander Fleming's hypothesis? How could you test his hypothesis? (Hint: See page 13.)

BIGIDEA
CHEMISTRY AS THE CENTRAL SCIENCE

22. Do the steps in scientific methodology always need to be followed in the same order? Explain.

1.4 Problem Solving in Chemistry

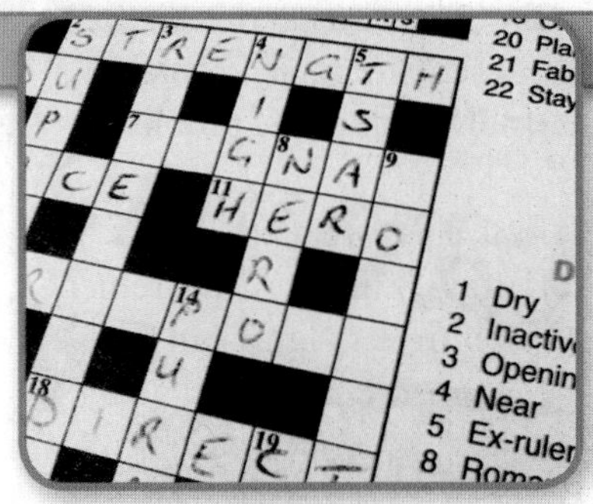

CHEMISTRY & YOU

Q: How does a plan make solving problems easier? Have you ever tried to solve a crossword puzzle? Figuring out a strategy before you begin can help you. You may try to fill in all the "down" clues before you try the "across" clues. You may try to complete the fill-in-the-blank clues first and then move on to more difficult ones. You can also use strategies to solve problems in chemistry.

Key Questions

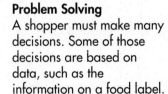

What is a general approach to solving a problem?

What are the steps for solving numeric problems?

What are the steps for solving nonnumeric problems?

Skills Used in Solving Problems

You are in a supermarket. Do you buy a name brand or the store brand of peanut butter? Do you buy the 1 liter bottle or the 2 liter bottle of water? Which checkout line will move the fastest? Problem solving is a skill you use all the time.

When you solve a problem, you might be able to look at a data table, a graph, or some other kind of visual. The shopper in the photo below is reading the label on a container. Reading the label helps her decide whether she will buy the item. She may be allergic to some ingredients. She may also want to know how many Calories are in each serving.

The skills you use to solve a word problem in chemistry are not that different from those you use while shopping or cooking. Making a plan and then following that plan always helps you solve a problem effectively.

Key Question What is a general approach to solving a problem? **Creating a plan and then following that plan helps you solve a problem effectively.**

Problem Solving
A shopper must make many decisions. Some of those decisions are based on data, such as the information on a food label.

BUILD Connections

Have you ever had to memorize important dates for history class or lines from a Shakespearean play for English class? Memorization is a small part of learning chemistry. To be successful in chemistry, you must become a good problem solver.

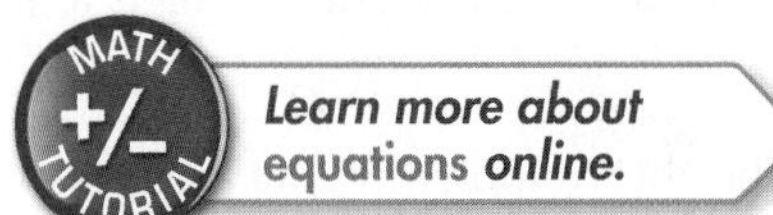

Learn more about equations *online.*

Solving Numeric Problems

Measurements are very important in chemistry. That is why most word problems in chemistry involve math. In this book, the solutions to the sample numeric problems are organized into a three-step problem-solving approach. The three steps are analyze, calculate, and evaluate. You will find this approach helpful when working on numeric problems in this textbook. The figure below shows the three steps in the process. Sample Problem 1.1 on the next page shows how the steps work to solve a numeric problem.

❶ Analyze To solve a word problem, first figure out what you know. Then, figure out what you want to know. You might know a measurement or an equation. If you expect the answer to be a number, figure out what unit(s) the answer should have.

After you identify what you know (the known) and what you want to find out (the unknown), you need to make a plan. A diagram might help you see a relationship between the known and the unknown. A table or a graph may help you identify data or identify a relationship between a known quantity and the unknown. You may need to select an equation that you can use to calculate the unknown.

❷ Calculate If you plan well, doing the calculations is usually easy. For some problems, you will have to change a measurement from one unit to another. For other problems, you may need to rearrange an equation before you can solve for an unknown. You will be taught these math skills as you need them.

❸ Evaluate After you calculate an answer, evaluate it. Does the answer make sense? If not, reread the word problem. Did you copy the data correctly? Did you choose the right equations?

Check that your answer has the correct unit(s) and the correct number of significant figures. You may need to use scientific notation in your answer. You will study significant figures and scientific notation in Chapter 3.

Key Question What are the steps for solving numeric problems? **The steps for solving a numeric word problem are analyze, calculate, and evaluate.**

Solving Numeric Problems
This flowchart shows the steps for solving a numeric problem.

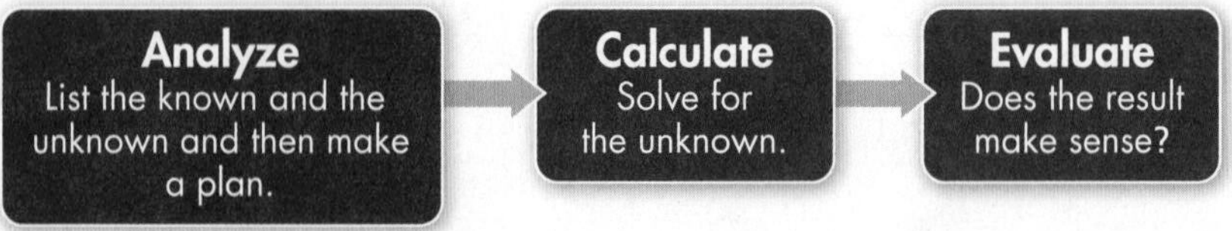

CHEMISTRY TUTORIAL

Sample Problem 1.1

Estimating Walking Time

You are visiting a city. You want to catch an afternoon performance at a local theater. The shortest route from your hotel to the theater is eight blocks. How many minutes will the trip take if you can walk 1 mile in 20 minutes? Assume that 10 blocks equals 1 mile.

❶ Analyze List the knowns and the unknown.

KNOWNS	UNKNOWN
distance to be traveled = 8 blocks	time of trip = ? minutes
walking speed = 1 mile/20 minutes	
1 mile = 10 blocks	

❷ Calculate Solve for the unknown.

Divide the distance to be traveled (in blocks) by the number of blocks in 1 mile to get the distance of the trip in miles. Then, multiply the number of miles by the time it takes to walk 1 mile.

The relationship 1 mile = 10 blocks can be interpreted as "1 mile per 10 blocks."

Divide the number of blocks to be traveled by the number of blocks in 1 mile.

$$8\,\cancel{\text{blocks}} \times \frac{1\text{ mile}}{10\,\cancel{\text{blocks}}} = 0.8\text{ mile}$$

Multiply the number of miles by the time it takes to walk 1 mile.

$$0.8\,\cancel{\text{mile}} \times \frac{20\text{ minutes}}{1\,\cancel{\text{mile}}} = 16\text{ minutes}$$

Notice how the units cancel.

❸ Evaluate Does the result make sense? It takes you 16 minutes to walk eight blocks. This answer seems reasonable and has the correct unit.

Practice Problems

23. How many minutes will it take to walk to an ice cream shop that is six blocks away from your hotel? Use the information in the sample problem.

KNOWNS	UNKNOWN
distance to be traveled = 6 blocks	time of trip = ? minutes
walking speed = 1 mile/20 minutes	
1 mile = 10 blocks	

❶ Analyze List the knowns and the unknown.

❷ Calculate Solve for the unknown.

❸ Evaluate Does the result make sense?

24. Challenge How many blocks can be walked in 48 minutes? Use the information in the sample problem.

Solving Nonnumeric Problems

You do not need to use numbers or equations in every word problem in chemistry. In some problems, you apply ideas you are studying to a new situation. A nonnumeric problem is a problem without numbers. The problem-solving approach is different for problems without numbers. There are only two steps for solving a nonnumeric problem: analyze and solve. The figure below shows the steps in this process.

1 Analyze To solve a nonnumeric problem, you still need to identify what is known and what is unknown. Most importantly, you need to make a plan for getting from the known to the unknown.

2 Solve It might help you to draw a picture or make a flowchart to solve a problem without numbers. Building a model might also be useful. If your answer is not a number, you do not need to check the units, make an estimate, or check your calculations.

Key Question What are the steps for solving nonnumeric problems? **The steps for solving a nonnumeric problem are analyze and solve.**

Solving Nonnumeric Problems
This flowchart shows the steps for solving a nonnumeric problem.

Analyze
Identify the relevant concepts and make a plan.
Solve
Apply the concepts to the problem.

1.4 LessonCheck

Key Concept Check

25. **Review** What are the two general steps needed to solve a problem?

26. **List** What are the three steps for solving problems with numbers?

27. **List** What are the two steps for solving problems without numbers?

Think Critically

28. **Compare and Contrast** How are the processes for solving numeric and nonnumeric problems similar? In what way are they different?

29. **Calculate** Read the following problem and then answer the questions: "There are 3600 seconds in one hour. How many seconds are there in one day?"

- **a.** What is the known? What is the unknown?
- **b.** What relationship between the known and unknown do you need to solve the problem?
- **c.** What is the answer to the problem?
- **d.** Does your answer make sense? Explain why or why not.

CHEMISTRY & YOU

30. Pick a game you like to play or a puzzle you enjoy solving. How does having a plan make playing the game or solving the puzzle easier? (Hint: See page 17.)

Accidental Chemistry

Chemists usually do research with a certain goal in mind. However, scientists sometimes accidentally stumble upon a discovery that they did not intend to find.

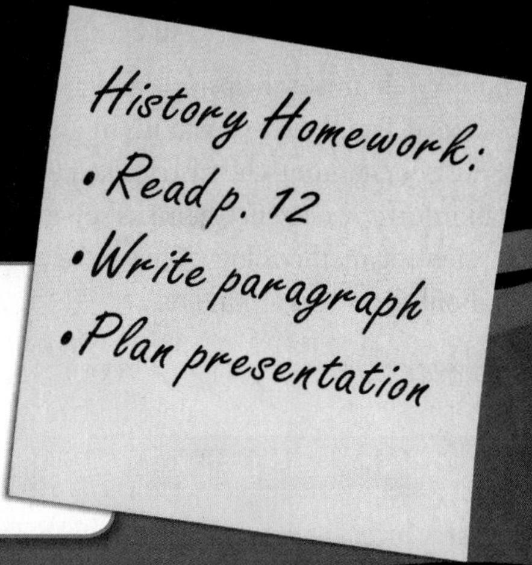

History Homework:
• Read p. 12
• Write paragraph
• Plan presentation

Sticky Notes In 1968, a chemist named Spencer Silver made a glue, or adhesive. The problem was, it was only slight sticky. In 1974, his coworker, Art Fry, was singing in his church choir. He thought that the adhesive would be great for making bookmarks to mark his songbook.

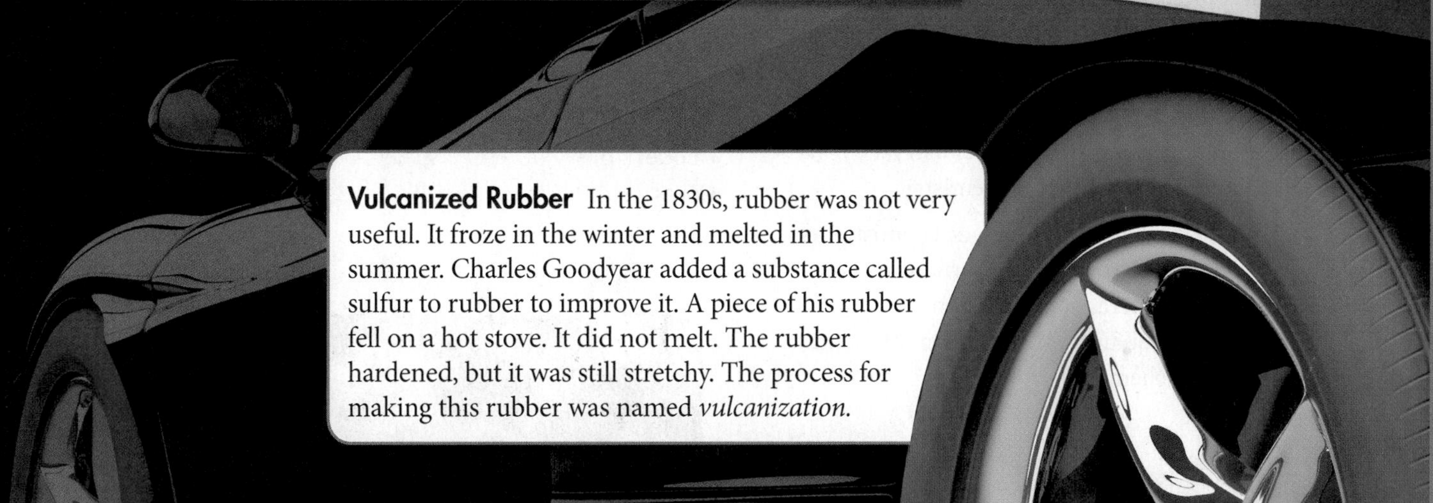

Vulcanized Rubber In the 1830s, rubber was not very useful. It froze in the winter and melted in the summer. Charles Goodyear added a substance called sulfur to rubber to improve it. A piece of his rubber fell on a hot stove. It did not melt. The rubber hardened, but it was still stretchy. The process for making this rubber was named *vulcanization.*

Sugar Substitute

Saccharin In 1879, Constantine Fahlberg was looking for new ways to use coal tar. One day, he forgot to wash his hands after work. Later, he noticed that his bread tasted sweet. The sweet taste came from his hands. The material on his hands was saccharine.

Take It Further

1. Identify Coal tar contains carbon. What type of chemistry was Fahlberg doing?

2. Form an Opinion Are the inventions described examples of technology? Explain why or why not.

1 Study Guide

BIGIDEA
CHEMISTRY AS THE CENTRAL SCIENCE

Understanding chemistry helps you understand other areas of science. People in many kinds of jobs use chemistry. Understanding chemistry also helps you to become an informed citizen. Chemists solve problems by using scientific methodology. They develop theories about the world around us.

1.1 The Scope of Chemistry

Chemistry affects all parts of life as well as most things in nature. All living and nonliving things are composed of matter.

Five traditional areas of study are organic chemistry, inorganic chemistry, biochemistry, analytical chemistry, and physical chemistry.

Some big ideas in chemistry include chemistry as the central science; electrons and the structure of atoms; bonding and interactions; reactions; kinetic theory; the mole and quantifying matter; matter and energy; and carbon chemistry.

- matter (4)
- chemistry (4)
- organic chemistry (5)
- inorganic chemistry (5)
- biochemistry (5)
- analytical chemistry (5)
- physical chemistry (5)

1.2 Chemistry and You

Chemistry helps explain the natural world, prepare people for careers, and produce informed citizens.

Modern research in chemistry leads to technologies that help the environment, conserve and produce energy, improve our lives, and help us learn more about the universe.

- technology (9)

1.3 Thinking Like a Scientist

Lavoisier helped change chemistry from a science of observation to the science of measurement that it is today.

Scientific methodology involves making observations, proposing and testing hypotheses, and developing theories.

When scientists communicate and work together, a successful outcome is more likely.

- scientific methodology (12)
- observation (12)
- hypothesis (13)
- experiment (13)
- independent variable (13)
- dependent variable (13)
- model (13)
- theory (14)
- scientific law (14)

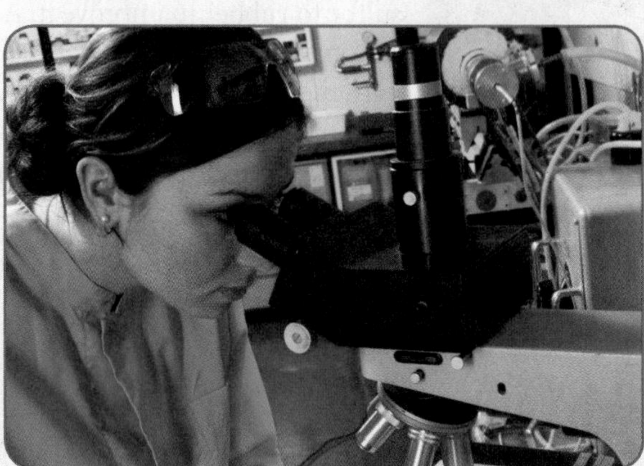

1.4 Problem Solving in Chemistry

Creating a plan and then following that plan helps you solve a problem effectively.

The steps for solving a numeric word problem are analyze, calculate, and evaluate.

The steps for solving a nonnumeric problem are analyze and solve.

1 Assessment

★ Solutions appear in Appendix D

Lesson by Lesson

1.1 The Scope of Chemistry

31. Explain why air is classified as matter.

★**32.** The Chinese characters for chemistry literally mean "change study." Why are these appropriate characters to represent chemistry?

33. Describe the main difference between inorganic chemistry and organic chemistry.

1.2 Chemistry and You

★**34.** Why would a firefighter or a reporter need to understand chemistry?

35. How do chemists help medical doctors treat patients?

★**36.** How can scientists study what distant stars are made of?

1.3 Thinking Like a Scientist

★**37.** What is the most powerful tool that any scientist can have?

38. What is the purpose of an experiment?

★**39.** Which of the following is not involved in scientific methodology?

a. hypothesis
b. experiment
c. guess
d. theory

40. How is an independent variable different from a dependent variable?

★**41.** You perform an experiment and get unexpected results. According to scientific methodology, what should you do next?

42. List two general reasons why scientists are likely to collaborate.

1.4 Problem Solving in Chemistry

★**43.** Identify the statements that correctly describe good problem solvers.

a. read a problem only once
b. check their work
c. look up missing facts
d. look for relationships among the data

44. What do effective problem-solving strategies have in common?

45. In which step of the three-step problem-solving approach for numeric problems is a problem-solving strategy developed?

46. If your heart beats at an average rate of 72 times per minute, how many times will your heart beat in an hour? How many times will your heart beat in a day?

★**47.** How many days would it take you to count a million pennies if you could count one penny each second?

Understand Concepts

★**48.** Match each area of chemistry with a numbered statement.

a. physical chemistry
b. organic chemistry
c. analytical chemistry
d. inorganic chemistry
e. biochemistry

(1) measure the level of lead in blood
(2) study non-carbon-based chemicals in rocks
(3) investigate changes that occur as food is digested in the stomach
(4) study carbon-based chemicals in coal
(5) explain the energy transfer that occurs when ice melts

49. Explain why chemistry might be useful in a career you are thinking of pursuing.

50. Describe a situation in which you used at least two steps in scientific methodology to solve a problem.

Think Critically

*51. **Calculate** Four beakers have a total weight of 2.0 lb. Each beaker weighs 0.5 lb. Describe two different methods you could use to calculate the weight of two beakers. Then, try both methods and compare the answers.

*52. **Interpret Diagrams** The air you breathe is about 20 percent oxygen and 80 percent nitrogen. Use your problem-solving skills to decide which drawing best represents a sample of air and then explain your choice.

a.
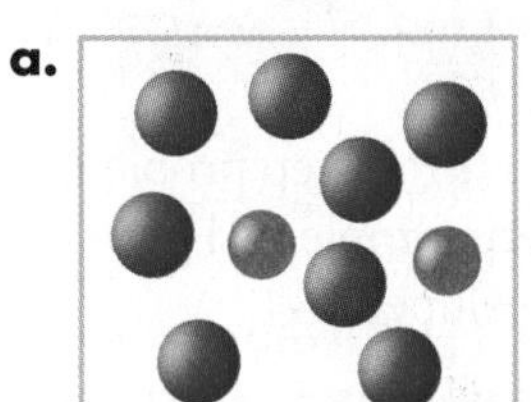

c.
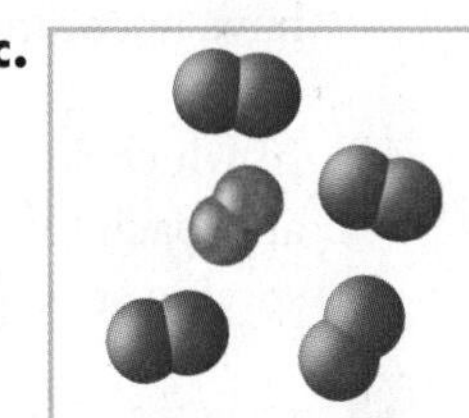

b.
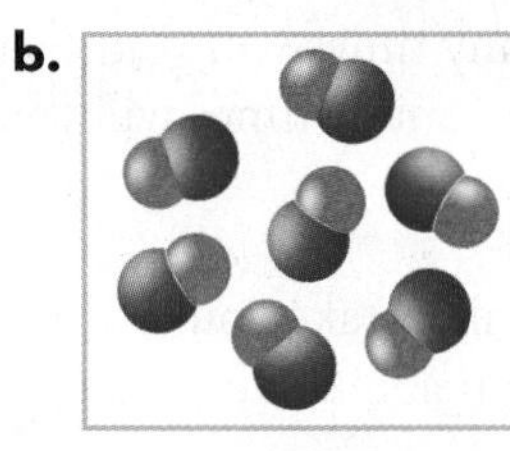

d.

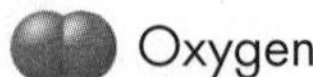

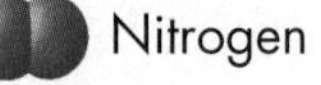

FOUNDATIONS Wrap-Up

Stirring Up Chemistry

1. **Draw Conclusions** At the beginning of this chapter, you mixed food coloring into water. Explain what this activity had to do with chemistry.

Concept Check

Now that you have finished studying Chapter 1, answer these questions. Use your own words.

2. What kind of chemist would test the water in a lake to see if it were polluted?
3. Why would you study chemistry if you wanted to be an astronaut?
4. You notice that sugar dissolves faster in hot tea than it does in iced tea. What step of the scientific method are you using?
5. Explain the steps you would take to solve a problem that uses numbers.

Write About Science

53. **Explain** Pick one activity that you can do faster or with less effort because of technology. Write a paragraph in which you describe the activity, identify the technology, and explain how the technology affects the activity.

54. **Relate Cause and Effect** Write a paragraph that explains how you can learn about the research that is done by scientists. Then, explain how this information could help you be an informed citizen.

CHEMYSTERY

Is Bio Better?

When you return home from the store, you go online to search for "bioplastics." You learn that the products you found at the store were most likely made from polylactic acid (PLA). You like that PLA products come from natural resources, such as corn, and that less energy is used in making PLA than other plastics. However, you are concerned that it would be difficult to find a facility that would be able to compost the cups and utensils when you and your friends are finished with them.

*55. **Relate Cause and Effect** What factors will affect your decision as to whether to purchase the picnic products made from PLA? Explain your answer.

56. **Connect to the BIGIDEA** How would a knowledge of chemistry help you make an informed decision?

Standardized Test Prep

For help with answering test questions, go to your Chemistry Skills and Math Workbook.

Select the choice that best answers each question or completes each statement.

1. The branch of chemistry that studies chemicals containing carbon is ______ chemistry.
   (A) physical
   (B) inorganic
   (C) analytical
   (D) organic
2. An analytical chemist is most likely to
   (A) explain why paint is stirred before it is used.
   (B) explain what keeps paint attached to the steel frame of an automobile.
   (C) identify the type of paint chips found at the scene of a hit-and-run accident.
   (D) investigate the effect of leaded paint on the development of a young child.
3. Chemists who work in the biotechnology field are most likely to work with
   (A) X-ray technicians.
   (B) geologists.
   (C) physicians.
   (D) physicists.

Read the following conversion problem and then answer Questions 4–6.

A basketball player made 3 out of every 7 shots attempted last season. If the player attempted 350 shots during the season, how many baskets did she make?

4. What are the knowns and the unknown?
5. What is the answer to the problem?
6. Does your answer make sense? Explain.

Use the flowchart to answer Question 7.

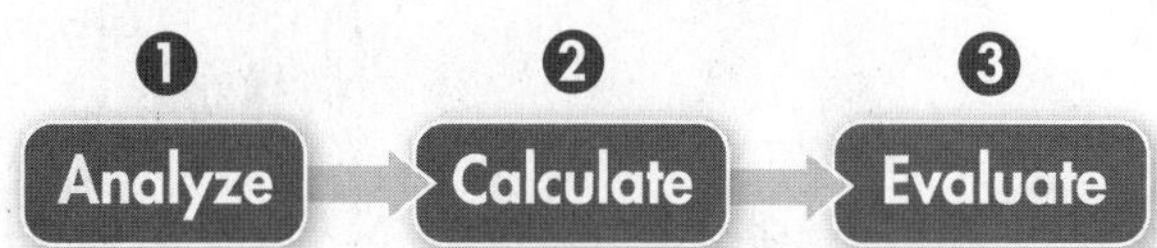

7. What should you do before you calculate an answer to a numeric problem, and what should you do after you calculate the answer?

Use this paragraph to answer Questions 8–10.

(A) One day, your car does not start. **(B)** You say, "The battery is dead!" **(C)** Your friend uses a battery tester and finds that the battery has a full charge. **(D)** Your friend sees corrosion on the battery terminals. **(E)** Your friend says, "Maybe corrosion is causing a bad connection in the electrical circuit, preventing the car from starting." **(F)** Your friend cleans the terminals, and the car starts.

8. Which statements are observations?
9. Which statements are hypotheses?
10. Which statements describe experiments?

Tips for Success

True-False Questions When the word *because* is placed between two statements, you must first decide if the statements are both true, both false, or if one statement is true and the other false. If both are true, you must decide if the second statement is a correct explanation for the first.

For each question, there are two statements. Decide whether each statement is true or false. Then, decide whether Statement II is a correct explanation for Statement I.

	Statement I		Statement II
11.	A hypothesis may be rejected after an experiment.	BECAUSE	Experiments are used to test hypotheses.
12.	Theories help you make mental models of objects that cannot be seen.	BECAUSE	Theories summarize the results of many observations and experiments.
13.	All Internet sites that provide scientific information are equally reliable.	BECAUSE	All information on these sites is reviewed by qualified scientists.

If You Have Trouble With . . .

Question	1	2	3	4	5	6	7	8	9	10	11	12	13
See Lesson	1.1	1.1	1.2	1.4	1.4	1.4	1.4	1.3	1.3	1.3	1.3	1.3	1.3

2 Matter and Change

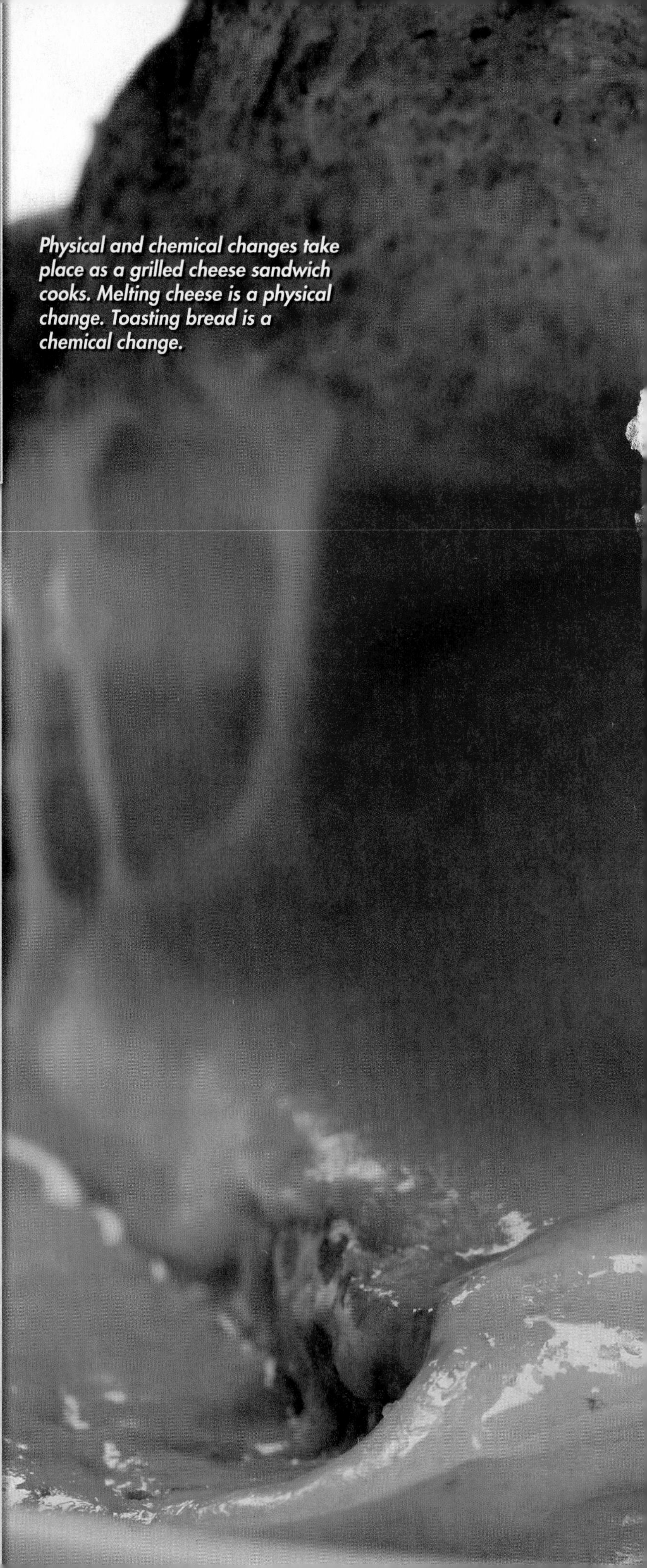

Physical and chemical changes take place as a grilled cheese sandwich cooks. Melting cheese is a physical change. Toasting bread is a chemical change.

FOUNDATIONS for Learning

Classifying Matter

1. Use a self-adhesive label and pen to label two clear containers "Baking Soda" and "Flour."
2. Add half a cup of water to each container.
3. Add half a teaspoon of baking soda to one container. Add half a teaspoon of flour to the other container. Do not stir the mixtures. Record what you observe.
4. Use a stirring rod to stir both mixtures for 45 seconds. Record what you observe.

Form a Hypothesis Explain whether mixing the solids and water caused a change.

PearsonChem.com

UntamedScience™

Take a video field trip with the Untamed Science crew to find out how old tires can be recycled both physically and chemically.

BIGIDEA

CHEMISTRY AS THE CENTRAL SCIENCE

Essential Questions:

1. *What properties are used to describe matter?*
2. *How can matter change its form?*

CHEMYSTERY

Which One Is Not Like the Others?

There are more than 300 geysers in Yellowstone National Park. Water and steam shoot out of the ground when a geyser erupts.

The bottoms of glaciers go through melting and freezing cycles in Glacier National Park. These cycles produce valleys that are scoured into a U-shape. These valleys lie between steep sides of earth.

The leaves on the trees change color each fall in Acadia National Park. The leaves go from green to red, orange, or yellow.

All three of these sights are amazing to see. They all result from changes. Are they physical or chemical changes? One of them is not like the others. But which one is different and why?

▶ Connect to the **BIGIDEA** As you read about matter, think about how matter is altered by physical and chemical changes.

2.1 Properties of Matter

CHEMISTRY & YOU

Q: Why are windows made of glass? You look through windows every day at home or at school. Most windows are made of glass. Glass is transparent, meaning you can see through it. Glass is smooth and hard. It is also easy to shatter. Transparency, smoothness, and hardness are properties of glass. In this lesson, you will learn how properties can be used to classify and identify matter.

Key Questions

Why do all samples of a substance have the same intensive properties?

What are three states of matter?

How can physical changes be classified?

BUILD Vocabulary

mass the amount of matter in an object

volume the amount of space an object takes up

extensive property a property that depends on the amount of matter

intensive property a property that depends on the type of matter, not the amount

RELATED WORD FORMS

The word *extent* means "a range." You can think of extensive properties as having a range of values that depend on the amount of matter.

Describing Matter

What properties do you observe when you examine matter? Is a solid hard or soft? Is a liquid clear or cloudy? Does a gas have an odor or not? The properties used to describe matter can be classified as either extensive or intensive properties.

Extensive Properties Matter is anything that has mass and takes up space. **Mass** is a measure of the amount of matter in an object. The watering can in the picture below has more matter than the soda can does. So the mass of the watering can is greater than the mass of the soda can. The **volume** of an object is a measure of the space the object takes up. The watering can takes up more space than the soda can does. So the watering can has a greater volume. Mass and volume are both examples of extensive properties. An **extensive property** is a property that depends on the amount of matter in a sample.

Intensive Properties The watering can and the soda can are made of different materials. The soda can is mostly aluminum. The watering can is mostly copper. Each of these materials has different properties. Aluminum is silver in color. Copper is reddish-yellow. Color is an example of an intensive property. An **intensive property** is a property that depends on the type of matter in a sample. An intensive property does not depend on the amount of matter in the sample.

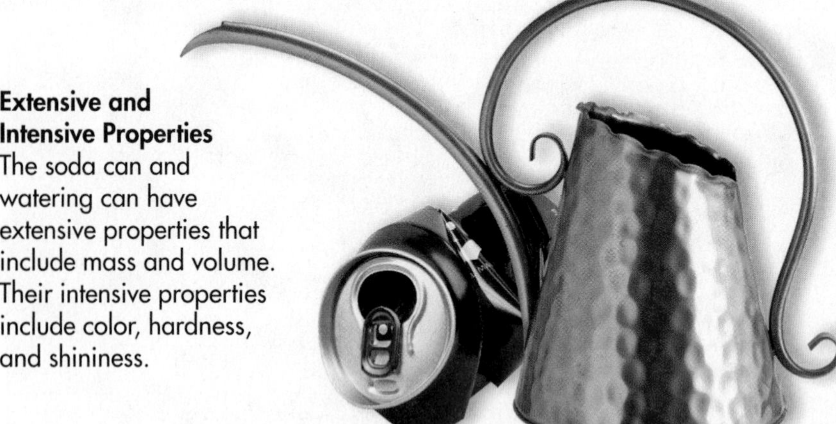

Extensive and Intensive Properties
The soda can and watering can have extensive properties that include mass and volume. Their intensive properties include color, hardness, and shininess.

Identifying a Substance The soda can and the watering can have different chemical makeups, or compositions. Matter that has a uniform and definite composition is called a **substance.** Aluminum and copper are examples of substances. Substances are sometimes called pure substances. Every sample of a substance has the same intensive properties. For example, a copper watering can has the same intensive properties as a piece of copper wire.

Aluminum and copper share some properties. They are both malleable, which means they can be hammered into sheets without breaking. They are also both shiny. Aluminum and copper have some different properties. They are different in color. Pure copper is harder than pure aluminum. Copper is a better conductor of heat and electricity than aluminum. Malleability, shininess, color, hardness, and conductivity are physical properties. A **physical property** is a quality or condition of a substance that can be observed or measured without changing the substance's composition.

The table below lists some physical properties for a few substances. The table shows the state of each substance at room temperature, the color of each substance, and the melting and boiling points. Physical properties can help you to identify substances. Notice that water is a colorless liquid at room temperature that boils at 100°C and melts at 0°C. Could a liquid that boils at 78°C and melts at −117°C be water? No, it has different properties from water. According to the table, this substance is ethanol.

Key Question Why do all samples of a substance have the same intensive properties? **Every sample of a given substance has identical intensive properties because every sample has the same composition.**

substance matter that has a uniform and definite composition

physical property a property that can be observed or measured without changing the identity of the substance

WORD ORIGINS

The word *substance* comes from a Latin word that means "material." A substance is made of material.

Identifying Substances This table shows properties that can be used to help identify substances.

Go to your Chemistry Skills and Math Workbook to practice interpreting tables.

Physical Properties of Some Substances

Substance	State	Color	Melting point (°C)	Boiling point (°C)
Neon	Gas	Colorless	−249	−246
Oxygen	Gas	Colorless	−218	−183
Chlorine	Gas	Greenish-yellow	−101	−34
Ethanol	Liquid	Colorless	−117	78
Mercury	Liquid	Silvery-white	−39	357
Bromine	Liquid	Reddish-brown	−7	59
Water	Liquid	Colorless	0	100
Sulfur	Solid	Yellow	115	445
Aluminum	Solid	Silver	660	2519
Sodium chloride	Solid	White	801	1413
Gold	Solid	Yellow	1064	2856
Copper	Solid	Reddish-yellow	1084	2562

BUILD Vocabulary

solid matter that has a definite shape and volume

liquid matter that has a definite volume but not a definite shape

gas matter that does not have a definite shape or volume

vapor the gaseous state of a substance that is a liquid or solid at room temperature

physical change a change in the properties of a substance that does not change the composition of the substance

MULTIPLE MEANINGS

In chemistry, the word *state* refers to the form of matter. In everyday life, you probably think of a state as one of the areas that make up the United States.

States of Matter

What words can you use to describe water? You might use ice, water, and steam. These words describe three different physical states of water. Ice is solid water. Water that flows and feels wet is a liquid. Steam is vaporized water. It is produced when water boils. Like water, most substances can be in three states. These three states of matter have certain characteristics. The figure to the right shows a model of each state of matter.

Solids A **solid** is a form of matter that has a definite shape and volume. Its shape does not depend on the shape of its container. The particles in a solid are packed together tightly, often in an orderly way. As a result, solids are almost incompressible. They cannot be easily squeezed into a smaller volume. Solids also expand only slightly when heated.

Liquids The particles in a liquid are in close contact with one another. However, they are not held together in a rigid or orderly way. Particles in a liquid flow from one place to another. This is why a liquid takes the shape of its container. The volume of the liquid does not change as its shape changes. A **liquid** is a form of matter that has a definite volume but not a definite shape. Liquids are almost incompressible. Most liquids expand slightly when heated.

Gases Like a liquid, a gas takes the shape of its container. However, a gas can expand to fill any volume. A **gas** is a form of matter that does not have a definite shape or volume. The particles in a gas are often much farther apart than the particles in a liquid. Because of the space between particles, gases are easily compressed into a smaller volume. The table below compares the three states of matter.

The word vapor is sometimes used to mean gas. But these two words have different meanings. The term *gas* is used for substances like oxygen that exist in the gaseous state at room temperature. (Gaseous is the adjective form of gas.) **Vapor** describes the gaseous state of a substance that is usually a solid or a liquid at room temperature, like water vapor.

Key Question What are three states of matter? **Three states of matter are solid, liquid, and gas.**

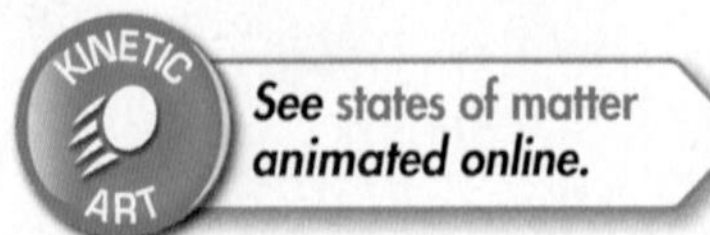

KINETIC ART
See states of matter animated online.

Properties of Solids, Liquids, and Gases

	Solids	Liquids	Gases
Fixed shape	Yes	No	No
Fixed volume	Yes	Yes	No
Space between particles	Touching	Small	Large
Particle movement	Fixed	Flowing	Free
Compressible	No	No	Yes
Expands when heated	Slightly	Slightly	Yes

Solid Particles are packed closely together so that they form a definite shape.

Liquid Particles are close together, but they can flow freely past one another.

Gas Particles are far apart and can move freely.

Physical Changes

The state of ice changes when ice melts, but ice and water are the same substance. Melting is a physical change. A **physical change** alters some properties of a material, but it does not change the composition of the material.

Physical changes can be classified as reversible or irreversible. Words such as freeze, melt, and condense are used to describe reversible physical changes. If you cool liquid water below its melting point, it will turn into ice. If you warm the ice above its melting point, it will change back into a liquid. Changes of state are physical changes that are reversible. Words such as tear, break, cut, and crush describe irreversible physical changes. When you break an egg or a window, you can't put it back together.

Key Question How can physical changes be classified? **They can be classified as reversible or irreversible.**

BUILD Connections

You've probably seen your breath fog up a windshield. This can happen easily if it's cold outside. Water vapor in your breath condenses and changes to water droplets. If the air inside the car is warm, the droplets quickly change back to water vapor.

2.1 LessonCheck

Key Concept Check

1. **Review** Explain why all samples of a given substance have the same intensive properties.
2. **Identify** Name three states of matter.
3. **Describe** Describe the two categories used to classify physical changes.

Think Critically

4. **Compare and Contrast** In what way are liquids and gases alike? In what way are liquids and solids different from one another?

CHEMISTRY & YOU

5. Glass is used to make windows. Copper is used to make electrical wires. What properties of glass make it useful for windows? Why wouldn't you use copper to make windows? (Hint: See page 29.)

BIGIDEA
CHEMISTRY AS THE CENTRAL SCIENCE

6. How is understanding the properties of matter helpful in fields other than chemistry?

2.2 Mixtures

CHEMISTRY & YOU

Q: Why aren't there coffee grounds in a cup of coffee? Coffee is often brewed by mixing hot water with ground coffee beans. But how are grounds kept out of a coffee cup? In this lesson, you will learn how to classify and separate mixtures.

Key Questions

How can mixtures be classified?

How can mixtures be separated?

BUILD Vocabulary

mixture a physical blend of two or more parts

heterogeneous mixture a mixture that has a composition that is not uniform

homogeneous mixture a mixture that has a uniform composition

solution a homogeneous mixture

phase the part of a sample with a uniform composition

PREFIXES

The prefix *hetero-* means "different." One part of a heterogeneous mixture is different from another part of the mixture. The prefix *homo-* means "the same." Every part of a homogeneous mixture is the same as every other part of the mixture.

Classifying Mixtures

You can find lettuce, tomatoes, cheese, green peppers, and many other items at a salad bar like the one below. You can choose which foods you want in your salad and how much of each food to add. When complete, your salad mixture will probably have several different types and amounts of food. A **mixture** is a physical blend of two or more components, or parts.

Most types of matter that you see are mixtures. Some mixtures are easier to recognize than others. It is easy to see that chicken noodle soup is a mixture of chicken, noodles, and broth. It is harder to see that air is a mixture of gases. Chicken noodle soup and air represent two different types of mixtures—heterogeneous mixtures and homogeneous mixtures.

Heterogeneous Mixtures The ingredients in the chicken noodle soup are not evenly distributed throughout the mixture. There are usually different amounts of chicken and noodles in each spoonful. A mixture that does not have a uniform composition throughout is a **heterogeneous mixture.**

Salads Are Mixtures You can choose the amount of each item you want from a salad bar. Your salad is unlikely to have the same composition as other salads containing the same items.

Two Types of Mixtures Olive oil and vinegar are homogeneous mixtures. Mixing olive oil and vinegar forms a heterogeneous mixture with two distinct phases.

Homogeneous Mixtures The olive oil in the figure above does not look like a mixture, but it is. It is made of substances that are evenly spread throughout the mixture. The same is true for the vinegar. Olive oil and vinegar are homogeneous mixtures. A **homogeneous mixture** is a mixture that has a uniform composition throughout. Another name for a homogeneous mixture is a **solution.** Many solutions are liquids. Some are gases, like air. Others are solids, like steel.

The term **phase** is used to describe any part of a sample with uniform composition and properties. A homogeneous mixture has a single phase. A heterogeneous mixture has at least two phases. Each layer in the heterogeneous oil and vinegar mixture is a phase.

Key Question How can mixtures be classified? **Mixtures can be classified as heterogeneous mixtures or as homogeneous mixtures based on the distribution of their components.**

Quick Lab

Purpose To separate a mixture using paper chromatography

Materials

- green marking pen
- filter paper strip
- metric ruler
- clear plastic tape
- pencil
- rubbing alcohol
- clear plastic drinking cup
- clear plastic wrap

Separating Mixtures

Procedure

1. Use the marking pen to draw a line across a strip of filter paper, as shown in the picture. The line should be 2 cm from one end of the strip.
2. Tape the unmarked end of the filter paper to the center of a pencil. The strip should hang down when the pencil is held horizontally.
3. Working in a well-ventilated room, pour rubbing alcohol into a plastic cup to a depth of 1 cm.
4. Rest the pencil on the cup. The strip should touch the alcohol's surface, but the ink should not. Cover the cup with plastic wrap.
5. Observe the setup for 15 minutes.

Analyze and Conclude

1. **Identify** How did the appearance of the filter paper change during the procedure?
2. **Analyze Data** What evidence is there that green ink is a mixture?
3. **Apply Concepts** How could you use this procedure to identify an unknown type of green ink?

filtration a process that separates a solid from a liquid in a heterogeneous mixture

distillation a process that separates a liquid from a mixture by boiling

WORD ORIGINS

The word *distill* comes from the Latin word *distillare,* meaning "to trickle down in small drops."

Separating Mixtures

You can use a fork to remove the parts you do not like in a salad. Many mixtures are not as easy to separate. Consider a mixture of oil and vinegar. You might have noticed that oil floats on vinegar. To separate this mixture, you can carefully pour off the oil layer. You can also separate the parts by cooling the mixture. Since oil and vinegar freeze at different temperatures, you can remove the frozen part from the liquid part.

Filtration A coffee filter separates ground coffee beans from brewed coffee. The liquid coffee passes through the paper filter. The solid coffee grounds stay in the filter because they are too big to pass through. The filter paper used to separate mixtures in laboratories is like a coffee filter. A mixture is poured into a funnel lined with filter paper. Solid particles that are too big to go through the filter stay in the funnel. The liquid passes through the filter paper. The process that separates a solid from a liquid in a heterogeneous mixture is called **filtration.**

Distillation Tap water is a homogeneous mixture of water and dissolved substances. Distillation is one way to separate the water from these other substances. During a **distillation,** a liquid is boiled to produce a vapor that is then condensed back into a liquid. The figure below shows a distillation. Tap water is heated to make water vapor. Pure water is collected at the end. The substances dissolved in tap water have much higher boiling points than the water itself. These substances are left behind in the distillation flask.

Key Question How can mixtures be separated? **Differences in physical properties can be used to separate mixtures.**

Distillation

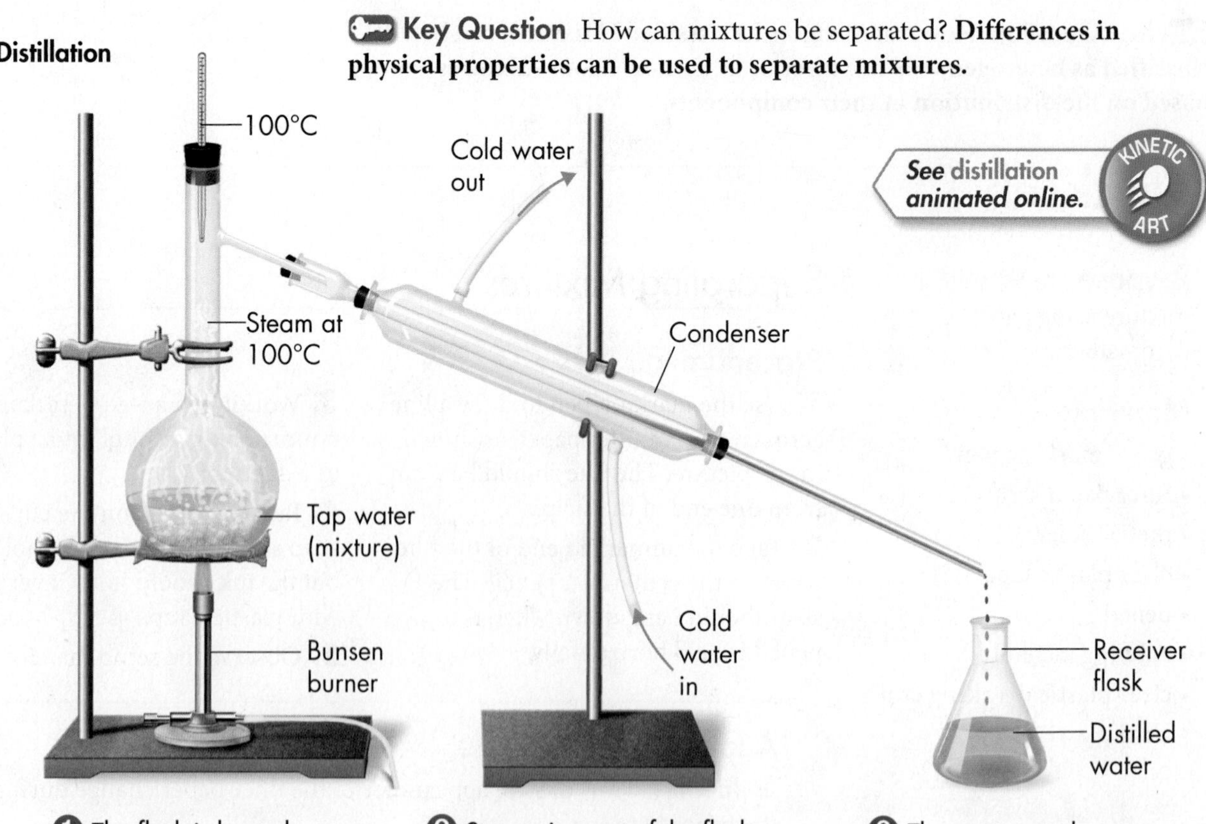

❶ The flask is heated. Liquid water changes into water vapor. The other substances in the tap water stay in the flask.

❷ Steam rises out of the flask and flows into a glass tube in the condenser. Cold water is piped into the condenser around this tube to cool the steam.

❸ The steam condenses on the inside of the glass tube. This liquid water drips into the receiver flask. The water is now distilled.

Sample Problem 2.1

Separating a Heterogeneous Mixture

How could a mixture of aluminum nails and iron nails be separated?

❶ Analyze Identify the relevant concepts. You need to know properties of both aluminum and iron to find a way to separate the nails.

❷ Solve Apply concepts to this situation.

List the properties of each substance in the mixture.

Aluminum	Iron
• metal	• metal
• gray color	• gray color
• doesn't dissolve in water	• doesn't dissolve in water
• not attracted to magnet	• attracted to magnet

Identify a property that can be used to separate the different substances from one another.

Iron is attracted to a magnet. Aluminum is not attracted to a magnet. You could use a magnet to remove the iron nails from a mixture of iron and aluminum.

Practice Problem

7. Air is mainly a mixture of nitrogen and oxygen, with small amounts of other gases such as argon and carbon dioxide. What property could you use to separate the gases in air?

2.2 LessonCheck

Key Concept Check

8. Identify How are mixtures classified?

9. List What type of properties can be used to separate mixtures?

Vocabulary Check *Choose a highlighted word from the lesson to complete the sentence correctly.*

10. A mixture with an uneven distribution of parts is a(n) ________.

Think Critically

11. Compare and Contrast How are a substance and a solution similar? How are they different?

12. What process is used to separate ground coffee beans from brewed coffee? (Hint: See page 34.)

BIGIDEA CHEMISTRY AS THE CENTRAL SCIENCE

13. Give three examples of mixtures you have separated at home and explain how you separated them.

2.3 Elements and Compounds

CHEMISTRY & YOU

Q: Why does burned toast taste so bad? Bread that is toasted to a nice golden brown color can be a tasty part of breakfast. But most people would agree that bread that is burned and black tastes bad. There is a fine line between toasting or grilling food and burning it. Adding intense heat causes some compounds in foods to break down to their simpler chemical building blocks.

Key Questions

How are elements and compounds different?

How can substances and mixtures be distinguished?

What do chemists use to represent elements and compounds?

Why is a periodic table useful?

element the simplest form of matter that has a unique set of properties

compound a substance that contains two or more elements that are chemically combined

chemical change a change that results in a substance with a different composition

MULTIPLE MEANINGS

You might have heard your English teacher use the word *compound* to describe words. For example, *basketball* is a compound word made up of the words *basket* and *ball*. Similarly, chemical compounds are made up of at least two or more elements.

Distinguishing Elements and Compounds

Substances can be classified as elements or compounds. An **element** is the simplest form of matter that has a unique set of properties. Oxygen and hydrogen are two of more than 100 known elements. Elements cannot be broken down into simpler substances. Compounds, however, can be broken down into simpler substances.

Compounds A **compound** is a substance that contains two or more elements that are chemically combined. The elements in a compound are combined in a fixed proportion. One example of a compound is sucrose, or table sugar. Carbon, oxygen, and hydrogen are chemically combined in table sugar. Every sample of table sugar contains twice as much hydrogen as oxygen. This means that the proportion of hydrogen to oxygen is fixed.

Chemical Change Physical methods cannot break compounds into simpler substances. For example, the act of boiling water cannot break the water into oxygen and hydrogen. Physical methods cannot cause a chemical change. A **chemical change** is a change that produces matter with a different composition than that of the original matter.

Chemical Change

❶ Adding too much heat to table sugar causes a chemical change.

❷ The table sugar reacts with oxygen in air to form carbon dioxide, water, and solid carbon.

When a compound breaks into simpler substances, a chemical change takes place. Heating can break down some compounds into simpler substances. The pictures on the previous page show how you can heat a layer of sugar in a pan until the sugar breaks down into solid carbon, carbon dioxide, and water vapor. Can these new substances also be broken down?

Carbon cannot break down any further because it is an element. Heat will not cause water to break down, but electricity will. When electricity passes through water, oxygen and hydrogen are produced.

Properties of Compounds The properties of a compound are often very different from those of the elements that make it up. For example, sugar is a sweet-tasting white solid made of carbon, hydrogen, and oxygen. Carbon is a black solid that has no taste. Hydrogen is a gas that burns in the presence of oxygen. Oxygen is a colorless gas that you breathe. The figure below shows some properties of the elements sodium and chlorine. You would not want to handle either element. Sodium is a soft, gray metal that reacts violently with water. Chlorine is a pale, yellow-green, poisonous gas. However, when combined, these elements make table salt, a white solid you can eat.

Key Question How are elements and compounds different? **Compounds can be broken down into simpler substances by chemical means, but elements cannot.**

BUILD Understanding

T-Chart Make a T-chart for elements and compounds. In the left column, write Elements. In the right column, write Compounds. Use this chart to compare these two classes of substances.

Comparing Properties of Elements and Compounds

Sodium
The vapor of this element produces the light in some street lamps.

Chlorine
This element can be used to kill harmful organisms in swimming pools.

Sodium chloride
This compound is used to season and preserve food.

Distinguishing Substances and Mixtures

Can you tell if a sample of matter is a substance or a mixture based only on how it looks? That could be difficult. After all, homogeneous mixtures and substances both appear to be made of only one kind of matter. Sometimes you can decide by thinking about whether there is more than one kind of the material in question. For example, you can buy whole milk, low fat milk, skim milk, light cream, or heavy cream. You could conclude that milk and cream are mixtures because there are many different kinds. You might infer that these mixtures are different because they contain different amounts of fat.

You can use the general characteristics of substances and mixtures to tell them apart. The flowchart below shows how to tell if matter is an element, compound, or mixture.

Key Question How can substances and mixtures be distinguished? **If the composition of a material is fixed, the material is a substance. If the composition of a material may vary, the material is a mixture.**

Flowchart for Elements, Compounds, and Mixtures
The flowchart shows how you can decide whether matter is an element, compound, or mixture.

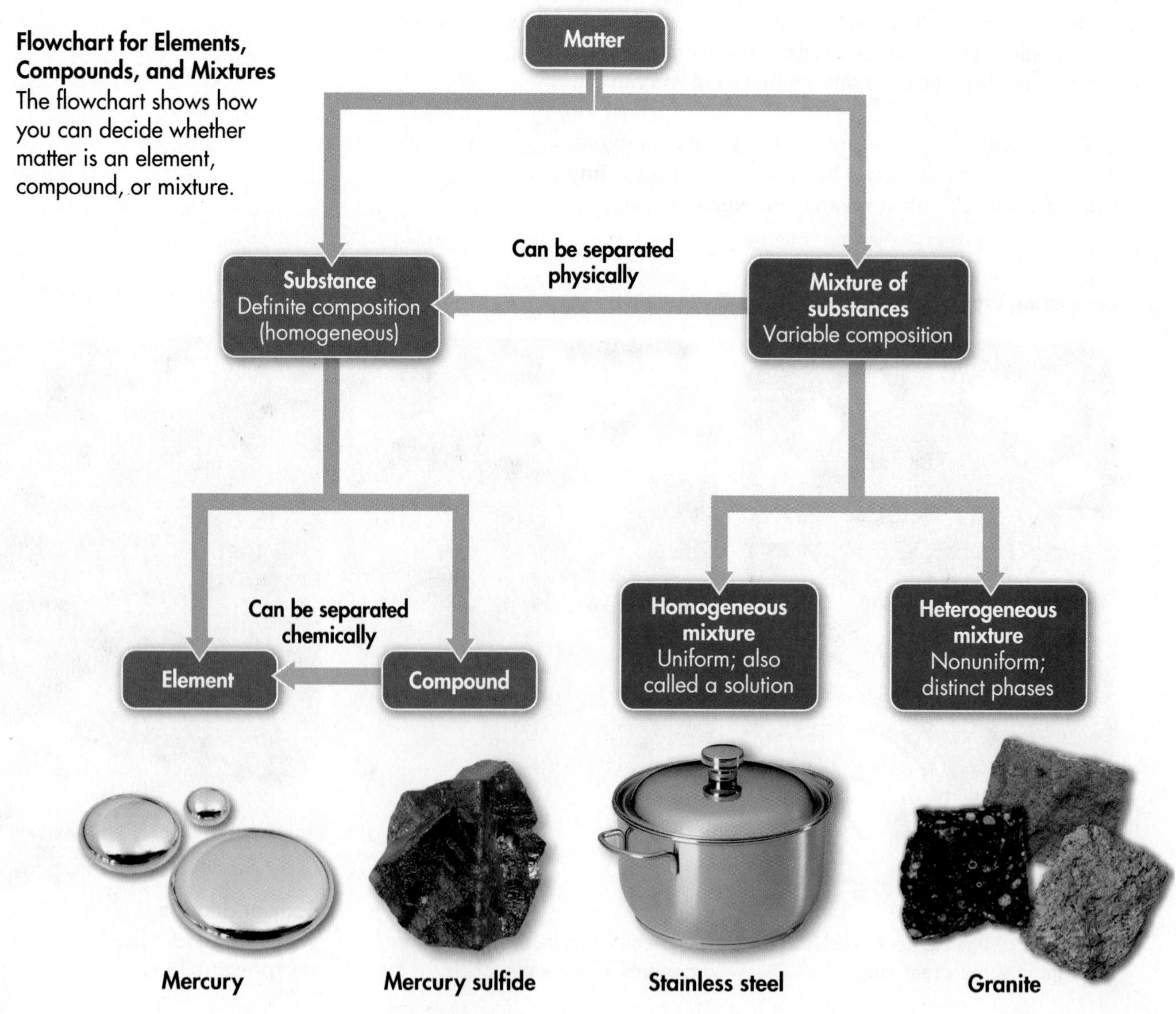

Sample Problem 2.2

Classifying Materials

When a blue-green solid is heated, a colorless gas and a black solid form. All three materials are substances. Is it possible to classify these substances as elements or compounds?

❶ Analyze Identify the relevant concepts. A compound can be broken down into simpler substances by a chemical change, but an element cannot. Heating can cause a chemical change.

A compound is made of two or more elements that are chemically combined.

❷ Solve Apply concepts to this situation.

List the known facts and important concepts.

- A blue-green solid is heated.
- A colorless gas and a black solid appear.

Determine if the substances are elements or compounds.

Blue-green solid: Two substances were produced by heating one substance. It is likely the blue-green solid was broken down. It is a compound.

Colorless gas and black solid: They could be elements or compounds. More tests are needed.

Practice Problems

14. Liquid A and Liquid B are clear liquids. They are placed in open containers and are allowed to evaporate. When evaporation is complete, there is a white solid in Container B. There is no solid in Container A. What can you infer about the two liquids?

Hint: Evaporation is a way of physically separating matter.

15. A clear liquid in an open container is allowed to evaporate. After three days, a solid is left in the container. Was the clear liquid an element, a compound, or a mixture? How do you know?

Symbols and Formulas

The names water and table salt do not tell you anything about the chemical composition of these substances. Words are not the best way to show what happens to matter during a chemical change. Chemists use chemical symbols to show the elements that make up matter.

People have used symbols to represent different kinds of matter for thousands of years. Today, each element has a **chemical symbol** that is made of one or two letters. The first letter of a chemical symbol is always capitalized. If there is a second letter, it is lowercase. Jöns Jacob Berzelius (1779–1848) thought of using letters from the Latin names of elements as symbols. The table below shows some symbols that do not match the English names of the elements.

Symbols and Latin Names for Some Elements

Name	Symbol	Latin name
Sodium	Na	*natrium*
Potassium	K	*kalium*
Antimony	Sb	*stibium*
Copper	Cu	*cuprum*
Gold	Au	*aurum*
Silver	Ag	*argentum*
Iron	Fe	*ferrum*
Lead	Pb	*plumbum*
Tin	Sn	*stannum*

Chemical symbols are a quick way to write the chemical formulas of compounds. The symbols for carbon and hydrogen are C and H. The symbol for oxygen is O. The formula shown below is for sucrose, or table sugar. The subscripts tell you how many atoms of each type of element are in each unit of the compound. The formula for a given compound is always the same.

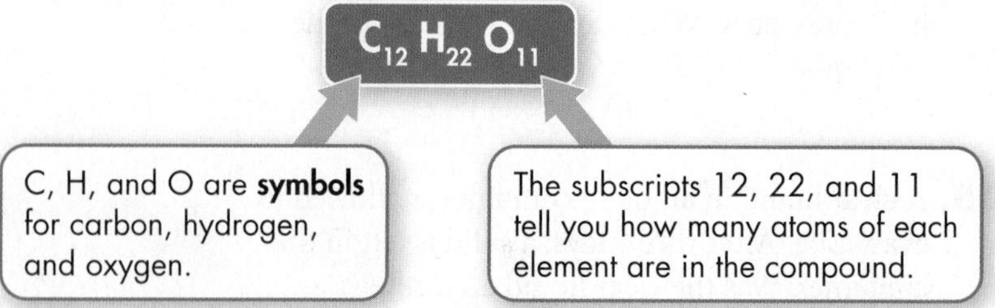

$C_{12}H_{22}O_{11}$
C, H, and O are **symbols** for carbon, hydrogen, and oxygen.
The subscripts 12, 22, and 11 tell you how many atoms of each element are in the compound.

Key Question What do chemists use to represent elements and compounds? **Chemists use chemical symbols to represent elements and chemical formulas to represent compounds.**

The Periodic Table—A Preview

All the known elements are organized in a special table called the periodic table. A **periodic table** is an arrangement of elements in which the elements are placed into groups based on their properties. You can use the periodic table to compare the properties of elements.

The figure below shows the modern periodic table. The symbol for each element is placed in a square. The atomic number for each element is placed at the top of each square. You can find that number above the symbol. The elements are listed in order of their atomic number. You can see that these numbers increase from left to right across a row. They also increase from the top to the bottom of a column. You will learn more about atomic numbers in Chapter 4. Hydrogen (H) has an atomic number of 1. This element is at the top left corner of the table. Helium (He) has an atomic number of 2. It is at the top right. You can use the atomic number or symbol to find any element in the table.

Elements are organized into periods and groups in the periodic table. Each row is a period. Each column is a group. Periods are numbered 1–7. Groups are numbered 1A–8A or 1B–8B.

chemical symbol one or two letters used to represent an element

periodic table an organized grouping of the elements

USING PRIOR KNOWLEDGE

You have probably heard the words *chemical* and *symbol* used separately. The word chemical is used to refer to substances. The word symbol is used to refer to something that represents something else. A chemical symbol is one or two letters that represent an element.

The Periodic Table Elements are arranged by atomic number in the periodic table.

Hydrogen
Symbol: H
Atomic number: 1

Helium
Symbol: He
Atomic number: 2

	1A	2A	3B	4B	5B	6B	7B	8B	8B	8B	1B	2B	3A	4A	5A	6A	7A	8A
1	1 H																	2 He
2	3 Li	4 Be											5 B	6 C	7 N	8 O	9 F	10 Ne
3	11 Na	12 Mg											13 Al	14 Si	15 P	16 S	17 Cl	18 Ar
4	19 K	20 Ca	21 Sc	22 Ti	23 V	24 Cr	25 Mn	26 Fe	27 Co	28 Ni	29 Cu	30 Zn	31 Ga	32 Ge	33 As	34 Se	35 Br	36 Kr
5	37 Rb	38 Sr	39 Y	40 Zr	41 Nb	42 Mo	43 Tc	44 Ru	45 Rh	46 Pd	47 Ag	48 Cd	49 In	50 Sn	51 Sb	52 Te	53 I	54 Xe
6	55 Cs	56 Ba	71 Lu	72 Hf	73 Ta	74 W	75 Re	76 Os	77 Ir	78 Pt	79 Au	80 Hg	81 Tl	82 Pb	83 Bi	84 Po	85 At	86 Rn
7	87 Fr	88 Ra	103 Lr	104 Rf	105 Db	106 Sg	107 Bh	108 Hs	109 Mt	110 Ds	111 Rg	112 Cn	113 Uut	114 Fl	115 Uup	116 Lv	117 Uus	118 Uuo

57 La	58 Ce	59 Pr	60 Nd	61 Pm	62 Sm	63 Eu	64 Gd	65 Tb	66 Dy	67 Ho	68 Er	69 Tm	70 Yb
89 Ac	90 Th	91 Pa	92 U	93 Np	94 Pu	95 Am	96 Cm	97 Bk	98 Cf	99 Es	100 Fm	101 Md	102 No

period a row in the periodic table

group a column in the periodic table

MULTIPLE MEANINGS

You probably think of a *period* as the amount of time you have to spend in class. It can mean "a block of time." In chemistry, period refers to rows in the periodic table. These rows have repeating, or periodic, properties.

Periods and Groups in the Periodic Table
Each row of the periodic table is called a period.
Each column is called a group.

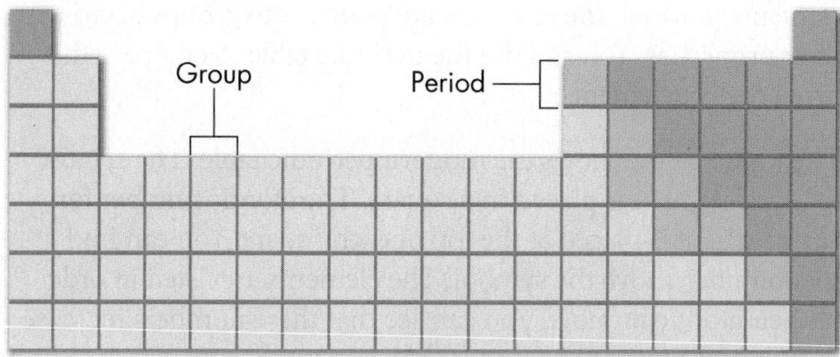

Periods Each row of the periodic table is called a **period.** The properties of the elements change as you move across each period.

Groups Each column of the periodic table is called a **group,** or family. Elements in the same group have similar chemical and physical properties. You will learn more about trends in the periodic table in Chapter 6.

Key Question Why is the periodic table useful? **The periodic table allows you to compare the properties of one element (or group of elements) to another element (or group of elements).**

2.3 LessonCheck

Key Concept Check

16. **Compare** How is a compound different from an element?

17. **Compare** How can you distinguish a substance from a mixture?

18. **Identify** What are chemical symbols and chemical formulas used for?

19. **Explain** What makes the periodic table such a useful tool?

Vocabulary Check

Choose a highlighted word from the lesson to complete the sentence correctly.

20. A(n) __________ can be broken down into simpler substances.

21. Each column of the periodic table is called a(n) __________.

Think Critically

22. **Classify** Classify each of the following as an element, compound, or mixture.
a. table sugar **b.** tap water

23. **Identify** Write the chemical symbol for each of the following elements:
a. lead **b.** silver **c.** hydrogen

24. **Identify** Name two elements that have properties similar to those of the element calcium (Ca).

CHEMISTRY & YOU

25. What happens to the compounds in bread when it is overcooked? Why does this change the taste of the bread? (Hint: See page 37.)

2.4 Chemical Reactions

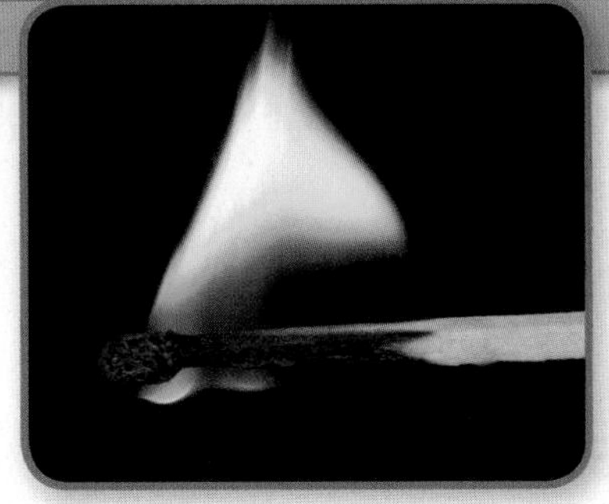

CHEMISTRY & YOU

Q: What happened to the match? Matches are often used to light candles on a birthday cake. A match is lit at the tip, and the fire burns down the match. A lit match is different from an unlit match. In this lesson, you will learn whether burning a match is a chemical change or a physical change.

Key Questions

What always happens during a chemical change?

What are four possible clues that a chemical change has taken place?

How are the mass of the reactants and the mass of the products of a chemical reaction related?

chemical property the ability of a substance to undergo a chemical change

USING PRIOR KNOWLEDGE

Properties describe the characteristics of materials. Chemical properties describe the chemical characteristics of substances.

Chemical Changes

Iron forms a new substance when it rusts. That substance is iron oxide, or Fe_2O_3. You have heard words such as rust, burn, rot, bubble, and explode. These words often mean that a chemical change is happening. The ability of a substance to undergo a specific chemical change is called a **chemical property.** For example, when iron comes in contact with oxygen, a chemical reaction occurs that forms rust. The ability to form rust is a chemical property of iron. Chemical properties can be used to identify a substance. But chemical properties can be observed only when a chemical change happens.

Physical Versus Chemical Changes The figure below compares a physical change and a chemical change. Breaking charcoal into smaller pieces is a physical change. The smaller pieces of charcoal are made of the same substances as the larger pieces. The composition of matter never changes during a physical change. The composition of matter always changes during a chemical change. A chemical change happens when the charcoal is heated and burned. The substances in the charcoal react with oxygen in the air to form other substances.

Physical and Chemical Changes

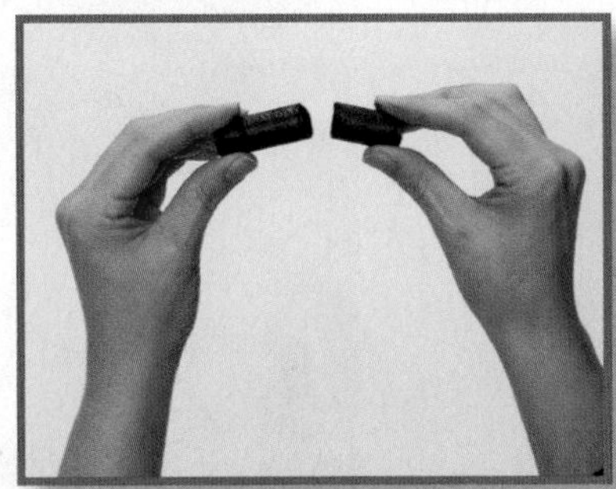

Physical Change Breaking charcoal into smaller pieces is a physical change.

Chemical Change Burning charcoal is a chemical change.

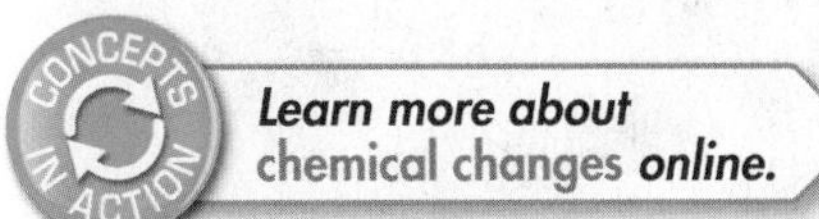

Learn more about chemical changes *online.*

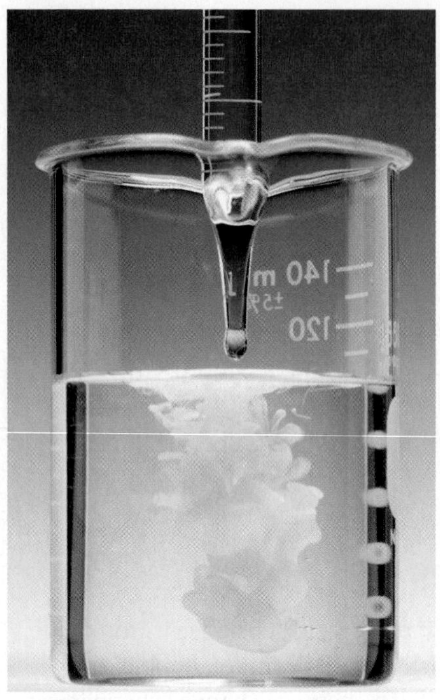

Chemical Reaction
Solid silver chloride forms when you mix solutions of silver nitrate and sodium chloride.

Chemical Reactions A chemical change is also called a chemical reaction. One or more substances change into one or more new substances during a **chemical reaction.** A substance that is present at the start of the reaction is called a **reactant.** Reactants change during the reaction. A substance that is produced during the reaction is called a **product.** The figure to the left shows a chemical reaction. A white solid forms when two clear liquids are mixed together. The liquids are solutions of silver nitrate and sodium chloride. These are the reactants. The solid is silver chloride. It is a product of the reaction.

Key Question What always happens during a chemical change? **The composition of matter always changes.**

Recognizing Chemical Changes

How can you tell whether a chemical change has taken place? There are four clues that can serve as a guide. These clues include a transfer of energy, a change in color, the formation of a precipitate, or the production of a gas.

Energy Transfer Every chemical change involves a transfer of energy. Think of what happens when you cook food. Energy stored in fuel is used to cook the food. The fuel chemically combines with oxygen in the air when the burner is lit. This reaction gives off energy as heat and light, as shown in the figure below. The food absorbs some of the heat. The energy causes chemical changes to take place in the food.

Transfer of Energy
Energy transferred from burning fuel causes these eggs to undergo a chemical change.

Signs of a Chemical Change

Color Change
A test strip is dipped in a solution. The color change is used to determine if the solution is acidic.

Formation of a Precipitate
A reaction during cheese making causes milk to separate into solid curds and liquid whey.

Production of a Gas
Bubbles of carbon dioxide gas form when antacid tablets are dropped into a glass of water.

Color Change Food may change color and brown as it cooks. A color change is another sign that chemical changes are happening. The above left figure shows a color change. A substance on the paper changes from blue to red when it is placed in the solution. It reacts with the acid in the solution.

Formation of a Precipitate You can see other clues of a chemical change when you clean a bathtub. The ring of soap scum that forms in a bathtub is a precipitate. A **precipitate** is a solid that forms when two liquids react. The above center figure shows a precipitate that forms when cheese is made.

Production of a Gas You can also see another clue when you use a bathroom cleaner to remove soap scum. Many cleaners start to bubble when you spray them on the scum. The bubbles are produced because a gas is released by the chemical change that is happening. The above right figure of the antacid tablets also shows a reaction that forms a gas.

You need to be careful when you see clues of a chemical change. Just because you see one of the clues does not mean that a chemical change has taken place. The clue may be the result of a physical change. For example, energy is transferred when matter changes state. Bubbles form when you boil water or open a soda bottle. The only way to be sure that a chemical change has happened is to test the composition of a sample before and after the change.

Key Question What are four clues that a chemical change has taken place? **Clues to a chemical change include a transfer of energy, a change in color, the formation of a precipitate, or the production of a gas.**

chemical reaction when one or more substances change into one or more new substances

reactant a substance present at the start of a reaction

product a substance produced during a reaction

precipitate a solid that forms when two liquids react

ROOT WORDS

The root word in *reactant* is *react*. To react means "to undergo a change." A reactant is the substance that changes during a chemical reaction.

law of conservation of mass states that matter is conserved in any physical or chemical change

ROOT WORDS

The root word in *conservation* is *conserve*. The verb conserve means "to stay constant." So conservation of mass means that the mass stays constant, or the same.

Conservation of Mass

When wood burns, substances in the wood combine with oxygen from the air. You can see the ash pile that forms during this reaction, and it seems smaller than the wood. The reaction seems to reduce the amount of matter. It actually does not. You cannot see the carbon dioxide and water vapor that are released into the air when wood burns. The mass of these gases plus the mass of the ashes is the same as the mass of the wood and oxygen. In other words, the total mass of the products is always the same as the total mass of the reactants. The **law of conservation of mass** states that mass is conserved in any physical change or chemical change. So mass is neither created nor destroyed. The photos below show how conservation of mass can be observed for chemical changes in a closed container.

Key Question How are the mass of the reactants and the mass of the products of a chemical reaction related? **During any chemical reaction, the mass of the products is always equal to the mass of the reactants.**

Conservation of Mass During a Chemical Reaction

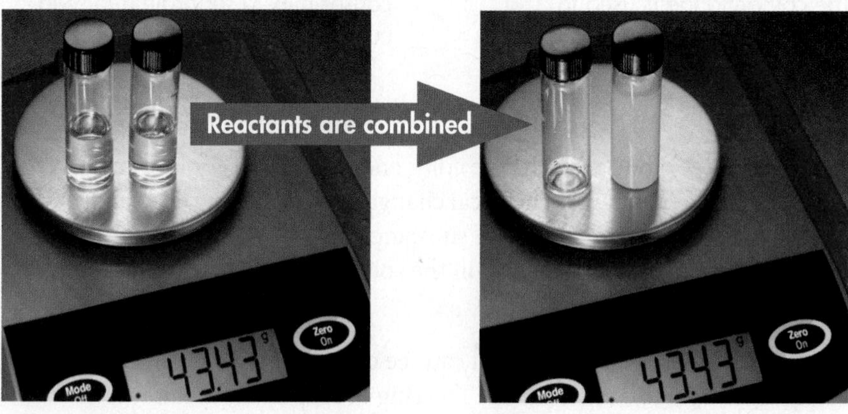

❶ The mass of the reactants is measured.

❷ Mass does not change when products form.

2.4 LessonCheck

Key Concept Check

26. Explain How does a chemical change affect the composition of matter?

27. List Name four possible clues that a chemical change has taken place.

28. Compare In a chemical reaction, how does the mass of the reactants compare with the mass of the products?

Vocabulary Check *Choose a highlighted word from the lesson to complete the sentence correctly.*

29. A(n) __________ forms during a chemical reaction.

Think Critically

30. Classify Classify the following changes as physical or chemical changes.

a. Water boils. **b.** A metal rusts.

31. Explain When is mass conserved according to the law of conservation of mass?

CHEMISTRY & YOU

32. Are the changes that happen to a burning match chemical or physical changes? How do you know? (Hint: See page 44.)

2 Study Guide

BIGIDEA

CHEMISTRY AS THE CENTRAL SCIENCE

Physical and chemical properties are used to describe matter. Physical properties include melting point and boiling point. Chemical properties include the ability to burn or rust. Matter may be made of elements or compounds. Elements and compounds are pure substances but can be physically combined to make heterogeneous or homogeneous mixtures. These different forms of matter may undergo physical or chemical changes.

2.1 Properties of Matter

Every sample of a given substance has identical intensive properties because every sample has the same composition.

Three states of matter are solid, liquid, and gas.

Physical changes can be classified as reversible or irreversible.

- mass (28)
- volume (28)
- extensive property (28)
- intensive property (28)
- substance (29)
- physical property (29)
- solid (30)
- liquid (30)
- gas (30)
- vapor (30)
- physical change (31)

2.2 Mixtures

Mixtures can be classified as heterogeneous mixtures or as homogeneous mixtures based on the distribution of their components.

Differences in physical properties can be used to separate mixtures.

- mixture (32)
- heterogeneous mixture (32)
- homogeneous mixture (33)
- solution (33)
- phase (33)
- filtration (34)
- distillation (34)

2.3 Elements and Compounds

Compounds can be broken down into simpler substances by chemical means, but elements cannot.

If the composition of a material is fixed, the material is a substance. If the composition may vary, the material is a mixture.

Chemists use chemical symbols to represent elements and chemical formulas to represent compounds.

The periodic table allows you to easily compare the properties of one element (or group of elements) to another element (or group of elements).

- element (36)
- compound (36)
- chemical change (36)
- chemical symbol (40)
- periodic table (41)
- period (42)
- group (42)

2.4 Chemical Reactions

During a chemical change, the composition of matter always changes.

Four possible clues to chemical change include a transfer of energy, a change in color, the formation of a precipitate, or the production of a gas.

During any chemical reaction, the mass of the products is always equal to the mass of the reactants.

- chemical property (43)
- chemical reaction (44)
- reactant (44)
- product (44)
- precipitate (45)
- law of conservation of mass (46)

2 Assessment

★ Solutions appear in Appendix D.

Lesson by Lesson

2.1 Properties of Matter

33. Describe the difference between an extensive property and an intensive property. Give an example of each.

34. List three physical properties of copper.

35. Name two physical properties that could be used to distinguish between water and ethanol.

★36. Name one physical property that could not be used to distinguish chlorine from oxygen.

37. What is the physical state of each of these materials at room temperature?

a. gold
b. gasoline
c. oxygen
d. neon
e. olive oil
f. sulfur
g. mercury

★38. Fingernail polish remover is mostly acetone. It is a liquid at room temperature. Would you describe acetone in the gaseous state as a vapor or a gas? Explain your answer.

39. Compare the arrangements of individual particles in solids, liquids, and gases.

★40. Explain why sharpening a pencil is a different type of physical change than freezing water to make ice cubes.

2.2 Mixtures

41. What is the difference between homogeneous mixtures and heterogeneous mixtures?

42. How many phases does a solution have? Explain your answer.

43. What is the goal of a distillation? Describe briefly how this goal is accomplished.

★44. Classify each of the following as a homogeneous or heterogeneous mixture.

a. chocolate chip ice cream
b. green ink
c. cake batter
d. cooking oil
e. granite rock
f. salt water
g. paint

2.3 Elements and Compounds

45. How could you distinguish an element from a compound?

★46. Classify the following materials as an element, compound, or mixture. Give reasons for your answers.

a. table salt (NaCl)
b. salt water
c. sodium (Na)

47. Describe the relationship between the three items in each of the following groups. Identify each item as an element, compound, or mixture.

a. hydrogen, oxygen, and water
b. nitrogen, oxygen, and air
c. sodium, chlorine, and table salt

48. Name the elements found in each of the following compounds.

a. ammonia (NH_3)
b. potassium oxide (K_2O)
c. sucrose ($C_{12}H_{22}O_{11}$)
d. calcium sulfide (CaS)

★49. What does the formula H_2O tell you about the composition of water?

2.4 Chemical Reactions

*50. Classify each of the following as a physical or chemical change. For any chemical change, list at least one clue to support your answer.

a. A copper wire is bent.

b. Charcoal burns in a grill.

c. Sugar dissolves in water.

51. Which type of property cannot be observed without changing the composition of a substance?

*52. The products formed when ammonium nitrate (NH_4NO_3) explodes are nitrogen, oxygen, and water. When 40 grams of ammonium nitrate explode, 14 grams of nitrogen and 8 grams of oxygen form. How many grams of water form?

Understand Concepts

*53. Explain why mass cannot be used as a property to identify a sample of matter.

54. Is malleability an extensive property or an intensive property? Explain.

*55. Use the arrangement of particles in solids and gases to explain why solids are not as easy to compress as gases.

56. Identify each of the following items as a mixture or compound. Classify the mixtures as homogenous or heterogeneous.

a. raw egg

b. gasoline

c. blood

57. Classify the following properties of the element silicon as chemical or physical properties:

a. blue-gray color

b. doesn't dissolve in water

c. melts at 1410°C

d. reacts vigorously with fluorine

58. Identify each of the following as an element, a compound, or a mixture:

a. distilled water

b. laundry detergent

c. sulfur

59. In photograph A, a coil of zinc metal is in a solution of sulfuric acid. In photograph B, a yellow solution of sodium chromate is being added to a colorless solution of silver nitrate. What clues in the photographs indicate that a chemical change is probably occurring?

A.

B.

*60. Describe clues you might observe during the following events that could support the conclusion that a chemical change is occurring.

a. An antacid tablet is dropped into water.

b. A ring of scum forms around a bathtub.

c. Iron rusts.

d. A firecracker explodes.

e. Bubbles form when hydrogen peroxide is poured onto an open wound.

f. A hamburger cooks.

FOUNDATIONS Wrap-Up

Classifying Matter

1. **Draw Conclusions** At the beginning of this chapter, you observed what happened when you added flour and baking soda to water. What type of change happened for each substance? How do you know?

Concept Check

Now that you've finished studying Chapter 2, answer these questions.

2. How is ice different from liquid water?
3. Is guacamole a heterogeneous mixture or a homogeneous mixture? Explain.
4. Is an ice cube melting a physical change or a chemical change?

61. Classify each of the following as a chemical change or a physical change.

a. Wood is burned to generate electricity.

b. Your body digests a cereal bar.

c. Water in a rain puddle evaporates.

62. Explain why the production of a gas does not always mean that a chemical reaction has occurred.

*63. The wax seems to disappear as a candle burns. How can the law of conservation of mass apply to this reaction?

CHEMYSTERY

Which One Is Not Like the Others?

The eruption of geysers in Yellowstone National Park is caused by a physical change. Underground water is heated to temperatures hot enough to turn the water into steam. This steam causes pressure underground to increase. The steam is at first unable to escape. The geyser erupts when the pressure reaches a critical level.

The shaping of valleys is also caused by physical changes. The melting and refreezing of water is a physical change. A physical change also happens as the earth underneath the glacier is broken apart and moved.

The changing of the color of leaves is the result of chemical changes. Chemical changes happen in the leaves as the temperature and hours of sunlight change in the fall. Leaves changing color is not like the physical changes of geysers erupting or glaciers moving.

64. **Identify** Are the physical changes in the mystery reversible or irreversible physical changes? Explain your answer.

65. **Connect to the BIGIDEA** Why is it important for rangers at national parks to understand physical and chemical changes?

Think Critically

*66. **Apply Concepts** Make a plan to separate sand from a mixture of charcoal, sand, sugar, and water.

67. **Apply Concepts** A change in odor can also be a clue that a chemical change has occurred. Describe at least one situation in which you might be likely to detect such a change in odor in a kitchen.

68. **Explain** When powdered iron is left exposed to the air, it rusts. Explain why the mass of the rust is greater than the mass of the powdered iron.

*69. **Interpret Graphs** Five elements that make up 98% of the mass of the human body are oxygen (61%), carbon (23%), hydrogen (10.0%), nitrogen (2.6%), and calcium (1.4%). How do the elements in the human body compare to the most abundant elements in Earth's crust, oceans, and atmosphere, as shown in the circle graph?

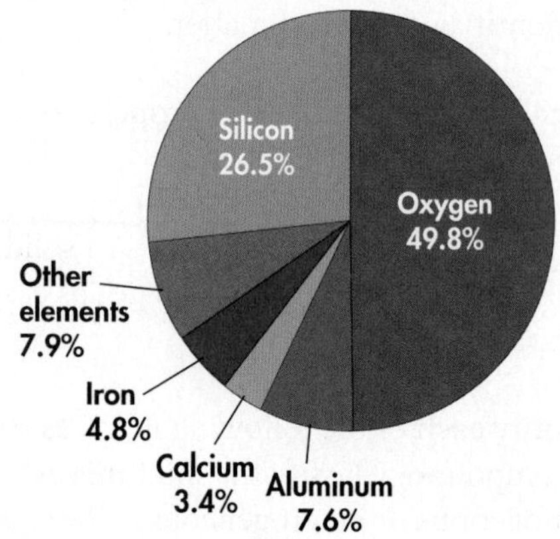

Write About Science

70. **Explain** Write a paragraph that supports the statement: "Dry tea is a mixture, not a substance." Include at least two pieces of evidence to support your argument.

71. **Explain** Lavoisier proposed the law of conservation of mass in 1789. Write a paragraph describing, in general, what Lavoisier must have done before he proposed this law. Use what you have learned about the scientific method.

72. **Connect to the BIGIDEA** Compare elements and compounds by saying how they are alike. Then contrast elements and compounds by describing how they are different.

Standardized Test Prep

For help with answering test questions, go to your Chemistry Skills and Math Workbook.

Select the choice that best answers each question or completes each statement.

1. Which of the following is not a chemical change?
   (A) paper being shredded
   (B) steel rusting
   (C) charcoal burning
   (D) a newspaper yellowing in the sun

2. Which phrase best describes an apple?
   (A) heterogeneous mixture
   (B) homogeneous compound
   (C) heterogeneous substance
   (D) homogeneous mixture

3. Which element is paired with the wrong symbol?
   (A) sulfur, S
   (B) potassium, P
   (C) nitrogen, N
   (D) calcium, Ca

4. Which of these properties could not be used to distinguish between table salt and table sugar?
   (A) boiling point
   (B) melting point
   (C) density
   (D) color

5. The state of matter characterized by a definite volume and an indefinite shape is a
   (A) solid.   (C) mixture.
   (B) liquid.   (D) gas.

The lettered choices below refer to Questions 6–9. A lettered choice may be used once, more than once, or not at all.

(A) compound
(B) heterogeneous mixture
(C) element
(D) homogeneous mixture

Which description correctly identifies each of the following materials?

6. air
7. carbon monoxide
8. zinc
9. mushroom pizza

Tips for Success

Using Models To answer some test questions, you will be asked to use visual models. At first, the models may look very similar. Decide which information will help you answer the question. The number of particles, their colors, or their shapes may or may not be important.

Use the atomic windows to answer Question 10.

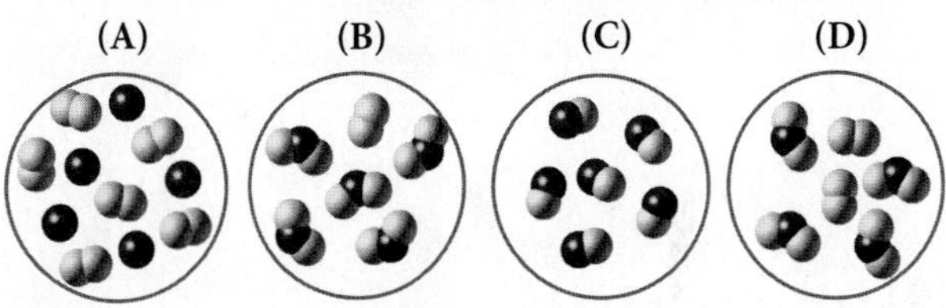

10. The species in window A react. Use the law of conservation of mass to determine which window best represents the reaction products.

Use the data table to answer Questions 11–14.

Mass of magnesium (g)	Mass of oxygen (g)	Mass of magnesium oxide (g)
5.0	3.3	8.3
6.5	(a)	10.8
13.6	9.0	(b)
(c)	12.5	31.5

11. Magnesium metal burns vigorously in oxygen to produce the compound magnesium oxide. Use the law of conservation of mass to identify the masses labeled (a), (b), and (c) in the table.

12. Use the data in the completed table to construct a graph with mass of magnesium on the *x*-axis and mass of magnesium oxide on the *y*-axis.

13. How many grams of magnesium oxide form when 8.0 g of magnesium are burned?

14. How many grams of magnesium and oxygen react to form 20.0 g of magnesium oxide?

If You Have Trouble With . . .

Question	1	2	3	4	5	6	7	8	9	10	11	12	13	14
See Lesson	2.4	2.2	2.3	2.1	2.1	2.3	2.3	2.3	2.3	2.4	2.4	2.4	2.4	2.4

3 Scientific Measurement

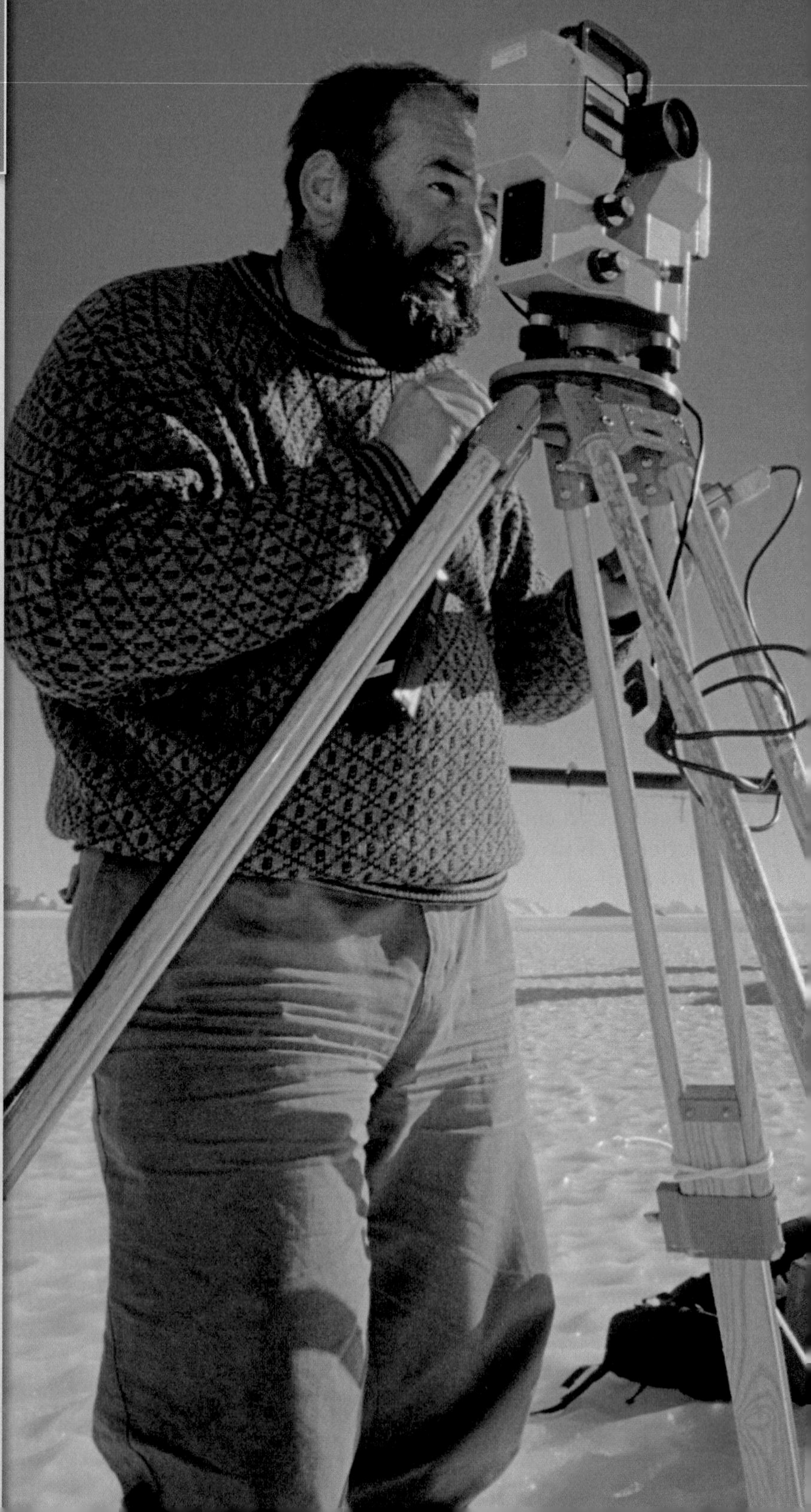

Exploring Density 

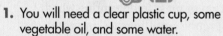

1. You will need a clear plastic cup, some vegetable oil, and some water.
2. Pour some vegetable oil into the cup.
3. Predict what will happen if you add water to the cup. Which liquid do you think will be on the top?
4. Now, add some water to the cup. Were your predictions correct?

Form a Hypothesis Suggest an explanation for the order of the two liquid layers.

PearsonChem.com

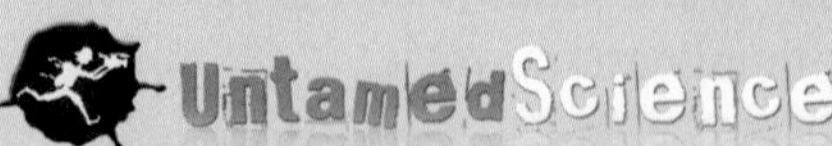

Take a video field trip with the Untamed Science crew to discover why accurate and precise measurements are important for communicating results with other scientists.

A surveyor in Antarctica uses a device called a theodolite to measure the landscape for a future airstrip.

QUANTIFYING MATTER

Essential Questions:

1. *How do scientists express the degree of uncertainty in their measurements?*
2. *How is dimensional analysis used to solve problems?*

Just Give Me a Sign

Imagine you get lost while traveling in a foreign country, as many tourists do. But then you spot these signs along the road. If you know the distance to your destination, you can find your way. However, the distances on these signs are listed as numbers with no units attached. For example, is Preston 8 kilometers away or 8 miles away? Is there any way to know for sure?

▶ Connect to the **BIGIDEA** As you read this chapter, try to familiarize yourself with common metric units used in science.

3.1 Using and Expressing Measurements

CHEMISTRY & YOU

Q: How do you measure a photo finish? You probably know that a 100-meter dash is timed in seconds. However, measuring each runner's time to the nearest second in a close finish will not tell you who won. That's why sprint times are often measured to the nearest hundredth of a second (0.01 s). Chemistry also requires making accurate and often very small measurements.

Key Questions

How do you write numbers in scientific notation?

How do you evaluate accuracy and precision?

Why must measurements be reported to the correct number of significant figures?

BUILD Vocabulary

measurement a quantity given as a number and a unit

scientific notation a number written as the product of a coefficient and 10 raised to a power

ACADEMIC WORDS

The word *notation* means the "process of using a special system of signs or symbols for a special purpose." For example, musicians use musical notations. Editors use marginal notations. Scientists use scientific notation.

Scientific Notation

Everyone makes and uses measurements. A **measurement** is a quantity that has a number and a unit. Your height (66 inches) and age (15 years) are measurements.

Measurements are fundamental to experimental sciences. In chemistry, you will see very large numbers and very small numbers. For example, a single gram of hydrogen contains about 602,000,000,000,000,000,000,000 hydrogen atoms. An example of a very small number you may see is 0.000 000 000 000 000 000 000 327 grams. This number is the mass of an atom of gold. Writing and using such large or small numbers is cumbersome. It is easy to make mistakes when working with such large and small numbers. You can work more easily with these numbers by writing them in scientific notation.

In **scientific notation**, a given number is written as the product of two numbers: a coefficient and 10 raised to a power. For example, the number 602,000,000,000,000,000,000,000 can be written in scientific notation as 6.02×10^{23}. The coefficient is 6.02. The power of 10, or exponent, is 23. In scientific notation, the coefficient is always a number greater than or equal to 1 and less than 10. The coefficient is multiplied by 10 to a power, or exponent.

$$6.02 \times 10^{23}$$

The coefficient is always greater than or equal to 1 and less than 10.

The exponent tells you how many times the number must be multiplied or divided by 10.

To find the exponent to use when writing a number in scientific notation, you count the number of places the decimal point must be moved to give a single digit to the left of the decimal point. The value of the exponent is the number of places the decimal point has been moved. The exponent is positive when the decimal point moves to the left. It's negative if the decimal point moves to the right.

A positive exponent indicates how many times the coefficient must be multiplied by 10. A negative exponent indicates how many times the coefficient must be divided by 10.

Learn more about scientific notation online.
MATH
+/–
TUTORIAL

When writing numbers greater than 10 in scientific notation, move the decimal point to the left until the coefficient is greater than or equal to 1 and less than 10. Count the number of places you moved the decimal point. Then, write the number of places as a positive exponent of 10. Below are two examples.

$$6{,}300{,}000. = 6.3 \times 10^6 \qquad 94{,}700. = 9.47 \times 10^4$$

When writing numbers less than 1 in scientific notation, move the decimal point to the right until the number is greater than or equal to 1 and less than 10. Count the number of places you moved the decimal point. Then, write the number of places as a negative exponent of 10 as shown below.

$$0.000\,008 = 8.0 \times 10^{-6} \qquad 0.00736 = 7.36 \times 10^{-3}$$

To change a number from scientific notation into standard form, move the decimal point to the right if the exponent is positive. Move the decimal point to the left if the exponent is negative. The number of spaces the decimal point moves equals the exponent.

Multiplication and Division To multiply numbers written in scientific notation, multiply the coefficients. Then add the exponents as shown below.

$$(3 \times 10^4) \times (2 \times 10^2) = (3 \times 2) \times 10^{4+2} = 6 \times 10^6$$

$$(2.1 \times 10^3) \times (4.0 \times 10^{-7}) = (2.1 \times 4.0) \times 10^{3+(-7)} = 8.4 \times 10^{-4}$$

To divide numbers written in scientific notation, divide the coefficients. Then subtract the exponent in the denominator from the exponent in the numerator. Here's an example:

$$\frac{(3.0 \times 10^5)}{(6.0 \times 10^2)} = \left(\frac{3.0}{6.0}\right) \times 10^{5-2} = 0.50 \times 10^3 = 5.0 \times 10^2$$

After multiplying or dividing the coefficients, check that the coefficient is still greater than or equal to 1 and less than 10. If it is not, you will need to move the decimal point and adjust the exponent of 10.

Addition and Subtraction If you want to add or subtract numbers expressed in scientific notation, the exponents must be the same. In other words, the decimal points must be aligned before you add or subtract. Look at the example below. First, rewrite the second number so the exponent is 3. To get the exponent to 3, move the decimal point one place to the left so you can add 1 to the exponent. Then add the numbers.

$$\begin{aligned}(5.4 \times 10^3) + (8.0 \times 10^2) &= (5.4 \times 10^3) + (0.80 \times 10^3)\\ &= (5.4 + 0.80) \times 10^3\\ &= 6.2 \times 10^3\end{aligned}$$

Key Question How do you write numbers in scientific notation? **In scientific notation, a number is written as the product of a coefficient and 10 raised to a power. The coefficient must be greater than or equal to 1 and less than 10.**

Just a Hair

A hair's width expressed in meters is a very small measurement.

$0.00007\text{ m} = 7 \times 10^{-5}\text{ m}$

Decimal point moves 5 places to the right. Exponent is –5

Go to your Chemistry Skills and Math Workbook for more practice using scientific notation.

Sample Problem 3.1

Using Scientific Notation

Solve the following problem. Express the answer in scientific notation.

$$(8.0 \times 10^2) \times (7.0 \times 10^{-5})$$

1 Analyze Identify the relevant concepts. To multiply numbers in scientific notation, multiply the coefficients. Then add the exponents.

2 Solve Apply the concepts to this problem.

Multiply the coefficients.

$(8.0 \times 10^2) \times (7.0 \times 10^{-5})$

$(8.0 \times 7.0) = 56$

Then add the exponents.

$(8.0 \times 10^2) \times (7.0 \times 10^{-5}) = 56 \times 10^{2+(-5)}$

$= 56 \times 10^{-3}$

Move the decimal point and adjust the exponent so that the answer is in scientific notation.

$= 5.6 \times 10^{-2}$

Practice Problems

1. Solve the following problem. Express the answer in scientific notation.

$$(8.4 \times 10^{-2}) \div (2.1 \times 10^{-6})$$

1 Analyze Identify the relevant concepts.

2 Solve Apply the concepts to this problem.

TO GET YOU STARTED...

Divide the coefficients first:

$8.4 \div 2.1 = 4.0$

Now subtract the exponents.

2. Solve the following problem and express the solution in scientific notation:

$$(6.6 \times 10^{-8}) + (5.0 \times 10^{-9})$$

Remember: To add or subtract numbers in scientific notation, the exponents must be the same.

3. Solve the following problem. Express the answer in scientific notation.

$$(9.4 \times 10^2) - (2.1 \times 10^2)$$

Accuracy, Precision, and Error

To be successful in chemistry and other activities, you must make reliable measurements. Reliable measurements are those that are correct and reproducible.

Accuracy and Precision The measuring cups and teaspoons you use in a kitchen have some degree of error. Every scientific measurement made in a lab also has the potential for error. Scientists evaluate the accuracy and precision of every measurement. In science, correct measurements are described as accurate. Reproducible measurements are described as precise. Some people use the words accuracy and precision as if they mean the same thing. However, accuracy and precision do not have the same meanings in chemistry. **Accuracy** is a measure of how close a measurement comes to the actual or true value of whatever is measured. **Precision** is a measure of how close a series of measurements are to one another. Measurements can be precise even if they are not accurate.

The darts on the dartboards below show accuracy and precision in measurements. Let the bull's-eye of each dartboard be the true, or correct, value of what you are measuring. The closeness of a dart to the bull's-eye corresponds to the degree of accuracy. The closeness of several darts to one another corresponds to the degree of precision.

accuracy the closeness of a measurement to the true value of what is being measured

precision the closeness of a set of measurements taken under the same conditions

WORD ORIGINS

The word *accuracy* comes from the Latin word *curare*. Curare means "to arrange." An accurate measurement is one that is "arranged" as close to the true value as possible.

Accuracy Versus Precision
The arrangement of darts shows the difference between accuracy and precision.

Good accuracy/good precision
Closeness to the bull's-eye indicates a high degree of accuracy. The closeness of the darts to one another indicates high precision.

Poor accuracy/good precision
Precision is high because the darts are close together. The results are reproducible, but inaccurate.

Poor accuracy/poor precision
The darts land far from each other and from the bull's-eye. The results are neither accurate nor precise.

accepted value the correct value for the measurement based on reliable references

experimental value the value measured in the lab

error the difference between the experimental value and the accepted value

percent error the relative error of a measurement

WORD ORIGINS

The word *error* comes from the Latin word *errare*, which means "to stray." The error is the amount that the experimental value "strays" from the accepted value for the measurement.

Determining Error Suppose you use a thermometer to measure the boiling point of pure water at standard pressure. The thermometer reads 99.1°C. But, the boiling point of pure water at standard pressure is actually 100.0°C. Why doesn't the thermometer read 100.0°C?

The accepted and experimental values often differ. The **accepted value** is the correct value for the measurement based on reliable references. The **experimental value** is the value measured in the lab. The difference between the experimental value and the accepted value is called the **error.**

$$\text{Error} = \text{experimental value} - \text{accepted value}$$

Error can be positive or negative. Error is positive if the experimental value is greater than the accepted value. Error is negative if the experimental value is less than the accepted value. The magnitude, or size, of the error shows how much the experimental value differs from the accepted value. For the boiling point measurement, the error is 99.1°C − 100°C, or −0.9°C.

You can use the error to calculate the relative error, or percent error. The **percent error** of a measurement is the absolute value of the error divided by the accepted value and then multiplied by 100%. This equation is shown below.

|error| is the absolute value of error

$$\text{Percent error} = \frac{|\text{error}|}{\text{accepted value}} \times 100\%$$

correct value based on reliable references

Key Question How do you evaluate accuracy and precision? **You can evaluate the accuracy of a measurement by comparing the measured value to the accepted value. You can evaluate the precision of a measurement by comparing the values of two or more repeated measurements.**

Measurements and Accuracy
The measuring instrument you select determines the accuracy of your measurement. Calipers can be used to measure the tomato's height with a small amount of error.

Sample Problem 3.2

Calculating Percent Error

The boiling point of pure water is measured to be 99.1°C. The accepted value for the boiling point of pure water is 100°C. Calculate the percent error.

KNOWNS	UNKNOWN
boiling point of water = 100.0°C	percent error = ?
measured temperature = 99.1°C	

1 Analyze List the knowns and the unknown. Use the equations for error and percent error to solve the problem.

2 Calculate Solve for the unknown.

Start with the equation for percent error.

$$\text{percent error} = \frac{|\text{error}|}{\text{accepted value}} \times 100\%$$

Substitute the equation for error.

$$\text{percent error} = \frac{|\text{experimental value} - \text{accepted value}|}{\text{accepted value}} \times 100\%$$

Plug in the known values and solve.

$$= \frac{|99.1^\circ\text{C} - 100.0^\circ\text{C}|}{100.0^\circ\text{C}} \times 100\%$$

$$= \frac{0.9\cancel{^\circ\text{C}}}{100.0\cancel{^\circ\text{C}}} \times 100\% = 0.9\%$$

3 Evaluate Does the result make sense? The experimental value was off by about 1°C, or $\frac{1}{100}$ of the accepted value. The answer makes sense.

Practice Problems

4. A student measures the depth of a swimming pool to be 2.04 meters at its deepest end. The accepted value is 2.00 meters. What is the student's percent error?

1 Analyze List the knowns and the unknown.

2 Calculate Solve for the unknown.

3 Evaluate Does the result make sense?

KNOWNS	UNKNOWN
experimental value = 2.04 m	percent error = ?
accepted value = 2.00 m	

5. A technician measures the boiling point of octane to be 124.1°C. The actual boiling point of octane is 125.7°C. Calculate the percent error.

KNOWNS	UNKNOWN
experimental value =	percent error = ?
accepted value =	

Degrees Celsius
The temperature shown on this Celsius thermometer can be reported to three significant figures.

BUILD Vocabulary

significant figures all the digits in a measurement that are known plus a last digit that is estimated

MULTIPLE MEANINGS
The word *figure* has many meanings. In history, *figure* can refer to a person, such as a famous figure in history. In math, we refer to triangles as plane figures. We even use *figure* informally when we say "I never figured on going."

Significant Figures

The thermometer above has a scale with lines, called calibrations. This thermometer is calibrated in 1°C intervals. You can read the temperature to the nearest degree. You can also estimate the temperature to the nearest tenth of a degree by noting the closeness of the red liquid inside to the calibrations. Notice that the liquid is above 22°C but does not come up to the calibration for 23°C. So, you can estimate that the temperature is about 22.9°C.

The value 22.9°C has three digits. The first two digits (2 and 2) are known with certainty. But the last digit (9) is an estimate. This digit has some uncertainty because you cannot know if the estimate is correct. These reported digits provide useful information and are called significant figures. The **significant figures** in a measurement include all the digits that are known plus a last digit that is estimated. When you make calculations with measurements, the precision of a calculated answer is limited by the least precise measurement used in the calculation. If the least precise measurement in your calculation has two significant figures, then your calculated answer can have at most two significant figures.

As shown below, instruments differ in the number of significant figures that can be obtained from their use.

Increasing Precision
Three differently calibrated meter sticks are used to measure a trunk's width. The meter stick calibrated in 0.1 m (1 dm) intervals is more precise than the one calibrated in 1 m intervals. However, the meter stick calibrated in 0.1 m intervals is less precise than one calibrated in 0.01 m (1 cm) intervals.

Learn more on precision in measurements *online.*

Determining Significant Figures in Measurements To determine whether a digit in a measured value is significant, you need to apply the following rules.

1. Every nonzero digit in a reported measurement is assumed to be significant.

24.7 meters
0.743 meter
714 meters

Each of these measurements has three significant figures.

2. Zeros between nonzero digits are significant.

7003 meters
40.79 meters
1.503 meters

Each of these measurements has four significant figures.

3. Leftmost zeros in front of nonzero digits are not significant. They act as placeholders. You can eliminate such placeholding zeros by writing the measurements in scientific notation.

0.0071 meter = 7.1×10^{-3} meter
0.42 meter = 4.2×10^{-1} meter
0.000099 meter = 9.9×10^{-5} meter

Each of these measurements has only two significant figures.

4. Zeros at the end of a number and to the right of a decimal point are always significant.

43.00 meters
1.010 meters
9.000 meters

Each of these measurements has four significant figures.

5. Zeros that act as placeholders to show the magnitude of a number are not significant. These zeros are found at the rightmost end of a measurement. They lie to the left of an understood decimal point.

300 meters (one significant figure)
7000 meters (one significant figure)
27,210 meters (four significant figures)

The zeros in these measurements are not significant.

When such zeros are known measured values, they are significant. Writing the value in scientific notation makes it clear that these zeros are significant.

300 meters = 3.00×10^{2} meters
(three significant figures)

The zeros in this measurement are significant.

6. There are two situations in which a number has an unlimited number of significant figures. The first situation involves counting. Counted numbers are exact.

23 people in your classroom

This measurement is a counted value, so it has an unlimited number of significant figures.

The second situation involves exactly defined quantities. Numbers found within a system of measurement are exact.

60 min = 1 hr
100 cm = 1 m

Each of these numbers has an unlimited number of significant figures.

Sample Problem 3.3

Counting Significant Figures in Measurements

How many significant figures are in each measurement?

a. 123 m
b. 40,506 mm
c. 9.8000×10^4 m
d. 22 meter sticks
e. 98,000 m
f. 0.070 80 m

❶ Analyze Identify the relevant concepts. The locations of each zero and the decimal point in the measurement determine which of the rules apply for determining significant figures. These locations are known by inspecting each measurement value.

❷ Solve Apply the concepts to this problem.

For all numbers, apply rule 1.

a. 123 m — By rule 1, there are **three** significant figures.

For numbers that contain zeros, apply rules 2 through 6.

b. 40,506 mm — By rule 2, there are **five** significant figures.

c. 9.8000×10^4 m — By rule 4, there are **five** significant figures.

d. 22 meter sticks — By rule 6, there are **unlimited** significant figures.

e. 98,000 m — By rule 5, there are **two** significant figures.

For some numbers, you may need to apply multiple rules.

f. 0.07080 m — By rules 2, 3, and 4, there are **four** significant figures.

Practice Problems

Hint: Reread the rules for significant figures before beginning these problems.

6. Count the significant figures in each measured length.
a. 0.05730 meter **b.** 8765 meters

❶ Analyze Identify the relevant concepts.

❷ Solve Apply the concepts to each problem.

7. Count the significant figures in each measured length.
a. 0.00073 meter **b.** 40.007 meters

8. Challenge How many significant figures are in 8.750×10^{-2} gram?

Significant Figures in Calculations Suppose you measure a floor. You find that the floor is 7.7 m (meters) long by 5.4 m wide. Each of these measurements has two significant figures. The measurements are precise to only two significant figures.

When you multiply the length times the width, you find that the area is 41.58 square meters. However, the length and width are expressed to only two significant figures. So the answer has to be expressed to two significant figures, or 42 m^2. A calculated value cannot be more precise than the least precise measurement used to calculate it. You must round each calculated value so that it shows the correct number of significant figures.

▶ **Rounding** To round a number, first decide how many significant figures the answer should have. This decision depends on the given measurements and on the type of calculation used to find the answer.

Look at the number to the right of your last significant digit. If this number is less than 5, drop the digit. The value of the last significant digit stays the same. If the number to the right is 5 or greater, increase the value of the digit in the last significant place by 1. For example:

> To round each number to three significant digits, count three digits that are significant, starting from the leftmost nonzero digit:
>
> 14,732   0.08727   23.009
>
> Look at the digit immediately to the right of the significant digits:
>
> 14,732   0.08727   23.009
>
> If the nonsignificant digit is lower than 5, do not round up. If the nonsignificant digit is 5 or higher, round up. Be sure the final number has the correct number of significant figures:
>
> 14,700   0.0873   23.0
>
> Whole numbers ending in multiple zeros should be written in scientific notation. So 14,700 should be written as 1.47×10^4.

▶ **Addition and Subtraction** Round the answer to the same number of decimal places as the measurement with the least number of decimal places. You will practice rounding with addition and subtraction in Sample Problem 3.5.

▶ **Multiplication and Division** Ignore the decimal point in the answer when rounding during multiplication and division. Instead, round the answer to the same number of significant figures as the measurement with the least number of significant figures. You can practice rounding with multiplication and division in Sample Problem 3.6 and in your *Chemistry Skills and Math Workbook.*

Key Question Why must measurements be reported to the correct number of significant figures? **Measurements must always be reported to the correct number of significant figures. Calculated answers often depend on the number of significant figures in the values used in the calculation.**

BUILD Understanding

Compare/Contrast Table
Addition and subtraction have different rules for determining the number of significant figures than multiplication and division have. Use a compare/contrast table to identify the differences and similarities between the two sets of rules.

Sample Problem 3.4

Rounding Measurements

Round each measurement to the number of significant figures shown in parentheses. Write the answers in scientific notation.

a. 314.721 meters (four) **b.** 0.001775 meter (two)

1 Analyze **Identify the relevant concepts.** Use the rules for determining significant figures to round the number in each measurement. Then apply the rules for expressing numbers in scientific notation.

2 Solve **Apply the concepts to this problem.**

Starting from the left, count the desired number of significant digits for each value.

a. 314.721 meters (four) | **b.** 0.001775 meter (two)

Apply the rules for rounding.

314.721 meters
↑
2 is less than 5, so you do not round up.

0.001775 meter
↑
7 is greater than 5, so round up.

Write each correctly rounded number in scientific notation.

314.7 meters $= 3.147 \times 10^2$ meters

0.0018 meter $= 1.8 \times 10^{-3}$ meter

Practice Problems

9. Round each measurement to three significant figures. Write your answers in scientific notation.

a. 87.073 meters

b. 4.3621×10^8 meters

1 Analyze **Identify the relevant concepts.**

2 Solve **Apply the concepts to this problem.**

Hint: Before you round your measurement, remember to look at the digit that follows the desired last significant figure.

10. Round each measurement to two significant figures. Write your answers in scientific notation.

a. 0.01552 meter

b. 9009 meters

Sample Problem 3.5

Significant Figures in Addition and Subtraction

Perform the following addition and subtraction operations. Give each answer to the correct number of significant figures.

a. 12.52 m + 349.0 m + 8.24 m **b.** 74.626 m − 28.34 m

❶ Analyze Identify the relevant concepts. Perform the specified math operation. Then round the answer to match the measurement with the least number of decimal places.

❷ Solve Apply the concepts to this problem.

	a.	b.
Align the decimal points. Then do the operation.	12.52 m 349.0 m + 8.24 m 369.76 m	74.626 m − 28.34 m 46.286 m
Identify the measurement with the least number of decimal places.	349.0 (1 decimal place)	28.34 (2 decimal places)
Round to the least number of decimal places.	369.76 m → 369.8 m	46.286 m → 46.29 m
Report the answer in scientific notation.	369.8 m = 3.698×10^2 m	46.29 m = 4.629×10^1 m

Practice Problems

11. Perform each operation. Express your answers to the correct number of significant figures.

a. 9.44 meters − 2.11 meters

b. 1.36 meters + 10.17 meters

❶ Analyze Identify the relevant concepts.

❷ Solve Apply the concepts to this problem.

12. Challenge Perform each operation. Express your answers to the correct number of significant figures and in scientific notation.

a. 61.2 meters + 9.35 meters + 8.6 meters

b. 14.2 grams + 8.73 grams + 0.912 gram

CHEMISTRY TUTORIAL

Sample Problem 3.6

Significant Figures in Multiplication and Division

Perform the following operations. Give the answers to the correct number of significant figures.

a. 7.85 meters × 0.44 meter **b.** 2.4526 meters^2 ÷ 8.4 meters

❶ Analyze Identify the relevant concepts. Perform the specified math operation. Then round the answer to match the measurement with the least number of significant figures.

❷ Solve Apply the concepts to this problem.

	a.	b.
Perform the operation. Be sure to include the units in your calculations.	a. $7.85\ m \times 0.44\ m = 3.454\ m^2$	b. $2.4526\ m^2 \div 8.4\ m = 0.291976\ m$
Identify the measurement with the least number of significant figures.	0.44 m (2 significant figures)	8.4 m (2 significant figures)
Round the answer to the least number of significant figures in the starting measurements.	$3.454\ m^2 \rightarrow$ **$3.5\ m^2$**	$0.291976\ m \rightarrow$ **$0.29\ m$**

Practice Problems

13. Solve the problems below. Give each answer to the correct number of significant figures.

a. 8.3 meters × 2.22 meters

b. 2.10 meters × 0.70 meter

c. 0.365 meter^2 ÷ 0.0200 meter

❶ Analyze Identify the relevant concepts.

❷ Solve Apply the concepts to the problem.

14. Challenge Solve the following problems. Give each answer to the correct number of significant figures and in scientific notation:

a. 8432 meters^2 ÷ 12.5 meters

b. 22.4 meters × 11.3 m × 5.2 meters

Quick Lab

Purpose To measure the dimensions of an object as accurately and precisely as possible and to apply rules for rounding answers calculated from the measurements

Materials

- 3-inch × 5-inch index card
- metric ruler

Accuracy and Precision

Procedure

1. Use a metric ruler to measure in centimeters the length and width of an index card as accurately as you can. Estimate the hundredths place in your measurement.

2. Calculate the area ($A = l \times w$) and the perimeter [$P = 2 \times (l + w)$] of the index card. Write both your unrounded answers and your correctly rounded answers on the chalkboard.

Analyze and Conclude

1. Identify How many significant figures are in your measurements of length and of width?

2. Compare How do your measurements compare with those of your classmates?

3. Explain How many significant figures are in your calculated value for the area? In your calculated value for the perimeter? Do your rounded answers have as many significant figures as your classmates' measurements?

4. Evaluate Assume that the correct (accurate) length and width of the card are 12.70 cm and 7.62 cm, respectively. Calculate the percent error for each of your two measurements.

3.1 LessonCheck

Key Concept Check

15. **Review** How can you express a number in scientific notation?

16. **Review** How are accuracy and precision evaluated?

17. **Explain** Why must a given measurement always be reported to the correct number of significant figures?

Think Critically

18. **Calculate** Solve the following. Express each answer in scientific notation with the correct number of significant figures.

a. $(5.3 \times 10^4) + (1.3 \times 10^4)$
b. $(7.2 \times 10^{-4}) \div (1.8 \times 10^3)$

19. **Evaluate** Determine the number of significant figures in each of the following measurements.

a. 11 soccer players
b. 0.070 020 meter
c. 10,800 meters
d. 5.00 cubic meters

20. The winner of a 100-meter dash finishes the race in 9.98 seconds. The second place runner has a time of 10.05 seconds. Is one measurement more precise than the other? Explain your answer. (Hint: See page 57.)

BIGIDEA QUANTIFYING MATTER

21. Write a brief paragraph explaining the differences between the accuracy, the precision, and the error of a measurement.

3.2 Units of Measurement

CHEMISTRY & YOU

Q: What is the forecast for tomorrow—hot or cold? The temperatures in this weather forecast are in degrees but do not have a temperature scale. Will the high tomorrow be 28°C, which is very warm? Or 28°F, which is very cold? Without the correct units, you cannot be sure. When you make a measurement, you must assign the correct units to the number. Without the units, it's impossible to explain the measurement clearly to others.

Key Questions

What makes metric units easy to use?

What temperature units do scientists commonly use?

What determines the density of a substance?

International System of Units (SI) the revised version of the metric system

ACADEMIC WORDS

The word *derive* means "to get or receive from a source." Base SI units are the source for derived units. For example, the unit for volume (cubic meter) is derived from the base unit for length (meter).

CONCEPTS IN ACTION
Learn more about SI units online.

Using SI Units

All measurements need units. But not just any units will do. Suppose you and a friend measured the length of a wall using your shoes. Your friend says the wall is 11 shoes long. You say the wall is 13 shoes long. Both of you might be right if your shoe is a different size than your friend's shoe. Units used in science must have standard values. Using units with standard values means that the unit will have the same meaning for everyone.

The standards of measurement used in science are those of the metric system. The metric system is important because it is simple and easy to use. All metric units are based on multiples of 10. As a result, you can more easily convert between units. The metric system began in France in 1795. The **International System of Units** (or SI, after the French name, *Le Système International d'Unités*) is a revised version of the metric system. In 1960, the SI was accepted internationally.

There are seven SI base units, which are listed in the table below. You can derive, or obtain, other units from these base units. Derived units are used for such measurements as volume, density, and pressure. All measured quantities can be reported in SI units. Sometimes, however, non-SI units are preferred for convenience or practical reasons. In this book, you will learn about SI and non-SI units.

SI Base Units

Quantity	SI base unit	Symbol
Length	meter	m
Mass	kilogram	kg
Temperature	kelvin	K
Time	second	s
Amount of substance	mole	mol
Luminous intensity	candela	cd
Electric current	ampere	A

Commonly Used Metric Prefixes				
Prefix	**Symbol**	**Meaning**	**Factor**	**Example relationship**
mega	M	1 million times larger	10^6	1 Mm = 1,000,000 m
kilo	k	1000 times larger	10^3	1 km = 1,000 m
deci	d	10 times smaller	10^{-1}	10 dm = 1 m
centi	c	100 times smaller	10^{-2}	100 cm = 1 m
milli	m	1000 times smaller	10^{-3}	1000 mm = 1 m
micro	μ	1 million times smaller	10^{-6}	1,000,000 μm = 1 m
nano	n	1 billion times smaller	10^{-9}	1,000,000,000 nm = 1 m

Writing Metric Units Sometimes, a metric base unit is not the most convenient way to describe an item. When this happens, you can modify the unit by adding a prefix. The table above lists common metric prefixes. For example, the prefix *milli-* means 1/1000. You can add *milli-* to meter to get a millimeter (mm), or 1/1000 of a meter (0.001 m) A hyphen (-) measures about 1 mm. The prefix *centi-* means 1/100. So a centimeter (cm) is 1/100 of a meter, or 0.01 m.

meter (m) SI unit of length

MULTIPLE MEANINGS

Meter also refers to a pattern or measure. In poetry, the meter refers to the poem's rhythmic pattern. In music, a meter is a time value given to each note.

Units of Length Size is an important property of matter. In SI, the basic unit of length is the **meter** (m). All measurements of length can be expressed in meters. The length of a page in this book is about one fourth of a meter. Small items that are visible with the naked eye may be reported in units of millimeters (mm). Even smaller items, such as the diameter of a cell, may be reported in micrometers (μm). (The symbol for micro, μ, is the twelfth letter in the Greek alphabet, mu.) Large distances are usually expressed in kilometers (km). A standard marathon distance race is about 42,000 m. This distance is more conveniently expressed as 42 km (42 × 1000 m). The table below summarizes the relationships among metric units of length.

Metric Units of Length				
Unit	**Symbol**	**Relationship**	**Example**	
Kilometer	km	1 km = 10^3 m	length of about five city blocks	≈ 1 km
Meter	m	base unit	height of doorknob from the floor	≈ 1 m
Decimeter	dm	10^1 dm = 1 m	diameter of large orange	≈ 1 dm
Centimeter	cm	10^2 cm = 1 m	diameter of shirt button	≈ 1 cm
Millimeter	mm	10^3 mm = 1 m	thickness of dime	≈ 1 mm
Micrometer	μm	10^6 μm = 1 m	diameter of bacterial cell	≈ 1 μm
Nanometer	nm	10^9 nm = 1 m	thickness of RNA molecule	≈ 1 nm

Units of Volume The space occupied by a sample of matter is called its volume. You can calculate the volume of any cubic or rectangular solid by multiplying its length by its width by its height. Length, width, and height are all expressed in meters—the SI unit of length. So, the unit for volume is derived from units of length. The SI unit of volume is a cubic meter (m^3). This is the amount of space taken up by a cube that is 1 m along each edge. An automatic dishwasher has a volume of about 1 m^3.

A more convenient unit of volume for everyday use is the liter—a non-SI unit. A **liter** (L) is the volume of a cube that is 10 centimeters (10 cm) along each edge (10 cm × 10 cm × 10 cm = 1000 cm^3 = 1 L). A smaller non-SI unit of volume is the milliliter (mL). Liquid medicines are sometimes prescribed in units of milliliters. One milliliter is 1/1000 of a liter. Thus, there are 1000 mL in 1 L. Because 1 L is the same as 1000 cm^3, 1 mL and 1 cm^3 are the same volume. The units milliliter and cubic centimeter can be used in place of each other. The table below gives the relationships of some metric units of volume.

There are many devices for measuring liquid volumes, including graduated cylinders, pipets, burets, volumetric flasks, and syringes. The volume of any solid, liquid, or gas will change with temperature. The change is most dramatic in gases. For this reason, accurate volume-measuring devices are calibrated at a given temperature. This temperature is usually 20°C, which is about normal room temperature.

Metric Units of Volume

Unit	Symbol	Relationship	Example
Liter	L	base unit	quart of milk ≈ 1 L
Milliliter	mL	10^3 mL = 1 L	20 drops of water ≈ 1 mL
Cubic centimeter	cm^3	1 cm^3 = 1 mL	cube of sugar ≈ 1 cm^3
Microliter	μL	10^6 μL = 1 L	crystal of table salt ≈ 1 μL

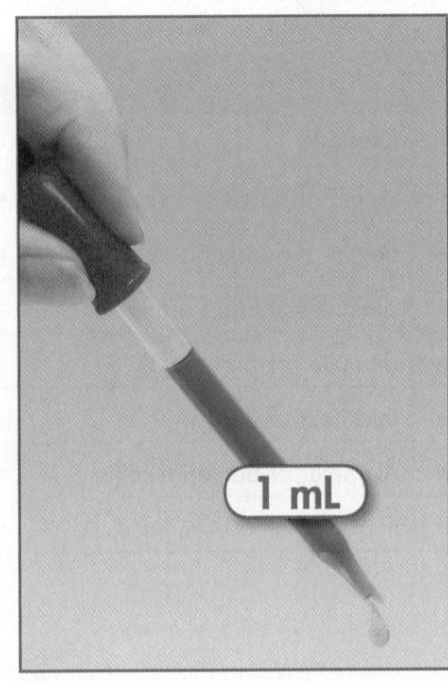

Units of Volume
The volume of liquids is often expressed in the units milliliters (mL) and liters (L). The volume of solids is often expressed in units such as cubic centimeters (cm^3).

Units of Mass The SI unit for mass is the **kilogram** (kg). A kilogram is the basic SI unit of mass. A kilogram was originally defined as the mass of 1 liter of liquid water at 4°C. A cube of water at 4°C measuring 10 cm on each edge would have a volume of 1 L and a mass of 1000 grams (g), or 1 kg. A **gram** (g) is 1/1000 of a kilogram. The relationships among units of mass are shown in the table below.

Metric Units of Mass

Unit	Symbol	Relationship	Example
Kilogram	kg	1 kg = 10^3 g	small textbook ≈ 1 kg
Gram	g	1 g = 10^{-3} kg	dollar bill ≈ 1 g
Milligram	mg	10^3 mg = 1 g	ten grains of salt ≈ 1 mg
Microgram	μg	10^6 μg = 1 g	particle of baking powder ≈ 1 μg

You can use an instrument called a balance to measure the mass of an object. The object is placed on one side of the balance. Standard masses are added to the other side until the balance beam is level. The unknown mass is equal to the sum of the standard masses.

Mass Versus Weight Weight—a measure of force—is different from mass. **Weight** is a force that measures the pull on a given mass by gravity. In other words, weight is a measure of the amount of matter and the effect of Earth's gravity. Mass is the measure of the quantity of matter. The weight of an object can change with its location because the force of gravity changes with location. For example, an astronaut on the moon weighs one-sixth of what he or she weighs on Earth because the force of Earth's gravity is about six times greater than that of the moon. It is possible for an object to become weightless if it is not acted on by the force of gravity. However, an object can never be massless because it is made of matter. All matter has mass.

Units of Energy The capacity to do work or to produce heat is called **energy**. Like any other quantity, energy can be measured. The SI unit of energy is the **joule** (J). You may be more familiar with a **calorie** (cal), a common non-SI unit of energy. One calorie is the quantity of heat that raises the temperature of 1 g of pure water by 1°C. Conversions between joules and calories can be carried out by using the following relationships:

$$1 \text{ J} = 0.2390 \text{ cal} \qquad 1 \text{ cal} = 4.184 \text{ J}$$

In this book, you will see energy values expressed in joules and calories. You'll also see them expressed in kilojoules (kJ) and kilocalories (kcal).

Key Question What makes metric units easy to use? **All metric units are based on multiples of 10. As a result, you can easily convert between units.**

liter (L) unit of volume

kilogram (kg) SI unit of mass

gram (g) unit of mass; 1/1000 of a kilogram

weight force that measures the pull of gravity on a given mass

energy the capacity to do work or to produce heat

joule (J) SI unit of energy

calorie (cal) unit of energy

WORD ORIGINS

The word *calorie* comes from the Latin word *calor,* which means "heat." One calorie is the amount of heat necessary to raise the temperature of one gram of pure water by one degree Celsius.

temperature the measure of how hot or cold an object is

Celsius scale a temperature scale that sets the freezing point of water at 0 degrees and the boiling point of water at 100 degrees

Kelvin scale a temperature scale that sets absolute zero as the 0 point on the scale

absolute zero 0 K or −273.15°C

WORD ORIGINS

Temperature comes from the Latin word *temperatura,* which means "fever." You've probably had a fever before and used a thermometer to measure your temperature, or how hot you were.

Temperature Scales

When you hold a glass of hot water, the glass feels warm because heat transfers from the glass to your hand. When you hold an ice cube, it feels cold because heat transfers from your hand to the ice cube. **Temperature** is a measure of how hot or cold an object is.

Almost all substances expand with an increase in temperature and contract as temperature decreases. (Water is a very important exception.) The common bulb thermometer is based on these properties. The liquid in the bulb of the thermometer expands when temperature increases. The liquid contracts when the temperature decreases. As the liquid expands and contracts, the height of the column of liquid inside the thermometer changes.

Celsius Scale Scientists commonly use two equivalent units of temperature: the degree Celsius and the kelvin. The Celsius scale is named after the Swedish astronomer Anders Celsius. This scale uses two easily determined temperatures as reference temperature values: the freezing point and the boiling point of water. The **Celsius scale** sets the freezing point of water at 0°C and the boiling point of water at 100°C. The distance between these two fixed points is divided into 100 equal intervals called degrees. Temperatures measured in this scale are reported as degrees Celsius (°C).

Kelvin Scale Another temperature scale used in the physical sciences is the Kelvin scale. On the **Kelvin scale**, the freezing point of water is 273.15 kelvins (K), and the boiling point is 373.15 K. Notice that with the Kelvin scale, the degree sign is not used.

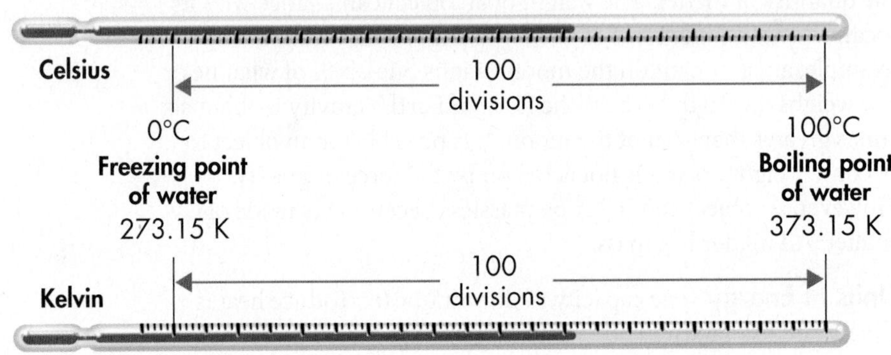

Celsius and Kelvin Scales
In the Celsius scale and the Kelvin scale, there are 100 equal intervals between the freezing point and boiling point of water.

As you can see in the figure above, a change of 1 degree on the Celsius scale is equal to 1 kelvin on the Kelvin scale. The zero point on the Kelvin scale is 0 K, or absolute zero. **Absolute zero** is equal to −273.15°C. You can round −273.15°C to −273°C for problems in this book. To convert between degrees Celsius and kelvins, add or subtract 273 as shown below.

$$K = °C + 273$$
$$°C = K - 273$$

Key Question What temperature units do scientists commonly use? **Scientists commonly use two equivalent units of temperature: the degree Celsius and the kelvin.**

CHEMISTRY TUTORIAL

SampleProblem 3.7

Converting Between Temperature Scales

Normal human body temperature is 37°C. What is this temperature in kelvins (K)?

1 Analyze List the known and the unknown. Use the known value and the equation K = °C + 273 to calculate the temperature in kelvins.

KNOWN	UNKNOWN
Temperature in °C = 37°C	Temperature in K = ? K

2 Calculate Solve for the unknown.

Write the equation to be used to convert °C to K.	K = °C + 273
Substitute the known value for °C.	K = 37 + 273
Solve for the temperature in kelvins.	K = 37 + 273 = 310 K

3 Evaluate Does the result make sense? The freezing point of water is 273 K and the boiling point of water is 373 K. You should expect a temperature in this range because normal body temperature is between these two values.

Practice Problems

22. The element silver melts at 962°C and boils at 2212°C. Express these temperatures in kelvins.

1 Analyze List the knowns and the unknowns.

2 Calculate Solve for the unknowns.

3 Evaluate Does this result make sense?

KNOWNS	UNKNOWNS
T_{melt} = 962°C	T_{melt} = ? K
T_{boil} = 2212°C	T_{boil} = ? K

23. Liquid nitrogen boils at 77.2 K. What is this temperature in degrees Celsius?

KNOWN	UNKNOWN
T_{boil} =	T_{boil} = ? °C

24. Challenge Which temperature is higher: −12°C or 206 K?

Floating on Water
Cranberries are less dense than water, so they float. Farmers make use of this property when it's time to harvest the crop.

density the ratio of the mass to the volume of an object

ROOT WORDS

The root word of density is *dense.* Density is the noun form; dense is the adjective form.

Density

Have you ever wondered why some things float in water while others sink? If you think that the cranberries in the photo above float because they are lightweight, you are partly correct. The relationship between an object's mass and its volume tells you whether it will float or sink. This relationship is called density. **Density** is the ratio of the mass of an object to its volume. Notice that when mass is measured in grams and volume in cubic centimeters, density has units of grams per cubic centimeter (g/cm^3). The SI unit of density is kilograms per cubic meter, or kg/m^3.

$$\text{Density} = \frac{\text{mass}}{\text{volume}}$$

Density is an intensive property that depends only on the composition of a substance, not on the size of the sample. With a mixture, density can vary because the composition of a mixture can vary.

Density of Liquids What happens when vegetable oil is poured into a container of water? The table below shows that the density of vegetable oil is less than the density of water. For that reason, the oil floats on top of the water. Look at the beaker that shows different liquids forming distinct layers. These liquids form layers in the beaker due to differences in density. For example, the corn syrup (colored red) sinks below the water (colored green) because the density of corn syrup is greater than the density of water.

Liquid Layers
When liquids of different densities are placed in a container, they separate into layers.

Go to your Chemistry Skills and Math Workbook to practice interpreting data.

Densities of Some Common Liquids

Material	Density at 20°C (g/cm^3)
Vegetable oil	≈ 0.91
Water (4°C)	1.000
Dish soap	≈ 1.03
Corn syrup	≈ 1.33
Honey	≈ 1.36

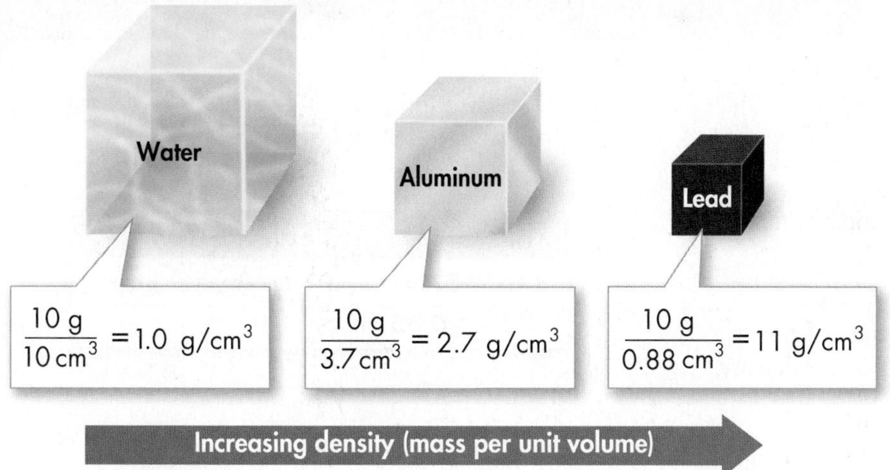

Comparing Densities
Look at the samples of water, aluminum, and lead. Note that each 10 g sample has a different volume. The 10 g sample of pure aluminum has a smaller volume than 10 g of water but a larger volume than 10 g of lead. The volumes vary because the substances have different densities.

Density of Gases You have probably seen a helium-filled balloon rapidly rise into the air when it is released. A gas-filled balloon will rise if the gas is less dense than air. The gas-filled balloon will sink if the density of the gas is greater than the density of air. Helium is less dense than air, so a helium-filled balloon rises. The table below shows the densities of some common gases. Notice that for gases, the units are grams per liter (g/L).

Densities of Some Common Gases

Material	Density at 20°C (g/L)
Carbon dioxide	1.83
Oxygen	1.33
Air	1.20
Nitrogen	1.17
Methane	0.665
Helium	0.166
Hydrogen	0.084

Density and Temperature What happens to the density of a substance as its temperature increases? Experiments show that the volume of most substances increases as the temperature increases. Meanwhile, the mass remains the same despite the temperature and volume changes. Remember that density is the ratio of an object's mass to its volume. So if the volume changes with temperature (while the mass remains constant), then the density must also change with temperature. The density of a substance generally decreases as its temperature increases.

As you will learn in Chapter 15, water is an important exception. At some range of temperatures, the volume of water increases as its temperature decreases. Ice, or solid water, floats because it is less dense (0.917 g/cm^3) than liquid water (1.000 g/cm^3).

Key Question What determines the density of a substance? **Density is an intensive property that depends on the composition of a substance, but not on the size of the sample. Density can be calculated by using the substance's volume and mass.**

Floating in Air
The density of air decreases as altitude increases. These helium balloons will stop rising when the density of the air is equal to or less than the density of helium.

Sample Problem 3.8

Calculating Density

A copper penny has a mass of 3.1 g and a volume of 0.35 cm^3. What is the density of copper?

KNOWNS	UNKNOWN
mass = 3.1 g	density = ? g/cm^3
volume = 0.35 cm^3	

1 Analyze List the knowns and the unknown. Use the known values and the equation for density.

2 Calculate Solve for the unknown.

Start with the equation for density.

$$\text{Density} = \frac{\text{mass}}{\text{volume}}$$

Substitute the known values in the equation and then solve.

$$\text{Density} = \frac{3.1\ \text{g}}{0.35\ \text{cm}^3} = 8.8571\ \text{g/cm}^3$$

Round to the correct number of significant figures.

Your answer has to have two significant figures.
Use the rules for rounding:
$8.8571\ \text{g/cm}^3 \rightarrow 8.9\ \text{g/cm}^3$

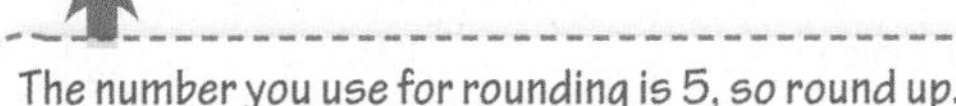

The number you use for rounding is 5, so round up.

3 Evaluate Does the answer make sense? The copper penny has a volume of approximately 0.3 cm^3 and a mass of about 3 grams. A piece of copper with three times the volume of the penny should have a mass three times larger—about 9 grams. One cubic centimeter (1 cm^3) is about three times the volume of 0.3. This estimate is close to the calculated result.

Practice Problems

25. A bar of silver has a mass of 68.0 g and a volume of 6.48 cm^3. What is the density of silver?

KNOWNS	UNKNOWN
mass = 68.0 g	density = ? g/cm^3
volume = 6.48 cm^3	

1 Analyze List the knowns and the unknown.

2 Calculate Solve for the unknown.

3 Evaluate Does this result make sense?

26. Challenge A student finds a shiny piece of metal that she thinks is aluminum. She determines that the metal has a volume of 245 cm^3 and a mass of 612 g. Calculate the density of the metal. Is the metal aluminum? The density of aluminum is 2.70 g/cm^3.

KNOWNS	UNKNOWNS
mass =	density = ? g/cm^3
volume =	Is this metal aluminum?
density of aluminum =	

CHEMISTRY & YOU: GREEN CHEMISTRY

Carbon Footprints

To measure a footprint, you might use such units as centimeters or inches. But what about a carbon footprint? A carbon footprint is a measure of how much greenhouse gas is released into the atmosphere by a person, country, or industry. Such greenhouse gases as carbon dioxide (CO_2) and methane (CH_4) are gases that contribute to global warming.

Any activity that involves the burning of fossil fuels results in CO_2 emissions. Car and air travel, home heating and cooling, and electricity usage add to an individual's carbon footprint. Your carbon footprint is the total mass of CO_2 that you put into the atmosphere over the course of a year. This quantity can be expressed in metric tons (t) of CO_2 per year. A metric ton equals 1000 kg. The units of your carbon footprint can be abbreviated as t CO_2/yr or 10^3 kg CO_2/yr.

FOOTPRINT UNITS The carbon footprint of fresh produce can be expressed in g CO_2 per serving. Cars require different units: kg CO_2 per gallon of gasoline.

Take It Further

Infer What factors do you think determine the carbon footprint of an apple? Why might the carbon footprints of two apples in the same store differ substantially?

3.2 LessonCheck

Key Concept Check

27. Review Why are metric units easy to use?

28. Identify What temperature units do scientists commonly use?

29. Review What determines density?

Vocabulary Check *Choose a highlighted word from the lesson to complete the sentence correctly.*

30. An object's ________ can be affected by a change in its location.

Think Critically

31. Identify Write the name and symbol of the SI units for mass, length, volume, and temperature.

32. Calculate Surgical instruments may be sterilized by heating at 170°C for 1.5 hr. Convert 170°C to kelvins.

33. Apply Concepts A 68 g bar of gold is cut into three equal pieces. How does the density of each piece compare to the density of the original gold bar?

CHEMISTRY & YOU

34. In a few countries, such as the United States, metric units are not commonly used in everyday measurements. What temperature units are used for a typical weather forecast in the United States? What about for a country that uses the metric system, such as Australia or Japan? (Hint: See page 72.)

3.3 Solving Conversion Problems

CHEMISTRY & YOU

Q: How can you convert U.S. dollars to euros? You may know that different countries have different currencies, or money. For example, the euro is the basic unit of money for many countries in Europe. The yen is the basic currency in Japan. Because each country's currency compares differently with the U.S. dollar, knowing how to convert currency units correctly is important if you plan to travel outside the United States. Conversion problems are easily solved by a problem-solving approach called dimensional analysis.

Key Questions

What happens when a measurement is multiplied by a conversion factor?

What kinds of problems can you solve by using dimensional analysis?

BUILD Vocabulary

conversion factor a ratio of equivalent measurements

dimensional analysis a method of problem solving that uses the units that are part of a measurement to solve a problem

RELATED WORDS
The word *conversion* is related to the word *convert*, which means "to change forms." Conversion factors are ratios that are used to change a value from one form to another.

Conversion Factors

Many everyday quantities can be expressed in several different ways. For example, consider money such as $1:

1 dollar = 4 quarters = 10 dimes = 20 nickels = 100 pennies

These are all ways to describe the same amount of money. The same thing is true of scientific quantities. For example, think about a length that measures exactly 1 meter:

1 meter = 100 centimeters = 1000 millimeters

These are different ways to express the same length. Whenever two measurements are equivalent, or equal, a ratio of the two measurements written as a fraction will equal 1. As you can see below, you can divide both sides of the equation 1 m = 100 cm by 1 m or by 100 cm.

$$\frac{1\text{ m}}{1\text{ m}} = \frac{100\text{ cm}}{1\text{ m}} = 1 \quad \text{or} \quad \frac{1\text{ m}}{100\text{ cm}} = \frac{100\text{ cm}}{100\text{ cm}} = 1$$

conversion factors

The ratios 100 cm/1 m and 1 m/100 cm are examples of conversion factors. A **conversion factor** is a ratio of equivalent measurements. The measurement in the numerator (on the top) is equivalent to the measurement in the denominator (on the bottom). The conversion factors shown above are read "one hundred centimeters per meter" and "one meter per hundred centimeters."

Conversion factors within a system of measurement are defined quantities or exact quantities. Therefore, they have an unlimited number of significant figures. They also do not affect the rounding of a calculated answer.

1 meter 100 centimeters

1 m = 10 20 30 40 50 60 70 80 90

Smaller quantity → **1 m** ← Larger unit

Larger quantity → **100 cm** ← Smaller unit

Conversion Factor
The two parts of a conversion factor—the numerator and denominator—are equal.

See conversion factors *animated online.*

The figure above shows another way to look at the relationships in a conversion factor. Notice that the smaller quantity is part of the measurement with the larger unit. That is, a meter is physically larger than a centimeter. The larger quantity is part of the measurement with the smaller unit. You can also use conversion factors to convert between units that do not have the same base unit. For example, volume can be given in units of milliliters or cubic centimeters. The relationship 1 mL = 1 cm^3 yields the following conversion factors:

$$\frac{1\ \text{mL}}{1\ \text{cm}^3} \quad \text{and} \quad \frac{1\ \text{cm}^3}{1\ \text{mL}}$$

You can write a conversion factor any time you have an equation that shows two things to be equivalent.

Key Question What happens when a measurement is multiplied by a conversion factor? **When a measurement is multiplied by a conversion factor, the numerical value and units are changed. However, the size of the quantity remains the same.**

Dimensional Analysis

You can solve some problems by using algebra. For example, you can convert kelvins to degree Celsius by using the equation °C = K − 273. Other problems can be solved by using dimensional analysis. **Dimensional analysis** is a way to solve problems by using the units, or dimensions, of measurements.

Simple Unit Conversions In chemistry, you may need to express a measurement in a unit that is different from the given unit. Dimensional analysis allows you to convert the units of a measurement into an equivalent measurement with another unit. Recall that you can cancel quantities and units that are found in the numerator and denominator of a fraction. Dimensional analysis uses conversion factors that allow you to cancel in this way. You cancel like units and leave the desired unit for your answer.

Multistep Problems Many complex tasks are best handled by breaking them down into smaller parts. Suppose you were cleaning a car. You might first vacuum the inside and then wash and dry the exterior. Many complex word problems are more easily solved by breaking the problem down into steps too. When converting between units, sometimes you must use more than one conversion factor. Go to your *Chemistry Skills and Math Workbook* for practice.

Key Question What kinds of problems can you solve by using dimensional analysis? **You can use dimensional analysis for solving conversion problems in which a measurement with one unit is changed to an equivalent measure with another unit.**

BUILD Connections

You might not realize it, but you do dimensional analysis all the time. For example, you know that one-half hour is 30 minutes:

$$0.5\ \cancel{\text{hr}} \times \frac{60\ \text{min}}{1\ \cancel{\text{hr}}} = 30\ \text{min}$$

This is dimensional analysis!

Using Dimensional Analysis

The directions for an experiment ask each student to measure 1.84 g of copper (Cu) wire. The teacher has a spool of copper wire with a mass of 50.0 g. How many students can do the experiment?

KNOWNS	UNKNOWN
mass of copper available = 50.0 g Cu	number of students = ?
Each student needs 1.84 grams of copper.	

1 Analyze **List the knowns and the unknown.**

2 Calculate **Solve for the unknown.** The desired conversion is mass of copper ⟶ number of students.

You know that each student needs 1.84 g of copper. Write two conversion factors based on that relationship.

$$\frac{1.84 \text{ g Cu}}{1 \text{ student}} \text{ and } \frac{1 \text{ student}}{1.84 \text{ g Cu}}$$

Select the conversion factor needed to convert from units of mass to units of students.

$$\frac{1 \text{ student}}{1.84 \text{ g Cu}}$$

Hint: You cannot have a fraction of a student, so round down your answer to a whole number.

Multiply the mass of copper by the conversion factor.

$$50.0 \cancel{\text{g Cu}} \times \frac{1 \text{ student}}{1.84 \cancel{\text{g Cu}}} = 27.174 \text{ students} = 27 \text{ students}$$

3 Evaluate **Does the result make sense?** The unit of the answer (students) is the one desired. You can estimate the answer by using the conversion factor of 1 student to 2 g of Cu. Multiplying the conversion factor by 50 g Cu gives the approximate answer of 25 students, which is close to the calculated answer.

Practice Problems

35. An experiment requires that each student use an 8.5 cm length of magnesium ribbon. How many students can do the experiment if there is a 570 cm length of magnesium ribbon available?

1 Analyze **List the knowns and the unknown.**

2 Calculate **Solve for the unknown.**

3 Evaluate **Does the result make sense?**

KNOWNS	UNKNOWN
length of magnesium ribbon available = 570 cm	number of students = ?
Each student needs 8.5 cm magnesium ribbon.	

36. Challenge An atom of gold has a mass of 3.271×10^{-22} g. How many atoms of gold are in 5.00 g of gold?

KNOWNS	UNKNOWN
mass of 1 atom of gold = mass of gold =	number of gold atoms = ?

Sample Problem 3.10

Converting Between Metric Units: Simple Unit Conversions

Convert 750 dg to g. (Refer to the table on page 69 if you need to review metric prefixes.)

1 Analyze **List the knowns and the unknown.** The desired conversion is decigrams ⟶ grams. Multiply the given units by the correct conversion factor. Use the relationship 1 g = 10 dg to write the conversion factor.

KNOWNS	UNKNOWN
mass = 750 dg	mass = ? g
1 g = 10 dg	

2 Calculate **Solve for the unknown.**

Use the relationship 1 g = 10 dg to write the correct conversion factor.

$$\frac{1\ g}{10\ dg}$$

Notice that the known unit (dg) is in the denominator and the unknown unit (g) is in the numerator.

Multiply the known mass by the conversion factor.

$$750\ \cancel{dg} \times \frac{1\ g}{10\ \cancel{dg}} = 75\ g$$

3 Evaluate **Does the result make sense?** A gram is a larger mass than a decigram. So it makes sense that the number of grams is less than the given number of decigrams. The answer has the correct unit and the correct number of significant figures.

Practice Problems

37. Convert the following:

a. 15 cm^3 to liters **b.** 7.38 g to kilograms

KNOWNS	UNKNOWNS
a. volume = 15 cm^3	volume = ? L
b. mass = 7.38 g	mass = ? kg

1 Analyze **List the knowns and the unknowns.**

2 Calculate **Solve for the unknowns.**

3 Evaluate **Do the results make sense?**

38. Challenge The diameter of a sewing needle is 0.073 centimeters (cm). What is the diameter in micrometers (μm)?

You can use a two-step conversion to change centimeters to micrometers. First, change centimeters to meters. Then, change meters to micrometers.

SampleProblem 3.11

Using Density as a Conversion Factor

What is the volume of a pure silver coin that has a mass of 14 g? The density of silver (Ag) is 10.5 g/cm^3.

❶ Analyze List the knowns and the unknown. You need to convert the mass of the coin into a corresponding volume. The density gives you the following relationship between volume and mass: 1 cm^3 Ag = 10.5 g Ag. Multiply the mass by the proper conversion factor to get an answer in cm^3.

KNOWNS	UNKNOWN
mass = 14 g	volume of coin = ? cm^3
density of silver = 10.5 g/cm^3	

❷ Calculate Solve for the unknown.

Use the relationship 1 cm^3 Ag = 10.5 g Ag to write two conversion factors.

$$\frac{10.5\text{ g Ag}}{1\text{ cm}^3\text{ Ag}} \text{ and } \frac{1\text{ cm}^3\text{ Ag}}{10.5\text{ g Ag}}$$

Choose the conversion factor needed to convert from mass to volume.

$$\frac{1\text{ cm}^3\text{ Ag}}{10.5\text{ g Ag}}$$

Notice that the known unit (g) is in the denominator and the unknown unit (cm^3) is in the numerator.

Multiply the mass of the coin by the conversion factor.

$$14\,\cancel{\text{g Ag}} \times \frac{1\text{ cm}^3\text{ Ag}}{10.5\,\cancel{\text{g Ag}}} = 1.3333\text{ cm}^3\text{ Ag}$$

Round your answer to the appropriate number of significant figures.

Your answer must have two significant figures.

$1.3333\text{ cm}^3\text{ Ag} \longrightarrow 1.3\text{ cm}^3\text{ Ag}$

❸ Evaluate Does the result make sense? A mass of 10.5 g of silver has a volume of 1 cm^3. So it makes sense that 14.0 g of silver should have a volume slightly larger than 1 cm^3. The answer has two significant figures because the given mass has two significant figures.

Density can be used to write two conversion factors. To figure out which one you need, consider the units of your given quantity and the units needed in your answer.

Practice Problems

39. Use dimensional analysis and the given density to make the following conversion: 14.8 g of boron to cm^3 of boron. The density of boron is 2.34 g/cm^3.

❶ **Analyze** **List the knowns and the unknown.**

❷ **Calculate** **Solve for the unknown.**

❸ **Evaluate** **Does this result make sense?**

KNOWNS	UNKNOWN
mass = 14.8 g	volume = ? cm^3
density = 2.34 g/cm^3	

40. Use dimensional analysis and the given density to make the following conversion: 4.62 g of mercury to cm^3 of mercury. The density of mercury is 13.5 g/cm^3.

KNOWNS	UNKNOWN
mass =	volume = ? cm^3
density =	

41. Challenge Rework Problems 39 and 40 by applying the following equation.

$$\text{Density} = \frac{\text{mass}}{\text{volume}}$$

3.3 LessonCheck

Key Concept Check

42. **Review** What happens to the numerical value of a measurement that is multiplied by a conversion factor? What happens to the actual size of the quantity?

43. **Review** What types of problems can be solved by using dimensional analysis?

Think Critically

44. Identify What conversion factor would you use to convert between these pairs of units?

a. minutes to hours

b. grams to milligrams

c. cubic centimeters to milliliters

45. Calculate Make the following conversions. Express your answers in scientific notation.

a. 14.8 g = ? μg

b. 3.72 g = ? kg

c. 66.3 L = ? cm^3

d. 7.5×10^4 J = ? kJ

e. 3.9×10^5 mg = ? dg

f. 2.1×10^{-4} dL = ? μL

CHEMISTRY & YOU

46. Use the Internet to find the exchange rate of U.S. dollars to euros. Write a conversion factor that allows you to convert from U.S. dollars to euros. How many euros could you buy with $50? (Hint: See page 79.)

3 Study Guide

BIGIDEA QUANTIFYING MATTER

Scientists express the degree of uncertainty in their measurements and calculations by using significant figures. In general, a calculated answer cannot be more precise than the least precise measurement from which it was calculated. Dimensional analysis is a problem-solving method that involves analyzing the units of the given measurement and the unknown to plan a solution.

3.1 Using and Expressing Measurements

In scientific notation, a number is written as the product of a coefficient and 10 raised to a power. The coefficient must be greater than or equal to 1 and less than 10.

You can evaluate the accuracy of a measurement by comparing the measured value to the correct value. You can evaluate the precision of a measurement by comparing the values of two or more repeated measurements.

Measurements must always be reported to the correct number of significant figures. Calculated answers often depend on the number of significant figures in the values used in the calculation.

- measurement (54)
- scientific notation (54)
- accuracy (57)
- precision (57)
- accepted value (58)
- experimental value (58)
- error (58)
- percent error (58)
- significant figures (60)

Key Equations

$$\text{Error} = \text{experimental value} - \text{accepted value}$$

$$\text{Percent error} = \frac{|\text{error}|}{\text{accepted value}} \times 100\%$$

3.2 Units of Measurement

All metric units are based on multiples of 10. As a result, you can easily convert between units.

Scientists commonly use two equivalent units of temperature: the degree Celsius and the kelvin.

Density is an intensive property that depends only on the composition of a substance, not on the size of the sample. Density can be calculated by using the substance's volume and mass.

- International System of Units (SI) (68)
- meter (m) (69)
- liter (L) (70)
- kilogram (kg) (71)
- gram (g) (71)
- weight (71)
- energy (71)
- joule (J) (71)
- calorie (cal) (71)
- temperature (72)
- Celsius scale (72)
- Kelvin scale (72)
- absolute zero (72)
- density (74)

Key Equations

$$K = {}^{\circ}C + 273$$

$${}^{\circ}C = K - 273$$

$$\text{Density} = \frac{\text{mass}}{\text{volume}}$$

3.3 Solving Conversion Problems

When a measurement is multiplied by a conversion factor, the numerical value and units are changed. However, the actual size of the quantity remains the same.

You can use dimensional analysis for solving conversion problems in which a measurement with one unit is changed to an equivalent measure with another unit.

- conversion factor (78)
- dimensional analysis (79)

Math Tune-Up: Conversion Problems

Problem	❶ Analyze	❷ Calculate	❸ Evaluate
A grocer is selling oranges at 3 for \$2. How much would it cost to buy a dozen oranges?	Knowns: 3 oranges = \$2 1 dozen = 12 Unknown: cost of 12 oranges = ? The desired conversion is oranges ⟶ \$.	Use the relationship 3 oranges = \$2 to write the correct conversion factor: $\frac{\$2}{3 \text{ oranges}}$ Multiply the known quantity by the conversion factor: $12 \cancel{\text{oranges}} \times \frac{\$2}{3 \cancel{\text{oranges}}} = \$8$	A dozen is larger than the number 3, so the cost should exceed \$2. The known unit (oranges) cancels, and the answer has the correct unit (\$).
Convert the volume 865 cm^3 to liters.	Knowns: volume = 865 cm^3 10^3 cm^3 = 1 L Unknown: volume = ? L The desired conversion is cm^3 ⟶ L.	Use the relationship 10^3 cm^3 = 1 L to write the correct conversion factor: $\frac{1 \text{ L}}{10^3 \text{ cm}^3}$ Multiply the known volume by the conversion factor: $865 \cancel{\text{cm}^3} \times \frac{1 \text{ L}}{10^3 \cancel{\text{cm}^3}} = 0.865 \text{ L}$	A cubic centimeter is much smaller than a liter, so the answer should be numerically smaller than the given measurement. The known unit (cm^3) cancels, and the answer has the correct unit (L).
Express the length 8.2×10^{-4} μm in centimeters.	Knowns: length = 8.2×10^{-4} μm 10^6 μm = 1 m 1 m = 10^2 cm Unknown: length = ? cm The desired conversion is μm ⟶ cm. First, change μm to m and then change m to cm: μm ⟶ m ⟶ cm.	Use the relationship 10^6 μm = 1 m to write the first conversion factor: $\frac{1 \text{ m}}{10^6 \text{ μm}}$ Use the relationship 1 m = 10^2 cm to write the second conversion factor: $\frac{10^2 \text{ cm}}{1 \text{ m}}$ Multiply the known length by the conversion factors: $8.2 \times 10^{-4} \cancel{\text{μm}} \times \frac{1 \cancel{\text{m}}}{10^6 \cancel{\text{μm}}} \times \frac{10^2 \text{ cm}}{1 \cancel{\text{m}}}$ $= 8.2 \times 10^{-8}$ cm	A micrometer is smaller than a centimeter, so the answer should be numerically smaller than the given measurement. The known unit (μm) cancels, and the answer has the correct unit (cm). Hint: For a multistep problem, do one conversion at a time.

3 Assessment

★ Solutions appear in Appendix D.

Lesson by Lesson

3.1 Using and Expressing Measurements

47. Three students found the mass of a copper cylinder four times—each using a different balance. Describe the accuracy and precision of each student's measurements if the correct mass of the cylinder is 47.32 g.

Mass of Cylinder (g)			
	Colin	Travis	Kivrin
Weighing 1	47.13	47.45	47.95
Weighing 2	47.94	47.39	47.91
Weighing 3	46.83	47.42	47.89
Weighing 4	47.47	47.41	47.93

48. How many significant figures are in each underlined measurement?

a. <u>60 s</u> = 1 min
b. <u>47.70 g</u> of copper
c. 1 km = <u>1000 m</u>

49. Round off each of these measurements to three significant figures.

a. 98.473 L
b. 0.000 763 21 cg
c. 12.17°C
d. $0.007\,498\,3 \times 10^4$ mm

★**50.** Round off each of the answers correctly.

a. 8.7 g + 15.43 g + 19 g = 43.13 g
b. 4.32 cm × 1.7 cm = 7.344 cm^2
c. 853.2 L − 627.443 L = 225.757 L
d. 38.742 m^2 ÷ 0.421 m = 92.023 75 m

51. How are the error and the percent error of a measurement calculated?

3.2 Units of Measurement

52. Write the SI base unit of measurement for each of these quantities.

a. time
b. length
c. temperature
d. mass
e. energy
f. amount of substance

★**53.** Order these units from smallest to largest: cm, μm, km, mm, m, nm, dm. Then, give each measurement in terms of meters.

54. The melting point of tin is 232 °C. Express this temparature in kelvins.

55. What equation is used to determine the density of an object?

★**56.** A shiny, gold-colored bar of metal has a mass of 57.3 g. It has a volume of 4.7 cm^3. Is the bar of metal pure gold? (Hint: Gold has a density of 19.3 g/cm^3.)

3.3 Solving Conversion Problems

57. What must be true for a ratio of two measurements to be a conversion factor?

58. How do you know which unit of a conversion factor must be in the denominator?

★**59.** Make the following conversions.

a. 157 seconds to minutes
b. 42.7 L to milliliters
c. 261 nm to millimeters
d. 0.065 km to decimeters

★**60.** Make the following conversions.

a. 0.44 mL/min to microliters per second
b. 7.86 g/cm^2 to milligrams per square millimeter
c. 1.54 kg/L to grams per cubic centimeter

61. How many milliliters are contained in 1 m^3?

★**62.** Complete this table so all the measurements in each row have the same value.

mg	g	cg	kg
a. ____	b. ____	28.3	c. ____
6.6×10^3	d. ____	e. ____	f. ____
g. ____	2.8×10^{-4}	h. ____	i. ____

Understand Concepts

63. Rank these numbers from smallest to largest.

a. 5.3×10^4
b. 57×10^3
c. 4.9×10^{-2}
d. 0.0057
e. 5.1×10^{-3}
f. 0.0072×10^2

64. Comment on the accuracy and precision of these basketball free-throw shooters.

a. 99 of 100 shots are made.
b. 99 of 100 shots hit the front of the rim and bounce off.
c. 33 of 100 shots are made; the rest miss.

65. Write six conversion factors involving these units of measure: $1 \text{ g} = 10^2 \text{ cg} = 10^3 \text{ mg}$.

***66.** A 2.00 kg sample of bituminous coal is composed of 1.30 kg of carbon, 0.20 kg of ash, 0.15 kg of water, and 0.35 kg of a volatile (gas-forming) material. Using this information, determine how many kilograms of carbon are in 125 kg of this coal.

***67.** The density of dry air measured at 25°C is $1.19 \times 10^{-3} \text{ g/cm}^3$. What is the volume of 50.0 g of air?

***68.** A watch loses 0.15 s every minute. How many minutes will the watch lose in one day?

***69.** Earth is approximately 1.5×10^8 km from the sun. How many minutes does it take light to travel from the sun to Earth? (The speed of light is 3.0×10^8 m/s.)

***70.** A tank measuring 28.6 cm by 73.0 mm by 0.72 m is filled with olive oil. The oil in the tank has a mass of 1.38×10^4 g. What is the density of olive oil in kilograms per liter?

FOUNDATIONS Wrap-Up

Exploring Density

1. Draw Conclusions At the beginning of this chapter, you placed two different liquids in a cup. Explain why the liquids formed layers the way they did.

Concept Check

Now that you've finished studying Chapter 3, answer these questions:

2. Which SI unit would you use to express the length of your hand?

3. Explian how derived units are different from base units.

4. Suppose water gets in a car's fuel tank. Will the water be on the top or the bottom of the tank? (Assume that the two liquids do not mix into one another.) The density of water is 1.000 g/cm^3, and the density of gasoline is about 0.67 g/cm^3.

5. An airline has a weight limit of 23 kg for one suitcase. If your suitcase weighs 55 pounds, can you take it?

Think Critically

*71. **Calculate** One of the first mixtures of metals—called an amalgam—was used by dentists for tooth fillings. Amalgams consisted of 26.0 g of silver, 10.8 g of tin, 2.4 g of copper, and 0.8 g of zinc. How much silver is in a 25.0 g sample of this amalgam?

72. **Describe** What if ice were more dense than water? It would certainly be easier to pour water from a pitcher of ice cubes and water. Think of another situation that would differ.

CHEMYSTERY

Just Give Me a Sign

The road signs point to locations in England. Although England has adopted metric units for many everyday quantities, distances shown on road signs are not among them. The road signs above list distances in miles—a nonmetric unit. Speed limit signs in England are typically expressed in miles per hour—also nonmetric. However, in the same country, gasoline is sold by metric units of volume (liters), fabric is measured in metric units of area (square meters), and the local weather report uses metric units of temperature (°C).

73. **Calculate** The relationship between kilometers and miles (mi) is 1 km = 0.621 mi. How far it is to Chipping in kilometers?

74. **Calculate** Suppose you encounter the road signs above while cycling. If your average speed is 18 km/h, how many minutes will it take you to reach Preston?

75. **Connect to the BIGIDEA** Describe two ways in which the road signs above might be considered examples of "uncertainty in measurement."

*76. **Calculate** A cheetah can run 112 km/h over a 100 m distance. What is this speed in meters per second?

77. **Graph** Plot these data that show how the mass of sulfur increases with an increase in volume. Determine the density of sulfur from the slope of the line.

Volume of sulfur (cm^3)	Mass of sulfur (g)
11.4	23.5
29.2	60.8
55.5	115
81.1	168

Write About Science

78. **Describe** For one of the topics below, write a short paragraph that identifies metric and nonmetric units that are commonly used to communicate information.
    a. measurements used in cooking
    b. measurements used in sports
    c. measurements used in transportation

79. **Connect to the BIGIDEA** Explain how the three-step problem-solving approach defined in Chapter 1 (Analyze, Calculate, Evaluate) applies to problems that involve dimensional analysis.

Standardized Test Prep

For help with answering test questions, go to your Chemistry Skills and Math Workbook.

Select the choice that best answers each question or completes each statement.

1. Which of these series of units is ordered from smallest to largest?
   (A) μg, cg, mg, kg
   (B) mm, dm, m, km
   (C) μs, ns, cs, s
   (D) nL, mL, dL, cL
2. Which answer represents the measurement 0.00428 g rounded to two significant figures?
   (A) 4.28×10^3 g
   (B) 4.3×10^3 g
   (C) 4.3×10^{-3} g
   (D) 4.0×10^{-3} g
3. An over-the-counter medicine has 325 mg of its active ingredient per tablet. How many grams does this mass represent?
   (A) 325,000 g
   (B) 32.5 g
   (C) 3.25 g
   (D) 0.325 g
4. If 10^4 μm = 1 cm, how many μm^3 = 1 cm^3?
   (A) 10^4
   (B) 10^6
   (C) 10^8
   (D) 10^{12}
5. If a substance contracts when it freezes, its
   (A) density will remain the same.
   (B) density will increase.
   (C) density will decrease.
   (D) change in density cannot be predicted.

For Questions 6–7, identify the knowns and the unknown. Include units in your answers.

6. The density of water is 1.0 g/mL. How many deciliters of water will fill a 0.5 L bottle?
7. A graduated cylinder contains 44.2 mL of water. A 48.6 g piece of metal is carefully dropped into the cylinder. When the metal is completely covered with water, the water rises to the 51.3 mL mark. What is the density of the metal?

Tips for Success

Interpret Diagrams Before you answer questions about a diagram, study the diagram carefully. Ask: What is the diagram showing? What does it tell me?

Use the diagrams below to answer Questions 8 and 9.

The atomic windows represent particles of the same gas occupying the same volume at the same temperature. The systems differ only in the number of gas particles per unit volume.

a.
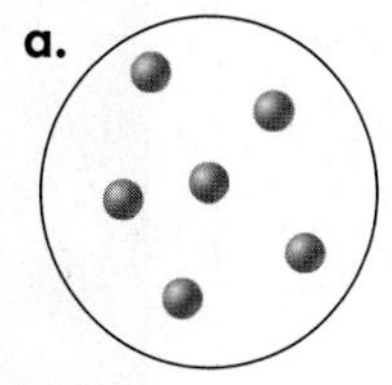
b.
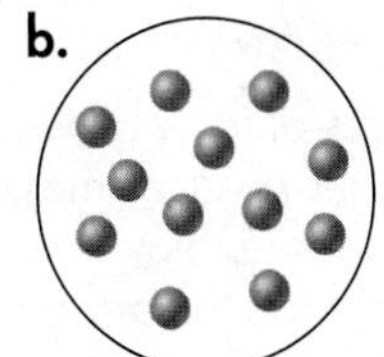
c.
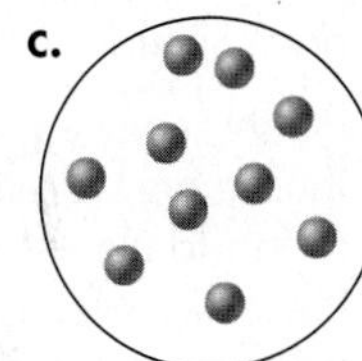

8. List the windows in order of decreasing density.
9. Compare the density of the gas in window (a) to the density of the gas in window (b).

For each question, there are two statements. Decide whether each statement is true or false. Then, decide whether Statement II is a correct explanation for Statement I.

	Statement I		Statement II
10.	There are five significant figures in the measurement 0.00450 m.	BECAUSE	All zeros to the right of a decimal point in a measurement are significant.
11.	Precise measurements will always be accurate measurements.	BECAUSE	A value that is measured 10 times in a row must be accurate.
12.	A temperature in kelvins is always numerically larger than the same temperature in degrees Celsius.	BECAUSE	A temperature in kelvins equals a temperature in degrees Celsius plus 273.

If You Have Trouble With . . .

Question	1	2	3	4	5	6	7	8	9	10	11	12
See Lesson	3.2	3.1	3.3	3.3	3.2	3.3	3.2	3.2	3.2	3.1	3.1	3.2

4

Atomic Structure

FOUNDATIONS for Learning

Electric Charge

1. Firmly stick two 25 cm pieces of clear plastic tape side-by-side to your desktop, about 10 cm apart. Leave 2 to 3 cm of tape sticking over the edge of the desk.
2. Grasp the free ends of the tape pieces and pull sharply upward to peel the tape off the desk. Slowly bring the pieces, which have similar charges, toward one another.
3. Pull two more pieces of tape between your thumb and forefinger several times, as if trying to clean each one. Slowly bring these two pieces of tape toward one another. What do you observe?

Form a Hypothesis Do you think the tape pieces used in Step 2 have the same charge as those used in Step 3? Test your hypothesis.

PearsonChem.com

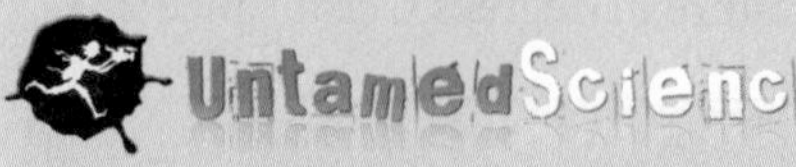

Take a video field trip as the Untamed Science crew re-enacts a crime scene to explore how isotopes can be used as evidence to solve crimes.

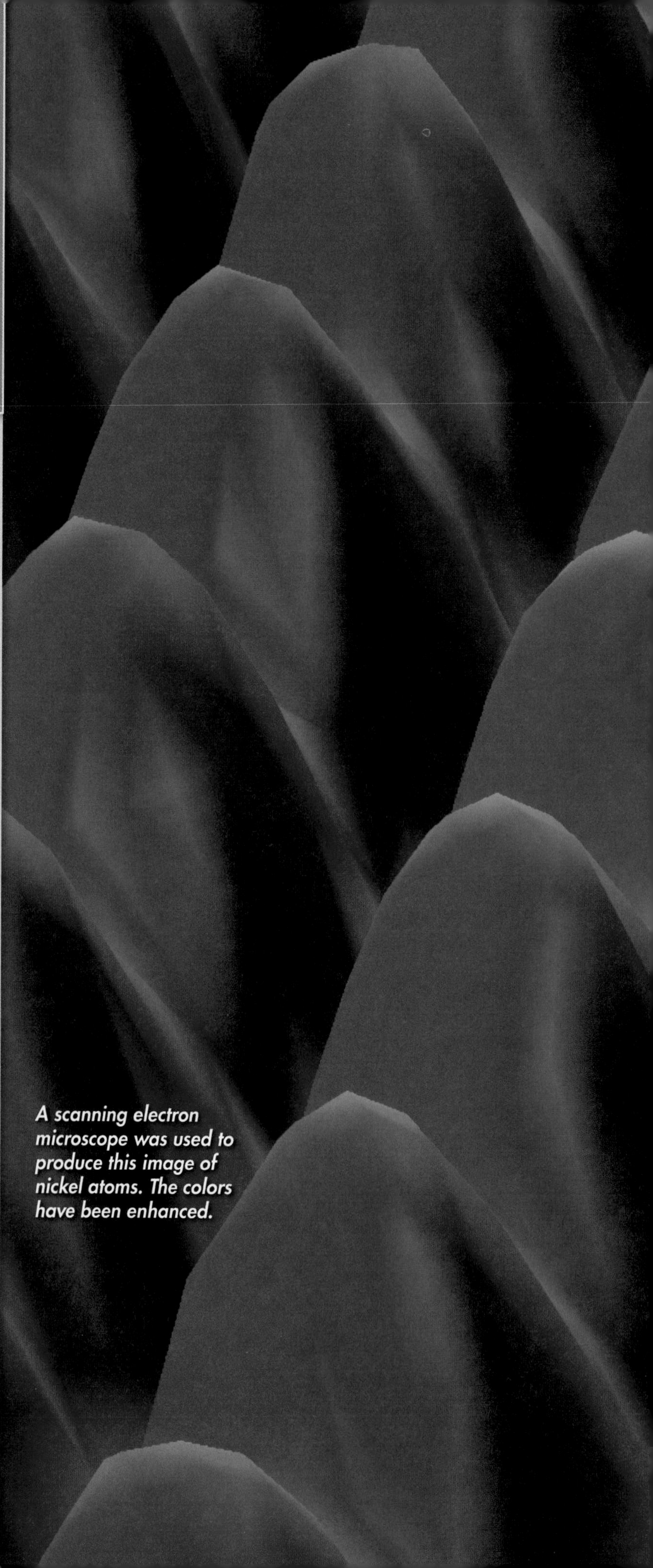

A scanning electron microscope was used to produce this image of nickel atoms. The colors have been enhanced.

BIGIDEA

ELECTRONS AND THE STRUCTURE OF ATOMS

Essential Questions:

1. *What components make up an atom?*
2. *How are atoms of one element different from atoms of another element?*

CHEMYSTERY

Artifact or Artifake?

Crystal skulls are shaped like human skulls and carved from quartz crystal. Crystal skulls are thought to have originated from pre-Columbian Central American cultures. If so, then crystal skulls would have been carved several hundred, or even thousands, of years ago. They would probably have been carved using primitive stone, wooden, and bone tools.

Although crystal skulls are displayed in museums throughout the world, none of them were found in an actual archaeological dig. This unusual circumstance has led to some debate about the skulls' history. People have questioned whether crystal skulls were ever carved by people from ancient civilizations. Are these sculptures true artifacts that were carved in the pre-Columbian era, or are they just fakes?

▶ Connect to the BIGIDEA As you read about the structure of atoms, think about how scientists could identify whether a crystal skull originated from an ancient civilization or is just a fake.

4.1 Defining the Atom

CHEMISTRY & YOU

Q: How do you study something that you cannot see? Sometimes it is fun to try to guess what is inside a present before you open it. You might examine the shape or weight of the box. Or you might shake the box a little to find out if anything moves around or makes noise inside of it. Similar to how you might study a wrapped present, scientists study things that cannot be seen with the naked eye. In this lesson, you will learn how scientists studied atoms without being able to see them.

Key Questions

How did John Dalton further Democritus's ideas on atoms?

What instruments are used to observe individual atoms?

BUILD Vocabulary

atom the smallest particle of matter that retains the identity of an element in a chemical reaction

Dalton's atomic theory an early theory relating chemical changes to events at the atomic level

WORD ORIGINS

Atom comes from the Greek word *atomos*, meaning "indivisible."

Early Models of the Atom

Using your unaided eyes, you cannot see the tiny particles that make up matter. Yet, all matter is made up of such particles, which are called atoms. An **atom** is the smallest particle of an element that keeps the element's identity in a chemical reaction.

Many early scholars were curious about the idea of the atom. They wanted to know what the smallest and most basic units of matter looked like and how they acted. Though these philosophers and scientists did not have the tools to see individual atoms, they were able to suggest ideas about the structure of atoms.

Democritus's Atomic Philosophy The Greek philosopher Democritus (460 B.C.–370 B.C.) was one of the first people to suggest the existence of atoms. Democritus reasoned that atoms were indivisible and indestructible. Democritus's ideas were based on observations of matter with the unaided eye. Democritus and people of his time did not have the tools to study or experiment with matter. His ideas agreed with later scientific theory, but they did not explain the chemical behavior of matter. Democritus's ideas were not supported by experiments, because his ideas were philosophical. Democritus used a thoughtful approach to study matter instead of using techniques based on the scientific method.

Dalton's Atomic Theory A better understanding of atoms and chemical behavior developed more than 2,000 years after Democritus's death. John Dalton (1766–1844), an English chemist and school teacher, used experimental methods to look into Democritus's ideas on atoms.

Dalton's Atomic Theory
Dalton's atomic theory explains atoms' characteristics and how atoms can interact.

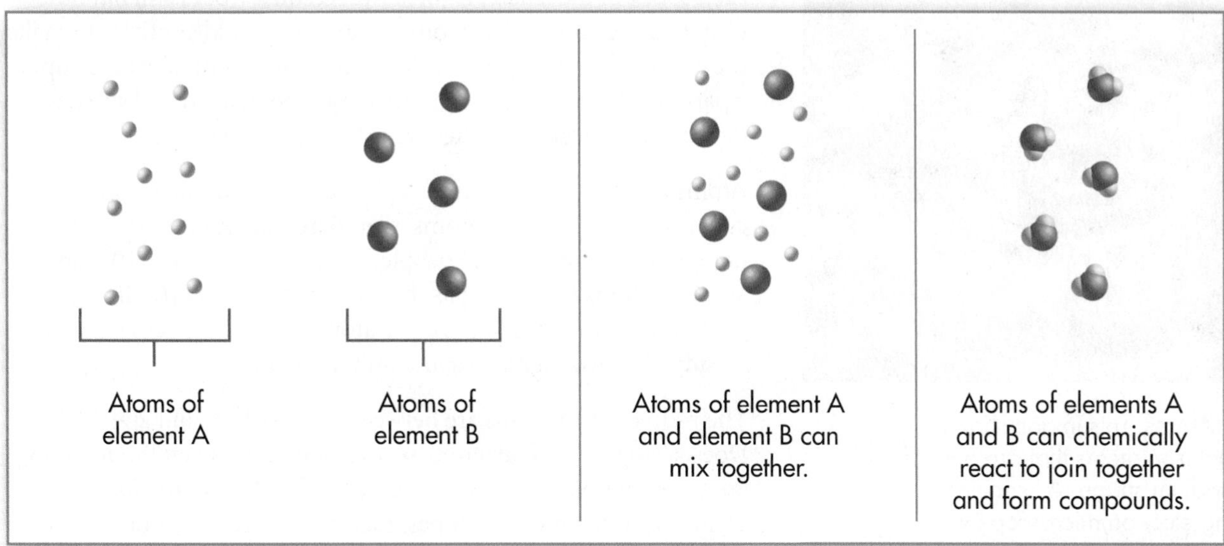

Atoms of element A
Atoms of element B
Atoms of element A and element B can mix together.
Atoms of elements A and B can chemically react to join together and form compounds.

Over many years, Dalton tested hypotheses and developed theories to explain his observations of chemistry. The result of his work is known as **Dalton's atomic theory.** Dalton's atomic theory includes the ideas listed below. They are also illustrated in the figure above.

1. All elements are composed of tiny indivisible particles called atoms. Atoms of the same element are identical. The atoms of any one element are different from those of any other element.
2. Atoms of different elements can physically mix together or can chemically combine in simple whole-number ratios to form compounds.
3. Chemical reactions occur when atoms are rearranged so that atoms are attached in a different arrangement. Atoms of one element, however, are never changed into atoms of another element as a result of a chemical reaction.

Key Question How did John Dalton further Democritus's ideas on atoms? **Democritus reasoned that atoms were indivisible and indestructible. Dalton conducted experiments to study the nature of atoms and to develop a scientific theory about them.**

Drops of Mercury
This petri dish contains drops of liquid mercury. Every drop of mercury, no matter its size, has the same properties. Even if you could make a drop the size of one atom, it would still have the chemical properties of mercury.

Sizing Up the Atom

The liquid mercury shown in the petri dish to the right illustrates Dalton's atomic theory. Whether the drops of mercury are large or small, all of the drops have the same properties. All of the drops are made of the same kind of atoms.

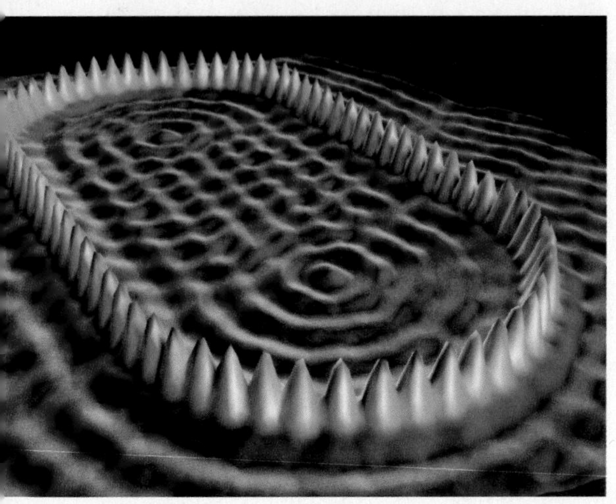

Moving Atoms This image shows individual iron atoms that are positioned into a stadium shape. A scanning tunnelling electron microscope was used to observe these atoms.

Another example is to think of a coin made of the element copper (Cu). If you were to grind the copper coin into a fine dust, each speck in the small pile of shiny red dust would still have the properties of copper. If by some means you could continue to make the copper dust particles smaller, you would eventually come upon a particle of copper that could no longer be divided and still have copper's chemical properties. This final particle is an atom.

Atoms are very small. A pure copper coin the size of a penny contains about 2×10^{22} atoms. Compare that number to Earth's population, about 7×10^{9} people. There are about 3×10^{12} times as many atoms in the coin as there are people on Earth. If you could line up 100,000,000 copper atoms (or 10^{8} copper atoms) side by side, they would make a line only 1 cm long!

The radii of most atoms are between 5×10^{-11} m and 2×10^{-10} m. Does seeing individual atoms seem impossible? Even though they are small, atoms can be seen with specialized instruments such as scanning electron microscopes. Electron microscopes have a higher resolution and can be used to view much smaller objects than light microscopes.

With the help of electron microscopes, individual atoms can even be moved around and put in patterns as in the figure on the left. The ability to move atoms may one day allow us to make atomic-sized devices, such as electronic circuits and computer chips.

Key Question What instruments are used to observe individual atoms? **Individual atoms can be seen with instruments such as scanning electron microscopes.**

4.1 LessonCheck

Key Concept Check

1. **Review** How did Democritus characterize atoms?
2. **Explain** How did Dalton advance the atomic philosophy proposed by Democritus?
3. **Identify** What instrument can be used to observe individual atoms?

Vocabulary Check *Choose a highlighted word from the lesson to complete each sentence correctly.*

4. One of the ideas in __________ is that all elements are composed of tiny indivisible particles called atoms.
5. The smallest particle of an element that keeps its identity in a chemical reaction is a(n) __________.

Think Critically

6. **Explain** In your own words, explain the main ideas of Dalton's atomic theory.
7. **Calculate** A sample of copper with a mass of 63.5 g contains 6.02×10^{23} atoms. Calculate the mass of a single copper atom.

CHEMISTRY & YOU

8. Dalton studied atoms by observing the ratios in which elements combine in chemical reactions. How is this similar to figuring out what is inside a present before opening it? (Hint: See page 93.)

BIGIDEA

ELECTRONS AND THE STRUCTURE OF ATOMS

9. According to Dalton's theory, is it possible to convert atoms of one element into atoms of another? Explain.

4.2 Structure of the Nuclear Atom

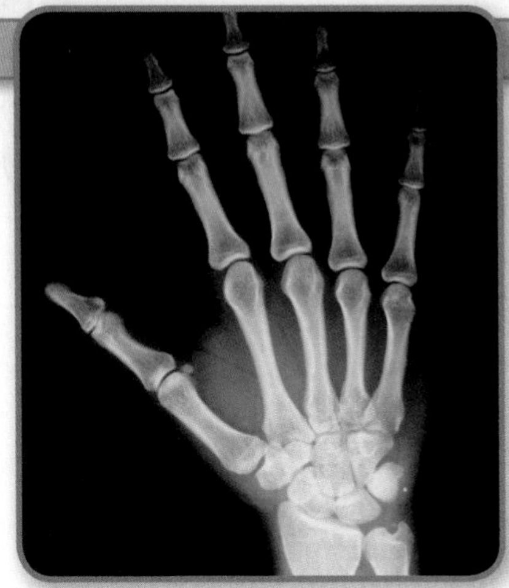

CHEMISTRY & YOU

Q: You can X-ray a person's hand to see inside it—but how can you see inside an atom? Doctors often use X-rays to see bones and other structures that cannot be seen through the skin. Scientists tried to determine what was inside an atom without being able to see inside it. In this lesson, you will learn about the methods scientists used to "see" inside an atom.

Key Questions

What are three kinds of subatomic particles?

How can you describe the structure of the nuclear atom?

BUILD Vocabulary

electron a negatively charged subatomic particle

cathode ray a stream of electrons produced at the negative electrode (cathode) of a tube containing gas at low pressure

Subatomic Particles

In the previous lesson, you learned about Dalton's atomic theory. Dalton's atomic theory discussed properties and interactions of atoms. Even though Dalton's atomic theory is almost 200 years old, most of the theory is still accepted today. One important change, however, is that atoms are now known to be divisible. They can be broken down into even smaller, more fundamental particles, called subatomic particles. Three kinds of subatomic particles are electrons, protons, and neutrons.

Electrons In 1897, the English physicist J. J. Thomson (1856–1940) discovered the electron. **Electrons** are negatively charged subatomic particles. Electrons were the first subatomic particles to be discovered.

▶ **Thomson's Experiment** Thomson performed experiments that involved passing an electric current through a gas at low pressure. He sealed the gas in a glass tube fitted at both ends with metal disks called electrodes. The electrodes were connected to a source of electricity, as shown below. One electrode, the anode, became positively charged. The other electrode, the cathode, became negatively charged. The result was a glowing beam, or **cathode ray,** that traveled from the cathode to the anode.

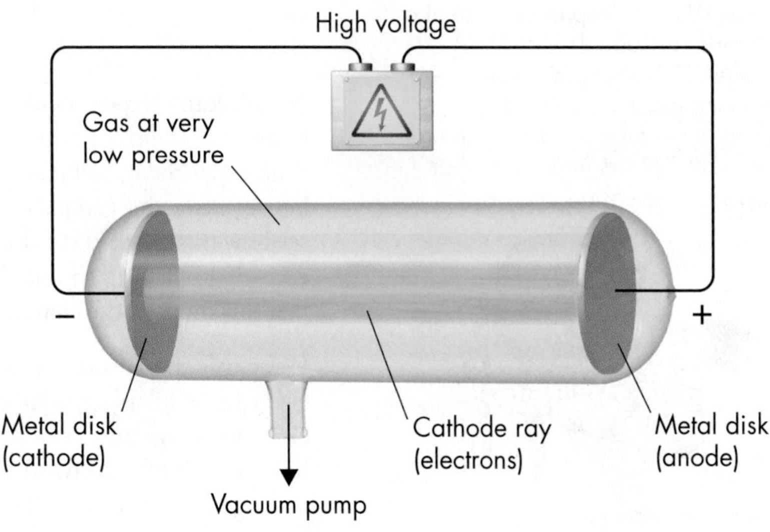

Cathode-Ray Tube Electrons were discovered using cathode-ray tubes. The cathode-ray is attracted to the metal plate that has a positive charge.

Thomson's Experiment
Thomson found that the cathode ray is deflected by a metal plate that has a negative plate and attracted to a metal plate that has a positive charge. A cathode ray can also be deflected by a magnet.

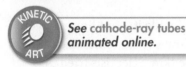

See cathode-ray tubes animated online.

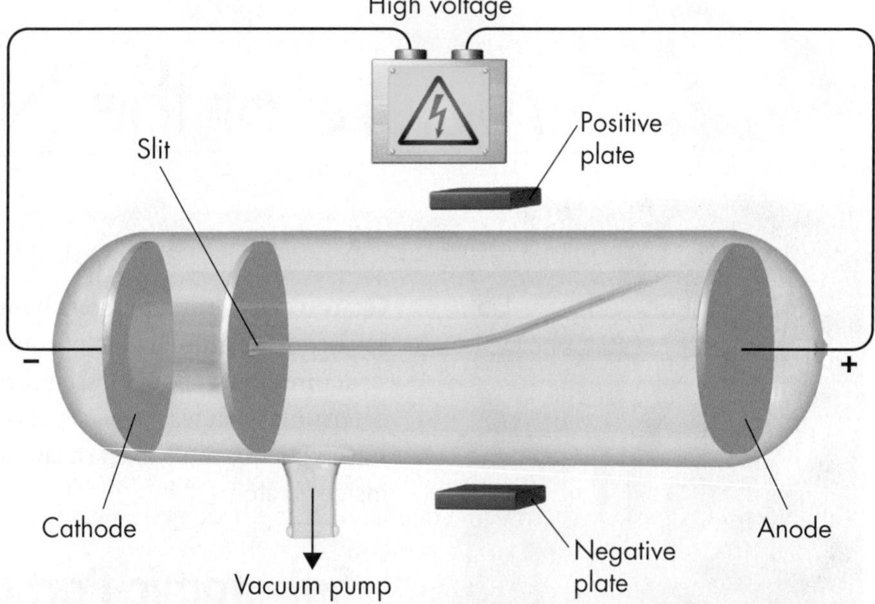

BUILD Connections

LCD and plasma televisions are often called flat-screen TVs. However, before LCD and plasma televisions became popular, the most common televisions were CRT TVs, or cathode-ray tube televisions. These TVs are deep in order to fit a cathode ray tube. In CRT TVs, images on screen are created by shooting electrons within the cathode ray tube toward a screen. The screen glows in patterns that appear as television images.

Thomson found that a positively charged plate attracts the cathode ray, while a negatively charged plate repels it. This is shown in the figure above. Thomson knew that opposite charges attract and like charges repel. So he hypothesized that a cathode ray is a stream of tiny negatively charged particles moving at high speed. These tiny particles are electrons.

To test his hypothesis, Thomson set up an experiment to measure the ratio of an electron's charge to its mass. He found this ratio to be constant no matter what kind of gas he used or what type of metal he used for the electrodes. He concluded that electrons are a component of the atoms of all elements.

▶ **Millikan's Experiment** The American physicist Robert A. Millikan (1868–1953) did experiments to find the charge of an electron. In his oil drop experiment, Millikan suspended negatively charged oil droplets between two charged plates. Then, he changed the voltage on the plates to see how this affected the droplets' rate of fall. He found that the charge on each oil droplet was a multiple of 1.60×10^{-19} coulomb. Millikan concluded that this must be the charge of an electron.

Using this charge value and Thomson's charge-to-mass ratio of an electron, Millikan calculated an electron's mass. Millikan's values for electron charge and mass are similar to those accepted today. An electron has one unit of negative charge, and its mass is 1/1840 the mass of a hydrogen atom.

Protons If cathode rays are electrons given off by atoms, then what are the atoms like that have lost the electrons? For example, after a hydrogen atom (the lightest kind of atom) loses an electron, what is left? Consider four things that scientists knew about atoms and electric charges:

1. Atoms have no net electric charge. Atoms are electrically neutral.
2. Electric charges are carried by particles of matter.
3. Electric charges always exist in whole-number multiples of a single basic unit. There are no fractions of charges.
4. When a given number of negatively charged particles combines with an equal number of positively charged particles, an electrically neutral particle is formed.

When you consider the information above, it makes sense that a particle with one unit of positive charge should remain when a hydrogen atom loses an electron. Evidence for such a positively charged particle was found in 1886. Eugen Goldstein (1850–1930) observed a cathode-ray tube and found rays traveling in the direction opposite to that of the cathode rays. These positively charged subatomic particles are called **protons.** Each proton has a mass about 1,840 times that of an electron.

Neutrons In 1932, the English physicist James Chadwick (1891–1974) found yet another subatomic particle: the neutron. **Neutrons** are subatomic particles with no charge, but with a mass almost the same as a proton's mass. The table below gives the properties of these subatomic particles. Even though protons and neutrons are very small, physicists think that they are made up of even smaller particles called *quarks.*

Key Question What are three kinds of subatomic particles? **Three kinds of subatomic particles are electrons, protons, and neutrons.**

proton a positively charged subatomic particle

neutron a neutral subatomic particle

RELATED WORD FORMS
The word *neutral* means "having no charge." A neutron is a subatomic particle that has neither a positive nor negative charge.

Properties of Subatomic Particles

Particle	Symbol	Relative charge	Relative mass (mass of proton = 1)	Actual mass (g)
Electron	e^-	1–	1/1840	9.11×10^{-28}
Proton	p^+	1+	1	1.67×10^{-24}
Neutron	n^0	0	1	1.67×10^{-24}

Learn more about the size of the atom ***online.***

The Atomic Nucleus

When subatomic particles were discovered, scientists wondered how the particles were put together in an atom. Scientists, including Thomson, thought that electrons were evenly distributed throughout an atom filled with positively charged material. This model became known as the "plum-pudding model" because it was thought that electrons were stuck into a lump of positive charge. This is similar to how raisins are stuck in the dough of plum pudding. However, this model was short-lived. A new model was soon to be proposed by a former student of Thomson's by the name of Ernest Rutherford (1871–1937).

nucleus central core of an atom; an atom's nucleus contains protons and neutrons

MULTIPLE MEANINGS
You may remember the word *nucleus* from when you learned about cells. Nucleus is also the name of a cell part that contains DNA inside eukaryotic cells.

Rutherford's Gold Foil Experiment In 1911, Rutherford and his co-workers devised an experiment to test the plum-pudding model of atomic structure. Their experiment used alpha particles, which are helium atoms that have lost their two electrons. Alpha particles have a double positive charge because of the two protons. In the experiment, shown below, a beam of alpha particles was directed at a very thin sheet of gold foil. If the plum-pudding model was correct, the alpha particles should have passed easily through the gold foil. The particles should only have had slight deflections due to the positive charges spread throughout the gold atoms.

Rutherford's results showed that most alpha particles did pass straight through the gold foil or were slightly deflected. However, a small fraction of the alpha particles bounced off the gold foil at very large angles. Some even bounced straight back toward the source. This was a big surprise!

The Rutherford Atomic Model Based on the results of his experiment, Rutherford came up with a new model of the atom. He proposed that the atom is mostly empty space. This explains why most of the alpha particles were not deflected much by the gold foil. He concluded that all the positive charge and almost all the mass are concentrated in a small region. Only in this region was positive charge great enough to account for the large deflection of some of the alpha particles. He called this region the nucleus. The **nucleus** is the tiny central core of an atom and is composed of protons and neutrons.

The Rutherford atomic model is known as the nuclear atom. In the nuclear atom, protons and neutrons are located in the positively charged nucleus. The electrons are distributed around the nucleus and occupy almost all the volume of the atom. The nucleus is very small and dense compared to the atom as a whole. If an atom were the size of a football stadium, the nucleus would be about the size of a marble.

Rutherford's Experiment

Experimental Set-Up Rutherford aimed a beam of alpha particles at a sheet of gold foil surrounded by a fluorescent screen. Most of the particles passed through the foil with no deflection at all. A few particles were greatly deflected.

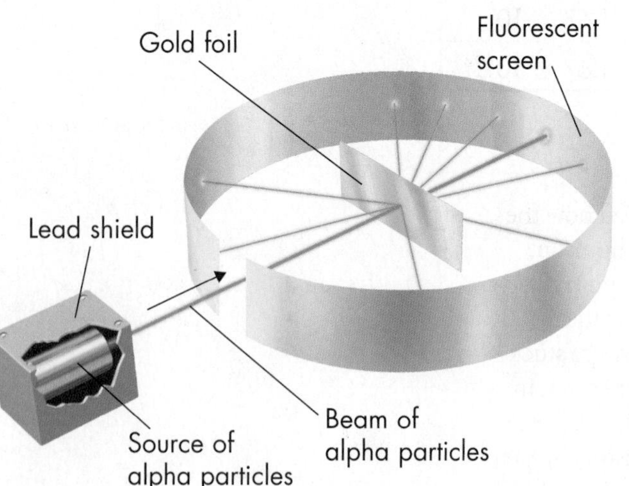

Rutherford's Conclusions Most of the alpha particles passed through the gold foil because the atom is mostly empty space. The mass and positive charge are concentrated in a small region of the atom called the nucleus. Particles that approach the nucleus closely are greatly deflected. Particles that do not come close to the nucleus move straight through or are slightly deflected.

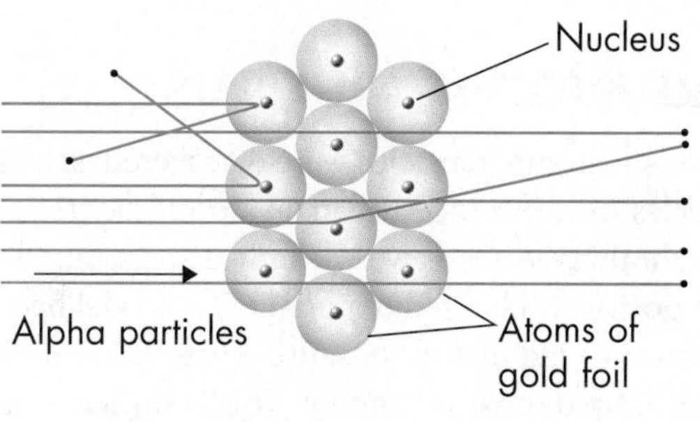

See Rutherford's gold-foil experiment ***animated online.***

Rutherford's model turned out to be incomplete. In Chapter 5, you will learn how the Rutherford atomic model was revised to explain the chemical properties of elements.

Key Question How can you describe the structure of the nuclear atom? **In the nuclear atom, the protons and neutrons are located in the positively charged nucleus. The electrons are distributed around the nucleus and occupy almost all of the atom's volume.**

Quick Lab

Purpose To determine the shape of a fixed object inside a sealed box without opening the box

Materials

- **box containing a regularly shaped object fixed in place and a loose marble**

Using Inference: The Black Box

Procedure

1. Do not open the box.
2. Manipulate the box so that the marble moves around the fixed object.
3. Gather data (clues) that describe the marble's movement.
4. Sketch a picture of the object in the box, showing its shape, size, and location within the box.
5. Repeat this activity with a different box containing a different object.

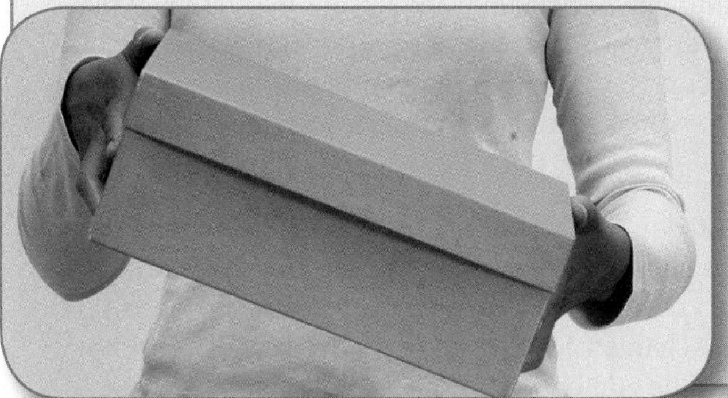

Analyze and Conclude

1. **Compare** Find a classmate who had a box with the same letter as yours, and compare your findings.
2. **Apply Concepts** Think about the experiments that have contributed to a better understanding of the atom. Which experiment does this activity remind you of?

4.2 LessonCheck

Key Concept Check

10. **Review** What are three types of subatomic particles?

11. **Explain** How does the Rutherford model describe the structure of atoms?

Vocabulary Check *Choose a highlighted word from the lesson to complete each sentence correctly.*

12. A(n) __________ is a positively charged subatomic particle.

13. Protons and neutrons are located in the __________ of an atom.

Think Critically

14. **Review** What are the charges and relative masses of the three main subatomic particles?

15. **Explain** Describe Thomson's and Millikan's contributions to atomic theory.

16. **Compare and Contrast** Compare Rutherford's expected outcome of the gold-foil experiment with the actual outcome.

17. How did scientists "see" inside an atom to determine the structures inside of it? (Hint: See page 98.)

4.3 Distinguishing Among Atoms

CHEMISTRY & YOU

Q: How can there be different varieties of atoms? Some things exist in many different varieties. For example, dogs can differ in many ways, such as color, size, ear shape, and length of hair. Just as there are many types of dogs, atoms come in different varieties, too.

Key Questions

What makes one element different from another?

How do isotopes of an element differ?

How do you calculate the atomic mass of an element?

BUILD Vocabulary

atomic number the number of protons in an atom

USING PRIOR KNOWLEDGE Remember that the atomic number identifies an atom. The number that is unique to each atom is the number of protons. So, the atomic number is equal to the number of protons in an atom.

Atomic Number and Mass Number

Atoms are made up of protons, neutrons, and electrons. Protons and neutrons are in the nucleus. Electrons surround the nucleus. How, then, are atoms of hydrogen, for example, different from atoms of oxygen?

Atomic Number Look at the table below. You can see that a hydrogen atom has one proton, but an oxygen atom has eight protons. Elements are different because they contain different numbers of protons. An element's **atomic number** is the number of protons in an atom of that element. Since all hydrogen atoms have one proton, the atomic number of hydrogen is 1. All oxygen atoms have eight protons, so the atomic number of oxygen is 8. An element's atomic number identifies that element.

For each element listed in the table, the number of protons equals the number of electrons. Remember that atoms are electrically neutral. To be neutral, the number of negatively charged particles must equal the number of positively charged particles. In other words, the number of electrons must equal the number of protons.

Atoms of the First Ten Elements

Name	Symbol	Atomic number	Protons	Neutrons*	Mass number	Electrons
Hydrogen	H	1	1	0	1	1
Helium	He	2	2	2	4	2
Lithium	Li	3	3	4	7	3
Beryllium	Be	4	4	5	9	4
Boron	B	5	5	6	11	5
Carbon	C	6	6	6	12	6
Nitrogen	N	7	7	7	14	7
Oxygen	O	8	8	8	16	8
Fluorine	F	9	9	10	19	9
Neon	Ne	10	10	10	20	10

* Number of neutrons in the most abundant isotope. Isotopes are introduced later in Lesson 4.3.

Sample Problem 4.1

Understanding Atomic Number

The element nitrogen (N) has an atomic number of 7. How many protons and electrons are in a neutral nitrogen atom?

❶ Analyze Identify the relevant concepts. The atomic number gives the number of protons. In a neutral atom, the number of protons equals the number of electrons.

❷ Solve Apply the concepts to this problem.

Identify the atomic number. → The atomic number of nitrogen is 7.

Use the atomic number to find the number of protons. → The atomic number is 7, so a nitrogen atom has 7 protons.

Use the number of protons to find the number of electrons. → The number of protons is 7, so a nitrogen atom has 7 electrons.

Remember: Nitrogen is a neutral atom, so the number of protons must equal the number of electrons.

Practice Problems

18. How many protons and electrons are in each atom?

a. fluorine (atomic number = 9)
b. calcium (atomic number = 20)
c. aluminum (atomic number = 13)
d. potassium (atomic number = 19)

❶ Analyze Identify the relevant concepts.

❷ Solve Apply the concepts to this problem.

19. Challenge Complete the table.

Element	Atomic number	Protons	Electrons
Br	35	**a.** ____	35
S	16	**b.** ____	**c.** ____
V	**d.** ____	23	**e.** ____
f. ____	**g.** ____	**h.** ____	5

Mass Number Most of an atom's mass is found in its nucleus. The mass of an atom depends on the number of protons and neutrons. The total number of protons and neutrons in an atom is called the **mass number.** For example, a helium atom has two protons and two neutrons, so its mass number is 4. A carbon atom has six protons and six neutrons, so its mass number is 12.

Finding the Number of Neutrons If you know the atomic number and mass number of an atom of any element, you can determine the atom's composition. The number of neutrons in an atom is the difference between the mass number and the atomic number.

Number of neutrons = mass number − atomic number

Mass number is the total number of protons and neutrons.

Atomic number is the number of protons for the element.

mass number the total number of protons and neutrons in an atom

USING PRIOR KNOWLEDGE
Remember that the mass of an object is a measure of matter contained in that object. An atom's mass comes from its protons and neutrons.

The table on page 100 shows that a fluorine atom has an atomic number of 9 and a mass number of 19. The atomic number equals the number of protons, which also equals the number of electrons. A fluorine atom has nine protons and nine electrons. The difference between the mass number and the atomic number is ten $(19 - 9 = 10)$, so the fluorine atom has ten neutrons.

Representing the Composition of an Atom The composition of any atom can be written in shorthand notation using the atomic number and the mass number. The shorthand notation for gold is in the figure below. The chemical symbol for gold is Au. The symbol appears with two numbers written to its left. The atomic number is the bottom number. The mass number is the top number. You can also refer to atoms by using the mass number and the name of the element. For example, $^{197}_{79}Au$ may be written as gold-197.

Key Question What makes one element different from another? **Elements are different from one another because they contain different numbers of protons.**

Representing Atoms The atomic number and mass number can be used to write the shorthand notation for an element.

Mass Number
the combined number of protons and neutrons in an atom of an element

Atomic Number
the number of protons in an atom of an element (You can find the atomic number on the periodic table.)

Go to your Chemistry Skills and Math Workbook to practice determining the composition of atoms.

Determining the Composition of an Atom

How many protons, electrons, and neutrons are in each atom?

a. $^{9}_{4}Be$ **b.** $^{20}_{10}Ne$ **c.** $^{23}_{11}Na$

KNOWNS	UNKNOWNS
• Beryllium (Be) atomic number = 4 mass number = 9 • Neon (Ne) atomic number = 10 mass number = 20 • Sodium (Na) atomic number = 11 mass number = 23	number of: protons = ? electrons = ? neutrons = ?

❶ Analyze List the knowns and the unknowns. The atomic number and mass number is in each chemical symbol.

❷ Calculate Solve for the unknowns. Use the definitions of atomic number and mass number to calculate the numbers of protons, electrons, and neutrons.

Use the atomic number to find the number of protons.

atomic number = number of protons
a. 4 b. 10 c. 11

Use the atomic number to find the number of electrons.

atomic number = number of electrons
a. 4 b. 10 c. 11

Use the mass number and atomic number to find the number of neutrons.

number of neutrons = mass number − atomic number
a. number of neutrons = 9 − 4 = 5
b. number of neutrons = 20 − 10 = 10
c. number of neutrons = 23 − 11 = 12

Hint: Check your math. For each atom, the mass number equals the number of protons plus the number of neutrons.

Practice Problems

20. How many protons, electrons and neutrons are in each atom?

a. $^{80}_{35}Br$ **b.** $^{32}_{16}S$

❶ Analyze List the knowns and unknowns.

❷ Calculate Solve for the unknowns.

KNOWNS	UNKNOWNS
Bromine (Br) atomic number = 35 mass number = 80	number of: protons = ? electrons = ? neutrons = ?
Sulfur (S) atomic number = mass number =	number of: protons = ? electrons = ? neutrons = ?

21. How many electrons and neutrons are in each atom?

a. $^{108}_{47}Ag$ **b.** $^{207}_{82}Pb$

22. Challenge Use the table on page 100 to express the composition of each atom below in shorthand form.

a. carbon-12 **c.** beryllium-9
b. boron-11 **d.** oxygen-16

isotopes atoms of the same element that have the same atomic number but different mass numbers

PREFIXES

The prefix *iso-* is from the Greek word *isos*, which means "equal." Each isotope of an element has the same number of protons as the other isotopes of the element. Isotopes of an element are different in the number of neutrons they have.

Isotopes

Look at the figure below. It shows that there are three different kinds of neon atoms. How do these atoms differ? All have the same number of protons (10) and electrons (10), but they each have different numbers of neutrons. The atoms in the figure are all isotopes of neon. **Isotopes** are atoms of the same element that have the same number of protons but a different number of neutrons. Because isotopes of the same element have a different number of neutrons, they also have different mass numbers.

Even though isotopes have different numbers of neutrons, isotopes are chemically alike. They are alike because the isotopes of elements have identical numbers of protons and electrons, which are the subatomic particles responsible for chemical behavior. Remember the dogs at the beginning of the lesson. Their color or size does not change the fact that they are all dogs. Similarly, the number of neutrons in isotopes of an element doesn't change which element it is because the atomic number doesn't change.

There are three isotopes of neon. Look at the figure below to see models of each neon isotope. Each neon isotope has ten protons in its nucleus. The most common neon isotope has ten neutrons. It has a mass number of 20 and is called neon-20 ($^{20}_{10}Ne$). The second isotope in the figure has 11 neutrons and a mass number of 21. It is called neon-21 ($^{21}_{10}Ne$). The third isotope has 12 neutrons and a mass number of 22. This isotope is called neon-22 ($^{22}_{10}Ne$).

Key Question How do isotopes of an element differ? **Isotopes of an element have different numbers of neutrons, so they also have different mass numbers.**

Isotopes of Neon
Each isotope of neon has 10 protons and 10 electrons. The number of neutrons is different in each isotope.

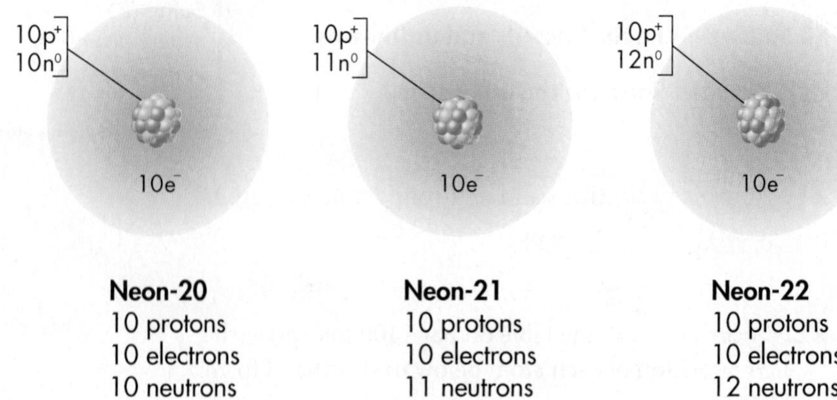

Neon-20
10 protons
10 electrons
10 neutrons

Neon-21
10 protons
10 electrons
11 neutrons

Neon-22
10 protons
10 electrons
12 neutrons

Sample Problem 4.3

Writing Chemical Symbols for Isotopes

Diamonds are a naturally occurring form of elemental carbon. Two stable isotopes of carbon are carbon-12 and carbon-13. Write the symbol for each isotope using superscripts and subscripts to represent the mass number and the atomic number.

1 Analyze Identify the relevant concepts. Isotopes are atoms that have the same number of protons but different numbers of neutrons.

2 Solve Apply the concepts to this problem.

Use the table on page 100 to identify the symbol and the atomic number for carbon.	The symbol for carbon is C. The atomic number of carbon is 6.
Look at the name of the isotope to find the mass number.	For carbon-12, the mass number is 12. For carbon-13, the mass number is 13.
Write the symbol for the atom. Directly to the left of the symbol, write the mass number at the top and the atomic number at the bottom.	For carbon-12, the symbol is $^{12}_{6}C$. For carbon-13, the symbol is $^{13}_{6}C$.

Practice Problems

23. Three isotopes of oxygen are oxygen-16, oxygen-17, and oxygen-18. Write the symbol for each, including the atomic number and mass number.

1 Analyze Identify the relevant concepts.

2 Solve Apply the concepts to this problem.

24. Three isotopes of hydrogen are hydrogen-1, hydrogen-2, and hydrogen-3. Write the symbol for each, including the atomic number and mass number.

25. Challenge Three chromium isotopes are chromium-50, chromium-52, and chromium-53. How many neutrons are in each isotope, given that chromium has an atomic number of 24? Write the symbol for each isotope of chromium.

Check that the atomic number of each isotope is the same.

BUILD Vocabulary

atomic mass unit (amu) a standard unit of mass equal to one-twelfth of the mass of a carbon-12 atom

atomic mass the weighted average mass of the atoms of an element in a naturally occurring sample

USING PRIOR KNOWLEDGE

Almost all measurements are reported with units. To show the importance of units, take and list some measurements of a common object. Report the measurements to a classmate without saying the units of each measurement, and see if the person can identify the object.

Atomic Mass

The mass of a proton or a neutron is very small (1.67×10^{-24} g). The mass of an electron is 9.11×10^{-28} g, which is negligible in comparison to a proton or neutron. With these values, the mass of even the largest atom is incredibly small. Since the 1920s, it has been possible to determine these tiny masses by using an instrument called a mass spectrometer. Scientists used this instrument and found that the mass of a fluorine atom is 3.155×10^{-23} g, and the mass of an arsenic atom is 1.244×10^{-22} g.

Atomic Mass Units Knowing the real masses of individual atoms is sometimes useful. However, values this small are difficult to work with. Instead, it is more useful to compare the relative masses of atoms using a reference isotope as a standard. Scientists chose the isotope carbon-12 as the reference isotope. They assigned carbon-12 as having a mass of exactly 12 atomic mass units.

$$\text{mass of carbon-12 atom} = 12 \text{ amu}$$

So, a single **atomic mass unit** (amu) is defined as one-twelfth of the mass of a carbon-12 atom.

$$1 \text{ amu} = \tfrac{1}{12} \text{ mass of carbon-12 atom}$$

Using these units, a helium-4 atom has one-third of the mass of a carbon-12 atom. On the other hand, a nickel-60 atom has five times the mass of a carbon-12 atom.

A carbon-12 atom has six protons and six neutrons in its nucleus, and its mass is set as 12 amu. The six protons and six neutrons account for nearly all of the mass of the carbon-12 atom. Therefore, the mass of a single proton or a single neutron is about one-twelfth of 12 amu, or about 1 amu. Because the mass of any single atom depends mainly on the number of protons and neutrons in the nucleus of the atom, you might predict that the atomic mass of an element should be a whole number. However, that is not usually the case.

Relative Abundance of Isotopes In nature, most elements are found as a mixture of two or more isotopes. Isotopes of an element do not occur in even or equal amounts. Instead, each isotope appears at a certain percent, called a natural percent abundance.

Think about the isotopes of hydrogen. There are three isotopes of hydrogen. According to the table on the next page, almost all naturally occurring hydrogen (99.985 percent) is hydrogen-1. The other two isotopes are present in trace amounts. Notice that the atomic mass of hydrogen listed in the table (1.0079 amu) is very close to the mass of hydrogen-1 (1.0078 amu). The slight difference takes into account the larger masses, but much smaller amounts, of the other two isotopes of hydrogen.

Percent Abundance and Atomic Mass of Isotopes
The atomic mass of an element is calculated using the percent abundance and the mass of its isotopes. The difference in mass between each isotope of an element is due to the number of neutrons.

Go to your Chemistry Skills and Math Workbook to practice interpreting data.

Natural Percent Abundance of Stable Isotopes of Some Elements

Name	Symbol	Natural percent abundance	Mass (amu)	Atomic mass (amu)
Hydrogen	${}^{1}_{1}H$ ${}^{2}_{1}H$ ${}^{3}_{1}H$	99.985 0.015 negligible	1.0078 2.0141 3.0160	1.0079
Helium	${}^{3}_{2}He$ ${}^{4}_{2}He$	0.0001 99.9999	3.0160 4.0026	4.0026
Carbon	${}^{12}_{6}C$ ${}^{13}_{6}C$	98.89 1.11	12.000 13.003	12.011
Nitrogen	${}^{14}_{7}N$ ${}^{15}_{7}N$	99.63 0.37	14.003 15.000	14.007
Oxygen	${}^{16}_{8}O$ ${}^{17}_{8}O$ ${}^{18}_{8}O$	99.759 0.037 0.204	15.995 16.995 17.999	15.999
Chlorine	${}^{35}_{17}Cl$ ${}^{37}_{17}Cl$	75.77 24.23	34.969 36.966	35.453

▶ **Relative Abundance and Atomic Mass** Now consider the two stable isotopes of chlorine listed in the table above: chlorine-35 and chlorine-37. If you calculate the arithmetic mean, or average, of these two masses ((34.969 amu + 36.966 amu)/2), you get an average atomic mass of 35.968 amu. However, this value is higher than the actual atomic mass value of 35.453 amu. Why is there a difference?

To explain this difference, you need to know the natural percent abundance of the isotopes of chlorine. Chlorine-35 accounts for about 75 percent of the naturally occurring chlorine atoms. Chlorine-37 accounts for only about 25 percent. The **atomic mass** of an element is a weighted average mass of the atoms in a naturally occurring sample of the element. Since there is more chlorine-35 naturally occurring, the atomic mass of chlorine is closer to chlorine-35 than to chlorine-37. A weighted average mass reflects both the mass and the relative abundance of the isotopes as they are found in nature.

The atomic mass of an element can sometimes give you a clue about the relative abundance of isotopes. For example, copper has an atomic mass of 63.546 amu. The two isotopes of copper are copper-63 and copper-65. Using the atomic mass as a clue, which isotope do you think is the most abundant? Compare the atomic mass to the mass of each isotope. The atomic mass of 63.546 amu is closer to 63 than it is to 65. Since the atomic mass is a weighted average of the isotopes, copper-63 must be more abundant than copper-65.

BUILD Understanding

Preview Visuals Look at the table to the left. There is a lot of information in the table, but you can apply some methods to make reading the table easier. Start by reading the table's title. The title tells you what information you can expect to find. Next, read each column head. Make sure you understand what each head means.

BUILD Connections

Your teacher may use a concept similar to relative abundance to calculate your class grade. For example, your test score may be a larger percentage of your grade than your homework score.

Test score = 85
(70% of grade)
Homework score = 96
(30% of grade)
Your grade= 88.3 B

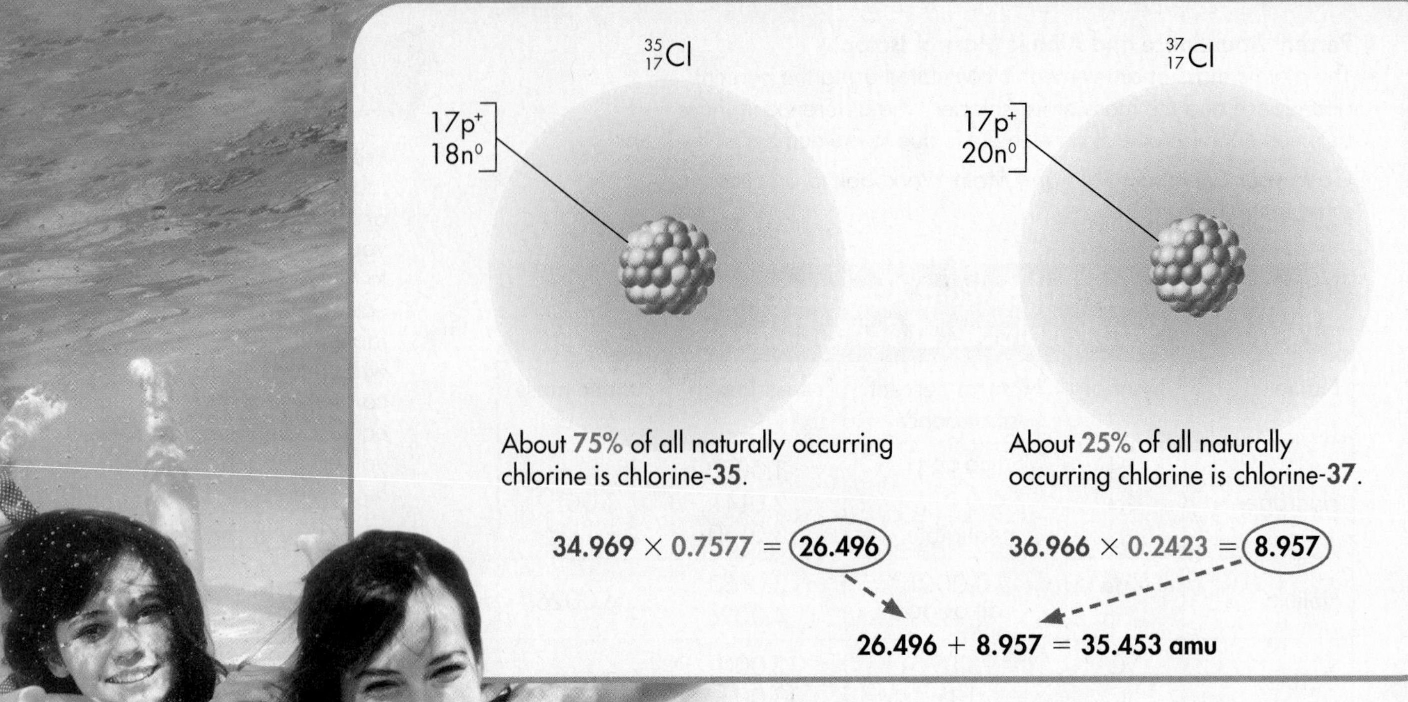

Isotopes of Chlorine Chlorine is a reactive element used to disinfect swimming pools. Chlorine occurs as two isotopes: chlorine-35 and chlorine-37.

MATH TUTORIAL **Learn more about weighted averages online.**

Calculating Atomic Mass You can find atomic mass if you know three things: the number of stable isotopes of the element, the mass of each isotope, and the natural percent abundance of each isotope. To calculate the atomic mass of an element, multiply the mass of each isotope by its natural abundance in decimal form, and then add the products. The sum is the weighted average mass of the atoms of the element as they occur in nature.

For example, the figure above shows how you calculate the atomic mass of chlorine. The mass of chlorine-35 is multiplied by the decimal form of its relative abundance (0.7577). The mass of chlorine-37 is multiplied by the decimal form of its relative abundance (0.2423). Then, the products are added together to find the atomic mass of chlorine (35.453 amu).

Look at another example. Carbon has two stable isotopes: carbon-12, which has a natural abundance of 98.89 percent, and carbon-13, which has a natural abundance of 1.11 percent. The mass of carbon-12 is 12.000 amu; the mass of carbon-13 is 13.003 amu. The atomic mass of carbon is calculated as follows:

$$\begin{aligned}\text{Atomic mass of carbon} &= (12.000 \text{ amu} \times 0.9889) + (13.003 \text{ amu} \times 0.0111)\\ &= (11.867 \text{ amu}) + (0.144 \text{ amu})\\ &= 12.011 \text{ amu}\end{aligned}$$

Key Question How do you calculate the atomic mass of an element? **To calculate the atomic mass of an element, multiply the mass of each isotope by its natural abundance, expressed as a decimal, and then add the products.**

Calculating Atomic Mass

Element X has two naturally occurring isotopes. The isotope with a mass of 10.012 amu (^{10}X) has a relative abundance of 19.91 percent. The isotope with a mass of 11.009 amu (^{11}X) has a relative abundance of 80.09 percent. Calculate the atomic mass of element X.

❶ Analyze List the knowns and the unknown.
The mass each isotope contributes to the element's atomic mass can be calculated by multiplying the isotope's mass by its relative abundance. The atomic mass of the element is the sum of these products.

KNOWNS	UNKNOWN
• Isotope ^{10}X: mass = 10.012 amu; relative abundance = 19.91%	atomic mass of X = ?
• Isotope ^{11}X: mass = 11.009 amu; relative abundance = 80.09%	

❷ Calculate Solve for the unknown.

Find the decimal form of each percent abundance. Divide the relative abundance of each isotope by 100%.

$$\frac{19.91\cancel{\%}}{100\cancel{\%}} = \frac{19.91}{100} = 0.1991$$

$$\frac{80.09\cancel{\%}}{100\cancel{\%}} = \frac{80.09}{100} = 0.8009$$

Use the atomic mass and the decimal form of the percent abundance to find the mass contributed by each isotope.

for ^{10}X: 10.012 amu × 0.1991 = 1.993 amu
for ^{11}X: 11.009 amu × 0.8009 = 8.817 amu

Add the atomic mass contributions for all the isotopes.

For element X, atomic mass = 1.993 amu + 8.817 amu
= 10.810 amu

❸ Evaluate Does the result make sense?
The calculated value is closer to the mass of the more abundant isotope, as would be expected.

Practice Problems

26. The element copper has naturally occurring isotopes with mass numbers of 63 and 65. The relative abundance and atomic masses are 69.2% for copper-63 (mass = 62.93 amu) and 30.8% for copper-65 (mass = 64.93 amu). Calculate the atomic mass of copper.

KNOWNS	UNKNOWN
Copper-63 mass = 62.93 amu relative abundance = 69.2%	atomic mass of Cu = ?
Copper-65 mass = 64.93 amu relative abundance = 30.8%	

❶ **Analyze** **List the knowns and unknown.**

❷ **Calculate** **Solve for the unknown.**

❸ **Evaluate** **Does the result make sense?**

27. Calculate the atomic mass of bromine. The two isotopes of bromine have atomic masses and relative abundances of 78.92 amu (50.69%) and 80.92 amu (49.31%).

KNOWNS	UNKNOWN
Bromine-79 mass = relative abundance =	atomic mass of Br = ?
Bromine-81 mass = relative abundance =	

28. Challenge Gallium has two isotopes: gallium-69 and gallium-71. Which is more abundant, given that the atomic mass of gallium is 69.723 amu?

4.3 LessonCheck

Key Concept Check

29. Explain What distinguishes the atoms of one element from the atoms of another?

30. Compare and Contrast How do the isotopes of a given element differ from one another?

31. Explain How is atomic mass calculated?

Vocabulary Check *Choose a highlighted word from the lesson to complete the sentence correctly.*

32. The __________ is the number of protons in an atom and the __________ is the total number of protons and neutrons.

Think Critically

33. Use Models What does the number represent in the isotope platinum-194?

34. Explain The atomic masses of elements are generally not whole numbers. Explain why.

35. Calculate List the number of protons, neutrons, and electrons in each pair of isotopes.

a. $^{6}_{3}\text{Li}$, $^{7}_{3}\text{Li}$ **b.** $^{42}_{20}\text{Ca}$, $^{44}_{20}\text{Ca}$ **c.** $^{78}_{34}\text{Se}$, $^{80}_{34}\text{Se}$

CHEMISTRY & YOU

36. There are many different atoms. In what ways can atoms be different from one another? (Hint: See page 100.)

4 Study Guide

BIGIDEA ELECTRONS AND THE STRUCTURE OF ATOMS

Atoms are the smallest particles of an element that still have the chemical properties of that element. Atoms have positively charged protons and neutral neutrons inside a nucleus, and negatively charged electrons outside the nucleus. Atoms of the same element have the same number of protons, which is equal to an atom's atomic number. But atoms of the same element can have different numbers of neutrons. Atoms of the same element with different numbers of neutrons are isotopes.

4.1 Defining the Atom

Democritus reasoned that atoms were indivisible and indestructible. Dalton conducted experiments to study the nature of atoms and develop a scientific theory about atoms.

Scientists can observe individual atoms by using instruments such as scanning electron microscopes.

- atom (92)
- Dalton's atomic theory (93)

4.2 Structure of the Nuclear Atom

Three kinds of subatomic particles are electrons, protons, and neutrons.

In the nuclear atom, the protons and neutrons are located in the positively charged nucleus. The electrons are distributed around the nucleus and occupy almost the entire volume of the atom.

- electron (95)
- cathode ray (95)
- proton (97)
- neutron (97)
- nucleus (98)

4.3 Distinguishing Among Atoms

Elements are different because they contain different numbers of protons.

Isotopes of an element have different numbers of neutrons, so they also have different mass numbers.

To calculate the atomic mass of an element, multiply the mass of each isotope by its natural abundance, expressed as a decimal, and then add the products.

- atomic number (100)
- mass number (102)
- isotope (104)
- atomic mass unit (amu) (106)
- atomic mass (107)

Key Equation

$$\text{number of neutrons} = \text{mass number} - \text{atomic number}$$

4 Assessment

★ Solutions appear in Appendix D.

Lesson by Lesson

4.1 Defining the Atom

37. What is an atom?

38. What were the limitations of Democritus's ideas about atoms?

39. With which of these statements would John Dalton have agreed in the early 1800s? Explain why or why not for each one.

- **a.** Atoms are the smallest particles of matter.
- **b.** The mass of an iron atom is different from the mass of a copper atom.
- **c.** Every atom of silver is identical to every other atom of silver.
- **d.** A compound is composed of atoms of two or more different elements.

40. Use Dalton's atomic theory to describe how atoms interact during a chemical reaction.

4.2 Structure of the Nuclear Atom

41. What experimental evidence did Thomson have for each statement?

- **a.** Electrons have a negative charge.
- **b.** Atoms of all elements contain electrons.

★**42.** Would you expect two electrons to attract or repel each other?

43. How do the charge and mass of a neutron compare to the charge and mass of a proton?

44. Why does it make sense that if an atom loses electrons, it is left with a positive charge?

45. Describe the location of the electrons in Thomson's "plum-pudding" model of the atom.

★**46.** How did the results of Rutherford's gold-foil experiment differ from his expectations?

47. What is the charge, positive or negative, of the nucleus of every atom?

48. In the Rutherford atomic model, which subatomic particles are located in the nucleus?

4.3 Distinguishing Among Atoms

49. Why is an atom electrically neutral?

50. What does the atomic number of each atom represent?

51. How many protons are in the nuclei of the following atoms?

- **a.** phosphorus (P)
- **b.** molybdenum (Mo)
- **c.** aluminum (Al)
- **d.** cadmium (Cd)
- **e.** chromium (Cr)
- **f.** lead (Pb)

52. What is the difference between the mass number and the atomic number of an atom?

★**53.** Complete the following table.

Atomic number	Mass number	Number of protons	Number of neutrons
9	**a.** ____	**b.** ____	10
c. ____	**d.** ____	14	15
e. ____	47	**f.** ____	25
g. ____	55	25	**h.** ____

54. Name two ways that isotopes of an element differ.

★**55.** Lithium has two isotopes, lithium-6 (atomic mass = 6.015, relative abundance = 7.5%) and lithium-7 (atomic mass = 7.016, relative abundance = 92.5%). Calculate the atomic mass of lithium.

Understand Concepts

*56. How can there be more than 1,000 different atoms when there are only about 100 different elements?

57. What data must you know about the isotopes of an element to calculate the element's atomic mass?

58. Compare the size and density of an atom with its nucleus.

*59. You are standing on the top of a boron-11 nucleus. Describe the numbers and kinds of subatomic particles you see looking down into the nucleus, and those you see looking out from the nucleus.

60. What parts of Dalton's atomic theory no longer agree with the current picture of the atom?

*61. The four isotopes of lead are shown below, each with its percent by mass abundance and the composition of its nucleus. Using these data, calculate the approximate atomic mass of lead.

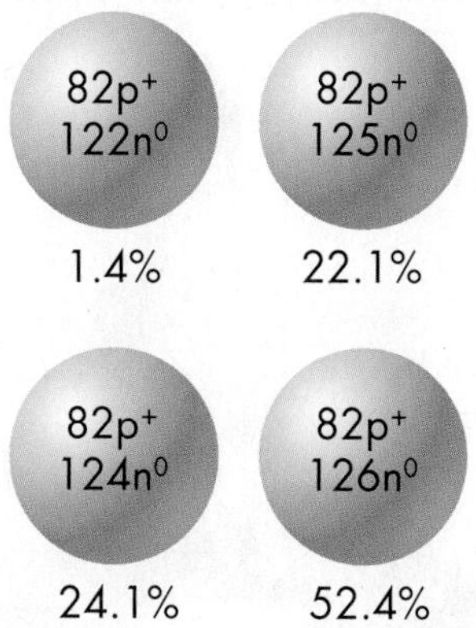

62. How is an average mass different from a weighted average mass?

63. If you know the atomic number and mass number of an atom of an element, how can you determine the number of protons, neutrons, and electrons in that atom?

64. If isotopes are chemically alike, but physically different, propose which subatomic particles are responsible for determining an element's chemical reactivity.

Think Critically

65. **Interpret Diagrams** The diagram below shows gold atoms being bombarded with fast-moving alpha particles.

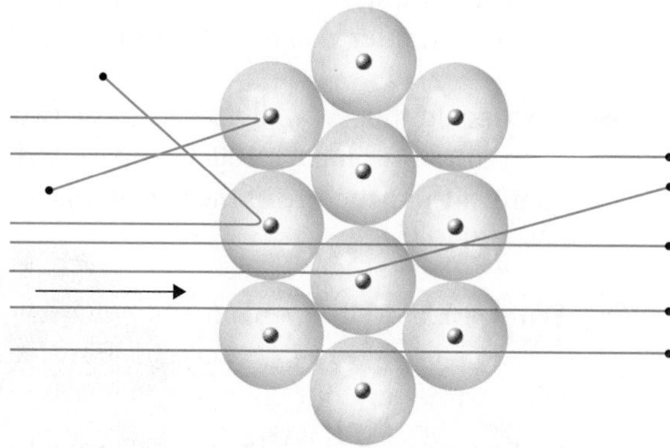

a. The large yellow spheres represent gold atoms. What do the small gray spheres represent?

b. List at least two characteristics of the small gray spheres.

c. Which subatomic particle cannot be found in the area represented by the gray spheres?

66. **Apply Concepts** The law of conservation of mass was introduced in Chapter 2. Use Dalton's atomic theory to explain this law.

*67. **Calculate** Lithium has two naturally occurring isotopes. Lithium-6 has an atomic mass of 6.015 amu; lithium-7 has an atomic mass of 7.016 amu. The atomic mass of lithium is 6.941 amu. Using these data, show that the relative abundance of lithium-7 is 92.5%.

FOUNDATIONS Wrap-Up

Electric Charge

1. **Draw Conclusions** Think about the pieces of tape in the activity at the beginning of the chapter. What subatomic particles do you think could cause the tapes' behavior?

Concept Check

Now that you've finished studying Chapter 4, answer these questions.

2. How is a proton different from an electron?
3. In Rutherford's experiments, why did some of the particles deflect at large angles back toward the source of the particles?

Write About Science

68. Communicate Explain how Rutherford's gold-foil experiment yielded new evidence about atomic structure. *Hint:* First, describe the setup of the experiment. Then, explain how Rutherford interpreted his experimental data.

69. Connect to the BIGIDEA Choose two atoms from the table on page 100. Compare and contrast the structure of the two atoms.

CHEMYSTERY

Artifact or Artifake?

There are currently no crystal skulls that have been proven to be from ancient civilizations. The Linnean Society of London is a research institute specializing in taxonomy and natural history. They have used electron microscopy to view the surface of crystal skulls, including a crystal skull that is part of the Smithsonian collection. Images from the scanning electron microscope reveal circular patterns on the surface of the skulls. These patterns indicate the skulls were likely carved using a modern carving device with a rotary wheel. Ancient civilizations would not have had such devices. Therefore, all the crystal skulls that are known today appear to be "artifakes," not artifacts.

70. Infer Why would electron microscopes be able to provide more information about an object than a light microscope?

71. Connect to the BIGIDEA How has knowledge of atomic structure aided in the development of the electron microscope?

Cumulative Review

72. How does a scientific law differ from a scientific theory? (See Lesson 1.3 for help.)

73. The temperature in a science classroom is 24°C. In which state of matter do each of the following substances occur at that temperature? (See Lesson 2.1 for help.)

Physical Properties of Some Substances

Substance	Melting point (°C)	Boiling point (°C)
Ethanol	−117	78
Neon	−249	−246
Mercury	−39	357
Aluminum	660	2519
Chlorine	−101	−34
Sulfur	115	445
Water	0	100
Copper	1084	2562

74. Classify each as an element, a compound, or a mixture. (See Lessons 2.2 and 2.3 for help.)

***75.** Oxygen and hydrogen react explosively to form water. In one reaction, 6 g of hydrogen combines with oxygen to form 54 g of water. How much oxygen was used? (See Lesson 2.4 for help.)

***76.** What is the mass of 4.42 cm^3 of platinum? The density of platinum is 22.5 g/cm^3. (See Lesson 3.2 for help.)

77. An aquarium measures 54.0 cm × 1.10 m × 80.0 cm. How many cubic centimeters of water will this aquarium hold? (See Lesson 3.3 for help.)

Standardized Test Prep

For help with answering test questions, go to your Chemistry Skills and Math Workbook.

Select the choice that best answers each question or completes each statement.

1. The smallest particle of an element that retains its identity in a chemical reaction is a:
(A) proton.
(B) neutron.
(C) atom.
(D) compound.

2. Which of these descriptions is *incorrect*?
(A) proton: positive charge, in nucleus, mass of ≈ 1 amu
(B) electron: negative charge, mass of ≈ 0 amu, in nucleus
(C) neutron: mass of ≈ 1 amu, no charge

3. Thallium has two isotopes, thallium-203 and thallium-205. Thallium's atomic number is 81, and its atomic mass is 204.38 amu. Which statement about the thallium isotopes is true?
(A) There is more thallium-203 in nature.
(B) Atoms of both isotopes have 81 protons.
(C) Thallium-205 atoms have fewer neutrons.
(D) The most common atom of thallium has a mass of 204.38 amu.

4. Which atom is composed of 16 protons, 16 electrons, and 16 neutrons?
(A) ${}^{48}_{16}S$
(B) ${}^{16}_{32}Ge$
(C) ${}^{32}_{16}S$
(D) ${}^{16}_{32}S$

Use the art below to answer Question 5.

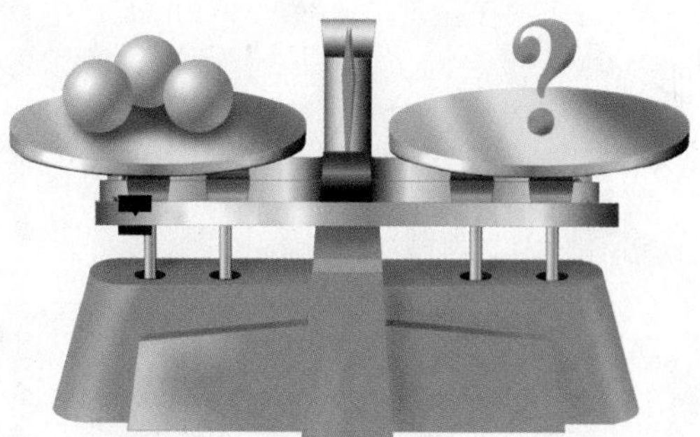

5. How many nitrogen-14 atoms (${}^{14}N$) would you need to place on the right pan to balance the three calcium-42 atoms (${}^{42}Ca$) on the left pan of the "atomic balance" above? Describe the method you used to determine your answer, including any calculations.

Tips for Success

Connectors Sometimes two phrases in a true/false question are connected by a word such as *because* or *therefore*. These words imply a relationship between one part of the sentence and another. Statements that include such words can be false even if both parts of the statement are true by themselves.

For each question below, there are two statements. Decide whether each statement is true or false. Then decide whether Statement II is a correct explanation for Statement I.

	Statement I		Statement II
6.	Every aluminum-27 atom has 27 protons and 27 electrons.	**BECAUSE**	The mass number of aluminum-27 is 27.
7.	Isotopes of an element have different atomic masses.	**BECAUSE**	The nuclei of an element's isotopes contain different numbers of protons.
8.	An electron is repelled by a negatively charged particle.	**BECAUSE**	An electron has a negative charge.
9.	In an atom, the number of neutrons is generally equal to or greater than the number of protons.	**BECAUSE**	The mass number is generally equal to or greater than the atomic number.

If You Have Trouble With . . .

Question	1	2	3	4	5	6	7	8	9
See Lesson	4.1	4.2	4.3	4.3	4.3	4.3	4.3	4.2	4.2

5 Electrons in Atoms

FOUNDATIONS for Learning

Light from a Mint

1. You will need a wintergreen mint and a pair of pliers.
2. Break the mint in half. **CAUTION** *Never taste anything in the lab, including candy.*
3. Turn off the lights.
4. Watch the mint's broken edge as you carefully crush it between the pliers' jaws.

Observe Describe what you saw when you crushed the mint.

PearsonChem.com

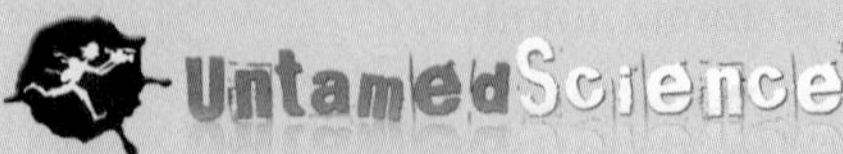

Take a video field trip with the Untamed Science crew to discover the chemistry behind fireworks of different colors.

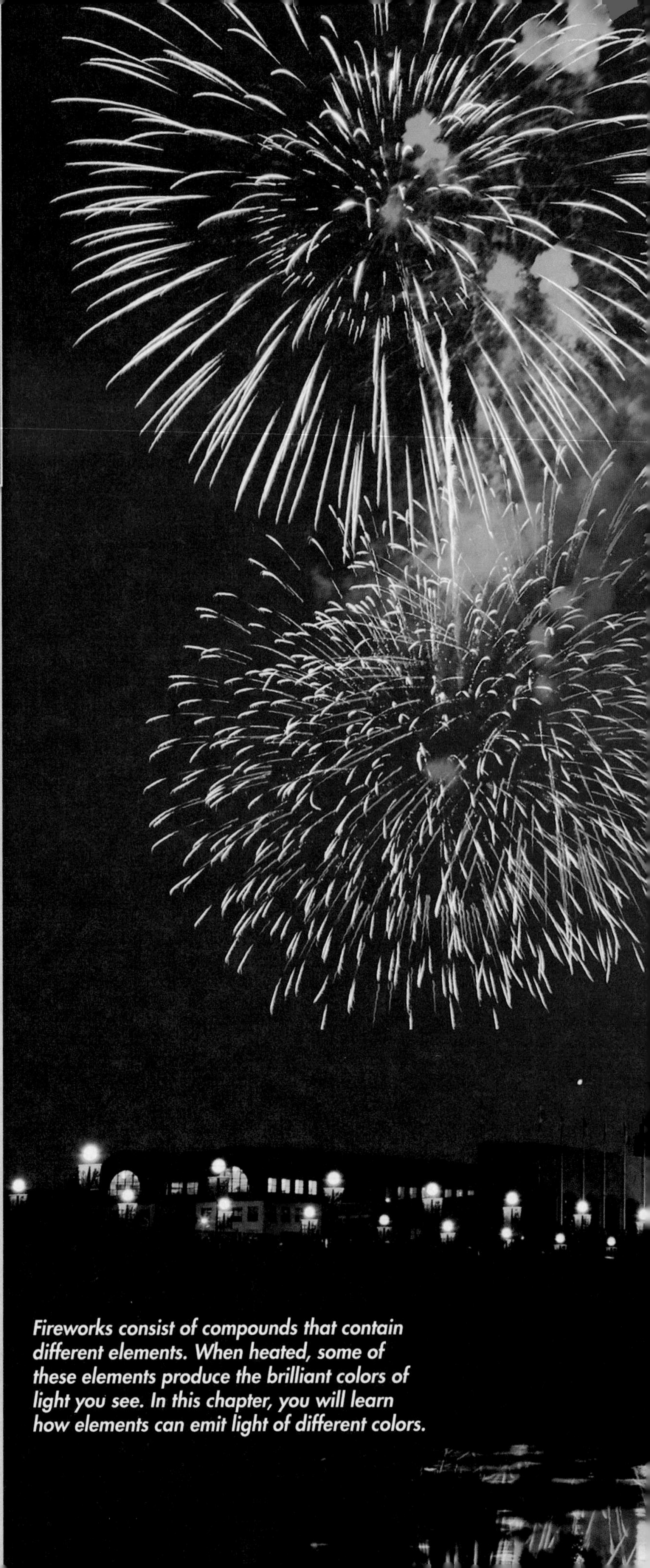

Fireworks consist of compounds that contain different elements. When heated, some of these elements produce the brilliant colors of light you see. In this chapter, you will learn how elements can emit light of different colors.

BIGIDEA

ELECTRONS AND THE STRUCTURE OF ATOMS

Essential Questions:

1. *How does the quantum mechanical model describe electron arrangement in atoms?*
2. *What happens when electrons in atoms absorb or release energy?*

CHEMYSTERY

Now You See It . . . Now You Don't

Young Liam loves to go outside at night to gaze at the stars. For his birthday, his parents gave him star stickers that glow in the dark. He put the stars on his ceiling so he could look at them from the comfort of his bed.

Liam looked at the constellations he had created on his ceiling while he drifted off to sleep. He woke up very disturbed a few hours later. The stars no longer glowed even though it was still dark in his room. He turned on his bedroom light and ran down the hall to wake his parents. Liam brought his parents back to his room and turned off the light. To his surprise, the stars started to glow again. Why did the stars stop glowing and then light up again later?

▶ Connect to the BIGIDEA As you read about electrons in atoms, think about how stickers that glow in the dark might work.

5.1 Revising the Atomic Model

CHEMISTRY & YOU

Q: Why do scientists use mathematical models to describe the position of electrons in atoms? Wind tunnels and models simulate the forces from the moving air on a design. This photo shows a life-sized model of a speed skier. It is a physical model. However, not all models are physical. In fact, the current atomic model is a mathematical model.

Key Questions

What did Bohr propose in his model of the atom?

What does the quantum mechanical model determine about the electrons in an atom?

How do the sublevels of principal energy levels differ from each other?

Energy Levels in Atoms

In the 1800s and early 1900s, scientists tried to determine what atoms look like. They used models to describe their findings. So far, the atomic model you've seen in this textbook shows atoms that have a nucleus surrounded by motionless electrons. Ernest Rutherford used existing ideas about the atom and his discovery of the nucleus to propose another atomic model. In this model, the electrons revolve around the nucleus like planets revolve around the sun.

Limitations of Rutherford's Atomic Model Rutherford's atomic model explained only a few simple properties of atoms. It could not explain certain properties of elements. For example, it could not explain why metals or compounds of metals give off certain colors of light when heated in a flame. It also could not explain why an object such as the iron scroll shown below glows different colors at different temperatures. First, the iron glows dull orange. As it is heated to higher temperatures, it glows yellow and then white. Rutherford's atomic model was too simple to explain these color changes. A better atomic model was needed to explain this behavior.

Glowing Metal
The iron scroll glows when it is heated to very high temperatures.
The iron that is glowing yellow is hotter than iron that is glowing orange.

The Bohr Atomic Model Niels Bohr—Rutherford's student—developed a new atomic model in 1913. He changed Rutherford's model to include newer discoveries about how an atom's energy changes. The atom's energy changes when the atom absorbs or emits light. Bohr proposed that an electron exists only in specific circular paths, or orbits, around the nucleus.

Each possible electron orbit in his model has a fixed energy. The fixed energies that an electron can have are called **energy levels.** You can think of the energy levels as being like the rungs of a ladder. The lowest rung represents the lowest energy level. You can climb up or down the ladder by stepping from rung to rung. Similarly, an electron can move from one energy level to another.

▶ **Quantized Energy Levels** To climb a ladder, you must step just the right distance to go from rung to rung. The situation is similar for an electron. It must gain or lose just the right amount of energy to change energy levels. A **quantum** of energy is the amount of energy required to move an electron from one energy level to another energy level. Therefore, an electron's energy is said to be quantized.

For a particular atom, the amount of energy an electron gains or loses is not always the same. Look at the figure below. The energy levels in an atom are not equally spaced like the rungs on the ladder on the left. Instead, the energy levels are more like the ladder on the right. The higher energy levels are closer together. An electron needs less energy to move to the next higher energy level when it is already in a high energy level.

Key Question What did Bohr propose in his model of the atom? **Bohr proposed that an electron exists only in specific circular paths, or orbits, around the nucleus.**

energy level the specific energy that an electron can have

quantum the amount of energy needed to move an electron from one energy level to another energy level

WORD ORIGINS

Quantum comes from the Latin word *quantus*, which means "how much."

Energy Levels

A ladder's rungs are somewhat like electron energy levels.

In an ordinary ladder, the rungs have equal spacing. Your feet cannot float between the rungs. Similarly, an electron cannot exist between energy levels.

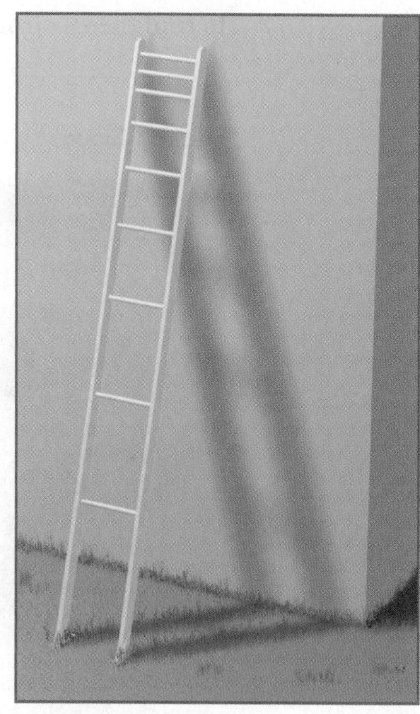

The energy levels in atoms have unequal spacing like the rungs in this unusual ladder. The higher energy levels are closer together.

quantum mechanical model a mathematical model that describes the behavior of electrons in atoms

ACADEMIC WORDS
The word *mechanical* in quantum mechanical model indicates motion. This model describes how electrons move in an atom.

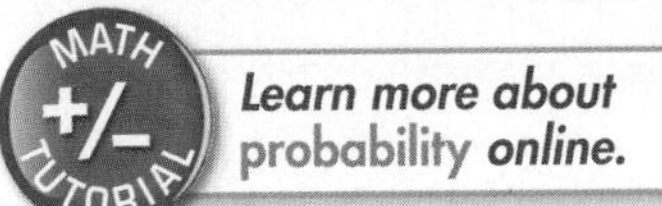

Learn more about probability online.

The Quantum Mechanical Model

The Rutherford and Bohr physical models of the atom described the path of a moving electron in the same way you would describe the path of a large moving object. Later experimental results did not support this way of describing electron motion. In 1926, Erwin Schrödinger developed a mathematical equation that described the behavior of the electron in a hydrogen atom. The **quantum mechanical model**—the modern model of electrons in atoms—emerged from the Schrödinger equation.

Like the Bohr model, the quantum mechanical model requires electrons to have certain energies. Unlike the Bohr model, the quantum mechanical model does not require the electron to take an exact path around the nucleus. Instead, the quantum mechanical model shows how likely it is to find the electron in various locations around the nucleus.

Probability Probability describes how likely it is to find an electron in a particular location around an atom's nucleus. Suppose you picked a marble from a bag without looking. The bag contains three red marbles and one green marble. The probability of picking the green marble is one in four, or 25 percent. The probability of picking a red one is 75 percent.

Electron Cloud The quantum mechanical model describes the motion of electrons—just like you can describe a windmill's moving blades. Look at the photo below. The windmill blades have some probability of being anywhere in the blurry region. You cannot know a blade's exact location at any point in time. Similarly, you cannot know an electron's exact location at any instant. An electron has a probability of being in a given volume of space around the nucleus. A fuzzy cloudlike region like the one shown below represents this probability. The cloud is more dense where the probability of finding the electron is high. It is less dense where the probability is low.

Key Question What does the quantum mechanical model determine about the electrons in an atom? **The quantum mechanical model describes the allowed energies an electron can have. It also describes how likely it is to find the electron in various locations around an atom's nucleus.**

Electron Cloud You can compare a windmill's blades to an electron cloud.

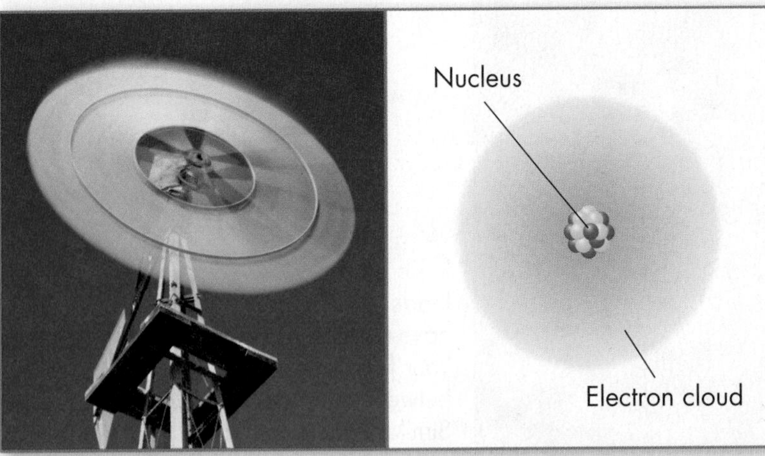

The windmill blades are somewhere in the blurry region.

The electron cloud shows where the electrons are likely to be found.

CHEMISTRY & YOU: HISTORY

Development of Atomic Models

The atomic model changed as scientists learned more about the atom's structure through experiments and calculations.

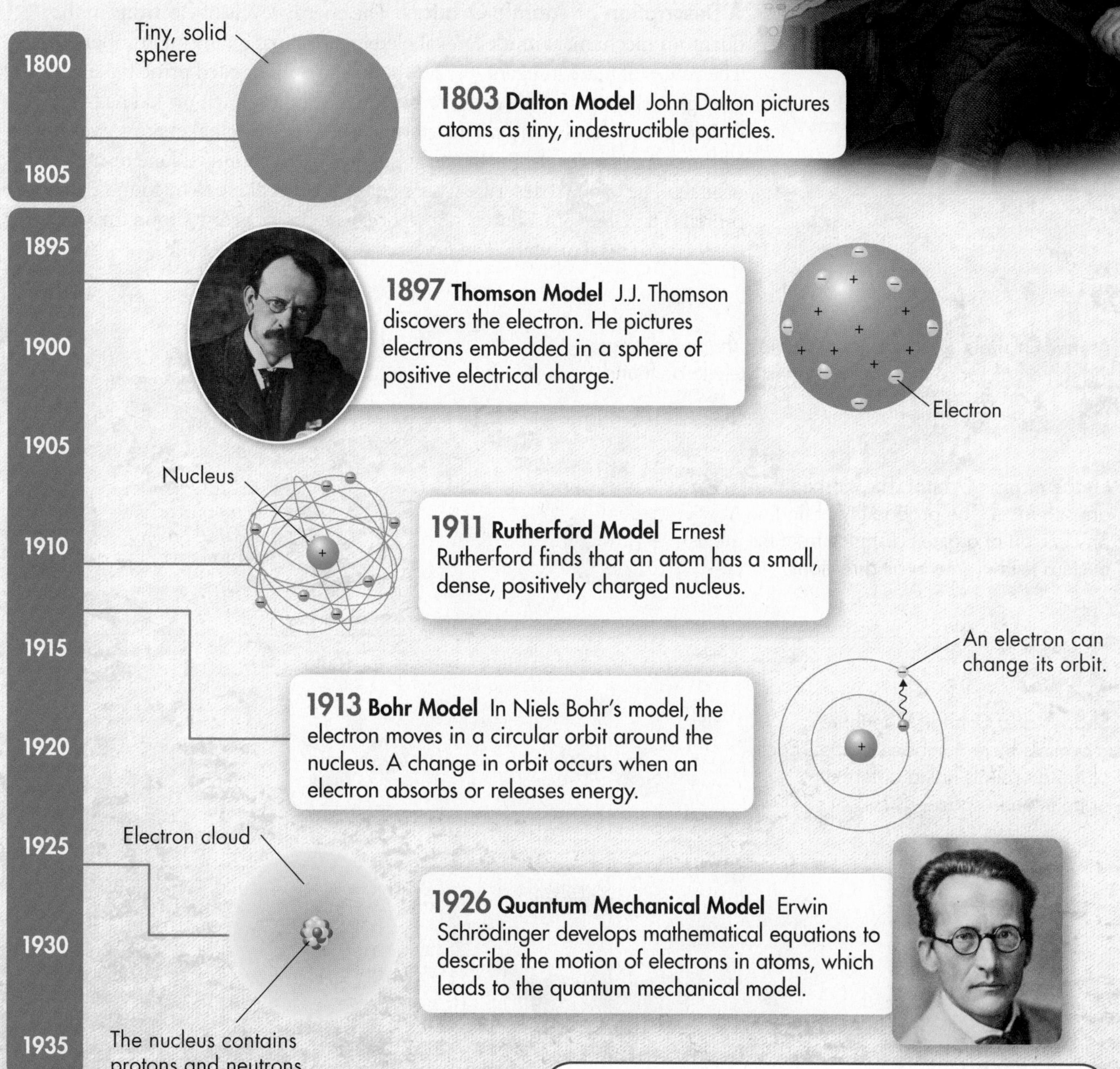

1800
1805
Tiny, solid sphere
1803 Dalton Model John Dalton pictures atoms as tiny, indestructible particles.
1895
1900
1897 Thomson Model J.J. Thomson discovers the electron. He pictures electrons embedded in a sphere of positive electrical charge.
Electron
1905
Nucleus
1910
1911 Rutherford Model Ernest Rutherford finds that an atom has a small, dense, positively charged nucleus.
1915
An electron can change its orbit.
1913 Bohr Model In Niels Bohr's model, the electron moves in a circular orbit around the nucleus. A change in orbit occurs when an electron absorbs or releases energy.
1920
1925
Electron cloud
1926 Quantum Mechanical Model Erwin Schrödinger develops mathematical equations to describe the motion of electrons in atoms, which leads to the quantum mechanical model.
1930
1935
The nucleus contains protons and neutrons.

Take It Further

1. Summarize For each scientist, list a major contribution related to understanding the atom: Dalton, Thomson, Rutherford, Bohr, and Schrödinger.

2. Describe Have you ever needed to identify something you could not see? Explain.

atomic orbital
a mathematical expression that describes where you might find an electron

ROOT WORDS

The root word of atomic is atom. It comes from the Greek word *atomos*, meaning "cannot divide any more."

Atomic Orbitals

Solutions to the Schrödinger equation give the energy levels an electron can have. For each energy level, the Schrödinger equation also leads to a mathematical expression called an atomic orbital. An **atomic orbital** describes the probability of finding an electron at various locations around the nucleus. You can draw atomic orbitals as diagrams. Each orbital diagram shows the region of space where you are likely to find an electron.

A Description of Atomic Orbitals The energy levels of electrons in the quantum mechanical model are labeled by principal quantum numbers (n). The values of n are integers—1, 2, 3, 4, and so on. For each principal energy level greater than 1, there are several atomic orbitals. Each orbital has a different shape and energy. The energy levels in a principal energy level are called energy sublevels. Each energy sublevel corresponds to one or more orbitals. The orbitals describe where an electron is likely to be found. Each orbital is labeled with a letter: *s*, *p*, *d*, or *f*. The figure below shows the shapes for the *s*, *p*, and *d* orbitals. The *f* orbitals are more complicated.

Atomic Orbitals Each orbital diagram's shape indicates the region of space that an electron is likely to be found.

Shape of an *s* Orbital The *s* orbitals are spherical. The probability of finding an electron at a given distance from the nucleus is the same in all directions.

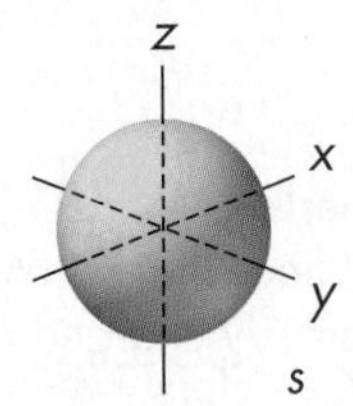

Shapes of *p* Orbitals The three *p* orbitals have dumbbell shapes. Each of these orbitals has a different orientation in space.

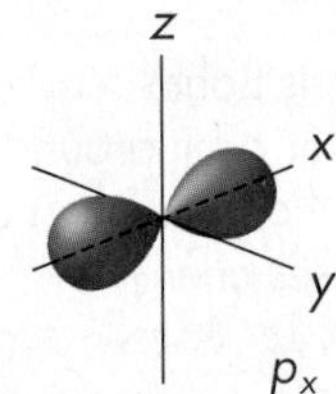

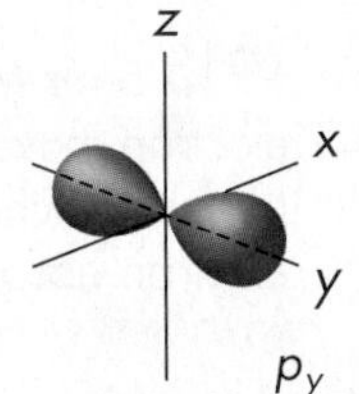

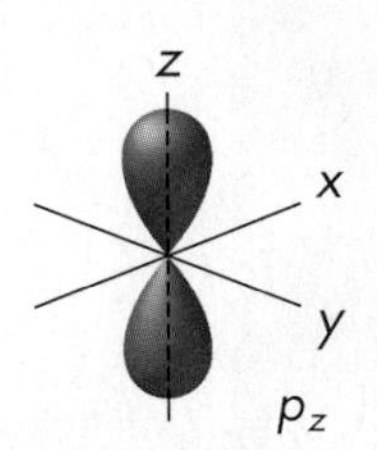

Shapes of *d* Orbitals Four of the five kinds of *d* orbitals look like four-leaf clovers. They all have different orientations in space.

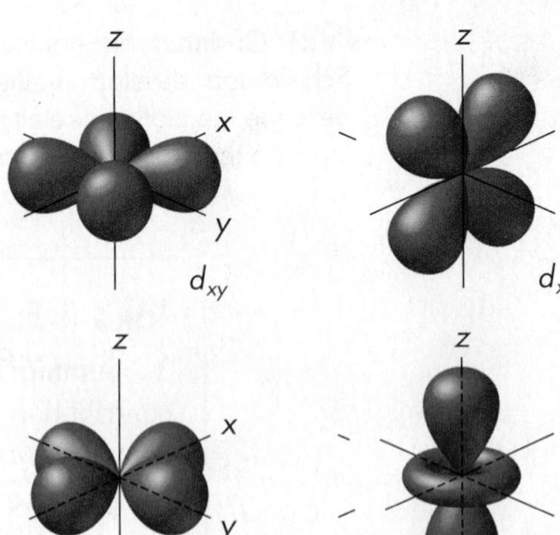

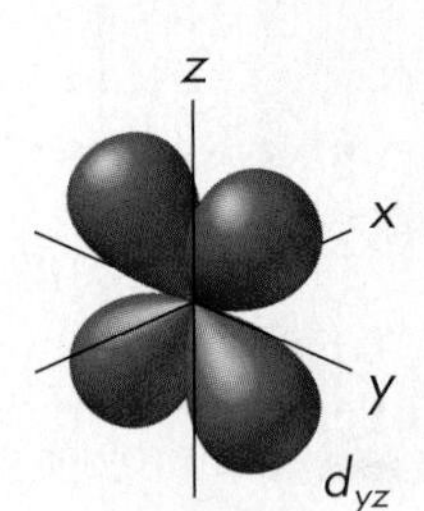

Summary of Principal Energy Levels and Sublevels			
Principal Energy Level	Number of Sublevels	Type of Sublevel	Maximum Number of Electrons
$n = 1$	1	1*s* (1 orbital)	2
$n = 2$	2	2*s* (1 orbital), 2*p* (3 orbitals)	8
$n = 3$	3	3*s* (1 orbital), 3*p* (3 orbitals), 3*d* (5 orbitals)	18
$n = 4$	4	4*s* (1 orbital), 4*p* (3 orbitals), 4*d* (5 orbitals), 4*f* (7 orbitals)	32

Learn more about probability and atomic structure *online.* CONCEPTS IN ACTION

Types of Atomic Orbitals in Each Principal Energy Level The number and types of atomic orbitals depend on the principal energy level. Compare the first and second columns in the table above. Notice that the principal quantum number equals the number of sublevels. The lowest principal energy level ($n = 1$) has one sublevel: 1*s*. The second principal energy level ($n = 2$) has two sublevels: 2*s* and 2*p*. The 2*p* sublevel has three *p* orbitals with equal energy.

The third principal energy level has a total of nine orbitals: one 3*s*, three 3*p*, and five 3*d* orbitals. The fourth principal energy level ($n = 4$) has 16 orbitals: one 4*s*, three 4*p*, five 4*d*, and seven 4*f* orbitals. The number of orbitals in any principal energy level is equal to n^2.

Key Question How do sublevels of principal energy levels differ from each other? **Each energy sublevel corresponds to one or more orbitals of different shapes. The orbitals describe where an electron is likely to be found.**

BUILD Connections

Belt colors in karate indicate a student's expertise. Beginners wear white belts; experts wear black belts. Several belt colors are between these two levels. Some belt colors have sublevels, just like principal energy levels have sublevels.

5.1 LessonCheck

Key Concept Check

1. **Review** What was the basic proposal in the Bohr atom model?
2. **Describe** What does the quantum mechanical model determine about electrons in atoms?
3. **Review** How do two sublevels of the same principal energy level differ from each other?

Vocabulary Check *Choose a highlighted word from the lesson to complete each sentence correctly.*

4. The amount of energy needed to move an electron from one energy level to another is a(n) ________.
5. The ________ are the specific energies than an electron in an atom can have.

Think Critically

6. **Apply Concepts** How many orbitals are in the 3*p* sublevel? The 2*s* sublevel?

CHEMISTRY & YOU

7. Previous atomic models were physical models based on the motion of large objects. Why do scientists no longer use physical models to describe electron motion? (Hint: See page 120.)

BIGIDEA
ELECTRONS AND THE STRUCTURE OF ATOMS

8. How do Bohr's model and the quantum mechanical model differ?

5.2 Electron Arrangement in Atoms

CHEMISTRY & YOU

Q: What makes an atom's electron configuration stable? Unstable arrangements tend to become more stable by losing energy. The yoga position shown here is unstable. The yogi would have less energy if she falls, and her new position would be more stable. Energy and stability also play an important role in determining electron configurations in an atom.

Key Question

What are the three rules for writing the electron configurations of elements?

electron configuration the way electrons are arranged in orbitals

aufbau principle the rule that says electrons are added to the lowest energy level first

WORD ORIGINS

The word *aufbau* is a German word meaning "building up." The aufbau principle describes how to build up, or fill in, electrons in energy levels.

Electron Configurations

In an atom, electrons and the nucleus interact to make the most stable arrangement possible. An **electron configuration** is the electron arrangement in the orbitals around an atom's nucleus. The aufbau principle, the Pauli exclusion principle, and Hund's rule are the three rules you can use to find an atom's electron configuration.

Aufbau Principle You can obtain an atom's electron configuration by filling in atomic orbitals one electron at a time. The **aufbau principle** states that orbitals are filled in order of increasing energy, starting with the lowest energy. The figure below shows the ordering of orbital energy levels. Each box in the figure represents an atomic orbital.

Aufbau Diagram

This diagram shows the relative energy levels of the first several atomic orbitals. Orbitals at the bottom have less energy than orbitals at the top.

Increasing energy

6s 6p 5d 4f

5s 5p 4d

4s 4p 3d

3s 3p

2s 2p

1s

Remember, the s sublevel has the lowest energy in each principal energy level.

Pauli Exclusion Principle The **Pauli exclusion principle** states that an atomic orbital may contain no more than two electrons. For example, either one or two electrons can occupy an *s* orbital or a *p* orbital. Two electrons in the same orbital must have opposite spins. **Spin** is a quantum mechanical property of electrons. Think about spin as clockwise or counterclockwise.

Hund's Rule According to **Hund's rule**, electrons occupy orbitals of the same energy in a way that maximizes the number of electrons with the same spin direction. For example, three electrons occupy three orbitals of equal energy with spins equal in direction. Any additional electrons then occupy each orbital so that their spins are opposite in direction compared to the first electron in the orbital.

Orbital Diagrams Orbital diagrams are one way to show electron arrangement in atomic orbitals. You use the three rules to make orbital diagrams. The boxes in the table below show the diagrams for a few elements. The arrows represent electrons and the direction of their spins (↑ or ↓). Look at the diagrams for hydrogen and helium. The one electron in hydrogen goes into the lowest energy orbital (1*s*) according to the aufbau principle. Helium has two electrons. Both electrons go into the 1*s* orbital. You write an orbital that has a pair of electrons as [↑↓]. Notice that the spins are opposite.

Now look at the orbital diagram for oxygen. Oxygen has eight electrons. To write the orbital diagram for oxygen, fill the 1*s* orbital first and then the 2*s* orbital. Each of these *s* orbitals has two electrons with opposite spins, following the Pauli exclusion principle. Next, add one electron to each of the three 2*p* orbitals. Write three electrons in three orbitals of equal energy as [↑][↑][↑], following Hund's rule. The last electron in oxygen pairs with an electron in one of the 2*p* orbitals. The other two 2*p* orbitals are only half filled, with one electron each.

Pauli exclusion principle no more than two electrons may be in an atomic orbital

spin a property of electrons that may be thought of as clockwise or counterclockwise

Hund's rule the number of electrons with the same spin is as large as possible in orbitals of the same energy

USING PRIOR KNOWLEDGE

The word *spin* may make you think about a wheel turning or a dancer twirling. Think about electrons turning clockwise or counterclockwise when you think about electron spin.

Electron Configurations of Selected Elements

Element	1s	2s	$2p_x$	$2p_y$	$2p_z$	3s	Electron configuration
H	[↑]	[ ]	[ ]	[ ]	[ ]	[ ]	$1s^1$
He	[↑↓]	[ ]	[ ]	[ ]	[ ]	[ ]	$1s^2$
Li	[↑↓]	[↑]	[ ]	[ ]	[ ]	[ ]	$1s^2 2s^1$
C	[↑↓]	[↑↓]	[↑]	[↑]	[ ]	[ ]	$1s^2 2s^2 2p^2$
N	[↑↓]	[↑↓]	[↑]	[↑]	[↑]	[ ]	$1s^2 2s^2 2p^3$
O	[↑↓]	[↑↓]	[↑↓]	[↑]	[↑]	[ ]	$1s^2 2s^2 2p^4$
F	[↑↓]	[↑↓]	[↑↓]	[↑↓]	[↑]	[ ]	$1s^2 2s^2 2p^5$
Ne	[↑↓]	[↑↓]	[↑↓]	[↑↓]	[↑↓]	[ ]	$1s^2 2s^2 2p^6$
Na	[↑↓]	[↑↓]	[↑↓]	[↑↓]	[↑↓]	[↑]	$1s^2 2s^2 2p^6 3s^1$

BUILD Connections

Electron configurations are often written in shorthand. Do you ever use a shorthand way to communicate? How about when you send a text message? You may use numbers and symbols in place of words. Your friends still know what you mean because they understand the shorthand being used.

Writing Electron Configurations The last column of the table on the previous page shows the atoms' electron configurations. You can write the electron configuration in shorthand. You indicate the number of electrons in each sublevel with a superscript. Hydrogen has one electron in a 1*s* orbital. Write its electron configuration as $1s^1$. Helium has two electrons in a 1*s* orbital. Its configuration is $1s^2$. Oxygen has two electrons in a 1*s* orbital, two electrons in a 2*s* orbital, and four electrons in 2*p* orbitals. The electron configuration of oxygen is $1s^2 2s^2 2p^4$.

The sublevels in the same principal energy level are usually written together in electron configurations. Sometimes, this order differs from the order shown in the aufbau diagram. For example, you would write the electron configuration for bromine as $1s^2 2s^2 2p^6 3s^2 3p^6 3d^{10} 4s^2 4p^5$. You write the 3*d* sublevel before the 4*s* sublevel even though the 4*s* sublevel has a lower energy.

Exceptional Electron Configurations The pitcher in the below photo is made of copper. Copper has an electron configuration that is an exception to the aufbau principle. Using the aufbau principle for copper, you would end up with this incorrect electron configuration:

$$1s^2 2s^2 2p^6 3s^2 3p^6 3d^9 4s^2$$

The correct electron configuration for copper is as follows. Notice how the numbers of electrons in 3*d* and 4*s* sublevels are different from those predicted by the aufbau principle.

$$1s^2 2s^2 2p^6 3s^2 3p^6 3d^{10} 4s^1$$

Copper has a filled *d* sublevel in this arrangement of electrons. Filled energy sublevels are more stable than partly filled sublevels. There are other exceptions to the aufbau principle for higher energy levels. However, the aufbau principle applies to most of the electron configurations you will write.

Key Question What are the three rules for writing the electron configurations of elements? **The aufbau principle, the Pauli exclusion principle, and Hund's rule tell you how to find electron configurations.**

Copper
Copper is a shiny metal. The electron configuration of copper does not follow the aufbau principle.

Sample Problem 5.1

Writing Electron Configurations

The atomic number for phosphorus is 15. Write the orbital diagram and electron configuration for a phosphorus atom.

1 Analyze **Identify the relevant concepts.** Phosphorus has 15 electrons. These electrons follow the aufbau principle, the Pauli exclusion principle, and Hund's rule when they fill atomic orbitals.

2 Solve **Apply the concepts to this problem.**

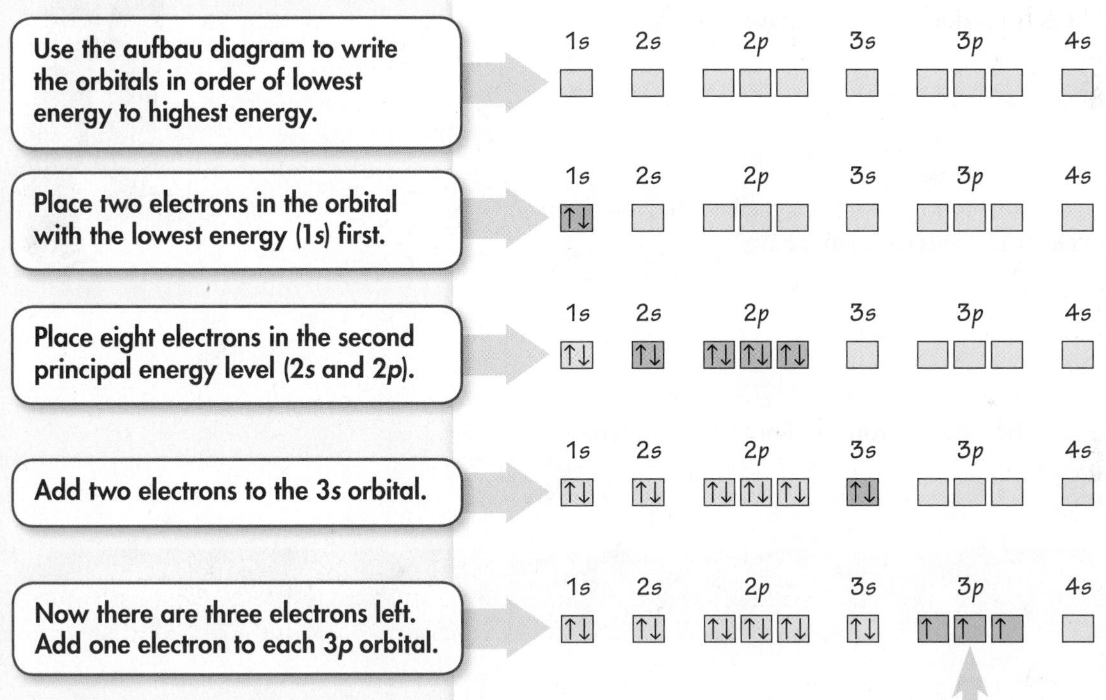

Use the aufbau diagram to write the orbitals in order of lowest energy to highest energy.
1s 2s 2p 3s 3p 4s
Place two electrons in the orbital with the lowest energy (1s) first.
1s 2s 2p 3s 3p 4s
Place eight electrons in the second principal energy level (2s and 2p).
1s 2s 2p 3s 3p 4s
Add two electrons to the 3s orbital.
1s 2s 2p 3s 3p 4s
Now there are three electrons left. Add one electron to each 3p orbital.
1s 2s 2p 3s 3p 4s
Hund's rule says that electrons fill orbitals of equal energy so the maximum number of spins are in the same direction.

Write the symbol of each sublevel with a superscript showing the number of electrons.

The electron configuration of phosphorus is $1s^2 2s^2 2p^6 3s^2 3p^3$.

Note: The sum of the superscripts equals the number of electrons: $2 + 2 + 6 + 2 + 3 = 15$

Practice Problems

When you write each configuration, group the sublevels within the same principal energy level.

9. Write the electron configuration for each atom.
  a. carbon
  b. boron

❶ **Analyze** **Identify the relevant concepts.**

❷ **Solve** **Apply the concepts to this problem.**

10. Write the electron configuration for each atom. How many unpaired electrons does each atom have?
  a. silicon
  b. sulfur

11. Write the electron configuration for each atom. How many unpaired electrons does each atom have?
  a. argon
  b. calcium

12. Challenge Write the electron configuration for krypton.

5.2 LessonCheck

Key Concept Check

13. **List** What are the three rules for writing the electron configurations of elements?

Vocabulary Check

Choose a highlighted word from the lesson to complete each sentence correctly.

14. According to the __________, electrons fill energy levels starting with the lowest energy first.

15. The arrangement of electrons in an atom's orbitals is called the __________.

16. An electron's __________ is a property that may be thought of as clockwise or counterclockwise.

Think Critically

17. Sequence Use the aufbau diagram to arrange the following sublevels in order of decreasing energy: $2p$, $4s$, $3s$, $3d$, and $3p$.

18. Apply Concepts The atomic number for arsenic is 33. What is the electron configuration of an arsenic atom?

CHEMISTRY & YOU

19. Explain why the correct electron configuration for oxygen is $1s^2 2s^2 2p^4$ and not $1s^2 2s^2 2p^3 3s^1$. (Hint: See page 126.)

5.3 Atomic Emission Spectra and the Quantum Mechanical Model

CHEMISTRY & YOU

Q: What gives gas-filled lights their colors? You've likely seen lighted signs in shop windows or along busy streets. Glass tubes bent in various shapes form these signs. An electric current passing through the gas in each tube makes the gas glow with its own characteristic color.

Key Questions

What causes atomic emission spectra?

How did Einstein explain the photoelectric effect?

How are the frequencies of light emitted by an atom related to changes of electron energies?

How does quantum mechanics differ from classical mechanics?

BUILD Vocabulary

amplitude the height of a wave from zero to the crest

wavelength (λ) the distance between the crests of a wave

frequency (ν) the number of wave cycles that pass by a point in a given amount of time

hertz (Hz) the unit for frequency that is equal to cycles per second

WORD ORIGINS

The hertz is named for Heinrich Hertz, who measured the length and the speed of electromagnetic waves.

Light and Atomic Emission Spectra

The previous lessons in this chapter introduced you to some ideas about how electrons in atoms are arranged in atomic orbitals. You learned how each orbital has a particular energy level. You also learned how to write electron configurations. You will now get a closer look at what led to the Schrödinger equation and the quantum mechanical model.

The Nature of Light The quantum mechanical model grew out of the study of light. Isaac Newton tried to explain the behavior of light by describing light as being made up of particles. Later, experimental evidence convinced scientists that light was best described as waves.

▶ **Waves Properties** You can describe a wave by its amplitude, its wavelength, and its frequency. The figure below shows these properties. The **amplitude** is the wave's height from zero to the top of the wave, or the crest. The **wavelength** is the distance between the two adjacent crests. The symbol λ (the Greek letter lambda) represents wavelength. The **frequency** is the number of wave cycles to pass a given point in a certain amount of time. The symbol ν (the Greek letter nu) represents frequency. The units of frequency are usually cycles per second. A **hertz** (Hz) is the SI unit of cycles per second. You can also write a hertz as a reciprocal second (s^{-1}).

Wave Properties The blue curve shows one complete wave cycle; the red curve shows another. This wave has a frequency of 2 Hz because two cycles pass in one second. Notice how you measure a wave's wavelength and amplitude.

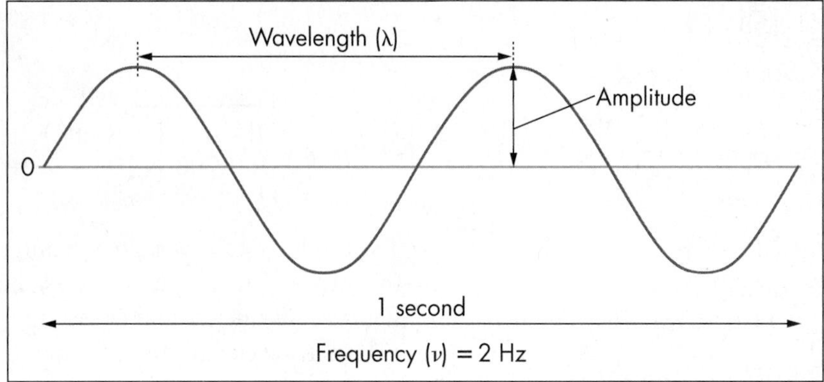

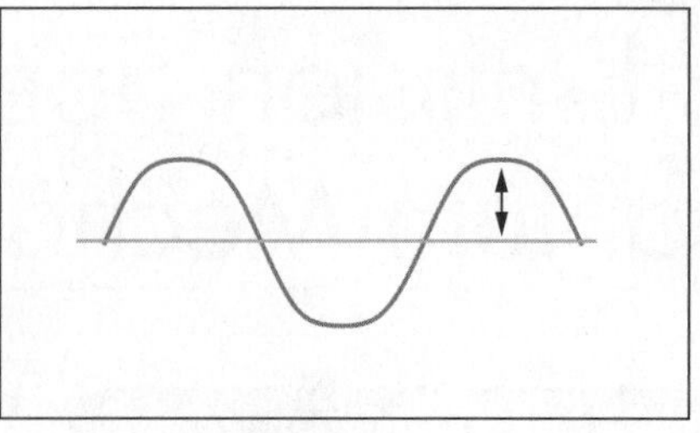

Low Amplitude You can think of amplitude as the height of the wave.

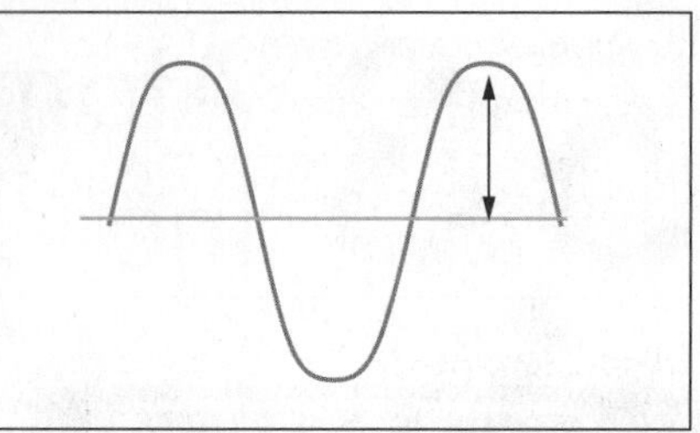

High Amplitude The amplitude of this wave is almost double the amplitude of the wave to the left.

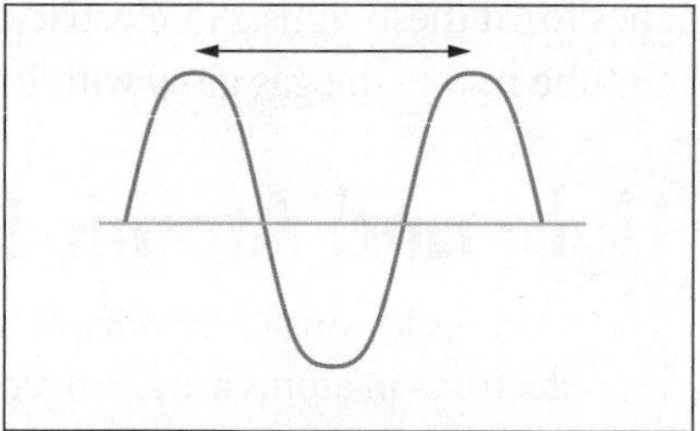

Long Wavelength You can find wavelength by measuring the distance from one crest to the next.

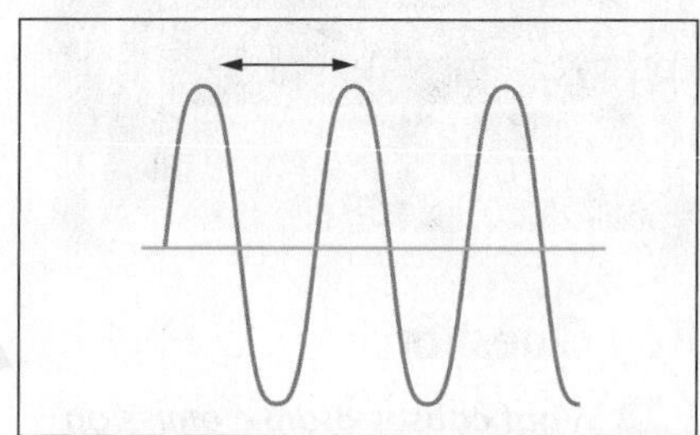

Short Wavelength The wavelength of this wave is about one half the wavelength of the wave to the left.

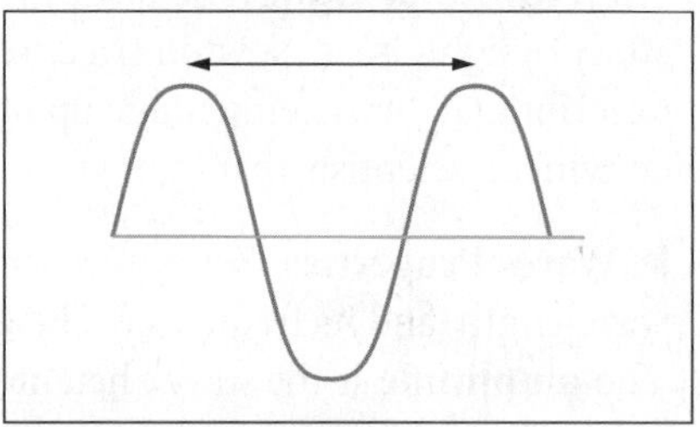

Low Frequency A wave vibrating at one cycle per second has a frequency of 1 Hz.

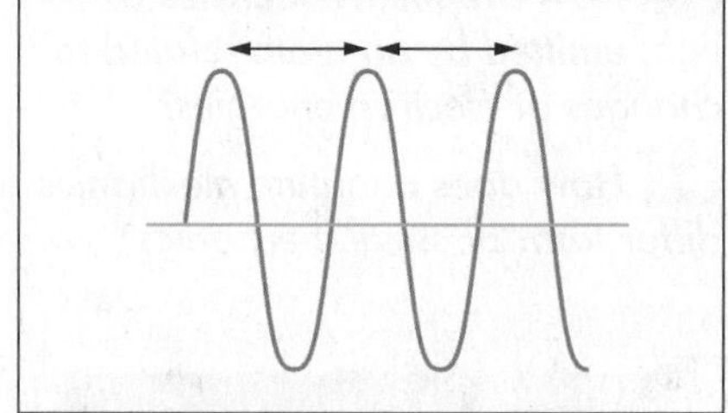

High Frequency A wave vibrating at two cycles per second has a frequency of 2 Hz.

The figure above shows how wave properties can vary. Light waves can have different amplitudes, wavelengths, and frequencies. However, all light waves travel at the same speed—the speed of light. The speed of light (c) is a constant. In a vacuum, the speed of light is 2.998×10^8 m/s. Frequency and wavelength are related by the speed of light, as this equation shows.

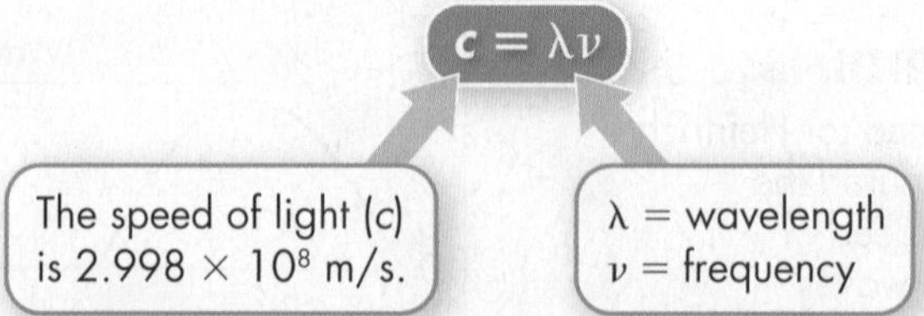

The product of the wavelength and the frequency equals a constant. Thus, as the wavelength of light increases, the frequency decreases. Look again at the figures of frequency and wavelength. Notice that the high-frequency wave has a shorter wavelength than the low-frequency wave.

Electromagnetic Waves
Electromagnetic radiation can have different wavelengths. The visible light portion of this range is very small. It is in the 10^{-7} m wavelength range and the 10^{15} Hz (s^{-1}) frequency range.

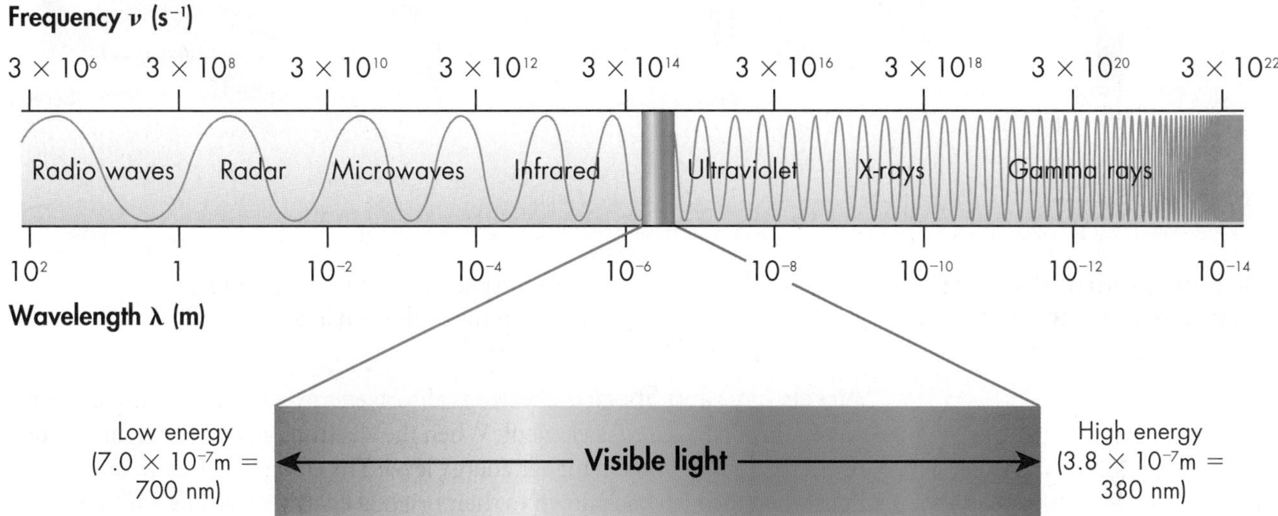

▶ **Electromagnetic Radiation** Light waves are electromagnetic waves. **Electromagnetic radiation** includes radio waves, microwaves, infrared waves, visible light, ultraviolet waves, X-rays, and gamma rays. In a vacuum, each of these waves travels at the speed of light. The figure above shows the wavelengths and frequencies of each kind of electromagnetic wave. Notice that each type has a certain range of wavelengths and frequencies. Radio waves have the longest wavelengths. Gamma rays have the shortest wavelengths.

Visible light includes all the colors you can see. The wavelength and frequency of each color of light are characteristic of that color. For example, the reddest light has a wavelength of 7.0×10^{-7} m, or 700 nm. The sun gives off visible light of all the wavelengths and frequencies. You see this light as white light. When this white light passes through a prism, the different wavelengths separate into a **spectrum** of colors. The rainbow in the photo below is an example of a spectrum of visible light from the sun.

electromagnetic radiation energy waves that travel at the speed of light

spectrum wavelengths of visible light that are separated by a prism

PREFIXES
The prefix *electro-* is used to describe something electric. Electromagnetic radiation consists of changing electric and magnetic fields.

Rainbow
Each tiny droplet of water in the air acts as a prism to produce the spectrum you see in a rainbow. Each color blends into the next in this order: red, orange, yellow, green, blue, and violet.

Comparing Spectra

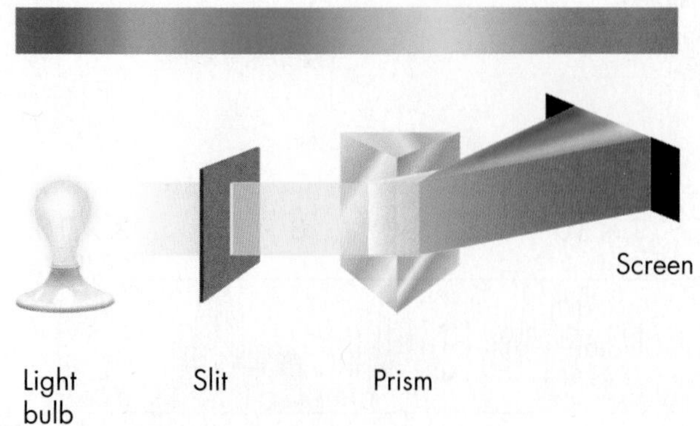

White light spectrum White light produces a rainbow of colors.

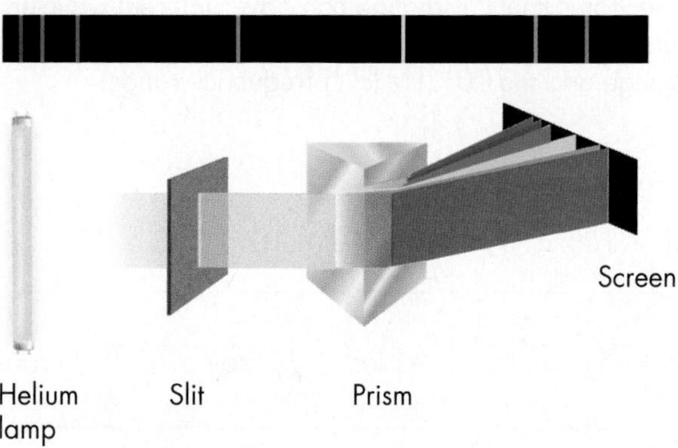

Helium spectrum Light from a helium lamp produces discrete lines.

Atomic Emission Spectra Electrons absorb energy when an electric current passes through a gaseous element. When the electrons absorb the right amount of energy, they move to a higher energy level. The electrons give off, or emit, light when they fall back down to their original energy level. The emitted light's energy is equal to the amount of energy the electrons absorb.

atomic emission spectrum the wavelengths of light emitted by an element

WORD ORIGINS

The word *emission* comes from a Latin word that means "to send out." *Spectrum* is the Latin word for "appearance." An atomic emission spectrum allows the light sent out from an atom to be seen.

Look at the figure above that shows the spectrum of white light. Notice that it includes all the wavelengths of visible light. Now look at the figure that shows the spectrum of light given off by helium. The light given off by a single element contains only a few colors. These colors show up as narrow lines of light. They are characteristic of the element. The colors of light an element emits compose its **atomic emission spectrum**. Each line in an atomic emission spectrum corresponds to a wavelength of light emitted by the electrons of that element.

The atomic emission spectrum of each element is like a person's fingerprint. No two elements have the same atomic emission spectrum. Atomic emission spectra are useful for identifying elements. The figure below shows the colors emitted by sodium and by mercury.

Key Question What causes atomic emission spectra? **Electrons move to higher energy levels when atoms absorb energy. These electrons lose energy by emitting light when they return to lower energy levels.**

Atomic Emission

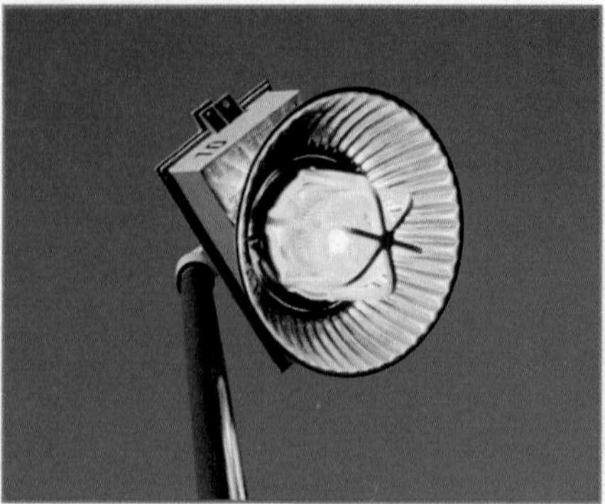

Sodium Lamps filled with sodium vapor give off yellow light.

Mercury Lamps filled with mercury vapor give off blue light.

Sample Problem 5.2

Calculating the Wavelength of Light

Calculate the wavelength of the yellow light emitted by a sodium lamp. The frequency of the light is 5.09×10^{14} Hz ($5.09 \times 10^{14}\ s^{-1}$).

KNOWNS	UNKNOWN
$\nu = 5.09 \times 10^{14}\ s^{-1}$	$\lambda = ?\ m$
$c = 2.998 \times 10^{8}\ m/s$	

1 Analyze **List the knowns and the unknown.**

2 Calculate **Solve for the unknown.**

Write the equation that relates light's frequency and wavelength.

$$c = \lambda\nu$$

Rearrange the equation to solve for λ.

Isolate λ by dividing both sides by ν.

$$\frac{c}{\nu} = \frac{\lambda\nu}{\nu}$$

Rewrite the equation so the unknown is on the left.

$$\lambda = \frac{c}{\nu}$$

Substitute the knowns. Cancel the units and then solve.

$$\lambda = \frac{2.998 \times 10^{8}\ m/s}{5.09 \times 10^{14}\ s^{-1}} = 5.89 \times 10^{-7}\ m$$

Note: The unit s^{-1} is the same as 1/s. Here's how the seconds in the units cancel out:

$$\frac{\left(\frac{m}{s}\right)}{\left(\frac{1}{s}\right)} = \frac{m}{s} \times \frac{s}{1}$$

3 Evaluate **Does the result make sense?** Look back at the figure of electromagnetic waves. You can estimate that yellow light has a wavelength close to 6×10^{-7} m. The answer is close to this value.

Practice Problems

20. What is the wavelength of radiation with a frequency of 1.50×10^{13} Hz? Does this radiation have a longer or shorter wavelength than red light?

KNOWNS	UNKNOWN
$\nu = 1.50 \times 10^{13}\ s^{-1}$	$\lambda = ?\ m$
$c = 2.998 \times 10^{8}\ m/s$	

1 Analyze **List the knowns and the unknown.**

2 Calculate **Solve for the unknown.**

3 Evaluate **Does the result make sense?**

21. Challenge What is the frequency of radiation with a wavelength of 5.00×10^{-8} m? What kind of electromagnetic radiation is this?

KNOWNS	UNKNOWN
$\lambda =$	$\nu = ?\ s^{-1}$
$c =$	

Quick Lab

Purpose To determine the identity of the metal in an unknown solution based on its characteristic color when heated in a flame

Materials

- six small test tubes
- sodium chloride ($NaCl$) solution
- calcium chloride ($CaCl_2$) solution
- lithium chloride ($LiCl$) solution
- copper(II) chloride ($CuCl_2$) solution
- potassium chloride (KCl) solution
- unknown solution
- six cotton swabs
- gas burner

Flame Tests

Procedure

1. Make a two-column data table. Label the columns "Metal" and "Flame Color." Enter the metal's name for each solution in the first column.

2. Label each of five test tubes with a solution's name. Label the sixth tube "Unknown." Add 1 mL of each solution to the appropriately labeled test tube.

3. Dip an end of a cotton swab into the sodium chloride solution and then briefly hold it in the burner flame. Record the color of the flame. Do not leave the swab in the flame too long or it may melt or catch fire.

4. Repeat step 3 for each of the remaining solutions by using a new cotton swab each time.

5. Perform a flame test with the unknown solution. Note the color of the flame.

Analyze and Conclude

1. Identify What is the metal in the unknown?

2. Draw Conclusions Each solution produces a unique color. Would you expect this result based on the atom's modern view? Explain.

3. Predict Some fireworks contain chemicals that produce colors. What element do you think produces crimson red? Yellow?

Planck's constant (h) the constant with the value 6.626×10^{-34} J·s

ACADEMIC WORDS

You might use the word *constant* to describe something that stays the same—no matter what. It has a similar meaning in science. A constant is a number that has a fixed value. It is always the same.

The Quantum Concept and Photons

Classical physics does not explain the emission spectra of atoms. It predicts that an atomic emission spectrum would contain all colors, not just a few.

The Quantization of Energy In 1900, German physicist Max Planck wanted to describe why substances produce the colors they do when heated. He could explain the color changes if he assumed that the energy changes only in small discrete units. A quantum is one of these discrete energy units. The equation below shows how the energy (E) of a single quantum relates to the frequency of radiation (ν).

$$E = h\nu$$

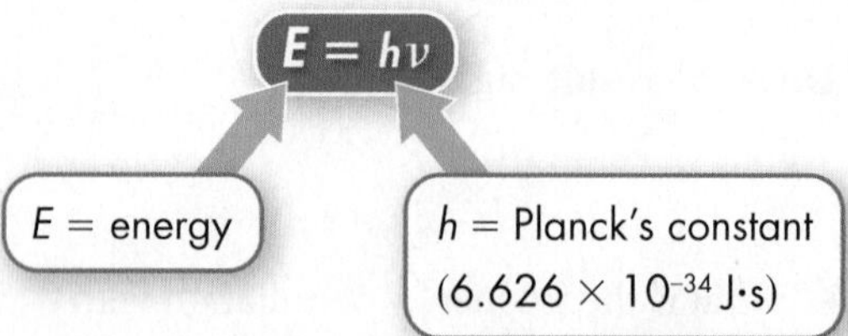

Planck's constant is the constant h. It has a value of 6.626×10^{-34} J·s. The equation shows that the energy of a quantum equals $h\nu$. The emission or absorption of a small quantum of energy involves a low frequency. The emission or absorption of a large quantum of energy involves a high frequency.

Sample Problem 5.3

Calculating the Energy of a Quantum

What is the energy of a quantum of microwave radiation with a frequency of $3.20 \times 10^{11}\ s^{-1}$?

1 Analyze **List the knowns and the unknown.**

KNOWNS	UNKNOWN
$\nu = 3.20 \times 10^{11}\ s^{-1}$	$E = ?\ J$
$h = 6.626 \times 10^{-34}\ J{\cdot}s$	

2 Calculate **Solve for the unknown.**

Write the equation that relates energy and frequency.

$$E = h\nu$$

Substitute the knowns and then cancel the units.

$$E = (6.626 \times 10^{-34}\ J{\cdot}\cancel{s}) \times (3.20 \times 10^{11}\ \cancel{s^{-1}})$$

Solve the equation.

$$E = 2.12 \times 10^{-22}\ J$$

3 Evaluate **Does the result make sense?** The units cancel to give joules (a unit of energy), which is what you want. Individual quanta have very small energies, so the answer seems reasonable.

Practice Problems

22. Calculate the energy of a quantum of radiant energy with a frequency of $5.00 \times 10^{11}\ s^{-1}$.

1 Analyze **List the knowns and the unknown.**

2 Calculate **Solve for the unknown.**

3 Evaluate **Does the result make sense?**

KNOWNS	UNKNOWN
$\nu = 5.00 \times 10^{11}\ s^{-1}$	$E = ?\ J$
$h = 6.626 \times 10^{-34}\ J{\cdot}s$	

23. Challenge A type of light you cannot see has a wavelength of 260 nm. What is the energy of this light in joules?

Hint: Use the equation $c = \lambda\nu$ to find the frequency of light from the wavelength. Then, calculate the energy.

KNOWNS	UNKNOWNS
$\lambda =$	$\nu = ?\ s^{-1}$
$c =$	$E = ?\ J$
$h =$	

photoelectric effect certain frequencies of light cause electrons to eject from a metal

photon a quantum of light

PREFIXES

The prefix *photo-* means light. Any word that begins with *photo-* is related to light in some way. One such word is *photosynthesis*. A photon is a unit of light, and light causes the photoelectric effect.

The Photoelectric Effect Scientists could use Planck's theory to explain many observations that classical physics could not explain. In 1905, Albert Einstein used Planck's quantum theory to explain the photoelectric effect. The **photoelectric effect** results when light shines on a metal and causes electrons to be ejected. Only light above a certain frequency will cause the photoelectric effect. For example, a very bright red light will not cause potassium to eject electrons, but a very weak yellow light will cause potassium to eject electrons.

The classical wave theory of light cannot explain the photoelectric effect. Classical physics correctly describes light as a form of energy. However, if light followed the rules of classical physics, any frequency of light would cause an electron to eject. This does not happen.

Photons Einstein proposed that you could describe light as quanta of energy that behave like particles. These light quanta are called **photons**. The equation $E = h\nu$ describes quantizing photon energy. All photons of light that have the same frequency have the same energy. Einstein recognized that for a photoelectric effect to occur, it needs a minimum energy value. This minimum energy is the threshold frequency. The figure below shows how the photoelectric effect depends on the frequency of light. No electrons eject if the photon's frequency is too low. Frequencies of light above the threshold frequency will cause the photoelectric effect.

The photoelectric effect shows that light can be described as particles. Some other behaviors of light show that light can be described as waves. Therefore, scientists use both particle models and wave models to describe light.

Key Question How did Einstein explain the photoelectric effect? **To explain the photoelectric effect, Einstein proposed that you could describe light as quanta of energy that behave as if they were particles.**

Photoelectric Effect

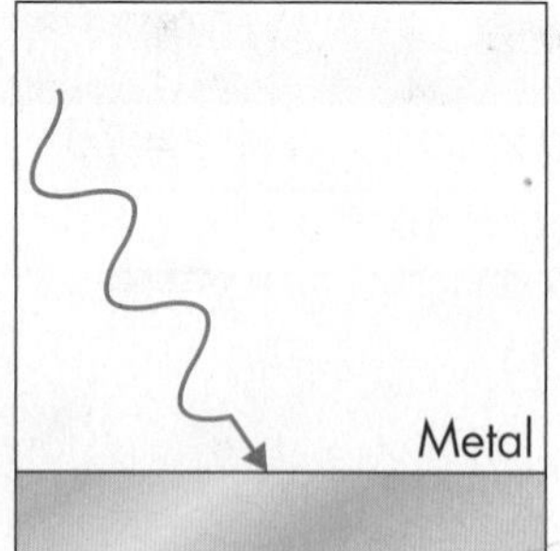

1 No electrons are ejected because the frequency of the light is below the threshold frequency.

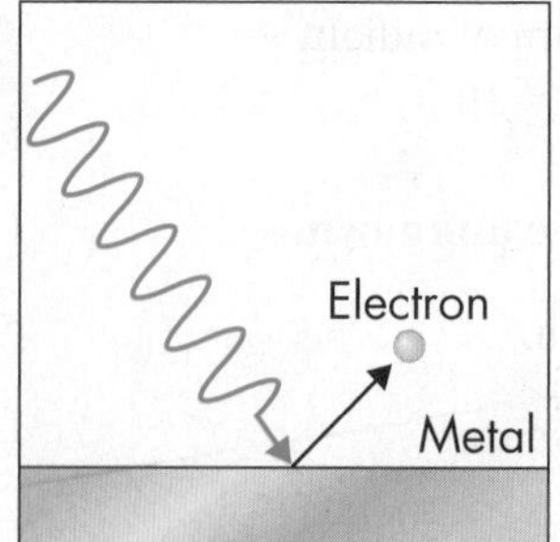

2 If the frequency is increased to be above the threshold frequency, electrons are ejected.

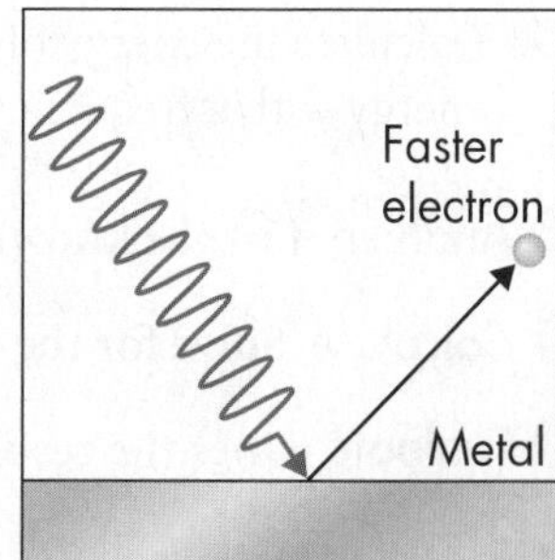

3 If the frequency is increased again, the ejected electrons will travel faster.

An Explanation for Atomic Spectra

Bohr proposed that electrons are in circular orbits that have specific energies. Scientists knew about atomic emission spectra before Bohr proposed his model. Bohr applied quantum theory to electron energy levels in atoms to explain hydrogen's atomic emission spectrum. His model explained why hydrogen's atomic emission spectrum consists of specific frequencies of light. The values of these frequencies predicted by his model agreed with the experimental results.

Electron Excitation In the Bohr model, the one electron in the hydrogen atom can have only certain specific energies. When the electron has its lowest possible energy, the atom is in its **ground state**. The principal quantum number (n) is 1 for hydrogen's ground state. An electron is said to be excited when it absorbs energy and moves to a higher energy level. The figure below shows what happens when an electron becomes excited. The absorbed photon's energy determines which energy level the electron will occupy. An electron can move to an exited state with $n = 2, 3, 4$, etc.

An electron dropping back to a lower energy level emits a quantum of energy in the form of light (a photon). Bohr already knew that energy relates to the frequency of the emitted light by the equation $E = h\nu$. The light emitted by an electron moving from a higher to a lower energy level has a certain frequency. This frequency depends on the energy change of the electron. Therefore, each transition produces a line of a specific frequency in the spectrum. An upper limit exists for each set of lines in a spectrum. This upper limit exists because an electron with enough energy will completely escape the atom.

Bohr's model explained hydrogen's atomic emission spectrum. However, it could not explain the emission spectra of atoms that contain more than one electron. Also, it did not explain how atoms bond to form molecules. So the quantum mechanical model replaced the Bohr model.

Key Question How are the frequencies of light emitted by an atom related to the changes of electron energies? **The light emitted by an electron moving from a higher to a lower energy level has a frequency that depends on the electron's energy change.**

ground state an electron's lowest energy state

USING PRIOR KNOWLEDGE

You have the lowest possible energy when you lie on the ground. Electrons have the lowest possible energy when they are in the ground state.

Learn more about the **hydrogen spectrum.**

Electron Excitation

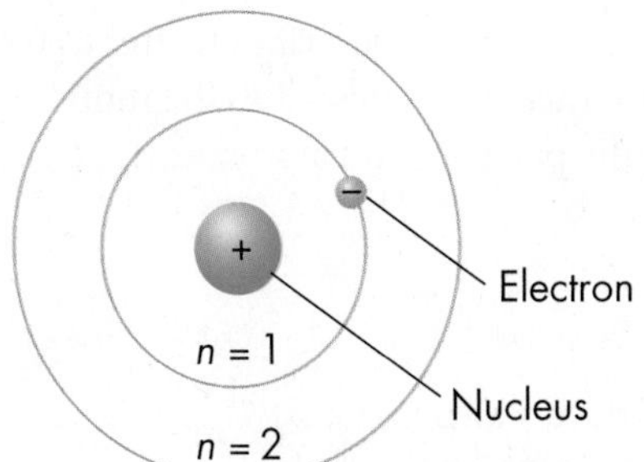

Ground State The ground state of an electron is the energy level that an electron normally occupies. This state is the most stable.

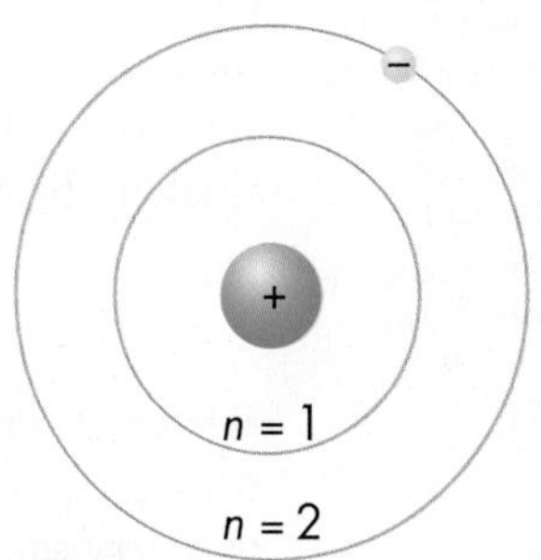

Excited State An electron becomes excited when it absorbs energy, such as a photon. It will temporarily move to a higher energy level.

BUILD Understanding

T-Chart As you read, make a t-chart to compare how matter behaves as waves and how it behaves as particles. List the properties and types of matter that each description can explain.

Quantum Mechanics

In 1924, Louis de Broglie asked an important question: Given that light behaves as waves and particles, can particles of matter behave as waves? He developed a mathematical expression for the wavelength of a moving particle to answer his question.

The Wavelike Nature of Matter De Broglie proposed that matter moves in a wavelike way. This idea would not have gained acceptance unless experiments supported it. Experiments by Clinton Davisson and Lester Germer at Bell Labs in New Jersey did just that. The two scientists had been striking metal with electron beams. Some of the electrons bounced off the metal surface. The scientists noticed that the reflected electrons produced curious patterns. The patterns were like those obtained when X-rays reflect from metal surfaces. They believed that the electrons were particles but reflected as if they were waves! De Broglie received the Nobel Prize for his work on the wave nature of matter. Davisson also received the Nobel Prize for his experiments that showed the wave nature of electrons.

The wavelike properties of electrons are useful in looking at objects that you cannot see with an optical microscope. The electron beams in an electron microscope have much smaller wavelengths than visible light. These smaller wavelengths allow a much clearer enlarged image of a very small object than is possible with an ordinary microscope. The figure below shows how a grain of pollen looks when using an electron microscope.

De Broglie's equation predicts that all moving objects behave like waves. Why do ordinary objects, such as golf balls, not seem to travel as waves? The object's mass must be very small in order for its wavelength to be large enough to observe. For example, a 50 gram golf ball traveling at 40 m/s has a wavelength of only 3×10^{-34} m. This wavelength is much too small to detect. On the other hand, an electron has a mass of only 9.11×10^{-28} g. If it were moving at a velocity of 40 m/s, it would have a wavelength of 2×10^{-5} m. This wavelength is easy to measure.

De Broglie's prediction that matter shows wave and particle properties brought on a new way of describing the motions of subatomic particles and atoms. The newer theory is quantum mechanics. The older theory is classical mechanics. Classical mechanics can describe the motion and behavior of larger objects. It describes matter as being composed of particles. Quantum mechanics describes the motions of smaller objects, such as subatomic particles and atoms, as waves.

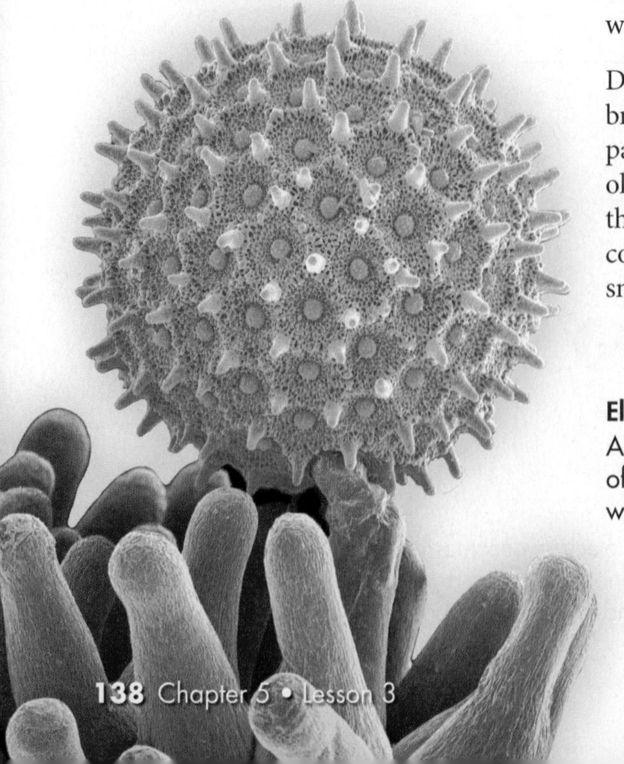

Electron Micrograph
An electron microscope can produce sharp images of a very small pollen grain because of the small wavelength of a moving electron.

The Heisenberg Uncertainty Principle Physicist Werner Heisenberg proposed the **Heisenberg uncertainty principle**, which states that it is impossible to know the exact velocity and the exact position of a particle at the same time. This principle applies to particles of all sizes, but the effect is not noticable for large objects, such as cars. It is important when studying small particles, such as electrons.

Consider how you determine an object's location. To find a set of keys in a dark room, you can use a flashlight. You see the keys when the light bounces off them and into your eyes. In a similar way, you might hit an electron with a photon of light to find the electron. However, the electron has a very small mass. Hitting it with a photon affects its motion in a way that you cannot accurately predict. The very act of measuring the electron's position changes its velocity, making its velocity uncertain.

Key Question How does quantum mechanics differ from classical mechanics? **Classical mechanics describes the motions of bodies much larger than atoms. Quantum mechanics describes the motions of subatomic particles and atoms as waves.**

Heisenberg uncertainty principle you cannot know the exact velocity and the exact position of a particle at the same time

USING PRIOR KNOWLEDGE

When you are not sure about the correct answer on a test, you are uncertain. According to the Heisenberg uncertainty principle, you cannot be sure about an electron's velocity and position at the same time.

5.3 LessonCheck

Key Concept Check

24. **Describe** What is the origin of an element's atomic emission spectrum?

25. **Review** What was Einstein's explanation for the photoelectric effect?

26. **Explain** How is the change in electron energy related to the frequency of light emitted by an atom?

27. **Explain** How does quantum mechanics differ from classical mechanics?

Vocabulary Check

Choose a highlighted word from the lesson to complete each sentence correctly.

28. The distance between neighboring crests in a wave is the wave's __________.

29. The characteristic wavelengths emitted by an element is an element's __________.

30. The h in the equation $E = h\nu$ is called __________.

31. A(n) __________ is a quantum of light energy.

Think Critically

32. **Sequence** Arrange these in order of decreasing wavelength: infrared radiation from a heat lamp, dental X-rays, and a radio station signal.

33. **Calculate** What is the energy of a quantum of blue light with a wavelength of 460 nm?

CHEMISTRY & YOU

34. The glass tubes in lighted signs contain helium, neon, argon, krypton, xenon gas, or a mixture of these gases. Why do the colors of the light depend on the gases? (Hint: See page 137.)

BIGIDEA

ELECTRONS AND THE STRUCTURE OF ATOMS

35. A strontium compound emits red light when heated in a flame. A barium compound emits yellow-green light when heated in a flame. Explain why these colors are emitted.

5 Study Guide

BIGIDEA ELECTRONS AND THE STRUCTURE OF ATOMS

The quantum mechanical model comes from solutions to the Schrödinger equation. Solutions to the Schrödinger equation give the energies an electron can have and the atomic orbitals, which describe the regions of space where an electron may be found. Electrons can absorb energy to move from one energy level to a higher energy level. When an electron moves from a higher energy level back down to a lower energy level, light is emitted.

5.1 Revising the Atomic Model

Bohr proposed that an electron is found only in specific circular paths, or orbits, around the nucleus.

The quantum mechanical model determines the allowed energies an electron can have. It also determines how likely it is to find the electron in various locations around an atom's nucleus.

Each energy sublevel corresponds to one or more orbitals of different shapes. The orbitals describe where an electron is likely to be found.

- energy level (119)
- quantum (119)
- quantum mechanical model (120)
- atomic orbital (122)

5.2 Electron Arrangement in Atoms

The aufbau principle, the Pauli exclusion principle, and Hund's rule tell you how to find electron configurations.

- electron configuration (124)
- aufbau principle (124)
- Pauli exclusion principle (125)
- spin (125)
- Hund's rule (125)

5.3 Atomic Emission Spectra and the Quantum Mechanical Model

Electrons move to higher energy levels when atoms absorb energy. These electrons lose energy by emitting light when they return to lower energy levels.

To explain the photoelectric effect, Einstein proposed that you could describe light as quanta of energy that behave as if they were particles.

The light emitted by an electron moving from a higher to a lower energy level has a frequency that depends on the electron's energy change.

Classical mechanics describes the motions of bodies much larger than atoms. Quantum mechanics describes the motions of subatomic particles and atoms as waves.

- amplitude (129)
- wavelength (129)
- frequency (129)
- hertz (129)
- electromagnetic radiation (131)
- spectrum (131)
- atomic emission spectrum (132)
- Planck's constant (134)
- photoelectric effect (136)
- photon (136)
- ground state (137)
- Heisenberg uncertainty principle (139)

Key Equations

$$c = \lambda\nu$$

$$E = h\nu$$

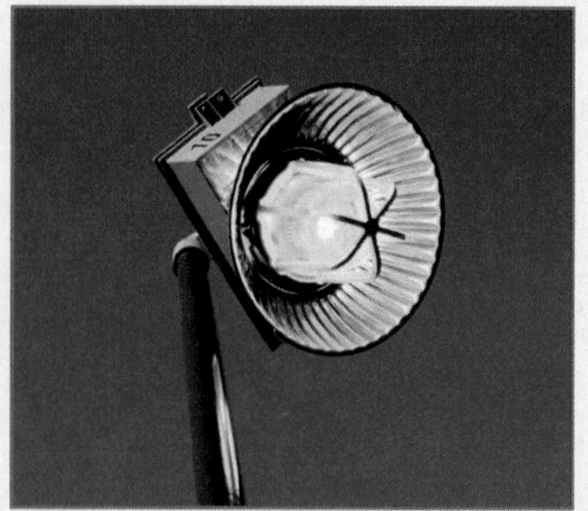

Math Tune-Up: Atomic Emission Spectra and Photons

Problem	❶ Analyze	❷ Calculate	❸ Evaluate
Calculate the wavelength of radiation with a frequency of 8.43×10^9 Hz ($8.43 \times 10^9\ s^{-1}$). In what region of the electromagnetic spectrum is this radiation?	Knowns: $\nu = 8.43 \times 10^9\ s^{-1}$ $c = 2.998 \times 10^8$ m/s Unknown: $\lambda = ?$ m Use the equation that relates the frequency and wavelength of light: $c = \lambda\nu$	Solve for λ, cancel the units, and then calculate. $\lambda = \frac{c}{\nu}$ $\lambda = \frac{2.998 \times 10^8\ m/\cancel{s}}{8.43 \times 10^9\ \cancel{s^{-1}}}$ $\lambda = 3.56 \times 10^{-2}$ m The radiation is in the radar region of the electromagnetic spectrum.	The magnitude of the frequency of the radiation is larger than the value for the speed of light, so the answer should be less than 1. Hint: Review Sample Problem 5.2 if you have trouble with converting between wavelength and frequency.
What is the energy of a quantum of X-ray radiation with a frequency of $7.49 \times 10^{18}\ s^{-1}$?	Knowns: $\nu = 7.49 \times 10^{18}\ s^{-1}$ $h = 6.626 \times 10^{-34}$ J·s Unknown: E = ? J Use the equation that relates the energy of a photon of radiation and the frequency of the radiation: $E = h\nu$	Substitute the known values for ν and h into the equation, cancel units, and then calculate. $E = (6.626 \times 10^{-34}\ J\cdot\cancel{s}) \times (7.49 \times 10^{18}\ \cancel{s^{-1}})$ $E = 4.96 \times 10^{-15}$ J	Individual photons have very small energies, so the answer is reasonable.

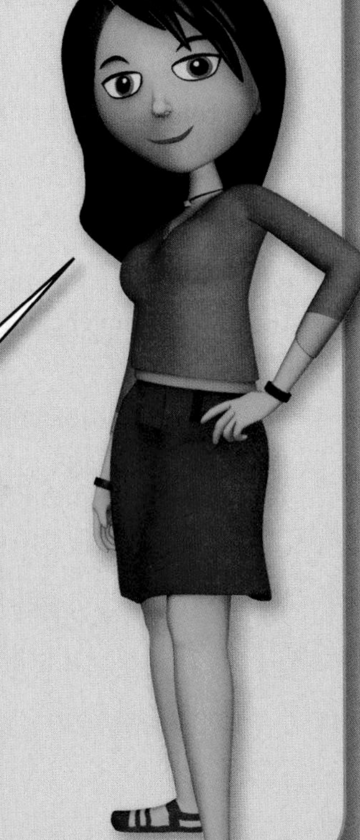

Refer to Sample Problem 5.3 if you have trouble with finding the energy of a quantum.

5 Assessment

★ Solutions appear in Appendix D.

Lesson by Lesson

5.1 Revising the Atomic Model

36. Describe Rutherford's atom model and then compare it with the model proposed by Bohr.

37. What is an atomic orbital?

38. Sketch 1*s*, 2*s*, and 2*p* orbitals, using the same scale for each. (Hint: The 2*s* orbital has a larger diameter than the 1*s* orbital because it has a higher energy.)

★39. How many orbitals are in the 2*p* sublevel?

★40. How many sublevels do each of these principal energy levels contain?

a. $n = 1$
b. $n = 2$
c. $n = 3$
d. $n = 4$

5.2 Electron Arrangement in Atoms

★41. What are the three rules that govern filling atomic orbitals with electrons?

★42. Arrange the following sublevels in order of increasing energy: 3*d*, 2*s*, 4*s*, 3*p*.

★43. Which of these orbital designations are invalid?

a. 4*s*
b. 2*d*
c. 3*f*
d. 3*p*

44. What is the maximum number of electrons that can go into each of the following sublevels?

a. 2*s*
b. 4*p*
c. 3*p*
d. 3*d*

★45. What is meant by $3p^3$?

46. Write electron configurations for the elements that have these atomic numbers.

a. 7
b. 9
c. 12
d. 36

47. Give electron configurations for atoms from these elements.

a. Na
b. K
c. I
d. Ne

★48. How many electrons are in the highest occupied energy level of these atoms?

a. barium
b. aluminum
c. sodium
d. oxygen

49. How many electrons are in the second energy level of an atom for these elements?

a. chlorine
b. phosphorus
c. potassium

5.3 Atomic Emission Spectra and the Quantum Mechanical Model

50. Use a diagram to illustrate each term for a wave.

a. wavelength
b. amplitude
c. cycle

51. What is meant by a wave's frequency? What are the units of frequency? Describe the relationship between frequency and wavelength.

52. List the colors of the visible spectrum in order of increasing wavelength.

★53. Consider the following regions of the electromagnetic spectrum: ultraviolet, X-ray, visible, infrared, radio wave, and microwave.

a. Arrange the regions in order of decreasing wavelength. (Hint: See page 131.)
b. How does the order in part (a) differ from that of decreasing frequency?

54. How did Planck influence the development of modern atomic theory?

Understand Concepts

55. Give the symbol for the atom that corresponds to each electron configuration.

a. $1s^2 2s^2 2p^6 3s^2 3p^6$
b. $1s^2 2s^2 2p^6 3s^2 3p^6 3d^{10} 4s^2 4p^6 4d^7 5s^1$
c. $1s^2 2s^2 2p^6 3s^2 3p^6 3d^{10} 4s^2 4p^6 4d^{10} 4f^7 5s^2 5p^6 5d^1 6s^2$

★56. Write the electron configuration for an arsenic atom. Calculate the total number of electrons in each energy level and then state which energy levels are not full.

★57. Give the symbols and names of the elements that correspond to these configurations of atoms.

a. $1s^2 2s^2 2p^6 3s^1$
b. $1s^2 2s^2 2p^3$
c. $1s^2 2s^2 2p^6 3s^2 3p^6 3d^2 4s^2$

58. An AM radio station broadcasts at a frequency of 1150 kHz. What is the wavelength of this radiation in centimeters?

★59. A mercury lamp, such as the one below, emits radiation with a wavelength of 4.36×10^{-7} m.

a. In what region of the electromagnetic spectrum is this radiation?
b. Calculate this radiation's frequency.

60. You use a microwave oven to heat your dinner. The frequency of the radiation is $2.37 \times 10^9\ s^{-1}$. What is the energy of one photon, or quantum, of this radiation?

Think Critically

★61. Compare Explain the difference between an orbit in the Bohr model and an orbital in the quantum mechanical model.

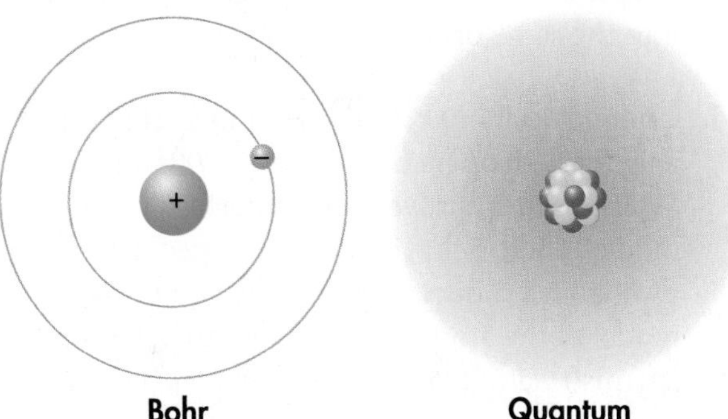

Bohr model

Quantum mechanical model

62. Evaluate and Revise Orbital diagrams for the ground states of two elements are shown below. Each diagram shows something that is incorrect. Identify the error in each diagram and then draw the correct diagram.

a. Nitrogen

1s	2s	2p		
↑↓	↑↓	↑↓	↑	

b. Magnesium

1s	2s	2p			3s
↑↓	↑↓	↑↓	↑↓	↑↓	

FOUNDATIONS Wrap-Up

Light from a Mint

1. Draw Conclusions At the beginning of this chapter, you saw light coming from a mint as you crushed it. Describe the process through which the mint gave off light.

Concept Check

Now that you have finished studying Chapter 5, answer these questions:

2. What type of electromagnetic radiation did the mint give off? How do you know?

3. How are different colors of gas-filled signs possible? Why are they all not the same color?

Write About Science

***63.** **Explain** What happens when you try to place two bar magnets pointing in the same direction alongside each other? Write a brief description of how that is like trying to place two electrons into the same orbital.

64. Connect to the **BIG**IDEA Rapid changes in chemistry happened in the late 1800s and early 1900s. Bohr improved on Rutherford's atom model. Then, Schrödinger developed a quantum mechanical model. Explain why you think a model of the atom is crucial to understanding chemistry and to explaining matter's behavior.

CHEMYSTERY

Now You See It . . . Now You Don't

Liam eventually realized that his star stickers would always stop glowing after a period of time. He discovered that he could "recharge" the stickers by turning on the lights. After he turned off the lights, the stars would glow again. However, after a few hours, the stars would eventually stop glowing.

Glow-in-the-dark objects contain compounds that react with light. When these objects are exposed to light, the electrons in the compounds absorb energy and become excited. As the electrons drop back down to a lower energy level, they emit light. This process, called phosphorescence, occurs more slowly in the compounds contained in glow-in-the-dark objects than in other compounds.

65. **Infer** Do Liam's glow-in-the-dark stars glow when the lights are on? Explain.

***66.** Connect to the **BIG**IDEA Light emitted from an incandescent lightbulb is in the visible region of the electromagnetic spectrum (about 400 nm to 700 nm). What does this information tell you about the energy of the photons absorbed by the electrons in glow-in-the-dark objects?

Cumulative Review

67. Hamburger undergoes a chemical change when cooked on a grill. All chemical changes are subject to the law of conservation of mass. But a cooked hamburger will weigh less than the uncooked meat patty. Explain.
(Hint: See Lesson 2.4 for help.)

68. This photo shows a magnified view of a piece of granite. Is granite a substance or a mixture?
(Hint: See Lesson 2.3 for help.)

69. Express the following measurements in scientific notation.
(Hint: See Lesson 3.1 for help.)

a. 0.000039 kg
b. 784 L
c. 0.0830 g
d. 9,700,000 ng

***70.** When a piece of copper with a mass of 36.4 g is placed into a graduated cylinder containing 20.00 mL of water, the water level rises to 24.08 mL—completely covering the copper. What is the copper's density?
(Hint: See Lesson 3.2 for help.)

***71.** Which has more mass: a 28.0 cm^3 piece of lead or a 16.0 cm^3 piece of gold? The density of lead is 11.3 g/cm^3; the density of gold is 19.3 g/cm^3.
(Hint: See Lesson 3.3 for help.)

72. Give the number of protons and electrons in each of the following.
(Hint: See Lesson 4.3 for help.)

a. Cs
b. Ag
c. Cd
d. Se

Standardized Test Prep

For help with answering test questions, go to your Chemistry Skills and Math Workbook.

Select the choice that best answers each question or completes each statement.

Tips for Success

Eliminate Wrong Answers If you do not know which response is correct, start by eliminating those you know are wrong. If you can rule out some choices, you will have fewer left to consider, and you will increase your chances of choosing the correct answer.

1. Select the correct electron configuration for silicon (atomic number 14).
 (A) $1s^22s^22p^23s^23p^23d^24s^2$
 (B) $1s^22s^22p^43s^23p^4$
 (C) $1s^22s^62p^6$
 (D) $1s^22s^22p^63s^23p^2$

2. Which two orbitals have the same shape?
 (A) 2*s* and 2*p*
 (B) 2*s* and 3*s*
 (C) 3*p* and 3*d*
 (D) More than one is correct.

3. Which of these statements characterize the nucleus of every atom?
 I. It has a positive charge.
 II. It is very dense.
 III. It is composed of protons, electrons, and neutrons.
 (A) I and II only
 (B) II and III only
 (C) I and III only
 (D) I, II, and III

4. As the wavelength of light increases,
 (A) the frequency increases.
 (B) the speed of light increases.
 (C) the energy decreases.
 (D) the intensity increases.

5. In an atom's third energy level,
 (A) there are two energy sublevels.
 (B) the *f* sublevel has seven orbitals.
 (C) there are three *s* orbitals.
 (D) a maximum of 18 electrons are allowed.

The lettered choices below refer to Questions 6–10. A lettered choice may be used once, more than once, or not at all.

(A) ns^2np^6 (B) ns^2np^2 (C) ns^2 (D) ns^4np^1 (E) ns^2np^4

Which configuration is the configuration of the highest occupied energy level for each of these elements?

6. sulfur

7. germanium

8. beryllium

9. krypton

10. strontium

Use the drawings to answer Questions 11–14. Each drawing represents an electromagnetic wave.

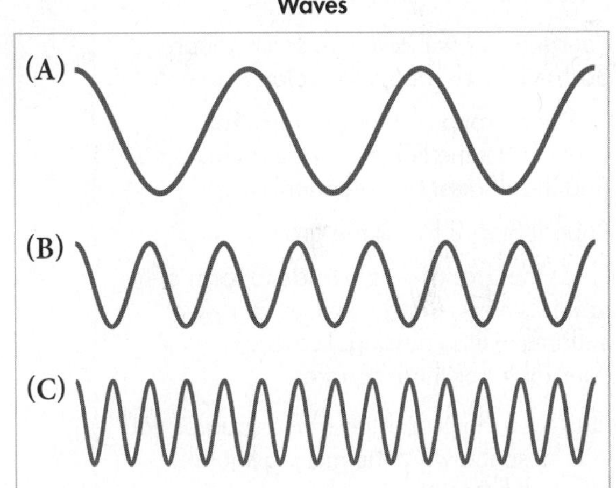

11. Which wave has the longest wavelength?

12. Which wave has the highest energy?

13. Which wave has the lowest frequency?

14. Which wave has the highest amplitude?

Write a short essay to answer Question 15.

15. Explain the rules that determine how electrons are arranged around the nuclei of atoms.

If You Have Trouble With . . .

Question	1	2	3	4	5	6	7	8	9	10	11	12	13	14	15
See Lesson	5.2	5.1	5.1	5.3	5.1	5.2	5.2	5.2	5.2	5.2	5.3	5.3	5.3	5.3	5.2

6 The Periodic Table

FOUNDATIONS for Learning

Organize by Properties

1. Your teacher will give you some squares. Sort them into groups by color.
2. Use one group of squares to make a column. Put the lightest shade at the top and the darkest at the bottom.
3. Repeat Step 2 for all the groups.
4. Place the groups side by side to form a table with rows and columns. Hint: Two squares will be missing. Leave spaces in your table for these squares.

Predict Use the properties of the squares you have to describe what the missing squares should look like.

PearsonChem.com

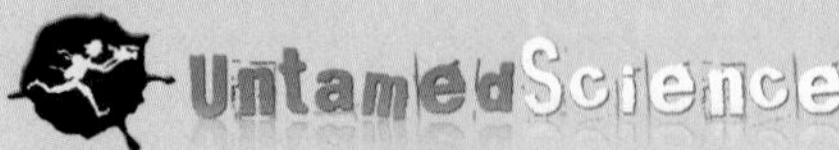

Take a trip with the Untamed Science crew to a game show about the periodic table.

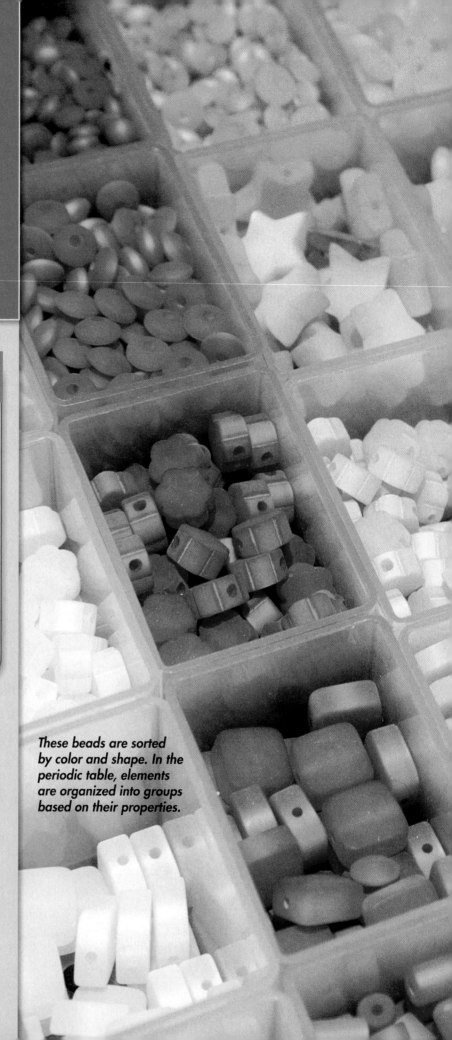

These beads are sorted by color and shape. In the periodic table, elements are organized into groups based on their properties.

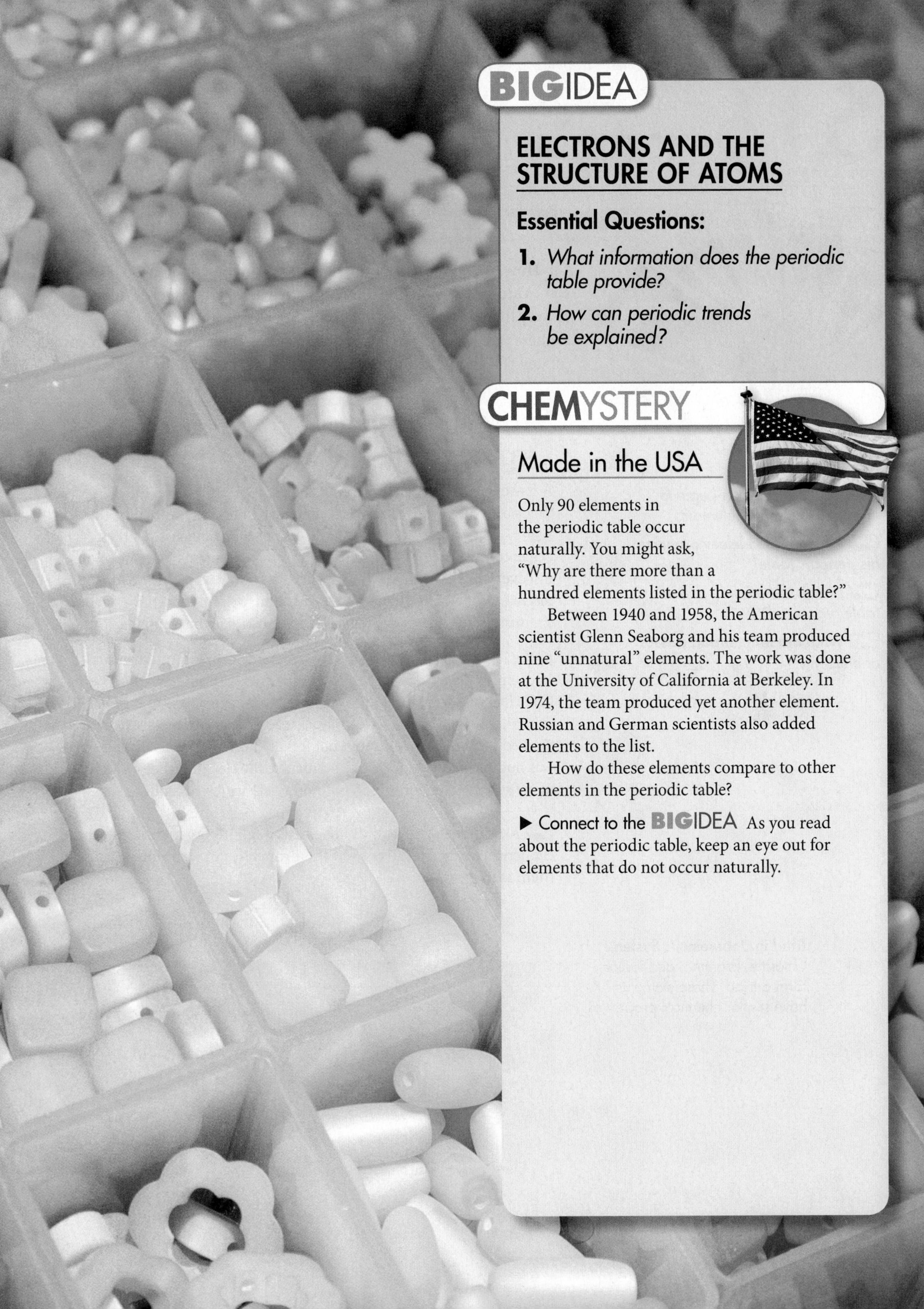

BIGIDEA

ELECTRONS AND THE STRUCTURE OF ATOMS

Essential Questions:

1. *What information does the periodic table provide?*
2. *How can periodic trends be explained?*

CHEMYSTERY

Made in the USA

Only 90 elements in the periodic table occur naturally. You might ask, "Why are there more than a hundred elements listed in the periodic table?"

Between 1940 and 1958, the American scientist Glenn Seaborg and his team produced nine "unnatural" elements. The work was done at the University of California at Berkeley. In 1974, the team produced yet another element. Russian and German scientists also added elements to the list.

How do these elements compare to other elements in the periodic table?

▶ Connect to the BIGIDEA As you read about the periodic table, keep an eye out for elements that do not occur naturally.

6.1 Organizing the Elements

CHEMISTRY & YOU

Q: How can you organize and classify elements? When you begin some card games, you probably organize your cards. Maybe you classify them by color or number. In this lesson, you will learn how elements are arranged in the periodic table and what that arrangement can tell you about the elements.

Key Questions

How did chemists begin to organize the known elements?

How did Mendeleev organize his periodic table?

How is the modern periodic table organized?

What are three broad classes of elements?

Searching for an Organizing Principle

A few elements, such as gold and silver, have been known for thousands of years. Yet only 13 elements had been identified by the year 1700. Chemists expected to discover other elements. As they began to use scientific methods to search for elements, the rate of discovery increased. How would chemists know when they had discovered all the elements? To begin to answer this question, chemists needed to find a logical way to organize the elements.

In the 1820s, J. W. Dobereiner tried grouping elements into triads. In chemistry, a triad is a set of three elements with similar properties. Chlorine, bromine, and iodine formed one triad because they behave in similar ways. For example, they all react easily with metals. Triads worked for some elements, but not for all known elements. Dobereiner was not the only person to try to organize the elements. Before 1869, many systems were proposed but none were widely accepted.

Key Question How did chemists begin to organize the known elements? **Early chemists used the properties of elements to sort them into groups.**

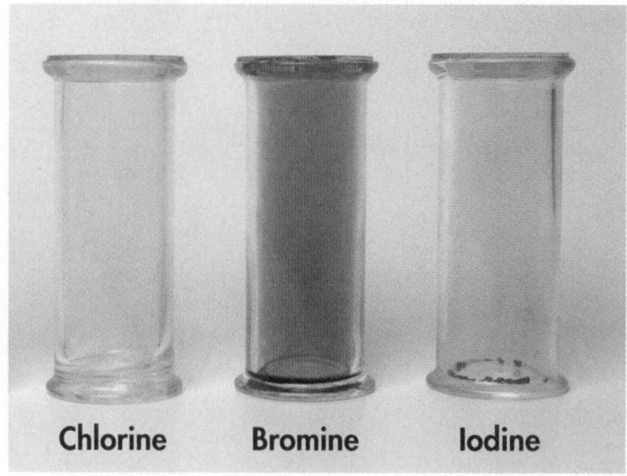

Triad in Dobereiner's System Chlorine, bromine, and iodine form a triad. These elements have similar chemical properties.

но въ ней, мнѣ кажется, уже ясно выражается примѣнимость выставляемаго мною начала ко всей совокупности элементовъ, пай которыхъ извѣстенъ съ достовѣрностію. На этотъ разъ я и желалъ преимущественно найдти общую систему элементовъ. Вотъ этотъ опытъ:

			Ti=50	Zr=90	?=180.
			V=51	Nb=94	Ta=182.
			Cr=52	Mo=96	W=186.
			Mn=55	Rh=104,4	Pt=197,4
			Fe=56	Ru=104,4	Ir=198.
			Ni=Co=59	Pl=106,6	Os=199.
H=1			Cu=63,4	Ag=108	Hg=200.
	Be=9,4	Mg=24	Zn=65,2	Cd=112	
	B=11	Al=27,4	?=68	Ur=116	Au=197?
	C=12	Si=28	?=70	Sn=118	
	N=14	P=31	As=75	Sb=122	Bi=210
	O=16	S=32	Se=79,4	Te=128?	
	F=19	Cl=35,5	Br=80	I=127	
Li=7	Na=23	K=39	Rb=85,4	Cs=133	Tl=204
		Ca=40	Sr=87,6	Ba=137	Pb=207.
		?=45	Ce=92		
		?Er=56	La=94		
		?Yt=60	Di=95		
		?In=75,6	Th=118?		

Mendeleev's Periodic Table Mendeleev arranged the known elements in order of increasing atomic mass. He left spaces for elements that had not yet been discovered.

Mendeleev's Periodic Table

By the 1860s, more than 60 elements were known. At that time, Dmitri Mendeleev, a Russian chemist, was working on a textbook. He wanted a way to show his students how all the known elements were related. He wrote the properties of each element on a separate note card. He moved the cards around until he found an organization that worked. He chose a table in which the elements were arranged in order by atomic mass.

Look at the table above. In each column, the elements are arranged from lowest to highest atomic mass. The column breaks allow elements with similar properties to end up side by side in the same row. Find the column that begins with Ti = 50. Note the two question marks between zinc (Zn) and arsenic (As). Mendeleev predicted that elements with those atomic masses would be discovered. He also predicted what their properties would be.

The missing elements were gallium and germanium. Gallium was discovered in 1875. Germanium was discovered in 1886. There was a close match between the predicted properties of these elements and their real properties. This match helped convince chemists that Mendeleev's periodic table was a powerful tool.

Key Question How did Mendeleev organize his periodic table? **Mendeleev arranged the elements in his periodic table in order of increasing atomic mass.**

Period																																
1	1 H																															2 He
2	3 Li	4 Be																									5 B	6 C	7 N	8 O	9 F	10 Ne
3	11 Na	12 Mg																									13 Al	14 Si	15 P	16 S	17 Cl	18 Ar
4	19 K	20 Ca															21 Sc	22 Ti	23 V	24 Cr	25 Mn	26 Fe	27 Co	28 Ni	29 Cu	30 Zn	31 Ga	32 Ge	33 As	34 Se	35 Br	36 Kr
5	37 Rb	38 Sr															39 Y	40 Zr	41 Nb	42 Mo	43 Tc	44 Ru	45 Rh	46 Pd	47 Ag	48 Cd	49 In	50 Sn	51 Sb	52 Te	53 I	54 Xe
6	55 Cs	56 Ba	57 La	58 Ce	59 Pr	60 Nd	61 Pm	62 Sm	63 Eu	64 Gd	65 Tb	66 Dy	67 Ho	68 Er	69 Tm	70 Yb	71 Lu	72 Hf	73 Ta	74 W	75 Re	76 Os	77 Ir	78 Pt	79 Au	80 Hg	81 Tl	82 Pb	83 Bi	84 Po	85 At	86 Rn
7	87 Fr	88 Ra	89 Ac	90 Th	91 Pa	92 U	93 Np	94 Pu	95 Am	96 Cm	97 Bk	98 Cf	99 Es	100 Fm	101 Md	102 No	103 Lr	104 Rf	105 Db	106 Sg	107 Bh	108 Hs	109 Mt	110 Ds	111 Rg	112 Cn	113 Uut	114 Fl	115 Uup	116 Lv	117 Uus	118 Uuo

Modern Periodic Table
In this table, the elements are arranged by increasing atomic number. As you move from sodium (Na) to argon (Ar) in Period 3, the properties of the elements change. When you move from potassium (K) to krypton (Kr) in Period 4, this pattern of properties will repeat.

Today's Periodic Table

Using atomic mass to organize the periodic table did not work for all the elements. For example, the atomic mass of iodine (I) is 126.90. The atomic mass of tellurium (Te) is 127.60. In a periodic table based on atomic mass, iodine should come before tellurium because iodine has the smaller atomic mass. Yet, based on its properties, iodine belongs in a group with bromine and chlorine. So Mendeleev had to ignore the atomic masses and place iodine after tellurium in his table.

The placement of iodine and tellurium makes sense when the elements are arranged in order of atomic number. Remember that the atomic number of an element is equal to the number of protons in its atoms. The atomic number is unique for each element. The modern periodic table starts with hydrogen (H), which has an atomic number of 1.

Periods in the Table There are seven rows, or periods, in the table. Period 1 has 2 elements, Period 2 has 8 elements, Period 4 has 18 elements, and Period 6 has 32 elements. Each period corresponds to a principal energy level. Remember that higher energy levels have more orbitals. That is why there are more elements in periods with higher numbers.

Repeating Properties The properties of the elements in a period change as you move from left to right across the period. This pattern of change repeats as you move from one period to the next. The pattern gives rise to the **periodic law:** When elements are arranged in order of increasing atomic number, there is a periodic repetition of their physical and chemical properties. Arranging the elements into periods has an important outcome. Elements that have similar chemical and physical properties end up in the same column in the periodic table.

Key Question How is the modern periodic table organized? **In the modern periodic table, elements are arranged in order of increasing atomic number.**

periodic law when elements are arranged in order of increasing atomic number, there is a periodic repetition of their properties

WORD ORIGINS
Periodic comes from the Greek roots *peri,* meaning "around" and *hodos,* meaning "path." In a periodic table, properties repeat when the path is from left to right across each period.

Metals | Metalloids | Nonmetals

	1 IA 1A	2 IIA 2A	3 IIIA 3B	4 IVA 4B	5 VA 5B	6 VIA 6B	7 VIIA 7B	8 VIIIA 8B	9 VIIIA 8B	10 VIIIA 8B	11 IB 1B	12 IIB 2B	13 IIIB 3A	14 IVB 4A	15 VB 5A	16 VIB 6A	17 VIIB 7A	18 VIIIB 8A
1	1 H																	2 He
2	3 Li	4 Be											5 B	6 C	7 N	8 O	9 F	10 Ne
3	11 Na	12 Mg											13 Al	14 Si	15 P	16 S	17 Cl	18 Ar
4	19 K	20 Ca	21 Sc	22 Ti	23 V	24 Cr	25 Mn	26 Fe	27 Co	28 Ni	29 Cu	30 Zn	31 Ga	32 Ge	33 As	34 Se	35 Br	36 Kr
5	37 Rb	38 Sr	39 Y	40 Zr	41 Nb	42 Mo	43 Tc	44 Ru	45 Rh	46 Pd	47 Ag	48 Cd	49 In	50 Sn	51 Sb	52 Te	53 I	54 Xe
6	55 Cs	56 Ba	71 Lu	72 Hf	73 Ta	74 W	75 Re	76 Os	77 Ir	78 Pt	79 Au	80 Hg	81 Tl	82 Pb	83 Bi	84 Po	85 At	86 Rn
7	87 Fr	88 Ra	103 Lr	104 Rf	105 Db	106 Sg	107 Bh	108 Hs	109 Mt	110 Ds	111 Rg	112 Cn	113 Uut	114 Fl	115 Uup	116 Lv	117 Uus	118 Uuo

57 La	58 Ce	59 Pr	60 Nd	61 Pm	62 Sm	63 Eu	64 Gd	65 Tb	66 Dy	67 Ho	68 Er	69 Tm	70 Yb
89 Ac	90 Th	91 Pa	92 U	93 Np	94 Pu	95 Am	96 Cm	97 Bk	98 Cf	99 Es	100 Fm	101 Md	102 No

Classifying Elements
Periodic tables are sometimes color-coded to classify certain kinds of elements. This periodic table classifies elements as metals (yellow), nonmetals (blue), and metalloids (green).

Metals, Nonmetals, and Metalloids

Most periodic tables are laid out like the one shown above. Some elements from Periods 6 and 7 have been placed below the table. This arrangement makes the periodic table more compact with less wasted space. It also reflects the atomic structure of the periodic table, which you will study in Lesson 6.2.

Each column in the table is a group. Note that each group has two labels. The labels shown in red divide the groups into "A" groups and "B" groups. The red labels are used mainly in the United States.

Look at the labels shown in black. They number the groups from left to right 1 through 18. This is the standard numbering system used by chemists from around the world. So when chemists in the United States communicate with chemists in other countries, they often refer to the groups in the periodic table as Group 1 through Group 18.

Dividing the elements into groups is not the only way to classify them based on their properties. The elements can be sorted into three broad classes based on their general properties. These three classes of elements are metals, nonmetals, and metalloids. Across a period, the properties of elements become less metallic and more nonmetallic. Turn the page to learn more about these classes of elements.

BUILD Connections

Do you know that a piano keyboard has a repeating pattern of notes? To hear the pattern, start at middle C and play seven white keys in order from left to right. The next note is another C. All the C notes sound similar, but not exactly the same. In the same way, elements in a group on the periodic table have similar, but not identical, properties.

Metals and Nonmetals
The properties of metals and nonmetals determine how they are used.

Carbon (C) and Phosphorus (P)
A diamond, which is made of carbon, is very hard. Some match heads are coated with phosphorus, a brittle solid. Carbon and phosphorus are nonmetals.

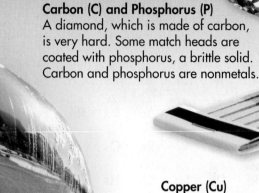

Copper (Cu)
Copper is flexible and second only to silver as a conductor of electric current. This metal is used in electrical cables.

Iron (Fe)
This sculpture in Chicago, Illinois, is called Cloud Gate. It is covered in stainless steel, which contains the metals iron and chromium (Cr). The shiny surface reflects part of the Chicago skyline.

BUILD Vocabulary

metals elements that are good conductors of heat and electric current; they tend to be ductile, malleable, and shiny

nonmetals elements that tend to have properties that are opposite to those of metals

metalloid an element that has some properties in common with metals and some in common with nonmetals

PREFIXES AND SUFFIXES

The prefix *non-* means "not." The suffix *-oid* means "like." A nonmetal is not a metal, but a metalloid is like a metal in some ways.

Metals Most elements are metals—about 80 percent. **Metals** are good conductors of heat and electric current. A freshly cleaned or cut surface of a metal will have a high luster, or be shiny. The luster is caused by the metal's ability to reflect light. All metals are solids at room temperature, except for mercury (Hg).

Many metals are ductile, meaning that they can be drawn into wires. Most metals are malleable, and can be hammered into thin sheets without breaking. The properties of metals determine how people use them.

Nonmetals Look for all the nonmetals except hydrogen in the upper-right corner of the periodic table. Most nonmetals are gases at room temperature. Two examples are the major gases in air—nitrogen and oxygen. A few are solids, such as sulfur and phosphorus. One nonmetal, bromine, is a dark-red liquid.

There is more variation in physical properties among nonmetals than among metals. This variation makes it hard to describe a set of general properties for all nonmetals. However, nonmetals tend to have properties that are opposite to those of metals. In general, **nonmetals** are poor conductors of heat and electric current. Carbon is one exception. It is a good conductor of electric current. Solid nonmetals tend to be brittle, meaning that they will shatter if hit with a hammer.

Metalloid
Silicon is a metalloid. Silicon dioxide is the main compound in glass. Melted glass can be poured into a mold. It can also be shaped by a glass blower as it cools.

Metalloids Look again at the periodic table on page 151. Note the heavy black stair-step line that separates the metals from the nonmetals. Find the elements that are shaded green. These elements are metalloids. A **metalloid** generally has some properties that are similar to those of metals and some that are similar to nonmetals.

At times, a metalloid may behave like a metal. At other times, it may behave like a nonmetal. Sometimes scientists can change how a metalloid behaves. Here is one example. Like most nonmetals, pure silicon is a poor conductor of electric current. However, when a small amount of boron is mixed with silicon, the mixture is a good conductor of electric current. In fact, this mixture is used to make computer chips.

Key Question What are three broad classes of elements? **Three broad classes of elements are metals, nonmetals, and metalloids.**

BUILD Understanding

Compare and Contrast Make a table to compare metals and nonmetals. Describe the general properties of these classes, not the properties of one element.

6.1 LessonCheck

Key Concept Check

1. **Explain** What did early chemists use to organize elements into groups?
2. **Identify** What property did Mendeleev use to organize his periodic table?
3. **Explain** How are elements arranged in the modern periodic table?
4. **List** Name the three broad classes of elements.

Vocabulary Check *Choose a highlighted word from the lesson to complete the sentence correctly.*

5. ______ tend to be poor conductors of heat and electric current.

Think Critically

6. **Compare** Which set of elements have similar properties?
   a. oxygen (O), carbon (C), boron (B)
   b. strontium (Sr), magnesium (Mg), calcium (Ca)
   c. nitrogen (N), neon (Ne), nickel (Ni)

CHEMISTRY & YOU

7. Mendeleev made a separate note card for each element. How did these note cards help Mendeleev organize the elements? (Hint: See page 149.)

BIGIDEA
ELECTRONS AND THE STRUCTURE OF ATOMS

8. Why is atomic number better than atomic mass for organizing the elements in the periodic table?

6.2 Classifying the Elements

Key Questions

What information can be shown in a periodic table?

How can elements be classified based on electron configurations?

CHEMISTRY & YOU

Q: What can you learn about each element from the periodic table? A driver's license is one form of identification, or ID. An ID has information about a person. It usually has the person's name, address, and age. It may have other facts, such as a person's height, eye color, and sex.

The periodic table contains a square for each element with facts about that element. In this lesson, you will learn the kinds of information that are usually listed in a periodic table.

Reading the Periodic Table

The periodic table is a very useful tool if you know how to read it. Look at the figure below. It shows the element square for aluminum from the large periodic table on pages 156 and 157.

In the center of the square is the symbol for aluminum (Al). The atomic number for aluminum (13) is above the symbol. The element name and atomic mass are below the symbol.

Find the vertical column with the numbers 2, 8, and 3. These numbers tell you the number of electrons in each occupied energy level of an aluminum atom.

Periodic Table Square
An element square provides facts about an element.

The wrappers on chocolate "coins" contain aluminum.

Look at the four element squares below. Note that each element symbol is printed in a different color. Three of the colors are used to show the state of an element at room temperature. The Si for silicon is printed in black because silicon is a solid. The He for helium is printed in red because helium is a gas. The Br for bromine is printed in blue because bromine is one of the two elements that are liquids. The other liquid is mercury (Hg). Gray is used for elements that are not found in nature, such as plutonium (Pu). In Chapter 25, you will learn how scientists produce those elements.

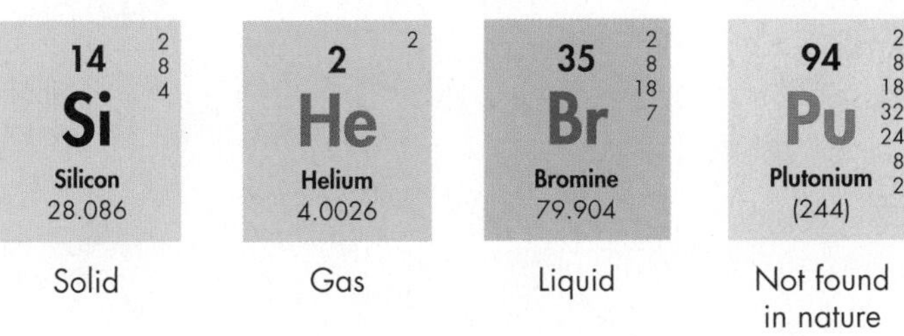

The background colors of the squares are used to show which elements have similar properties. For example, two shades of orange are used for the metals in Group 1A and Group 2A. The elements in Group 1A are **alkali metals.** The elements in Group 2A are **alkaline earth metals.**

Groups 1A and 2A are not the only groups with both a group number and a name. The nonmetals of Group 7A are called **halogens.** The name halogen comes from the Greek word *hals*, meaning "salt," and the Latin word *genesis*, meaning "to be born." Salts are a general class of chemical compounds. One common salt is table salt, which is a compound of sodium and chlorine. Chlorine, bromine, and iodine can be prepared from their salts.

7A

17 Cl Chlorine 35.453 2 8 7

35 Br Bromine 79.904 2 8 18 7

53 I Iodine 126.90 2 8 18 18 7

Key Question What information can be shown in a periodic table? **The periodic table usually shows the symbols and names of the elements, along with information about the structure of their atoms.**

alkali metal any metal in Group 1A of the periodic table

alkaline earth metal any metal in Group 2A of the periodic table

halogen any nonmetal in Group 7A of the periodic table

WORD ORIGINS

The name alkali comes from the Arabic *al aqali*, meaning "the ashes." These are the ashes that are left after wood burns. Wood ash is rich in compounds of the Group 1A metals sodium and potassium.

Periodic Table of the Elements

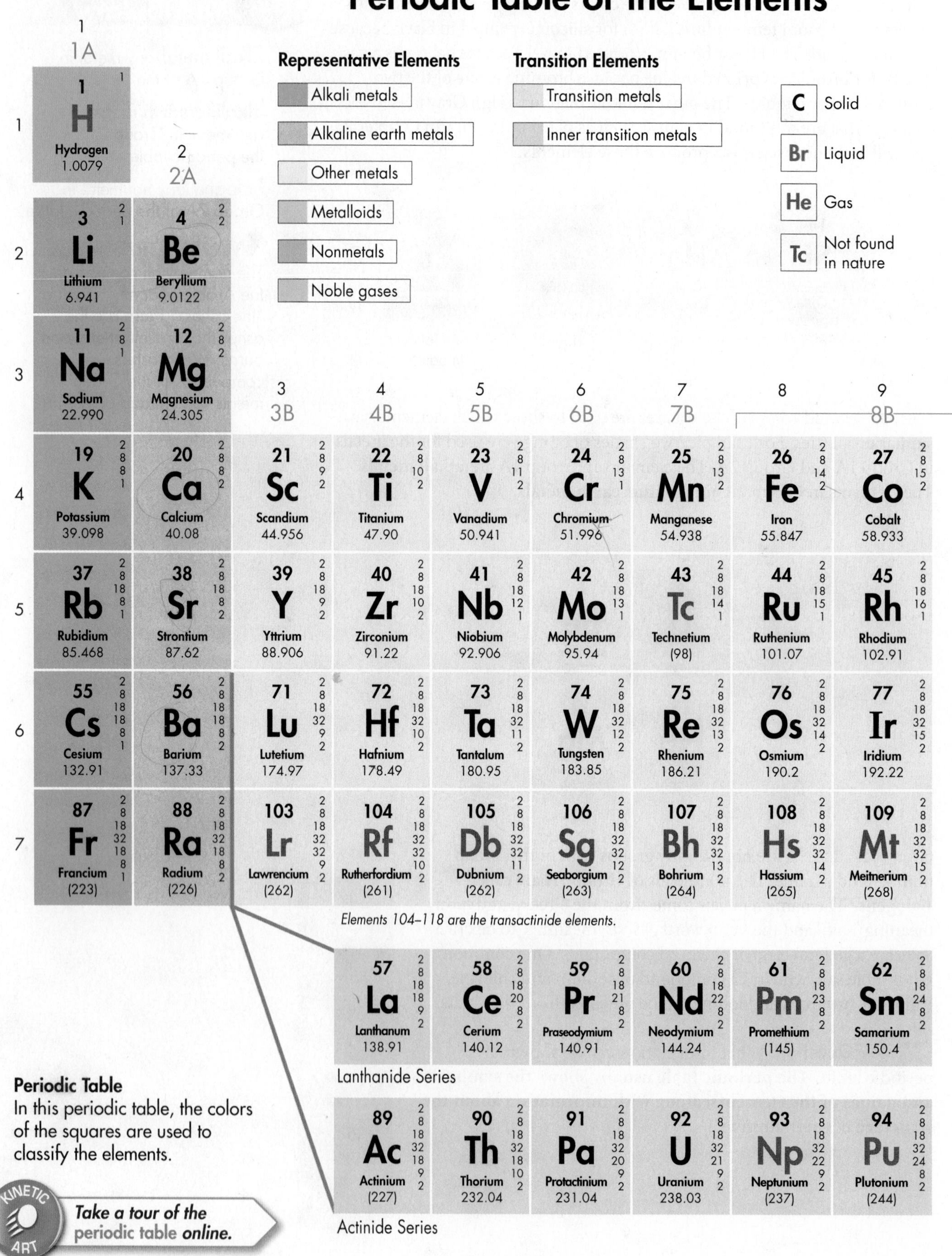

Representative Elements
- Alkali metals
- Alkaline earth metals
- Other metals
- Metalloids
- Nonmetals
- Noble gases

Transition Elements
- Transition metals
- Inner transition metals

Symbol	State
C	Solid
Br	Liquid
He	Gas
Tc	Not found in nature

Period	1 1A	2 2A	3 3B	4 4B	5 5B	6 6B	7 7B	8 8B	9 8B
1	1 H Hydrogen 1.0079 (1)								
2	3 Li Lithium 6.941 (2 1)	4 Be Beryllium 9.0122 (2 2)							
3	11 Na Sodium 22.990 (2 8 1)	12 Mg Magnesium 24.305 (2 8 2)							
4	19 K Potassium 39.098 (2 8 8 1)	20 Ca Calcium 40.08 (2 8 8 2)	21 Sc Scandium 44.956 (2 8 9 2)	22 Ti Titanium 47.90 (2 8 10 2)	23 V Vanadium 50.941 (2 8 11 2)	24 Cr Chromium 51.996 (2 8 13 1)	25 Mn Manganese 54.938 (2 8 13 2)	26 Fe Iron 55.847 (2 8 14 2)	27 Co Cobalt 58.933 (2 8 15 2)
5	37 Rb Rubidium 85.468 (2 8 18 8 1)	38 Sr Strontium 87.62 (2 8 18 8 2)	39 Y Yttrium 88.906 (2 8 18 9 2)	40 Zr Zirconium 91.22 (2 8 18 10 2)	41 Nb Niobium 92.906 (2 8 18 12 1)	42 Mo Molybdenum 95.94 (2 8 18 13 1)	43 Tc Technetium (98) (2 8 18 14 1)	44 Ru Ruthenium 101.07 (2 8 18 15 1)	45 Rh Rhodium 102.91 (2 8 18 16 1)
6	55 Cs Cesium 132.91 (2 8 18 18 8 1)	56 Ba Barium 137.33 (2 8 18 18 8 2)	71 Lu Lutetium 174.97 (2 8 18 32 9 2)	72 Hf Hafnium 178.49 (2 8 18 32 10 2)	73 Ta Tantalum 180.95 (2 8 18 32 11 2)	74 W Tungsten 183.85 (2 8 18 32 12 2)	75 Re Rhenium 186.21 (2 8 18 32 13 2)	76 Os Osmium 190.2 (2 8 18 32 14 2)	77 Ir Iridium 192.22 (2 8 18 32 15 2)
7	87 Fr Francium (223) (2 8 18 32 18 8 1)	88 Ra Radium (226) (2 8 18 32 18 8 2)	103 Lr Lawrencium (262) (2 8 18 32 32 9 2)	104 Rf Rutherfordium (261) (2 8 18 32 32 10 2)	105 Db Dubnium (262) (2 8 18 32 32 11 2)	106 Sg Seaborgium (263) (2 8 18 32 32 12 2)	107 Bh Bohrium (264) (2 8 18 32 32 13 2)	108 Hs Hassium (265) (2 8 18 32 32 14 2)	109 Mt Meitnerium (268) (2 8 18 32 32 15 2)

Elements 104–118 are the transactinide elements.

Lanthanide Series

57	58	59	60	61	62
La Lanthanum 138.91 (2 8 18 18 9 2)	Ce Cerium 140.12 (2 8 18 20 8 2)	Pr Praseodymium 140.91 (2 8 18 21 8 2)	Nd Neodymium 144.24 (2 8 18 22 8 2)	Pm Promethium (145) (2 8 18 23 8 2)	Sm Samarium 150.4 (2 8 18 24 8 2)

Actinide Series

89	90	91	92	93	94
Ac Actinium (227) (2 8 18 32 18 9 2)	Th Thorium 232.04 (2 8 18 32 18 10 2)	Pa Protactinium 231.04 (2 8 18 32 20 9 2)	U Uranium 238.03 (2 8 18 32 21 9 2)	Np Neptunium (237) (2 8 18 32 22 9 2)	Pu Plutonium (244) (2 8 18 32 24 8 2)

Periodic Table
In this periodic table, the colors of the squares are used to classify the elements.

KINETIC ART *Take a tour of the periodic table online.*

13	Atomic number
2 8 3	Electrons in each energy level
Al	Element symbol
Aluminum	Element name
26.982	Atomic mass†

†*The atomic masses in parentheses are the mass numbers of the longest-lived isotope of elements for which a standard atomic mass cannot be defined.*

10	11 1B	12 2B	13 3A	14 4A	15 5A	16 6A	17 7A	18 8A
								2 **He** Helium 4.0026 2
			5 **B** Boron 10.81 2 3	6 **C** Carbon 12.011 2 4	7 **N** Nitrogen 14.007 2 5	8 **O** Oxygen 15.999 2 6	9 **F** Fluorine 18.998 2 7	10 **Ne** Neon 20.179 2 8
			13 **Al** Aluminum 26.982 2 8 3	14 **Si** Silicon 28.086 2 8 4	15 **P** Phosphorus 30.974 2 8 5	16 **S** Sulfur 32.06 2 8 6	17 **Cl** Chlorine 35.453 2 8 7	18 **Ar** Argon 39.948 2 8 8
28 **Ni** Nickel 58.71 2 8 16 2	29 **Cu** Copper 63.546 2 8 18 1	30 **Zn** Zinc 65.38 2 8 18 2	31 **Ga** Gallium 69.72 2 8 18 3	32 **Ge** Germanium 72.59 2 8 18 4	33 **As** Arsenic 74.922 2 8 18 5	34 **Se** Selenium 78.96 2 8 18 6	35 **Br** Bromine 79.904 2 8 18 7	36 **Kr** Krypton 83.80 2 8 18 8
46 **Pd** Palladium 106.4 2 8 18 18	47 **Ag** Silver 107.87 2 8 18 18 1	48 **Cd** Cadmium 112.41 2 8 18 18 2	49 **In** Indium 114.82 2 8 18 18 3	50 **Sn** Tin 118.69 2 8 18 18 4	51 **Sb** Antimony 121.75 2 8 18 18 5	52 **Te** Tellurium 127.60 2 8 18 18 6	53 **I** Iodine 126.90 2 8 18 18 7	54 **Xe** Xenon 131.30 2 8 18 18 8
78 **Pt** Platinum 195.09 2 8 18 32 17 1	79 **Au** Gold 196.97 2 8 18 32 18 1	80 **Hg** Mercury 200.59 2 8 18 32 18 2	81 **Tl** Thallium 204.37 2 8 18 32 18 3	82 **Pb** Lead 207.2 2 8 18 32 18 4	83 **Bi** Bismuth 208.98 2 8 18 32 18 5	84 **Po** Polonium (209) 2 8 18 32 18 6	85 **At** Astatine (210) 2 8 18 32 18 7	86 **Rn** Radon (222) 2 8 18 32 18 8
110 **Ds** Darmstadtium (269) 2 8 18 32 32 17 1	111 **Rg** Roentgenium (272) 2 8 18 32 32 18 1	112 **Cn** Copernicium (277) 2 8 18 32 32 18 2	113 **Uut*** Ununtrium (284) 2 8 18 32 32 18 3	114 **Fl** Flerovium (289) 2 8 18 32 32 18 4	115 **Uup*** Ununpentium (288) 2 8 18 32 32 18 5	116 **Lv** Livermorium (293) 2 8 18 32 32 18 6	117 **Uus*** Ununseptium (294) 2 8 18 32 32 18 7	118 **Uuo*** Ununoctium (299) 2 8 18 32 32 18 8

*Discovery reported but not verified

63 **Eu** Europium 151.96 2 8 18 25 8 2	64 **Gd** Gadolinium 157.25 2 8 18 25 9 2	65 **Tb** Terbium 158.93 2 8 18 27 8 2	66 **Dy** Dysprosium 162.50 2 8 18 28 8 2	67 **Ho** Holmium 164.93 2 8 18 29 8 2	68 **Er** Erbium 167.26 2 8 18 30 8 2	69 **Tm** Thulium 168.93 2 8 18 31 8 2	70 **Yb** Ytterbium 173.04 2 8 18 32 8 2
95 **Am** Americium (243) 2 8 18 32 25 8 2	96 **Cm** Curium (247) 2 8 18 32 25 9 2	97 **Bk** Berkelium (247) 2 8 18 32 27 8 2	98 **Cf** Californium (251) 2 8 18 32 28 8 2	99 **Es** Einsteinium (252) 2 8 18 32 29 8 2	100 **Fm** Fermium (257) 2 8 18 32 30 8 2	101 **Md** Mendelevium (258) 2 8 18 32 31 8 2	102 **No** Nobelium (259) 2 8 18 32 32 8 2

noble gas an element in Group 8A of the periodic table

representative element an element in Groups 1A through 7A

ACADEMIC WORDS

The adjective *representative* can mean "having all the expected properties for a given group." So elements can be called "representative" if, as a group, they have all the possible properties of elements.

Electron Configurations in Groups

Many of the properties of elements depend on the behavior of electrons. So there should be a connection between an element's electron configuration and its place in the periodic table. The elements can be sorted into four classes based on their electron configurations. Refer to the large periodic table as you read about these classes of elements.

The Noble Gases The elements in Group 8A of the periodic table are known as **noble gases.** These gases are sometimes called inert gases because they rarely take part in reactions. The photos on this page show two uses of noble gases. The electron configurations for the first four noble gases in Group 8A are listed below.

Element	Configuration
Helium (He)	$1s^2$
Neon (Ne)	$1s^22s^22p^6$
Argon (Ar)	$1s^22s^22p^63s^23p^6$
Krypton (Kr)	$1s^22s^22p^63s^23p^63d^{10}4s^24p^6$

Look at the part of each configuration that is marked in yellow. This part describes the highest occupied energy level. In each case, the *s* and *p* sublevels are filled with electrons. There are two electrons in the *s* sublevel and six electrons in the *p* sublevel. The noble gases are the only elements whose highest occupied energy levels are completely filled.

Noble Gases
Balloons are often filled with helium to give them "lift." Neon and argon produce the colors in this sign.

	1A	2A	3A	4A	5A	6A	7A
1	1 H Hydrogen 1.0079						
2	3 Li Lithium 6.941	4 Be Beryllium 9.0122	5 B Boron 10.81	6 C Carbon 12.011	7 N Nitrogen 14.007	8 O Oxygen 15.999	9 F Fluorine 18.998
3	11 Na Sodium 22.990	12 Mg Magnesium 24.305	13 Al Aluminum 26.982	14 Si Silicon 28.086	15 P Phosphorus 30.974	16 S Sulfur 32.06	17 Cl Chlorine 35.453
4	19 K Potassium 39.098	20 Ca Calcium 40.08	31 Ga Gallium 69.72	32 Ge Germanium 72.59	33 As Arsenic 74.922	34 Se Selenium 78.96	35 Br Bromine 79.904
5	37 Rb Rubidium 85.468	38 Sr Strontium 87.62	49 In Indium 114.82	50 Sn Tin 118.69	51 Sb Antimony 121.75	52 Te Tellurium 127.60	53 I Iodine 126.90
6	55 Cs Cesium 132.91	56 Ba Barium 137.33	81 Tl Thallium 204.37	82 Pb Lead 207.2	83 Bi Bismuth 208.98	84 Po Polonium (209)	85 At Astatine (210)
7	87 Fr Francium (223)	88 Ra Radium (226)					

Representative Elements
The elements in Groups 1A through 7A have a wide range of properties. Aluminum and sulfur are representative elements.

The Representative Elements The figure above shows the part of the periodic table with Groups 1A through 7A. Elements in these groups are often called **representative elements.** As a group, these elements have a wide range of physical and chemical properties. Some of the elements are metals, some are nonmetals, and some are metalloids. Most are solids, a few are gases, and one is a liquid.

In atoms of representative elements, the *s* and *p* sublevels of the highest occupied energy level are not filled. Look at the configurations for lithium, sodium, and potassium. These elements are in Group 1A. Atoms of these elements have only one electron in the highest occupied energy level. The electron is in an s sublevel.

Element	Configuration
Lithium (Li)	$1s^22s^1$
Sodium (Na)	$1s^22s^22p^63s^1$
Potassium (K)	$1s^22s^22p^63s^23p^64s^1$

Carbon, silicon, and germanium are in Group 4A. Atoms of elements in Group 4A have four electrons in the highest occupied energy level.

Element	Configuration
Carbon (C)	$1s^22s^22p^2$
Silicon (Si)	$1s^22s^22p^63s^23p^2$
Germanium (Ge)	$1s^22s^22p^63s^23p^63d^{10}4s^24p^2$

For any representative element, its group number is equal to the number of electrons in the highest occupied energy level. So for Group 3A, the number of electrons is three, and for Group 6A, the number is six.

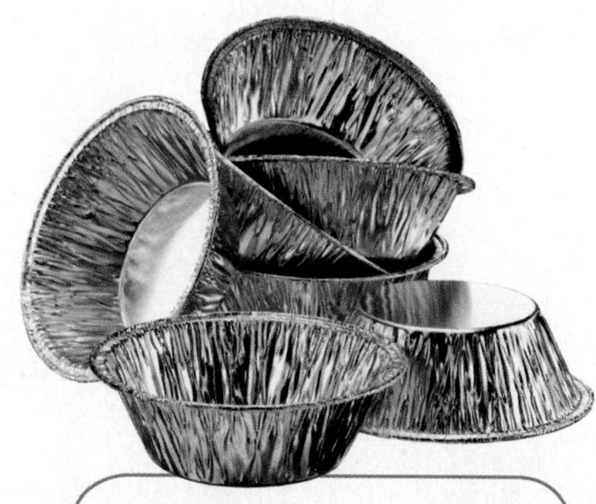

Aluminum (Al)
Aluminum is a metal that can be shaped into a thin sheet.

Sulfur (S)
Some volcanoes release high amounts of sulfur vapors. The sulfur cools and is deposited as a solid yellow powder.

transition metal one of the Group B elements that is usually displayed in the main body of a periodic table

inner transition metal an element in the lanthanide or actinide series

MULTIPLE MEANINGS

In some sports, the change between offense and defense is called a transition. In music, a transition is a passage that moves from one key to another key. On the periodic table, transition elements fall between the representative elements on the left of the table and those on the right.

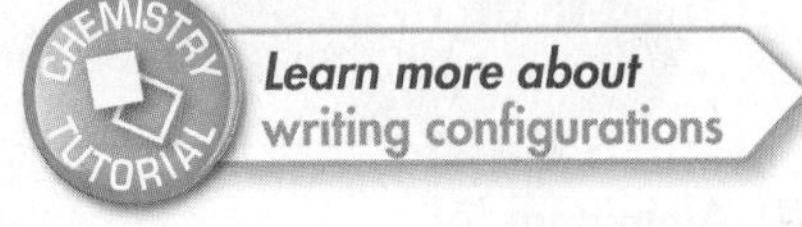

Learn more about writing configurations

Transition Elements In the periodic table, elements in the B groups separate the A groups on the left side of the table from the A groups on the right side. Elements in the B groups are called transition elements. They are divided into transition metals and inner transition metals based on their electron configurations.

The **transition metals** are the Group B elements in the main body of a periodic table. Copper, silver, and iron are transition metals. In atoms of a transition metal, the highest occupied *s* sublevel and a nearby *d* sublevel contain electrons. Having electrons in these *d* orbitals sets transition metals apart from other elements.

The **inner transition metals** are the elements that appear below the main body of the periodic table. In atoms of these elements, the highest occupied *s* sublevel and a nearby *f* sublevel generally contain electrons. Having electrons in these *f* orbitals sets inner transition metals apart from other elements. Uranium is an inner transition metal.

Blocks of Elements A pattern appears when you compare where elements are in the periodic table and their electron configurations. The periodic table in the diagram below is divided into four colored blocks. The *s* block has the elements in Groups 1A and 2A, plus helium. The *p* block has the elements in Groups 3A, 4A, 5A, 6A, 7A, and 8A, except for helium. The transition metals are in the *d* block, and the inner transition metals are in the *f* block.

Remember that a period corresponds to a principal energy level. Also, the principal energy level for electrons in a *d* sublevel is one less than the period number. For electrons in an *f* sublevel, the principal energy level is two less than the period number.

The block diagram can help you find an electron configuration. See the examples for sulfur and nickel on the next page.

Electron Configurations

This diagram classifies elements into blocks based on the electrons in the highest occupied sublevels. The label above each group tells you the number of electrons in the highest occupied sublevel for that group.

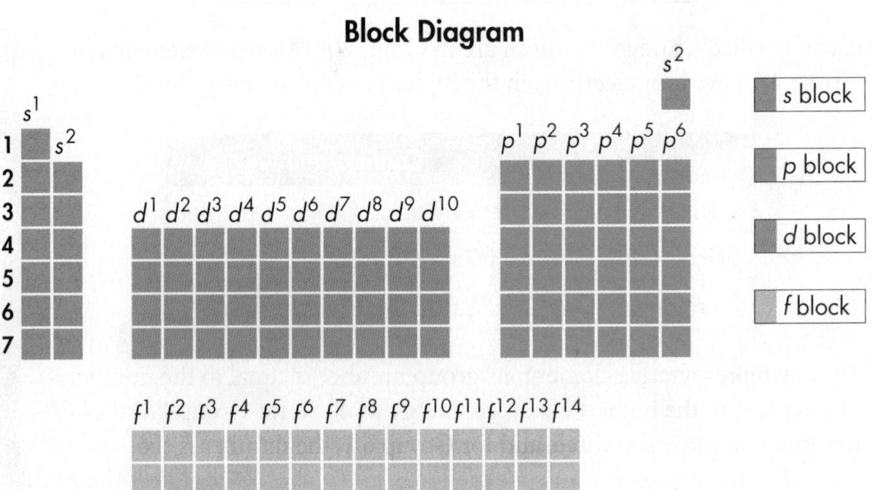

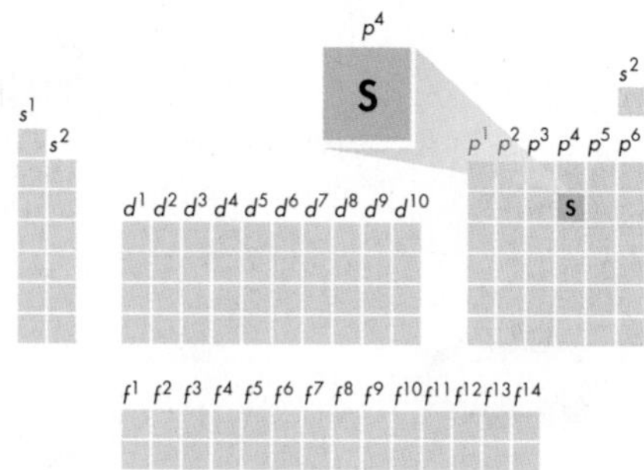

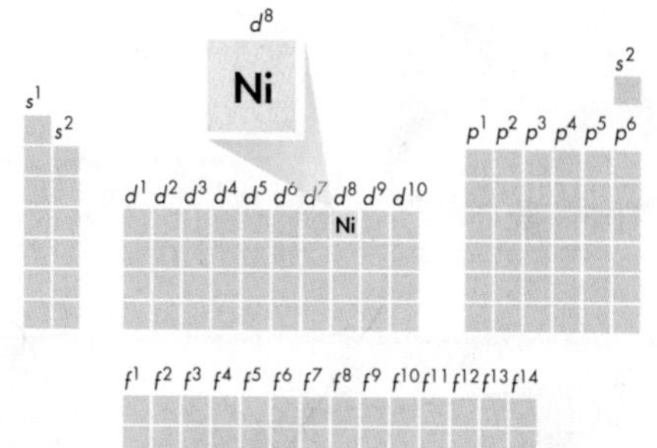

Sulfur Sulfur is in Group 6A of Period 3. It has 16 electrons. Elements in Period 3 have three occupied energy levels. Before electrons are added to the third level, the *s* and *p* sublevels in energy levels 1 and 2 are filled. The configuration must start as follows.

$$1s^22s^22p^6$$

The *s* sublevel in a period is filled before the *p* sublevel. Group 6A is in the *p* block. So the 3*s* sublevel must be filled. Add $3s^2$ to the configuration.

$$1s^22s^22p^63s^2$$

Find the p^4 label above Group 6A. The configuration must end with $3p^4$. To check the configuration, add up the electrons (2 + 2 + 6 + 2 + 4 = 16). This total matches the atomic number for sulfur.

$$1s^22s^22p^63s^23p^4$$

Nickel The transition element nickel is in Period 4. It has 28 electrons. It has four occupied energy levels. The *s* and *p* sublevels in energy levels 1, 2, and 3 are filled. The configuration starts as follows.

$$1s^22s^22p^63s^23p^6$$

Nickel is in the *d* block of Period 4. So the 4*s* sublevel must be filled. Add $4s^2$.

$$1s^22s^22p^63s^23p^64s^2$$

Find the d^8 label above nickel's group. These electrons are in energy level 3. Add $3d^8$ to the configuration.

$$1s^22s^22p^63s^23p^63d^84s^2$$

Key Question How can elements be classified based on electron configurations? **Elements can be sorted into noble gases, representative elements, transition metals, or inner transition metals based on their electron configurations.**

6.2 LessonCheck

Key Concept Check

9. **Identify** What kinds of information can you find in a periodic table?

10. **List** Into what four classes can elements be sorted based on their electron configurations?

Think Critically

11. **Explain** How do you know that potassium and sodium have similar chemical properties?

12. **Classify** Identify each element as an alkali metal, an alkaline earth metal, or a halogen.
    a. barium
    b. chlorine
    c. lithium
    d. beryllium

13. **Classify** Based on their electron configurations, identify each element as a representative element, transition metal, or noble gas.
    a. $1s^22s^22p^63s^23p^63d^{10}4s^24p^6$
    b. $1s^22s^22p^63s^23p^63d^64s^2$
    c. $1s^22s^22p^63s^23p^2$

14. **Describe** How many electrons are in the highest occupied energy level of an element in Group 5A?

15. **Identify** Which of these elements are transition metals: Cu, Sr, Cd, Au, Al, Ge, Co?

CHEMISTRY & YOU

16. How is an element square in the periodic table like a driver's license? (Hint: See page 154.)

6.3 Periodic Trends

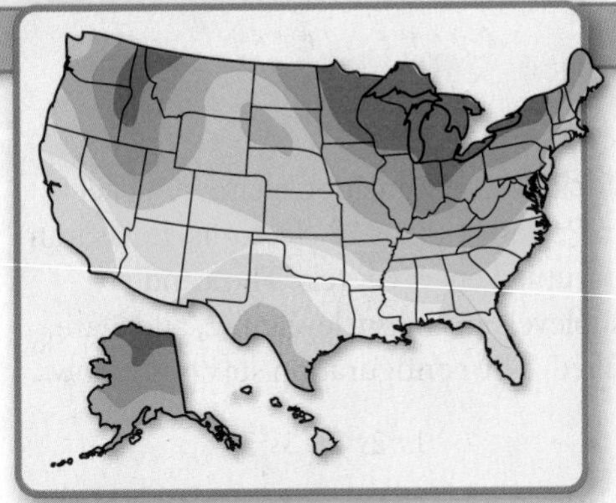

CHEMISTRY & YOU

Q: How are trends in the weather and trends in the properties of elements similar? The weather you experience depends on where you are on Earth. Florida has a higher average temperature than Minnesota. A rain forest receives more rain than a desert. In the same way, the properties of an element are related to where the element is located in the periodic table.

Key Questions

What are the trends among the elements for atomic size?

How do ions form?

What are the trends among the elements for first ionization energy, ionic size, and electronegativity?

BUILD Vocabulary

atomic radius one half of the distance between the nuclei of two atoms of the same element when the atoms are joined

WORD ORIGINS

Radius comes from the Latin word *ray*, meaning "spoke of a wheel." In a bicycle wheel, the spokes run from the hub, or center, of the wheel to the rim, or outer edge. The nucleus is the "hub" of an atom. The highest occupied energy level is the "rim."

Trends in Atomic Size

Atoms have different sizes. Scientists can use the units that form when atoms of the same element join to determine atomic size. These units are called molecules. In the diagram of a molecule below, the atoms are the same. The distance between the nuclei of these atoms can be used to find an atomic radius. (Nuclei is the plural of nucleus.) The **atomic radius** is one half of the distance between the nuclei of two atoms of the same element when the atoms are joined.

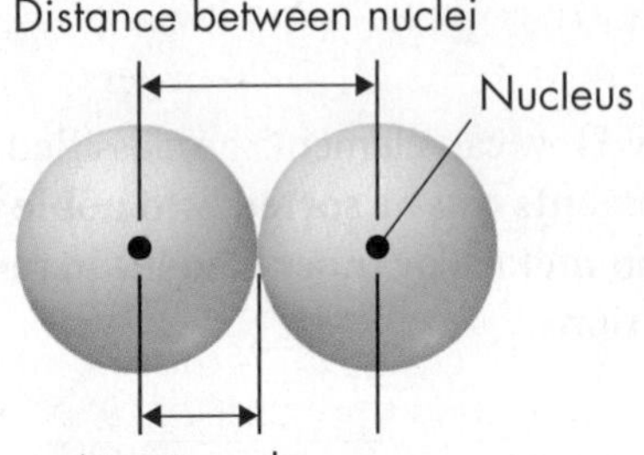

Atoms are very small. The atomic radius is often given in picometers (pm). There are one trillion, or 10^{12}, picometers in a meter. Use the models below to compare the sizes of atoms in four halogens.

Atomic Radii

This diagram compares the atomic radii of four nonmetals. Radii is the plural of radius.

Fluorine (F_2)
62 pm

Chlorine (Cl_2)
102 pm

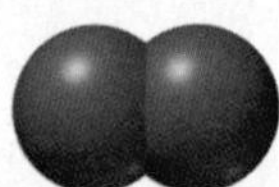

Bromine (Br_2)
120 pm

Iodine (I_2)
140 pm

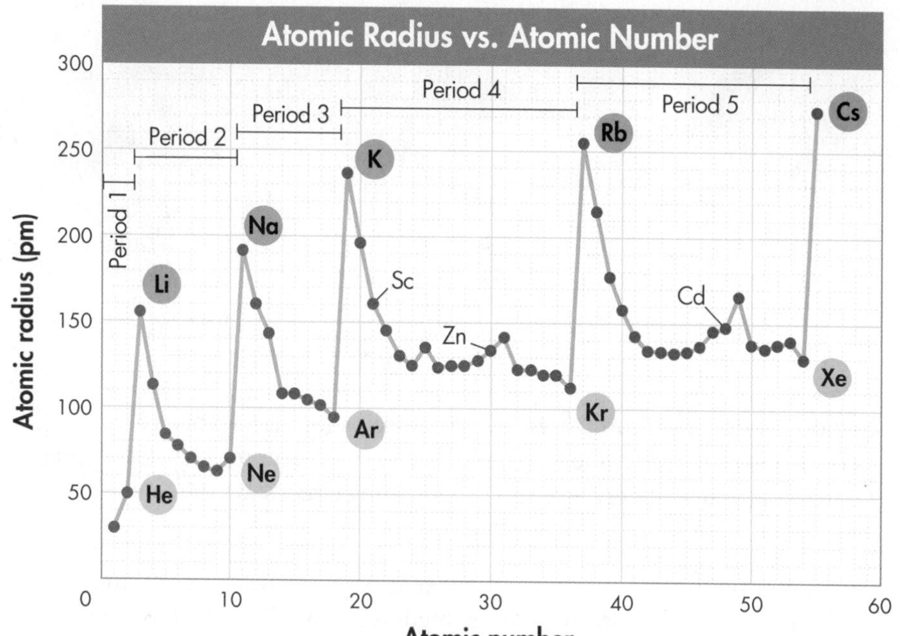

Atomic Radii
This graph plots the atomic radius versus the atomic number for elements 1 through 55.

Go to your Chemistry Skills and Math Workbook to practice interpreting graphs.

Group Trends in Atomic Size On the graph, each point stands for an atomic radius. The orange circles mark the points for the alkali metals. The purple circles mark the points for the noble gases. Follow each set of circles across the graph. In each group, the atomic radius increases as the atomic number increases. This increase is an example of a trend.

The structure of an atom changes as the atomic number increases. One change is an increase in the number of protons. With more protons, the nucleus has a greater positive charge. Remember that electrons have a negative charge. So they are attracted to the protons in the nucleus. A larger positive charge draws the electrons closer to the nucleus. If the number of protons were the only change, the atomic radius would decrease in a group.

As the atomic number increases in a group, the number of occupied energy levels increases. The electrons in the lower levels act as a screen, or shield, between the charge on the nucleus and the electrons in the highest level. This effect is called the shielding effect.

As each energy level is added, the protons have less of a pull on the electrons in the highest level. The distance from the nucleus increases, and so does the atomic size. The art below illustrates this trend for Group 1A.

BUILD Connections

Use a magnet to hold a card on a metal surface. Then try to hold two cards. Add cards one by one until the magnet can no longer hold up the cards. The cards shield the surface from the magnet's pull. The magnet is like a nucleus. The cards represent electrons in lower energy levels. The surface represents electrons in the highest occupied level.

Electron Shielding in Group 1A
The increase in occupied energy levels explains the increase in atomic size from lithium to potassium.

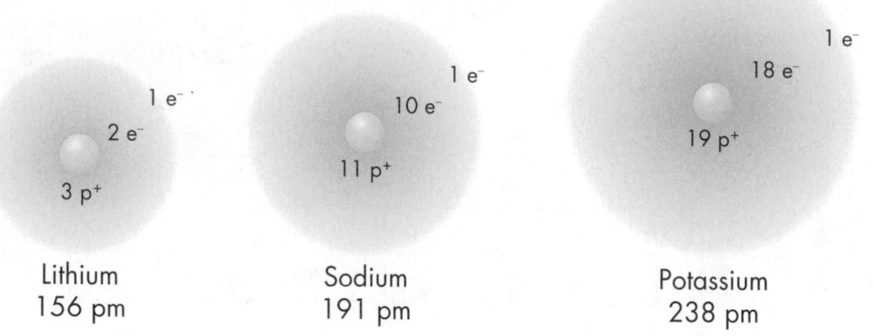

Trend for Atomic Size in Period 3
Phosphorus, sulfur, and chlorine are Period 3 elements. Their atoms are similar in size because they have the same number of inner electrons. Adding protons causes the slight decrease in atomic size from phosphorus to chlorine.

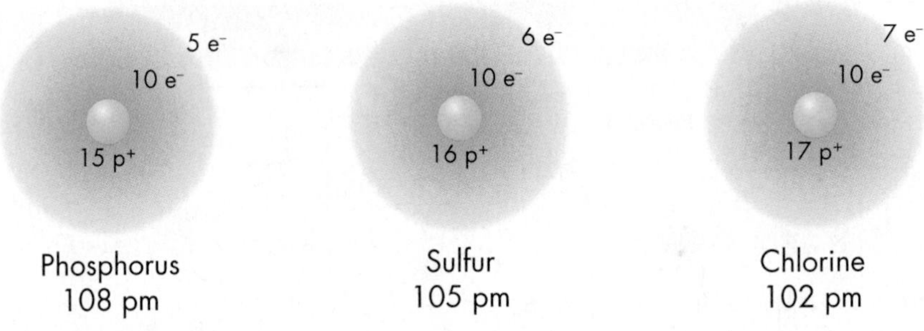

Period Trends in Atomic Size As the atomic number increases across a period, one proton and one electron is added to each atom. The electrons are added to the same energy level. So the shielding effect stays the same. This means that atomic size is not affected.

The charge on the nucleus does affect atomic size. As the charge on the nucleus increases, the electrons in the highest occupied energy level are drawn closer to the nucleus. Because the electrons are closer to the nucleus, the atomic size decreases.

Look at the drawing above, which compares the size of three atoms from Period 3—phosphorus, sulfur, and chlorine. The size of the atoms decreases only a little as a proton is added to the nucleus because the shielding effect stays the same.

The figure below summarizes the group and period trends in atomic size. Note how the color changes in the arrows. In the horizontal arrow, the color changes from dark red to light red. This shows that atomic size is decreasing. In the vertical arrow, the color changes from light red to dark red. This shows that atomic size is increasing.

Key Question What are the trends among the elements for atomic size? **In general, atomic size increases from top to bottom within a group and decreases from left to right across a period.**

Trends in Atomic Size
The size of atoms tends to decrease from left to right across a period.
The size of atoms tends to increase from top to bottom in a group.

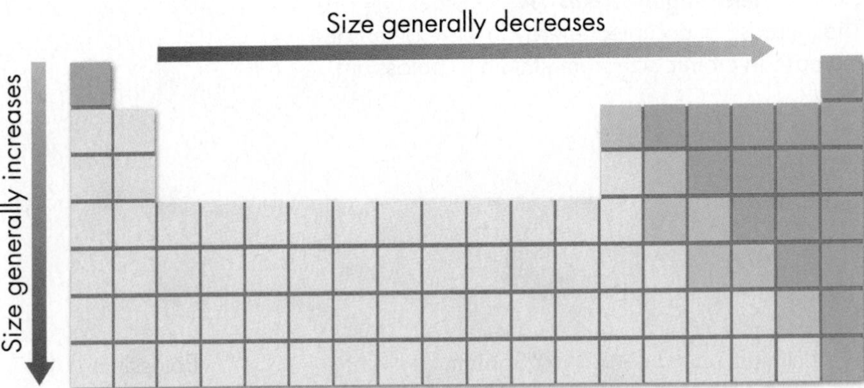

Ions

Remember that an atom is neutral because it has equal numbers of protons, which have a positive charge, and electrons, which have a negative charge. Some compounds are made of neutral atoms. Other compounds are made of particles called ions. An **ion** is an atom or group of atoms that has a positive or negative charge. Ions form when electrons are transferred between atoms.

Atoms of metals, such as sodium, tend to form ions by losing one or more electrons. The drawing below compares the atomic structure of a sodium atom and a sodium ion. In the ion, the number of electrons (10) is not equal to the number of protons (11). Because there are more protons than electrons, the ion has a positive charge. An ion with a positive charge is called a **cation.**

Atoms of nonmetals, such as chlorine, tend to form ions by gaining one or more electrons. The drawing below also compares the atomic structure of a chlorine atom and a chloride ion. In the ion, the number of electrons (18) is not equal to the number of protons (17). Because there are more electrons than protons, the ion has a negative charge. An ion with a negative charge is called an **anion.**

ion any atom or group of atoms that has a positive or negative charge

cation any atom or group of atoms with a positive charge

anion any atom or group of atoms with a negative charge

PREFIXES

The prefix *ana-* means "up." In an anion, the number of electrons goes up compared to a neutral atom. One meaning of the prefix *cata-* is "down." In a cation, the number of electrons goes down.

Key Question How do ions form? **Positive and negative ions form when electrons are transferred between atoms.**

Formation of Cations and Anions

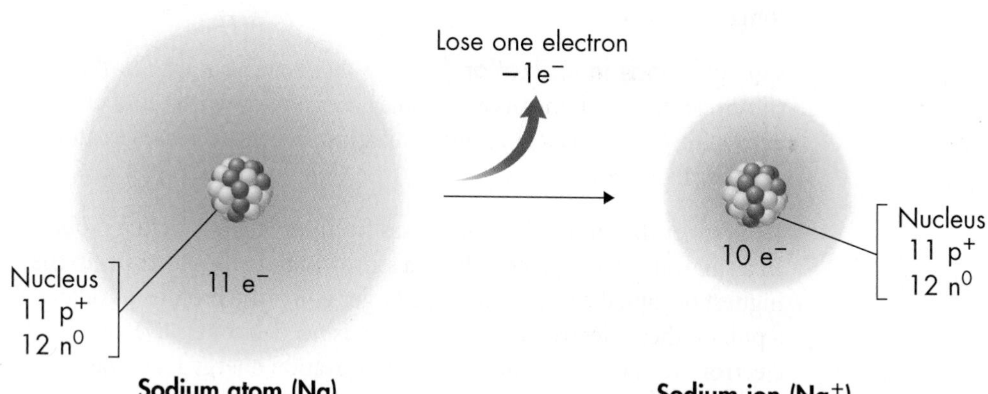

Sodium atom (Na) **Sodium ion (Na^+)**

Cation Formation Cations form when atoms lose electrons. The charge for a cation is written as a number followed by a plus sign. If the charge is 1+, the 1 is omitted from the symbol. The symbol for a sodium ion is Na^+.

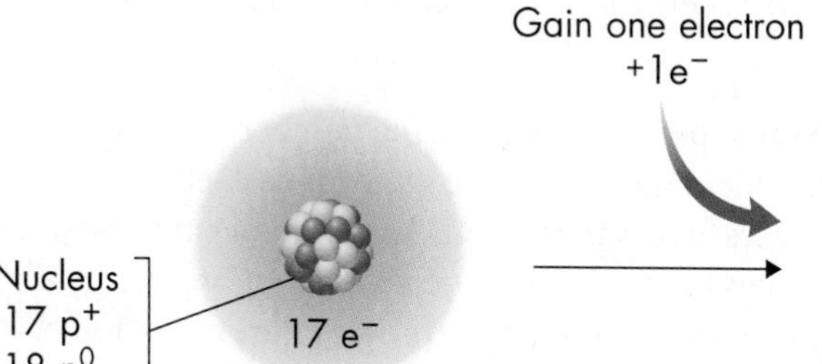

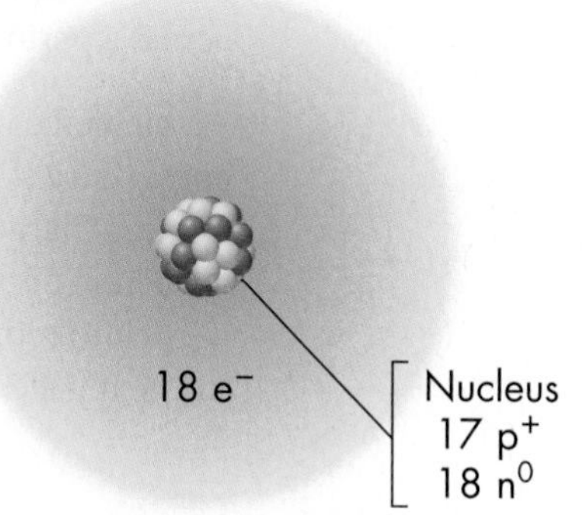

Chlorine atom (Cl) **Chloride ion (Cl^-)**

Anion Formation When an atom gains an electron, it becomes a negatively charged ion. The charge for an anion is written as a number followed by a minus sign. The symbol for a chloride ion is Cl^-.

First Ionization Energy
This graph plots first ionization energy against atomic number for 55 elements. The unit used for energy is kJ/mol. A mole (mol) is an amount of matter equal to the atomic mass of an element in grams.

Go to your Chemistry Skills and Math Workbook to practice interpreting graphs.

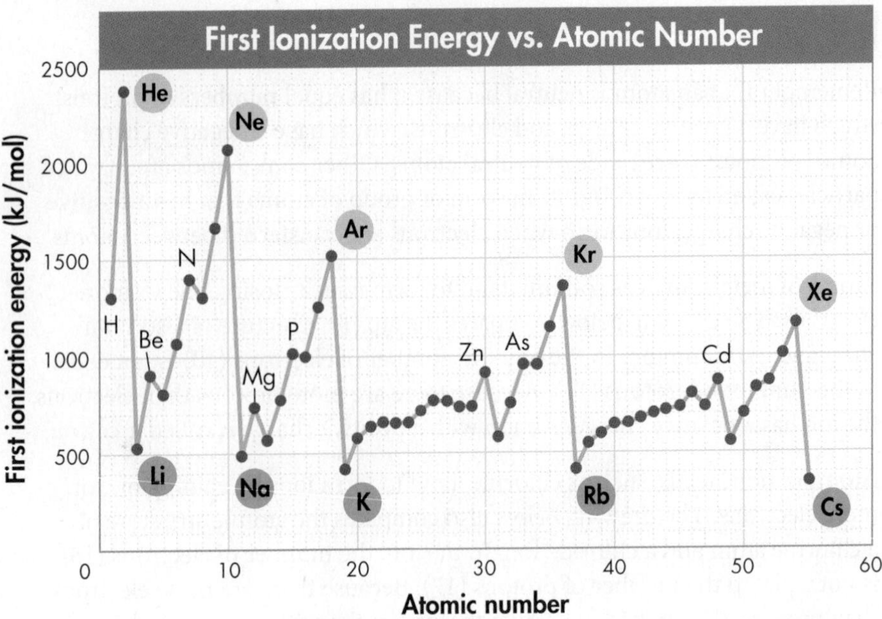

ionization energy the energy required to remove an electron from an atom

To *ionize* means to change into an ion. To describe the result of this action, you can add the suffix *-ation* to form *ionization*.

Trends in Ionization Energy

When atoms absorb energy, electrons can move to higher energy levels. Sometimes an electron gains enough energy to escape the attraction of the protons in the nucleus. The energy required to remove an electron from an atom is called **ionization energy.** The energy needed to remove the first electron from an atom is called the first ionization energy.

Group Trends in Ionization Energy Look at the graph above. Find the circles for alkali metals and noble gases. Follow each set of circles across the graph. In each group, ionization energy decreases as atomic number increases.

Remember that atomic size increases from top to bottom in a group. In a small atom, the protons have a strong pull on the electrons in the highest occupied energy level. In a larger atom, the protons have less of a pull on these electrons. So less energy is needed to remove an electron from that level, and the first ionization energy is smaller.

Period Trends in Ionization Energy Look again at the graph. Follow the points in Period 2 from lithium (Li) to neon (Ne). Notice that the first ionization energy tends to increase from left to right across a period.

All elements in the same period have the same number of occupied energy levels. So the shielding effect is the same for each element. The nuclear charge increases across the period. As the charge increases, the attraction of the nucleus for an electron increases. So more energy is needed to remove an electron from an atom. The figure at the top of the next page shows trends for first ionization energy.

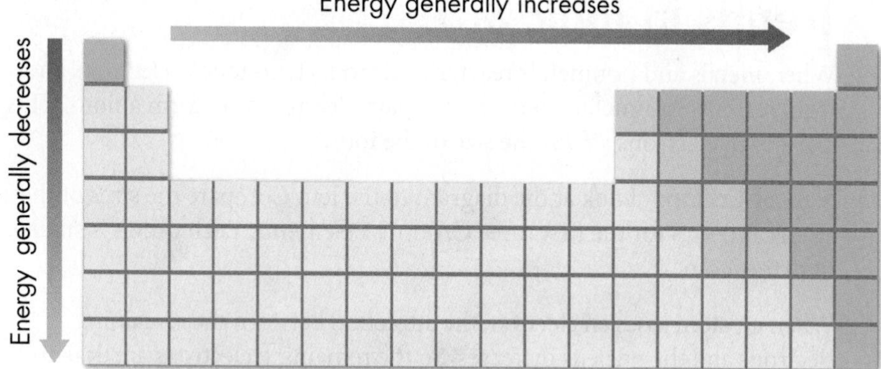

Trends in First Ionization Energy First ionization energy tends to increase from left to right across a period. It tends to decrease from top to bottom in a group.

Second and Third Ionization Energies Sometimes more than one electron can be removed from an atom. The energy needed to remove a second electron is called the second ionization energy. The energy needed to remove a third electron is called the third ionization energy.

Look at the data in the table below. For each element, the second ionization energy is larger than the first. The third is larger than the second. This pattern occurs because a cation forms when the first electron is removed. More energy is needed to remove an electron from an ion with a 1+ charge. It is even harder to remove an electron from an ion with a 2+ charge.

Ionization energies can help you predict the ions an element will form. Look at the data for lithium (Li) and sodium (Na). In each case, the second ionization energy is much larger than the first. Removing a second electron from these atoms is difficult. So Group 1A metals tend to form ions with a 1+ charge.

Key Question What are the trends among the elements for ionization energy? **First ionization energy tends to decrease from top to bottom within a group and increase from left to right across a period.**

Ionization Energies of First 14 Elements (kJ/mol)

Symbol	First	Second	Third
H	1312		
He (noble gas)	2372	5247	
Li	520	7297	11,810
Be	899	1757	14,840
B	801	2430	3659
C	1086	2352	4619
N	1402	2857	4577
O	1314	3391	5301
F	1681	3375	6045
Ne (noble gas)	2080	3963	6276
Na	496	4565	6912
Mg	738	1450	7732
Al	578	1816	2744
Si	786	1577	3229

Ionization Energies The table compares ionization energies for elements 1 through 14. The red lines mark the points at which the value for a first, second, or third ionization energy makes a dramatic drop before it starts to rise again.

Go to your Chemistry Skills and Math Workbook to practice interpreting data.

Trends in Ionic Size

Comparing Atomic and Ionic Sizes
This drawing compares the sizes of atoms and ions for some elements in Group 1A and Group 7A. The numbers are the measurements for the radii in picometers (pm).

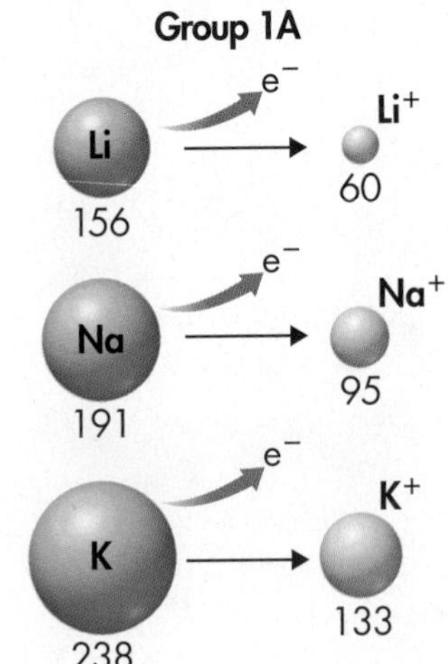

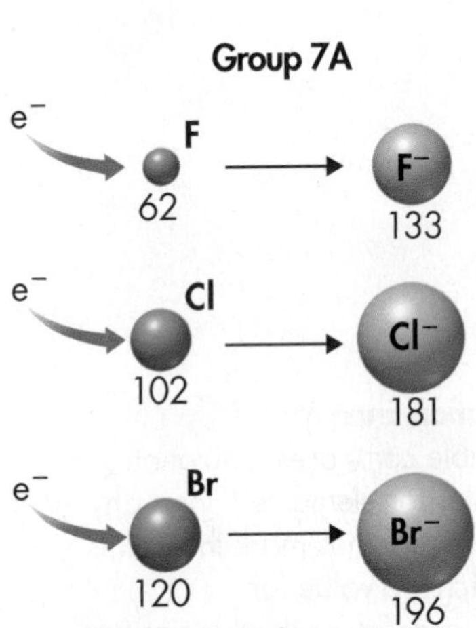

When metals and nonmetals react, metal atoms tend to lose electrons and form cations. Nonmetal atoms tend to gain electrons and form anions. This transfer of electrons affects the size of the ions.

Size of Cations Look at the diagram to the left. Compare the sizes of the atoms and ions for the first three Group 1A elements. Each cation is smaller than the atom.

When an atom loses an electron, the attraction between the remaining electrons and the nucleus increases. So the remaining electrons are drawn closer to the nucleus. Cations are smaller than the atoms from which they form.

Size of Anions Look again at the diagram. Compare the sizes of the atoms and ions for the first three Group 7A elements. In each case, the anion is larger than the atom.

As the number of electrons increases, the attraction of the nucleus for any one electron decreases. So anions are larger than the atoms from which they form.

Group Trends in Ionic Size Ionic size tends to increase from top to bottom in a group. This is true whether the ions are smaller than their atoms as in Group 1A or larger than their atoms as in Group 7A. This trend for ionic size matches the group trend for atomic size.

Period Trends in Ionic Size Look at the figure below. The two arrows across the top show the period trends for ionic size. The size of cations decreases from left to right across a period. The size of anions also decreases from left to right across a period. The drawing also summarizes the group trends in ionic size.

Key Question What are the trends among the elements for ionic size? **Ionic size tends to increase from top to bottom within a group. Generally, the size of cations and anions decreases from left to right across a period.**

Trends in Ionic Size
The ionic size of cations and anions increases from top to bottom in groups. The size decreases from left to right across periods.

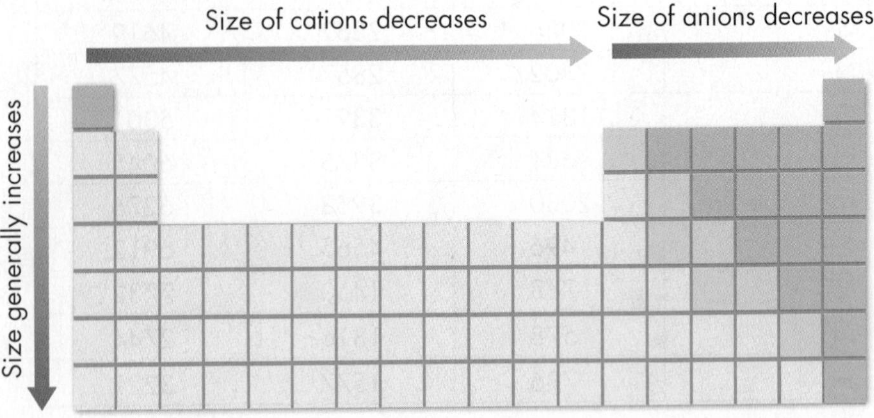

Quick Lab

Periodic Trends in Ionic Radii

Purpose To use a graph to identify period and group trends

Materials

- graph paper

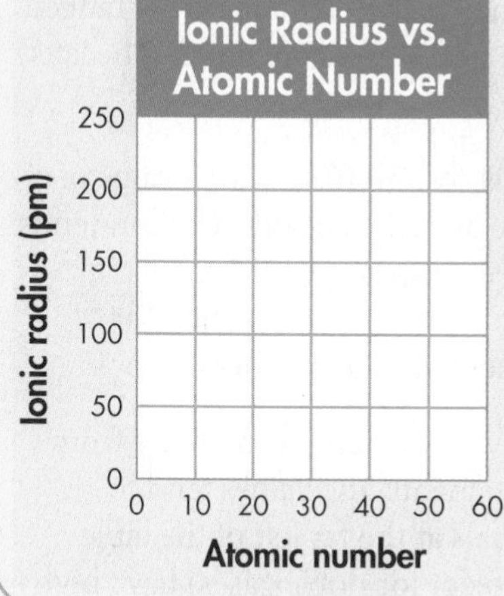

Procedure

Use the data in the table below to plot ionic radius versus atomic number for the representative elements in Periods 1 through 5. Begin with Element 1 and end with Element 54.

Analyze and Conclude

1. **Compare** How does its size change when an atom forms a cation? How does its size change when an atom forms an anion?
2. **Describe** How do the ionic radii change within a group of metals? How do they change within a group of nonmetals?
3. **Describe** Look at the part of your graph that corresponds to Period 2. What is the shape of this part?
4. **Compare and Contrast** Is the trend across a period similar or different for Periods 3, 4, and 5?

Atomic and Ionic Radii
The atomic radius is in the upper-right corner of each element square. The ionic radius is in the lower-left corner. The circle in the lower-right corner tells you the type of ion and its charge.

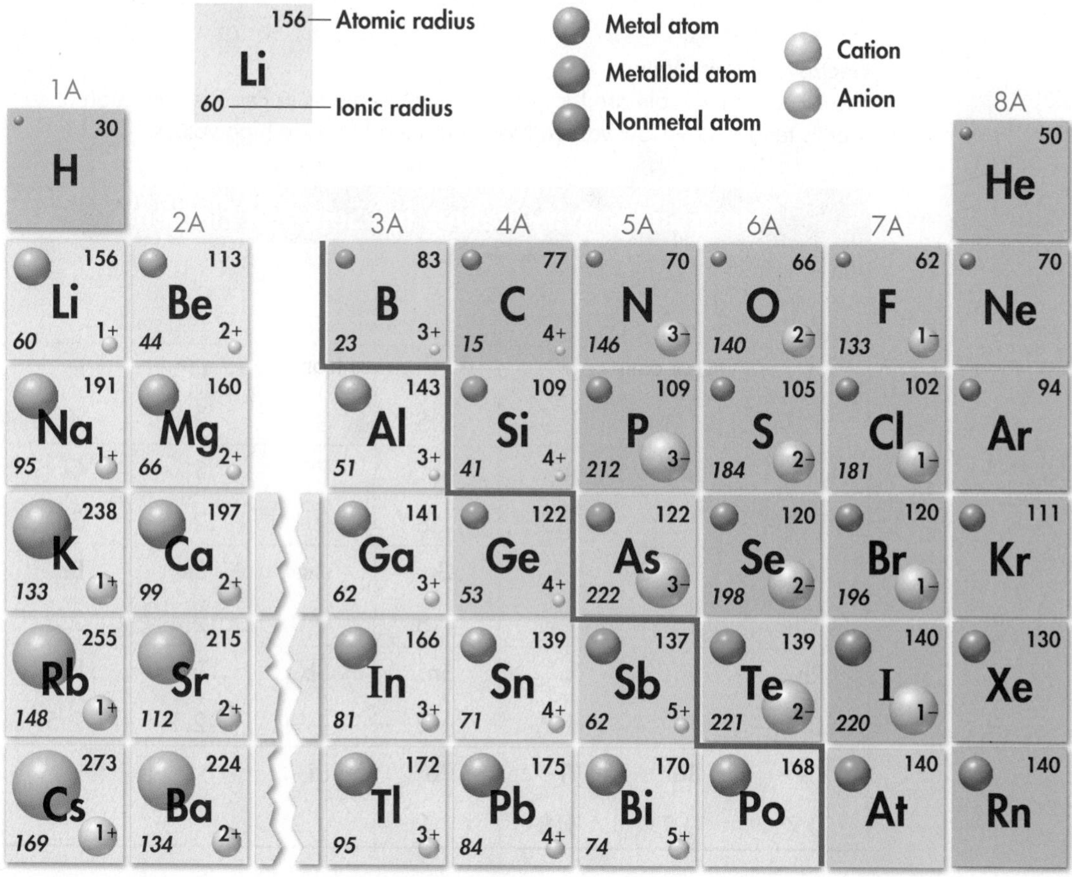

electronegativity the ability of an atom to attract electrons when the atom is in a compound

RELATED WORD FORMS

The word *electronegative* is an adjective. It is used to describe a particle that has a negative charge. It can be used to describe an electron.

Trends in Electronegativity

In Chapters 7 and 8, you will study two kinds of bonds that can form in compounds. Electrons take part in both kinds of bonds. There is a property that can be used to predict the kind of bond that will form. That property is called electronegativity. **Electronegativity** is the ability of an atom of an element to attract electrons when the atom is in a compound.

Electronegativity Values The table below lists electronegativity values for representative elements in Groups 1A through 7A. The elements are arranged in the same order as in the periodic table. The noble gases are omitted because they do not form many compounds.

The least electronegative element in the table is cesium (Cs), with a value of 0.7. Of the elements listed, it is the least able to attract electrons. Cesium tends to lose electrons and form cations. The most electronegative element is fluorine (F), with a value of 4.0. Fluorine has a very strong attraction for electrons. So when it reacts with another element, it tends to form anions.

Group and Period Trends Electronegativity values tend to decrease from top to bottom in a group. For representative elements, the values tend to increase from left to right across a period. Metals at the far left of the table have low values. Nonmetals at the far right (except for noble gases) have high values. The values among the transition metals are not as predictable.

Key Question What are the trends among the elements for electronegativity? **In general, electronegativity values decrease from top to bottom within a group. For representative elements, the values tend to increase from left to right across a period.**

Electronegativity Values
The values in the table are for representative elements in Periods 1 through 6. Metals tend to have low values. Nonmetals tend to have high values.

Electronegativity Values for Selected Elements						
H 2.1						
Li 1.0	**Be** 1.5	**B** 2.0	**C** 2.5	**N** 3.0	**O** 3.5	**F** 4.0
Na 0.9	**Mg** 1.2	**Al** 1.5	**Si** 1.8	**P** 2.1	**S** 2.5	**Cl** 3.0
K 0.8	**Ca** 1.0	**Ga** 1.6	**Ge** 1.8	**As** 2.0	**Se** 2.4	**Br** 2.8
Rb 0.8	**Sr** 1.0	**In** 1.7	**Sn** 1.8	**Sb** 1.9	**Te** 2.1	**I** 2.5
Cs 0.7	**Ba** 0.9	**Tl** 1.8	**Pb** 1.9	**Bi** 1.9		

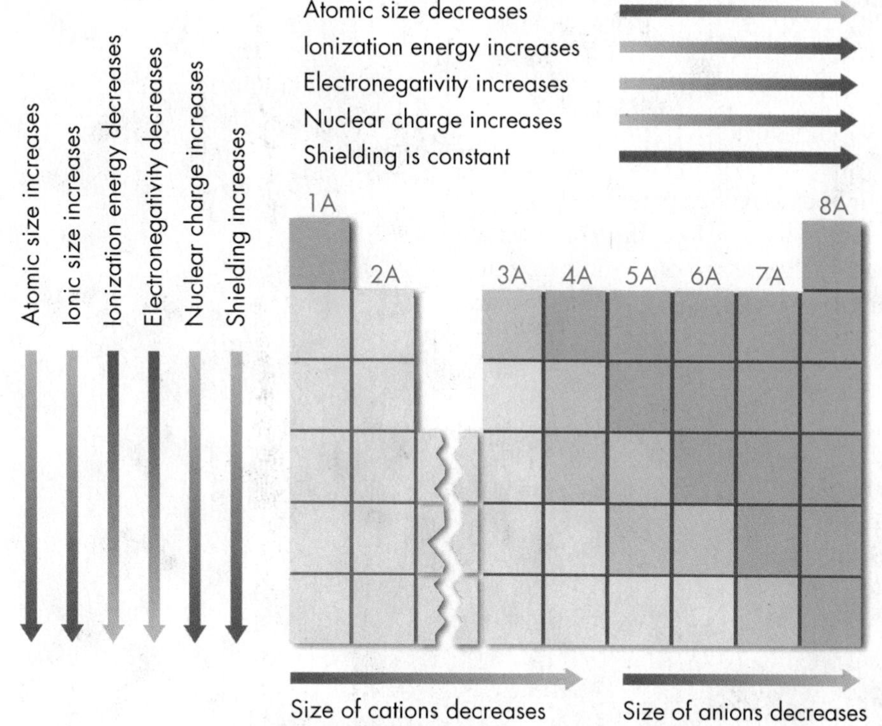

Summary of Trends
Use this figure to review the group and period trends you studied in this lesson. Remember that an arrow that changes from light red to dark red shows an increase in a trend. An arrow that changes from dark red to light red shows a decrease.

See periodic trends animated online.

Summary of Periodic Trends Look at the figure above. It summarizes the trends for atomic size, ionic size, ionization energy, and electronegativity. The elements shown are representative elements and noble gases. Also note the trends for nuclear charge and shielding.

The increase in nuclear charge in groups and across periods explains many of the trends. In groups, the number of occupied energy levels has a major effect on each trend. When more energy levels are occupied, shielding increases.

6.3 LessonCheck

Key Concept Check

17. **Review** How does atomic size change in groups and across periods?

18. **Explain** When do ions form?

19. **Summarize** What is the trend for first ionization energy in groups and across periods?

20. **Describe** Compare the size of ions to the size of the atoms from which they form.

21. **Review** How do electronegativity values change in groups and across periods?

Think Critically

22. **Sequence** Arrange these elements in order of decreasing atomic size: sulfur, chlorine, aluminum, and sodium. Does your sequence show a period trend or a group trend?

23. **Identify** Which element in each pair has the larger first ionization energy?

a. sodium, potassium

b. magnesium, phosphorus

CHEMISTRY & YOU

24. You have seen maps that show the yearly amount of rain at different locations. In what way is a periodic table like those maps? (Hint: See page 162.)

CHEMISTRY & YOU: EVERYDAY MATTER

Elements of Life

Like everything else in the universe, your body is made up of elements. Your body uses these elements for different functions. Roughly 97 percent of your body is made up of just four elements: oxygen, carbon, hydrogen, and nitrogen. The remaining 3 percent contains about 20 other elements that are needed for life.

CIRCULATORY SYSTEM Iron plays an important role in the circulatory system. Because red blood cells contain iron, they are able to carry oxygen from the lungs to cells throughout the body. The cells use oxygen to release energy from food. Two other elements—copper and cobalt—are needed for red blood cells to form.

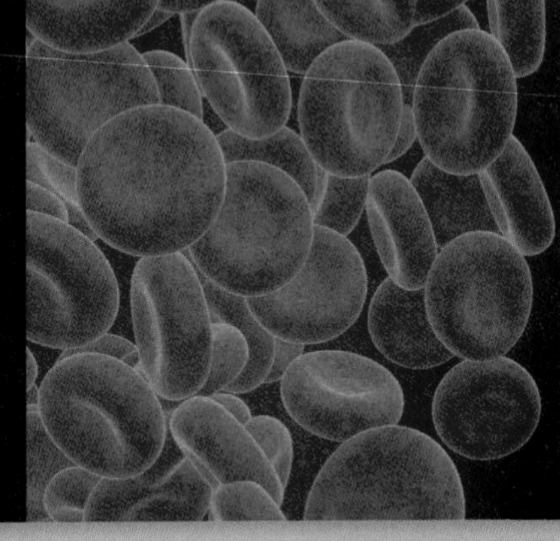

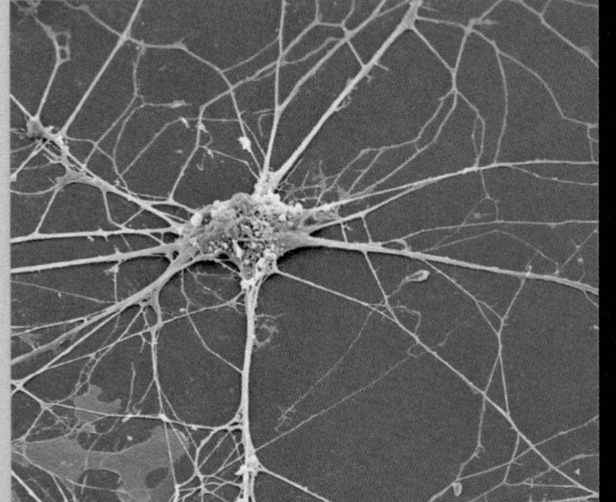

NERVOUS SYSTEM Sodium and potassium are needed for your nervous system to work properly. These elements help your brain to communicate with other parts of your body. The messages are carried by nerve cells. Other elements that your nervous system needs are calcium, chlorine, zinc, and magnesium.

SKELETAL SYSTEM Your bones and teeth are two parts of the skeletal system. They are largely made up of calcium and phosphorus. These elements give bones and teeth their strength. Fluorine, boron, magnesium, and silicon are also important for bone growth and for keeping bones strong.

Take It Further

1. Classify Are the four elements that make up about 97 percent of the human body metals, nonmetals, or metalloids?

2. Predict The elements sodium and potassium are present in nerve cells as ions. What is the charge on these ions?

3. Predict Which is larger, a sodium ion or a potassium ion? Which is larger, a potassium ion or a calcium ion? Give a reason for your answers.

6 Study Guide

BIGIDEA ELECTRONS AND THE STRUCTURE OF ATOMS

Periodic tables may contain each element's name, symbol, atomic number, atomic mass, and number of electrons in each energy level. The electron configuration of an element can be determined based on the location of an element in the periodic table. Atomic size, ionization energy, ionic size, and electronegativity are trends that vary across periods and groups of the periodic table. These trends can be explained by variations in atomic structure. The increase in nuclear charge within groups and across periods explains many trends. Within groups, an increase in electron shielding has a significant effect on these trends.

6.1 Organizing the Elements

Early chemists used the properties of elements to sort them into groups.

Mendeleev arranged the elements in his periodic table in order of increasing atomic mass.

In the modern periodic table, elements are arranged in order of increasing atomic number.

Three classes of elements are metals, nonmetals, and metalloids.

- periodic law (150)
- metal (152)
- nonmetal (152)
- metalloid (153)

6.2 Classifying the Elements

The periodic table usually shows the symbols and names of elements, along with information about the structure of their atoms.

Elements can be sorted into noble gases, representative elements, transition metals, or inner transition metals based on their electron configurations.

- alkali metal (155)
- alkaline earth metal (155)
- halogen (155)
- noble gas (158)
- representative element (159)
- transition metal (160)
- inner transition metal (160)

6.3 Periodic Trends

In general, atomic size increases from top to bottom within a group and decreases from left to right across a period.

Positive and negative ions form when electrons are transferred between atoms.

First ionization energy tends to decrease from top to bottom within a group and increase from left to right across a period.

Ionic size tends to increase from top to bottom within a group. Generally, the size of cations and anions decreases from left to right across a period.

In general, electronegativity values decrease from top to bottom within a group. For representative elements, the values tend to increase from left to right across a period.

- atomic radius (162)
- ion (165)
- cation (165)
- anion (165)
- ionization energy (166)
- electronegativity (170)

6 Assessment

★ Solutions appear in Appendix D

Lesson by Lesson

6.1 Organizing the Elements

25. Why did Mendeleev leave spaces in his periodic table?

★26. What effect did the discovery of gallium have on the acceptance of Mendeleev's table?

27. What pattern is revealed when the elements are arranged in a periodic table in order of increasing atomic number?

28. Based on their locations in the periodic table, would you expect carbon and silicon to have similar properties? Explain your answer.

29. Identify each property below as more typical of a metal or a nonmetal.

a. gas at room temperature
b. brittle
c. malleable
d. poor conductor of electric current
e. shiny

30. In general, how are metalloids different from metals and nonmetals?

6.2 Classifying the Elements

31. Where are the alkali metals, the alkaline earth metals, the halogens, and the noble gases located in the periodic table?

32. Use this element square to answer the following questions about nitrogen.

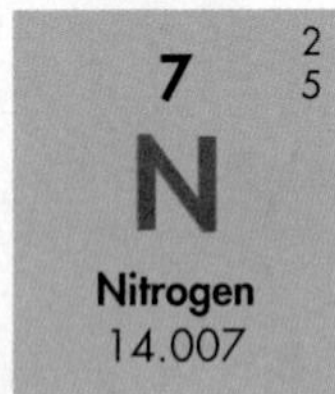

a. How many protons does its atoms have?
b. Is nitrogen a solid, liquid, or gas at room temperature?
c. How many of its energy levels are occupied?

33. Which of the following are symbols for representative elements: Na, Mg, Fe, Ni, Cl?

34. Use the block diagram on page 160 to write the electron configurations of these elements.

a. the noble gas in Period 3
b. the metalloid in Period 3
c. the alkaline earth metal in Period 3

6.3 Periodic Trends

★35. Which element in each pair has atoms with a larger atomic radius?

a. sodium, lithium
b. strontium, magnesium
c. carbon, germanium
d. selenium, oxygen

36. Explain the difference between the first and second ionization energy of an element.

37. Which element in each pair has a larger first ionization energy?

a. lithium, boron
b. magnesium, strontium
c. cesium, aluminum

★38. How does the ionic radius of a typical metal compare with its atomic radius?

39. Which particle has the larger radius in each pair of atoms and ions?

a. Na, Na^+
b. S, S^{2-}
c. I, I^-
d. Al, Al^{3+}

★40. When the elements in each pair react, which element has a greater attraction for electrons?

a. Ca or O
b. O or F
c. H or O
d. K or S

41. Locate each of the following elements in the periodic table. Decide whether its atoms are likely to form anions or cations.

a. sodium
b. oxygen
c. iodine
d. calcium

Understand Concepts

42. Write the symbol of the element or elements that fit each description.

a. a nonmetal in Group 4A

b. the inner transition metal with the lowest atomic number

c. a metal in Group 5A

★43. In which pair of elements are the chemical properties of the elements most similar? Explain your reasoning.

a. sodium and chlorine

b. nitrogen and phosphorus

c. boron and oxygen

44. For which of these properties does lithium have a larger value than potassium?

a. first ionization energy

b. atomic radius

c. electronegativity

d. ionic radius

45. Explain why fluorine has a smaller atomic radius than both oxygen and chlorine.

46. Would you expect metals or nonmetals in the same period to have higher ionization energies? Give a reason for your answer.

47. The bar graph shows the relationship between atomic and ionic radii for Group 1A elements.

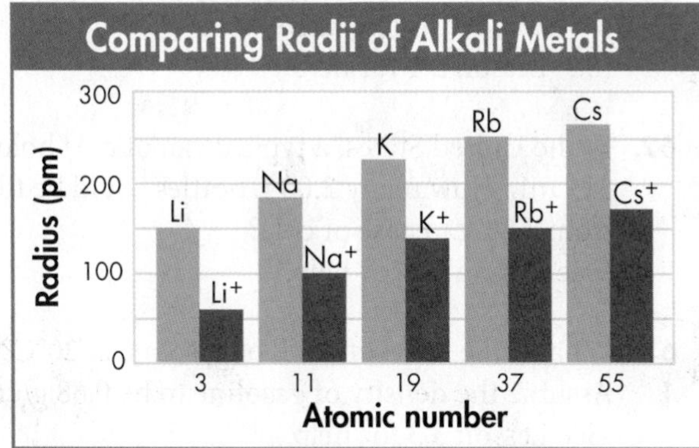

a. Describe and explain the trend in atomic radius within the group.

b. Explain the difference between the size of the atoms and the size of the ions.

Think Critically

48. Predict Do you think there are more elements left to discover? If so, what is the lowest atomic number a new element could have? Explain.

★49. Apply Concepts Why does it take more energy to remove a 4*s* electron from zinc than calcium?

50. Sequence The following spheres represent Ca, Ca^{2+}, and Mg^{2+}. Which one is which? Explain.

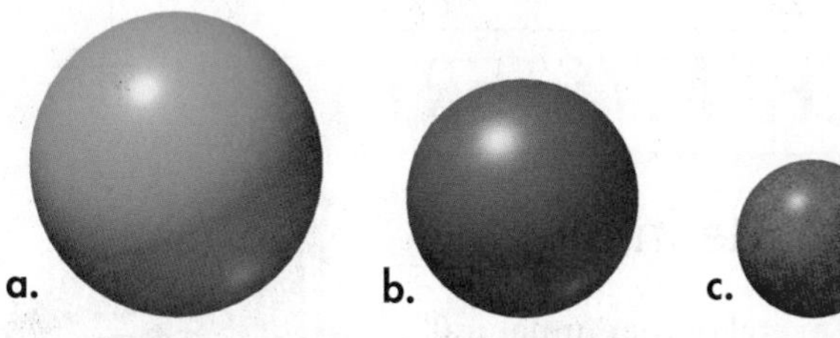

51. Interpret Diagrams Use the periodic table and the Block Diagram to identify these elements:

a. has its outermost electron in $7s^1$

b. contains only one electron in a *d* orbital

52. Make Generalizations Why is the first ionization energy of a nonmetal much higher than that of an alkali metal?

FOUNDATIONS Wrap-Up

Organize by Properties

1. Use Analogies At the beginning of the chapter, you organized colored squares based on their properties. How is what you did similar to what Mendeleev did?

Concept Check

Now that you have finished studying Chapter 6, answer these questions.

2. How does knowing the properties of magnesium (Mg) help you predict the properties of calcium (Ca)?

3. Why do jewelers work with gold or silver?

4. Some cooking pots have a copper bottom. What property of copper do these pots make use of?

Write About Science

53. **Explain** Why does the size of an atom tend to increase from top to bottom within a group? Why does the size of an atom tend to decrease from left to right across a period?

54. **Summarize** Describe the general properties of metals, nonmetals, and metalloids. Also describe where these classes of elements are located on the periodic table.

CHEMYSTERY

Made in the USA

Several of the "unnatural" elements were in fact "made in the USA." For example, elements with atomic numbers 94 through 102 were first artificially prepared in California. Three of these elements have names to prove it—americium, berkelium, and californium. Elements such as these are labeled on the periodic table as "Not found in nature" in this book and as "Artificially prepared" in some others.

Most of the artificially prepared elements are transition elements in Period 7. Atoms of these elements have an unstable nucleus. In an unstable nucleus, particles will break into smaller parts. This process continues until the nucleus is stable.

55. **Infer** The elements with atomic numbers 99, 101, 104, and 107 were named to honor famous scientists. Identify the scientist that each element is meant to honor.

56. **Connect to the BIGIDEA** Which element in Period 5 is not found in nature?

Cumulative Review

57. Explain why science today depends less on chance discoveries than it did in the past. (See Lesson 1.3 for help.)

*58. Identify each process as a chemical change or a physical change. (See Lesson 2.1 for help.)

a. melting of iron
b. lighting a match
c. grinding corn
d. souring of milk

59. Describe two methods to separate a mixture of small copper and iron beads. (See Lessons 2.2 and 2.3 for help.)

60. The volume of the liquid in the cylinder is reported as 31.8 mL. (See Lesson 3.1 for help.)

a. How many significant figures are there in the measurement?
b. In which digit is there uncertainty?

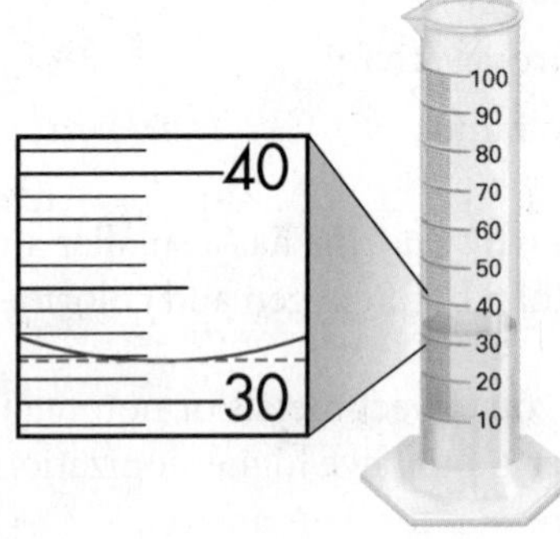

61. A jeweler determines the density of a sample of pure gold to be 20.3 g/cm^3. The accepted value is 19.3 g/cm^3. What is the percent error of the jeweler's density measurement? (See Lesson 3.1 for help.)

62. In the United States, a typical can of cola holds 355 mL. How many 2.00 L bottles could be filled from a 24-can case of cola? (See Lesson 3.3 for help.)

63. What is the mass of 7.7 L of gasoline at 20°C? Assume the density of gasoline to be 0.68 g/cm^3. (See Lesson 3.3 for help.)

*64. How many filled *p* orbitals do atoms of these elements contain? (See Lesson 5.2 for help.)

a. carbon
b. phosphorus
c. oxygen
d. nitrogen

Standardized Test Prep

For help with answering test questions, go to your Chemistry Skills and Math Workbook.

Select the choice that best answers each question or completes each statement.

1. Which of the following properties increases as you move across a period from left to right?

I. electronegativity

II. ionization energy

III. atomic radius

(A) I and II only **(C)** II and III only
(B) I and III only **(D)** I, II, and III

2. List the symbols for sodium, sulfur, and cesium in order of increasing atomic radii.
(A) Na, S, Cs **(C)** S, Na, Cs
(B) Cs, Na, S **(D)** Cs, S, Na

3. The electron configuration for an element in the halogen group should always end with
(A) ns^2np^6. **(C)** ns^2np^4.
(B) ns^2np^5. **(D)** ns^2np^2.

Use the spheres to answer Questions 4 and 5.

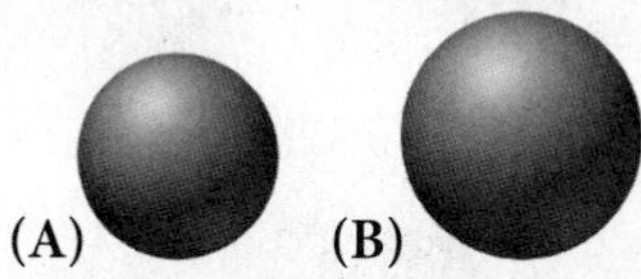

4. If the spheres represent a potassium atom and a potassium ion, which best represents the ion?

5. If the spheres represent an atom and an anion of the same element, which sphere represents the atom and which represents the anion?

Tips for Success

Interpreting Data Tables Tables can present a large amount of data in a small space. Before you try to answer questions based on a table, look at the table. Read the title, if there is one, and the column headings. Then read the questions. As you read each question, decide which data you will need to use in order to answer the question.

Use the data table to answer Questions 6–8.

Alkali metal	Atomic radius (pm)	First ionization energy (kJ/mol)	Electronegativity value
Li	152	520	1.0
Na	186	495.8	0.9
K	227	418.8	0.8
Rb	244	250	0.8
Cs	262	210	0.7

6. If you plot atomic radius versus first ionization energy, would the graph reveal a direct or inverse relationship?

7. If you plot atomic radius versus electronegativity, would the graph reveal a direct or inverse relationship?

8. If you plot first ionization energy versus electronegativity, would the graph reveal a direct or inverse relationship?

For each question, there are two statements. Decide whether each statement is true or false. Then decide whether Statement II is a correct explanation for Statement I.

	Statement I		Statement II
9.	Electronegativity values are higher for metals than for nonmetals.	**BECAUSE**	Atoms of nonmetals are among the largest atoms.
10.	A calcium atom is larger than a calcium ion.	**BECAUSE**	Ions are always larger than the atoms from which they are formed.
11.	The element hydrogen is a metal.	**BECAUSE**	Hydrogen is on the left in the periodic table.
12.	Among all the elements in a period, the noble gas always has the smallest ionization energy.	**BECAUSE**	Within any period, atomic radii tend to decrease moving from right to left.

If You Have Trouble With . . .

Question	1	2	3	4	5	6	7	8	9	10	11	12
See Lesson	6.3	6.3	6.2	6.3	6.3	6.3	6.3	6.3	6.3	6.3	6.1	6.3

7

Ionic and Metallic Bonding

FOUNDATIONS for Learning

Comparing Crystals

1. You will need table salt, some Epsom salts, colored paper, and a magnifying lens.
2. Place a small amount of table salt on one side of the paper and a small amount of Epsom salts on the other side of the paper.
3. Use a magnifying lens to look at the crystals more closely.

Compare and Contrast How are the crystals the same? How are they different?

PearsonChem.com

UntamedScience

Take a video field trip with the Untamed Science crew to observe intricate mineral formations and to learn how they can be used in everyday products.

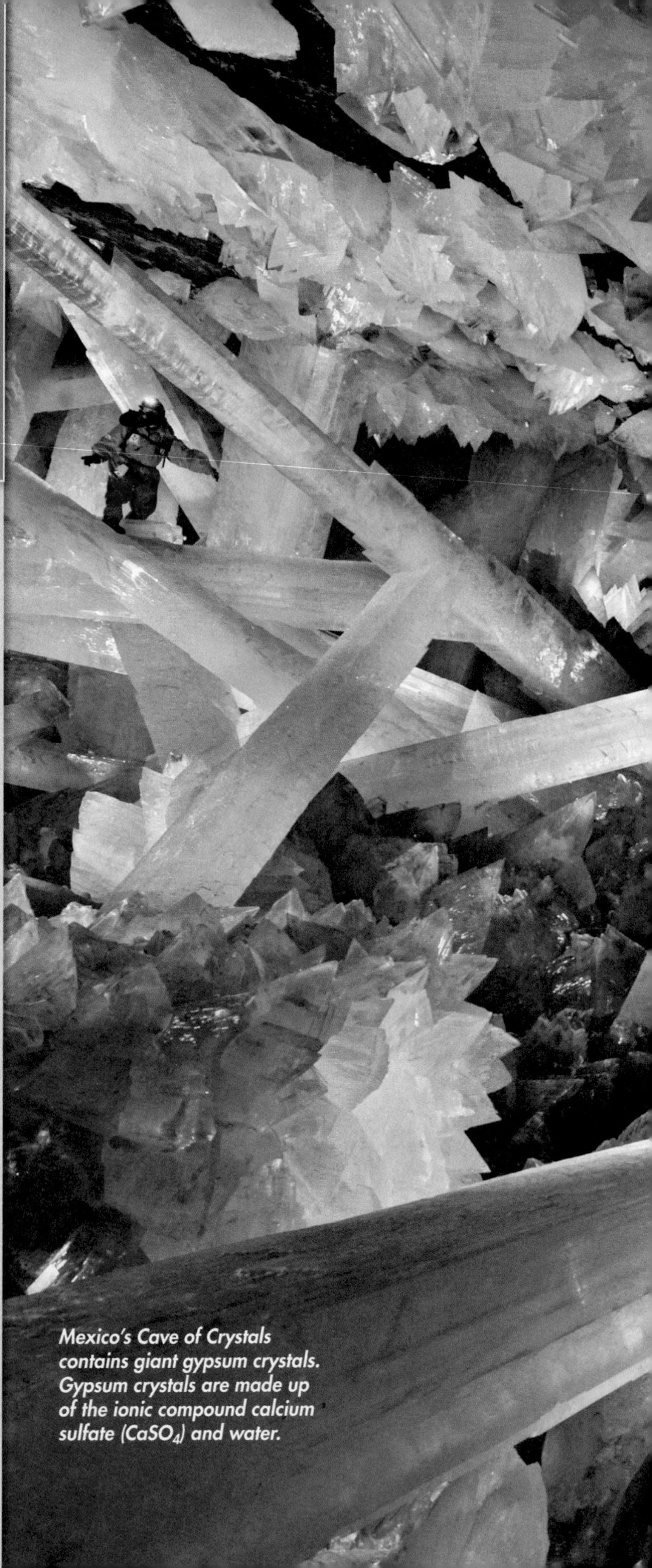

Mexico's Cave of Crystals contains giant gypsum crystals. Gypsum crystals are made up of the ionic compound calcium sulfate ($CaSO_4$) and water.

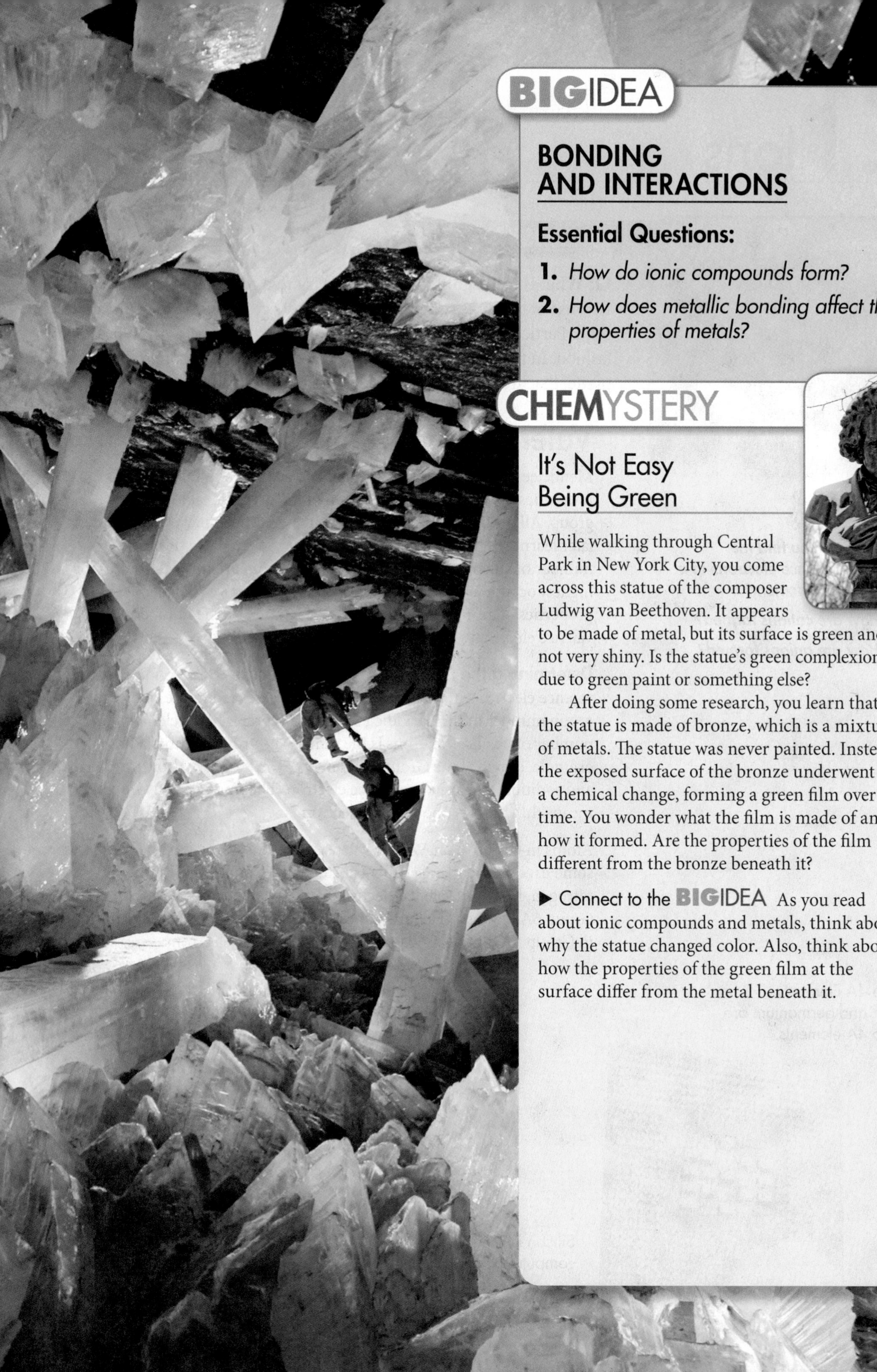

BIGIDEA

BONDING AND INTERACTIONS

Essential Questions:

1. *How do ionic compounds form?*
2. *How does metallic bonding affect the properties of metals?*

CHEMYSTERY

It's Not Easy Being Green

While walking through Central Park in New York City, you come across this statue of the composer Ludwig van Beethoven. It appears to be made of metal, but its surface is green and not very shiny. Is the statue's green complexion due to green paint or something else?

After doing some research, you learn that the statue is made of bronze, which is a mixture of metals. The statue was never painted. Instead, the exposed surface of the bronze underwent a chemical change, forming a green film over time. You wonder what the film is made of and how it formed. Are the properties of the film different from the bronze beneath it?

▶ Connect to the BIGIDEA As you read about ionic compounds and metals, think about why the statue changed color. Also, think about how the properties of the green film at the surface differ from the metal beneath it.

7.1 Ions

CHEMISTRY & YOU

Q: What is fool's gold? Pyrite (FeS_2) is often mistaken for gold. Because of that, it is sometimes called "fool's gold." Pyrite is a crystalline solid. Particles in crystalline solids are arranged in an orderly, repeating fashion. In this chapter, you will learn about crystalline solids, like pyrite, that are made up of ions that are bonded together.

Key Questions

How do you find the number of valence electrons in a representative element?

How are cations formed?

How are anions formed?

Valence Electrons

Mendeleev organized his periodic table based on similarities in the properties of elements. Each column of the periodic table is called a group. All of the elements in each group react in similar ways. Scientists later learned that all of the elements in each group have the same number of valence electrons. **Valence electrons** are the electrons in the highest occupied energy level of an element's atoms. The chemical properties of an element are largely determined by the number of valence electrons.

Determining the Number of Valence Electrons The number of valence electrons in an atom of an element is related to the element's group number in the periodic table. For a representative element, the number of valence electrons is the same as its group number. For example, atoms of the Group 1A elements (including hydrogen, lithium, and sodium) all have one valence electron. The number 1 in Group 1A means that there is one valence electron.

Atoms in Group 4A have four valence electrons. The figure below shows some uses of Group 4A elements. Atoms in Group 5A, including nitrogen, have five valence electrons. Oxygen and sulfur atoms, in Group 6A, have six. Helium is the only exception to the rule. Helium is in Group 8A, but helium atoms have two valence electrons.

Group 4A Elements
Silicon and germanium are Group 4A elements.

Silicon is used to make computer chips.

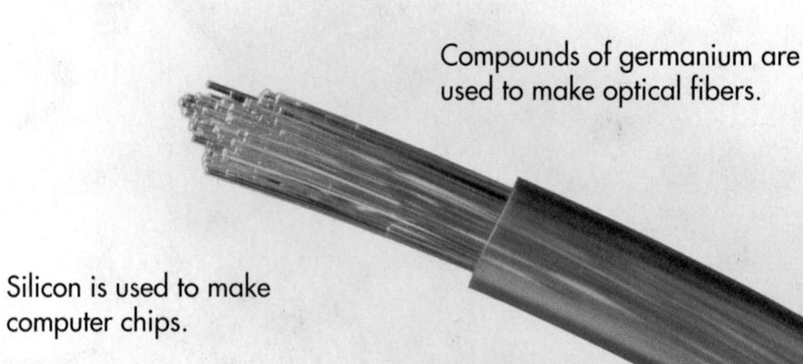

Compounds of germanium are used to make optical fibers.

Electron Dot Structures of Some Group A Elements								
	Group							
Period	1A	2A	3A	4A	5A	6A	7A	8A
1	H·							He:
2	Li·	·Be·	·B·	·C·	·N·	:O·	:F·	:Ne:
3	Na·	·Mg·	·Al·	·Si·	·P·	:S·	:Cl·	:Ar:
4	K·	·Ca·	·Ga·	·Ge·	·As·	:Se·	:Br·	:Kr:

Electron dot structures are diagrams that show an atom's valence electrons as dots. In general, only valence electrons are involved in chemical bonds. Electrons in lower energy levels are usually not involved in bonds. The table above shows electron dot structures for atoms of some Group A elements. Notice that all of the elements in a group (with the exception of helium) have the same number of electron dots in their structures.

The Octet Rule You learned in Chapter 6 that noble gases, such as neon, are generally nonreactive. That is, they are stable. In 1916, the chemist Gilbert Lewis used this fact to explain why atoms form certain kinds of ions and molecules. Recall that atoms of each of the noble gases (except helium) have eight valence electrons. The general electron configuration for these atoms is $ns^2 np^6$. A set of eight is an octet. Lewis explained that atoms tend to form compounds in a way that allows them to have eight electrons in their highest occupied energy level. He called his explanation the **octet rule.**

Atoms of metals tend to lose their valence electrons, leaving an octet in the next lowest energy level. Atoms of some nonmetals tend to gain or share electrons with another atom or atoms to form an octet. Although exceptions occur, the octet rule applies to atoms in most compounds.

Key Question How do you find the number of valence electrons in a representative element? **For a representative element, the number of valence electrons is the same as its group number.**

valence electron electron in the highest occupied energy level of an element's atoms

electron dot structure diagram that shows valence electrons as dots

octet rule in a chemical reaction, atoms gain or lose electrons to acquire the electron structure of a noble gas

WORD ORIGINS

Octet comes from the Greek word *okto*, meaning "eight." There are eight electrons in the highest occupied energy level of the noble gases, except for helium.

Formation of Cations

An atom is electrically neutral because it has an equal number of protons and electrons. An ion forms when an atom or molecule loses or gains electrons. A positively charged ion is called a cation. A cation forms when an atom loses one or more valence electrons. For metals, the cation's name is the same as the element's name. For example, a sodium atom (Na) forms a sodium cation (Na^+). Although their names are the same, metals and their cations have many important chemical differences. Sodium metal reacts explosively with water. Sodium cations, however, are quite nonreactive. Sodium cations are in table salt, a compound that is very stable in water.

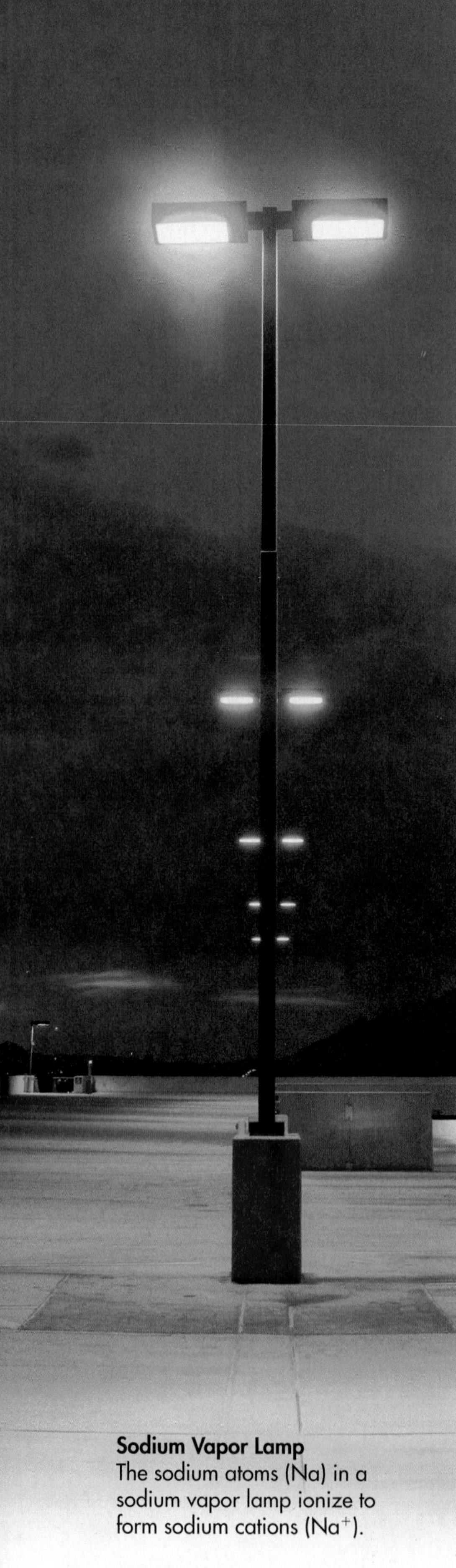
Sodium Vapor Lamp
The sodium atoms (Na) in a sodium vapor lamp ionize to form sodium cations (Na^+).

Metallic Cations The most common cations are those formed by the loss of valence electrons from metal atoms. Most of these atoms have one to three valence electrons. These valence electrons are easily removed. When an atom loses electrons, it becomes positively charged because the number of positively charged protons is now greater than the number of negatively charged electrons. As an example, think about sodium.

▶ **Losing Electrons to Form a Cation** Sodium belongs to Group 1A. A sodium atom can lose one electron to form a cation with a charge of 1+. The sodium ion is positive because once the electron is lost, the number of protons (11) is greater than the number of electrons (10). Sodium atoms become sodium ions in a sodium vapor lamp. This kind of lamp is shown in the photo to the left.

▶ **Representing Ionization** Formation of an ion is called ionization. You can show the ionization by writing the complete electron configuration of the atom and of the ion formed.

$$\text{Na}\ \ 1s^22s^22p^63s^1 \xrightarrow{-e^-} \text{Na}^+\ \ 1s^2\underbrace{2s^22p^6}_{\text{octet}}$$

Notice that the electron configuration of the sodium ion ($1s^2 2s^2 2p^6$) is the same as the electron configuration of a neon atom.

$$\text{Ne}\ \ 1s^2\underbrace{2s^22p^6}_{\text{octet}}$$

The diagrams below help illustrate this point.

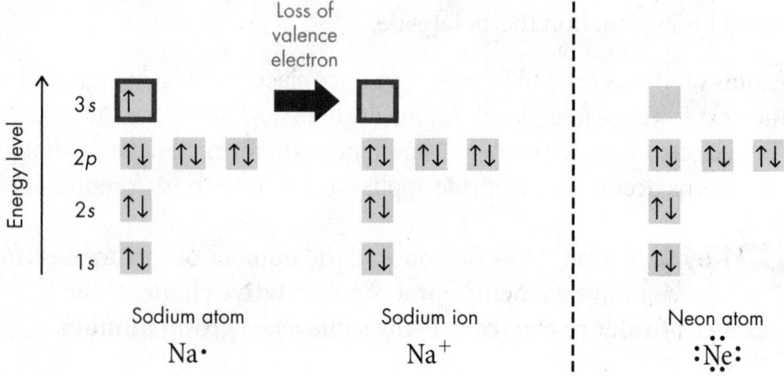

Both the sodium ion and the neon atom have eight valence electrons. Using electron dot structures, you can show the ionization more simply.

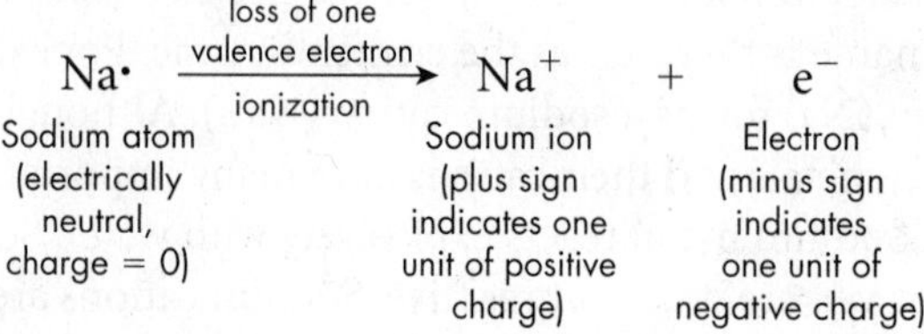

Group 2A Cations Magnesium belongs to Group 2A of the periodic table, so magnesium atoms have two valence electrons. A magnesium atom can lose both valence electrons to form a cation with a charge of 2+. This cation has the same electron configuration as a neon atom.

$$\cdot Mg\cdot \xrightarrow{\text{loss of two valence electrons}} Mg^{2+} + 2e^-$$

·Mg·		Mg^{2+}	+	$2e^-$
Magnesium atom (electrically neutral, charge = 0)		Magnesium ion (2+ indicates two units of positive charge)		Electrons (2 in front of e^- indicates two units of negative charge)

The figure on the right lists the cations formed by metals in Groups 1A and 2A. Cations of Group 1A elements always have a charge of 1+. Cations of Group 2A elements always have a charge of 2+.

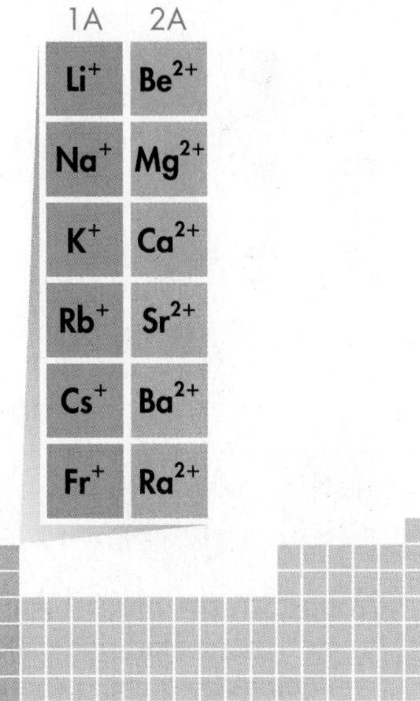

Groups 1A and 2A Cations Cations of Group 1A elements have a charge of 1+. Cations of Group 2A elements have a charge of 2+.

Transition Metal Cations The charges of cations of the transition metals may vary. An iron atom, for example, may lose two electrons to form the Fe^{2+} cation. Alternatively, it may lose three electrons to form the Fe^{3+} cation.

▶ **Octet Rule Exceptions** Some ions formed by transition metals do not have noble gas electron configurations. They are exceptions to the octet rule. Copper is one exception to the rule. To achieve the structure of argon, the noble gas before copper, a copper atom would have to lose 11 electrons. To acquire the electron configuration of krypton, the noble gas after copper, a copper atom would have to gain seven electrons. Ions with charges of three or more are not common. Thus, copper does not form a noble-gas configuration when forming an ion.

▶ **Pseudo Noble Gas Electron Configuration** A copper atom may not be able to attain noble-gas configuration, but it can still form a cation. If a copper atom loses its $4s^1$ electron, as shown below, the copper cation has 18 electrons in the highest occupied energy level. All of the orbitals are filled. So it is relatively stable. Such a configuration is known as a pseudo noble-gas electron configuration. Other elements that act in a similar way are found to the right of the transition metal block of the periodic table.

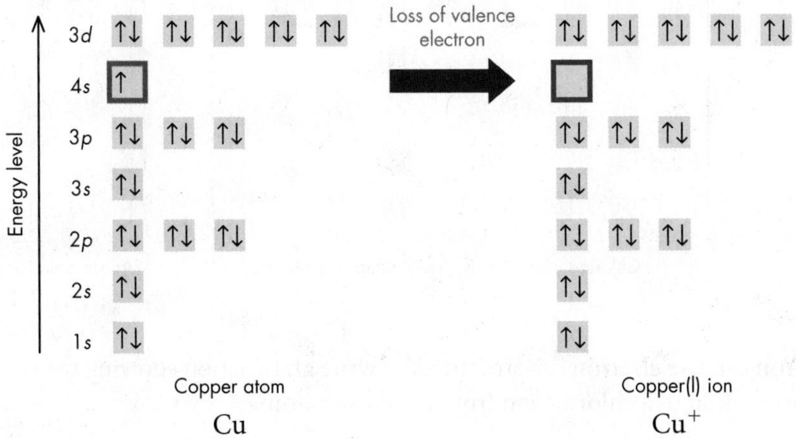

Key Question How are cations formed? **A positively charged ion, or a cation, is produced when an atom loses one or more valence electrons.**

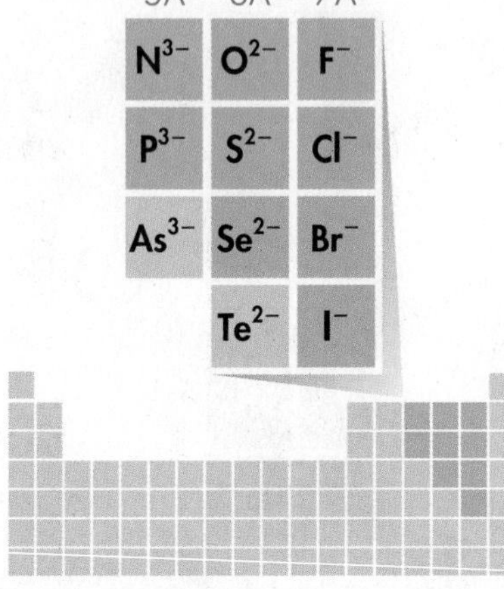

Groups 5A, 6A, and 7A Anions
Atoms of nonmetals and metalloids form anions by gaining enough valence electrons to attain the electron configuration of the nearest noble gas.

Formation of Anions

An anion is an atom or molecule with a negative charge. An anion forms when an atom gains one or more electrons. When an atom gains electrons, it becomes negatively charged because the number of negatively charged electrons is greater than the number of positively charged protons. The name of an anion of a nonmetallic element is *not* the same as the element name. The name of the anion ends in *-ide*. A chlorine atom (Cl) forms a chloride anion (Cl^-), and an oxygen atom (O) forms an oxide anion (O^{2-}). The figure on the left shows some anions formed by elements in Groups 5A, 6A, and 7A. The table lists some common anions.

Some Common Anions		
Name	**Symbol**	**Charge**
Fluoride	F^-	1−
Chloride	Cl^-	1−
Bromide	Br^-	1−
Iodide	I^-	1−
Oxide	O^{2-}	2−
Sulfide	S^{2-}	2−
Nitride	N^{3-}	3−
Phosphide	P^{3-}	3−

Gaining Electrons to Form an Anion Atoms of nonmetallic elements have relatively full valence shells. For example, chlorine belongs in Group 7A and has seven valence electrons. Such atoms form noble gas electron configurations by gaining electrons instead of losing them.

Representing Ionization A gain of one electron gives a chlorine atom an octet and converts a chlorine atom into a chloride ion.

$$\text{Cl} \quad 1s^22s^22p^63s^23p^5 \xrightarrow{+e^-} \text{Cl}^- \quad 1s^22s^22p^6\underbrace{3s^23p^6}_{\text{octet}}$$

The chloride ion has a single negative charge. Notice that the electron configuration of the chloride ion ($1s^2 2s^2 2p^6 3s^2 3p^6$) is the same as that of an argon atom.

$$\text{Ar} \quad 1s^22s^22p^6\underbrace{3s^23p^6}_{\text{octet}}$$

Chlorine atoms need one more valence electron to get the electron configuration of the nearest noble gas. The diagrams below show how both the chloride ion and the argon atom have an octet of electrons in their highest occupied energy levels.

Gain of valence electron

Energy level: 3p, 3s, 2p, 2s, 1s

Chlorine atom :Cl·
Chloride ion :Cl:⁻
Argon atom :Ar:

You can use electron dot structures to write an equation showing the formation of a chloride ion from a chlorine atom.

$$:\!\ddot{\underset{..}{\text{Cl}}}\cdot \;+\; e^- \xrightarrow{\text{gain of one valence electron}} :\!\ddot{\underset{..}{\text{Cl}}}\!:^-$$

Chlorine atom — Electron — Chloride ion

Examples of Anions Atoms of nonmetals and some metalloids form anions. Anions of chlorine and other halogens are called **halide ions.** All halogen atoms have seven valence electrons and need to gain only one electron to get the electron configuration of a noble gas. Thus, all halide ions (F^-, Cl^-, Br^-, and I^-) have a charge of 1−. The seawater in the photo contains many different ions. Most of the anions are chloride ions.

Oxygen is in Group 6A, and an oxygen atom has six valence electrons. An oxygen atom gets the electron configuration of neon by gaining two electrons, as shown below.

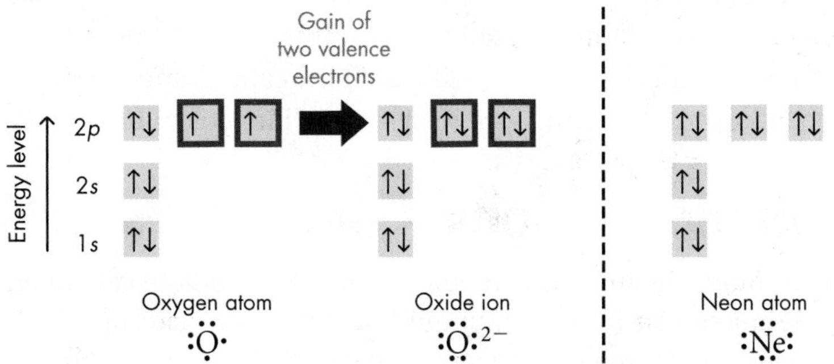

The oxide anion (O^{2-}) that forms when oxygen gains two electrons has a charge of 2−. You can write the equation for the formation of oxide anions by using electron dot structures.

$$:\ddot{\underset{..}{O}}\cdot + 2e^- \longrightarrow :\ddot{\underset{..}{O}}:^{2-}$$

Key Question How are anions formed? **An anion is produced when an atom gains one or more valence electrons.**

Ions in Seawater
Chloride (Cl^-), sodium (Na^+), magnesium (Mg^{2+}), calcium (Ca^{2+}), and potassium (K^+) ions are abundant in seawater.

halide ion an anion that forms when a halogen atom gains a valence electron

ROOT WORD

The words *halide* and *halogen* use the root word *hals*, which means "salt" in Greek. Halogens, found in Group 7A, form halide ions. When they form compounds, halide ions form salts.

7.1 LessonCheck

Key Concept Check

1. **Explain** How can you determine the number of valence electrons in an atom of a representative element?
2. **Describe** How do cations form?
3. **Describe** How do anions form?

Vocabulary Check *Choose a highlighted word from the lesson to complete each sentence correctly.*

4. An electron in the highest energy level of an element's atoms is called a(n) ________.
5. According to the ________, atoms gain or lose electrons to get the electron configuration of a noble gas.

Think Critically

6. **Make Generalizations** Atoms of which elements tend to gain electrons? Atoms of which elements tend to lose electrons?
7. **Apply Concepts** How many valence electrons are in a potassium atom? An oxygen atom?
8. **Infer** Identify the charge of the ion formed when a potassium atom loses one electron.

CHEMISTRY & YOU

9. Fool's gold is composed of iron(II) cations (Fe^{2+}), and disulfide anions (S_2^{2-}). Write the electron configuration of the Fe^{2+} ion. (Hint: See page 182.)

7.2 Ionic Bonds and Ionic Compounds

CHEMISTRY & YOU

Q: Where does table salt come from? People have used sodium chloride, or table salt, for thousands of years. It adds flavor and helps preserve food. In some countries, people farm salt from the evaporation of seawater. In other countries, salt is mined from rock deposits deep underground. In this lesson, you will learn how cations and anions combine to form stable compounds such as sodium chloride.

Key Questions

What is the electrical charge of an ionic compound?

What are three properties of ionic compounds?

BUILD Vocabulary

ionic compound a compound made up of cations and anions

ionic bond the bond that holds ions in ionic compounds together

chemical formula an expression of the number of atoms of each element in the smallest representative unit of a substance

formula unit the lowest whole number ratio of ions in an ionic compound

USING PRIOR KNOWLEDGE

You are probably already familiar with several chemical formulas. NaCl is the chemical formula for table salt, and H_2O is the chemical formula for water.

Formation of Ionic Compounds

Sodium chloride is an ionic compound made up of sodium cations and chloride anions. An **ionic compound** is a compound made up of cations and anions. Ionic compounds are electrically neutral. The total positive charge of the cations equals the total negative charge of the anions.

Ionic Bonds Ions are examples of charged particles. Charged particles exert forces on one another. These forces are called electrostatic forces. Like charges repel; opposite charges attract. Anions and cations have opposite charges, so they attract one another. The electrostatic forces that hold ions together in ionic compounds are called **ionic bonds.**

Sodium chloride provides an example of how ionic bonds are formed. Think about the reaction between a sodium atom and a chlorine atom. The sodium atom has a single valence electron that it can lose. The chlorine atom has seven valence electrons. Therefore, chlorine can gain one electron. When sodium and chlorine react to form a compound, the sodium atom transfers its one valence electron to the chlorine atom. So sodium and chlorine atoms combine in a one-to-one ratio, and both resulting ions have stable octets.

$$\text{Na}\cdot \quad \cdot\ddot{\underset{\cdot\cdot}{\text{Cl}}}: \longrightarrow \text{Na}^+ \quad :\ddot{\underset{\cdot\cdot}{\text{Cl}}}:^-$$

$$1s^22s^22p^6\,3s^1 \quad 1s^22s^22p^63s^23p^5 \qquad 1s^22s^22p^6\ (\text{octet}) \qquad 1s^22s^22p^63s^23p^6\ (\text{octet})$$

$$\text{Ne} \qquad \text{Ar}$$

$$1s^22s^22p^6\ (\text{octet}) \qquad 1s^22s^22p^63s^23p^6\ (\text{octet})$$

Note how each ion obtains a noble-gas electron configuration. The electron configuration of the sodium cation is the same as that of a neon atom. The electron configuration of the chloride anion is the same as that of an argon atom.

The ratio of cations to anions in an ionic compound is not always 1:1. For example, the elements magnesium and chlorine react to form the ionic compound magnesium chloride. Each magnesium atom has two valence electrons to lose. Each chlorine atom has seven valence electrons and readily gains one additional electron. So, when magnesium and chlorine react, two chlorine atoms combine with each magnesium atom.

Go online to learn more about ionic bonds. CONCEPTS IN ACTION

Formula Units The ionic compound sodium chloride is made up of equal numbers of sodium cations (Na^+) and chloride anions (Cl^-). You can describe the composition of substances by writing chemical formulas. A **chemical formula** shows the numbers of atoms of each element in the smallest representative unit of a substance. For example, NaCl is the chemical formula for sodium chloride.

Ionic compounds do not exist as single separate units. Instead, they exist as collections of positively and negatively charged ions arranged in repeating patterns. The figure below shows how sodium cations and chloride anions are arranged in an orderly three-dimensional pattern in sodium chloride.

The chemical formula of an ionic compound refers to a ratio known as the formula unit. A **formula unit** is the lowest whole-number ratio of ions in an ionic compound. For sodium chloride, the lowest whole number ratio of the ions is 1:1 (one Na^+ ion to one Cl^- ion). This means the formula unit for sodium chloride is NaCl. Although ionic charges are not shown in a formula unit, you should always interpret them as a ratio of oppositely charged ions.

In magnesium chloride, the ratio of magnesium cations to chloride anions is 1:2 (one Mg^{2+} ion to two Cl^- ions), so the formula unit is $MgCl_2$. Like sodium chloride, magnesium chloride is electrically neutral.

Key Question What is the electrical charge of an ionic compound? **Ionic compounds are composed of ions. However, the compounds are electrically neutral.**

Sodium Chloride Crystals

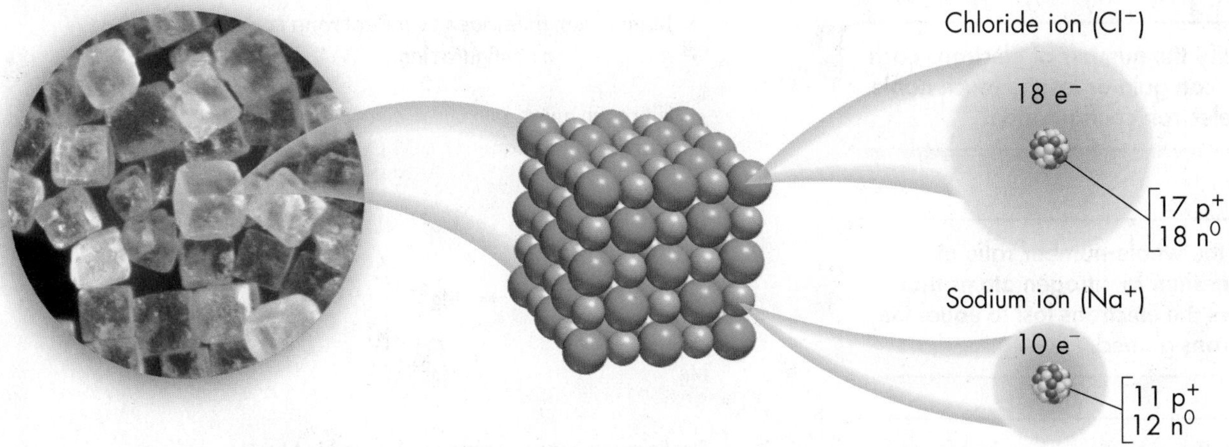

Crystals of sodium chloride

Na^+ ions and Cl^- ions are arranged in an orderly pattern and form a crystal.

Because there are the same number of anions as cations, sodium chloride (NaCl) is electrically neutral.

CHEMISTRY TUTORIAL

Sample Problem 7.1

Predicting Formulas of Ionic Compounds

Use electron dot structures to predict the formulas of the ionic compounds formed from the following elements:

a. potassium and oxygen **b.** magnesium and nitrogen

❶ Analyze **Identify the relevant concepts.** Atoms of metals lose valence electrons when forming an ionic compound. Atoms of nonmetals gain electrons. The final product is electrically neutral.

❷ Solve **Apply the concepts to this problem.**

Draw the electron dot structure of the starting elements.

a. K· and ·Ö: (oxygen with 6 dots)

Identify the number of electrons each atom can gain or lose to reach noble gas electron configuration.

K· Potassium must lose one electron to reach noble gas electron configuration.

·Ö: Oxygen must gain two electrons to reach noble gas configuration.

Find the whole-number ratio of potassium to oxygen atoms that allows the electrons lost to equal the electrons gained.

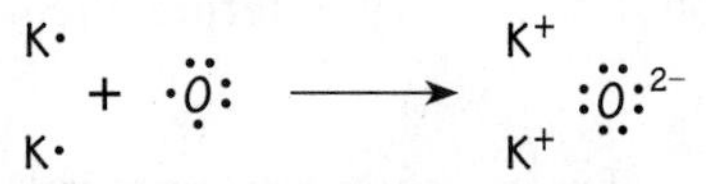

K· + K· + ·Ö: ⟶ K^+ K^+ $:\ddot{O}:^{2-}$

Write the ratio as a chemical formula.

The formula of the compound formed is K_2O.

Draw the electron dot structure of the starting elements.

b. Mg and ·N: (magnesium with 2 dots, nitrogen with 5 dots)

Identify the number of electrons each atom can gain or lose to reach noble gas electron configuration.

Mg Magnesium must lose two electrons to reach noble gas electron configuration.

·N: Nitrogen must gain three electrons to reach noble gas configuration.

Find the whole-number ratio of magnesium to nitrogen atoms that allows the electrons lost to equal the electrons gained.

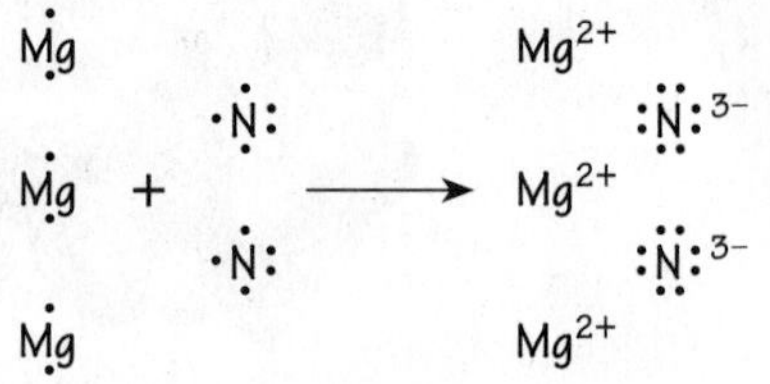

Mg Mg Mg + ·N: ·N: ⟶ Mg^{2+} Mg^{2+} Mg^{2+} $:\ddot{N}:^{3-}$ $:\ddot{N}:^{3-}$

Write the ratio as a chemical formula.

The formula of the compound formed is Mg_3N_2.

BUILD Math Skills

Recognizing Patterns What do most ionic compounds have in common? Atoms gain or lose electrons to achieve a noble-gas configuration. Noble gases have stable electron configurations. Stability is related to the number of valence electrons. Here are the electron dot structures for two noble gases.

Neon atom	Argon atom
:N̈e:	:Är:

How many electrons do the atoms of sodium and oxygen need gain or lose to have stable electron configurations?

Sodium atom	Oxygen atom
Na·	:Ö·

Go to your Chemistry Skills and Math Workbook for more practice problems.

Practice Problems

10. Use electron dot structures to determine the formula of the ionic compound formed when potassium reacts with iodine.

❶ Analyze Identify the relevant concepts.

❷ Solve Apply the concepts to this problem.

TO GET YOU STARTED...

Here is the electron dot structure for potassium:

K· Potassium must lose one electron to reach noble gas electron configuration.

11. Use electron dot structures to determine the formula of the ionic compound formed when lithium reacts with fluorine.

Hint: Find each element on the periodic table to determine the number of valence electrons.

12. What is the formula of the ionic compound composed of calcium cations and chloride anions?

13. Challenge Use electron dot structures to determine the formula of the ionic compound formed when aluminum reacts with oxygen.

Properties of Ionic Compounds

Most ionic compounds are crystalline solids at room temperature. The ions in such crystals are arranged in repeating three-dimensional patterns. In solid sodium chloride, each sodium ion is surrounded by six chloride ions, and each chloride ion is surrounded by six sodium ions. In this arrangement, each ion is attracted strongly to each of its neighbors. The large attractive forces mean that crystalline solids have a very stable structure. The stable structure of NaCl means that a lot of heat energy is needed to change the compound from its solid to its liquid form. The melting point of NaCl is about 800°C. Ionic compounds generally have high melting points. The photos below show the crystals of some other ionic compounds.

Crystalline Solids
The beauty of crystalline solids, such as these, comes from the orderly arrangement of their component ions.

Fluorite (CaF_2)

Grossularite ($Ca_3Al_2(SiO_4)_3$)

Aragonite ($CaCO_3$)

Barite ($BaSO_4$)

Wulfenite ($PbMoO_4$)

Beryl ($Be_3Al_2(SiO_3)_6$)

Hematite (Fe_2O_3)

Cinnabar (HgS)

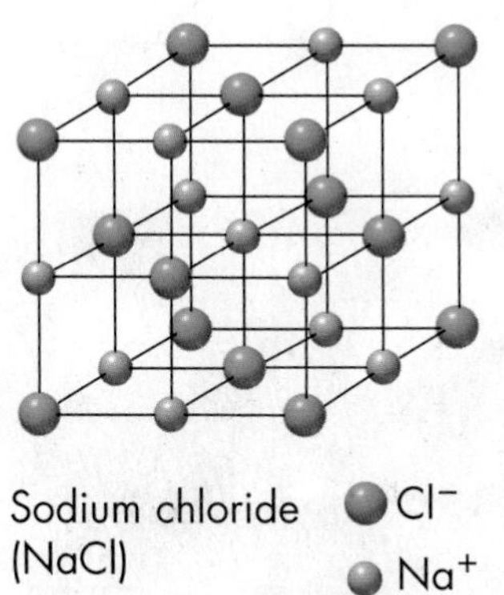

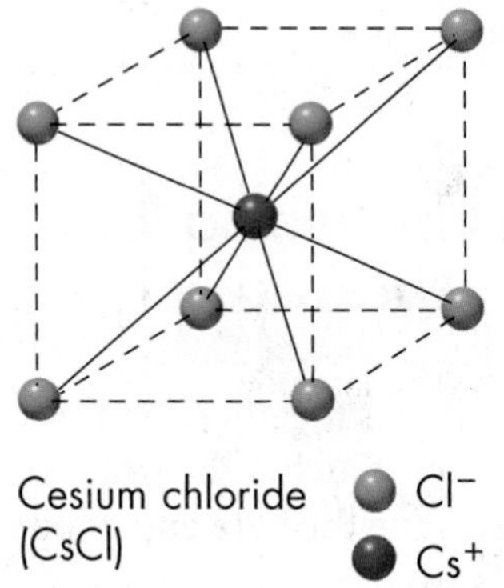

Comparing NaCl and CsCl Sodium chloride and cesium chloride both form cubic crystals, but the arrangement of ions within each crystal is different.

See crystal structures of ionic compounds online.
KINETIC
ART

The crystal structure of an ionic compound is determined by the arrangement of its ions. The figure above shows the three-dimensional arrangement of ions in NaCl and in CsCl. In both NaCl and CsCl, the ions are in one-to-one ratios. However, the ions are arranged differently in each compound.

Another characteristic property of ionic compounds is that they can conduct an electric current when melted or dissolved in water. When sodium chloride is melted or dissolved, the crystal structure breaks down and ions are free to move. Look at the figure below. If a voltage is applied across the molten salt, cations move to the negative electrode and anions move to the positive electrode. This movement of ions allows electric current to flow between the electrodes through an external wire. For a similar reason, ionic compounds also conduct electric current if they are dissolved in water.

Key Question What are three properties of ionic compounds? **Ionic compounds are crystalline solids at room temperature, have high melting points, and can conduct an electric current when melted or dissolved in water.**

Molten NaCl Sodium chloride melts at about 800°C. If a voltage is applied to molten NaCl, positive sodium ions move to the negative electrode, and negative chloride ions move to the positive electrode.

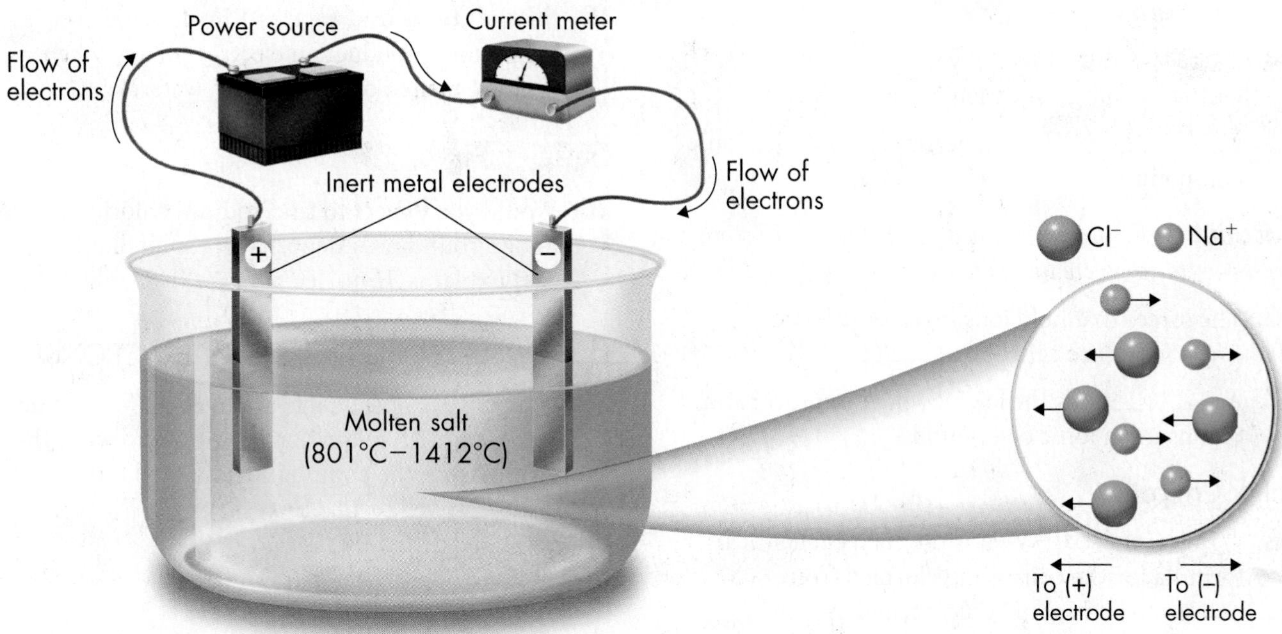

Quick Lab

Purpose To show that ions in solution conduct an electric current

Materials
- 3 D-cell batteries
- masking tape
- 2 30 cm lengths of bell wire with ends scraped bare
- clear plastic cup
- distilled water
- tap water
- vinegar (acetic acid, $C_2H_4O_2$)
- table sugar (sucrose, $C_{12}H_{22}O_{11}$)
- table salt (sodium chloride, NaCl)
- baking soda (sodium hydrogen carbonate, $NaHCO_3$)

Solutions Containing Ions

Procedure

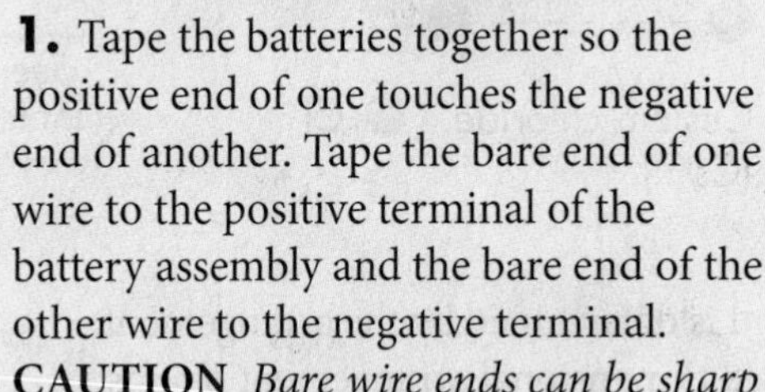

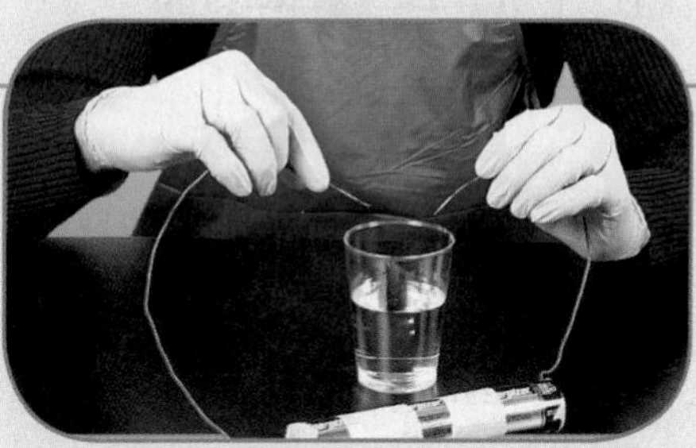

1. Tape the batteries together so the positive end of one touches the negative end of another. Tape the bare end of one wire to the positive terminal of the battery assembly and the bare end of the other wire to the negative terminal. **CAUTION** *Bare wire ends can be sharp and scratch skin. Handle with care.*

2. Half fill the cup with distilled water. Hold the bare ends of the wires close together in the water.

3. Look for the production of bubbles. They are a sign that the solution conducts electric current.

4. Repeat Steps 2 and 3 with tap water, vinegar, and concentrated solutions of table sugar, table salt, and baking soda.

Analyze and Conclude

1. Observe Which samples produced bubbles of gas? Which samples did not produce bubbles of gas?

2. Draw Conclusions Which samples conducted an electric current? What do these samples have in common?

3. Predict Would you expect the same results if you used only one battery? If you used six batteries? Explain your answers.

7.2 LessonCheck

Key Concept Check

14. **Describe** How can you describe the electrical charge of an ionic compound?

15. **Identify** What properties characterize ionic compounds?

Vocabulary Check *Choose a highlighted word from the lesson to complete the sentence correctly.*

16. The forces that hold ions together in ionic compounds are called ________.

17. A ________ is the lowest whole-number ratio of ions in an ionic compound.

Think Critically

18. **Apply Concepts** What is the correct chemical formula for the compounds formed from potassium and sulfur? Calcium and oxygen?

19. **Relate Cause and Effect** Why do ionic compounds conduct an electric current when they are melted or dissolved in water?

CHEMISTRY & YOU

20. Would you expect to find sodium chloride in underground rock deposits as a solid, liquid, or gas? Explain. (*Hint:* See page 190.)

BIGIDEA BONDING AND INTERACTIONS

21. Which pairs of elements are likely to form ionic compounds? Explain your choices and write the formulas for the compounds that will form:

a. Cl, Br
b. K, He
c. Li, Cl
d. I, Na

7.3 Bonding in Metals

CHEMISTRY & YOU

Q: What are some properties that are unique to metals? Decorative fences are often made of a metal called wrought iron. Wrought iron is a form of iron that contains trace amounts of carbon. It is tough, malleable, ductile, and corrosion-resistant; and it melts at a very high temperature. These properties are due to the way that metal ions form bonds with one another.

Key Questions

How can you model the valence electrons of metal atoms?

Why are alloys important?

metallic bond the force of attraction that holds free valence electrons and metal cations together

USING PRIOR KNOWLEDGE

There are three main types of bonds between atoms: ionic bonds, metallic bonds, and covalent bonds. You learned about ionic bonds in the previous section. You will learn about covalent bonds in the next chapter.

Metallic Bonds and Metallic Properties

Metals are not made up of neutral atoms. Instead, metals consist of closely packed cations and loosely held valence electrons. The valence electrons of atoms in a pure metal can be modeled as a sea of electrons. That is, the valence electrons can move freely from one part of the metal to another. **Metallic bonds** are the forces of attraction between the free-floating valence electrons and the positively charged metal ions. These bonds hold metals together.

Properties of Metals The motion of electrons in metals explains many physical properties of metals. Metals are ductile. This means that metals can be drawn into wires, as shown in the figure below. Metals are also malleable, which means that they can be hammered or pressed into shapes. The free-floating valence electrons give metals their ductility and malleability. The positive charges of the metal cations do not repel each other because they are insulated by the negative charges of the free-floating valence electrons. Metals are also good conductors of electric current because electrons flow freely in the metal.

Comparing Metals and Ionic Crystals

A metal rod can be forced through a narrow opening to produce wire.

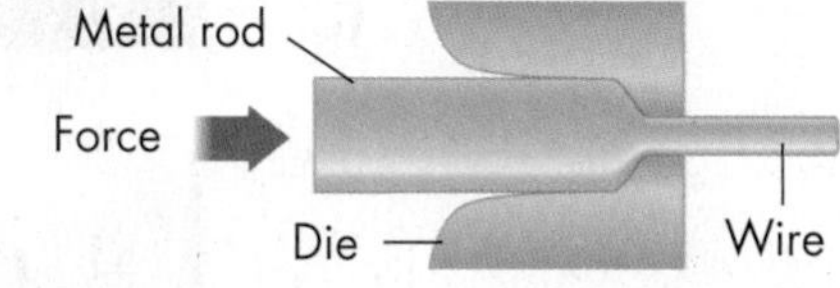

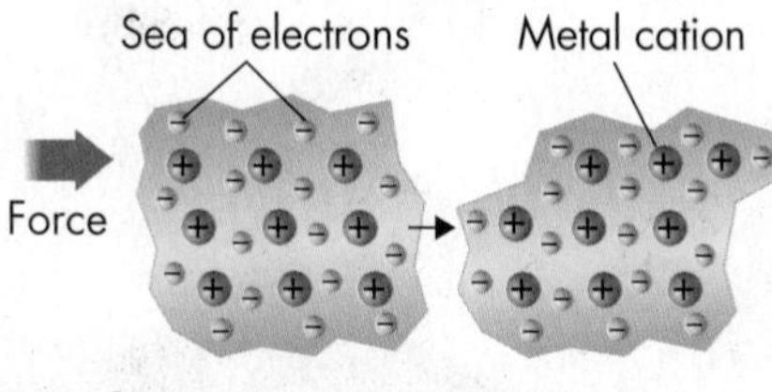

Metal The metal changes shape but remains in one piece.

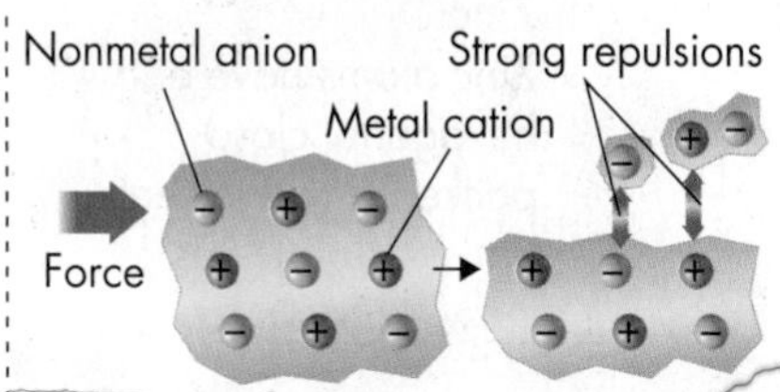

Ionic crystal An ionic crystal would shatter instead.

Go online to review the properties of metals.

BUILD Understanding

Two-Column Chart Draw a two-column chart. In the left column, write the properties of metals. In the right column, write an explanation of how the property is caused by the free-floating electrons of metals.

Crystalline Structure of Metals You may be surprised to learn that metals are crystalline. In fact, metal atoms are arranged in very compact and orderly patterns. The figures below show three common arrangements of metal atoms.

The metallic element chromium crystallizes in a body-centered cubic pattern. In this structure, each atom has eight neighbors. Gold forms a face-centered cubic structure. In this arrangement, every atom has twelve neighbors. In a hexagonal close-packed arrangement, every atom also has twelve neighbors. However, unlike the face-centered cubic structure, the atoms form a hexagonal shape. Zinc has a hexagonal close-packed crystal structure. Other examples include magnesium and cadmium.

Key Question How can you model the valence electrons of metal atoms? **The valence electrons in a pure metal can be modeled as a sea of electrons.**

Chromium
Chromium atoms have a body-centered cubic arrangement.

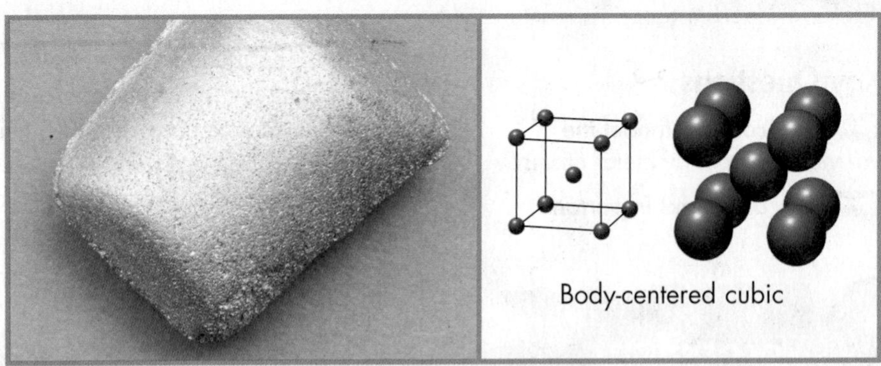
Body-centered cubic

Gold
Gold atoms have a face-centered cubic arrangement.

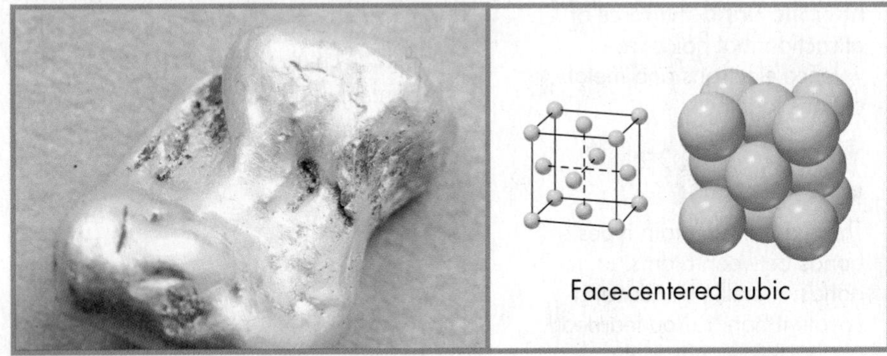
Face-centered cubic

Zinc
Zinc atoms have a hexagonal close-packed arrangement.

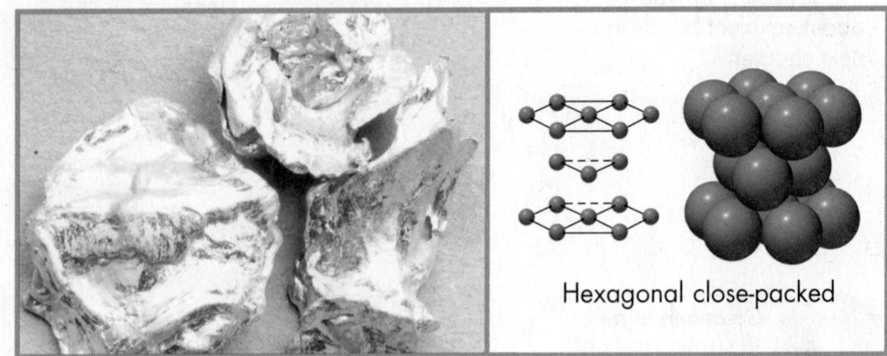
Hexagonal close-packed

Alloys

You use metallic items, such as spoons and forks, every day. Very few of these objects are made out of a single kind of metal. Instead, most of the metals you use are alloys. **Alloys** are mixtures of two or more elements, at least one of which is a metal. Brass, for example, is an alloy of copper and zinc. Alloys are important because their properties are often superior to those of their component elements. Bronze is another alloy. Bronze is usually made up of seven parts copper to one part tin. Bronze is harder than copper and is easier to cast into molds. For this reason, bronze is often used to make coins.

The most important alloys today are steels. Most steels are made of iron, carbon, and small amounts of metals, such as chromium and manganese. Steels have many useful properties, such as corrosion resistance, ductility, hardness, and toughness. Below are two items made of common alloys. Read the Build Connections at right to learn about another common alloy.

Alloys can form from their component atoms in different ways. If the atoms of the components in an alloy are about the same size, they can replace each other in the crystal. If the atomic sizes are quite different, the smaller atoms can fit into the spaces between the larger atoms. In steels, for example, carbon atoms occupy the spaces between the iron atoms.

Key Question Why are alloys important? **Alloys are important because their properties are often superior to those of their components.**

Common Alloys

alloy a mixture of two or more elements, at least one of which is a metal

WORD ORIGINS

The word *alloy* is based on the Latin word *alligare,* which means "to mix things together."

BUILD Connections

Sterling silver is an alloy. It is 92.5% silver and 7.5% copper. Sterling silver is harder and more durable than pure silver, yet it is still soft enough to be made into jewelry.

CHEMISTRY & YOU: EVERYDAY MATTER

Ionic Crystals

Crystals of ionic compounds, such as sodium chloride, can be grown by a process called nucleation. During nucleation, the ionic compound that is to be crystallized is dissolved in a solvent, such as water. In the dissolution process, the positive and negative ions break away from each other. As the solvent is removed, the ions join together again to form a repeating three-dimensional pattern. Sodium chloride has a cubic crystal structure, but different ionic compounds form crystals with different shapes.

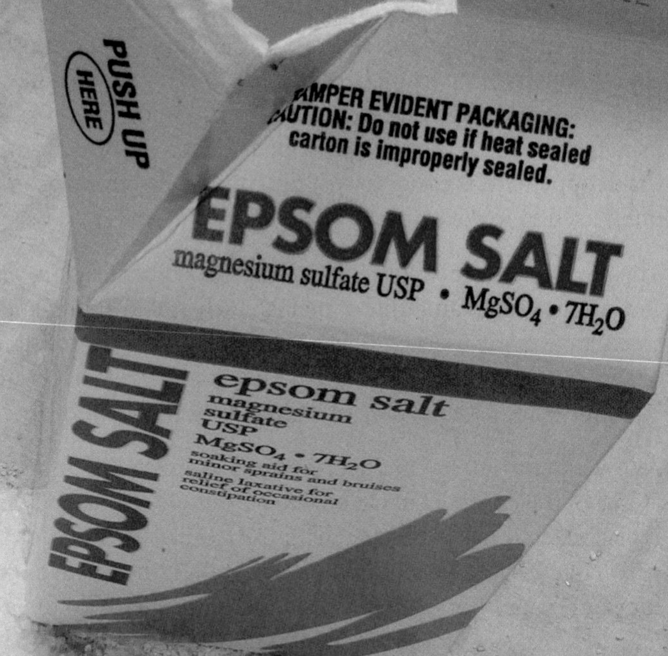

Think About It

1. Identify Epsom salts are magnesium sulfate ($MgSO_4$) crystals. A magnesium sulfate formula unit consists of a magnesium cation and a sulfate (SO_4^{2-}) anion. What is the charge on the magnesium cation?

2. Form a Hypothesis What factors do you think affect crystal growth during nucleation? Form a hypothesis identifying two possible factors.

7.3 LessonCheck

Key Concept Check

22. Describe How do chemists model the valence electrons of metal atoms?

23. Explain Why are alloys more useful than pure metals?

Think Critically

24. Explain What do the terms *ductile* and *malleable* mean?

25. Relate Cause and Effect Why is it possible to bend metals but not ionic crystals?

26. Describe Name two widely used alloys and describe some of their uses.

27. How are metals and ionic compounds different? How are they similar? (Hint: See page 193.)

BIGIDEA BONDING AND INTERACTIONS

28. Describe how the sea-of-electrons model is used to explain the physical properties of metals.

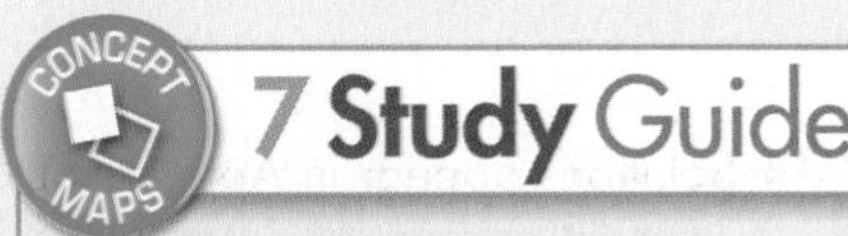

BIGIDEA
BONDING AND INTERACTIONS

Atoms form positive ions (cations) by losing valence electrons and form negative ions (anions) by gaining valence electrons. The electrostatic forces between the oppositely charged ions hold the cations and anions together in an ionic compound. Ionic compounds generally have high melting points and can conduct an electric current in solution and in the molten state. Metals are made up of closely packed cations surrounded by a sea of electrons. The sea-of-electrons model explains why metals are good conductors of electric current and why they are ductile and malleable.

7.1 Ions

For a representative element, the number of valence electrons is the same as its group number.

A positively charged ion, or cation, is produced when an atom loses one or more valence electrons.

An anion is produced when an atom gains one or more valence electrons.

- valence electron (180)
- electron dot structure (181)
- octet rule (181)
- halide ion (185)

7.2 Ionic Bonds and Ionic Compounds

Ionic compounds are composed of ions. However, the compounds are electrically neutral.

Ionic compounds are crystalline solids at room temperature, have high melting points, and can conduct an electric current when melted or dissolved in water.

- ionic compound (186)
- ionic bond (186)
- chemical formula (187)
- formula unit (187)

7.3 Bonding in Metals

The valence electrons of atoms in a pure metal can be modeled as a sea of electrons.

Alloys are important because their properties are often superior to those of their component elements.

- metallic bond (193)
- alloy (195)

7 Assessment

★ Solutions appear in Appendix D

Lesson by Lesson

7.1 Ions

29. What is a valence electron?

★30. To which group in the periodic table does each of the following elements belong? How many valence electrons do atoms of each element have?

a. nitrogen
b. lithium
c. phosphorus
d. barium
e. bromine
f. carbon

31. Write electron dot structures for each of the following elements:

a. Cl
b. S
c. Al
d. Li

32. Describe two ways that an ion forms from an atom.

★33. How many electrons must an atom of each element lose to attain a noble gas electron configuration?

a. Ca
b. Al
c. Li
d. Ba

34. Why do nonmetal atoms tend to form anions when they react to form compounds?

★35. How many electrons must be gained by each of the following atoms to achieve a stable electron configuration?

a. N
b. S
c. Cl
d. P

★36. What is the formula of the ions formed when atoms of the following elements gain or lose valence electrons and attain noble gas configurations?

a. sulfur
b. sodium
c. fluorine
d. phosphorus

7.2 Ionic Bonds and Ionic Compounds

37. Define an ionic bond.

38. Explain why ionic compounds are electrically neutral.

★39. Which of the following pairs of atoms would you expect to combine chemically to form an ionic compound?

a. Li and S
b. O and S
c. Al and O
d. F and Cl
e. I and K
f. H and N

40. How can you represent the composition of an ionic compound?

★41. Identify the ions that form each ionic compound.

a. calcium fluoride, CaF_2
b. aluminum bromide, $AlBr_3$
c. lithium oxide, Li_2O
d. aluminum sulfide, Al_2S_3
e. potassium nitride, K_3N

42. Write the formulas for the ions in the following compounds:

a. KCl
b. BaS
c. $MgBr_2$
d. Li_2O

43. Why are most ionic substances brittle?

44. Explain why molten $MgCl_2$ conducts an electric current while crystalline $MgCl_2$ does not.

7.3 Bonding in Metals

★45. How can you describe the arrangement of atoms in metals?

46. Explain briefly why metals are good conductors of electric current.

★47. Name the three crystal arrangements of closely packed metal atoms. Give an example of a metal that crystallizes in each arrangement.

48. Name some alloys that you have used or seen.

49. Explain why the properties of all steels are not identical.

Understand Concepts

*50. In terms of electrons, why does a cation have a positive charge?

51. The spheres below represent the relative diameters of atoms or ions. Rearrange the sequences in (a) and (b) so the relative sizes of the particles correspond to the increasing size of the particles as shown in the illustration.

a. oxygen atom, oxide ion, sulfur atom, sulfide ion
b. sodium atom, sodium ion, potassium atom, potassium ion

*52. Write the name and symbol of the ion formed when
a. a sulfur atom gains two electrons.
b. an aluminum atom loses three electrons.
c. a nitrogen atom gains three electrons.
d. a calcium atom loses two electrons.

*53. Write electron configurations for the following atoms and ions, and comment on the result.
a. Ar
b. Cl^-
c. S^{2-}
d. P^{3-}

54. If ionic compounds are composed of charged particles (ions), why isn't every ionic compound either positively or negatively charged?

*55. Which of the following compounds are most likely not ionic?
a. H_2O
b. Na_2O
c. CO_2
d. CaS
e. SO_2
f. NH_3

56. The properties of all samples of brass are not identical. Explain.

Think Critically

*57. **Make Generalizations** What is the relationship between the number of electrons in the valence shells in an electron configuration diagram for an atom and the number of dots in the corresponding electron dot structure?

58. **Interpret Diagrams** How atoms and ions are arranged in crystals is not just dependent on size. The spheres in each atomic window below are identical in size. The windows have exactly the same area. In which window are the spheres more closely packed? Explain your reasoning.

a.
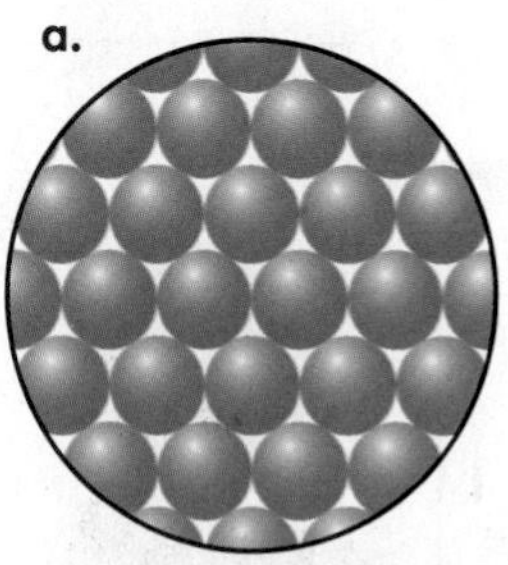

b.
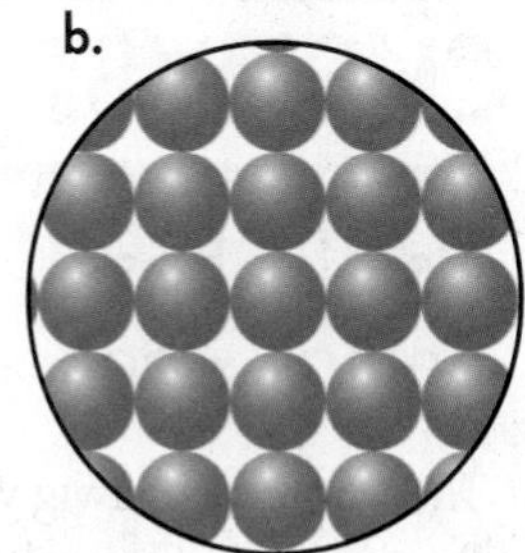

*59. **Compare and Contrast** Describe the similarities and differences between ionic compounds and metals in terms of their physical and chemical characteristics.

FOUNDATIONS Wrap-Up

Observing Crystals

1. **Draw Conclusions** At the beginning of the chapter you looked at table salt and Epsom salt crystals with a magnifying lens. Explain why the crystals looked the way they did.

Concept Check

Now that you've finished studying Chapter 7, answer these questions.

2. What cation and anion make up table salt?
3. Explain why crystals do not all have the same appearance.

Write About Science

60. Compare Describe the formation of a cation that is an exception to the octet rule. In your description, compare the electron configuration of the cation to the electron configurations of the nearest noble gases.

61. Research Go online and research X-ray diffraction crystallography. How are the samples prepared? How are the X-rays generated and detected? How is this technique used to study the structure of crystalline substances?

CHEMYSTERY

It's Not Easy Being Green

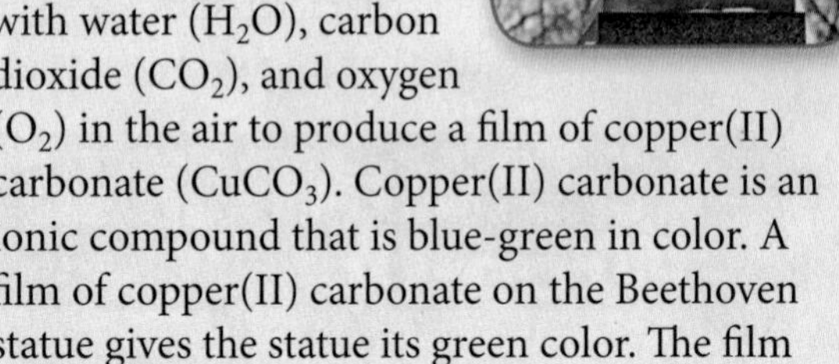

The statue of Ludwig van Beethoven in Central Park is bronze. Bronze is an alloy containing copper and tin.

When bronze is exposed to the elements, it reacts with water (H_2O), carbon dioxide (CO_2), and oxygen (O_2) in the air to produce a film of copper(II) carbonate ($CuCO_3$). Copper(II) carbonate is an ionic compound that is blue-green in color. A film of copper(II) carbonate on the Beethoven statue gives the statue its green color. The film also protects the metal against further corrosion.

***62. Apply Concepts** A copper atom can lose one or two electrons to form a Cu^+ ion or a Cu^{2+} ion, respectively. The charge of the copper ion in $CuCO_3$ is 2+. Write the electron configuration of this cation.

63. Form an Opinion Why do you think bronze is often used to create statues?

64. Connect to the BIGIDEA How are the properties of the copper(II) carbonate film on the statue different from the properties of the bronze beneath the film? Explain how these properties are a result of the type of bonding present.

Cumulative Review

***65.** What physical state(s) can each of the following substances become as you raise its temperature? (See Lesson 2.1 for help.)

a. silver
b. gasoline
c. ice
d. wax

***66.** Classify the following actions as chemical or physical changes. (See Lesson 2.4 for help.)

a. Cookies are baked.
b. A firefly emits light.
c. A figure is carved from wood.
d. Caramel is made from sugar.

67. Round each measurement to the number of significant figures indicated in parentheses. (See Lesson 3.1 for help.)

a. 56.55 g (3)
b. 0.004849 m (2)
c. 1.8072 L (3)
d. 4.007×10^3 mg (2)

68. Determine the number of protons, electrons, and neutrons in each of the three isotopes of oxygen. (See Lesson 4.3 for help.)

***69.** How many orbitals are in the following sublevels? (See Lesson 5.2 for help.)

a. 4*s* sublevel
b. 2*p* sublevel
c. 3*s* sublevel
d. 4*d* sublevel

***70.** A beam of electromagnetic radiation has a wavelength of 500 nm. (See Lesson 5.3 for help.)

a. What is this wavelength in meters?
b. In what region of the spectrum is this?

***71.** Give the symbol of the element and the complete electron configuration of the element found at each location in the periodic table. (See Lesson 6.2 for help.)

a. Group 1A, Period 4
b. Group 3A, Period 3
c. Group 6A, Period 3
d. Group 2A, Period 6

72. Give the name and symbol of two elements that have properties similar to those of potassium. (See Lesson 6.2 for help.)

Standardized Test Prep

For help with answering test questions, go to your Chemistry Skills and Math Workbook.

Tips for Success

Review All the Answer Choices Even if you find an answer that looks correct, continue reading until you have looked at *every* answer. There may be more than one correct response, or one may be better than another. Also, "all of the above" may be a possible answer. If you stop reading as soon as you find an answer that is correct, you won't notice this option.

Select the choice that best answers each question or completes each statement.

1. Which of these is not an ionic compound?
   (A) KF
   (B) SiO_2
   (C) Na_2SO_4
   (D) Na_2O

2. Which statements are correct when barium and oxygen react to form an ionic compound?
   I. Each barium atom loses 2 electrons and forms a cation.
   II. Oxygen atoms form oxide anions (O^{2-}).
   III. The ions are present in a one-to-one ratio in the compound.
   (A) I and II only
   (B) II and III only
   (C) I and III only
   (D) I, II, and III

The lettered choices below refer to Questions 3–6. A lettered choice may be used once, more than once, or not at all.

(A) gains two electrons
(B) loses two electrons
(C) gains three electrons
(D) loses one electron
(E) gains one electron

Which choice describes what likely happens as each of the following elements forms an ion?

3. iodine
4. magnesium
5. cesium
6. phosphorus

7. How many valence electrons does arsenic have?
   (A) 5
   (B) 4
   (C) 3
   (D) 2

8. Which electron configuration represents a nitride ion?
   (A) $1s^2 2s^2 3s^2 4s^2$
   (B) $1s^2 2s^2 2p^6$
   (C) $1s^2 2s^2 2p^3$
   (D) $1s^2$

9. When a bromine atom gains an electron
   (A) a bromide ion is formed.
   (B) the ion formed has a 1– charge.
   (C) the ion formed is an anion.
   (D) all the above are correct.

Use the description and the graph to answer Questions 10–12.

Lattice energy is the energy required to change one mole (6.02×10^{23} formula units) of a crystalline, ionic solid to gaseous ions. The graph below shows the lattice energies for ionic compounds formed between selected alkali metals and halogens.

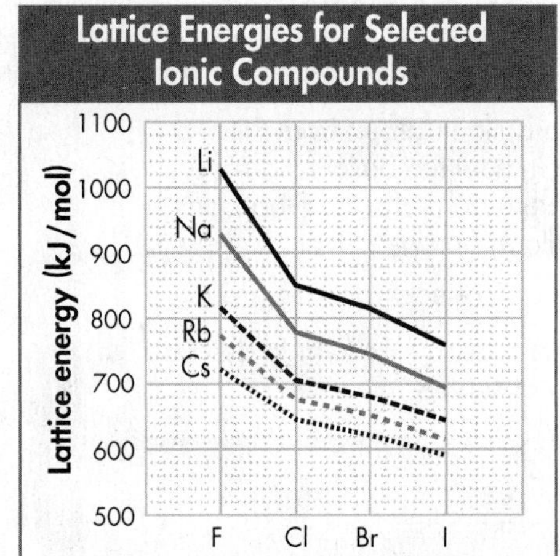

10. For a given alkali metal, what is the trend in lattice energy as the atomic radius of the halogen increases?

11. For a given halogen, what is the trend in lattice energy as the atomic radius of the alkali metal increases?

12. Complete this sentence: "As the atomic radius of either the halogen or the alkali metal increases, the lattice energy ________."

If You Have Trouble With . . .

Question	1	2	3	4	5	6	7	8	9	10	11	12
See Lesson	7.2	7.2	7.1	7.1	7.1	7.1	7.1	7.1	7.1	7.2	7.2	7.2

8 Covalent Bonding

FOUNDATIONS for Learning

Shapes of Molecules

1. Blow up nine round balloons to the same size and then tie them off.
2. Tightly tie the ends of two balloons together with a piece of string. Repeat to form groups of three and four balloons.
3. Hold the two-balloon group from the tied ends. Observe how the balloons arrange themselves. Repeat for the three-balloon and four-balloon groups.
4. Sketch the shape of each balloon group.

Identify Choose a geometric term to describe each shape you observed.

PearsonChem.com

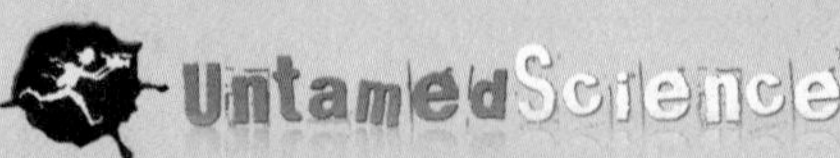

Tag along with the Untamed Science crew to explore how covalent bonding and powder coating can produce a sweet ride.

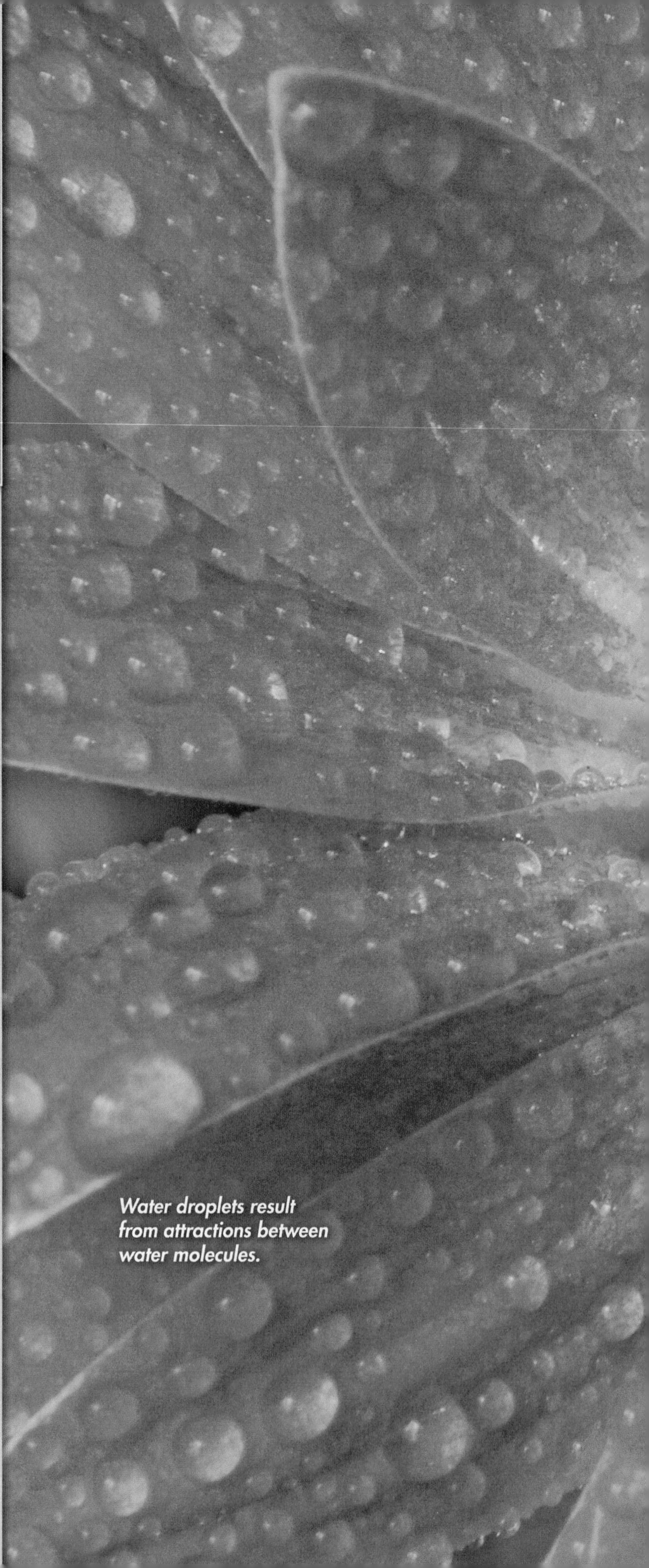

Water droplets result from attractions between water molecules.

BIGIDEA

BONDING AND INTERACTIONS

Essential Questions:

1. *How is the bonding in molecular compounds different from the bonding in ionic compounds?*
2. *How do electrons affect the shape of a molecule?*
3. *Which factors affect the properties of molecules?*

CHEMYSTERY

What's That Alarm?

A family woke up in the middle of the night to the sound of a loud alarm. The family thought it must be the fire alarm. They quickly evacuated the house and called 9-1-1. While they waited for the fire department to arrive, the family members looked for signs of fire. But they didn't see any—not even smoke.

The fire department inspected the home. A fire inspector told the family that a compound containing carbon and oxygen atoms caused the alarm. Carbon dioxide (CO_2) is made of carbon and oxygen, but the fire department confirmed that it was not carbon dioxide. Are there other molecules besides carbon dioxide made of carbon and oxygen? What was this mystery substance, and why would it set off an alarm?

▶ Connect to the **BIGIDEA** As you read about covalent bonding, think about how there could be different molecules made of carbon and oxygen atoms.

8.1 Molecular Compounds

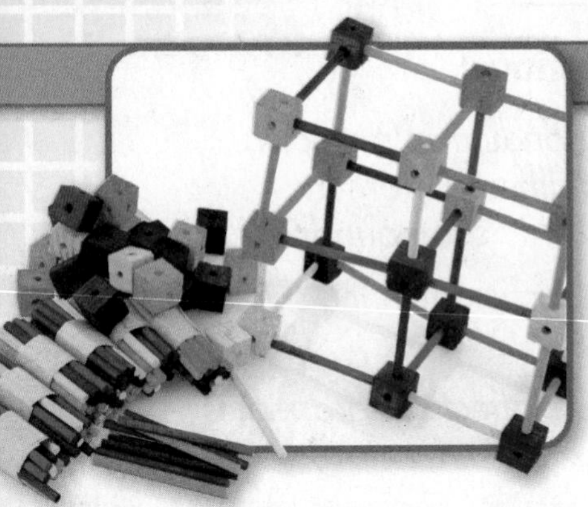

CHEMISTRY & YOU

Q: How are atoms joined together to make compounds with different structures? This toy model is made from cubes that are joined together with sticks. The pieces in this model are limited to cubes and sticks. But you can make many different models based on how many pieces you use and how you arrange them. In this lesson, you will learn how atoms are joined together to form units called molecules.

Key Questions

What information does a molecular formula provide?

What representative units define molecular compounds and ionic compounds?

Molecules and Molecular Compounds

The noble gases, such as helium and neon, exist as uncombined atoms in nature. They are described as monatomic because they consist of single atoms. Many elements are not monatomic. For example, a portion of the air you breathe is oxygen gas (O_2). As you might guess from the chemical formula, O_2 consists of two oxygen atoms that are bonded together.

In Chapter 7, you learned about ionic compounds. Ionic compounds are generally crystalline solids with high melting points. Other types of compounds have very different properties. For example, water (H_2O) is a liquid at room temperature. Carbon dioxide (CO_2) and nitrous oxide (N_2O) are both gases at room temperature. The bonds that hold the atoms together in O_2, H_2O, CO_2, and N_2O are not ionic bonds. Their bonds do not involve the transfer of electrons. The figure below shows two examples of gases that have bonds that are not ionic bonds.

Comparing Gas Particles

Scuba divers breathe compressed air—a mixture of gases that includes oxygen.

Dentists sometimes use nitrous oxide (also known as laughing gas) as a mild anesthetic.

Sharing Electrons Recall that ionic bonds form when the combining atoms give up or accept electrons. Atoms can also combine by sharing electrons. Atoms that share electrons are joined by a **covalent bond.** In a covalent bond, a "tug of war" for electrons takes place between the atoms. This tug of war joins the atoms together.

Look again at the models of oxygen and nitrous oxide on the previous page. Each model represents a molecule of the substance. A **molecule** is a neutral group of atoms joined together by covalent bonds. Oxygen gas consists of oxygen molecules. Each oxygen molecule is made of two covalently bonded oxygen atoms. An oxygen molecule is an example of a diatomic molecule. A **diatomic molecule** is a molecule that contains two atoms. Other elements that exist as diatomic molecules include hydrogen, nitrogen, and the halogens.

Molecules can also be made of atoms of different elements. A compound made of molecules is called a **molecular compound.** Water is an example of a molecular compound. The molecules in water are all the same. Each water molecule is a tightly bound unit of two hydrogen atoms and one oxygen atom.

Representing Molecules A **molecular formula** is the chemical formula of a molecular compound. A molecular formula shows how many atoms of each element a molecule of a substance contains. The molecular formula of water is H_2O. The subscript written after an element's symbol shows the number of atoms of that element in the molecule. If there is only one atom, you do not include the subscript 1. The molecular formula of water, H_2O, tells you that each molecule contains two hydrogen atoms and one oxygen atom.

Some molecular formulas have subscripts that are not lowest whole number ratios. For example, the molecular formula for butane is C_4H_{10}. A molecule of butane has four carbon atoms and ten hydrogen atoms. If you rewrite this formula by using the lowest whole number ratio of the two elements, you would get C_2H_5. This molecular formula no longer represents butane.

A molecular formula does not tell you about a molecule's structure. It does not show the arrangement of the atoms in space. It also does not show which atoms are covalently bonded to one another. Diagrams and models such as the ones shown below can be used to show a molecule's structure.

covalent bond a bond formed by the sharing of electrons between atoms

molecule a neutral group of atoms joined together by covalent bonds

diatomic molecule a molecule that consists of two atoms

molecular compound a compound that is composed of molecules

molecular formula a chemical formula that shows the kind and number of atoms in a molecule of a compound

PREFIXES

The prefix *co-* often means that two or more people or things share the same task—like coanchors in a newscast. In a covalent bond, two atoms share electrons.

Representations of an Ammonia Molecule
The formula NH_3 tells you only what atoms make up an ammonia molecule. Other representations provide more information.

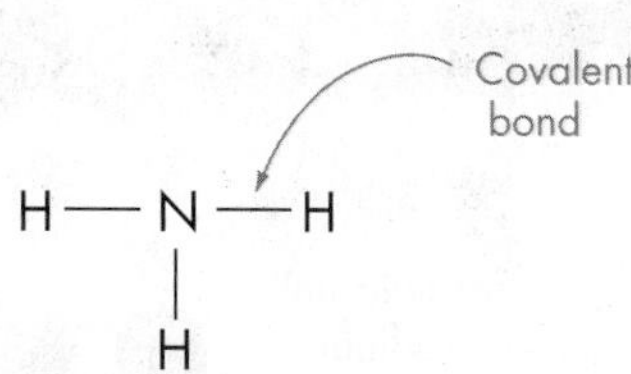

Structural formula This formula shows the order in which the atoms are bonded together.

Space-filling model This molecular model shows how the atoms are arranged in three-dimensional space.

Ball-and-stick model This molecular model shows the three-dimensional structure and the bonds between the atoms.

Molecular Formulas and Structures The formula of a molecular compound identifies the number and kind of atoms in each molecule of the compound.

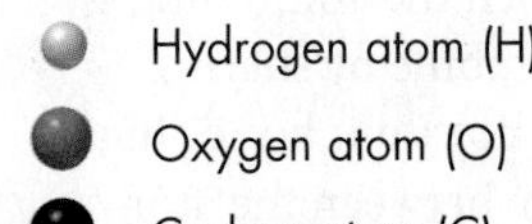

Carbon dioxide (CO_2)
1 molecule of CO_2 contains
2 oxygen atoms
1 carbon atom

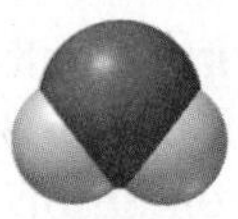

Water (H_2O)
1 molecule of H_2O contains
2 hydrogen atoms
1 oxygen atom

The figure above shows the chemical formulas and structures of two molecular compounds. The arrangement of the atoms within a molecule is called its molecular structure. The molecular structure of carbon dioxide shows how the three atoms are arranged in a row. It also shows that the carbon atom in each molecule is between the two oxygen atoms. The molecular structure of water shows that the oxygen atom is between the two hydrogen atoms. However, the atoms in water are not arranged in a row. Instead, the hydrogen atoms are mainly on one side of the water molecule.

Key Question What information does a molecular formula provide? **A molecular formula shows how many atoms of each element a molecule of a substance contains.**

Comparing Molecular and Ionic Compounds

Now you've seen how formulas can be used to describe molecular compounds and ionic compounds. The formulas describe different representative units for each compound type. The formula of a molecular compound describes its molecule. The formula of an ionic compound describes its formula unit. It is important not to confuse molecules with formula units. The figure below can help you understand why.

Molecular and Ionic Compounds Water is a molecular compound. The three atoms in a molecule of water act as a single unit. Sodium chloride is an ionic compound. The ions in its formula unit do not act as a unit. They exist as an array of ions.

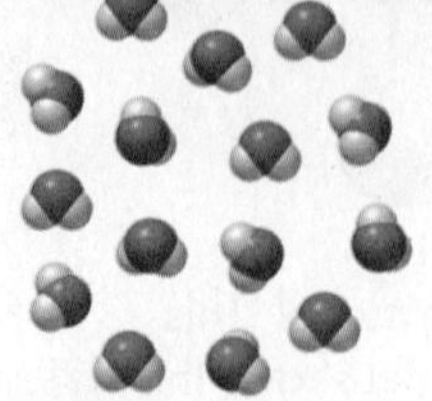

Collection of water molecules

Molecule of water:

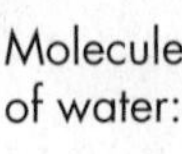

Chemical formula: H_2O

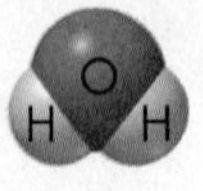

Array of sodium ions and chloride ions

Formula unit of sodium chloride:

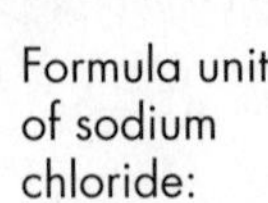

Chemical formula: NaCl

Molecular compounds usually have lower melting and boiling points than ionic compounds. Many molecular compounds are gases or liquids at room temperature. Ionic compounds form when a metal and a nonmetal combine, but most molecular compounds are composed of atoms of two or more nonmetals. The table below compares several characteristics of molecular and ionic compounds.

Key Question What representative units define molecular compounds and ionic compounds? **The representative unit of a molecular compound is a molecule. The representative unit of an ionic compound is a formula unit.**

Characteristics of Molecular and Ionic Compounds

Characteristic	Molecular compound	Ionic compound
Representative unit	Molecule	Formula unit
Bond formation	Sharing of electrons between atoms	Transfer of one or more electrons between atoms
Type of elements	Nonmetallic	Metallic and nonmetallic
Physical state	Solid, liquid, or gas	Solid
Melting point	Low (usually below 300°C)	High (usually above 300°C)
Solubility in water	High to low	Usually high
Electrical conductivity in aqueous solution	Poor to nonconducting	Good conductor

8.1 LessonCheck

Key Concept Check

1. **Identify** What information does a molecular formula provide?

2. **Compare** How is the representative unit of a molecular compound different from the representative unit of an ionic compound?

Vocabulary Check

Choose a highlighted word from the lesson to complete each sentence correctly.

3. Atoms that share electrons are held together by ________.

4. A neutral group of atoms joined together by covalent bonds is called a(n) ________.

Think Critically

5. **Compare** How do the molecules whose formulas are NO and N_2O differ?

6. **Apply Concepts** Give an example of a diatomic molecule found in Earth's atmosphere.

7. **Identify** What information does a molecular structure give?

CHEMISTRY & YOU

8. You can make different types of toy models from simple pieces of wood or plastic. Similarly, there are many different types of molecules. How are atoms joined together to make compounds with different structures? (Hint: See page 206.)

8.2 The Nature of Covalent Bonding

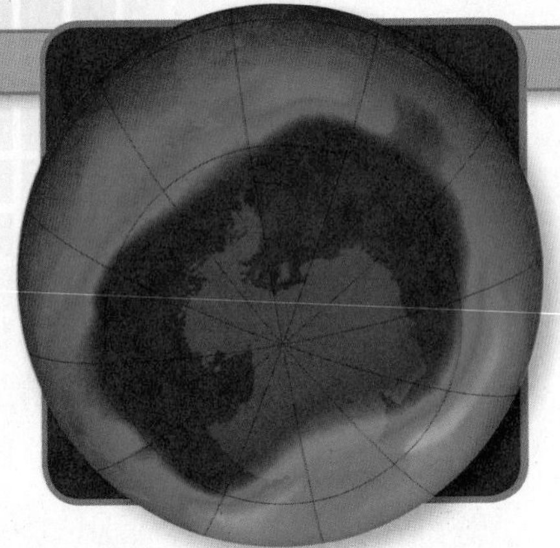

CHEMISTRY & YOU

Q: What is the difference between the oxygen you breathe and the oxygen in ozone? Earth's atmosphere has two different molecules that are both made of oxygen atoms. One is the form of oxygen that our cells need to survive. The other molecule is called ozone. Ozone provides protection from the sun, but it also causes smog. The colors in this map indicate the concentrations of ozone in various parts of the atmosphere. In this lesson, you will learn how oxygen atoms join to form the oxygen you breathe and how they also join to form ozone.

Key Questions

What is the result of electron sharing in a covalent bond?

How do coordinate covalent bonds differ from other covalent bonds?

What are some exceptions to the octet rule?

How is the strength of a covalent bond related to its bond dissociation energy?

How are resonance structures used?

The Octet Rule in Covalent Bonding

When ionic compounds form, electrons are transferred between ions. This transfer of electrons allows each ion to acquire a noble gas electron configuration. A similar rule applies for covalent bonds. In covalent bonds, atoms share electrons so each atom has a noble gas electron configuration. For example, a single hydrogen atom has one electron. A pair of hydrogen atoms shares electrons to form a covalent bond in a diatomic hydrogen molecule. Each hydrogen atom attains the electron configuration of helium—a noble gas with two electrons.

Atoms of the nonmetals and metalloids in Groups 4A, 5A, 6A, and 7A of the periodic table often form covalent bonds. These bonded atoms usually acquire a total of eight electrons, or an octet, by sharing electrons. So the octet rule that you studied in the previous chapter also applies to molecular compounds.

Reviewing Electron Dot Structures You were introduced to electron dot structures in Chapter 7. An atom's electron dot structure can help you identify how many bonds an atom can form with other atoms. The group number in the periodic table tells you how many valence electrons are in an atom's electron dot structure, as shown below.

Drawing Electron Dot Structures Carbon is in Group 4, so you draw four electrons in its electron dot structure. This structure shows that a carbon atom can form four covalent bonds.

	4A	5A	6A	7A
Periodic table square	6 C Carbon	7 N Nitrogen	8 O Oxygen	9 F Fluorine
Electron dot structure	·Ċ̣·	·Ṇ̈·	:Ö̤·	:F̤̈·

Single Covalent Bonds In a molecule, there is an attraction between the shared electrons and the positive nuclei of the atoms. This attraction holds the atoms in the molecule together. Two atoms that are held together by sharing one pair of electrons are joined by a **single covalent bond.**

▶ **Hydrogen** Hydrogen gas consists of diatomic molecules. The atoms in each molecule share one pair of electrons, forming a single covalent bond. Look below to see the electron dot structure for the hydrogen molecule. The two dots between the symbols for hydrogen represent the electrons of the covalent bond.

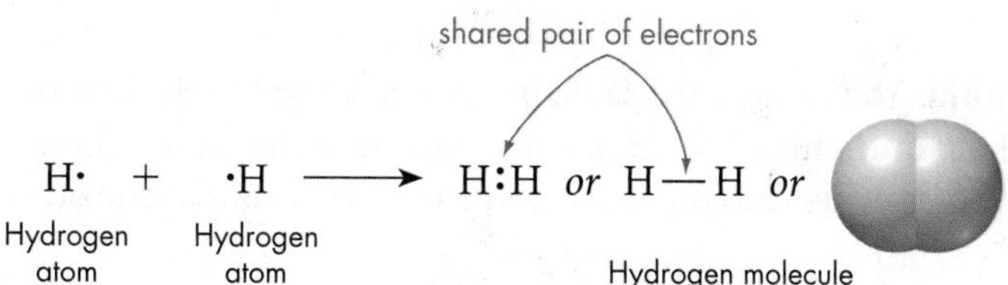

The pair of shared electrons that forms the covalent bond can also be shown as a dash. For example, a hydrogen molecule is written as H—H. A **structural formula** shows the covalent bonds as dashes and shows the arrangement of covalently bonded atoms. In contrast, the molecular formula of hydrogen (H_2) shows only the number of hydrogen atoms in each molecule.

▶ **Fluorine** The halogens also form diatomic molecules with single covalent bonds. Fluorine is one example of a halogen. Each fluorine atom below has seven valence electrons. Each atom needs one more electron to reach the electron configuration of a noble gas. The two fluorine atoms share a pair of electrons and form a single covalent bond to reach the electron configuration of neon.

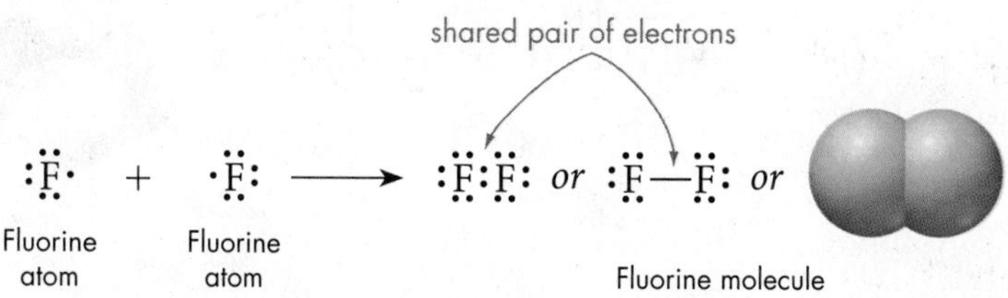

In an F_2 molecule, each fluorine atom shares one electron to complete the octet. Look above at the electron dot structures for F_2. Notice that the two fluorine atoms share only one pair of valence electrons. Each fluorine atom has three other pairs of valence electrons that it does not share. A pair of valence electrons that is not shared between atoms is called an **unshared pair**. An unshared pair is also known as a lone pair or a nonbonding pair.

single covalent bond a bond formed when two atoms share a pair of electrons

structural formula a formula that shows the arrangement of atoms in a molecule

unshared pair a pair of valence electrons that is not shared between atoms

USING PRIOR KNOWLEDGE

A diagram of a building's structure shows how the parts, such as the roof and the walls, are put together. A molecule's structural formula shows how the atoms are put together.

▶ Water A water molecule (H_2O) has three atoms and two single covalent bonds. An oxygen atom has six valence electrons. It needs two electrons to complete its octet. Each of the two hydrogen atoms shares an electron with the oxygen atom. Look at the electron dot structures below. Notice that all three atoms have noble gas configurations. Also notice that the oxygen atom in water has two unshared pairs of valence electrons.

KINETIC ART *See covalent bonding animated online.*

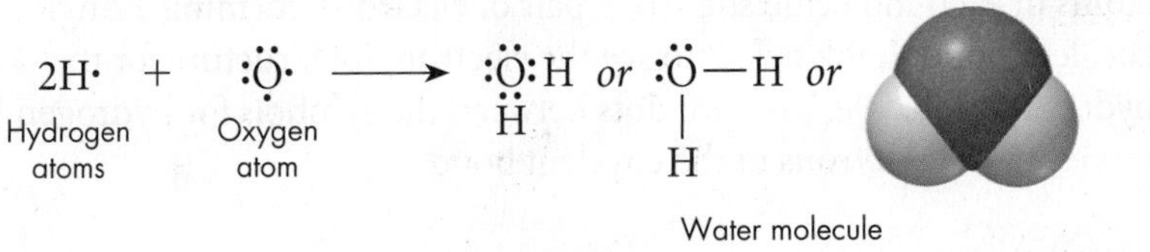

▶ Ammonia You can use the same method to draw the electron dot structure for ammonia gas (NH_3). An ammonia molecule has three single covalent bonds. It also has one unshared pair of electrons as shown below.

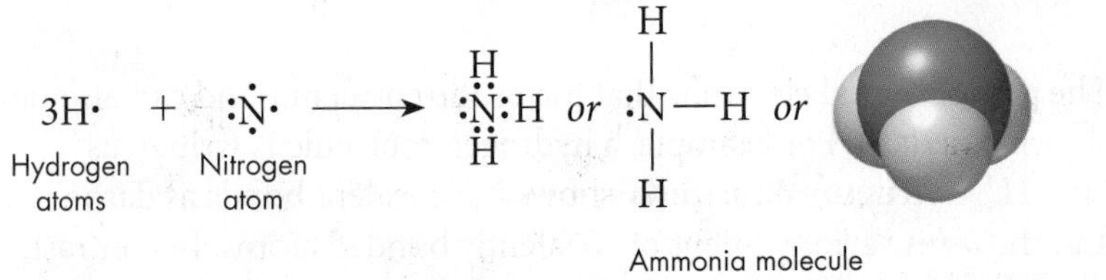

▶ Methane The stove shown below is fueled by natural gas, which is mostly methane (CH_4). A methane molecule has four single covalent bonds as shown below. A carbon atom has four valence electrons. It needs four more electrons to complete its octet. Each of the four hydrogen atoms shares electrons with the carbon atom to form four identical bonds. A methane molecule has no unshared pairs of electrons.

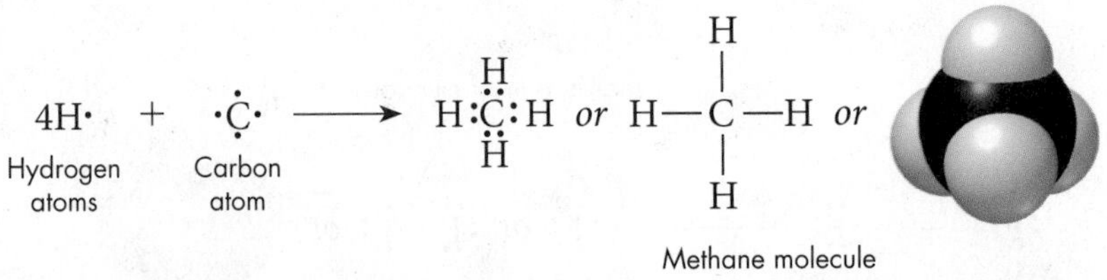

Methane
Methane is the main ingredient of natural gas. Natural gas is often used as a fuel for stoves, water heaters, dryers, and furnaces.

Sample Problem 8.1

Drawing an Electron Dot Structure

Hydrochloric acid is prepared by dissolving the gas hydrogen chloride (HCl) in water. Hydrogen chloride is a diatomic molecule with a single covalent bond. Draw the electron dot structure for HCl.

1 Analyze Identify the relevant concepts. In a single covalent bond, a hydrogen atom and a chlorine atom must share a pair of electrons. Each atom must contribute one electron to the bond.

2 Solve Apply the concepts to this problem.

Draw the electron dot structure for each atom.

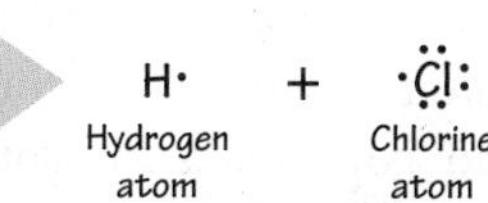

Determine the number of electrons needed for each atom to have a noble gas configuration.

Hydrogen needs one electron to reach the electron configuration of helium.

Chlorine needs one electron to reach the electron configuration of argon.

Draw the electron dot structure for the molecule, indicating the shared electrons.

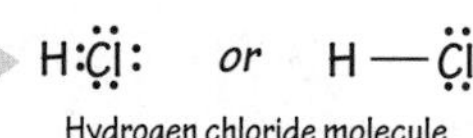

Through electron sharing, both atoms have noble gas electron configurations.

Practice Problems

9. Draw the electron dot structure for the diatomic molecule chlorine (Cl_2).

1 Analyze Identify the relevant concepts.

2 Solve Apply the concepts to this problem.

10. Challenge Draw the electron dot structure for hydrogen peroxide (H_2O_2).

Hint: Hydrogen peroxide has three single covalent bonds.

double covalent bond a bond in which two atoms share two pairs of electrons

triple covalent bond a bond in which two atoms share three pairs of electrons

coordinate covalent bond a covalent bond in which one atom provides both bonding electrons

USING PRIOR KNOWLEDGE

You are familiar with the words *double* and *triple*. Use this knowledge to remember the meanings of double and triple covalent bonds.

Double Covalent Bonds Sometimes, atoms must share two or three pairs of electrons to reach a noble gas configuration. A **double covalent bond** is a bond that involves two shared pairs of electrons. A carbon dioxide (CO_2) molecule has double covalent bonds. A carbon dioxide molecule contains two oxygen atoms as shown below. Each oxygen atom shares two electrons with carbon to form a total of two double covalent bonds.

:Ö· + ·Ċ· + ·Ö: ⟶ :Ö::C::Ö: *or* :Ö=C=Ö: *or*

Oxygen atom | Carbon atom | Oxygen atom

Carbon dioxide molecule

Triple Covalent Bonds A bond formed by sharing three pairs of electrons is a **triple covalent bond.** The diatomic molecule nitrogen (N_2) has a triple covalent bond. Nitrogen is a major part of Earth's atmosphere, shown in the photo below. Look at the equation below. A nitrogen atom has five valence electrons. Each nitrogen atom in the molecule must share three electrons to have a complete octet.

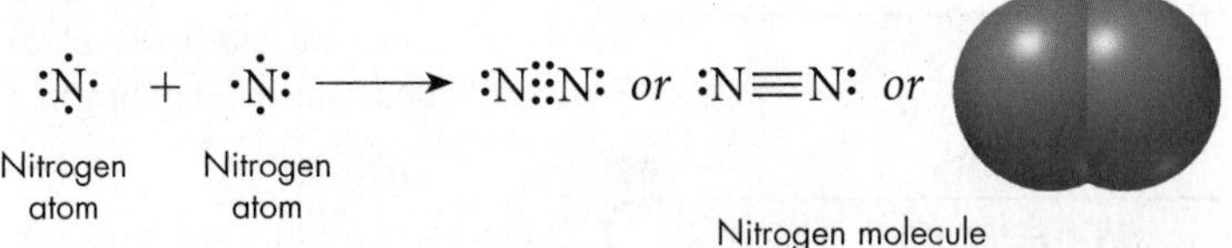

Key Question What is the result of electron sharing in a covalent bond? **In a covalent bond, electron sharing usually occurs so that each atom reaches the electron configuration of a noble gas. Atoms form single, double, or triple covalent bonds by sharing one, two, or three pairs of electrons, respectively.**

Nitrogen
Earth's atmosphere is mostly nitrogen. Three pairs of electrons are shared in a nitrogen molecule, forming a triple covalent bond.

Coordinate Covalent Bonds

There is another type of covalent bond that is different from the bonds in water, ammonia, methane, carbon dioxide, and nitrogen. The carbon and oxygen atoms in carbon monoxide gas (CO) are held together by this type of bond. To see how this bond forms, begin by looking at the equation below. The carbon atom needs to gain four electrons to have the electron configuration of neon. The oxygen atom needs two electrons. The two atoms can share two pairs of electrons to form a double covalent bond.

·C·	+	·O:	⟶	:C::O:
Carbon atom		Oxygen atom		Carbon monoxide molecule

With this double bond in place, the oxygen has a stable configuration, but the carbon does not. To solve this problem, the oxygen atom can donate one of its unshared pairs of electrons to form a third bond as shown below.

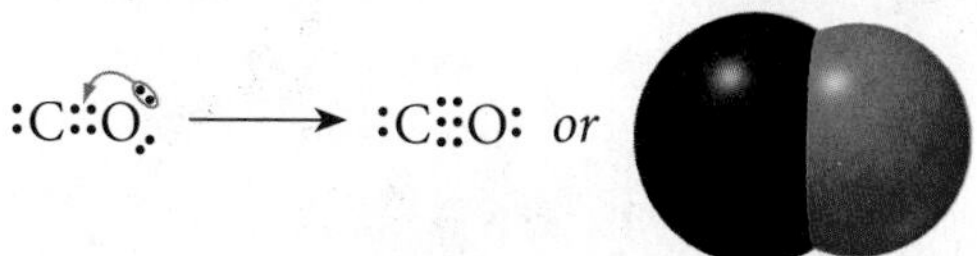

Carbon monoxide molecule

This type of bond is called a **coordinate covalent bond**—a covalent bond in which one atom supplies both bonding electrons. Once a coordinate covalent bond is formed, it is like any other covalent bond.

Drawing Coordinate Covalent Bonds In a structural formula, you can show a coordinate covalent bond as an arrow. The arrow must point from the atom donating the pair of electrons to the atom receiving them. Look at the structural formula of carbon monoxide in the table below. The formula shows two covalent bonds and one coordinate covalent bond. Notice that the arrow points from the oxygen atom to the carbon atom.

BUILD Connections

Coordinate covalent bonding can be similar to going on a movie date. You may pay for your own ticket and your date's ticket, but you both enjoy the movie together. In a coordinate covalent bond, one atom supplies both the electrons and then both atoms enjoy the bond together.

Some Common Diatomic Molecules and Molecular Compounds

Name	Chemical Formula	Structural Formula	Properties and uses
Hydrogen	H_2	H—H	Hydrogen is a colorless, odorless, tasteless gas.
Nitrogen	N_2	:N≡N:	Nitrogen is a colorless, odorless, tasteless gas. Earth's atmosphere is almost 80 percent nitrogen by volume.
Carbon monoxide	CO	:C⇚O:	Carbon monoxide is a colorless toxic gas. It is a major air pollutant present in tobacco smoke and vehicle exhaust.
Carbon dioxide	CO_2	:Ö=C=Ö:	Carbon dioxide is a colorless unreactive gas. It is essential for plant growth and is exhaled in the breath of animals.
Sulfur dioxide	SO_2	:Ö=S: → :Ö:	Sulfur dioxide is produced in the combustion of petroleum products and coal. It is a major air pollutant in industrial areas and can cause respiratory problems.

Ammonia Fertilizers
The polyatomic ammonium ion (NH_4^+) is an important component of fertilizer for home gardens, field crops, and potted plants.

polyatomic ion a tightly bound group of atoms that has either a positive or negative charge and behaves as a unit

PREFIXES
The prefix *poly-* means "many" or "several." A polyatomic ion contains several atoms. For example, a sulfate ion (SO_4^{2-}) has five atoms.

Coordinate Covalent Bonds in Ions An ammonium ion (NH_4^+) is found in many fertilizers, like the one shown above. This ion is made of atoms joined by covalent bonds, including a coordinate covalent bond. As shown below, the ammonium ion forms when a hydrogen ion attaches to the unshared pair of electrons in an ammonia molecule. Ions such as NH_4^+ are polyatomic ions. A **polyatomic ion** is a tightly bound group of atoms that has a positive or negative charge and behaves as a unit.

unshared electron pair; coordinate covalent bond

$$H^+ + :\underset{\ddot{H}}{\overset{H}{\ddot{N}}}:H \longrightarrow \left[H:\underset{\ddot{H}}{\overset{H}{\ddot{N}}}:H\right]^+ \quad or \quad H\leftarrow\underset{H}{\overset{H}{N^+}}—H$$

Hydrogen ion; Ammonia molecule (NH_3); Ammonium ion (NH_4^+)

Most polyatomic cations and anions contain covalent and coordinate covalent bonds. In addition, polyatomic ions form ionic bonds with ions of the opposite charge. So compounds that have polyatomic ions have both ionic bonds and covalent bonds.

The charge of a positive polyatomic ion equals the difference between the total number of valence electrons of the atoms and the number of electrons in the ion. For example, the charge of an ammonium ion is $9 - 8 = 1+$.

A negative polyatomic ion has a greater number of electrons than the number of valence electrons in the atoms. The charge of a negative polyatomic ion equals the number of these extra electrons.

Key Question How are coordinate covalent bonds different from other covalent bonds? **In a coordinate covalent bond, the shared electron pair comes from a single atom.**

Sample Problem 8.2

Drawing the Electron Dot Structure of a Polyatomic Ion

The H_3O^+ ion forms when a hydrogen ion is attracted to an unshared electron pair in a water molecule. Draw the electron dot structure of the hydronium ion.

❶ Analyze **Identify the relevant concepts.** Each atom must share electrons to obey the octet rule.

❷ Solve **Apply the concepts to this problem.**

Draw the electron dot structures of the hydrogen ion and the water molecule.

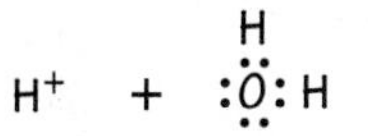

H^+ + H:Ö:H (with H above O)

Hydrogen ion — Water molecule (H_2O)

Determine the total number of valence electrons contributed by the two reactants.

Hydrogen ion:	0 electrons
Water molecule:	8 electrons
Total	8 electrons

Combine the two electron dot structures.

H:Ö:H (with H above O)

The oxygen atom contributes both bonding electrons.

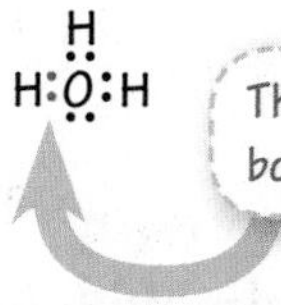

Correctly indicate the charge on the electron dot structure for the hydronium ion.

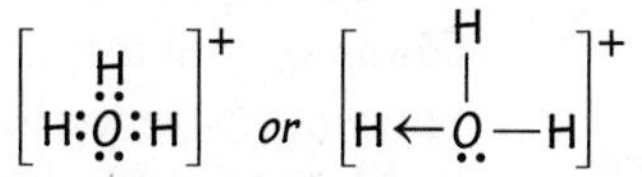

$[H:\ddot{O}:H]^+$ (with H above O) *or* $[H \leftarrow \ddot{O} — H]^+$ (with H above O)

Hydronium ion (H_3O^+)

Hint: In any reaction, the net charge of the reactants must equal the net charge of the products.

Practice Problems

11. Draw the electron dot structure for the hydroxide ion (OH^-).

❶ Analyze **Identify the relevant concepts.**

❷ Solve **Apply the concepts to this problem.**

12. Challenge Draw the electron dot structure for the sulfate ion (SO_4^{2-}).

Hint: In the sulfate ion, each oxygen atom bonds to the sulfur atom.

Nitrogen Dioxide
During a lightning strike, nitrogen and oxygen in the atmosphere can combine to produce nitrogen dioxide.

Exceptions to the Octet Rule

The octet rule provides guidance for drawing electron dot structures. But for some molecules and ions, it is impossible to draw structures that satisfy the octet rule. For example, the octet rule does not work for molecules whose total number of valence electrons is an odd number. There are also some molecules that have atoms with less, or more, than a complete octet of valence electrons.

Molecules With Odd Numbers of Valence Electrons Lightning strikes, such as the one shown to the left, produce nitrogen dioxide (NO_2). A molecule of NO_2 has an odd number of valence electrons—seventeen, to be exact. Two possible electron dot structures for a NO_2 molecule are shown below. Both of these electron dot structures fail to satisfy the octet rule. It is impossible to draw a structure for NO_2 that obeys the octet rule for all the atoms.

:Ö—Ṅ=Ö:

:Ö=Ṅ—Ö:

Nitrogen dioxide molecule

Molecules With Atoms That Reduce the Octet to Less Than 8 Some molecules have an even number of valence electrons yet still fail to follow the octet rule. One example is boron trifluoride (BF_3). Look at the electron dot structure below. The boron atom in BF_3 only has six electrons. Therefore, this molecule is an exception to the octet rule.

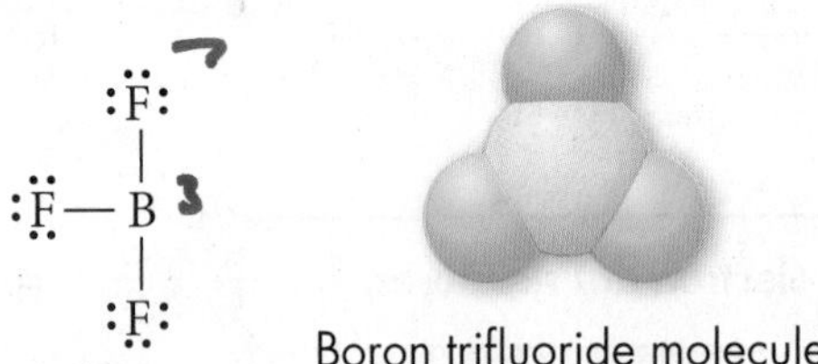

Boron trifluoride molecule

Molecules With Atoms That Expand the Octet to More Than 8 Some atoms expand the octet to more than eight electrons. One example is phosphorus pentachloride (PCl_5). In this molecule, the phosphorus atom bonds to five chlorine atoms. The electron dot structure below shows that phosphorus has ten valence electrons. Another example is sulfur hexafluoride (SF_6). The electron dot structure for SF_6 shows that sulfur has twelve valence electrons. Both of these molecules are exceptions to the octet rule.

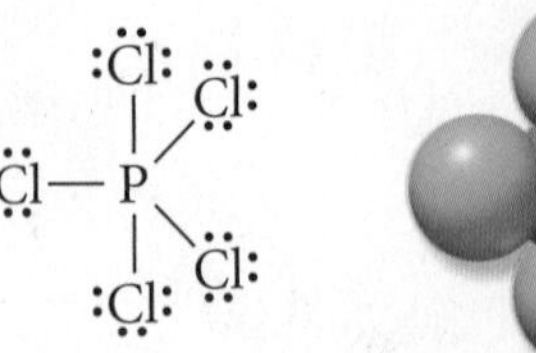

Phosphorus pentachloride molecule

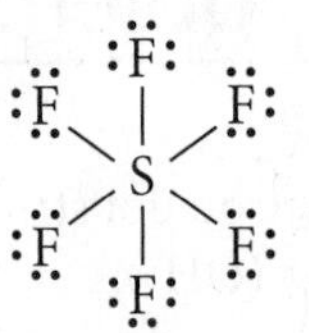

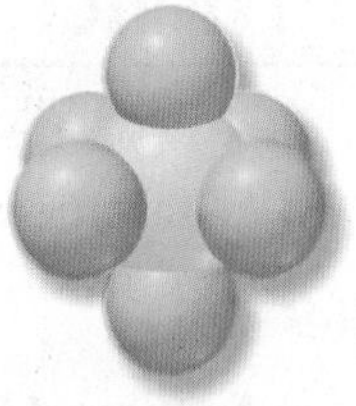

Sulfur hexafluoride molecule

Key Question What are some exceptions to the octet rule? **The octet rule is not satisfied in molecules whose total number of valence electrons is an odd number. There are also molecules that have atoms with less, or more, than a complete octet of valence electrons.**

Bond Dissociation Energies

When two atoms combine to form a bond, energy is released. This release of energy suggests that the product is more stable than the reactants. To break the bond, you would need to supply energy. The energy needed to break the bond between two covalently bonded atoms is the **bond dissociation energy**. Chemists usually express bond dissociation energies in units of kJ/mol. This unit means the amount of energy needed to break one mole (abbreviated mol) of bonds. You'll study the mole in Chapter 12. A mole of bonds is 6.02×10^{23}.

Comparing Bond Dissociation Energies The larger the bond dissociation energy, the stronger the bond. Compare the bond dissociation energies for a carbon-carbon single bond and a carbon-carbon double bond in the table below. It takes more energy to break the double bond (657 kJ/mol compared to 347 kJ/mol). The triple carbon-carbon bond has an even higher bond dissociation energy (908 kJ/mol). Now compare the bond lengths for the three carbon-carbon bonds. Notice that as the bond dissociation energy increases, the length of the bond decreases.

Bond Stability Strong carbon-carbon bonds help explain why carbon compounds are so stable. Compounds with only C—C and C—H covalent bonds are usually unreactive. Methane, which consists of C—H bonds, is an unreactive molecule. Compounds such as methane are unreactive partly because the dissociation energies for their bonds are high.

Key Question How is the strength of a covalent bond related to its bond dissociation energy? **A large bond dissociation energy corresponds to a strong covalent bond.**

Bond Dissociation Energies and Bond Lengths for Covalent Bonds

Bond	Bond dissociation energy (kJ/mol)	Bond length (pm)
H—H	435	74
C—H	393	109
C—O	356	143
C=O	736	121
C≡O	1074	113
C—C	347	154
C=C	657	133
C≡C	908	121
C—N	305	147
Cl—Cl	243	199
N—N	209	140
O—H	464	96
O—O	142	132

bond dissociation energy
the energy needed to break the covalent bond(s) between two atoms

PREFIXES
The prefix *dis-* can mean "to undo." The bond dissociation energy is the energy it takes to undo the bond.

resonance structure one of the two or more equally valid electron dot structures of a molecule or polyatomic ion

RELATED WORDS

The word *resonance* is related to the verb *resonate*. To resonate means to be in harmony or agreement. Two resonance structures are in agreement with one another.

Resonance

Ozone (O_3) in the upper atmosphere blocks harmful ultraviolet radiation from the sun. At lower levels, ozone contributes to the smog in the photo below. The ozone molecule has two possible electron dot structures. Notice you can convert one structure to the other by shifting electron pairs. You can do this without changing the positions of the oxygen atoms.

$$:\underset{\cdot\cdot}{\ddot{O}}:\ddot{O}::\ddot{O} \longleftrightarrow \ddot{O}::\ddot{O}:\underset{\cdot\cdot}{\ddot{O}}:$$

These electron dot structures suggest that ozone has two different types of bonds—one single coordinate covalent bond and one double covalent bond. If this were true, you would expect ozone to have two bonds of different lengths. However, measurements show that the two bonds are the same length. The bonding in the ozone molecule is the average of the two structures.

Electron dot structures, such as the two shown for ozone, are called resonance structures. **Resonance structures** occur when it is possible to draw two or more valid electron dot structures for a molecule by using the same number of electron pairs. Resonance structures can also be drawn for some ions. Chemists use resonance structures to "see" the bonding in molecules that cannot be fully described by a single structural formula.

Look again at the two resonance structures for ozone. Notice a double-headed arrow connecting them. Earlier chemists believed that the electrons flipped back and forth within the molecule. For this reason, they drew double-headed arrows between two resonance structures. Chemists now know that no back-and-forth changes occur, but they continue to use double-headed arrows to connect resonance structures.

Key Question How do chemists use resonance structures? **Chemists use resonance structures to model the bonding in molecules that cannot be described by a single structural formula.**

Ground-Level Ozone
The ozone high above the ground forms a protective layer that absorbs ultraviolet radiation from the sun. But at ground level, ozone is a pollutant that can cause smog. The smog shown here is in Los Angeles, California.

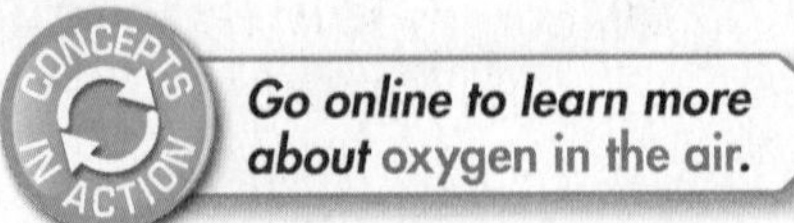

Go online to learn more about oxygen in the air.

Quick Lab

Purpose To compare and contrast the stretching of rubber bands and the dissociation energy of covalent bonds

Materials

- one 170 g (6 oz) can of food
- two 454 g (16 oz) cans of food
- three No. 25 rubber bands
- metric ruler
- metal coat hanger
- plastic grocery bag
- paper clip
- graph paper

Strengths of Covalent Bonds

Procedure 

1. Bend the coat hanger to fit over the top of a door. The hook should hang down on one side of the door. Measure the lengths of the rubber bands (in cm). Hang a rubber band on the coat hanger hook.

2. Place the 170 g can in the plastic bag. Use the paper clip to fasten the bag to the end of the rubber band. Lower the bag gently until it is suspended from the end of the rubber band. Measure and record the length of the stretched rubber band. Using different combinations of food cans, repeat this process three times with the following masses: 454 g, 624 g, and 908 g.

3. Repeat Step 2, using two rubber bands to connect the hanger and the paper clip. Then, repeat by using three rubber bands.

4. Graph the length difference: (stretched rubber band) − (unstretched rubber band) on the *y*-axis versus mass (kg) on the *x*-axis for one, two, and three rubber bands. Estimate and draw a best-fit line for each set of data. Your graph should have three separate straight lines. Each line should pass through the origin. The lines should extend past 1 kg on the *x*-axis. Find the slope of each line in cm/kg.

Analyze and Conclude

1. Analyze Experimental Results Assuming the rubber bands are models for covalent bonds, what can you conclude about the relative strengths of single, double, and triple bonds?

2. Evaluate How does the behavior of the rubber bands differ from that of covalent bonds?

8.2 LessonCheck

Key Concept Check

13. Identify What electron configurations do atoms usually achieve by sharing electrons to form covalent bonds?

14. Compare How is a coordinate covalent bond different from other covalent bonds?

15. List What are three ways the octet rule is sometimes broken?

16. Explain How is the strength of a covalent bond related to its bond dissociation energy?

17. Review Why are resonance structures used to represent some molecules?

Vocabulary Check

Choose a highlighted word from the lesson to complete the sentence correctly.

18. The energy required to break the bond between two covalently bonded atoms is the _______.

Think Critically

19. Infer When are two atoms likely to form a double bond between them? A triple bond?

20. Compare Which bond is stronger: the bond in H_2 or a C—C bond? Explain your reasoning.

CHEMISTRY & YOU

21. How do the oxygen you breathe and the oxygen in atmospheric ozone differ? (Hint: See page 218.)

8.3 Bonding Theories

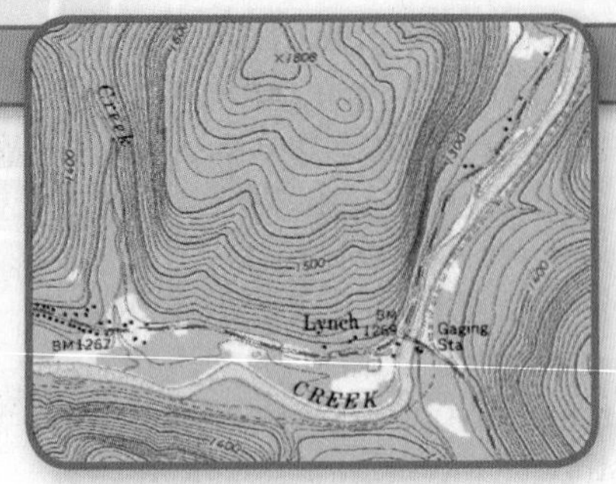

CHEMISTRY & YOU

Q: How can you predict where an electron is most likely to be found in a molecule? If you go hiking, you might use a topographic map like the one shown here. The lines on a topographic map show you where elevations change. In this lesson, you will learn how to read electron "maps" that show where you are most likely to find electrons.

Key Questions

How are atomic and molecular orbitals related?

What do scientists use the VSEPR theory for?

In what ways is orbital hybridization useful in describing molecules?

Molecular Orbitals

The model you have been using for covalent bonding assumes the orbitals are those of the individual atoms. There is another model that describes bonding in a different way—the quantum mechanical model of bonding. In this model, the atomic orbitals of two atoms overlap to produce a molecular orbital. A **molecular orbital** is an orbital that applies to the entire molecule. As seen in the figure below, the atomic orbitals combine to form a molecular orbital of a different shape.

Atomic orbitals and molecular orbitals are somewhat similar. Just as an atomic orbital belongs to a particular atom, a molecular orbital belongs to a particular molecule. An atomic orbital is filled if it contains two electrons. A molecular orbital also contains two electrons. A molecular orbital that can be occupied by two electrons of a covalent bond is a **bonding orbital**.

In general, covalent bonding results from an imbalance between the attractions and repulsions of the nuclei and electrons. The positive nuclei and negative electrons attract each other because their charges have opposite signs. Two nuclei repel one another because their charges have the same sign. Two electrons also repel one another for the same reason. However, two atoms can bond to form a molecule. Bonds in molecules are possible because the attractions involved are stronger than the repulsions involved.

Key Question How are atomic and molecular orbitals related? **Just as an atomic orbital belongs to a particular atom, a molecular orbital belongs to a molecule as a whole.**

Molecular Orbital Two atomic orbitals can combine to form a molecular orbital. The molecular orbital's shape indicates a high probability of finding the electrons between the two nuclei.

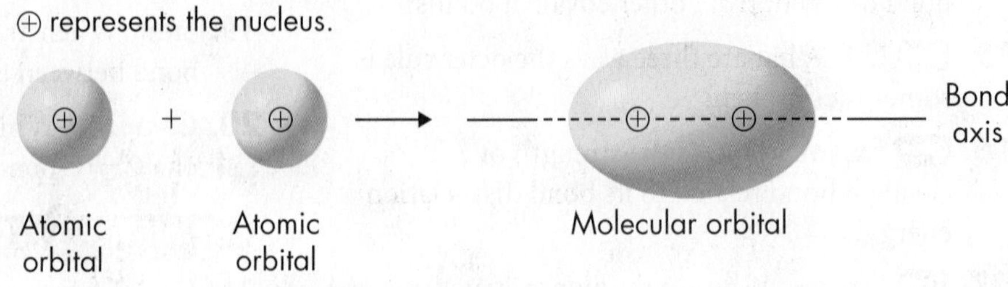

Molecular Shapes
Five common molecular shapes are shown here.

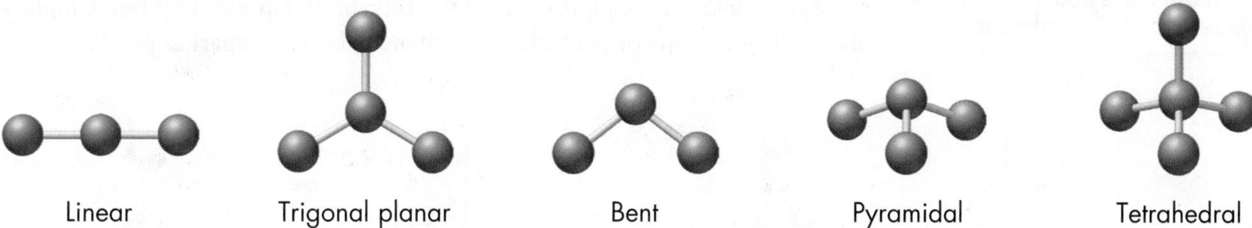

VSEPR Theory

A two-dimensional sketch of you may fail to show what you truly look like. Similarly, an electron dot structure sometimes fails to show the three-dimensional shape of a molecule. In order to predict the three-dimensional shapes of molecules, scientists use valence-shell electron-pair repulsion theory (VSEPR theory). **VSEPR theory** states that the repulsion between electron pairs causes molecular shapes to adjust so the valence-electron pairs stay as far apart as possible. Five of the possible molecular shapes are shown above.

BUILD Vocabulary

molecular orbital an orbital that applies to the entire molecule

bonding orbital a molecular orbital that can be occupied by two electrons of a covalent bond

VSEPR theory theory that states that the repulsion between electron pairs causes molecular shapes that allow for the greatest distance between valence-electron pairs

RELATED WORD FORMS

The word *molecular* is related to the word *molecule.* A molecular orbital is an orbital in a molecule. In the same way, an atomic orbital is an orbital in an atom.

Linear: The Simplest Molecular Shape In the simplest molecular shape, the valence-electron pairs are furthest apart when they are arranged as a straight line, or a linear shape. Carbon dioxide (CO_2) is an example of a molecule with a linear shape. The double bonds joining the oxygens to the carbon are farthest apart when the O=C=O bond angle is 180°. As a result, CO_2 is a linear molecule.

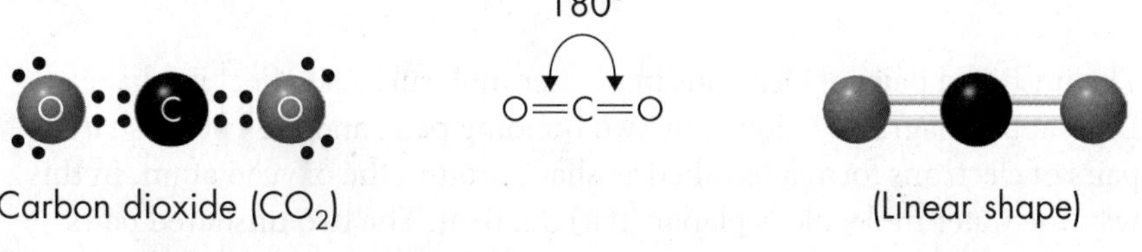

Carbon dioxide (CO_2) (Linear shape)

More Complex Molecular Shapes Some molecules must be three-dimensional in shape to separate their valence-electron pairs as much as possible. Methane (CH_4) is one such example. The electron dot structure and structural formula of methane show the molecule as if it were flat and two-dimensional.

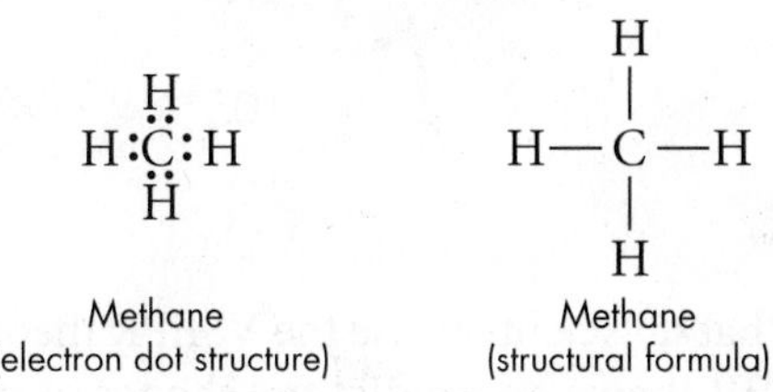

Methane (electron dot structure) Methane (structural formula)

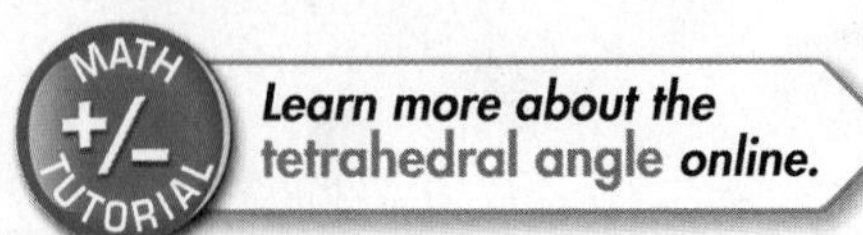

MATH
+/–
TUTORIAL
Learn more about the tetrahedral angle online.

In reality, methane molecules are three-dimensional. The diagrams below show that the hydrogen atoms in a methane molecule are at the four corners of a shape called a regular tetrahedron. In this arrangement, the H—C—H bond angles are 109.5°. This angle is called the **tetrahedral angle**. This bond angle allows the four pairs of electrons in methane to be as far apart as possible.

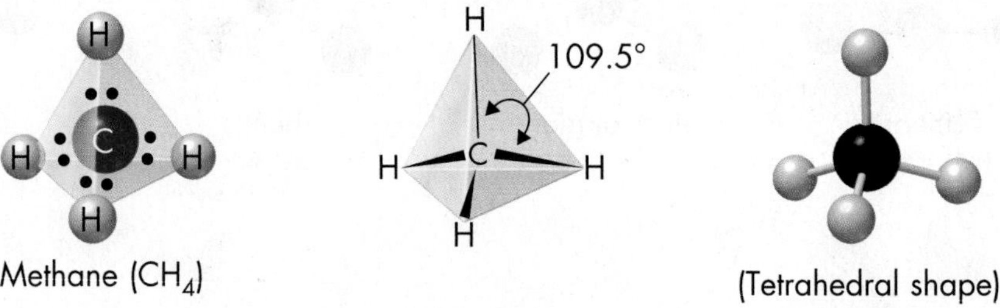

Methane (CH_4)

(Tetrahedral shape)

BUILD Understanding

Cause and Effect Diagram As you read, make a two-column chart. In the first column, draw each type of molecular shape you read about. In the second column, write the reason a molecule would have this shape.

The Effect of Unshared Pairs on Molecular Shapes Unshared pairs of electrons are also important in predicting the shapes of molecules. As shown below, the nitrogen in ammonia (NH_3) is surrounded by four pairs of valence electrons. One of these electron pairs is an unshared pair. No bonding atom attracts these unshared electrons. So they are held closer to the nitrogen than the three bonding pairs. The unshared pair strongly repels the bonding pairs, pushing them together into a pyramidal shape. The measured H—N—H bond angle in NH_3 is 107°.

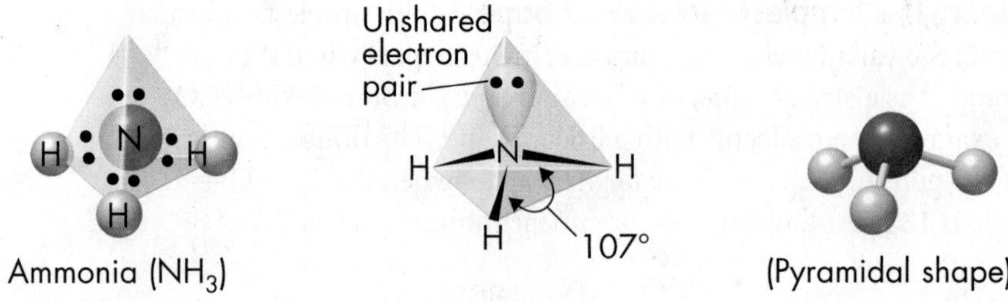

Ammonia (NH_3)

(Pyramidal shape)

The unshared pairs of electrons in a water molecule also affect its shape. Look at the diagrams below. The two bonding pairs and the two unshared pairs of electrons form a tetrahedral shape around the oxygen atom. In this way, the water molecule is planar (flat) but bent. The two unshared pairs repel the two bonding pairs. As a result, the H—O—H bond angle is reduced to about 105°.

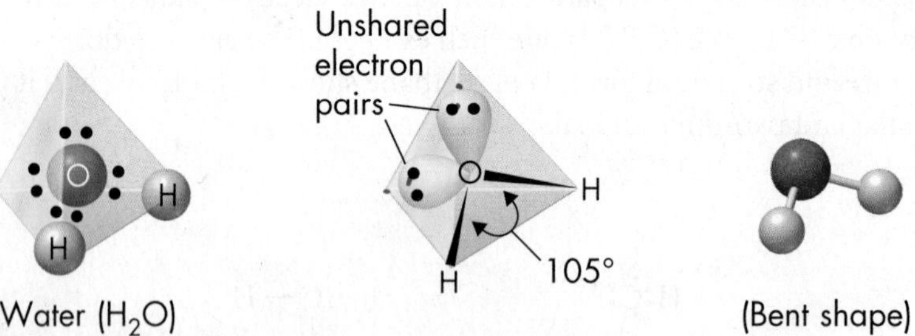

Water (H_2O)

(Bent shape)

Key Question What do scientists use the VSEPR theory for? **Scientists use the VSEPR theory to predict the shapes of molecules.**

Hybrid Orbitals

The VSEPR theory works well for explaining molecular shapes. But it does not help much in describing the types of bonds in a molecule. Orbital hybridization provides information about both molecular bonding and molecular shape. In **hybridization**, several atomic orbitals mix to form the same total number of equivalent hybrid orbitals.

The carbon atom's outer electron configuration is $2s^2 2p^2$. This configuration has two unpaired electrons as shown below. These unpaired electrons can combine with unpaired electrons of other atoms to form two covalent bonds.

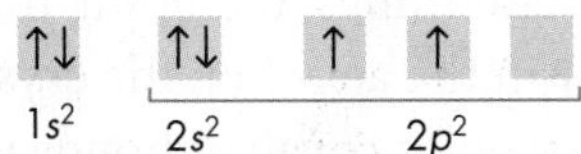

However, in a methane molecule, a carbon atom bonds to four hydrogen atoms. How can these two extra bonds form? Look at the diagram below. One of carbon's 2*s* electrons is promoted to the empty 2*p* orbital. The atom then has four unpaired electrons. This promotion allows the carbon atom to covalently bond to four hydrogen atoms to form methane.

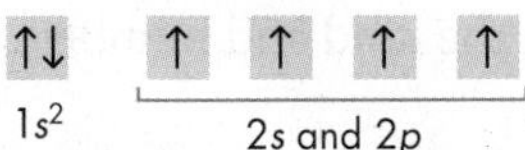

You might think that one bond would be different from the other three. But all the bonds are the same. The one 2*s* orbital and three 2*p* orbitals mix to form four identical hybrid orbitals, called sp^3 hybrid orbitals.

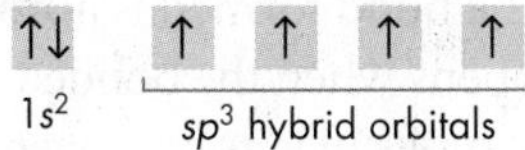

Key Question In what ways is orbital hybridization useful in describing molecules? **Orbital hybridization provides information about both molecular bonding and molecular shape.**

hybridization the mixing of several atomic orbitals to form the same total number of equivalent hybrid orbitals

tetrahedral angle bond angle of 109.5° that results when a central atom forms four bonds directed to the center of a regular tetrahedron

WORD ORIGINS

Tetrahedron comes from *tetra,* the Greek word for "four," and *hedron,* the Greek word for "side." A tetrahedron has four sides.

8.3 LessonCheck

Key Concept Check

22. Review How are atomic orbitals and molecular orbitals related?

23. Explain How do scientists use VSEPR theory?

24. Identify How is orbital hybridization useful in describing molecules?

Vocabulary Check *Choose a highlighted word from the lesson to complete the sentence correctly.*

25. According to ______, the shape of a molecule adjusts so that the valence electron pairs are as far apart as possible.

Think Critically

26. Explain Molecules of carbon dioxide and water have different shapes, even though they both have three atoms. Use VSEPR theory to explain why.

27. Classify The BF_3 molecule is planar. A fluoride ion can attach to the boron in BF_3 to form the BF_4^- ion. What is the geometric shape of this ion?

28. Models and drawings are often used to help you visualize where something can be found. How can a drawing show you where an electron is most likely to be found? (Hint: See page 220.)

8.4 Polar Bonds and Molecules

CHEMISTRY & YOU

Q: How does a snowflake get its shape? Each individual snowflake is formed from as many as 100 ice crystals. The size and shape of each crystal depends on several things, including the air temperature and the amount of water vapor in the air when the crystal is forming. In this lesson, you will see how polar covalent bonds in water molecules influence the shape of a snowflake.

Key Questions

How do electronegativity values determine the charge distribution in a polar bond?

How do the strengths of intermolecular attractions compare with the strengths of ionic and covalent bonds?

Why are the properties of molecular compounds so diverse?

Bond Polarity

In a covalent bond, the bonded atoms share electrons. Covalent bonds can differ in how the atoms share the electrons. The properties of a molecule depend on the kind and number of atoms and how the atoms share electrons.

Nonpolar Covalent Bonds The pair of electrons in a covalent bond are pulled between the nuclei of the atoms that share the electrons. As illustrated below, the forces on the electrons are much like a game of tug of war. When the two atoms pull equally, they share the bonding electrons equally and the bond formed is a **nonpolar covalent bond.** This equal sharing happens when the bonded atoms are identical. For example, such diatomic molecules as hydrogen (H_2) and oxygen (O_2) have nonpolar covalent bonds.

Polar Covalent Bonds A polar covalent bond, or a **polar bond**, is a covalent bond between atoms in which the electrons are shared unequally. In a polar bond, the more electronegative atom attracts the electrons more strongly. So it gains a slightly negative charge. The less electronegative atom has a slightly positive charge.

Electron Tug of War
The nuclei of atoms pull on the shared electrons, much as the knot in the rope is pulled toward opposing sides in a game of tug of war.

▶ **Describing Polar Covalent Bonds** Recall that electronegativity is the ability of an atom to attract electrons when the atom is in a compound. Refer to page 170 in Chapter 6 to see the electronegativity values for some elements.

Consider the hydrogen chloride (HCl) molecule. Hydrogen has an electronegativity of 2.1. Chlorine has an electronegativity of 3.0. These values are different, so the two pulling forces on the bonding electrons are not equal. Thus, the covalent bond in HCl is a polar bond. The chlorine atom has a slightly negative charge because it attracts the electrons more strongly. The hydrogen atom has a slightly positive charge. These charges are also called partial charges because they are less than the full charges that result from the complete transfer of an electron.

Two ways to represent polar bonds are shown below. In the left structure, the lowercase Greek letter delta (δ) shows that the individual atoms have only a partial positive charge (δ+) or partial negative charge (δ–). In the right structure, an arrow that points to the more electronegative atom shows the polar nature of the bond.

$$\overset{\delta+}{\mathrm{H}}\!-\!\overset{\delta-}{\mathrm{Cl}} \quad or \quad \overset{+\!\longrightarrow}{\mathrm{H}\!-\!\mathrm{Cl}}$$

▶ **Predicting Bond Type** The electronegativity difference between two atoms reveals what kind of bond is likely to form. Look at the table below. Notice that as the electronegativity difference between two atoms increases, the polarity of the bond increases. If the difference is greater than 2.0, the electrons will likely be pulled away completely by one of the atoms. In that case, an ionic bond will form.

Electronegativity Differences and Bond Types

Electronegativity difference range	Most probable type of bond	Example
0.0–0.4	Nonpolar covalent	H—H (0.0)
0.4–1.0	Moderately polar covalent	$\overset{\delta+}{\mathrm{H}}$—$\overset{\delta-}{\mathrm{Cl}}$ (0.9)
1.0–2.0	Very polar covalent	$\overset{\delta+}{\mathrm{H}}$—$\overset{\delta-}{\mathrm{F}}$ (1.9)
≥2.0	Ionic	$Na^{+}Cl^{-}$ (2.1)

▶ **Describing Molecules with Polar Covalent Bonds** The presence of a polar bond in a molecule often makes the entire molecule polar. In a **polar molecule**, one end of the molecule is slightly negative, and the other end is slightly positive. The hydrogen chloride molecule is a polar molecule. In this molecule, the partial charges on the hydrogen and chlorine atoms result in electrically charged ends called poles. A molecule that has two poles is called a dipolar molecule, or **dipole**. The hydrogen chloride molecule is a dipole.

nonpolar covalent bond covalent bond between two atoms that share the electrons equally

polar bond covalent bond between two atoms that share the electrons unequally

polar molecule a molecule in which one end is slightly negative and the other end is slightly positive

dipole a molecule that has two poles of opposite charge

USING PRIOR KNOWLEDGE

You know that Earth has a North Pole and a South Pole. The word *pole* refers to one of the opposite ends of an object. A dipole is a molecule with two oppositely charged ends.

See polar molecules animated online.

Sample Problem 8.3

Identifying Bond Type

Which type of bond (nonpolar covalent, moderately polar covalent, very polar covalent, or ionic) will form between each of the following pairs of atoms?

a. N and H **b.** Al and Cl

❶ **Analyze** **Identify the relevant concepts.** The types of bonds depend on the electronegativity differences between the bonding elements.

❷ **Solve** **Apply the concepts to this problem.**

Step	a	b
Identify the electronegativities of each atom by using the table on page 170.	**a.** N: 3.0; H: 2.1	**b.** Al: 1.5; Cl: 3.0
Find the difference between the two electronegativity values.	$3.0 - 2.1 = 0.9$	$3.0 - 1.5 = 1.5$
Use the table on the previous page to determine the bond type.	0.9 is between 0.4 and 1.0, so the bond is moderately polar covalent.	1.5 is between 1.0 and 2.0, so the bond is very polar covalent.

Practice Problems

29. Classify the bonds between atoms of each pair of elements as nonpolar covalent, moderately polar covalent, very polar covalent, or ionic.

a. H and Br
b. K and Cl
c. C and O
d. Cl and F
e. Li and O
f. Br and Br

❶ **Analyze** **Identify the relevant concepts.**

❷ **Solve** **Apply the concepts to this problem.**

Write the electronegativity difference as the absolute value. This way, the difference will never be a negative number.

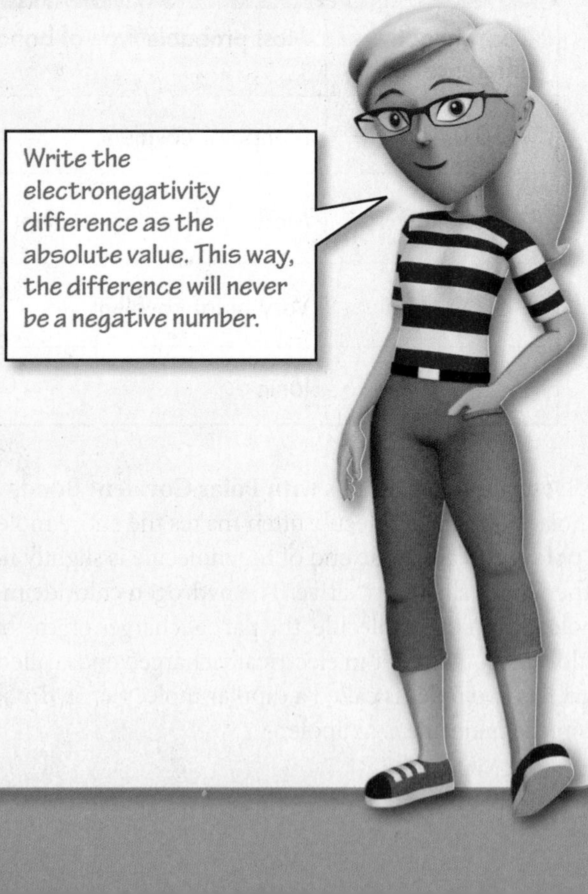

30. Challenge Place the following covalent bonds in order from least polar to most polar:

a. H—Cl
b. H—Br
c. H—S
d. H—C

Powder Coating

Have you ever admired a new car's glossy, smooth paint? Car manufacturers use a special process to apply paint to a car. This process is called powder coating or electrostatic spray painting. Powder coating isn't just for cars though. The process has many different applications, including the painting of motorcycles and outdoor furniture.

In powder coating, a custom-designed spray nozzle is connected to an electric power supply. The power supply gives a negative charge to the paint droplets as they exit the spray gun. The negatively charged paint droplets are attracted to the positively charged metal surface.

An eye-catching paint finish is not the only benefit of powder coating. This process is also environmentally friendly. Because the paint is actually attracted to its intended surface, the amount of wasted paint is much lower compared to traditional spray painting. Also, the amount of toxic volatile organic compounds (VOCs) released is minimal—if there are any at all.

APPLYING THE PAINT This worker is using an electrostatic spray gun to apply paint to the metal. Once the paint is applied, the part is baked in an oven to cure the paint.

GLOSSY FINISH Powder coating can produce a smooth, glossy paint finish.

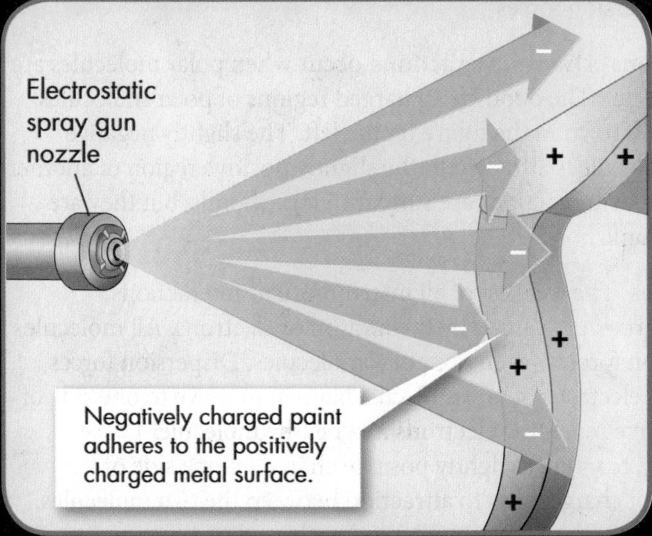
Electrostatic spray gun nozzle
Negatively charged paint adheres to the positively charged metal surface.

ATTRACTIVE PAINT The paint almost wraps around the metal, sticking to any available charged surface.

Take It Further

1. **Analyze Benefits** Powder coating is being used for more and more applications, partly because of its many benefits. Research other advantages of powder coating that are not mentioned here.
2. **Infer** Powder coating results in a smooth surface, usually without drips and runs. Why do you think drips and runs are avoided during powder coating?

van der Waals forces the two weakest intermolecular attractions: dipole interactions and dispersion forces

dipole interactions forces that result from the attraction of oppositely charged regions of polar molecules

dispersion forces attractions caused by the electron motion in one molecule affecting the motion of electrons in another molecule

hydrogen bond attractive forces in which a hydrogen atom that is covalently bonded to a very electronegative atom is also weakly bonded to an unshared electron pair of another electronegative atom

WORD ORIGINS

Disperse comes from a Latin word meaning "to scatter." Dispersion forces are a result of moving electrons, causing other electrons to scatter because they repel each other.

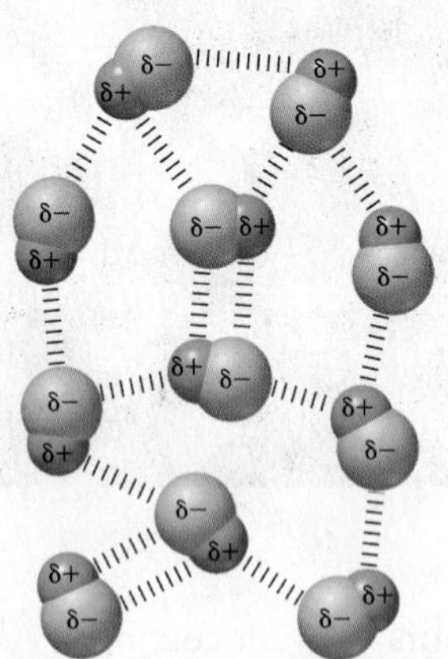

Dipole Interactions
Polar molecules are attracted to one another by dipole interactions—a type of van der Waals force.

▶ **Determining Molecular Polarity** Some molecules that have polar bonds are not polar. The effect of polar bonds on the polarity of an entire molecule depends on the shape of the molecule. It also depends on the orientation of the polar bonds. Look at the water molecule below. The highly electronegative oxygen atom partially pulls the bonding electrons away from the two hydrogen atoms. The bent shape of the water molecule gives two oppositely charged ends. So the water molecule is polar.

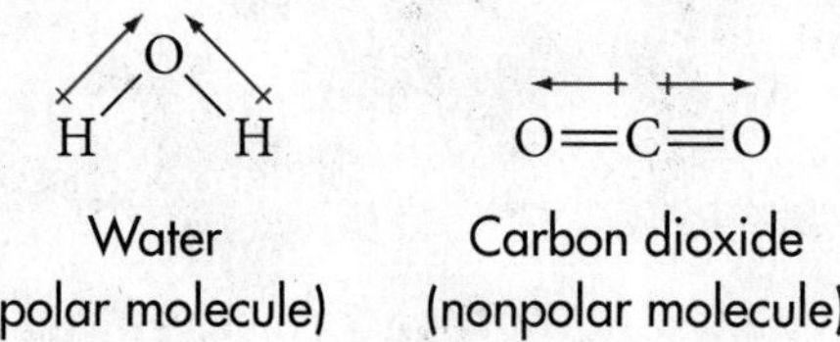

Water (polar molecule)

Carbon dioxide (nonpolar molecule)

The carbon dioxide molecule also has two polar bonds. However, the carbon and oxygen atoms lie along the same axis. Their bond polarities cancel because the bonds are oriented in opposite directions. Carbon dioxide is therefore a nonpolar molecule even though it has polar bonds.

Key Question How do electronegativity values determine the charge distribution in a polar bond? **In a polar bond, the more electronegative atom attracts electrons more strongly and gains a slightly negative charge. The less electronegative atom has a slightly positive charge.**

Attractions Between Molecules

Molecules can be attracted to each other by a variety of different forces. These attractive forces are weaker than ionic bonds and covalent bonds. However, these attractions—called intermolecular attractions—are important. Among other things, these attractions are responsible for determining whether a molecular compound is a gas, a liquid, or a solid at a given temperature.

Van der Waals Forces The two weakest intermolecular attractions form a category called **van der Waals forces.** These forces are named after the Dutch chemist Johannes van der Waals. Van der Waals forces include dipole interactions and dispersion forces.

▶ **Dipole Interactions** **Dipole interactions** occur when polar molecules are attracted to one another. The oppositely charged regions of polar molecules attract each other, as shown in the figure on the left. The slightly negative region of a polar molecule is attracted to the slightly positive region of another polar molecule. Dipole interactions are similar to ionic bonds, but they are much weaker than ionic bonds.

▶ **Dispersion Forces** The weakest of all intermolecular interactions, called **dispersion forces,** are caused by the motion of electrons. All molecules experience dispersion forces—even nonpolar molecules. Dispersion forces occur when moving electrons of one molecule happen to move to one side of a molecule. Their force repels the electrons in a nearby molecule. Those electrons move away, forming a slightly positive charge on one side of the molecule. The shift of charge leads to attraction between the two molecules. Dispersion forces are similar to, but much weaker than, dipole interactions.

Halogen diatomic molecules attract each other mainly by means of dispersion forces. Fluorine and chlorine are gases at room temperature because of their weak dispersion forces. A greater number of electrons allows stronger dispersion forces. Bromine has more electrons than fluorine and chlorine. As a result, bromine molecules attract each other enough that bromine is a liquid at room temperature. Iodine, which has an even greater number of electrons, is a solid at room temperature.

Hydrogen Bonds: A Special Case of Dipole Interactions The dipole interactions in water produce an attraction between water molecules. Each O—H bond in the water molecule is highly polar. The oxygen has a slightly negative charge because of its greater electronegativity. The hydrogen atoms have a slightly positive charge. The positive region of one water molecule attracts the negative region of another water molecule, as shown below.

This attraction—called a hydrogen bond—is strong compared to other dipole interactions. **Hydrogen bonds** are attractive forces in which a hydrogen atom that is covalently bonded to a very electronegative atom is also weakly bonded to an unshared electron pair of another electronegative atom. Hydrogen bonds are the strongest of the intermolecular forces, but they have only about 5 percent of the strength of an average covalent bond. You may guess from the name that hydrogen bonding always involves hydrogen. Hydrogen is the only reactive element with valence electrons that are not shielded from the nucleus by other electrons.

You can find hydrogen bonds in other molecules besides water. Hydrogen bonds form only under certain conditions. A covalent bond must already exist between a hydrogen atom and a highly electronegative atom, such as oxygen, nitrogen, or fluorine. The combination of this highly polar bond and the lack of a shielding effect in the hydrogen atom is responsible for the strength of hydrogen bonds. They are very important in determining the properties of water and biological molecules, such as proteins.

Key Question How do the strengths of intermolecular attractions compare with the strengths of ionic and covalent bonds? **Intermolecular attractions are weaker than ionic bonds and covalent bonds.**

BUILD Connections

Have you ever seen a bug walk on water? This is possible because of hydrogen bonding in water. The attractions between the molecules at the water's surface are so strong that they keep the bug from sinking.

Hydrogen Bonds in Water
The hydrogen bonding between water molecules accounts for many properties of water, including the fact that water is a liquid at room temperature.

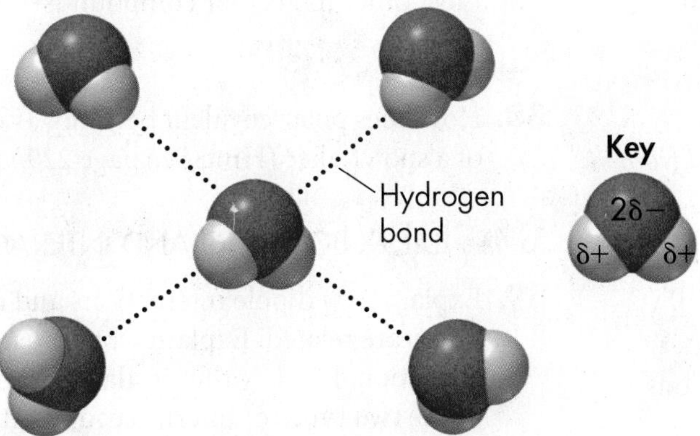

network solid a solid in which all atoms are covalently bonded to one another

USING PRIOR KNOWLEDGE

The word *network* in the term *network solid* should be familiar to you. In common usage, it is an interconnected set of things. For example, you have a network of friends.

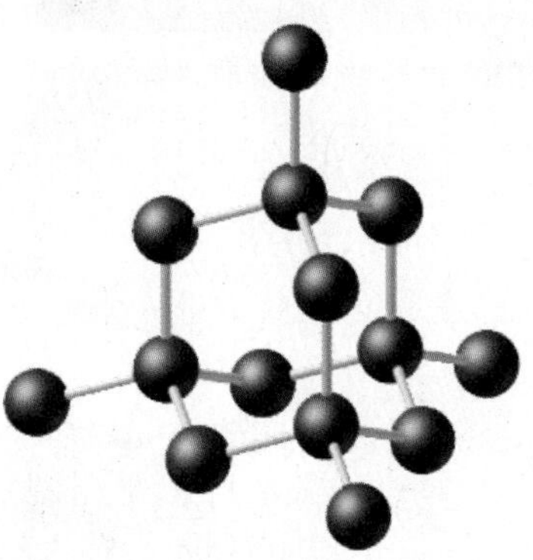

Diamond
Diamond is a network solid form of carbon.

Intermolecular Attractions and Molecular Properties

At room temperature, some compounds are gases, some are liquids, and some are solids. The physical properties of a compound depend on the type of bonding it displays—mostly on whether the bonding is ionic or covalent. A huge range of physical properties exists among molecular compounds. This diversity of physical properties exists mainly because of the widely varying intermolecular attractions the molecules display.

The melting and boiling points of most molecular compounds are low compared with those of ionic compounds. To melt most molecular solids, only the weak attractions between the molecules need to be broken. Others are so stable that they do not melt until the temperature reaches 1000°C or higher. Most of these very stable substances are network solids (or network crystals). In a **network solid**, all the atoms are covalently bonded to each other. Melting a network solid requires breaking covalent bonds throughout the solid.

Diamond is an example of a network solid. Each carbon atom in a diamond is covalently bonded to four other carbon atoms, as shown in the figure on the left. All the carbon atoms throughout the diamond are connected by covalent bonds. Cutting a diamond requires breaking many of these bonds. Diamond does not melt. Instead, it vaporizes to a gas at 3500°C and above. You can think of samples of diamond and other network solids as single molecules.

Key Question Why are the properties of molecular compounds so diverse? **The diversity of physical properties among molecular compounds is mainly due to widely varying intermolecular attractions.**

8.4 LessonCheck

Key Concept Check

31. Explain How do electronegativity values influence the charge distribution in a polar bond?

32. Compare How do the strengths of intermolecular attractions compare to the strengths of ionic bonds and covalent bonds?

33. Explain Why are the properties of molecular compounds so diverse?

Vocabulary Check
Choose a highlighted word from the lesson to complete each sentence correctly.

34. In a(n) _______, one end of the molecule is slightly positive, and the other end is slightly negative.

35. The strongest of all intermolecular attractions are _______.

Think Critically

36. Explain Explain this statement: Not every molecule with polar bonds is polar. Use CCl_4 as an example.

37. Compare How does a network solid differ from most other molecular compounds?

CHEMISTRY & YOU

38. How does polar covalent bonding affect the shape of a snowflake? (Hint: See page 229.)

BIGIDEA BONDING AND INTERACTIONS

39. Explain how dipole interactions and dispersion forces are related. Explain what causes each attraction. Identify the similarities and differences in the two types of intermolecular attractions.

8 Study Guide

BIGIDEA

BONDING AND INTERACTIONS

In molecular compounds, bonding occurs when atoms share electrons. In ionic compounds, bonding occurs when electrons are transferred between atoms. Shared electrons and the valence electrons that are not shared affect the shape of a molecular compound, as the valence electrons stay as far apart from each other as possible. The properties of a molecule are affected by intermolecular attractions.

8.1 Molecular Compounds

A molecular formula shows how many atoms of each element a molecule of a substance contains.

The representative unit of a molecular compound is a molecule. The representative unit of an ionic compound is a formula unit.

- covalent bond (205)
- molecule (205)
- diatomic molecule (205)
- molecular compound (205)
- molecular formula (205)

8.2 The Nature of Covalent Bonding

In covalent bonds, electron sharing usually occurs so atoms attain configurations of noble gases.

In a coordinate covalent bond, the shared electron pair comes from a single atom.

The octet rule is not satisfied in molecules whose total number of valence electrons is an odd number. There are also molecules that have atoms with less, or more, than a complete octet of valence electrons.

A large bond dissociation energy corresponds to a strong covalent bond.

Chemists use resonance structures to model the bonding in molecules that cannot be described by a single structural formula.

- single covalent bond (209)
- structural formula (209)
- unshared pair (209)
- double covalent bond (212)
- triple covalent bond (212)
- coordinate covalent bond (213)
- polyatomic ion (214)
- bond dissociation energy (217)
- resonance structure (218)

8.3 Bonding Theories

Just as an atomic orbital belongs to a particular atom, a molecular orbital belongs to a molecule as a whole.

Scientists use the VSEPR theory to predict the shapes of molecules.

Orbital hybridization provides information about both molecular bonding and molecular shape.

- molecular orbital (220)
- bonding orbital (220)
- VSEPR theory (221)
- tetrahedral angle (222)
- hybridization (223)

8.4 Polar Bonds and Molecules

In a polar bond, the more electronegative atom attracts electrons more strongly and gains a slightly negative charge. The less electronegative atom has a slightly positive charge.

Intermolecular attractions are weaker than ionic bonds and covalent bonds.

The diversity of physical properties among molecular compounds is mainly due to widely varying intermolecular attractions.

- nonpolar covalent bond (224)
- polar bond (224)
- polar molecule (225)
- dipole (225)
- van der Waals forces (228)
- dipole interactions (228)
- dispersion forces (228)
- hydrogen bond (229)
- network solid (230)

8 Assessment

★ Solutions appear in Appendix D.

Lesson by Lesson

8.1 Molecular Compounds

40. The melting point of a compound is 1240°C. Is this compound most likely an ionic compound or a molecular compound?

41. Identify the numbers and kinds of atoms in a molecule of ascorbic acid (vitamin C), $C_6H_8O_6$.

42. Which of the following gases in Earth's atmosphere would you expect to find as molecules and which as individual atoms? Explain.

a. nitrogen
b. oxygen
c. argon

43. Describe the differences between molecular formulas and structural formulas.

8.2 The Nature of Covalent Bonding

44. Explain why neon is monatomic but chlorine is diatomic.

45. Classify the following compounds as ionic or molecular.

a. $MgCl_2$
b. Na_2S
c. H_2O
d. H_2S

46. Describe the differences between an ionic and a covalent bond.

47. How many electrons do two atoms in a double covalent bond share? How many in a triple covalent bond?

★48. Describe a coordinate covalent bond and then give an example.

49. Draw possible electron dot structures for the following substances. Each substance contains only single covalent bonds.

a. I_2
b. OF_2
c. H_2S
d. NI_3

50. Draw the electron dot structure for the hydrogen carbonate ion (HCO_3^-). Carbon is the central atom, and hydrogen is attached to oxygen in this polyatomic ion.

★51. Which of these compounds contains elements that do not follow the octet rule? Explain.

a. NF_3
b. PCl_2F_3
c. SF_4
d. SCl_2

52. Explain what is meant by bond dissociation energy.

53. When a sulfur atom forms a covalent bond to achieve an octet of electrons, how many electrons are in shared pairs?

★54. Draw the electron dot structures for each of these molecules.

a. NH_3
b. BrCl
c. H_2O_2
d. SiH_4

8.3 Bonding Theories

★55. Use VSEPR theory to predict the shapes of the following compounds.

a. CO_2
b. $SiCl_4$
c. SO_3
d. SCl_2
e. CO
f. H_2Se

8.4 Polar Bonds and Molecules

56. How must the electronegativities of two atoms compare if a covalent bond between them is to be polar?

57. What is a hydrogen bond?

58. Why do compounds with strong intermolecular attractive forces have higher boiling points than compounds with weak intermolecular attractive forces?

59. Which of these molecules is least likely to form a hydrogen bond with a water molecule? Explain your reasoning.

a. NH_3
b. CH_3Cl
c. HF
d. H_2O_2

Understand Concepts

60. Explain why each of the following electron dot structures is incorrect. Replace each structure with one that is more acceptable.

a. $[:C::\dot{N}:]^-$

b. $:\ddot{F}:\ddot{P}::\ddot{F}:$
$\quad\;\; :\ddot{F}:$

61. Use VSEPR theory to predict the geometry of each of the following substances.

a. $SiCl_4$ **c.** CCl_4
b. CO_3^{2-} **d.** SCl_2

62. What term describes the geometry around the central atom in each of these simple molecules?

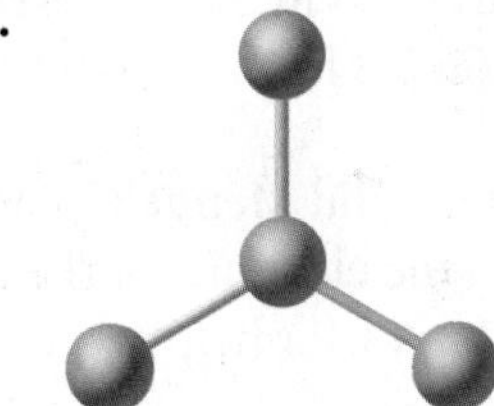

b.

c.

d.

63. Vinegar contains the compound ethanoic acid, whose molecular formula is CH_3COOH.

a. Draw the electron dot structure of ethanoic acid. (Hint: The two carbon atoms are bonded to each other, and the two oxygen atoms are bonded to the same carbon.)

b. Is the bonding between each of the oxygen atoms and the carbon the same?

c. Is the bonding between the carbon atom and each oxygen atom a polar or nonpolar bond?

d. Is ethanoic acid a polar molecule?

Think Critically

★64. Explain Ethyl alcohol (CH_3CH_2OH) and dimethyl ether (CH_3OCH_3) each have the same molecular formula: C_2H_6O. Ethyl alcohol has a much higher boiling point (78°C) than dimethyl ether (−25°C). Offer an explanation for this difference.

65. Evaluate Although the relative positions of the atoms are correct in each of these molecules, there are one or more incorrect bonds in each of the electron dot structures. Identify the incorrect bonds. Draw the correct electron dot structure for each molecule.

a. H=C=C=H
b. :F—O—H
c. :I:::Cl:
d. H—N:::N—H

★66. Predict What shape do you expect for a molecule with a central atom and the following electron pairings?

a. two bonding pairs of electrons and two nonbonding pairs of electrons
b. four bonding pairs of electrons and zero nonbonding pairs of electrons
c. three bonding pairs of electrons and one nonbonding pair of electrons

FOUNDATIONS Wrap-Up

Shapes of Molecules

1. Draw Conclusions At the beginning of this chapter, you formed clusters of two, three, and four balloons. Explain how the balloons behaved like atoms in a molecule.

Concept Check

Now that you've finished studying Chapter 8, answer these questions.

2. Table salt (NaCl) melts at a much higher temperature than table sugar ($C_{12}H_{22}O_{11}$) does. Why is this so?

3. When in an elevator, you likely move so you are separated from your neighbors as much as possible. How is this situation similar to how electron pairs arrange themselves in a molecule?

Write About Science

67. **Explain** Describe what a molecular compound is. Explain how a molecular formula is the chemical formula of a molecular compound.

68. **Research a Problem** Research how chemists know that an oxygen molecule has unpaired electrons. Write a brief report on what you find.

CHEMYSTERY

What's That Alarm?

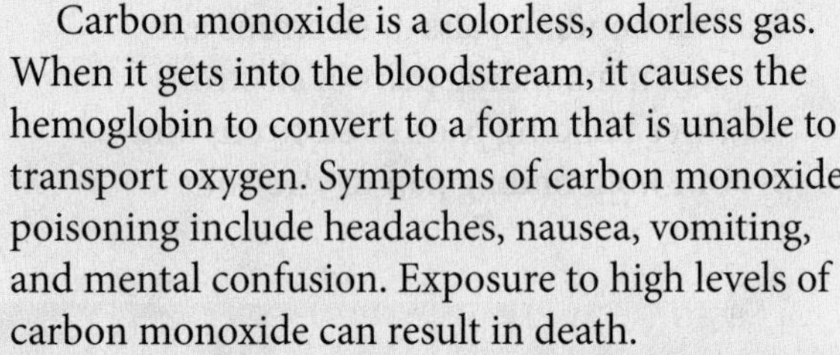

The family realized that the alarm was caused by carbon monoxide (CO). In carbon monoxide, the carbon and oxygen atom are joined by a triple covalent bond. Although carbon monoxide and carbon dioxide are both made of carbon and oxygen atoms, they have very different properties.

Carbon monoxide is a colorless, odorless gas. When it gets into the bloodstream, it causes the hemoglobin to convert to a form that is unable to transport oxygen. Symptoms of carbon monoxide poisoning include headaches, nausea, vomiting, and mental confusion. Exposure to high levels of carbon monoxide can result in death.

Fuel-burning appliances, such as water heaters, fireplaces, furnaces, and gas stoves, produce carbon monoxide. If the appliance is not working properly, it may release unsafe amounts of carbon monoxide. If a home has one of these appliances, the homeowners should install carbon monoxide detectors because people cannot detect the gas by sight or smell.

69. **Use Models** Draw the electron dot structures of carbon monoxide and carbon dioxide.

70. **Connect to the BIGIDEA** How does covalent bonding allow different molecular compounds composed of the same kinds of atoms?

Cumulative Review

71. Name three indicators of chemical change. (See Lesson 2.4 for help.)

*72. Make the following conversions. (See Lesson 3.3 for help.)
   a. 66.5 mm to micrometers
   b. 4×10^{-2} g to centigrams
   c. 5.62 mg/mL to decigrams per liter
   d. 85 km/h to meters per second

73. How many neutrons are in each atom? (See Lesson 4.3 for help.)
   a. silicon-30
   b. magnesium-24
   c. nitrogen-15
   d. chromium-50

74. What does the 5 in $3d^5$ represent? (See Lesson 5.2 for help.)

75. What criteria did Mendeleev and Moseley use to arrange the elements in the periodic table? (See Lesson 6.1 for help.)

*76. Identify the larger atom of each pair. (See Lesson 6.3 for help.)
   a. calcium and barium
   b. silicon and sulfur
   c. sodium and nitrogen

77. How many valence electrons does each atom have? (See Lesson 7.1 for help.)
   a. argon
   b. aluminum
   c. selenium
   d. beryllium

*78. Which of the following ions has the same number of electrons as a noble gas? (See Lesson 7.1 for help.)
   a. Al^{3+}
   b. O^{2-}
   c. Br^-
   d. N^{3-}

79. Which element is likely to form an ionic compound with chlorine? (See Lesson 7.2 for help.)
   a. iodine
   b. cesium
   c. helium

Standardized Test Prep

For help with answering test questions, go to your Chemistry Skills and Math Workbook.

Select the choice that best answers each question or completes each statement.

1. A bond in which two atoms share a pair of electrons is not
(A) a coordinate covalent bond.
(B) a polar covalent bond.
(C) an ionic bond.
(D) a nonpolar covalent bond.

2. How many valence electrons are in a molecule of phosphoric acid (H_3PO_4)?
(A) 7 (C) 24
(B) 16 (D) 32

3. Which of these molecules can form a hydrogen bond with a water molecule?
(A) N_2 (C) O_2
(B) NH_3 (D) CH_4

4. Which substance contains both covalent and ionic bonds?
(A) NH_4NO_3 (C) LiF
(B) CH_3OCH_3 (D) $CaCl_2$

5. Which of these bonds is most polar?
(A) H—Cl (C) H—F
(B) H—Br (D) H—I

Use the description and data table below to answer Questions 6–9.

The table relates molecular shape to the number of bonding and nonbonding electron pairs in molecules.

Bonding pairs	Non-bonding pairs	Arrangement of electron pairs	Molecular shape	Example
4	0	tetrahedral	tetrahedral	CH_4
3	1	tetrahedral	pyramidal	NCl_3
2	2	tetrahedral	bent	H_2S
1	3	tetrahedral	linear	HF

6. Draw the electron dot structure for each example molecule.

7. Explain why the arrangement of electron pairs is tetrahedral in each molecule.

8. H_2S has two hydrogen atoms bonded to a sulfur atom. Why is the molecule not linear?

9. What is the arrangement of electron pairs in PBr_3? Predict the molecular shape of a PBr_3 molecule.

For Questions 10–11, identify the type of intermolecular forces represented by the dotted lines in the drawings.

10. H_2O

11. BrCl

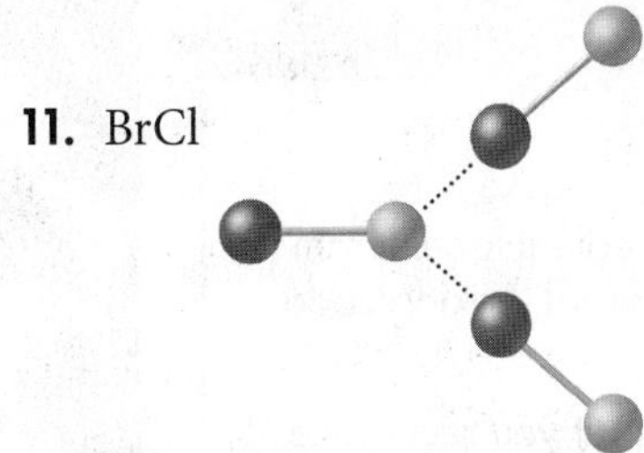

Tips for Success

Connectors Sometimes, two phrases in a true/false question are connected by a word such as *because*. The word implies that one thing caused another thing to happen. Statements that include such words can be false even if both parts of the statement are true by themselves.

In Questions 12–14, a statement is followed by an explanation. Decide if each statement is true and then decide if the explanation given is correct.

12. A carbon monoxide molecule has a triple covalent bond because carbon and oxygen atoms have an unequal number of valence electrons.

13. Xenon has a lower boiling point than neon because dispersion forces between xenon atoms are stronger than those between neon atoms.

14. The nitrate ion has three resonance structures because the nitrate ion has three single bonds.

If You Have Trouble With . . .

Question	1	2	3	4	5	6	7	8	9	10	11	12	13	14
See Lesson	8.2	8.2	8.4	8.3	8.1	8.3	8.2	8.2	8.2	8.2	8.4	8.4	8.4	8.2

9 Chemical Names and Formulas

FOUNDATIONS for Learning

Element Name Search

1. Select a variety of ingredient labels from such items as bread, cereal, baking soda, soap, and shampoo.
2. List all the ingredients that you recognize. Do not be discouraged by the many unfamiliar names.
3. With the help of a periodic table, list all the ingredient names that contain or come from the name of an element.

Identify Circle the names of all the elements on your list that are metals.

PearsonChem.com

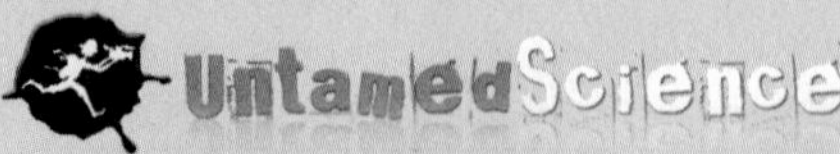

Take a video field trip and travel back in time with the Untamed Science crew as two sailors are introduced to the new language of chemistry.

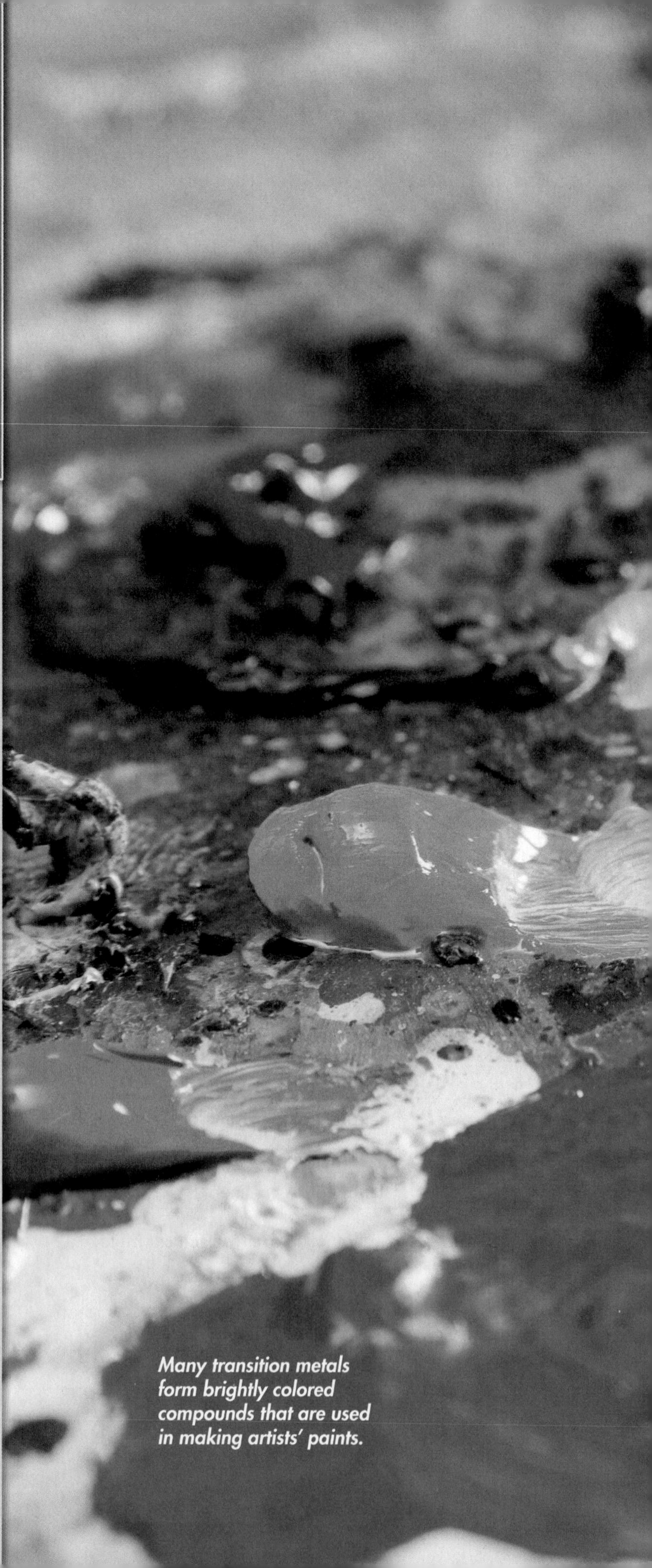

Many transition metals form brightly colored compounds that are used in making artists' paints.

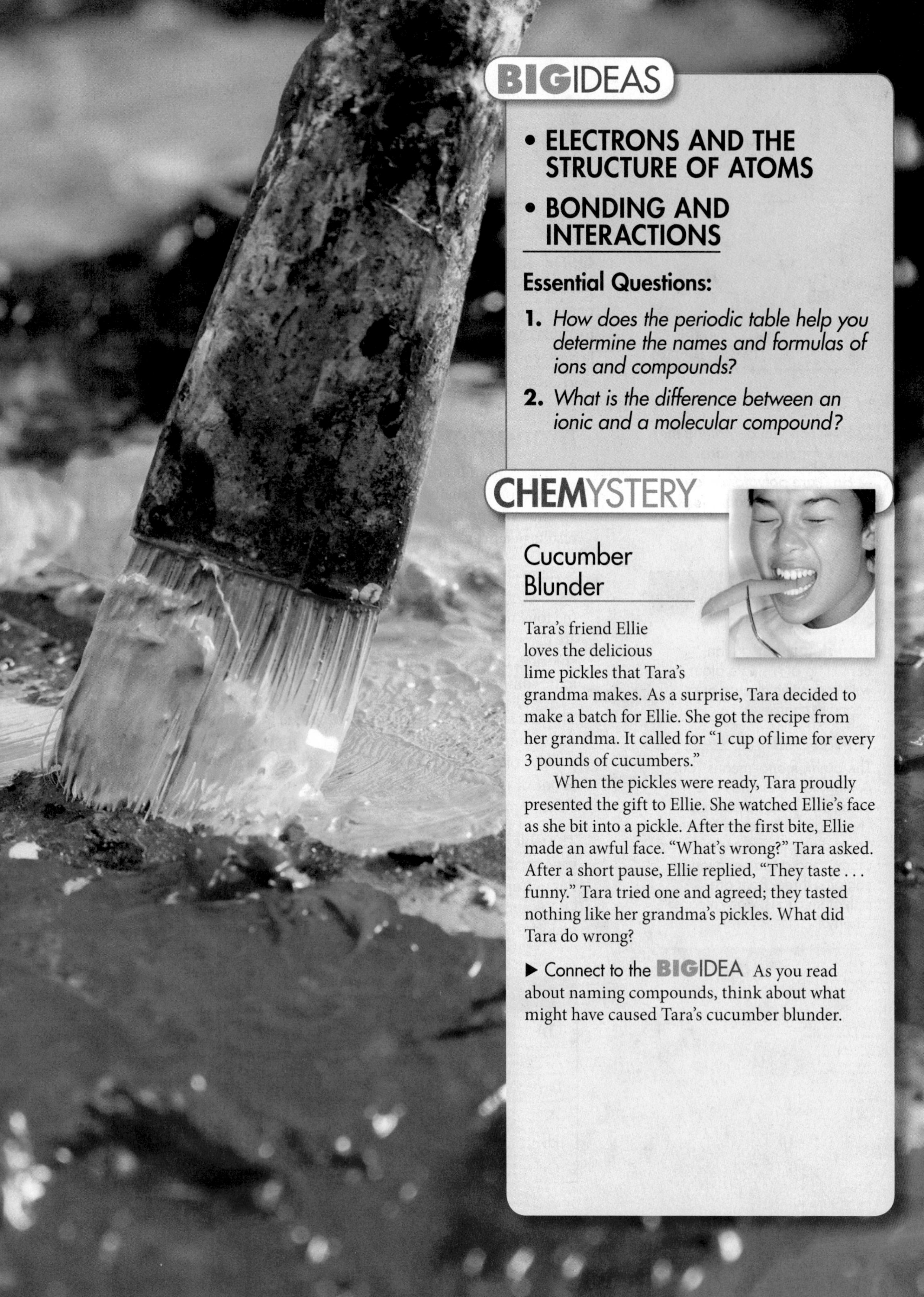

BIGIDEAS

- **ELECTRONS AND THE STRUCTURE OF ATOMS**
- **BONDING AND INTERACTIONS**

Essential Questions:

1. *How does the periodic table help you determine the names and formulas of ions and compounds?*
2. *What is the difference between an ionic and a molecular compound?*

CHEMYSTERY

Cucumber Blunder

Tara's friend Ellie loves the delicious lime pickles that Tara's grandma makes. As a surprise, Tara decided to make a batch for Ellie. She got the recipe from her grandma. It called for "1 cup of lime for every 3 pounds of cucumbers."

When the pickles were ready, Tara proudly presented the gift to Ellie. She watched Ellie's face as she bit into a pickle. After the first bite, Ellie made an awful face. "What's wrong?" Tara asked. After a short pause, Ellie replied, "They taste . . . funny." Tara tried one and agreed; they tasted nothing like her grandma's pickles. What did Tara do wrong?

▶ Connect to the **BIGIDEA** As you read about naming compounds, think about what might have caused Tara's cucumber blunder.

9.1 Naming Ions

CHEMISTRY & YOU

Q: Do you speak the language of chemistry? Look at the label on a bottle of window cleaner or dishwashing liquid. Do the ingredient names make sense? Every substance has a unique chemical name and formula. Naming compounds is an important skill in chemistry. In this lesson, you learn how to name ions. Then, in the next lesson, you will learn how to name ionic compounds.

Key Questions

How can you determine the charges of monatomic ions?

How are polyatomic ions different from monatomic ions and how are they similar?

BUILD Vocabulary

monatomic ion an ion consisting of a single atom with a positive charge or a negative charge

PREFIXES

The prefix *mono-* means "one." A monatomic ion has one atom. The prefix *di-* means "two," and *tri-* means "three." So, a diatomic ion contains two atoms, and a triatomic ion contains three. Both are polyatomic ions. *Poly-* means "many."

Monatomic Ions

Ionic compounds are made up of positive ions and negative ions. The positive ion is usually a metal. The negative ion is often a nonmetal. In an ionic compound, oppositely charged ions combine in a way that results in a net charge of zero.

Sodium chloride (NaCl) is an ionic compound. It contains one sodium ion (Na^+) and one chloride ion (Cl^-). The total positive charge equals the total negative charge. So, the net charge of the compound is zero. You are probably familiar with the name and chemical formula of sodium chloride. But how do you determine the names and formulas of other ionic compounds?

The first step is to learn more about ions. The simplest ions are monatomic ions. A **monatomic ion** consists of a single atom with a positive or negative charge. The ion's charge results from the loss or gain of one or more valence electrons. A loss of electrons yields a positively charged ion. A gain of electrons yields a negatively charged ion.

The table below shows the ion symbols for some Group A elements. The superscript after each element symbol indicates the charge of the ion. For example, Li^+ is a monatomic ion with a one unit of positive charge. O^{2-} is a monatomic ion with two units of negative charge. Note that the majority of elements in Groups 4A and 8A usually do not form ions.

Ion Symbols for Some Group A Elements

1A	2A	3A	4A	5A	6A	7A	8A
Li^+	Be^{2+}			N^{3-}	O^{2-}	F^-	
Na^+	Mg^{2+}	Al^{3+}		P^{3-}	S^{2-}	Cl^-	
K^+	Ca^{2+}			As^{3-}	Se^{2-}	Br^-	
Rb^+	Sr^{2+}					I^-	
Cs^+	Ba^{2+}						

Cations Metallic elements tend to lose valence electrons to form cations. The figure to the right identifies several metals whose ionic charges can be obtained from their positions in the periodic table. When the metals in Groups 1A, 2A, and 3A lose electrons, they form cations with positive charges equal to their group number.

For example, lithium, sodium, and potassium are metals in Group 1A. These metals lose one electron to form cations with a 1+ charge: Li^+, Na^+, and K^+. Magnesium and calcium are Group 2A metals. They tend to lose two electrons to form cations with a 2+ charge: Mg^{2+} and Ca^{2+}. Aluminum is the only common Group 3A metal. As you might expect, aluminum atoms lose three electrons and form a 3+ cation: Al^{3+}.

The names of the cations of the Group 1A, Group 2A, and Group 3A metals are the name of the metal, followed by the word *ion* or *cation*. So, Na^+ is the sodium ion (or sodium cation), Ca^{2+} is the calcium ion (or calcium cation), and Al^{3+} is the aluminum ion (or aluminum cation).

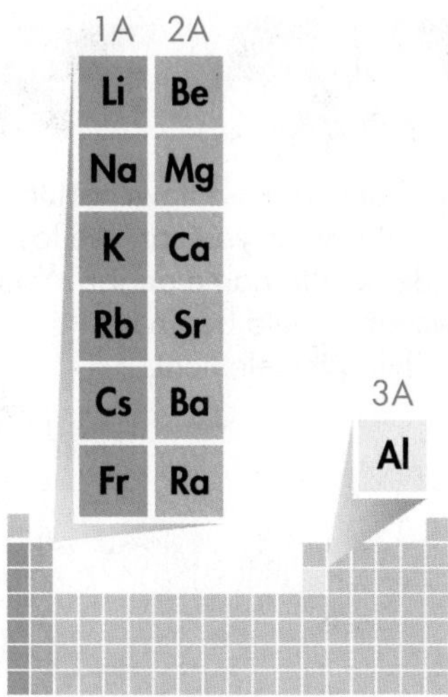

Elements That Form Cations
These representative elements form positive ions with charges equal to their group number.

Anions Nonmetals tend to gain electrons to form anions. So, the charge of a nonmetal ion is negative. To find the charge of any ion of a Group A nonmetal, subtract 8 from the group number. The elements in Group 7A form anions with a 1− charge ($7 - 8 = -1$). Anion names start with the stem of the element name and end in *-ide*. For example, two elements in Group 7A are fluorine and chlorine. Their anions are the fluor*ide* ion (F^-) and chlor*ide* ion (Cl^-).

Anions of nonmetals in Group 6A have a 2− charge ($6 - 8 = -2$). Oxygen and sulfur are Group 6A elements. Oxygen forms the ox*ide* anion (O^{2-}), and sulfur forms the sulf*ide* anion (S^{2-}). The first three elements in Group 5A—nitrogen, phosphorus, and arsenic—form anions with a 3− charge. These anions have the symbols N^{3-}, P^{3-}, and As^{3-}. They are called nitr*ide* ion, phosph*ide* ion, and arsen*ide* ion, respectively. The figure at right shows common Group A elements that form anions.

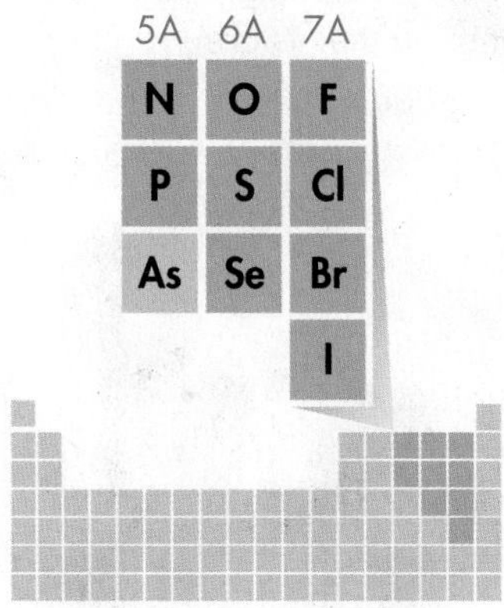

Elements That Form Anions
These representative elements form negative ions with charges equal to the group number of the element minus 8.

Metals That Form More Than One Ion Some metallic elements can form more than one cation with different ionic charges. These include certain transition metals in Groups 1B through 8B. The charges of the cations of many transition metals must be determined from the number of electrons lost. For example, iron is a transition metal that forms two common cations. If an iron atom loses two electrons, it forms the Fe^{2+} cation. If the atom loses three electrons, it forms the Fe^{3+} cation. Cations of tin and lead can also have more than one common ionic charge. The figure to the right identifies some of the metallic elements that form more than one cation.

▶ **Stock System** There are two methods for naming cations that can have more than one charge. The preferred method is the Stock system. In the Stock system, the charge on the ion is shown by a Roman numeral in parentheses after the name of the element. For example, Fe^{2+} is named iron(II) ion. You read the name as "iron two ion." The cation Fe^{3+} is named iron(III) ion, which is read as "iron three ion." Note that there is no space between the element name and the Roman numeral in parentheses.

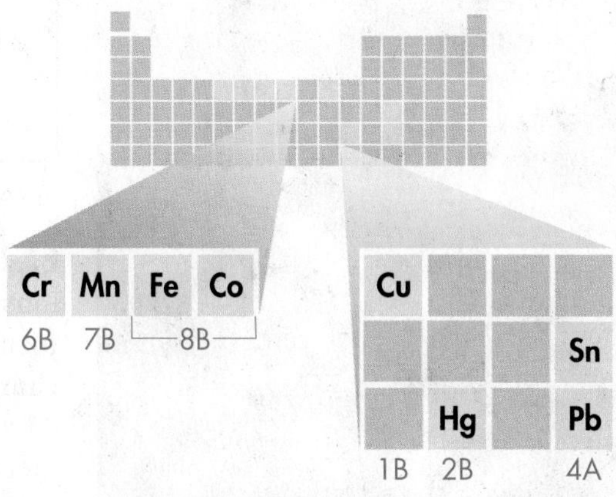

Elements That Form More Than One Ion
These metallic elements form more than one positive ion.

BUILD Understanding

Flowchart Make a flowchart that shows the steps you can use to decide how to name an ion. Your flowchart should begin by classifying the element.

▶ **Classical Names** An older, less useful method for naming cations uses a root word followed by different suffixes. The classical name of the element is used to form the root word. For example, *ferrum* is Latin for iron. So, *ferr-* is the root name for iron. The suffix *-ous* is used to name the cation with the lower of the two ionic charges. The suffix *-ic* is used with the higher of the two ionic charges. In this system, Fe^{2+} is the ferrous ion and Fe^{3+} is the ferric ion.

Classical Names of Iron Cations

Symbol	Element	Root	Suffix	Name (root + suffix)
Fe^{2+}	Iron	*ferr-*	*-ous*	Ferrous ion
Fe^{3+}	Iron	*ferr-*	*-ic*	Ferric ion

A major disadvantage of using classical names for ions is that they do not tell you the actual charge of the ion. The table below lists the Stock names and classical names of common metal ions with more than one charge.

Symbols and Names of Common Metal Ions With More Than One Ionic Charge

Symbol	Stock name	Classical name
Cu^{+}	Copper(I) ion	Cuprous ion
Cu^{2+}	Copper(II) ion	Cupric ion
Fe^{2+}	Iron(II) ion	Ferrous ion
Fe^{3+}	Iron(III) ion	Ferric ion
*Hg_2^{2+}	Mercury(I) ion	Mercurous ion
Hg^{2+}	Mercury(II) ion	Mercuric ion
Pb^{2+}	Lead(II) ion	Plumbous ion
Pb^{4+}	Lead(IV) ion	Plumbic ion
Sn^{2+}	Tin(II) ion	Stannous ion
Sn^{4+}	Tin(IV) ion	Stannic ion
Cr^{2+}	Chromium(II) ion	Chromous ion
Cr^{3+}	Chromium(III) ion	Chromic ion
Mn^{2+}	Manganese(II) ion	Manganous ion
Mn^{3+}	Manganese(III) ion	Manganic ion

*A diatomic elemental ion

Key Question How can you determine the charges of monatomic ions? **When the metals in Groups 1A, 2A, and 3A lose electrons, they form cations with positive charges equal to their group number. The charge of any ion of a Group A nonmetal is determined by subtracting 8 from the group number. The charges of cations of many transition metal ions can be determined from the number of electrons lost.**

Transition Metal Ions Compounds and solutions that contain ions of transition metals are often strongly colored.

SampleProblem 9.1

Naming Cations and Anions

Name the ion formed by each of these elements.

a. potassium **b.** sulfur

❶ **Analyze** **Identify the relevant concepts.** Use the periodic table to determine the charge of Group A elements. Cations have positive charges; anions have negative charges. Metal cations take the name of the metal. The names of nonmetallic anions end in *-ide*.

❷ **Solve** **Apply the concepts to this problem.**

Write the symbol for the element.	**a.** K	**b.** S
Determine the charge of the ion formed by the element.	1+	2−
Determine whether the ion is a cation or an anion.	K^+ is a cation.	S^{2-} is an anion.
Apply the appropriate rules for naming the ion. Use a Roman numeral if necessary.	Following the rules for naming metal cations, K^+ is named potassium ion.	Following the rules for naming nonmetal anions, S^{2-} is named sulfide ion.

Practice Problems

1. Name the ions formed by these elements.

a. selenium **c.** barium

b. phosphorus **d.** iodine

❶ **Analyze** **Identify the relevant concepts.**

❷ **Solve** **Apply the concepts to this problem.**

2. How many electrons were lost or gained to form these ions?

a. Fe^{3+} **b.** O^{2-} **c.** Cu^+ **d.** Sr^{2+}

3. Challenge Name the ion formed when a lead atom loses 4 electrons.

Remember: You can use the periodic table to determine the ionic charge of a Group A element.

Hint: In Problem 3, use a Roman numeral to indicate the numerical value of the charge of the lead ion.

Polyatomic Ions
These molecular models show the arrangement of atoms in four common polyatomic ions.

Ammonium ion (NH_4^+)

Nitrate ion (NO_3^-)

Sulfate ion (SO_4^{2-})

Phosphate ion (PO_4^{3-})

Common Polyatomic Ions

Charge	Formula	Name
1–	$H_2PO_4^-$	Dihydrogen phosphate
	$C_2H_3O_2^-$	Ethanoate
	HSO_3^-	Hydrogen sulfite
	HSO_4^-	Hydrogen sulfate
	HCO_3^-	Hydrogen carbonate
	NO_2^-	Nitrite
	NO_3^-	Nitrate
	CN^-	Cyanide
	OH^-	Hydroxide
	MnO_4^-	Permanganate
	ClO^-	Hypochlorite
	ClO_2^-	Chlorite
	ClO_3^-	Chlorate
	ClO_4^-	Perchlorate
2–	HPO_4^{2-}	Hydrogen phosphate
	$C_2O_4^{2-}$	Oxalate
	SO_3^{2-}	Sulfite
	SO_4^{2-}	Sulfate
	CO_3^{2-}	Carbonate
	CrO_4^{2-}	Chromate
	$Cr_2O_7^{2-}$	Dichromate
	SiO_3^{2-}	Silicate
3–	PO_3^{3-}	Phosphite
	PO_4^{3-}	Phosphate
1+	NH_4^+	Ammonium

Polyatomic Ions

Not all ions consist of a single atom. For example, the sulfate anion consists of one sulfur atom and four oxygen atoms. These five atoms together make up a single anion with an overall 2– charge. The formula is written as SO_4^{2-}.

Sulfate is an example of a polyatomic ion. Unlike a monatomic ion, a polyatomic ion is composed of more than one atom. But like a monatomic ion, a polyatomic ion behaves as a unit and carries a charge. The figure above shows the structures of four common polyatomic ions. The atoms in each polyatomic ion are held together by covalent bonds.

Naming Polyatomic ions The table to the left lists the names and formulas of common polyatomic ions. You can see that the names of most polyatomic anions end in *-ite* or *-ate*. For example, notice the endings of the names of the hypochlor*ite* ion (ClO^-) and the nitr*ate* ion (NO_3^-).

Sometimes, the same two or three elements combine in different ratios to form different polyatomic ions. You should be able to find several examples in the table. Look for pairs of ions for which there is an *-ite* and an *-ate* ending. One such pair is sulfite and sulfate. You should be able to discern a pattern in the naming convention.

-ite	***-ate***
SO_3^{2-}, sulfite	SO_4^{2-}, sulfate
NO_2^-, nitrite	NO_3^-, nitrate
ClO_2^-, chlorite	ClO_3^-, chlorate

The charge on each polyatomic ion in a given pair is the same. The *-ite* ending indicates one less oxygen atom than the *-ate* ending. However, the ending does not tell you the actual number of oxygen atoms in the ion. For example, the nitrite ion has two oxygen atoms, and the sulfite ion has three oxygen atoms. All anions with names ending in *-ite* or *-ate* contain oxygen.

Three important polyatomic ions do not have names ending in *-ite* or *-ate*. The CN^- anion is called the cyan*ide* ion. The OH^- anion is called the hydrox*ide* ion. And the NH_4^+ cation is called the ammon*ium* ion. Notice that the ammonium ion is the only common polyatomic ion with a positive charge.

Polyatomic Ions That Contain Hydrogen When the formula for a polyatomic ion begins with H (hydrogen), you can think of the H as representing a hydrogen ion (H^+) combined with another polyatomic ion. For example, HCO_3^- is a combination of H^+ and CO_3^{2-}. The charge on the new ion is the sum of the ionic charges of the two ions that combine.

H^+	+	CO_3^{2-}	$\longrightarrow$	HCO_3^-
Hydrogen ion (1+ charge)		Carbonate ion (2– charge)		Hydrogen carbonate ion (1– charge)

H^+	+	PO_4^{3-}	$\longrightarrow$	HPO_4^{2-}
Hydrogen ion (1+ charge)		Phosphate ion (3– charge)		Hydrogen phosphate ion (2– charge)

The hydrogen carbonate anion (HCO_3^-) and the hydrogen phosphate anion HPO_4^{2-} are essential components of living systems.

Key Question How do polyatomic ions differ from monatomic ions and how are they similar? **Unlike a monatomic ion, a polyatomic ion is composed of more than one atom. But like a monatomic ion, a polyatomic ion behaves as a unit and carries a charge.**

BUILD Connections

Human blood is mostly water by volume. Blood also contains many dissolved ionic compounds, some of which contain polyatomic ions. Essential ions in your blood include the hydrogen carbonate anion (HCO_3^-), the hydrogen phosphate anion (HPO_4^{2-}), and the dihydrogen phosphate anion ($H_2PO_4^-$).

9.1 LessonCheck

Key Concept Check

4. Explain How can you determine the charges of Group A metal cations? Of nonmetal anions? Of transition metal cations?

5. Compare How are polyatomic ions and monatomic ions similar? How are they different?

Think Critically

6. Identify What are the charges on ions of Group 1A, Group 3A (aluminum), and Group 5A (nonmetals)?

7. Describe Write the symbol for the ion of each element. Classify the ion as an anion or a cation, and then name the ion.

a. potassium
b. oxygen
c. bromine
d. tin (2 electrons lost)
e. beryllium
f. cobalt (3 electrons lost)

8. Describe Write the symbol or formula (including charge) for each of these ions.

a. ammonium ion
b. chromium(II) ion
c. chromate ion
d. nitrate ion

CHEMISTRY & YOU

9. Suppose you were trying to teach someone how to name ions. Which rules about the "language of chemistry" would you emphasize? (Hint: See pages 239–240 and 242–243.)

BIGIDEA
ELECTRONS AND THE STRUCTURE OF ATOMS

10. How does the electron configuration of an ion of a Group 1A or Group 7A element compare to that of the nearest noble gas? How do the charges of the two ions compare?

9.2 Naming and Writing Formulas for Ionic Compounds

CHEMISTRY & YOU

Q: What is the name of the secret ingredient? If you leave peach or pineapple slices out to dry for several days, the fruit can turn an ugly brown. But if you follow a recipe and use a certain ingredient, the fruit slices will keep their color for a long period of time. For a recipe to make sense, you need to be able to identify the ingredients by name. In the chemistry laboratory, you will need to be able to identify chemicals by name. In this lesson, you learn how to name ionic compounds.

Key Questions

How do you determine the formula and name of a binary ionic compound?

How do you determine the formula and name of a compound with a polyatomic ion?

BUILD Vocabulary

binary compound a compound composed of two elements

WORD ORIGINS

Binary comes from the Latin word *bini*, which means "two by two."

Binary Ionic Compounds

Many substances have common names that refer to a property of the substance or its source. Consider baking soda. The common name, *baking soda,* tells you how the compound is used. It helps make breads and cake mixes rise during baking. The chemical formula of baking soda is $NaHCO_3$.

Potash (K_2CO_3) is another example. It is an ionic compound that can be obtained by boiling wood ashes in iron pots. Hence, the name *potash.* The photo below shows a substance with the common name *cinnabar.* Can you tell what elements are in cinnabar just from looking at the name? Unfortunately, such names do not tell you anything about the chemical composition of the compound.

French chemist Antoine-Laurent Lavoisier (1743–1794) determined the composition of many compounds in his experiments. As more and more compounds were identified, Lavoisier found it hard to memorize all the unrelated compound names. Together with other chemists, he developed a systematic method for naming chemical compounds.

Writing Formulas for Binary Ionic Compounds *Potassium chloride* is the name of a common ionic compound. It consists of potassium cations (K^+) and chloride anions (Cl^-). A compound composed of two elements is called a **binary compound**. Potassium chloride is an example of a binary ionic compound. Note that some molecular compounds can also be binary compounds.

If you know the name of a binary ionic compound, you can write its formula. To write the formula of a binary ionic compound, first write the symbol of the cation, and then the anion. Then, add subscripts as needed to balance the charges. The ions must be combined in the lowest whole-number ratio.

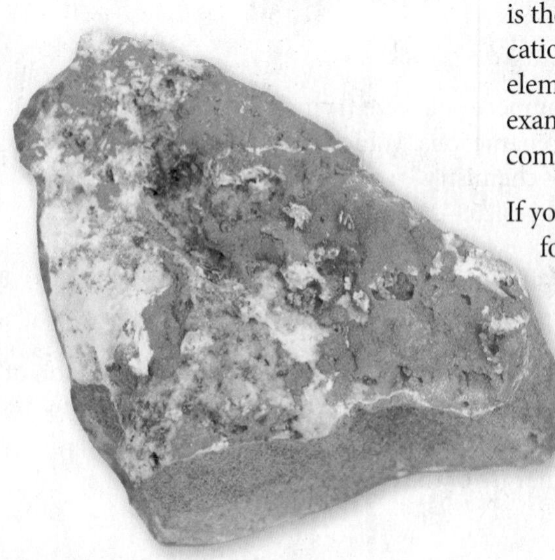

Cinnabar
The red substance that is deposited in this rock is commonly called cinnabar. Its chemical formula is HgS.

▶ Balancing the Charges In an ionic compound, the positive charge of the cation(s) balances the negative charge of the anion(s). So, the net ionic charge of the formula unit is zero.

Name	Cation	Anion	Ratio of Ions	Formula
Potassium chloride	K^+	Cl^-	1:1	KCl
Calcium bromide	Ca^{2+}	Br^-	1:2	$CaBr_2$
Iron(III) oxide	Fe^{3+}	O^{2-}	2:3	Fe_2O_3

The table above lists three binary ionic compounds. Start with potassium chloride. The 1+ charge of each potassium cation (K^+) is balanced by the 1− charge of each chloride anion (Cl^-). So, in potassium chloride, the potassium and chloride ions combine in a 1:1 ratio. The formula is KCl. The net ionic charge of the formula unit is zero.

Calcium bromide is made up of calcium cations (Ca^{2+}) and bromide anions (Br^-). The two ions do not have equal charges. Each calcium ion has a 2+ charge, so it combines with two negative charges. Each bromide ion has a 1− charge. So, the ions combine in a 1:2 ratio. The formula for calcium bromide is $CaBr_2$.

The figure to the right shows a steel factory, where steel is made from iron ore. Hematite, a common iron ore, contains iron(III) oxide. Iron(III) oxide consists of iron(III) cations (Fe^{3+}) and oxide anions (O^{2-}). How can you balance a 3+ charge and a 2− charge? First, you must find the least common multiple of the numbers 3 and 2, which is 6. Now look at each ion. How many Fe^{3+} cations give you a 6+ charge? You need two. How many O^{2-} anions give you a 6− charge? You need three. So, two Fe^{3+} cations balance three O^{2-} anions. The correct formula is Fe_2O_3.

Steelworks
In the process for making steel, iron is extracted from hematite, an ore containing iron(III) oxide.

▶ The Crisscross Method Another way to write a balanced formula for a binary ionic compound is the crisscross method. The numerical value of the charge of each ion is crossed over and becomes the subscript for the other ion. Notice how the signs of the charges are dropped.

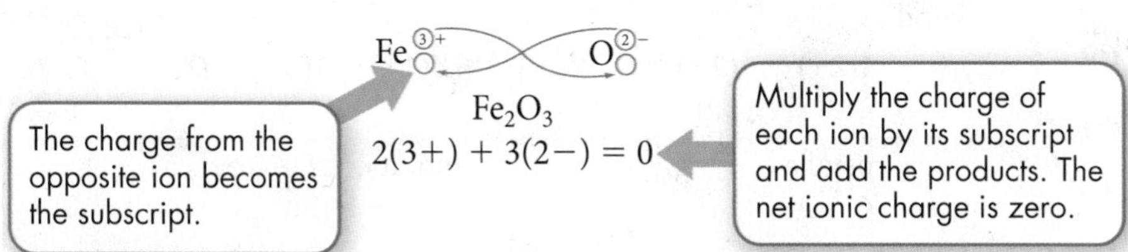

Fe 3+ O 2−
Fe_2O_3
$2(3+) + 3(2-) = 0$
The charge from the opposite ion becomes the subscript.
Multiply the charge of each ion by its subscript and add the products. The net ionic charge is zero.

If you use the crisscross method to write the formula for calcium sulfide (Ca^{2+} and S^{2-}), you obtain Ca_2S_2. However, the 2:2 ratio of calcium and sulfide ions is not the lowest whole number ratio. If you divide this ratio by 2, you get 1:1. The correct formula for calcium sulfide is CaS.

Ca^{2+} S^{2-}

Ca_2S_2 reduces to CaS

$1(2+) + 1(2-) = 0$

For any binary ionic compound in which the magnitudes of the charges are the same, the ions combine in a 1:1 ratio.

CHEMISTRY TUTORIAL

Sample Problem 9.2

Writing Formulas for Binary Ionic Compounds

Write formulas for these binary ionic compounds.

a. copper(II) sulfide **b.** potassium nitride

1 Analyze Identify the relevant concepts. Binary ionic compounds are composed of a monatomic cation and a monatomic anion. The symbol for the cation appears first in the formula for the compound. The ionic charges in an ionic compound must balance, and the ions must be combined in the lowest whole-number ratio.

Hint: The subscript after an element's symbol in a chemical formula indicates the number of atoms. If there is only one atom, the subscript 1 is omitted.

2 Solve Apply the concepts to this problem.

Write the symbol and charge for each ion in the compound—the cation first and then the anion.	**a.** Cu^{2+} and S^{2-}	**b.** K^{+} and N^{3-}
	The crisscross method is used in these solutions.	
Balance the formula by using appropriate subscripts.	Cu ②+ ⟷ S ②− Cu_2S_2	K ①+ ⟷ N ③− K_3N
If necessary, reduce subscripts to the lowest whole-number ratio.	A 2:2 ratio of copper(II) ions to sulfide ions is not the lowest whole-number ratio. Cu_2S_2 reduces to CuS.	The subscripts are expressed in the lowest whole number ratio (3:1) in K_3N.
Check that the charges of the two ions add up to zero.	$1(2+) + 1(2-) = 0$	$3(1+) + 1(3-) = 0$

Remember: If the magnitudes of the charges of the cation and anion are equal, the ions combine in a 1:1 ratio. In copper(II) sulfide, one copper(II) cation (2+ charge) is balanced by one sulfide anion (2− charge). So, the correct formula is CuS.

BUILD Math Skills

Chemical Formulas as Ratios When you write formulas for binary ionic compounds, the subscripts tell you the ratio in which the two ions combine. The subscripts also tell you the ratio of the ionic charges. For example, the formula for potassium nitride is K_3N. You can interpret the subscripts in the formula as follows:

3:1 = 3 potassium cations:1 nitride anion
3:1 = 3(1+ charge):1(3− charge)

Note that when you interpret the formula in terms of ionic charge, the total positive charge of the cations equals the total negative charge of the anions.

$$3(1+) + 1(3-) = 0$$

Go to your *Chemistry Skills and Math Workbook* for more practice problems.

Practice Problems

11. Write formulas for compounds formed from these pairs of ions.

a. Ba^{2+}, S^{2-} **c.** Ca^{2+}, N^{3-}
b. Li^{+}, O^{2-} **d.** Cu^{2+}, I^{-}

❶ **Analyze Identify the relevant concepts.**

❷ **Solve Apply the concepts to this problem.**

12. Write the formula for each ionic compound.

a. sodium iodide
b. potassium sulfide

13. Write formulas for these ionic compounds.

a. stannous chloride
b. calcium iodide

14. Challenge Which of the following formulas are incorrect? Explain your answer.

a. $AsRb_3$ **b.** $BeCl_3$ **c.** NaF

Make sure to check your formula by adding up the charges. The net ionic charge of the formula unit should be zero.

Naming Binary Ionic Compounds If you know the formula for a binary ionic compound, you can write its name. Remember that a binary ionic compound consists of a monatomic metal cation and a monatomic nonmetal anion. To name a binary ionic compound, place the cation name first, followed by the anion name. The table below shows some examples.

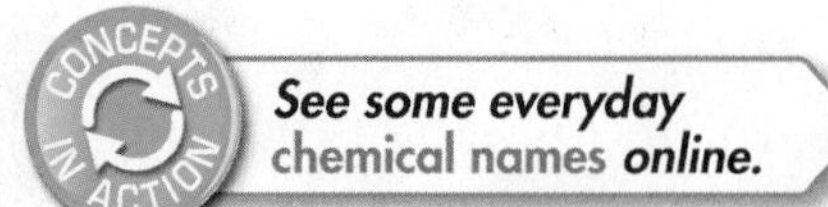

CONCEPTS IN ACTION
See some everyday chemical names online.

Formula	Cation	Anion	Ratio of Ions	Name
NaBr	Na^+	Br^-	1:1	Sodium bromide
SnF_2	Sn^{2+}	F^-	1:2	Tin(II) fluoride
SnO_2	Sn^{4+}	O^{2-}	1:2	Tin(IV) oxide

▶ **Compounds With Elements That Form One Ion** The compound NaBr is composed of the metal sodium and the nonmetal fluorine. Sodium and bromine are Group A elements that have only one charge. Sodium forms a cation with a 1+ charge. Bromine forms an anion with a 1− charge. So, the name of NaBr is sodium bromide.

▶ **Compounds With Elements That Form More Than One Ion** Another example of a binary ionic compound is SnF_2. Following the same rule, you would name this compound *tin fluoride*. However, the name *tin fluoride* is incomplete. Tin is a metal that forms two common ions: Sn^{2+} and Sn^{4+}. The names of these ions are tin(II) ion and tin(IV) ion, respectively. Which of these ions forms SnF_2? The formula tells you the answer. In SnF_2, the tin cation and the fluoride anion combine in a 1:2 ratio. Fluorine is a Group 7A element, so the charge of the fluoride ion is 1−. To balance the 2− charge of two fluoride ions, the charge of the tin cation must be 2+. So, the name of SnF_2 is *tin(II) fluoride*. If the metallic element in a binary ionic compound has more than one common ionic charge, a Roman numeral must be included in the cation name.

In the compound SnO_2, the tin cation and the oxide anion also combine in a 1:2 ratio. But oxygen is a Group 6A element, so the charge on the oxide ion is 2−. To balance the 4− charge of two oxide ions, the charge of the tin cation must be 4+. The name of SnO_2 is *tin(IV) oxide*. The figure below shows common uses of tin(II) fluoride and tin(IV) oxide.

Key Question How do you determine the formula and name of a binary ionic compound? **To write the formula of a binary ionic compound: (1) Write the symbol of the cation and then the anion. (2) Add subscripts as needed to balance the charges. To name a binary ionic compound: (1) Place the cation name first, followed by the anion name. (2) If the metal in a binary ionic compound has more than one ionic charge, a Roman numeral must be included in the cation name.**

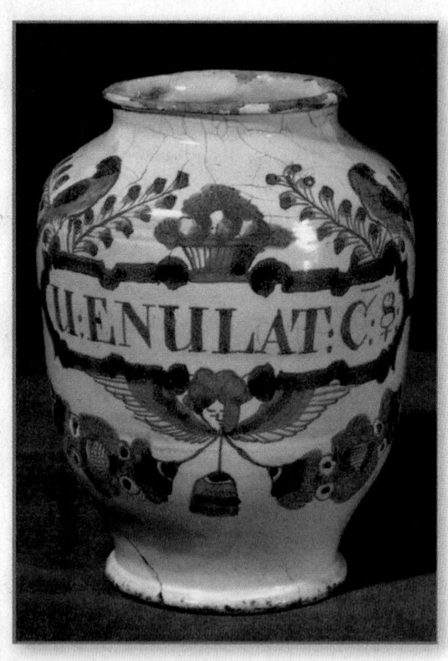

U:ENULAT:C

Tin Compounds
Tin(II) fluoride and tin(IV) oxide have different compositions and uses. Tin(II) fluoride is added to some toothpastes to prevent cavities. Tin(IV) oxide is used in glazes for pottery.

Sample Problem 9.3

Naming Binary Ionic Compounds

Name these binary ionic compounds.

a. CoI_2 **b.** Li_2Se

❶ Analyze **Identify the relevant concepts.** Confirm that the compound is a metal combined with a nonmetal. To name the compound, name the ions in the order written in the formula—the cation name, followed by the anion name. The name of a metal ion that has more than one common ionic charge must include a Roman numeral indicating the charge.

❷ Solve **Apply the concepts to this problem.**

Step	a.	b.
Use the formula to identify the elements. If you find two elements, the compound is binary.	CoI_2 contains cobalt cations and iodide anions.	Li_2Se contains lithium cations and selenide anions.
If the metal in the compound forms more than one ion, identify each cation.	Cobalt forms two cations: Co^{2+} and Co^{3+}.	Lithium forms one cation: Li^{+}.
If the metal has more than one common ionic charge, use the nonmetal anion to determine which cation is indicated by the formula.	The iodide ion is I^{-}. Two iodide ions have a charge of 2−. So, the cobalt ion must be Co^{2+} to balance the charge.	This step is not needed for Li_2Se because the lithium ion has only one common charge.
Write the name of the cation, followed by the name of the anion. Include Roman numerals as needed.	cobalt(II) iodide	lithium selenide

Practice Problems

15. Name these binary ionic compounds.

a. ZnS **c.** BaO

b. KCl **d.** AlF_3

❶ Analyze **Identify the relevant concepts.**

❷ Solve **Apply the concepts to this problem.**

16. Challenge Write the names for these binary ionic compounds.

a. CaO **c.** FeS

b. Cu_2Se **d.** $CuBr_2$

Check each answer by writing the formula by using the ions from the name.

Sea Shells
The shells of marine organisms are composed of calcium carbonate ($CaCO_3$).

Go to your Chemistry Skills and Math Workbook to practice writing formulas for ionic compounds.

Compounds With Polyatomic Ions

The seashells shown to the left are made of calcium carbonate ($CaCO_3$). Calcium carbonate contains more than two elements, so it is not a binary compound. Remember that an *-ate* or *-ite* ending on the name of a compound indicates that the compound contains a polyatomic anion. These suffixes also tell you that the polyatomic ion contains oxygen. Calcium carbonate contains one monatomic ion (Ca^{2+}) and one polyatomic ion (CO_3^{2-}).

Writing Formulas for Compounds With Polyatomic Ions How do you write the formula for an ionic compound that has a polyatomic ion? The procedure is very similar to the one you used for binary ionic compounds. To write the formula for a compound with a polyatomic ion, first write the symbol (or formula) for the cation followed by the symbol (or formula) for the anion. Then, add subscripts as needed to balance the charges.

For example, calcium nitrate is composed of a calcium cation (Ca^{2+}) and a polyatomic nitrate anion (NO_3^-). In calcium nitrate, two nitrate anions, each with a 1− charge, are needed to balance the 2+ charge of each calcium cation.

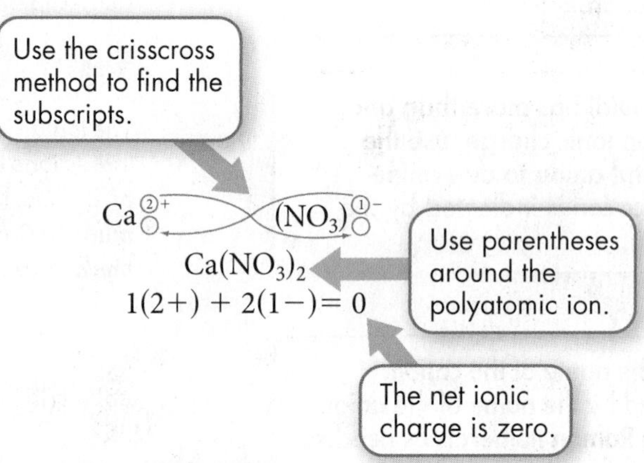

The charge is balanced and the ions are expressed in the lowest whole-number ratio, so the formula is correct. Notice the parentheses around the nitrate ion in the formula. The subscript 2 after the parentheses shows that the compound contains two nitrate anions. Whenever more than one polyatomic ion is needed to balance the charges in an ionic compound, use parentheses to set off the polyatomic ion in the formula.

Lithium carbonate is composed of lithium cations (Li^+) and polyatomic carbonate anions (CO_3^{2-}). In the formula for lithium carbonate, two lithium cations, each with a 1+ charge, balance the 2− charge of one carbonate anion. Parentheses are not needed to set off the polyatomic carbonate anion.

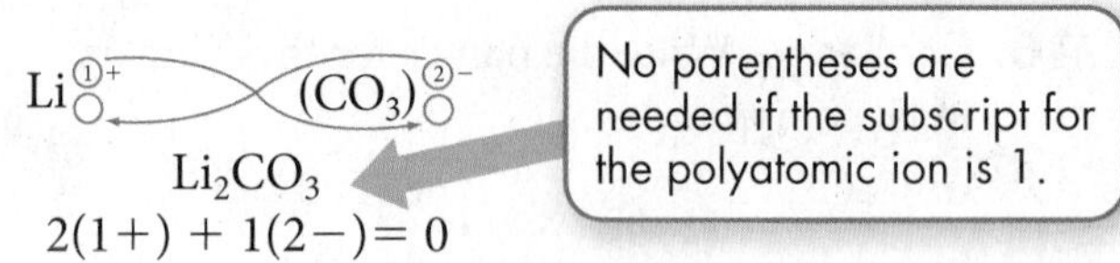

BUILD Connections

Most car engines start up with the help of a lead storage battery. Inside the battery, an energy-producing reaction takes place. This reaction yields the ionic compound lead(II) sulfate ($PbSO_4$), which consists of the monatomic ion Pb^{2+} and the polyatomic ion SO_4^{2-}.

Sample Problem 9.4

Writing Formulas for Compounds With Polyatomic Ions

What are the formulas for these ionic compounds?

a. magnesium hydroxide **b.** potassium sulfate

❶ Analyze Identify the relevant concepts. Write the symbol or formula for each ion in the order listed in the name. Use subscripts to balance the charges. The ions must be combined in the lowest whole-number ratio. If more than one polyatomic ion is needed to balance a formula, place the polyatomic ion formula in parentheses, followed by the appropriate subscript.

❷ Solve Apply the concepts to this problem.

Write the symbol or formula for each ion in the compound—the cation first and then the anion. Include the charge for each ion.	**a.** cation: Mg^{2+} anion: OH^{-}	**b.** cation: K^{+} anion: SO_4^{2-}
Balance the formula by using appropriate subscripts.	Mg^{2+} $(OH)^{1-}$ $Mg(OH)_2$	K^{1+} $(SO_4)^{2-}$ K_2SO_4
Make sure that the formula expresses the lowest whole-number ratio of ions.	1:2 is the lowest whole-number ratio.	2:1 is the lowest whole-number ratio.
Check that the charges of the two ions add up to zero.	$1(2+) + 2(1-) = 0$	$2(1+) + 1(2-) = 0$

Remember: Use parentheses only when there is more than one polyatomic ion in the balanced formula.

Practice Problems

17. Write formulas for compounds formed from these pairs of ions.

a. Na^{+}, SO_3^{2-}

b. calcium ion, phosphate ion

18. Write formulas for these compounds.

a. lithium hydrogen sulfate

b. chromium(III) nitrite

19. Challenge A student writes the formula for magnesium sulfate as $Mg_2(SO_4)_3$. Explain why this formula is incorrect, and then write the correct formula for the compound.

Sodium Hypochlorite
The compound NaClO is often added to laundry water to brighten white fabrics.

Go to your Chemistry Skills and Math Workbook to practice naming ionic compounds.

Naming Compounds With Polyatomic Ions You have learned to write formulas for compounds containing polyatomic ions when given their names. Now, if you were given the formulas for these compounds, could you name them? When naming compounds containing polyatomic ions, you must first identify any polyatomic ions in the formula for the compound. If the polyatomic ion is unfamiliar, find its name in the table on page 242.

To name a compound containing a polyatomic ion, first write the cation name and then the anion name. If the cation is a metallic element that has more than one common ionic charge, include a Roman numeral in the cation name.

If you look at a bleach bottle, such as the one shown in the figure above, you may see an ingredient listed as NaClO. This compound is used as a disinfectant for swimming pools and as a stain remover for laundry. In NaClO, the cation is the sodium ion (Na^+). The anion is the hypochlorite ion (ClO^-). So, the name for NaClO is sodium hypochlorite.

The table below lists the formulas and names of some compounds containing polyatomic ions. Read Sample Problem 9.5 to practice the method used to name such compounds.

Formula	Cation	Anion	Ratio of Ions	Name
NaClO	Na^+	ClO^-	1:1	sodium hypochlorite
$SnCrO_4$	Sn^{2+}	CrO_4^{2-}	1:1	tin(II) chromate
$(NH_4)_3PO_4$	NH_4^+	PO_4^{3-}	3:1	ammonium phosphate

Key Question How do you determine the formula and name of a compound with a polyatomic ion? **To write the formula for a compound with a polyatomic ion: (1) Write the symbol (or formula) for the cation, followed by the symbol (or formula) for the anion. (2) Add subscripts as needed to balance the charges, and use parentheses as needed to set off the polyatomic ion in the formula. To name a compound containing a polyatomic ion: (1) State the cation name first and then the anion name. (2) If the cation is a metallic element that has more than one common ionic charge, include a Roman numeral in the cation name.**

Sample Problem 9.5

Naming Compounds With Polyatomic Ions

Name these ionic compounds.

a. $(NH_4)_2C_2O_4$ **b.** $Fe(ClO_3)_3$

1 Analyze **Identify the relevant concepts.** Determine whether there is a polyatomic ion in the formula. To name the compound, list the ion names in the order written in the formula—cation and then the anion. If the cation has more than one ionic charge, include a Roman numeral in the cation name.

2 Solve **Apply the concepts to this problem.**

Step	a.	b.
Identify any polyatomic ions.	**a.** NH_4^+ and $C_2O_4^{2-}$	**b.** ClO_3^-
Determine if any metal ions in the compound have more than one common ionic charge. If so, use the nonmetal anion to determine which cation is indicated by the formula.	This step is not needed because there is no metal ion in this compound.	Iron forms two common cations: Fe^{2+} and Fe^{3+}. Chlorate ion is ClO_3^-. Three chlorate ions give a charge of 3−. So, the iron ion must be Fe^{3+} to balance the charge.
Write the name of the cation and then the anion. Include Roman numerals as needed.	ammonium oxalate	iron(III) chlorate

Practice Problems

20. Name these ionic compounds.

a. CaC_2O_4 **c.** $KMnO_4$

b. $KClO$ **d.** Li_2SO_3

1 Analyze **Identify the relevant concepts.**

2 Solve **Apply the concepts to this problem.**

21. Write the names for these ionic compounds.

a. $Al(OH)_3$ **c.** $Sn_3(PO_4)_2$

b. $NaClO_3$ **d.** Na_2CrO_4

Hint: Check each answer by writing the formula using the ions from the name.

22. Challenge Why is it not fair to be asked to write the formula for a compound named *lead chromate*?

Quick Lab

Purpose To mix solutions containing cations and anions to make ionic compounds

Materials

- 9 small test tubes
- test tube rack
- paper, pencil, ruler
- 6 droppers
- solution A (Fe^{3+} ion)
- solution B (Ag^{+} ion)
- solution C (Pb^{2+} ion)
- solution X (CO_3^{2-} ion)
- solution Y (OH^{-} ion)
- solution Z (PO_4^{3-} ion)

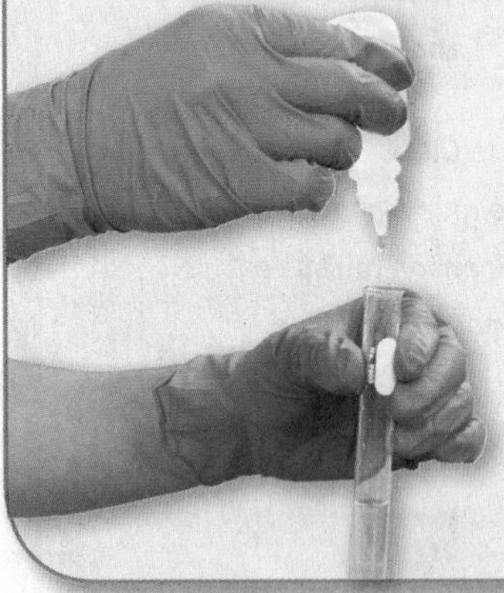

Making Ionic Compounds

Procedure

1. Label three test tubes *A*, three test tubes *B*, and three test tubes *C*.

2. Add 10 drops (approximately 0.5 mL) of solution *A* to the test tubes that are labeled *A*. Add 10 drops of solution *B* to the test tubes that are labeled *B*. Repeat this step with solution *C*.

3. Add 10 drops of solution *X* to one test tube of *A*, 10 drops to one test tube of *B*, and 10 drops to one test tube of *C*. Observe each test tube for the formation of a solid.

4. Make a 3-by-3 inch grid to record your observations. Label the rows *A*, *B*, and C. Label the columns *X*, *Y*, and *Z*. Describe any solid material you observe.

5. Repeat Step 3, adding 10 drops of solution *Y* to test tubes *A*, *B*, and *C*. Record your observations.

6. Repeat Step 3, adding 10 drops of solution *Z* to test tubes *A*, *B*, and *C*. Record your observations.

Analyze and Conclude

1. Infer Some ionic compounds are insoluble in water. What did you observe? How many of the compounds formed were insoluble?

2. Identify Write the formula for each ionic compound formed.

3. Describe Name each ionic compound formed.

4. Draw Conclusions Will mixing any cation with any anion always lead to the formation of an insoluble ionic compound? Explain your answer.

9.2 LessonCheck

Key Concept Check

23. Summarize Describe the procedures for writing the formulas and names of binary ionic compounds.

24. Review How do you write the formulas and the names of compounds with polyatomic ions?

Think Critically

25. Apply Concepts Write the formula for these binary ionic compounds.
- **a.** beryllium chloride
- **b.** cesium sulfide
- **c.** sodium iodide
- **d.** strontium oxide

26. Apply Concepts Write the formula for these compounds containing polyatomic ions.
- **a.** chromium(III) nitrite
- **b.** sodium perchlorate

27. Explain When do you use parentheses in writing a chemical formula?

28. Describe Name these ionic compounds.
- **a.** LiF
- **b.** SnS_2
- **c.** $MnCO_3$
- **d.** $Sr(H_2PO_4)_2$

CHEMISTRY & YOU

29. Many food manufacturers use sodium sulfite to keep dried fruit looking delicious. Write the formula for sodium sulfite. (Hint: See page 250.)

Algal Blooms

Have you ever seen a lake or river covered with what looks like green or blue-green paint? This "paint" is actually algae that have reproduced rapidly. This event is called an *algal bloom*. Freshwater algal blooms often occur when there is an excess of phosphate compounds, commonly called *phosphates*, in the water. Phosphates are nutrients that algae need to survive. However, when phosphate levels are too high, algae grow and reproduce at unusually rapid rates.

Although most algal blooms are not harmful, some release toxins that are dangerous to humans and animals. Even nontoxic algal blooms may cause problems. For example, they may deplete the amount of oxygen in water and block sunlight. These are resources that underwater plants need to live. In addition, algal blooms may alter the taste and odor of the water.

Phosphates are found in fertilizers, detergents, and other cleaning products. These products can enter waterways by direct dumping and runoff. To help reduce the occurrence of algal blooms, government agencies and industries work together to provide cleaning products that are more environmentally friendly. Next time you go to the store, notice that many detergents have a label stating they are "Phosphate Free."

CONTAMINATION Some blue-green algae, such as this *Microcystis* species, can produce toxins that may contaminate drinking water.

Take It Further

1. Identify Sodium phosphate is one example of a phosphate compound. It was once widely used in detergents. Write the formula for this compound.

2. Infer How might an algal bloom affect aquatic grasses?

3. Research a Problem There are several other factors that can contribute to an algal bloom. Research this topic and then identify at least two other factors that contribute to algal blooms.

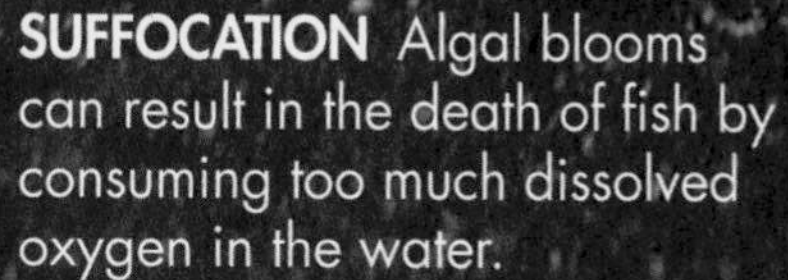

SUFFOCATION Algal blooms can result in the death of fish by consuming too much dissolved oxygen in the water.

9.3 Naming and Writing Formulas for Molecular Compounds

CHEMISTRY & YOU

Q: What numerical prefixes are used in chemistry? You already know words that contain numerical prefixes. For example, the word *triathlon* contains the prefix *tri-*, meaning *three*. Athletes sometimes compete in multisport events—pentathlons, heptathlons, decathlons, and so on. The prefix in each name tells you the number of sports in the event. Chemistry uses prefixes too. In this lesson, you learn how prefixes in the name of a binary molecular compound tell you its composition.

Key Question

What guidelines are used to write the name and formula of a binary molecular compound?

Binary Molecular Compounds

In the previous lesson, you learned about binary ionic compounds. Binary ionic compounds are composed of the ions of two elements: a metal and a nonmetal.

Binary molecular compounds are also composed of two elements, but both elements are nonmetals. The nonmetal atoms that make up a binary molecular compound are not ions joined by ionic bonds. Instead, the atoms within each molecule share electrons, forming one or more covalent bonds.

You previously used ionic charges to name and write formulas for binary ionic compounds. But binary molecular compounds do not contain ions. So, you will need to learn a different system to name and write formulas for these compounds.

Comparing CO and CO_2 When two nonmetallic elements combine, they often do so in more than one way. For example, how would you name a binary compound formed by the combination of carbon and oxygen atoms? The elements carbon and oxygen combine to form the two compounds shown below.

CO molecule

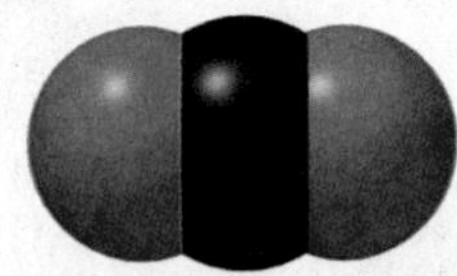

CO_2 molecule

The formulas for these compounds are CO and CO_2. One possible name for these compounds would be *carbon oxide*. However, the two "carbon oxides" are very different compounds. The bubbles in the fizzy drink pictured at left contain CO_2 gas. Sitting in a room with small amounts of CO_2 in the air would not present any problems. You exhale CO_2 as a product of your body chemistry. So, CO_2 is normally present in the air you breathe.

Carbonated Beverage
CO_2 is soluble in water and is used to "carbonate" many beverages. A CO_2 molecule has two carbon-oxygen double bonds.

Vehicle Emissions
Most car engines burn gasoline. The products of the reaction include carbon *dioxide* (CO_2) and carbon *monoxide* (CO). CO is a poisonous gas. The car's exhaust system contains a device called a catalytic converter, which converts most of the CO to CO_2.

On the other hand, if the CO_2 in a normal room were replaced by the same amount of CO, you could suffocate. The binary compound CO is a poisonous gas that interferes with your blood's ability to carry oxygen to body cells. Car emissions, pictured above, contain trace amounts of CO. As you can see, the properties of these two "carbon oxides" are very different. A naming system is needed to distinguish one from the other.

Naming Binary Molecular Compounds Chemists use prefixes in the names of binary molecular compounds to indicate the number of each kind of atom. The table at right lists the prefixes used to name binary molecular compounds. The prefix tells you how many atoms of an element are present in a molecule of the compound. According to the table, the prefix *mono-* would describe the single oxygen atom in CO. The prefix *di-* would describe the two oxygen atoms in CO_2.

Prefixes Used in Naming Binary Molecular Compounds

Prefix	Number
mono-	1
di-	2
tri-	3
tetra-	4
penta-	5
hexa-	6
hepta-	7
octa-	8
nona-	9
deca-	10

To name a binary molecular compound, use the following guidelines.

1. Write the names of the elements in the order listed in the formula.
2. Use prefixes to indicate the number of each kind of atom. You do not need to use the prefix *mono-* for the first element. The vowel at the end of a prefix is sometimes dropped when the name of the element begins with a vowel.
3. End the name of the second element with the suffix *-ide*.

Following these guidelines, CO is named carbon *mono*xide and CO_2 is named carbon *di*oxide. What about the compound Cl_2O_8? This binary molecular compound consists of two chlorine atoms and eight oxygen atoms. The correct name is *di*chlorine *oct*oxide.

Remember: Before you apply the steps listed above, you must confirm that the compound is a binary molecular compound. For more practice, read through Sample Problem 9.6 on the next page.

Naming Binary Molecular Compounds

Name these binary molecular compounds.

a. N_2O **b.** PCl_3

1 Analyze **Identify the relevant concepts.** Confirm that the compound is a binary molecular compound—a compound composed of two nonmetals. To name the compound, name the elements in the order written in the formula. Use prefixes as needed to indicate the number of each kind of atom. Use the suffix *-ide* in the name of the second element.

2 Solve **Apply the concepts to this problem.**

	a.	b.
Identify the elements in the compound.	N_2O is composed of two nonmetals: nitrogen and oxygen.	PCl_3 is composed of two nonmetals: phosphorus and chlorine.
Identify the number of atoms of each element in a molecule of the compound.	Each molecule of N_2O has 2 nitrogen atoms and 1 oxygen atom.	Each molecule of PCl_3 has 1 phosphorus atom and 3 chlorine atoms.
Write the names of the elements in the order they are written in the formula. Add prefixes to show the number of atoms of each element. Use the suffix *-ide* in the name of the second element.	dinitrogen monoxide	phosphorus trichloride

Practice Problems

30. Name these binary molecular compounds.

a. OF_2 **c.** SO_3

b. S_2F_{10} **d.** SF_6

1 Analyze **Identify the relevant concepts.**

2 Solve **Apply the concepts to this problem.**

31. Challenge The name a student gives for the molecular compound $SiCl_4$ is *monosilicon trichloride*. Is this name correct? Explain your answer.

Is the prefix *mono-* used with the first element indicated in the formula? If you are not sure, review the naming guidelines on the previous page.

Writing Formulas for Binary Molecular Compounds How would you write the chemical formula for a binary molecular compound if you know its name? To write the formula of a binary molecular compound, first use the prefixes in the name to tell you the subscript of each element in the formula. Then, write the correct symbols for the two elements with the appropriate subscripts. If you are not sure of the symbol of either element, refer to the periodic table. Here are a couple of examples for practice.

▶ **Tetraphosphorus trisulfide** The compound tetraphosphorus trisulfide is used in certain matches. The name *tetraphosphorus trisulfide* has the prefixes *tetra-* and *tri-*, so the subscripts of phosphorus and sulfur must be 4 and 3, respectively. The symbol for phosphorus is P. The symbol for sulfur is S. The formula for tetraphosphorus trisulfide is P_4S_3.

▶ **Nitrogen trifluoride** In the name *nitrogen trifluoride,* only the second element (fluorine) has a prefix: *tri-*. Each molecule of nitrogen trifluoride has 1 nitrogen atom and 3 fluorine atoms. So, nitrogen does not require a subscript, but fluorine requires a subscript of 3. The symbol for nitrogen is N. The symbol for fluorine is F. The formula for nitrogen trifluoride is NF_3.

Key Question What guidelines are used to write the name and formula of a binary molecular compound? **To name a binary molecular compound: (1) Write the names of the elements in the order listed in the formula. (2) Use prefixes appropriately to indicate the number of each kind of atom, and end the name of the second element with the suffix *-ide*. To write the formula of a binary molecular compound: (1) Use the prefixes in the name to tell you the subscript of each element in the formula. (2) Then, write the correct symbols for the two elements with the appropriate subscripts.**

BUILD Understanding

Two-Column Chart Create a two-column chart to use as a reference for writing the names and formulas of binary molecular compounds. In the left column, list the guidelines for naming binary molecular compounds. In the right column, list the guidelines for writing formulas for binary molecular compounds.

9.3 LessonCheck

Key Concept Check

32. **Review** Explain how to write the name and formula of a binary molecular compound.

Think Critically

33. **Describe** Write the names of these molecular compounds.
    a. NCl_3 c. NI_3 e. N_2H_4
    b. BCl_3 d. SO_3 f. N_2O_3

34. **Apply Concepts** Write the formulas for these binary molecular compounds.
    a. phosphorus pentachloride
    b. iodine heptafluoride
    c. chlorine trifluoride
    d. iodine dioxide

35. **Describe** Write the formulas or names for these molecular compounds.
    a. CS_2 c. carbon tetrabromide
    b. Cl_2O_7 d. diphosphorus trioxide

CHEMISTRY & YOU

36. How does a triathlon differ from a pentathlon? How does phosphorus trifluoride differ from phosphorus pentafluoride? (Hint: See page 257.)

BIGIDEA BONDING AND INTERACTIONS

37. What is the difference between an ionic compound and a molecular compound?

9.4 Naming and Writing Formulas for Acids and Bases

CHEMISTRY & YOU

Q: What's the name of the acid responsible for the crisp taste in this drink? There's an acid that gives many soft drinks a crisp, enjoyable taste. In this lesson, you will learn the names and formulas of some important acids, including one found in many soft drinks.

Key Question

How do you determine the names and formulas of acids and bases?

BUILD Vocabulary

acid a compound that contains at least one hydrogen atom and that produces hydrogen ions when dissolved in water

base a compound that produces hydroxide ions when dissolved in water

MULTIPLE MEANINGS

To a chemist, the word *base* refers to a class of compounds with unique properties. But the same word can be interpreted very differently by a chef who uses a soup *base*, an officer who works at a military *base*, or a shortstop who throws to second *base*.

Acids and Bases

Acids are a group of ionic compounds with unique properties. An **acid** is a compound that contains at least one hydrogen atom and that produces hydrogen ions in a water solution. You will learn more about the properties of acids in Chapter 19.

Naming Acids Acids are a bit trickier to name than other ionic compounds. To name an acid, think of it as an anion combined with one or more hydrogen ions. The anion combines with enough hydrogen ions to make the acid molecule electrically neutral.

The general formula for an acid is H_nX. In this formula, X is an anion and *n* is a subscript indicating the number of hydrogen ions combined with the anion. Three rules can help you name any acid with the general formula H_nX. Notice that the naming system depends on the name of the anion (X).

1. When the name of the anion ends in *-ide,* the acid name begins with the prefix *hydro-*. The stem of the anion has the suffix *-ic* and is followed by the word *acid.* For example, HCl (X = chloride) is named *hydro*chlor*ic acid.*
2. When the anion name ends in *-ite,* the acid name is the stem of the anion with the suffix *-ous,* followed by the word *acid.* For example, H_2SO_3 (X = sulfite) is named sulfur*ous acid.*
3. When the anion name ends in *-ate,* the acid name is the stem of the anion with the suffix *-ic,* followed by the word *acid.* For example, HNO_3 (X = nitrate) is named nitr*ic acid.*

The table below summarizes each of these rules.

Naming Common Acids

Anion ending	Example	Acid name	Example
-ide	chlor*ide*, Cl^-	*hydro*-(stem)-*ic acid*	*hydro*chlor*ic acid*
-ite	sulf*ite*, SO_3^{2-}	(stem)-*ous acid*	sulfur*ous acid*
-ate	nitr*ate*, NO_3^-	(stem)-*ic acid*	nitr*ic acid*

Writing Formulas of Acids A list of some common acids that you will use in the laboratory is shown at right. If you know the name of an acid, you can write its formula. Just use the reverse of the rules for naming acids. Then, balance the charges as you would for any ionic compound. For example, hydrobromic acid is a combination of hydrogen ion (H^+) and bromide ion (Br^-), according to Rule 1. The formula for hydrobromic acid is HBr.

Using Rule 2, phosphorous acid is a combination of hydrogen ions and a phosphite ion (PO_3^{3-}). Three hydrogen ions balance the 3– charge of the phosphite anion. The formula for phosphorous acid is H_3PO_3.

Using Rule 3, sulfuric acid is a combination of hydrogen ions and a sulfate ion (SO_4^{2-}). Two hydrogen ions balance the 2– charge of the sulfate anion. The formula for sulfuric acid is H_2SO_4.

Common Acids	
Name	**Formula**
Hydrochloric acid	HCl
Sulfuric acid	H_2SO_4
Nitric acid	HNO_3
Ethanoic acid	$HC_2H_3O_2$
Phosphoric acid	H_3PO_4
Carbonic acid	H_2CO_3

Naming and Writing Formulas for Bases A **base** is an ionic compound that produces hydroxide ions when dissolved in water. Bases are named by following the rules for ionic compounds; the name of the cation is followed by the name of the anion. For example, sodium hydroxide is a base that is often used in paper factories like the one shown below. Sodium hydroxide (NaOH) is made up of sodium cations (Na^+) and hydroxide anions (OH^-).

To write the formula for a base, first write the symbol for the metal cation followed by the formula for the hydroxide ion. Then, balance the ionic charges just as you would for any ionic compound. For example, aluminum hydroxide consists of the aluminum cation (Al^{3+}) and the hydroxide anion (OH^-). Three hydroxide ions balance the 3+ charge of the aluminum cation. So, the formula is $Al(OH)_3$.

Key Question How do you determine the names and formulas of acids and bases? **Rules for naming acids: (1) When the anion name ends in *-ide,* the acid name begins with the prefix *hydro-*. The stem of the anion has the suffix *-ic* and is followed by the word *acid.* (2) When the anion name ends in *-ite,* the acid name is the stem of the anion with the suffix *-ous,* followed by *acid.* (3) When the anion name ends in *-ate,* the acid name is the stem of the anion with the suffix *-ic,* followed by *acid.* Bases are named in the same way as other ionic compounds; the name of the cation is followed by the name of the anion.**

Use of Sodium Hydroxide
In the first step of papermaking, manufacturers use NaOH to break down recycled paper and wood to make pulp.

Sample Problem 9.7

Naming Acids and Bases

Name these compounds as acids or bases.

a. HClO **b.** HCN **c.** KOH

Naming Acids

❶ Analyze Identify the relevant concepts. The compounds in parts (a) and (b) are acids. The anion of the acid determines the acid name based on the following rules: (1) If the anion name ends in *-ide*, name the acid by using the stem of the anion with the prefix *hydro-* and the suffix *-ic*, followed by the word *acid*. (2) If the anion name ends in *-ite*, name the acid by using the stem of the anion with the suffix *-ous*, followed by *acid*. (3) If the anion name ends in *-ate*, name the acid by using the stem of the anion with the suffix *-ic*, followed by *acid*.

❷ Solve Apply the concepts to this problem.

Identify the ions in the acid.	**a.** H^+ and ClO^-	**b.** H^+ and CN^-
Identify the suffix in the anion name.	hypochlor*ite*	cyan*ide*
Use the rules above to determine the appropriate prefix (if any) and suffix.	If the anion ends in *-ite*, use the suffix *-ous*. (Rule 2)	If the anion ends in *-ide*, use the prefix *hydro-* and the suffix *-ic*. (Rule 1)
Add the prefix (if any) and suffix to the anion stem, followed by the word *acid*.	hypochlorous acid	hydrocyanic acid

Practice Problems

38. Name these acids.

a. HF **b.** HNO_3 **c.** H_2SO_3

❶ Analyze Identify the relevant concepts.

❷ Solve Apply the concepts to this problem.

39. Challenge Write formulas for these acids.

a. perchloric acid
b. hydroiodic acid
c. chlorous acid

Hint: For Problem 39, use the corresponding naming rules in reverse. Then, balance the charges to write the correct formula.

Naming Bases

❶ **Analyze Identify the relevant concepts.** The compound in part (c), KOH, is a base. Bases are named like other ionic compounds; the name of the cation is followed by the name of the anion.

❷ **Solve Apply the concepts to this problem.**

First, identify the cation and the anion in the compound. → c. cation: K^+
anion: OH^-

Now write the name of the cation, followed by the name of the anion. → potassium hydroxide

Practice Problems

40. Name these bases.

a. $Ba(OH)_2$ **b.** $Ca(OH)_2$ **c.** $Fe(OH)_2$

❶ **Analyze Identify the relevant concepts.**

❷ **Solve Apply the concepts to this problem.**

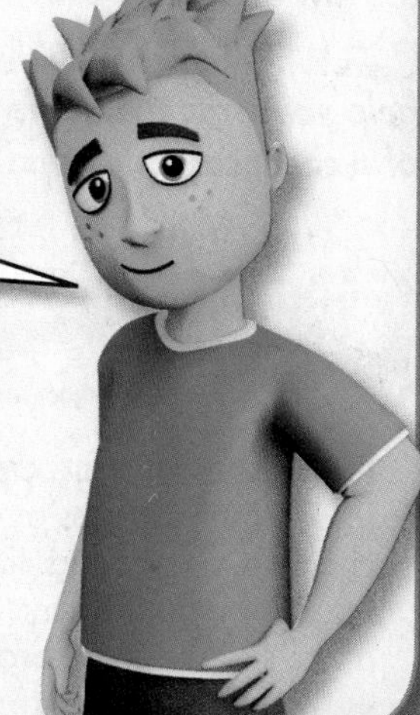

Remember: You need to include a Roman numeral if the metal ion can have different ionic charges.

41. Challenge Write formulas for these bases.

a. cesium hydroxide
b. beryllium hydroxide
c. manganese(III) hydroxide

9.4 LessonCheck

Key Concept Check

42. Review Explain how to determine the name and formula of an acid.

43. Review How are names and formulas determined for bases?

Vocabulary Check

Choose the highlighted word from the lesson to complete the sentence correctly.

44. The chemical formula of a(n) __________ can be described by using the general form H_nX.

Think Critically

45. Identify Give the names of these acids.

a. HNO_2
b. $HMnO_4$
c. HBr
d. H_2S

46. Identify Write the names of these bases.

a. LiOH
b. $Pb(OH)_2$
c. $Mg(OH)_2$
d. $Al(OH)_3$

CHEMISTRY & YOU

47. An acid that provides the crisp taste in many soft drinks has the formula H_3PO_4. What is the name of this acid? (Hint: See page 260.)

9.5 The Laws Governing How Compounds Form

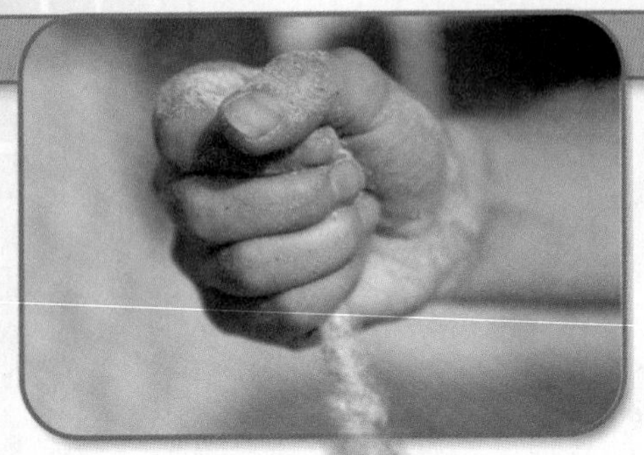

CHEMISTRY & YOU

Q: Did you know that sand from a beach can be used to make glass? Sand contains the compound silicon dioxide, which is used in glassmaking. One unit of silicon dioxide has one silicon atom and two oxygen atoms. In this lesson, you learn why the ratio of silicon to oxygen atoms in silicon dioxide is always the same.

Key Questions

How are experimental data used to show that a compound obeys the law of definite proportions?

What general guidelines can help you write the name and formula of a chemical compound?

BUILD Vocabulary

law of definite proportions in different samples of a given chemical compound, the masses of the elements are always in the same proportions

law of multiple proportions whenever the same two elements form more than one compound, the different masses of one element that combine with the same mass of the other element are in the ratio of small whole numbers

ACADEMIC WORDS

The word *definite* means "fixed." The word *proportion* refers to a ratio. Another way to state the law of definite proportions is to say that the *ratio* of elements in a compound is always *fixed.*

Definite and Multiple Proportions

Two laws—the law of definite proportions and the law of multiple proportions—describe how elements combine to form compounds. The fact that compounds obey these rules allows you to write the names and formulas of compounds.

Law of Definite Proportions Magnesium sulfide (MgS) is a binary ionic compound composed of magnesium cations and sulfide anions. Suppose you had 100.0 g of magnesium sulfide. If you could break it down into its elements, you would get 43.13 g of magnesium and 56.87 g of sulfur.

$$100.00 \text{ g MgS} \longrightarrow 43.13 \text{ g Mg} + 56.87 \text{ g S}$$

The Mg:S ratio of these masses can be calculated as follows.

$$\frac{43.13 \text{ g Mg}}{55.87 \text{ g S}} = \frac{0.758}{1} = 0.758{:}1$$

The **law of definite proportions** states that in samples of any chemical compound, the masses of the elements are always in the same proportions. You can demonstrate that a compound obeys the law of definite proportions by showing that in different samples of the compound, the elements combine in the same ratio by mass. The table below lists mass data for different samples of MgS.

Mass of MgS (g)	Mass of Mg (g)	Mass of S (g)	Mg:S (by Mass)
25.00	10.78	14.22	0.758:1
100.00	43.13	56.87	0.758:1
563.65	243.05	320.60	0.758:1

You can see that the Mg:S mass ratio does not change despite the size of the sample. Like all compounds, MgS obeys the law of definite proportions. This law is consistent with Dalton's atomic theory. Recall that Dalton postulated that atoms combine in simple whole-number ratios. If the ratio of atoms of each element in a compound is fixed, then it follows that the ratio of their masses is also fixed.

CuCl and $CuCl_2$
a. Copper(I) chloride (CuCl) contains the elements copper and chlorine. This compound is green.
b. Copper(II) chloride ($CuCl_2$) contains the same two elements as copper(I) chloride—copper and chlorine. But the compound is blue.

Law of Multiple Proportions In the early 1800s, John Dalton and others studied the properties of many compounds. Some pairs of compounds contained the same elements but had different properties. For example, the photo above shows two binary compounds formed by the elements copper and chlorine. Copper(I) chloride (CuCl) is a green ionic solid. Copper(II) chloride ($CuCl_2$) is a blue ionic solid. Each compound obeys the law of definite proportions. The table below shows mass data for a sample of each compound.

Compound	Mass of Sample (g)	Mass of Cu (g)	Mass of Cl (g)	Cl:Cu (by Mass)
CuCl	100.0	64.2	35.8	0.56:1
$CuCl_2$	100.0	47.2	52.8	1.12:1

You can interpret this data as follows. In every sample of CuCl, 0.56 g of chlorine is present for each gram of copper. In every sample of $CuCl_2$, 1.12 g of chlorine are present for each gram of copper. You can use this data to compare the relative mass of Cl in each compound.

$$\frac{1.12 \text{ g Cl (per 1 g Cu in CuCl}_2\text{)}}{0.56 \text{ g Cl (per 1 g Cu in CuCl)}} = \frac{2}{1} = 2{:}1$$

Go online for more practice calculating mass ratios.

For any given mass of copper, there is always twice the mass of chlorine in $CuCl_2$ as there is in CuCl. Using the results from these kinds of studies, Dalton stated the **law of multiple proportions**: Whenever the same two elements form more than one compound, the different masses of one element that combine with the same mass of the other element are in the ratio of small whole numbers.

See the law of multiple proportions *animated online.*

Key Question How are experimental data used to show that a compound obeys the law of definite proportions? **You can demonstrate that a compound obeys the law of definite proportions by showing that in different samples of the compound, the elements combine in the same ratio by mass.**

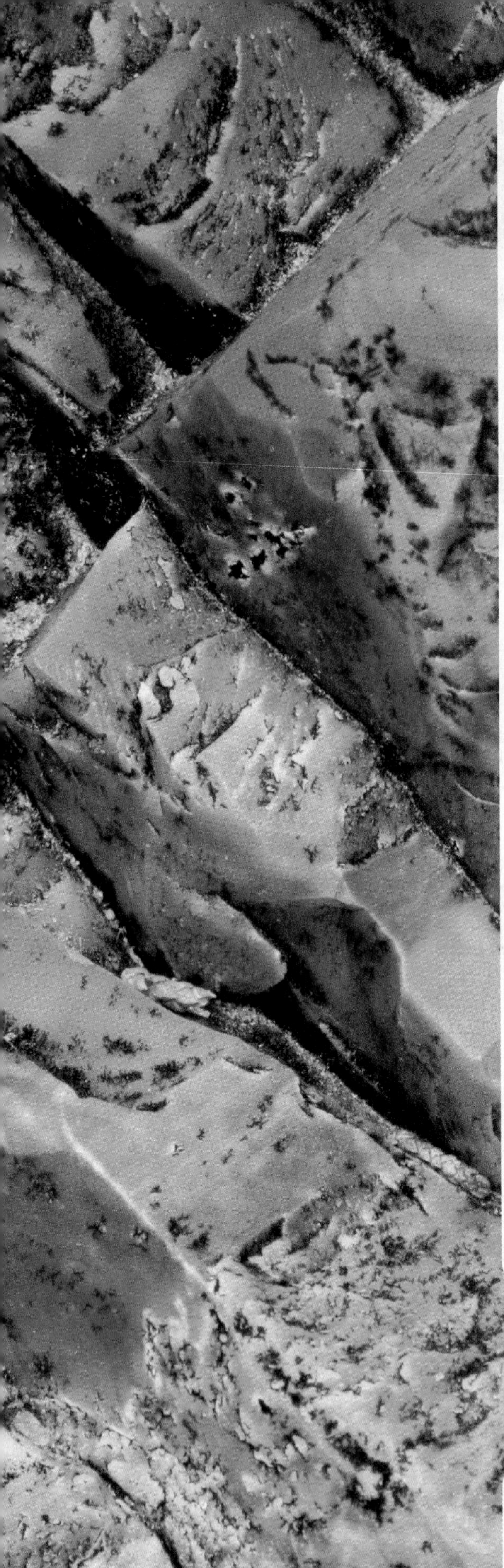

Practicing Skills: Chemical Names and Formulas

In the average home, you can find hundreds of different chemicals. Where are they exactly? In lots of places. You can find them under the kitchen sink, near the washing machine, in a medicine cabinet, or in the garage.

Many of these products have warning labels that tell about their possible dangers. Most people would not know what to do if a child ate or drank one of these chemicals. A phone call to an emergency center can provide lifesaving information. But to get the right information, the caller must provide the names of the product's ingredients.

Naming Chemical Compounds One of the skills that you learned in this chapter is how to name a compound based on its chemical formula. It takes practice to master this skill. Here are some guidelines to help you name compounds correctly:

1. Follow the rules for naming acids when the H is the first element in the formula.
2. If the compound is a binary ionic compound, the name generally ends with the suffix *-ide*. If the compound is a molecular binary compound, use prefixes to indicate the number of atoms of each element.
3. When a polyatomic ion that includes oxygen is in the formula, the compound name generally ends in *-ite* or *-ate*.
4. If the compound contains a metal cation that can have different ionic charges, use a Roman numeral to indicate the numerical value of the ionic charge in the compound.

The flowchart on the next page provides you with a road map for following these guidelines. The flowchart gives you a sequence of questions. Follow the arrows and answer each question to help you narrow down the naming rules that apply to a given compound.

The formula of the compound should be written in the general form Q_xR_y. The letters Q and R each represent an atom, monatomic ion, or polyatomic ion. You can see how the flowchart works by using it to name two different examples: HNO_3 and N_2O_3.

Petrified Wood
When wood ages, certain compounds from sediment can replace the dead tissue in the wood. The process is called *petrification*. Some of these compounds are colored and provide the various colors in the petrified wood.

Naming Compounds
This flowchart will help you name compounds when given a chemical formula. Begin with the letters Q and R in the general formula Q_xR_y.

Q_xR_y

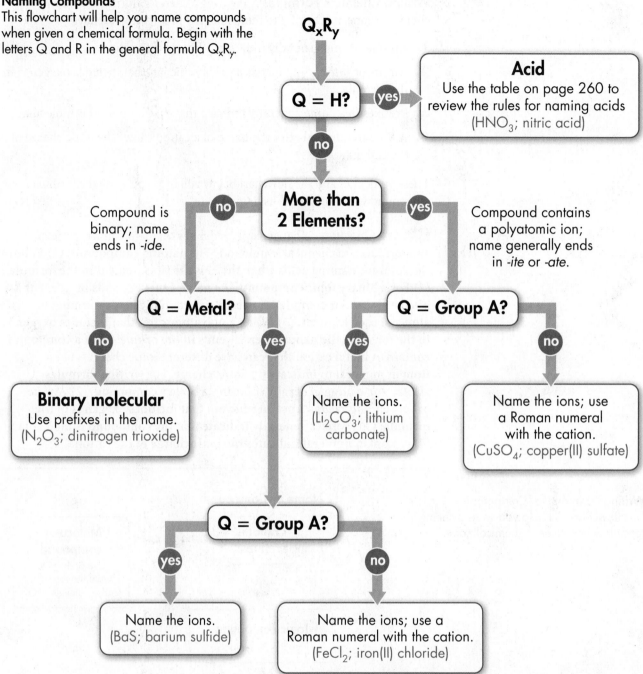

Q = H? → yes → **Acid** Use the table on page 260 to review the rules for naming acids (HNO_3; nitric acid)

Q = H? → no → **More than 2 Elements?**

More than 2 Elements? → no → Compound is binary; name ends in *-ide*. → **Q = Metal?**

- Q = Metal? → no → **Binary molecular** Use prefixes in the name. (N_2O_3; dinitrogen trioxide)
- Q = Metal? → yes → **Q = Group A?**
  - yes → Name the ions. (BaS; barium sulfide)
  - no → Name the ions; use a Roman numeral with the cation. ($FeCl_2$; iron(II) chloride)

More than 2 Elements? → yes → Compound contains a polyatomic ion; name generally ends in *-ite* or *-ate*. → **Q = Group A?**

- yes → Name the ions. (Li_2CO_3; lithium carbonate)
- no → Name the ions; use a Roman numeral with the cation. ($CuSO_4$; copper(II) sulfate)

▶ **Example: HNO_3** To find the name of HNO_3, let Q represent hydrogen and let R represent the nitrate ion. So, Q = H and R = NO_3. The first question is "Q = H?" You can read this as "Does Q represent hydrogen?" The answer is yes, so the box to the right tells you that the compound is an acid. You can then follow the rules for naming acids. HNO_3 is named *nitric acid.*

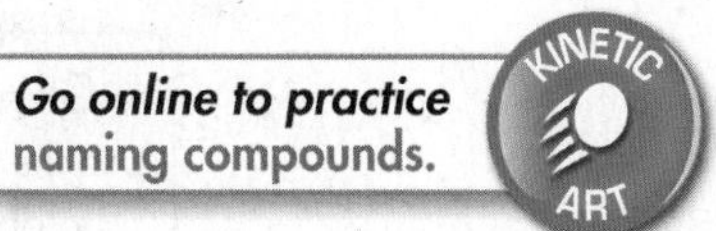

▶ **Example: N_2O_3** To name N_2O_3, let Q represent nitrogen and R represent oxygen. So, Q = N and R = O. The answer to the first question is no, so you follow the arrow down. Does the compound have more than two elements? The answer is again no, so you follow the arrow to the left. Is Q a metal? The answer is no, so N_2O_3 is a binary molecular compound. You must use prefixes in the name for N_2O_3. The correct name is *di*nitrogen *tri*oxide.

Writing Chemical Formulas In writing a chemical formula from a chemical name, it is helpful to remember the following guidelines:

1. An *-ide* ending generally indicates a binary compound.
2. An *-ite* or *-ate* ending means a polyatomic ion that includes oxygen is in the formula.
3. Prefixes in a name generally indicate that the compound is molecular.
4. A Roman numeral after the name of a cation shows the ionic charge of the cation.

These guidelines and the flowchart below will help you write the formula for a compound when you know its name.

Key Question What general guidelines can help you write the name and formula of a chemical compound? **For naming compounds: (1) Follow the rules for naming acids when the H is the first element in the formula. (2) For a binary ionic compound, the name generally ends in *-ide*. For a binary molecular compound, use prefixes to indicate the number of atoms of each element. (3) When a polyatomic ion that includes oxygen is in the formula, the name generally ends in *-ite* or *-ate*. (4) If a compound contains a metal cation that can have different ionic charges, use a Roman numeral to indicate the ionic charge. For writing formulas: (1) An *-ide* ending generally indicates a binary compound. (2) An *-ite* or *-ate* ending means a polyatomic ion that includes oxygen is in the formula. (3) Prefixes generally indicate that the compound is molecular. (4) A Roman numeral indicates the ionic charge of the cation.**

Writing Formulas for Compounds
This flowchart will help you write a chemical formula when given a chemical name.

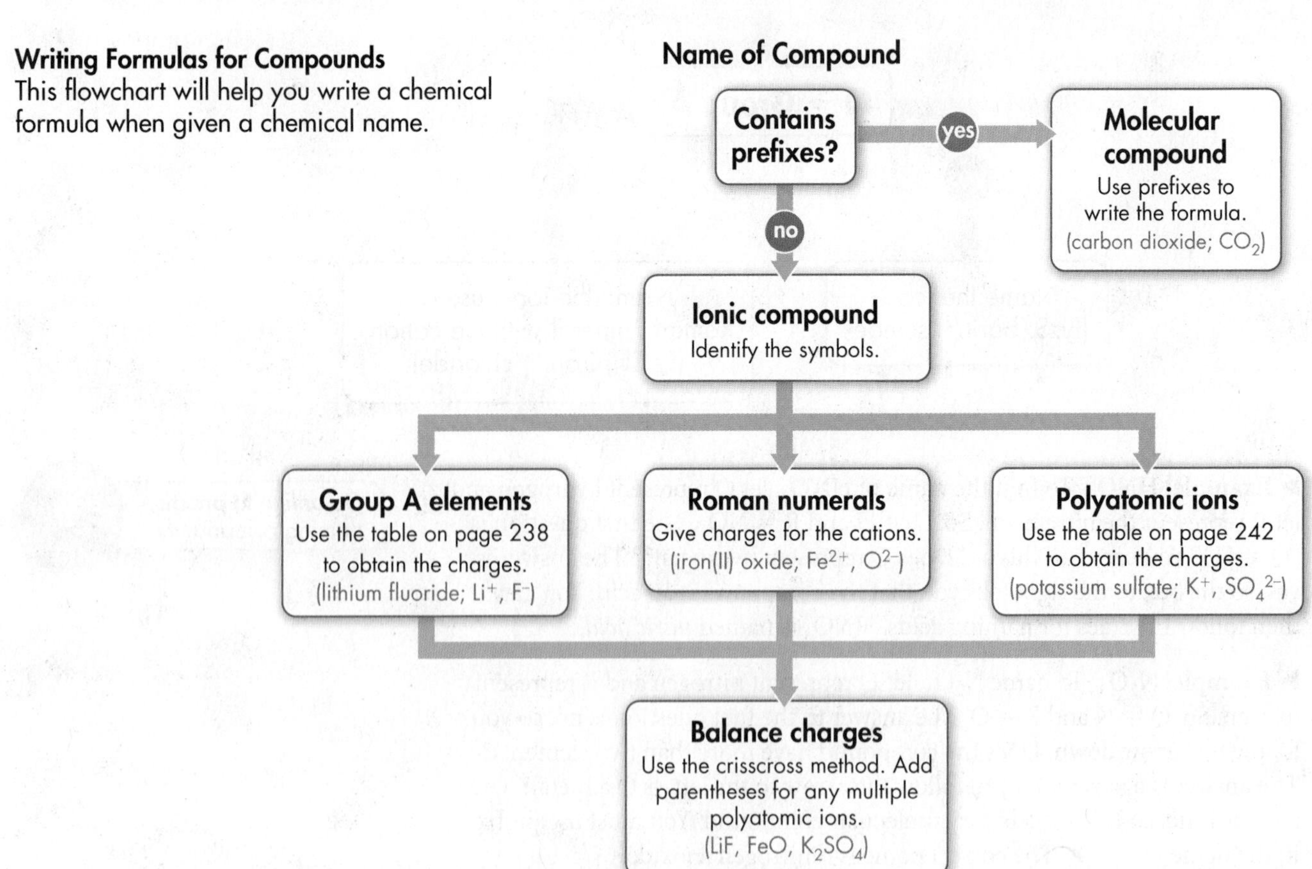

CHEMISTRY & YOU: CAREERS

Sports Nutrition Advisor

Athletes have different nutrition requirements than the average person. As a result, many professional athletes hire nutrition advisors who specialize in athlete nutrition.

Sports nutrition advisors create programs that help athletes match their food to their activities. This improves performance and recovery in athletes. The program might describe how to maintain an energy balance through the day and how to avoid dehydration. Programs also describe which vitamins and minerals to take to maintain proper body chemistry.

It is important that the advisors understand the "language of chemistry." They must understand the ingredient labels on products. Registered advisors take classes in nutrition. They also study chemistry, biochemistry, anatomy, physiology, and statistics.

COMPETITIVE IN THE COLD Winter athletes, such as snowboarders, must maintain their energy stores to train and compete at peak levels.

Take It Further

1. Infer How might understanding chemistry help a sports nutrition advisor develop a meal plan for an athlete?

2. List Choose five foods or supplements from your home. Read the ingredient labels on each product. Make a list of the compounds whose names you understand. Classify each as an ionic compound, molecular compound, acid, or base.

9.5 LessonCheck

Key Concept Check

48. **Review** How is the law of definite proportions consistent with Dalton's atomic theory?

49. **List** What general guidelines can help you write the name and formula of a compound?

Think Critically

50. **Compare** Carbon reacts with oxygen to form two compounds.

Compound A: 2.41 g C and 3.22 g O
Compound B: 6.71 g C and 17.9 g O

What is the lowest whole-number mass ratio of carbon that combines with a given mass of oxygen?

51. **Identify** Name these compounds.

a. $CaCO_3$ b. $PbCrO_4$ c. $SnCr_2O_7$

52. **Describe** Write the chemical formulas for these compounds.

a. tin(II) hydroxide
b. barium fluoride
c. tetraiodide nonoxide
d. iron(III) oxalate

CHEMISTRY & YOU

53. Use the flowchart on page 268 to help you write the formula for silicon dioxide.

BIGIDEA BONDING AND INTERACTIONS

54. Explain why the chemical composition of water (H_2O) is always the same.

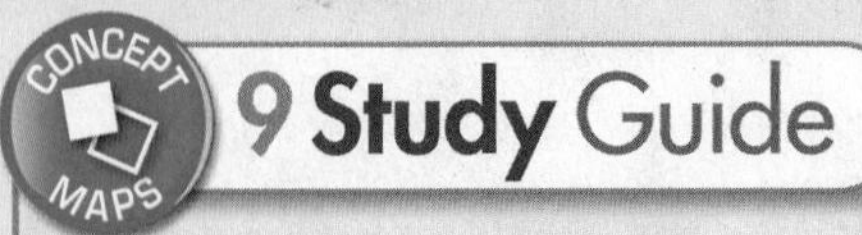

9 Study Guide

BIGIDEAS THE STRUCTURE OF ATOMS; BONDING AND INTERACTIONS

An element's position in the periodic table supplies information on ion formation and bonding tendencies, which is used to write the names and formulas of ions and compounds. Ionic and molecular compounds differ in composition, Ions form ionic compounds; molecules form molecular compounds.

9.1 Naming Ions

When metals in Groups 1A, 2A, and 3A lose electrons, they form cations with positive charges equal to their group number. The charge of any ion of a Group A nonmetal is determined by subtracting 8 from the group number. The charges of the cations of many transition metals must be determined from the number of electrons lost.

A polyatomic ion is composed of more than one atom that behaves as a unit and carries a charge.

- monatomic ion (238)

9.2 Naming and Writing Formulas for Ionic Compounds

To write the formula of a binary ionic compound, write the symbol of the cation and then the anion. Then, balance the charges. The name of an ionic compound is the cation and then the anion.

To write formulas for compounds with polyatomic ions, write the symbol for the cation followed by the symbol for the anion. Then, balance the charges. To name a compound containing a polyatomic ion, state the cation name, followed by the anion name.

- binary compound (244)

9.3 Naming and Writing Formulas for Molecular Compounds

To name a binary molecular compound, write the names of the elements in the order listed in the formula. Use a prefix to indicate the number of each atom. End the name of the second element with *-ide*.

To write the formula of a binary molecular compound, use the prefixes to determine the subscript of each element. Write the symbols for the elements with the subscripts.

9.4 Naming and Writing Formulas for Acids and Bases

If the anion name ends in *-ide,* the acid name begins with the prefix *hydro-*. The stem of the anion has the suffix *-ic* and is followed by the word *acid.* If the anion name ends in *-ite,* the acid name is the stem of the anion, with the suffix *-ous,* followed by the word *acid.* If the anion name ends in *-ate,* the acid name is the stem of the anion, with the suffix *-ic,* followed by the word *acid.* To write the formula for an acid, use the rule for writing the name of the acid in reverse.

Bases are named like other ionic compounds. To write the formula for a base, write the symbol for the metal cation, followed by that of the hydroxide ion. Then, balance the ionic charges.

- acid (260)
- base (261)

9.5 The Laws Governing How Compounds Form

You can demonstrate that a compound obeys the law of definite proportions by showing that in different samples of the compound, the elements combine in the same ratio by mass.

Follow the rules for naming acids when H is the first element. If the compound is binary, the name generally ends with *-ide*. For a molecular binary compound, use prefixes to indicate the numbers of atoms. When a polyatomic ion with oxygen is in the formula, the compound name ends in *-ite* or *-ate*. If the compound contains a metal cation that can have different ionic charges, include a Roman numeral. An *-ite* or *-ate* ending indicates a polyatomic ion with oxygen. Prefixes usually indicate a molecular compound. A Roman numeral after the name of a cation shows the ionic charge of the cation.

- law of definite proportions (264)
- law of multiple proportions (265)

Skills Tune-Up: Names and Formulas

Problem	❶ Analyze	❷ Solve
Write the name for the binary ionic compound CrI_2.	Name the ions in the order written in the formula. Use a Roman numeral if the metal cation in the compound can have more than one common ionic charge. Hint: Refer to Sample Problems 9.2–9.3 if you have trouble identifying binary ionic compounds.	CrI_2 contains chromium cations and iodide anions. Chromium forms two common cations: Cr^{2+} and Cr^{3+}. The compound CrI_2 is electrically neutral. Iodide ion is I^- and the formula CrI_2 specifies two iodide ions, which give a charge of 2–. So, the chromium ion must be Cr^{2+}. The name of the compound is chromium(II) iodide.
Write the name for the binary molecular compound N_2O_5. Hint: Review Sample Problem 9.6 if you need help naming binary molecular compounds.	Name the elements in the order written in the formula. Use prefixes as necessary to indicate the number of each kind of atom. Use the suffix *-ide* in the name of the second element.	N_2O_5 is composed of two nitrogen atoms and five oxygen atoms. The name of the compound is dinitrogen pentoxide.
Write the formula for the ionic compound aluminum sulfate.	Write the symbol or formula for each ion in the order written in the name. Use subscripts to balance the charges. The ions must be combined in the lowest whole-number ratio. Use parentheses if more than one polyatomic ion is needed to balance a formula.	Aluminum sulfate contains Al^{3+} cations and $SO_4{}^{2-}$ anions.  The formula for aluminum sulfate is $Al_2(SO_4)_3$. Remember: Use parentheses when there is more than one polyatomic ion in the balanced formula.
Write the formula for the binary molecular compound selenium dioxide. Remember: The number 1 is never used as a subscript in a formula.	The prefixes in the name indicate the subscript of each element in the formula. Write the symbols for the two elements with the appropriate subscripts.	Selenium dioxide is composed of one selenium atom and two oxygen atoms. The formula for selenium dioxide is written as SeO_2.

9 Assessment

★ Solutions appear in Appendix D.

Lesson by Lesson

9.1 Naming Ions

55. Give the expected charges on the ions of elements of these groups of the periodic table.

a. Group 6A **c.** Group 7A
b. Group 1A **d.** Group 3A

★**56.** Give the expected charge of the cations of these elements.

a. Sr **b.** Ca **c.** Al **d.** Cs

57. Name these ions. (Use the table on page 240 if necessary.)

a. Ba^{2+} **b.** I^- **c.** Ag^+ **d.** Hg^{2+}

58. Name these ions.

a. OH^- **b.** Pb^{4+} **c.** SO_4^{2-} **d.** O^{2-}

9.2 Naming and Writing Formulas for Ionic Compounds

59. What is the net charge of every ionic compound? Explain.

★**60.** How do you determine the charge of a transition metal cation from the formula of an ionic compound containing that cation?

61. How are formulas written for ionic compounds with polyatomic ions, given their names? How is the reverse done?

62. Complete the table by writing correct formulas for the compounds formed by combining positive and negative ions. Then, name each compound.

	NO_3^-	CO_3^{2-}	CN^-	PO_4^{3-}
NH_4^+	a.____	e.____	i.____	m.____
Sn^{4+}	b.____	f.____	j.____	n.____
Fe^{3+}	c.____	g.____	k.____	o.____
Mg^{2+}	d.____	h.____	l.____	p.____

63. When must parentheses be used in a formula for a compound?

9.3 Naming and Writing Formulas for Molecular Compounds

64. What are the components of a binary molecular compound?

★**65.** What prefix indicates each of the following numbers of atoms in the formula of a binary molecular compound?

a. 3 **b.** 1 **c.** 2 **d.** 6 **e.** 5 **f.** 4

66. Write the formula or name for these compounds.

a. P_2O_5
b. CCl_4
c. boron trichloride
d. dinitrogen tetrahydride

9.4 Naming and Writing Formulas for Acids and Bases

67. Give the name or the formula for these acids.

a. HCl **c.** sulfuric acid
b. HNO_3 **d.** ethanoic acid

68. Write formulas for these compounds.

a. nitrous acid
b. aluminum hydroxide
c. hydroselenic acid
d. strontium hydroxide

★**69.** Write names or formulas for these compounds.

a. $Pb(OH)_2$ **c.** copper(II) hydroxide
b. $Co(OH)_2$ **d.** iron(II) hydroxide

9.5 The Laws Governing How Compounds Form

70. What is the law of definite proportions?

71. Describe the law of multiple proportions.

★**72.** Nitrous oxide (laughing gas) is used as an anesthetic in dentistry. The mass ratio of nitrogen to oxygen is 7:4. A 68 g sample of a compound composed of nitrogen and oxygen contains 42 g of nitrogen. Is the sample nitrous oxide?

Understand Concepts

73. Write formulas for these compounds.

a. potassium permanganate
b. calcium hydrogen carbonate
c. dichlorine heptoxide
d. trisilicon tetranitride

74. Write formulas for these compounds.

a. magnesium sulfide **d.** copper(II) nitrite
b. sodium phosphite **e.** potassium sulfite
c. barium hydroxide **f.** calcium carbonate

75. Name each substance.

a. $LiClO_4$ **d.** CaO **g.** $SrSO_4$
b. Cl_2O **e.** $Ba_3(PO_4)_2$ **h.** $CuC_2H_3O_2$
c. HgF_2 **f.** I_2 **i.** $SiCl_4$

76. Write formulas for these compounds.

a. calcium bromide **e.** tin(IV) cyanide
b. silver chloride **f.** lithium hydride
c. aluminum carbide **g.** strontium ethanoate
d. nitrogen dioxide **h.** sodium silicate

***77.** A compound of general formula Q_xR_y contains no hydrogen, and Q and R are elements. Neither Q nor R is a metal. Is Q_xR_y an acid, a binary ionic compound, or a binary molecular compound?

***78.** Two compounds contain only tin and chlorine. The ratio of the masses of chlorine combined with 1.00 g of tin in the two compounds is 2:1. If one compound has the formula $SnCl_2$, what is the formula for the other compound?

79. Analysis of two compounds shows that they contain only lead and iodine in these amounts:

Compound A: 22.48 g Pb and 27.52 g I
Compound B: 5.80 g Pb and 14.20 g I

a. Determine the ratio of lead contained in the two compounds for every 1 g of iodine.
b. Use your ratio and your knowledge of ionic charges to write the formulas and the names of the two compounds.

Think Critically

80. Compare and Contrast How does the information conveyed by a molecular formula differ from that given by a formula unit of a compound?

***81. Use Models** Nitrogen and oxygen form a number of stable chemical compounds. In the models below, nitrogen is blue; oxygen is red. Write the molecular formula and name of each.

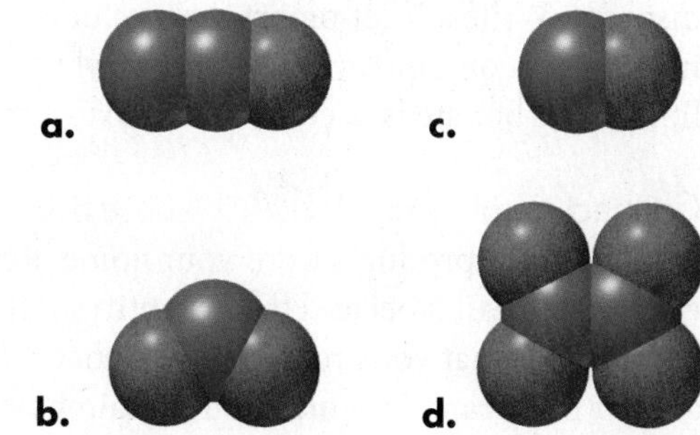

***82. Evaluate and Revise** Explain what is wrong with each formula.

a. $CsCl_2$ **c.** ZnO_2
b. LiNe **d.** Ba_2S_2

FOUNDATIONS Wrap-Up

Element Name Search

1. Infer In the beginning of this chapter, you listed chemical names found on product labels. Can you identify any of the chemicals as ionic compounds? Explain your answer, using at least two examples.

Concept Check

Now that you have finished studying Chapter 9, answer these questions:

2. How can you determine the charge of a monatomic ion?

3. What guidelines can help you write the name of a chemical compound?

4. What guidelines can you use for writing chemical formulas of compounds?

Write About Science

83. Research a Problem Sodium ions (Na^+) and potassium ions (K^+) are needed for the human body to function. Deficiencies in these ions can have adverse effects on your health. Research where these ions are most likely to be found in the body and the roles they play. Write a brief essay describing your findings.

84. Explain Investigate the role of lithium carbonate in the successful treatment of bipolar disorder. Write a brief report that includes information on bipolar disorder and why lithium carbonate is used to treat it.

85. Connect to the BIGIDEA Choose five personal-care products from your home. Read each ingredient label and then identify all the compounds that you are able to decipher. Write a short paragraph in which you explain how learning to name chemical compounds has helped you decipher these ingredient labels.

CHEMYSTERY

Cucumber Blunder

Tara called her grandmother to find out what she did wrong. She started to describe what she had done.

When Tara mentioned squeezing limes, her grandmother interrupted and explained: Lime, in this case, meant pickling lime, not the citrus fruit. "Pickling lime? I've never heard of that!" Tara exclaimed.

Her grandmother fetched a package of pickling lime from the cupboard to look at the ingredient label. She read aloud "food-grade calcium hydroxide." Her grandmother elaborated, "That's what makes the pickles crunchy like you like 'em."

86. Compare *Lime* is the common name for *calcium hydroxide*. What are the advantages and disadvantages of each name?

***87. Connect to the BIGIDEA** Is calcium hydroxide an ionic or a molecular compound? Write the formula.

Cumulative Review

88. List five properties of the chair you are sitting on. Classify each as physical or chemical. (See Lesson 2.1 and 2.4 for help.)

89. Determine the sum of the following measurements to the correct number of significant figures. (See Lesson 3.1 for help.)

$$1.55 \text{ cm} + 0.235 \text{ cm} + 3.4 \text{ cm}$$

90. Compare neutrons and protons with respect to charge, mass, and position in the atom. (See Lesson 4.2 for help.)

***91.** The diagrams below show two models of the atom. (See Lessons 4.2 and 5.1 for help.)

a. Which model is more accurate?

(1)

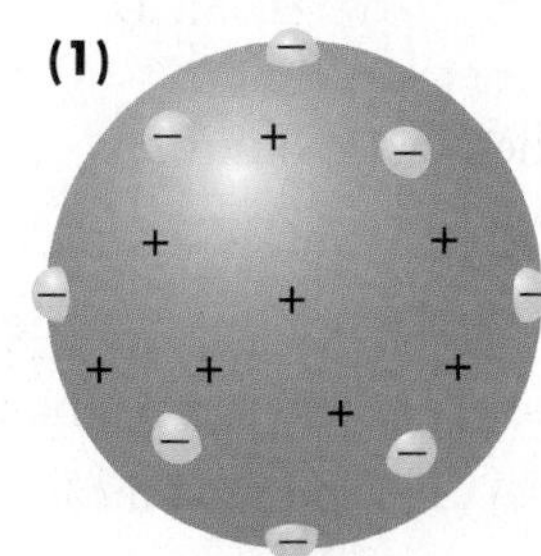

(2)

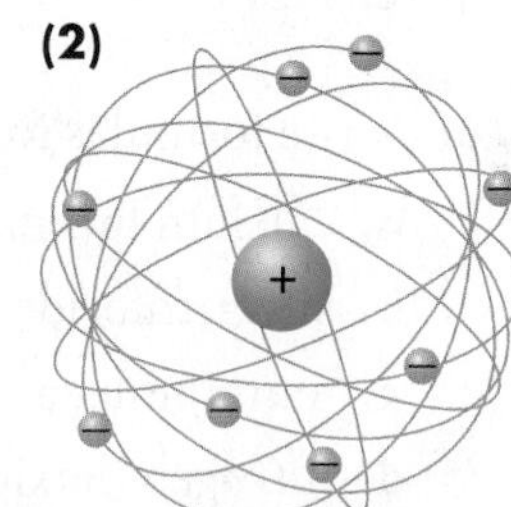

b. What do the positively charged particles represent? The negatively charged particles?

c. What major subatomic particle is missing in both of these models?

***92.** What elements have these electron configurations? (See Lesson 5.2 for help.)

a. $1s^2 2s^2 2p^6$ **c.** $1s^2 2s^2 2p^1$

b. $1s^2 2s^2 2p^2$ **d.** $1s^2$

***93.** How many valence electrons are in each atom? (See Lesson 7.1 for help.)

a. lithium **c.** neon

b. sulfur **d.** calcium

94. Write the electron configuration for the element neon. Identify three ions that have the same electron configuration. (See Lesson 7.2 for help.)

***95.** Which of the following compounds would you expect to contain covalent bonds? Why? (See Lesson 8.2 for help.)

a. KCl **b.** PBr_3 **c.** ClBr **d.** NaI

Standardized Test Prep

For help with answering test questions, go to your Chemistry Skills and Math Workbook.

Select the choice that best answers each question or completes each statement.

1. Identify the pair in which the formula does not match the name.
   (A) sulfite, SO_3^{2-}
   (B) nitrite, NO_3^-
   (C) hydroxide, OH^-
   (D) dichromate, $Cr_2O_7^{2-}$

2. Which of these compounds are ionic?
   I. $CaSO_4$ II. N_2O_4 III. NH_4NO_3 IV. CaS
   (A) I and II only
   (B) II and III only
   (C) III and IV only
   (D) I, III, and IV only

3. What is the name of $AlCl_3$?
   (A) aluminum trichloride
   (B) aluminum(III) chloride
   (C) aluminum chlorite
   (D) aluminum chloride

4. The Roman numeral in manganese(IV) sulfide indicates the
   (A) group number on the periodic table.
   (B) positive charge on the manganese ion.
   (C) number of manganese ions in the formula.
   (D) number of sulfide ions needed in the formula.

Tips for Success

Eliminate Wrong Answers If you do not know which choice is correct, start by eliminating those you know are wrong. If you can rule out some choices, you will increase your chances of choosing the correct answer.

5. Which of these statements does not describe every binary molecular compound?
   (A) Molecules of binary molecular compounds are composed of two atoms.
   (B) The names of binary molecular compounds contain prefixes.
   (C) The names of binary molecular compounds end in the suffix *-ide*.
   (D) Binary molecular compounds are composed of two nonmetals.

6. What is the formula of ammonium carbonate?
   (A) NH_4CO_3
   (B) $(NH_4)_2CO_3$
   (C) NH_3CO_4
   (D) NH_4CO_2

The lettered choices below refer to Questions 7–10.
(A) QR (B) QR_2 (C) Q_2R (D) Q_2R_3

Which formula shows the correct ratio of ions in the compound formed by each pair of elements?

	Element Q	Element R
7.	aluminum	sulfur
8.	potassium	oxygen
9.	lithium	chlorine
10.	strontium	bromine

Use the data table to answer Questions 11–12. The table gives formulas for some of the ionic compounds formed when cations (M, N, P) combine with anions (A, B, C, D).

Cation	Anion			
	A	B	C	D
M	MA_2	(1)	(2)	MD
N	(3)	N_2B	(4)	(5)
P	PA_3	(6)	PC	P_2D_3

11. Use the given formulas to determine the ionic charge of each cation and anion.

12. Write formulas for compounds (1) through (6).

Use the atomic windows to answer Question 13.

13. Classify the contents as elements only, compounds only, or elements and compounds.

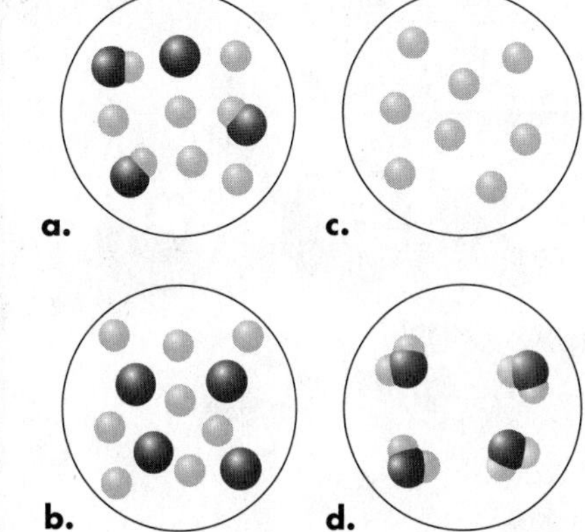

If You Have Trouble With . . .

Question	1	2	3	4	5	6	7	8	9	10	11	12	13
See Lesson	9.1	9.2	9.2	9.2	9.3	9.2	9.2	9.2	9.2	9.2	9.2	9.2	9.3

10 Chemical Quantities

FOUNDATIONS for Learning

Chalk Full of Moles

1. You will need some soft chalk, sandpaper, and a balance.
2. Use the balance to find the chalk's mass.
3. Use the chalk to write your name on the sandpaper.
4. Find the chalk's mass again.
5. Calculate the difference between the two measurements.

Form a Hypothesis One mole of chalk, or calcium carbonate, has a mass of 100 grams. How many moles of chalk did you use to write your name?

PearsonChem.com

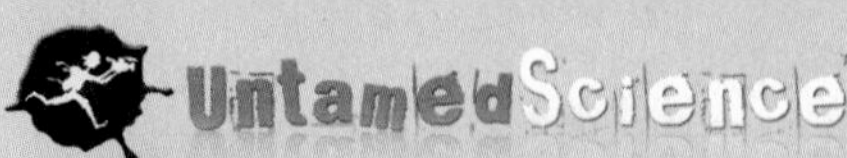

Take a video field trip with a member of the Untamed Science crew to a tutoring session about the mole with Amedeo Avogadro.

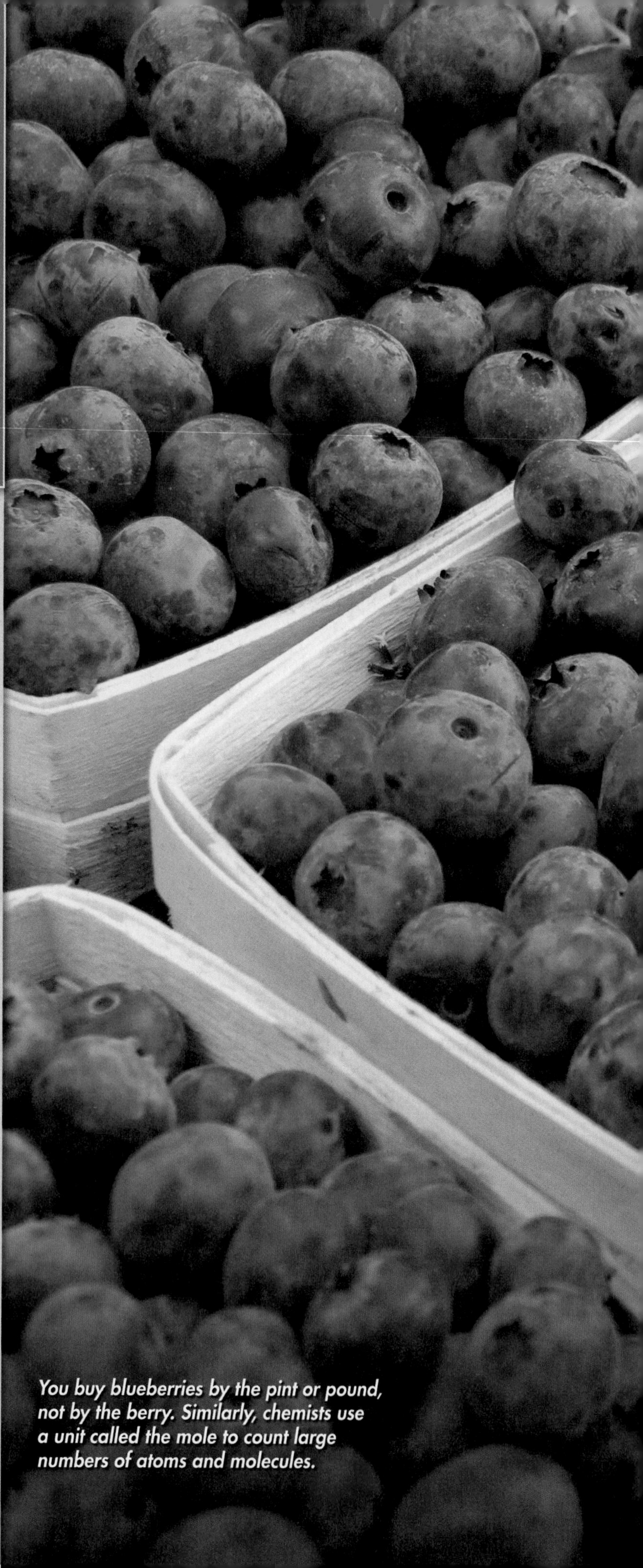

You buy blueberries by the pint or pound, not by the berry. Similarly, chemists use a unit called the mole to count large numbers of atoms and molecules.

BIGIDEA

THE MOLE AND QUANTIFYING MATTER

Essential Questions:

1. *Why is the mole an important measurement in chemistry?*
2. *How can the molecular formula of a compound be determined experimentally?*

CHEMYSTERY

A Formula for Cheating

Anabolic steroids are compounds that increase muscle size and strength. Stories are often in the news about professional athletes who have used steroids to enhance their performance. These athletes have included baseball players, football players, cyclists, and track stars.

More than 100 different types of anabolic steroids have been developed. Each of these substances is illegal in the United States without a prescription. Steroids have also been banned by many sports organizations because of their dangerous side effects and because they give users unfair advantages.

Athletes are often tested for steroid use. How can steroids in the body be detected?

▶ Connect to the BIGIDEA As you read about the mole and chemical quantities, think about how the molar mass and molecular formula of a compound can be determined and used to identify the presence of steroids in the body.

10.1 The Mole: A Measurement of Matter

CHEMISTRY & YOU

Q: How can you measure the amount of sand in a sand sculpture? Have you ever gone to the beach and made a sand castle? You could measure the amount of sand in the castle by counting the grains of sand. Is there an easier way to measure the amount of sand? Chemists measure the amount of a substance by using a unit called the mole.

Key Questions

How can you convert among the count, mass, and volume of something?

How do chemists count the number of atoms, molecules, or formula units in a substance?

How do you determine the molar mass of an element and of a compound?

Measuring Matter

One way to measure matter is to count how many of something you have. For example, a recipe for apple pie might call for four, six, or eight apples. Each of these measurements is a count. Another way to measure matter is to find its mass. You could use a balance to measure the mass of apples in kilograms. You can also measure matter by volume. For instance, at an orchard, you can find apples priced by the bushel. A bushel is a unit of volume.

Some measuring units stand for a specific number of items. For example, a pair means two, and a dozen means 12. Suppose you have a dozen average-sized apples. Each of the different ways to measure apples—by count, by mass, and by volume—can be equated to a dozen apples:

$$1 \text{ dozen apples} = \underset{\text{(a count)}}{12 \text{ apples}} = \underset{\text{(a mass)}}{2.0 \text{ kg apples}} = \underset{\text{(a volume)}}{0.20 \text{ bushel apples}}$$

Knowing how the count, mass, and volume of an item relate to a common unit allows you to convert among these units. For example, based on the relationships given above, you can calculate the mass of 90 apples. First you must convert from numbers of apples to dozens of apples. Then you must convert dozens of apples to kilograms of apples. The conversion factors you need are:

$$\frac{1 \text{ dozen apples}}{12 \text{ apples}} \text{ and } \frac{2.0 \text{ kg apples}}{1 \text{ dozen apples}}$$

Multiply the two conversion factors by the count to find the mass:

$$90 \cancel{\text{apples}} \times \frac{1 \cancel{\text{dozen apples}}}{12 \cancel{\text{apples}}} \times \frac{2.0 \text{ kg apples}}{1 \cancel{\text{dozen apples}}} = 15 \text{ kg apples}$$

Ninety apples have a total mass of 15 kg.

Notice the units cancel to give kilograms, which is the unit you need.

Key Question How can you convert among the count, mass, and volume of something? **Knowing how the count, mass, and volume of an item relate to a common unit allows you to convert among these units.**

What Is a Mole?

For apples and other large objects, it is reasonable to measure by counting. What would happen if you tried to count the grains of sand in a sand castle? It would be an endless job. Recall that matter is composed of atoms, molecules, or ions. These particles are much smaller than grains of sand. Counting these particles one by one would be impossible.

Counting With Moles Eggs usually come in a package that holds 12 eggs, or a dozen. If you buy a total of 36 eggs, you are likely to say, "I bought three dozen eggs." Chemists use a unit called the mole in much the same way.

A **mole** (mol) of a substance is 6.02×10^{23} representative particles of that substance. The mole is the SI unit for measuring the amount of a substance by number of particles. The number 6.02×10^{23} is also called **Avogadro's number** in honor of the Italian scientist Amedeo Avogadro di Quaregna (1776–1856).

Representative Particles The term **representative particle** refers to the kinds of particles present in a substance. These particles could be atoms, molecules, or formula units. The representative particle of most elements is the atom. Iron is composed of iron atoms. Helium is composed of helium atoms. There are seven elements that normally exist as diatomic molecules (H_2, N_2, O_2, F_2, Cl_2, Br_2, and I_2). The representative particle of these elements is the molecule.

For all molecular compounds, the molecule is the representative particle. For example, water is composed of molecules that each have two hydrogen atoms and one oxygen atom. The representative particle of water is the H_2O molecule, not the individual atoms. A mole of a molecular compound contains 6.02×10^{23} molecules.

For ionic compounds, such as calcium chloride ($CaCl_2$), the representative particle is the formula unit. Remember that the formula unit shows the ratio of ions. The representation of a formula unit, such as $CaCl_2$, shows the number of ions of each element in its lowest whole number ratio. A mole of an ionic compound contains 6.02×10^{23} formula units.

Converting Between Particles and Moles You can use the conversion factors shown below to convert the number of representative particles in a substance to moles or to convert moles to the number of representative particles in a substance.

$$\frac{1 \text{ mol}}{6.02 \times 10^{23} \text{ representative particles}} \text{ and } \frac{6.02 \times 10^{23} \text{ representative particles}}{1 \text{ mol}}$$

Key Question How do chemists count the number of atoms, molecules, or formula units in a substance? **The mole allows chemists to count the number of representative particles in a substance.**

BUILD Vocabulary

mole (mol) the amount of a substance that contains 6.02×10^{23} representative particles of that substance

Avogadro's number the number of representative particles in 1 mol: 6.02×10^{23}

representative particle the kind of particles present in a substance, such as atoms, molecules, or formula units

ACADEMIC WORDS
The word *representative* describes something or someone who serves as a symbol for a group. A representative in Congress acts in place of many people.

BUILD Connections

Avogadro's number is a standard unit that is used for measuring particles. Another standard unit you use every day is the dozen. For example, when you buy a dozen eggs, you are buying a carton of 12 eggs.

Sample Problem 10.1

Converting Moles to Number of Atoms

Propane is a gas used for cooking and heating. How many representative particles and how many atoms are there in 2.12 mol of propane (C_3H_8)?

1 Analyze **List the known and the unknowns.**

KNOWN	UNKNOWNS
number of moles = 2.12 mol C_3H_8	number of representative particles = ?
	number of atoms = ? atoms

2 Calculate **Solve for the unknowns.**
The representative particle of propane is a propane molecule. The desired conversions are: moles ⟶ molecules and molecules ⟶ atoms.

First, state the relationship between moles and the number of molecules.

$$1 \text{ mol } C_3H_8 = 6.02 \times 10^{23} \text{ molecules } C_3H_8$$

Write the conversion factor needed to convert moles to number of molecules.

$$\frac{6.02 \times 10^{23} \text{ molecules } C_3H_8}{1 \text{ mol } C_3H_8}$$

Note: Molecules are the representative particles of C_3H_8. You are solving for the number of representative particles here.

Multiply the number of moles by the conversion factor.

$$2.12 \text{ mol } C_3H_8 \times \frac{6.02 \times 10^{23} \text{ molecules } C_3H_8}{1 \text{ mol } C_3H_8}$$

$$= 1.28 \times 10^{24} \text{ molecules } C_3H_8$$

Now state the relationship between the number of molecules and the number of atoms.

$$1 \text{ molecule } C_3H_8 = 11 \text{ atoms}$$

Hint: Use the chemical formula to find the number of atoms. In C_3H_8, there are 3 carbon atoms and 8 hydrogen atoms.

Write the conversion factor needed to convert molecules to atoms.

$$\frac{11 \text{ atoms}}{1 \text{ molecule } C_3H_8}$$

Multiply the number of molecules by the conversion factor.

$$1.28 \times 10^{24} \text{ molecules } C_3H_8 \times \frac{11 \text{ atoms}}{1 \text{ molecule } C_3H_8}$$

$$= 1.41 \times 10^{25} \text{ atoms}$$

3 Evaluate **Does the result make sense?** There are 11 atoms in each molecule of propane and more than 2 mol of propane, so the number of atoms should be more than 20 times Avogadro's number of propane molecules.

BUILD Math Skills

Using Conversion Factors You use a conversion factor to change the units in a calculation. The conversion factor is written as a fraction. The numerator and denominator have terms that are equal. Multiplying by the conversion factor is the same as multiplying by 1.

$$2\ \cancel{\text{dozen eggs}} \times \frac{12\ \text{eggs}}{1\ \cancel{\text{dozen eggs}}} = 24\ \text{eggs}$$

12 = 1 dozen, so the conversion factor equals 1.

Include all the units when you set up a problem with conversion factors. Make sure to cancel out the units, leaving the answer with the correct unit.

Practice Problems

1. How many representative particles and how many atoms are in 1.14 mol of sulfur trioxide (SO_3)?

❶ Analyze List the known and the unknowns.

❷ Calculate Solve for the unknowns.

❸ Evaluate Does the result make sense?

KNOWN	UNKNOWNS
number of moles = 1.14 mol SO_3	number of representative particles = ?
	number of atoms = ? atoms

2. How many moles is 2.80×10^{24} atoms of silicon?

KNOWN	UNKNOWN
number of atoms =	number of moles = ? mol Si

3. How many moles is 2.17×10^{23} representative particles of bromine?

Hint: Bromine is a diatomic molecule, so the representative particle of bromine is Br_2.

4. Challenge How many carbon atoms are in 2.12 mol of propane? How many hydrogen atoms are in 2.12 mol of propane?

Molar Mass

Atomic mass is expressed in atomic mass units (amu). Atomic masses are relative values based on the mass of the most common isotope of carbon, which is carbon-12. An average carbon atom has an atomic mass of 12.0 amu and is 12 times heavier than an average hydrogen atom. An average hydrogen atom has an atomic mass of 1.0 amu.

The table below compares carbon and hydrogen atoms. The mass ratio of one carbon atom to one hydrogen atom is 12:1, or just 12. What happens when you have ten of each of these atoms? Ten carbon atoms are 12 times heavier than ten hydrogen atoms. In fact, any number of carbon atoms will be 12 times heavier than the same number of hydrogen atoms. The mass ratio will always be 12:1. If you think about it, that means 12.0 g of carbon atoms and 1.0 g of hydrogen atoms must contain the same number of atoms.

Look closely at the table below. Based on the information in the table, can you determine the mass of 50 carbon atoms? One carbon atom has a mass of 12 amu. Fifty carbon atoms must have a mass of 600 amu:

$$\frac{12 \text{ amu}}{1 \text{ \sout{carbon atom}}} \times 50 \text{ \sout{carbon atoms}} = 600 \text{ amu}$$

The atomic masses of the elements in the periodic table are not whole numbers. For example, the atomic mass of carbon is not exactly 12 times the mass of hydrogen. This is because atomic masses are weighted average masses of the isotopes of each element.

Comparing Atomic Masses
When the number of atoms of carbon and hydrogen are equal, the mass ratio of carbon to hydrogen stays the same.

Go to your Chemistry Skills and Math Workbook to practice interpreting data.

Carbon Atoms		Hydrogen Atoms		Mass Ratio
Number	Mass (amu)	Number	Mass (amu)	$\frac{\text{Mass carbon}}{\text{Mass hydrogen}}$
●	12	●	1	$\frac{12 \text{ amu}}{1 \text{ amu}} = \frac{12}{1}$
●●	24 (2 × 12)	●●	2 (2 × 1)	$\frac{24 \text{ amu}}{2 \text{ amu}} = \frac{12}{1}$
●●●●●●●●●●	120 (10 × 12)	●●●●●●●●●●	10 (10 × 1)	$\frac{120 \text{ amu}}{10 \text{ amu}} = \frac{12}{1}$
50 ●	600 (50 × 12)	50 ●	50 (50 × 1)	$\frac{600 \text{ amu}}{50 \text{ amu}} = \frac{12}{1}$
Avogadro's number	$(6.02 \times 10^{23}) \times (12)$	Avogadro's number	$(6.02 \times 10^{23}) \times (1)$	$\frac{(6.02 \times 10^{23}) \times (12)}{(6.02 \times 10^{23}) \times (1)} = \frac{12}{1}$

Molar Mass of an Element
The mass of one mole of each element is different.

The Mass of a Mole of an Element When you are performing an experiment in your chemistry lab, do you count the number of particles of the substance you are measuring? No! There are usually far too many particles to count. It is a lot easier to measure substances using mass, not the number of particles. Quantities measured in grams are easy to work with, so chemists use molar masses to express quantities of a substance.

The **molar mass** of a substance is the mass in grams of one mole of representative particles in that substance. The photo shows one mole each of carbon, sulfur, and iron. The molar mass of carbon is 12.0 g. The molar mass of sulfur is 32.1 g. The molar masses of any two elements contain the same number of representative particles. How many atoms are contained in the molar mass of an element? You already know the answer to this question. The molar mass of any element contains one mole, or 6.02×10^{23} atoms, of that element.

You can also think about moles and molar mass in this way: You know that 12.0 g is the molar mass of carbon-12. So, you know that 12.0 g of carbon is one mole of carbon atoms. The same relationship applies to other elements. The molar mass of any element is the mass of 6.02×10^{23} of its atoms.

molar mass the mass in grams of one mole of an element or compound

RELATED WORDS
The word *molar* comes from the unit *mole*. Molar is used to describe the mass of one mole of an element or compound.

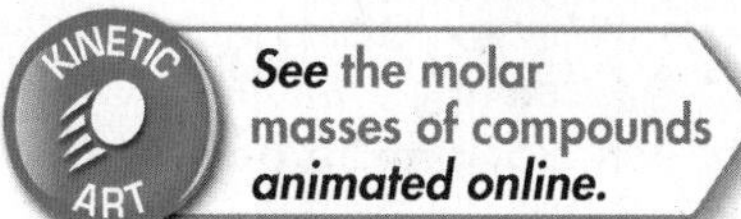

KINETIC ART
See the molar masses of compounds ***animated online.***

Molar Mass of a Compound You need to know the formula of a compound in order to find the molar mass of the compound.

Go to your Chemistry Skills and Math Workbook to practice finding the molar mass of a compound.

Flowchart A flowchart is a way to show the steps in a process. Make a flowchart as you review Sample Problem 10.2.

The Mass of a Mole of a Compound The mass of a molecule or formula unit is the sum of the masses of the atoms that make up the molecule or formula unit. For example, the formula of sulfur trioxide is SO_3. A molecule of SO_3 is composed of one sulfur atom and three oxygen atoms. You can calculate the mass of a molecule of SO_3 by adding the atomic masses of its atoms. You can find atomic masses on the periodic table. The mass of sulfur is 32.1 amu. The mass of three oxygen atoms is three times the atomic mass of one oxygen atom:

$$3 \times 16.0 \text{ amu} = 48.0 \text{ amu}$$

That means the mass of one molecule of SO_3 is:

$$32.1 \text{ amu} + 48.0 \text{ amu} = 80.1 \text{ amu}$$

The molar mass of any compound is the mass in grams of one mole of that compound. That means that one mole, or 6.02×10^{23} molecules, of SO_3 has a mass of 80.1 g. This is the molar mass of sulfur trioxide.

$$1 \text{ mol } SO_3 = 80.1 \text{ g} = 6.02 \times 10^{23} \text{ molecules of } SO_3$$

Key Question How do you determine the molar mass of an element and of a compound? **The atomic mass of an element expressed in grams is the mass of a mole of the element. To calculate the molar mass of a compound, find the number of grams of each element in one mole of the compound. Then, add the masses of the elements in the compound.**

Sample Problem 10.2

Finding the Molar Mass of a Compound

The decomposition of hydrogen peroxide (H_2O_2) provides enough energy to launch a rocket. What is the molar mass of hydrogen peroxide?

1 Analyze List the knowns and the unknown.

KNOWNS	UNKNOWN
chemical formula = H_2O_2	molar mass = ? g/mol
mass of 1 mol H = 1.0 g H	
mass of 1 mol O = 16.0 g O	

2 Calculate Solve for the unknown. Convert moles of atoms to grams by using conversion factors (g/mol) based on the molar mass of each element. The sum of the masses of the elements is the molar mass.

Use the chemical formula to find the number of moles of H and O in 1 mol of H_2O_2.

For each mole of H_2O_2, there are 2 mol H atoms and 2 mol O atoms.

Write the conversion factor needed to convert from moles of H to grams of H.

$$\frac{1.0\text{ g H}}{1\text{ mol H}}$$

Multiply the number of moles by the conversion factor.

$$2\ \cancel{\text{mol H}} \times \frac{1.0\text{ g H}}{1\ \cancel{\text{mol H}}} = 2.0\text{ g H}$$

Write the conversion factor needed to convert from moles of O to grams of O.

$$\frac{16.0\text{ g O}}{1\text{ mol O}}$$

Multiply the number of moles by the conversion factor.

$$2\ \cancel{\text{mol O}} \times \frac{16.0\text{ g O}}{1\ \cancel{\text{mol O}}} = 32.0\text{ g O}$$

Add the results to find the molar mass of H_2O_2.

mass of 1 mol H_2O_2 = 2.0 g H + 32.0 g O = 34.0 g

molar mass of H_2O_2 = 34.0 g/mol

3 Evaluate Does the result make sense? The answer is the sum of two times the molar mass of hydrogen plus oxygen (2 × 17.0 g/mol = 34.0 g/mol). The answer is expressed to the tenths place because the numbers being added are expressed to the tenths place.

When you write moles in your answer, use the abbreviation *mol* instead of the word *moles.*

Practice Problems

Hint: One mole of PCl_3 has 1 mol of P atoms and 3 mol of Cl atoms.

5. Find the molar mass of PCl_3.

1 Analyze List the knowns and the unknown.

2 Calculate Solve for the unknown.

3 Evaluate Does the result make sense?

KNOWNS	UNKNOWN
chemical formula = PCl_3	molar mass = ? g/mol
mass of 1 mol P = 31.0 g P	
mass of 1 mol Cl = 35.5 g Cl	

6. What is the mass of 1.00 mol of sucrose ($C_{12}H_{22}O_{11}$)?

KNOWNS	UNKNOWN
chemical formula =	molar mass = ? g/mol
mass of 1 mol C =	
mass of 1 mol H =	
mass of 1 mol O =	

7. Challenge What is the mass of 1.00 mol of sodium hydrogen carbonate?

10.1 LessonCheck

Key Concept Check

8. Review What do you need to know to convert among the count, mass, and volume of something?

9. Describe How do chemists count the number of representative particles in a substance?

10. Explain How do you determine the molar mass of an element? How do you determine the molar mass of a compound?

Vocabulary Check *Choose a highlighted term from the lesson to complete each sentence correctly.*

11. The __________ is the SI unit for measuring the number of particles of a substance.

12. The mass of one mole of representative particles of a substance is called the __________ of the substance.

Think Critically

13. Calculate How many atoms are in 1.75 mol of $CHCl_3$?

14. Calculate What is the molar mass of $CaSO_4$?

15. What are the different ways you can measure the amount of sand in a sand sculpture? (Hint: See pages 278 and 279.)

10.2 Mole–Mass and Mole–Volume Relationships

CHEMISTRY & YOU

Q: How can you calculate the moles of a substance in a given mass or volume? You entered and won a contest to guess how many pennies are in a container. First, you estimated the thickness and diameter of a penny to find its approximate volume. Then, you estimated the volume of the container. You did the arithmetic and made your guess. In a similar way, chemists use the relationships between the mole and other quantities, such as mass, volume, and number of particles, to solve problems.

Key Questions

How do you convert the mass of a substance to the number of moles of the substance?

How do you convert the volume of a gas at STP to the number of moles of the gas?

The Mole–Mass Relationship

You learned that the molar mass of a substance is the mass in grams of one mole of that substance. This applies to all substances—elements, molecular compounds, and ionic compounds.

Sometimes, the term *molar mass* may be unclear. For example, suppose you were asked for the molar mass of oxygen. This could mean the molar mass of oxygen atoms (O), which is 16.0 g/mol. It could also mean the molar mass of molecular oxygen (O_2), which is 32.0 g/mol. To avoid confusion, use the formula of the substance. In this case, it is O or O_2.

Suppose you need a given number of moles of a substance for an experiment. How can you measure this amount? If you know the number of moles and want to find the mass, use this equation:

$$\text{mass} = \text{number of moles} \times \frac{\text{molar mass}}{1\ \text{mol}}$$

Suppose instead that you obtain a certain mass of a substance in a laboratory experiment. How many moles is this? If you know the mass and want to find the number of moles, then use this equation:

$$\text{number of moles} = \text{mass} \times \frac{1\ \text{mol}}{\text{molar mass}}$$

Key Question How do you convert the mass of a substance to the number of moles of the substance? **Use the molar mass of an element or compound to convert between the mass of a substance and the moles of the substance.**

SampleProblem 10.3

Converting Moles to Mass

Items made from aluminum, such as aircraft parts and cookware, resist corrosion because the aluminum reacts with oxygen in the air. This reaction forms a coating of aluminum oxide (Al_2O_3). The tough, resistant coating prevents any further corrosion. What is the mass, in grams, of 9.45 mol of aluminum oxide?

❶ Analyze List the known and the unknown.

KNOWN	UNKNOWN
number of moles = 9.45 mol Al_2O_3	mass = ? g Al_2O_3

❷ Calculate Solve for the unknown. The mass of the compound is calculated from the known number of moles of the compound. The desired conversion is moles ⟶ mass.

First, determine the mass of 1 mol of Al_2O_3.

$$2\ \cancel{\text{mol Al}} \times \frac{27.0\text{ g Al}}{1\ \cancel{\text{mol Al}}} = 54.0\text{ g Al}$$

$$3\ \cancel{\text{mol O}} \times \frac{16.0\text{ g O}}{1\ \cancel{\text{mol O}}} = 48.0\text{ g O}$$

$$1\text{ mol } Al_2O_3 = 54.0\text{ g Al} + 48.0\text{ g O} = 102.0\text{ g } Al_2O_3$$

Note: This is the molar mass of Al_2O_3.

Identify the conversion factor relating moles of Al_2O_3 to grams of Al_2O_3.

$$\frac{102.0\text{ g } Al_2O_3}{1\text{ mol } Al_2O_3}$$

Multiply the given number of moles by the conversion factor.

$$9.45\ \cancel{\text{mol } Al_2O_3} \times \frac{102.0\text{ g } Al_2O_3}{1\ \cancel{\text{mol } Al_2O_3}}$$

$$= 9.45 \times 102.0\text{ g } Al_2O_3$$

$$= 964\text{ g } Al_2O_3$$

❸ Evaluate Does the result make sense? The number of moles of Al_2O_3 is approximately ten, and each has a mass of approximately 100 g. The answer should be close to 1000 g.

BUILD Math Skills

Using Molar Mass as a Conversion Factor

Molar mass is the mass of one mole of a substance. It is a useful conversion factor. You can write the conversion factor for the molar mass of Al_2O_3 in two ways:

$$\frac{102.0\ g\ Al_2O_3}{1\ mol\ Al_2O_3} \quad or \quad \frac{1\ mol\ Al_2O_3}{102.0\ g\ Al_2O_3}$$

Both are the same—except the numerator and denominator are switched. Use the first conversion factor when you are solving for the mass of Al_2O_3. Use the second conversion factor when you are solving for moles of Al_2O_3.

Practice Problems

16. Calculate the mass, in grams, of 2.50 mol of iron(II) hydroxide ($Fe(OH)_2$).

1 Analyze List the known and the unknown.

2 Calculate Solve for the unknown.

3 Evaluate Does the result make sense?

KNOWN	UNKNOWN
number of moles = 2.50 mol $Fe(OH)_2$	mass = ? g $Fe(OH)_2$

17. Find the mass, in grams, of 4.52×10^{-3} mol of $C_{20}H_{42}$.

KNOWN	UNKNOWN
number of moles =	mass = ? g $C_{20}H_{42}$

18. Challenge Find the mass, in grams, of 3.75 mol of sucrose ($C_{12}H_{22}O_{11}$).

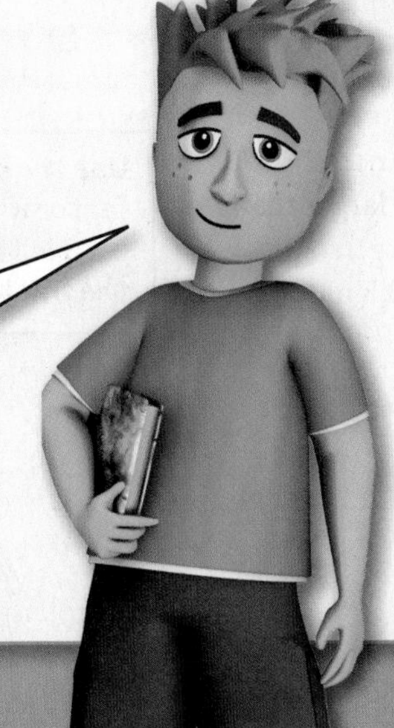

Start by determining the molar mass of the compound.

SampleProblem 10.4

Converting Mass to Moles

When iron is exposed to air, it corrodes to form red-brown rust. Rust is iron(III) oxide (Fe_2O_3). How many moles of iron(III) oxide are contained in 92.2 g of pure Fe_2O_3?

1 Analyze List the known and the unknown.

KNOWN	UNKNOWN
mass = 92.2 g Fe_2O_3	number of moles = ? mol Fe_2O_3

2 Calculate Solve for the unknown. The number of moles of the compound is calculated from the known mass of the compound. The conversion is mass ⟶ moles.

First, determine the mass of 1 mol of Fe_2O_3.

$$2\ \cancel{\text{mol Fe}} \times \frac{55.8\ \text{g Fe}}{1\ \cancel{\text{mol Fe}}} = 111.6\ \text{g Fe}$$

$$3\ \cancel{\text{mol O}} \times \frac{16.0\ \text{g O}}{1\ \cancel{\text{mol O}}} = 48.0\ \text{g O}$$

$$1\ \text{mol Fe}_2\text{O}_3 = 111.6\ \text{g Fe} + 48.0\ \text{g O} = 159.6\ \text{g Fe}_2\text{O}_3$$

Identify the conversion factor relating grams of Fe_2O_3 to moles of Fe_2O_3.

$$\frac{1\ \text{mol Fe}_2\text{O}_3}{159.6\ \text{g Fe}_2\text{O}_3}$$

Multiply the given mass by the conversion factor.

$$92.2\ \cancel{\text{g Fe}_2\text{O}_3} \times \frac{1\ \text{mol Fe}_2\text{O}_3}{159.6\ \cancel{\text{g Fe}_2\text{O}_3}} = \frac{92.2\ \text{mol Fe}_2\text{O}_3}{159.6} = 0.578\ \text{mol Fe}_2\text{O}_3$$

Use the conversion factor with the units you need in the numerator of the fraction.

3 Evaluate Does the result make sense? The given mass (about 90 g) is slightly larger than the mass of 0.5 mol of Fe_2O_3 (about 80 g), so the answer should be slightly larger than 0.5 mol.

BUILD Math Skills

Rounding It is important to answer chemistry problems with the correct number of significant figures. Once you have determined how many significant figures your answer should have, round to that many digits. If the digit to the right of the last significant digit is less than 5, drop it. If the number to the right is greater than or equal to 5, drop the number and then add 1 to the number before it. Study these two examples that are each rounded to three significant figures.

25.03 → 25.0

3 is less than 5, so leave the 0 as it is.

25.07 → 25.1

7 is between 5 and 9, so round the 0 up to 1.

Go to your Chemistry Skills and Math Workbook for more practice.

Practice Problems

19. Find the number of moles in 3.70×10^{-1} g of boron.

1 Analyze List the known and the unknown.

2 Calculate Solve for the unknown.

3 Evaluate Does the result make sense?

KNOWN	UNKNOWN
mass = 3.70×10^{-1} g B	number of moles = ? mol B

20. Find the number of moles in 26.7 g of hydrogen peroxide (H_2O_2).

KNOWN	UNKNOWN
mass =	number of moles = ? mol H_2O_2

21. Challenge Calculate the number of moles in 75.0 g of dinitrogen trioxide (N_2O_3).

Hint: Start by finding the molar mass.

Volume of Gases
Gas particles move quickly and randomly to fill the space available.

Small Molecules
Eight small gas molecules occupy this space.

Large Molecules
Eight large gas molecules occupy the same space.

BUILD Vocabulary

Avogadro's hypothesis equal volumes of gases at the same temperature and pressure contain equal numbers of particles

standard temperature and pressure (STP) 0°C and 101.3 kPa

molar volume 22.4 L, or the volume occupied by one mole of a gas at STP

ACADEMIC WORDS

The word *standard* is often used to mean "regularly or widely used." The use of *standard* in *standard temperature and pressure* (STP) is more specific. Standard temperature and pressure have specific numerical values, which are 0°C and 101.3 kPa, respectively.

The Mole–Volume Relationship

The volumes of one mole of solid and of liquid substances can be very different. The volume of one mole of glucose or one mole of *para*-dichlorobenzene is much larger than that of one mole of water. What about the volumes of gases? The volume of one mole of any gas is much more predictable than the volumes of liquids or solids.

Avogadro's Hypothesis In 1811, Amedeo Avogadro proposed a hypothesis to explain the relationship between the moles and the volumes of gases. **Avogadro's hypothesis** states that equal volumes of gases at the same temperature and pressure contain equal numbers of particles. It does not matter whether the gases are made from the same substance or different substances.

The particles that make up different gases are not the same size. However, there is a great distance between particles of all gases. As shown in the figures above, a collection of relatively large particles does not require more space than the same number of smaller particles.

The volume of a gas varies with a change in temperature or a change in pressure. Due to these variations with temperature and pressure, the volume of a gas is usually measured at a standard temperature and pressure. **Standard temperature and pressure (STP)** describes a temperature of 0°C and a pressure of 101.3 kPa, or 1 atmosphere. At STP, one mole of any gas occupies a volume of 22.4 L. This quantity, 22.4 L, is called the **molar volume** of a gas. It is the volume of 6.02×10^{23} representative particles of the substance. With gases, these particles are usually atoms or molecules.

Calculating the Volume and Moles of a Gas at STP You can use molar volume to convert a known number of moles of a gas to the volume of the gas at STP. If you know the number of moles and want to find the volume at STP, use this equation:

$$\text{volume} = \text{number of moles} \times \frac{22.4\ \text{L}}{1\ \text{mol}}$$

You can also use molar volume to convert a known volume of gas at STP to the number of moles of the gas. If you know the volume at STP and want to find the number of moles, use this equation:

$$\text{number of moles} = \text{volume} \times \frac{1\ \text{mol}}{22.4\ \text{L}}$$

Key Question How do you convert the volume of a gas at STP to the number of moles of the gas? **The molar volume is used to convert between the number of moles of gas and the volume of the gas at STP.**

Mole Road Map
The mole is at the center of chemical calculations. To convert from one unit to another, you must use the mole. The conversion factor you need to use is based on what you know and what you want to find.

KINETIC ART **See the mole road map animated online.**

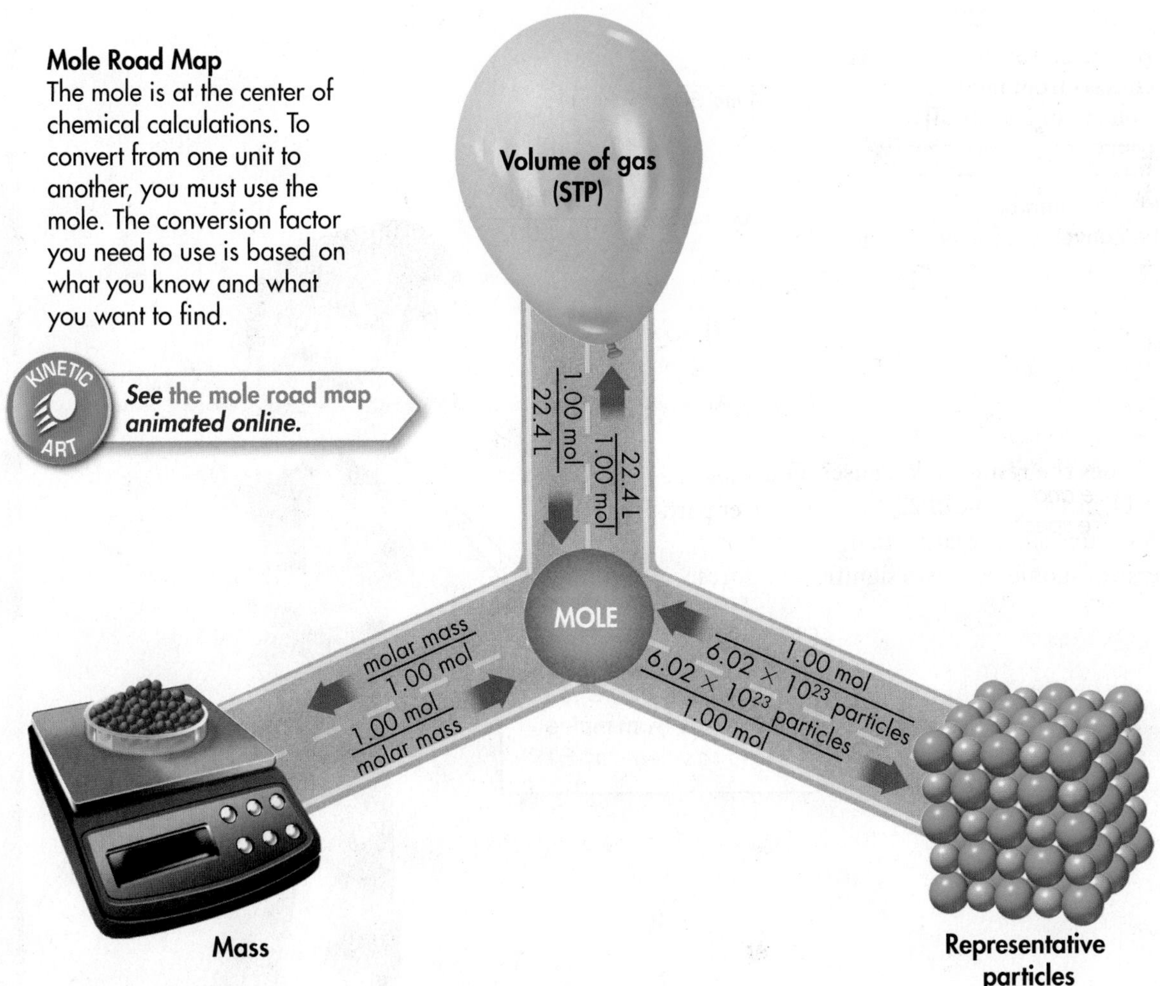

Sample Problem 10.5

Calculating Gas Quantities at STP

Sulfur dioxide (SO_2) is a gas produced by burning coal. It is an air pollutant and one of the causes of acid rain. Determine the volume, in liters, of 0.60 mol of SO_2 gas at STP.

1 Analyze **List the known and the unknown.**

KNOWN	UNKNOWN
number of moles = 0.60 mol SO_2	volume = ? L SO_2

2 Calculate **Solve for the unknown.** Sulfur dioxide is a gas, so the volume at STP can be calculated from the known number of moles.

State the relationship between moles of SO_2 and the volume of SO_2 at STP.

$$1 \text{ mol } SO_2 = 22.4 \text{ L } SO_2 \text{ at STP}$$

Write the conversion factor needed to convert from moles of SO_2 to the volume of SO_2 at STP.

$$\frac{22.4 \text{ L } SO_2}{1 \text{ mol } SO_2}$$

Multiply the given number of moles by the conversion factor.

$$0.60 \cancel{\text{mol } SO_2} \times \frac{22.4 \text{ L } SO_2}{1 \cancel{\text{mol } SO_2}}$$

$$= 0.60 \times 22.4 \text{ L } SO_2$$

$$= 13 \text{ L } SO_2$$

3 Evaluate **Does the result make sense?** One mole of any gas at STP has a volume of 22.4 L, so 0.60 mol should have a volume slightly larger than 0.5 mol, or 11.2 L. The answer should have two significant figures.

Use the conversion factor that allows you to convert from moles of gas to volume at STP.

Practice Problems

22. What is the volume of 3.70 mol of N_2 gas at STP?

1 Analyze **List the known and the unknown.**

2 Calculate **Solve for the unknown.**

3 Evaluate **Does the result make sense?**

KNOWN	UNKNOWN
number of moles = 3.70 mol N_2	volume = ? L N_2

23. At STP, how many moles are in 0.880 L of He gas?

KNOWN	UNKNOWN
volume =	number of moles = ? mol He

24. Challenge Two gases are at STP: 3.20×10^{-3} mol of CO_2 and 0.960 mol of CH_4. Which gas has the larger volume?

10.2 LessonCheck

Key Concept Check

25. Describe How do you convert between the mass and the number of moles of a substance?

26. Describe How do you convert between the volume of a gas at STP and the number of moles of the gas?

Vocabulary Check *Choose a highlighted term from the lesson to complete each sentence correctly.*

27. __________ refers to the conditions of 0°C and 101.3 kPa.

28. According to __________, equal volumes of any gas at a given temperature and pressure will have the same number of particles.

Think Critically

29. Calculate Find the number of moles in 508 g of ethanol (C_2H_6O).

30. Calculate What is the volume, in liters, of 1.50 mol of Cl_2 at STP?

CHEMISTRY & YOU

31. How can you calculate the moles of a substance in a given mass? How can you calculate the moles of a gas in a given volume at STP? (Hint: See pp. 287 and 293.)

BIGIDEA
THE MOLE AND QUANTIFYING MATTER

32. A chemist collects 2.94 L of carbon monoxide (CO) gas at STP during an experiment. Explain how she can determine the mass of gas that she collected. Why is the mole important for this calculation?

10.3 Percent Composition and Chemical Formulas

Key Questions

How do you calculate the percent composition of a compound?

How can you calculate the empirical formula of a compound?

How does the molecular formula of a compound compare with the empirical formula?

percent composition the percent by mass of each element in a compound

WORD ORIGINS

The word *percent* comes from the Latin phrase meaning "by the hundred." One percent is one part of 100 equal parts.

Learn more about circle graphs *online.*

CHEMISTRY & YOU

Q: What does the percent composition of a compound tell you? A tag sewn into the seam of a shirt usually tells you what fibers were used to make the cloth. It also tells you the percentage of each type of fiber. It helps to know the percentages of the fibers in the shirt because they affect how warm the shirt is, whether it will need to be ironed, and how it should be cleaned. Similarly, in chemistry, it is important to know the percentages of the elements in a compound.

Percent Composition of a Compound

In lawn care, the relative amount of each nutrient in fertilizer is important. In spring, you may use a fertilizer with a higher percent of nitrogen to "green" the grass. In fall, you may use a fertilizer with a higher percent of potassium to strengthen the roots. Knowing the relative amounts of the components of a mixture or compound is useful.

Relative amounts of elements in a compound are expressed as percent composition. **Percent composition** is the percent by mass of each element in a compound. The figures below show the percent composition of two different compounds containing potassium, chromium, and oxygen. No matter how much of a particular compound is present, the percent by mass of each element in the compound is always the same.

Percent Composition

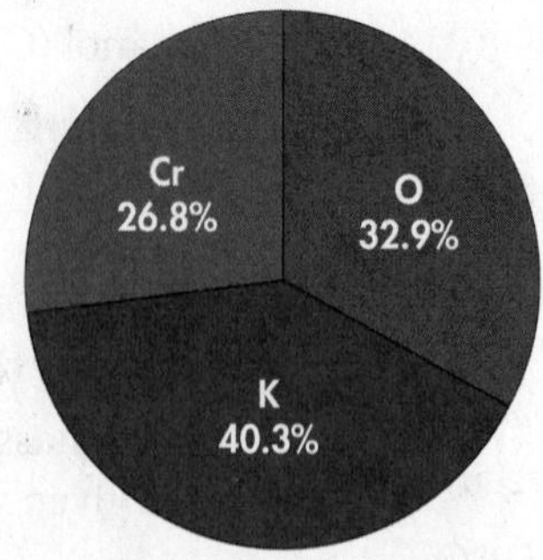

Potassium chromate (K_2CrO_4) is composed of 40.3% potassium, 26.8% chromium, and 32.9% oxygen. The sum of the percentages is 100%.

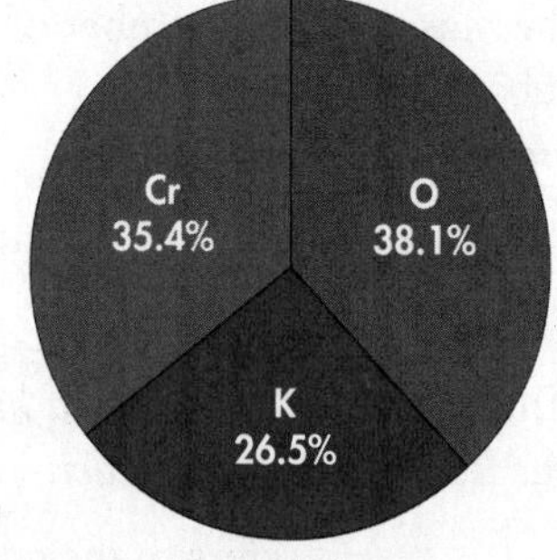

Potassium dichromate ($K_2Cr_2O_7$) is composed of 26.5% potassium, 35.4% chromium, and 38.1% oxygen. The sum of the percentages is 100%.

Percent Composition From Mass Data If you know the relative mass of each element in a compound, you can calculate the percent composition of the compound. The percent by mass of an element in a compound is the number of grams of the element divided by the mass in grams of the compound multiplied by 100%:

$$\% \text{ by mass of element} = \frac{\text{mass of element}}{\text{mass of compound}} \times 100\%$$

Percent Composition From the Chemical Formula You can also calculate the percent composition of a compound using its chemical formula. The subscripts in the chemical formula are used to calculate the mass of each element in a mole of that compound. Using the individual masses of the elements and the molar mass, you can calculate the percent by mass of each element:

$$\% \text{ by mass of element} = \frac{\text{mass of element in 1 mol compound}}{\text{molar mass of compound}} \times 100\%$$

Percent Composition as a Conversion Factor You can use percent composition to calculate the number of grams of any element in a specific mass of a compound. To do this, multiply the mass of the compound by a conversion factor based on the percent composition of the element in the compound.

Here is an example: Propane is a fuel used in gas grills. It comes from petroleum refining or natural-gas processing. Propane has a percent composition of 81.8% carbon and 18.2% hydrogen. That means that in a 100 g sample of propane, you would have 81.8 g of carbon and 18.2 g of hydrogen. You can use the following conversion factors to solve for the mass of carbon or hydrogen contained in a specific amount of propane:

$$\frac{81.8 \text{ g C}}{100 \text{ g } C_3H_8} \text{ and } \frac{18.2 \text{ g H}}{100 \text{ g } C_3H_8}$$

If you wanted to find the mass of carbon in a sample of propane, you would use the first conversion factor. If you wanted to find the mass of hydrogen in a sample of propane, you would use the second conversion factor.

Key Question How do you calculate percent composition of a compound? **The percent by mass of an element in a compound is the number of grams of the element divided by the mass in grams of the compound multiplied by 100%.**

BUILD Connections

Before you take off in a large airliner, the flight attendant shows how to use the oxygen mask. The mask will drop in front of you if the plane's cabin loses too much air pressure. On some airplanes, this oxygen is produced by a chemical reaction. Chemists use the percent composition of the compounds to determine how much of each chemical is necessary to produce the correct amount of oxygen.

Learn more about percent composition *online.*

SampleProblem 10.6

Calculating Percent Composition From Mass Data

When a 13.60 g sample of a compound containing only magnesium and oxygen is decomposed, 5.40 g of oxygen is obtained. What is the percent composition of this compound?

1 Analyze **List the knowns and the unknowns.**

KNOWNS	UNKNOWNS
mass of compound = 13.60 g $Mg_?O_?$	percent by mass of O = ?% O
mass of oxygen = 5.40 g O	percent by mass of Mg = ?% Mg

2 Calculate **Solve for the unknowns.** The percent by mass of an element in a compound is the mass of that element divided by the mass of the compound, multiplied by 100%.

Find the mass of magnesium in the compound.

$$\text{mass of Mg} = \text{mass of compound} - \text{mass of O}$$
$$= 13.60\text{ g compound} - 5.40\text{ g O}$$
$$= 8.20\text{ g Mg}$$

Write the equation for percent by mass of an element.

$$\%\text{ by mass of element} = \frac{\text{mass of element}}{\text{mass of compound}} \times 100\%$$

Find the percent by mass of oxygen in the compound.

$$\%\text{O} = \frac{5.40\text{ g}}{13.60\text{ g}} \times 100\%$$
$$= 39.7\%\text{ O}$$

Find the percent by mass of magnesium in the compound.

$$\%\text{Mg} = \frac{8.20\text{ g}}{13.60\text{ g}} \times 100\%$$
$$= 60.3\%\text{ Mg}$$

3 Evaluate **Does the result make sense?**

The percentages of the elements add up to 100%: 39.7% + 60.3% = 100%.

Check your answer by adding the percentages of all the elements. The total should equal 100%.

BUILD Math Skills

Percents Remember that a percent refers to the number of parts per 100. There are three ways you can write a percent:

50%		$\frac{50}{100}$		0.50
percent form	or	fraction form	or	decimal form

When you use a percent in a calculation, you must first convert it to either its fraction value or its decimal value. Then, you can multiply or divide.

Go to your Chemistry Skills and Math Workbook for more practice.

Practice Problems

33. A compound is formed when 9.03 g of Mg combines completely with 3.48 g of N. What is the percent composition of this compound?

❶ Analyze List the knowns and the unknowns.

❷ Calculate Solve for the unknowns.

❸ Evaluate Does the result make sense?

KNOWNS	UNKNOWNS
mass of magnesium = 9.03 g Mg	percent by mass of Mg = ?% Mg
mass of nitrogen = 3.48 g N	percent by mass of N = ?% N

34. When a 14.2 g sample of mercury(II) oxide is decomposed into its elements by heating, 13.2 g of Hg is obtained. What is the percent composition of the compound?

KNOWNS	UNKNOWNS
mass of compound =	percent by mass of Hg = ?% Hg
mass of mercury =	percent by mass of O = ?% O

35. In a reaction between two gases, 28.0 g of N_2 combines with 6.0 g of H_2 to form ammonia (NH_3). What is the percent composition of ammonia?

36. Challenge Compare the percent composition of formaldehyde (CH_2O) to that of glucose ($C_6H_{12}O_6$).

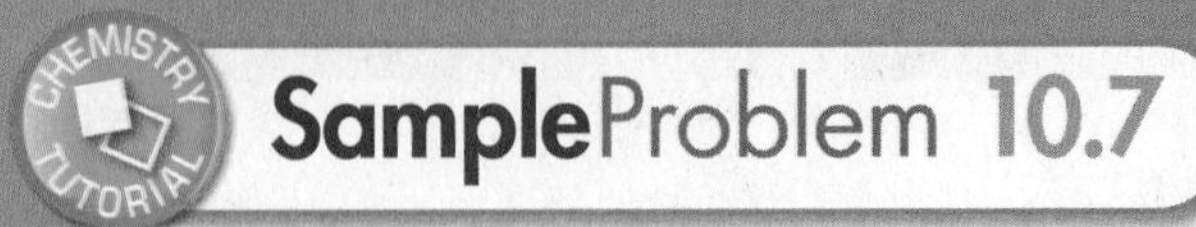

Calculating Percent Composition From a Formula

Propane (C_3H_8), the fuel commonly used in gas grills, is one of the compounds obtained from petroleum. Calculate the percent composition of propane.

❶ Analyze List the known and the unknowns.

KNOWN	UNKNOWNS
chemical formula = C_3H_8	percent by mass of C = ?% C
	percent by mass of H = ?% H

❷ Calculate Solve for the unknowns. Calculate the percent by mass of each element by dividing the mass of that element in one mole of the compound by the molar mass of the compound and then multiplying by 100%.

Determine the mass of C and H in 1 mol of C_3H_8.

$$3\ \text{mol C} \times \frac{12.0\ \text{g C}}{1\ \text{mol C}} = 36.0\ \text{g C}$$

$$8\ \text{mol H} \times \frac{1.0\ \text{g H}}{1\ \text{mol H}} = 8.0\ \text{g H}$$

Determine the molar mass of C_3H_8.

$$1\ \text{mol}\ C_3H_8 = 36.0\ \text{g C} + 8.0\ \text{g H} = 44.0\ \text{g}\ C_3H_8$$

Determine the percent by mass of C in C_3H_8.

$$\%\text{C} = \frac{\text{mass of C in 1 mol } C_3H_8}{\text{molar mass of } C_3H_8} \times 100\% = \frac{36.0\ \text{g}}{44.0\ \text{g}} \times 100\% = 81.8\%\ \text{C}$$

Determine the percent by mass of H in C_3H_8.

$$\%\text{H} = \frac{\text{mass of H in 1 mol } C_3H_8}{\text{molar mass of } C_3H_8} \times 100\% = \frac{8.0\ \text{g}}{44.0\ \text{g}} \times 100\% = 18\%\ \text{H}$$

❸ Evaluate Does the result make sense? The percentages of the elements add up to 100%: 82% + 18% = 100%

Note: The percentages add up to 100% when rounded to whole numbers.

Practice Problems

37. Calculate the percent by mass of nitrogen in NH_3.

❶ Analyze List the known and the unknown.

❷ Calculate Solve for the unknown.

❸ Evaluate Does the result make sense?

KNOWN	UNKNOWN
chemical formula = NH_3	percent by mass of N = ?% N

38. Challenge Calculate the percent composition of sodium hydrogen sulfate ($NaHSO_4$).

Sample Problem 10.8

Using Percent Composition as a Conversion Factor

Calculate the mass of carbon in 82.0 g of propane (C_3H_8).

KNOWN	UNKNOWNS
mass of C_3H_8 = 82.0 g	% by mass of carbon = ?% C
	mass of carbon = ? g C

1 Analyze **List the known and the unknowns.**

2 Calculate **Solve for the unknowns.** Use the conversion factors based on the percent composition of propane to make the following conversion: grams of $C_3H_8 \longrightarrow$ grams of C.

Determine the percent by mass of C in C_3H_8.

$$\%\,C = \frac{\text{mass of C in 1 mol } C_3H_8}{\text{molar mass of } C_3H_8} \times 100\% = \frac{36.0\,\cancel{g}}{44.0\,\cancel{g}} \times 100\%$$

$$= 81.8\%\,C$$

Make a conversion factor by writing the percent by mass as a fraction.

$$\frac{81.8\text{ g C}}{100\text{ g } C_3H_8}$$

Note: Percent means "per hundred," which is a fraction.

Multiply the mass of C_3H_8 by the conversion factor.

$$82.0\,\cancel{g\,C_3H_8} \times \frac{81.8\text{ g C}}{100\,\cancel{g\,C_3H_8}} = 67.1\text{ g C}$$

3 Evaluate **Does the result make sense?** Although there are more hydrogen atoms than carbon atoms, the carbon atoms are much more massive. Therefore, it makes sense that 67.1 g of the sample consists of carbon.

Practice Problems

39. Calculate the mass of nitrogen in 125 g of NH_3.

1 Analyze **List the known and the unknown.**

2 Calculate **Solve for the unknown.**

3 Evaluate **Does the result make sense?**

KNOWN	UNKNOWN
mass of NH_3 = 125 g	mass of N = ? g N

40. Calculate the mass of hydrogen in 350 g of ethane (C_2H_6).

KNOWN	UNKNOWN
mass of C_2H_6 =	mass of H = ? g H

41. Challenge Calculate the mass of each element in 20.2 g of sodium hydrogen sulfate ($NaHSO_4$).

Quick Lab

Purpose To measure the percent of water in a series of crystalline compounds called hydrates

Materials

- three medium test tubes
- balance
- spatula
- hydrated compounds of copper(II) sulfate, calcium chloride, and sodium sulfate
- test tube holder
- gas burner

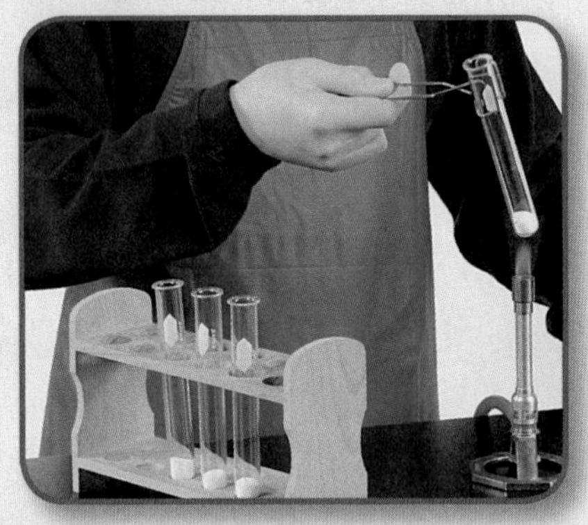

Percent Composition

Procedure

1. Label each test tube with the name of a compound. Measure and record the masses of the test tubes.

2. Add 2–3 g of each compound to the correct test tube. Measure and record the mass of each test tube and the compound.

3. Using a test tube holder, hold one of the tubes at a 45° angle and then gently heat its contents over the burner, slowly passing it in and out of the flame. Note any change in the appearance of the solid compound.

4. As moisture begins to condense in the upper part of the test tube, gently heat the entire length of the tube. Continue heating until all the moisture is driven from the tube. This process may take 2–3 minutes. Repeat Steps 3 and 4 for the other two tubes.

5. Allow each tube to cool. Then, measure and record the mass of each test tube and the heated compound.

Analyze and Conclude

1. Organize Data Set up a data table so you can subtract the mass of the empty tube from the mass of the compound and the test tube—before and after heating.

2. Calculate Find the difference between the mass of each compound before and after heating. This difference represents the amount of water lost by the hydrated compound due to heating.

3. Calculate Determine the percent by mass of water lost by each compound.

BUILD Vocabulary

empirical formula the formula with the lowest whole-number ratio of elements in a compound

WORD ORIGINS

The word *empirical* is from a Greek word that refers to experimental methods. Today, the word is often used to describe scientific inquiry. Empirical science is observational and experimental science.

Empirical Formulas

A useful formula for cooking rice is to use one cup of rice and two cups of water. If you need twice the amount of cooked rice, you need two cups of rice and four cups of water. Like the cooked rice, the formulas for some compounds also show a basic ratio of elements. Multiplying that ratio by any factor can produce the formulas for other compounds.

The **empirical formula** of a compound gives the lowest whole-number ratio of the atoms or moles of the elements in the compound. An empirical formula may or may not be the same as a molecular formula. The whole number ratio of hydrogen to oxygen in hydrogen peroxide is 1:1. The empirical formula of hydrogen peroxide is HO. However, the molecular formula of hydrogen peroxide is H_2O_2. The molecular formula of this compound has twice as many atoms as the empirical formula. For some compounds, the empirical and molecular formulas are the same. This is true for carbon dioxide, which is always CO_2. Look at the figure on the next page for help interpreting formulas.

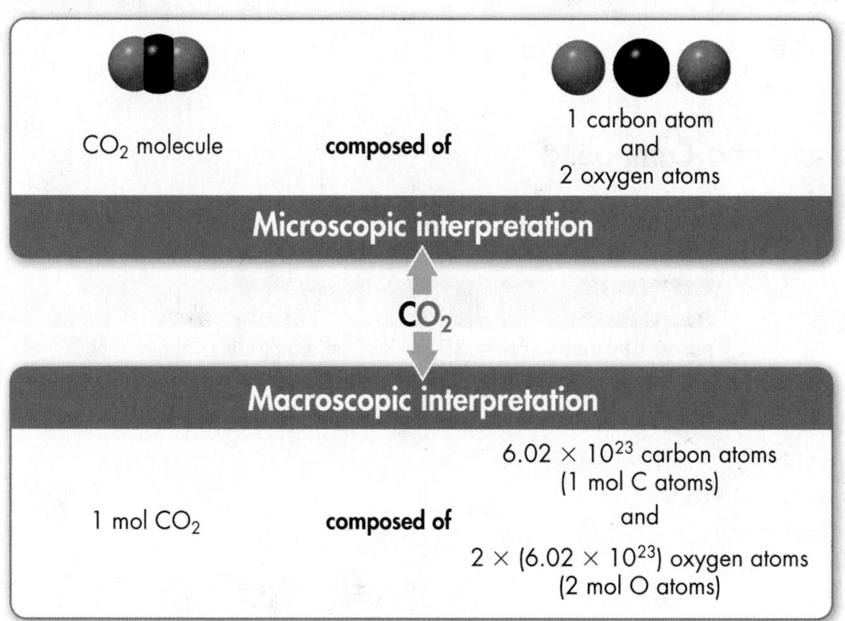

Interpreting Formulas
A formula can be interpreted on a microscopic level in terms of atoms or on a macroscopic level in terms of moles of atoms.

The photographs below show two compounds of carbon and hydrogen that have the same empirical formula but different molecular formulas.

The percent composition of a compound can be used to calculate the empirical formula of that compound. The percent composition shows the ratio of masses of the elements in a compound. The ratio of masses can be changed to a ratio of moles using conversion factors based on the molar mass of each element. The mole ratio is then reduced to the lowest whole-number ratio to obtain the empirical formula of the compound.

Key Question How can you calculate the empirical formula of a compound? **The percent composition of a compound can be used to calculate the empirical formula of that compound.**

Empirical vs. Molecular Formulas Even though the empirical formula for these compounds is the same, they have different molecular formulas and different properties.

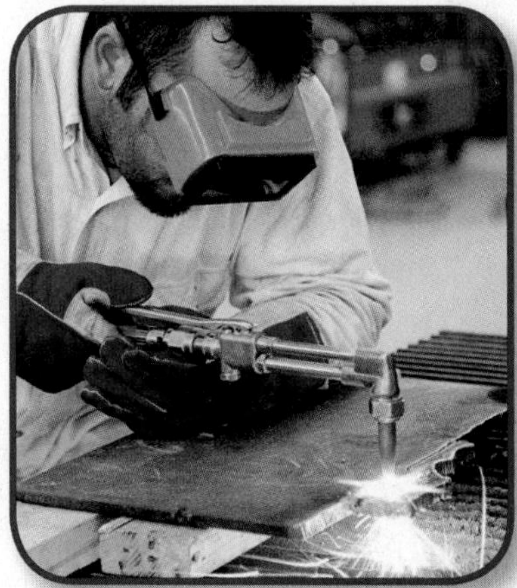

Ethyne (C_2H_2) is a gas used in welders' torches.

Styrene (C_8H_8) is an oily liquid used in making polystyrene packing materials.

Determining the Empirical Formula of a Compound

A compound is analyzed and found to contain 25.9% nitrogen and 74.1% oxygen. What is the empirical formula of the compound?

❶ Analyze **List the knowns and the unknown.**

KNOWNS	UNKNOWN
percent by mass of N = 25.9% N	empirical formula = $N_?O_?$
percent by mass of O = 74.1% O	

❷ Calculate **Solve for the unknown.**
The percent composition gives the ratio of the mass of nitrogen atoms to the mass of oxygen atoms in the compound. Change the ratio of masses to a ratio of moles and then reduce to the lowest whole-number ratio.

Convert the percent by mass of each element to mass.

$$25.9\% \text{ by mass N} = \frac{25.9 \text{ g N}}{100} = 25.9 \text{ g N}$$

$$74.1\% \text{ by mass O} = \frac{74.1 \text{ g O}}{100} = 74.1 \text{ g O}$$

Convert the mass of each element to moles.

$$25.9 \cancel{\text{g N}} \times \frac{1 \text{ mol N}}{14.0 \cancel{\text{g N}}} = 1.85 \text{ mol N}$$

$$74.1 \cancel{\text{g O}} \times \frac{1 \text{ mol O}}{16.0 \cancel{\text{g O}}} = 4.63 \text{ mol O}$$

Divide each molar quantity by the smallest number of moles to get 1 mol for the element with the smallest number of moles.

$$\frac{1.85 \text{ mol N}}{1.85} = 1 \text{ mol N}$$

$$\frac{4.63 \text{ mol O}}{1.85} = 2.50 \text{ mol O}$$

The mole ratio of N to O is now $N_1O_{2.5}$.

Multiply each part of the ratio by the smallest whole number that will convert both subscripts to whole numbers.

$$1 \text{ mol N} \times 2 = 2 \text{ mol N}$$

$$2.5 \text{ mol O} \times 2 = 5 \text{ mol O}$$

Write the empirical formula.

The empirical formula is N_2O_5.

❸ Evaluate **Does the result make sense?** The subscripts are whole numbers, and the percent composition of this empirical formula equals the percents given in the original problem.

BUILD Math Skills

Unit Ratios When you calculate empirical formulas, you use the moles of each element to find unit ratios. A unit ratio is a fraction that has 1 as the denominator. In the example on the previous page, you used the number of moles of the element with the fewest atoms—nitrogen—to find a unit ratio. For nitrogen, the unit ratio was 1.00/1. For oxygen, the unit ratio was 2.50/1. Using the unit ratio made it easier to find the lowest whole-number ratio.

Practice Problems

42. Calculate the empirical formula of a compound that is 94.1% O and 5.9% H.

1 Analyze **List the knowns and the unknown.**

2 Calculate **Solve for the unknown.**

3 Evaluate **Does the result make sense?**

KNOWNS	UNKNOWN
percent by mass of H = 5.9% H	empirical formula = $H_?O_?$
percent by mass of O = 94.1% O	

43. Calculate the empirical formula of a compound that is 67.6% Hg, 10.8% S, and 21.6% O.

KNOWNS	UNKNOWN
percent by mass of Hg =	empirical formula = $Hg_?S_?O_?$
percent by mass of S =	
percent by mass of O =	

44. Challenge 1,6-diaminohexane is used to make nylon. What is the empirical formula of this compound if its percent composition is 62.1% C, 13.8% H, and 24.1% N?

Hint: Start by converting the percent by mass of each element to moles.

Compounds with Empirical Formula CH_2O The molecular formulas for ethanoic acid, methanal, and glucose are all multiples of the empirical formula CH_2O.

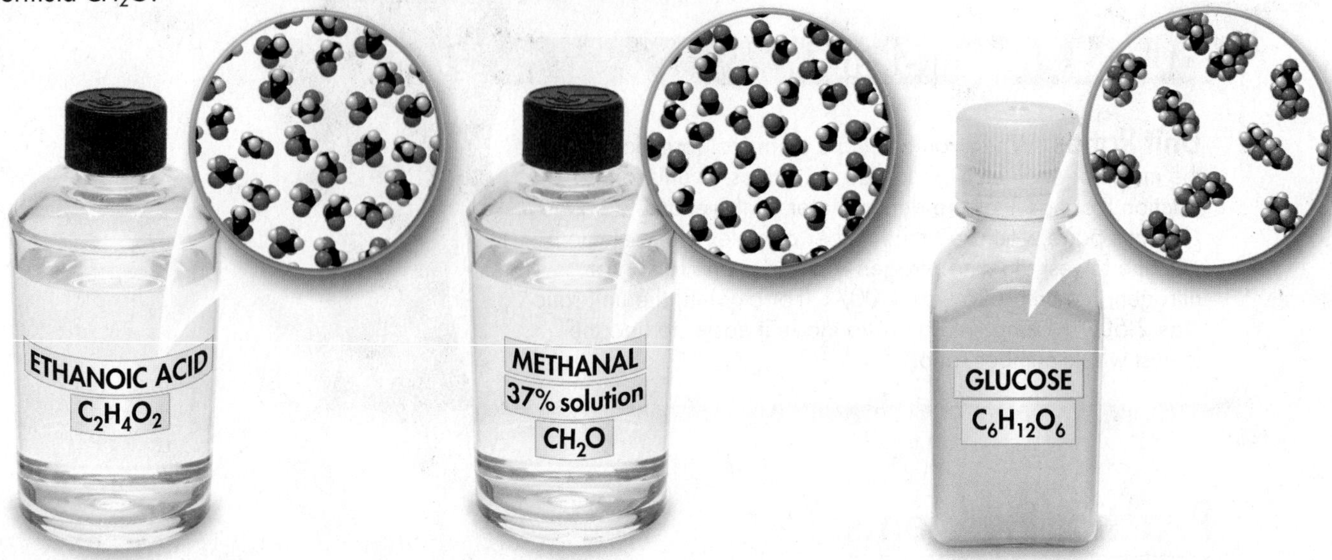

Molecular Formulas

Look at the figure above. Ethanoic acid, methanal, and glucose have the same empirical formula: CH_2O. These three compounds have different molecular formulas that are simple whole-number multiples of the molar masses of the empirical formula CH_2O.

To find the molecular formula of a compound, divide the experimentally determined molar mass by the empirical formula mass. This gives you the number of empirical formula units in a molecule of the compound. Multiply the number of atoms of each element in the empirical formula by this number to find the molecular formula.

Key Question How does the molecular formula of a compound compare with the empirical formula? **The molecular formula of a compound is either the same as its experimentally determined empirical formula or it is a simple whole-number multiple of its empirical formula.**

10.3 LessonCheck

Key Concept Check

45. **Review** How do you calculate the percent by mass of an element in a compound?

46. **Identify** What information can you use to calculate the empirical formula of a compound?

47. **Explain** How is the molecular formula of a compound related to its empirical formula?

CHEMISTRY & YOU

48. What information can you obtain from the percent composition of a compound? (Hint: See page 297.)

BIGIDEA
THE MOLE AND QUANTIFYING MATTER

49. The percent composition of methyl butanoate is 58.8% C, 9.8% H, and 31.4% O. What is its empirical formula?

Ion Mobility Spectrometry

In 2001, a terrorist boarded an airline flight with explosives inside his shoes. Since that time, Americans have had to remove their shoes during airport security checks. However, newer airport security devices, known as "puffer portals," allow airport security to scan for minute traces of explosives on a person's body and clothing—without the person having to remove any clothing or shoes.

The puffer portal looks like a standard airport metal detector. There are vents and nozzles on the walls and ceiling of the portal. When a passenger steps inside, the doors close, and the instrument sends sharp bursts of air to dislodge particles from his or her body, hair, and clothing. The air sample is then passed through a chemical analysis system called an ion mobility spectrometer (IMS). The IMS identifies compounds based on the amount of time it takes for ions to pass through an electrified field in a tube filled with a nonreactive gas (drift gas). This "drift time" is then compared to a database of drift times of different compounds. In this way, molecules of known explosive or narcotic materials can be detected and identified. If even a picogram of an explosive is detected, an alarm sounds.

A Closer Look

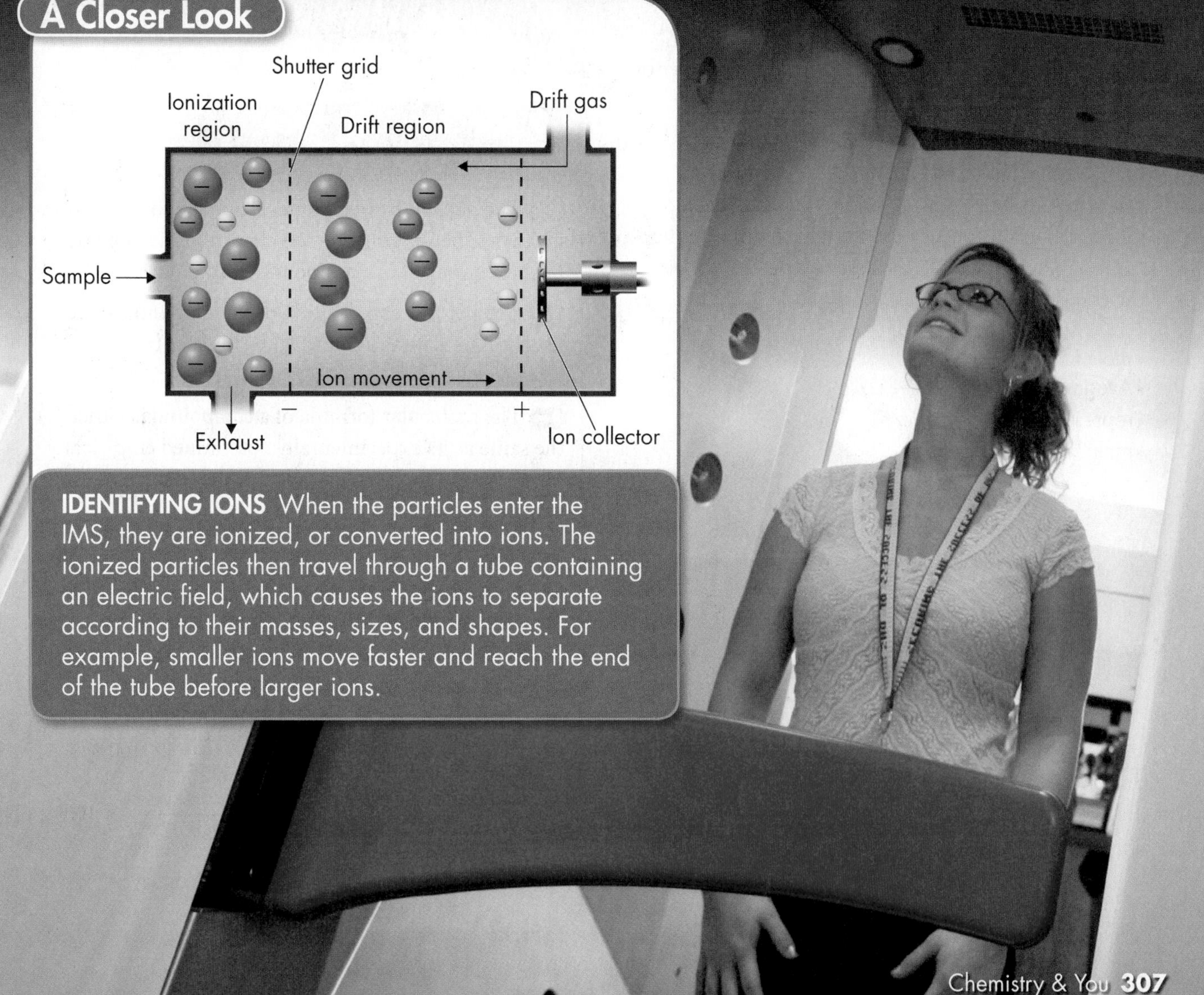

IDENTIFYING IONS When the particles enter the IMS, they are ionized, or converted into ions. The ionized particles then travel through a tube containing an electric field, which causes the ions to separate according to their masses, sizes, and shapes. For example, smaller ions move faster and reach the end of the tube before larger ions.

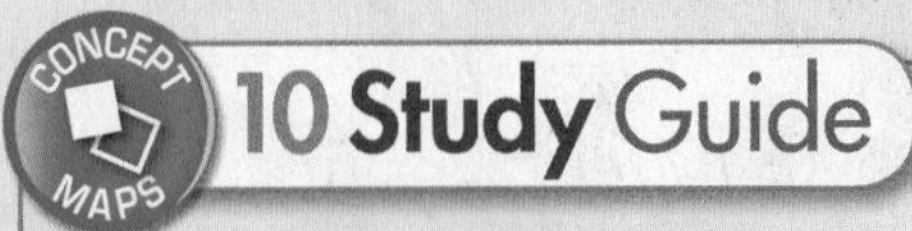

10 Study Guide

BIGIDEA
THE MOLE AND QUANTIFYING MATTER

The mole is an important measurement in chemistry. The mole allows you to convert among the amount of representative particles in a substance, the mass of a substance, and the volume of a gas at STP. The molecular formula of a compound can be determined by first finding the percent composition of the compound and then determining the empirical formula. Using the empirical formula mass and the molar mass of the compound, the molecular formula can be determined.

10.1 The Mole: A Measurement of Matter

Knowing how the count, mass, and volume of an item relate to a common unit allows you to convert among these units.

The mole allows chemists to count the number of representative particles in a substance.

The atomic mass of an element expressed in grams is the mass of a mole of the element. To calculate the molar mass of a compound, find the number of grams of each element in one mole of the compound. Then, add the masses of the elements in the compound.

- mole (279)
- Avogadro's number (279)
- representative particle (279)
- molar mass (283)

10.2 Mole–Mass and Mole–Volume Relationships

Use the molar mass of an element or compound to convert between the mass of a substance and the moles of the substance.

The molar volume is used to convert between the number of moles of gas and the volume of the gas at STP.

- Avogadro's hypothesis (292)
- standard temperature and pressure (STP) (292)
- molar volume (292)

Key Equations

$$\text{number of moles} = \text{mass} \times \frac{1 \text{ mol}}{\text{molar mass}}$$

$$\text{number of moles of a gas at STP} = \text{volume} \times \frac{1 \text{ mol}}{22.4 \text{ L}}$$

10.3 Percent Composition and Chemical Formulas

The percent by mass of an element in a compound is the number of grams of the element divided by the mass in grams of the compound multiplied by 100%.

The percent composition of a compound can be used to calculate the empirical formula of that compound.

The molecular formula of a compound is either the same as its experimentally determined empirical formula or it is a simple whole-number multiple of its empirical formula.

- percent composition (296)
- empirical formula (302)

Key Equations

$$\text{\% by mass of element} = \frac{\text{mass of element}}{\text{mass of compound}} \times 100\%$$

$$\text{\% by mass of element} = \frac{\text{mass of element in 1 mol compound}}{\text{molar mass of compound}} \times 100\%$$

Math Tune-Up: Mole Problems

Problem	❶ Analyze	❷ Calculate	❸ Evaluate
How many moles of lithium (Li) is 4.81×10^{24} atoms of lithium?	Knowns: number of atoms = 4.81×10^{24} atoms Li 1 mol Li = 6.02×10^{23} atoms Li Unknown: moles = ? mol Li The desired conversion is atoms ⟶ moles.	Use the correct conversion factor to convert from atoms to moles. $4.81 \times 10^{24}\ \cancel{\text{atoms Li}} \times \dfrac{1\ \text{mol Li}}{6.02 \times 10^{23}\ \cancel{\text{atoms Li}}} = 7.99\ \text{mol Li}$	The given number of atoms is about 8 times Avogadro's number, so the answer should be around 8 mol of atoms.
Calculate the mass in grams of 0.160 mol of H_2O_2.	Known: number of moles = 0.160 mol H_2O_2 Unknown: mass = ? g H_2O_2 The desired conversion is moles ⟶ mass.	Determine the molar mass of H_2O_2 and then use the correct conversion factor to convert from moles to grams. $1\ \text{mol}\ H_2O_2 = (2\ \cancel{\text{mol}})(1.0\ \text{g}/\cancel{\text{mol}}) + (2\ \cancel{\text{mol}})(16.0\ \text{g}/\cancel{\text{mol}}) = 34.0\ \text{g}\ H_2O_2$ $0.160\ \cancel{\text{mol}\ H_2O_2} \times \dfrac{34.0\ \text{g}\ H_2O_2}{1\ \cancel{\text{mol}\ H_2O_2}} = 5.44\ \text{g}\ H_2O_2$	The number of moles of H_2O_2 is about 0.2, and the molar mass is about 30 g/mol. The answer should be around 6 g.
What is the volume of 1.25 mol of He at STP?	Knowns: number of moles = 1.25 mol He 1 mol He at STP = 22.4 L He Unknown: volume = ? L He The desired conversion is moles ⟶ volume at STP.	Use the correct conversion factor to convert from moles to volume at STP. $1.25\ \cancel{\text{mol He}} \times \dfrac{22.4\ \text{L He}}{1\ \cancel{\text{mol He}}} = 28.0\ \text{L}$	One mole of gas at STP has a volume of 22.4 L, so 1.25 mol should have a volume larger than 22.4 L.
What is the percent composition of the compound formed when 29.0 g of Ag combines completely with 4.30 g of S?	Knowns: mass of Ag = 29.0 g Ag mass of S = 4.30 g S mass of compound = 29.0 g + 4.30 g = 33.3 g Unknowns: percent by mass of Ag = ?% Ag percent by mass of S = ?% S Use the equation: % by mass of element = $\dfrac{\text{mass of element}}{\text{mass of compound}} \times 100\%$	Calculate the percent by mass of Ag and S in the compound. $\%\text{Ag} = \dfrac{29.0\ \text{g}}{33.3\ \text{g}} \times 100\%$ %Ag = 87.1% Ag $\%\text{S} = \dfrac{4.30\ \text{g}}{33.3\ \text{g}} \times 100\%$ %S = 12.9% S	The percents of the elements add up to 100%.

Hint: Review Sample Problem 10.1 if you have trouble converting between the number of representative particles and moles.

Remember: A mole of any gas at STP occupies a volume of 22.4 L.

Hint: Review Sample Problems 10.6 and 10.7 if you have trouble calculating the percent composition of a compound.

10 Assessment

⋆ Solutions appear in Appendix D.

Lesson by Lesson

10.1 The Mole: A Measurement of Matter

⋆**50.** Name the representative particle (atom, molecule, or formula unit) of each substance.

a. oxygen gas
b. sodium sulfide
c. sulfur dioxide
d. potassium

51. Describe the relationship between Avogadro's number and one mole of any substance.

⋆**52.** Find the number of moles in each substance.

a. 2.41×10^{24} formula units of NaCl
b. 9.03×10^{24} atoms of Hg
c. 4.65×10^{24} molecules of NO_2

⋆**53.** Find the number of representative particles in each substance.

a. 3.00 mol Sn
b. 0.400 mol KCl
c. 7.50 mol SO_2
d. 4.80×10^{-3} mol NaI

54. What is the molar mass of chlorine?

55. List the steps you would take to calculate the molar mass of any compound.

⋆**56.** Calculate the molar mass of each substance.

a. H_3PO_4
b. N_2O_3
c. $(NH_4)_2SO_4$
d. $C_4H_9O_2$

57. Calculate the mass of 1.00 mol of each of these substances.

a. silicon dioxide (SiO_2)
b. diatomic nitrogen (N_2)
c. iron(III) hydroxide ($Fe(OH)_3$)
d. copper (Cu)

10.2 Mole–Mass and Mole–Volume Relationships

58. Find the mass of each substance.

a. 1.50 mol C_5H_{12}
b. 14.4 mol F_2
c. 0.780 mol $Ca(CN)_2$
d. 7.00 mol H_2O_2
e. 5.60 mol NaOH
f. 3.21×10^{-2} mol Ni

59. How many moles is each of the following?

a. 15.5 g SiO_2
b. 0.0688 g AgCl
c. 79.3 g Cl_2
d. 5.96 g KOH
e. 937 g $Ca(C_2H_3O_2)_2$
f. 0.800 g Ca

60. What is the volume of one mole of any gas at STP?

⋆**61.** Calculate the volume of each of the following gases at STP.

a. 7.64 mol Ar
b. 1.34 mol SO_2
c. 0.442 mol C_2H_6
d. 2.45×10^{-3} mol H_2S

10.3 Percent Composition and Chemical Formulas

62. What is the percent composition of the compound formed when 2.70 g of aluminum combine with oxygen to form 5.10 g of aluminum oxide?

⋆**63.** Calculate the percent composition when 13.3 g of Fe combine completely with 5.7 g of O.

⋆**64.** Calculate the percent composition of each compound.

a. H_2S
b. $(NH_4)_2C_2O_4$
c. $Mg(OH)_2$
d. Na_3PO_4

65. Which of the following can be classified as an empirical formula?

a. S_2C_{12}
b. $C_6H_{10}O_4$
c. Na_2SO_3

66. Which pair of molecules has the same empirical formula?

a. $C_2H_4O_2$ and $C_6H_{12}O_6$
b. $NaCrO_4$ and $Na_2Cr_2O_7$

⋆**67.** Which of the following molecular formulas are also empirical formulas?

a. ribose ($C_5H_{10}O_5$)
b. ethyl butyrate ($C_6H_{12}O_2$)
c. chlorophyll ($C_{55}H_{72}MgN_4O_5$)
d. DEET ($C_{12}H_{17}ON$)

Understand Concepts

*68. Table sugar, or sucrose, has the chemical formula $C_{12}H_{22}O_{11}$.

a. How many atoms are in 1.00 mol of sucrose?
b. How many atoms of C are in 2.00 mol of sucrose?
c. How many atoms of H are in 2.00 mol of sucrose?
d. How many atoms of O are in 3.65 mol of sucrose?

69. Which of the following contains the largest number of atoms?

a. 82.0 g Kr
b. 0.842 mol C_2H_4
c. 36.0 g N_2

*70. Calculate the grams of oxygen in 90.0 g of Cl_2O.

71. Determine the empirical formula of a compound composed of 42.9% C and 57.1% O.

*72. A fictitious "atomic balance" is shown below. Fifteen atoms of boron on the left side of the balance are balanced by six atoms of an unknown element E on the right side.

a. What is the atomic mass of element E?
b. What is the identity of element E?

*73. What mass of helium is needed to inflate a balloon to a volume of 5.50 L at STP?

74. Calculate the empirical formula for a compound consisting of 0.40 mol Cu and 0.80 mol Br.

75. Calculate the empirical formula for a compound with 4 atoms of carbon for every 12 atoms of hydrogen.

76. How many water molecules are in a 1.00 L bottle of water? The density of water is 1.00 g/mL.

Think Critically

*77. **Infer** What is the empirical formula of a compound that has three times as many hydrogen atoms as carbon atoms but only half as many oxygen atoms as carbon atoms?

78. **Apply Concepts** How are the empirical and molecular formulas of a compound related?

79. **Compare** Why does one mole of carbon have a smaller mass than one mole of sulfur? How are the atomic structures of these elements different?

80. **Analyze Data** One mole of any gas at STP equals 22.4 L of that gas. It is also true that different elements have different atomic volumes, or diameters. How can you reconcile these two statements?

FOUNDATIONS Wrap-Up

Chalk Full of Moles

1. **Draw Conclusions** At the beginning of this chapter, you found the mass of chalk needed to write your name on a piece of sandpaper. You then calculated the number of moles of chalk used. How are grams and moles related?

Concept Check

Now that you have finished studying Chapter 10, answer these questions. Use your own words.

2. Suppose you have a mole of apples. How many apples do you have?
3. You blow up a balloon so that it has a volume of 5.5 L at STP. How many moles of air did you blow into the balloon?
4. Butane is a gas used as a fuel for cooking and camping. The molecular formula for butane is C_4H_{10}. What is the empirical formula for butane?

Write About Science

81. Research Research the history of Avogadro's number. What elements other than carbon have been used to define a mole? Write a report that summarizes your findings.

82. Explain Elite athletes often monitor their own lactic acid buildup and determine their lactate threshold. Research the use of the concept of lactate threshold in intense athletic training and then write a brief paragraph that explains it.

CHEMYSTERY

A Formula for Cheating

Typically, steroids can be detected in an athlete's urine. A urine sample is collected and is first injected into an instrument that separates the chemical compounds in the urine.

The separated compounds are then analyzed by using a mass spectrometer. The mass spectrometer provides such information as the molar mass of the compounds present in the urine sample and the molecular structure of these compounds. These structures can be compared with a database of known compounds to identify the presence of steroids in the sample.

***83. Calculate** Analysis of an athlete's urine found the presence of a compound with a molar mass of 312 g/mol. How many moles of this compound are contained in 30.0 mg? How many molecules of the compound is this?

84. Connect to the BIGIDEA The compound found in the athlete's urine is the steroid THG. This compound has a percent composition of 80.8% carbon, 8.97% hydrogen, and 10.3% oxygen. What is the empirical formula of THG?

Cumulative Review

***85.** Classify each of the following as a physical change or a chemical change. (See Lessons 2.1 and 2.4 for help.)

a. An aspirin tablet is crushed to a powder.
b. A red rose turns brown.
c. Grape juice turns to wine.
d. Fingernail polish remover evaporates.
e. A bean seed sprouts.

86. A student writes down the density of table sugar as 1.59 and the density of carbon dioxide as 1.83. Can these values be correct? Explain. (See Lesson 3.2 for help.)

***87.** Convert each of the following. (See Lesson 3.3 for help.)

a. 4.72 g to mg
b. 2.7×10^3 cm/s to km/h

***88.** How many protons, electrons, and neutrons are in each isotope? (See Lesson 4.3 for help.)

a. zirconium-90
b. palladium-108
c. bromine-81
d. antimony-123

***89.** Write the complete electron configuration for each atom. (See Lesson 5.2 for help.)

a. fluorine **b.** lithium **c.** rubidium

90. Why do the elements magnesium and barium have similar chemical and physical properties? (See Lesson 6.2 for help.)

91. How can the periodic table be used to infer the number of valence electrons in an atom? (See Lesson 7.1 for help.)

92. How does a molecule differ from an atom? (See Lesson 8.1 for help.)

93. Explain how you can use electronegativity values to classify a bond as nonpolar covalent, polar covalent, or ionic. (See Lesson 8.4 for help.)

***94.** Identify any incorrect formulas among the following. (See Lesson 9.2 for help.)

a. H_2O_2
b. $NaIO_4$
c. SrO
d. CaS_2
e. $CaHPO_4$
f. $BaOH$

Standardized Test Prep

For help with answering test questions, go to your Chemistry Skills and Math Workbook.

Tips for Success

Wear a Watch Be aware of how many questions you have to answer and how much time you have to answer them. Look at your watch or a clock frequently to keep track of your progress.

1. Choose the term that best completes the second relationship.
   a. dozen : eggs
      mole : ____
   (A) atoms (C) size
   (B) 6.02×10^{23} (D) grams
   b. mole : Avogadro's number
      molar volume : ____
   (A) mole (C) STP
   (B) water (D) 22.4 L

Select the choice that best answers each question or completes each statement.

2. Calculate the molar mass of ammonium phosphate ($(NH_4)_3PO_4$).
   (A) 113.0 g/mol (C) 149.0 g/mol
   (B) 121.0 g/mol (D) 242.0 g/mo
3. Based on the structural formula below, what is the empirical formula for tartaric acid, a compound found in grape juice?

```
HO—CH—COOH
     |
HO—CH—COOH
```

   (A) $C_2H_3O_3$ (C) CHO
   (B) $C_4H_6O_6$ (D) $C_1H_{1.5}O_{1.5}$
4. How many hydrogen atoms are in six molecules of ethylene glycol ($C_2H_6O_2$)?
   (A) 6 (C) $6 \times (6.02 \times 10^{23})$
   (B) 36 (D) $36 \times (6.02 \times 10^{23})$
5. Which of these compounds has the largest percent by mass of nitrogen?
   (A) N_2O (D) N_2O_3
   (B) NO (E) N_2O_4
   (C) NO_2
6. Which of these statements is true of a balloon filled with 1.00 mol $N_2(g)$ at STP?
   I. The balloon has a volume of 22.4 L.
   II. The contents of the balloon have a mass of 14.0 g.
   III. The balloon contains 6.02×10^{23} molecules.
   (A) I only (C) I and III only
   (B) I and II only (D) I, II, and III
7. Allicin ($C_6H_{10}S_2O$) is the compound that gives garlic its odor. A sample of allicin contains 3.0×10^{21} atoms of carbon. How many hydrogen atoms does this sample contain?
   (A) 10 (C) 1.8×10^{21}
   (B) 1.0×10^{21} (D) 5.0×10^{21}

The lettered choices below refer to Questions 8–11. A lettered choice may be used once, more than once, or not at all.

(A) CH (B) CH_2 (C) C_2H_5 (D) CH_3 (E) C_2H_3

Which of the formulas is the empirical formula for each of the following compounds?

8. C_8H_{12}
9. C_6H_6
10. C_2H_6
11. C_4H_{10}

For Questions 12–14, write the molecular formula for each compound whose structural formula is shown. Then, calculate the compound's molar mass.

12.
```
   H  OH H
   |  |  |
H—C—C—C—H
   |  |  |
   H  H  H
```

13.
```
      H  O
      |  ||
H2N—C—C—OH
      |
      H
```

14.
```
   H  H      O
   |  |      ||
H—C—C—O—C—H
   |  |
   H  H
```

If You Have Trouble With . . .

Question	1	2	3	4	5	6	7	8	9	10	11	12	13	14
See Lesson	10.2	10.1	10.3	10.1	10.3	10.2	10.1	10.3	10.3	10.3	10.3	10.1	10.1	10.1

11 Chemical Reactions

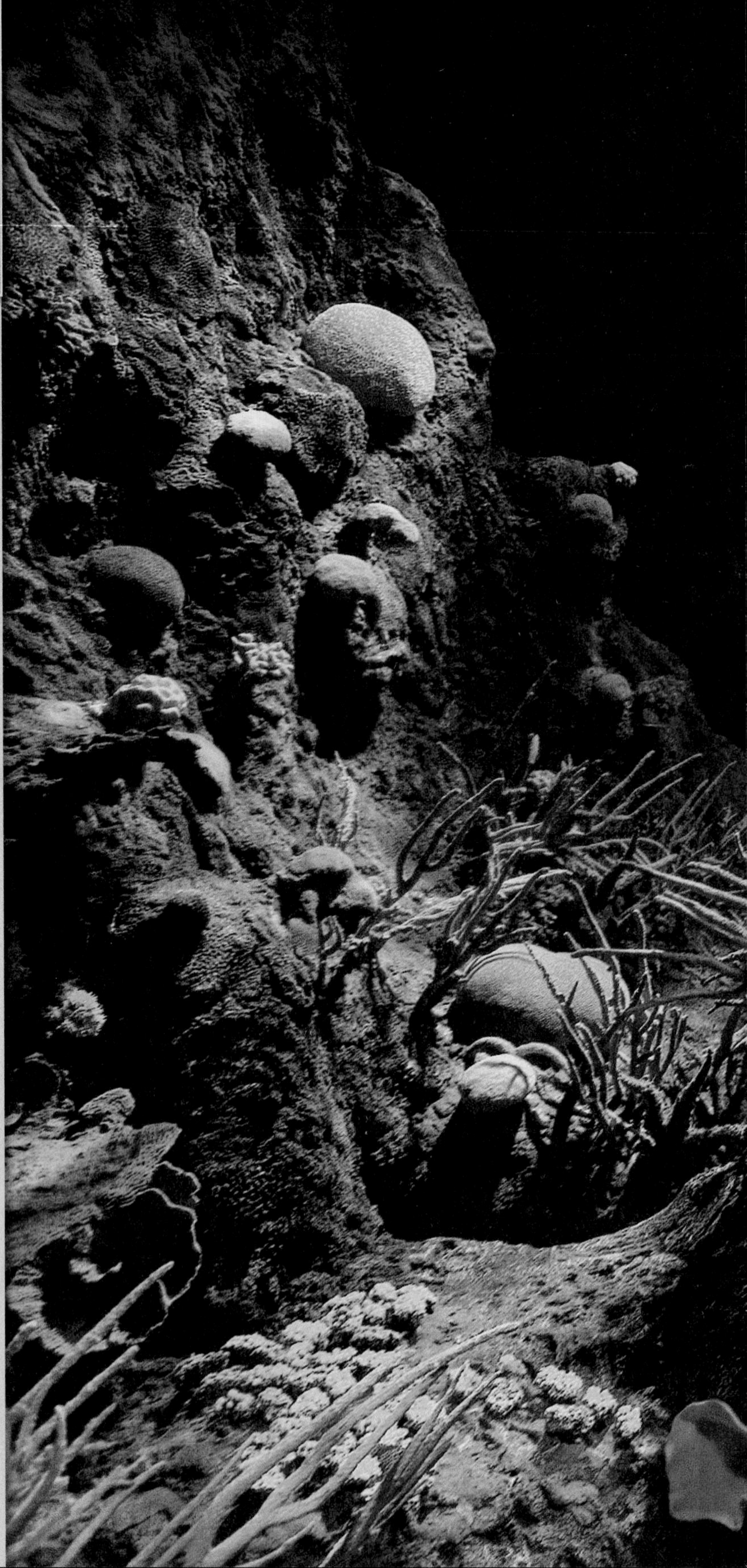

Marine animals such as snails and coral need calcium. In a reef aquarium, calcium is added to the water in the form of an aqueous solution of calcium hydroxide.

FOUNDATIONS for Learning

A Fizzy Reaction 

1. You will need baking soda, vinegar, a plastic bottle, and a balloon.
2. Pour 5 g of baking soda into the plastic bottle. Then pour 15 mL of vinegar into the empty balloon.
3. Carefully stretch the opening of the balloon over the top of the bottle. As you seal the bottle, try not to spill any vinegar into it.
4. Now, hold the balloon vertically so that the vinegar drains into the bottle. Observe what happens.

Form a Hypothesis What caused the volume of the balloon to change?

PearsonChem.com

 **UntamedScience**

Take a video field trip with the Untamed Science crew to "meet" some winners of the Nobel Prize in Chemistry.

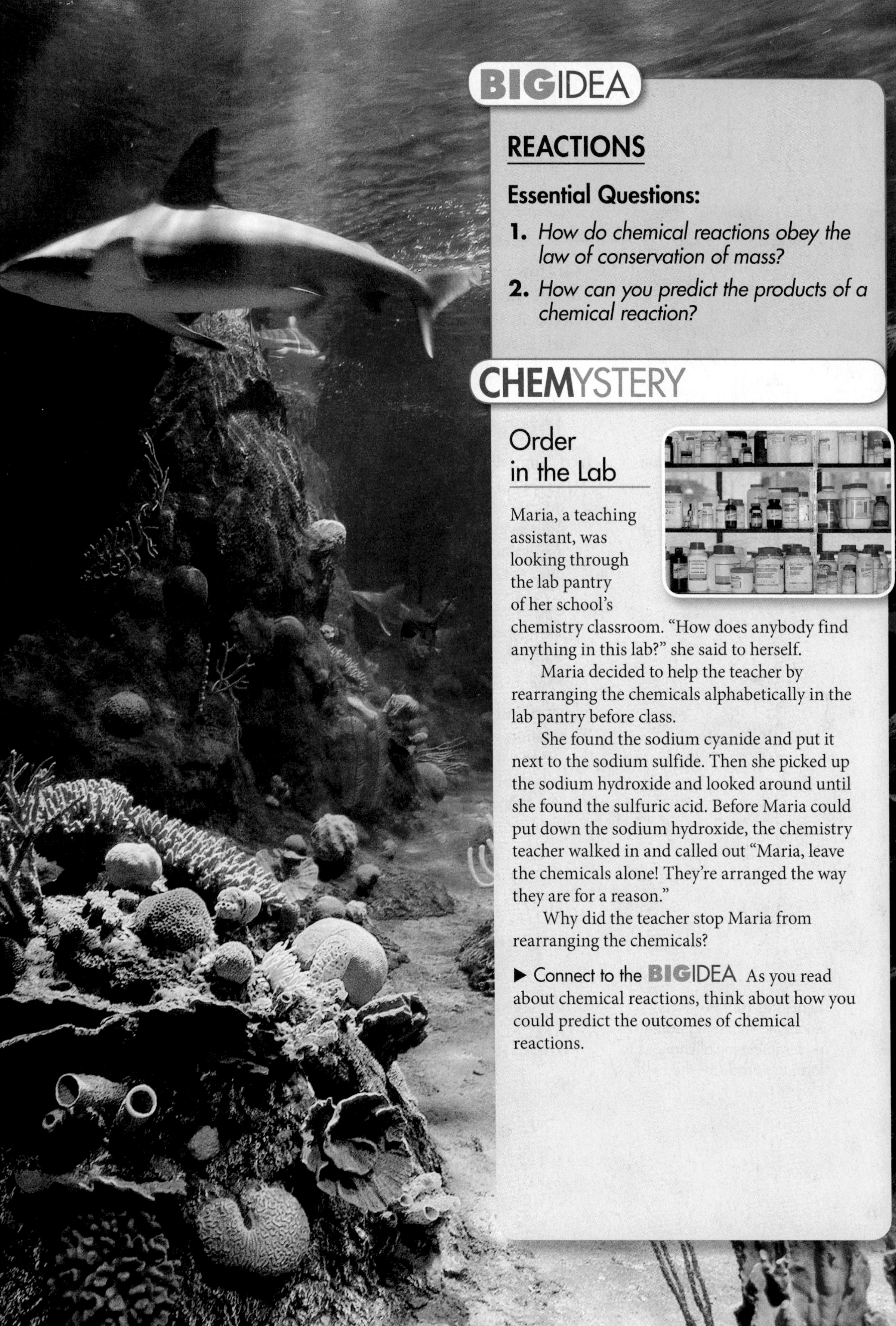

BIGIDEA

REACTIONS

Essential Questions:

1. *How do chemical reactions obey the law of conservation of mass?*
2. *How can you predict the products of a chemical reaction?*

CHEMYSTERY

Order in the Lab

Maria, a teaching assistant, was looking through the lab pantry of her school's chemistry classroom. "How does anybody find anything in this lab?" she said to herself.

Maria decided to help the teacher by rearranging the chemicals alphabetically in the lab pantry before class.

She found the sodium cyanide and put it next to the sodium sulfide. Then she picked up the sodium hydroxide and looked around until she found the sulfuric acid. Before Maria could put down the sodium hydroxide, the chemistry teacher walked in and called out "Maria, leave the chemicals alone! They're arranged the way they are for a reason."

Why did the teacher stop Maria from rearranging the chemicals?

▶ Connect to the **BIGIDEA** As you read about chemical reactions, think about how you could predict the outcomes of chemical reactions.

11.1 Describing Chemical Reactions

CHEMISTRY & YOU

Q: How is a chemical reaction going to change the way you drive? You've probably heard about fuel-cell cars. Fuel cells produce electricity through a chemical reaction. But, instead of gasoline, the "fuel" used in a fuel cell is hydrogen gas. In this lesson, you'll learn how to write and balance the equations that represent chemical reactions.

Key Questions

How do you write a skeleton equation?

What are the steps for writing and balancing a chemical equation?

Introduction to Chemical Equations

Chemical reactions take place all the time—both inside you and around you. After a meal, a series of chemical reactions takes place as your body digests food. Chemical reactions also take place inside plants during photosynthesis. In order to grow, a plant uses sunlight, carbon dioxide, and water. The reactions involved in photosynthesis and digestion are different. But both sets of chemical reactions are needed to sustain life.

Cooking food always involves chemical reactions. The photo below shows three baked muffins next to some of the ingredients used—flour, eggs, brown sugar, and butter. The recipe tells you which ingredients to mix together and how much of each to use.

All chemical reactions involve changing substances. In a chemical reaction, one or more reactants change into one or more products. When you make muffins, reactants in the ingredients change as they are mixed together and heated in an oven. The product is baked muffins. The recipe gives you information on how they are made. Chemists have their own kind of recipe. It's called a chemical equation.

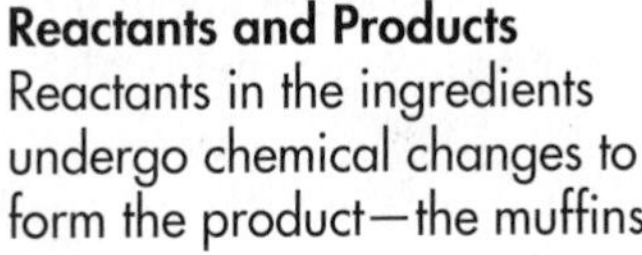

Reactants and Products
Reactants in the ingredients undergo chemical changes to form the product—the muffins.

Examples of Chemical Reactions

Iron turns to red-brown rust (iron(III) oxide) in the presence of oxygen.
Iron + oxygen ⟶ iron(III) oxide

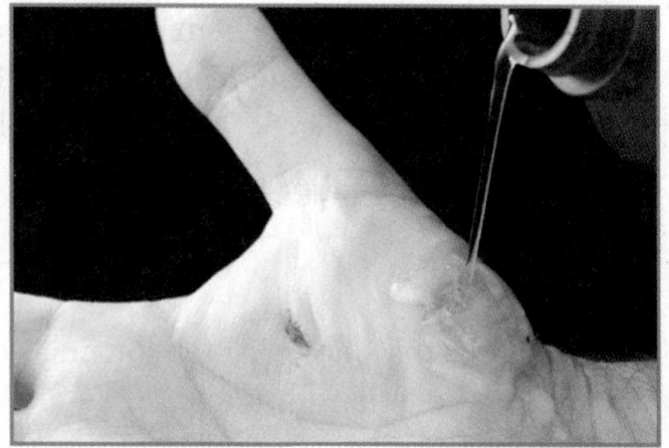

Water and oxygen form when hydrogen peroxide is poured on a cut.
Hydrogen peroxide ⟶ water + oxygen

Word Equations How do you describe what happens in a chemical reaction? There is a shorthand method for writing a description of a chemical reaction. In this method, the reactants are written on the left and the products are written on the right. An arrow separates them. You read the arrow as *yields, gives,* or *reacts to produce.*

Reactants ⟶ products

The photos above show two examples of chemical reactions. How could you describe the rusting of the iron truck? You could say: "Iron reacts with oxygen to produce iron(III) oxide (rust)." That is a perfectly good description, but it's quicker to identify the reactants and product in a word equation.

Iron + oxygen ⟶ iron(III) oxide

To make a word equation, write the names of the reactants, separated by plus signs, to the left of the arrow. Write the names of the products, also separated by plus signs, to the right of the arrow. Notice that no plus sign is needed on the product side of this equation because iron(III) oxide is the only product.

Have you ever poured hydrogen peroxide on an open cut? Bubbles of oxygen gas form rapidly. The production of gas is evidence of a chemical change. Two new substances are produced in this reaction, oxygen gas and liquid water. You could describe this reaction by saying, "Hydrogen peroxide decomposes to form water and oxygen gas." You could also write a word equation.

Hydrogen peroxide ⟶ water + oxygen

Another example of a chemical reaction is the burning of methane. Methane is the main component of natural gas, a common fuel for heating homes and cooking food. Burning a substance requires oxygen, so methane and oxygen are the reactants. The products are water and carbon dioxide. The word equation is as follows:

Methane + oxygen ⟶ carbon dioxide + water

BUILD Connections

When you turn on a gas stove, you are controlling a chemical reaction that gives off heat. In a modern gas stove, natural gas (about 90% methane) is mixed with air (21% oxygen). When you turn on the burner, an electric spark ignites the mixture. The reactants change into carbon dioxide and water, and heat is released.

chemical equation a representation of a chemical reaction that uses chemical formulas and symbols

skeleton equation chemical equation that does not show relative amounts of reactants or products

catalyst a substance that speeds up a reaction but is not used up in the reaction

MULTIPLE MEANINGS
A *catalyst* can also refer to something (or someone) that brings about a major change. For example, a coach might be the catalyst who inspires a sports team to victory.

Chemical Equations Word equations describe chemical reactions well, but they are cumbersome. It's easier to use the formulas for the reactants and products to write chemical equations. A **chemical equation** is a representation of a chemical reaction. The formulas of the reactants are connected by an arrow with the formulas of the products. Here is a chemical equation for rusting:

$$Fe + O_2 \longrightarrow Fe_2O_3$$

Equations that show just the formulas of the reactants and products are called skeleton equations. A **skeleton equation** is a chemical equation that does not indicate the relative amounts of the reactants and products. To write a skeleton equation, write the chemical formulas for the reactants to the left of the yields sign (arrow) and the formulas for the products to the right of it.

To make the equation more complete, you can add other symbols. See the table below for symbols commonly used in chemical equations. For example, here is the unbalanced equation for rusting with symbols for the physical states added:

$$Fe(s) + O_2(g) \longrightarrow Fe_2O_3(s)$$

In many chemical reactions, a catalyst is added to the reaction mixture. A **catalyst** is a substance that speeds up the reaction but is not used up in the reaction. A catalyst is neither a reactant nor a product, so its formula is written above the arrow in a chemical equation. For example, an aqueous solution of hydrogen peroxide ($H_2O_2(aq)$) decomposes to produce water and oxygen. The reaction happens slowly, but can be sped up by adding manganese(IV) oxide.

$$H_2O_2(aq) \xrightarrow{MnO_2} H_2O(l) + O_2(g)$$

Placing "MnO_2" above the arrow indicates that MnO_2 is a catalyst.

Key Question How do you write a skeleton equation? **To write a skeleton equation, write the chemical formulas for the reactants to the left of the yields sign and the formulas for the products to the right of it.**

Symbols Used in Chemical Equations

Symbol	Explanation
$+$	Separates two reactants or two products
$\longrightarrow$	"Yields"; separates reactants from products
$\rightleftharpoons$	Used in place of $\longrightarrow$ for reversible reactions
(s), (l), (g)	Designates a reactant or product in the solid state, liquid state, or gaseous state; placed after the formula
(aq)	Designates an aqueous solution, meaning the substance is dissolved in water; placed after the formula
$\xrightarrow{\Delta}$ $\xrightarrow{heat}$	Indicates that heat is supplied to the reaction
$\xrightarrow{Pt}$	A formula written above or below the yields sign indicates its use as a catalyst (in this example, platinum).

Sample Problem 11.1

Writing a Skeleton Equation

Hydrochloric acid reacts with solid sodium hydrogen carbonate. The products formed are aqueous sodium chloride, water, and carbon dioxide gas. Write a skeleton equation for this chemical reaction.

❶ Analyze Identify the relevant concepts.

Write the correct formula for each substance in the reaction. Indicate the state of each substance. Separate the reactants from the products with an arrow. Use plus signs to separate the reactants and the products.

❷ Solve Apply the concepts to this problem.

Start with the names of reactants and products. Include their physical states.

Write the correct formula for each reactant and each product.

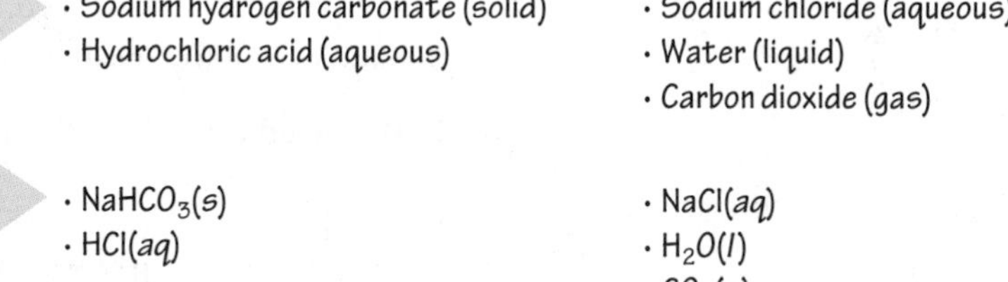

Reactants
• Sodium hydrogen carbonate (solid)
• Hydrochloric acid (aqueous)
Products
• Sodium chloride (aqueous)
• Water (liquid)
• Carbon dioxide (gas)
• $NaHCO_3(s)$
• $HCl(aq)$
• $NaCl(aq)$
• $H_2O(l)$
• $CO_2(g)$

Place the reactants to the left of the arrow and the products to the right. Use plus signs to separate the two reactants and each of the three products.

$$NaHCO_3(s) + HCl(aq) \longrightarrow NaCl(aq) + H_2O(l) + CO_2(g)$$

Practice Problems

1. Heating copper(II) sulfide in the presence of diatomic oxygen produces pure copper and sulfur dioxide gas. Write a skeleton equation for this chemical reaction.

❶ Analyze Identify the relevant concepts.

❷ Solve Apply the concepts to this problem.

> **TO GET YOU STARTED...**
>
> Identify the reactants and products.
>
> | Reactants | Products |
> |---|---|
> | Copper(II) sulfide (solid) | Copper (solid) |
> | Oxygen (gas) | Sulfur dioxide (gas) |

2. Sulfur burns in oxygen to form sulfur dioxide. Write a skeleton equation for this chemical reaction.

3. Challenge Write a sentence that describes the following skeleton equation.

$$NaHCO_3(s) \xrightarrow{\Delta} Na_2CO_3(s) + CO_2(g) + H_2O(l)$$

Balancing Chemical Equations

How would you write a simple word equation for the manufacture of bicycles? Start by limiting yourself to four major components: frames, wheels, handlebars, and pedals. Your word equation for making a bicycle could read like this.

$$\underset{\text{Reactants}}{\text{Frame} + \text{wheels} + \text{handlebar} + \text{pedals}} \longrightarrow \underset{\text{Product}}{\text{bicycle}}$$

Using Coefficients Your word equation shows the reactants (the kinds of parts) and the product (a bicycle). However, the equation does not indicate the quantity of each part needed to make one bicycle.

▶ **Skeleton Equation** A standard bicycle has one frame (F), two wheels (W), one handlebar (H), and two pedals (P). The formula for a bicycle would be FW_2HP_2. You can now write a skeleton equation.

$$F + W + H + P \longrightarrow FW_2HP_2$$

This equation is unbalanced. An unbalanced equation does not indicate the quantity of the reactants needed to make the product.

▶ **Balanced Equation** The balanced equation for making a bicycle looks like this.

$$F + 2W + H + 2P \longrightarrow FW_2HP_2$$

The balanced equation tells you that one frame, two wheels, one handlebar, and two pedals yield one bicycle. The number of each part on the reactant side is the same as the number of that part on the product side.

To balance the equation, the number 2 was placed in front of *wheels* and *pedals*. These numbers are called **coefficients**—small whole numbers that are placed in front of the formulas in an equation in order to balance it. The number 1 is understood to be in front of *frame, handlebar,* and *bicycle*. If a reactant has a coefficient of 1, you may omit the coefficient from the equation.

Counting Atoms Chemists use balanced equations to describe reactions. A **balanced equation** is a chemical equation in which each side of the equation has the same number of atoms of each element.

Recall that John Dalton's atomic theory states that as reactants are converted to products, the bonds holding the atoms together break, and new bonds form. The atoms themselves are neither created nor destroyed. Instead, they are rearranged. In any chemical change, atoms and mass are conserved.

Representing a chemical reaction by a balanced chemical equation is often a two-step process. First, write the skeleton equation. Then, use coefficients to balance the equation so that it obeys the law of conservation of mass. In every balanced equation, each side of the equation has the same number of atoms of each element.

coefficient a small whole number that is placed in front of a formula to balance a chemical equation

balanced equation a chemical equation in which each side of the equation has the same number of atoms of each element

USING PRIOR KNOWLEDGE

You may already know the word *coefficient* from your math class. Coefficients are placed in front of variables in algebraic equations.

▶ **Step 1: Write a Skeleton Equation** When hydrogen and oxygen are mixed, a spark will initiate a rapid reaction. The product of the reaction is water. The skeleton equation is as follows.

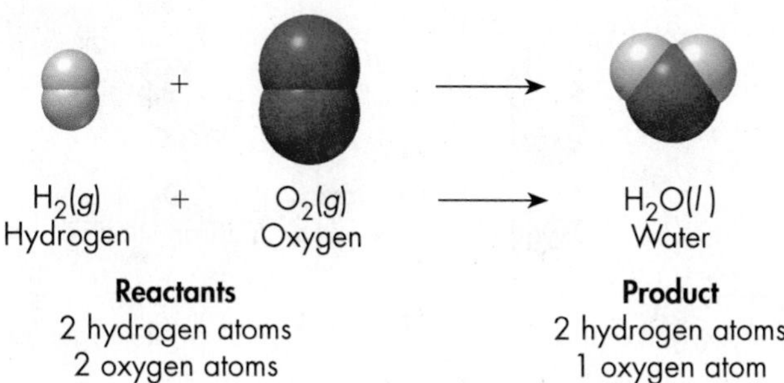

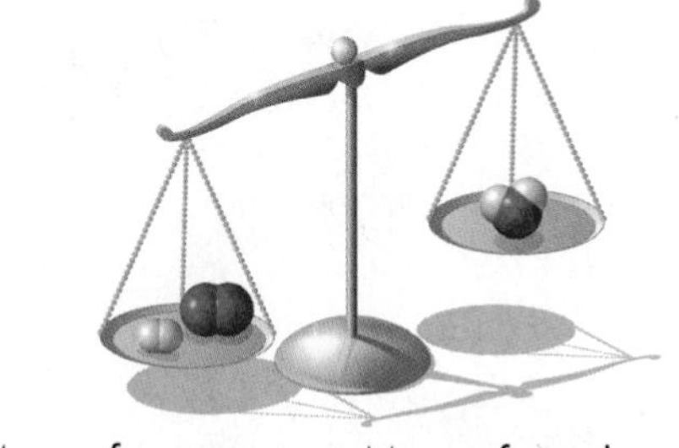
Mass of reactants ≠ Mass of products

The formulas for all the reactants and the product are correct, but this equation is not balanced. Count the atoms on both sides of the equation. Two oxygen atoms are on the reactant (left) side of the equation and only one oxygen atom is on the product (right) side. If you could put the reactants and products on a balance, it would look like the figure to the right.

As written, the unbalanced equation does not obey the law of conservation of mass. In order to quantitatively describe what really happens, you must balance the equation. What can you do to balance it?

▶ **Step 2: Balance the Equation** In the skeleton equation, hydrogen is balanced, but oxygen is not.

$$H_2(g) + O_2(g) \longrightarrow H_2O(l)$$

If you put the coefficient 2 in front of H_2O, the oxygen will be balanced.

$$H_2(g) + O_2(g) \longrightarrow 2H_2O(l)$$

But now there are twice as many hydrogen atoms in the product (four atoms) as there are in the reactants (two atoms). The equation is still not balanced. To correct the equation, put the coefficient 2 in front of H_2.

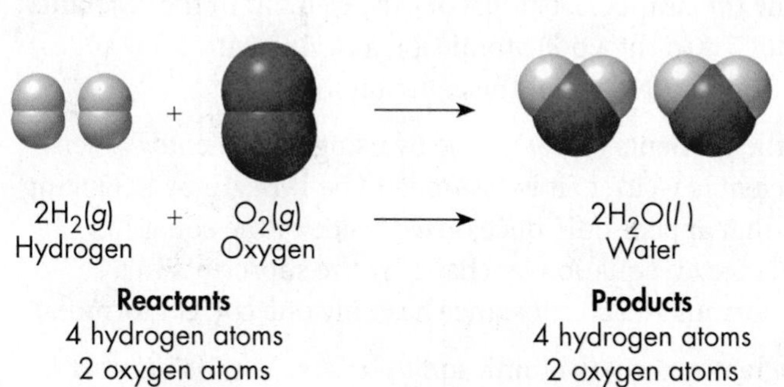

Mass of reactants = Mass of products

Now you have four hydrogen atoms and two oxygen atoms on each side of the equation. The equation is balanced. If you could put the reactants and products on a balance, it would look like the figure to the right.

Go to your Chemistry Skills and Math Workbook to practice writing and balancing equations.

▶ **Balanced Skeleton Equation** Sometimes a skeleton equation may already be balanced. For example, carbon burns in the presence of oxygen to produce carbon dioxide.

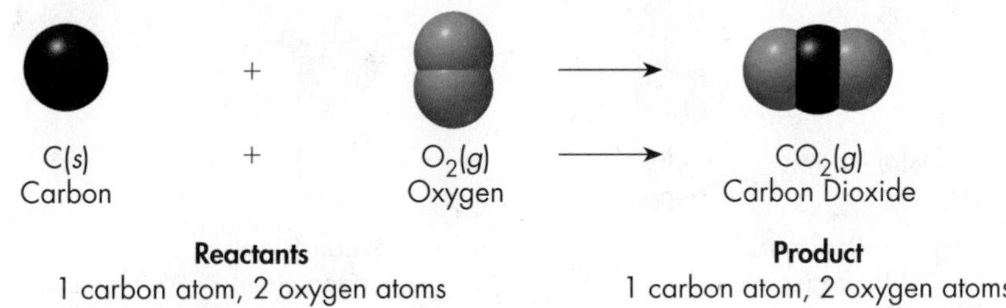

$C(s)$ Carbon	+	$O_2(g)$ Oxygen	⟶	$CO_2(g)$ Carbon Dioxide

Reactants
1 carbon atom, 2 oxygen atoms

Product
1 carbon atom, 2 oxygen atoms

This equation is balanced. One carbon atom and two oxygen atoms are on each side of the equation. You do not need to change the coefficients. They are all understood to be 1.

Some useful guidelines for writing and balancing equations are listed in the table below.

Key Question What are the steps for writing and balancing a chemical equation? **To write a balanced chemical equation, first write the skeleton equation. Then use coefficients to balance the equation so that the same number of each atom appears on both sides of the equation.**

Rules for Writing and Balancing Equations

1. Determine the correct formula for each reactant and product.
2. Write the skeleton equation by placing the formulas for the reactants on the left and the formulas for the products on the right with a yields sign (⟶) in between. If two or more reactants or products are involved, separate their formulas with plus signs.
3. Determine the number of atoms of each element in the reactants and products. Count a polyatomic ion as a single unit if it appears unchanged on both sides of the equation.
4. Balance the elements one at a time by using coefficients. When no coefficient is written, it is assumed to be 1. Begin by balancing elements that appear only once on each side of the equation. Never balance an equation by changing the subscripts in a chemical formula. Each substance has only one correct formula.
5. Check each atom or polyatomic ion to be sure that its number is equal on both sides of the equation.
6. Make sure all the coefficients are in the lowest possible ratio.

Balancing a Chemical Equation

Students suspended copper wire in an aqueous solution of silver nitrate. They noticed a deposit of silver crystals on the copper wire when the copper reacted with the silver nitrate. They recorded the equation for this reaction but didn't balance it. Balance their equation.

$$AgNO_3(aq) + Cu(s) \longrightarrow Cu(NO_3)_2(aq) + Ag(s)$$

1 Analyze **Identify the relevant concepts.**

Apply the rules for balancing equations. Because the polyatomic nitrate ion appears as a reactant and a product, this ion can be balanced as a unit.

2 Solve **Apply the concepts to this problem.**

Use the skeleton equation to identify which atoms or ions are balanced, and which are not.

$$AgNO_3(aq) + Cu(s) \longrightarrow Cu(NO_3)_2(aq) + Ag(s)$$

Ag is balanced.
Cu is balanced.
NO_3^- is not balanced.

Balance the nitrate ion. Put a coefficient 2 in front of $AgNO_3(aq)$. Recount the atoms and ions on both sides to check if the equation is balanced.

$$2AgNO_3(aq) + Cu(s) \longrightarrow Cu(NO_3)_2(aq) + Ag(s)$$

Ag is not balanced.
Cu is balanced.
NO_3^- is balanced.

Balance the silver. Put a coefficient 2 in front of $Ag(s)$. Recount the atoms and ions on both sides to check if the equation is balanced.

$$2AgNO_3(aq) + Cu(s) \longrightarrow Cu(NO_3)_2(aq) + 2Ag(s)$$

Ag is balanced.
Cu is balanced.
NO_3^- is balanced.

Practice Problems

4. Balance the equation:
$C(s) + O_2(g) \longrightarrow CO(g)$

1 Analyze **Identify the relevant concepts.**

2 Solve **Apply the concepts to this problem.**

5. Balance the equation:
$Mg(s) + AgNO_3(aq) \longrightarrow Ag(s) + Mg(NO_3)_2(aq)$

6. Challenge Balance the following equation.
$CO(g) + Fe_2O_3(s) \longrightarrow Fe(s) + CO_2(g)$

Remember: You can balance polyatomic ions as a unit when they appear on both sides of a chemical equation.

SampleProblem 11.3

Balancing a Chemical Equation

Aluminum is a good choice for outdoor furniture because it reacts with oxygen in the air to form a thin protective coat of aluminum oxide. Balance the equation for this reaction.

$$Al(s) + O_2(g) \longrightarrow Al_2O_3(s)$$

❶ Analyze **Identify the relevant concepts.**

Apply the rules for balancing equations. Notice the odd number of oxygen atoms in the product.

❷ Solve **Apply the concepts to this problem.**

BUILD Math Skills

Even and Odd Numbers A situation that often occurs in balancing equations is the "even-odd problem." Any whole-number coefficient placed in front of a diatomic molecule (such as O_2) gives you an even number of that atom on one side of the equation. If the other side contains an odd number of the same atom, how do you balance them? The simplest way is to multiply the formula with the odd number of atoms by 2. See how this is done below for Al_2O_3.

Use the skeleton equation to identify which atoms are balanced, and which are not.

$$Al(s) + O_2(g) \longrightarrow Al_2O_3(s)$$

Al is not balanced.
O is not balanced.

Balance the aluminum by placing the coefficient 2 in front of Al(*s*). Recount the atoms on both sides.

$$2Al(s) + O_2(g) \longrightarrow Al_2O_3(s)$$

Al is balanced.
O is not balanced.

Multiply the formula with the odd number of oxygen atoms (on the right) by 2 to get an even number of oxygen atoms on the right. Recount the atoms.

$$2Al(s) + O_2(g) \longrightarrow 2Al_2O_3(s)$$

Al is not balanced.
O is not balanced.

Balance the oxygen. Put a coefficient of 3 in front of $O_2(g)$. Recount the atoms.

$$2Al(s) + 3O_2(g) \longrightarrow 2Al_2O_3(s)$$

Al is not balanced.
O is balanced.

Rebalance the aluminum by changing the coefficient of Al(*s*) from 2 to 4. Recount the atoms to check if the equation is balanced.

$$4Al(s) + 3O_2(g) \longrightarrow 2Al_2O_3(s)$$

Al is balanced.
O is balanced.

Remember: A coefficient in front of a formula for a compound multiplies each subscript. So, $2Al_2O_3$ contains 4 aluminum atoms and 6 oxygen atoms.

PracticeProblems

7. Balance the equation:
$FeCl_3 + NaOH \longrightarrow Fe(OH)_3 + NaCl$

❶ Analyze **Identify the relevant concepts.**

❷ Solve **Apply the concepts to this problem.**

8. Challenge Write a balanced equation for the reaction below.
Sodium + water $\longrightarrow$ sodium hydroxide + hydrogen

Quick Lab

Materials

- aluminum foil, 20 cm × 20 cm
- large beaker or glass pan
- tarnished silver fork
- sodium hydrogen carbonate
- plastic tablespoon
- hot water

Removing Silver Tarnish

Procedure 

1. Fill the beaker about three-quarters full of hot water and add 2 tablespoons of sodium hydrogen carbonate ($NaHCO_3$).
2. Crush the aluminum foil into a loose ball and place it in the beaker.
3. Write a brief description of the tarnished fork. Place it in the beaker so that it is touching the aluminum foil ball.
4. Allow the beaker to stand undisturbed for 30 minutes.
5. Remove the fork and aluminum foil ball and rinse them with water.

Analyze and Conclude

1. **Observe** Look at the silver fork after you take it out of the beaker. What changes do you observe?
2. **Explain** Did a chemical reaction occur? How do you know?
3. **Identify** The tarnish on the silver fork is silver sulfide (Ag_2S). Silver becomes tarnished when it is exposed to air, egg yolk, or rubber bands. Each of these substances contains sulfur. Look for a pale yellow precipitate of aluminum sulfide on the bottom of the beaker. Write the formula for aluminum sulfide.
4. **Apply Concepts** The word equation for the reaction you observed is shown below. Write a balanced chemical equation for this reaction.

$$\text{Silver sulfide} + \text{aluminum} \longrightarrow \text{aluminum sulfide} + \text{silver}$$

11.1 LessonCheck

Key Concept Check

9. **Explain** How do you write a skeleton equation?

10. **Summarize** Describe the steps in writing a balanced chemical equation.

Vocabulary Check

Choose a highlighted word from the lesson to complete each sentence correctly.

11. A(n) __________ speeds up a reaction but isn't a reactant or product.

12. A whole number placed in front of a formula in an equation is a(n) __________.

Think Critically

13. **Apply Concepts** Balance the following equations:
    a. $SO_2(g) + O_2(g) \longrightarrow SO_3(g)$
    b. $Fe_2O_3(s) + H_2(g) \longrightarrow Fe(s) + H_2O(l)$
    c. $P(s) + O_2(g) \longrightarrow P_4O_{10}(s)$

14. **Describe** Write a balanced equation for the following reaction: Iron metal and chlorine gas react to form solid iron(III) chloride.

15. The reaction between oxygen and hydrogen in a fuel cell produces the energy to power a car. What is the product of the reaction in a fuel cell that makes the fuel-cell car a zero-emission car? (Hint: See page 321.)

11.2 Types of Chemical Reactions

CHEMISTRY & YOU

Q: What happens to the wax when you burn a candle? You probably have noticed that you have less candle after burning than before, but you may not know that a candle will not burn unless oxygen is present. When you burn a candle, a chemical reaction called *combustion* takes place. In this lesson, you will learn that if you can recognize the type of reaction, you may be able to predict the products of the reaction.

Key Question

What are the five general types of reactions?

BUILD Vocabulary

combination reaction a chemical change in which two or more substances react to form a single new substance

SUFFIXES

The suffix *-ation* means "the act of." The verb *combine* plus *-ation* gives you *combination*, or "the act of combining." A combination reaction refers to the act of chemically combining two or more reactants.

Classifying Reactions

By classifying chemical reactions, you can more easily predict what products are likely to form. One classification system identifies five general types. The five general types of reactions include combination, decomposition, single-replacement, double-replacement, and combustion. The table below lists examples of each type that you will learn about in the lesson.

Types of Chemical Reactions

Type	Example
Combination	$2Mg(s) + O_2(g) \longrightarrow 2MgO(s)$
Decomposition	$2HgO(s) \longrightarrow 2Hg(l) + O_2(g)$
Single-replacement	$2K(s) + 2H_2O(l) \longrightarrow 2KOH(aq) + H_2(g)$
Double-replacement	$2KI(aq) + Pb(NO_3)_2(aq) \longrightarrow PbI_2(s) + 2KNO_3(aq)$
Combustion	$CH_4(g) + 2O_2(g) \longrightarrow CO_2(g) + 2H_2O(g)$

Not all chemical reactions fit into just one category. Sometimes a reaction may fit equally well into two categories. Even so, recognizing a reaction as a particular type is useful. Understanding patterns of chemical behavior will allow you to predict the products of many reactions.

Combination Reactions The first type of reaction is the combination, or synthesis, reaction. A **combination reaction** is a chemical change in which two or more substances react to form a single new substance.

The figure at the top of the next page shows the reaction of magnesium metal and oxygen gas. These two elements combine to form the compound magnesium oxide.

$$2Mg(s) + O_2(g) \longrightarrow 2MgO(s)$$

Combination Reaction
When ignited, magnesium ribbon reacts with oxygen in the air to form magnesium oxide, a white solid.

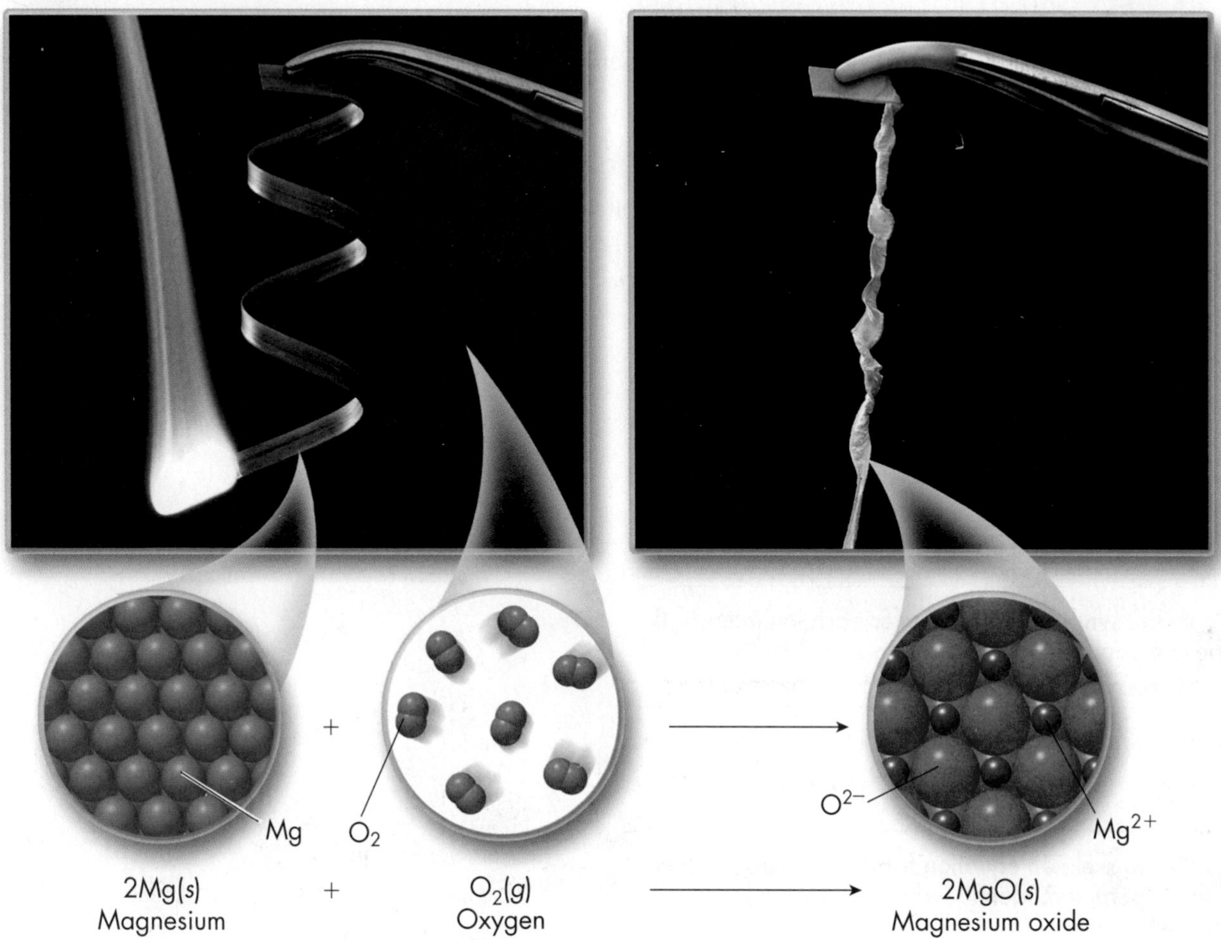

Notice that in this reaction, as in all combination reactions, the product is a single substance (MgO), which is a compound. The reactants in this combination reaction (Mg and O_2) are two elements, which is often the case. But two compounds may also combine to form a single substance.

When a Group A metal and a nonmetal react, the product is a binary ionic compound.

$$2K(s) + Cl_2(g) \longrightarrow 2KCl(s)$$

When two nonmetals react in a combination reaction, more than one product is often possible.

$$S(s) + O_2(g) \longrightarrow SO_2(g) \text{ sulfur dioxide}$$
$$2S(s) + 3O_2(g) \longrightarrow 2SO_3(g) \text{ sulfur trioxide}$$

More than one product may also result from the combination reaction of a transition metal and a nonmetal.

$$Fe(s) + S(s) \longrightarrow FeS(s) \text{ iron(II) sulfide}$$
$$2Fe(s) + 3S(s) \longrightarrow Fe_2S_3(s) \text{ iron(III) sulfide}$$

Sample Problem 11.4

Writing Equations for Combination Reactions

Write a balanced equation for the combination of copper and sulfur.

$$Cu(s) + S(s) \longrightarrow \text{(two reactions possible)}$$

1 Analyze Identify the relevant concepts. Two combination reactions are possible because copper is a transition metal and has more than one common ionic charge (Cu^{+} and Cu^{2+}). The two chemical equations must be balanced separately.

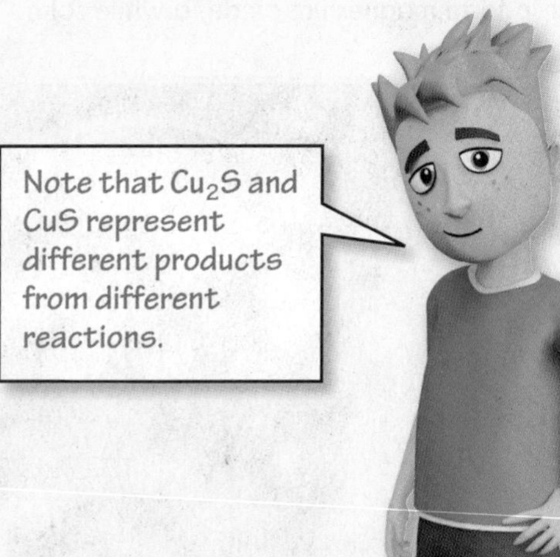

Note that Cu_2S and CuS represent different products from different reactions.

2 Solve Apply the concepts to this problem.

Identify the two binary ionic compounds that can be formed by the combination of copper and sulfur.

Copper(I) sulfide
Copper(II) sulfide

Write the symbol and charge for each ion in each of the compounds. Write the cation first, then the anion.

Cu^{+} and S^{2-}
Cu^{2+} and S^{2-}

Write the formula for each product.

Cu_2S
CuS

Write the skeleton equation for the reaction involving the copper(I) ion. Identify which atoms are balanced and which are not.

For copper(I) sulfide:

$$Cu(s) + S(s) \longrightarrow Cu_2S(s)$$

Cu is not balanced.
S is balanced.

Balance the copper. Put a coefficient of 2 in front of Cu(*s*). Recount the atoms to check whether the equation is balanced.

$$2Cu(s) + S(s) \longrightarrow Cu_2S(s)$$

Cu is balanced.
S is balanced.

Write the skeleton equation for the reaction involving the copper(II) ion. Identify which atoms are balanced and which are not.

For copper(II) sulfide:

$$Cu(s) + S(s) \longrightarrow CuS(s)$$

Cu is balanced.
S is balanced.

Note: For copper(II) sulfide, the skeleton equation is already balanced.

BUILD Math Skills

Arithmetic Operations To balance a chemical equation, you need to know the total number of each kind of atom on each side of the equation. When counting atoms, you must consider the coefficients in front of the chemical formulas and any subscripts that appear in the formulas.

Suppose you encounter the term $3Ba(NO_3)_2$ while balancing an equation. How many oxygen atoms are there? Begin with the subscript 3 in the polyatomic ion NO_3^-. The nitrate ion contains 3 oxygen atoms. Each formula unit of $Ba(NO_3)_2$ contains two nitrate ions. So multiply 3 oxygen atoms by 2, the subscript outside the parentheses. You now have 6 oxygen atoms. Multiply this by 3, the coefficient in front of the formula, to get 18 oxygen atoms. The steps below summarize the calculation.

NO_3^- contains 3 oxygen atoms.
$Ba(NO_3)_2$ contains $3 \times 2 = 6$ oxygen atoms.
$3Ba(NO_3)_2$ contains $6 \times 3 = 18$ oxygen atoms.

Go to your Chemistry Skills and Math Workbook for more practice problems.

Practice Problems

16. Write the balanced chemical equation for the reaction of solid lithium and oxygen gas to form solid lithium oxide.

$$Li(s) + O_2(g) \longrightarrow Li_2O(s)$$

❶ **Analyze Identify the relevant concepts.**

❷ **Solve Apply the concepts to this problem.**

17. Write a balanced equation for the following combination reaction.

$$\text{Hydrogen} + \text{bromine} \longrightarrow$$

18. Write the balanced chemical equation for the reaction of solid tetraphosphorus decoxide and water to produce phosphoric acid.

$$P_4O_{10}(s) + H_2O(l) \longrightarrow H_3PO_4(aq)$$

19. Challenge Write and balance the equation for the formation of magnesium nitride (Mg_3N_2) from its elements.

Hint: The representative particle of nitrogen gas is the diatomic molecule N_2.

decomposition reaction a chemical change in which a single compound breaks down into two or more products

ROOT WORDS

The root word of *decomposition* is *decompose.* To decompose means to break down. During a decomposition reaction, a substance breaks down into simpler products.

Decomposition Reactions Some chemical reactions are the opposite of combination reactions. These kinds of reactions are called decomposition reactions. When mercury(II) oxide is heated, it decomposes, or breaks down, into two simpler substances, as shown in the figure below.

$$2HgO(s) \longrightarrow 2Hg(l) + O_2(g)$$

A **decomposition reaction** is a chemical change in which a single compound breaks down into two or more simpler products. Decomposition reactions involve only one reactant and two or more products. The products can be any combination of elements and compounds. It is usually difficult to predict the products of decomposition reactions. However, when a simple binary compound, such as HgO, breaks down, the products are most likely two elements. Most decomposition reactions require energy in the form of heat, light, or electricity.

Did you know that a decomposition reaction happens when an automobile air bag inflates? A device that can trigger the reaction is placed into the air bag along with sodium azide (NaN_3) pellets. When the device is triggered by a collision, the sodium azide pellets decompose and release nitrogen gas, which inflates the air bag quickly.

$$2NaN_3(s) \longrightarrow 2Na(s) + 3N_2(g)$$

Decomposition Reaction
When orange-colored mercury(II) oxide is heated, it decomposes into its constituent elements: liquid mercury and gaseous oxygen.
Go to your Chemistry Skills and Math Workbook to practice balancing equations for decomposition reactions.

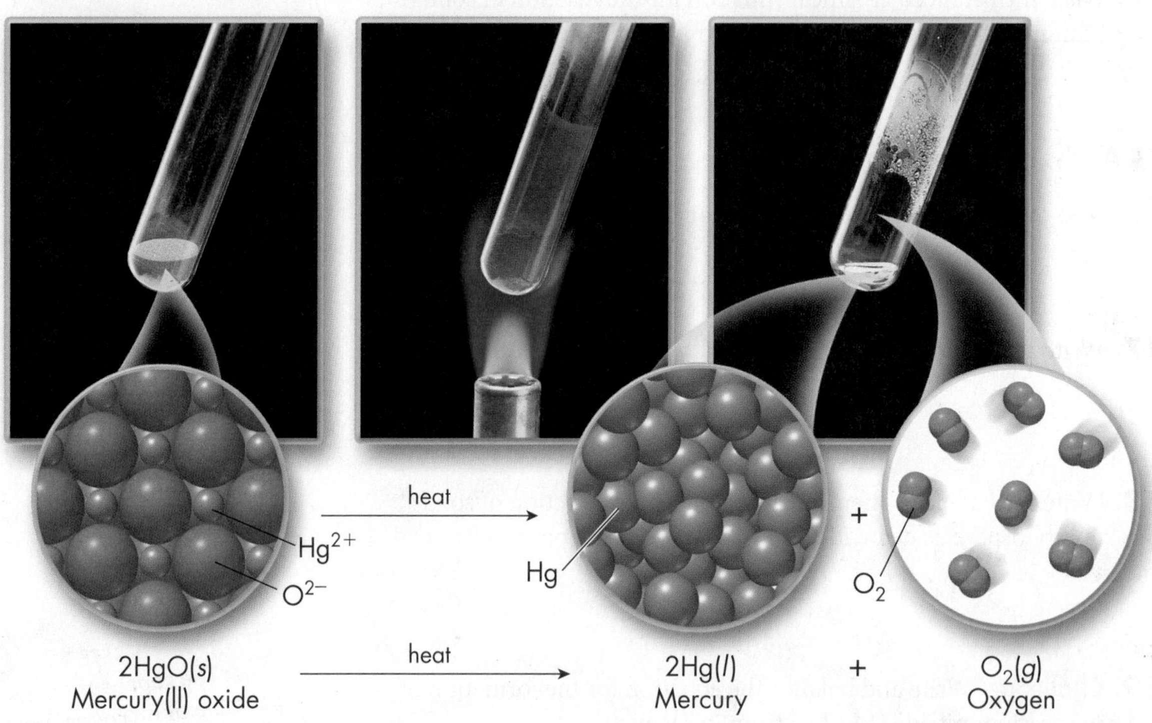

Solid mercury(II) oxide contains mercury(II) cations and oxide anions held together in a repeating pattern.

Liquid mercury contains mercury atoms that move freely around each other.

Oxygen gas is made up of diatomic molecules.

Sample Problem 11.5

Writing Equations for Decomposition Reactions

Write a balanced equation for the decomposition of water.

$$H_2O(l) \xrightarrow{\text{electricity}}$$

1 Analyze **Identify the relevant concepts.** The constituent elements of water are hydrogen and oxygen. Both products are found as diatomic molecules.

2 Solve **Apply the concepts to this problem.**

Write the formula of each product.

$H_2(g)$

$O_2(g)$

Write the skeleton equation for the reaction. Identify which atoms are balanced, and which are not.

$H_2O(l) \xrightarrow{\text{electricity}} H_2(g) + O_2(g)$

H is balanced.
O is not balanced.

Balance the oxygen. Put a coefficient of 2 in front of $H_2O(l)$. Recount the atoms.

$2H_2O(l) \xrightarrow{\text{electricity}} H_2(g) + O_2(g)$

H is not balanced.
O is balanced.

Rebalance the hydrogen. Put a coefficient of 2 in front of $H_2(g)$. Recount the atoms to check whether the equation is balanced.

$2H_2O(l) \xrightarrow{\text{electricity}} 2H_2(g) + O_2(g)$

H is balanced.
O is balanced.

Practice Problems

20. Complete and balance the following decomposition reaction.

$$HI \longrightarrow$$

1 Analyze **Identify the relevant concepts.**

2 Solve **Apply the concepts to this problem.**

21. Write the formula for the binary compound that decomposes to form the products H_2 and Br_2.

22. Challenge Balance the decomposition equation:

$$Al(OH)_3(s) \longrightarrow Al_2O_3(s) + H_2O(l)$$

Single-Replacement Reaction The alkali metal potassium replaces hydrogen in water and forms a solution of potassium hydroxide in a single-replacement reaction.

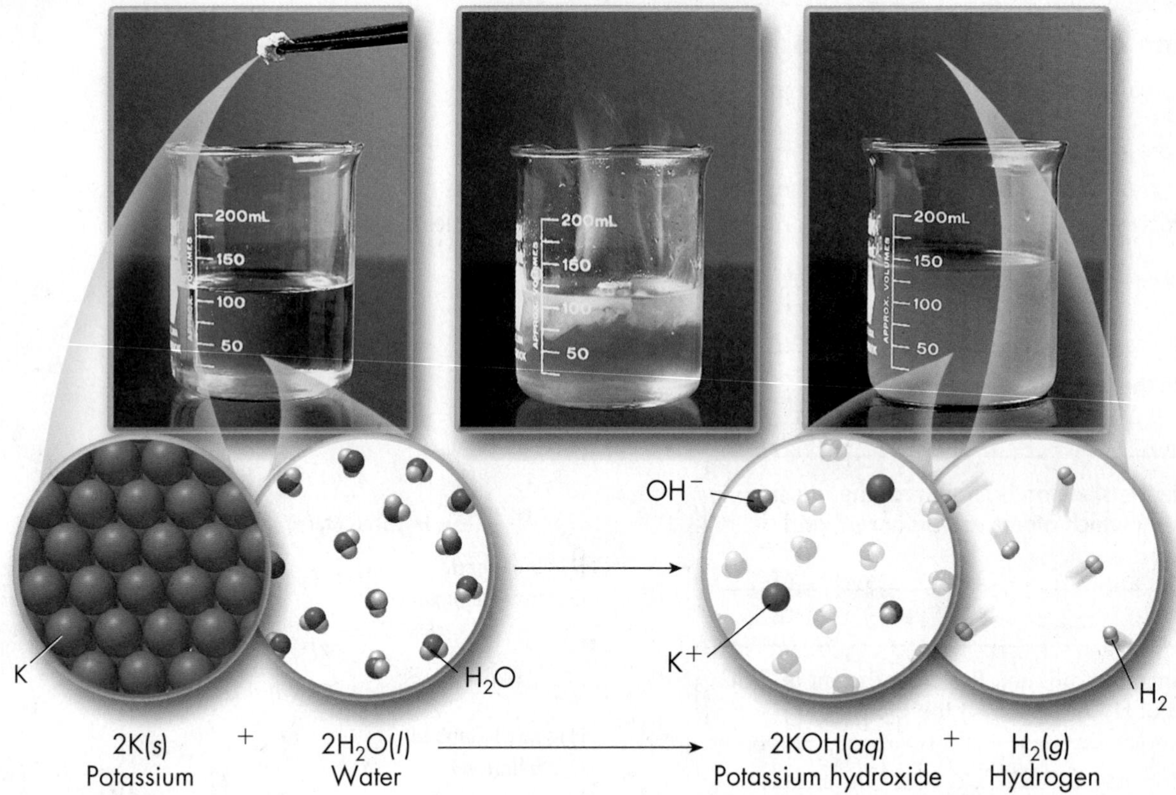

single-replacement reaction a chemical change in which one element replaces a second element in a compound

activity series a list of elements in order of decreasing activity

ACADEMIC WORDS

A *series* is a group of related things that are arranged in a sequence. Numbers can be arranged in a series. So can comic books or podcasts.

Single-Replacement Reactions Dropping a small piece of potassium into a beaker of water creates a vigorous reaction. The reaction produces hydrogen gas and a large quantity of heat. The released hydrogen gas can ignite explosively, as shown above. The reaction is described as follows.

$$2K(s) + 2H_2O(l) \longrightarrow 2KOH(aq) + H_2(g)$$

Note in the equation how potassium and hydrogen change places. The reacting element K replaces H in the reactant compound H_2O. The products are the diatomic molecule H_2 and the compound KOH.

A **single-replacement reaction** is a chemical change in which one element replaces a second element in a compound. In a single-replacement reaction, both the reactants and the products consist of an element and a compound.

The **activity series** of metals, shown on the facing page, lists metals in order of decreasing reactivity. Whether one metal will displace another metal from a compound depends upon the relative reactivities of the two metals. A reactive metal will replace any metal that is less reactive.

A halogen can also replace another halogen from a compound. The activity of the halogens decreases as you go down Group 7A of the periodic table—fluorine, chlorine, bromine, and iodine. Bromine is more active than iodine, so this reaction occurs:

$$Br_2(aq) + 2NaI(aq) \longrightarrow 2NaBr(aq) + I_2(aq)$$

But bromine is less active than chlorine, so this reaction does not occur:

$$Br_2(aq) + NaCl(aq) \longrightarrow \text{No reaction}$$

Sample Problem 11.6

H_2O H_2 O_2

Writing Equations for Single-Replacement Reactions

Write a balanced equation for the following single-replacement reaction.

$$Cl_2(aq) + NaBr(aq) \longrightarrow$$

Remember: In a single-replacement reaction, one element replaces a second element in a compound. Both the reactants and products consist of an element and a compound.

1 Analyze Identify the relevant concepts. Chlorine is more reactive than bromine and replaces bromine in its compounds.

2 Solve Apply the concepts to this problem.

Write the skeleton equation for the reaction. Identify which atoms or ions are balanced and which are not.

$Cl_2(aq) + NaBr(aq) \longrightarrow NaCl(aq) + Br_2(aq)$

Cl is not balanced.
Na^+ is balanced.
Br is not balanced.

Balance the chlorine. Put a coefficient of 2 in front of NaCl(*aq*). Recount the atoms.

$Cl_2(aq) + NaBr(aq) \longrightarrow 2NaCl(aq) + Br_2(aq)$

Cl is balanced.
Na^+ is not balanced.
Br is not balanced.

Balance the sodium. Put a coefficient of 2 in front of NaBr(*aq*). Recount the atoms and ions to check that the equation is balanced.

$Cl_2(aq) + 2NaBr(aq) \longrightarrow 2NaCl(aq) + Br_2(aq)$

Cl is balanced.
Na^+ is balanced.
Br is balanced.

Practice Problems

Complete the equations for these single-replacement reactions in aqueous solution. Balance each equation. Write "no reaction" if a reaction does not occur.

23. $Mg(s) + Pb(NO_3)_2(aq) \longrightarrow$

1 Analyze Identify the relevant concepts.

2 Solve Apply the concepts to this problem.

24. $Zn(s) + H_2SO_4(aq) \longrightarrow$

25. Challenge

a. $Cl_2(aq) + NaI(aq) \longrightarrow$
b. $Ca(s) + H_2O(l) \longrightarrow$

Activity Series of Metals

Name	Symbol	
Lithium	Li	Will replace H from acids and water
Potassium	K	
Calcium	Ca	
Sodium	Na	
Magnesium	Mg	Will replace H from acids only
Aluminum	Al	
Zinc	Zn	
Iron	Fe	
Lead	Pb	
(Hydrogen)	(H)	
Copper	Cu	
Mercury	Hg	
Silver	Ag	

Decreasing activity ↓

Double-Replacement Reaction Aqueous solutions of potassium iodide and lead(II) nitrate react to form lead(II) iodide, the yellow-orange precipitate.

Go to your Chemistry Skills and Math Workbook to practice writing balanced equations for single- and double-replacement reactions.

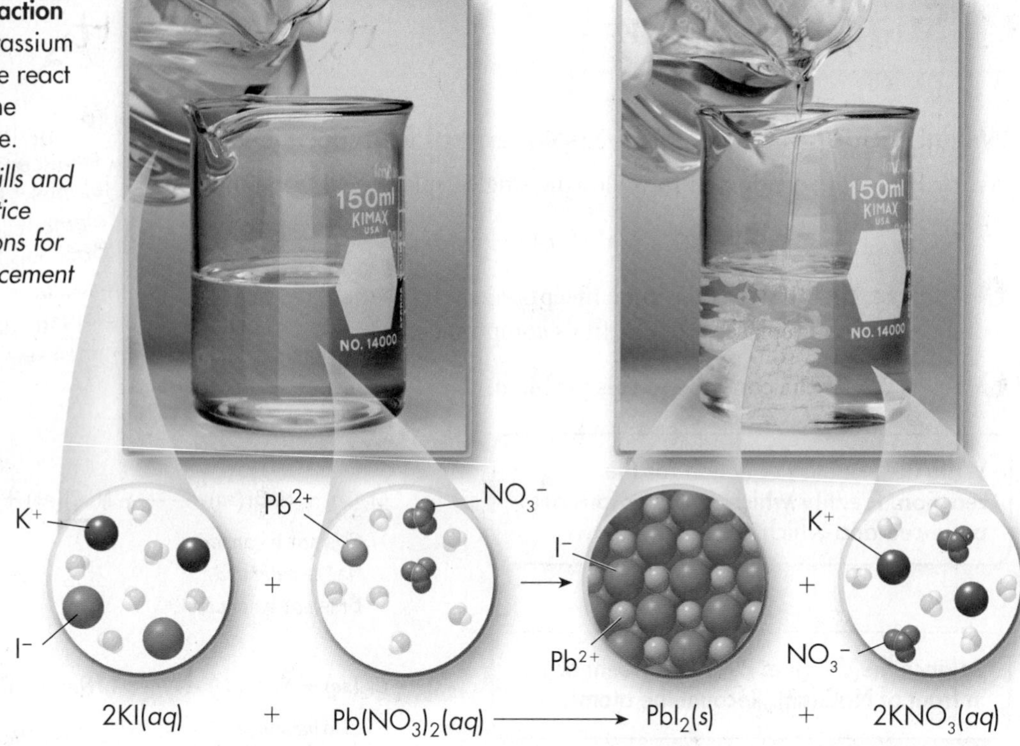

Double-Replacement Reactions Sometimes, when two solutions of ionic compounds are mixed, nothing happens. At other times, the ions in the two solutions react. The figure above shows the reaction that happens when aqueous solutions of potassium iodide and lead(II) nitrate are mixed. The reaction results in the formation of a yellow-orange precipitate of lead(II) iodide. Potassium nitrate, the other product of the reaction, remains in solution.

double-replacement reaction a chemical change in which two positive ions change places between two compounds

This reaction is a **double-replacement reaction,** which is a chemical change involving an exchange of positive ions between two compounds. The reactions generally take place in aqueous solution. They often produce a precipitate, a gas, or a molecular compound such as water. For a double-replacement reaction to happen, one of the following is usually true:

1. One of the products is only slightly soluble and precipitates from solution. For example, the reaction of aqueous solutions of sodium sulfide and cadmium nitrate produces a yellow precipitate of cadmium sulfide.

$$Na_2S(aq) + Cd(NO_3)_2(aq) \longrightarrow CdS(s) + 2NaNO_3(aq)$$

2. One of the products is a gas. Poisonous hydrogen cyanide gas is produced when aqueous sodium cyanide is mixed with sulfuric acid.

$$2NaCN(aq) + H_2SO_4(aq) \longrightarrow 2HCN(g) + Na_2SO_4(aq)$$

3. One product is a molecular compound such as water. Combining solutions of calcium hydroxide and hydrochloric acid produces water.

$$Ca(OH)_2(aq) + 2HCl(aq) \longrightarrow CaCl_2(aq) + 2H_2O(l)$$

Writing Equations for Double-Replacement Reactions

A precipitate of barium carbonate is formed when an aqueous solution of barium chloride reacts with aqueous potassium carbonate. Write a balanced chemical equation for the double-replacement reaction.

$$K_2CO_3(aq) + BaCl_2(aq) \longrightarrow$$

1 Analyze Identify the relevant concepts. The driving force behind the reaction is the formation of a precipitate. Write the correct formulas of the products using ionic charges. Then, balance the equation.

2 Solve Apply the concepts to this problem.

Write the skeleton equation for the reaction.

$K_2CO_3(aq) + BaCl_2(aq) \longrightarrow KCl(aq) + BaCO_3(s)$

Identify which atoms are balanced and which are not.

K^+ is not balanced.
CO_3^{2-} is balanced.
Ba^{2+} is balanced.
Cl^- is not balanced.

Balance the chlorine. Put a coefficient of 2 in front of KCl.

$K_2CO_3(aq) + BaCl_2(aq) \longrightarrow 2KCl(aq) + BaCO_3(s)$

Recount the atoms to check whether the equation is balanced.

K^+ is balanced.
CO_3^{2-} is balanced.
Ba^{2+} is balanced.
Cl^- is balanced.

Practice Problems

26. Write a balanced equation for the following double-replacement reaction.

$NaOH(aq) + Fe(NO_3)_3(aq) \longrightarrow$ (Iron(III) hydroxide is a precipitate.)

1 Analyze Identify the relevant concepts.

2 Solve Apply the concepts to this problem.

27. Write a balanced equation for the following reaction.

$KOH(aq) + H_3PO_4(aq) \longrightarrow$ (Water is formed.)

28. Challenge Balance the following chemical equation.

$Ba(NO_3)_2(aq) + H_3PO_4(aq) \longrightarrow$ (Barium phosphate is a precipitate.)

Hint: First, identify the products of the double-replacement reaction. Then, balance the equation.

combustion reaction a chemical change in which an element or compound reacts with oxygen, resulting in the release of light and heat energy

RELATED WORDS

The verb *combust* means "to catch fire." A *combustion reaction* is one in which an element or compound catches fire.

Combustion Reactions The flames of a campfire, candle, or gas grill are evidence that a combustion reaction is taking place. A **combustion reaction** is a chemical change in which an element or a compound reacts with oxygen, often producing energy in the form of heat and light.

Oxygen is always one of the reactants in a combustion reaction. Often the other reactant is a hydrocarbon, which is a compound composed of hydrogen and carbon. The complete combustion of a hydrocarbon produces carbon dioxide and water. But if the supply of oxygen is limited during a reaction, the combustion will not be complete. Elemental carbon (soot) and toxic carbon monoxide gas may be additional products.

The complete combustion of a hydrocarbon releases a large amount of energy as heat. That's why hydrocarbons such as methane (CH_4), propane (C_3H_8), and butane (C_4H_{10}) are important fuels. The combustion of methane is shown in the figure below. Gasoline is a mix of hydrocarbons that can be approximated by the formula C_8H_{18}. The complete combustion of gasoline in a car engine is shown by this equation:

$$2C_8H_{18}(l) + 25O_2(g) \longrightarrow 16CO_2(g) + 18H_2O(g)$$

Key Question What are the five general types of reactions? **The five general types of reactions include combination, decomposition, single-replacement, double-replacement, and combustion.**

Combustion Reaction
Methane gas reacts with oxygen from the surrounding air in a combustion reaction to produce carbon dioxide and water.

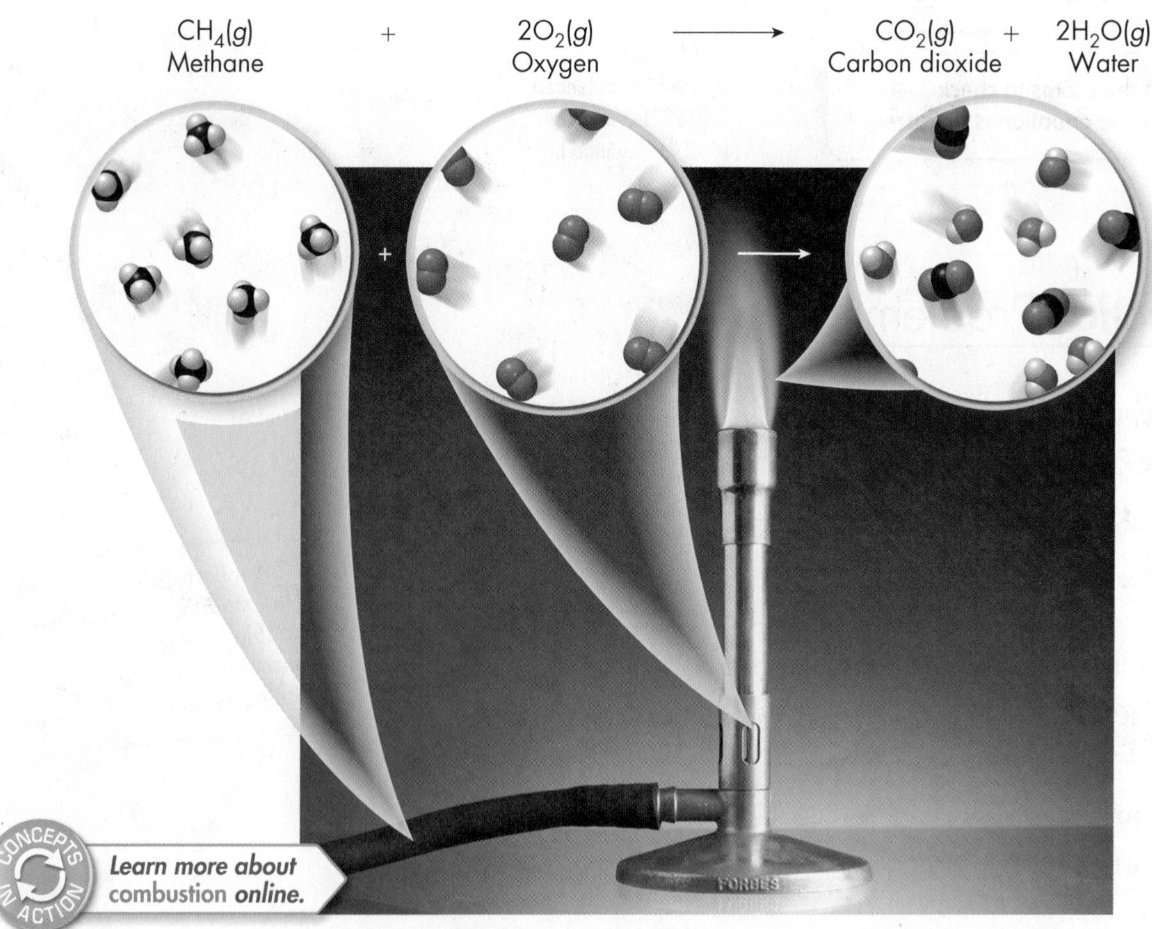

CONCEPTS IN ACTION *Learn more about combustion **online**.*

Sample Problem 11.8

Writing Equations for Combustion Reactions

An alcohol lamp often uses ethanol as its fuel. Write a balanced equation for the complete combustion of ethanol.

$$C_2H_6O(l)$$

1 Analyze **Identify the relevant concepts.** Oxygen is the other reactant in a combustion reaction. The products are CO_2 and H_2O.

2 Solve **Apply the concepts to this problem.**

Write the skeleton equation for the reaction. Identify which atoms are balanced and which are not.

$C_2H_6O(l) + O_2(g) \longrightarrow CO_2(g) + H_2O(g)$

C is not balanced.
H is not balanced.
O is balanced.

Balance the elements one at a time by using coefficients.

$C_2H_6O(l) + O_2(g) \longrightarrow 2CO_2(g) + H_2O(g)$

$C_2H_6O(l) + O_2(g) \longrightarrow 2CO_2(g) + 3H_2O(g)$

$C_2H_6O(l) + 3O_2(g) \longrightarrow 2CO_2(g) + 3H_2O(g)$

Recount the atoms to check whether the equation is balanced.

C is balanced.
H is balanced.
O is balanced.

Practice Problems

29. Write a balanced equation for the complete combustion of formaldehyde. The chemical formula is $CH_2O(g)$.

1 Analyze **Identify the relevant concepts.**

2 Solve **Apply the concepts to this problem.**

30. Write a balanced equation for the complete combustion of heptane ($C_7H_{16}(l)$).

31. Challenge Write a balanced equation for the complete combustion of acetone ($C_3H_6O(l)$).

Remember: A combustion reaction always involves oxygen as a reactant.

① Combination Reaction

General Equation: $R + S \longrightarrow RS$

Reactants: Generally two elements, or two compounds (in which at least one compound is a molecular compound)

Probable Products: A single compound

Example: Burning magnesium in air

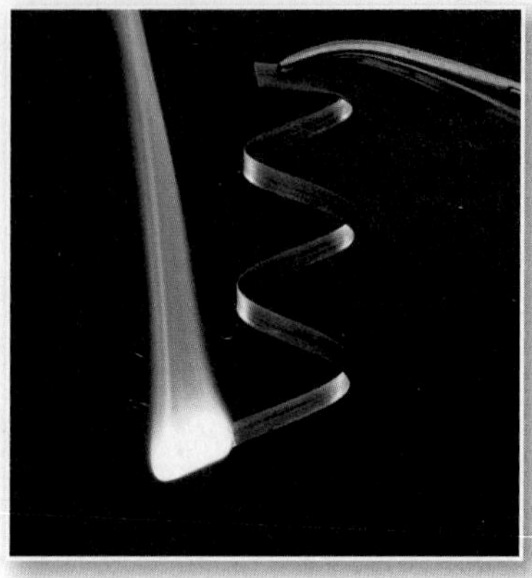

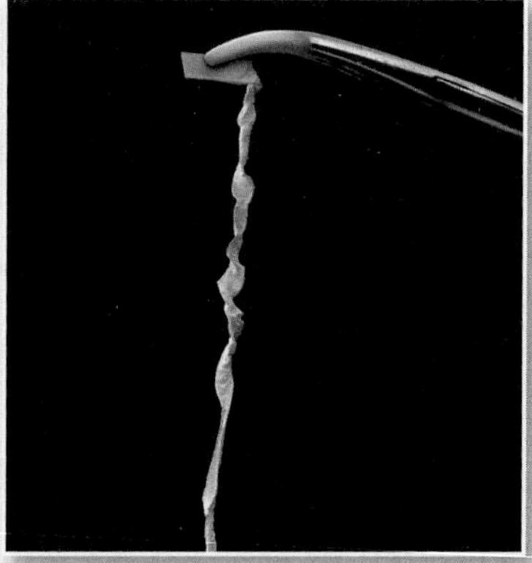

$2Mg(s) + O_2(g) \longrightarrow 2MgO(s)$

② Decomposition Reaction

General Equation: $RS \longrightarrow R + S$

Reactants: Generally a single binary compound or a compound with a polyatomic ion

Probable Products: Two elements (for a binary compound), or two or more elements and/or compounds (for a compound with a polyatomic ion)

Example: Heating mercury(II) oxide

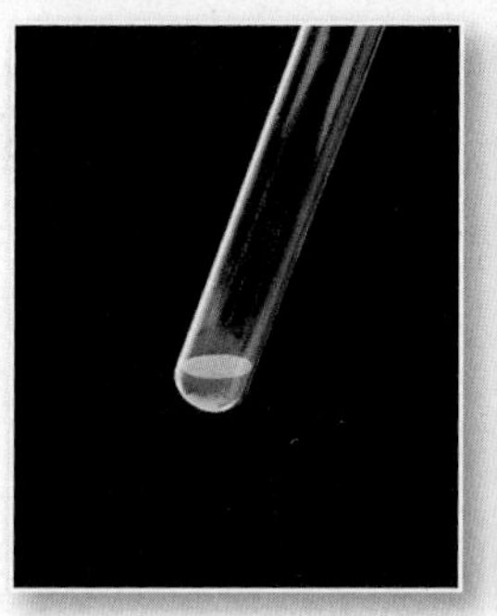

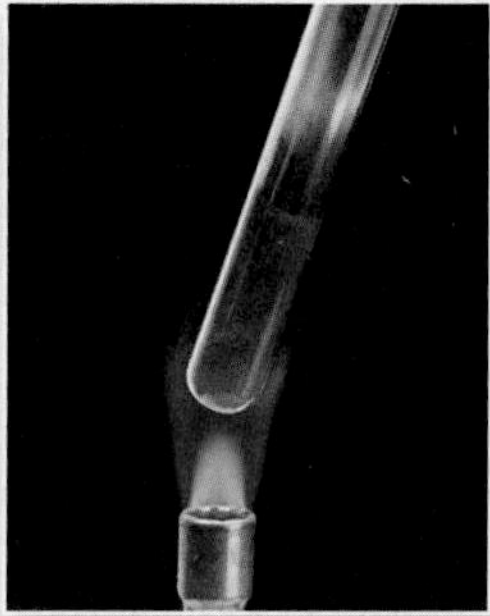

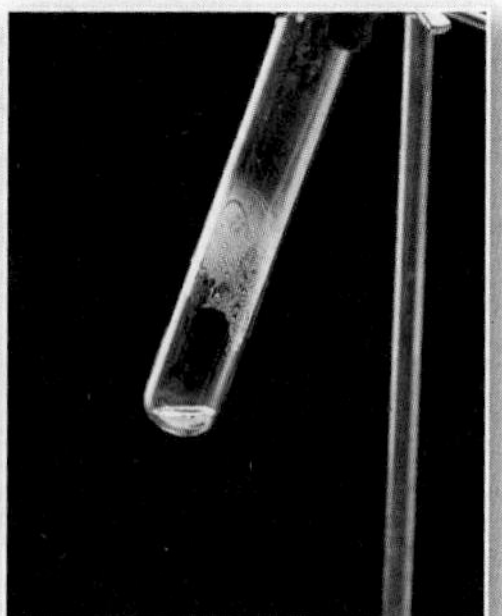

$2HgO(s) \longrightarrow 2Hg(l) + O_2(g)$

③ Single-Replacement Reaction

General Equation: $T + RS \longrightarrow TS + R$

Reactants: An element and a compound

In a single-replacement reaction, an element replaces another element from a compound in aqueous solution. For a single-replacement reaction to occur, the element that is replaced must be less active than the element that is doing the replacing.

Probable Products: A different element and a new compound

Example: Potassium in water

$2K(s) + 2H_2O(l) \longrightarrow 2KOH(aq) + H_2(g)$

4 Double-Replacement Reaction

General Equation: $R^+S^- + T^+U^- \longrightarrow R^+U^- + T^+S^-$

Reactants: Two ionic compounds
In a double-replacement reaction, two ionic compounds react by exchanging cations to form two different compounds.

Probable Products: Two new compounds
Double-replacement reactions are driven by the formation of a precipitate, a gaseous product, or water.

Example: Reaction of aqueous solutions of potassium iodide and lead(II) nitrate

$2KI(aq) + Pb(NO_3)_2(aq) \longrightarrow PbI_2(s) + 2KNO_3(aq)$

5 Combustion Reaction

General Equation: $C_xH_y + (x + y/4)O_2 \longrightarrow xCO_2 + (y/2)H_2O$

Reactants: Oxygen and a compound of C, H, (O)
When oxygen reacts with an element or compound, combustion may occur.

Probable Products: CO_2 and H_2O
With incomplete combustion, C and CO may also be products.

Example: The combustion of methane gas in air

$CH_4(g) + 2O_2(g) \longrightarrow CO_2(g) + 2H_2O(g)$

11.2 LessonCheck

Key Concept Check

32. **Review** What are five types of reactions?

Think Critically

33. **Identify** Which of the five general types of reaction would most likely occur, given each set of reactants? What are the probable products?
- **a.** an aqueous solution of two ionic compounds
- **b.** a single compound

34. **Apply Concepts** Balance each equation below.
- **a.** $Al(s) + Cl_2(g) \longrightarrow$
- **b.** $Ag(s) + HCl(aq) \longrightarrow$
- **c.** $C_2H_2(g) + O_2(g) \longrightarrow$

CHEMISTRY & YOU

35. When a candle burns, hydrocarbons in the wax react with oxygen in the air. One of the hydrocarbons found in candle wax has the formula $C_{25}H_{52}$. What possible products are formed as a candle burns? (Hint: See page 336.)

BIGIDEA REACTIONS

36. After wood burns, the ash weighs much less than the original wood. Explain why the law of conservation of mass is not violated in this situation.

11.3 Reactions in Aqueous Solution

CHEMISTRY & YOU

Q: How did soda straws get into limestone caves? These "soda straws" are really stalactites in a limestone cave. "Soda straw" stalactites grow on cave ceilings as thin-walled hollow tubes that result from chemical reactions involving water. In this lesson, you will learn about the formation of precipitates and the reactions that produce them.

Key Questions

What does a net ionic equation show?

How can you predict the formation of a precipitate in a double-replacement reaction?

BUILD Understanding

Compare/Contrast Table
Choose one of the reactions discussed in the lesson. Then create a compare/contrast table that shows the differences between the conventional chemical equation and the net ionic equation for the reaction.

Net Ionic Equations

Your world is based on water. More than 70 percent of Earth's surface is covered by water. Also, about 66 percent of the adult human body is water. It is not surprising, then, that many important chemical reactions take place in water. Chemical reactions that take place in water are said to take place in aqueous solution.

The figure below shows aqueous solutions of silver nitrate and sodium chloride reacting to form solid silver chloride and aqueous sodium nitrate. This is a double-replacement reaction.

$$AgNO_3(aq) + NaCl(aq) \longrightarrow AgCl(s) + NaNO_3(aq)$$

The equation above was written according to the rules for balancing equations described in Lesson 11.1. However, the equation does not give you the full picture of what's happening in aqueous solution. $AgNO_3$, NaCl, and $NaNO_3$ are ionic compounds that separate into cations and anions when they dissolve in water. Recall that cations are positively-charged ions, and anions are negatively-charged ions.

Precipitate in a Double-Replacement Reaction
A precipitate of silver chloride forms when aqueous solutions of silver nitrate and sodium chloride are mixed.

Write Out the Dissociated Ions When sodium chloride dissolves in water, it separates into sodium ions ($Na^+(aq)$) and chloride ions ($Cl^-(aq)$). Likewise, when silver nitrate dissolves in water, it separates into silver ions ($Ag^+(aq)$) and nitrate ions ($NO_3^-(aq)$). Both compounds are said to have *dissociated* into ions.

You can use these ions to write a **complete ionic equation,** an equation that shows all dissolved ionic compounds as dissociated free ions.

$$Ag^+(aq) + NO_3^-(aq) + Na^+(aq) + Cl^-(aq) \longrightarrow AgCl(s) + Na^+(aq) + NO_3^-(aq)$$

Remove the Spectator Ions Notice that the nitrate ions and the sodium ions appear unchanged on both sides of the equation. The equation can be simplified by removing these ions because they don't participate in the reaction.

$$Ag^+(aq) + \cancel{NO_3^-(aq)} + \cancel{Na^+(aq)} + Cl^-(aq) \longrightarrow AgCl(s) + \cancel{Na^+(aq)} + \cancel{NO_3^-(aq)}$$

An ion that appears on both sides of an equation and is not directly involved in the reaction is called a **spectator ion.**

When you rewrite an equation leaving out the spectator ions, you have the net ionic equation. The **net ionic equation** is an equation that shows only those particles that are directly involved in the chemical change.

$$Ag^+(aq) + Cl^-(aq) \longrightarrow AgCl(s)$$

Balance the Ionic Charges In writing balanced net ionic equations, you must make sure that the ionic charge is balanced. In the previous reaction, the net ionic charge on each side of the equation is zero. So, the equation is balanced. But consider the skeleton equation for the reaction of lead with silver nitrate.

$$Pb(s) + AgNO_3(aq) \longrightarrow Ag(s) + Pb(NO_3)_2(aq)$$

The nitrate ion is the spectator ion. The net ionic equation is as follows:

$$Pb(s) + Ag^+(aq) \longrightarrow Ag(s) + Pb^{2+}(aq) \text{ (unbalanced)}$$

Why is this equation unbalanced? There is one unit of positive charge on the reactant side of the equation and two units of positive charge on the product side. Placing the coefficient 2 in front of $Ag^+(aq)$ balances the charge. A coefficient of 2 in front of $Ag(s)$ rebalances the atoms.

$$Pb(s) + 2Ag^+(aq) \longrightarrow 2Ag(s) + Pb^{2+}(aq) \text{ (balanced)}$$

Key Question What does a net ionic equation show? **A net ionic equation shows only those particles involved in the reaction and is balanced in both mass and charge.**

complete ionic equation a chemical equation that shows dissolved ionic compounds as dissociated free ions

spectator ion an ion that appears on both sides of an equation and is not directly involved in the reaction

net ionic equation a chemical equation that shows only those particles that are directly involved in the chemical change

RELATED WORD FORMS

You may think of sports when you hear the word *spectator.* A spectator is someone who watches an event but does not participate in it.

CHEMISTRY TUTORIAL

Sample Problem 11.9

Writing and Balancing Net Ionic Equations

Aqueous solutions of iron(III) chloride and potassium hydroxide are mixed. A precipitate of iron(III) hydroxide forms. Write a balanced net ionic equation for the reaction.

1 Analyze **Identify the relevant concepts.** Write the complete ionic equation. Eliminate aqueous ions that appear in both the reactants and products. Then balance the equation with respect to both mass and charge.

2 Solve **Apply the concepts to this problem.**

Write the skeleton equation for the reaction.

$$FeCl_3(aq) + KOH(aq) \longrightarrow Fe(OH)_3(s) + KCl(aq)$$

Write the complete ionic equation for the reaction, showing any soluble ionic compounds as individual ions. Balance the atoms as needed.

$$Fe^{3+}(aq) + 3Cl^-(aq) + 3K^+(aq) + 3OH^-(aq) \longrightarrow Fe(OH)_3(s) + 3K^+(aq) + 3Cl^-(aq)$$

Eliminate aqueous ions that appear as both reactants and products. The spectator ions are K^+ and Cl^-.

$$Fe^{3+}(aq) + \cancel{3Cl^-}(aq) + \cancel{3K^+}(aq) + 3OH^-(aq) \longrightarrow Fe(OH)_3(s) + \cancel{3K^+}(aq) + \cancel{3Cl^-}(aq)$$

Count the atoms and charges to check whether the equation is balanced.

$$Fe^{3+}(aq) + 3OH^-(aq) \longrightarrow Fe(OH)_3(s)$$

Fe^{3+} is balanced.
OH^- is balanced.
Charges are balanced.

Practice Problems

37. Write a balanced net ionic equation for this reaction.

$$H_3PO_4(aq) + NaOH(aq) \longrightarrow Na_3PO_4(aq) + H_2O(l)$$

1 Analyze **Identify the relevant concepts.**

2 Solve **Apply the concepts to this problem.**

38. Challenge Write the complete ionic equation and net ionic equation for the reaction of aqueous calcium hydroxide with phosphoric acid. The products are calcium phosphate and water.

Note: Of the five types of reactions identified in this chapter, both single- and double-replacement reactions can be written as net ionic equations.

Predicting the Formation of a Precipitate

You have seen that mixing solutions of two ionic compounds can sometimes result in the formation of an insoluble salt called a precipitate. Some combinations of solutions produce precipitates. Others do not. Whether or not a precipitate forms depends upon the solubility of the new compounds that form. By using the general rules for solubility of ionic compounds, you can predict the formation of a precipitate. These general rules are shown in the table below.

Will a precipitate form when aqueous solutions of $Na_2CO_3(aq)$ and $Ba(NO_3)_2(aq)$ are mixed? You can apply the solubility rules to find out.

$$2Na^+(aq) + CO_3^{2-}(aq) + Ba^{2+}(aq) + 2NO_3^-(aq) \longrightarrow ?$$

Examine the Reactant Ions When these four ions are mixed, the cations could change partners. If they do, the two new compounds that would form are $NaNO_3$ and $BaCO_3$. These are the only new combinations of cation and anion possible.

Apply the Solubility Rules Recall that sodium is an alkali metal. Refer to Rules 1 and 2. They tell you that sodium nitrate will not form a precipitate because alkali metal salts and nitrate salts are soluble. So, Na^+ and NO_3^- are spectator ions. Rule 5 of the table tells you that carbonates in general are insoluble. So, barium carbonate will precipitate. The net ionic equation for this reaction is as follows:

$$Ba^{2+}(aq) + CO_3^{2-}(aq) \longrightarrow BaCO_3(s)$$

The photo to the right shows the reaction of aqueous solutions of sodium sulfate and barium nitrate. The products are sodium nitrate, which is soluble (Rules 1 and 2), and barium sulfate, which is insoluble (Rule 3).

Key Question How can you predict the formation of a precipitate in a double-replacement reaction? **By using the general rules for solubility of ionic compounds, you can predict the formation of a precipitate.**

Formation of a Precipitate
A precipitate forms when aqueous solutions of sodium sulfate and barium nitrate are mixed. The net ionic equation is written as:
$Ba^{2+}(aq) + SO_4^{2-}(aq) \longrightarrow BaSO_4(s)$
Go to your Chemistry Skills and Math Workbook to practice writing net ionic equations.

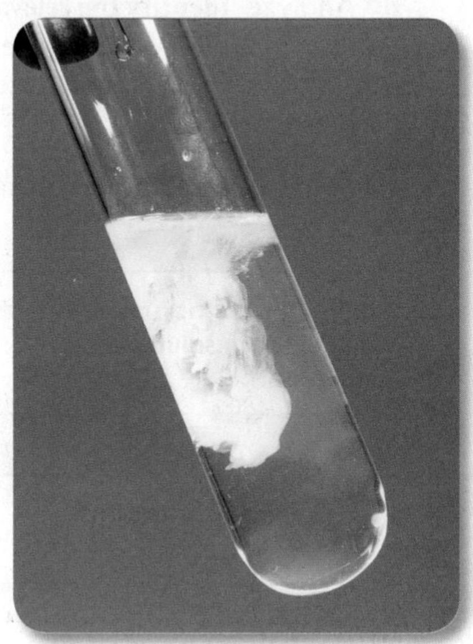

Solubility Rules for Ionic Compounds

Compounds	Solubility	Exceptions
1. Salts of alkali metals and ammonia	Soluble	Some lithium compounds
2. Nitrate salts and chlorate salts	Soluble	Few exceptions
3. Sulfate salts	Soluble	Compounds of Pb, Ag, Hg, Ba, Sr, and Ca
4. Chloride salts	Soluble	Compounds of Ag and some compounds of Hg and Pb
5. Carbonates, phosphates, chromates, sulfides, and hydroxides	Most are insoluble.	Compounds of the alkali metals and of ammonia

CHEMISTRY TUTORIAL

SampleProblem 11.10

Predicting the Formation of a Precipitate

Aqueous potassium carbonate reacts with aqueous strontium nitrate. Identify the precipitate formed and write the net ionic equation for the reaction.

Hint: Use the solubility rules in the table on the previous page to identify the precipitate formed.

❶ Analyze **Identify the relevant concepts.** Write the reactants, showing each as dissociated free ions. Look at possible new pairings of cation and anion that produce an insoluble substance. Eliminate the spectator ions.

❷ Solve **Apply the concepts to this problem.**

Identify the dissociated ions that make up each soluble ionic compound.

$K_2CO_3(aq) = 2K^+(aq) + CO_3^{2-}(aq)$

$Sr(NO_3)_2(aq) = Sr^{2+}(aq) + 2NO_3^-(aq)$

Write out the reactants as individual ions.

$2K^+(aq) + CO_3^{2-}(aq) + Sr^{2+}(aq) + 2NO_3^-(aq) \longrightarrow ?$

Identify the possible products of the reaction. These are new pairings of the reactant ions.

KNO_3 and $SrCO_3$

Use the solubility rules to determine which of the possible products is soluble, and which is insoluble.

Of the two possible combinations, KNO_3 is soluble (Rules 1 and 2), and $SrCO_3$ is insoluble (Rule 5).

Write the complete balanced ionic equation for the reaction.

$$2K^+(aq) + CO_3^{2-}(aq) + Sr^{2+}(aq) + 2NO_3^-(aq) \longrightarrow 2K^+(aq) + 2NO_3^-(aq) + SrCO_3(s)$$

Remove the two spectator ions, K^+ and NO_3^-.

$$\cancel{2K^+}(aq) + CO_3^{2-}(aq) + Sr^{2+}(aq) + \cancel{2NO_3^-}(aq) \longrightarrow \cancel{2K^+}(aq) + \cancel{2NO_3^-}(aq) + SrCO_3(s)$$

Balance the atoms and charges as needed until you have the net ionic equation.

$$CO_3^{2-}(aq) + Sr^{2+}(aq) \longrightarrow SrCO_3(s)$$

CO_3^{2-} is balanced.
Sr^{2+} is balanced.
Charges are balanced.

Practice Problems

39. Identify the precipitate formed when solutions of these compounds are mixed. Write the net ionic equation.

$$NH_4Cl(aq) + Pb(NO_3)_2(aq) \longrightarrow$$

❶ Analyze **Identify the relevant concepts.**

❷ Solve **Apply the concepts to this problem.**

40. Identify the precipitate formed and write the net ionic equation for the following reaction.

$$Na_3PO_4(aq) + FeCl_3(aq) \longrightarrow$$

41. Write the balanced net ionic equation for the following reaction.

$$(NH_4)_2S(aq) + Co(NO_3)_2(aq) \longrightarrow$$

42. **Challenge** Write a complete ionic equation and a net ionic equation for the reaction of aqueous solutions of iron(III) nitrate and sodium hydroxide.

11.3 LessonCheck

Key Concept Check

43. **Review** What is a net ionic equation?

44. **Explain** How can you predict the formation of a precipitate in a double-replacement reaction?

Think Critically

45. **Apply Concepts** Write a balanced net ionic equation for each reaction.

a. $Pb(NO_3)_2(aq) + H_2SO_4(aq) \longrightarrow PbSO_4(s) + HNO_3(aq)$

b. $Pb(C_2H_3O_2)_2(aq) + HCl(aq) \longrightarrow PbCl_2(s) + HC_2H_3O_2(aq)$

46. **Identify** List the precipitate formed when solutions of these ionic compounds are mixed.

a. $H_2SO_4(aq) + BaCl_2(aq) \longrightarrow$

b. $Al_2(SO_4)_3(aq) + NH_4OH(aq) \longrightarrow$

47. **Apply Concepts** Hard water contains calcium and magnesium ions. One way to soften water is to add sodium phosphate. Write complete and net ionic equations for the reaction of these two alkaline earth ions with aqueous sodium phosphate.

CHEMISTRY & YOU

48. How did the "soda straws," which are composed of calcium carbonate, get into the cave? (Hint: See page 343.)

11 Study Guide

BIGIDEA REACTIONS

The law of conservation of mass states that mass is neither created nor destroyed. When describing a reaction, you can write a balanced equation to show how mass is conserved during the reaction. You can predict the products of most chemical reactions by identifying the reaction type. To determine the reaction type, consider the number of reacting elements and compounds.

11.1 Describing Chemical Reactions

To write a skeleton equation, write the formulas for the reactants to the left of the yields sign and the formulas for the products to the right.

To write a balanced chemical equation, first write the skeleton equation. Then use coefficients to balance the equation so that the same number of each atom appears on both sides of the equation.

- chemical equation (318)
- skeleton equation (318)
- catalyst (318)
- coefficient (320)
- balanced equation (320)

11.2 Types of Chemical Reactions

The five general types of reactions are combination, decomposition, single-replacement, double-replacement, and combustion.

- combination reaction (326)
- decomposition reaction (330)
- single-replacement reaction (332)
- activity series (332)
- double-replacement reaction (334)
- combustion reaction (336)

11.3 Reactions in Aqueous Solution

A net ionic equation shows only those particles involved in the reaction and is balanced in mass and charge.

By using the general rules for solubility of ionic compounds, you can predict the formation of a precipitate.

- complete ionic equation (341)
- spectator ion (341)
- net ionic equation (341)

Skills Tune-Up: Balancing Chemical Equations

Problem	❶ Analyze	❷ Solve
Write the balanced equation for the following reaction: $C_2H_4 + O_2 \longrightarrow$	The reactants are a hydrocarbon (C_2H_4) and oxygen (O_2). The reactants suggest a combustion reaction. The products of the complete combustion of a hydrocarbon are CO_2 and H_2O.	First write a skeleton equation. $C_2H_4 + O_2 \longrightarrow CO_2 + H_2O$ (unbalanced) Balance the C atoms and the H atoms first. $C_2H_4 + O_2 \longrightarrow 2CO_2 + 2H_2O$ (unbalanced) Balance the O atoms next. $C_2H_4 + 3O_2 \longrightarrow 2CO_2 + 2H_2O$ (balanced)
Write the balanced equation for the following reaction: $Al + Cu(NO_3)_2 \longrightarrow$	$Cu(NO_3)_2$ is an ionic compound, and Al is an element. This is a single-replacement reaction. Check the table on page 333 to be sure a reaction will take place.	First write a skeleton equation. $Al + Cu(NO_3)_2 \longrightarrow Al(NO_3)_3 + Cu$ (unbalanced) Balance the equation. $2Al + 3Cu(NO_3)_2 \longrightarrow 2Al(NO_3)_3 + 3Cu$ (balanced)
Write the balanced equation for the following reaction: $Na(OH)(aq) + Ba(NO_3)_2(aq) \longrightarrow$	Both reactants are ionic compounds in aqueous solution, so this is a double-replacement reaction. In a double-replacement reaction, two compounds exchange positive ions. They often produce a gas, a precipitate, or another molecular compound such as water.	Write the reactants, showing each as dissociated free ions. $Na^+(aq) + OH^-(aq) + Ba^{2+}(aq) + 2NO_3^-(aq) \longrightarrow$ Look at the possible new pairings of cation and anion that yield an insoluble substance. Of the two possible combinations, $NaNO_3$ is soluble and $Ba(OH)_2$ is insoluble. Balance the equation. $2NaOH(aq) + Ba(NO_3)_2(aq) \longrightarrow 2NaNO_3(aq) + Ba(OH)_2(s)$ (balanced)

Hint: A subscript in a polyatomic ion moves with the ion. So the 3 in NO_3 stays with the ion. But the 2 in $Cu(NO_3)_2$ is there only to balance the charges. It is not part of the ion and doesn't move with it.

Hint: Use the solubility rules in the table on page 343 to determine whether a precipitate forms.

11 Assessment

* Solutions appear in Appendix D.

Lesson by Lesson

11.1 Describing Chemical Reactions

49. Identify the reactants and products in each chemical reaction.

a. Hydrogen gas and sodium hydroxide are formed when sodium is dropped into water.
b. In photosynthesis, carbon dioxide and water react to form oxygen gas and glucose.

50. Write sentences that completely describe each of the chemical reactions shown in these skeleton equations.

a. $NH_3(g) + O_2(g) \xrightarrow{Pt} NO(g) + H_2O(g)$
b. $H_2SO_4(aq) + BaCl_2(aq) \longrightarrow BaSO_4(s) + HCl(aq)$
c. $N_2O_3(g) + H_2O(l) \longrightarrow HNO_2(aq)$

51. The equation for the formation of water from its elements, $H_2(g) + O_2(g) \longrightarrow H_2O(l)$, can be "balanced" by changing the formula of the product to H_2O_2. Explain why this is incorrect.

***52.** Balance the following equations:

a. $PbO_2(s) \longrightarrow PbO(s) + O_2(g)$
b. $Fe(OH)_3(s) \longrightarrow Fe_2O_3(s) + H_2O(g)$
c. $(NH_4)_2CO_3(s) \longrightarrow NH_3(g) + H_2O(g) + CO_2(g)$
d. $CaCl_2(aq) + H_2SO_4(aq) \longrightarrow CaSO_4(s) + HCl(aq)$

11.2 Types of Chemical Reactions

***53.** Write balanced chemical equations for the following combination reactions:

a. $Mg(s) + O_2(g) \longrightarrow$
b. $P(s) + O_2(g) \longrightarrow$ diphosphorus pentoxide
c. $Ca(s) + S(s) \longrightarrow$

54. Write a balanced chemical equation for each decomposition reaction.

a. $Ag_2O(s) \xrightarrow{\Delta}$
b. ammonium nitrate $\xrightarrow{\Delta}$ dinitrogen monoxide + water

55. Use the activity series of metals to write a balanced chemical equation for each single-replacement reaction.

a. $Au(s) + KNO_3(aq) \longrightarrow$
b. $Zn(s) + AgNO_3(aq) \longrightarrow$
c. $Al(s) + H_2SO_4(aq) \longrightarrow$

56. Write a balanced equation for each of the following double-replacement reactions:

a. $H_2C_2O_4(aq) + KOH(aq) \longrightarrow$
b. $CdBr_2(aq) + Na_2S(aq) \longrightarrow$
(Cadmium sulfide is a precipitate.)

57. Write a balanced equation for the complete combustion of each compound.

a. butene (C_4H_8) **b.** propanal (C_3H_6O)

58. Balance each equation and identify its type.

a. $Hf(s) + N_2(g) \longrightarrow Hf_3N_4(s)$
b. $Mg(s) + H_2SO_4(aq) \longrightarrow MgSO_4(aq) + H_2(g)$
c. $C_2H_6(g) + O_2(g) \longrightarrow CO_2(g) + H_2O(g)$
d. $Pb(NO_3)_2(aq) + NaI(aq) \longrightarrow PbI_2(s) + NaNO_3(aq)$

59. What is a distinguishing feature of every decomposition reaction?

11.3 Reactions in Aqueous Solution

60. What is a spectator ion?

***61.** Write a balanced net ionic equation for the following reactions:

a. $HCl(aq) + Ca(OH)_2(aq) \longrightarrow$
b. $AgNO_3(aq) + AlCl_3(aq) \longrightarrow$
(Silver chloride is a precipitate.)

62. Complete each equation and then write a net ionic equation.

a. $Al(s) + H_2SO_4(aq) \longrightarrow$
b. $HCl(aq) + Ba(OH)_2(aq) \longrightarrow$
c. $Au(s) + HCl(aq) \longrightarrow$

Understand Concepts

63. Each equation is incorrect. Find the errors, then rewrite and balance each equation.

a. $Cl_2 + NaI \longrightarrow NaCl_2 + I$
b. $NH_3 \longrightarrow N + H_3$
c. $Na + O_2 \longrightarrow NaO_2$

***64.** Write a balanced chemical equation for each combination reaction.

a. sodium oxide + water ⟶ sodium hydroxide
b. dichlorine heptoxide + water ⟶ perchloric acid

65. Write a balanced chemical equation for each single-replacement reaction that takes place in aqueous solution.

a. Steel wool (iron) is placed in sulfuric acid. (Assume that iron forms Fe^{2+} ion.)
b. Bromine reacts with aqueous barium iodide.

***66.** Pieces of sodium and magnesium are dropped into separate water-filled test tubes (*A* and *B*). There is vigorous bubbling in Tube *A* but not in Tube *B*.

a. Which tube contains the sodium metal?
b. Write an equation for the reaction in the tube containing the sodium metal. What type of reaction is occurring in this tube?

67. Write a balanced equation for the complete combustion of each compound. Assume that the products are carbon dioxide and water.

a. octane (C_8H_{18})
b. glucose ($C_6H_{12}O_6$)
c. ethanoic acid ($HC_2H_3O_2$)

68. Write a balanced net ionic equation for each reaction. The product that is not ionized is given.

a. $H_2C_2O_4 + KOH \longrightarrow [H_2O]$
b. $Na_2S + HCl \longrightarrow [H_2S]$

***69.** A yellow precipitate formed when aqueous solutions of sodium sulfide and cadmium nitrate were mixed in a beaker.

a. Write the formula of the yellow precipitate.
b. Identify the spectator ions in the solution.
c. Write the net ionic equation for the reaction.

Think Critically

70. **Interpret Photos** The photos show various types of reactions.

(1)
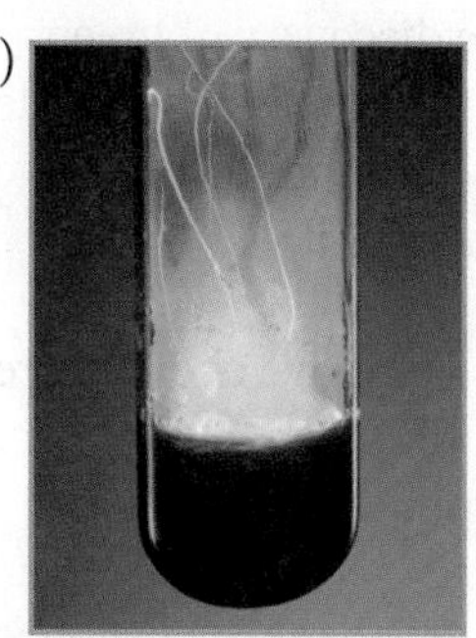
(2)
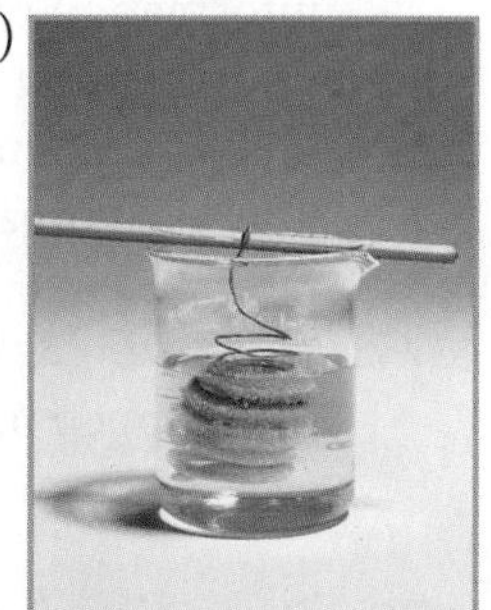
(3)

(4)

(1) Aluminum reacts with bromine.

(2) Copper reacts with aqueous silver nitrate.

(3) Propane (C_3H_8) reacts with oxygen.

(4) Aqueous lead(II) nitrate reacts with aqueous potassium iodide.

a. Identify each type of reaction.
b. Write the equation for each reaction.

FOUNDATIONS Wrap-Up

A Fizzy Reaction

1. Explain The reaction you observed at the start of the chapter can be described as:

$$NaHCO_3(aq) + HC_2H_3O_2(aq) \longrightarrow CO_2(g) + H_2O(l) + NaC_2H_3O_2(aq)$$

What caused the balloon to inflate?

Concept Check

Now that you've finished studying Chapter 11, answer these questions.

2. Is the equation above balanced? Explain.

3. Why is it important to know how to balance chemical equations?

Write About Science

71. **Explain** Research organisms such as fireflies and jellyfish that use bioluminescence, including information on the discovery of green fluorescent protein (GFP). In a pamphlet or poster, explain how bioluminescence works and how each organism uses it.

72. **Observe** Make a list of five chemical reactions that happen in your kitchen. Describe and name each reaction on your list.

*73. **Draw Conclusions** When pale yellow chlorine gas is bubbled through a clear, colorless solution of sodium iodide, the solution turns brown. Write a sentence identifying the type of reaction and the products that form. Then write the net ionic equation.

CHEMYSTERY

Order in the Lab

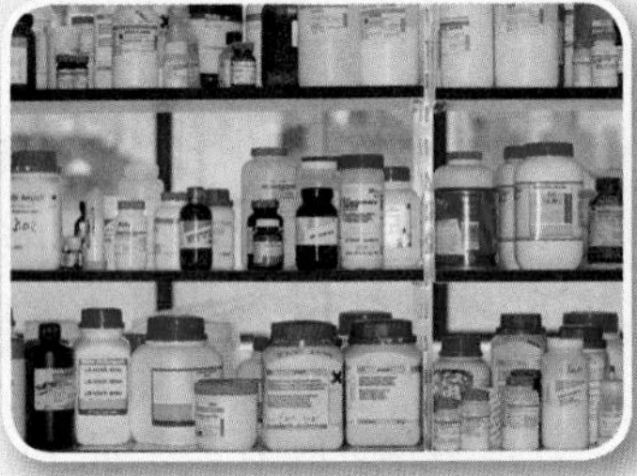

Chemicals should not be stored in alphabetical order because some chemicals that will react if mixed could end up next to each other. For example, acids should not be stored near cyanides, sulfides, and other chemicals that produce toxic gases when combined. Acids should also not be stored near bases or active metals. Reactions between acids and bases produce heat. Acids and active metals react to produce gases and heat. Acids and flammables should have separate, dedicated storage areas.

74. **Connect to the BIGIDEA** Should sulfuric acid be stored next to sodium hydroxide? Explain your answer. If they should not be stored next to each other, write a balanced chemical equation to support your answer.

Cumulative Review

*75. List the number of protons, neutrons, and electrons in this isotope of titanium: $^{50}_{22}Ti$. (See Lesson 4.3 for help.)

*76. Give the name or formula for the following compounds: (See Lesson 9.2 for help.)

a. potassium chromate
b. sodium hydrogen sulfite
c. $HMnO_4$
d. $K_2C_2O_4$

77. The graph shows the percent composition of two different compounds formed by the elements iron, oxygen, and sulfur. (See Lesson 10.3 for help.)

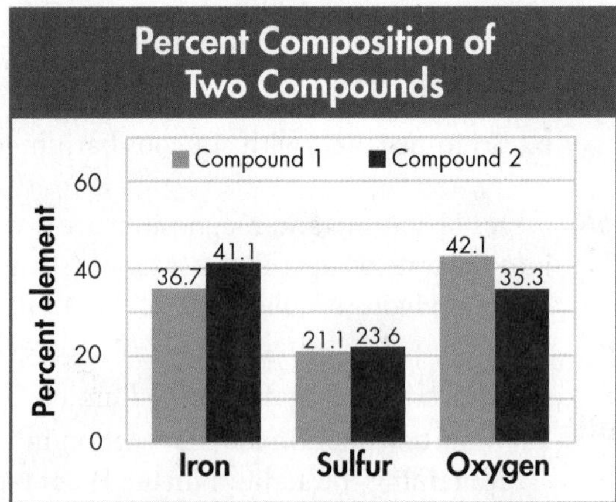

a. Using the data on the graphs, calculate the empirical formula of each compound.
b. Name each compound.

78. Calcium chloride is a white solid used as a drying agent. The maximum amount of water absorbed by different quantities of $CaCl_2$ is given in the table. (See Lesson 10.2 for help.)

$CaCl_2$ (g)	$CaCl_2$ (mol)	H_2O (g)	H_2O (mol)
17.3	a.____	5.62	e.____
48.8	b.____	15.8	f.____
124	c.____	40.3	g.____
337	d.____	109	h.____

a. Complete the table. Then plot moles of water absorbed (y-axis) versus moles of $CaCl_2$.
b. Based on your graph, how many molecules of water does each formula unit of $CaCl_2$ absorb?

Standardized Test Prep

For help with answering test questions, go to your Chemistry Skills and Math Workbook.

Select the choice that best answers each question or completes each statement.

1. When the equation $Fe_2O_3 + H_2 \longrightarrow Fe + H_2O$ is balanced using whole-number coefficients, what is the coefficient of H_2?
   (A) 6 (B) 3 (C) 2 (D) 1

2. Identify a spectator ion in this reaction.
   $Ba(OH)_2(aq) + H_2SO_4(aq) \longrightarrow BaSO_4(s) + H_2O(l)$
   (A) Ba^{2+}
   (B) SO_4^{2-}
   (C) OH^-
   (D) H^+
   (E) There is no spectator ion.

3. Magnesium ribbon reacts with an aqueous solution of copper(II) chloride in a single-replacement reaction. Which are the products of the balanced net ionic equation for the reaction?
   (A) $Mg^{2+}(aq) + 2Cl^-(aq) + Cu(s)$
   (B) $Mg^+(aq) + Cl^-(aq) + Cu^+(aq)$
   (C) $Mg^{2+}(aq) + Cu(s)$
   (D) $Cu(s) + 2Cl^-(aq)$

Use the following description and data table to answer Questions 4–6.

Dropper bottles labeled P, Q, and R contain one of three aqueous solutions: potassium carbonate, K_2CO_3; hydrochloric acid, HCl; and calcium nitrate, $Ca(NO_3)_2$. The table shows what happens when pairs of solutions are mixed.

Solution	P	Q	R
P	—	Precipitate	No reaction
Q	Precipitate	—	Gas forms.
R	No reaction	Gas forms.	—

4. Identify the contents of each dropper bottle.
5. Write the net ionic equation for the formation of the precipitate.
6. Write the complete ionic equation for the formation of the gas.

7. Which are the expected products of the decomposition reaction of potassium oxide, K_2O?
   (A) $K^+(s)$ and $O^{2-}(g)$
   (B) $K^+(s)$ and $O_2(g)$
   (C) $K(s)$ and $O_2^{2-}(g)$
   (D) $K(s)$ and $O_2(g)$

Tips for Success

Interpreting Diagrams Before you answer questions about a diagram, study the diagram carefully. Read all captions and labels. Look at all the information in the diagram and think about how it all interrelates.

Use the diagram to answer Questions 8–11.

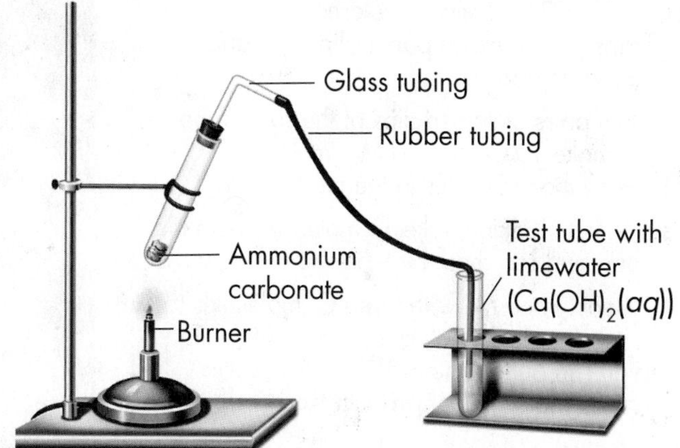

8. When ammonium carbonate is heated, water, ammonia, and carbon dioxide are produced. What type of chemical reaction is occurring?
9. Write formulas for the reaction products.
10. Write a balanced equation for the reaction. Include states for reactants and products.
11. Limewater is used to test for the presence of carbon dioxide gas. The products of the reaction of $Ca(OH)_2$ with CO_2 are calcium carbonate and water. Write a balanced equation for the reaction.

If You Have Trouble With . . .

Question	1	2	3	4	5	6	7	8	9	10	11
See Lesson	11.1	11.3	11.3	11.3	11.3	11.3	11.2	11.2	11.1	11.1	11.1

12 Stoichiometry

FOUNDATIONS for Learning

How Many Can You Make?

1. Obtain 20 identically colored paper clips (C), 20 metal paper clips (M), and a plastic bag.
2. Join pairs of paper clips of the same type to make 10 C_2 and 10 M_2 "molecules." Place the molecules in the plastic bag.
3. Without looking, take 15 molecules from the bag and sort them by type into two rows.
4. "React" one M_2 with three C_2 molecules to form two MC_3 molecules. Continue until you run out of one of the reactants. How many molecules of product did you form?

Predict Would your results be the same if you repeated the experiment? Explain.

PearsonChem.com

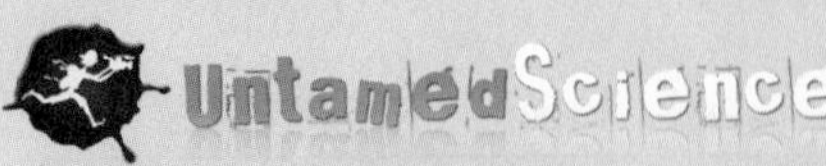

Travel back in time with the Untamed Science crew as Amedeo Avogadro uses stoichiometry to solve a baking crisis.

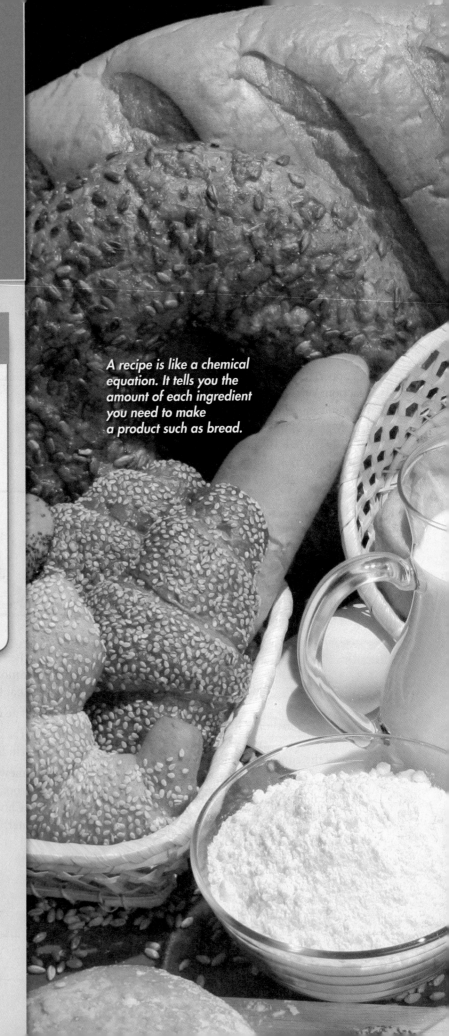

A recipe is like a chemical equation. It tells you the amount of each ingredient you need to make a product such as bread.

BIG IDEAS

- THE MOLE
- REACTIONS

Essential Questions:

1. *How are balanced chemical equations used in stoichiometric calculations?*
2. *How can you calculate amounts of reactants and products in a chemical reaction?*

CHEMYSTERY

Cookie Crumbles

Jack wanted to make cookies to sell at the school bake sale. The recipe he chose called for specific amounts of butter, flour, sugar, and eggs. Jack wanted to make sure that his cookies were delicious and sweet. He didn't think the recipe had enough sugar. So he added twice as much sugar as the recipe called for.

Jack mixed the ingredients and put balls of the dough on a cookie sheet. He then placed them in the oven to bake. Jack was very disappointed when he took them out of the oven. His cookies were brown, hard, and crumbly. They were not sweet and delicious. What happened? He checked the oven temperature and the amount of time that the cookies were in the oven. The time and temperature matched the directions in the recipe. Why didn't Jack's cookies turn out as he expected?

▶ Connect to the BIGIDEA As you read about quantifying chemical reactions, consider what could have happened to Jack's cookies.

12.1 The Arithmetic of Equations

CHEMISTRY & YOU

Q: How do you determine how much starting material you need to make a finished product? When making bikes, you need such parts as wheels, handlebars, pedals, and frames. To make 200 bikes, you would need to calculate how many of each part you need to produce that many bikes. In this lesson, you will learn how chemists determine how much of each reactant is needed to make a certain amount of product.

Key Questions

How do chemists use balanced chemical equations?

In terms of what quantities can you interpret a balanced chemical equation?

BUILD Vocabulary

stoichiometry the calculation of amounts of substances in chemical reactions

WORD ORIGINS

Stoichiometry comes from the combination of the Greek words *stoikheioin,* meaning "element," and *metron,* meaning "to measure." Stoichiometry is the calculation of amounts of substances involved in chemical reactions.

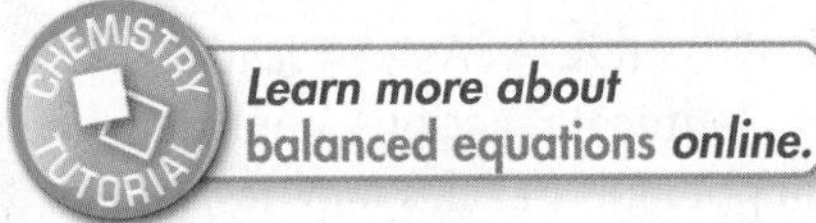

*Learn more about balanced equations **online.***

*Learn more about stoichiometry **online.***

Using Equations

Recall from Chapter 11 that you can use a balanced equation to represent the parts needed to make one bicycle. Each bicycle requires one frame, two wheels, one handlebar, and two pedals:

$$F + 2W + H + 2P \longrightarrow FW_2HP_2$$

If you want to make two bikes, then you can double the amounts of all the parts needed to make one bike. You can think of the parts of the bicycle as the reactants and the bike as the product.

Balanced Chemical Equations A balanced chemical equation tells you what amounts of reactants to mix and what amount of a product to expect. Chemists use balanced chemical equations as a basis to calculate how much reactant is needed or how much product will be formed in a reaction. Nearly everything you use is manufactured from chemicals. In manufacturing, chemists use balanced equations to help them carry out chemical processes economically so reactants are not wasted.

If you know the quantity of one substance, you can calculate the quantity of any other substance consumed or created in the reaction. Quantity usually means the amount of a substance expressed in grams or moles. A quantity could also be expressed in liters, tons, or molecules.

The calculation of quantities in chemical reactions is called **stoichiometry.** Calculations using balanced equations are called stoichiometric calculations. Stoichiometry is a form of bookkeeping for chemists. Accountants track income, money spent, and profits for a business by counting the amounts of each in dollars and cents. Chemists use stoichiometry to count the amounts of reactants and products. To make their counts, chemists use ratios of moles or representative particles derived from chemical equations.

Key Question How do chemists use balanced chemical equations? **Chemists use balanced chemical equations to calculate how much reactant is needed or how much product will be formed in a reaction.**

Chemical Equations

Fertilizers are often used to improve the growth of gardens, such as the flower garden shown at right. Ammonia (NH_3) is widely used to make fertilizers. In industry, ammonia is produced by the reaction of nitrogen with hydrogen:

$$N_2(g) + 3H_2(g) \longrightarrow 2NH_3(g)$$

This chemical equation is balanced. It tells you the relative amounts of reactants and product in the reaction. However, you can express these quantities in different ways, including the number of atoms, the number of molecules, the number of moles, the mass, and the volume. As you study stoichiometry, you will learn how to interpret a chemical equation in terms of any of these quantities.

Number of Atoms A balanced equation shows the number and types of atoms that are rearranged to make the product or products. Remember that the number and types of atoms are not changed in a reaction. There are two atoms of nitrogen and six atoms of hydrogen that react in the synthesis of ammonia. These eight atoms recombine to form the product ammonia. Notice that there are also two atoms of nitrogen and six atoms of hydrogen on the product side of the equation:

$$N_2(g) + 3H_2(g) \longrightarrow 2NH_3(g)$$
$$2 \text{ atoms N} + 6 \text{ atoms H} \longrightarrow 2 \text{ atoms N} + 6 \text{ atoms H}$$
$$8 \text{ atoms} \longrightarrow 8 \text{ atoms}$$

Number of Molecules A balanced equation also shows the number of molecules in a reaction. The equation for ammonia synthesis shows that one molecule of nitrogen reacts with three molecules of hydrogen to form two molecules of ammonia. Nitrogen and hydrogen will always react to form ammonia in a 1:3:2 ratio of molecules. If 10 molecules of nitrogen react with 30 molecules of hydrogen, you would expect to get 20 molecules of ammonia. Of course, it is not practical to count such small numbers of molecules. However, you could take Avogadro's number of nitrogen molecules and make them react with three times Avogadro's number of hydrogen molecules. The ratio of nitrogen molecules to hydrogen molecules is still 1:3. The reaction forms two times Avogadro's number of ammonia molecules:

$$1 \times \begin{matrix} 6.02 \times 10^{23} \\ \text{molecules } N_2 \end{matrix} + 3 \times \begin{matrix} 6.02 \times 10^{23} \\ \text{molecules } H_2 \end{matrix} \longrightarrow 2 \times \begin{matrix} 6.02 \times 10^{23} \\ \text{molecules } NH_3 \end{matrix}$$

The ratio of nitrogen to hydrogen to ammonia will always be 1:3:2.

Uses of Ammonia
Gardeners use ammonium salts as fertilizer. Plants need the nitrogen in these salts to grow.

Number of Moles Avogadro's number of representative particles of a substance is equal to one mole of a substance. Therefore, a balanced chemical equation tells you the number of moles as well as the number of representative particles. The coefficients of a balanced chemical equation indicate the relative numbers of moles of reactants and products in a chemical reaction. These numbers are the most important pieces of information that a balanced chemical equation provides. In the synthesis of ammonia, one mole of nitrogen molecules reacts with three moles of hydrogen molecules to form two moles of ammonia molecules. Notice that the total number of moles of reactants does not have to equal the total number of moles of product:

$$\begin{aligned} N_2(g) + 3H_2(g) &\longrightarrow 2NH_3(g) \\ 1\text{ mol } N_2 + 3\text{ mol } H_2 &\longrightarrow 2\text{ mol } NH_3 \\ 4\text{ mol} &\longrightarrow 2\text{ mol} \end{aligned}$$

Mass A balanced chemical equation also shows that chemical reactions follow the law of conservation of mass. This law states that mass can be neither created nor destroyed in an ordinary chemical or physical process. The number and type of atoms do not change in a chemical reaction. Therefore, the total mass of the atoms in the reaction does not change. You can use the mole relationship to relate mass to the number of atoms in the chemical equation. The mass of one mole of nitrogen (28.0 g) plus the mass of three moles of hydrogen (6.0 g) react to form the mass of two moles of ammonia (34.0 g). The number of moles of reactants does not equal the number of moles of product. However, the total number of grams of reactants does equal the total number of grams of product:

$$\begin{aligned} (1 \times 28.0\text{ g } N_2) + (3 \times 2.0\text{ g } H_2) &\longrightarrow (2 \times 17.0\text{ g } NH_3) \\ 28.0\text{ g } N_2 + 6.0\text{ g } H_2 &\longrightarrow 34.0\text{ g } NH_3 \\ 34.0\text{ g} &\longrightarrow 34.0\text{ g} \end{aligned}$$

Volume A balanced equation also tells you about the volumes of gases if you assume standard temperature and pressure (STP). Recall that one mole of any gas at STP has a volume of 22.4 L. The equation below indicates that 22.4 L of N_2 react with 67.6 L (3 × 22.4 L) of H_2. This reaction forms 44.8 L (2 × 22.4 L) of NH_3:

$$\begin{aligned} (1 \times 22.4\text{ L } N_2) + (3 \times 22.4\text{ L } H_2) &\longrightarrow (2 \times 22.4\text{ L } NH_3) \\ 22.4\text{ L } N_2 + 67.2\text{ L } H_2 &\longrightarrow 44.8\text{ L } NH_3 \end{aligned}$$

Sample Problem 12.1

Interpreting a Balanced Chemical Equation

Hydrogen sulfide smells like rotten eggs. It is found in volcanic gases. Here is the balanced equation for the burning of hydrogen sulfide:

$$2H_2S(g) + 3O_2(g) \longrightarrow 2SO_2(g) + 2H_2O(g)$$

Interpret this equation in terms of

a. the numbers of representative particles and moles.

b. the total masses of reactants and products.

Remember: Atoms and molecules are representative particles. In this equation, all the reactants and products are molecules. So, all the representative particles are molecules.

1 Analyze **Identify the relevant concepts.** The coefficients in the balanced equation give the relative numbers of representative particles and moles of reactants and products. A balanced chemical equation obeys the law of conservation of mass.

2 Solve **Apply concepts to this problem.** You do not need to do any calculations to interpret the number of representative particles and moles. You only need to use the coefficients of the balanced equation.

Use the coefficients in the balanced equation to identify the number of molecules and moles.

$$2H_2S(g) + 3O_2(g) \longrightarrow 2SO_2(g) + 2H_2O(g)$$

a. 2 molecules H_2S + 3 molecules O_2 $\longrightarrow$ 2 molecules SO_2 + 2 molecules H_2O

2 mol H_2S + 3 mol O_2 $\longrightarrow$ 2 mol SO_2 + 2 mol H_2O

Use the periodic table to calculate the molar mass of each reactant and product.

b. 1 mol H_2S = 34.1 g H_2S

1 mol O_2 = 32.0 g O_2

1 mol SO_2 = 64.1 g SO_2

1 mol H_2O = 18.0 g H_2O

Multiply the number of moles of each reactant and product by its molar mass.

2 mol H_2S + 3 mol O_2 $\longrightarrow$ 2 mol SO_2 + 2 mol H_2O

$$\left(2\,\cancel{\text{mol } H_2S} \times \frac{34.1\text{ g } H_2S}{1\,\cancel{\text{mol } H_2S}}\right) + \left(3\,\cancel{\text{mol } O_2} \times \frac{32.0\text{ g } O_2}{1\,\cancel{\text{mol } O_2}}\right) \longrightarrow$$

$$\left(2\,\cancel{\text{mol } SO_2} \times \frac{64.1\text{ g } SO_2}{1\,\cancel{\text{mol } SO_2}}\right) + \left(2\,\cancel{\text{mol } H_2O} \times \frac{18.0\text{ g } H_2O}{1\,\cancel{\text{mol } H_2O}}\right)$$

Add the masses of the reactants and then add the masses of the products.

68.2 g H_2S + 96.0 g O_2 $\longrightarrow$ 128.2 g SO_2 + 36.0 g H_2O

164.2 g $\longrightarrow$ 164.2 g

Hint: The mass of the reactants equals the mass of the products. The law of conservation of mass is obeyed.

BUILD Math Skills

Dimensional Analysis Remember from Lesson 3.3 that dimensional analysis is a way to analyze and solve problems by using the units of the measurements involved. When you interpret equations in terms of different quantities, you are performing dimensional analysis.

The units that may be interpreted from the coefficients of a balanced equation are representative particles and moles. Using dimensional analysis and the molar mass of a substance you can interpret, or calculate, the amount of grams of a substance. Using dimensional analysis and the volume of a gas at STP you can interpret, or calculate, the amount of liters of a gas.

Practice Problems

1. Interpret this equation for the formation of water from its elements in terms of the numbers of molecules and moles and volumes of gases at STP.

$$2H_2(g) + O_2(g) \longrightarrow 2H_2O(g)$$

❶ Analyze Identify the relevant concepts.

❷ Solve Apply the concepts to this problem.

2. Interpret this equation in terms of the relative numbers of moles and masses of reactants and products:

$$C_2H_5OH(l) + 3O_2(g) \longrightarrow 2CO_2(g) + 3H_2O(g)$$

3. Interpret this equation for the reaction of ammonia and oxygen in terms of Avogadro's number of molecules and volumes of gases at STP:

$$4NH_3(g) + 5O_2(g) \longrightarrow 4NO(g) + 6H_2O(l)$$

4. Challenge Balance this equation:

$$C_2H_4(g) + O_2(g) \longrightarrow CO_2(g) + H_2O(g)$$

Interpret the balanced equation in terms of the relative numbers of moles, volumes of gas at STP, and masses of reactants and products.

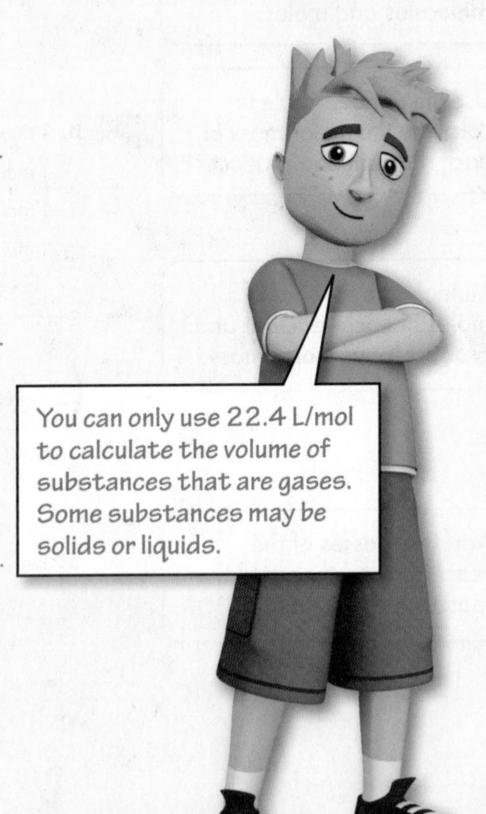

You can only use 22.4 L/mol to calculate the volume of substances that are gases. Some substances may be solids or liquids.

Interpreting the Balanced Equation for Ammonia The figure below shows all the information that the balanced chemical equation for the formation of ammonia provides. Notice that the mass of the reactants equals the mass of the products. The number of atoms of each type in the reactants also equals the number of atoms of each type in the product. Mass and atoms are conserved in every chemical reaction. Molecules, formula units, moles, and volumes are not always conserved.

Interpreting a Balanced Chemical Equation The balanced chemical equation for the formation of ammonia can be interpreted in several ways.

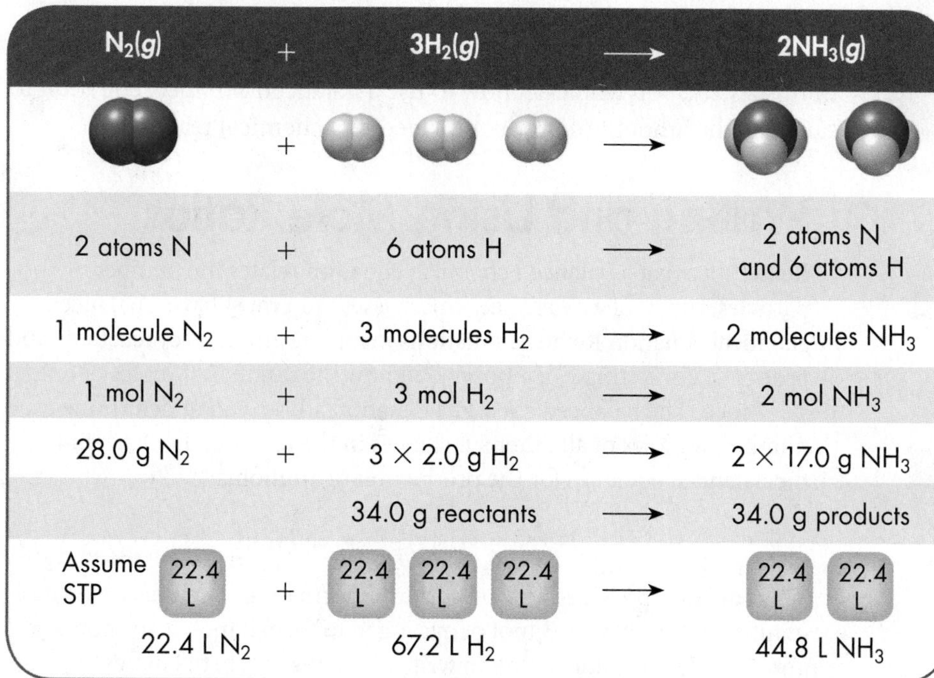

$N_2(g)$	+	$3H_2(g)$	$\longrightarrow$	$2NH_3(g)$
	+		$\longrightarrow$	
2 atoms N	+	6 atoms H	$\longrightarrow$	2 atoms N and 6 atoms H
1 molecule N_2	+	3 molecules H_2	$\longrightarrow$	2 molecules NH_3
1 mol N_2	+	3 mol H_2	$\longrightarrow$	2 mol NH_3
28.0 g N_2	+	3×2.0 g H_2	$\longrightarrow$	2×17.0 g NH_3
		34.0 g reactants	$\longrightarrow$	34.0 g products
Assume STP 22.4 L	+	22.4 L 22.4 L 22.4 L	$\longrightarrow$	22.4 L 22.4 L
22.4 L N_2		67.2 L H_2		44.8 L NH_3

See balancing chemical equations animated online. KINETIC ART

Key Question In terms of what quantities can you interpret a balanced chemical equation? **A balanced chemical equation can be interpreted in terms of number of atoms, number of molecules, number of moles, mass, and volume.**

12.1 LessonCheck

Key Concept Check

5. Explain How do chemists use balanced equations?

6. Identify Chemical reactions can be described in terms of what quantities?

Think Critically

7. Explain How is a balanced chemical equation similar to a recipe?

8. Apply Concepts Interpret this equation in terms of the relative number of representative particles, the number of moles, and the masses of reactants and products:

$$2K(s) + 2H_2O(l) \longrightarrow 2KOH(aq) + H_2(g)$$

CHEMISTRY & YOU

9. How can you determine the amount of each reactant you need to make a product? (Hint: See page 354.)

12.2 Chemical Calculations

CHEMISTRY & YOU

Q: How do manufacturers know how to make enough of their desired product? Chemical plants combine nitrogen and hydrogen to produce ammonia. Ammonia may be wasted if too much is produced. If too little is produced, there may not be enough for all the customers. In this lesson, you will learn how to use a balanced chemical equation to calculate the amount of product formed in a chemical reaction.

Key Questions

How are mole ratios used in chemical calculations?

What is the general procedure for solving a stoichiometric problem?

BUILD Vocabulary

mole ratio a conversion factor obtained by interpreting the coefficients of a balanced chemical equation in terms of moles

USING PRIOR KNOWLEDGE

Remember that a ratio shows the relationship between two quantities. So, a mole ratio shows the relationship between the amount of moles of two substances.

Writing and Using Mole Ratios

Remember that a balanced chemical equation relates the number of particles, moles of a substance, and masses. You must have a balanced chemical equation for all calculations involving amounts of reactants and products. For example, suppose you know the number of moles of one substance. The balanced chemical equation allows you to determine the number of moles of all other substances in the reaction. Look again at the balanced equation for the production of ammonia:

$$N_2(g) + 3H_2(g) \longrightarrow 2NH_3(g)$$

This equation provides very important information. It tells us that 1 mol of nitrogen reacts with 3 mol of hydrogen to form 2 mol of ammonia. You can use this information to write ratios that relate the moles of the substances. A **mole ratio** is a conversion factor obtained by interpreting the coefficients of a balanced chemical equation in terms of moles. In chemical calculations, mole ratios are used to convert between a given number of moles of one substance to moles of a different substance. Here are three mole ratios derived from the above balanced equation:

$$\frac{1\ \text{mol}\ N_2}{3\ \text{mol}\ H_2} \quad \frac{2\ \text{mol}\ NH_3}{1\ \text{mol}\ N_2} \quad \frac{3\ \text{mol}\ H_2}{2\ \text{mol}\ NH_3}$$

Mole-Mole Calculations You can calculate the number of moles of one substance if you know the moles of another substance. Multiply the given number of moles by the mole ratio as shown below. In the ratio below, W is the unknown quantity you want to find and G is the given quantity. The values a and b are the coefficients from the balanced equation.

The amount of G is x moles.

The mole ratio comes from the balanced equation.

Solve $\frac{xb}{a}$ to find the number of moles of W.

$$x\ \text{mol}\ G \times \frac{b\ \text{mol}\ W}{a\ \text{mol}\ G} = \frac{xb}{a}\ \text{mol}\ W$$

Given — Mole ratio — Calculated

SampleProblem 12.2

Calculating Moles of a Product

How many moles of NH_3 are produced when 0.60 mol of nitrogen reacts with hydrogen?

❶ Analyze List the known and the unknown.

KNOWN	UNKNOWN
moles of nitrogen = 0.60 mol N_2	moles of ammonia = ? mol NH_3

❷ Calculate Solve for the unknown. The calculation requires a balanced chemical equation. To determine the number of moles of NH_3, multiply the moles of N_2 by the form of the mole ratio that allows the moles of N_2 to cancel.

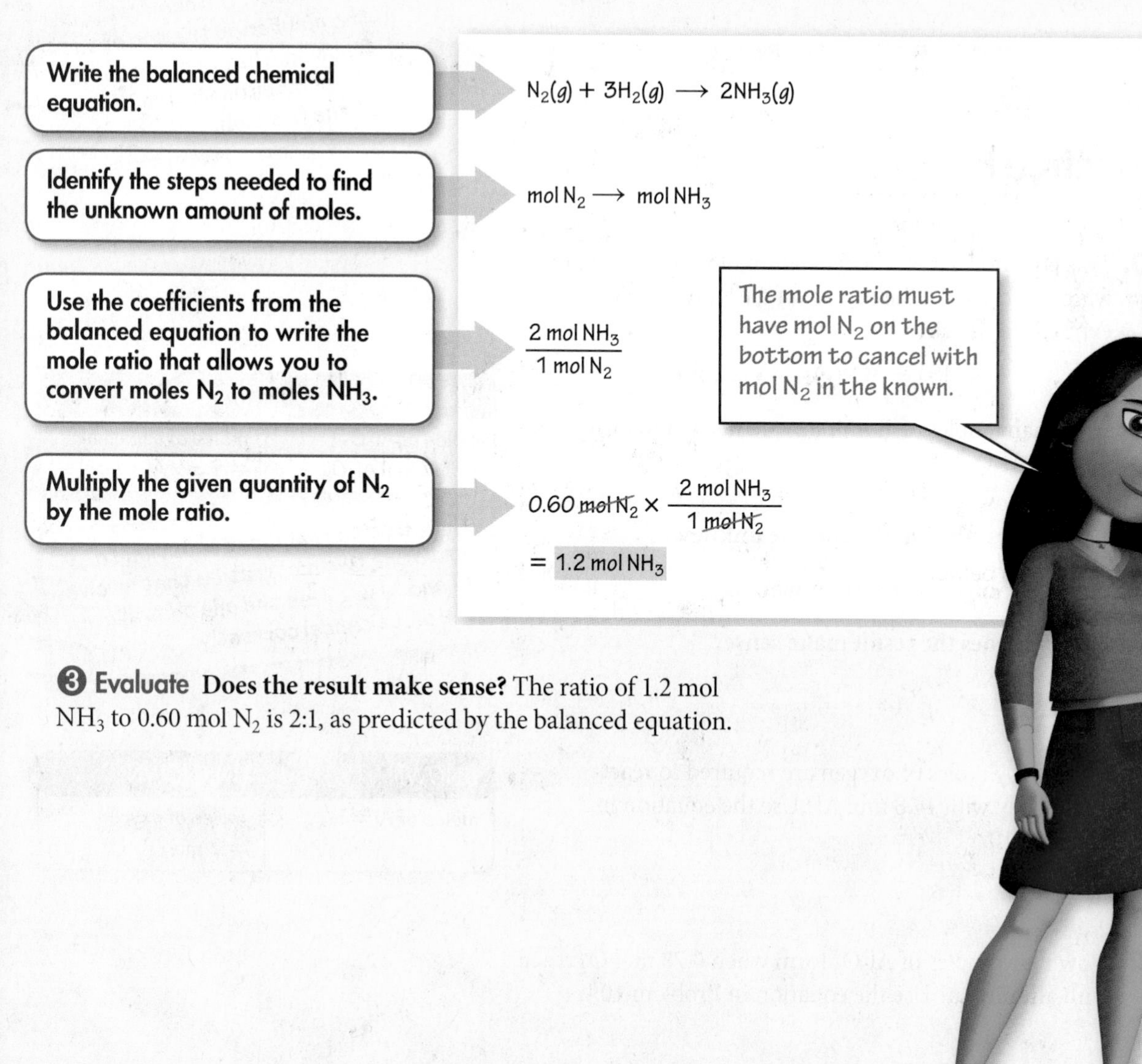

Write the balanced chemical equation.

$N_2(g) + 3H_2(g) \longrightarrow 2NH_3(g)$

Identify the steps needed to find the unknown amount of moles.

$\text{mol } N_2 \longrightarrow \text{mol } NH_3$

Use the coefficients from the balanced equation to write the mole ratio that allows you to convert moles N_2 to moles NH_3.

$$\frac{2 \text{ mol } NH_3}{1 \text{ mol } N_2}$$

The mole ratio must have mol N_2 on the bottom to cancel with mol N_2 in the known.

Multiply the given quantity of N_2 by the mole ratio.

$$0.60 \cancel{\text{mol } N_2} \times \frac{2 \text{ mol } NH_3}{1 \cancel{\text{mol } N_2}} = 1.2 \text{ mol } NH_3$$

❸ Evaluate Does the result make sense? The ratio of 1.2 mol NH_3 to 0.60 mol N_2 is 2:1, as predicted by the balanced equation.

BUILD Math Skills

Using Ratios Mole ratios can help you find the moles of any substance in a reaction—but only if you use the correct ratio. Make sure the substance you want to find is in the numerator of the ratio. For example, consider the following reaction.

$$N_2 + 3H_2 \longrightarrow 2NH_3$$

Using the balanced equation, you can write two mole ratios for the relationship between the number of moles of H_2 used and the number of moles of NH_3 produced.

$$\frac{3 \text{ mol } H_2}{2 \text{ mol } NH_3} \quad \frac{2 \text{ mol } NH_3}{3 \text{ mol } H_2}$$

Use the first ratio if you know the moles of NH_3 and want to find the moles of H_2. Use the second ratio if you know the moles of H_2 and want to find the moles of NH_3.

Go to your Chemistry Skills and Math Workbook for more practice.

Remember: The numerator is the number on the top of the fraction. The denominator is the number on the bottom of the fraction.

Practice Problems

10. This equation shows the formation of aluminum oxide, which is found on the surface of aluminum objects exposed to the air:

$$4Al(s) + 3O_2(g) \longrightarrow 2Al_2O_3(s)$$

How many moles of aluminum are needed to form 3.7 mol Al_2O_3?

KNOWN	UNKNOWN
moles of Al_2O_3 = 3.7 mol Al_2O_3	moles of aluminum = ? mol Al

Hint: Use the balanced equation to write the two mole ratios that involve Al and Al_2O_3. Use the one that allows the units cancel correctly.

1 Analyze List the known and the unknown.

2 Calculate Solve for the unknown.

3 Evaluate Does the result make sense?

11. How many moles of oxygen are required to react completely with 14.8 mol Al? Use the equation in Problem 10.

KNOWN	UNKNOWN
moles of Al =	moles of oxygen = ? mol O_2

12. How many moles of Al_2O_3 form when 0.78 mol O_2 reacts with aluminum? Use the equation in Problem 10.

Mass-Mass Calculations A balanced chemical equation allows you to calculate the mass of any substance in a given chemical equation from the mass of another substance. To do this conversion, you use a mole ratio from the balanced equation. If the given sample is measured in grams, convert the mass to moles by using its molar mass. Then use the mole ratio from the balanced equation to calculate the number of moles of unknown. Determine the mass of the unknown by multiplying the number of moles of the unknown by its molar mass. The known and the unknown can be a reactant or product.

In mass-mass problems, you will have a given mass (G) and have to find an unknown mass (W). Use the steps below to solve these types of problems.

1. Change the mass of G to moles of G (mass $G \longrightarrow$ mol G) by using the molar mass of G:

$$\text{mass } G \times \frac{1 \text{ mol } G}{\text{molar mass } G} = \text{mol } G$$

2. Change the moles of G to moles of W (mol $G \longrightarrow$ mol W) by using the mole ratio from the balanced equation:

$$\text{mol } G \times \frac{b \text{ mol } W}{a \text{ mol } G} = \text{mol } W$$

3. Change the moles of W to grams of W (mol $W \longrightarrow$ mass W) by using the molar mass of W:

$$\text{mol } W \times \frac{\text{molar mass } W}{1 \text{ mol } W} = \text{mass } W$$

The figure below shows the steps for mass-mass stoichiometric calculations. For a mole-mass problem, skip the first conversion (from mass to moles). For a mass-mole problem, skip the last conversion (from moles to mass).

Key Question How are mole ratios used in chemical calculations? **In chemical calculations, mole ratios are used to convert between a given number of moles of a reactant or product to moles of a different reactant or product.**

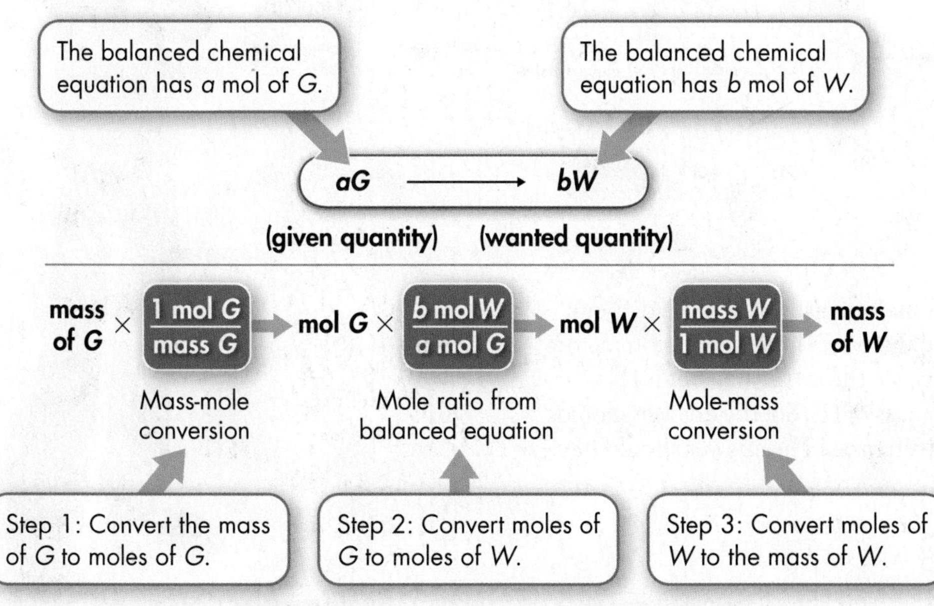

The balanced chemical equation has a mol of G.
The balanced chemical equation has b mol of W.
aG ⟶ bW
(given quantity) (wanted quantity)
mass of G × 1 mol G / mass G → mol G × b mol W / a mol G → mol W × mass W / 1 mol W → mass of W
Mass-mole conversion
Mole ratio from balanced equation
Mole-mass conversion
Step 1: Convert the mass of G to moles of G.
Step 2: Convert moles of G to moles of W.
Step 3: Convert moles of W to the mass of W.

Mass-Mass Conversion Steps This diagram shows the steps necessary to solve a mass-mass stoichiometry problem: Convert mass to moles, use the mole ratio, and then convert moles to mass.

Go to your Chemistry Skills and Math Workbook to practice calculating the mass of a product.

Sample Problem 12.3

Calculating the Mass of a Product

Calculate the number of grams of NH_3 produced by the reaction of 5.40 g of hydrogen with an excess of nitrogen. The balanced equation is:

$$N_2(g) + 3H_2(g) \longrightarrow 2NH_3(g)$$

1 Analyze List the knowns and the unknown. Note that the mole ratio is derived from the balanced equation.

KNOWNS	UNKNOWN
mass of hydrogen = 5.40 g H_2	mass of ammonia = ? g NH_3
mole ratio = 2 mol NH_3/3 mol H_2	
molar mass of H_2 = 2.0 g H_2/1 mol H_2	
molar mass of NH_3 = 17.0 g NH_3/ 1 mol NH_3	

2 Calculate Solve for the unknown. Use the mass of hydrogen to find the mass of ammonia. The coefficients of the balanced equation show that 3 mol H_2 reacts with 1 mol N_2 to produce 2 mol NH_3.

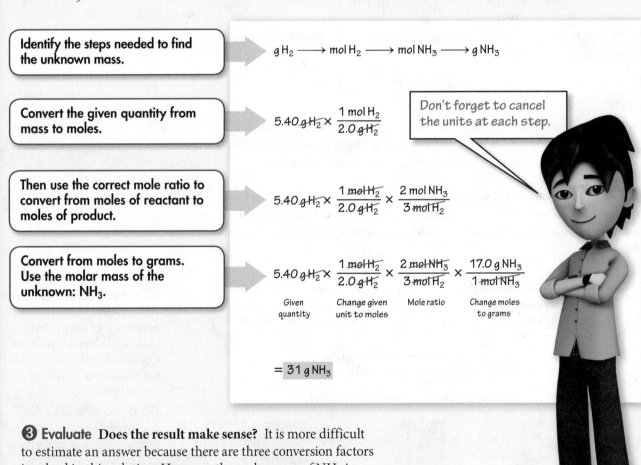

Identify the steps needed to find the unknown mass.

$$g\ H_2 \longrightarrow mol\ H_2 \longrightarrow mol\ NH_3 \longrightarrow g\ NH_3$$

Convert the given quantity from mass to moles.

$$5.40\ \cancel{g\ H_2} \times \frac{1\ mol\ H_2}{2.0\ \cancel{g\ H_2}}$$

Then use the correct mole ratio to convert from moles of reactant to moles of product.

$$5.40\ \cancel{g\ H_2} \times \frac{1\ \cancel{mol\ H_2}}{2.0\ \cancel{g\ H_2}} \times \frac{2\ mol\ NH_3}{3\ \cancel{mol\ H_2}}$$

Convert from moles to grams. Use the molar mass of the unknown: NH_3.

$$5.40\ \cancel{g\ H_2} \times \frac{1\ \cancel{mol\ H_2}}{2.0\ \cancel{g\ H_2}} \times \frac{2\ \cancel{mol\ NH_3}}{3\ \cancel{mol\ H_2}} \times \frac{17.0\ g\ NH_3}{1\ \cancel{mol\ NH_3}}$$

Given quantity; Change given unit to moles; Mole ratio; Change moles to grams

$$= 31\ g\ NH_3$$

Don't forget to cancel the units at each step.

3 Evaluate Does the result make sense? It is more difficult to estimate an answer because there are three conversion factors involved in this solution. However, the molar mass of NH_3 is much greater than the molar mass of H_2. So, the answer should have a larger mass than the given mass. The answer should have two significant figures.

Practice Problems

13. Acetylene gas (C_2H_2) is produced by adding water to calcium carbide (CaC_2):

$$CaC_2(s) + 2H_2O(l) \longrightarrow C_2H_2(g) + Ca(OH)_2(aq)$$

How many grams of acetylene are produced by adding water to 5.00 g CaC_2?

1 Analyze **List the knowns and the unknown.**

KNOWNS	UNKNOWN
mass of CaC_2 = 5.00 g CaC_2	mass of C_2H_2 = ? g C_2H_2
mole ratio from balanced equation = 1 mol CaC_2/1 mol C_2H_2	
molar mass of C_2H_2 = 26.0 g C_2H_2/1 mol C_2H_2	
molar mass of CaC_2 = 64.1 g CaC_2/ 1 mol CaC_2	

2 Calculate **Solve for the unknown.**

3 Evaluate **Does the result make sense?**

14. The reaction of fluorine with ammonia produces dinitrogen tetrafluoride and hydrogen fluoride:

$$5F_2(g) + 2NH_3(g) \longrightarrow N_2F_4(g) + 6HF(g)$$

How many grams of N_2F_4 can be produced from 225 g F_2?

KNOWNS	UNKNOWN
mass of F_2 =	mass of N_2F_4 = ? g N_2F_4
mole ratio from balanced equation =	
molar mass of F_2 =	
molar mass of N_2F_4 =	

15. Use the chemical equation in Problem 14 to determine how many grams of NH_3 are required to produce 4.65 g HF?

Decomposition of Water
In this decomposition reaction, water molecules are broken down into hydrogen and oxygen molecules. Hydrogen gas is produced in the right test tube. Oxygen gas is produced in the left test tube.

Other Stoichiometric Calculations

You have seen how to find mole ratios from a balanced chemical equation. You can also use mole ratios to calculate any measurement unit that is related to the mole. For example, you may be asked to find quantities expressed as the number of representative particles, units of mass, or volumes of gases at STP. The problems can include mass-volume, particle-mass, and volume-volume calculations.

The photo on the left shows a decomposition reaction. Water is being broken down into hydrogen and oxygen molecules. You can use stoichiometry to relate the moles, mass, particles, and volumes of water, oxygen, and hydrogen in this reaction. In most stoichiometric problems, the given quantity is first converted to moles. Then, the mole ratio from the balanced equation is used to calculate the number of moles of the wanted substance. Finally, the moles are converted to any other unit of measurement related to the unit mole.

The Mole-Mass Relationship The molar mass of any substance equals the mass of one mole of the substance, so 1 mol = molar mass. You have learned how to use this relationship to solve mass-mass, mass-mole, and mole-mass stoichiometric problems.

The mole-mass relationship gives you two conversion factors. The conversion factor you use depends on whether you need to convert mass to moles or moles to mass.

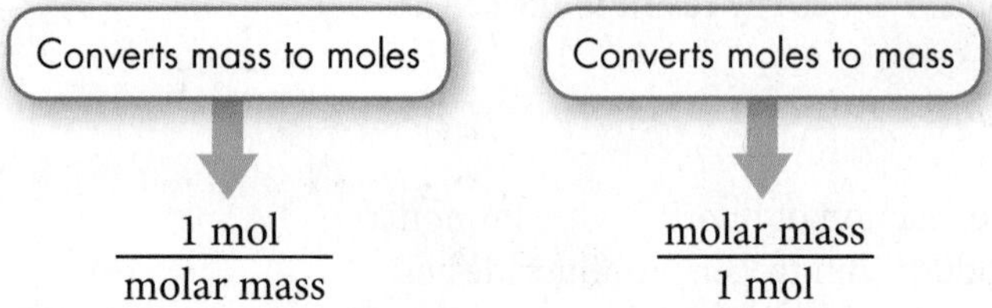

$$\frac{1 \text{ mol}}{\text{molar mass}} \qquad \frac{\text{molar mass}}{1 \text{ mol}}$$

The Mole-Particle Relationship Remember that the mole can also be related to other quantities. Recall from Chapter 10 that 1 mol = 6.02×10^{23} representative particles. Representative particles may be molecules, atoms, or formula units. You can use the relationship between moles and the number of representative particles to solve stoichiometric calculations. Again, the conversion factor you use depends on whether you need to find the number of moles or the number of particles.

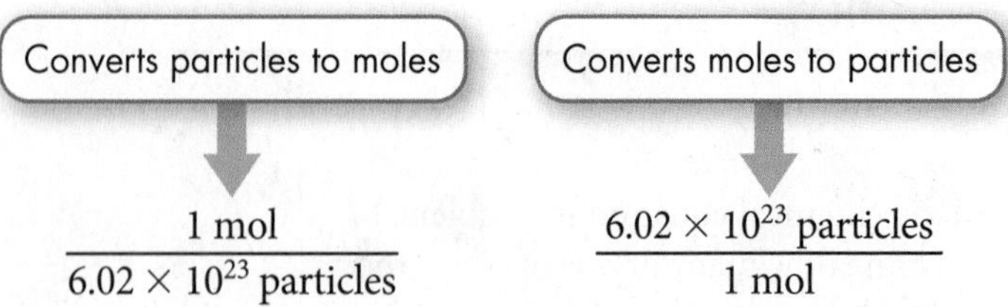

$$\frac{1 \text{ mol}}{6.02 \times 10^{23} \text{ particles}} \qquad \frac{6.02 \times 10^{23} \text{ particles}}{1 \text{ mol}}$$

Sample Problem 12.4

Calculating Molecules of a Product

How many molecules of oxygen are produced when 29.2 g of water is decomposed by electrolysis according to this balanced equation?

$$2H_2O(l) \xrightarrow{\text{electricity}} 2H_2(g) + O_2(g)$$

1 Analyze List the knowns and the unknown. The mole ratio is derived from the balanced equation.

KNOWNS	UNKNOWN
mass of water = 29.2 g H_2O	molecules of oxygen = ? molecules O_2
mole ratio = 1 mol O_2/2 mol H_2O	
molar mass of H_2O = 18.0 g H_2O/1 mol H_2O	
molecules per mole of O_2 = 6.02×10^{23} molecules O_2/1 mol of O_2	

2 Calculate Solve for the unknown. Use the mass of water to find the molecules of oxygen. The appropriate mole ratio relating mol O_2 to mol H_2O from the balanced equation is 1 mol O_2/2 mol H_2O.

Identify the conversion steps needed to find the number of molecules.

$$\text{g } H_2O \longrightarrow \text{mol } H_2O \longrightarrow \text{mol } O_2 \longrightarrow \text{molecules } O_2$$

Convert the given quantity from mass to moles.

$$29.2 \text{ g } H_2O \times \frac{1 \text{ mol } H_2O}{18.0 \text{ g } H_2O}$$

Then convert from moles of reactant to moles of product.

$$29.2 \text{ g } H_2O \times \frac{1 \text{ mol } H_2O}{18.0 \text{ g } H_2O} \times \frac{1 \text{ mol } O_2}{2 \text{ mol } H_2O}$$

Finally convert from moles to molecules.

$$29.2 \text{ g } H_2O \times \frac{1 \text{ mol } H_2O}{18.0 \text{ g } H_2O} \times \frac{1 \text{ mol } O_2}{2 \text{ mol } H_2O} \times \frac{6.02 \times 10^{23} \text{ molecules } O_2}{1 \text{ mol } O_2}$$

Given quantity | Change to moles | Mole ratio | Change to molecules

$$= 4.88 \times 10^{23} \text{ molecules } O_2$$

Remember: Start your calculations with the given quantity, even if the given quantity is a product in the reaction.

3 Evaluate Does the result make sense? The given mass of water should produce a little less than 1 mol of oxygen—or a little less than Avogadro's number of molecules. The answer should have three significant figures.

BUILD Math Skills

On some calculators, the exponent key is "Exp" instead of "EE"

Using Scientific Notation With Calculators The number of molecules in stoichiometric equations should be reported by using scientific notation. To enter Avogadro's number on your calculator, use the exponent key [EE] as shown here:

6.02 [EE] 23

You may need to press the button on your calculator that changes the display to scientific notation to view your answer in scientific notation.

Practice Problems

16. How many molecules of oxygen are produced by the decomposition of 6.54 g of potassium chlorate ($KClO_3$)?

$$2KClO_3(s) \longrightarrow 2KCl(s) + 3O_2(g)$$

KNOWNS	UNKNOWN
mass of $KClO_3$ = 6.54 g $KClO_3$	molecules of oxygen = ? molecules O_2
mole ratio from balanced equation = 3 mol O_2/2 mol $KClO_3$	
molecules per mole of O_2 = 6.02×10^{23} molecules O_2/1 mol O_2	
molar mass of $KClO_3$ = 122.6 g $KClO_3$/1 mol $KClO_3$	

1 Analyze **List the knowns and the unknown.**

2 Calculate **Solve for the unknown.**

3 Evaluate **Does the result make sense?**

17. The last step in the production of nitric acid is the reaction of nitrogen dioxide with water:

$$3NO_2(g) + H_2O(l) \longrightarrow 2HNO_3(aq) + NO(g)$$

How many molecules of nitric acid are produced when 43.2 g of water reacts with nitrogen dioxide?

KNOWNS	UNKNOWN
mass of water =	molecules of nitric acid = ? molecules HNO_3
mole ratio from balanced equation =	
molecules per mole of HNO_3 =	
molar mass of water =	

18. Challenge Use the equation in Problem 17. How many grams of nitrogen dioxide must react with water to produce 5.00×10^{22} molecules of nitrogen monoxide?

The Mole-Volume Relationship You can also use stoichiometry to relate volumes to moles of gaseous reactants and products in a reaction. For a gas, 1 mol = 22.4 L at STP:

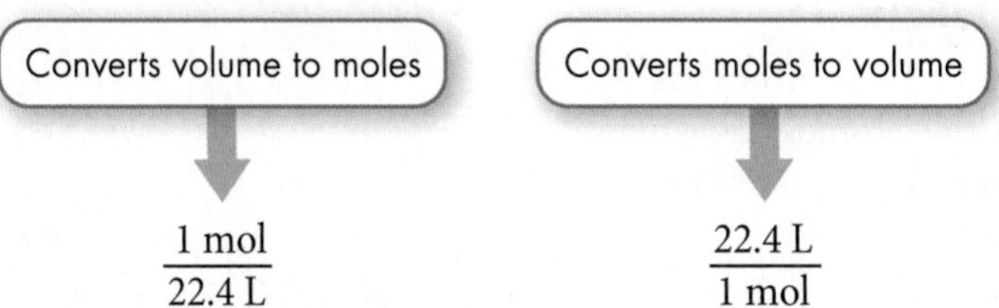

$$\frac{1 \text{ mol}}{22.4 \text{ L}} \qquad \frac{22.4 \text{ L}}{1 \text{ mol}}$$

Steps for a Stoichiometric Problem The figure below summarizes the steps for a typical stoichiometric problem. Notice that the units of the given quantity will not necessarily be the same as the units of the wanted quantity. For example, you might be given the mass of *G* and asked to calculate the volume of *W* at STP. Also, your final answer may not be in moles even though you used the mole ratio to convert between quantities.

Key Question What is the general procedure for solving a stoichiometric problem? **In a typical stoichiometric problem, the given quantity is first converted to moles. Then, the mole ratio from the balanced equation is used to calculate the number of moles of the wanted substance. Finally, the moles are converted to any other unit of measurement related to the unit mole, as the problem requires.**

BUILD Connections

How is stoichiometry related to the air bags in a car? During a car crash, a reaction produces nitrogen gas, which fills up the car's air bags. Air bags must inflate enough during a collision to protect you but not so much as to hurt you. Engineers use stoichiometry to determine the exact amount of each reactant needed to produce the correct volume of gas.

Solving Stoichiometric Problems
You can solve a variety of stoichiometric problems if you know how to use conversion factors. This diagram shows the steps needed to solve different types of problems.

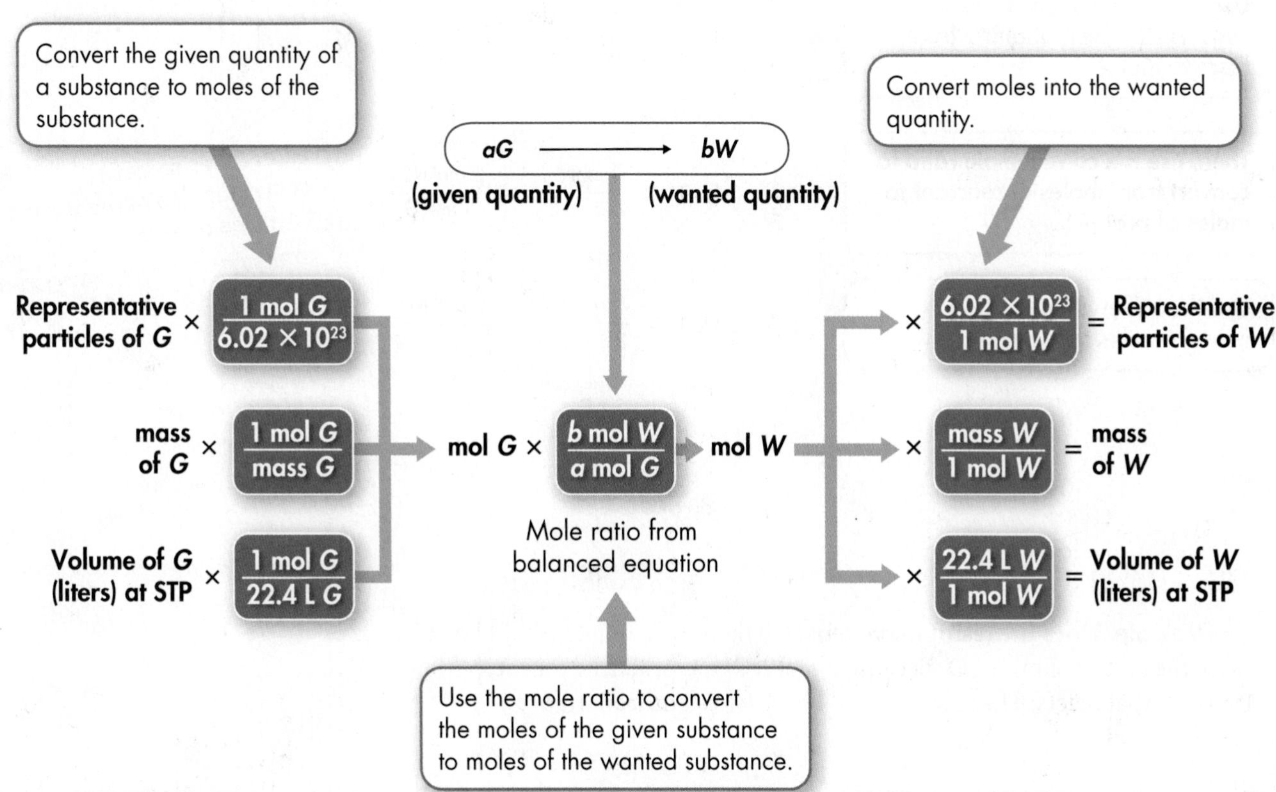

Sample Problem 12.5

Volume-Volume Stoichiometric Calculations

Nitrogen monoxide and oxygen gas combine to form the brown gas nitrogen dioxide, which contributes to photochemical smog. How many liters of nitrogen dioxide are produced when 34 L of oxygen react with an excess of nitrogen monoxide? Assume conditions are at STP:

$$2NO(g) + O_2(g) \longrightarrow 2NO_2(g)$$

1 Analyze List the knowns and the unknown. Note that the mole ratio is derived from the balanced equation.

KNOWNS	UNKNOWN
volume of oxygen = 34 L O_2	volume of nitrogen dioxide = ? L NO_2
mole ratio = 2 mol NO_2/1 mol O_2	
liters O_2 per mole O_2 = 22.4 L O_2/1 mol O_2	
liters NO_2 per mole NO_2 = 22.4 L NO_2/1 mol NO_2	

2 Calculate Solve for the unknown.
Start with the volume of oxygen to convert to the volume of nitrogen dioxide. For gaseous reactants and products at STP, 1 mol of a gas has a volume of 22.4 L.

Identify the conversions that need to be made to find the volume.

$$\text{L } O_2 \longrightarrow \text{mol } O_2 \longrightarrow \text{mol } NO_2 \longrightarrow \text{L } NO_2$$

Use the mole-volume ratio to convert the given quantity from liters to moles.

$$34 \text{ L } O_2 \times \frac{1 \text{ mol } O_2}{22.4 \text{ L } O_2}$$

Then, use the correct mole ratio to convert from moles of reactant to moles of product.

$$34 \text{ L } O_2 \times \frac{1 \text{ mol } O_2}{22.4 \text{ L } O_2} \times \frac{2 \text{ mol } NO_2}{1 \text{ mol } O_2}$$

Hint: Don't forget to convert moles of reactant to moles of product.

Use the mole-volume ratio to convert moles to liters.

$$34 \text{ L } O_2 \times \frac{1 \text{ mol } O_2}{22.4 \text{ L } O_2} \times \frac{2 \text{ mol } NO_2}{1 \text{ mol } O_2} \times \frac{22.4 \text{ L } NO_2}{1 \text{ mol } NO_2}$$

Given quantity | Change to moles | Mole ratio | Change to liters

$$= 68 \text{ L } NO_2$$

3 Evaluate Does the result make sense? The volume of NO_2 should be twice the given volume of O_2 because 2 mol NO_2 are produced for each 1 mol O_2 that reacts. The answer should have two significant figures.

BUILD Math Skills

Tips on Conversions Some stoichiometric calculations include many terms. Simplify the terms before you perform the calculations. Remove any units that cancel out. You may also notice other numbers that cancel out, such as 22.4, as shown below.

$$34\,\cancel{L\,O_2} \times \frac{1\,\cancel{mol\,O_2}}{\cancel{22.4}\,\cancel{L\,O_2}} \times \frac{2\,\cancel{mol\,NO_2}}{1\,\cancel{mol\,O_2}} \times \frac{\cancel{22.4}\,L\,NO_2}{1\,\cancel{mol\,NO_2}}$$

Go to your Chemistry Skills and Math Workbook for more practice.

Practice Problems

19. The equation for the combustion of carbon monoxide is:

$$2CO(g) + O_2(g) \longrightarrow 2CO_2(g)$$

How many liters of oxygen are required to burn 3.86 L of carbon monoxide?

KNOWNS	UNKNOWN
volume of carbon monoxide = 3.86 L CO	volume of oxygen = ? L O_2
mole ratio from balanced equation = 1 mol O_2/2 mol CO	
liters O_2 per mole O_2 = 22.4 L O_2/1 mol O_2	
liters CO per mole CO = 22.4 L CO/1 mol CO	

1 Analyze **List the knowns and the unknown.**

2 Calculate **Solve for the unknown.**

3 Evaluate **Does the result make sense?**

20. Phosphorus and hydrogen can be combined to form phosphine (PH_3).

$$P_4(s) + 6H_2(g) \longrightarrow 4PH_3(g)$$

How many liters of phosphine are formed when 0.42 L of hydrogen reacts with phosphorus?

KNOWNS	UNKNOWN
volume of hydrogen =	volume of phosphine = ? L PH_3
mole ratio from balanced equation =	
liters H_2 per mole H_2 =	
liters PH_3 per mole PH_3 =	

21. **Challenge** Use the chemical equation in Problem 20. What is the total liters of hydrogen needed to produce 11.2 L of PH_3?

Sample Problem 12.6

Finding the Volume of a Gas Needed for a Reaction

Assuming STP, how many milliliters of oxygen are needed to produce 20.4 mL SO_3 according to this balanced equation?

$$2SO_2(g) + O_2(g) \longrightarrow 2SO_3(g)$$

1 Analyze List the knowns and the unknown.

In Sample Problem 12.5 the 22.4 L/mol factors canceled out. This will always be true in a volume-volume problem. The coefficients in a balanced chemical equation indicate the relative number of moles. The coefficients also indicate relative volumes of each gas. The volume can be expressed in any unit. Use volume ratios in the same way you have used mole ratios.

KNOWNS	UNKNOWN
volume of sulfur trioxide = 20.4 mL	volume of oxygen = ? mL O_2
volume ratio from balanced equation = 1 ml O_2/2 mL SO_3	

Hint: A volume ratio is derived from the balanced equation the same way that a mole ratio is derived.

2 Calculate Solve for the unknown.

Multiply the given volume by the appropriate volume ratio.

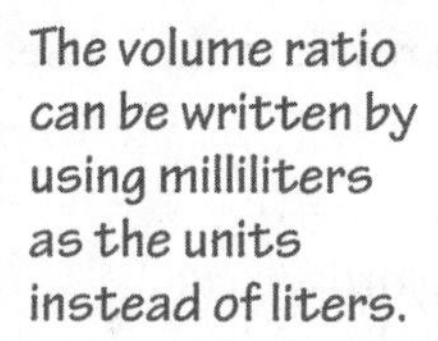

$$20.4\ \cancel{mL\ SO_3} \times \frac{1\ mL\ O_2}{2\ \cancel{mL\ SO_3}} = 10.2\ mL\ O_2$$

The volume ratio can be written by using milliliters as the units instead of liters.

3 Evaluate Does the result make sense?

The volume ratio is two volumes of SO_3 to one volume of O_2. So, the volume of O_2 should be half the volume of SO_3. The answer should have three significant figures.

Practice Problems

Use this chemical equation to answer the problems below:

$$CS_2(l) + 3O_2(g) \longrightarrow CO_2(g) + 2SO_2(g)$$

22. Calculate the volume of sulfur dioxide, in milliliters, produced when 27.9 mL O_2 reacts with carbon disulfide.

1 Analyze **List the knowns and the unknown.**

2 Calculate **Solve for the unknown.**

3 Evaluate **Does the result make sense?**

KNOWNS	UNKNOWN
volume of oxygen = 27.9 mL	volume of sulfur dioxide = ? mL SO_2
volume ratio from balanced equation = 2 mL SO_2/3 mL O_2	

23. Use the equation in Problem 22 to determine how many liters of carbon dioxide are produced when 42 L SO_2 are formed?

KNOWNS	UNKNOWN
volume of sulfur dioxide =	volume of carbon dioxide = ? L CO_2
volume ratio from balanced equation =	

24. Challenge Use the equation in Problem 22 to determine how many deciliters of carbon dioxide are produced when 0.38 L SO_2 is formed?

12.2 LessonCheck

Key Concept Check

25. Explain How are mole ratios used in chemical calculations?

26. Sequence Outline the sequence of steps needed to solve a typical stoichiometric problem.

Think Critically

27. Calculate The combustion of acetylene gas is represented by this equation:

$$2C_2H_2(g) + 5O_2(g) \longrightarrow 4CO_2(g) + 2H_2O(g)$$

a. How many moles of H_2O are produced when 64.0 g C_2H_2 burn in oxygen?

b. How many grams of CO_2 and grams of H_2O are produced when 52.0 g C_2H_2 burn in oxygen?

28. Apply Concepts Write the 12 mole ratios for this equation for the combustion of isopropyl alcohol:

$$2C_3H_7OH(l) + 9O_2(g) \longrightarrow 6CO_2(g) + 8H_2O(g)$$

CHEMISTRY & YOU

29. How do you think air bag manufacturers know how to get the right amount of gas in an inflated air bag? (Hint: See page 369.)

BIGIDEA
THE MOLE AND QUANTIFYING MATTER

30. Use what you have learned about stoichiometric calculations to explain the following statement: Stoichiometric calculations are not possible without a balanced chemical equation.

12.3 Limiting Reagent and Percent Yield

CHEMISTRY & YOU

Q: What determines how much product you can make? A carpenter could not build two four-legged tables with only two tabletops and seven table legs. The first table would require four of the legs. Only three legs would be left for the second table. In this case, the number of table legs limits the number of four-legged tables that can be made. In this lesson, you will learn how the amount of product is limited in a chemical reaction.

Key Questions

How is the amount of product in a reaction affected by an insufficient quantity of any of the reactants?

What does the percent yield of a reaction measure?

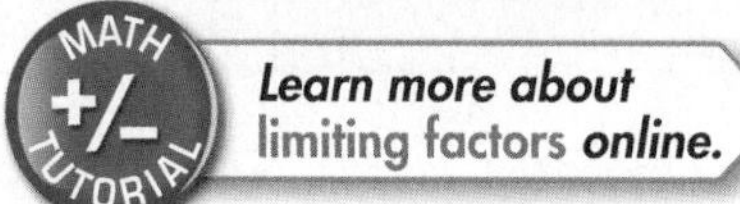

Learn more about limiting factors *online.*

Limiting and Excess Reagents

Many cooks follow a recipe when they make a new dish. They know that they must have enough of all the ingredients in order to follow the recipe. Suppose you want to make tacos like the ones shown below. You have more than enough meat, cheese, lettuce, and salsa. These are excess ingredients. However, you have only two taco shells. The number of taco shells you have will limit the number of tacos you can make. Thus, the taco shells are the limiting ingredient in this meal. A chemist often faces a similar situation. In a chemical reaction, an insufficient quantity of any of the reactants will limit the amount of product that forms.

Limiting Ingredients The amount of product is determined by the amount of the limiting reagent. In this example, the taco shells are the limiting reagent. No matter how much of the other ingredients you have, you can make only two tacos if you have only two taco shells.

Limiting ingredient
- taco shells

Excess ingredients
- salsa
- lettuce
- ground beef
- cheese

Identifying Limiting Reagents A balanced chemical equation is a chemist's recipe. You can interpret the recipe in terms of individual particles or in terms of moles. The coefficients used to write the balanced equation give the ratio of representative particles and the mole ratio. The figure below shows how to interpret the equation for the synthesis of ammonia in terms of molecules and moles. Notice that this "recipe" calls for three molecules of H_2 for every one molecule of N_2.

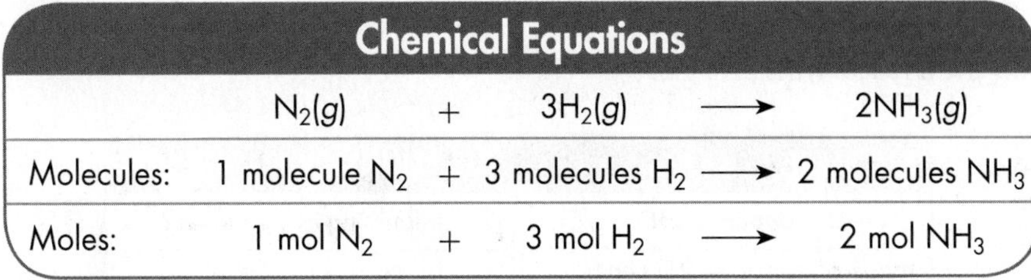

Chemical Equations

	$N_2(g)$	+	$3H_2(g)$	⟶	$2NH_3(g)$
Molecules:	1 molecule N_2	+	3 molecules H_2	⟶	2 molecules NH_3
Moles:	1 mol N_2	+	3 mol H_2	⟶	2 mol NH_3

Two molecules of NH_3 are produced when one molecule of N_2 reacts with three molecules of H_2. What would happen if two molecules of N_2 reacted with three molecules of H_2? Would more than two molecules of NH_3 be formed? The figure below shows the molecules that are present before and after the reaction.

Experimental Conditions

	Reactants		Products
Before reaction	2 molecules N_2	3 molecules H_2	0 molecules NH_3
After reaction	1 molecule N_2	0 molecules H_2	2 molecules NH_3

Before the reaction takes place, nitrogen and hydrogen are present in a 2:3 molecule ratio. The molecule ratio is the same as the mole ratio. The reaction follows the balanced equation. One molecule of N_2 reacts with three molecules of H_2 to produce two molecules of NH_3. At this point, the reaction stops because all the hydrogen has been used up. One molecule of unreacted nitrogen is left, along with the two molecules of NH_3 that have been produced.

In this reaction, only the hydrogen is completely used up. Hydrogen is the limiting reagent. The **limiting reagent** is the reactant that determines the amount of product that can be formed by a reaction. The reaction stops when the limiting reagent is used up. The reactant that is not completely used up in a reaction is called the **excess reagent.** In this example, some nitrogen is left over. Nitrogen is the excess reagent.

BUILD Vocabulary

limiting reagent the reactant that determines the amount of product that forms

excess reagent the reactant that is not completely used up

RELATED WORDS

You have probably heard the word *excessive*. Excessive is used to describe things that go beyond what is normal. You can think of excess reagents as being present in amounts beyond what is used. The limiting reagent limits the amounts of product formed because it runs out first.

See limiting reagents **animated online.**

CHEMISTRY TUTORIAL

Sample Problem 12.7

Determining the Limiting Reagent in a Reaction

The balanced equation for the reaction of copper with sulfur to form copper(I) sulfide is:

$$2Cu(s) + S(s) \longrightarrow Cu_2S(s)$$

What is the limiting reagent when 80.0 g Cu reacts with 25.0 g S?

1 Analyze List the knowns and the unknown. The mole ratio is derived from the balanced equation.

KNOWNS	UNKNOWN
mass of copper = 80.0 g Cu	limiting reagent = ?
mass of sulfur = 25.0 g S	
mole ratio = 1 mol S/2 mol Cu	

2 Calculate Solve for the unknown. Find the number of moles of each reactant first. Then use the balanced equation to calculate the number of moles of one reactant needed to react with the given amount of the other reactant.

Use the molar mass to convert from mass to moles for one of the reactants.

$$80.0\ \text{g Cu} \times \frac{1\ \text{mol Cu}}{63.5\ \text{g Cu}} = 1.26\ \text{mol Cu}$$

Then, convert the mass of the other reactant to moles.

$$25.0\ \text{g S} \times \frac{1\ \text{mol S}}{32.1\ \text{g S}} = 0.779\ \text{mol S}$$

Now use the mole ratio to find the number of moles of S needed to react with 1.26 moles of Cu.

$$\underset{\text{Given quantity}}{1.26\ \text{mol Cu}} \times \underset{\text{Mole ratio}}{\frac{1\ \text{mol S}}{2\ \text{mol Cu}}} = \underset{\text{Needed amount}}{0.630\ \text{mol S}}$$

Compare the amount of sulfur needed with the given amount of sulfur.

0.630 mol S (amount needed to react) < 0.779 mol S (given amount)

Identify the limiting reagent.

There is more sulfur than needed. Copper is the limiting reagent.

Hint: It does not matter which reactant you use. You could use the actual number of moles of S to find the amount of Cu needed. You would still find that Cu is the limiting reagent.

3 Evaluate Does the result make sense? The ratio of the given moles of Cu to moles of S was less than the mole ratio (2:1) from the balanced equation. So, copper should be the limiting reagent.

BUILD Math Skills

Significant Figures and Moles The number of moles of a substance is an exact quantity. Exact quantities have an unlimited number of significant figures. You should ignore exact quantities when determining the number of significant figures in your final answer. Take a look at this example:

$$32\ g\ Cu \times \frac{1\ mol\ Cu}{63.5\ g\ Cu} = 0.50\ mol\ Cu$$

This is a multiplication and division calculation. Its answer has only as many significant figures as the number in the calculation with the fewest significant figures. We do not use the 1 in the numerator of the molar mass to determine significant figures because 1 mol Cu is an exact quantity. So the number with the fewest significant figures is 32 g Cu. Thus, the answer has only two significant figures.

Go to your Chemistry Skills and Math Workbook for more practice.

Practice Problems

31. The equation for the complete combustion of ethene (C_2H_4) is:

$$C_2H_4(g) + 3O_2(g) \longrightarrow 2CO_2(g) + 2H_2O(g)$$

Identify the limiting reagent when 2.70 mol C_2H_4 reacts with 6.30 mol O_2.

❶ Analyze List the knowns and the unknown.

❷ Calculate Solve for the unknown.

❸ Evaluate Does the result make sense?

KNOWNS	UNKNOWN
moles of ethene = 2.70 mol C_2H_4	limiting reagent = ?
moles of oxygen = 6.30 mol O_2	
mole ratio from balanced equation = 1 mol C_2H_4/3 mol O_2	

32. Hydrogen gas can be produced by the reaction of magnesium metal with hydrochloric acid:

$$Mg(s) + 2HCl(aq) \longrightarrow MgCl_2(aq) + H_2(g)$$

Identify the limiting reagent when 6.00 g HCl reacts with 5.00 g Mg.

KNOWNS	UNKNOWN
mass of hydrochloric acid =	limiting reagent = ?
mass of magnesium =	
mole ratio from balanced equation =	

Hint: For Problem 32, make sure you convert mass to moles. The reactant with the smallest mass or volume is not always the limiting reactant.

33. The equation for the reaction of phosphoric acid with sodium hydroxide is:

$$H_3PO_4(aq) + 3NaOH(aq) \longrightarrow Na_3PO_4(aq) + 3H_2O(l)$$

Identify the limiting reagent when 1.75 mol H_3PO_4 reacts with 5.00 mol NaOH.

BUILD Connections

Does your car have an excess reagent? Car engines need oxygen to burn gasoline. They also need just the right ratio of oxygen to fuel. Leftover fuel forms pollutants when oxygen is the limiting reagent. Other pollutants form when oxygen is in excess. How did engineers solve this problem? Cars have oxygen sensors that help the engine run efficiently. These sensors control the amount of oxygen that mixes with fuel.

Finding the Amount of a Product A reaction stops once the limiting reagent is used up. No more products are made. So, the limiting reagent determines the amount of product that is formed. You may have noticed that the mass of copper used in the reaction in Sample Problem 12.7 was greater than the mass of sulfur. However, copper was the limiting reagent. The reactant that is present in the smaller amount by mass or volume is not necessarily the limiting reagent. You must first convert the amount of each reactant to moles if the amounts are given in other units, such as grams. Then use mole ratios to determine the limiting reagent and the amount of product formed. You may also have to convert moles of product into another unit for some problems.

Key Question How is the amount of product in a reaction affected by an insufficient quantity of any of the reactants? **In a chemical reaction, an insufficient quantity of any of the reactants will limit the amount of product that forms.**

Quick Lab

Purpose To illustrate the concept of a limiting reagent in a chemical reaction

Materials

- **graduated cylinder**
- **balance**
- **three 250 mL Erlenmeyer flasks**
- **three rubber balloons**
- **4.2 g magnesium ribbon**
- **300 mL 1.0*M* hydrochloric acid**

Limiting Reagents

Procedure

1. Add 100 mL of the hydrochloric acid solution to each flask.

2. Weigh out 0.6 g, 1.2 g, and 2.4 g of magnesium ribbon. Place each sample into its own balloon.

3. Stretch the end of each balloon over the mouth of each flask. Do not allow the magnesium ribbon in the balloon to fall into the flask.

4. Magnesium reacts with hydrochloric acid to form hydrogen gas. You will generate a certain volume of hydrogen gas when you mix the magnesium with the hydrochloric acid in Step 5. How do you think the volume of hydrogen produced in each flask will compare?

5. Lift up on each balloon and shake the magnesium into each flask. Observe the volume of gas produced until the reaction in each flask is completed. Record your observations.

Analyze and Conclude

1. Analyze Data Based on the size of the balloons, how did the volumes of hydrogen gas produced compare? Did the results agree with your prediction?

2. Apply Concepts Write a balanced equation for the reaction you observed.

3. Calculate The 100 mL of hydrochloric acid contained 0.10 mol HCl. Show by calculation why the balloon with 1.2 g Mg inflated to about twice the size of the balloon with 0.60 g Mg.

4. Calculate Show by calculation why the balloons with 1.2 g and 2.4 g Mg inflated to approximately the same volume. What was the limiting reagent when 2.4 g Mg was added to the acid?

Sample Problem 12.8

Using a Limiting Reagent to Find the Quantity of a Product

What is the maximum number of grams of Cu_2S that can be formed when 80.0 g Cu reacts with 25.0 g S?

$$2Cu(s) + S(s) \longrightarrow Cu_2S(s)$$

❶ Analyze List the knowns and the unknown. Note that the mole ratio is derived from the balanced equation.

KNOWNS	UNKNOWN
limiting reagent = 1.26 mol Cu	yield = ? g Cu_2S
molar mass Cu_2S = 159.1 g Cu_2S/ 1 mol Cu_2S	
mole ratio from balanced equation =1 mol Cu_2S /2 mol Cu	

❷ Calculate Solve for the unknown.

Identify the limiting reagent. → The limiting reagent was determined in Sample Problem 12.7. It is Cu.

Determine the steps needed to find the product in grams. → mol Cu $\longrightarrow$ mol Cu_2S $\longrightarrow$ g Cu_2S

Use the mole ratio to convert the moles of the limiting reagent to moles of the product. → $1.26\ \cancel{\text{mol Cu}} \times \frac{1\ \text{mol } Cu_2S}{2\ \cancel{\text{mol Cu}}}$

Hint: The quanity of each reactant is the same as in Sample Problem 12.7. So, you already know that 80.0 g of Cu is equal to 1.26 mol of Cu.

Use the molar mass to convert from moles of the product to mass of the product. → $1.26\ \cancel{\text{mol Cu}} \times \frac{1\ \cancel{\text{mol } Cu_2S}}{2\ \cancel{\text{mol Cu}}} \times \frac{159.1\ \text{g } Cu_2S}{1\ \cancel{\text{mol } Cu_2S}}$

$= 1.00 \times 10^2\ \text{g } Cu_2S$

❸ Evaluate Does the result make sense? Copper is the limiting reagent in this reaction. Copper is combining with sulfur to form Cu_2S. So, the maximum number of grams of Cu_2S produced should be more than the mass of copper that initially reacted. However, the mass of Cu_2S produced should be less than the total mass of the reactants (105.0 g) because sulfur was in excess.

BUILD Math Skills

Calculations With Fractions You should be familiar with how to enter fractions on your calculator. However, you can save time by knowing how to work with fractions that contain a 1. Look at the example below. A fraction with a 1 in the denominator is equal to the number in the numerator.

$$2.5 \times \frac{20}{1} = 2.5 \times 20 = 50$$

But when the 1 is in the numerator of the fraction, divide by the number in the denominator.

$$50 \times \frac{1}{5} = \frac{50}{5} = 10$$

Practice Problems

34. This equation shows the incomplete combustion of ethene:

$$C_2H_4(g) + 2O_2(g) \longrightarrow 2CO(g) + 2H_2O(g)$$

In a reaction, 2.70 mol C_2H_4 reacts with 6.30 mol O_2.

a. Identify the limiting reagent.

b. Calculate the moles of water produced.

1 Analyze **List the knowns and the unknowns.**

2 Calculate **Solve for the unknowns.**

3 Evaluate **Do the results make sense?**

KNOWNS	UNKNOWNS
moles of C_2H_4 = 2.70 mol C_2H_4	limiting reagent = ?
moles of O_2 = 6.30 mol O_2	yield of H_2O = ? mol H_2O
mole ratio from balanced equation = 1 mol C_2H_4 / 2 mol O_2	

35. The heat from an acetylene torch is produced by burning acetylene (C_2H_2) in oxygen:

$$2C_2H_2(g) + 5O_2(g) \longrightarrow 4CO_2(g) + 2H_2O(g)$$

How many grams of water can be produced by the reaction of 2.40 mol C_2H_2 with 7.40 mol O_2?

KNOWNS	UNKNOWNS
moles of C_2H_2 =	limiting reagent = ?
moles of O_2 =	yield of H_2O = ? g H_2O
mole ratio from balanced equation =	

36. Challenge Silicon dioxide reacts with carbon to form silicon carbide and carbon monoxide.

$$SiO_2(s) + 3C(s) \xrightarrow{\Delta} SiC(s) + 2CO(g)$$

How many grams of CO gas are made by the reaction of 50.0 g SiO_2 with 40.0 g C?

Percent Yield

Does every student in your class get a grade of 100% when your teacher gives a test to the class? They could, but this probably never happens. Instead, there is a range of grades in the class. Your test grade is a ratio. The numerator of the ratio is the number of questions you answered correctly. The denominator is the total number of questions. The ratio is often expressed as a percentage. The grade compares how well you performed with how well you could have performed. If you missed one or more questions, then your grade would be less than 100%. Chemists use similar ratios when the amount of product from a chemical reaction is less than expected.

Calculating Percent Yield Chemists use balanced chemical equations to calculate the amount of product that can form during a reaction. This calculated amount is the theoretical yield. The **theoretical yield** is the maximum amount of product that could be formed from given amounts of reactants. The **actual yield** is the amount of product that is actually formed during the reaction in the laboratory. Chemists measure this amount after the reaction is completed. The **percent yield** is the ratio of the actual yield to the theoretical yield expressed as a percent.

$$\text{Percent yield} = \frac{\text{actual yield}}{\text{theoretical yield}} \times 100\%$$

The actual yield of a chemical reaction is usually less than the theoretical yield. So, the percent yield is often less than 100%. The percent yield is a measure of the efficiency of a reaction carried out in the laboratory. This yield is similar to an exam score measuring your efficiency of learning. It is also similar to a batting average measuring your efficiency of hitting a baseball or softball. Baseball and softball players, like the one shown in the figure below, have a batting average. The batting average is the number of hits a player makes divided by the number of times the player is at bat.

Stoichiometry and conservation of mass tell us that percent yields of greater than 100% are not possible. However, errors and lack of knowledge can result in a yield that appears to be greater than 100%. Suppose oxygen is a reactant in a reaction. More product may be formed than expected if air leaks into a system.

Batting Average A batting average is similar to a percent yield. A batting average is calculated by dividing the number of hits a batter has had (actual yield) by the number of times she bats (theoretical yield).

BUILD Vocabulary

theoretical yield the maximum amount of product that could be formed from given amounts of reactants

actual yield the amount of product that actually forms by a reaction

percent yield the ratio of the actual yield to the theoretical yield expressed as a percent

ACADEMIC WORDS

You might think of the word *yield* as meaning "to give up." In chemistry, *yield* is used as a noun that means "the amount of product." Theoretical yield is calculated by using stoichiometry.

Sample Problem 12.9

Calculating the Theoretical Yield of a Reaction

Calcium carbonate decomposes when heated. The balanced equation for this reaction is:

$$CaCO_3(s) \xrightarrow{\Delta} CaO(s) + CO_2(g)$$

What is the theoretical yield of CaO if 24.8 g $CaCO_3$ is heated?

1 Analyze List the knowns and the unknown. The mole ratio is derived from the balanced equation.

KNOWNS	UNKNOWN
mass of calcium carbonate = 24.8 g $CaCO_3$	theoretical yield = ? g CaO
mole ratio = 1 mol CaO/1 mol $CaCO_3$	

2 Calculate Solve for the unknown. Calculate the theoretical yield by using the mass of the reactant.

Identify the steps needed to find the mass of product in grams.

$$\text{g } CaCO_3 \longrightarrow \text{mol } CaCO_3 \longrightarrow \text{mol CaO} \longrightarrow \text{g CaO}$$

Use the molar mass to convert the mass of the reactant to moles of the reactant.

$$24.8 \text{ g } CaCO_3 \times \frac{1 \text{ mol } CaCO_3}{100.1 \text{ g } CaCO_3}$$

Next, use the correct mole ratio to convert to moles of the product.

$$24.8 \text{ g } CaCO_3 \times \frac{1 \text{ mol } CaCO_3}{100.1 \text{ g } CaCO_3} \times \frac{1 \text{ mol CaO}}{1 \text{ mol } CaCO_3}$$

Use the molar mass of the product to convert from moles to mass of the product.

$$24.8 \text{ g } CaCO_3 \times \frac{1 \text{ mol } CaCO_3}{100.1 \text{ g } CaCO_3} \times \frac{1 \text{ mol CaO}}{1 \text{ mol } CaCO_3} \times \frac{56.1 \text{ g CaO}}{1 \text{ mol CaO}}$$

$$= 13.9 \text{ g CaO}$$

3 Evaluate Does the result make sense? The mole ratio of CaO to $CaCO_3$ is 1:1. The ratio of their masses in the reaction should be the same as the ratio of their molar masses, which is slightly greater than 1:2. The resulting mass of CaO is slightly greater than half the mass of $CaCO_3$.

BUILD Math Skills

Percents Percents are ratios multiplied by 100. For example, suppose you answer 4 out of 5 questions correct. You can write the ratio as $\frac{4}{5}$. This ratio is equal to 0.80. Find the percent by multiplying by 100.

$$0.80 \times 100\% = 80\%$$

So, $\frac{4}{5}$, 0.80, and 80% are all different ways to express the same value.

Go to your Chemistry Skills and Math Workbook for more practice.

Practice Problems

Hint: If there is an excess of a reactant, then there is more than enough of that reactant. It will not limit the yield of the reaction.

37. When 84.8 g of iron(III) oxide reacts with an excess of carbon monoxide, iron is produced:

$$Fe_2O_3(s) + 3CO(g) \longrightarrow 2Fe(s) + 3CO_2(g)$$

What is the theoretical yield of iron?

1 Analyze List the knowns and the unknown.

2 Calculate Solve for the unknown.

3 Evaluate Does the result make sense?

KNOWNS	UNKNOWN
mass of iron(III) oxide = 84.8 g Fe_2O_3	theoretical yield of iron = ? g Fe
mole ratio from balanced equation = 2 mol Fe/1 mol Fe_2O_3	

38. What is the theoretical yield of Cu_2S when 20.0 g Cu reacts with excess S?

$$2Cu(s) + S(s) \longrightarrow Cu_2S(s)$$

KNOWNS	UNKNOWN
mass of copper =	theoretical yield of Cu_2S = ? g Cu_2S
mole ratio from balanced equation =	

39. Silicon carbide is produced when silicon dioxide reacts with carbon:

$$SiO_2(s) + 3C(s) \xrightarrow{\Delta} SiC(s) + 2CO(g)$$

What is the theoretical yield when 62.4 g C reacts with 73.1 g SiO_2?

40. Challenge When 5.00 g of copper reacts with excess silver nitrate, silver metal and copper(II) nitrate are produced. What is the theoretical yield of silver in this reaction?

Hint: Write a balanced equation for the reaction of copper and silver nitrate before starting your calculations.

Flowchart Create a flowchart that shows the steps needed to determine percent yield.

Determining Percent Yield You can calculate the theoretical yield before you carry out a reaction. However, an actual yield is an experimental value that must be measured. The figure below shows a typical laboratory procedure for determining the actual yield of a product of a decomposition reaction.

Once you have determined the actual yield for a reaction, you can calculate the percent yield. This calculated value can be used to predict the actual yield that will form if the reaction is repeated under the same conditions.

Factors That Affect Percent Yield Many factors can cause percent yields to be less than 100%. Reactions do not always go to completion. A reaction that is incomplete produces less than the calculated amount of product. Impure reactants and competing side reactions may cause unwanted products to form. Laboratory procedures also affect percent yield. Products may also be lost during filtration or when transferring materials between containers. A percent yield of 100% is also unlikely if reactants or products have not been carefully measured.

Key Question What does the percent yield of a reaction measure? **The percent yield is a measure of the efficiency of a reaction carried out in the laboratory.**

Determining Percent Yield
Sodium hydrogen carbonate ($NaHCO_3$) will decompose when heated.

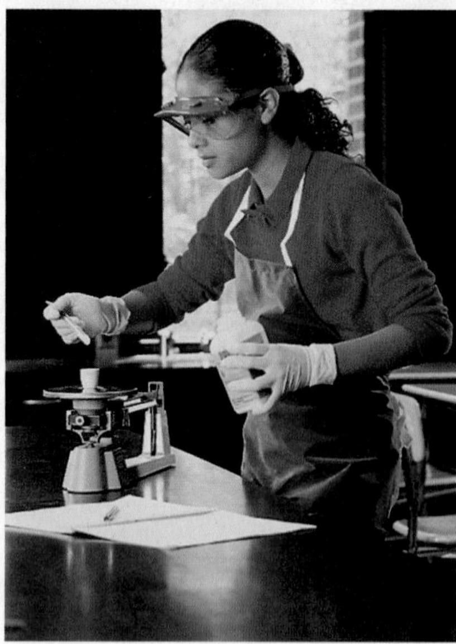

❶ The mass of $NaHCO_3$, the reactant, is measured.

❷ The reactant is heated. $NaHCO_3$ decomposes to yield sodium carbonate (Na_2CO_3).

❸ The mass of Na_2CO_3 is measured. The percent yield is calculated once the actual yield is determined.

Success Stats

You may not use the term *percent yield* outside of chemistry class. However, there are many examples of percent yield in your life. In chemistry, percent yield refers to the amount of product formed in a reaction compared to how much product was possible. In school, percent yield could refer to the graduation rate or a score on a test. In sports, percent yield could refer to the percentage of shots that make it into a goal. The actual performance of a product compared to its advertised performance is also an example of percent yield.

Percent yield is a way to measure how successfully something or someone has performed. The next time you calculate the percent yield of a chemical reaction, think about how this skill could be used in other situations outside of chemistry class.

85% PERFORMANCE

Actual Yield: 153 minutes during which a drink stayed hot in thermos

Theoretical Yield: 180 minutes, as advertised by the thermos manufacturer

Take It Further

1. Calculate Sara's car is advertised to get 43 miles per gallon. Sara calculated her gas mileage over the last month. It was 39 miles per gallon. What is the percent yield of Sara's gas mileage?

2. Identify The percent yield of a reaction may be different each time the reaction occurs. Similarly, the performance of an athlete may vary. What are some factors that might affect percent yield?

38% SHOT-CONVERSION RATE

Actual Yield: 8 goals scored

Theoretical Yield: 21 shots on goal

95% GRADUATION RATE

Actual Yield: 305 students graduate

Theoretical Yield: 321 students in the senior class

SampleProblem 12.10

Calculating the Percent Yield of a Reaction

What is the percent yield if 13.1 g CaO is actually produced when 24.8 g $CaCO_3$ is heated?

$$CaCO_3(s) \xrightarrow{\Delta} CaO(s) + CO_2(g)$$

The theoretical yield of CaO was calculated in Sample Problem 12.9.

❶ Analyze List the knowns and the unknown.

KNOWNS	UNKNOWN
actual yield = 13.1 g CaO	percent yield = ?%
theoretical yield = 13.9 g CaO	

❷ Calculate Solve for the unknown. Use the equation for percent yield.

Write the equation for percent yield.

$$\text{percent yield} = \frac{\text{actual yield}}{\text{theoretical yield}} \times 100\%$$

Substitute the values for actual yield and theoretical yield into the equation for percent yield.

$$\text{percent yield} = \frac{13.1\ \cancel{g\,CaO}}{13.9\ \cancel{g\,CaO}} \times 100\%$$

Solve the equation.

$$\text{percent yield} = 94.2\%$$

❸ Evaluate Does the result make sense? In this example, the actual yield is slightly less than the theoretical yield. Therefore, the percent yield should be slightly less than 100%.

Practice Problems

41. If 50.0 g of silicon dioxide is heated with an excess of carbon, 27.9 g of silicon carbide is produced.

$$SiO_2(s) + 3C(s) \xrightarrow{\Delta} SiC(s) + 2CO(g)$$

What is the percent yield of this reaction?

Hint: Calculate the theoretical yield first. Then you can calculate the percent yield.

❶ Analyze List the knowns and the unknowns.

❷ Calculate Solve for the unknowns.

❸ Evaluate Do the results make sense?

KNOWNS	UNKNOWNS
actual yield = 27.9 g SiC	theoretical yield = ? g SiC
mass of SiO_2 = 50.0 g SiO_2	percent yield = ?%

42. Use the chemical equation in Problem 41. When 50.0 g of silicon dioxide is heated with an excess of carbon, 32.2 g of silicon carbide is produced. What is the percent yield of this reaction?

KNOWNS	UNKNOWNS
actual yield =	theoretical yield = ? g SiC
mass of SiO_2 =	percent yield = ?%

43. When 202 g of iron(III) oxide reacts with 186 g of carbon monoxide, 118 g of iron is produced:

$$Fe_2O_3(s) + 3CO(g) \longrightarrow 2Fe(s) + 3CO_2(g)$$

What is the percent yield of iron?

44. Challenge If 15.0 g of nitrogen reacts with 15.0 g of hydrogen, 10.5 g of ammonia is produced. What is the percent yield of this reaction?

12.3 LessonCheck

Key Concept Check

45. Relate Cause and Effect In a chemical reaction, how is the amount of product formed affected by having an insufficient quantity of one of the reactants?

46. Explain How can you gauge the efficiency of a reaction carried out in the laboratory?

Vocabulary Check

Choose a highlighted term from the lesson to complete each sentence correctly.

47. The __________ is the calculated amount of product that could be produced by a reaction.

48. The reactant that is left over after the reaction is the __________.

Think Critically

49. Calculate How many grams of SO_3 are produced when 20.0 g FeS_2 reacts with 16.0 g O_2 according to this balanced equation?

$$4FeS_2(s) + 15O_2(g) \longrightarrow 2Fe_2O_3(s) + 8SO_3(g)$$

50. Calculate What is the percent yield if 4.65 g of copper is produced when 1.87 g of aluminum reacts with an excess of copper(II) sulfate?

$$2Al(s) + 3CuSO_4(aq) \longrightarrow Al_2(SO_4)_3(aq) + 3Cu(s)$$

51. What determines how much product you can make in a chemical reaction? (Hint: See page 375.)

12 Study Guide

BIGIDEAS
THE MOLE; REACTIONS

Balanced chemical equations are the basis for stoichiometric calculations. The coefficients of a balanced equation indicate the number of particles, moles, or volumes of gas in the reaction. Mole ratios from the balanced equation are used to calculate the amount of a reactant or product in a chemical reaction from a given amount of one of the reactants or products.

12.1 The Arithmetic of Equations

Chemists use balanced chemical equations to calculate how much reactant is needed or product is formed in a reaction.

A balanced chemical equation can be interpreted in terms of numbers of atoms, numbers of molecules, numbers of moles, mass, and volume.

- stoichiometry (354)

12.2 Chemical Calculations

In chemical calculations, mole ratios are used to convert between a given number of moles of a reactant or product to moles of a different reactant or product.

In a typical stoichiometric problem, the given quantity is first converted to moles. Then, the mole ratio from the balanced equation is used to calculate the number of moles of the wanted substance. Finally, the moles are converted to any other unit of measurement related to the unit mole, as the problem requires.

- mole ratio (360)

Key Equation

mole-mole relationship for $aG \rightarrow bW$:

$$x \text{ mol } G \times \frac{b \text{ mol } W}{a \text{ mol } G} = \frac{xb}{a} \text{ mol } W$$

12.3 Limiting Reagent and Percent Yield

In a chemical reaction, an insufficient quantity of any of the reactants will limit the amount of product that forms.

The percent yield is a measure of the efficiency of a reaction performed in the laboratory.

- limiting reagent (375)
- excess reagent (375)
- theoretical yield (381)
- actual yield (381)
- percent yield (381)

Key Equation

$$\text{percent yield} = \frac{\text{actual yield}}{\text{theoretical yield}} \times 100\%$$

Math Tune-Up: Stoichiometry Problems

Problem

Iron metal (Fe) can be obtained from iron ore (Fe_2O_3).

$$Fe_2O_3(s) + 3CO(g) \longrightarrow 2Fe(s) + 3CO_2(g)$$

How much iron ore is needed to obtain 92.8 grams of iron metal?

Sodium hydroxide reacts with carbon dioxide according to the balanced equation below.

$$2NaOH(s) + CO_2(g) \longrightarrow Na_2CO_3(s) + H_2O(l)$$

What is the limiting reagent when 3.50 mol NaOH reacts with 2.00 mol CO_2?

1 Analyze

Knowns:
mass of iron = 92.8 g Fe
mole ratio from balanced equation =
1 mol Fe_2O_3/2 mol Fe
molar mass of iron = 55.8 g Fe/1 mol Fe
molar mass of iron ore = 159.6 g Fe_2O_3/1 mol Fe_2O_3

Unknown:
Mass of iron ore = ? g Fe_2O_3

Knowns:
moles of NaOH = 3.50 mol NaOH
moles of CO_2 = 2.00 mol CO_2

Unknown:
limiting reagent = ?

2 Calculate

Perform the following steps:
g Fe ⟶ mol Fe ⟶ mol Fe_2O_3 ⟶ g Fe_2O_3

$$92.8\ \cancel{g\ Fe} \times \frac{1\ \cancel{mol\ Fe}}{55.8\ \cancel{g\ Fe}} \times \frac{1\ \cancel{mol\ Fe_2O_3}}{2\ \cancel{mol\ Fe}} \times \frac{159.6\ g\ 1\ mol\ Fe_2O_3}{1\ \cancel{mol\ Fe_2O_3}}$$

$$= 133\ g\ Fe_2O_3$$

Hint: Review Sample Problem 12.3 if you have trouble with calculating the mass of a reactant.

Determine how many moles of CO_2 are needed to react with 3.50 mol NaOH.

$$3.50\ \cancel{mol\ NaOH} \times \frac{1\ mol\ CO_2}{2\ \cancel{mol\ NaOH}}$$

$$= 1.75\ mol\ CO_2$$

Only 1.75 mol CO_2 are needed to react with 3.50 mol NaOH. Because there are 2.00 mol CO_2, there is excess CO_2. Therefore, NaOH is the limiting reagent.

3 Evaluate

The molar mass of the iron ore is more than twice the molar mass of iron metal. So, it makes sense that the mass of the iron ore would be greater than the mass of the iron metal produced.

Check your work. You could start with the given amount of moles of CO_2 and solve for how many moles of NaOH are needed.

Hint: Review Sample Problem 12.7 if you have trouble identifying the limiting reagent.

12 Assessment

∗ Solutions appear in Appendix D.

Lesson by Lesson

12.1 The Arithmetic of Equations

52. Interpret each chemical equation in terms of interacting particles.

a. $2KClO_3(s) \longrightarrow 2KCl(s) + 3O_2(g)$
b. $4NH_3(g) + 6NO(g) \longrightarrow 5N_2(g) + 6H_2O(g)$
c. $4K(s) + O_2(g) \longrightarrow 2K_2O(s)$

53. Interpret each equation in Problem 52 in terms of interacting numbers of moles of reactants and products.

54. Calculate and compare the mass of the reactants with the mass of the products for each equation in Problem 52. Show that each balanced equation obeys the law of conservation of mass.

55. Balance this equation:

$$C_5H_{12}(g) + O_2(g) \longrightarrow CO_2(g) + H_2O(g)$$

Interpret the balanced equation in terms of the relative numbers of moles, volumes of gas at STP, and masses of reactants and products.

12.2 Chemical Calculations

56. Explain the term *mole ratio* in your own words. When would you use this term?

57. What ratio is used to carry out each conversion?

a. mol CH_4 to g CH_4
b. L $CH_4(g)$ to mol $CH_4(g)$ (at STP)
c. molecules CH_4 to mol CH_4

∗58. Carbon disulfide is an important industrial solvent. It is prepared by the reaction of coke (carbon) with sulfur dioxide:

$$5C(s) + 2SO_2(g) \longrightarrow CS_2(l) + 4CO(g)$$

a. How many moles of CS_2 form when 2.7 mol C reacts?
b. How many moles of carbon are needed to react with 5.44 mol SO_2?

59. What information about a reaction is derived from the coefficients in a balanced equation?

60. Rust is produced when iron reacts with oxygen:

$$4Fe(s) + 3O_2(g) \longrightarrow 2Fe_2O_3(s)$$

How many grams of Fe_2O_3 are produced when 12.0 g of iron rusts?

∗61. Lithium nitride reacts with water to form ammonia and aqueous lithium hydroxide:

$$Li_3N(s) + 3H_2O(l) \longrightarrow NH_3(g) + 3LiOH(aq)$$

a. What mass of water is needed to react with 32.9 g Li_3N?
b. When the above reaction takes place, how many molecules of NH_3 are produced?
c. Calculate the number of grams of Li_3N that must be added to an excess of water to produce 15.0 L NH_3 (at STP).

12.3 Limiting Reagent and Percent Yield

62. What is the significance of the limiting reagent in a reaction? What happens to the amount of any reagent that is present in an excess?

63. How would you identify a limiting reagent in a chemical reaction?

∗64. In a reaction chamber, 3.0 mol of aluminum is mixed with 5.3 mol Cl_2, and they react. This balanced chemical equation describes the reaction:

$$2Al(s) + 3Cl_2(g) \longrightarrow 2AlCl_3(s)$$

a. Identify the limiting reagent for the reaction.
b. Calculate the number of moles of product formed.
c. Calculate the number of moles of excess reagent remaining after the reaction.

∗65. Heating an ore of antimony (Sb_2S_3) in the presence of iron gives the element antimony and iron(II) sulfide:

$$Sb_2S_3(s) + 3Fe(s) \longrightarrow 2Sb(s) + 3FeS(s)$$

When 15.0 g Sb_2S_3 reacts with an excess of Fe, 9.84 g Sb is produced. What is the percent yield of this reaction?

Understand Concepts

66. If 75.0 g of silderite ore ($FeCO_3$) is heated with an excess of oxygen, 45.0 g of ferric oxide (Fe_2O_3) is produced:

$$4FeCO_3(s) + O_2(g) \longrightarrow 2Fe_2O_3(s) + 4CO_2(g)$$

What is the percent yield of this reaction?

★67. Hydrazine (N_2H_4) is used as rocket fuel. It reacts with oxygen to form nitrogen and water:

$$N_2H_4(l) + O_2(g) \longrightarrow N_2(g) + 2H_2O(g)$$

a. How many liters of N_2 (at STP) form when 1.0 kg N_2H_4 reacts with 1.2 kg O_2?
b. How many grams of the excess reagent remain after the reaction?

68. If the reaction below proceeds with a 96.8% yield, how many kilograms of $CaSO_4$ are formed when 5.24 kg SO_2 reacts with an excess of $CaCO_3$ and O_2?

$$2CaCO_3(s) + 2SO_2(g) + O_2(g) \longrightarrow 2CaSO_4(s) + 2CO_2(g)$$

★69. Hydrogen gas can be made by reacting methane (CH_4) with high-temperature steam:

$$CH_4(g) + H_2O(g) \longrightarrow CO(g) + 3H_2(g)$$

How many hydrogen molecules are produced when 158 g of methane reacts with steam?

70. Suppose hydrogen gas and iodine vapor react to give gaseous hydrogen iodide.

a. Write the balanced equation for the reaction.
b. In the atomic window below, which reactant is the limiting reagent?
c. How many molecules of the limiting reagent need to be added to the atomic window so all the reactants will react to form products?

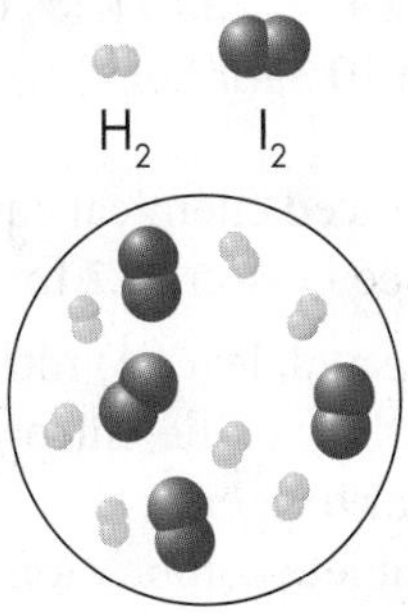

Think Critically

71. Evaluate You have a certain quantity of reactant. You calculate that a particular reaction should produce 55 g of a product. When you perform the reaction, you find you have produced 63 g of product. What is your percent yield? What could have caused a percent yield greater than 100%?

72. Apply Concepts A car gets 9.2 kilometers to a liter of gasoline. How many liters of air will be needed to burn the gasoline for a 1250 km trip? Assume that gasoline is 100% octane (C_8H_{18}) and undergoes complete combustion. The density of octane is 0.69 g/cm^3. Air is 21% oxygen by volume at STP.

★73. Calculate Liquid sulfur difluoride reacts with fluorine gas to form gaseous sulfur hexafluoride.

a. Write the balanced equation for the reaction.
b. How many fluorine molecules are required to react with 5.00 mg of sulfur difluoride?
c. What volume of fluorine gas at STP is required to react completely with 6.66 g of sulfur difluoride?

FOUNDATIONS Wrap-Up

How Many Can You Make?

1. Draw Conclusions At the beginning of this chapter, you used paper clips to build models of molecules. Which type of paper clip was the limiting reagent? Explain.

Concept Check

Now that you've finished studying Chapter 12, answer these questions.

2. What information can you get from a balanced chemical equation?
3. What are the steps for finding the mass of a product if you know the mass of the limiting reagent?
4. Explain whether the reactant with the greatest mass is always the excess reagent.
5. Why would you not expect a reaction you carry out in the lab to have a percent yield greater than 100%?

Write About Science

74. Explain Explain this statement: "Mass and atoms are conserved in every chemical reaction, but moles are not necessarily conserved."

75. Explain Review the "mole road map" that is in Lesson 10.2. Explain how this road map ties into the summary of steps for the stoichiometric problems shown in Lesson 12.2.

76. Explain In an air bag reaction, sodium azide (NaN_3) decomposes to solid sodium and nitrogen gas. The nitrogen gas causes the air bag to inflate. Explain why the quantity of NaN_3 is important to air bag performance in terms of limiting reagents and percent yield.

CHEMYSTERY

Cookie Crumbles

Jack tried to make cookies that were extra sweet by adding more sugar than was in the recipe. What Jack didn't realize is that a recipe is like a balanced chemical equation. The reactants, or ingredients, must be combined in specific ratios to get the desired product.

Jack changed the amount of sugar, but he didn't change any of the other ingredients. Therefore, he changed the ratios of the ingredients. Balanced chemical equations are important in baking and in many other fields.

77. Infer Jack's recipe calls for 2.5 cups of flour and 2 eggs. Jack wants to increase the number of cookies produced from the recipe by 50%. How much flour and eggs will he need?

78. Connect to the BIGIDEA How does Jack's baking experience illustrate the concept of a limiting reagent?

Cumulative Review

79. When comparing ultraviolet and visible electromagnetic radiation, which has
- **a.** a higher frequency?
- **b.** a higher energy?
- **c.** a shorter wavelength?

(See Lesson 5.3 for help.)

80. Write electron dot formulas for the following atoms. (See Lesson 7.1 for help.)
- **a.** Cs
- **b.** Br
- **c.** Ca
- **d.** P

81. Can a compound have both ionic and covalent bonds? Explain your answer. (See Lesson 8.2 for help.)

82. Name each substance. (See Lessons 9.2 and 9.4 for help.)
- **a.** K_2SO_4
- **b.** H_2CO_3

83. Write the formula for each compound. (See Lesson 9.2 for help.)
- **a.** aluminum carbonate
- **b.** potassium sulfide
- **c.** manganese(II) chromate

84. What is the mass, in grams, of a molecule of benzene (C_6H_6)? (See Lesson 10.2 for help.)

85. How many moles do the following have? (See Lesson 10.2 for help.)
- **a.** 47.8 g KNO_3
- **b.** 2.22 L SO_2 (at STP)
- **c.** 2.25×10^{22} molecules PCl_3

★86. What is the molecular formula of oxalic acid, molar mass 90 g/mol? Its percent composition is 26.7% C, 2.2% H, and 71.1% O. (See Lesson 10.3 for help.)

87. Write a balanced chemical equation for each reaction. (See Lesson 11.2 for help.)
- **a.** When heated, lead(II) nitrate decomposes to form lead(II) oxide, nitrogen dioxide, and molecular oxygen.
- **b.** The complete combustion of isopropyl alcohol (C_3H_7OH) produces carbon dioxide and water vapor.

Standardized Test Prep

For help with answering test questions, go to your Chemistry Skills and Math Workbook.

Tips for Success

Anticipate the answer. Use what you know to predict what you think the answer should be. Then, look to see if your answer or one much like it is given as an option.

Select the choice that best answers each question or completes each statement.

1. Nitric acid is formed by the reaction of nitrogen dioxide with water.

$$3NO_2(g) + H_2O(l) \longrightarrow NO(g) + 2HNO_3(aq)$$

How many moles of water are needed to react with 8.4 mol NO_2?

(A) 2.8 mol
(B) 3.0 mol
(C) 8.4 mol
(D) 25 mol

2. Phosphorus trifluoride is formed from its elements:

$$P_4(s) + 6F_2(g) \longrightarrow 4PF_3(g)$$

How many grams of fluorine are needed to react with 6.20 g of phosphorus?

(A) 2.85 g
(B) 5.70 g
(C) 11.4 g
(D) 37.2 g

3. Magnesium nitride is formed in the reaction of magnesium metal with nitrogen gas.

$$3Mg(s) + N_2(g) \longrightarrow Mg_3N_2(s)$$

The reaction of 4.0 mol of nitrogen with 6.0 mol of magnesium produces

(A) 2.0 mol of Mg_3N_2 and no excess N_2.
(B) 2.0 mol of Mg_3N_2 and 2.0 mol of excess N_2.
(C) 4.0 mol of Mg_3N_2 and 1.0 mol of excess Mg.
(D) 6.0 mol of Mg_3N_2 and 3.0 mol of excess N_2.

Use the reaction below to answer Questions 4 and 5.

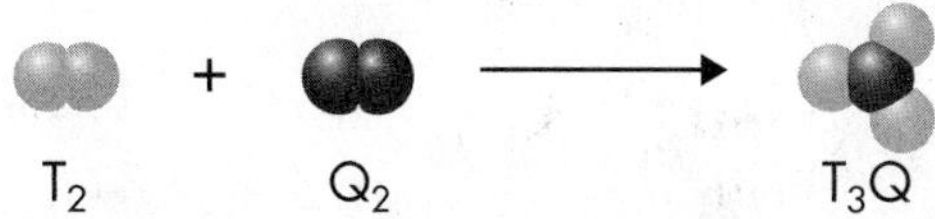

4. Write a balanced equation for the reaction between element T and element Q.

5. Based on the atomic windows below, identify the limiting reagent.

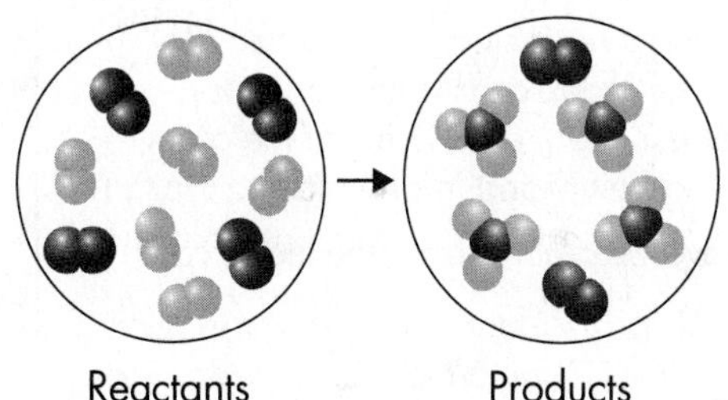

For each question, there are two statements. Decide whether each statement is true or false. Then decide whether Statement II is a correct explanation for Statement I.

	Statement I		Statement II
6.	Every stoichiometry calculation uses a balanced equation.	**BECAUSE**	Every chemical reaction obeys the law of conservation of mass.
7.	A percent yield is always greater than 0% and less than 100%.	**BECAUSE**	The actual yield in a reaction is never more than the theoretical yield.
8.	The amount of the limiting reagent left after a reaction is zero.	**BECAUSE**	The limiting reagent is completely used up in a reaction.
9.	The coefficients in a balanced equation represent the relative masses of the reactants and products.	**BECAUSE**	The mass of the reactants must equal the mass of the products in a chemical reaction.
10.	A mole ratio is always written with the larger number in the numerator.	**BECAUSE**	A mole ratio will always be greater than 1.

If You Have Trouble With . . .

Question	1	2	3	4	5	6	7	8	9	10
See Lesson	12.2	12.2	12.3	12.1	12.3	12.1	12.3	12.3	12.1	12.2

13 States of Matter

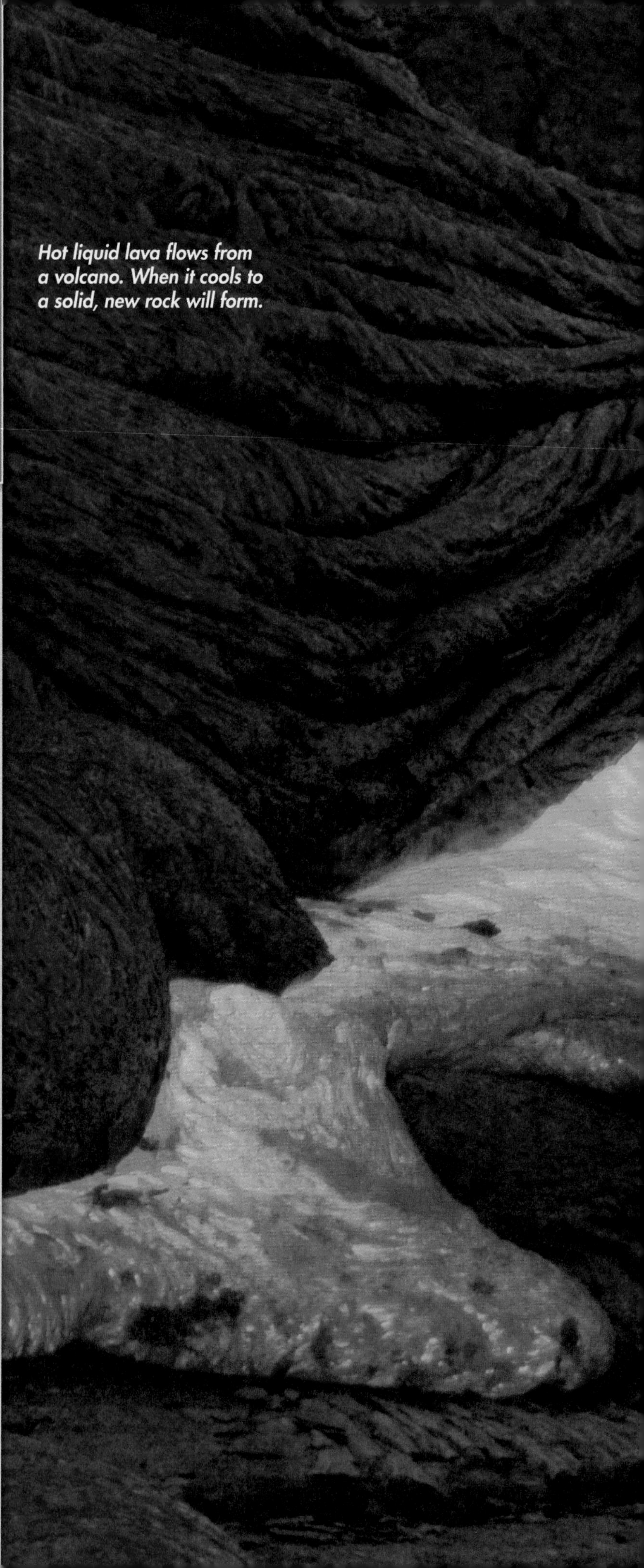

Hot liquid lava flows from a volcano. When it cools to a solid, new rock will form.

FOUNDATIONS for Learning

Observing Gas Pressure

1. Fill a small glass to its rim with water.
2. Place an index card on top of the glass.
3. Working over a sink, use one hand to press the index card firmly to the top of the glass. Then, quickly invert the glass, keeping your hand in one place.
4. Remove your hand from the index card.

Form a Hypothesis Explain why you think the water doesn't fall out of the inverted glass.

PearsonChem.com

Take a video field trip with the Untamed Science crew as they explore the unique properties of fullerenes.

BIGIDEA

KINETIC THEORY

Essential Questions:

1. *What factors determine the physical state of a substance?*
2. *What are the characteristics that distinguish gases, liquids, and solids?*
3. *How do substances change from one state to another?*

CHEMYSTERY

Foggy Car Windows

It's a cold, rainy day in September. You and a friend are going to a movie. When you first get into your mom's car, you can see nearby trees swaying in the wind. Your mom starts the car, and the glass fogs up. You cannot see outside.

Your mom turns on the heat. The heat only makes the foggy windows worse. Then, she turns on the air conditioner. The fog is gone in seconds. Why do car windows fog up when it is cold or raining outside? Why does the fog go away when you turn on the air conditioner?

▶ Connect to the BIGIDEA As you read about states of matter, think about what might cause car windows to fog.

13.1 The Nature of Gases

CHEMISTRY & YOU

Q: What factors most strongly affect the weather? You've probably seen a weather map on TV. A weather map shows areas of high and low pressure. It may also show temperature readings. These data describe a gas—Earth's atmosphere. In this lesson, you will learn how temperature and pressure affect gas particles.

Key Questions

What are the three assumptions of the kinetic theory as it applies to gases?

How does kinetic theory explain gas pressure?

What is the relationship between the temperature in kelvins and the average kinetic energy of particles?

BUILD Vocabulary

kinetic energy the energy an object has because of its motion

kinetic theory the theory that says all matter is made of particles in constant motion

gas pressure pressure that results from the force exerted by a gas on an object

vacuum an empty space with no particles and no pressure

atmospheric pressure pressure that results from collisions of atoms and molecules in air with objects

pascal (Pa) SI unit of pressure

WORD ORIGINS

The word *kinetic* is derived from the Greek word that means "to move." *Kinetic* refers to motion.

Kinetic Theory and a Model for Gases

The word *kinetic* refers to motion. The energy an object has because of its motion is called **kinetic energy**. The **kinetic theory** says that all matter is made of tiny particles that are in constant motion. The particles in a gas are usually molecules or atoms. The kinetic theory makes three assumptions about gases:

1. The particles in a gas are small, hard spheres with an insignificant volume.
2. The motion of gas particles is rapid, constant, and random.
3. All collisions between gas particles are perfectly elastic.

The diagram on the next page illustrates these assumptions.

Particle Size Gas particles are considered to be spheres that are so small that they take up almost no space. In a liquid or solid, the particles are close together. In a gas, though, the particles are far apart and have empty space between them. According to the kinetic theory, no attractive or repulsive forces exist between the particles in a gas.

Particle Motion Gas particles move constantly. They travel in straight-line paths until they collide with other particles or other objects. The particles change direction only when they rebound from a collision. As a result, gases fill their containers. A gas that is not in a container will spread out forever.

Particle Collisions All collisions between particles in a gas are perfectly elastic. During an elastic collision, kinetic energy is transferred without loss from one particle to another. As a result, the total kinetic energy remains constant.

Key Question What are three assumptions of the kinetic theory as it applies to gases? **The particles of gas are small, hard spheres with an insignificant volume. The motion of the particles in a gas is rapid, constant, and random. All collisions between gas particles are perfectly elastic.**

Characteristics of a Gas

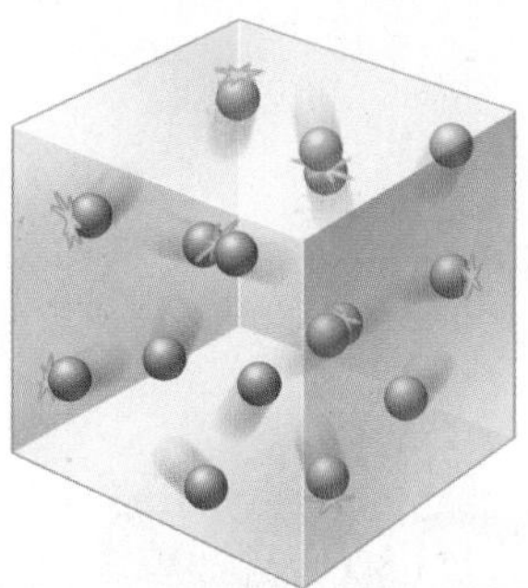

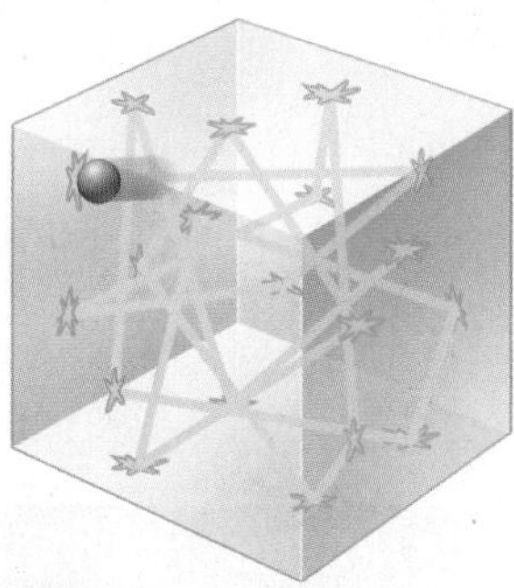

❶ Gas particles move constantly. In a container, they often collide with each other and with the walls of the container.

❷ Gas particles travel in a straight line between collisions.

❸ A gas fills all of the available space in its container.

Gas Pressure

A balloon filled with helium or hot air keeps its shape because of the pressure of the gas inside it. **Gas pressure** results from the force exerted by a gas per unit surface area of an object. In other words, pressure is the amount of force exerted on a given area. What causes this force? Moving bodies exert a force when they collide with other bodies. A single moving particle in a gas exerts an extremely small force. But when many particles collide with the same object at the same time, the pressure is measurable. Gas pressure is the result of billions of rapidly moving gas particles colliding with an object at the same time. If there are no particles in a given space, there is no gas pressure. An empty space with no particles and no pressure is called a **vacuum.**

The air you breathe is a mixture of gases. The collisions of gas particles in air with objects result in **atmospheric pressure.** This pressure changes with altitude. As you climb a mountain, the density of Earth's atmosphere decreases. As a result, atmospheric pressure decreases.

Measuring Gas Pressure A barometer is an instrument used to measure atmospheric pressure. As particles in the air collide with the surface of the mercury in the dish, the mercury level in the tube rises. The pressure of the atmosphere depends on weather and on altitude. In fair weather at sea level, the atmospheric pressure will support a mercury column 760 mm high. The figure at right shows an early type of mercury barometer.

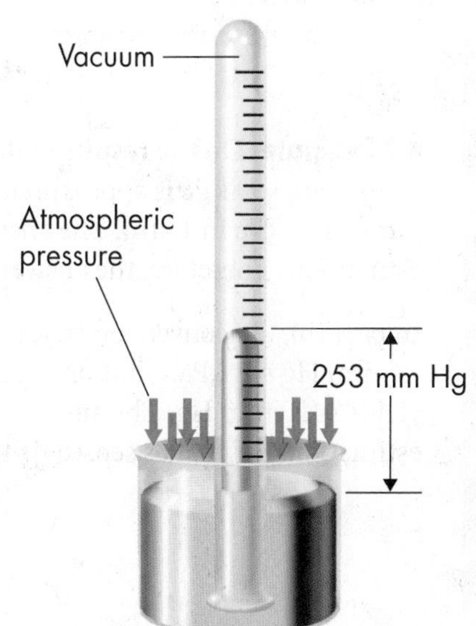

Barometer Mount Everest is 9000 m above sea level. Atmospheric pressure is lower than at sea level. Here, the pressure supports a mercury column only 253 mm high.

Units of Gas Pressure The SI unit of pressure is the **pascal** (Pa). A pascal represents a very small amount of pressure. Normal atmospheric pressure is about 100,000 Pa, or 100 kilopascals (kPa). Two older units of pressure are still used. These units are millimeters of mercury (mm Hg) and atmospheres. One standard atmosphere (atm) is the pressure needed to support 760 mm of mercury in a mercury barometer at 25°C. The relationships among the three units are:

$$1 \text{ atm} = 760 \text{ mm Hg} = 101.3 \text{ kPa}$$

Key Question How does kinetic theory explain gas pressure? **Gas pressure is the result of billions of rapidly moving particles in a gas simultaneously colliding with an object.**

SampleProblem 13.1

Converting Between Units of Pressure

A pressure gauge records a pressure of 450 kPa. Convert this measurement to

a. atmospheres.
b. millimeters of mercury.

❶ Analyze **List the knowns and the unknowns.**

KNOWNS	UNKNOWNS
pressure = 450 kPa	pressure = ? atm
101.3 kPa = 1 atm	pressure = ? mm Hg
101.3 kPa = 760 mm Hg	

❷ Calculate **Solve for the unknowns.** Convert the given pressure into the desired unit by multiplying by the proper conversion factor.

Identify the appropriate conversion factor to convert kPa to atm.

a. $\frac{1\ \text{atm}}{101.3\ \text{kPa}}$

Multiply the given pressure by the conversion factor.

$$450\ \cancel{\text{kPa}} \times \frac{1\ \text{atm}}{101.3\ \cancel{\text{kPa}}} = 4.4\ \text{atm}$$

Identify the appropriate conversion factor to convert kPa to mm Hg.

b. $\frac{760\ \text{mm Hg}}{101.3\ \text{kPa}}$

Multiply the given pressure by the conversion factor.

$$450\ \cancel{\text{kPa}} \times \frac{760\ \text{mm Hg}}{101.3\ \cancel{\text{kPa}}} = 3400\ \text{mm Hg}$$

❸ Evaluate **Do the results make sense?**
In part (a), 450 kPa is approximately 4.5 times the number of kPa in 1 atm. The answer is close to this estimation. Therefore, the answer makes sense.

In part (b), the conversion factor is approximately 7.6 mm Hg per kPa. Multiplying 7.6 by 450 kPa yields 3420 mm Hg. The answer is close to this estimation and makes sense.

When selecting the appropriate conversion factor, choose the one that allows you to cancel out the units correctly.

BUILD Math Skills

Check That Units Cancel When you use conversion factors, it's important to remember to use the correct units. You may find that your problem will include different kinds of units as you calculate. If you see the same unit in both the numerator and the denominator, you can cancel that unit. Taking this step helps make certain that your conversion factor is set up correctly. It also ensures that your answer will have the correct units.

Practice Problems

1. What pressure, in kilopascals and in atmospheres, does a gas exert at 385 mm Hg?

❶ **Analyze** **List the knowns and the unknowns.**

❷ **Calculate** **Solve for the unknowns.**

❸ **Evaluate** **Do the results make sense?**

KNOWNS	UNKNOWNS
pressure = 385 mm Hg	pressure = ? atm
760 mm Hg = 101.3 kPa	pressure = ? kPa
760 mm Hg = 1 atm	

2. What pressure, in atmospheres and in mm Hg, does a gas exert at 22.8 kPa?

KNOWNS	UNKNOWNS
pressure = 22.8 kPa	pressure = ? atm
101.3 kPa = 1 atm	pressure = ? mm Hg
101.3 kPa = 760 mm Hg	

Remember: Before you make your calculations, double-check that you have set up the conversion factor correctly.

3. What pressure, in kPa and in mm Hg, does a gas exert at 0.57 atm?

4. Challenge The pressure at the top of Mount Everest is 33.7 kPa. Is that pressure greater or less than 0.25 atm?

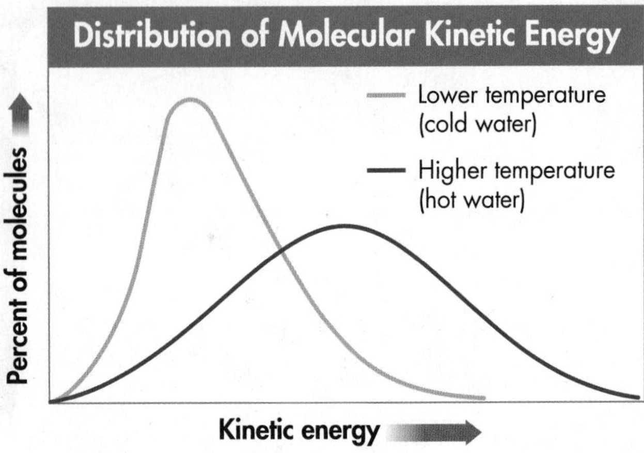

Distribution of Molecular Kinetic Energy The green and purple curves show the kinetic energy distribution of a typical collection of molecules at two different temperatures.

Go to your Chemistry Skills and Math Workbook to practice interpreting graphs.

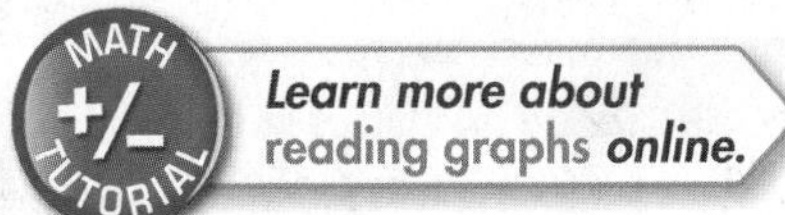

MATH
+/–
TUTORIAL
Learn more about reading graphs online.

Kinetic Energy and Temperature

As a substance is heated, its particles absorb energy. Some of the energy is stored in the particles. The stored energy, or potential energy, does not raise the temperature of the substance. The remaining absorbed energy speeds up the particles. In other words, it increases the particle's kinetic energy. This increase in kinetic energy results in an increase in temperature.

The particles in any collection of atoms or molecules at a given temperature have a wide range of kinetic energies. Most of the particles have kinetic energies somewhere in the middle of this wide range, as shown in the graph at left. Scientists use average kinetic energy to discuss the kinetic energy of a collection of particles in a substance. At any given temperature, the particles of all substances have the same average kinetic energy. The physical state of the particles doesn't matter. For example, the ions in solid table salt, the molecules in liquid water, and the atoms in gaseous helium all have the same average kinetic energy at room temperature.

The average kinetic energy of the particles in a substance is directly proportional to the substance's temperature in kelvins. An increase in the average kinetic energy of the particles causes the temperature of a substance to rise. As a substance cools, the particles tend to move more slowly. In other words, their average kinetic energy decreases.

Key Question What is the relationship between the temperature in kelvins and the average kinetic energy of particles? **The Kelvin temperature of a substance is directly proportional to the average kinetic energy of the particles of the substance.**

13.1 LessonCheck

Key Concept Check

5. Describe Briefly describe what the kinetic theory assumes about gases.

6. Explain Use kinetic theory to explain what causes gas pressure.

7. Explain How is the Kelvin temperature of a substance related to the average kinetic energy of its particles?

Vocabulary Check *Choose a highlighted term from the lesson to complete the sentences correctly.*

8. The __________ says that all matter is made of particles in constant motion.

9. __________ is the energy an object has because of its motion.

Think Critically

10. Predict A cylinder of oxygen gas is cooled from 300 K (27°C) to 150 K (–123°C). By what factor does the average kinetic energy of the oxygen molecules in the cylinder decrease?

CHEMISTRY & YOU

11. A low pressure system moving into your region usually means a storm is coming. What happens to the column of mercury in a barometer as a storm approaches? Why? (Hint: See page 397.)

BIGIDEA KINETIC THEORY

12. Why does a gas take the shape and volume of its container?

13.2 The Nature of Liquids

CHEMISTRY & YOU

Q: Why are many hot drinks more fragrant than cold drinks? The smell of hot coffee or hot cocoa fills a room, but the smell of iced coffee or chocolate milk doesn't. You can smell a hot drink because some molecules change from the liquid state to the gaseous state. In this lesson, you will learn why this process takes place more quickly in a warmer liquid.

Key Questions

What factors determine the physical properties of a liquid?

What is the relationship between evaporation and kinetic energy?

When can a dynamic equilibrium exist between a liquid and its vapor?

Under what conditions does boiling occur?

A Model for Liquids

According to the kinetic theory, the particles in gases and the particles in liquids have kinetic energy. This energy allows the particles to flow past one another. Substances that can flow are called fluids. The ability of gases and liquids to flow makes them take the shape of their containers, as shown in the figures below. According to the kinetic theory, the particles in a liquid are attracted to each other while particles in a gas are not. These attractions keep the particles in a liquid close together. That is why liquids have a definite volume.

The physical properties of liquids are determined by two opposing factors: the tendency for the particles to flow and the attractions that keep the particles close together.

Key Question What factors determine the physical properties of a liquid? **Two opposing forces—the motions of particles in a liquid and the attractions among the particles—determine the physical properties of liquids.**

Comparing Gases and Liquids

Properties of Gases

- Gases conform to the shapes of their containers.
- Volume changes with the container.
- Particles are not attracted to each other.
- Gases are less dense than liquids.
- Adding pressure decreases the volume of gases.

Properties of Liquids

- Liquids conform to the shapes of their containers.
- Volume remains constant—no matter the container.
- Particles are attracted to each other.
- Liquids are denser than gases.
- Adding pressure has very little effect on the volume of liquids.

BUILD Vocabulary

vaporization the conversion of a liquid to a gas

evaporation the conversion of a nonboiling liquid to a gas

vapor pressure the measure of the force exerted by a gas above a liquid in a sealed container

WORD ORIGINS

Evaporation and *vaporization* come from the Latin word for steam. In both processes, some particles have enough kinetic energy to change from liquid to gas, as water does to form steam.

Evaporation

Water in an open system, such as an open container, eventually escapes into the air as water vapor. That's why a puddle on a driveway will eventually dry up. The water becomes a vapor and enters the air around it. The change of a liquid to a gas or vapor is called **vaporization.** When this conversion happens at the surface of a liquid that is not boiling, the process is called **evaporation.**

Molecules of a liquid are attracted to one another. Only those molecules that have a certain minimum kinetic energy can escape the liquid through evaporation. Most of the molecules in a liquid don't have enough kinetic energy to overcome the forces that hold them together.

Evaporation and Temperature You may have noticed that a liquid evaporates faster when it is heated. Heating the liquid increases the average kinetic energy of its particles. The added energy helps more particles overcome the attractive forces that keep them in the liquid state. As evaporation occurs, the particles with the highest kinetic energy escape first. The particles left in the liquid have a lower average kinetic energy than the particles that have escaped. The process is like removing the fastest runner from a race. The remaining runners have a lower average speed. As evaporation takes place, the liquid's temperature decreases. Therefore, evaporation is a cooling process.

You can observe the cooling effects of evaporation on a hot day. The man in the photo below is sweating. When you sweat, water molecules in your sweat absorb heat from your body. The molecules with the highest kinetic energy evaporate, cooling the liquid that remains on your skin.

Key Question What is the relationship between evaporation and kinetic energy? **During evaporation, only those molecules with a certain minimum kinetic energy can escape from the surface of the liquid.**

Sweat
The evaporation of sweat helps to cool your skin when you exercise.

Vapor Pressure

The evaporation of a liquid in a closed system differs from evaporation in an open system, as shown in the photos at right. In a closed system, no particles can escape into the outside air. When a partially filled container of liquid is sealed, some of the particles at the surface of the liquid vaporize. These particles collide with the walls of the sealed container, producing pressure. A measure of the force exerted by a gas above a liquid is called **vapor pressure.** Over time, the number of particles entering the vapor increases, and some of the particles return to the liquid state. When particles change from vapor to liquid, the process is called condensation. The following equation summarizes the relationship between evaporation and condensation:

$$\text{Liquid} \underset{\leftarrow \text{condensation}}{\overset{\text{evaporation} \rightarrow}{\rightleftharpoons}} \text{Vapor (gas)}$$

Eventually, the number of particles condensing will equal the number of particles vaporizing. The vapor pressure will then remain constant because the system is balanced, or at equilibrium. At equilibrium, the particles in the system continue to evaporate and condense, but no net change occurs in the number of particles in the liquid or vapor.

Vapor Pressure and Temperature Change An increase in the temperature of a contained liquid increases the vapor pressure. This happens because the particles in the warmed liquid have increased kinetic energy. More of the particles will reach the minimum kinetic energy they need to escape from the surface of the liquid. After the particles escape the liquid, they collide with the walls of the container at a greater frequency. The table below gives the vapor pressures of some common liquids. Liquids with higher vapor pressure will evaporate more easily.

Evaporation in Open and Closed Systems

Open System In an open system, molecules that evaporate can escape from the system.

Closed System In a closed system, the molecules cannot escape. They collect as a vapor above the liquid. Some molecules condense back into a liquid.

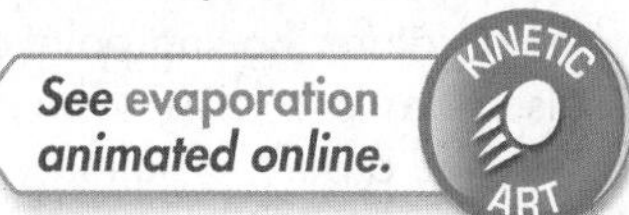

See evaporation animated online.

Vapor Pressure (in kPa) of Three Substances at Different Temperatures						
Substance	**0°C**	**20°C**	**40°C**	**60°C**	**80°C**	**100°C**
Water	0.61	2.33	7.37	19.92	47.34	101.33
Ethanol	1.63	5.85	18.04	47.02	108.34	225.75
Diethyl ether	24.70	58.96	122.80	230.65	399.11	647.87

Go to your Chemistry Skills and Math Workbook to practice interpreting data.

Measuring Vapor Pressure With a Manometer

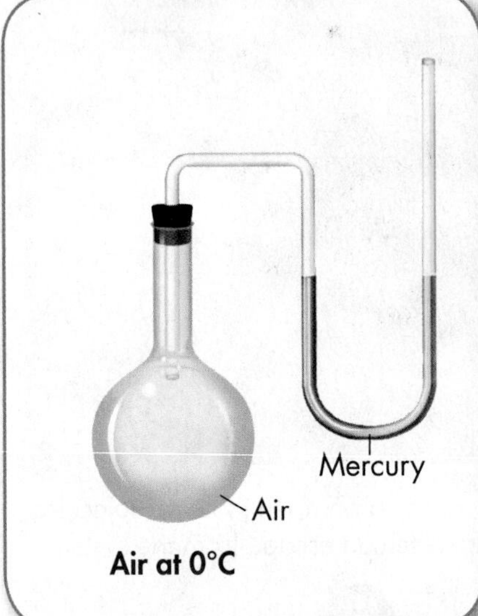

When the container holds only air, the mercury levels are the same on both sides of the tube.

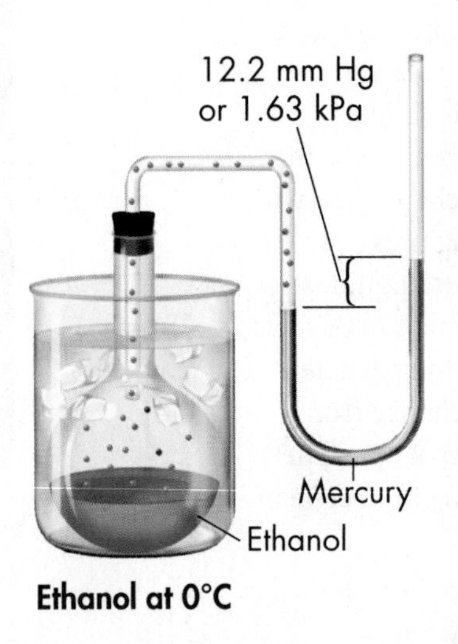

When a liquid is added to the container, the vapor pressure rises. The difference between the two levels of mercury is the vapor pressure.

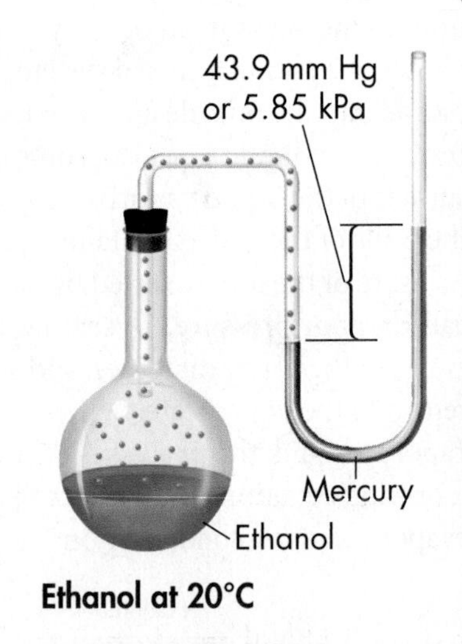

As the temperature rises, so does the vapor pressure.

BUILD Vocabulary

boiling point the temperature at which the vapor pressure of a liquid is just equal to the external pressure on the liquid

MULTIPLE MEANINGS
Boiling point refers to a liquid's temperature. Boiling point can also refer to a crisis: "The tension reached a boiling point."

Vapor Pressure Measurements You can determine the vapor pressure of a liquid with a manometer. The figure above shows how a simple manometer works. One end of a U-shaped tube containing mercury is attached to a closed container. The other end of the tube is open to the atmosphere.

When there is only air in the container, the pressure is the same on both sides of the tube. The mercury level is the same in each arm of the tube. When a liquid is added to the container, as shown in the center image, the pressure in the container increases. The vapor pressure of the liquid pushes the mercury down on the container side of the U-shaped tube. You can determine the vapor pressure in mm of Hg by measuring the difference between the two levels of mercury.

As shown above on the right, the vapor pressure increases as temperature increases. In other words, the gas in the closed container exerts more pressure on the liquid as temperature rises. The vapor pressure of the warmer liquid pushes the mercury down even farther on the container side of the U-shaped tube.

Key Question When can a dynamic equilibrium exist between a liquid and its vapor? **In a system at constant vapor pressure, a dynamic equilibrium exists between the vapor and the liquid. The system is in equilibrium because the rate of evaporation of liquid equals the rate of condensation of vapor.**

Boiling Point

The rate of evaporation of a liquid from an open container increases as the liquid is heated. Heating allows a greater number of particles at the liquid's surface to escape from the liquid. The remaining particles in the liquid move faster and faster as they absorb the added energy. The average kinetic energy of the particles in the liquid increases. Thus, the temperature of the liquid rises. As the temperature increases, the vapor pressure increases. When a liquid is heated until particles throughout the liquid have enough energy to vaporize, the liquid boils. The **boiling point** (bp) is the temperature at which the vapor pressure of the liquid is just equal to the external pressure on the liquid. Bubbles of vapor form throughout the liquid. These bubbles rise to the surface and escape into the air.

Look at the graph at right. The boiling point of each liquid at standard pressure (101.3 kPa) is the temperature where the curve crosses the dashed line. For example, the boiling point of water at standard pressure is 100°C.

Boiling Point and Pressure Changes Liquids do not always boil at the same temperature. Boiling points decrease at higher altitudes. For example, in Denver—which is 1600 m above sea level—the average atmospheric pressure is 85.3 kPa. Here, water boils at about 95°C.

As shown below, the boiling point is lower at a lower external pressure. The particles in the liquid need less kinetic energy to escape from the liquid. At a higher external pressure, the boiling point increases. The particles in the liquid need more kinetic energy to escape from the liquid.

Vapor Pressure Versus Temperature As temperature increases, so does vapor pressure.

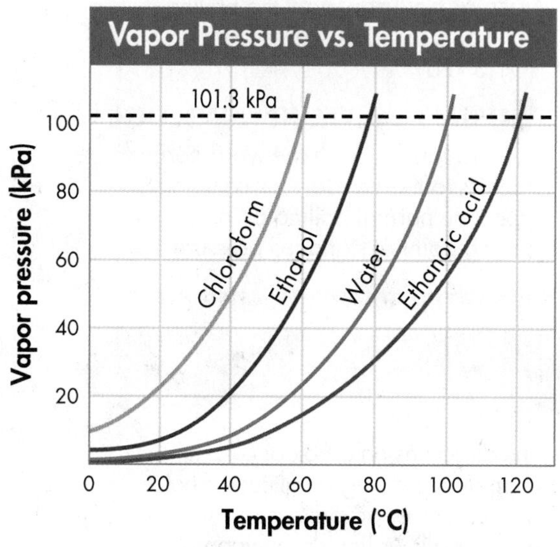

Boiling Point and Altitude A substance's boiling point varies with altitude.

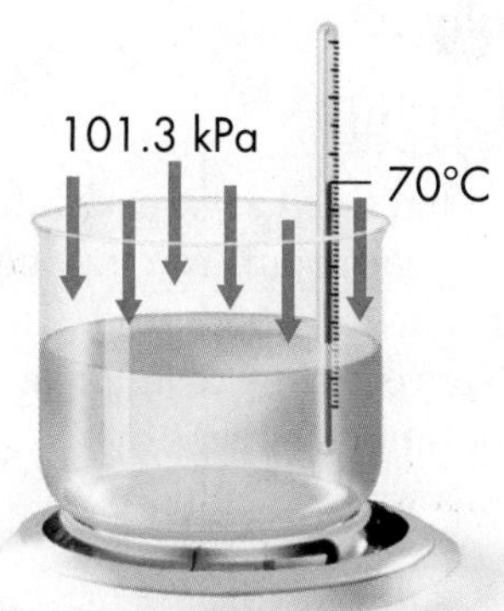

Sea Level at 70°C Atmospheric pressure at the surface of water at 70°C is greater than its vapor pressure.

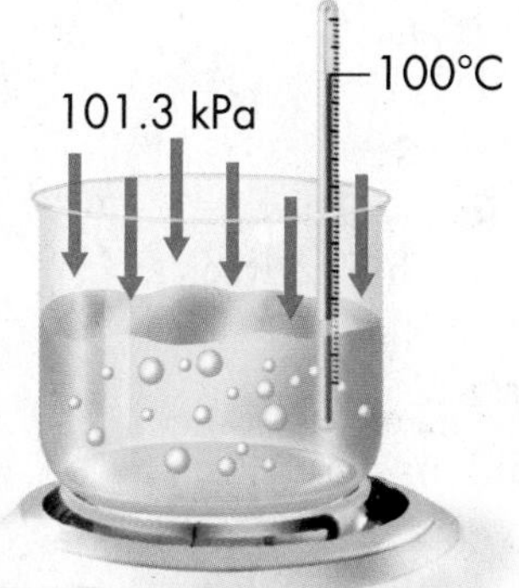

Sea Level at 100°C At the boiling point, the vapor pressure is equal to atmospheric pressure.

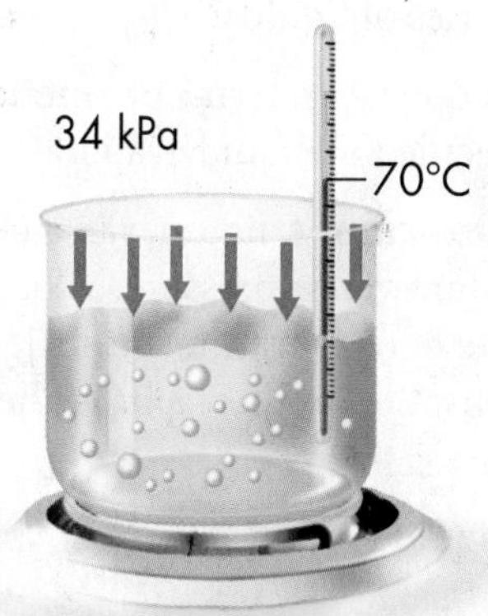

Atop Mount Everest at 70°C At higher altitudes, the atmospheric pressure is lower, so the water boils at a lower temperature.

BUILD Vocabulary

normal boiling point the boiling point of a liquid at a pressure of 101.3 kPa

USING PRIOR KNOWLEDGE

You are familiar with the word *normal.* It refers to the standard or common type. The normal boiling point is the boiling point at standard pressure.

BUILD Connections

The directions on a box of cake mix change depending on altitude. That's because lower air pressure at high altitudes allows liquids to evaporate more quickly. Cakes collapse as liquids evaporate.

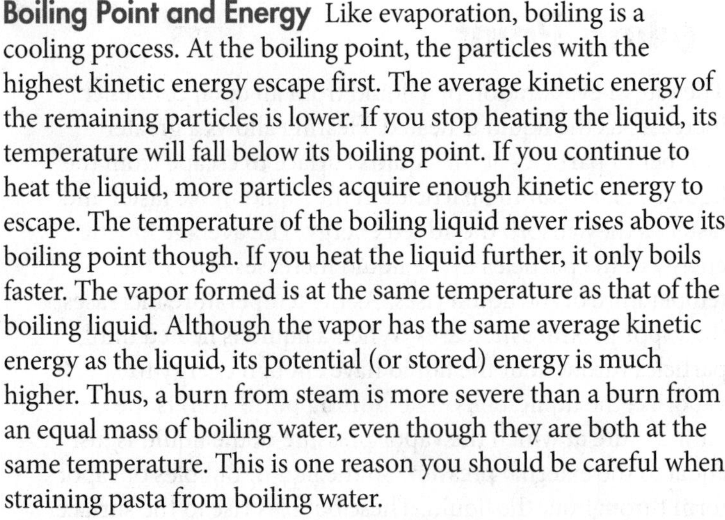

Boiling Point and Energy Like evaporation, boiling is a cooling process. At the boiling point, the particles with the highest kinetic energy escape first. The average kinetic energy of the remaining particles is lower. If you stop heating the liquid, its temperature will fall below its boiling point. If you continue to heat the liquid, more particles acquire enough kinetic energy to escape. The temperature of the boiling liquid never rises above its boiling point though. If you heat the liquid further, it only boils faster. The vapor formed is at the same temperature as that of the boiling liquid. Although the vapor has the same average kinetic energy as the liquid, its potential (or stored) energy is much higher. Thus, a burn from steam is more severe than a burn from an equal mass of boiling water, even though they are both at the same temperature. This is one reason you should be careful when straining pasta from boiling water.

Normal Boiling Point A liquid can have various boiling points depending on external pressure. The **normal boiling point** is defined as the boiling point of a liquid at a pressure of 101.3 kPa. The normal boiling point of water is 100°C. However, at the top of Mount Everest, the external pressure is 34 kPa. The boiling point of water at this elevation is 71°C.

Key Question Under what conditions does boiling occur? **When a liquid is heated to a temperature at which particles throughout the liquid have enough energy to vaporize, the liquid begins to boil.**

13.2 LessonCheck

Key Concept Check

13. **Identify** What factors help determine the physical properties of liquids?

14. **Explain** In terms of kinetic energy, explain how a molecule in a liquid evaporates.

15. **Describe** A liquid is in a closed container and has a constant vapor pressure. What is the relationship between the rate of evaporation of the liquid and the rate of condensation of the vapor in the container?

16. **Relate Cause and Effect** What conditions must exist for a liquid to boil?

Vocabulary Check *Choose a highlighted term from the lesson to complete the sentences correctly.*

17. The temperature at which the vapor pressure of a liquid and the external pressure are equal is the liquid's ________.

18. The conversion of a liquid to a gas or vapor is called ________.

Think Critically

CHEMISTRY & YOU

19. You can often smell a warm drink from across the room. You may not be able to smell a similar cold drink until you're very close to it. Explain why evaporation happens more quickly in a warmer liquid. (Hint: See page 403.)

BIGIDEA KINETIC THEORY

20. Why does a liquid take the shape but not the volume of its container?

13.3 The Nature of Solids

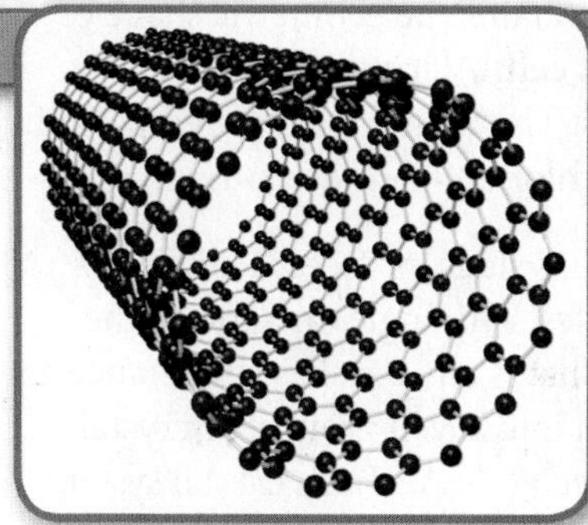

CHEMISTRY & YOU

Q: What is the strongest material in the world? It's not steel or even diamond. It's a form of carbon called fullerene nanotubes. These structures form when carbon atoms link together in hexagonal, or six-sided, patterns. They are over 300 times stronger than steel! Nanotechnology is a new kind of science that involves the study of these fullerene nanotubes. Scientists are studying how to use these very strong and very small structures.

Key Questions

How are the structure and properties of solids related?

What determines the shape of a crystal?

BUILD Vocabulary

melting point the temperature at which a solid changes into a liquid

freezing point the temperature at which a liquid changes into a solid

USING PRIOR KNOWLEDGE

You have seen ice melt. Solid ice changes to liquid water when the temperature is above 0°C. This same process occurs at the melting point of any substance—the solid changes into a liquid.

A Model for Solids

The particles in liquids are relatively free to move. However, the particles in solids are not. In most solids, the atoms, ions, or molecules are packed tightly together. These solids are dense. They are not easy to compress. Particles in solids tend to vibrate about fixed points. Therefore, solids do not flow. The orderly arrangement of the particles and the fixed location of the particles are reflected in the physical properties of solids.

Melting Point and Freezing Point Heating any substance increases the kinetic energy of its particles. When you heat a solid, the organization of the particles within the solid breaks down. At a certain temperature, the solid melts. The **melting point** (mp) is the temperature at which a solid changes into a liquid. The **freezing point** (fp) is the temperature at which a liquid changes into a solid. The melting and freezing points of a substance are at the same temperature. For example, liquid water freezes at 0°C, and frozen water melts at the same temperature: 0°C.

At that temperature, the number of particles melting is equal to the number of particles freezing. The following equation summarizes this process:

$$\text{Solid} \underset{\leftarrow \text{freezing}}{\overset{\text{melting} \rightarrow}{\rightleftharpoons}} \text{Liquid}$$

In general, ionic solids have higher melting points than molecular solids have. The forces holding ionic solids together are stronger than the forces holding molecular solids together.

Key Question How are the structure and properties of solids related? **The general properties of solids reflect the orderly arrangement of their particles and the fixed locations of their particles.**

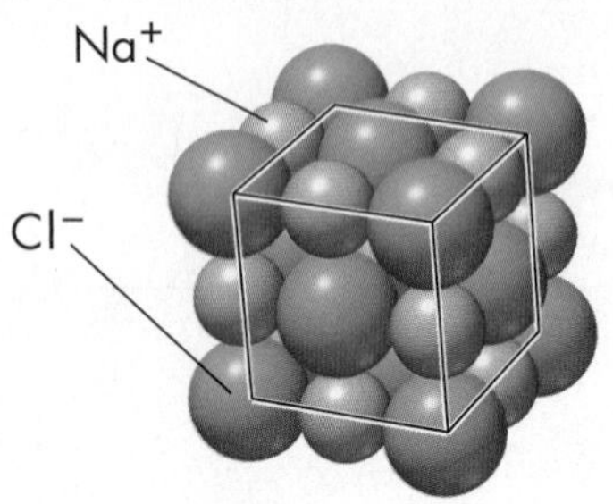

Ionic Crystal
In sodium chloride (NaCl), sodium ions (Na^+) and chloride ions (Cl^-) are closely packed in a regular pattern. The ions vibrate about fixed points on the crystal.

Crystal Structure and Unit Cells

Most solid substances are crystalline. In a **crystal**, the particles are arranged in an orderly, repeating, three-dimensional pattern. The shape of a crystal depends on the arrangement of the particles within it. The smallest group of particles within a crystal that retains the geometric shape of the crystal is known as a **unit cell**. A crystal lattice is a repeating pattern of unit cells. The figure at left shows part of the crystal lattice in sodium chloride.

Crystal Systems A crystal has sides, or faces. These faces come together at specific angles. The angles are always the same for a given substance. That is what makes a substance unique. Crystals are classified into seven groups, or crystal systems. Each group has a special shape. Each crystal system can be composed of up to four types of unit cells. The figure below shows six crystal systems.

Crystal Systems
These mineral crystals have an orderly arrangement of particles.

Learn more about crystal structures of solids *online.* CONCEPTS IN ACTION

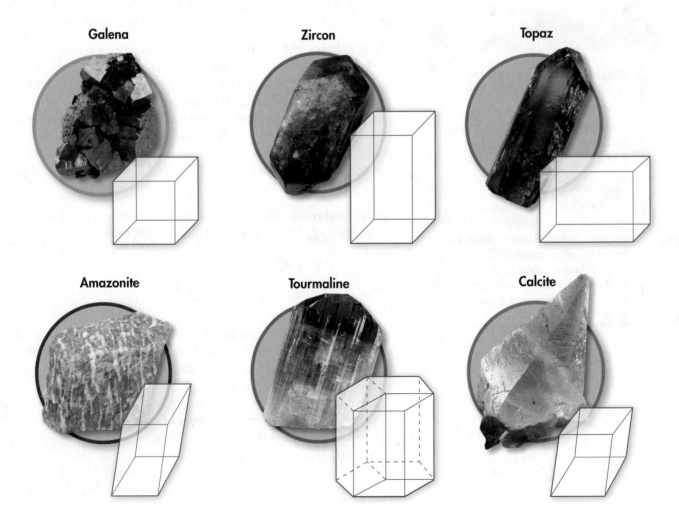

Galena

Zircon

Topaz

Amazonite

Tourmaline

Calcite

Allotropes of Carbon

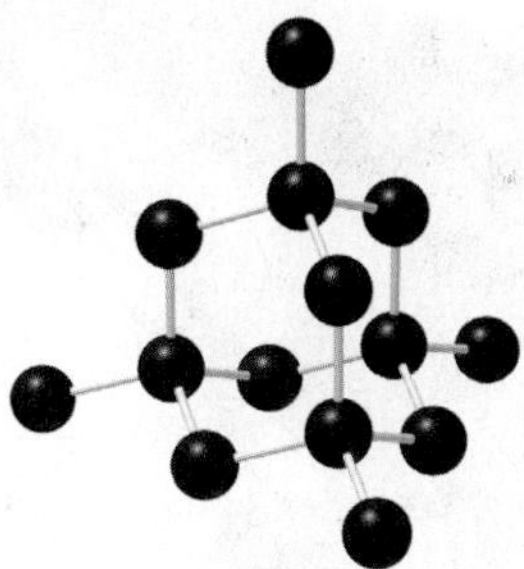

Diamond In diamond, each carbon atom inside the diamond is strongly bonded to four others. The crystal is rigid and compact.

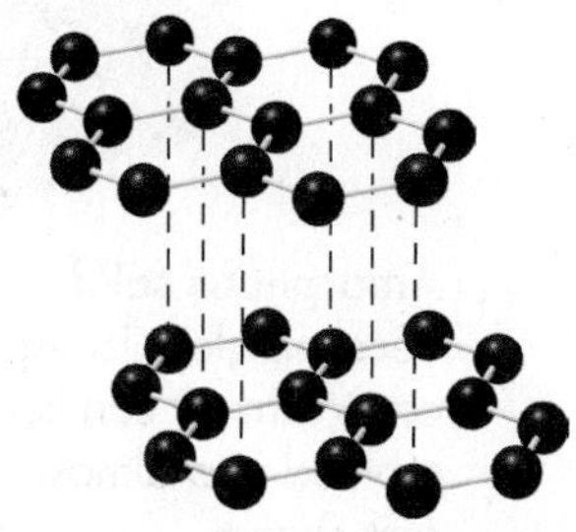

Graphite In graphite, the carbon atoms are linked in widely spaced, hexagonal (six-sided) layers.

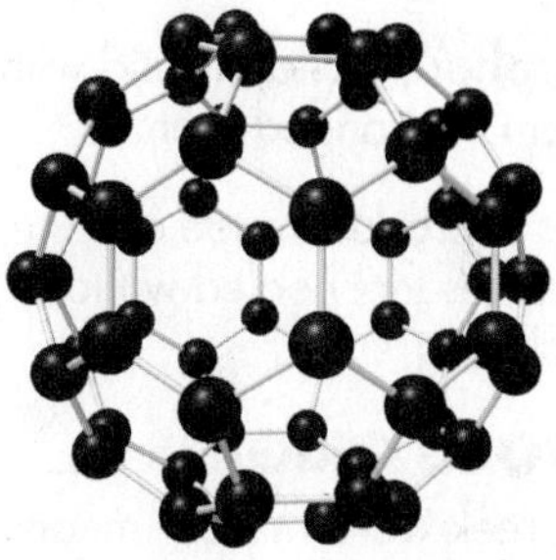

Fullerene In buckminsterfullerene, 60 carbon atoms form a hollow sphere. The carbons are arranged in pentagons and hexagons.

Allotropes Some solid substances can exist in more than one form. **Allotropes** are two or more different molecular forms of the same element in the same physical state. Allotropes are made of atoms of the same element. But because their structures are different, they have different properties. Only a few elements have allotropes. Phosphorus, sulfur, and oxygen have allotropes. Carbon also has several allotropes. The figure above shows the structure of three allotropes of carbon.

Diamond is one crystalline form of carbon. It forms when carbon crystallizes under tremendous pressure. Diamond has a high density and is very hard. Graphite is a different crystalline form of carbon. The lead in a pencil is not the element lead but graphite. In graphite, the carbon atoms are packed in sheets. Graphite has a relatively low density and is much softer than diamond.

In 1985, a third crystalline form of carbon was discovered in soot. This form of carbon is called buckminsterfullerene. The carbon atoms form a hollow sphere, or cage. The cage is known as a buckyball. The atoms are arranged in a pattern of hexagons and pentagons on the surface of the cage. Their pattern looks like the surface of a soccer ball. Since 1985, other molecules in which carbon forms hollow cages have been discovered. All these similar forms of carbon are called fullerenes. The hollow-cage structures that form fullerenes give them great strength and rigidity.

crystal solid in which the particles are arranged in an orderly way

unit cell the smallest group of particles in a crystal that retains the geometric shape of the crystal

allotropes two or more different molecular forms of the same element

The root word *allos-* means "different" or "other." In different allotropes, atoms of the same element are bonded in different ways.

amorphous solid a solid with randomly arranged atoms

glass a product made of substances that cooled without crystallizing

WORD ORIGINS

The Greek word *morph-* means "form" or "shape." The prefix *a-* means "not." *Amorphous* literally means "without a shape or form."

BUILD Connections

Car windows are made of layers of plastic between layers of glass. The combination of the amorphous solids plastic and glass stops the windows from shattering during an accident.

Amorphous solid
Because glass is not crystalline, it can be molded into almost any shape.

Noncrystalline Solids Not all solids are crystalline in form. Some solids, such as the solid in the figure above, are amorphous. An **amorphous solid** does not have an ordered internal structure. Rubber, plastic, and asphalt are amorphous solids. Their atoms are arranged randomly. Glasses, such as the bowl above, are also amorphous solids. A **glass** is made of inorganic substances that have cooled to a rigid state without crystallizing. Glasses are sometimes called supercooled liquids.

The internal structures of glasses are intermediate between a crystalline solid and a free-flowing liquid. Glasses do not melt at a definite temperature. Instead, they gradually soften when heated. When a crystalline solid is shattered, the fragments have the same surface angles as the original solid. When an amorphous solid, such as glass, is shattered, the fragments have irregular angles and jagged edges.

Key Question What determines the shape of a crystal? **The shape of a crystal reflects the arrangement of the particles within the solid.**

13.3 LessonCheck

Key Concept Check

21. **Describe** In general, how are the particles arranged in solids?

22. **Explain** What does the shape of a crystal tell you about the structure of a crystal?

Vocabulary Check *Choose a highlighted word from the lesson to complete the sentences correctly.*

23. A solid changes into a liquid at its ________.

24. Two molecular forms of the same element at the same physical state are called ________.

Think Critically

25. How do allotropes of an element differ?

CHEMISTRY & YOU

26. What structural properties make fullerene nanotubes the strongest material in the world? (Hint: See page 409.)

BIGIDEA KINETIC THEORY

27. Why does a solid have a definite shape and a definite volume?

13.4 Changes of State

CHEMISTRY & YOU

Q: Where does rainwater go when a puddle dries up? Water cycles through much of the matter on Earth. It falls as liquid rain or solid snow. Then, it collects in oceans, rivers, and glaciers. It returns to the air as a gas through evaporation. All living organisms use water. Then, they release it into the air. In this section, you will learn what conditions can control the state of a substance.

Key Questions

When can sublimation occur?

What do the curved lines on a phase diagram represent?

BUILD Vocabulary

sublimation the change of a solid to a vapor without passing through the liquid state

MULTIPLE MEANINGS

When a substance goes directly from the solid state to the gaseous state, it is said to sublime. As an adjective, the word *sublime* means "lofty," "supreme," or "noble."

Sublimation

Suppose you hang wet laundry on a clothesline on a very cold day. The water in the clothes quickly freezes to ice. If the day is sunny, the clothes become dry. But the ice never thaws. The ice changes directly to water vapor without melting and passing through the liquid state. Solids, like liquids, have vapor pressures. At or near room temperature, solids with vapor pressures above atmospheric pressure may change from the solid state directly to the gaseous state. Particles with sufficient energy escape the surface of a solid and become gaseous. The change of a substance from a solid to a vapor without passing through the liquid state is called **sublimation.** Sublimation can occur because solids, like liquids, have a vapor pressure.The figure below illustrates the process of sublimation.

Gaseous particles can change directly to solid particles through deposition. Eventually, the rate of sublimation is equal to the rate of deposition. The equation below summarizes this process:

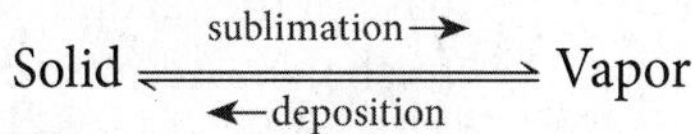

$$\text{Solid} \underset{\text{deposition}}{\overset{\text{sublimation}}{\rightleftharpoons}} \text{Vapor}$$

Sublimation When iodine crystals are heated, they undergo sublimation. The crystals go directly from the solid to the gaseous state. When the vapor cools, it goes directly from the gaseous to the solid state.

Iodine also undergoes sublimation. This violet-black solid ordinarily changes into a purple vapor without passing through a liquid state. When solid iodine is heated, some of the particles change directly to gas. When these gas particles come in contact with a cool surface, they change directly to solid.

Sublimation has useful applications. If freshly brewed coffee is frozen and the water vapor is removed, the result is freeze-dried coffee. Solid carbon dioxide (dry ice) is used to cool goods that must remain frozen during shipment. Dry ice has a low temperature of −78°C. Because it sublimes, it does not produce a liquid. Solid air fresheners contain a variety of substances that sublime at room temperature. The gaseous particles then move throughout the room. Sublimation is also useful for separating certain substances.

Key Question When can sublimation occur? **Sublimation occurs in solids with vapor pressures that exceed atmospheric pressure at or near room temperature.**

Quick Lab

Purpose To observe the sublimation of air freshener

Materials

- small pieces of solid air freshener
- small shallow container
- two clear 8-oz plastic cups
- hot tap water
- ice
- three thick cardboard strips

Sublimation

Procedure

1. Place a few pieces of air freshener in one of the cups. **CAUTION** *Work in a well-ventilated room.*

2. Bend the cardboard strips and then place them over the rim of the cup that has the air freshener pieces.

3. Place the second cup inside the first. The base of the second cup should not touch the air freshener. Adjust the cardboard as necessary. This assembly is your sublimator.

4. Fill the top cup with ice. Do not get any ice or water in the bottom cup.

5. Fill the shallow container about one-third full with hot tap water.

6. Carefully place your sublimator in the hot water. Observe what happens.

Analyze and Conclude

1. Define What is sublimation?

2. Predict What do you think would happen if the water in the shallow container were at room temperature? If it were boiling?

3. Explain Why is it possible to separate the substances in some mixtures by sublimation?

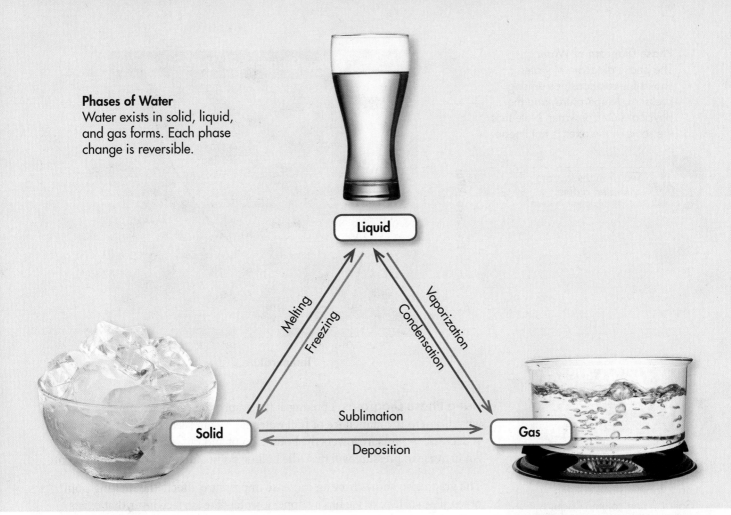

Phases of Water
Water exists in solid, liquid, and gas forms. Each phase change is reversible.

Liquid
Melting
Freezing
Vaporization
Condensation
Solid
Sublimation
Deposition
Gas

Phase Diagrams

The simple diagram above shows the relationships between different phases of matter and the processes that change the phase of matter. You can see that each phase change is reversible. Matter changes between phases according to temperature and pressure. The relationships among the solid, liquid, and vapor states (or phases) of a substance in a sealed container can also be shown in a single graph, called a **phase diagram**. A phase diagram gives the conditions of temperature and pressure at which a substance exists as solid, liquid, or gas (vapor). Phase diagrams are quantitative. They indicate the specific temperatures and pressures at which phase changes occur. You can show where two phases exist in equilibrium by drawing a line on the phase diagram to separate the two regions that represent phases.

Interpreting Phase Diagrams Look at the phase diagram for water on the next page. In each of the colored regions of the phase diagram, water is in a single phase. The curving line that separates water's vapor phase from its liquid phase shows where water can change its state from liquid to vapor or from vapor to liquid. The same line shows that the vapor pressure of water changes with temperature. The other two lines describe the conditions for equilibrium between liquid water and ice and between water vapor and ice. The point on the diagram at which all three lines meet is called the triple point. The **triple point** describes the only set of conditions at which all three phases can exist in equilibrium with one another. As you can see in the graph, water's triple point occurs at 0.61 kPa and 0.016°C. At this point, water exists as liquid, vapor, and ice.

phase diagram a graph that shows relationships between the solid, liquid, and gas states of a substance

triple point the conditions at which all three phases exist in equilibrium with each other

RELATED WORDS
The word *triple* describes anything with three parts or something with three times as much as something else. The triple point is the point at which all three phases of a substance exist in equilibrium.

Phase Diagram of Water
The phase diagram of water shows the relationships among pressure, temperature, and the physical states of water. Note that the scale of the axes is not linear.

KINETIC ART
See changes in state animated online.

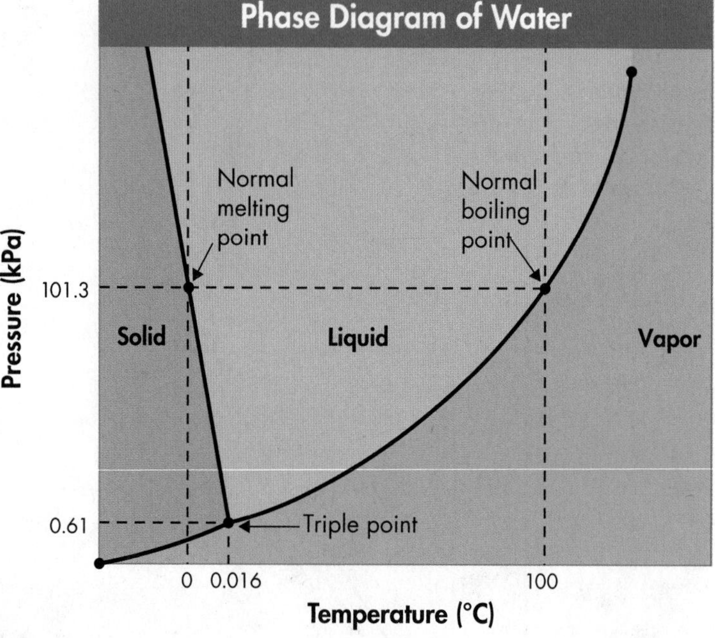

BUILD Understanding

Compare and Contrast
As a review, draw a simple chart, labeling one column "Solids," one column "Liquids," and the third column "Gases." Under each column, list the properties of the different states of matter. Include information about particle position, volume, and compressibility.

Using Phase Diagrams Looking at the graph, you can determine what happens if you melt ice or boil water at pressures less than 101.3 kPa. A decrease in pressure lowers the boiling point and raises the melting point. An increase in pressure will raise the boiling point and lower the melting point.

The graph also shows how an increase in pressure affects the melting point of ice. The surface of ice has a slippery, water-like surface layer that exists well below ice's melting point. Even ice that is at –129°C has this layer. The liquid-like surface layer provides the lubrication needed for smooth skating and skiing.

Key Question What do the curved lines on a phase diagram represent? **The curved lines on a phase diagram represent the temperatures and pressures at which two phases exist in equilibrium.**

13.4 LessonCheck

Key Concept Check

28. **Identify** What properties must a solid have to undergo sublimation?

29. **Explain** What do the curved lines on a phase diagram represent?

Vocabulary Check *Choose a highlighted term from the lesson to complete the sentences correctly.*

30. A substance goes through __________ when it changes from a solid to a vapor without becoming a liquid.

31. A graph that shows the relationships between a substance's physical states is called a __________.

Think Critically

32. Using the phase diagram for water shown at the top of the page, estimate the boiling point of water at a pressure of 50 kPa.

CHEMISTRY & YOU

33. Describe how water might move from Earth's surface to Earth's atmosphere and back again as part of the water cycle. In your description, be sure to include any phase changes that occur. (Hint: See page 413.)

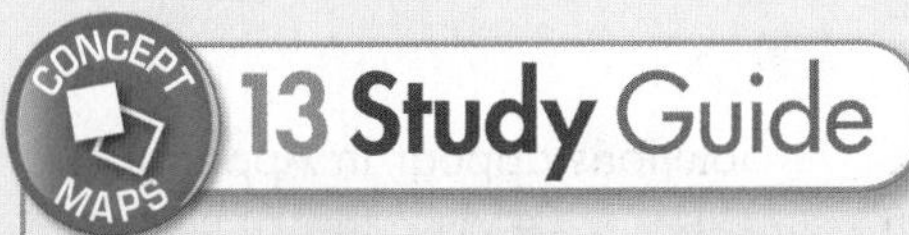

13 Study Guide

BIGIDEA KINETIC THEORY

The state of a substance is determined by conditions of pressure and temperature. Low pressures and high temperatures favor gases in which particles move randomly in constant, high-speed motion. At higher pressures and lower temperatures, the particles slow down and exert attractive forces on one another, producing a liquid. At still higher pressures and lower temperatures, the particles become fixed in orderly arrangements, producing solids. A substance changes state when there is a change in the balance between the random motion of its particles and the attractions among those particles.

13.1 The Nature of Gases

Particles in a gas are considered to be small, hard spheres with an insignificant volume. The motion of the particles in a gas is rapid, constant, and random. All collisions between particles in a gas are perfectly elastic.

Gas pressure is the result of billions of rapidly moving particles in a gas simultaneously colliding with an object.

The Kelvin temperature of a substance is directly proportional to the average kinetic energy of the particles of the substance.

- kinetic energy (396)
- kinetic theory (396)
- gas pressure (397)
- vacuum (397)
- atmospheric pressure (397)
- pascal (Pa) (397)

13.2 The Nature of Liquids

Two opposing forces—the motions of particles in a liquid and the attractions among the particles—determine the physical properties of liquids.

During evaporation, only those molecules with a certain minimum kinetic energy can escape from the surface of the liquid.

In a system at constant vapor pressure, a dynamic equilibrium exists between the vapor and the liquid. The system is in equilibrium because the rate of evaporation of liquid equals the rate of condensation of vapor.

When a liquid is heated to a temperature at which particles throughout the liquid have enough energy to vaporize, the liquid begins to boil.

- vaporization (402)
- evaporation (402)
- vapor pressure (403)
- boiling point (405)
- normal boiling point (406)

13.3 The Nature of Solids

The general properties of solids reflect the orderly arrangement of their particles and the fixed locations of their particles.

The shape of a crystal reflects the arrangement of the particles within the solid.

- melting point (407)
- freezing point (407)
- crystal (408)
- unit cell (408)
- allotropes (409)
- amorphous solid (410)
- glass (410)

13.4 Changes of State

Sublimation occurs in solids with vapor pressures that exceed atmospheric pressure at or near room temperature.

The curved lines on a phase diagram represent the temperatures and pressures at which two phases exist in equilibrium.

- sublimation (411)
- phase diagram (413)
- triple point (413)

13 Assessment

★ Solutions appear in Appendix D.

Lesson by Lesson

13.1 The Nature of Gases

34. Which of these statements is characteristic of matter in the gaseous state?
- **a.** Gases fill their containers completely.
- **b.** Gases exert pressure.
- **c.** Gases have mass.
- **d.** The pressure of a gas is independent of the temperature.
- **e.** Gases are compressible.

35. List the various units used to measure pressure and then identify the SI unit.

36. Convert 1656 kPa to atm.

★**37.** Convert 190 mm Hg to kPa and atm.

38. Explain the relationship between the Kelvin temperature of a substance and the kinetic energy of its particles.

39. How is the average kinetic energy of water molecules affected when you pour hot water into cups at the same temperature as the water?

13.2 The Nature of Liquids

40. Explain why liquids and gases differ in density and the ability to be compressed.

41. Compare evaporation of a liquid in a closed container with that of a liquid in an open container.

42. Explain why increasing the temperature of a liquid increases its rate of evaporation.

43. Describe the effect that increasing temperature has on the vapor pressure of a liquid.

44. Distinguish between the boiling point and the normal boiling point of a liquid.

★**45.** Explain how boiling is a cooling process.

46. According to the graph below, what is the vapor pressure of water at 40°C?

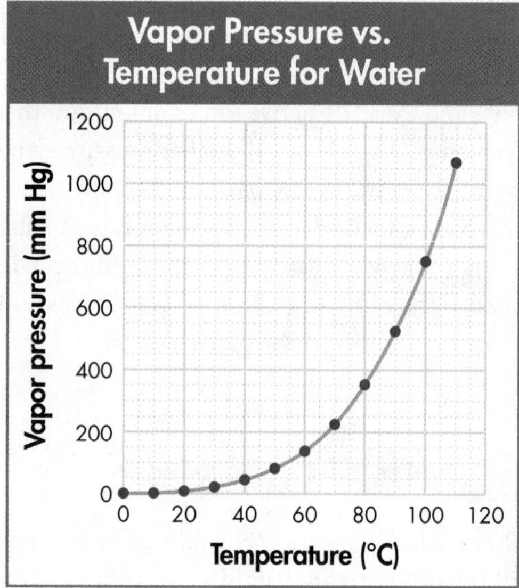

13.3 The Nature of Solids

47. Describe what happens when a solid is heated to its melting point.

★**48.** Explain why molecular solids usually have lower melting points than ionic solids.

13.4 Changes of State

★**49.** When you remove the lid from a food container that has been left in a freezer for several months, you discover a large collection of ice crystals on the underside of the lid. Explain what has happened.

50. Explain why a liquid stays at a constant temperature while it is boiling.

Understand Concepts

*51. What happens to the average kinetic energy of the water molecules in your body when you have a fever?

52. Describe the evaporation process, vapor pressure, and boiling point.

53. Why is the equilibrium that exists between a liquid and its vapor in a closed container called a dynamic equilibrium?

*54. In a series of liquids, as the intermolecular forces of attraction strengthen, would you expect the vapor pressure to increase or decrease? Explain.

55. Predict the physical state of each substance at the specified temperature. Use the melting point and boiling point data from the table below.
a. phenol at 99°C
b. ammonia at –25°C
c. methanol in an ice-water bath
d. methanol in a boiling-water bath
e. ammonia at –100°C
f. phenol at 25°C

Substance	Melting Point (°C)	Boiling Point (°C)
Ammonia	–77.7	–33.4
Methanol	–97.7	64.7
Water	0	100
Phenol	40.9	181.9

56. Why is atmospheric pressure much lower on the top of a mountain than it is at sea level?

*57. A fully inflated raft is left outside overnight. The next morning, the raft is not fully inflated. As the air temperature rises during the day, the raft expands to the size it was the night before. Assuming that the amount of air inside the raft did not change, use kinetic theory to explain why the size of the raft changes.

Think Critically

58. **Relate Cause and Effect** What role does atmospheric pressure play when someone is drinking a liquid through a straw?

59. **Explain** Is the average kinetic energy of the particles in a block of ice at 0°C the same as or different from the average kinetic energy of the particles in a gas-filled weather balloon at 0°C? Explain.

60. **Apply Concepts** How does perspiration help cool your body on a hot day?

61. **Relate Cause and Effect** Why do different liquids have different normal boiling points?

62. **Explain** A liquid-vapor equilibrium exists in a container. Explain why the equilibrium vapor pressure in the container is not affected when the volume of the container is changed.

FOUNDATIONS Wrap-Up

Observing Gas Pressure

1. **Draw Conclusions** At the beginning of this chapter, you saw a card "stick" to the glass because of air pressure. Explain how air pressure caused the card to stick to the glass.

Concept Check

Now that you've finished studying Chapter 13, answer these questions:

2. How are gases different from liquids and solids?
3. What makes a liquid evaporate? What makes a liquid boil?
4. Explain the freezing point and the melting point of a solid.
5. How do pressure and temperature affect how substances change state?

Write About Science

63. **Infer** What everyday evidence suggests to you that all matter is in constant motion? Think about all kinds of matter—solids, liquids, and gases. What do you know about the particles in them and how those particles behave?

*64. **Analyze Data** A teacher wants to demonstrate that unheated water can boil at room temperature in a beaker with a bell jar connected to a vacuum pump. However, the pump is not working correctly. It can reduce pressures only to 15 kPa. Can the teacher use this pump to perform the demonstration successfully? Explain your answer.

65. **Propose a Solution** A mixture of gases contains oxygen, nitrogen, and water vapor. What physical process could you use to remove the water vapor from the sample?

CHEMYSTERY

Foggy Car Windows

Car windows fog up because of condensation. When it is cold outside, your body and breath warm the air inside the car. Warm, moist air comes in contact with the cold surface of the car window. That causes it to fog up. Warm air can hold more water vapor than cold air. So, using a car heater increases the amount of moisture in the air. The amount of moisture in the air will also be higher on a rainy day because some of the water on the passengers evaporates. An air conditioner cools and removes moisture from the air.

66. **Explain** Describe why opening a window can also help defog a car windshield.

67. **Connect to the BIGIDEA** How does the average motion of the water molecules change as water vapor condenses on a car window? Why does the motion change?

Cumulative Review

68. How are the frequency and wavelength of light waves related? (See Lesson 5.3 for help.)

*69. Write the electron configuration for each ion. (See Lesson 7.1 for help.)
   a. Ca^{2+}
   b. S^{2-}

70. List the intermolecular attractions between molecules in order of increasing strength. (See Lesson 8.4 for help.)
   a. dispersion forces
   b. hydrogen bonds
   c. dipole interactions

71. Write a correct formula for each compound. (See Lessons 9.2 and 9.4 for help.)
   a. copper(I) sulfite
   b. nitrous acid

72. Write formulas for these ions. (See Lesson 9.1 for help.)
   a. iron(III) ions
   b. cadmium ions

73. How many moles are there in each sample? (See Lesson 10.2 for help.)
   a. 888 g of sulfur dioxide
   b. 8.6 L CO_2 (at STP)

74. Balance these equations. (See Lesson 11.1 for help.)
   a. $V_2O_5 + H_2 \longrightarrow V_2O_3 + H_2O$
   b. $(NH_4)_2Cr_2O_7 \longrightarrow Cr_2O_3 + N_2 + H_2O$

75. List the metal that ranks higher in the activity series of metals. (See Lesson 11.2 for help.)
   a. magnesium or mercury
   b. potassium or lithium

76. Classify each reaction as combination, decomposition, single replacement, double replacement, or combustion. (See Lesson 11.2 for help.)
   a. $2Li(s) + Br_2(l) \longrightarrow 2LiBr(s)$
   b. $2C_2H_6(g) + 7O_2(g) \longrightarrow 4CO_2(g) + 6H_2O(g)$

Standardized Test Prep

For help with answering test questions, go to your Chemistry Skills and Math Workbook.

Tips for Success

Interpreting Graphs A line graph helps you see the relationship between two variables. Before you answer a question about a graph, identify the variables and the general relationship between the variables based on the shape of the curve.

Use this graph to answer Questions 1 and 2.

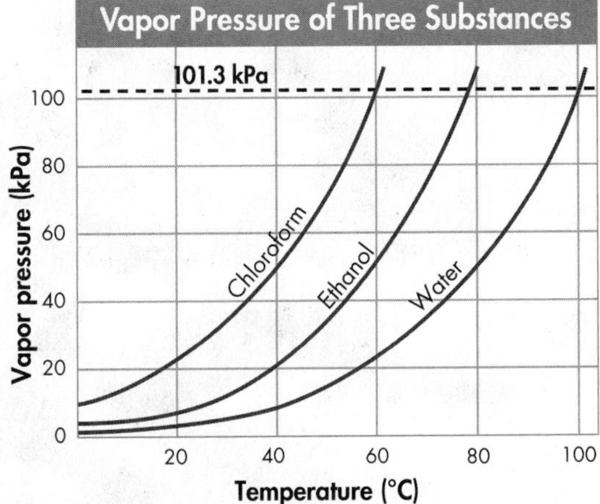

1. What is the normal boiling point of ethanol?
2. Can chloroform be heated to 90°C in an open container?

3. Which sequence has the states of CH_3OH correctly ordered in terms of increasing average kinetic energy?
   (A) $CH_3OH(s)$, $CH_3OH(g)$, $CH_3OH(l)$
   (B) $CH_3OH(g)$, $CH_3OH(l)$, $CH_3OH(s)$
   (C) $CH_3OH(l)$, $CH_3OH(g)$, $CH_3OH(s)$
   (D) $CH_3OH(s)$, $CH_3OH(l)$, $CH_3OH(g)$

Use this drawing to answer Questions 4–6. The same liquid is in each flask.

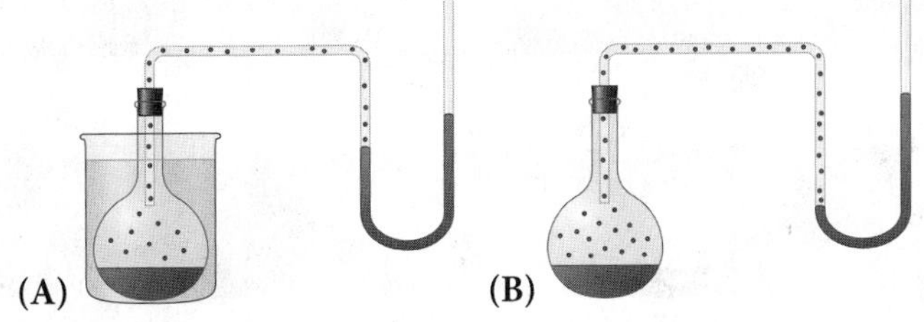

4. In which flask is the vapor pressure lower? Give a reason for your answer.
5. In which flask is the liquid at the higher temperature? Explain your answer.
6. How can the vapor pressure in each flask be determined?

For each question below, there are two statements. Decide whether each statement is true or false. Then, decide whether Statement II is a correct explanation for Statement I.

	Statement I		Statement II
7.	In an open container, the rate of evaporation of a liquid always equals the rate of condensation.	BECAUSE	A dynamic equilibrium exists between the liquid and its vapor in an open container.
8.	Water boils at a temperature below 100°C on top of a mountain.	BECAUSE	Atmospheric pressure decreases with an increase in altitude.
9.	The temperature of a substance always increases as heat is added to the substance.	BECAUSE	The average kinetic energy of the particles in a substance increases with an increase in temperature.
10.	Solids have a fixed volume.	BECAUSE	Particles in a solid cannot move.
11.	Gases are more compressible than liquids.	BECAUSE	There is more space between particles in a gas than between particles in a liquid.

If You Have Trouble With . . .

Question	1	2	3	4	5	6	7	8	9	10	11
See Lesson	13.1	13.2	13.4	13.2	13.2	13.2	13.2	13.2	13.1	13.3	13.1

14 The Behavior of Gases

FOUNDATIONS for Learning

Hot and Cold Balloons

1. Work with a partner. You will need two round non-latex balloons, a bowl of ice water, and a bowl of hot water.
2. Blow up both balloons to the same size.
3. Predict what will happen if you put one balloon in each bowl.
4. Then put one balloon in the cold water and one in the hot water. Were your predictions correct?

Form a Hypothesis Explain why you think the balloons changed as they did.

PearsonChem.com

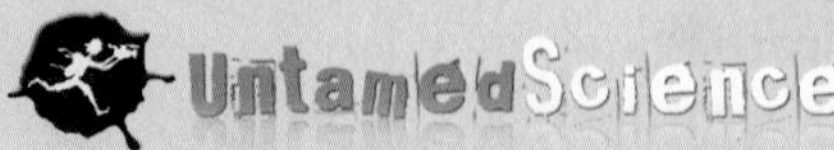

Take a video field trip with the Untamed Science crew as they talk with experts who are working on new ways to keep fruits and vegetables fresher longer.

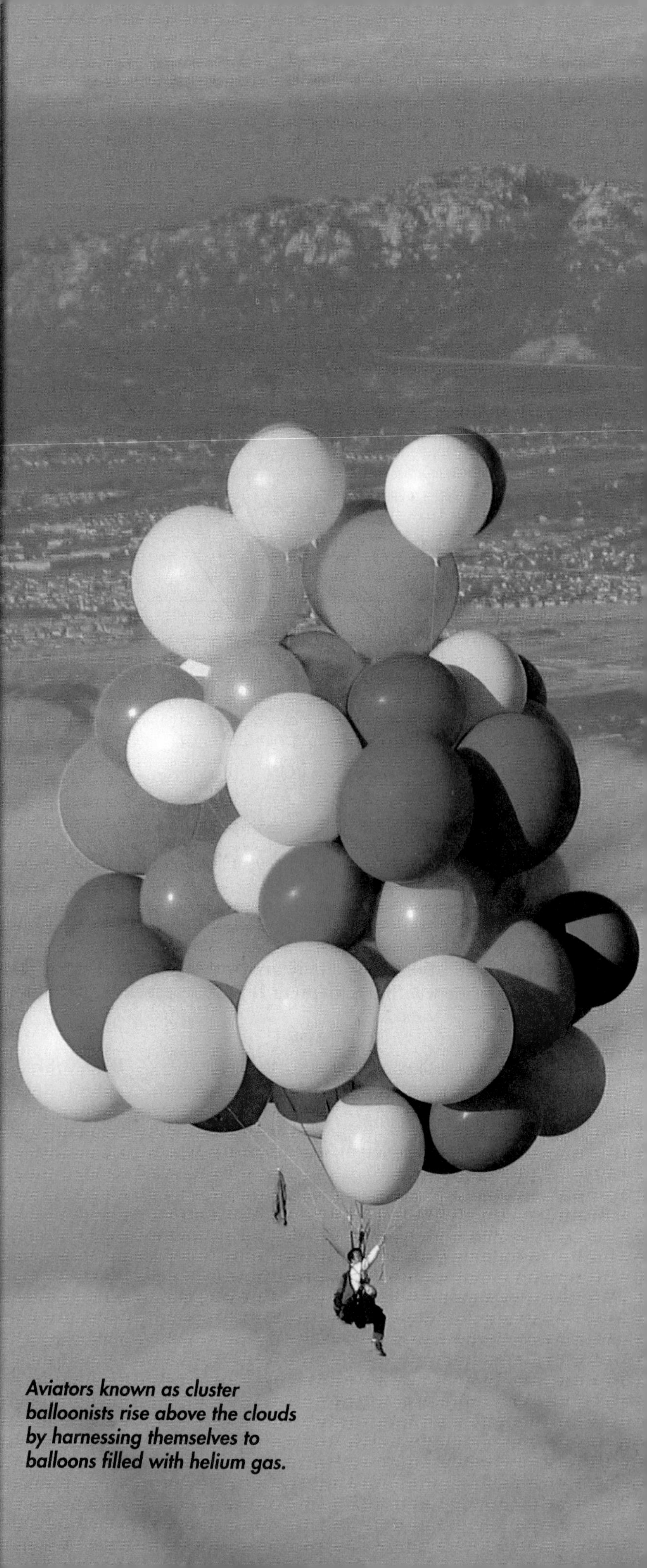

Aviators known as cluster balloonists rise above the clouds by harnessing themselves to balloons filled with helium gas.

KINETIC THEORY

Essential Questions:

1. *How do gases respond to changes in pressure, volume, and temperature?*
2. *Why is the ideal gas law useful even though ideal gases do not exist?*

CHEMYSTERY

Under Pressure

Just after 2 P.M., Becki completes her eighth scuba dive over a four-day period off the coast of Belize. After the dive, she feels fine.

A few hours later at dinner, Becki feels tired. She thinks that her fatigue is probably due to the many hours she spent swimming during her vacation. But she also begins to feel itchy and notices a blotchy rash on her skin. Did she get stung by a sea creature during her last dive? Becki decides to go back to her hotel room to get some rest. As she is walking, she begins to feel severe pains in the joints of her arms and legs and feels achy all over her body. Becki feels like she is coming down with the flu, but she realizes that her symptoms are related to her dives. What is wrong with Becki?

▶ Connect to the **BIG**IDEA As you read about the behavior of gases, think about what may have caused Becki's symptoms.

14.1 Properties of Gases

CHEMISTRY & YOU

Q: Why is there a recommended pressure range for the air inside a soccer ball? In organized soccer, there are rules about the equipment used in a game. For example, in international competitions, the ball's mass must be between 410 and 450 grams. The pressure of the air inside the ball must be between 0.6 and 1.1 atmospheres. In this lesson, you'll study variables that affect gas pressure.

Key Questions

Why are gases easier to compress than solids or liquids?

What are the three factors that affect gas pressure?

compressibility a measure of how much the volume of matter decreases under pressure

USING PRIOR KNOWLEDGE

The word *press* is in the middle of the word *compressibility*. You know that press means to push against. Compressibility is how easily something gives when you push against it.

Compressibility

You've learned that a gas expands to fill its container. A gas is also easy to compress, or squeeze, into a smaller space. **Compressibility** is a measure of how much the volume of matter decreases under pressure.

Compressibility of a gas is important in auto safety. As you know, cars have seat belts and air bags. When a car stops suddenly, the people in the car keep moving forward unless they are wearing seat belts. Air bags are a second line of defense. When the car stops suddenly, the rapid change in movement triggers a chemical reaction inside the air bag. One product of the reaction is nitrogen gas. As shown in the figure below, nitrogen gas causes the bag to inflate.

Why does colliding with an inflated air bag hurt less than colliding with a steering wheel or dashboard? A collision with an air bag makes the molecules of gas inside the bag move closer together. The figure at the top of the next page shows a person colliding with an air bag. The compression of the gas absorbs much of the impact's energy.

Air Bag
When the sensor detects a crash, an electrical signal causes the air bag to rapidly fill with nitrogen gas.

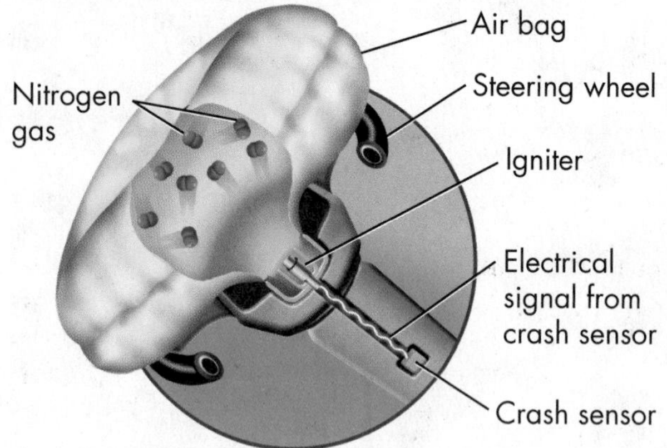

Compression of a Gas
Because gases can be compressed, the air bag absorbs some of the energy from the impact of a collision.

Kinetic theory explains why gases compress more easily than liquids or solids. Remember that the volume of the particles in a gas is small compared to the overall volume of the gas. So the distance between particles in a gas is much greater than the distance between particles in a liquid or solid. Under increased pressure, the particles in a gas are forced closer together, or compressed.

The figure below shows two air samples in different containers. The air samples are identical—8 nitrogen molecules and 2 oxygen molecules. In the larger container, the molecules are farther apart. In the smaller container, the air sample is compressed. So the molecules are closer together.

Key Question Why are gases easier to compress than solids or liquids? **Gases are easily compressed because the space between particles in a gas is greater than in a solid or a liquid.**

Modeling Air at Two Different Pressures

The molecules in this sample are far apart.

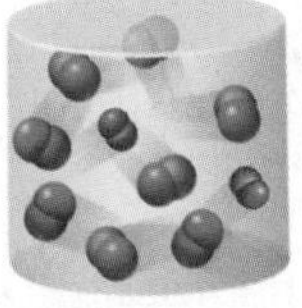

The molecules in this sample are closer together because the gas is compressed.

Factors Affecting Gas Pressure

Kinetic theory explains other properties of gases. Gases have the ability to expand. They also take the shape and volume of their container. Each gas particle moves in a straight line until it collides with another gas particle or with a wall of its container. Gas particles are always moving, and their motion is random. Kinetic theory assumes that there are no major forces of attraction or repulsion among particles in a gas. This assumption means gas particles move around freely.

Four variables are used to describe a gas. The four variables are pressure, volume, temperature, and number of moles. The table below shows the symbol and units for each variable.

Gas in a Flexible Container As air is added to the raft, the pressure inside the raft increases. The pressure keeps the raft inflated.

Variable	Symbol	Units
pressure	P	kilopascals (kPa)
volume	V	liters (L)
temperature	T	kelvins (K)
number of moles	n	moles (mol)

Amount of Gas Scientists can use kinetic theory to predict and explain how gases will respond to a change of conditions. Think about adding air to an inflatable raft, such as the one shown above. As you add air, the pressure inside the raft increases. The gas molecules collide with the raft's walls. These collisions cause pressure inside the raft. Adding air to the raft increases the amount of gas. Increasing the amount of gas increases the number of collisions. So the pressure increases. The figure below shows what happens when a gas is added to a rigid container.

Gas in a Rigid Container

❶ The volume of the gas is constant because the container is rigid. The temperature also stays the same.

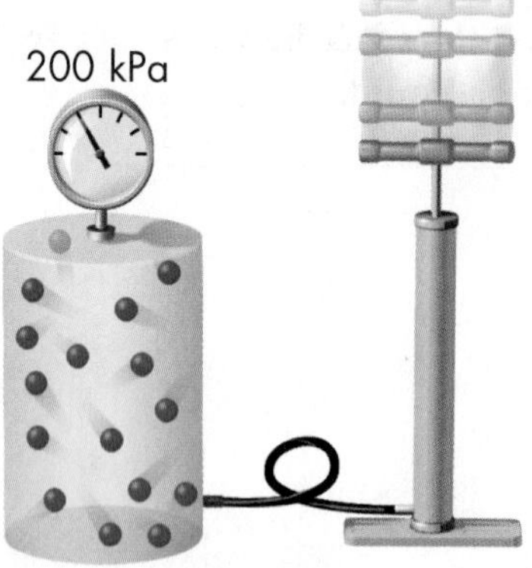

❷ When you add more gas particles, the pressure in the container increases. If you double the number of particles, the pressure will double.

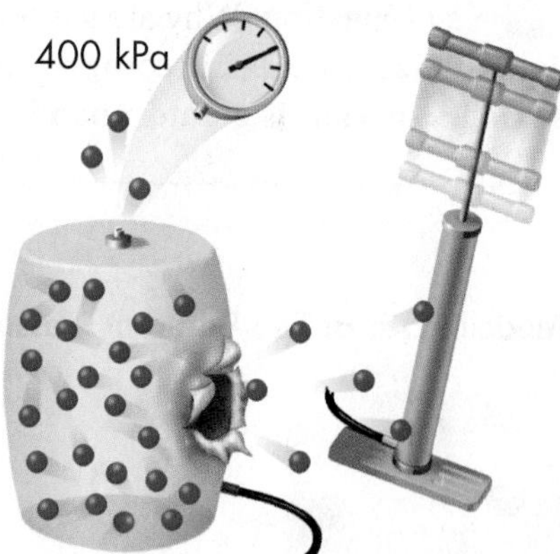

❸ If you add too much gas, the container can burst. The container bursts because the pressure is greater than the strength of the container.

If the pressure of a gas in a sealed container is lower than the outside air pressure, air will rush into the container when it's opened. This movement causes the whoosh you hear when you open a vacuum-packed jar. Read the Build Connections to learn more about why a vacuum-sealed jar makes a sound when you open it.

Aerosol cans depend on the movement of gas. The gas in an aerosol can is stored at a high pressure. The air outside the can is at a lower pressure. When you push the spray button, you create an opening. The gas flows through the opening to the lower pressure area outside. The movement of the gas forces the contents out of the can.

Volume You can increase the pressure exerted by a contained gas by reducing its volume. When a gas is in a cylinder, such as in a car engine, a piston can be used to reduce its volume.

The figure below shows a cylinder of gas under two different conditions. The temperature and the amount of gas are constant. Initially, the first cylinder has a volume of 1 L and a pressure of 100 kPa. If you decrease the volume by half to 0.5 L, you double the pressure to 200 kPa. Increasing the volume of the gas has the opposite effect. If you double the volume, the particles can expand into a volume that is twice the size. With the same amount of gas in twice the volume, the pressure is cut in half.

BUILD Connections

Are you familiar with the "button" on lids of vacuum-sealed jars of salsa or spaghetti sauce? These buttons are pressed in, and they pop up when you open the jar. The pressure inside the jar is lower than the atmospheric pressure. When you open the jar, air rushes in and makes the button on the lid pop up.

Pressure and Volume

Volume = 1 L
Pressure = 100 kPa

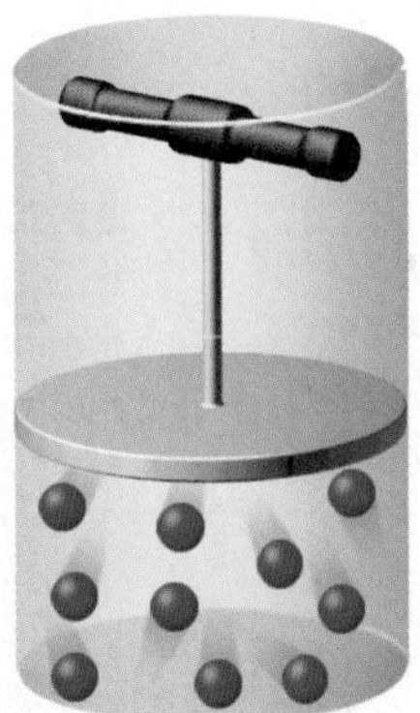

Volume = 0.5 L
Pressure = 200 kPa

❶ The particles of gas in the cylinder are moving. The particles colliding with the walls of the container create pressure.

❷ If you push the piston down, you decrease the volume. The same number of particles crowd into a smaller space.

❸ The same amount of gas now takes up a smaller space. The gas particles collide with the walls more often. So the pressure increases.

Potato Chip Bag If you leave a sealed potato chip bag near a sunny window, it can bulge. The gas in the bag gets warmer, so the pressure increases.

Temperature You can use kinetic theory to explain why a bag of potato chips bulges when left in a sunny window. Look at the photo to the left. The sun heats the gas inside the bag. As the temperature of the gas goes up, the gas molecules move faster. The faster moving molecules hit the bag's walls with more energy. So the pressure inside the bag goes up.

Look at the figure below. The volume and the amount of gas are constant. When the Kelvin temperature of the gas doubles from 300 K to 600 K, the pressure doubles from 100 kPa to 200 kPa. A contained gas can create a lot of pressure when heated. The container can burst if heated enough.

Key Question What are the three factors that affect gas pressure? **The amount of gas, the volume, and the temperature are factors that affect gas pressure.**

Pressure and Temperature

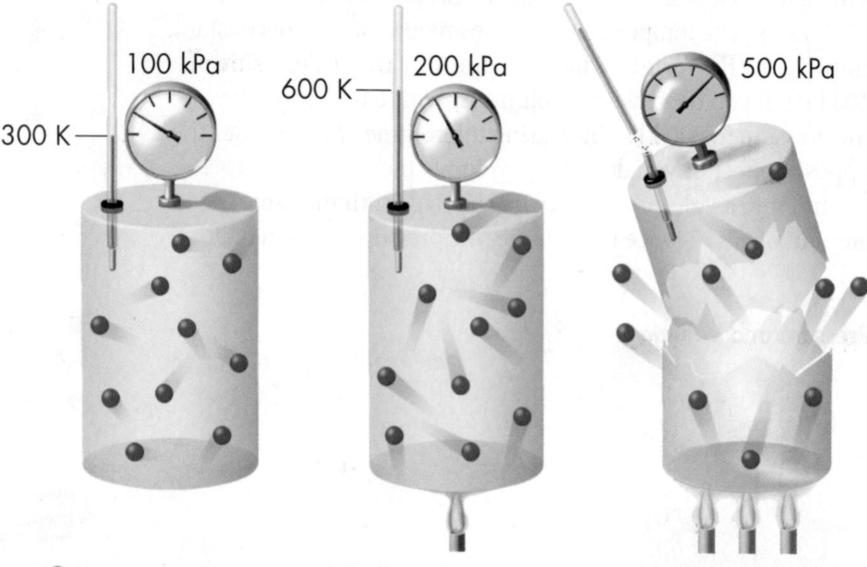

❶ Adding heat to a gas increases the kinetic energy of the molecules.

❷ Faster-moving molecules hit the wall with more energy. So the pressure increases.

❸ When temperature increases enough, the pressure may cause the container to burst.

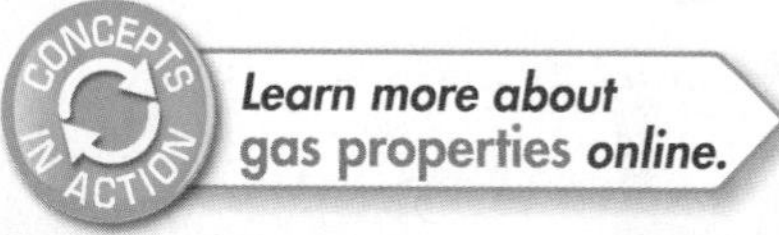

CONCEPTS IN ACTION
Learn more about gas properties online.

14.1 LessonCheck

Key Concept Check

1. **Review** Why is a gas easy to compress?
2. **Identify** Which three factors affect gas pressure?

Think Critically

3. **Compare and Contrast** Why does colliding with an air bag hurt less than colliding with a steering wheel?

CHEMISTRY & YOU

4. Which would travel farther if kicked with the same amount of force: a properly inflated soccer ball or an underinflated soccer ball? Explain your reasoning. (Hint: See page 424.)

BIGIDEA KINETIC THEORY

5. Use the kinetic theory of gases to explain why a gas can be easily squeezed into a smaller volume.

14.2 The Gas Laws

CHEMISTRY & YOU

Q: How do you fill up a hot air balloon? A hot air balloon works on the principle that warm air is less dense than cooler air. To make a hot air balloon rise, the pilot heats the air inside the balloon. To make the balloon descend, the pilot releases hot air through a vent in the top of the balloon. In this lesson, you'll study the laws that allow you to predict gas behavior.

Key Question

How are the pressure, volume, and temperature of a gas related?

Boyle's law the volume of a gas varies inversely with the pressure applied to it when temperature is constant

ACADEMIC WORDS

The term *varies inversely* tells you that an increase in one variable causes a decrease in the other. This just means that as one thing goes up, the other goes down.

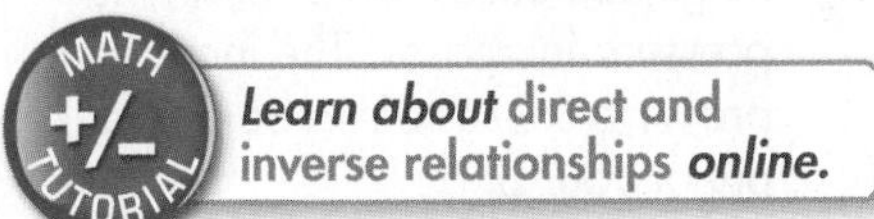

MATH +/– TUTORIAL
Learn about direct and inverse relationships online.

Boyle's Law

Robert Boyle was the first to study the relationship between the pressure and the volume of a gas. **Boyle's law** states that if the temperature of a gas is constant, the volume varies inversely with the pressure.

Boyle's law describes that when the volume of a gas changes, the pressure changes in the opposite way. If you push down on the plunger of a bicycle pump, for example, the volume of air inside the pump cylinder gets smaller, or decreases. As a result, the pressure inside the cylinder increases.

As you might expect, the reverse is also true. As the pressure of a gas decreases, the volume increases. When two variables are inversely proportional, the graph of the relationship is always a curve. The graph below shows an inverse relationship.

Boyle's Law As pressure increases, the volume decreases. The temperature does not change.
Go to your Chemistry Skills and Math Workbook to practice interpreting graphs.

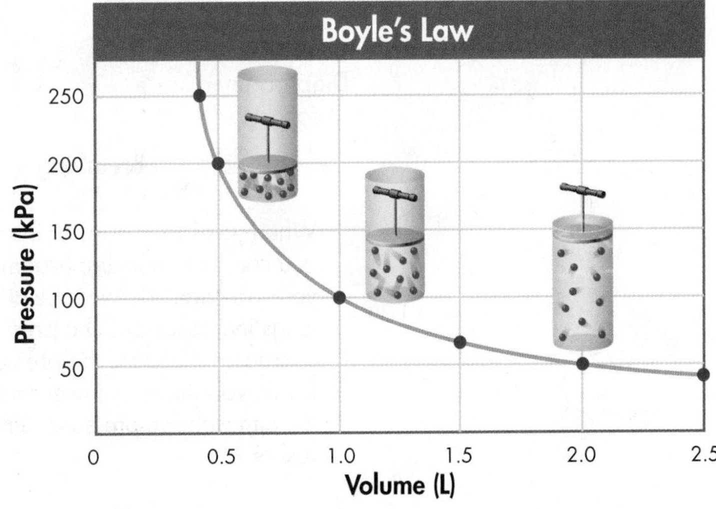

BUILD Connections

Twist the ends of a plastic straw tightly but in different directions. Twist until you can't twist anymore. Ask a friend to flick the middle of the straw with their fingernail. You should hear the straw snap.

By forcing the air inside the straw into a smaller volume, you increase the pressure. It doesn't take much to make the straw burst.

The equation below expresses Boyle's law mathematically.

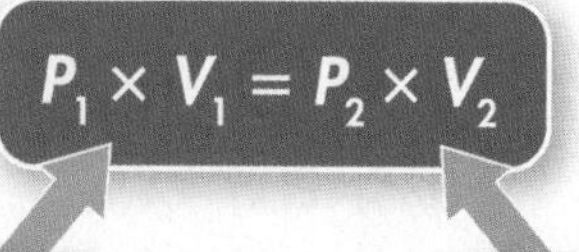

P_1 and V_1 are the pressure and volume of a gas before a change.

P_2 and V_2 are the pressure and volume of a gas after a change.

The figure below shows how breathing illustrates Boyle's law. Your lungs have properties that are similar to balloons. Take a deep breath and pay attention to what happens. When you inhale, your lungs get bigger. Because the volume increases, the pressure inside your lungs decreases and air enters. When you exhale, your lungs return to their original volume. As a result, the pressure inside your lungs increases, and the air rushes out. Try the activity described in the Build Connections to help you understand how the pressure and volume of a gas are related.

Key Question How are the pressure and volume of a gas related? **If the temperature is constant, as the pressure of a gas increases, the volume decreases.**

Volume-Pressure Changes in Breathing

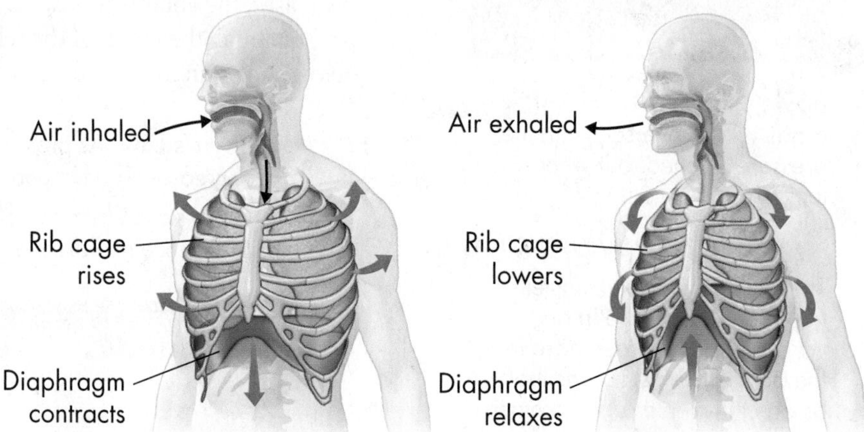

When you breathe in, or inhale, you contract your diaphragm and your rib cage. The volume of your lungs increases and the pressure decreases. Because the pressure inside your lungs is lower than the atmospheric pressure, air rushes in.

When you breathe out, or exhale, you relax your diaphragm and your rib cage. The volume of your lungs decreases. As a result, the pressure increases. The increase in pressure causes air to be pushed out of your body.

SampleProblem 14.1

Using Boyle's Law

A balloon contains 30.0 L of helium gas at 103 kPa. What is the volume of the helium when the balloon rises to an altitude where the pressure is only 25.0 kPa? (Assume that the temperature remains constant.)

1 Analyze List the knowns and the unknown.

KNOWNS	UNKNOWN
$P_1 = 103\text{ kPa}$	$V_2 = ?\text{ L}$
$V_1 = 30.0\text{ L}$	
$P_2 = 25.0\text{ kPa}$	

2 Calculate Solve for the unknown. Use Boyle's law to find V_2.

Start with Boyle's law.

$$P_1 \times V_1 = P_2 \times V_2$$

Rearrange the equation to isolate V_2.

Isolate V_2 by dividing both sides by P_2.

$$\frac{P_1 \times V_1}{P_2} = \frac{\cancel{P_2} \times V_2}{\cancel{P_2}}$$

Rewrite the equation so that your unknown is on the left.

$$V_2 = \frac{P_1 \times V_1}{P_2}$$

Now substitute the knowns into the equation, and cancel units.

$$V_2 = \frac{103\ \cancel{\text{kPa}} \times 30.0\text{ L}}{25.0\ \cancel{\text{kPa}}}$$

Solve the equation.

$$V_2 = \frac{103 \times 30.0\text{ L}}{25.0} = \frac{3090\text{ L}}{25.0} = 124\text{ L or } 1.24 \times 10^2\text{ L}$$

3 Evaluate Does the result make sense? You know that Boyle's law states an inverse relationship. So if the pressure decreases, the volume must increase. The pressure decreased from 103 kPa to 25.0 kPa. The answer shows that the volume increased from 30.0 L to 1.24×10^2 L. This answer agrees with the pressure-volume relationship and with kinetic theory.

Check your work by putting the answer into the original equation ($P_1 \times V_1 = P_2 \times V_2$). Both sides must be the same.

BUILD Math Skills

Isolating a Variable To solve an equation, you must isolate the variable. You do this by getting the variable alone on one side of the equation.

You can use any operation to isolate the variable. But remember that whatever you do to one side of the equation, you have to do to the other.

Go to your Chemistry Skills and Math Workbook for more practice.

Practice Problems

6. The pressure on 2.50 L of N_2O changes from 105 kPa to 40.5 kPa. If the temperature does not change, what will the new volume be?

1 Analyze **List the knowns and the unknown.**

2 Calculate **Solve for the unknown.**

3 Evaluate **Does the result make sense?**

KNOWNS	UNKNOWN
P_1 = 105 kPa	V_2 = ? L
V_1 = 2.50 L	
P_2 = 40.5 kPa	

7. A gas with a volume of 4.00 L at a pressure of 205 kPa expands to a volume of 12.0 L. What is the pressure in the container if the temperature remains constant?

KNOWNS	UNKNOWN
P_1 =	P_2 = ? kPa
V_1 =	
V_2 =	

Hint: Expands means to spread out.

8. A gas with a volume of 4.0 L at 90.0 kPa expands until the pressure drops to 20.0 kPa. What is its new volume if the temperature doesn't change?

9. Challenge A gas sample at constant temperature has a volume of 250 mL at 355 kPa. What volume (in L) will the sample occupy if the pressure is changed to 157 kPa?

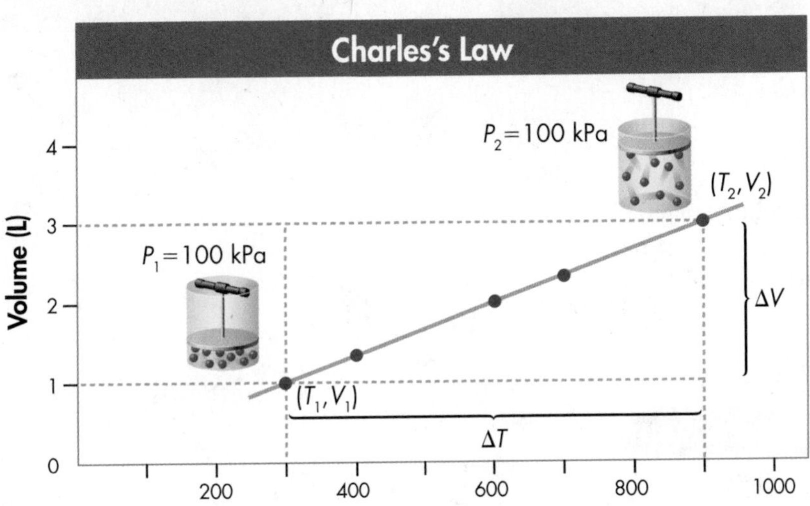

Charles's Law This graph shows a direct relationship. As temperature increases, volume increases. The pressure stays the same.

Go to your Chemistry Skills and Math Workbook to practice interpreting graphs.

See Charles's law *animated online.* KINETIC ART

Charles's Law

Jacques Charles studied the relationship between the temperature and the volume of a gas. Charles observed that the temperature and volume of a gas increase together. **Charles's law** states that the volume of a gas is directly proportional to its Kelvin temperature if the pressure is constant.

For each gas Charles studied, he observed a volume-temperature graph that was a straight line. Use the blue dashed lines in the graph above to help you read the graph. When the temperature is 300 K, the volume is 1 L. When the temperature is 900 K, the volume is 3 L. In both cases, the ratio V/T is the same, 1/300. The ratio is the same at all conditions of T and V when the pressure is constant. The equation below expresses Charles's law mathematically.

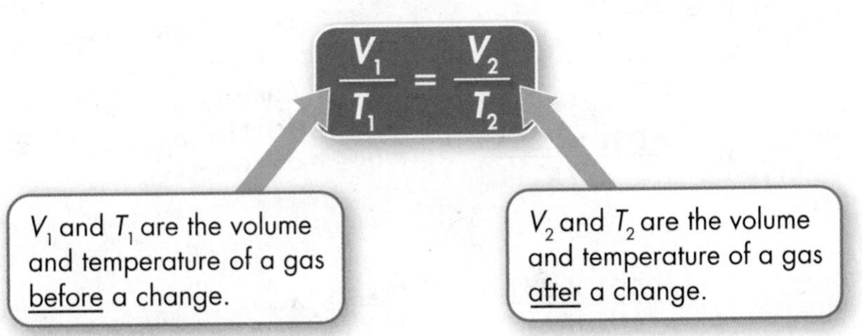

$\frac{V_1}{T_1} = \frac{V_2}{T_2}$
V_1 and T_1 are the volume and temperature of a gas before a change.
V_2 and T_2 are the volume and temperature of a gas after a change.

The ratio V/T is always the same if the temperatures are expressed in kelvins. If the temperatures are expressed in degrees Celsius, the ratio V/T changes. So when you solve gas law problems, remember to express the temperatures in kelvins.

Key Question How are the temperature and volume of a gas related? **As the temperature of an enclosed gas increases, the volume increases if the pressure is constant.**

Charles's law the volume and Kelvin temperature of a gas are directly proportional at constant pressure

ACADEMIC WORDS

Directly proportional describes a relationship where both variables increase or decrease together. If one variable goes up, the other variable goes up.

CHEMISTRY TUTORIAL

SampleProblem 14.2

Using Charles's Law

A balloon inflated in a room at 24°C has a volume of 4.00 L. The balloon is then heated to a temperature of 58°C. What is the new volume if the pressure is constant?

❶ Analyze **List the knowns and the unknown.**

KNOWNS	UNKNOWN
$V_1 = 4.00\ L$	$V_2 = ?\ L$
$T_1 = 24°C$	
$T_2 = 58°C$	

❷ Calculate **Solve for the unknown.** Use Charles's law to find V_2.

Start by expressing the temperatures in kelvins.

To convert temperature in °C to kelvins, add 273.

$T_1 = 24°C + 273 = 297\ K$

$T_2 = 58°C + 273 = 331\ K$

Write the equation for Charles's law.

$$\frac{V_1}{T_1} = \frac{V_2}{T_2}$$

Rearrange the equation to isolate V_2.

Isolate V_2 by multiplying both sides by T_2.

$$T_2 \times \frac{V_1}{T_1} = \frac{V_2}{\cancel{T_2}} \times \cancel{T_2}$$

Rewrite the equation so that your unknown is on the left.

$$V_2 = \frac{V_1 \times T_2}{T_1}$$

Substitute the knowns into the equation, and cancel units.

$$V_2 = \frac{4.00\ L \times 331\ \cancel{K}}{297\ \cancel{K}}$$

Solve the equation.

$$V_2 = \frac{4.00\ L \times 331}{297} = \frac{1324\ L}{297} = 4.46\ L$$

Remember: Including units can help you get the right answer. Cancel out a unit when it's on the top and the bottom of a fraction.

❸ Evaluate **Does the result make sense?** You know that Charles's law states a direct relationship. So if the temperature increases, the volume must increase. The temperature increased from 297 K to 331 K. The original volume was 4.00 L, and the answer shows an increase to 4.46 L. This answer agrees with the temperature-volume relationship and with kinetic theory.

BUILD Math Skills

Significant Figures in Multiplication and Division It is important to round your answers to the correct number of significant figures. You can call them "sig figs" for short. To find the correct number of sig figs, examine the values that you will use in the calculation. Find the value with the fewest significant figures. Your answer must have the same number of significant figures as this value. Look at this example:

3.1 (2 sig figs) ⟵ fewest sig figs
× 12.60 (4 sig figs)
39.06 (answer from calculator)

Round the answer to 39 (2 sig figs).

Go to your Chemistry Skills and Math Workbook for more practice.

Practice Problems

10. If a sample of gas occupies 6.80 L at 325°C, what will its volume be at 25.0°C if the pressure does not change?

Hint: Don't forget to change °C to K by adding 273 to °C before you use Charles's law.

1 Analyze List the knowns and the unknown.

2 Calculate Solve for the unknown.

3 Evaluate Does the result make sense?

KNOWNS	UNKNOWN
V_1 = 6.80 L	V_2 = ? L
T_1 = 325°C	
T_2 = 25.0°C	

11. Exactly 5.00 L of air at −50.0°C is warmed to 100.0°C. What is the new volume if the pressure remains constant?

KNOWNS	UNKNOWN
V_1 =	V_2 = ? L
T_1 =	
T_2 =	

12. When the temperature of a fixed amount of gas doubles from 20 K to 40 K, what happens to the volume at constant pressure?

13. Challenge At 20°C, the volume of a balloon is 3.79 L. At what temperature will the balloon's volume reach 4.50 L if the pressure is constant?

Gay-Lussac's law the pressure and the Kelvin temperature of a gas are directly proportional if the volume is constant

ACADEMIC WORDS

The word *constant* simply means that the variable doesn't change.

Gay-Lussac's Law

300 K

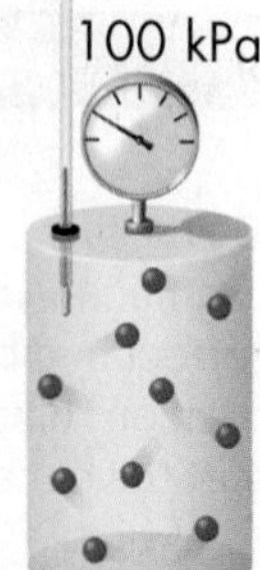

If you increase the temperature of an enclosed gas, you increase the pressure.

600 K

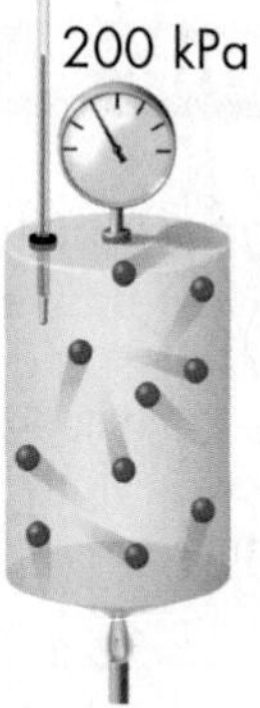

The particles of gas move faster and collide with the container wall more often. So the pressure increases.

Gay-Lussac's Law

In 1802, Joseph Gay-Lussac discovered the relationship between the pressure and temperature of a gas. The gas law that describes this relationship bears his name. **Gay-Lussac's law** states that the pressure of a gas is directly proportional to the Kelvin temperature if the volume remains constant.

Look at the figure above. When the temperature is 300 K, the pressure is 100 kPa. When the temperature is doubled to 600 K, the pressure doubles to 200 kPa. Gay-Lussac's law involves direct proportions. So the ratios P_1/T_1 and P_2/T_2 are equal at constant volume. You can express Gay-Lussac's law mathematically as follows.

$$\frac{P_1}{T_1} = \frac{P_2}{T_2}$$

P_1 and T_1 are the pressure and temperature of a gas before a change.

P_2 and T_2 are the pressure and temperature of a gas after a change.

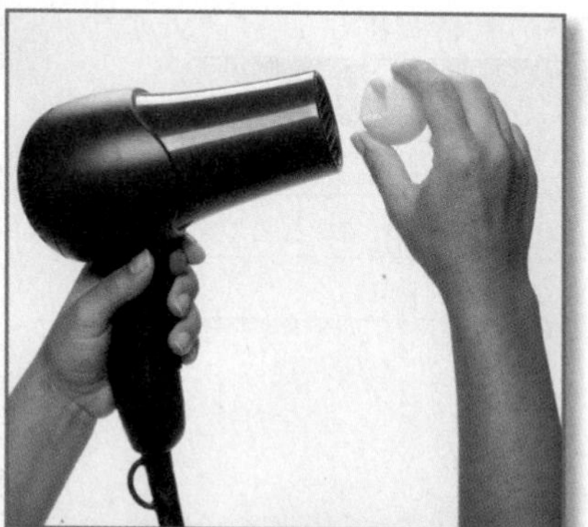

Repairing a Dented Ball Heating a table tennis ball causes the particles of gas inside the ball to move faster. The pressure increases, causing the dent to pop out.

You can use this pressure-temperature relationship in your life. Instead of throwing a dented table tennis ball away, you can use the principles of Gay-Lussac's law to fix it. Look at the photo. Increasing the temperature of the gas inside the ball causes the pressure of the gas to increase. The increase in pressure restores the ball's shape.

Key Question How are the pressure and temperature of a gas related? **As the temperature of an enclosed gas increases, the pressure increases if the volume is constant.**

SampleProblem 14.3

CHEMISTRY TUTORIAL

Using Gay-Lussac's Law

Aerosol cans have labels that warn you not to burn the cans or store them above a certain temperature. This problem will show why it is dangerous to dispose of aerosol cans in a fire. The gas in a used aerosol can is at a pressure of 103 kPa at 25°C. If the can is thrown onto a fire, what will the pressure be when the temperature reaches 928°C?

❶ Analyze List the knowns and the unknown.

KNOWNS	UNKNOWN
P_1 = 103 kPa	P_2 = ? kPa
T_1 = 25°C	
T_2 = 928°C	

❷ Calculate Solve for the unknown.
Use Gay-Lussac's law to calculate the unknown pressure (P_2).

Start by expressing the temperatures in kelvins.

$T_1 = 25°C + 273 = 298\ K$
$T_2 = 928°C + 273 = 1201\ K$

Write the equation for Gay-Lussac's law.

$$\frac{P_1}{T_1} = \frac{P_2}{T_2}$$

Rearrange the equation to isolate P_2.

Isolate P_2 by multiplying both sides by T_2.

$$T_2 \times \frac{P_1}{T_1} = \frac{P_2}{\cancel{T_2}} \times \cancel{T_2}$$

Remember: Multiplying both sides by T_2 lets you cancel out T_2 on the right side. This leaves P_2 by itself. Then P_2 is isolated.

Rewrite the equation so that your unknown is on the left.

$$P_2 = \frac{P_1 \times T_2}{T_1}$$

Substitute the knowns into the equation, and cancel units.

$$P_2 = \frac{103\ kPa \times 1201\ \cancel{K}}{298\ \cancel{K}}$$

Solve the equation.

$$P_2 = \frac{103\ kPa \times 1201}{298} = \frac{123{,}703\ kPa}{298} = 415 \text{ or } 4.15 \times 10^2\ kPa$$

❸ Evaluate Does the result make sense? Gay-Lussac's law states a direct relationship. So if the temperature increases, the pressure will increase. The temperature increased from 298 K to 1201 K. The answer shows that the pressure increased from 103 kPa to 4.15 × 10^2 kPa (415 kPa). This answer agrees with the temperature-pressure relationship and with kinetic theory. This extreme increase in pressure will cause the aerosol can to explode, which could injure someone standing near the fire.

BUILD Math Skills

Canceling Units If you solve a problem and cancel units correctly, the units of your answer should be what you expect. If they are not, reason through the problem again. You may have expressed one of the values in the wrong form. Or you may have canceled units incorrectly.

Practice Problems

14. A sealed cylinder of gas contains nitrogen gas at 1.00×10^3 kPa pressure and a temperature of 20°C. When the cylinder is left in the sun, the temperature of the gas increases to 50°C. What is the new pressure in the cylinder?

Remember: 1.00×10^3 kPa is the same as 1000 kPa.

1 Analyze **List the knowns and the unknown.**

2 Calculate **Solve for the unknown.**

3 Evaluate **Does the result make sense?**

KNOWNS	UNKNOWN
$P_1 = 1.00 \times 10^3$ kPa	$P_2 = ?$ kPa
$T_1 = 20°C$	
$T_2 = 50°C$	

15. The pressure in a sealed plastic container is 108 kPa at 41°C. What is the pressure when the temperature drops to 22°C? Assume that the volume has not changed.

KNOWNS	UNKNOWN
$P_1 =$	$P_2 = ?$ kPa
$T_1 =$	
$T_2 =$	

16. The pressure in a car tire is 198 kPa at 27°C. After a long drive, the pressure is 225 kPa. What is the temperature of the air in the tire? Assume that the volume is constant.

Hint: To isolate T_2 in Problem 16, first multiply both sides by T_2. Then, multiply both sides by T_1/P_1. Finally, cancel out the like terms.

17. Challenge A gas sample has a pressure of 6580 Pa at 266°C. If the volume doesn't change, what will the pressure be at −62.0°C? Express your answer in kilopascals.

The Combined Gas Law

The **combined gas law** combines Boyle's law, Charles's law, and Gay-Lussac's law. You can use the combined gas law when the pressure, volume, and temperature vary. The combined gas law equation is expressed mathematically as follows.

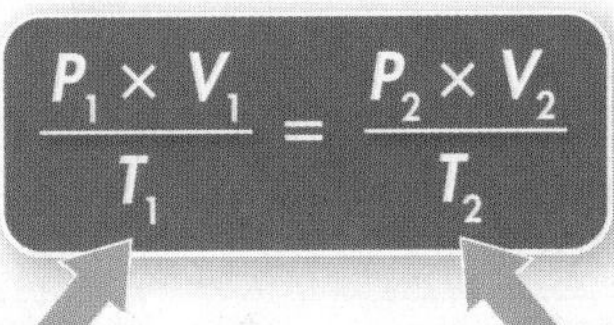

$$\frac{P_1 \times V_1}{T_1} = \frac{P_2 \times V_2}{T_2}$$

P_1, V_1, and T_1 are the pressure, volume, and temperature before a change.

P_2, V_2, and T_2 are the pressure, volume, and temperature after a change.

combined gas law the law that describes the relationships between the pressure, volume, and temperature of a gas

ACADEMIC WORDS
Look up the word *law* in your dictionary. Then explain how the scientific meaning differs from the everyday meaning.

Weather balloons, like the one in the photo below, carry data-gathering instruments up into the atmosphere. At an altitude of about 27,000 meters, the balloon bursts. The combined gas law can help to explain this situation. The temperature and pressure drop as the balloon rises. These changes have opposite effects on the weather balloon's volume. A drop in temperature causes the volume to decrease. A drop in pressure causes the volume to increase. The balloon bursts, so you know the drop in pressure must affect the volume more than the drop in temperature does.

Key Question How are the pressure, volume, and temperature of a gas related? **When only the amount of gas is constant, the combined gas law describes the relationships between pressure, volume, and temperature.**

Weather Balloon
Meteorologists use weather balloons to gather data about Earth's atmosphere.

CHEMISTRY TUTORIAL

SampleProblem 14.4

Using the Combined Gas Law

The volume of a gas-filled balloon is 30.0 L at 313 K and 153 kPa. What is the volume at standard temperature and pressure (STP)? (Hint: STP = 273 K and 101.3 kPa.)

1 Analyze List the knowns and the unknown.

KNOWNS	UNKNOWN
$V_1 = 30.0\text{ L}$	$V_2 = ?\text{ L}$
$T_1 = 313\text{ K}$	
$P_1 = 153\text{ kPa}$	
$T_2 = 273\text{ K}$	
$P_2 = 101.3\text{ kPa}$	

2 Calculate Solve for the unknown.

Use the combined gas law to calculate V_2.

Start by writing the combined gas law.

$$\frac{P_1 \times V_1}{T_1} = \frac{P_2 \times V_2}{T_2}$$

Rearrange the equation to isolate V_2.

To isolate V_2, first multiply both sides by T_2.

$$T_2 \times \frac{P_1 \times V_1}{T_1} = \frac{P_2 \times V_2}{\cancel{T_2}} \times \cancel{T_2}$$

Now, divide both sides by P_2.

$$\frac{P_1 \times V_1 \times T_2}{P_2 \times T_1} = \frac{\cancel{P_2} \times V_2}{\cancel{P_2}}$$

Rewrite the equation so that your unknown is on the left.

$$V_2 = \frac{P_1 \times V_1 \times T_2}{P_2 \times T_1}$$

Substitute the knowns into the equation, and cancel units.

$$V_2 = \frac{153\,\cancel{\text{kPa}} \times 30.0\text{ L} \times 273\,\cancel{\text{K}}}{101.3\,\cancel{\text{kPa}} \times 313\,\cancel{\text{K}}}$$

Solve the equation.

$$V_2 = \frac{153 \times 30.0\text{ L} \times 273}{101.3 \times 313} = \frac{1,253,070\text{ L}}{31,707} = 39.5\text{ L}$$

3 Evaluate Does the result make sense? A decrease in temperature and a decrease in pressure have opposite effects on the volume. To evaluate the increase in volume, multiply V_1 (30.0 L) by the ratio P_1/P_2 (1.51) and the ratio T_2/T_1 (0.872). The result is 39.5 L.

Practice Problems

18. At STP, a gas sample has a volume of 20.0 L. What would the volume be at 75.0 K and 200.0 kPa? (Hint: STP = 273 K and 101.3 kPa.)

1 Analyze **List the knowns and the unknown.**

2 Calculate **Solve for the unknown.**

3 Evaluate **Does the result make sense?**

KNOWNS	UNKNOWN
V_1 = 20.0 L	V_2 = ? L
T_1 = 273 K	
P_1 = 101.3 kPa	
T_2 = 75.0 K	
P_2 = 200.0 kPa	

19. A gas at 155 kPa and 25°C has an initial volume of 1.00 L. The pressure of the gas increases to 605 kPa as the temperature is raised to 125°C. What is the new volume?

KNOWNS	UNKNOWN
V_1 =	V_2 = ? L
T_1 =	
P_1 =	
T_2 =	
P_2 =	

20. Challenge A 2.35 mol sample of He gas occupies 57.9 L at 300.0 K and 1.00 atm. What is the volume of this sample at 423 K and 2.00 atm?

Hint: Don't be fooled! Problem 20 gives you extra information. You do not need to know the amount of gas (2.35 mol) to solve the problem.

14.2 LessonCheck

Key Concept Check

21. **Review** How are the pressure and volume of a gas related at constant temperature?

22. **Review** If pressure is constant, how does a change in temperature affect the volume of a gas?

23. **Review** What is the relationship between the temperature and pressure of a gas at constant volume?

24. **Describe** When is the combined gas law useful?

Vocabulary Check *Choose a highlighted word from the lesson to complete the sentence correctly.*

25. The law that shows the relationship between a gas's volume and pressure at constant temperature is __________.

Think Critically

CHEMISTRY & YOU

26. A hot air balloon has a propane burner onboard to heat the air inside the balloon. What happens to the volume of the balloon as the air is heated? (Hint: See page 431.)

BIGIDEA KINETIC THEORY

27. Use the kinetic theory of gases to explain Gay-Lussac's law.

Atmospheric Chemist

Earth's atmosphere is the mixture of gases that surround Earth. These gases include oxygen, nitrogen, water vapor, carbon dioxide, methane, and ozone. Each gas can affect life on Earth in a different way.

Atmospheric chemists study the amounts of different gases in the atmosphere. They also study how these gases affect one another. Some atmospheric chemists study the effect of fossil fuels and other pollutants on the air you breathe, the climate, and living things. Other atmospheric chemists study hot gases and dust from volcanoes. Atmospheric chemists can also study other planets' atmospheres with the help of telescopes.

Scientists from different backgrounds often work together in atmospheric research. These different backgrounds might include chemistry, physics, climatology, and oceanography. Atmospheric chemists typically have a bachelor's degree in chemistry or atmospheric science. Many also have a graduate degree.

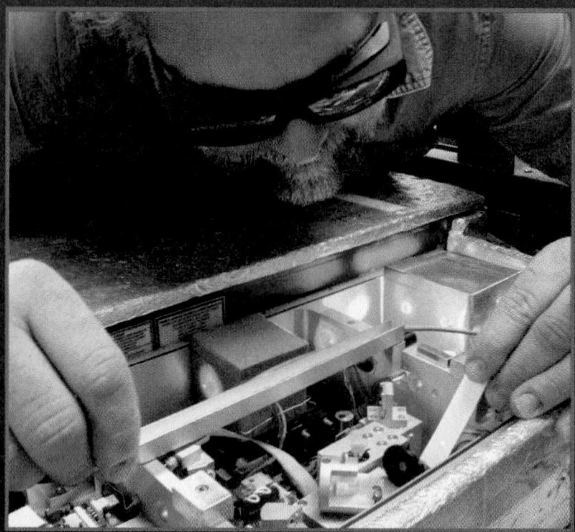

TOOLS AND TECHNOLOGY
An atmospheric chemist adjusts a device used to analyze gases in the atmosphere.

AIR QUALITY Tailpipe and smokestack emissions can cause a form of pollution called smog. Atmospheric chemists can help communities better understand how human activities impact local air quality.

Take It Further

1. Infer What kinds of data do you think atmospheric chemists collect to study gases in the atmosphere?

2. Research a Problem Ozone (O_3) is one of many gases that atmospheric chemists study. Research the ozone layer and describe how atmospheric ozone levels have changed over time.

14.3 Ideal Gases

CHEMISTRY & YOU

Q: How can you make fog indoors? Carbon dioxide freezes at −78.5°C, which is much colder than the ice in your freezer. Solid carbon dioxide, or dry ice, can be used to make stage fog. Dry ice does not melt—it sublimes. As solid carbon dioxide changes to gas, water vapor in the air condenses and forms a white fog. Dry ice can exist because gases do not obey the assumptions of kinetic theory at all conditions. In this lesson, you will learn how real gases differ from the ideal gases on which the gas laws are based.

Key Questions

How can you calculate the amount of gas when the pressure, volume, and temperature are known?

Under what conditions do real gases differ most from ideal gases?

BUILD Vocabulary

ideal gas law the relationship of pressure, volume, temperature, and amount of gas, or $PV = nRT$

ideal gas constant (R) the constant with the value 8.31 (L•kPa)/(K•mol)

USING PRIOR KNOWLEDGE

Ideal means best case or perfect. *Ideal* is also imaginary. An ideal gas is a perfect but imaginary gas.

Ideal Gas Law

In the previous lesson, you learned to solve gas problems with three variables: pressure, volume, and temperature. In this lesson, you'll learn about another variable—the amount of gas. This variable is expressed as the number of moles and has the symbol n.

The **ideal gas law** includes all four variables: pressure, volume, temperature, and the number of moles. The equation below expresses the ideal gas law mathematically.

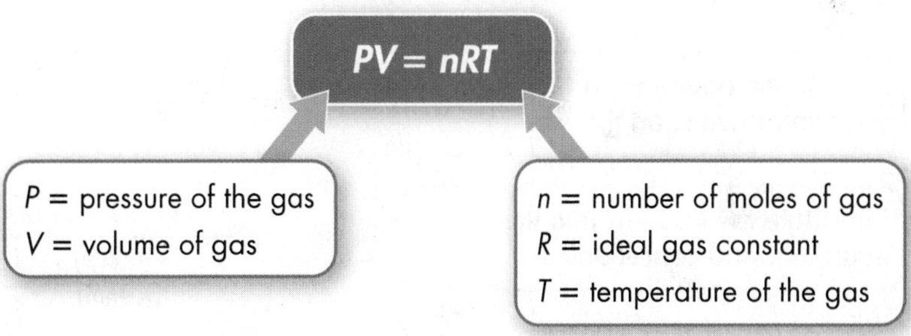

The equation $PV = nRT$ describes the physical behavior of an ideal gas. Although an ideal gas does not exist, the equation works well for real gases. You will learn more about real gases later in this lesson.

If you know the values for P, V, T, and n for one set of conditions, you can find a value for the constant, R. The numerical value of R depends on the units used. For this textbook, R, the **ideal gas constant,** has the value 8.31 (L•kPa)/(K•mol). Using this value for R and the ideal gas law, you can find the number of moles of gas, n, in a container.

Key Question How can you calculate the amount of gas when the pressure, volume, and temperature are known? **When the pressure, volume, and temperature of a gas are known, you can use the ideal gas law to calculate the number of moles of the gas.**

Using the Ideal Gas Law

At 34°C, the pressure inside a nitrogen-filled tennis ball is 212 kPa. The volume is 0.148 L. How many moles of nitrogen gas are in the tennis ball?

❶ Analyze List the knowns and the unknown.

KNOWNS	UNKNOWN
$P = 212\ \text{kPa}$	$n = ?\ \text{mol}\ N_2$
$V = 0.148\ \text{L}$	
$R = 8.31 \frac{\text{L} \cdot \text{kPa}}{\text{K} \cdot \text{mol}}$	
$T = 34°\text{C}$	

❷ Calculate Solve for the unknown. Use the ideal gas law to find *n*.

First, express the temperature in kelvins.

$T = 34°\text{C} + 273 = 307\ \text{K}$

Write the ideal gas law.

$P \times V = n \times R \times T$

Rearrange the equation to isolate *n*.

Isolate *n* by dividing both sides by $R \times T$.

$$\frac{P \times V}{R \times T} = \frac{n \times \cancel{R} \times \cancel{T}}{\cancel{R} \times \cancel{T}}$$

Rewrite the equation so that your unknown is on the left.

$$n = \frac{P \times V}{R \times T}$$

Substitute the knowns into the equation, and cancel units.

$$n = \frac{212\ \cancel{\text{kPa}} \times 0.148\ \cancel{\text{L}}}{8.31 \frac{(\cancel{\text{L}} \cdot \cancel{\text{kPa}})}{(\cancel{\text{K}} \cdot \text{mol})} \times 307\ \cancel{\text{K}}}$$

Remember: You can cancel out units when they are on both the top and the bottom of a fraction. In this case, everything cancels out except moles.

Solve the equation.

$$n = \frac{212 \times 0.148}{\frac{8.31}{\text{mol}} \times 307} = \frac{31.38\ \text{mol}}{2551}$$

$$= 0.0123 \text{ or } 1.23 \times 10^{-2}\ \text{mol}\ N_2$$

❸ Evaluate Does the result make sense? A tennis ball has a small volume and is not under great pressure. It is reasonable that the ball contains a small amount of nitrogen.

BUILD Math Skills

Reciprocals When you use the ideal gas law equation, it helps to understand reciprocals. Two fractions are reciprocals of each other if their product is 1.

This same property applies to units that are in fractions. Look at the last part of Step 2 on the previous page. After canceling the units, 1 is in the numerator and 1/mol is in the denominator. You can use the property of reciprocals to simplify this fraction. All you need to do is "flip" the fraction in the denominator from 1/mol to mol/1 and multiply it by the numerator.

$$\frac{1}{\left(\frac{1}{\text{mol}}\right)} \text{ is the same as } 1 \times \frac{\text{mol}}{1}.$$

The units are moles because the 1 cancels out.

$$\cancel{1} \times \frac{\text{mol}}{\cancel{1}} = \text{mol}$$

Practice Problems

28. When the temperature of a rigid hollow ball containing 685 L of helium gas is 621 K, the pressure of the gas is 1.89×10^3 kPa. How many moles of helium does the ball contain?

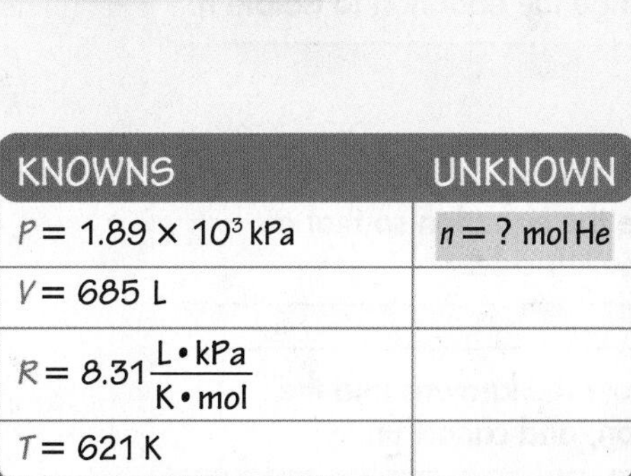

KNOWNS	UNKNOWN
$P = 1.89 \times 10^3$ kPa	$n = ?$ mol He
$V = 685$ L	
$R = 8.31 \frac{\text{L} \cdot \text{kPa}}{\text{K} \cdot \text{mol}}$	
$T = 621$ K	

1 Analyze List the knowns and the unknown.

2 Calculate Solve for the unknown.

3 Evaluate Does the result make sense?

29. What pressure will be exerted by 0.450 mol of a gas at 25°C if it is contained in a 0.650 L vessel?

KNOWNS	UNKNOWN
$V =$	$P = ?$ kPa
$n =$	
$R =$	
$T =$	

Hint: Be sure to isolate the unknown variable, pressure.

30. A 1.56 mol gas sample has a pressure of 135 kPa when the temperature is 27°C. What is the volume of the gas sample?

31. Challenge A 4.50 g sample of methane (CH_4) contains 0.281 mol of CH_4. The sample is in a 2.00 L container at 35°C. What is the pressure in the container?

SampleProblem 14.6

> Hint: Use the periodic table to find the molar mass of CH_4.
> molar mass$_C$ + 4(molar mass$_H$) = 12.0 g + 4(1.0 g) = 16.0 g

Using the Ideal Gas Law

A deep underground cavern contains 2.24×10^6 L of methane gas (CH_4) at a pressure of 1.50×10^3 kPa and a temperature of 315 K. How many kilograms of CH_4 does the cavern contain?

KNOWNS	UNKNOWNS
$P = 1.50 \times 10^3$ kPa	$n = ?$ mol CH_4
$V = 2.24 \times 10^6$ L	$m = ?$ kg CH_4
$R = 8.31 \dfrac{\text{L} \cdot \text{kPa}}{\text{K} \cdot \text{mol}}$	
$T = 315$ K	
molar mass$_{CH_4}$ = $16.0 \dfrac{\text{g}}{\text{mol}}$	

1 Analyze **List the knowns and the unknowns.**

2 Calculate **Solve for the unknowns.** Use the ideal gas law to find n. Use the molar mass of methane to convert moles to grams. Then convert grams to kilograms.

Write the ideal gas law.

$$P \times V = n \times R \times T$$

Rearrange the equation to isolate *n*.

Isolate n by dividing both sides by $R \times T$.

$$\frac{P \times V}{R \times T} = \frac{n \times \cancel{R} \times \cancel{T}}{\cancel{R} \times \cancel{T}}$$

Rewrite the equation so that *n* is on the left side.

$$n = \frac{P \times V}{R \times T}$$

Substitute the knowns into the equation, and cancel units.

$$n = \frac{(1.50 \times 10^3 \ \cancel{\text{kPa}}) \times (2.24 \times 10^6 \ \cancel{\text{L}})}{8.31 \dfrac{\cancel{\text{L}} \cdot \cancel{\text{kPa}}}{\cancel{\text{K}} \cdot \text{mol}} \times 315 \ \cancel{\text{K}}}$$

Solve the equation for the number of moles of methane.

$$n = \frac{(1.50 \times 10^3) \times (2.24 \times 10^6)}{\dfrac{8.31}{\text{mol}} \times 315} = \frac{3.36 \times 10^9}{\dfrac{2618}{\text{mol}}}$$

$$= 1.28 \times 10^6 \text{ mol } CH_4$$

Do a mole-mass conversion.

$$1.28 \times 10^6 \ \cancel{\text{mol } CH_4} \times \frac{16.0 \text{ g } CH_4}{1 \ \cancel{\text{mol } CH_4}} = 2.05 \times 10^7 \text{ g } CH_4$$

Convert from grams to kilograms.

$$2.05 \times 10^7 \ \cancel{\text{g}} \ CH_4 \times \frac{1 \text{ kg}}{1000 \ \cancel{\text{g}}} = \frac{2.05 \times 10^7 \text{ kg } CH_4}{1000}$$

$$= 2.05 \times 10^4 \text{ kg } CH_4$$

3 Evaluate **Does the result make sense?** Although the methane is compressed, its volume is still very large. So it is reasonable that the cavern contains a large mass of methane.

BUILD Math Skills

Scientific Notation Sometimes your answer is a very large or a very small number. Using scientific notation makes the number easier to read. To convert numbers to scientific notation, you move the decimal point to after the first number that isn't zero.

Suppose the answer is 0.000072. You move the decimal point five places to the right. When you move the decimal point to the right, the exponent is negative.

$$0.000072 = 7.2 \times 10^{-5}$$

5 places

Go to your Chemistry Skills and Math Workbook for more practice.

Practice Problems

32. A helium-filled weather balloon has a volume of 2.4×10^2 L at 99 kPa pressure and a temperature of 273 K. What is the mass (in grams) of the helium in the balloon?

1 Analyze **List the knowns and the unknowns.**

2 Calculate **Solve for the unknowns.**

3 Evaluate **Does the result make sense?**

KNOWNS	UNKNOWNS
$P = 99$ kPa	$n = ?$ mol He
$V = 2.4 \times 10^2$ L	$m = ?$ g He
$R = 8.31 \frac{\text{L} \cdot \text{kPa}}{\text{K} \cdot \text{mol}}$	
$T = 273$ K	
molar mass$_{He}$ = $4.0 \frac{\text{g}}{\text{mol}}$	

33. A 2.00 L tank is filled with methane (CH_4) at 35°C and a pressure of 360 kPa. How many grams of methane does the tank contain?

KNOWNS	UNKNOWNS
$P =$	$n = ?$ mol CH_4
$V =$	$m = ?$ g CH_4
$R =$	
$T =$	
molar mass$_{CH_4}$ =	

34. What volume will 12.0 g of oxygen gas (O_2) occupy at 298 K and a pressure of 52.7 kPa?

Hint: For Problem 34, you need to convert 12.0 g O_2 to moles O_2 before substituting it into the equation.

35. Challenge A child's lungs have a volume of 2.20 L. How many grams of air do her lungs hold at a pressure of 102 kPa and a body temperature of 37°C? Use a molar mass of 29 g for air, which is about 20% O_2 (32 g/mol) and 80% N_2 (28 g/mol).

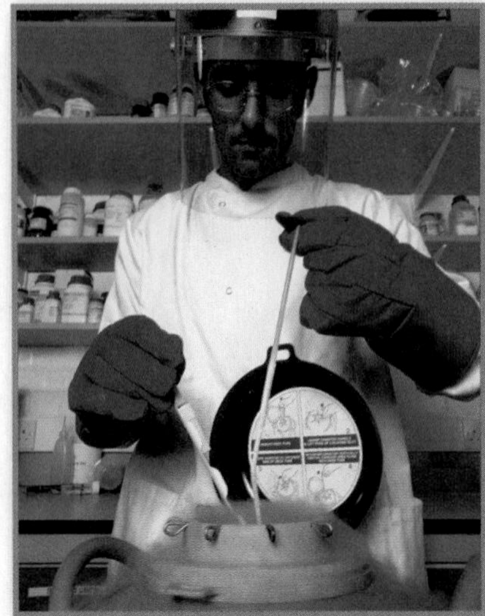

Liquid Nitrogen A lab technician places a cell sample into an insulated tank containing liquid nitrogen.

Ideal Gases and Real Gases

Ideal gases obey the gas laws at all pressures and temperatures. An ideal gas must therefore agree with the assumptions of kinetic theory. The particles in an ideal gas must have no volume and must have no attractions for one another. But ideal gases do not exist. Real gases do exist, and they sometimes behave like an ideal gas.

The particles in a real gas have volume and have attractions for one another. These attractions allow a gas to change to a liquid when it is compressed or cooled. If you cool water vapor to below 100°C, it condenses to a liquid. Other real gases behave similarly. Lower temperatures and greater pressures are needed to condense some real gases. For example, to produce liquid nitrogen from nitrogen gas, you need to lower the temperature to −196°C. The figure to the left shows how scientists use liquid nitrogen to cool materials to very low temperatures.

Quick Lab

Purpose To measure the amount of carbon dioxide gas given off when antacid tablets dissolve in water

Materials

- **6 effervescent antacid tablets**
- **3 round non-latex balloons**
- **plastic medicine dropper**
- **water**
- **clock or watch**
- **metric tape measure**
- **graph paper**

Carbon Dioxide from Antacid Tablets

Procedure 

1. Break six antacid tablets into small pieces. Keep the pieces from each tablet in a separate pile. Put the pieces from one tablet into the first balloon. Put the pieces from two tablets into a second balloon. Put the pieces from three tablets into a third balloon.

2. After you use the medicine dropper to squirt about 5 mL of cold water into each balloon, immediately tie off each balloon.

3. Shake the balloons to mix the contents. Allow the contents to warm to room temperature.

4. Measure and record the circumference of each balloon several times during the next 20 minutes.

5. Use the maximum circumference of each balloon to calculate its volume. (Hint: For the volume of a sphere, use $V = \frac{4}{3}\pi r^3$ and r = circumference/2π.)

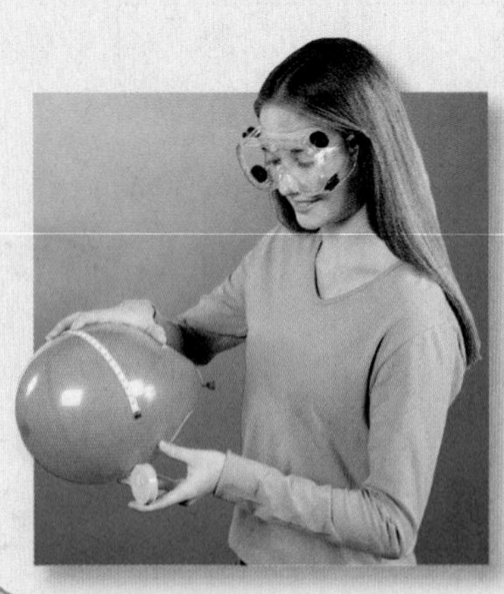

Analyze and Conclude

1. Graph Using your data from Step 5, make a graph of volume versus number of tablets in the balloons.

2. Explain Use your graph to describe the relationship between the number of tablets used and the volume of the balloons.

3. Calculate Assume the balloons are filled with carbon dioxide (CO_2) gas at 20°C and standard pressure. Calculate the mass and the number of moles of CO_2 in each balloon at maximum inflation.

Comparing Ideal Gases and Real Gases A real gas behaves very much like an ideal gas at high temperatures and low pressures. At other conditions, a real gas differs from an ideal gas. You can use the table below to compare ideal gases and real gases.

Question	Ideal Gas	Real Gas
Does it exist?	No, it's only a model.	Yes, all gases are real gases.
Does it obey the gas laws?	Yes, an ideal gas obeys the gas laws at all temperatures and pressures.	Sometimes, a real gas obeys the gas laws at high temperatures and low pressures.
How big are its particles?	Tiny, the size of a particle of an ideal gas isn't noticeable.	Small, but when compressed, the size of each particle is important.
Are there attractions between its particles?	No, there are no attractions between particles of an ideal gas.	Yes, but the particles move so fast that they usually do not "feel" the attractions. Lower temperatures cause the particles to slow down and feel the attractions.

Key Question Under what conditions do real gases differ most from ideal gases? **Real gases differ most from an ideal gas at low temperatures and high pressures.**

14.3 LessonCheck

Key Concept Check

36. **Review** How can you determine the number of moles of a contained gas when the pressure, volume, and temperature are known values?

37. **Identify** Under what conditions do real gases differ most from ideal gases?

Vocabulary Check *Choose a highlighted word from the lesson to complete each sentence correctly.*

38. The constant R used to solve gas problems is the ________.

39. The equation $PV = nRT$ summarizes the ________.

Think Critically

40. **Compare** What is the difference between a real gas and an ideal gas?

CHEMISTRY & YOU

41. Some fog machines use dry ice and water to create stage fog. Dry ice is added to hot water, which causes the dry ice to sublime. The cold carbon dioxide gas causes water vapor in the air to condense into small droplets. This causes a smoky fog. If water vapor behaved like an ideal gas at these conditions, would you expect to see the fog? Explain. (Hint: See page 446.)

BIGIDEA KINETIC THEORY

42. Use the kinetic theory of gases to explain why a real gas differs from an ideal gas at low temperatures and high pressures.

14.4 Gases: Mixtures and Movements

CHEMISTRY & YOU

Q: Why do balloons filled with helium deflate faster than balloons filled with air? You have probably seen party balloons filled with air or helium. The surface of a latex balloon has tiny holes that gas particles can pass through. These holes allow the balloon to deflate over time. How fast the balloon deflates depends on the gas it contains.

Key Questions

How is the total pressure of a gas mixture related to the partial pressures of the gases in the mixture?

How does a gas's molar mass affect the rate it diffuses or effuses?

partial pressure the contribution each gas in a mixture of gases makes to the total pressure

Dalton's law of partial pressures the total pressure of a mixture of gases equals the sum of the partial pressures of the gases in the mixture

ROOT WORDS

The word *partial* comes from the Latin word *part*. It means a piece of the whole. Partial pressure is part of the total, or whole, pressure.

Dalton's Law

Gas pressure is the result of particles in a gas colliding with an object, such as the walls of a container. More collisions cause the gas pressure to increase. Two things that can cause more collisions are an increase in the number of particles in a given volume and an increase in kinetic energy of the particles.

Gas pressure depends only on the number of particles in a given volume and on their average kinetic energy. All of the particles in a mixture of gases have the same average kinetic energy at a given temperature. The kind of particle is not important.

Partial Pressure In a mixture of gases, the total pressure is the sum of the pressures of all the gases. The contribution each gas in a mixture makes to the total pressure is called the **partial pressure** of that gas. The equation below relates the total pressure to the partial pressure of each gas in a mixture.

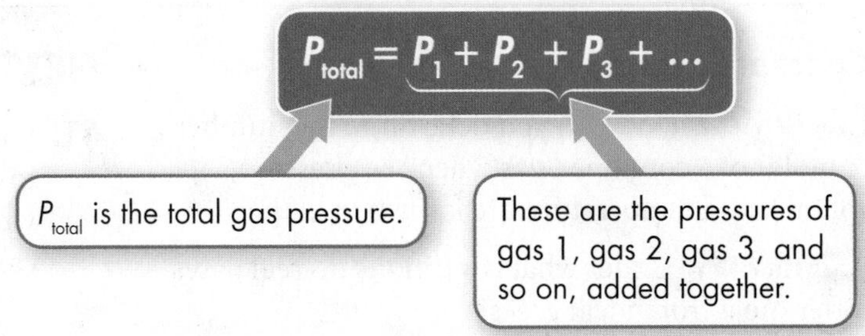

$P_{total} = P_1 + P_2 + P_3 + \ldots$
P_{total} is the total gas pressure.
These are the pressures of gas 1, gas 2, gas 3, and so on, added together.

This equation expresses a law proposed by a chemist named John Dalton. **Dalton's law of partial pressures** states that the total pressure of a mixture of gases is equal to the sum of the partial pressures of the gases. Dalton's law of partial pressures assumes that volume and temperature are constant. In a mixture of gases, each gas exerts its own pressure. Each gas's pressure is not affected by the pressures of other gases in the mixture.

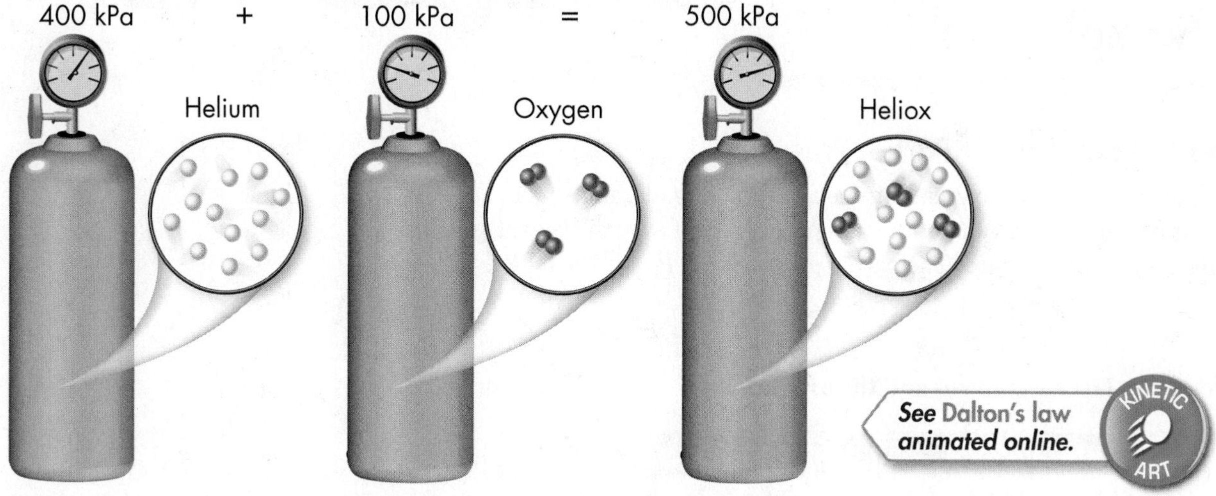

See Dalton's law animated online.

KINETIC ART

Dalton's Law of Partial Pressures
Heliox is a helium-oxygen gas mixture used for breathing under water. The pressure in the heliox tank is 500 kPa. In this mixture, the helium and oxygen gases exert partial pressures of 400 kPa and 100 kPa.

The figure above shows how the partial pressures of two gases affect the total pressure when the two gases are mixed. The pressure exerted by one gas in the mixture does not affect the pressure of the other gas. So the pressure in the heliox tank is the sum of the pressures in the tanks of oxygen and helium (400 kPa + 100 kPa = 500 kPa).

Percent Composition and Partial Pressures The table below shows the gases in dry air. Dry air is a mixture of gases. Nitrogen makes up 78.08 percent of the mixture. The total pressure of the mixture is 101.32 kPa. To calculate the partial pressure of nitrogen from the percent composition, follow these steps:

Step 1 Divide 78.08% by 100. $78.08\% \div 100 = 0.7808$

Step 2 Multiply by total pressure. $0.7808 \times 101.32 \text{ kPa} = 79.11 \text{ kPa}$

Key Question How is the total pressure of a gas mixture related to the partial pressures of the gases in the mixture? **In a mixture of gases, the total pressure is the sum of the partial pressures of the gases.**

Composition of Dry Air

Component	Volume (%)	Partial Pressure (kPa)
Nitrogen	78.08	79.11
Oxygen	20.95	21.23
Carbon dioxide	0.04	0.04
Argon and others	0.93	0.94
Total	**100.00**	**101.32**

Partial Pressures of Gases in Air
Partial pressures of gases in dry air add up to the total pressure.

Go to your Chemistry Skills and Math Workbook to practice interpreting data.

Using Dalton's Law of Partial Pressures

A sample of air contains oxygen, nitrogen, carbon dioxide, and small amounts of other gases. What is the partial pressure of oxygen (P_{O_2}) at 101.30 kPa of total pressure? The partial pressures are $P_{N_2} = 79.10$ kPa, $P_{CO_2} = 0.040$ kPa, and $P_{\text{others}} = 0.94$ kPa.

1 Analyze List the knowns and the unknown.

KNOWNS	UNKNOWN
$P_{\text{total}} = 101.30$ kPa	$P_{O_2} = ?$ kPa
$P_{N_2} = 79.10$ kPa	
$P_{CO_2} = 0.040$ kPa	
$P_{\text{others}} = 0.94$ kPa	

2 Calculate Solve for the unknown. Use the equation for Dalton's law of partial pressures to calculate P_{O_2}.

Start with the equation for Dalton's law of partial pressures.

$$P_{\text{total}} = P_{O_2} + P_{N_2} + P_{CO_2} + P_{\text{others}}$$

Rearrange the equation to isolate P_{O_2}.

Isolate P_{O_2} by subtracting P_{N_2}, P_{CO_2}, and P_{others} from both sides.

$$P_{\text{total}} - P_{N_2} - P_{CO_2} - P_{\text{others}} = P_{O_2} + \cancel{P_{N_2}} + \cancel{P_{CO_2}} + \cancel{P_{\text{others}}} - \cancel{P_{N_2}} - \cancel{P_{CO_2}} - \cancel{P_{\text{others}}}$$

Rewrite the equation so that the unknown is on the left side.

$$P_{O_2} = P_{\text{total}} - P_{N_2} - P_{CO_2} - P_{\text{others}}$$

Substitute the knowns into the equation.

$$P_{O_2} = 101.30 \text{ kPa} - 79.10 \text{ kPa} - 0.040 \text{ kPa} - 0.94 \text{ kPa}$$

Solve the equation.

$$P_{O_2} = 21.22 \text{ kPa}$$

Remember: You can check your work by adding up all the partial pressures to see if they equal 101.30 kPa.

21.22 kPa	(P_{O_2})
79.10 kPa	(P_{N_2})
0.040 kPa	(P_{CO_2})
+ 0.94 kPa	(P_{others})
101.30 kPa	(P_{total})

3 Evaluate Does the result make sense? The partial pressure of oxygen must be smaller than that of nitrogen because P_{total} is only 101.30 kPa. The other partial pressures are small, so the calculated answer of 21.22 kPa seems reasonable.

BUILD Math Skills

Significant Figures in Addition and Subtraction

Always report your answer to the correct number of significant figures. When using addition and subtraction, find the value with the least number of decimal places. Your answer should have the same number of decimal places as that value does. Study the example below.

15.98 (2 decimal places)
+ 2.4 (1 decimal place) ← fewest decimal places
18.38 (answer from calculator)

Round the answer to 18.4 (1 decimal place).

Go to your Chemistry Skills and Math Workbook for more practice.

Practice Problems

Hint: Check your work by substituting your answer for P_{CO_2} back into the original equation. Are both sides equal?

43. A gas mixture containing oxygen, nitrogen, and carbon dioxide has a total pressure of 32.9 kPa. If $P_{O_2} = 6.6$ kPa and $P_{N_2} = 23.0$ kPa, what is P_{CO_2}?

1 Analyze List the knowns and the unknown.

2 Calculate Solve for the unknown.

3 Evaluate Does the result make sense?

KNOWNS	UNKNOWN
P_{total} = 32.9 kPa	P_{CO_2} = ? kPa
P_{O_2} = 6.6 kPa	
P_{N_2} = 23.0 kPa	

44. Determine the total pressure of a gas mixture that contains oxygen, nitrogen, and helium. The partial pressures are $P_{O_2} = 20.0$ kPa, $P_{N_2} = 46.7$ kPa, and $P_{He} = 26.7$ kPa.

KNOWNS	UNKNOWN
P_{O_2} =	P_{total} = ? kPa
P_{N_2} =	
P_{He} =	

45. A mixture of oxygen, argon, and carbon dioxide exerts a total pressure of 2.54 atm. The partial pressures of oxygen and carbon dioxide are 1.52 atm and 0.68 atm. What is the partial pressure of argon in the mixture?

46. Challenge A heliox tank contains 20.0 percent helium and 80.0 percent oxygen. The total pressure is 650.0 kPa. What are the partial pressures of helium and oxygen?

Hint: For Problem 46, refer back to the section called "Percent Composition and Partial Pressures" on page 449.

Venn Diagram Create a Venn diagram to compare and contrast diffusion and effusion. Fill in the diagram as you read the lesson.

BUILD Vocabulary

diffusion the tendency of molecules to move toward areas of lower concentration until the concentration is uniform throughout

effusion the process that occurs when a gas escapes through a tiny hole in its container

PREFIXES

Diffusion and *effusion* come from a Latin word that means "to pour." They differ only in their prefixes. The prefix *dif-* means "apart." The prefix *ef-* means "out."

Graham's Law

What happens if you open a perfume bottle in one corner of a room? At some point, a person standing in the opposite corner will be able to smell the perfume. How does this happen?

Diffusion Molecules in the perfume evaporate and spread out through the air in the room. **Diffusion** is the tendency of molecules to move toward areas of lower concentration until the concentration is the same throughout.

The figure below shows the diffusion of orange bromine vapor. In the beginning, all the bromine molecules are at the bottom. The bromine molecules slowly diffuse. In the end, the concentration is the same in all parts of the container.

Diffusion

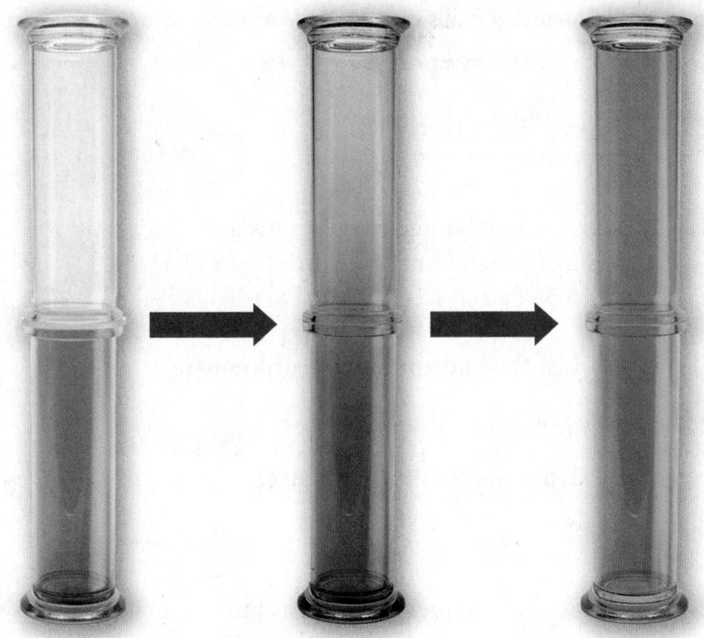

1. A tube of air and a tube of orange bromine vapor are sealed together. Bromine is on the bottom.
2. The bromine vapor diffuses upward through the air, moving toward the area with a lower concentration of bromine.
3. After several hours, bromine vapors are evenly spread throughout the sealed tubes.

Effusion Diffusion is not the only way that gases move. Gases also can move by effusion. During **effusion,** a gas escapes through a tiny hole in its container.

You may have noticed how a latex balloon filled with helium deflates after some time. The balloon deflates because of the process of effusion. There are tiny holes in latex balloons. The helium in the balloon slowly seeps out through these holes.

Blimps
The cigar-shaped part of a blimp is called the envelope. It is filled with helium gas. The envelope needs to be gastight so that the helium gas does not escape.

Comparing Diffusion and Effusion Rates How fast can gas particles effuse and diffuse? The answer depends on the type of particle. The lower the molar mass of the particle, the faster it diffuses and effuses.

Thomas Graham observed that a gas's rate of effusion is related to its molar mass. This observation makes sense. If two objects with different masses have the same kinetic energy, the lighter object must move faster. Gas particles that are at the same temperature have the same kinetic energy. So gas particles with a lower molar mass are lighter and will move faster than gas particles with a higher molar mass.

Blimps, like the one shown above, are often filled with helium because helium-filled blimps rise more easily than air-filled blimps. However, compared to air, helium is harder to keep inside the blimp. Kinetic theory can explain why.

Think of a latex party balloon. It can be filled with either helium or air. A helium-filled balloon will deflate faster than an air-filled balloon. Helium atoms are lighter than the oxygen or nitrogen molecules that make up air. So the molecules in air escape more slowly than helium atoms.

Key Question How does a gas's molar mass affect the rate it diffuses or effuses? **Gases of lower molar mass diffuse and effuse faster than gases of higher molar mass.**

14.4 LessonCheck

Key Concept Check

47. **Review** In a mixture of gases, how is the total pressure related to the partial pressures of all the gases in the mixture?

48. **Review** What is the effect of molar mass on rates of diffusion and effusion?

Vocabulary Check

Choose a highlighted word from the lesson to complete the sentence correctly.

49. Gases can escape through tiny holes in a container by the process of ________.

Think Critically

50. **Explain** How can you calculate the partial pressure of a gas in a mixture?

CHEMISTRY & YOU

51. Why do balloons filled with helium deflate faster than balloons filled with air? Use molar masses to explain your answer. (Hint: See page 453.)

14 Study Guide

BIGIDEA KINETIC THEORY

Ideal gases conform to the assumptions of kinetic theory. The behavior of ideal gases can be predicted by the gas laws. With the ideal gas law, the number of moles of a gas in a fixed volume at a known temperature and pressure can be calculated. Although an ideal gas does not exist, real gases behave ideally under a variety of temperature and pressure conditions.

14.1 Properties of Gases

Gases are easily compressed because the space between particles in a gas is greater than in a solid or a liquid.

The amount of gas, the volume, and the temperature are factors that affect gas pressure.

- compressibility (422)

14.2 The Gas Laws

If the temperature is constant, as the pressure of a gas increases, the volume decreases.

As the temperature of an enclosed gas increases, the volume increases if the pressure is constant.

As the temperature of an enclosed gas increases, the pressure increases if the volume is constant.

When only the amount of gas is constant, the combined gas law describes the relationships between pressure, volume, and temperature.

- Boyle's law (427)
- Charles's law (431)
- Gay-Lussac's law (434)
- combined gas law (437)

Key Equations

Boyle's law:
$$P_1 \times V_1 = P_2 \times V_2$$

Charles's law:
$$\frac{V_1}{T_1} = \frac{V_2}{T_2}$$

Gay-Lussac's law:
$$\frac{P_1}{T_1} = \frac{P_2}{T_2}$$

combined gas law:
$$\frac{P_1 \times V_1}{T_1} = \frac{P_2 \times V_2}{T_2}$$

14.3 Ideal Gases

When the pressure, volume, and temperature of a gas are known, you can use the ideal gas law to calculate the number of moles of the gas.

Real gases differ most from an ideal gas at low temperatures and high pressures.

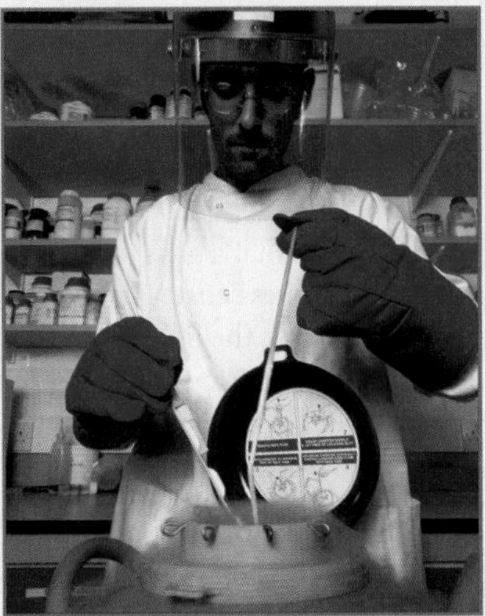

- ideal gas law (441)
- ideal gas constant (441)

Key Equation

ideal gas law:
$$P \times V = n \times R \times T$$

14.4 Gases: Mixtures and Movements

In a mixture of gases, the total pressure is the sum of the partial pressures of the gases.

Gases of lower molar mass diffuse and effuse faster than gases of higher molar mass.

- partial pressure (448)
- Dalton's law of partial pressures (448)
- diffusion (452)
- effusion (452)

Key Equation

Dalton's law: $P_{total} = P_1 + P_2 + P_3 + \ldots$

Math Tune-Up: Gas Law Problems

Problem	❶ Analyze	❷ Calculate	❸ Evaluate
A 2.50 L sample of nitrogen gas at a temperature of 308 K has a pressure of 1.15 atm. What is the new volume of the gas if the pressure is increased to 1.80 atm and the temperature is decreased to 286 K?	Knowns: $P_1 = 1.15$ atm $V_1 = 2.50$ L $T_1 = 308$ K $P_2 = 1.80$ atm $T_2 = 286$ K Unknown: $V_2 = ?$ Use the combined gas law: $\frac{P_1 \times V_1}{T_1} = \frac{P_2 \times V_2}{T_2}$	Isolate V_2 and calculate: $V_2 = \frac{P_1 V_1 T_2}{P_2 T_1}$ $V_2 = \frac{(1.15\ \cancel{\text{atm}})(2.50\ \text{L})(286\ \cancel{\text{K}})}{(1.80\ \cancel{\text{atm}})(308\ \cancel{\text{K}})}$ $V_2 = 1.48$ L	An increase in pressure causes the volume of a gas to decrease. Likewise, a decrease in temperature causes the volume of a gas to decrease. So V_2 should be smaller than V_1. The answer makes sense. Hint: Review Sample Problem 14.4 if you have trouble with the combined gas law.
How many moles of helium gas fill a 6.45 L balloon at a pressure of 105 kPa and a temperature of 278 K?	Knowns: $P = 105$ kPa $V = 6.45$ L $T = 278$ K $R = 8.31$ L·kPa/K·mol Unknown: $n = ?$ Use the ideal gas law: $PV = nRT$	Isolate n and calculate: $n = \frac{PV}{RT}$ $n = \frac{(105\ \cancel{\text{kPa}})(6.45\ \cancel{\text{L}})}{\left(8.31 \frac{\cancel{\text{L}} \cdot \cancel{\text{kPa}}}{\cancel{\text{K}} \cdot \text{mol}}\right)(278\ \cancel{\text{K}})}$ $n = 0.293$ mol	The gas is not at high pressure, nor is the volume large. So the number of moles in the balloon should be small. The answer is reasonable, and the units have canceled correctly.
A gas mixture containing argon, krypton, and helium has a total pressure of 376 kPa. If the partial pressures of argon and krypton are 92 kPa and 144 kPa, respectively, what is the partial pressure of helium?	Knowns: $P_{total} = 376$ kPa $P_{Ar} = 92$ kPa $P_{Kr} = 144$ kPa Unknown: $P_{He} = ?$ Dalton's law of partial pressures applies: $P_{total} = P_{Ar} + P_{He} + P_{Kr}$	Isolate P_{He} and calculate: $P_{He} = P_{total} - P_{Ar} - P_{Kr}$ $P_{He} = 376\ \text{kPa} - 92\ \text{kPa} - 144\ \text{kPa}$ $P_{He} = 140$ kPa $P_{He} = 1.40 \times 10^2$ kPa	The partial pressure of helium must be less than half the total pressure. The answer is reasonable. Dalton's law: The total pressure exerted by a mixture of gases (P_{total}) is equal to the sum of the partial pressures of the component gases.

14 Assessment

∗ Solutions appear in Appendix D.

Lesson by Lesson

14.1 Properties of Gases

52. What happens to the particles in a gas when the gas is compressed?

53. Explain why heating a contained gas that is held at a constant volume increases its pressure.

54. Describe what happens to the volume of a balloon when it is taken outside on a cold winter day. Then explain why it happens.

55. A metal cylinder contains 1 mole of nitrogen gas. What will happen to the pressure if another mole of gas is added to the cylinder, but the temperature and volume do not change?

56. If a gas is compressed from 4 L to 1 L and the temperature remains constant, what happens to the pressure?

57. Use the drawing to help explain why gas pressure decreases when gas is removed from a container with a fixed volume.

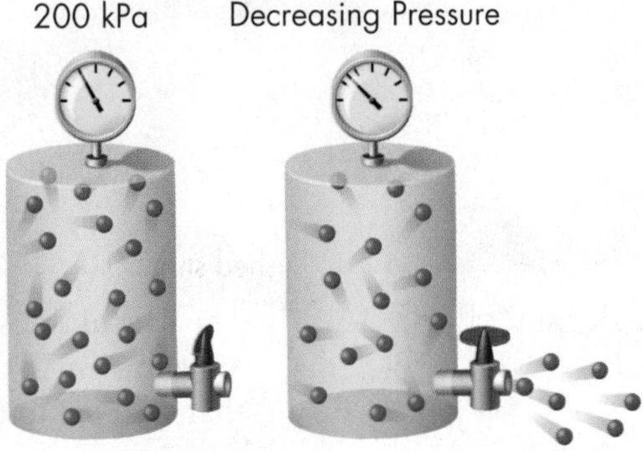

14.2 The Gas Laws

58. Write the mathematical equation for Charles's law and explain the symbols.

∗59. The gas in a closed container has a pressure of 3.00×10^2 kPa at 30°C (303 K). What will the pressure be if the temperature is lowered to −172°C (101 K)?

60. Calculate the volume of a gas (in L) at a pressure of 1.00×10^2 kPa if its volume at 1.20×10^2 kPa is 1.50×10^3 mL.

∗61. A gas with a volume of 3.00×10^2 mL at 150.0°C is heated until its volume expands to 6.00×10^2 mL. What is the new temperature of the gas if the pressure remains constant?

62. Write the mathematical expression for the combined gas law.

∗63. A sample of nitrogen gas has a pressure of 6.58 kPa at 539 K. If the volume does not change, what will the pressure be at 211 K?

∗64. A gas with a volume of 15 L at 327°C is cooled at constant pressure until the volume reaches 5 L. What is the new temperature of the gas?

14.3 Ideal Gases

65. Describe an ideal gas.

66. Explain why it is impossible for an ideal gas to exist.

∗67. What is the volume occupied by 1.24 mol of a gas at 35°C if the pressure is 96.2 kPa?

68. What volume will 12.0 g of oxygen gas (O_2) occupy at 25°C and a pressure of 52.7 kPa?

14.4 Gases: Mixtures and Movements

69. State Dalton's law of partial pressures in your own words.

70. Which gas effuses faster: hydrogen or chlorine? (Hint: Use information from the periodic table.)

Understand Concepts

71. How does kinetic theory explain the compressibility of gases?

72. A teacher adds enough water to cover the bottom of an empty metal can with a screw cap. The teacher heats the can with the cap off until the water boils, and then screws on the cap tightly. When the sealed can is dunked in cold water, the sides of the can immediately collapse inward. Use kinetic theory to explain why the can collapses inward.

73. Explain why aerosol containers carry the warning "Do not incinerate."

***74.** A 3.50 L gas sample at 20.0°C and a pressure of 86.7 kPa expands to a volume of 8.00 L. The final pressure of the gas is 56.7 kPa. What is the final temperature of the gas in degrees Celsius?

75. How would the number of particles of two gases compare if their partial pressures in a container were identical?

76. Explain why balloons filled with helium deflate faster than balloons filled with air.

Think Critically

***77. Analyze Data** A student collected the following data for a fixed volume of gas.

Temperature (°C)	Pressure (mm Hg)
10	726
20	750
40	800
70	880
100	960

a. Graph the data, using pressure as the dependent variable.
b. What is the pressure of the gas at 0°C?
c. Is the relationship between the variables directly or inversely proportional?
d. How does the pressure of the gas change with each degree Celsius change in the temperature?
e. Which gas law is illustrated by the data? Select two data points on your graph to confirm your answer.

FOUNDATIONS Wrap-Up

Hot and Cold Balloons

1. Draw Conclusions At the beginning of the chapter you placed balloons in hot water and cold water. Explain why the balloons changed the way they did.

Concept Check

Now that you've finished studying Chapter 14, answer these questions.

2. Why are some things easier to squeeze than others—for example, an inflated balloon and a lump of clay?

3. How can you change the pressure of a gas?

4. Why does a gas fill the entire container rather than gather in one small area?

5. If there is a tiny hole in a container that contains two different gases, which gas will leak out faster?

Write About Science

78. **Explain** Why does a tennis ball bounce higher in the summer than it does in the winter? Use what you know about gas behavior and kinetic theory to explain your answer.

79. **Research a Problem** Cars that run on natural gas or hydrogen require different fuel tanks and different refueling stations than cars that run on gasoline, which is a liquid at STP. Design a fuel tank for storing a gas. Explain how you would design a gas pump that pumped a gas instead of a liquid.

CHEMYSTERY

Under Pressure

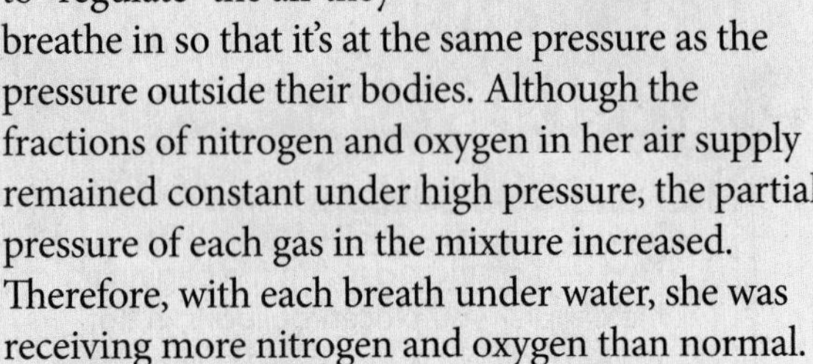

Becki realized that she had decompression sickness, also known as the bends. Recreational divers use regulators attached on their air tank to "regulate" the air they breathe in so that it's at the same pressure as the pressure outside their bodies. Although the fractions of nitrogen and oxygen in her air supply remained constant under high pressure, the partial pressure of each gas in the mixture increased. Therefore, with each breath under water, she was receiving more nitrogen and oxygen than normal.

As Becki ascended and the pressure on her body decreased, the excess nitrogen formed bubbles in her blood and tissues, causing pain and other symptoms. Serious cases of the bends require treatment in a high-pressure chamber. The pressure is reduced gradually so that the excess nitrogen can leave the body harmlessly.

80. **Infer** How could Becki have prevented getting the bends?

81. **Connect to the BIGIDEA** What would have happened if Becki held her breath while ascending from a dive? Use the gas laws to explain.

Cumulative Review

82. How many electrons, protons, and neutrons are there in an atom of lead-206? (See Lesson 4.3 for help.)

83. Which of these elements is a metal? (See Lesson 6.1 for help.)
  a. arsenic b. tungsten c. xenon

*84. Name each compound. (See Lesson 9.2.)
  a. $SnBr_2$
  b. $BaSO_4$
  c. $Mg(OH)_2$
  d. IF_5

*85. Calculate the molar mass of each substance. (See Lesson 10.1 for help.)
  a. $Ca(CH_3CO_2)_2$
  b. H_3PO_4
  c. $C_{12}H_{22}O_{11}$
  d. $Pb(NO_3)_2$

86. Explain why the volume 22.4 L is important. (See Lesson 10.2 for help.)

87. Which type of reaction is this: Calcium reacts with water to form calcium hydroxide and hydrogen gas? (See Lesson 11.2 for help.)

88. Write a balanced equation for this reaction: Tetraphosphorus decoxide reacts with water to form phosphoric acid. (See Lesson 11.1.)

*89. Aluminum oxide is formed from its elements. How many grams of Al(*s*) are needed to form 583 g $Al_2O_3(s)$? (See Lesson 12.2 for help.)

$$4Al(s) + 3O_2(g) \longrightarrow 2Al_2O_3(s)$$

90. Explain why a gas expands until it takes the shape and volume of its container. (See Lesson 13.1 for help.)

91. Use the drawings to explain how gas pressure is produced. (See Lesson 13.1 for help.)

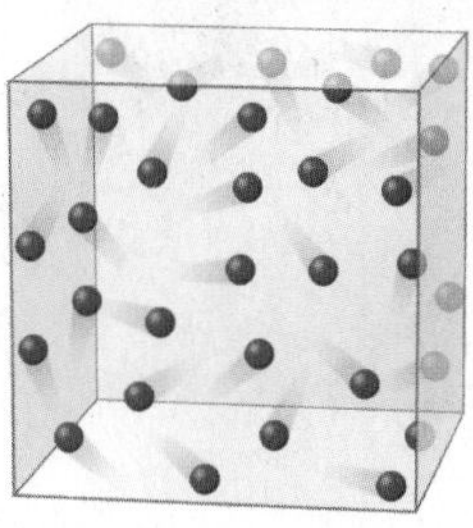

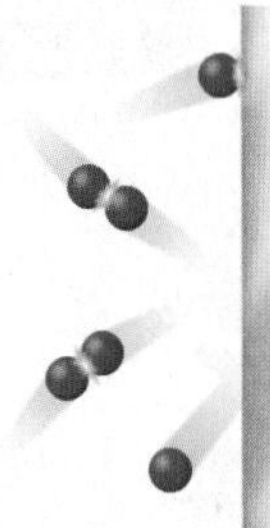

Standardized Test Prep

For help with answering test questions, go to your Chemistry Skills and Math Workbook.

Select the choice that best answers each question or completes each statement.

1. A gas in a balloon at constant pressure has a volume of 120.0 mL at −123°C. What is its volume at 27.0°C?
(A) 60.0 mL (C) 26.5 mL
(B) 240.0 mL (D) 546 mL

2. If the Kelvin temperature of a gas is tripled and the volume is doubled, the new pressure will be:
(A) 1/6 the original pressure.
(B) 2/3 the original pressure.
(C) 3/2 the original pressure.
(D) 5 times the original pressure.

3. Which of these gases effuses fastest?
(A) Cl_2 (C) NH_3
(B) NO_2 (D) N_2

4. All the oxygen gas from a 10.0 L container at a pressure of 202 kPa is added to a 20.0 L container of hydrogen at a pressure of 505 kPa. After the transfer, what are the partial pressures of oxygen and hydrogen?
(A) Oxygen's is 101 kPa; hydrogen's is 505 kPa.
(B) Oxygen's is 202 kPa; hydrogen's is 505 kPa.
(C) Oxygen's is 101 kPa; hydrogen's is 253 kPa.
(D) Oxygen's is 202 kPa; hydrogen's is 253 kPa.

5. Which of the following changes would increase the pressure of a gas in a closed container?

I. Part of the gas is removed.
II. The container size is decreased.
III. Temperature is increased.

(A) I and II only
(B) II and III only
(C) I and III only
(D) I, II, and III

6. A real gas behaves most nearly like an ideal gas:
(A) at high pressure and low temperature.
(B) at low pressure and high temperature.
(C) at low pressure and low temperature.
(D) at high pressure and high temperature.

Use the graphs to answer Questions 7–10. A graph may be used once, more than once, or not at all.

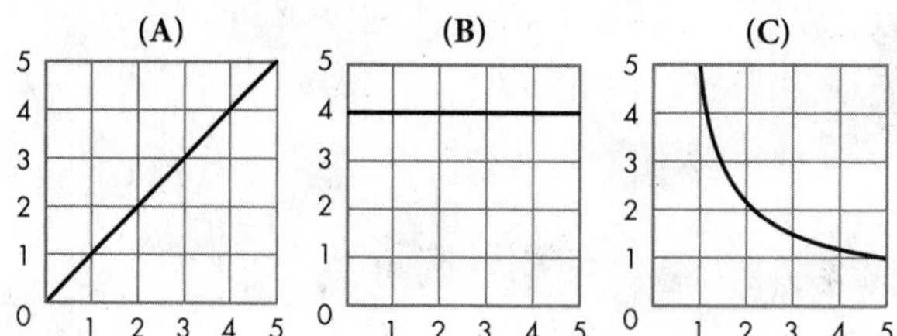

Which graph shows each of the following?

7. directly proportional relationship

8. graph with slope = 0

9. inversely proportional relationship

10. graph with a constant slope

Use the drawing to answer Questions 11 and 12.

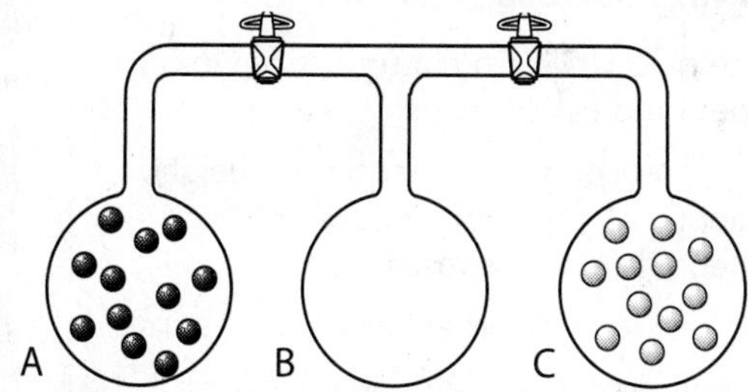

11. Bulb A and bulb C contain different gases. Bulb B contains no gas. If the valves between the bulbs are opened, how will the particles of gas be distributed when the system reaches equilibrium? Assume none of the particles are in the tubes that connect the bulbs.

Tips for Success

Constructing a Diagram If you are asked to draw a diagram, sketch lightly at first (so you can erase easily), or do a sketch on a separate piece of paper. Once you are sure of your answer, draw the final diagram.

12. Make a three-bulb drawing with 6 blue spheres in bulb A, 9 green spheres in bulb B, and 12 red spheres in bulb C. Then draw the setup to represent the distribution of gases after the valves are opened and the system reaches equilibrium.

If You Have Trouble With . . .

Question	1	2	3	4	5	6	7	8	9	10	11	12
See Lesson	14.2	14.2	14.4	14.3	14.1	14.3	14.2	14.2	14.2	14.2	14.4	14.4

15 Water and Aqueous Systems

Water has many unique properties. In this chapter, you will learn about the interactions between water molecules.

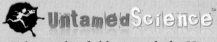

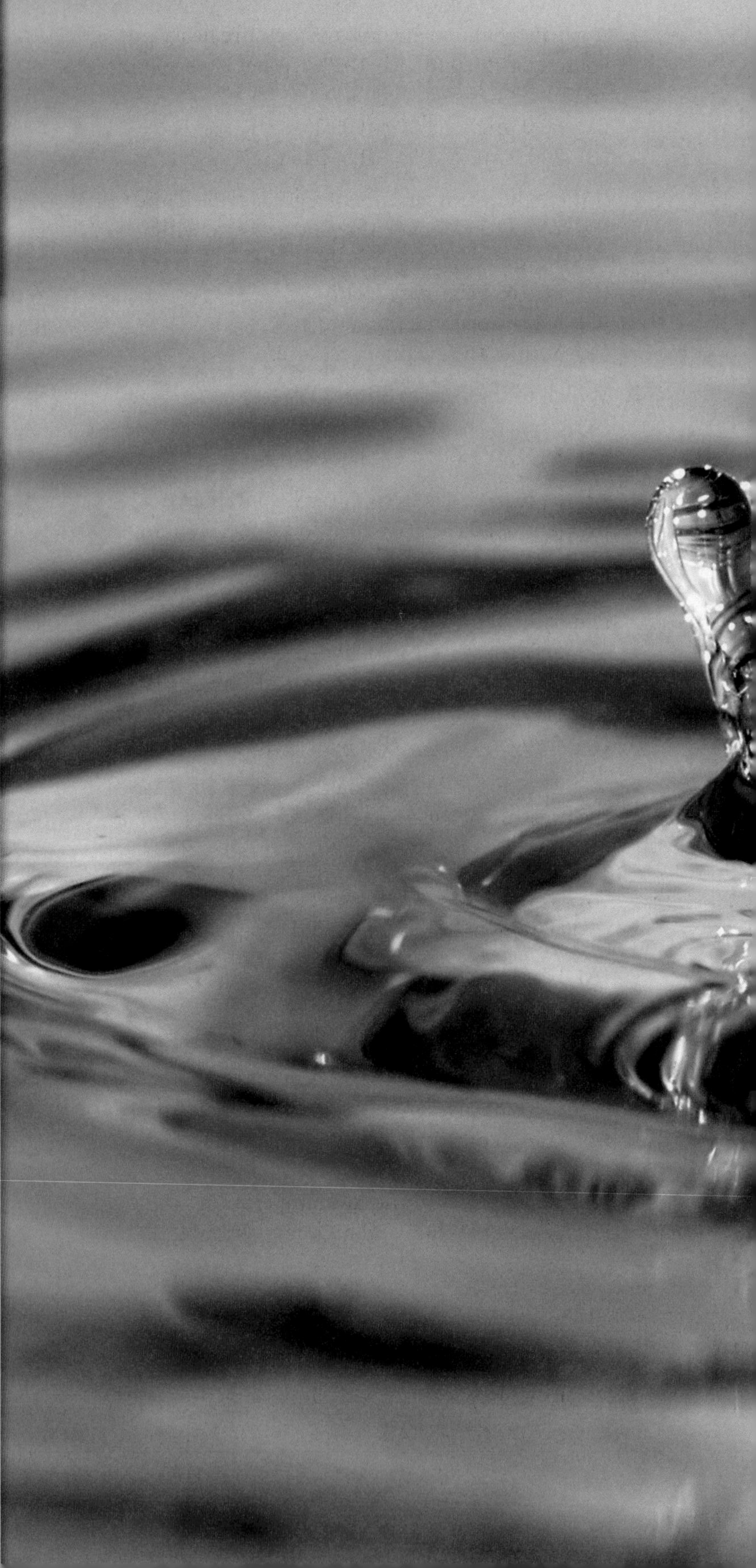

FOUNDATIONS for Learning

Observing Surface Tension

1. Place a 15 cm × 15 cm square of wax paper on a flat surface.
2. Drop $\frac{1}{4}$ teaspoon of water from a height of about 20 cm onto the center of the paper. Observe the result.
3. Mix 1 drop of detergent in $\frac{1}{2}$ cup of water.
4. Repeat Steps 1 and 2 using the diluted detergent in place of water.

Form a Hypothesis How do you think the detergent changed the physical properties of the water?

PearsonChem.com

Take a video field trip with the Untamed Science crew as they go behind the scenes to learn the chemistry behind making marshmallows.

BIGIDEA

BONDING AND INTERACTIONS

Essential Questions:

1. *How do the interactions between water molecules account for the unique properties of water?*
2. *How do aqueous solutions form?*

CHEMYSTERY

Coming Clean

It was a beautiful Saturday afternoon. Wes decided to take a long bike ride. He set off on the trails at a nearby park.

Wes got back from his bike ride and saw many stains on his socks. There was dirt from the trail and grease from the bicycle chain. Wes figured he could just clean the socks in the sink. He soaked the socks in water, but the dirt and the grease would not rinse off. Wes thought water was supposed to clean everything. He needed to know more about the chemistry of water. Then he might have tried something different to clean those dirty socks.

▶ Connect to the BIGIDEA As you read about water and aqueous systems, think about how Wes could remove the dirt and grease from his socks.

15.1 Water and Its Properties

CHEMISTRY & YOU

Q: What properties of water make it essential to life on Earth? When the Apollo 8 astronauts saw Earth from space, they called it the big blue marble. Water covers about three quarters of Earth's surface. Water makes up Earth's oceans, and solid water forms the polar ice caps. Water also moves through the atmosphere in the water cycle. Like all living things, the penguin in the photo below is made mostly of water.

Key Questions

What feature of water causes its high surface tension, low vapor pressure, and high boiling point?

How can you describe the structure of ice?

Water in the Liquid State

You could not live without water. All the plants and animals that share space with you on the "big blue marble" need water, too. Besides the water you can see on Earth's surface, huge reserves of water are found deep underground. Water in the form of ice and snow covers the polar regions of Earth. Water vapor from the evaporation of surface water is always present in Earth's atmosphere. Water vapor in the atmosphere also comes from steam spouted from geysers and volcanoes.

Polarity of Water Recall that water, H_2O, is a simple molecule consisting of three atoms. The structure of the water molecule is shown in the figure at the top of the facing page. The oxygen atom forms a covalent bond with each of the hydrogen atoms. Oxygen has a greater electronegativity than hydrogen. Therefore, the oxygen atom attracts the electron pair of the covalent O—H bond more than the hydrogen atom. Thus, the O—H bond is highly polar, and the oxygen atom takes on a partial negative charge ($\delta-$). The less electronegative hydrogen atoms take on partial positive charges ($\delta+$).

Water Is Vital to Life
The oceans supply penguins with plenty of food.

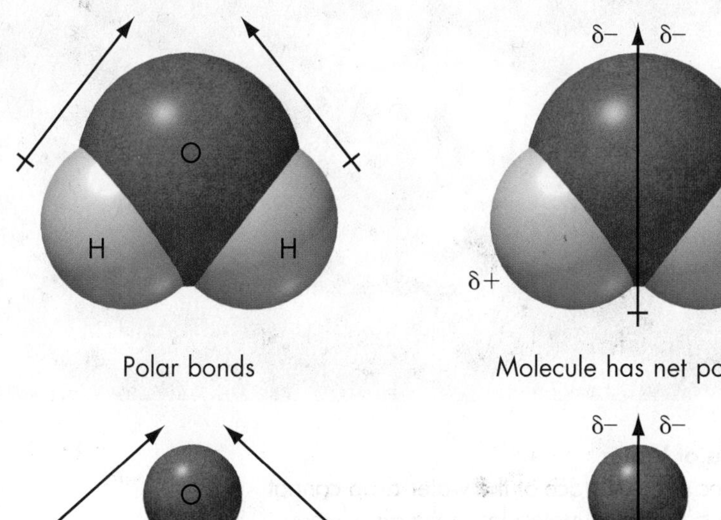

Polarity of H_2O
In a water molecule, the bond polarities are equal. The two poles do not cancel each other out because a water molecule is bent. The molecule as a whole is polar.

The shape of the water molecule determines the overall polarity of the molecule. If the water molecule were linear, the two opposite O—H bond polarities would cancel out and the molecule would be nonpolar. However, the bond angle of the water molecule is approximately 105°, which gives the molecule a bent shape. As a result, the two O—H bond polarities do not cancel out, so the water molecule as a whole is polar. The net polarity of the water molecule is shown in the figure above. The oxygen end of the molecule is slightly negative. The hydrogen end of the molecule is slightly positive.

Hydrogen Bonding Polar molecules are usually attracted to one another. The negative end of one molecule attracts the positive end of another molecule. In water, this attraction results in hydrogen bonding, as shown in the figure below. Hydrogen bonds are formed when a hydrogen atom that is covalently bonded to a very electronegative atom is attracted to another electronegative atom in a different molecule. Many properties of water result from hydrogen bonding. These properties include its high surface tension, low vapor pressure, and high boiling point.

Hydrogen Bonding in Water

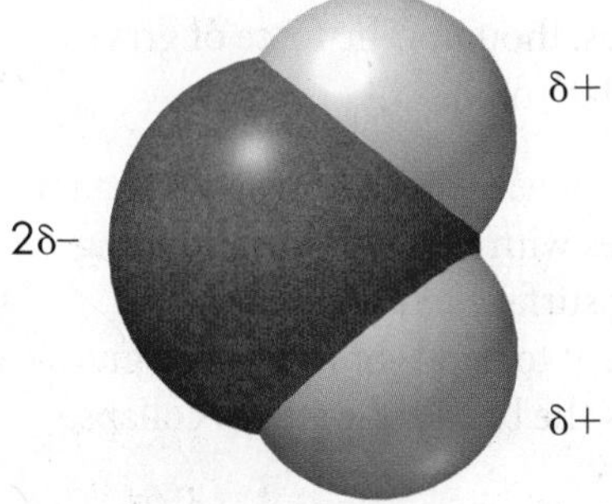

The oxygen atom has a partial negative charge. Each hydrogen atom has a partial positive charge.

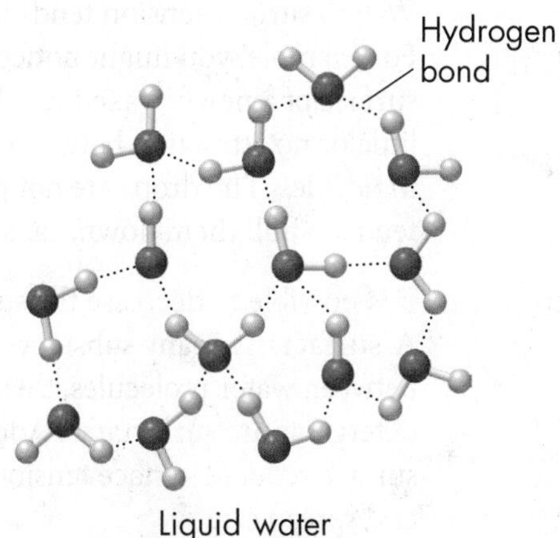

Hydrogen bonds form between a hydrogen atom of one water molecule and the oxygen atom of another water molecule.

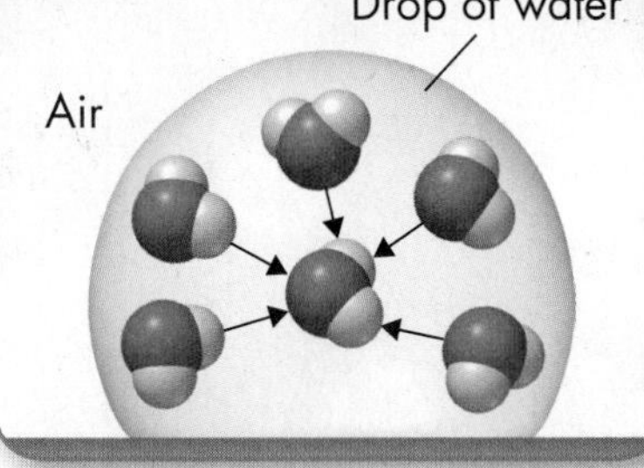

Surface Tension of Water
Water molecules at the surface of the water drop cannot form hydrogen bonds with molecules in the air, so they are pulled into the body of the liquid. As a result, water forms nearly spherical drops on a leaf.

BUILD Vocabulary

surface tension the inward force that makes the surface area of a liquid smaller

surfactant any substance that interferes with the hydrogen bonding between water molecules, thereby reducing surface tension

WORD ORIGINS

Both of these terms come from the French words *sur-*, "above,"and *face,* "outside." Both words apply to the molecules at the surface of a liquid that pull inward.

Surface Tension Have you ever seen a glass so full of water that the water surface is not flat, but bulges above the rim of the glass? Have you noticed that water forms nearly spherical drops on a leaf, as shown above? The surface of water acts like a skin. This property of water's surface is explained by hydrogen bonding. The water molecules within the liquid form hydrogen bonds with other molecules that surround them on all sides. The attractive forces on each of these molecules are balanced. However, water molecules at the surface of the liquid experience an unbalanced attraction. You can see in the figure above that the water molecules are hydrogen bonded on only the inside of the drop. As a result, water molecules at the surface tend to be pulled inward. The inward pull, or force, that makes the surface area of a liquid smaller is called **surface tension.**

All liquids have a surface tension, but water's surface tension is higher than most. This is why water beads up instead of spreading out on some surfaces. Water's surface tension tends to hold a drop of liquid in a spherical shape. For example, you might notice that water tends to form beads on the surface of a newly waxed car. The wax molecules are nonpolar. There is little or no attraction between the wax molecules and the polar water molecules. The drops are not perfect spheres, though. The force of gravity tends to pull them down, causing them to flatten.

It is possible to decrease the surface tension of water by adding a surfactant. A **surfactant** is any substance that interferes with the hydrogen bonding between water molecules, thereby reducing surface tension. Soaps and detergents are surfactants. Adding a detergent to beads of water on a greasy surface reduces surface tension. This causes the beads of water to collapse and spread out.

Vapor Pressure The vapor pressure of a liquid is the result of molecules escaping from the surface and entering the vapor phase. Water has a low vapor pressure compared to most other molecular compounds. A network of hydrogen bonds holds the molecules in liquid water to one another. These hydrogen bonds must be broken before water can change from a liquid to a vapor. As a result, the water molecules cannot easily escape the surface of the liquid, and evaporation is slow. What would happen if water had a higher vapor pressure? Lakes and oceans would quickly evaporate!

Boiling Point Molecular compounds with low molar masses are usually gases or liquids with low boiling points at normal atmospheric pressure. Ammonia (NH_3) is a molecular compound with a low molar mass. It has a molar mass of 17.0 g/mol and boils at about −33°C. Water has a molar mass of 18.0 g/mol, but it boils at 100°C. The higher boiling point of water is due to hydrogen bonding. Hydrogen bonding is more extensive in water than it is in ammonia. It takes much more energy in the form of heat to break the hydrogen bonds in water than it does in ammonia. If the hydrogen bonding in water were as weak as it is in ammonia, water would be a gas at the temperatures found on Earth.

Key Question What feature of water causes its high surface tension, low vapor pressure, and high boiling point? **Many unusual and important properties of water—including its high surface tension, low vapor pressure, and high boiling point—result from hydrogen bonding.**

Quick Lab

Purpose To observe an unusual surface property of water that results from hydrogen bonding

Materials

- **shallow dish or petri dish**
- **water**
- **paper clip**
- **rubber band, approximately 5 cm in diameter**
- **micropipettes or droppers (2)**
- **vegetable oil**
- **liquid dish detergent**

Surface Tension

Procedure 

1. Thoroughly clean and dry the dish.
2. Fill the dish almost full with water. Dry your hands.
3. Being careful not to break the surface, gently place the paper clip on the water. Observe what happens.
4. Repeat Steps 1 and 2.
5. Gently place the open rubber band on the water.
6. Slowly add the vegetable oil drop by drop onto the water encircled by the rubber band until that water is covered with a layer of oil. Observe the system for 15 seconds.
7. Allow one drop of dish detergent to fall onto the center of the oil layer. Observe the system for 15 seconds.

Analyze and Conclude

1. **Observe** What happened to the paper clip in Step 3? Why?
2. **Predict** If a paper clip becomes wet, does it float? Explain your answer.
3. **Observe** What shape did the rubber band take when the water inside it was covered with oil? Why did it take the observed shape?
4. **Describe** What happened when a drop of dish detergent was placed onto the layer of oil?

Density of Liquid Water and Ice	
Temperature (°C)	**Density (g/cm^3)**
100 (liquid water)	0.9584
50	0.9881
25	0.9971
10	0.9997
4	1.0000
0 (liquid water)	0.9998
0 (ice)	0.9168

Water in the Solid State

You have seen that water in the liquid state has some unique properties. The same is true for water in the solid state. For example, solid water has a lower density than liquid water. This is why ice cubes float in your glass of iced tea.

This situation is not usual for liquids. When a typical liquid cools, it contracts, and its density increases. The density increases because the molecules of the liquid move closer together so that a given volume of the liquid contains more molecules and thus more mass. As the cooling continues, the liquid becomes a solid. The density of the solid is greater than the density of the liquid. As a result, the solid sinks in its own liquid.

Density of Ice As water begins to cool, it behaves at first like a typical liquid. It contracts slightly and its density gradually increases, as shown in the table on the left. Notice that at 4°C, the density of water is at its highest value at 1.0000 g/cm^3. Below 4°C, the density of water actually starts to decrease. Below 4°C, water no longer behaves like a typical liquid. Ice forms at 0°C, and it has about a 10 percent lower density than liquid water at 0°C. You may have noticed that ice begins to form at the surface of a pond when the temperature reaches 0°C, but the ice does not sink. It floats at the surface, making ice skating and ice fishing possible. Ice is one of only a few solids that float in their own liquid.

Why is ice less dense than liquid water? As shown in the figure below, hydrogen bonds hold the water molecules in place in the solid phase. The structure of ice is a regular open framework of water molecules in a hexagonal arrangement. When ice melts, the framework collapses. Look back at the *Hydrogen Bonding in Water* figure on the second page of this lesson. You can see that the water molecules pack closer together in liquid water, making it more dense than ice.

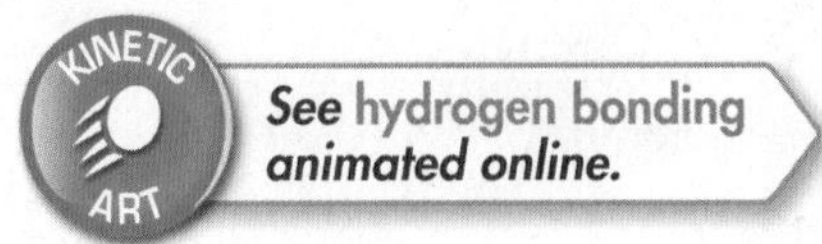

Structure of Ice The unique properties of ice are caused by hydrogen bonding.

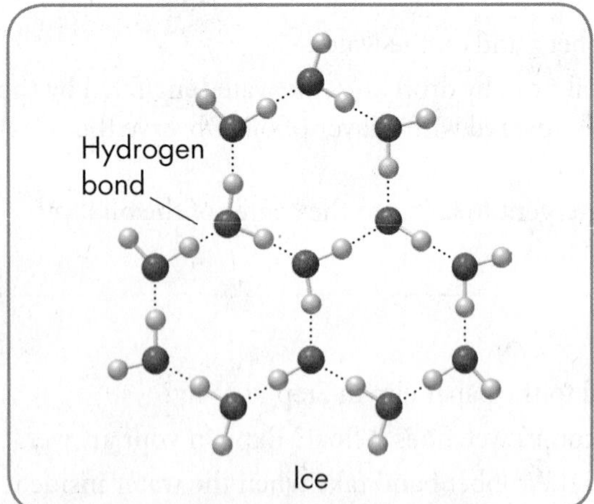

Hydrogen bonds in ice hold the water molecules farther apart in a more ordered arrangement than in liquid water.

The hexagonal symmetry of a snowflake reflects the structure of the ice crystal.

Ice in Natural Systems The fact that ice floats is very important for living things. Look at the photograph below. A layer of ice on the top of a body of water insulates the water beneath. It keeps the water from freezing solid except under extreme conditions. The liquid water at the bottom of an otherwise frozen body of water is warmer than 0°C. As a result, fish and other aquatic life are better able to survive. If ice were more dense than liquid water, ice would sink to the bottom. Bodies of water would freeze solid from the bottom up, destroying many types of living things.

Key Question How can you describe the structure of ice?
The structure of ice is a regular open framework of water molecules in a hexagonal arrangement.

Ice Floats in Liquid Water
Many animals that live in water would not survive if ice were more dense than liquid water.

15.1 LessonCheck

Key Concept Check

1. **Review** What causes the high surface tension, low vapor pressure, and high boiling point of water?
2. **Describe** How are water molecules arranged in ice?

Vocabulary Check *Choose a highlighted term from the lesson to complete each sentence correctly.*

3. Water forms spherical drops on leaves because water has a high __________.
4. Detergent is an example of a(n) __________.

Think Critically

5. **Explain** What causes surface tension in a liquid?
6. **Relate Cause and Effect** What effect does a surfactant have on the surface tension of water?
7. **Infer** Water (H_2O) and methane (CH_4) have similar molar masses. Methane changes from a liquid to a gas at -161°C. Water becomes a gas at 100°C. What could account for the difference?
8. **Apply Concepts** What causes water pipes to break in freezing weather?

CHEMISTRY & YOU

9. What properties of water that result from hydrogen bonding make it vital to life on Earth? (Hint: See pages 465 through 467.)

BIGIDEA BONDING AND INTERACTIONS

10. Describe how hydrogen bonding accounts for the properties of water.

15.2 Homogeneous Aqueous Systems

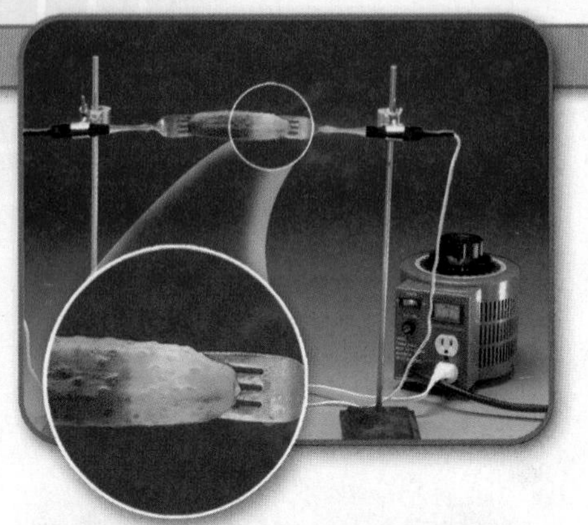

CHEMISTRY & YOU

Q: How can you make a pickle glow? Is it possible to read by the light of a glowing pickle? Although it sounds hard to believe, an ordinary dill pickle from the deli can be a source of light! Metal forks are inserted in the ends of the pickle and connected to a source of electric current. Over time, the pickle becomes hot, gives off steam, and begins to glow. The way the light is produced is not fully understood, but it is clear that conduction of electric current by the pickle is an important factor.

Key Questions

What types of substances dissolve most readily in water?

Why are all ionic compounds electrolytes?

Why do hydrates easily lose and regain water?

BUILD Vocabulary

aqueous solution water that contains dissolved substances

solvent the dissolving material in a solution

solute the dissolved particles in a solution

solvation the process by which the ions of an ionic solid become surrounded by solvent molecules

RELATED WORDS

Both *solvent* and *solute* come from the Latin *solvere*: "to loosen or dissolve." Typically, the *solvent* is a fluid. The *solute* is the material whose particles come loose and dissolve in the fluid.

Solutions

Water dissolves many of the substances with which it comes in contact. In fact, you cannot find chemically pure water in nature. Even the tap water you drink is a solution containing dissolved minerals and gases. An **aqueous solution** is water that contains dissolved substances.

Solvents and Solutes In a solution, the dissolving material is the **solvent.** The dissolved particles in a solution are the **solute.** A solvent dissolves the solute and the solute becomes dispersed in the solvent. Solvents and solutes may be gases, liquids, or solids.

Solutions are homogeneous, stable mixtures. For example, sodium chloride (NaCl) does not settle out even when its solutions are allowed to stand a long time. Solute particles can be atoms, ions, or molecules. Their average diameters are usually less than 1 nm (10^{-9} m). Solute particles are so small that if you filter a solution through filter paper, both the solute and the solvent will pass through the filter.

The Solution Process Water molecules are in constant motion because they have kinetic energy. When a crystal of sodium chloride is placed in water, the water molecules collide with the sodium chloride crystal.

A water molecule is polar. There is a partial negative charge on the oxygen atom and partial positive charges on the hydrogen atoms. The polar solvent molecules (H_2O) attract the solute ions (Na^+, Cl^-). The Na^+ ion is attracted to the negatively charged oxygen end of the water molecule. The Cl^- ion is attracted to the positively charged hydrogen end. As each solute ion breaks away from the crystal, it becomes surrounded by solvent molecules.

The ionic crystal dissolves when all of the solute ions are surrounded by solvent molecules. The process by which the positive and negative ions of an ionic solid become surrounded by solvent molecules is called **solvation.** The figure on the facing page shows a model of the solvation of sodium chloride, which is an ionic solid.

Solvation of an Ionic Solid When an ionic solid like NaCl dissolves, the ions become solvated, or surrounded by solvent molecules.

See solvation animated online.
KINETIC ART

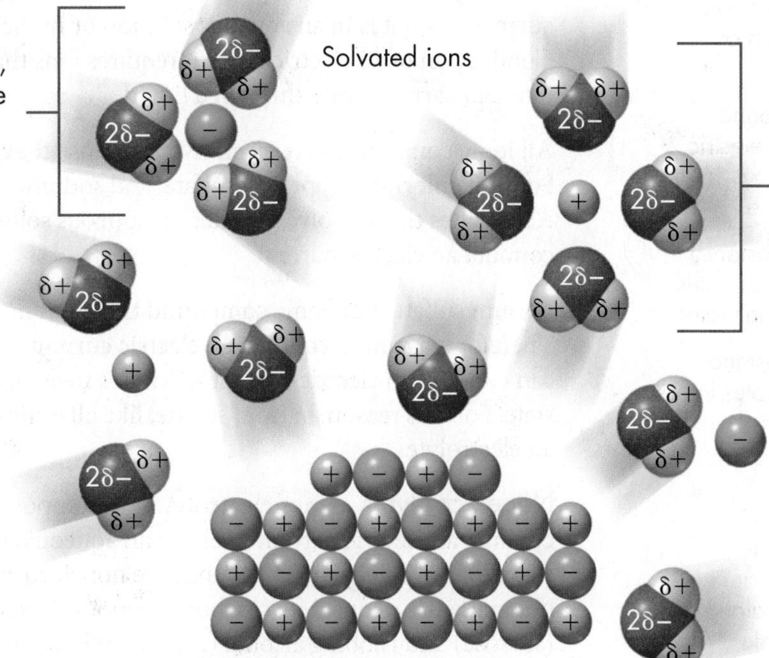

As a Cl⁻ ion breaks away from the crystal, it is surrounded by the positively charged ends of the polar water molecules.
Solvated ions
As a Na⁺ ion breaks away from the crystal, it is surrounded by the negatively charged ends of the polar water molecules.
Surface of solid NaCl

Substances That Dissolve in Water You know that a water molecule has a partially charged negative end (the oxygen atom) and a partially charged positive end (the hydrogen atoms). Water will tend to dissolve substances whose particles it can solvate. This includes ionic compounds such as sodium chloride and polar covalent compounds such as ethyl alcohol.

Substances That Do Not Dissolve in Water You know that oil and water do not mix. The compounds found in oil are nonpolar, while water molecules are polar. What about mixing oil with gasoline? Like oil, gasoline is composed of nonpolar molecules. The attractive forces that hold two molecules in oil together are similar in strength to the forces that hold two molecules in gasoline together. Molecules in oil can easily separate and replace molecules in gasoline to form a solution.

As a rule, polar solvents dissolve ionic compounds and polar compounds. Nonpolar solvents dissolve nonpolar compounds. This relationship can be summed up in the expression "like dissolves like."

There are exceptions to this rule. In some ionic compounds, the attractions among the ions in the crystals are stronger than the attractions of the water molecules for the ions. These compounds cannot be solvated. They are nearly insoluble. Barium sulfate ($BaSO_4$) and calcium carbonate ($CaCO_3$) are examples of nearly insoluble ionic compounds.

Key Question What types of substances dissolve most readily in water? **Substances that dissolve most readily in water include ionic compounds and polar covalent compounds.**

BUILD Connections

It is a hot day and you need a cold drink. You empty a package of powdered flavored drink mix into a pitcher of water and stir. You just made a solution. Water is the solvent. The powdered drink mix is the solute. The solute particles spread throughout the solvent.

electrolyte a compound that conducts an electric current when it is in an aqueous solution or in the molten state

nonelectrolyte a compound that does not conduct an electric current in either an aqueous solution or the molten state

strong electrolyte a substance that nearly completely dissociates into ions when dissolved in water

weak electrolyte a substance that only partially dissociates into ions when dissolved in water

USING PRIOR KNOWLEDGE

Ions carry electric charges. They are affected by electric fields and carry charges along as they move. Therefore, ionic compounds are *electrolytes*.

BUILD Connections

Why do lifeguards clear the pool when there is a thunderstorm nearby? Lightning is electricity. Pool water contains electrolytes. Therefore, pool water can conduct an electric current. Swimmers can be electrocuted if lightning strikes the water.

Electrolytes and Nonelectrolytes

Remember the glowing pickle? The pickle contained an electrolyte.

Electrolytes An **electrolyte** is a compound that conducts an electric current when it is in an aqueous solution or in the molten state. Conduction of an electric current requires ions that are mobile. Mobile ions can carry charges through a liquid.

All ionic compounds are electrolytes because they dissociate into ions. Sodium chloride, copper(II) sulfate, and sodium hydroxide are electrolytes that dissolve in water. In aqueous solutions, they can conduct an electric current.

Barium sulfate is an ionic compound that does not dissolve in water. Therefore, it cannot conduct an electric current in water. However, it can conduct an electric current when it is melted, or in the molten state. For this reason, barium sulfate, like all ionic compounds, is an electrolyte.

Nonelectrolytes A **nonelectrolyte** is a compound that does not conduct an electric current in either an aqueous solution or the molten state. Many molecular compounds are nonelectrolytes because they are not made up of ions. Most carbon compounds, such as table sugar (sucrose) and rubbing alcohol (2-propanol), are nonelectrolytes.

Some polar molecular compounds are nonelectrolytes in the pure state but become electrolytes when they dissolve in water. This change occurs because these compounds form ions in solution. For example, ammonia ($NH_3(g)$) is not an electrolyte in its pure state. The equation below shows how ammonia dissolves in water to form ions. An aqueous solution of ammonia conducts an electric current.

$$NH_3(g) + H_2O(l) \longrightarrow NH_4^+(aq) + OH^-(aq)$$

Ammonia dissolves in water to form an aqueous solution.

The solution conducts an electric current because ammonium ions and hydroxide ions form.

Hydrogen chloride ($HCl(g)$) is another compound that is not an electrolyte in its pure state. The equation below shows how hydrogen chloride produces ions in an aqueous solution. As a result, it too conducts an electric current.

$$HCl(g) + H_2O(l) \longrightarrow H_3O^+(aq) + Cl^-(aq)$$

Hydrogen chloride gas dissolves in water to form an aqueous solution.

The solution conducts an electric current because hydronium ions and chloride ions form.

Strengths of Electrolytes Not all electrolytes conduct an electric current to the same degree. Sodium chloride is a strong electrolyte because nearly all the sodium chloride dissolves to form separate Na^+ and Cl^- ions. In a solution that contains a **strong electrolyte,** all or nearly all of the solute is present as ions. The ions move in solution and can conduct an electric current. Most soluble ionic compounds, inorganic acids, and inorganic bases are strong electrolytes.

A **weak electrolyte** conducts an electric current poorly because only a small fraction of the solute is present as ions. Organic acids and bases are examples of weak electrolytes.

The table below summarizes what happens when a positively charged electrode and a negatively charged electrode are placed in an aqueous solution containing a strong electrolyte, a weak electrolyte, or a nonelectrolyte. Any positive ions present will move toward the negatively charged electrode. Any negative ions present will move toward the positively charged electrode. If ions are moving in the solution, the solution can conduct an electric current. Uncharged molecules will not be attracted to either the positively charged or negatively charged electrodes.

Key Question Why are all ionic compounds electrolytes? **All ionic compounds are electrolytes because they dissociate into ions.**

Behavior of Solutes in Aqueous Solutions

Type of solute	Example		Behavior in aqueous solution
Strong electrolyte	Sodium chloride (NaCl)	(+) (−)	NaCl almost completely dissociates in water. Na^+ ions (purple) move to the (−) electrode. Cl^- ions (green) move to the (+) electrode.
Weak electrolyte	Mercury(II) chloride ($HgCl_2$)	(+) 2+ (−)	$HgCl_2$ partially dissociates in water. Free Hg^{2+} ions (grey) move to the (−) electrode. Free Cl^- ions (green) move to the (+) electrode. Nondissociated $HgCl_2$ molecules are not attracted to the (+) or (−) electrodes.
Nonelectrolyte	Glucose ($C_6H_{12}O_6$)	(+) (−)	$C_6H_{12}O_6$ molecules do not dissociate in water. $C_6H_{12}O_6$ molecules are not attracted to the (+) or (−) electrodes.

Heating a Hydrate

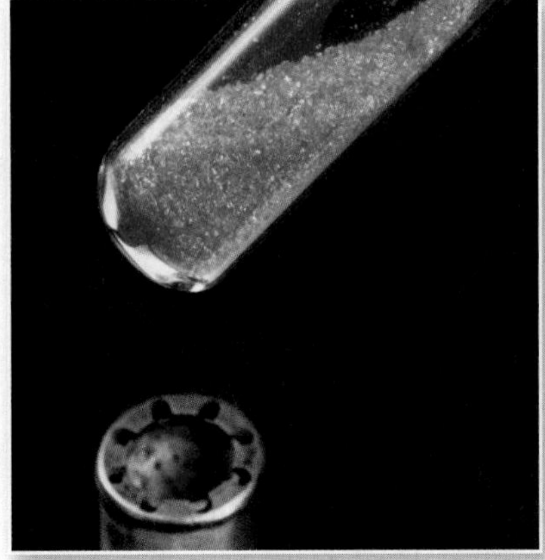

Heating of a sample of blue $CuSO_4 \cdot 5H_2O$ begins.

After time, much of the blue hydrate has been converted to white anhydrous $CuSO_4$.

BUILD Vocabulary

water of hydration water contained in a crystal

hydrate a compound that contains water of hydration

anhydrous a substance that does not contain water

ROOT WORDS

These terms all contain the root *hydr-*, which comes from the Greek *hydro* for water. They all refer to water in a crystal structure.

Hydrates

When an aqueous solution of copper(II) sulfate evaporates, blue crystals of copper(II) sulfate pentahydrate are left behind. Water molecules are a part of the crystal structure of copper(II) sulfate pentahydrate. However, the crystals are dry to the touch. The chemical formula for this compound is:

$$CuSO_4 \cdot 5H_2O$$

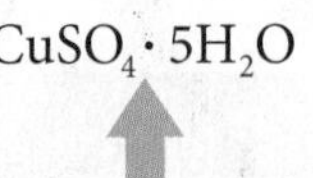

Use a dot to connect the formula unit and the number of water molecules per formula unit.

The water contained in a crystal is called the **water of hydration.** A **hydrate** is a compound that contains water of hydration.

The forces holding the water molecules in hydrates are not very strong, so the water is easily lost and regained. The photos above show how the hydrate $CuSO_4 \cdot 5H_2O$ loses its water of hydration when heated. It crumbles to a white anhydrous powder that has the formula $CuSO_4$. A substance that is **anhydrous** does not contain water.

Look at the chemical equation below. If you read the equation from left to right, you see how the blue copper(II) sulfate pentahydrate loses its water of hydration when heated. If you read the equation from right to left, you see that the blue copper(II) sulfate pentahydrate forms again when water is added to the white anhydrous copper(II) sulfate.

$$CuSO_4 \cdot 5H_2O(s) \underset{-\text{heat}}{\overset{+\text{heat}}{\rightleftharpoons}} CuSO_4(s) + 5H_2O(g)$$

Blue pentahydrate | White anhydrous powder

Some Common Hydrates		
Formula	**Chemical name**	**Common name**
$MgSO_4 \cdot 7H_2O$	Magnesium sulfate heptahydrate	Epsom salt
$CuSO_4 \cdot 5H_2O$	Copper(II) sulfate pentahydrate	Blue vitriol
$KAl(SO_4)_2 \cdot 12H_2O$	Potassium aluminum sulfate dodecahydrate	Alum
$Na_2B_4O_7 \cdot 10H_2O$	Sodium tetraborate decahydrate	Borax
$FeSO_4 \cdot 7H_2O$	Iron(II) sulfate heptahydrate	Green vitriol

The Percent by Mass of Water in a Hydrate Some hydrates are listed in the table above. Each one contains a fixed amount of water and has a definite composition.

To determine what percent by mass of a hydrate is water, first find the mass of water in one mole of the hydrate. Then find the molar mass of the hydrate. The percent by mass of water can be calculated using the equation below.

$$\text{Percent by mass } H_2O = \frac{\text{mass of water}}{\text{mass of hydrate}} \times 100\%$$

Efflorescent Hydrates Hydrates usually have a measurable vapor pressure because the water molecules in hydrates are held by weak forces. If a hydrate has a vapor pressure that is higher than the pressure of water vapor in the air, the hydrate will lose its water of hydration, or **effloresce.**

Copper(II) sulfate pentahydrate has a vapor pressure of about 1.0 kPa at room temperature. The pressure of water vapor at room temperature is about 1.3 kPa. When the vapor pressure drops below 1.0 kPa, copper(II) sulfate pentahydrate effloresces.

Hygroscopic Hydrates Hydrated ionic compounds that have a low vapor pressure can remove water from moist air. Hydrates and other compounds that remove moisture from air are **hygroscopic.**

Calcium chloride monohydrate is a hygroscopic substance. This compound takes up a second molecule of water from moist air, as shown in the equation below.

$$CaCl_2 \cdot H_2O(s) \xrightarrow{\text{moist air}} CaCl_2 \cdot 2H_2O(s)$$

Calcium chloride is used as a desiccant in the laboratory. A **desiccant** is a substance used to absorb moisture from the air and create a dry atmosphere.

A solid desiccant such as calcium sulfate ($CaSO_4$) can be added to a liquid solvent to keep it dry. A bottle labeled "dry ethanol" might have solid calcium sulfate at the bottom. The calcium sulfate does not dissolve much in the solvent, but it absorbs water from the ethanol. When a desiccant has absorbed all the water it can hold, it can be returned to its anhydrous state by heating.

effloresce to lose water of hydration

hygroscopic a term describing compounds that remove moisture from the air

desiccant a substance used to absorb moisture and create a dry atmosphere

USING PRIOR KNOWLEDGE

Small packets of silica gel are often found packaged with electronic equipment and leather goods. Although not a hydrate, silica gel is a hygroscopic material. Hygroscopic substances keep sensitive equipment and materials from being damaged by moisture.

BUILD Understanding

Cycle Diagram Complete a cycle diagram to describe the changes when a desiccant is used and reused. Use the terms *hydrate* and *anhydrous* in your description.

Sample Problem 15.1

Finding the Percent by Mass of Water in a Hydrate

Calculate the percent by mass of water in washing soda, sodium carbonate decahydrate ($Na_2CO_3 \cdot 10H_2O$).

1 Analyze List the known and the unknown.

KNOWN	UNKNOWN
formula of hydrate = $Na_2CO_3 \cdot 10H_2O$	percent by mass H_2O = ?%

2 Calculate Solve for the unknown. Divide the mass of water in one mol of the hydrate by the molar mass of the hydrate. Then, multiply by 100 percent.

Hint: From the formula, you know that for every mole of $Na_2CO_3 \cdot 10H_2O$, there are 10 mol of H_2O.

Start by writing the general equation for determining the percent by mass of water in a hydrate.

$$\text{Percent by mass } H_2O = \frac{\text{mass of water}}{\text{mass of hydrate}} \times 100\%$$

Calculate the mass of 1 mol of H_2O.

$$\text{mass of 1 mol } H_2O = \text{mass of 2 mol H} + \text{mass of 1 mol O} = (2 \times 1.0\,g) + (1 \times 16.0\,g) = 18.0\,g$$

Calculate the mass of 10 mol of H_2O (the mass of water in 1 mol of hydrate).

$$\text{mass of 10 mol } H_2O = 10 \times \text{mass of 1 mol } H_2O = 10 \times 18.0\,g = 180.0\,g$$

Calculate the mass of 1 mol of Na_2CO_3 (the mass of Na_2CO_3 in 1 mol of hydrate).

$$\text{mass of 1 mol } Na_2CO_3 = \text{mass of 2 mol Na} + \text{mass of 1 mol C} + \text{mass of 3 mol O} = (2 \times 23.0\,g) + (1 \times 12.0\,g) + (3 \times 16.0\,g) = 106.0\,g$$

Calculate the mass of 1 mol of hydrate, $Na_2CO_3 \cdot 10H_2O$.

$$\text{mass of 1 mol } Na_2CO_3 \cdot 10H_2O = \text{mass of 1 mol } Na_2CO_3 + \text{mass of 10 mol } H_2O = 106.0\,g + 180.0\,g = 286.0\,g$$

Calculate the percent by mass of water in the hydrate.

$$\text{Percent by mass } H_2O = \frac{\text{mass of 10 mol } H_2O}{\text{mass of 1 mol } Na_2CO_3 \cdot 10H_2O} \times 100\%$$

$$= \frac{180.0\,\cancel{g}}{286.0\,\cancel{g}} \times 100\% = 62.94\%$$

3 Evaluate Does the result make sense? The mass of the water accounts for more than half the molar mass of the compound, so a percentage greater than 50 percent is expected.

BUILD Math Skills

Order of Operations The order of math operations is important when you calculate molar masses. For example, when you calculate the molar mass of water, you must add the masses of two mol of H and one mol of O. Make sure that you multiply first and then add.

You can use the parentheses keys on your calculator to group the factors.

$$(2 \times 1.0\,g) + (1 \times 16.0\,g) = 18.0\,g$$

Without the parentheses, some calculators give an incorrect answer of 48.0 g.

$$2 \times 1.0\,g + 1 \times 16.0\,g = 48.0\,g$$

Go to your Chemistry Skills and Math Workbook for more practice.

Practice Problems

Hint: In Problem 11, start by determining the mass of 5 mol of water and the mass of 1 mol of the hydrate.

11. What is the percent by mass of water in $CuSO_4 \cdot 5H_2O$?

❶ **Analyze** **List the known and the unknown.**

❷ **Calculate** **Solve for the unknown.**

❸ **Evaluate** **Does the result make sense?**

KNOWN	UNKNOWN
formula of hydrate = $CuSO_4 \cdot 5H_2O$	percent by mass H_2O = ?%

12. What is the percent by mass of water in iron(II) sulfate heptahydrate ($FeSO_4 \cdot 7H_2O$)?

KNOWN	UNKNOWN
formula of hydrate =	percent by mass H_2O = ?%

13. Challenge If you need 5.00 g of anhydrous Na_2CO_3 for your reaction, how many grams of $Na_2CO_3 \cdot 10H_2O$ could you use instead?

Here's a tip to help you with Problem 13: You know from Sample Problem 15.1 that 62.94% of the hydrate is water.

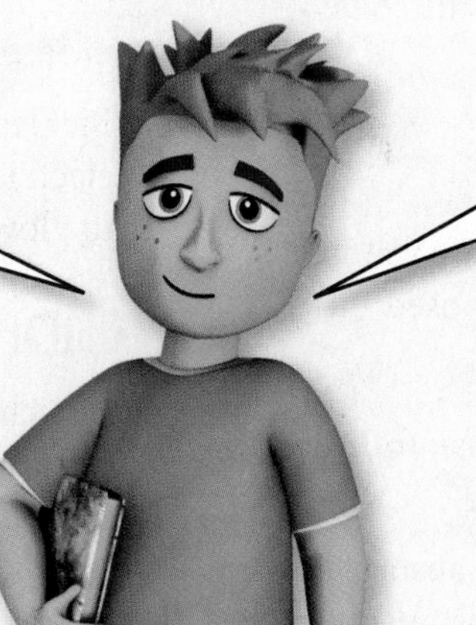

From this, you know that 37.06% of the hydrate is Na_2CO_3 (100% − 62.94% = 37.06%). This means that 37.06 g out of every 100 g of the hydrate is Na_2CO_3.

BUILD Vocabulary

deliquescent describes a substance that removes enough water from the air to form a solution

RELATED WORD FORMS
The adjective *deliquescent* and the verb *deliquesce* are related word forms. A substance that deliquesces is dissolving.

Deliquescent Compounds Some compounds are so hygroscopic that they become wet when they are exposed to normally moist air. These compounds are **deliquescent,** which means that they remove enough water from the air to dissolve completely and form solutions. The photos below show that pellets of sodium hydroxide are deliquescent. As a result, containers of sodium hydroxide and other deliquescent chemicals should always be tightly sealed. You should never allow deliquescent chemicals to come in contact with your skin.

Key Question Why do hydrates easily lose and regain water? **The forces holding the water molecules in hydrates are not very strong, so the water is easily lost and regained.**

Sodium Hydroxide

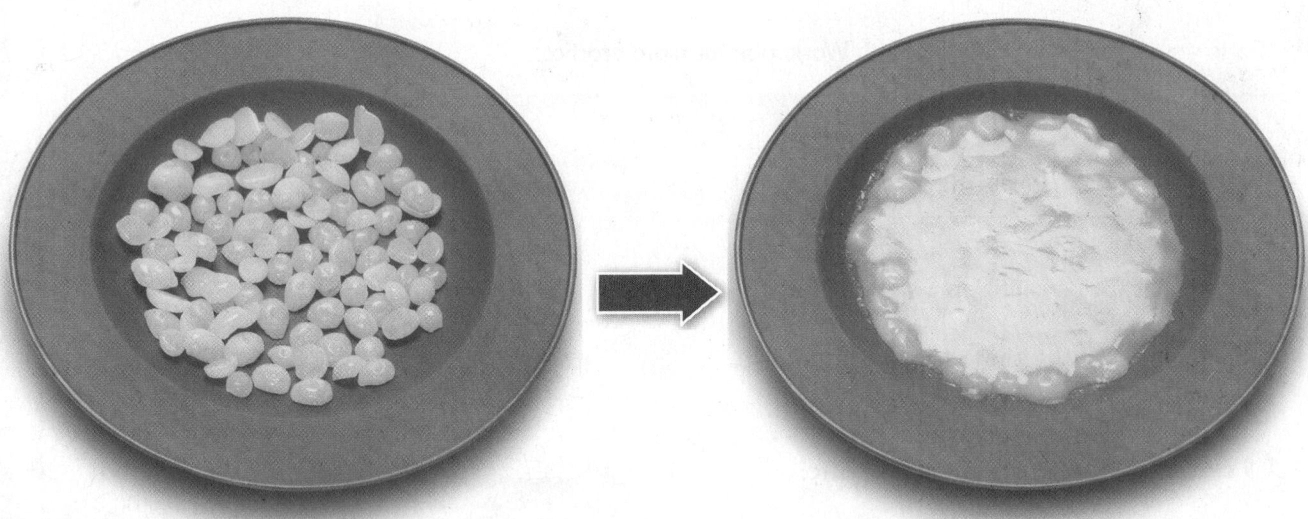

Sodium hydroxide pellets absorb moisture from the air.

Eventually a solution is formed.

15.2 LessonCheck

Key Concept Check

14. **Identify** What types of substances dissolve most readily in water?

15. **Review** What property of all ionic compounds make them electrolytes?

16. **Explain** Why do hydrates easily lose water when heated and regain water when exposed to moisture?

Vocabulary Check *Choose a highlighted term from the lesson to complete the sentence correctly.*

17. A(n) __________ is a substance used to absorb moisture from the air and create a dry atmosphere.

Think Critically

CHEMISTRY & YOU

18. Pickles contain table salt, NaCl. Why can electric current flow through a pickle, causing it to glow? (Hint: See pages 470 and 471.)

BIGIDEA BONDING AND INTERACTIONS

19. Which of the following substances dissolves to a significant extent in water? Explain your answer in terms of the polarities of water and the solute.

a. CH_4
b. KCl
c. $MgSO_4$
d. Sucrose ($C_{12}H_{22}O_{11}$)

15.3 Heterogeneous Aqueous Systems

CHEMISTRY & YOU

Q: Why are some sunsets red? The atmosphere contains particles of water and dust. Sunlight scatters as it passes through the particles, but not all wavelengths are scattered by the same amount. The shorter wavelengths of visible light (blue and green) are scattered more than the longer wavelengths (red and orange). At sunrise and sunset, the sun's light travels through more of Earth's atmosphere. The longer wavelengths are more visible because the shorter wavelengths are scattered out of the line of sight.

Key Questions

What is the difference between a suspension and a solution?

How does a colloid differ from a suspension and a solution?

BUILD Vocabulary

suspension a mixture from which particles settle out upon standing

ACADEMIC WORDS
The word *heterogeneous* means "made up of parts that are different." In a suspension, you can detect the presence of the different parts.

Suspensions

If you shake a container containing a piece of clay and water, the clay breaks into particles. The water becomes cloudy because the clay particles are suspended in the water. If you stop shaking the container, the particles settle out. A **suspension** is a mixture from which particles settle out upon standing.

A suspension is different from a solution. Solutions are homogeneous mixtures. Suspensions are heterogeneous because at least two substances in a suspension can be clearly identified. Also, the particles of a suspension are much larger. The particles in a suspension usually have a diameter greater than 1000 nm. The particle size in a solution is usually about 1 nm. The particles in a suspension do not stay suspended forever. The photos below show what happens when a solution and a suspension are filtered.

Key Question What is the difference between a suspension and a solution? **The particles of a suspension are much larger than the particles of a solution. Also, the particles of a suspension will settle out of the mixture and can be filtered.**

Solutions and Suspensions
A solution is a homogeneous mixture. A suspension is a heterogeneous mixture.

The small size of the solute particles in a solution lets them pass through filter paper.

The suspended particles in a suspension can be removed by filtration.

colloid a heterogeneous mixture containing particles that range in size between 1 nm to 1000 nm

SUFFIXES

The end of *colloid* comes from the Greek *-oeidēs,* which means "like." Many other words end in *-oid,* including cuboid, metalloid, and asteroid. In these words, *-oid* also means "like."

BUILD Connections

If you have ever squeezed a marshmallow, you may have been able to tell that it is filled with air. Marshmallows are formed from a mixture of gelatin and syrup. When the mixture is whipped vigorously, air becomes incorporated into the mixture. The air stays in the mixture as the marshmallow solidifies.

Colloids

Gelatin, paint, aerosol sprays, and smoke are all examples of a type of mixture called a colloid. A **colloid** is a heterogeneous mixture containing particles that range in size between 1 nm to 1000 nm. The particles are spread throughout the dispersion medium, which can be a solid, liquid, or gas. A dispersion medium is like a solvent. It holds and separates particles different from itself. The table below lists some common colloidal systems and gives examples of familiar colloids.

What is the difference between colloids, suspensions, and solutions? Many colloids look cloudy or milky, like suspensions, when they are concentrated. Colloids may look clear or almost clear, like solutions, when they are dilute. The important difference between colloids and solutions and between colloids and suspensions is in the size of the particles. Colloids have particles smaller than those in suspensions and larger than those in solutions. The particles in a colloid are small enough that they pass through filter paper. Also, the particles in a colloid do not settle out with time.

Some Colloidal Systems

System			
Dispersed phase	**Dispersion medium**	**Type**	**Example**
Gas	Liquid	Foam	Whipped cream
Gas	Solid	Foam	Marshmallow
Liquid	Liquid	Emulsion	Milk, mayonnaise
Liquid	Gas	Aerosol	Fog, aerosol
Solid	Gas	Smoke	Dust in air
Solid	Liquid	Sols, gels	Egg white, jelly, paint, blood, starch in water, gelatin

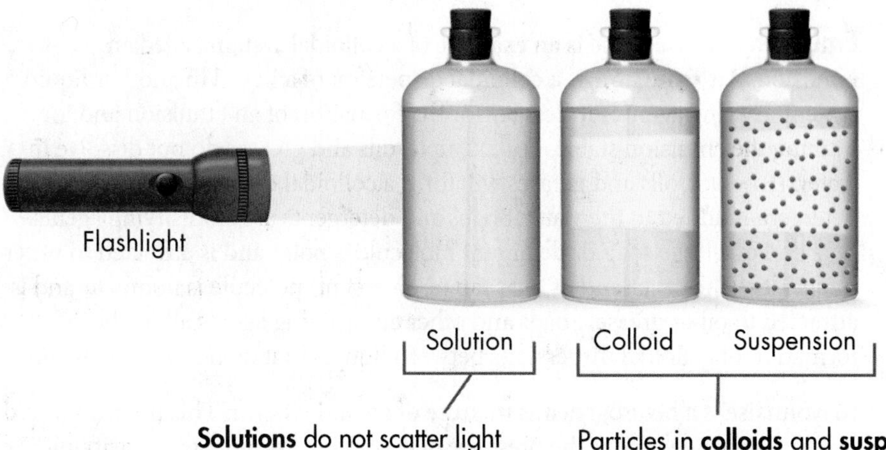

Scattering of Light
The path of light is visible only when the light is scattered by particles.

Solutions do not scatter light because their particles are too small.

Particles in **colloids** and **suspensions** scatter light in all directions. This is the Tyndall effect.

The Tyndall Effect You can only see a beam of sunlight if the light passes through particles of water (mist) or dust in the air. These particles scatter the sunlight. Similarly, a beam of light is visible as it passes through a colloid. The scattering of visible light by particles is called the **Tyndall effect.**

Suspensions also exhibit the Tyndall effect. Solutions do not exhibit the Tyndall effect because their particles are too small. The figure above shows the Tyndall effect. Notice the difference between a solution and a colloid and between a solution and a suspension.

Brownian Motion If you look at a colloid under a microscope, you will see flashes of light, which are called scintillations. Colloids scintillate because the particles move chaotically. The particles reflect and scatter light as they move. **Brownian motion** is the term used to describe the chaotic movement of colloidal particles. Brownian motion is caused by the molecules of the dispersion medium colliding with the small, dispersed colloidal particles. These collisions keep the colloidal particles from settling.

Coagulation Colloidal particles also tend to stay suspended because they become charged. Colloidal particles become charged by adsorbing ions from the dispersing medium onto their surface. Adsorption means to stick to a surface. Some colloidal particles become positively charged by adsorbing positively charged ions. Other colloidal particles become negatively charged by adsorbing negatively charged ions.

All the colloidal particles in the same colloidal system will have the same charge. However, the system will be neutral. Remember that like charges repel each other. The repulsion between like charges keeps the particles from sticking together and forming larger particles. The larger particles would have a greater tendency to settle out. A colloidal system can be destroyed, or coagulated, by adding electrolytes. The added ions neutralize the charged colloidal particles. Then, the particles can clump together to form heavier particles and settle out from the dispersion.

BUILD Connections

Why is it easier to see the light beam of a car on a foggy night than on a clear night? A beam of light is only visible when it is scattered by particles. Fog or mist is made of small water droplets, so fog exhibits the Tyndall effect.

Tyndall effect the scattering of visible light by particles

Brownian motion the chaotic movement of colloidal particles

WORD ORIGINS

Discoveries in science are often named for the first scientist to describe them. The *Tyndall effect* is named for 19th century physicist John Tyndall. *Brownian motion* was described by Robert Brown in the 19th century using pollen grains.

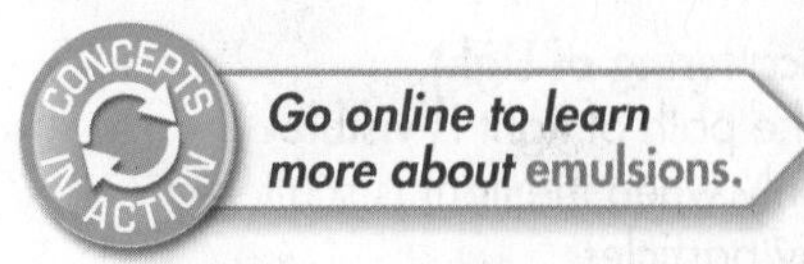
Go online to learn more about emulsions.

Emulsions Mayonnaise is an example of a colloidal system called an emulsion. An **emulsion** is a colloidal dispersion of a liquid in another liquid. An emulsifying agent is necessary for the formation of an emulsion and for keeping the emulsion stable. For example, oils and greases do not dissolve in water. However, oils and greases will form a colloidal dispersion if soap or detergent is added to the water. Soaps and detergents are emulsifying agents. One end of a large soap or detergent molecule is polar and is attracted to water molecules. The other end of the soap or detergent molecule is nonpolar and is attracted to oil or grease. Soaps and other emulsifying agents allow the formation of colloidal dispersions between liquids that do not ordinarily mix.

Mayonnaise is a heterogeneous mixture of oil and vinegar. This mixture would quickly separate without the presence of egg yolk, which is the emulsifying agent. Milk, margarine, and butter are also emulsions. Cosmetics, shampoos, and lotions are made with emulsifiers to maintain consistent quality. The table below summarizes the properties of solutions, colloids, and suspensions.

Key Question How does a colloid differ from a suspension and a solution? **Colloids have particles that are smaller than those in suspensions but larger than those in solutions.**

BUILD Vocabulary

emulsion a colloidal dispersion of a liquid in another liquid

WORD ORIGINS

The term *emulsion* comes from the Latin term *ēmuls(us)*, which means "to milk." In fact, milk is probably the most familiar example of an emulsion that you encounter from day to day.

Properties of Solutions, Colloids, and Suspensions

	System		
Property	**Solution**	**Colloid**	**Suspension**
Particle type	Ions, atoms, small molecules	Large molecules or particles	Large particles or aggregates
Particle size	0.1–1 nm	1–1000 nm	1000 nm and larger
Effect of light	No scattering	Exhibits Tyndall effect	Exhibits Tyndall effect
Effect of gravity	Stable, does not separate	Stable, does not separate	Unstable, sediment forms
Filtration	Particles not retained on filter	Particles not retained on filter	Particles retained on filter
Uniformity	Homogeneous	Heterogeneous	Heterogeneous

15.3 LessonCheck

Key Concept Check

20. **Describe** How is a suspension different from a solution?

21. **Explain** How is a colloid different from a suspension and a solution?

Vocabulary Check

Choose a highlighted term from the lesson to complete the sentence correctly.

22. The scattering of visible light by particles is called the ________.

Think Critically

23. **Apply Concepts** How can you determine through observation that a mixture is a suspension?

24. What would be the ideal conditions to see a red sunset? (Hint: See page 479.)

15 Study Guide

BIGIDEA

BONDING AND INTERACTIONS

Water molecules are held together by dipole interactions and the formation of hydrogen bonds. Hydrogen bonding in water can be used to explain the unique properties of water. These properties include a high surface tension, low vapor pressure, and high boiling point. Hydrogen bonding can also be used to explain why ice is less dense than liquid water. Many ionic compounds and polar covalent compounds dissolve in water to form aqueous solutions. Ionic compounds dissolve in water when the polar water molecules attract the ions of the solute. As a result, the individual solute ions break away from the ionic crystal.

15.1 Water and Its Properties

Many unusual and important properties of water—including its high surface tension, low vapor pressure, and high boiling point—result from hydrogen bonding.

The structure of ice is a regular open framework of water molecules in a hexagonal arrangement.

- surface tension (464)
- surfactant (464)

15.2 Homogeneous Aqueous Systems

Substances that dissolve most readily in water include ionic compounds and polar covalent compounds.

All ionic compounds are electrolytes because they dissociate into ions.

The forces holding the water molecules in hydrates are not very strong, so the water is easily lost and regained.

- aqueous solution (468)
- solvent (468)
- solute (468)
- solvation (468)
- electrolyte (470)
- nonelectrolyte (470)
- strong electrolyte (471)
- weak electrolyte (471)
- water of hydration (472)
- hydrate (472)
- anhydrous (472)
- effloresce (473)
- hygroscopic (473)
- desiccant (473)
- deliquescent (476)

Key Equation

$$\text{Percent by mass } H_2O = \frac{\text{mass of water}}{\text{mass of hydrate}} \times 100\%$$

15.3 Heterogeneous Aqueous Systems

The particles of a suspension are much larger than the particles of a solution. Also, the particles of a suspension will settle out of the mixture and can be filtered.

Colloids have particles that are smaller than those in suspensions but larger than those in solutions.

- suspension (477)
- colloid (478)
- Tyndall effect (479)
- Brownian motion (479)
- emulsion (480)

15 Assessment

⋆ Solutions appear in Appendix D.

Lesson by Lesson

15.1 Water and Its Properties

25. Explain why water molecules are polar.

⋆26. Why do the particles at the surface of a liquid behave differently from those in the bulk of the liquid?

27. Describe some observable effects that are produced by the surface tension of a liquid.

⋆28. What is a surfactant? Explain how it works.

29. How can the unusually low vapor pressure of water be explained?

⋆30. Explain why bodies of water with large surface areas, such as lakes and oceans, do not evaporate rapidly.

31. What characteristic of ice distinguishes it from other solid substances?

32. How does the structure of ice differ from the structure of liquid water?

⋆33. What would be some of the consequences if ice were denser than water?

15.2 Homogeneous Aqueous Systems

34. Distinguish between a solution in general and an aqueous solution.

35. How does the solvent differ from the solute in the formation of a solution?

⋆36. Identify the solvent and the solute in a solution of table sugar in water.

⋆37. Suppose an aqueous solution contains both table sugar and table salt. Can you separate either of these solutes from the water by filtration? Explain your reasoning.

⋆38. Describe the process of solvation.

39. Explain why gasoline does not dissolve in water.

⋆40. Which of the following substances dissolves appreciably in water? Give reasons for your choices.

a. HCl
b. K_2SO_4
c. NaI
d. C_2H_6
e. NH_3
f. $CaCO_3$

41. What particles must be present in a solution if it is to conduct an electric current?

⋆42. Why does molten sodium chloride conduct an electric current?

43. What is meant by a substance's water of hydration?

⋆44. Write formulas for these hydrates.

a. sodium sulfate decahydrate
b. calcium chloride dihydrate
c. barium hydroxide octahydrate

⋆45. Name each hydrate.

a. $SnCl_4 \cdot 5H_2O$
b. $FeSO_4 \cdot 7H_2O$
c. $BaBr_2 \cdot 4H_2O$
d. $FePO_4 \cdot 4H_2O$

⋆46. Epsom salt ($MgSO_4 \cdot 7H_2O$) changes to the monohydrate form at 150°C. Write an equation for this change.

⋆47. Explain why a hygroscopic substance can be used as a desiccant.

15.3 Heterogeneous Aqueous Systems

⋆48. Arrange colloids, suspensions, and solutions in order of increasing particle size.

⋆49. How could you distinguish through observation among a solution, a colloid, and a suspension?

50. Why don't solutions demonstrate the Tyndall effect?

⋆51. What are two circumstances that help keep colloidal particles in suspension?

52. How can a colloid be destroyed?

Understand Concepts

*53. Based on your knowledge of intermolecular forces, arrange these liquids in order of increasing surface tension: water (H_2O), hexane (C_6H_{14}), and ethanol (C_2H_6O).

*54. The graph below shows the density of water over the temperature range 0°C to 20°C.

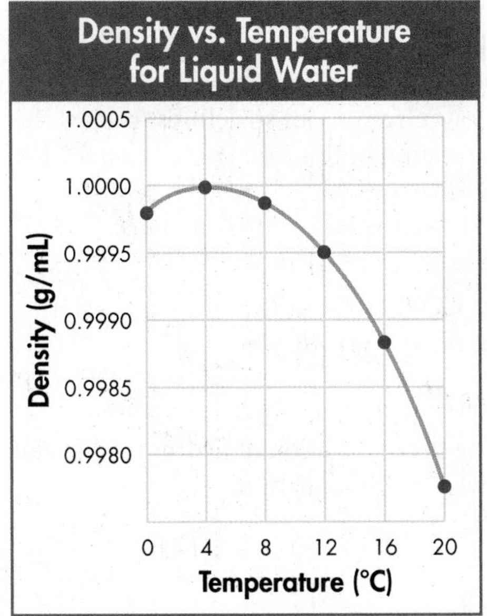

a. What is the maximum density of water?
b. At what temperature does the maximum density of water occur?
c. Would it be meaningful to expand the smooth curve to the left of the graph to temperatures below 0°C?

*55. Explain which properties of water are responsible for these occurrences.

a. Water in tiny cracks in rocks helps break up the rocks when it freezes.
b. Water beads up on a newly waxed car.
c. A longer time is needed for a teaspoon of water to evaporate than a teaspoon of alcohol.

*56. You have a solution containing either table sugar or table salt dissolved in water.

a. Can you tell which it is by looking at it? Explain.
b. Give two ways by which you could easily tell which it is, without tasting the solution.

*57. The diagrams below represent aqueous solutions of three different substances. Identify each substance as a strong electrolyte, weak electrolyte, or nonelectrolyte.

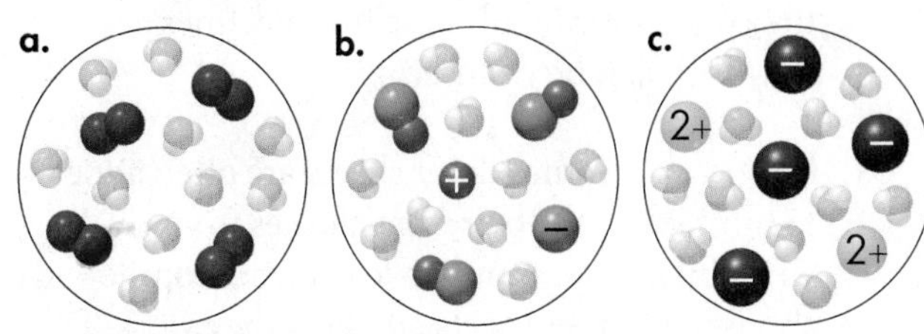

Think Critically

*58. **Predict** Describe what might happen if you put a sealed glass container full of water into a freezer.

*59. **Draw Conclusions** When the humidity is low and the temperature high, humans must take in large quantities of water or face serious dehydration. Why do you think water is so important for the proper functioning of your body?

FOUNDATIONS Wrap-Up

Observing Surface Tension

1. **Draw Conclusions** At the beginning of this chapter, you placed drops of plain water and soapy water on wax paper. Explain how the detergent changed the properties of the water.

Concept Check

Now that you have finished studying Chapter 15, answer these questions. Use your own words.

2. Why does ice float in liquid water?
3. Will an aqueous solution of sodium chloride conduct an electric current? Explain why or why not.
4. How could you tell if a mixture is a solution or a colloid?

Write About Science

60. Explain Research the importance of electrolytes in the body. Write a paragraph explaining why the concentration of these ions declines and how they can be restored.

61. Research Clothes dryer sheets are often added to tumble dryers to prevent clothes from wrinkling. Do research to learn what compounds are used in dryer sheets and how they work. Write a brief report of your findings.

CHEMYSTERY

Coming Clean

Wes's dirty socks finally did become clean, but only after being thrown into the washing machine with a load of his family's laundry. It was not just the machine that did the trick. It was also the laundry detergent that was added to the load.

Water alone cannot remove many common stains. The particles of dirt and grease on Wes's socks were trapped in the cloth fibers and could not be dissolved by water. Also, the water could not penetrate the fibers because of its high surface tension. Laundry detergents usually contain one or more surfactants. The surfactants reduce the surface tension of water so that it is able to wet and penetrate the fibers. The surfactants also act as emulsifiers. One end of the surfactant molecule is nonpolar and can dissolve the molecules in dirt and grease. The other end of the surfactant molecule is polar and can dissolve in water. Agitation provided by the washing machine helps pull the stain free from the cloth fibers.

***62. Infer** What happens to the molecules in the dirt and grease once they are lifted from the cloth fibers?

63. Connect to the BIGIDEA Explain how detergents remove stains from clothing by describing the interactions among the molecules in the detergent, the molecules in the stain, and the water molecules.

Cumulative Review

***64.** How many significant figures are in each measurement? (See Lesson 3.1 for help.)

a. 56.003 g
b. 750 mL
c. 0.0056 cm
d. 0.4005 dg

***65.** When a proton is attracted to the unshared electron pair of a water molecule, the polyatomic hydronium ion (H_3O^+) is formed. Draw electron dot structures to show the formation of this ion. (See Lesson 8.2 for help.)

***66.** Balance the following equations. (See Lesson 11.1 for help.)

a. $CO_2(g) + H_2O(l) \longrightarrow C_6H_{12}O_6(s) + O_2(g)$
b. $Na(s) + H_2O(l) \longrightarrow Na^+(aq) + OH^-(aq) + H_2(g)$

***67.** The decomposition of hydrogen peroxide is given by this equation.

$$2H_2O_2(l) \longrightarrow 2H_2O(l) + O_2(g)$$

Calculate the mass of water and the volume of oxygen at STP formed when 2.00×10^{-3} mol of hydrogen peroxide is decomposed. (See Lesson 12.2 for help.)

***68.** A mixture of 40 cm^3 of oxygen gas and 60 cm^3 of hydrogen gas at STP is ignited. (See Lesson 12.3 for help.)

a. Which gas is the limiting reagent?
b. What is the mass of water produced?
c. Which gas remains after the reaction?
d. What is the volume, at STP, of the remaining gas?

69. Explain how the following changes in the pressure on the surface of water affect the water's boiling point. (See Lesson 13.2 for help.)

a. an increase in pressure
b. a decrease in pressure

***70.** The temperature of 1 L of steam at constant volume and 1.00 atm pressure is increased from 100°C to 200°C. Calculate the final pressure of the steam in atmospheres, assuming the volume does not change. (See Lesson 14.2 for help.)

Standardized Test Prep

For help with answering test questions, go to your Chemistry Skills and Math Workbook.

Select the choice that best answers each question or completes each statement.

1. When a sugar cube completely dissolves in a glass of water, it forms
(A) a colloid.
(B) a suspension.
(C) an emulsion.
(D) a solution.

2. How many water molecules are tied up per formula unit of a compound that is an octahydrate?
(A) nine (B) eight (C) seven (D) six

3. Which property is characteristic of water?
(A) relatively high surface tension
(B) relatively high vapor pressure
(C) relatively low solvent ability
(D) relatively low polarity

Use the atomic windows to answer Question 4.

4. Atomic window (A) represents solute particles in a given volume of solution. Which window represents the solute particles in the same volume of solution when the amount of solvent is doubled?

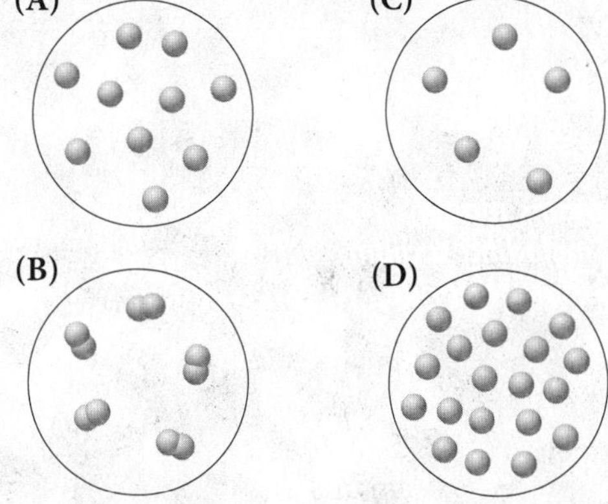

Tips for Success

Constructed Response You will probably answer most constructed response questions by writing a sentence or a paragraph. Put as much information into your answer as possible, but avoid unnecessary words. Be sure to address all the points asked for in the question.

Use the description and the data table to answer Questions 5–7.

A student measured the conductivity of six aqueous solutions. Each solution had equal concentrations of solute. The magnitude of the conductivity value is proportional to the number of ions in the solution. The SI conductivity unit is the microsiemens/cm (μS/cm). The table gives the student's results.

Solution	Conductivity (μS/cm)
Potassium chloride, KCl	2050
Aluminum chloride, $AlCl_3$	4500
Calcium chloride, $CaCl_2$	3540
Sodium hydroxide, $NaOH$	2180
Ethanol, C_2H_6O	0
Magnesium bromide, $MgBr_2$	3490

5. Why does the ethanol solution have zero conductivity?

6. Explain why two pairs of conducting solutions have similar conductivities.

7. The $AlCl_3$ solution has a conductivity that is about twice that of the KCl solution. Explain.

For each question, there are two statements. Decide whether each statement is true or false. Then decide whether Statement II is a correct explanation for Statement I.

	Statement I		Statement II
8.	Water has a relatively high surface tension.	BECAUSE	Water molecules form strong hydrogen bonds with other water molecules.
9.	Particles in a colloid settle out faster than particles in a solution.	BECAUSE	Particles in a colloid are larger than particles in a solution.
10.	Water molecules are polar.	BECAUSE	The bond between hydrogen and oxygen atoms in a water molecule is polar.

If You Have Trouble With . . .

Question	1	2	3	4	5	6	7	8	9	10
See Lesson	15.3	15.2	15.1	15.2	15.2	15.2	15.2	15.1	15.3	15.1

16 Solutions

FOUNDATIONS for Learning

Mixing Oil and Water

1. You will need a small jar with a lid, some water, and some salad oil.
2. Add water to the jar so it is one-quarter full. Add oil to the jar so it is one-half full. Put the lid on the jar.
3. Predict what will happen after you shake the jar and then let it sit.
4. Shake the jar and then let it sit for one minute. Were your predictions correct?

Form a Hypothesis Explain why you think the two substances acted as they did.

PearsonChem.com

Untamed Science

Take a video field trip as an Untamed Science "Truth Sleuth" digs into the details to find the truth about solutions.

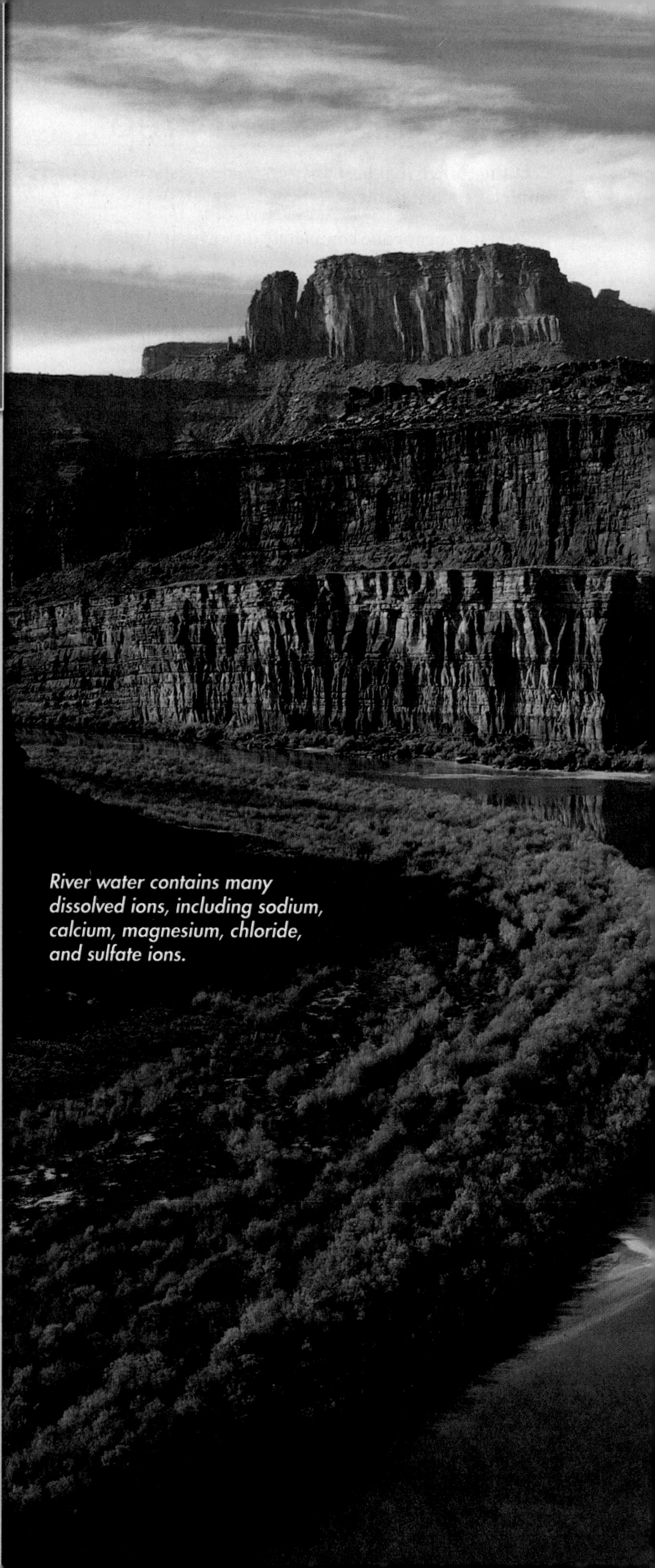

River water contains many dissolved ions, including sodium, calcium, magnesium, chloride, and sulfate ions.

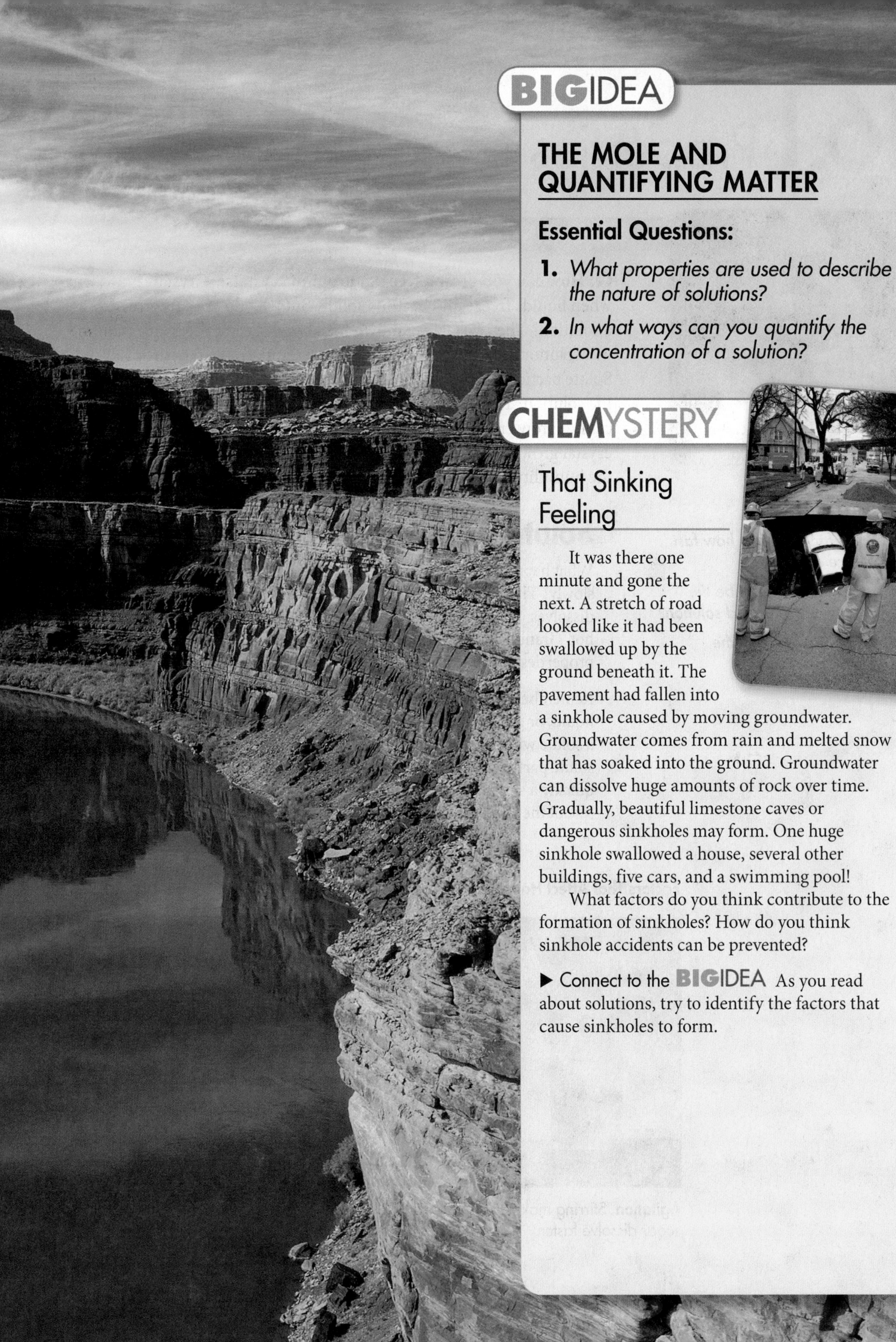

BIGIDEA

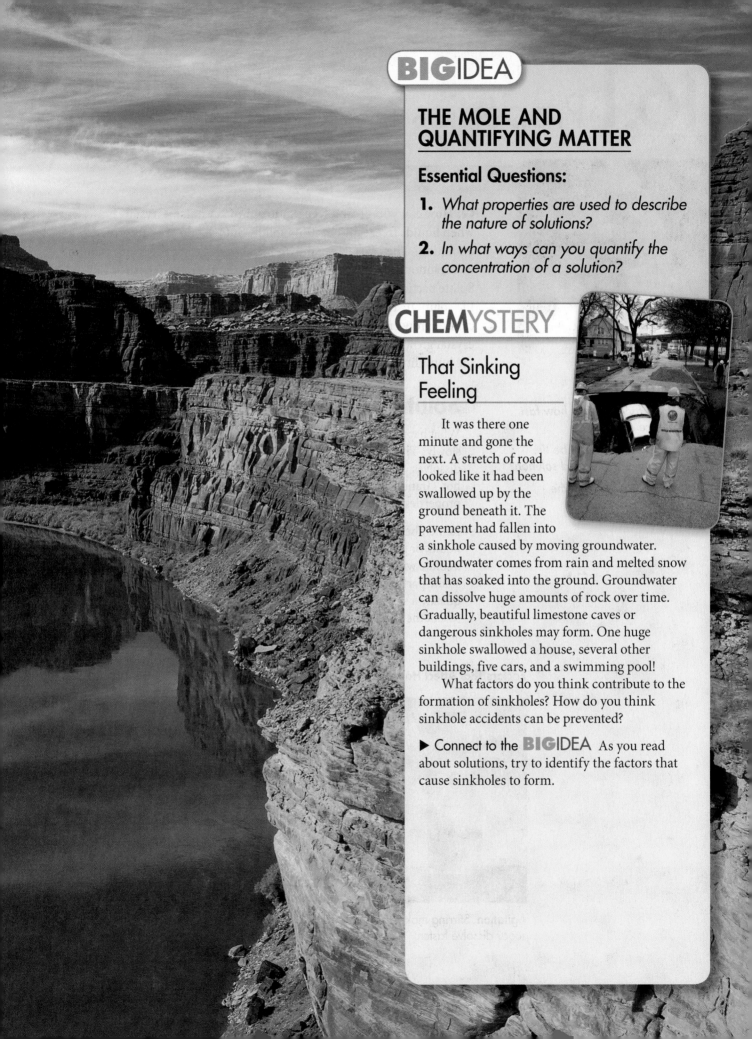

THE MOLE AND QUANTIFYING MATTER

Essential Questions:

1. *What properties are used to describe the nature of solutions?*
2. *In what ways can you quantify the concentration of a solution?*

CHEMYSTERY

That Sinking Feeling

It was there one minute and gone the next. A stretch of road looked like it had been swallowed up by the ground beneath it. The pavement had fallen into a sinkhole caused by moving groundwater. Groundwater comes from rain and melted snow that has soaked into the ground. Groundwater can dissolve huge amounts of rock over time. Gradually, beautiful limestone caves or dangerous sinkholes may form. One huge sinkhole swallowed a house, several other buildings, five cars, and a swimming pool!

What factors do you think contribute to the formation of sinkholes? How do you think sinkhole accidents can be prevented?

▶ Connect to the BIGIDEA As you read about solutions, try to identify the factors that cause sinkholes to form.

16.1 Properties of Solutions

CHEMISTRY & YOU

Q: How can you grow a tree made out of crystals? Crystals may form when liquids freeze and become solids. But why do crystals grow from a solution? The crystal tree shown here began as a paper trunk standing in a solution. The absorbent paper in the trunk soaked up the solution. Solute particles formed crystals on the paper as water evaporated from the solution. These crystals formed the delicate leaves of the tree. You cannot grow crystal trees from just any type of solution. The rate of crystal growth depends on the solute, the solvent, the temperature, and the humidity of the surroundings.

Key Questions

What factors affect how fast a substance dissolves?

How can you describe the equilibrium in a saturated solution?

What factors affect the solubility of a substance?

Solution Formation

What happens when you add sugar to tea? Does it dissolve quickly or slowly? The figure below shows factors that affect how quickly sugar dissolves. Sugar dissolves faster when you stir the tea or when the tea is hot. Granulated sugar dissolves faster than sugar cubes do. The properties of solutions help explain why you observe these differences.

Remember that solutions are homogeneous mixtures that may be solid, liquid, or gaseous. The properties of a solvent determine whether a solute will dissolve. How quickly a solute dissolves depends on how the solute particles interact with the solvent particles. Factors that affect how quickly a solute dissolves include agitation, temperature, and the particle size of the solute.

Factors That Affect How Fast Sugar Dissolves

Agitation Stirring makes sugar dissolve faster.

Temperature Sugar dissolves more quickly in hot tea than in cold tea.

Particle Size A cube of sugar dissolves more slowly than granulated sugar does.

Agitation Sugar dissolves slowly when it is placed in tea. Stirring the tea makes the sugar dissolve more quickly. Stirring speeds up the process because water in the tea interacts more with the surface of the sugar. Stirring and shaking are types of agitation. Agitation only affects how quickly a solid solute dissolves. It does not change the amount of solute that will dissolve.

Temperature Temperature affects how quickly a solute dissolves. Sugar dissolves faster in hot tea than in iced tea. Water molecules move faster at high temperatures than at low temperatures. Faster water molecules collide with the surfaces of sugar crystals more often and with more force. As a result, sugar dissolves faster.

Particle Size of the Solute The size of particles in a solute also affects how quickly the solute dissolves. The size of particles explains why a teaspoon of granulated sugar dissolves faster than a sugar cube. The teaspoon of sugar and the sugar cube have the same volume. However, the smaller particles in the granulated sugar have a larger surface area than the sides of the sugar cube do. Water molecules collide more quickly with more molecules in granulated sugar. This causes granulated sugar to dissolve faster.

Key Question What factors affect how fast a substance dissolves? **Agitation, temperature, and the particle size of the solute affect how fast a substance dissolves.**

BUILD Connections

How can some medicines work all day? In some extended release pills, the active ingredient is surrounded by a membrane that contains many tiny openings. Solvent in your body only comes into contact with the medicine through these openings. This allows the release of small doses of the medicine throughout the day.

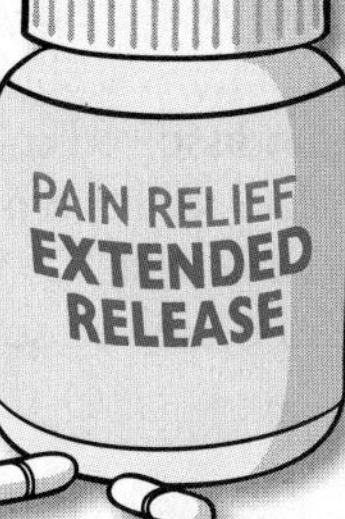

Quick Lab

Purpose To classify mixtures as solutions or colloids by using the Tyndall effect

Materials

- baking soda
- cornstarch
- stirring rod
- distilled water (or tap water)
- flashlight
- three jars with parallel sides
- teaspoon
- cup

Solutions and Colloids

Procedure

1. In a cup, mix 1/2 teaspoon of cornstarch with 4 teaspoons of water to make a paste.

2. Fill one jar with water. Add 1/2 teaspoon of baking soda to a second jar. Fill it with water. Stir to mix. Add the cornstarch paste to the third jar. Fill it with water. Stir to mix.

3. Turn out the lights in the room. Use the flashlight to shine a beam of light at each of the jars. Record your observations.

Analyze and Conclude

1. Observe In which of the jars in the experiment was it possible to see the path of the light beam?

2. Infer What made the light beam visible?

3. Explain What would you observe if you filtered the mixture that made the light beam visible and then used the flashlight to shine the light beam through that filtered mixture?

4. Predict What would you observe if you replaced the baking soda with sucrose (table sugar)? What would you observe if you replaced the cornstarch with diluted milk?

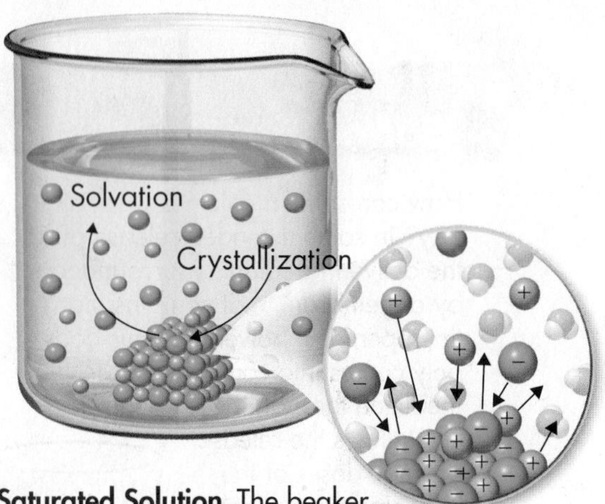

Saturated Solution The beaker contains a saturated solution and an undissolved solid. Particles move back and forth from solution to solid at the same rate. So the total amount of dissolved solute remains constant.

See a saturated solution animated online.

Solubility

What do you think would happen if you added a whole box of table salt to a glass of water? You need to know the solubility of the salt to answer this question. The **solubility** of a substance is the amount of solute that dissolves in a given quantity of solvent at a specified temperature and pressure. Solubility is often expressed in grams of solute per 100 g of solvent (g/100 g H_2O). Sometimes, the solubility of a gas is expressed in grams per liter of solution (g/L). So how much salt could you dissolve in a glass of water? If you add 36.2 g of sodium chloride (table salt) to 100 g of water at 25°C, all the salt will dissolve. Any extra salt will not dissolve—even if you stir the water for a long time. Why will the extra salt not dissolve?

Saturated and Unsaturated Solutions The figure shows a beaker containing a sodium chloride solution. Undissolved solid sodium chloride lies at the bottom of the beaker. You might expect all the solid particles to dissolve as water molecules interact with them. This does not happen. Particles do move from the solid into the solution. However, dissolved particles also move from the solution back into the solid.

These two processes occur at the same rate when the solution is saturated. A **saturated solution** contains the maximum amount of solute for a given quantity of solvent at a constant temperature and pressure. For example, a saturated solution forms at 25°C when 36.2 g of sodium chloride are dissolved in 100 g of water. If you add more salt to this solution, it will not dissolve. An equilibrium, or balance, exists in a saturated solution between the solution and the undissolved solute under given conditions.

An **unsaturated solution** contains less solute than a saturated solution does. You can add solute to an unsaturated solution and the solute will dissolve until the solution becomes saturated.

Miscible and Immiscible Liquids Some liquids are completely soluble in each other. For example, any amount of ethanol will dissolve in any amount of water. Pairs of liquids, such as water and ethanol, are described as miscible. Two liquids are **miscible** if they dissolve in each other in all proportions. The liquid that is present in the larger amount in the solution is considered to be the solvent. Liquids that are slightly soluble in each other are partially miscible. Liquids that are insoluble in each other are **immiscible.** Oil and water are examples of immiscible liquids. When you try to mix oil and water together, it is easy to see that neither one dissolves in the other one.

Key Question How can you describe the equilibrium in a saturated solution? **An equilibrium exists between the solution and the undissolved solute in a saturated solution under given conditions.**

solubility the amount of solute that can dissolve in a given amount of solvent

saturated solution a solution that cannot contain any more solute

unsaturated solution a solution that can contain more solute

miscible liquids that can dissolve in each other in all proportions

immiscible liquids that are insoluble in each other

supersaturated solution a solution that contains more solute than a saturated solution

PREFIXES

The prefix *un-* means "not." An unsaturated solution is not saturated. The prefix *super-* means "above" or "over." You can think of a supersaturated solution as being "oversaturated."

Factors Affecting Solubility

The solubility of a solute describes how much of the solute dissolves in a given amount of solvent. Temperature affects the solubility of solid and liquid solutes. Temperature and pressure affect the solubility of gaseous solutes.

Temperature and Solubility of Solids The graph shows how the solubility of a few substances varies with temperature. The solubility of most solid substances increases as the temperature of the solvent increases. For example, potassium nitrate (KNO_3) and potassium bromide (KBr) are more soluble at higher temperatures. The solubility of some substances decreases as temperature increases. For example, ytterbium sulfate ($Yb_2(SO_4)_3$) is more soluble at lower temperatures than at higher temperatures. The solubility of other substances changes very little with temperature. Sodium chloride (NaCl) is a good example of this type of substance.

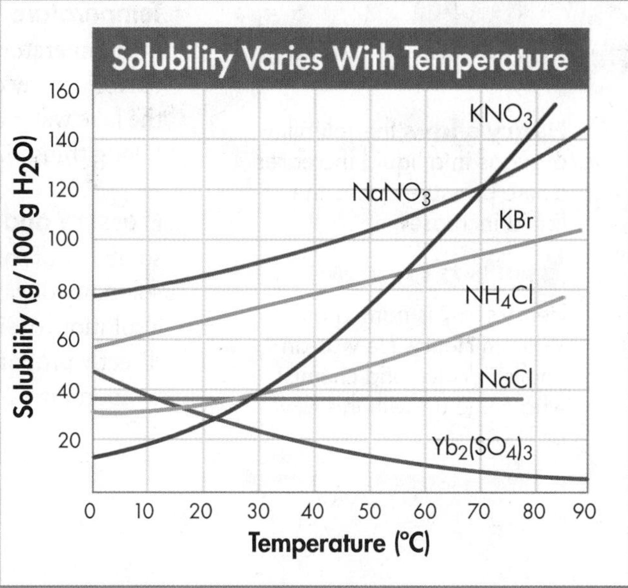

Solubility and Temperature The solubility of many substances increases as temperature increases. Go to your *Chemistry Skills and Math Workbook* to practice interpreting graphs.

The solubility of sodium acetate is greater at 30°C than at 25°C. Suppose you made a saturated solution of this compound at 30°C. Then you let the solution cool to 25°C without stirring it. What do you think would happen? You would probably expect to see crystals form in the solution as the temperature dropped. What if no crystals formed? You would have then made a supersaturated solution. A **supersaturated solution** contains more solute than it can theoretically hold at a given temperature. You can cause solid crystals to form in a supersaturated solution by adding a tiny crystal of solute, called a seed crystal. The photos show this process of crystallization.

Supersaturated Solution **Crystals in Solution**

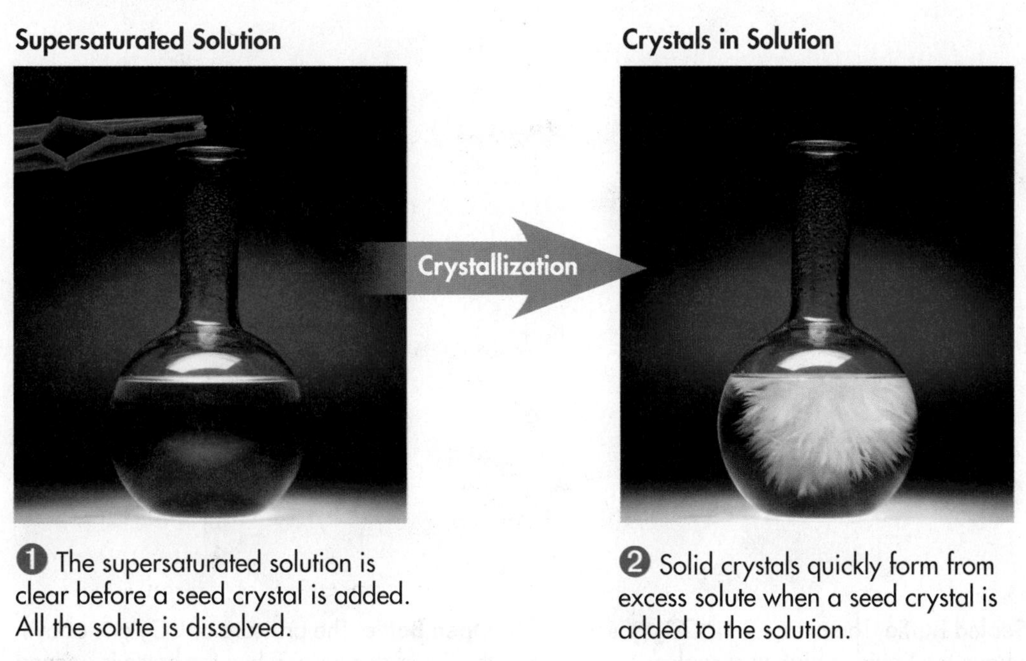

❶ The supersaturated solution is clear before a seed crystal is added. All the solute is dissolved.

❷ Solid crystals quickly form from excess solute when a seed crystal is added to the solution.

Henry's law the solubility of a gas in a liquid increases as the pressure above the liquid increases

WORD ORIGINS

Henry's law is named after William Henry. He was an English doctor and chemist who came up with this law in 1803.

Temperature and Gas Solubility The solubility of most gases decreases as the temperature of the solvent increases. This relationship can affect wildlife. Factories may dump heated water into lakes. This increases the temperature of the lake water and decreases the amount of dissolved oxygen in the water. Living things in the lake that need oxygen may be harmed.

Pressure and Gas Solubility Changes in pressure have little effect on the solubility of solids and liquids. However, pressure has a big effect on the solubility of gases. Henry's law describes the effects of pressure on gas in a solution. **Henry's law** states that the solubility (S) of a gas in a liquid is directly proportional to the pressure (P) of the gas above the liquid at a given temperature. This relationship is shown in this equation:

$$\frac{S_1}{P_1} = \frac{S_2}{P_2}$$

S_1 is the solubility at a certain pressure, P_1.

S_2 is the solubility at a different pressure, P_2.

You can see the principles of Henry's law in action when you open a carbonated beverage. Large amounts of carbon dioxide (CO_2) gas are forced into these drinks under pressure when they are bottled. The figure shows what happens when the bottle is opened. The pressure of CO_2 above the liquid decreases. Bubbles of CO_2 form in the liquid and escape from the open bottle. The concentration of dissolved CO_2 decreases when bubbles escape. The beverage loses most of its CO_2 and most of its fizz.

Key Question What factors affect the solubility of a substance? **Temperature affects the solubility of solid and liquid solutes in a solvent. Temperature and pressure affect the solubility of gaseous solutes.**

CO_2 in Solution

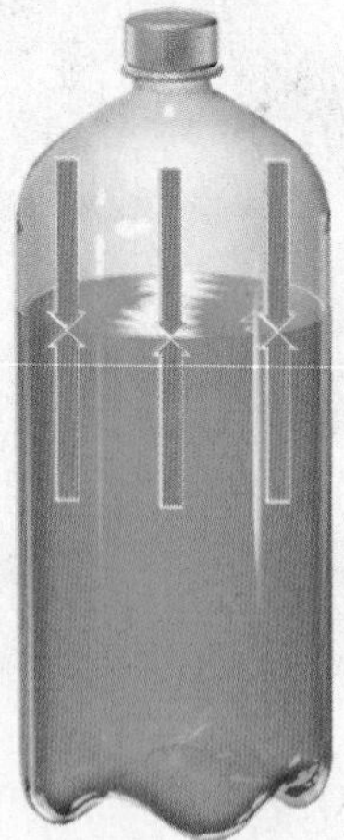

Sealed Bottle The pressure of CO_2 gas above the liquid is high in a sealed bottle. The CO_2 concentration in the solution is high.

Open Bottle The pressure of CO_2 gas above the liquid decreases when the bottle is opened. Carbon dioxide bubbles out of the liquid.

SampleProblem 16.1

Using Henry's Law

The solubility of a gas in water is 0.77 g/L at 3.5 atm of pressure. What is its solubility (in g/L) at 1.0 atm of pressure? The temperature is held constant at 25°C.

❶ Analyze List the knowns and the unknown.

KNOWNS	UNKNOWN
$P_1 = 3.5$ atm	$S_2 = ?$ g/L
$S_1 = 0.77$ g/L	
$P_2 = 1.0$ atm	

❷ Calculate Solve for the unknown.

Write the equation for Henry's law.

$$\frac{S_1}{P_1} = \frac{S_2}{P_2}$$

Isolate S_2 by multiplying both sides by P_2.

$$P_2 \times \frac{S_1}{P_1} = \frac{S_2}{\cancel{P_2}} \times \cancel{P_2}$$

Rewrite the equation so the unknown is on the left.

$$S_2 = \frac{S_1 \times P_2}{P_1}$$

Substitute the known values into the equation.

$$S_2 = \frac{0.77\ \text{g/L} \times 1.0\ \cancel{\text{atm}}}{3.5\ \cancel{\text{atm}}}$$

Solve the equation.

$$S_2 = \frac{0.77\ \text{g/L}}{3.5} = 0.22\ \text{g/L}$$

❸ Evaluate Does the result make sense? The new pressure is about one-third of the original pressure. So the new solubility should be about one-third of the original solubility. The answer is correctly expressed to two significant figures.

Remember that solubility is directly proportional to pressure. When pressure decreases, solubility also decreases.

Practice Problems

Hint: You are solving Henry's law for an unknown solubility in Problem 1. You are solving for an unknown pressure in Problem 2.

1. The solubility of a gas in water is 0.16 g/L at 104 kPa. What is the solubility when the pressure of the gas is increased to 288 kPa? Assume the temperature remains constant.

KNOWNS	UNKNOWN
P_1 = 104 kPa	S_2 = ? g/L
S_1 = 0.16 g/L	
P_2 = 288 kPa	

❶ **Analyze** **List the knowns and the unknown.**

❷ **Calculate** **Solve for the unknown.**

❸ **Evaluate** **Does the result make sense?**

2. A gas has a solubility in water at 0°C of 3.6 g/L at a pressure of 1.0 atm. What pressure is needed to produce an aqueous solution containing 9.5 g/L of the same gas at 0°C?

KNOWNS	UNKNOWN
P_1 =	P_2 = ? atm
S_1 =	
S_2 =	

3. The solubility of a gas is 0.58 g/L at a pressure of 104 kPa. What is its solubility if the pressure increases to 250 kPa at the same temperature?

4. **Challenge** The solubility of $CO_2(g)$ in a 2 L bottle of soft drink is 5.28 g/L at 4.0 atm. What is the difference in solubility if a similar soft drink is bottled at a pressure of 2.5 atm?

16.1 LessonCheck

Key Concept Check

5. **Review** What determines how fast a substance will dissolve?

6. **Describe** How can you describe the state of equilibrium in a saturated solution?

7. **Describe** What conditions affect solubilities of solid, liquid, and gaseous solutes in a solvent?

Vocabulary Check

Choose a highlighted word from the lesson to complete the sentence correctly.

8. Liquids that are insoluble in each other are ____________.

Think Critically

9. **Describe** What determines whether a substance will dissolve in a solvent?

10. **Explain** What could you do to change a saturated solution to an unsaturated solution?

CHEMISTRY & YOU

11. How do you think crystal growing kits work? Use what you know about solubility and saturated solutions to explain your answer. (Hint: See page 490.)

16.2 Concentrations of Solutions

CHEMISTRY & YOU

Q: How can you describe the concentration of a solution? Clean drinking water is important for all communities. How do you determine if water is clean? Even clear water may contain dissolved contaminants that you cannot see. Federal and state governments set standards that limit the amount of contaminants allowed in drinking water. These contaminants include metals, pesticides, and bacteria. Your drinking water must be tested continually to make sure that the concentrations of potentially dangerous substances are within established limits.

Key Questions

How do you calculate the molarity of a solution?

What effect does dilution have on the amount of solute?

How do percent by volume and percent by mass differ?

BUILD Vocabulary

concentration a measure of the amount of solute dissolved in a certain amount of solvent

dilute solution a solution that contains a small amount of solute

concentrated solution a solution that contains a large amount of solute

molarity (*M*) the number of moles of solute dissolved in one liter of solution

RELATED WORD FORMS

Molarity is related to the word *mole*. Remember that a mole is equal to 6.02×10^{23} particles.

Molarity

You can dissolve a pinch of table salt (NaCl) in a pot of water. You can also dissolve several tablespoons of salt in the same amount of water. These two solutions would contain different amounts of salt in the same volume of water. The **concentration** of a solution is a measure of the amount of solute that is dissolved in a given amount of solvent. A solution that contains a relatively small amount of solute is a **dilute solution.** The pot with the pinch of salt in it is a dilute solution. In contrast, a **concentrated solution** contains a large amount of solute. The pot with several tablespoons of salt in it is a concentrated solution.

Concentrated and dilute are qualitative descriptions that are used to compare solutions. How does a solution that is made by adding 1 g of NaCl to 100 g of water compare to a solution that is made by adding 30 g of NaCl to 100 g of water? The first solution might be called dilute. The second solution might be called concentrated. What if you compared the first solution to a solution that contains only 0.01 g of NaCl per 100 g of water? The solution that contains 1 g of NaCl might then be called concentrated.

Measuring Concentration Concentration can be more accurately expressed by using numbers. The most important unit of concentration you will use is molarity. **Molarity (*M*)** is the number of moles of solute dissolved in 1 liter of solution. Note that the volume involved is the total volume of the solution. It is not the volume of the solvent alone. Molarity is also known as molar concentration. When the symbol *M* is accompanied by a numerical value, it is read as "molar." For example, a 1.0*M* solution is read as a "one molar solution." A 1.0*M* solution has 1 mol of dissolved solute for every liter of solution.

How to Make a 0.5*M* Solution

❶ Add 0.5 mol of solute to a 1 L volumetric flask that is half filled with water.

❷ Swirl the flask carefully to dissolve the solute.

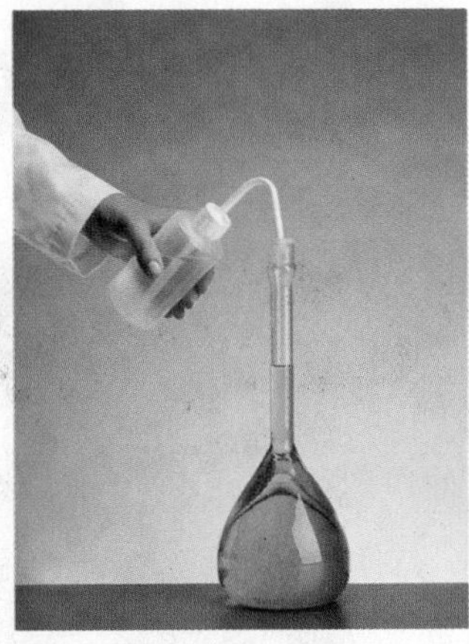

❸ Fill the flask with water exactly to the 1 L mark.

Making Molar Solutions The photos show how to make a 0.5*M* solution. To do this, you first need to measure the mass of 0.5 mol of solute. Then you can follow the instructions above to make 1 L of solution.

Calculating Molarity Molarity is equal to moles of solute divided by liters of solution. You can use the equation below to calculate molarity.

$$\text{Molarity } (M) = \frac{\text{moles of solute}}{\text{liters of solution}}$$

M is another way to express mol/L.

solute = the dissolved particles in the solution
solution = the mixture that contains the solute

Calculating Moles of Solute You can also use the equation above to find the moles of solute dissolved in a given volume of solution if you know the molarity. Rearrange the equation to solve for moles of solute. Then substitute known values for molarity and volume. The calculation below shows how to find the moles of lithium chloride (LiCl) in 2.00 L of a 2.5*M* solution.

$$\text{Molarity } (M) = \frac{\text{moles of solute}}{\text{liters of solution } (V)}$$

$$\text{Moles of solute} = \text{molarity } (M) \times \text{liters of solution } (V)$$

$$= 2.5M \times 2.00\text{ L} = \left(\frac{2.5\text{ mol}}{1\text{ }\cancel{\text{L}}}\right) \times 2.00\text{ }\cancel{\text{L}}$$

$$= 5.0\text{ mol}$$

So, 2.00 L of a 2.5*M* lithium chloride solution contains 5.0 mol of LiCl.

Key Question How do you calculate the molarity of a solution? **Divide the number of moles of solute by the volume of the solution in liters to calculate the molarity of a solution.**

SampleProblem 16.2

Calculating Molarity

Saline solutions are often given to patients in the hospital. One saline solution contains 0.90 g of NaCl in exactly 100 mL of solution. What is the molarity of the solution?

❶ Analyze List the knowns and the unknown.

KNOWNS	UNKNOWN
concentration = 0.90 g NaCl/100 mL	molarity = ?*M*
molar mass of NaCl = 58.5 g/mol	

❷ Calculate Solve for the unknown.

Start with the equation for molarity.

$$M = \frac{\text{moles of solute}}{\text{liters of solution}}$$

Use the molar mass to convert g of NaCl to mol of NaCl.

$$0.90\ \cancel{\text{g NaCl}} \times \frac{1\ \text{mol NaCl}}{58.5\ \cancel{\text{g NaCl}}} = 0.015\ \text{mol NaCl}$$

Convert volume units to liters.

$$100\ \cancel{\text{mL}} \times \frac{1\ \text{L}}{1000\ \cancel{\text{mL}}} = 0.100\ \text{L}$$

Hint: The relationship 1 L = 1000 mL gives you the conversion factor 1 L/1000 mL.

Substitute the knowns into the equation for molarity.

$$M = \frac{0.015\ \text{mol NaCl}}{0.100\ \text{L solution}}$$

Solve the equation to find molarity.

$$M = \frac{0.15\ \text{mol}}{\text{L}} = 0.15M$$

❸ Evaluate Does the result make sense? The answer should be less than 1*M* because a concentration of 0.90 g/100 mL is the same as 9.0 g/1000 mL (9.0 g/1 L). A mass of 9.0 g is less than 1 mol of NaCl. The answer is correctly expressed to two significant figures.

BUILD Math Skills

Identifying Conversion Factors You use conversion factors to change one unit into another unit. The conversion factor you choose depends on the final units you need. Conversion factors based on molar mass are used to convert moles to grams or to convert grams to moles. Use grams/1 mol when you need to change moles into grams. Use 1 mol/grams when you need to change grams into moles.

$$\frac{\text{grams}}{1\text{ mol}} \text{ and } \frac{1\text{ mol}}{\text{grams}}$$

Go to your Chemistry Skills and Math Workbook for more practice problems.

Practice Problems

12. A solution has a volume of 2.0 L and contains 36.0 g of glucose ($C_6H_{12}O_6$). The molar mass of glucose is 180 g/mol. What is the molarity of the solution?

1 Analyze **List the knowns and the unknown.**

2 Calculate **Solve for the unknown.**

3 Evaluate **Does the result make sense?**

Remember: Molarity is moles of solute per liter of solution.

KNOWNS	UNKNOWN
concentration = 36.0 g glucose/2.0 L	molarity = ?*M*
molar mass of glucose = 180 g/mol	

13. A solution has a volume of 250 mL and contains 0.70 mol of NaCl. What is its molarity?

KNOWNS	UNKNOWN
concentration =	molarity = ?*M*
molar mass of NaCl =	

14. Calculate the molarity of a solution that contains 0.50 g of NaCl dissolved in 100 mL of solution.

15. Challenge What is the molarity of a solution containing 400 g $CuSO_4$ in 4.00 L of solution?

Sample Problem 16.3

Calculating the Moles of Solute in a Solution

Household laundry bleach is a dilute aqueous solution of sodium hypochlorite (NaClO). How many moles of solute are present in 1.5 L of 0.70*M* NaClO?

KNOWNS	UNKNOWN
concentration (*M*) = 0.70*M* NaClO	moles of solute = ? mol
volume (*V*) = 1.5 L	

1 Analyze **List the knowns and the unknown.**

2 Calculate **Solve for the unknown.**

Write the equation for moles of solute. → moles of solute = $M \times V$

Substitute the knowns into the equation. → moles of solute = $\frac{0.70 \text{ mol NaClO}}{1 \cancel{L}} \times 1.5 \cancel{L}$

Solve the equation. → moles of solute = 0.70 mol NaClO × 1.5 = 1.1 mol NaClO

3 Evaluate **Does the result make sense?** The solution concentration is greater than 0.5 mol/L but less than 1.0 mol/L. With a volume of 1.5 L, the answer should be greater than 0.75 mol but less than 1.5 mol. The answer is correctly expressed to two significant figures.

Practice Problems

16. How many moles of sodium chloride (NaCl) are in 1.2 L of 0.75*M* NaCl?

KNOWNS	UNKNOWN
concentration (*M*) = 0.75*M* NaCl	moles of solute = ? mol
volume (*V*) = 1.2 L	

1 Analyze **List the knowns and the unknown.**

2 Calculate **Solve for the unknown.**

3 Evaluate **Does the result make sense?**

17. How many moles of ammonium nitrate (NH_4NO_3) are in 335 mL of 0.425*M* NH_4NO_3?

KNOWNS	UNKNOWN
concentration (*M*) =	moles of solute = ? mol
volume (*V*) =	

18. Challenge How many moles of solute are in 250 mL of 2.0*M* $CaCl_2$? How many grams of $CaCl_2$ is this?

Hint: Make sure your volume units cancel when you do these problems. If they do not, you are probably missing a conversion factor in your calculations.

Dilution

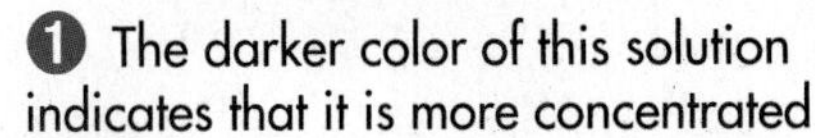
❶ The darker color of this solution indicates that it is more concentrated.

❷ Diluting a solution by adding solvent decreases the concentration.

BUILD Understanding

Cause and Effect Diagram After you finish reading this page, make a cause and effect diagram to show how making dilutions affects solutions.

Making Dilutions

Compare the solutions shown above. They contain the same amount of solute. However, they each contain different amounts of solvent. The solution that is darker blue is more concentrated than the one that is lighter blue. The darker solution also has the greater molarity. The lighter solution was made by adding more solvent to the darker solution. Diluting a solution reduces the number of moles of solute per unit volume. However, the total number of moles of solute in the solution does not change.

Diluting a solution changes the molarity and the volume of the solution. It does not change the number of moles of solute. The equation below shows that the total number of moles of solute is the same before and after dilution.

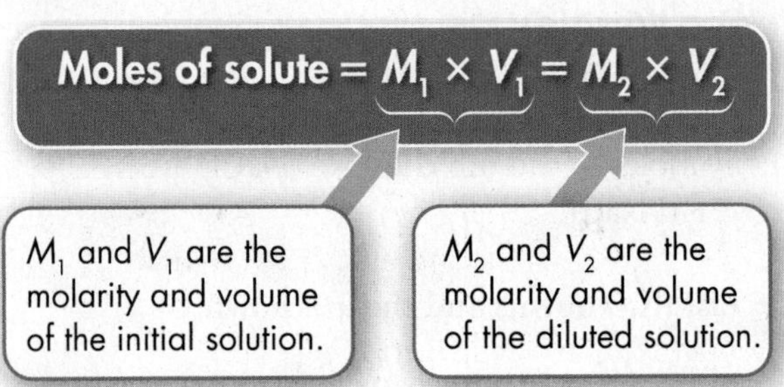

Moles of solute = $M_1 \times V_1 = M_2 \times V_2$
M_1 and V_1 are the molarity and volume of the initial solution.
M_2 and V_2 are the molarity and volume of the diluted solution.

The volumes can be in liters or milliliters. However, the same units must be used for both V_1 and V_2.

What tools could you use to dilute a solution? You could use a beaker or a graduated cylinder if you did not need a precise measurement. You could use a volumetric pipette or a buret to measure the volumes precisely.

Key Question What effect does dilution have on the amount of solute? **Diluting a solution reduces the number of moles of solute per unit volume. It does not change the total number of moles of solute in the solution.**

CHEMISTRY TUTORIAL

Sample Problem 16.4

Preparing a Dilute Solution

How many milliliters of aqueous 2.00*M* $MgSO_4$ solution must be diluted with water to prepare 100.0 mL of aqueous 0.400*M* $MgSO_4$?

KNOWNS	UNKNOWN
M_1 = 2.00*M* $MgSO_4$	V_1 = ? mL
M_2 = 0.400*M* $MgSO_4$	
V_2 = 100.0 mL	

1 Analyze List the knowns and the unknown.

2 Calculate Solve for the unknown.

Rearrange the dilution equation to isolate V_1.

To isolate V_1, divide both sides by M_1.

$$\frac{\cancel{M_1} \times V_1}{\cancel{M_1}} = \frac{M_2 \times V_2}{M_1}$$

Rewrite the equation so your unknown is on the left.

$$V_1 = \frac{M_2 \times V_2}{M_1}$$

Substitute the known values into the equation.

$$V_1 = \frac{0.400\cancel{M} \times 100.0\ \text{mL}}{2.00\cancel{M}}$$

Solve the equation.

$$V_1 = \frac{40.0\ \text{mL}}{2.00} = 20.0\ \text{mL}$$

3 Evaluate Does the result make sense? The initial concentration (2.00*M*) is five times larger than the dilute concentration (0.400*M*). The number of moles of solute does not change. So, the initial volume of solution should be one-fifth the final volume of the diluted solution.

Practice Problems

19. How many milliliters of a solution of 4.00*M* KI are needed to prepare 250.0 mL of 0.760*M* KI?

1 Analyze List the knowns and the unknown.

2 Calculate Solve for the unknown.

3 Evaluate Does the result make sense?

KNOWNS	UNKNOWN
M_1 = 4.00*M* KI	V_1 = ? mL
M_2 = 0.760*M* KI	
V_2 = 250.0 mL	

20. A dilute solution is prepared by adding water to 35.0 mL of 1.50*M* $MgSO_4$. The volume of the new solution is 100.0 mL. What is the molarity of the dilute solution?

KNOWNS	UNKNOWN
M_1 =	M_2 = ?*M* $MgSO_4$
V_1 =	
V_2 =	

BUILD Connections

You have probably seen food labels that tell you the percent composition of an ingredient. For example, the label on a fruit flavored drink often lists the "percent juice" contained in the product. Such information can be misleading unless the units are given. When you describe percent solutions, be sure to specify whether the concentration is % (v/v) or % (m/m).

Percent Solutions

You can use molarity to make a solution with a particular concentration. You can also make a solution with a particular concentration if you know the volume or mass of the solvent and solute.

Percent by Volume Suppose the solute and the solvent are liquids. An easy way to make the solution is to measure the volumes of the solute and the solution. You can express the concentration of the solute as a percent of the solution by volume.

The equation below shows how to calculate the percent by volume of a solution. The percent by volume of a solution is the ratio of the volume of solute to the volume of solution. Notice that you need to multiply by 100 to make the final result a percent by volume.

$$\text{Percent by volume } (\%(\text{v/v})) = \frac{\text{volume of solute}}{\text{volume of solution}} \times 100\%$$

You probably have rubbing alcohol in your bathroom. Rubbing alcohol is a solution of isopropyl alcohol that is 91 percent by volume. You could prepare this solution by diluting 91 mL of pure isopropyl alcohol with enough water to make 100 mL of solution. The concentration is written as 91 percent by volume, 91 percent (volume/volume), or 91% (v/v).

Percent by Mass Suppose the solute is a solid. An easy way to make the solution is to measure the mass of the solute and the mass of the solution. You can then express the concentration of the solution as a percent by mass, percent (mass/mass), or % (m/m). Percent by mass of a solution is the ratio of the mass of the solute to the mass of the solution. The equation below shows how to calculate percent by mass. Notice that the equation for percent by mass is similar to the equation for percent by volume.

$$\text{Percent by mass } (\%(\text{m/m})) = \frac{\text{mass of solute}}{\text{mass of solution}} \times 100\%$$

You can also define percent by mass as the number of grams of solute per 100 g of solution. For example, a solution that contains 7 g of sodium chloride in 100 grams of solution has a concentration of 7 percent by mass. You can also write this concentration as 7 percent (mass/mass) or 7% (m/m).

Key Question How do percent by volume and percent by mass differ? **Percent by volume of a solution is the ratio of the volume of solute to the volume of solution. Percent by mass of a solution is the ratio of the mass of the solute to the mass of the solution.**

Sample Problem 16.5

Calculating Percent by Volume

A solution is made by diluting 85 mL of ethanol (C_2H_6O) with water to a volume of 250 mL. What is the percent by volume of ethanol in the final solution?

1 Analyze **List the knowns and the unknown.**

KNOWNS	UNKNOWN
volume of solute = 85 mL	Percent by volume = ? % ethanol (v/v)
volume of solution = 250 mL	

2 Calculate **Solve for the unknown.**

State the equation for percent by volume.

$$\text{Percent by volume } (\% \text{ (v/v)}) = \frac{\text{volume of solute}}{\text{volume of solution}} \times 100\%$$

Substitute the known values into the equation.

$$\% \text{ (v/v)} = \frac{85 \cancel{\text{mL}} \text{ ethanol}}{250 \cancel{\text{mL}}} \times 100\%$$

Solve the equation.

$$\% \text{ (v/v)} = 0.34 \times 100\%$$
$$= 34\% \text{ ethanol (v/v)}$$

3 Evaluate **Does the result make sense?**
The volume of the ethanol is about one-third the volume of the solution. The answer is reasonable. The answer is correctly expressed to two significant figures.

You can follow the same steps to calculate percent by mass. You need to use the mass of the solute and the mass of the solution.

Practice Problems

21. A solution is made by diluting 10.0 mL of propanone (C_3H_6O, or acetone) with water. The total volume of the solution is 200 mL. What is the percent by volume of propanone in the solution?

KNOWNS	UNKNOWN
volume of solute = 10.0 mL	percent by volume = ? % propanone (v/v)
volume of solution = 200 mL	

1 Analyze List the knowns and the unknown.

2 Calculate Solve for the unknown.

3 Evaluate Does the result make sense?

22. What is the concentration in percent (v/v) of a solution containing 50 mL of diethyl ether ($C_4H_{10}O$) in 2.5 L of solution?

KNOWNS	UNKNOWN
volume of solute =	percent by volume = ? % diethyl ether (v/v)
volume of solution =	

23. Challenge A bottle of hydrogen peroxide (H_2O_2) is labeled 3.0% (v/v). How many mL of H_2O_2 are in a 400.0 mL bottle of this solution?

Hint: Rearrange the equation to solve for the volume of solute.

16.2 LessonCheck

Key Concept Check

24. Review How do you calculate the molarity of a solution?

25. Compare How does the number of moles of solute before a dilution compare with the number of moles of solute after the dilution?

26. Identify What are two ways of expressing the concentration of a solution as a percent?

Vocabulary Check *Choose a highlighted word from the lesson to complete the sentence correctly.*

27. A solution that contains a small amount of solute is a(n) __________ solution.

Think Critically

28. Calculate How many moles of solute are present in 50.0 mL of 0.20*M* KNO_3?

CHEMISTRY & YOU

29. What are three ways you can calculate the concentration of a solution? (Hint: See page 502.)

BIGIDEA
THE MOLE AND QUANTIFYING MATTER

30. What information would you need to convert molarity to percent by volume?

16.3 Colligative Properties of Solutions

CHEMISTRY & YOU

Q: Why do you need salt to make ice cream? Here is a hint—it is not because ice cream is supposed to taste salty. Temperatures below 0°C are needed to make ice cream. Ice cream makers add rock salt to ice so the mixture freezes at a few degrees below 0°C. In this lesson, you will discover how a solute can change the freezing point of a solution.

Key Question

What are three colligative properties of solutions?

colligative property
a property of solutions that depends only on the number of solute particles

RELATED WORD FORMS

The verb *colligate* means "to bind together." Colligative properties result from the attractions that hold the solute and solvent particles together.

Describing Colligative Properties

Physical properties of a solution differ from those of the pure solvent. For example, tea has different properties than pure water does. Some of the differences in properties do not depend on the identity of the solute. Instead, they depend on the number of solute particles in the solution.

A **colligative property** is a property of solutions that depends only on the number of solute particles. It does not depend on the identity of the particles. Three colligative properties of solutions are vapor pressure lowering, freezing point depression, and boiling point elevation.

Vapor Pressure Lowering Vapor pressure is the pressure exerted by a vapor above its liquid in a closed system. A solution that contains a nonvolatile solute always has a lower vapor pressure than the pure solvent. A nonvolatile solute is one that is not easily vaporized, such as sodium chloride or sugar. The figure below shows how the vapor pressure of a sugar solution is lower than the vapor pressure of pure water. Why do you think this is true?

Vapor Pressure Lowering

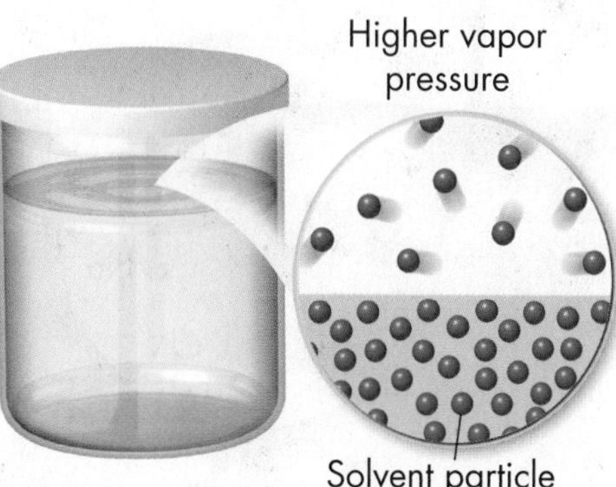

Pure Water The rate of solvent particles escaping the liquid is the same as the rate of particles leaving the vapor.

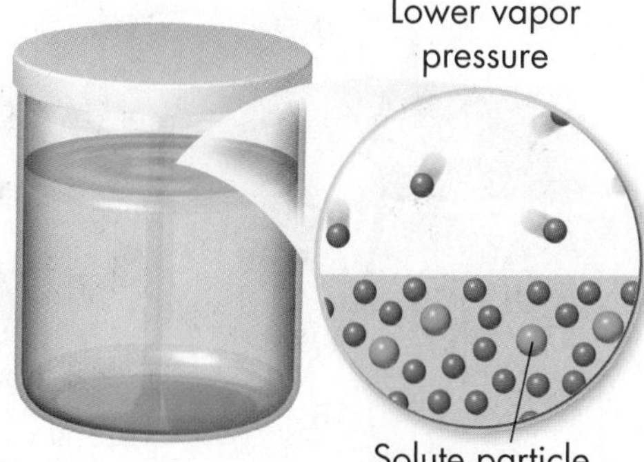

Solution Solute particles reduce the number of solvent particles that are able to escape the liquid. With fewer vapor particles, the vapor pressure is lower.

▶ Solute Concentration and Vapor Pressure Lowering

Sodium ions and chloride ions spread out when you dissolve table salt in water. Water molecules surrounding the ions are attracted to them. This causes the water molecules to slow down. Fewer water molecules have enough kinetic energy to escape the liquid and become vapor. As a result, the solution has a lower vapor pressure than pure water does at the same temperature.

The decrease in a solution's vapor pressure is proportional to the number of solute particles in a solution. The figure shows solute particles in solutions of glucose, sodium chloride, and calcium chloride. Glucose is made of molecules that do not break apart.

$$C_6H_{12}O_6(s) \xrightarrow{H_2O} C_6H_{12}O_6(aq)$$

Sodium chloride and calcium chloride are ionic solutes. They break apart into ions when they dissolve. Each formula unit of sodium chloride (NaCl) produces two particles in solution: a sodium ion and a chloride ion.

$$NaCl(s) \xrightarrow{H_2O} Na^+(aq) + Cl^-(aq)$$

Each formula unit of calcium chloride ($CaCl_2$) produces three particles:

$$CaCl_2(s) \xrightarrow{H_2O} Ca^{2+}(aq) + Cl^-(aq) + Cl^-(aq)$$

Ionic solutes have greater effects on vapor pressure than molecular solutes do because they produce more particles in solution. Suppose you dissolve an equal number of moles of glucose and calcium chloride in the same amount of water. The calcium chloride will lower the vapor pressure three times as much as the glucose will. Look at the figure to see how this happens.

Molecular vs. Ionic Solutes

Molecular Solutes in Solution Glucose does not dissociate. Three moles of glucose dissolved in water produce 3 mol of particles.

Ionic Solutes in Solution (NaCl) Each formula unit of NaCl dissociates into two ions. Three moles of sodium chloride dissolved in water produce 6 mol of particles.

Ionic Solutes in Solution ($CaCl_2$) Each formula unit of $CaCl_2$ dissociates into three ions. Three moles of calcium chloride dissolved in water produce 9 mol of particles.

Freezing Point Depression The particles in a solid form an orderly pattern when a substance freezes. The presence of a solute in water makes it more difficult for the water particles to form this pattern. More kinetic energy must be taken out of a solution before it freezes. As a result, the freezing point of a solution is lower than the freezing point of the pure solvent. The difference in temperature between the freezing point of a solution and the freezing point of the pure solvent is called the **freezing point depression**.

▶ **Solute Concentration and Freezing Point Depression** Freezing point depression is a colligative property. The size of the freezing point depression is proportional to the number of solute particles in solution. For example, sodium chloride produces twice as many particles as glucose produces in solution. As a result, a sodium chloride solution will freeze at a lower temperature than a glucose solution of equal concentration will. The freezing point depression caused by the sodium chloride will be twice as large as the change caused by glucose.

The freezing point depression of aqueous solutions helps keep travelers safe in cold, icy weather. Trucks spread a layer of salt on icy roads in winter to make the ice melt. The melted ice forms a solution that has a lower freezing point than pure water does. The photo below shows ice being removed from the wings of a plane. The solution of water and propylene glycol has a lower freezing point than pure water does.

BUILD Vocabulary

freezing point depression the difference in temperature between the freezing point of a solution and the freezing point of a pure solvent

USING PRIOR KNOWLEDGE

The phrase *freezing point depression* is really made up of two parts. Freezing point tells you the temperature where a substance turns to a solid. Depression refers to a decrease in that temperature.

Removing Ice
A mixture of water and propylene glycol is used to remove ice from planes.

Learn about freezing point depression ***online.*** CONCEPTS IN ACTION

Antifreeze The antifreeze used in a car's cooling system is a solution of water and ethylene glycol. The resulting mixture freezes below 0°C and boils above 100°C.

Boiling Point Elevation Boiling point is the temperature where the vapor pressure of a liquid is equal to atmospheric pressure. Adding a nonvolatile solute to a liquid solvent decreases the vapor pressure of the solvent. More kinetic energy must then be added to raise the vapor pressure of the solution to atmospheric pressure. As a result, the boiling point of a solution is higher than the boiling point of the pure solvent. **Boiling point elevation** is the difference in temperature between the boiling point of a solution and the boiling point of the pure solvent.

▶Solute Concentration and Boiling Point Elevation The photo shows antifreeze being poured into a car's cooling system. The antifreeze forms a solution with the water in the cooling system. It lowers the freezing point and elevates the boiling point. The lower freezing point keeps the solution in the engine from freezing in winter. The higher boiling point keeps the solution in the engine from boiling in summer. If the solution were to freeze or boil, the engine's cooling system would not work properly and the engine would be damaged.

Boiling point elevation is a colligative property. It does not depend on the identity of solute particles. It only depends on their concentration. The size of the boiling point elevation is proportional to the number of solute particles in the solution. For example, a 0.1*M* sodium chloride solution boils at a higher temperature than a 0.1*M* glucose solution does. The sodium chloride solution contains twice as many particles as the glucose solution does. Its boiling point elevation would be twice as high as the boiling point elevation of the glucose solution.

Key Question What are three colligative properties of solutions? **Three colligative properties of solutions are vapor pressure lowering, freezing point depression, and boiling point elevation.**

BUILD Vocabulary

boiling point elevation the difference in temperature between the boiling point of a solution and the boiling point of the pure solvent

ACADEMIC WORDS

Remember that the word *elevation* in boiling point elevation just means that the boiling point of a liquid goes up if something is dissolved in it.

16.3 LessonCheck

Key Concept Check

31. **Identify** Name three colligative properties of solutions.

Vocabulary Check

Choose a highlighted word from the lesson to complete the sentence correctly.

32. A property of solutions that depends only on the number of solute particles is a(n) ___________.

Think Critically

33. **Explain** Why does a solution have an elevated boiling point compared with the pure solvent?

34. **Compare** Would a dilute or a concentrated sodium fluoride solution have a higher boiling point? Explain.

35. **Compare** An equal number of moles of KI and MgI_2 are dissolved in equal volumes of water. Which solution has the higher

a. boiling point?

b. vapor pressure?

c. freezing point?

CHEMISTRY & YOU

36. Solutes other than NaCl could be used to produce the same freezing point depression in an ice cream maker. What factors do you think make NaCl a good choice? (Hint: See page 507.)

16.4 Calculations Involving Colligative Properties

Key Questions

What are two ways of expressing the ratio of solute to solvent in a solution?

How are freezing point depression and boiling point elevation related to molality?

molality (*m*) moles of solute per kilogram of solvent

RELATED WORDS
Be careful not to confuse molality with molarity. Molality depends on the mass of the solvent. Molarity depends on the volume of solution.

CHEMISTRY & YOU

Q: How hot is a pot of boiling pasta? Most people add a small amount of salt to the water when they cook dried pasta. They like the flavor of food cooked with salt. The dissolved salt can also increase the boiling point of the water. Suppose you added a tablespoon of salt to 2 L of water. A tablespoon of salt has a mass of about 18 g. Would the resulting boiling point increase be enough to shorten the time required for cooking? In this lesson, you will learn how to calculate the amount that the boiling point of the cooking water would rise.

Molality and Mole Fraction

Recall that colligative properties of solutions depend only on the number of solute particles dissolved in a given amount of solvent. Chemists use two ways to express the ratio of solute particles to solvent particles. They use molality and mole fraction.

Molality (*m*) is the number of moles of solute dissolved in 1 kilogram (1000 grams) of solvent. Molality is also called molal concentration.

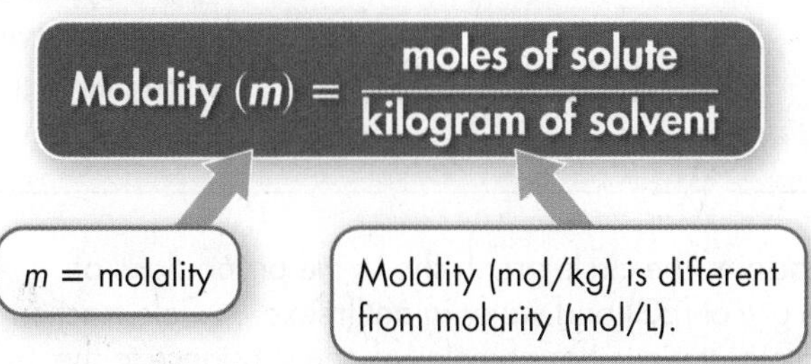

Molality (m) = moles of solute / kilogram of solvent
m = molality
Molality (mol/kg) is different from molarity (mol/L).

Comparing Molarity and Molality Note that molality is not the same as molarity. Molarity and molality depend on the moles of solute. However, molarity depends on the volume of solution. A one molar solution (1*M*) contains 1 mol of solute for every liter of solution. Molality depends on the mass of the solvent. A one molal solution (1*m*) contains 1 mol of solute for every kilogram of solvent.

You need to know the moles of solute and the mass of the solvent when you make a molal solution. For example, you can add 1 mol of glucose to 1 kg of water to make a 1*m* glucose solution. You can easily convert between mass and volume when you use water because 1 kg of water has a volume of 1 L.

mole fraction the ratio of the moles of solute to the total moles of solvent and solute

ACADEMIC WORDS

A *fraction* is a ratio expressed as one number divided by another number. A mole fraction is usually written as the decimal equivalent of the fraction.

Mole Fraction Mole fraction is another way to express the concentration of solutions. The **mole fraction** of a solute in a solution is the ratio of the moles of that solute to the total moles of solvent and solute. You can also find the mole fraction of the solvent. The equation below shows how to find the mole fraction (X) of a solute (A) and a solvent (B). Denominators in each equation are the same.

$$X_A = \frac{n_A}{n_A + n_B} \qquad X_B = \frac{n_B}{n_A + n_B}$$

X_A = mole fraction of the solute
n_A = moles of solute

X_B = mole fraction of the solvent
n_B = moles of solvent

The mole fraction of the solute (X_A) is found by dividing the moles of solute by the sum of the moles of solute and moles of solvent. The mole fraction of the solvent (X_B) is found by dividing the moles of solvent by the sum of the moles of solute and moles of solvent. Notice that you divide moles by moles. The units on the top of the equation cancel the units on the bottom. Mole fraction does not have units. The sum of the mole fractions of all the parts of a solution equals one.

The figure below shows how to calculate mole fractions of the solute and solvent for a solution of ethylene glycol in water. In this example, ethylene glycol is the solute and water is the solvent.

Key Question What are two ways of expressing the ratio of solute to solvent in a solution? **Chemists express the ratio of solute particles to solvent particles by using molality and mole fraction.**

Mole Fraction The circle graph shows the proportions of ethylene glycol (EG) and water in antifreeze. A mole fraction is the ratio of the number of moles of one substance to the total number of moles of all substances in the solution.

Total moles = Ⓐ+Ⓑ = 1.25 mol + 4.00 mol = 5.25 mol

$$\text{Mole fraction EG} = \frac{Ⓐ}{Ⓐ+Ⓑ} = \frac{1.25}{5.25} = 0.238$$

+

$$\text{Mole fraction } H_2O = \frac{Ⓑ}{Ⓐ+Ⓑ} = \frac{4.00}{5.25} = 0.762$$

1.000

You can calculate the mole fraction of the solute and the solvent. The mole fractions added together equal one.

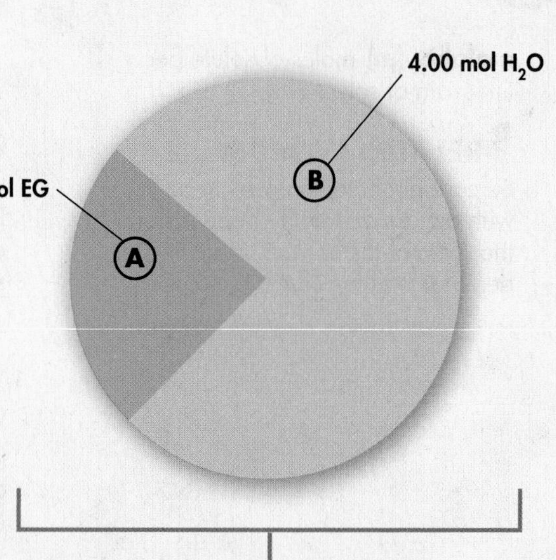

This circle graph shows how much of the solution is made up of each part. Ethylene glycol makes up about 25 percent of the solution. Water makes up about 75 percent.

Sample Problem 16.6

Using Molality

How many grams of potassium iodide must be dissolved in 500.0 g of water to produce a 0.060 molal KI solution?

1 Analyze **List the knowns and the unknown.**

KNOWNS	UNKNOWN
mass of water, or solvent = 500.0 g	mass of solute = ? g KI
molality = 0.060*m*	
molar mass of KI = 166.0 g/mol	

2 Calculate **Solve for the unknown.**

Write the molality of the solution in terms of mol of KI and kg of H_2O to use for conversion.

$$m = \frac{\text{moles of solute}}{\text{kilogram of solvent}} = \frac{0.060 \text{ mol KI}}{1.000 \text{ kg } H_2O}$$

Identify the conversion factor based on the molar mass of KI that allows you to convert from mol KI to g KI.

$$\frac{166.0 \text{ g KI}}{1 \text{ mol KI}}$$

Write the solvent mass in kilograms.

$$\text{mass of solvent} = 500.0 \cancel{\text{g}} \text{ } H_2O \times \frac{1 \text{ kg}}{1000 \cancel{\text{g}}} = 0.5000 \text{ kg } H_2O$$

Multiply the known solvent mass by the conversion factors.

$$0.5000 \cancel{\text{kg } H_2O} \times \frac{0.060 \cancel{\text{mol KI}}}{1.000 \cancel{\text{kg } H_2O}} \times \frac{166.0 \text{ g KI}}{1 \cancel{\text{mol KI}}}$$

Solve the equation.

mass of solute = 5.0 g KI

3 Evaluate **Does the result make sense?** A 1 molal KI solution is one molar mass of KI (166.0 g) dissolved in 1000 g of water. The desired molal concentration (0.060*m*) is about $\frac{1}{20}$ of that value. So, the mass of KI should be much less than the molar mass. The answer is correctly expressed to two significant figures.

BUILD Math Skills

Dimensional Analysis Dimensional analysis is a useful problem-solving skill. You use dimensional analysis with stuff you can count because anything you can count will have some unit of measure, which is the dimension. A unit could be hours in class, gallons of gas, or pizza slices per person. The great thing about dimensional analysis is that any number or expression can be multiplied by one without changing its value.

Another thing to remember is that units will be treated just like numbers. Units will be multiplied and divided, and if the units do not cancel out to what you are solving for, you will know something is wrong.

Go to your Chemistry Skills and Math Workbook for more practice problems.

Practice Problems

37. How many grams of sodium fluoride are needed to prepare a 0.400*m* NaF solution that contains 750 g of water?

❶ **Analyze List the knowns and the unknown.**

❷ **Calculate Solve for the unknown.**

❸ **Evaluate Does the result make sense?**

KNOWNS	UNKNOWN
mass of solvent = 750 g	mass of solute = ? g NaF
molality = 0.400*m*	
molar mass of NaF = 42.0 g/mol	

38. How many grams of sodium bromide (NaBr) must be dissolved in 400.0 g of water to produce a 0.500 molal solution?

KNOWNS	UNKNOWN
mass of solvent =	mass of solute = ? g NaBr
molality =	
molar mass of NaBr =	

39. Calculate the molality of a solution prepared by dissolving 10.0 g of NaCl in 600 g of water.

40. Challenge Calculate the molality of a glucose solution made by dissolving 60.0 g of glucose in 2.0 L of water.

Remember: Molality equals moles of solute dissolved per kilogram of solvent.

Freezing Point Depression and Boiling Point Elevation

Changes in freezing points and boiling points are usually very small. For example, the boiling point elevation caused by adding one tablespoon of salt to a pot of water would be much less than 1°C. You can calculate changes in freezing point and boiling point. To do this, you need to know the molality and have some reference data about the solvent.

Calculating Molal Freezing Point Depression An increase in the concentration of solute in a solution makes the freezing point depression (ΔT_f) even bigger. So freezing point depression is directly proportional to molal concentration (m). This holds true for molecular solutes. Use the equation below to calculate freezing point depression.

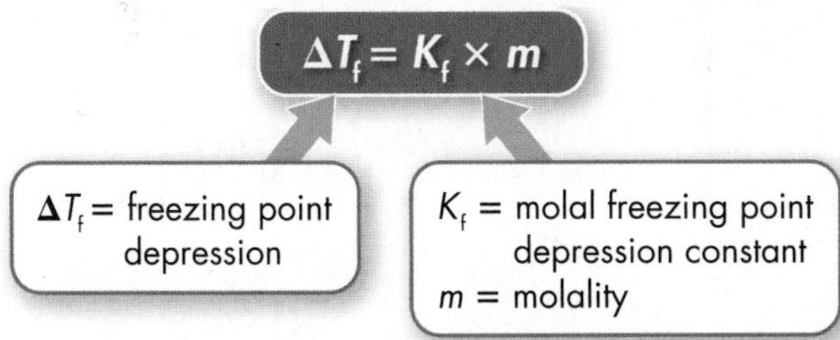

The constant K_f is the **molal freezing point depression constant.** It is equal to the change in freezing point for a 1 molal solution of a nonvolatile molecular solute. Its units are °C/m. The value of K_f depends on the solvent, not the solute. The table shows K_f values for common solvents. The value for water is 1.86 °C/m.

Calculating Molal Boiling Point Elevation Increasing the concentration of the solute also increases the boiling point elevation. Use the equation below to find the boiling point elevation of a solution.

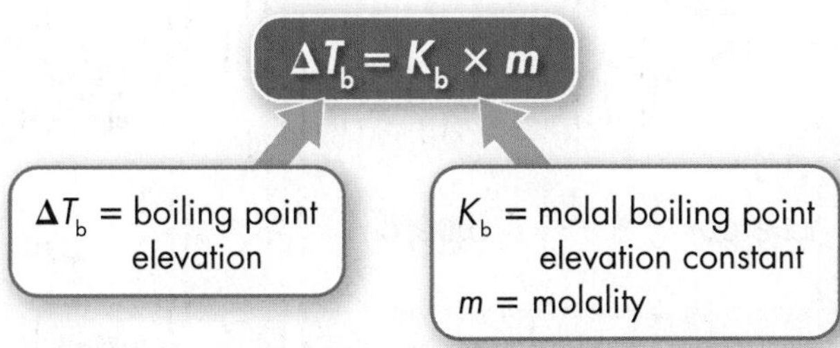

$\Delta T_b = K_b \times m$
ΔT_b = boiling point elevation
K_b = molal boiling point elevation constant
m = molality

The constant K_b is the **molal boiling point elevation constant.** It is equal to the change in boiling point for a 1 molal solution of a nonvolatile molecular solute. The table shows the K_b values for common solvents. K_b has units of °C/m. The value for water is 0.512°C/m.

The above equations work for molecular solutions. Sample Problem 16.8 shows how to solve for the ΔT_b of ionic solutions.

Key Question How are freezing point depression and boiling point elevation related to molality? **Freezing point depression and boiling point elevation of a solution are directly proportional to the molal concentration of molecular solutes.**

BUILD Vocabulary

molal freezing point depression constant the change in the freezing point for a one molal solution of a molecular solute

molal boiling point elevation constant the change in the boiling point for a one molal solution of a molecular solute

USING PRIOR KNOWLEDGE

You can use vocabulary words you have already learned to understand these constants. *Freezing point depression* describes a decrease in the freezing point. *Boiling point elevation* describes an increase in the boiling point.

K_f and K_b Values for Some Common Solvents

Solvent	K_f (°C/m)	K_b (°C/m)
Acetic acid	3.90	3.07
Benzene	5.12	2.53
Camphor	37.7	5.95
Cyclohexane	20.2	2.79
Ethanol	1.99	1.19
Nitrobenzene	7.00	5.24
Phenol	7.40	3.56
Water	1.86	0.512

CHEMISTRY TUTORIAL

Sample Problem 16.7

Calculating the Freezing Point Depression of a Solution

Antifreeze protects a car's engine from freezing. It also protects it from overheating. Calculate the freezing point depression of a solution containing exactly 100 g of ethylene glycol ($C_2H_6O_2$) antifreeze in 0.500 kg of water.

1 Analyze **List the knowns and the unknown.**

KNOWNS	UNKNOWN
mass of solute = 100 g $C_2H_6O_2$	ΔT_f = ?°C
mass of solvent = 0.500 kg H_2O	
K_f for H_2O = 1.86°C/m	
molar mass of $C_2H_6O_2$ = 62.0 g/mol	

2 Calculate **Solve for the unknown.**

Use the molar mass of $C_2H_6O_2$ to convert the mass of solute to moles.

$$100\ \text{g}\ C_2H_6O_2 \times \frac{1\ \text{mol}\ C_2H_6O_2}{62.0\ \text{g}\ C_2H_6O_2} = 1.61\ \text{mol}\ C_2H_6O_2$$

Write the equation for molality.

$$m = \frac{\text{moles of solute}}{\text{kilogram of solvent}}$$

Substitute the knowns into the equation and then solve for molality.

$$m = \frac{1.61\ \text{mol}}{0.500\ \text{kg}} = 3.22m$$

Write the equation for freezing point depression.

$$\Delta T_f = K_f \times m$$

Substitute the knowns into the equation and then solve for freezing point depression.

$$\Delta T_f = 1.86°\text{C}/m \times 3.22m = 5.99°\text{C}$$

Note: The freezing point of the solution is 0.00°C − 5.99°C = −5.99°C.

3 Evaluate **Does the result make sense?**
A 1 molal solution reduces the freezing temperature by 1.86°C. A decrease of 5.99°C for a solution that is a little more than 3 molal is reasonable.

BUILD Math Skills

Constants Be sure you can recognize the symbols used for constants. Constants may look like variables in equations. However, they are known values that do not change.

It is also important to choose the correct value for constants. Some constants only have one value. However, the constants K_f and K_b have different values depending on which solvent you use.

K_f for water = 1.86°C/*m*

K_f for benzene = 5.12°C/*m*

Go to your Chemistry Skills and Math Workbook for more practice problems.

Practice Problems

41. What is the freezing point depression of an aqueous solution of 10.0 g of glucose ($C_6H_{12}O_6$) in 50.0 g H_2O?

1 Analyze **List the knowns and the unknown.**

2 Calculate **Solve for the unknown.**

3 Evaluate **Does the result make sense?**

KNOWNS	UNKNOWN
mass of solute = 10.0 g $C_6H_{12}O_6$	ΔT_f = ?°C
mass of solvent = 50.0 g H_2O	
K_f for H_2O = 1.86°C/*m*	
molar mass of $C_6H_{12}O_6$ = 180.0 g/mol	

42. What is the freezing point depression of a solution of 12.0 g of naphthalene ($C_{10}H_8$) in 50.0 g of benzene?

KNOWNS	UNKNOWN
mass of solute =	ΔT_f = ?°C
mass of solvent =	
K_f for benzene =	
molar mass of $C_{10}H_8$ =	

43. Calculate the freezing point depression of a benzene solution containing 400 g of benzene and 200 g of the molecular compound acetone (C_3H_6O). K_f for benzene is 5.12°C/*m*.

44. Challenge What is the freezing point of an aqueous solution that contains 50.0 g of ethylene glycol ($C_2H_6O_2$) and 50.0 g of glucose ($C_6H_{12}O_6$) in 200.0 g of water?

Sample Problem 16.8

Calculating the Boiling Point of a Solution

What is the boiling point of a 1.50m NaCl solution?

❶ Analyze **List the knowns and the unknown.**

KNOWNS	UNKNOWN
solution concentration = 1.50m NaCl	boiling point = ?°C
K_b for H_2O = 0.512°C/m	
boiling point of pure water = 100°C	

❷ Calculate **Solve for the unknown.**

Write the equation that shows how each unit of NaCl dissociates into particles.

$$NaCl(s) \longrightarrow Na^+(aq) + Cl^-(aq)$$

Two particles are produced in solution, Na^+ and Cl^-.

Write the equation for effective molality.

effective molality = number of particles × solution molality

Substitute knowns into the equation to find effective molality.

effective molality = 2 × 1.50m = 3.00m

Hint: The effective molality is the molal concentration times the number of ions produced.

Write the equation for boiling point elevation.

$$\Delta T_b = K_b \times m$$

Substitute knowns into the equation to find the boiling point elevation.

$$\Delta T_b = 0.512°C/\cancel{m} \times 3.00\cancel{m} = 1.54°C$$

Calculate the boiling point of the solution.

$$T_b = 100°C + \Delta T_b$$
$$= 100°C + 1.54°C$$
$$= 101.54°C$$

❸ Evaluate **Does the result make sense?** The boiling point increases about 0.5°C for each mole of solute particles. So the total change is reasonable. Because the boiling point of water is defined as exactly 100°C, this value does not limit the number of significant figures in the solution of the problem.

Practice Problems

45. What is the boiling point of a solution that contains 1.25 mol of $CaCl_2$ in 1400 g of water?

❶ **Analyze** **List the knowns and the unknowns.**

❷ **Calculate** **Solve for the unknowns.**

❸ **Evaluate** **Does the result make sense?**

KNOWNS	UNKNOWNS
mass of solute = 1.25 mol $CaCl_2$	molality = ?m
mass of solvent = 1400 g H_2O	boiling point = ?°C
K_b for H_2O = 0.512°C/m	
boiling point of pure water = 100°C	

46. What is the boiling point of a solution that contains 2.00 mol of NaCl in 750 g of water?

KNOWNS	UNKNOWNS
mass of solute =	molality = ?m
mass of solvent =	boiling point = ?°C
K_b for solvent =	
boiling point of pure water =	

47. What is the boiling point of a solution of 12.0 g of naphthalene ($C_{10}H_8$) in 50.0 g of benzene? The boiling point of pure benzene is 80.1°C.

48. Challenge What mass of NaCl would have to be dissolved in 1.000 kg of water to raise the boiling point by 2.00°C?

16.4 LessonCheck

Key Concept Check

49. 🔑 **List** What are two ways of expressing the ratio of solute to solvent in a solution?

50. 🔑 **Explain** How are freezing point depression and boiling point elevation related to molality?

Vocabulary Check *Choose a highlighted word from the lesson to complete each sentence correctly.*

51. The ___________ of a solute is the ratio of the number of moles of solute to the total number of moles of solvent and solute.

52. The molal concentration is also called _________.

Think Critically

53. Predict What is the freezing point of a solution of 12.0 g of CCl_4 dissolved in 750.0 g of benzene? The freezing point of benzene is 5.48°C; K_f is 5.12°C/m.

CHEMISTRY & YOU

54. Calculate the boiling point elevation for the saltwater solution described at the beginning of the lesson. (Hint: See page 516.)

16 Study Guide

BIG IDEA
THE MOLE AND QUANTIFYING MATTER

Solubility, miscibility, concentration, and colligative properties are used to describe and characterize solutions. Solution concentration can be quantified in terms of molarity (moles of solute per liter of solution), molality (moles of solute per kilogram of solvent), percent by volume, and percent by mass.

16.1 Properties of Solutions

Agitation, temperature, and the particle size of the solute affect how fast a substance dissolves.

An equilibrium exists between solution and undissolved solute in saturated solutions under given conditions.

Temperature affects the solubility of solid and liquid solutes. Temperature and pressure affect the solubility of gaseous solutes.

- solubility (490)
- saturated solution (490)
- unsaturated solution (490)
- miscible (490)
- immiscible (490)
- supersaturated solution (491)
- Henry's law (492)

Key Equation

$$\text{Henry's law: } \frac{S_1}{P_1} = \frac{S_2}{P_2}$$

16.2 Concentrations of Solutions

Divide the number of moles of solute by the volume of the solution in liters to calculate the molarity of a solution.

Diluting a solution reduces the number of moles of solute per unit volume. It does not change the total number of moles of solute in solution.

Percent by volume is the ratio of the volume of solute to the volume of solution. Percent by mass is the ratio of the mass of solute to the mass of solution.

- concentration (495)
- dilute solution (495)
- concentrated solution (495)
- molarity (M) (495)

Key Equations

$$\text{Molarity } (M) = \frac{\text{moles of solute}}{\text{liters of solution}}$$

$$M_1 \times V_1 = M_2 \times V_2$$

$$\text{Percent by volume} = \frac{\text{volume of solute}}{\text{volume of solution}} \times 100\%$$

$$\text{Percent by mass} = \frac{\text{mass of solute}}{\text{mass of solution}} \times 100\%$$

16.3 Colligative Properties of Solutions

Three colligative properties of solutions are vapor pressure lowering, freezing point depression, and boiling point elevation.

- colligative property (505)
- freezing point depression (507)
- boiling point elevation (508)

16.4 Calculations Involving Colligative Properties

Chemists express the ratio of solute to solvent by using molality and mole fraction.

Freezing point depression and boiling point elevation of a solution are directly proportional to the molal concentration of molecular solutes.

- molality (m) (509)
- mole fraction (510)
- molal freezing point depression constant (K_f) (513)
- molal boiling point elevation constant (K_b) (513)

Key Equations

$$\text{Molality } (m) = \frac{\text{moles of solute}}{\text{kilogram of solvent}}$$

$$\text{Mole fractions: } X_A = \frac{n_A}{n_A + n_B} \quad X_B = \frac{n_B}{n_A + n_B}$$

$$\Delta T_f = K_f \times m$$

$$\Delta T_b = K_b \times m$$

Math Tune-Up: Solution Concentration Problems

Problem	❶ Analyze	❷ Calculate	❸ Evaluate
What volume of 12.00*M* sulfuric acid is required to prepare 1.00 L of 0.400*M* sulfuric acid?	Knowns: $M_1 = 12.00M\ H_2SO_4$ $M_2 = 0.400M\ H_2SO_4$ $V_2 = 1.00$ L of $0.400M\ H_2SO_4$ Unknown: $V_1 = ?$ L of $12.00M\ H_2SO_4$ Use the following equation to solve for the unknown initial volume of solution that is diluted: $M_1 \times V_1 = M_2 \times V_2$.	Solve the equation for V_1 and then substitute. $V_1 = \frac{M_2 \times V_2}{M_1}$ $V_1 = \frac{0.400\cancel{M} \times 1.00\text{ L}}{12.00\cancel{M}}$ $V_1 = 0.0333$ L	The concentration of the initial solution (12.00*M*) is 30 times larger than the concentration of the diluted solution (0.400*M*). So, the volume of the solution to be diluted should be one-thirtieth the final volume of the diluted solution.
Ethanol is mixed with gasoline to make a solution called *gasohol.* What is the percent by volume of ethanol in gasohol when 95 mL of ethanol is added to sufficient gasoline to make 1.0 L of gasohol?	Knowns: volume of ethanol = 95 mL volume of solution = 1.0 L Unknown: solution concentration = ? % (v/v) Use the equation for percent by volume: $\%\ (v/v) = \frac{\text{volume of solute}}{\text{volume of solution}} \times 100\%$	Make sure the known volumes are expressed in the same units. Then, calculate percent by volume of ethanol. $\%\ (v/v) = \frac{0.095\ \cancel{L}}{1.00\ \cancel{L}} \times 100\%$ $= 9.5\%\ (v/v)$	The volume of the solute is about one-tenth the volume of the solution, so the answer is reasonable. The answer is correctly expressed to two significant figures.
Calculate the molality of a solution prepared by mixing 5.40 g of LiBr with 444 g of water.	Knowns: mass of solute = 5.40 g mass of water = 444 g molar mass of LiBr = 86.8 g Unknown: solution concentration = ?*m* Use the equation for molal concentration: $\text{Molality} = \frac{\text{mol of solute}}{\text{kg of solvent}}$	Convert the mass of the solute to moles of solute. $5.40\ \cancel{\text{g LiBr}} \times \frac{1\text{ mol LiBr}}{86.8\ \cancel{\text{g LiBr}}} =$ 0.0622 mol LiBr Calculate molality. $\text{Molality} = \frac{0.0622\text{ mol LiBr}}{0.444\text{ kg }H_2O}$ $= 0.140m$	The answer has the correct units (mol of solute per kg of solvent) and is correctly expressed to three significant figures.

Remember: Molality is mol of solute per kg of solvent. Make sure you have the correct mass units in the denominator.

16 Assessment

★ Solutions appear in Appendix D.

Lesson by Lesson

16.1 Properties of Solutions

55. Name and distinguish between the two components of a solution.

56. Define the following terms: *solubility, saturated solution, unsaturated solution, miscible,* and *immiscible.*

57. Can a solution with undissolved solute be supersaturated? Explain.

58. If a saturated solution of sodium nitrate is cooled, what change might you observe?

59. What is the effect of pressure on the solubility of gases in liquids?

★60. The solubility of methane in water at 20°C and 1.00 atm pressure is 0.026 g/L. What will be the solubility of this gas at the following pressures? Assume the temperature does not change.

a. 0.60 atm

b. 1.80 atm

16.2 Concentrations of Solutions

61. Knowing the molarity of a solution is more meaningful than knowing whether a solution is dilute or concentrated. Explain.

62. Define molarity and then calculate the molarity of 1.0 mol of KCl in 750 mL of solution.

★63. How many milliliters of 0.500*M* KCl solution would you need to dilute to make 100.0 mL of 0.100*M* KCl?

★64. Calculate the molarity of a solution that contains 0.50 g of NaCl dissolved in 100 mL of solution.

65. Calculate the moles and grams of solute in each solution.

a. 1.0 L of 0.50*M* NaCl

b. 250 mL of 0.10*M* $CaCl_2$

★66. Calculate the grams of solute required to make the following solutions.

a. 2500 g of saline solution (0.90% NaCl (m/m))

b. 0.050 kg of 4.0% (m/m) $MgCl_2$

67. What is the percent by mass of sodium chloride in each of the following solutions?

a. 44 g of NaCl dissolved in 756 g of H_2O

b. 15 g of NaCl dissolved in 485 g of H_2O

★68. What is the concentration (in % (v/v)) of the following solutions?

a. 25 mL of ethanol (C_2H_6O) is diluted with water to a volume of 150 mL.

b. 175 mL of isopropyl alcohol (C_3H_8O) is diluted with water to a total volume of 275 mL.

16.3 Colligative Properties of Solutions

69. What are colligative properties? Identify three colligative properties and then explain why each occurs.

70. Which has the higher boiling point:

a. seawater or distilled water?

b. 0.100*M* of KCl or 0.100*M* of $MgCl_2$?

16.4 Calculations Involving Colligative Properties

71. Distinguish between a 1*M* solution and a 1*m* solution.

72. Describe how you would make an aqueous solution of methanol (CH_4O) in which the mole fraction of methanol is 0.40.

73. What is the boiling point of each solution?

a. 0.50 mol of glucose in 1000 g of H_2O

b. 1.50 mol of NaCl in 1000 g of H_2O

★74. What is the freezing point of each solution?

a. 1.40 mol of Na_2SO_4 in 1750 g of H_2O

b. 0.060 mol of $MgSO_4$ in 100 g of H_2O

Understand Concepts

75. Different numbers of moles of two different solutes—A and B—were added to identical quantities of water. The graph shows the freezing point of each of the solutions formed.

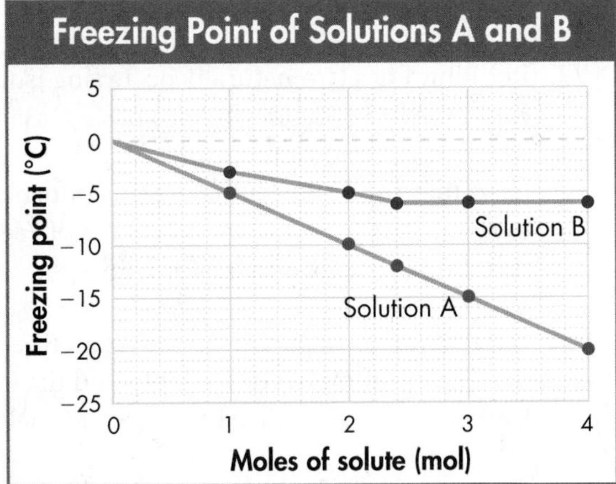

a. Explain the relative slopes of the two lines between 0 and 2 mol of solute added.

b. Why does the freezing point for solution B not continue to drop as amounts of solute B are added beyond 2.4 mol?

76. The solubility of sodium hydrogen carbonate ($NaHCO_3$) in water at 20°C is 9.6 g/100 g of H_2O. What is the mole fraction of $NaHCO_3$ in a saturated solution? What is the molality of the solution?

77. A solution is labeled 0.150*m* of NaCl. What are the mole fractions of the solute and solvent in this solution?

78. You are given a clear aqueous solution containing KNO_3. How would you determine experimentally if the solution is unsaturated, saturated, or supersaturated?

79. Calculate the freezing point and the boiling point of a solution that contains 15.0 g of urea (CH_4N_2O) in 250 g of water. Urea is a covalently bonded compound.

80. How many moles of ions are present when 0.10 mol of each compound is dissolved in water?

a. K_2SO_4

b. $Fe(NO_3)_3$

Think Critically

81. Apply Concepts Why might calcium chloride spread on icy roads be more effective at melting ice than sodium chloride?

82. Compare and Contrast Which will have a greater boiling point elevation: 3.00 g of $Ca(NO_3)_2$ in 60.0 g of water or 6.00 g of $Ca(NO_3)_2$ in 30.0 g of water?

***83. Analyze Data** A solution contains 26.5 g of NaCl in 75.0 g of H_2O at 20°C. Determine if the solution is unsaturated, saturated, or supersaturated. (The solubility of NaCl at 20°C is 36.0 g/100 g of H_2O.)

84. Infer An aqueous solution freezes at −2.47°C. What is its boiling point?

85. Calculate Percent (mass/volume), or % (m/v), is the number of grams of solute per 100 mL of solution. Hydrogen peroxide is often sold commercially as a 3.0% (m/v) aqueous solution.

a. If you buy a 250 mL bottle of 3.0% H_2O_2 (m/v), how many grams of hydrogen peroxide have you purchased?

b. What is the molarity of this solution?

FOUNDATIONS Wrap-Up

Mixing Oil and Water

1. Draw Conclusions At the beginning of this chapter, you added oil to water. Explain why the oil and water acted the way it did.

Concept Check

Now that you have finished studying Chapter 16, answer these questions:

2. What can you do to make a substance dissolve faster?

3. How can you describe the concentration of solutions?

4. Why do solutions boil at higher temperatures than pure solvents?

5. Would sugar or salt have a greater effect on the boiling point of water? Why?

Write About Science

86. **Describe** Find a recipe for rock candy online or in a cookbook. Write a short paragraph that describes how the recipe applies key concepts that you have learned about solutions. Use the terms *solute, solvent, solubility,* and *supersaturated solution* in your paragraph.

*87. **Sequence** Write a stepwise procedure for preparing 100 mL of 0.50*M* KCl, starting with a stock solution that is 2.0*M* KCl.

CHEMYSTERY

Although you cannot see it happening, the groundwater beneath your feet is slowly dissolving away rocks and minerals below ground. Eventually, enough of these mineral solutes will dissolve to hollow out underground cavities or caverns. A sinkhole occurs when the roof of an underground cavern depresses or collapses.

88. **Explain** Why do you think areas with salt beds below them are prone to sinkholes?

89. **Infer** As you read earlier in this chapter, agitation can speed up the dissolving of a solid in a liquid. What forces might cause the agitation of groundwater as it dissolves minerals underground?

90. **Connect to the BIGIDEA** Limestone, which contains mostly calcium carbonate ($CaCO_3$), is insoluble in water. But areas with limestone below them are prone to sinkholes. How do you think the "dissolving" of limestone differs from the movement of solute into solution?

Cumulative Review

91. Convert each of the following mass measurements to its equivalent in kilograms. (See Lesson 3.3 for help.)
    a. 347 g
    b. 73 mg
    c. 9.43 mg
    d. 877 mg

*92. Rubidium has two naturally occurring isotopes. Rubidium-85 (72.165 percent) has a mass of 84.912 amu, and rubidium-87 (27.835 percent) has a mass of 86.909 amu. Use this information to calculate the average atomic mass of rubidium. (See Lesson 4.3 for help.)

93. What is the most significant difference between the Thomson model of the atom and the Rutherford model? (See Lesson 5.1 for help.)

94. Name and give the symbol for the element in the following positions in the periodic table. (See Lesson 6.2 for help.)
    a. Group 7B, Period 4
    b. Group 3A, Period 5
    c. Group 1A, Period 7
    d. Group 6A, Period 6

95. Draw electron dot structures for the following atoms. (See Lesson 7.1 for help.)
    a. I
    b. Te
    c. Sb
    d. Sr

*96. What is the volume occupied by 1500 g of hydrogen gas (H_2) at STP? (See Lesson 10.2 for help.)

97. Indicate by simple equations how the following substances ionize or dissociate in water. (See Lesson 11.3 for help.)
    a. NH_4Cl
    b. $Cu(NO_3)_2$
    c. HNO_3
    d. $HC_2H_3O_2$
    e. Na_2SO_4
    f. $HgCl_2$

*98. A cylinder of nitrogen gas at 25°C and 101.3 kPa is heated to 45°C. What is the new pressure of the gas? (See Lesson 14.2 for help.)

99. When soap is shaken with water, which is formed: a solution, a suspension, or a colloid? Explain. (See Lesson 15.3 for help.)

Standardized Test Prep

For help with answering test questions, go to your Chemistry Skills and Math Workbook.

Select the choice that best answers each question or completes each statement.

1. An aqueous solution is 65% (v/v) rubbing alcohol. How many milliliters of water are in a 95 mL sample of this solution?
   (A) 62 mL (C) 33 mL
   (B) 1.5 mL (D) 30 mL

2. When 2.0 mol of methanol is dissolved in 45 g of water, the mole fraction of methanol is
   (A) 0.44. (C) 2.25.
   (B) 0.043. (D) 0.55.

The lettered choices below refer to Questions 3–6. A lettered choice may be used once, more than once, or not at all.

(A) moles/liter of solution
(B) grams/mole
(C) moles/kilogram of solvent
(D) °C/molal
(E) no units

Which of the above units is appropriate for each measurement?

3. molality
4. mole fraction
5. molar mass
6. molarity

Use the atomic windows to answer Questions 7–9. The windows show water and two aqueous solutions with different concentrations. Black spheres represent solute particles; gray spheres represent water.

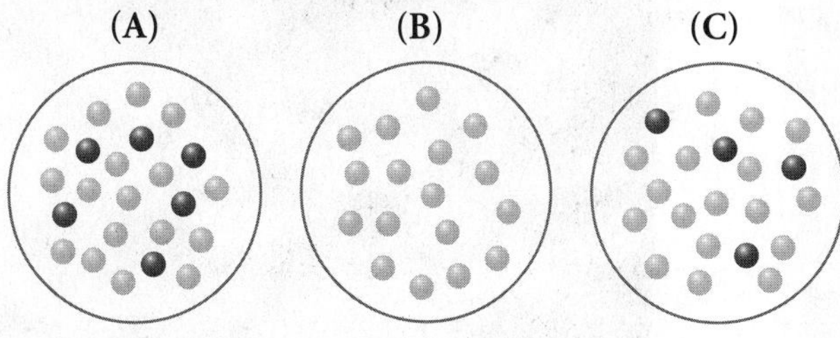

7. Which solution has the highest vapor pressure?
8. Which solution has the lowest vapor pressure?
9. Which solution has the lowest boiling point?

10. Which of these actions will cause more sugar to dissolve in a saturated sugar water solution?
    I. Add more sugar while stirring.
    II. Add more sugar and then heat the solution.
    III. Grind the sugar to a powder and then add while stirring.

    (A) I only (D) I and II only
    (B) II only (E) II and III only
    (C) III only

Tips for Success

Reading Data Tables Data tables are used to summarize data. When reading a table, try to figure out the relationships between the different columns and rows of information.

Use the description and the data table to answer Questions 11–14.

A student measured the freezing points of three different aqueous solutions at five different concentrations. The data are shown below.

Molarity (M)	Freezing Point Depression (°C)		
	NaCl	$CaCl_2$	C_2H_6O
0.5	1.7	2.6	0.95
1.0	3.5	5.6	2.0
1.5	5.3	8.3	3.0
2.0	7.2	11.2	4.1
2.5	9.4	14.0	5.3

11. Graph the data for all three solutes on the same graph, using molarity as the independent variable.
12. Summarize the relationship between molarity and freezing point depression.
13. Compare the slopes of the three lines and explain any difference.
14. If you collected similar data for KOH and then added a fourth line to your graph, which existing line would the new line approximate?

If You Have Trouble With . . .

Question	1	2	3	4	5	6	7	8	9	10	11	12	13	14
See Lesson	16.2	16.4	16.4	16.4	16.2	16.2	16.3	16.3	16.3	16.1	16.3	16.4	16.3	16.3

17 Thermochemistry

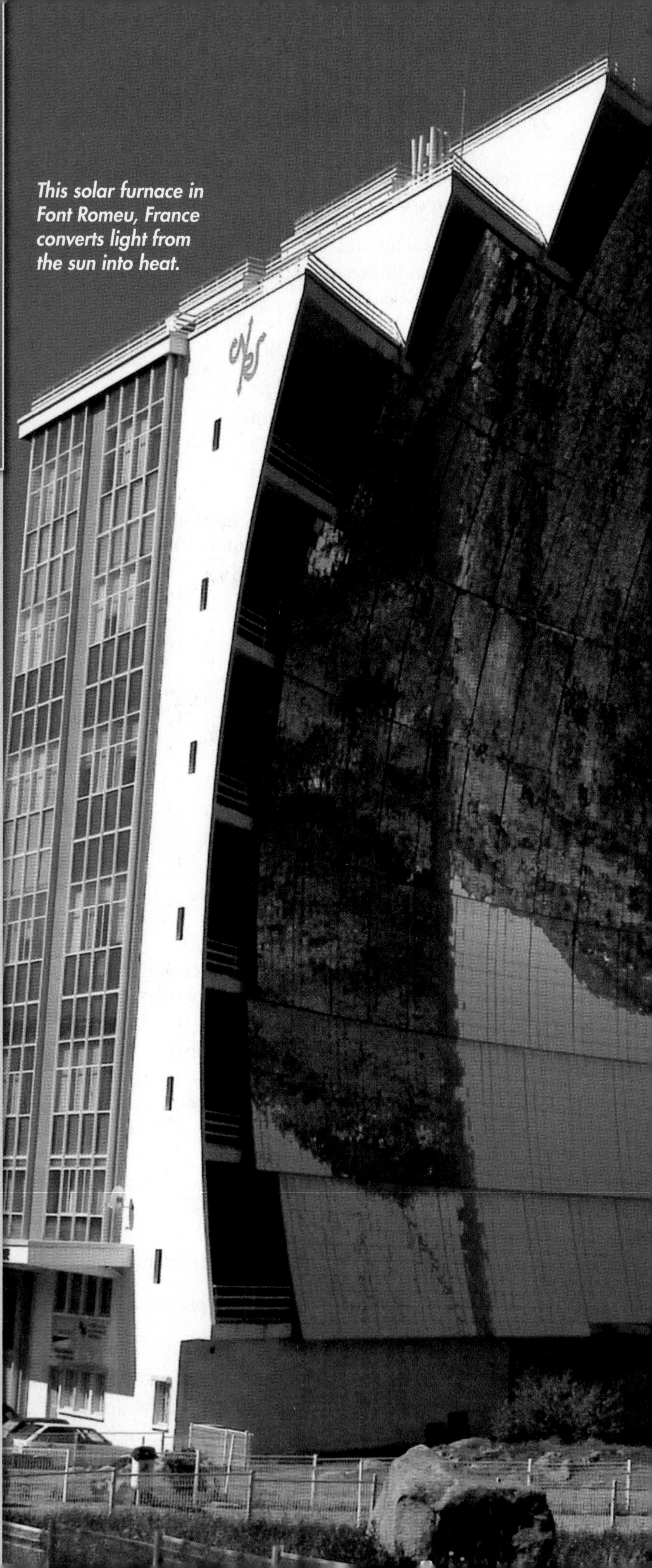

This solar furnace in Font Romeu, France converts light from the sun into heat.

FOUNDATIONS for Learning

Observing Heat Flow

1. You will need a clean rubber band. **CAUTION** *If you are allergic to latex, do not handle the rubber band.*
2. Without stretching the rubber band, place it against your skin. Note the temperature.
3. Move the rubber band away from your skin. Stretch the band quickly several times.
4. Relax the rubber band. Place it against your skin again. Note the temperature.

Form a Hypothesis Explain what you think caused the rubber band's change in temperature.

PearsonChem.com

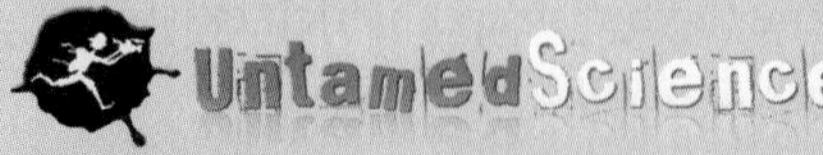

Take a video field trip and watch the Untamed Science crew explore different types of exothermic and endothermic chemical reactions.

MATTER AND ENERGY

Essential Questions:

1. *How is energy conserved in a chemical or physical process?*
2. *How can you determine the amount of energy absorbed or released in a chemical or physical process?*

CHEMYSTERY

Fighting Frost

It is a cold night in central Florida. Weather forecasters are predicting that temperatures will fall to −3°C. The citrus growers in the area are in a panic. Just an hour or two of temperatures below 0°C could be devastating to the citrus trees and fruit.

Citrus growers can use several methods to limit the damage caused by frost or freeze to their trees and fruit. Some growers install heaters to protect their crops. Other farmers use wind machines or helicopters to mix the layers of warm and cold air in the atmosphere. Mixing these layers raises the temperature near the ground. However, one of the most common methods of protecting citrus trees is to spray water on them. The freezing of the water protects the branches, leaves, and fruit.

▶ Connect to the **BIG**IDEA As you read about thermochemistry, think about how water freezing can protect citrus fruit and trees from frost.

17.1 The Flow of Energy

CHEMISTRY & YOU

Q: Why does lava cool faster in water than in air? Lava flowing out of an erupting volcano is very hot. Its temperature ranges between 550°C and 1400°C. As lava flows down the side of a volcano, it loses heat and begins to cool slowly. Sometimes, the lava may flow into the ocean, where it cools faster. In this lesson, you will learn about heat flow.

Key Questions

What happens to the energy of the universe during a chemical or physical process?

What are the ways in which energy changes can occur?

What factors affect heat capacity?

BUILD Vocabulary

thermochemistry the study of energy changes that occur during chemical reactions and changes in state

system the part of the universe on which you focus attention

surroundings everything in the universe outside of the system

law of conservation of energy in any chemical or physical process, energy is neither created nor destroyed

chemical potential energy the energy stored in the chemical bonds of a substance

Energy Transformations

Energy is the capacity for doing work or supplying heat. Unlike matter, energy has neither mass nor volume. You can detect energy only because of its effects. For example, a car moves because of the energy supplied by the fuel.

Thermochemistry is the study of energy changes that occur during chemical reactions and changes in state. In studying energy changes, you can define a **system** as the part of the universe on which you focus your attention. Everything else in the universe makes up the **surroundings.** In thermochemical experiments, you can consider the region relatively close to the system as the surroundings. Together, the system and its surroundings make up the universe.

Law of Conservation of Energy The **law of conservation of energy** states that in any chemical or physical process, energy is neither created nor destroyed. If the energy of the system increases during that process, the energy of the surroundings must decrease by the same amount. Also, if the energy of the system decreases during that process, the energy of the surroundings must increase by the same amount.

The Energy of Chemical Substances Every substance has a certain amount of energy stored inside it. The energy stored in the chemical bonds of a substance is called **chemical potential energy.** The kinds of atoms and the way they are arranged determine the amount of energy stored in the substance. During a chemical reaction, one substance transforms into another substance. The new substance has a different amount of chemical potential energy.

Key Question What happens to the energy of the universe during a chemical or physical process? **During any chemical or physical process, the energy of the universe stays the same.**

Endothermic and Exothermic Processes

When you buy gasoline, you are buying the stored potential energy it contains. The potential energy of gasoline is transformed into useful work that can be used to move a car when the gasoline is burned. However, heat is also produced at the same time, making the car's engine hot. Energy changes occur as either heat transfer or work, or a combination of both.

Heat, represented by *q*, is energy that transfers from one object to another because of a temperature difference between the objects. One possible effect of adding heat to an object is an increase in the object's temperature. Heat flows from a warmer object to a cooler object. If two objects remain in contact, heat will flow from the warmer object to the cooler object until the objects have the same temperature.

Direction of Heat Flow Most chemical and physical processes involve either the absorption or the release of heat. The direction of heat flow is given from the point of view of the system. An **endothermic process** absorbs heat from its surroundings. In an endothermic process, the system gains heat as the surroundings lose heat. In the photo below at left, the system is the body of the man listening to headphones. The system (the body) gains heat from its surroundings (the fire). Heat flowing into a system from its surroundings is defined as positive; *q* has a positive value.

An **exothermic process** releases heat to its surroundings. In an exothermic process, the system loses heat as the surroundings gain heat. In the photo below at right, the system (the body) loses heat to the surroundings (the sweat on the skin and the air). Heat flowing out of a system into its surroundings is defined as negative; *q* has a negative value.

heat (*q*) energy that transfers from one object to another because of a temperature difference between the objects

endothermic process a process in which heat is absorbed from the surroundings

exothermic process a process in which heat is released into the surroundings

PREFIXES

The prefix *endo-* means inside, and the prefix *exo-* means outside. The prefixes tell you the direction that heat flows.

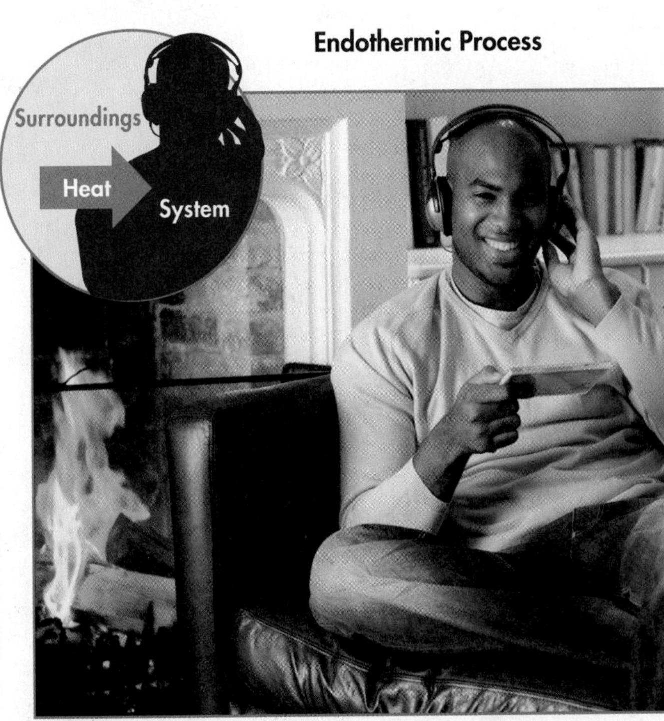

In an endothermic process, heat flows into the system from the surroundings.

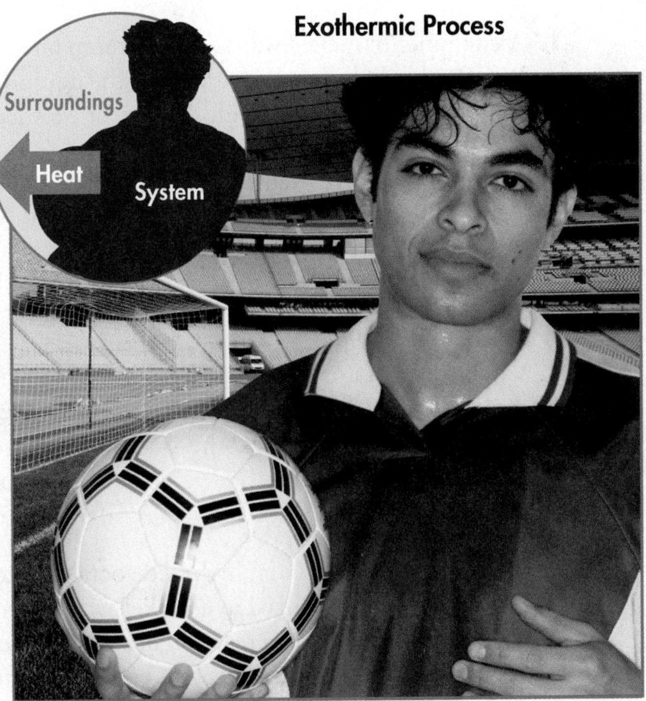

In an exothermic process, heat flows from the system to the surroundings.

Sample Problem 17.1

Recognizing Endothermic and Exothermic Processes

You bring a glass of water onto a rooftop on a winter day. Within hours, the water in the glass is frozen. Describe the direction of heat flow as the water freezes. Is this process endothermic or exothermic?

1 Analyze Identify the relevant concepts. Heat flows from a warmer object to a cooler object. An endothermic process absorbs heat from the surroundings. An exothermic process releases heat to the surroundings.

2 Solve Apply the concepts to this problem.

First, identify the system and the surroundings. → System: water
Surroundings: air

Determine the direction of heat flow. → The water in the glass is warmer than the surrounding air. Heat flows out of the water and into the air.

Determine if the process is endothermic or exothermic. → Heat is released from the system to the surroundings. The process is exothermic.

Practice Problems

1. A container of melted wax stands at room temperature. What is the direction of heat flow as the liquid wax solidifies? Is the process endothermic or exothermic?

1 Analyze Identify the relevant concepts.

2 Solve Apply the concepts to this problem.

2. You bake a potato in the oven for dinner. What is the direction of heat flow as the potato cooks? Is the process endothermic or exothermic?

3. Challenge When barium hydroxide octahydrate, $Ba(OH)_2 \cdot 8H_2O$, is mixed in a beaker with ammonium thiocyanate, NH_4SCN, a reaction occurs. The beaker becomes very cold. Is the reaction endothermic or exothermic?

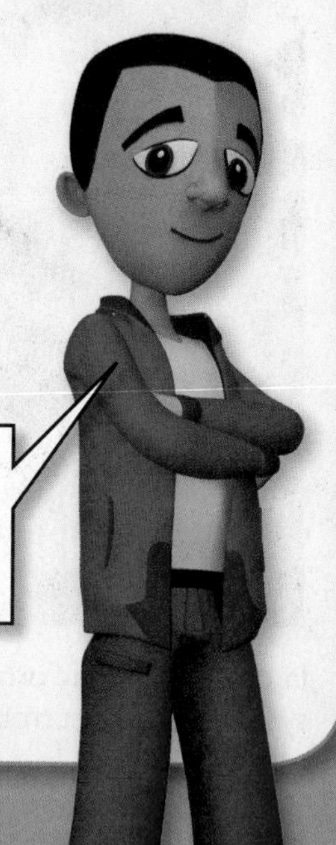

In a chemical reaction, the reactants are the system. Everything else is the surroundings.

Units for Measuring Heat Flow Even though heat and temperature are related, these measurements have different units. Heat flow is measured in two common units, the calorie and the joule. You have probably heard of someone exercising to "burn calories." During exercise, your body breaks down sugars and fats in a process that releases heat. There is not an actual fire burning the sugars and fats within your body, but chemical reactions have the same result. In breaking down 10 g of sugar, your body releases the same amount of energy that would be released as heat if 10 g of sugar were completely burned in a fire.

▶ **Calorie** A calorie (cal) is the quantity of heat needed to raise the temperature of 1 g of pure water 1°C. Write the word *calorie* with a small *c* except when referring to the energy contained in food. The dietary Calorie always refers to the energy in food. Use a capital *C* when referring to dietary Calories. One dietary Calorie is equal to one kilocalorie, or 1000 calories.

$$1 \text{ Calorie} = 1 \text{ kilocalorie} = 1000 \text{ calories}$$

▶ **Joule** The joule (J) is the SI unit of energy. One joule of heat raises the temperature of 1 g of pure water 0.2390°C. You can convert between calories and joules using the following relationships:

$$1 \text{ J} = 0.2390 \text{ cal} \qquad 4.184 \text{ J} = 1 \text{ cal}$$

Key Question What are the ways in which energy changes can occur? **Energy changes can occur as either heat transfer or work, or a combination of both.**

heat capacity the amount of heat needed to increase the temperature of an object exactly 1°C

RELATED WORDS

An object's capacity is the amount of something the object can take in before it is full. Think about how heat capacity fits this explanation of capacity.

Heat Capacity and Specific Heat

Suppose you put two identical pans on a stovetop. Now suppose you add a very small amount of water to one pan and a very large amount of water to the other pan. If you turn the burners on under both pans for the same length of time, what happens? The smaller amount of water will have a much greater change in temperature than the larger amount of water. This difference is due to heat capacity.

Heat Capacity The amount of heat needed to increase the temperature of an object exactly 1°C is the **heat capacity** of that object. The heat capacity of an object depends on both its mass and its composition. The greater the mass of the object, the greater its heat capacity. For example, one of the massive steel cables on the bridge in the photo to the right requires much more heat to raise its temperature 1°C than a small steel nail does. The steel cable has a greater heat capacity than the steel nail. Similarly, the larger volume of water on the stovetop has a greater heat capacity than the smaller volume of water.

Heat Capacity A massive steel cable has a higher heat capacity than a steel nail.

Different substances that have the same mass may have different heat capacities. A 20 kg puddle of water may be cool on a sunny day, while a nearby 20 kg iron sewer cover may be too hot to touch. This situation shows how different heat capacities affect the temperature of objects. If both the water and the iron absorb the same amount of energy from the sun, the temperature of the water changes less than the temperature of the iron. This is because the heat capacity of water is greater than the heat capacity of iron.

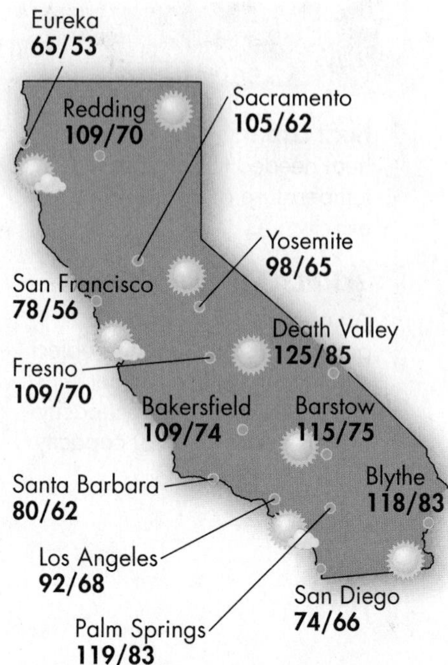

Temperature Moderation The high specific heat of the water in the ocean helps keep the temperatures in coastal cities much more moderate than those of cities farther inland.

Specific Heats of Some Common Substances

Substance	Specific heat	
	J/(g · °C)	cal/(g · °C)
Liquid water	4.18	1.00
Ethanol	2.4	0.58
Steam	1.9	0.45
Chloroform	0.96	0.23
Aluminum	0.90	0.21
Silver	0.24	0.057

Specific Heats The specific heat of a substance can be expressed in J/(g · °C) or cal/(g · °C).

Go to your Chemistry Skills and Math Workbook to practice interpreting data.

Specific Heat The specific heat capacity, or just the **specific heat** (C), of a substance is the amount of heat it takes to raise the temperature of 1 g of the substance 1°C. The table above gives specific heats for some common substances. Suppose you have equal masses of two substances that have different specific heats. Now suppose you apply a given amount of heat to both. The substance with the higher specific heat will have a lower final temperature than the substance with the lower specific heat.

▶ **Specific Heat of Water** Water has a high specific heat compared with the other substances in the table above. Just as it takes a lot of heat to raise the temperature of water, water also releases a lot of heat as it cools. Water in lakes and oceans absorbs heat from the air on hot days and releases it back into the air on cool days. As you can see on the weather map of California, the high specific heat of water causes moderate climates in coastal areas.

▶ **Calculating Specific Heat** You can calculate specific heat using the following mathematical equation.

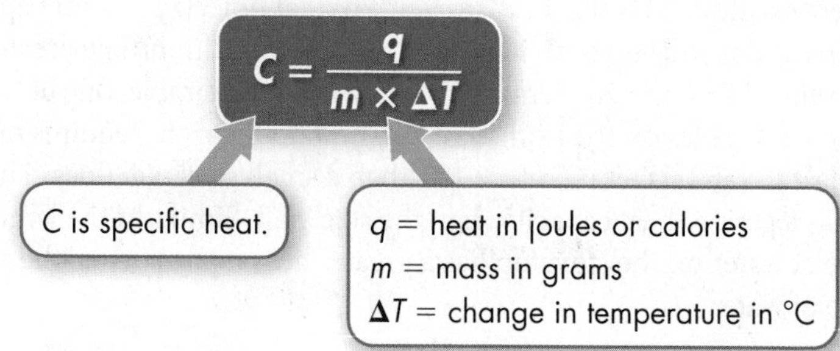

Heat may be expressed in terms of joules or calories. Therefore, the units of specific heat are either J/(g·°C) or cal/(g·°C).

Key Question What factors affect heat capacity? **Heat capacity is affected by the mass and composition of an object.**

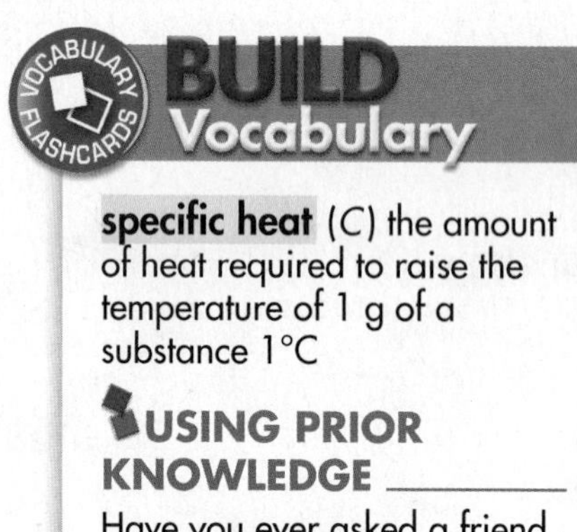

specific heat (C) the amount of heat required to raise the temperature of 1 g of a substance 1°C

USING PRIOR KNOWLEDGE

Have you ever asked a friend to "be specific"? If so, you wanted more details. Specific heat is *specific* for a certain mass and temperature change.

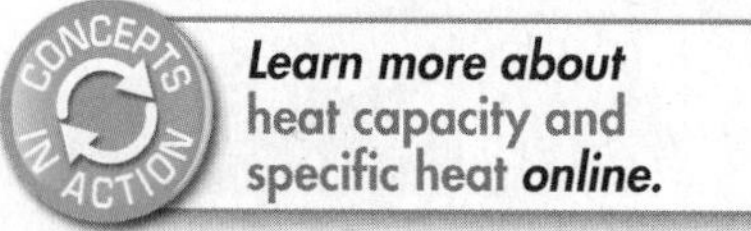

SampleProblem 17.2

Calculating the Specific Heat of a Substance

The temperature of a 95.4 g piece of copper increases from 25.0°C to 48.0°C when the copper absorbs 849 J of heat. What is the specific heat of copper?

1 Analyze **List the knowns and the unknown.**

KNOWNS	UNKNOWN
$m_{Cu} = 95.4\ g$	$C_{Cu} = ?\ J/(g\cdot°C)$
$T_f = 48.0°C$	
$T_i = 25.0°C$	
$q = 849\ J$	

2 Calculate **Solve for the unknown.** Use the known values and the definition of specific heat.

Start with the equation for specific heat.

$$C_{Cu} = \frac{q}{m_{Cu} \times \Delta T}$$

Find ΔT in units of °C.

$$\Delta T = T_f - T_i$$
$$\Delta T = 48.0°C - 25.0°C$$
$$\Delta T = 23.0°C$$

Substitute the knowns into the equation.

$$C_{Cu} = \frac{849\ J}{95.4\ g \times 23.0°C}$$

Solve the equation.

$$C_{Cu} = \frac{849\ J}{2194\ g\cdot°C} = 0.387\ J/(g\cdot°C)$$

When the denominator has multiple parts, multiply the parts of the denominator first. Then, divide the numerator by your answer.

3 Evaluate **Does the result make sense?** Remember that liquid water has a specific heat of 4.18 J/(g·°C). Metals have specific heats lower than water. Thus the calculated value of 0.387 J/(g·°C) for copper seems reasonable.

Practice Problems

4. When 435 J of heat is added to 3.4 g of olive oil at 21°C, the temperature increases to 85°C. What is the specific heat of the olive oil?

1 Analyze List the knowns and the unknown.

2 Calculate Solve for the unknown.

3 Evaluate Does the result make sense?

KNOWNS	UNKNOWN
$m_{olive\ oil}$ = 3.4 g	$C_{olive\ oil}$ = ? J/(g·°C)
T_f = 85°C	
T_i = 21°C	
q = 435J	

5. A chunk of silver has a heat capacity of 42.8 J/°C and a mass of 181 g. Calculate the specific heat of silver.

KNOWNS	UNKNOWN
m_{Ag} =	C_{Ag} = ? J/(g·°C)
$q/\Delta T$ =	

6. A 1.55 g piece of stainless steel absorbs 141 J of heat when its temperature increases by 178°C. What is the specific heat of the stainless steel?

7. Challenge How much heat is required to raise the temperature of 250.0 g of mercury 52°C? The specific heat of mercury is 0.14 J/(g·°C).

17.1 LessonCheck

Key Concept Check

8. Describe What happens to the energy of the universe during a chemical or physical process?

9. Review What are the ways that energy changes can occur?

10. List What two factors affect the heat capacity of an object?

Vocabulary Check

Choose a highlighted term from the lesson to complete the sentence correctly.

11. The heat needed to raise the temperature of a substance by 1°C is its __________.

Think Critically

12. Classify On a cold night you use an electric blanket to warm your body. Describe the direction of heat flow. Is this process endothermic or exothermic?

CHEMISTRY & YOU

13. Air has a smaller specific heat than water. Why does lava cool more quickly in water than in an equal mass of air? (Hint: See page 530.)

BIGIDEA MATTER AND ENERGY

14. How is the energy of the universe conserved during the combustion of gasoline in a car engine?

17.2 Measuring and Expressing Enthalpy Changes

CHEMISTRY & YOU

Q: How can you measure the amount of heat released when a match burns? When you light a match, heat is released to the surroundings. In addition to describing the direction of heat flow, you may also want to determine the quantity of heat that is transferred. Using specific heat allows you to measure heat flow in chemical and physical processes.

Key Questions

How can you measure the change in enthalpy of a reaction?

How can you express the enthalpy change for a reaction in a chemical equation?

BUILD Vocabulary

calorimetry the measurement of the heat flow into or out of a system during chemical or physical processes

enthalpy (*H*) an expression of the heat flow of a system at constant pressure

SUFFIXES

The suffix *-metry* means measurement. Calorimetry is the measurement of energy, which is sometimes reported in units of calories.

Calorimetry

In an endothermic process, the heat absorbed by the system equals the heat released by its surroundings. In an exothermic process, the heat released by a system equals the heat absorbed by its surroundings. Heat that is absorbed or released during many chemical reactions can be measured.

The technique used to measure heat absorbed or released is called calorimetry. **Calorimetry** is the measurement of the heat flow into or out of a system during chemical and physical processes.

Enthalpy Most chemical reactions and physical changes carried out in the laboratory are open to the atmosphere. The pressure from the atmosphere does not change. So the calorimetry measurement takes place at constant pressure. The **enthalpy** (*H*) of a system is an expression of the heat flow of the system at constant pressure.

The heat absorbed or released by a reaction at constant pressure is the same as the change in enthalpy, symbolized as ΔH. The value of ΔH of a reaction can be found by measuring the heat flow of the reaction at constant pressure. This textbook uses the terms *heat* and *enthalpy change* to mean the same thing because the reactions presented occur at constant pressure. In other words, $q = \Delta H$.

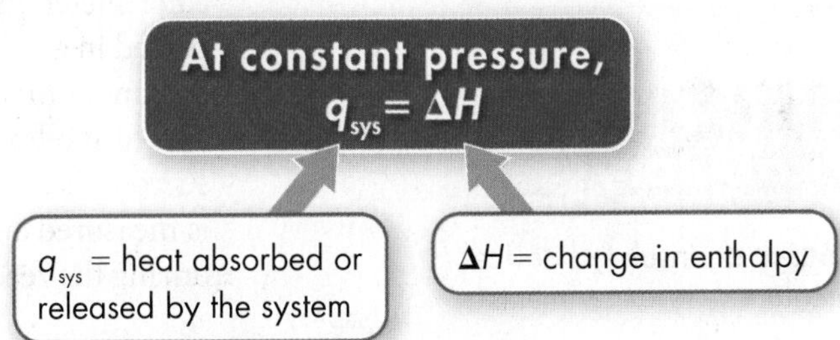

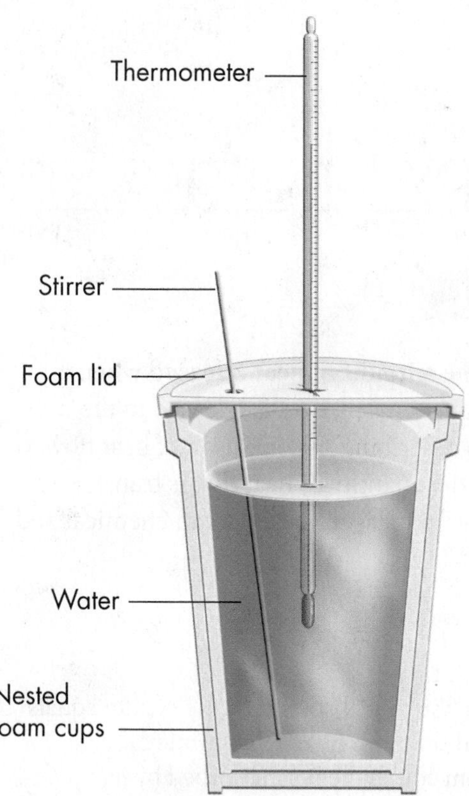

Constant Pressure Calorimeter A foam cup can be used as a simple calorimeter. A thermometer records the temperature change as chemicals react in water.

Measuring Heat Flow Calorimetry experiments can be performed at constant pressure or constant volume. The insulated device used in these experiments is called a **calorimeter.** Two types of calorimeters are described below.

▶ **Constant Pressure Calorimeters** The heat flows for many chemical reactions can be measured in a constant pressure calorimeter. Foam cups can be used as simple calorimeters like the one shown in the figure to the left. To carry out a constant pressure calorimetry experiment, dissolve the reacting chemicals (the system) in known volumes of water (the surroundings). Measure the initial temperature of each solution, and mix the solutions in the foam cup. After the reaction is complete, measure the final temperature of the solution in the cup. Then, you can calculate the heat absorbed or released by the surroundings (q_{surr}). To do this, use the equation for specific heat, the initial and final temperatures, and the heat capacity of water.

The heat absorbed by the surroundings is equal to, but has the opposite sign of, the heat released by the system. In other words, $q_{sys} = -q_{surr}$. Likewise, the heat released by the surroundings is equal to, but has the opposite sign of, the heat absorbed by the system. So the enthalpy change for the reaction (ΔH) can be written as follows:

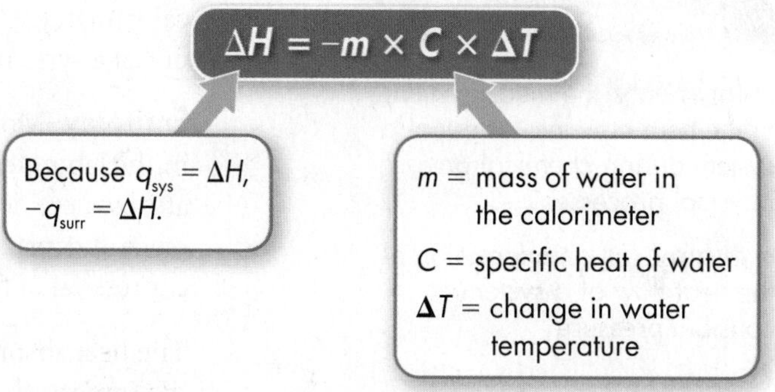

$\Delta H = -m \times C \times \Delta T$
Because $q_{sys} = \Delta H$, $-q_{surr} = \Delta H$.
m = mass of water in the calorimeter
C = specific heat of water
ΔT = change in water temperature

The sign of ΔH is positive for an endothermic reaction and negative for an exothermic reaction.

▶ **Constant Volume Calorimeters** Calorimetry experiments at constant volume are performed in a tool called a bomb calorimeter. In a bomb calorimeter, a sample of a compound is placed in a constant-volume chamber (the bomb). The sample is put under high pressure and burned in the presence of oxygen. The heat released during combustion warms water that surrounds the container. The temperature increase of the water is measured and used to calculate the quantity of heat released during the reaction.

Key Question How can you measure the change in enthalpy of a reaction? **The value of ΔH can be found by measuring the heat flow of the reaction at constant pressure.**

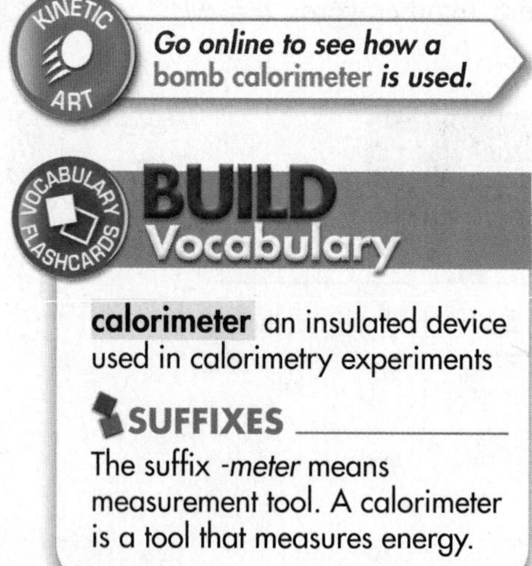

calorimeter an insulated device used in calorimetry experiments

SUFFIXES

The suffix *-meter* means measurement tool. A calorimeter is a tool that measures energy.

Enthalpy Change in a Calorimetry Experiment

When 25.0 mL of water containing 0.025 mol HCl at 25.0°C is mixed with 25.0 mL of water containing 0.025 mol NaOH at 25.0°C in a calorimeter, the temperature of the solution increases to 32.0°C. What is the enthalpy change (in kJ)? Assume the densities of the solutions are 1.00 g/mL and the final volume is 50.0 mL.

❶ Analyze List the knowns and the unknown.

KNOWNS	UNKNOWN
$C_{water} = 4.18\ J/(g·°C)$	$\Delta H = ?\ kJ$
$V_{final} = V_{HCl} + V_{NaOH}$ $= 25.0\ mL + 25.0\ mL$ $= 50.0\ mL$	
$T_i = 25.0°C$	
$T_f = 32.0°C$	
$density_{solution} = 1.00\ g/mL$	

❷ Calculate Solve for the unknown. Use dimensional analysis to find the mass of the water. Then calculate ΔT.

Write the enthalpy change equation.

$$\Delta H = -(m \times C \times \Delta T)$$

Use the density of water to calculate the mass of the water.

$$density = \frac{m}{V} \text{ so } m = V \times density$$

$$m_{water} = 50.0\ \cancel{mL} \times \frac{1.00\ g}{1\ \cancel{mL}} = 50.0\ g$$

Now, calculate ΔT.

$$\Delta T = T_f - T_i = 32.0°C - 25.0°C = 7.0°C$$

Substitute the known values into the equation to find ΔH.

$$\Delta H = -(50.0\ \cancel{g})(4.18\ J/(\cancel{g}·\cancel{°C}))(7.0\cancel{°C})$$
$$= -1500\ J$$

Convert the answer to the desired units using a conversion factor.

$$\Delta H = -1500\ \cancel{J} \times \frac{1\ kJ}{1000\ \cancel{J}} = -1.5\ kJ$$

Hint: Use the relationship 1 kJ = 1000 J to convert your answer from J to kJ.

❸ Evaluate Does the result make sense? The temperature of the solution increases, so the reaction is exothermic. For exothermic reactions, ΔH is negative. About 4 J of heat raises the temperature of 1 g of water 1°C, so 200 J of heat is required to raise 50 g of water 1°C. About 1400 J, or 1.4 kJ, are needed to raise the temperature of 50 g of water 7°C. This estimate is very close to the calculated value of −1.5 kJ for ΔH.

BUILD Math Skills

Algebraic Equations You can check that you've set up and solved your problem correctly by looking at units. Start by setting up the algebraic equation. Substitute the value and unit for each variable. Without calculating the numbers, just solve the equation for the units. If your solution ends in the units you want to find, your setup is correct. If not, revise your setup.

Practice Problems

15. When 50.0 mL of water containing 0.50 mol HCl at 22.5°C is mixed with 50.0 mL of water containing 0.50 mol NaOH at 22.5°C in a calorimeter, the temperature of the solution increases to 26.0°C. How much heat (in kJ) is released by this reaction?

Hint: Use the density of water to find the mass of the water. Then, substitute this value into the equation to find ΔH.

❶ **Analyze** **List the knowns and the unknown.**

❷ **Calculate** **Solve for the unknown.**

❸ **Evaluate** **Does the result make sense?**

KNOWNS	UNKNOWN
$C_{water} = 4.18\ J/(g\cdot°C)$	$\Delta H = ?\ kJ$
$V_{final} = V_{HCl} + V_{NaOH} = 50.0\ mL + 50.0\ mL = 100.0\ mL$	
$T_i = 22.5°C$	
$T_f = 26.0°C$	
$density_{solution} = 1.00\ g/mL$	

16. A sample of water containing 0.25 mol NaOH is mixed with a sample of water containing 1 mol H_3PO_4. The initial temperature of the solution is 21.7°C, and the final temperature of the solution is 25.5°C. The enthalpy change is −5.0 kJ. What is the total mass of the sample?

KNOWNS	UNKNOWN
$C_{water} =$	$m = ?\ g$
$\Delta H =$	
$T_i =$	
$T_f =$	

17. Challenge A small pebble is heated and placed in a foam cup calorimeter containing 25.0 mL of water at 25.0°C. The water reaches a maximum temperature of 26.4°C. How many joules of heat are released by the pebble?

Thermochemical Equations

The concrete in the photo below is a mixture of cement, water, and other materials. Cement contains calcium oxide and when it is mixed with water, the mixture becomes warm. This exothermic reaction produces calcium hydroxide, the main ingredient in concrete. In a chemical equation, the enthalpy change for the reaction can be written as either a reactant or a product. In the equation describing the exothermic reaction of calcium oxide and water, the enthalpy change is considered a product.

$$CaO(s) + H_2O(l) \longrightarrow Ca(OH)_2(s) + 65.2 \text{ kJ}$$

A chemical equation that includes the enthalpy change is called a **thermochemical equation.** You must include the physical states of the products and reactants in the thermochemical equation. Notice in the chemical equation above that each product and reactant is shown with its physical state in parentheses.

Heats of Reaction The **heat of reaction** is the enthalpy change for a chemical reaction exactly as it is written. Heats of reaction are reported as ΔH. ΔH is equal to the heat flow at a constant standard pressure of 101.3 kPa (1 atm).

▶ **Exothermic Processes** For exothermic processes, ΔH is negative. The reaction above is exothermic, so the heat of reaction, or ΔH, is -65.2 kJ. The graph below shows the enthalpy change of this exothermic process. In exothermic processes, the chemical potential energy of the reactants is higher than the chemical potential energy of the products.

BUILD Vocabulary

thermochemical equation a chemical equation that includes the change in enthalpy

heat of reaction the enthalpy change for a chemical equation exactly as it is written

ROOT WORDS

The root word *thermo-* refers to heat and temperature. So a thermochemical equation is an equation that shows both the heat and substances in a reaction.

BUILD Understanding

Compare/Contrast Table
Endothermic and exothermic reactions are both chemical processes. How are they different?

Exothermic Process Calcium oxide is one of the components of cement. The reaction of calcium oxide and water is an exothermic process because heat is released to the surroundings.

Enthalpy (H)

Reactants

$CaO(s) + H_2O(l)$

Energy is released
$\Delta H = -65.2$ kJ

Product

$Ca(OH)_2(s)$

Products

$Na_2CO_3(s) + H_2O(l) + CO_2(g)$

Enthalpy (H)

Energy is absorbed

$\Delta H = 85$ kJ

Reactant

$2NaHCO_3(s)$

Endothermic Process Muffin batter often contains baking soda, also known as sodium bicarbonate. The decomposition of sodium bicarbonate is an endothermic process.

▶ **Endothermic Processes** The system absorbs heat from the surroundings during endothermic processes, so ΔH is positive. The chemical potential energy of the products is higher than the chemical potential energy of the reactants. For example, baking soda (sodium bicarbonate) decomposes when it is heated. The carbon dioxide released in the reaction causes muffins such as the ones above to rise while baking. This process is endothermic, so the heat absorbed is considered to be a reactant.

$$2NaHCO_3(s) + 85\text{ kJ} \longrightarrow Na_2CO_3(s) + H_2O(l) + CO_2(g)$$

An enthalpy change problem is similar to a stoichiometry problem. The amount of heat released or absorbed during a reaction depends on the number of moles of the reactants. During this reaction, 2 mol sodium bicarbonate require 85 kJ of heat to decompose. So 4 mol sodium bicarbonate require twice as much heat, or 170 kJ, to decompose.

heat of combustion the heat of reaction for the complete burning of 1 mol of a substance

RELATED WORDS

The heat of combustion is a type of heat of reaction. Look back at the heat of reaction explanation earlier in this lesson.

Heats of Combustion The **heat of combustion** is the heat of reaction for the complete burning of 1 mol of a substance. Think about the combustion of methane (CH_4). This is an exothermic reaction.

$$CH_4(g) + 2O_2(g) \longrightarrow CO_2(g) + 2H_2O(l) + 890\text{ kJ}$$

You can also write a thermochemical equation as follows:

$$CH_4(g) + 2O_2(g) \longrightarrow CO_2(g) + 2H_2O(l) \qquad \Delta H = -890\text{ kJ}$$

Burning 1 mol of methane releases 890 kJ of heat. The heat of combustion (ΔH) for this reaction is -890 kJ per mol of methane burned.

Heats of combustion are reported as the enthalpy changes when the reactions are carried out at constant standard pressure and temperature.

Key Question How can you express the enthalpy change for a reaction in a chemical equation? **A thermochemical equation is a chemical equation that includes the enthalpy change for a reaction as a product or reactant.**

Sample Problem 17.4

Using the Heat of Reaction to Calculate Enthalpy Change

Decomposition is one type of chemical reaction. In decomposition, a reactant breaks down (decomposes) into other substances. Calculate the amount of heat (in kJ) required to decompose 2.24 mol $NaHCO_3(s)$.

$$2NaHCO_3(s) + 85\text{ kJ} \longrightarrow Na_2CO_3(s) + H_2O(l) + CO_2(g)$$

1 Analyze List the knowns and the unknown.

KNOWNS	UNKNOWN
amount of $NaHCO_3$ = 2.24 mol	ΔH = ? kJ for 2.24 mol
ΔH = 85 kJ for 2 mol	

2 Calculate Solve for the unknown. Write a conversion factor that relates kilojoules of heat to moles of $NaHCO_3$. Use the conversion factor to determine ΔH.

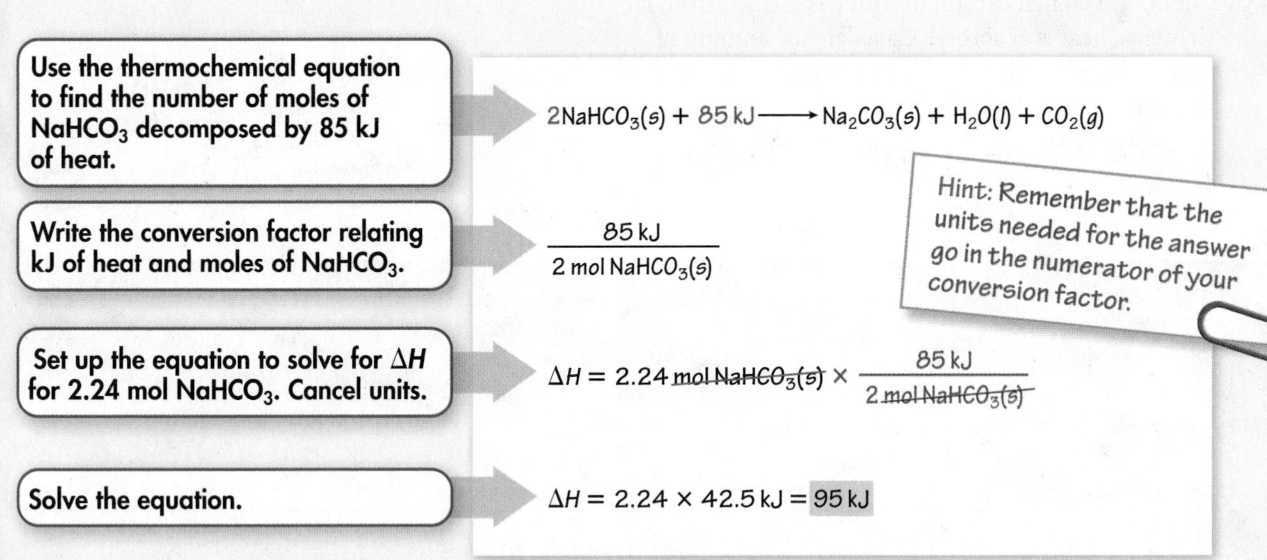

Use the thermochemical equation to find the number of moles of $NaHCO_3$ decomposed by 85 kJ of heat.

$$2NaHCO_3(s) + 85\text{ kJ} \longrightarrow Na_2CO_3(s) + H_2O(l) + CO_2(g)$$

Write the conversion factor relating kJ of heat and moles of $NaHCO_3$.

$$\frac{85\text{ kJ}}{2\text{ mol }NaHCO_3(s)}$$

Set up the equation to solve for ΔH for 2.24 mol $NaHCO_3$. Cancel units.

$$\Delta H = 2.24\ \cancel{\text{mol }NaHCO_3(s)} \times \frac{85\text{ kJ}}{2\ \cancel{\text{mol }NaHCO_3(s)}}$$

Solve the equation.

$$\Delta H = 2.24 \times 42.5\text{ kJ} = 95\text{ kJ}$$

Hint: Remember that the units needed for the answer go in the numerator of your conversion factor.

3 Evaluate Does the result make sense? The 85 kJ in the thermochemical equation refers to the decomposition of 2 mol $NaHCO_3(s)$. Therefore, the decomposition of 2.24 mol should absorb more heat than 85 kJ. The answer of 95 kJ is consistent with this estimate.

Practice Problems

18. The production of iron and carbon dioxide from iron(III) oxide and carbon monoxide is an exothermic reaction. How many kilojoules of heat are produced when 3.40 mol Fe_2O_3 reacts with an excess of CO?

$$Fe_2O_3(s) + 3CO(g) \longrightarrow 2Fe(s) + 3CO_2(g) + 26.3 \text{ kJ}$$

1 Analyze List the knowns and the unknown.

2 Calculate Solve for the unknown.

3 Evaluate Does the result make sense?

KNOWNS	UNKNOWN
amount of Fe_2O_3 = 3.40 mol	ΔH = ? kJ for 3.40 mol
ΔH = −26.3 kJ for 1 mol	

19. Water is decomposed to yield hydrogen gas and oxygen gas in an endothermic reaction. How many kilojoules of heat are required to decompose 114 mol H_2O?

$$H_2O(l) \longrightarrow H_2(g) + \tfrac{1}{2}O_2(g) \quad \Delta H = 285.8 \text{ kJ}$$

KNOWNS	UNKNOWN
amount of H_2O =	ΔH = ? kJ for 114 mol
ΔH =	

20. Challenge When carbon disulfide is formed from its elements, heat is absorbed. Calculate the amount of heat (in kJ) absorbed when 5.66 g of carbon disulfide is formed.

$$C(s) + 2S(s) \longrightarrow CS_2(l) \qquad \Delta H = 89.3 \text{ kJ}$$

Hint: To do Problem 20, first convert from mass of CS_2 to moles of CS_2.

17.2 LessonCheck

Key Concept Check

21. Describe How can you determine the value of ΔH of a reaction?

22. Review How are enthalpy changes expressed in chemical equations?

Vocabulary Check
Choose a highlighted term from the lesson to complete the sentence correctly.

23. ________ describes the heat flow of a system at constant pressure.

24. A ________ can be used to measure the heat released during a chemical reaction.

Think Critically

25. Describe When 2 mol of solid magnesium (Mg) combines with 1 mol of oxygen gas (O_2), 2 mol of solid magnesium oxide (MgO) are formed and 1204 kJ of heat are released. Write the thermochemical equation for this reaction.

26. What type of calorimeter would you use to measure the heat released when a match burns? Describe the experiment and how you would calculate the heat released. (Hint: See page 534.)

17.3 Heat in Changes of State

CHEMISTRY & YOU

Q: Why does sweating help cool you off? An athlete can burn a lot of calories during a game. These calories are used to do work or are released as heat. When your body heats up, you start to sweat. The evaporation of sweat is your body's way of cooling itself to a normal temperature.

Key Questions

What is the relationship between molar heat of fusion and molar heat of solidification?

What is the relationship between molar heat of vaporization and molar heat of condensation?

What thermochemical changes can occur when a solution forms?

BUILD Vocabulary

molar heat of fusion (ΔH_{fus}) the heat absorbed by 1 mol of a solid substance as it melts to a liquid at a constant temperature

MULTIPLE MEANINGS

The word *fusion* can mean melting, as in the molar heat of fusion, or combining together, as in jazz fusion—a combination of jazz and rock music styles.

Heats of Fusion and Solidification

What happens if you place an ice cube on a table in a warm room? The ice cube is the system, and the table and air around it are the surroundings. The ice absorbs heat from its surroundings and begins to melt. The heat does not raise the temperature of the liquid water right away, however. The temperature of the ice and the liquid water produced remains at 0°C until all of the ice has melted.

The same situation happens in a glass of ice water. If you measure the temperature with a thermometer, you will find that the temperature of the ice water remains at 0°C as long as both the water and ice are in the glass. Even though you might think that ice is colder than liquid water, both states of water exist at 0°C.

Heat of Fusion All solids absorb heat as they melt to become liquids. The gain of heat causes a change of state instead of a change in temperature. Whenever a gain or loss of heat causes a change of state, the temperature of the substance remains constant. The heat absorbed by 1 mol of a solid substance as it melts to a liquid at a constant temperature is the **molar heat of fusion** (ΔH_{fus}).

The melting of 1 mol of ice at 0°C to 1 mol of liquid water at 0°C requires the absorption of 6.01 kJ of heat. This quantity of heat is the molar heat of fusion of water. If more than 6.01 kJ of heat is added to 1 mol of ice, the temperature of the liquid water produced will rise above 0°C.

$$H_2O(s) \longrightarrow H_2O(l) \qquad \Delta H_{fus} = 6.01 \text{ kJ/mol}$$

Melting, or fusion, is an endothermic process because heat is absorbed by the system. Because fusion is endothermic, molar heats of fusion are reported as positive values.

Using the Heat of Fusion in Phase-Change Calculations

How many grams of ice at 0°C will melt if 2.25 kJ of heat are added? The thermochemical equation is

$$H_2O(s) + 6.01 \text{ kJ/mol} \longrightarrow H_2O(l)$$

❶ Analyze List the knowns and the unknown.

KNOWNS	UNKNOWN
$\Delta H_{fus} = 6.01$ kJ/mol	$m_{ice} = ?$ g
$\Delta H = 2.25$ kJ	
$T_i = 0°C$	
$T_f = 0°C$	

❷ Calculate Solve for the unknown. Find the number of moles of ice that can be melted by the addition of 2.25 kJ of heat. Convert moles of ice to grams of ice.

Start by expressing ΔH_{fus} as a conversion factor.

$$\frac{1 \text{ mol } H_2O(s)}{6.01 \text{ kJ}}$$

Express the molar mass of ice as a conversion factor.

$$\frac{18.0 \text{ g } H_2O(s)}{1 \text{ mol } H_2O(s)}$$

Multiply the known enthalpy change by the conversion factors.

$$m_{ice} = 2.25 \cancel{\text{kJ}} \times \frac{1 \cancel{\text{mol } H_2O(s)}}{6.01 \cancel{\text{kJ}}} \times \frac{18.0 \text{ g } H_2O(s)}{1 \cancel{\text{mol } H_2O(s)}}$$

Solve the equation.

$$m_{ice} = 2.25 \times 0.1664 \times 18.0 \text{ g } H_2O(s)$$
$$= 6.74 \text{ g } H_2O(s)$$

6.74 grams of ice will melt.

Cancel all like units before performing any mathematical operations.

❸ Evaluate Does the result make sense? To melt 1 mol of ice, 6.01 kJ of energy are required. Only about one third of this amount of heat (roughly 2 kJ) is available, so only about one-third mol of ice, or 18.0 g/3 = 6 g, should melt. This estimate is close to the calculated answer.

BUILD Math Skills

Significant Figures Unlike measurements, constants have unlimited significant figures. When a constant is multiplied by a measurement, the answer will have the same number of sig figs as the measurement. The example below shows what happens when you multiply a measurement with 5 sig figs by a constant such as a conversion factor.

$$\frac{1000\ g}{1\ kg} \times \underline{2.6924}\ kg = \underline{2692.4}\ g$$

Constants have unlimited sig figs.

The answer should have 5 sig figs.

Go to your Chemistry Skills and Math Workbook for more practice problems.

Practice Problems

27. How many grams of ice at 0°C could be melted by the addition of 0.400 kJ of heat?

1 Analyze **List the knowns and unknown.**

2 Calculate **Solve for the unknown.**

3 Evaluate **Does the result make sense?**

KNOWNS	UNKNOWN
ΔH_{fus} = 6.01 kJ/mol	m_{ice} = ? g
ΔH = 0.400 kJ	

28. Calculate the quantity of heat absorbed when 3.5 mol of ice melts at 0°C.

KNOWNS	UNKNOWN
ΔH_{fus} =	ΔH = ? kJ
amount of ice =	

29. A cup contains a sample of ice. When 8.50 g of water are added to the cup, the cup contains a total of 12.0 g. How many kilojoules of heat are required to melt the ice in the cup at 0°C?

30. Challenge How many kilojoules of heat are required to melt a 50.0 g popsicle at 0°C? Assume the popsicle has the same molar mass and heat of fusion as water.

Quick Lab

Purpose To estimate the heat of fusion of ice

Materials

- 100 mL graduated cylinder
- hot tap water
- foam cup
- thermometer
- ice

Heat of Fusion of Ice

Procedure

1. Fill the graduated cylinder with hot tap water. Let stand for 1 minute. Pour the water into the sink.

2. Measure 70 mL of hot water. Pour the water into the foam cup. Measure the temperature of the water.

3. Add an ice cube to the cup of water. Gently swirl the cup. Measure the temperature of the water as soon as the ice cube has completely melted.

4. Pour the water into the graduated cylinder and measure the volume.

Analyze and Conclude

1. Calculate Determine the mass of the ice. (Hint: Use the values for the increase in the volume of water and the density of water for this calculation.) Convert this mass into moles.

2. Calculate Determine the heat transferred from the water to the ice using the mass of the hot water, the specific heat of liquid water, and the change in temperature.

3. Calculate Determine ΔH_{fus} of ice (kJ/mol) by dividing the heat transferred from the water by the moles of ice melted.

4. Perform Error Analysis Compare your experimental value of ΔH_{fus} of ice with the accepted value of 6.01 kJ/mol. Account for any error.

BUILD Vocabulary

molar heat of solidification (ΔH_{solid}) the heat released when 1 mol of a liquid substance solidifies at a constant temperature

RELATED WORD FORMS

The word *molar* is the adjective form of the word *mole*. For example, *molar mass* means the mass of one mole.

Heat of Solidification The molar heat of fusion is the heat absorbed by a substance as it changes from solid to liquid. The substance releases the same amount of heat as it changes from a liquid to a solid. The **molar heat of solidification** (ΔH_{solid}) is the heat released when 1 mol of a liquid substance solidifies at a constant temperature.

The amount of heat absorbed by a melting solid is equal to the amount of heat released when the liquid solidifies. This relationship can be expressed mathematically as $\Delta H_{fus} = -\Delta H_{solid}$. So the conversion of 1 mol of liquid water at 0°C to 1 mol of ice at 0°C releases 6.01 kJ of heat. This quantity of heat is the molar heat of solidification of water.

$$H_2O(l) \longrightarrow H_2O(s) \qquad \Delta H_{solid} = -6.01 \text{ kJ/mol}$$

Key Question What is the relationship between molar heat of fusion and molar heat of solidification? **The quantity of heat absorbed by a melting solid is exactly the same as the quantity of heat released when the liquid solidifies.**

Heats of Vaporization and Condensation

Fusion and solidification are reverse processes that occur at a substance's melting point. Similarly, vaporization and condensation are reverse processes that occur at a substance's boiling point. Vaporization occurs when a liquid that absorbs heat at its boiling point becomes a vapor. Condensation occurs when a vapor releases heat at its boiling point, becoming a liquid. Like fusion and solidification, vaporization and condensation also have molar heats associated with them.

Heat of Vaporization The amount of heat required to vaporize 1 mol of a given liquid at a constant temperature is called its **molar heat of vaporization** (ΔH_{vap}). The table below lists the molar heats of vaporization for several substances at their normal boiling points.

Heats of Physical Change		
Substance	**ΔH_{fus} (kJ/mol)**	**ΔH_{vap} (kJ/mol)**
Ammonia (NH_3)	5.66	23.3
Ethanol (C_2H_6O)	4.93	38.6
Hydrogen (H_2)	0.12	0.90
Oxygen (O_2)	0.44	6.82
Water (H_2O)	6.01	40.7

The molar heat of vaporization of water is 40.7 kJ/mol. It takes 40.7 kJ of energy to convert 1 mol of liquid water to 1 mol of water vapor at the normal boiling point. The normal boiling point of water is 100°C at 101.3 kPa.

$$H_2O(l) \longrightarrow H_2O(g) \qquad \Delta H_{vap} = 40.7 \text{ kJ/mol}$$

Heat of Condensation Diethyl ether ($C_4H_{10}O$) has a boiling point of 34.6°C and a molar heat of vaporization (ΔH_{vap}) of 26.5 kJ/mol. If liquid diethyl ether is poured into a beaker on a warm, humid day, the ether will absorb heat from the beaker walls and evaporate rapidly. If the beaker loses enough heat, the water vapor in the air may condense on the beaker and freeze. The frozen water vapor forms a coating of frost on the outside of the beaker.

$$C_4H_{10}O(l) \longrightarrow C_4H_{10}O(g) \qquad \Delta H_{vap} = 26.5 \text{ kJ/mol}$$

Condensation is the opposite of vaporization. When a vapor condenses, heat is released. The amount of heat released when 1 mol of a vapor condenses at its normal boiling point is called the **molar heat of condensation** (ΔH_{cond}). The quantity of heat absorbed by a vaporizing liquid is exactly the same as the quantity of heat released when the vapor condenses; that is, $\Delta H_{vap} = -\Delta H_{cond}$.

molar heat of vaporization (ΔH_{vap}) the heat absorbed when 1 mol of a liquid substance vaporizes at a constant temperature

molar heat of condensation (ΔH_{cond}) the heat released when 1 mol of a vapor condenses at its normal boiling point

Vaporization, or changing state from a liquid to a gas, is also called evaporation.

Changes in State Enthalpy changes accompany changes in state. Fusion and vaporization are endothermic processes. Solidification and condensation are exothermic processes.

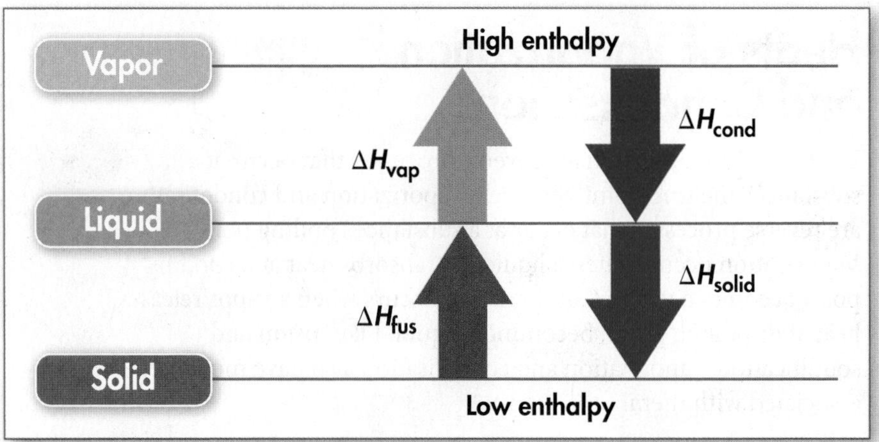

The figure above shows the relationships between the heats of vaporization, condensation, solidification, and fusion. Processes that absorb energy are represented by the arrows that point up. Processes that release energy are represented by the arrows that point down.

Look at the graph below. You should be able to see the enthalpy changes that occur as water changes from ice to liquid and then to vapor. On the graph, you should be able to see trends in the temperature and energy needs during changes of state. The large values for ΔH_{vap} and ΔH_{cond} are the reason hot vapors such as steam can be very dangerous. When steam touches your skin, the heat of condensation can cause a scalding burn.

Key Question What is the relationship between molar heat of vaporization and molar heat of condensation? **The quantity of heat absorbed by a vaporizing liquid is exactly the same as the quantity of heat released when the vapor condenses.**

Heating Curve for Water
A heating curve shows the enthalpy changes that take place during phase changes. Where the curve is flat, heat added does not cause a rise in temperature. Rather, the heat gained or lost is used to change the state of water.
Go to your Chemistry Skills and Math Workbook to practice interpreting graphs.

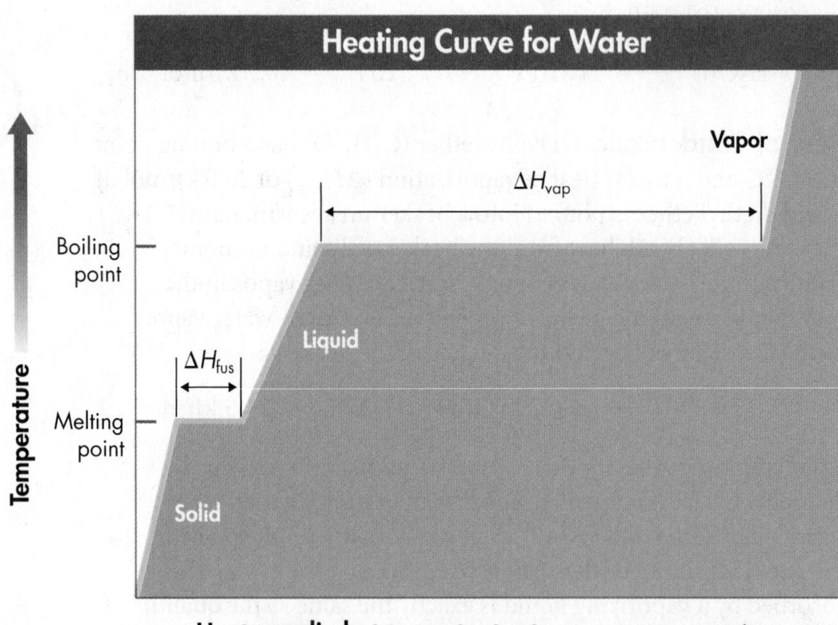

CHEMISTRY TUTORIAL

Sample Problem 17.6

Using the Heat of Vaporization in Phase-Change Calculations

How much heat (in kJ) is absorbed when 24.8 g $H_2O(l)$ at 100°C and 101.3 kPa is converted to $H_2O(g)$ at 100°C and 101.3 kPa?

1 Analyze List the knowns and the unknown.

KNOWNS	UNKNOWN
initial conditions = 100°C and 101.3 kPa	$\Delta H = ?$ kJ
final conditions = 100°C and 101.3 kPa	
$\Delta H_{vap} = 40.7$ kJ/mol	
$m_{water} = 24.8$ g	

2 Calculate Solve for the unknown. First, convert grams of water to moles of water. Then, find the amount of heat that is absorbed when the liquid water is converted to steam.

Start by expressing the molar mass of water as a conversion factor.

$$\frac{1 \text{ mol } H_2O(l)}{18.0 \text{ g } H_2O(l)}$$

Hint: Use the thermochemical equation $H_2O(l) + 40.7 \text{kJ/mol} \longrightarrow H_2O(g)$

Express ΔH_{vap} as a conversion factor.

$$\frac{40.7 \text{ kJ}}{1 \text{ mol } H_2O(l)}$$

Multiply the mass of water in grams by the conversion factors.

$$\Delta H = 24.8 \, \cancel{\text{g } H_2O(l)} \times \frac{1 \, \cancel{\text{mol } H_2O(l)}}{18.0 \, \cancel{\text{g } H_2O(l)}} \times \frac{40.7 \text{ kJ}}{1 \, \cancel{\text{mol } H_2O(l)}}$$

Solve the equation.

$$\Delta H = 24.8 \times 0.0556 \times 40.7 \text{ kJ} = 56.1 \text{ kJ}$$

56.1 kJ of heat are absorbed.

3 Evaluate Does the result make sense? Knowing that the molar mass of water is 18.0 g/mol, you can estimate that 24.8 g $H_2O(l)$ is somewhat less than 1.5 mol H_2O. The calculated enthalpy change should be a little less than 1.5 $\cancel{\text{mol}} \times 40$ kJ/$\cancel{\text{mol}} = 60$ kJ, and it is.

BUILD Math Skills

Multiplication and Division

When you multiply two measurements or constants you must multiply both the numerical values and the units. Look at the following examples of multiplying units:

$$\text{kJ} \times \text{g} = \text{kJ}\cdot\text{g}$$

$$\frac{\text{kJ}}{\cancel{\text{mol}}} \times \cancel{\text{mol}} = \text{kJ}$$

Check your answer by looking at its units. Does your answer have the units you expected? If not, make sure the problem is set up correctly and has the correct conversion factors.

Go to your Chemistry Skills and Math Workbook for more practice problems.

Practice Problems

31. How much heat is absorbed when 63.7 g $H_2O(l)$ at 100°C and 101.3 kPa is converted to $H_2O(g)$ at 100°C? Express your answer in kJ.

1 Analyze **List the knowns and the unknown.**

2 Calculate **Solve for the unknown.**

3 Evaluate **Does the result make sense?**

KNOWNS	UNKNOWN
ΔH_{vap} = 40.7 kJ/mol	ΔH = ? kJ
m_{water} = 63.7 g	

32. How many kilojoules of heat are required to vaporize 50.0 g of ethanol, C_2H_6O? The boiling point of ethanol is 78.3°C. Its molar heat of vaporization is 38.6 kJ/mol.

KNOWNS	UNKNOWN
ΔH_{vap} =	ΔH = ? kJ
$m_{ethanol}$ =	

33. Calculate the enthalpy change when 0.800 mol of ammonia gas condenses at its normal boiling point. Its molar heat of vaporization is 23.3 kJ/mol.

When choosing a conversion factor, be sure to choose the one that cancels out units.

34. Challenge How many kilojoules of heat are absorbed when 0.46 g of chloroethane (C_2H_5Cl, bp 12.3°C) vaporizes at its normal boiling point? The molar heat of vaporization of chloroethane is 24.7 kJ/mol.

Heat of Solution

If you have ever used a hot pack or a cold pack, then you have felt the enthalpy changes that happen when a solute dissolves in a solvent. The hot or cold pack changes temperature due to the formation of a solution. The solution process either releases or absorbs heat.

The enthalpy change that occurs when 1 mol of a substance dissolves is the **molar heat of solution** (ΔH_{soln}). For example, when 1 mol of sodium hydroxide, NaOH(*s*), is dissolved in water, the solution can become so hot that it steams. The heat from this process is released as the sodium ions and the hydroxide ions interact with the water. The temperature of the solution increases, releasing 44.5 kJ of heat as the molar heat of solution.

$$NaOH(s) \longrightarrow Na^+(aq) + OH^-(aq)$$

$$\Delta H_{soln} = -44.5 \text{ kJ/mol}$$

One example of an exothermic solution process is a hot pack. In a hot pack, calcium chloride, $CaCl_2(s)$, mixes with water and releases heat. The dissolution of ammonium nitrate, $NH_4NO_3(s)$, is an example of an endothermic process. When ammonium nitrate dissolves in water, the solution becomes so cold that frost may form on the outside of the container. Cold packs contain solid ammonium nitrate crystals and water. Once the solute dissolves in the solvent, the pack becomes cold. In this case, the solution process absorbs energy from the surroundings.

Key Question What thermochemical changes can occur when a solution forms? **During the formation of a solution, heat is either released or absorbed.**

molar heat of solution (ΔH_{soln}) the enthalpy change that occurs when 1 mol of a substance dissolves

A solution is made up of a solvent and a solute. The solvent is the substance that dissolves the solute.

17.3 LessonCheck

Key Concept Check

35. **Describe** How does the molar heat of fusion of a substance compare to its molar heat of solidification?

36. **Describe** How does the molar heat of vaporization of a substance compare to its molar heat of condensation?

37. **Identify** What enthalpy changes occur when a solute dissolves in a solvent?

Vocabulary Check *Choose a highlighted term from the lesson to complete the sentence correctly.*

38. The amount of heat absorbed by 1 mol of substance when it melts is called the ________.

Think Critically

39. **Calculate** How many kilojoules of heat are released when 25.0 g of NaOH(*s*) is dissolved in water?

CHEMISTRY & YOU

40. Explain why the evaporation of sweat off your body helps to cool you off. (Hint: See page 545.)

BIGIDEA MATTER AND ENERGY

41. Use what you know about hydrogen bonding to explain why water has such a large heat of vaporization. (Hint: Review Lesson 8.4.)

17.4 Calculating Heats of Reaction

Q: How much heat is released when a diamond changes into graphite? Diamonds are gemstones made up of carbon. Over a time period of millions and millions of years, diamond will break down into graphite, which is another form of carbon. How then can you determine the enthalpy change for the reaction?

Key Question

How can you calculate the heat of reaction when it cannot be directly measured?

Hess's law of heat summation if you add two or more thermochemical equations to give a final equation, then you also add the heats of reaction to give the final heat of reaction.

ROOT WORDS

Summation comes from the Latin word *summare,* which means "to add up."

Hess's Law

Sometimes it is hard to measure the enthalpy change for a reaction. The reaction might take place too slowly to measure the enthalpy change, or the reaction might be an intermediate step in a series of reactions. Fortunately, it is possible to determine a heat of reaction indirectly using Hess's law of heat summation. **Hess's law of heat summation** states that if you add two or more thermochemical equations to give a final equation, then you can also add the heats of reaction to give the final heat of reaction. In other words, Hess's law allows you to use known heats of reaction to determine an unknown heat of reaction.

Using Laws of Summation Laws of summation in chemistry can be compared to everyday events. Suppose you are wrapping a present and you have two lengths of paper. The first piece of paper is 50 cm long, and the second piece of paper is 25 cm long. When you lay the pieces end-to-end you have a length of paper that is 75 cm long. This is an example of summation.

Laws of summation allow you to use known values to solve for unknown values. The figure below shows how the law of summation works. The length of A is the summation of the lengths of B and C. If you know the lengths of B and C, you can use addition to solve for the length of A. Also, if you know the length of A and C, you can use subtraction to solve for the length of B.

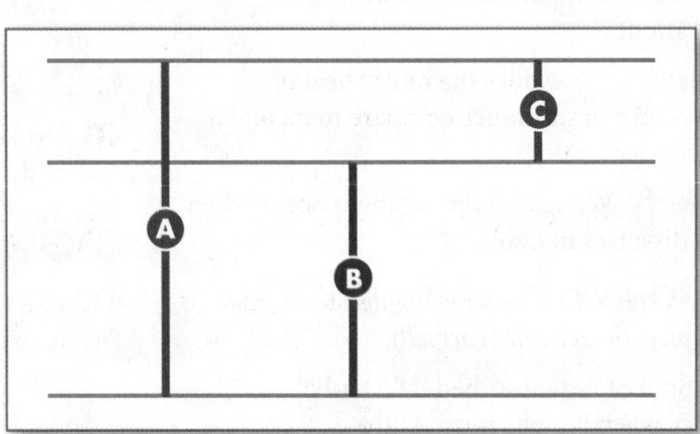

Laws of Summation
Using laws of summation, you can see that the lengths of B and C add up to the length of A.

Using Hess's Law The figure below shows the conversion of diamond to graphite. The overall reaction can be represented by the following reaction:

$$C(s, \text{diamond}) \longrightarrow C(s, \text{graphite})$$

The enthalpy change for this reaction cannot be measured directly. However, you can use Hess's law to find the enthalpy change for the conversion by using these reactions:

Equation 1 $C(s, \text{graphite}) + O_2(g) \longrightarrow CO_2(g) \quad \Delta H = -393.5 \text{ kJ}$

Equation 2 $C(s, \text{diamond}) + O_2(g) \longrightarrow CO_2(g) \quad \Delta H = -395.4 \text{ kJ}$

Notice that the reactions are combustion reactions, so the equations include $O_2(g)$ and $CO_2(g)$. These substances are not part of your original equation. That's okay, because you will cancel out both of these substances through your summation.

Now, write equation 1 in reverse to give:

Equation 3 $CO_2(g) \longrightarrow C(s, \text{graphite}) + O_2(g) \quad \Delta H = 393.5 \text{ kJ}$

When you write a reverse reaction, you must also change the sign of ΔH. Follow along below. If you add equations 2 and 3, you get the equation for the conversion of diamond to graphite. The $CO_2(g)$ and $O_2(g)$ terms on both sides of the summed equations cancel because they appear on opposite sides of the reaction arrows. Then add the values of ΔH for equations 2 and 3 together. The heat of reaction for the conversion of diamond to graphite is -1.9 kJ.

$$\begin{array}{ll} C(s, \text{diamond}) + \cancel{O_2(g)} \longrightarrow \cancel{CO_2(g)} & \Delta H = -395.4 \text{ kJ} \\ \cancel{CO_2(g)} \longrightarrow C(s, \text{graphite}) + \cancel{O_2(g)} & \Delta H = 393.5 \text{ kJ} \\ \hline C(s, \text{diamond}) \longrightarrow C(s, \text{graphite}) & \Delta H = -1.9 \text{ kJ} \end{array}$$

Key Question How can you calculate the heat of reaction when it cannot be directly measured? **Hess's law allows you to determine the heat of reaction indirectly using other known heats of reaction.**

Conversion of Diamond to Graphite Hess's law is used to determine the enthalpy change for the conversion of diamond to graphite.

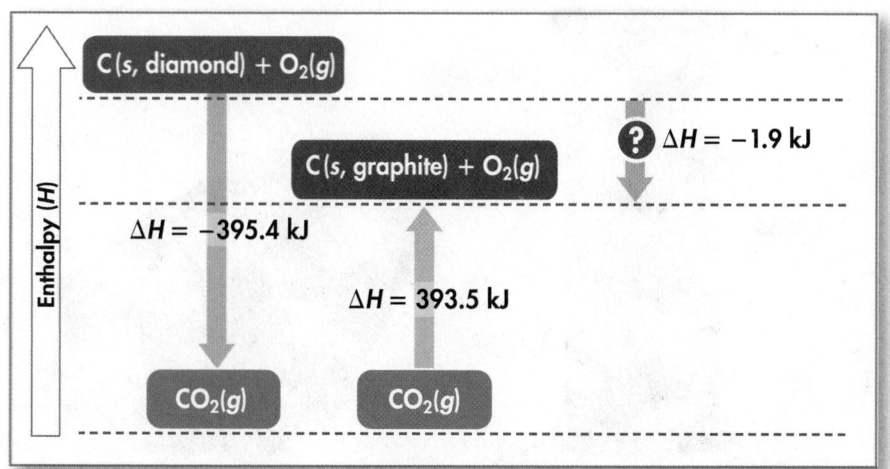

BUILD Connections

In a softball or baseball game, the number of runs scored is recorded per inning. A team's total score is found by adding the score for each inning. This is an example of summation.

Go online to see how Hess's law is used. KINETIC ART

standard heat of formation (ΔH_f°) the change in enthalpy that accompanies the formation of 1 mol of a compound from its elements with all substances in their standard states

USING PRIOR KNOWLEDGE

You have seen the word *standard* used many times in this chapter. The word indicates that the substance is in its standard condition.

Standard Heats of Formation

Enthalpy changes during a process depend on the conditions during the process. To compare enthalpy changes, scientists specify a common set of conditions. These conditions are called the standard state. Standard state conditions refer to the stable form of a substance at 25°C and 101.3 kPa (1 atm). The **standard heat of formation** (ΔH_f°) of a compound is the change in enthalpy that accompanies the formation of 1 mol of a compound from its elements with all substances in their standard states.

Standard Heat of Free Elements The ΔH_f° of a free element in its standard state has been assigned a value of zero. The elements hydrogen, nitrogen, oxygen, fluorine, chlorine, bromine, and iodine occur naturally as diatomic molecules. So $\Delta H_f^\circ = 0$ kJ/mol for $H_2(g)$, $N_2(g)$, $O_2(g)$, $F_2(g)$, $Cl_2(g)$, $Br_2(l)$, and $I_2(s)$.

Other elements are not diatomic molecules in their standard form. The standard form of carbon is solid graphite C(*s*, graphite). So $\Delta H_f^\circ = 0$ kJ/mol for the graphite form of carbon.

Standard Heat of Reactions Standard heats of formation provide another way to find a heat of reaction indirectly. When a reaction occurs at standard conditions, you can use standard heats of formation to calculate the heat of reaction. Such an enthalpy change is called the standard heat of reaction (ΔH°). You can calculate the standard heat of reaction using the equation:

$$\Delta H^\circ = \Delta H_f^\circ \text{ (products)} - \Delta H_f^\circ \text{ (reactants)}$$

ΔH_f° (products) means all of the standard heats of formation of the products added together.

ΔH_f° (reactants) means all the standard heats of formation of the reactants added together.

The standard heats of formation of substances are known values. Some standard heats of formation can be found in a table later in this section. Remember that for all elements in their standard state, $\Delta H_f^\circ = 0$ kJ/mol.

Bromine

Graphite

Bromine and Graphite
The standard heat of formations (ΔH_f°) for diatomic liquid bromine, $Br_2(l)$ and solid graphite, C(*s*, graphite) is 0.

Sample Problem 17.7

Calculating the Standard Heat of Reaction

What is the standard heat of reaction ($\Delta H°$) for the reaction of $CO(g)$ with $O_2(g)$ to form $CO_2(g)$? Use the following standard heats of formation:

$$\Delta H_f°CO(g) = -110.5 \text{ kJ/mol}$$
$$\Delta H_f°O_2(g) = 0 \text{ kJ/mol}$$
$$\Delta H_f°CO_2(g) = -393.5 \text{ kJ/mol}$$

1 Analyze List the knowns and the unknown.

KNOWNS	UNKNOWN
$\Delta H_f°CO(g) = -110.5$ kJ/mol	$\Delta H° = ?$ kJ
$\Delta H_f°O_2(g) = 0$ kJ/mol	
$\Delta H_f°CO_2(g) = -393.5$ kJ/mol	

2 Calculate Solve for the unknown. Write the balanced chemical equation. Then determine $\Delta H°$ using the standard heats of formation of the reactants and products.

First, write the equation for the standard heat of reaction.

$$\Delta H° = \Delta H_f°(\text{products}) - \Delta H_f°(\text{reactants})$$

Then, write the balanced equation.

$$2CO(g) + O_2(g) \longrightarrow 2CO_2(g)$$

Identify the reactants and products and the amount of each.

Reactants: $2CO(g)$ and $1O_2(g)$
Products: $2CO_2(g)$

Find the total $\Delta H_f°$ of all of the reactants.

$$\Delta H_f°(\text{reactants}) = [2 \text{ mol } CO(g) \times \Delta H_f°CO(g)] + [1 \text{ mol } O_2(g) \times \Delta H_f°O_2(g)]$$

$$= \left[2 \cancel{\text{mol } CO(g)} \times \frac{-110.5 \text{ kJ}}{1 \cancel{\text{mol } CO(g)}}\right] + \left[1 \cancel{\text{mol } O_2(g)} \times \frac{0 \text{ kJ}}{1 \cancel{\text{mol } O_2(g)}}\right]$$

$$= -221.0 \text{ kJ}$$

Find $\Delta H_f°$ of the product in a similar way.

$$\Delta H_f°(\text{products}) = 2 \text{ mol } CO_2(g) \times \Delta H_f°CO_2(g)$$

$$= 2 \cancel{\text{mol } CO_2(g)} \times \frac{-393.5 \text{ kJ}}{1 \cancel{\text{mol } CO_2(g)}}$$

$$= -787.0 \text{ kJ}$$

Now, substitute the knowns into the equation and solve.

$$\Delta H° = (-787.0 \text{ kJ}) - (-221.0 \text{ kJ})$$
$$= -566.0 \text{ kJ}$$

3 Evaluate Does the result make sense? The $\Delta H°$ is negative, so the reaction is exothermic. This outcome makes sense because combustion reactions always release heat.

BUILD Math Skills

Arithmetic Operations The order of operations of any math problem is as follows: Parentheses, Exponents, Multiplication, Division, Addition, and Subtraction. You may have been given this mnemonic device to remember this order:

Please excuse my dear aunt Sally.

Parentheses
Exponents
Multiplication
Division
Addition
Subtraction

In the problems below, remember the order of operations. You must multiply the number of moles of a substance by the heat of formation first. Then subtract the sum of $\Delta H_f°$(reactants) from the sum of $\Delta H_f°$(products).

Go to your Chemistry Skills and Math Workbook for more practice problems.

Practice Problems

42. Calculate $\Delta H°$ for the following reaction:

$$Br_2(g) \longrightarrow Br_2(l)$$

❶ Analyze **List the knowns and the unknown.**

❷ Calculate **Solve for the unknown.**

❸ Evaluate **Does the result make sense?**

KNOWNS	UNKNOWN
$\Delta H_f°Br_2(g) = 30.91$ kJ/mol	$\Delta H° = ?$ kJ
$\Delta H_f°Br_2(l) = 0$ kJ/mol	

43. What is the standard heat of reaction ($\Delta H°$) for the decomposition of hydrogen peroxide?

$$2H_2O_2(l) \longrightarrow 2H_2O(l) + O_2(g)$$

KNOWNS	UNKNOWN
$\Delta H_f°H_2O_2(l) =$	$\Delta H° = ?$ kJ
$\Delta H_f°H_2O(l) =$	
$\Delta H_f°O_2(g) =$	

44. What is the standard heat of reaction ($\Delta H°$) for the formation of carbon monoxide from carbon(s, graphite) and diatomic oxygen(g)?

$$2C(s, \text{graphite}) + O_2(g) \longrightarrow 2CO(g)$$

Hint: Find the standard heats of formation in the table on the next page.

45. Challenge What is the standard heat of reaction ($\Delta H°$) for the formation of $NO_2(g)$ from $NO(g)$ and $O_2(g)$?

Standard Heats of Formation ($\Delta H_f°$) at 25°C and 101.3 kPa					
Substance	**$\Delta H_f°$ (kJ/mol)**	**Substance**	**$\Delta H_f°$ (kJ/mol)**	**Substance**	**$\Delta H_f°$ (kJ/mol)**
$Al_2O_3(s)$	−1676.0	$F_2(g)$	0.0	$NO(g)$	90.37
$Br_2(g)$	30.91	$Fe(s)$	0.0	$NO_2(g)$	33.85
$Br_2(l)$	0.0	$Fe_2O_3(s)$	−822.1	$NaCl(s)$	−411.2
C(s, diamond)	1.9	$H_2(g)$	0.0	$O_2(g)$	0.0
C(s, graphite)	0.0	$H_2O(g)$	−241.8	$O_3(g)$	142.0
$CH_4(g)$	−74.86	$H_2O(l)$	−285.8	P(s, white)	0.0
$CO(g)$	−110.5	$H_2O_2(l)$	−187.8	P(s, red)	−18.4
$CO_2(g)$	−393.5	$I_2(g)$	62.4	S(s, rhombic)	0.0
$CaCO_3(s)$	−1207.0	$I_2(s)$	0.0	S(s, monoclinic)	0.30
$CaO(s)$	−635.1	$N_2(g)$	0.0	$SO_2(g)$	−296.8
$Cl_2(g)$	0.0	$NH_3(g)$	−46.19	$SO_3(g)$	−395.7

The table above shows standard heats of formation for several common substances. The heats of formation for other substances can be found in reference materials or through an online search.

Key Question How can you calculate the heat of reaction when it cannot be measured directly? **For a reaction that happens at standard conditions, you can calculate the heat of reaction by using the standard heats of formation.**

17.4 LessonCheck

Key Concept Check

46. Describe What are two ways the heat of reaction can be determined when it cannot be directly measured?

Think Critically

47. Calculate What is the enthalpy change (ΔH) in kJ for the following reaction?

$$2Al(s) + Fe_2O_3(s) \longrightarrow 2Fe(s) + Al_2O_3(s)$$

Use the enthalpy changes for the combustion of aluminum and iron:

$$2Al(s) + \tfrac{3}{2}O_2(g) \longrightarrow Al_2O_3(s) \quad \Delta H = -1676.0\text{ kJ}$$
$$2Fe(s) + \tfrac{3}{2}O_2(g) \longrightarrow Fe_2O_3(s) \quad \Delta H = -822.1\text{ kJ}$$

48. Explain How can you calculate the standard heat of reaction?

CHEMISTRY & YOU

49. How can you determine ΔH for the conversion of diamond to graphite without performing the reaction? (Hint: See page 551.)

BIGIDEA MATTER AND ENERGY

50. What is the standard heat of reaction ($\Delta H°$) for the decomposition of hydrogen peroxide?

$$2H_2O_2(l) \longrightarrow 2H_2O(l) + O_2(g)$$

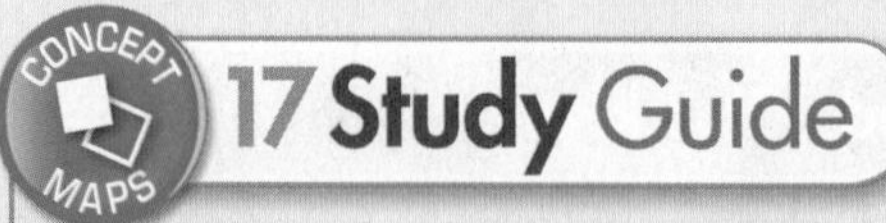

17 Study Guide

BIGIDEA MATTER AND ENERGY

During a chemical or physical process, the energy of the universe is conserved. If energy is absorbed by the system, the same amount of energy is released by the surroundings. If energy is released by the system, the same amount of energy is absorbed by the surroundings. The heat of a reaction or process can be determined experimentally through calorimetry. The heat of reaction can also be calculated by using the known heats of reaction of two or more thermochemical equations. The heat of reaction can also be calculated by using the standard heats of formation of the reactants and products.

17.1 The Flow of Energy

During any chemical or physical process, the energy of the universe stays the same.

Energy changes can occur as either heat transfer or work, or a combination of both.

Heat capacity is affected by the mass and composition of an object.

- thermochemistry (526)
- system (526) • surroundings (526)
- law of conservation of energy (526)
- chemical potential energy (526) • heat (527)
- endothermic process (527)
- exothermic process (527)
- heat capacity (529) • specific heat (530)

Key Equation

$$C = \frac{q}{m \times \Delta T}$$

17.2 Measuring and Expressing Enthalpy Changes

The value of ΔH can be found by measuring the heat flow of the reaction at constant pressure.

A thermochemical equation is a chemical equation that includes the enthalpy change for a reaction as a product or reactant.

- calorimetry (533)
- enthalpy (533)
- calorimeter (534)
- thermochemical equation (537)
- heat of reaction (537)
- heat of combustion (538)

Key Equation

$$\Delta H = -m \times C \times \Delta T$$

17.3 Heat in Changes of State

The quantity of heat absorbed by a melting solid is exactly the same as the quantity of heat released when the liquid solidifies.

The quantity of heat absorbed by a vaporizing liquid is exactly the same as the quantity of heat released when the vapor condenses.

During the formation of a solution, heat is either released or absorbed.

- molar heat of fusion (541)
- molar heat of solidification (544)
- molar heat of vaporization (545)
- molar heat of condensation (545)
- molar heat of solution (549)

17.4 Calculating Heats of Reaction

Hess's law allows you to determine the heat of reaction indirectly using other known heats of reaction.

For a reaction that happens at standard conditions, you can calculate the heat of reaction by using the standard heats of formation.

- Hess's law of heat summation (550)
- standard heat of formation (552)

Key Equation

$$\Delta H^\circ = \Delta H_f^\circ(\text{products}) - \Delta H_f^\circ(\text{reactants})$$

Math Tune-Up: Calculating Enthalpy Changes

Problem	❶ Analyze	❷ Calculate	❸ Evaluate
When 75.0 mL of water containing 0.100 mol HCl at 21.0°C is added to 75.0 mL of water containing 0.100 mol NaOH at 21.0°C in a foam cup calorimeter, the temperature of the solution increases to 29.6°C. Calculate the enthalpy change (in kJ) during this reaction.	Knowns: $C_{water} = 4.18\ J/(g \cdot °C)$ $V_{final} = V_{HCl} + V_{NaOH}$ $= 75.0\ mL + 75.0\ mL$ $= 150.0\ mL$ $\Delta T = T_f - T_i$ $= 29.6°C - 21.0°C$ $= 8.6°C$ $density_{solution} = 1.00\ g/mL$ Unknown: $\Delta H = ?\ kJ$ Use $\Delta H = -q_{surr}$ $= -m \times C \times \Delta T$	Calculate the mass of water. $m_{water} = 150.0\ \cancel{mL} \times \frac{1.00\ g}{1\ \cancel{mL}}$ $= 150.0\ g$ Use the values for m_{water}, C_{water}, and ΔT to calculate ΔH. $\Delta H = -(150.0\ \cancel{g})(4.18\ J/(\cancel{g} \cdot \cancel{°C}))$ $\times (8.6\cancel{°C})$ $= -5400\ J$ $\Delta H = -5.4\ kJ$	About 4 J of heat raises the temperature of 1 g of water 1°C, so 600 J of heat is required to raise the temperature of 150 g of water 1°C. To heat 150 g of water 9°C requires about 5400 J, or 5.4 kJ.
How much heat is absorbed when 54.9 g $H_2O(l)$ at 100°C and 101.3 kPa is converted to $H_2O(g)$ at 100°C?	Knowns: Initial and final conditions are 100°C and 101.3 kPa mass of liquid water converted to steam = 54.9 g $\Delta H_{vap} = 40.7\ kJ/mol$ Unknown: $\Delta H = ?\ kJ$ Refer to the thermochemical equation $H_2O(l) + 40.7\ kJ \longrightarrow H_2O(g)$	The required conversion factors come from the molar mass of water and ΔH_{vap}. $\frac{1\ mol\ H_2O(l)}{18.0\ g\ H_2O(l)}$ and $\frac{40.7\ kJ}{1\ mol\ H_2O(l)}$ Multiply the mass of water by the conversion factors. $\Delta H = 54.9\ \cancel{g\ H_2O(l)} \times \frac{1\ \cancel{mol\ H_2O(l)}}{18.0\ \cancel{g\ H_2O(l)}}$ $\times \frac{40.7\ kJ}{1\ \cancel{mol\ H_2O(l)}}$ $\Delta H = 124\ kJ$	The molar mass of water is 18.0 g/mol, so 54.9 g $H_2O(l)$ is about 3 mol H_2O. The calculated enthalpy change should be about 3 $\cancel{mol}$ × 40 kJ/$\cancel{mol}$ = 120 kJ, and it is.
What is the standard heat of reaction ($\Delta H°$) for the reaction of $SO_2(g)$ with $O_2(g)$ to form $SO_3(g)$?	Knowns: $\Delta H_f° SO_2(g) = -296.8\ kJ/mol$ $\Delta H_f° O_2(g) = 0\ kJ/mol$ $\Delta H_f° SO_3(g) = -395.7\ kJ/mol$ Unknown: $\Delta H° = ?\ kJ$ Use the standard heats of formation for the reactants and products to calculate $\Delta H°$. $\Delta H° = \Delta H_f°(products) - \Delta H_f°(reactants)$	Write the balanced equation. $2SO_2(g) + O_2(g) \longrightarrow 2SO_3(g)$ Find $\Delta H_f°$ of the reactants. $\Delta H_f°(reactants) = 2\ \cancel{mol\ SO_2(g)} \times \frac{-296.8\ kJ}{1\ \cancel{mol\ SO_2(g)}} + 0\ kJ = -593.6\ kJ$ Find $\Delta H_f°$ of the product. $\Delta H_f°(product) = 2\ \cancel{mol\ SO_3(g)} \times \frac{-395.7\ kJ}{1\ \cancel{mol\ SO_3(g)}} = -791.4\ kJ$ Calculate $\Delta H°$ for the reaction. $\Delta H° = (-791.4\ kJ) - (-593.6\ kJ)$ $\Delta H° = -197.8\ kJ$	The $\Delta H°$ is negative, so the reaction is exothermic. This makes sense because combustion reactions always release heat.

Note: For reactions in aqueous solutions, you can assume that the densities of the solutions are 1.00 g/mL.

Remember: The $\Delta H_f°$ of a free element in its standard state is 0 kJ/mol.

17 Assessment

★ Solutions appear in Appendix D

Lesson by Lesson

17.1 The Flow of Energy

51. Define *chemical potential energy.*

52. Why do you think it is important to define the system and the surroundings?

53. How do endothermic processes differ from exothermic processes?

★54. Two substances in a glass beaker chemically react, and the beaker becomes too hot to touch.

a. Is the reaction endothermic or exothermic?
b. If the two substances are defined as the system, what constitutes the surroundings?

★55. Classify these processes as endothermic or exothermic.

a. condensing steam
b. evaporating alcohol
c. burning alcohol

56. Describe the sign convention that is used when describing heat flow in a system.

57. What is the relationship between a calorie and a Calorie?

★58. Make the following conversions.

a. 8.50×10^2 cal to Calories
b. 444 cal to joules
c. 1.8 kJ to joules
d. 4.5×10^{-1} kJ to calories

59. What factors determine the heat capacity of an object?

★60. How much heat is required to raise the temperature of 400.0 g of silver 45°C?

17.2 Measuring and Expressing Enthalpy Changes

61. What is the function of a calorimeter?

62. What is the property that describes heat change at constant pressure?

63. What information is given in a thermochemical equation?

★64. The burning of magnesium is a highly exothermic reaction.

$$2Mg(s) + O_2(g) \longrightarrow 2MgO(s) + 1204 \text{ kJ}$$

How many kilojoules of heat are released when 0.75 mol of Mg burn in an excess of O_2?

65. Give the standard conditions for heat of combustion.

17.3 Heat in Changes of State

★66. Calculate the quantity of heat gained or lost in the following changes:

a. 0.44 mol of steam condenses at 100°C
b. 1.25 mol NaOH(*s*) dissolves in water

17.4 Calculating Heats of Reaction

67. Explain Hess's law of heat summation.

★68. A considerable amount of heat is required for the decomposition of aluminum oxide.

$$2Al_2O_3(s) \longrightarrow 4Al(s) + 3O_2(g)$$
$$\Delta H = 3352 \text{ kJ}$$

a. Find the enthalpy change for the formation of 1 mol of Al_2O_3 from its elements.
b. Is the reaction endothermic or exothermic?

★69. Calculate the enthalpy change for the formation of lead(IV) chloride by the reaction of lead(II) chloride with chlorine.

$$PbCl_2(s) + Cl_2(g) \longrightarrow PbCl_4(l)$$
$$\Delta H = ?$$

Use the following thermochemical equations:

$$Pb(s) + 2Cl_2(g) \longrightarrow PbCl_4(l)$$
$$\Delta H = -329.2 \text{ kJ}$$
$$Pb(s) + Cl_2(g) \longrightarrow PbCl_2(s)$$
$$\Delta H = -359.4 \text{ kJ}$$

Understand Concepts

*70. Equal masses of substance A and substance B absorb the same amount of heat. The temperature of substance A increases twice as much as the temperature of substance B. Which substance has the higher specific heat? Explain.

*71. Calculate the change in enthalpy (in kJ) for the following reactions using standard heats of formation (ΔH_f°):

a. $CH_4(g) + \frac{3}{2}O_2(g) \longrightarrow CO(g) + 2H_2O(l)$
b. $2CO(g) + O_2(g) \longrightarrow 2CO_2(g)$

72. The amounts of heat required to change different quantities of carbon tetrachloride, $CCl_4(l)$, into vapor are given in the table.

Mass of CCl_4	Heat	
(g)	(J)	(cal)
2.90	652	156
7.50	1689	404
17.0	3825	915
26.2	5894	1410
39.8	8945	2140
51.0	11453	2740

a. Graph the data, using heat (in cal) as the dependent variable.
b. What is the slope of the line?
c. The heat of vaporization of $CCl_4(l)$ is 53.8 cal/g. How does this value compare with the slope of the line?

*73. Find the enthalpy change for the formation of phosphorus pentachloride from its elements.

$$2P(s) + 5Cl_2(g) \longrightarrow 2PCl_5(s)$$

Use the following thermochemical equations:

$$PCl_5(s) \longrightarrow PCl_3(g) + Cl_2(g)$$

$$\Delta H = 156.5 \text{ kJ}$$

$$2P(s) + 3Cl_2(g) \longrightarrow 2PCl_3(g)$$

$$\Delta H = -574.0 \text{ kJ}$$

Think Critically

74. **Relate Cause and Effect** Your fingers quickly begin to feel cold when you touch an ice cube. What important thermochemical principle does this change illustrate?

*75. **Calculate** An ice cube with a mass of 40.0 g melts in water originally at 25.0°C.

a. How much heat does the ice cube absorb from the water when it melts? Report your answer in calories, kilocalories, and joules.
b. Calculate the number of grams of water that can be cooled to 0°C by the melting ice cube.

76. **Explain** Why is fusion an endothermic process, but freezing is an exothermic process?

*77. **Calculate** The sugar glucose ($C_6H_{12}O_6$) is an important nutrient for living organisms to meet their energy needs. The standard heat of formation (ΔH_f°) of glucose is −1260 kJ/mol. Calculate how much heat (in kJ) is released at standard conditions if 1 mol of glucose undergoes the following reaction:

$$C_6H_{12}O_6(s) + 6O_2(g) \longrightarrow 6CO_2(g) + 6H_2O(l)$$

FOUNDATIONS Wrap-Up

Observing Heat Flow

1. **Draw Conclusions** At the beginning of the chapter, you observed the temperature of a rubber band before and after stretching. Explain your observations.

Concept Check

Now that you're finished studying Chapter 17, answer these questions.

2. Define the system and surroundings of the rubber band experiment.
3. What happened to the energy of the universe during the experiment?
4. Which process is exothermic—the stretching of rubber or the relaxing of rubber?

Write About Science

78. **Explain** Use the concept of heat capacity to explain why on a sunny day, the concrete deck around an outdoor swimming pool becomes hot, while the water stays cool.

79. **Compare** Why is a burn from steam potentially far more serious than a burn from very hot water?

CHEMYSTERY

Fighting Frost

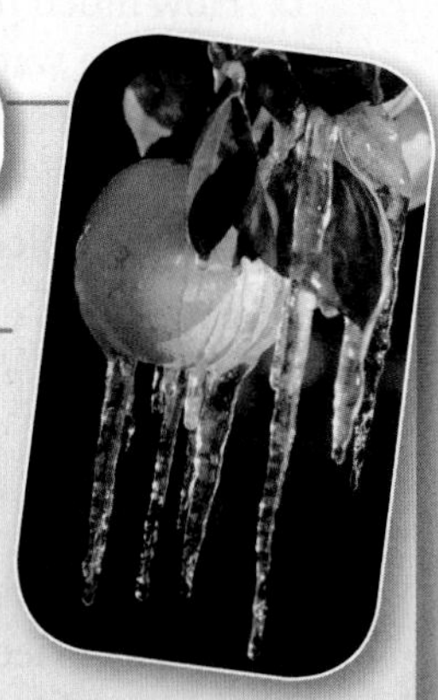

If the temperature of the branches, leaves, and fruit of a citrus tree falls below 0°C, severe damage can occur. When ice crystals form in the plant cells, water becomes unavailable to the plant tissues. This lack of fluids can kill a young tree. The fruit itself can also be damaged by frost. The juice vesicles inside the fruit rupture as ice crystals form within them. These ruptured vesicles cause the fruit to lose water and dry out. If fruit is not ready to harvest when frost is expected, citrus growers must find a way to protect their precious crops.

Spraying the trees with water throughout the duration of a frost is an effective way to prevent the trees and fruit from freezing. The water freezes directly on the branches, leaves, and fruit. Freezing is an exothermic process. As the water freezes, it releases heat and prevents the plant cells from reaching freezing temperatures.

80. **Apply Concepts** Identify the system and the surroundings when water freezes on a citrus fruit.

81. **Connect to the BIGIDEA** Explain, in terms of the law of conservation of energy, why the freezing of water on a citrus tree can cause the temperature of the tree to increase.

Cumulative Review

82. Write the correct chemical symbol for each element. (See Lesson 2.3 for help.)
    - **a.** chromium
    - **b.** copper
    - **c.** carbon

*83. Express the results of the following calculations with the correct number of significant figures. (See Lesson 3.1 for help.)
    - **a.** $6.723 \text{ m} \times 1.04 \text{ m}$
    - **b.** $8.934 \text{ g} + 0.2005 \text{ g} + 1.55 \text{ g}$
    - **c.** $864 \text{ m} \div 2.4 \text{ s}$

*84. When lightning flashes, nitrogen and oxygen combine to form nitrogen monoxide. The nitrogen monoxide reacts with oxygen to form nitrogen dioxide. Write equations for these two reactions. (See Lesson 11.1 for help.)

*85. A gas has a volume of 8.57 L at 273 K. What will be the volume at 355 K if its pressure does not change? (See Lesson 14.2 for help.)

Standardized Test Prep

For help with answering test questions, go to your Chemistry Skills and Math Workbook.

Select the choice that best answers each question or completes each statement.

Tips for Success

Eliminate Wrong Answers If you don't know which response is correct, start by eliminating those you know are wrong. If you can rule out some choices, you'll have fewer left to consider and you'll increase your chances of choosing the correct answer.

1. The ΔH_{fus} of ethanol (C_2H_6O) is 4.93 kJ/mol. How many kilojoules are required to melt 24.5 g of ethanol at its freezing point?
(A) 2.63 kJ **(C)** 9.27 kJ
(B) 4.97 kJ **(D)** 263 kJ

2. How much heat, in kilojoules, must be added to 178 g of liquid water to increase the temperature of the water by 5.0°C ?
(A) 890 kJ **(C)** 3.7 kJ
(B) 36 kJ **(D)** 0.093 kJ

3. The standard heat of formation of a free element in its standard state is always
(A) zero.
(B) positive.
(C) negative.
(D) higher for solids than for gases.

4. If ΔH for the reaction $2HgO(s) \longrightarrow 2Hg(l) + O_2(g)$ is 181.66 kJ, then ΔH for the reaction $Hg(l) + \frac{1}{2}O_2(g) \longrightarrow HgO(s)$ is
(A) 90.83 kJ. **(C)** −90.83 kJ.
(B) 181.66 kJ. **(D)** −181.66 kJ.

5. The specific heat capacity of ethanol is 10 times larger than the specific heat capacity of silver. A hot bar of silver with a mass of 55 g is dropped into an equal mass of cool alcohol. If the temperature of the silver bar drops 45°C, the temperature of the alcohol
(A) increases 45°C.
(B) decreases 4.5°C.
(C) increases 4.5°C.
(D) decreases 45°C.

6. Hydrogen gas and fluorine gas react to form hydrogen fluoride, HF. Calculate the enthalpy change (in kJ) for the conversion of 15.0 g of $H_2(g)$ to $HF(g)$ at constant pressure.

$$H_2(g) + F_2(g) \longrightarrow 2HF(g)$$
$$\Delta H = -536 \text{ kJ}$$

Use the graph and table to answer Questions 7–10. Assume 1.00 mol of each substance.

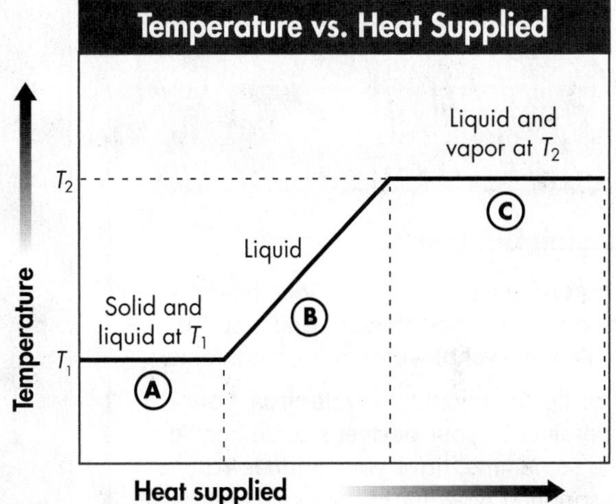

Substance	Freezing point (K)	ΔH_{fus} (kJ/mol)	Boiling point (K)	ΔH_{vap} (kJ/mol)
Ammonia	195.3	5.66	239.7	23.3
Benzene	278.7	9.87	353.3	30.8
Methanol	175.5	3.22	337.2	35.2
Neon	24.5	0.33	27.1	1.76

7. Calculate heat absorbed in region A for neon.

8. Calculate heat absorbed in region C for ammonia.

9. Calculate heat absorbed in region B for methanol (CH_4O). [specific heat = 2.53 J/(g·°C)]

10. Calculate heat absorbed in each region for benzene (C_6H_6). [specific heat = 1.74 J/(g·°C)]

If You Have Trouble With . . .

Question	1	2	3	4	5	6	7	8	9	10
See Lesson	17.3	17.1	17.4	17.4	17.1	17.2	17.3	17.3	17.3	17.3

18 Reaction Rates and Equilibrium

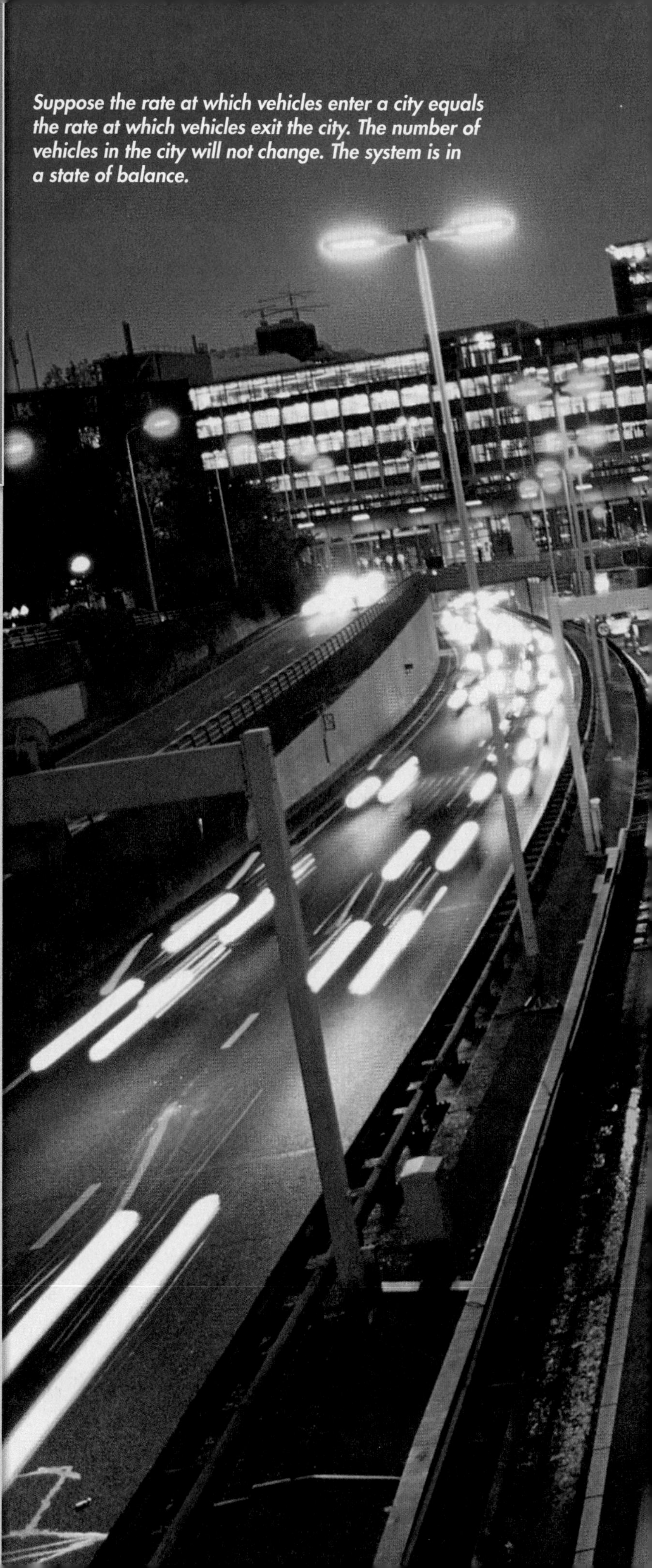

Suppose the rate at which vehicles enter a city equals the rate at which vehicles exit the city. The number of vehicles in the city will not change. The system is in a state of balance.

FOUNDATIONS for Learning

Changing but Constant

1. You and your partner will each have a small container of water and a spoon. Note the level of water in each container.
2. Transfer a spoonful of water from your container to your partner's container. At the same time, have your partner transfer a spoonful of water to your container.
3. Repeat Step 2 ten times.
4. Note the level of water in each container.

Form a Hypothesis Use your experience to explain how a system can change but still remain the same.

PearsonChem.com

Take a video field trip with Untamed Science to learn about the chemistry behind diabetes.

BIGIDEAS

- **REACTIONS**
- **MATTER AND ENERGY**

Essential Questions:

1. *How can the rate of a chemical reaction be controlled?*
2. *What is the role of energy in chemical reactions?*
3. *Why do some reactions occur naturally and others do not?*

CHEMYSTERY

Explosive Sugar

At a sugar refinery, sugar is treated until it is pure enough to sell to customers. Conveyor belts connect large storage towers to the packaging warehouse. In February 2008, workers at a refinery in Georgia heard a small explosion. The sound came from the spot where the conveyor belts entered the warehouse.

Five minutes later, a much larger explosion happened. This explosion destroyed the warehouse. The fire spread to the storage towers. Thirteen workers died, and dozens more were injured. It took 4 days for 232 firefighters to put out the fire in the warehouse. The fire in the towers took a few days longer to put out.

How did the first small explosion lead to the second, more destructive explosion?

▶ Connect to the **BIGIDEA** As you read about reaction rates, think about what could cause an explosion at a sugar refinery.

18.1 Rates of Reaction

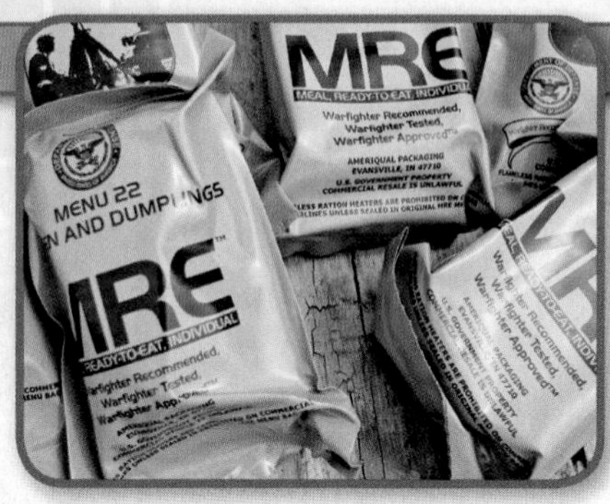

CHEMISTRY & YOU

Q: How can rusting be used to cook a meal? Sometimes, a soldier or hiker wants a hot meal but has no place to heat it. Rusting is a chemical change that produces heat. This change usually happens so slowly that the heat released could not be used to heat a meal. There are products that use the rusting of a mixture of iron powder, magnesium, and table salt to heat food. These products are known as Meals Ready to Eat, or MREs for short.

Key Questions

How is the rate of a chemical reaction expressed?

What four factors influence the rate of a chemical reaction?

Describing Reaction Rates

When you strike a match, a flame appears right away and the match burns quickly. Other reactions take place more slowly. For example, millions of years were needed for plants buried beneath Earth's surface to be changed to coal. These two examples show that the speed of chemical reactions can vary from very fast to very slow.

Describing Speed Speed is a familiar idea. In a race, speed decides the winner. The swimmers in the photo below are competing in a 100-meter race. You can use this equation to calculate the average speed for each swimmer:

$$\text{Average speed (m/s)} = \frac{\text{Distance (m)}}{\text{Time (s)}}$$

Each man swims the same distance (100 meters) in a different amount of time. The faster swimmer finishes the race in 54.5 seconds. His average speed is 100 m divided by 54.5 s, or 1.83 m/s. The slower swimmer takes 60.0 seconds to cover the same distance. His average speed is 100 m divided by 60.0 s, or 1.67 m/s. Both 1.83 m/s and 1.67 m/s are rates.

Describing Speed Speed is the distance traveled over a period of time. The average speed of a swimmer can be given in meters per second (m/s).

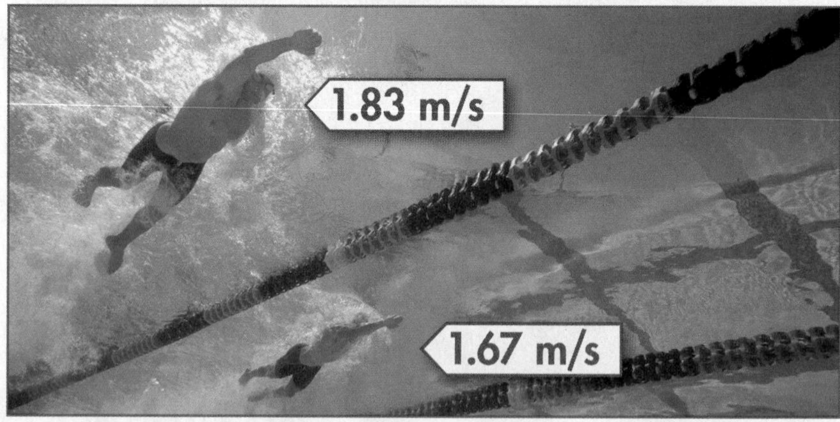

Rate of Change The height of a candle changes as the candle burns. The rate of burning depends on the compounds in the candle and the diameter of the candle.

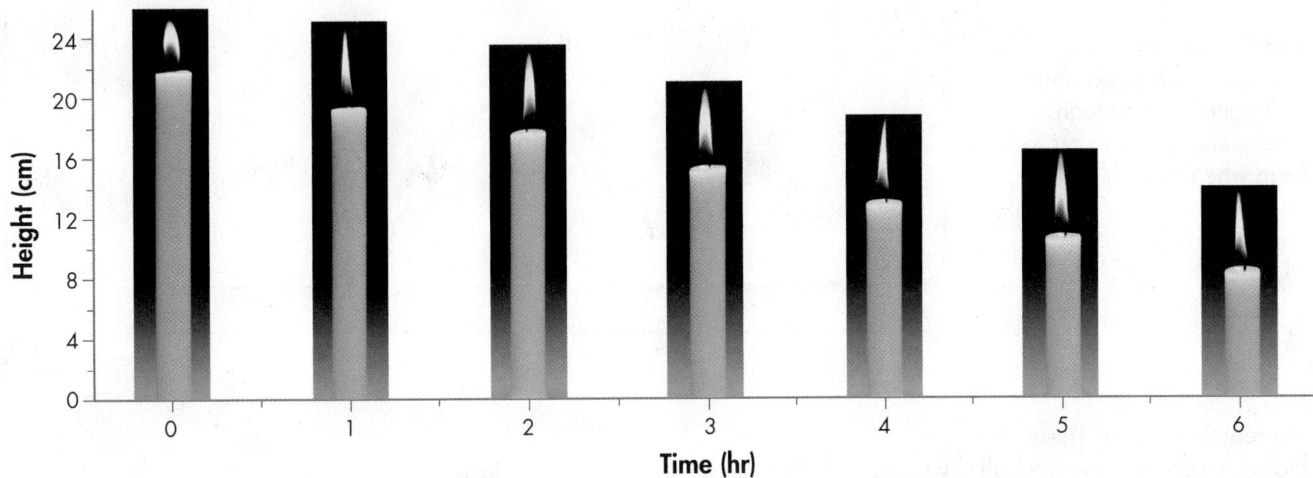

Rates of Change Speed is an example of a rate. A **rate** is a measure of how much something changes in a given amount of time. The graph above shows what happens to the height of a candle as it burns. The rate of burning is about 2.2 centimeters per hour. It would take about 10 hours for the candle to burn completely.

The rate of a chemical reaction, or the reaction rate, is usually given as the change in the amount of a reactant or a product over time. For example, a piece of iron has a mass of 55.8 g, which is 1 mol. One half of the iron turns to rust in one year. The rate at which the iron rusts is 0.5 mol/yr. This number is an average rate.

Reaction Progress The figure below shows the progress of a typical reaction. During the reaction, reactants are changed into products. The red squares stand for reactants. The blue circles stand for products. Look at the box on the far left. It shows the system just before the reaction begins. In the second box, the hand on the clock has moved, and some reactants have changed to products. In the box on the far right, almost all of the reactants have changed to products.

rate a measure of how much something changes in a given amount of time

MULTIPLE MEANINGS

A rate compares two quantities. Gas stations and grocery stores use a rate called *cost per unit.* For gasoline, the unit is a gallon. For potato salad, the unit is a pound. For rates of reaction, one unit is always time.

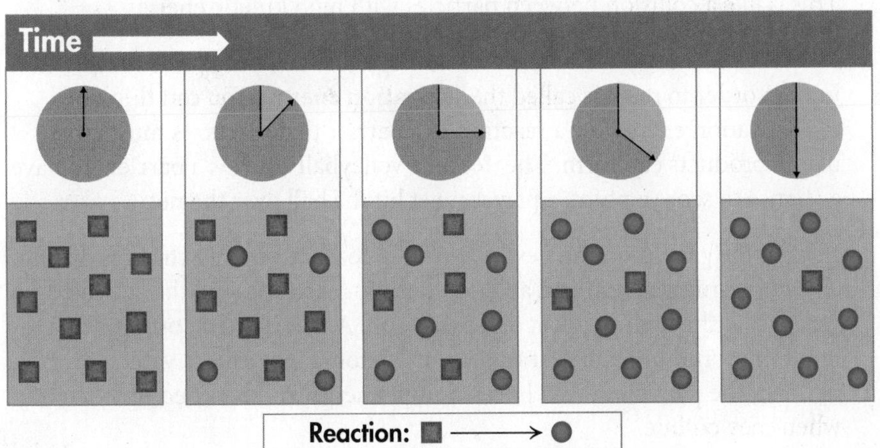

Reaction in Progress This figure shows what takes place over time during a typical reaction. As the amount of reactants decreases, the amount of products increases.

Collision Theory A reaction may or may not take place when molecules of hydrogen and oxygen collide.

Reaction occurs These molecules of oxygen and hydrogen have enough kinetic energy for water to form when they collide.

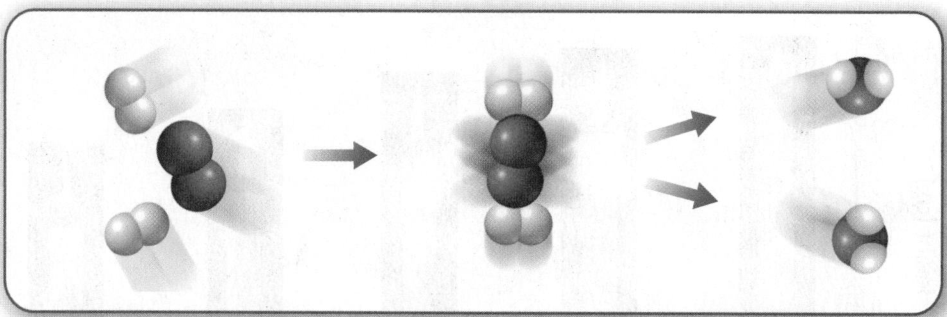

No reaction occurs These molecules do not have enough energy to react. They bounce apart without forming water.

Go online to see collision theory *animated.*

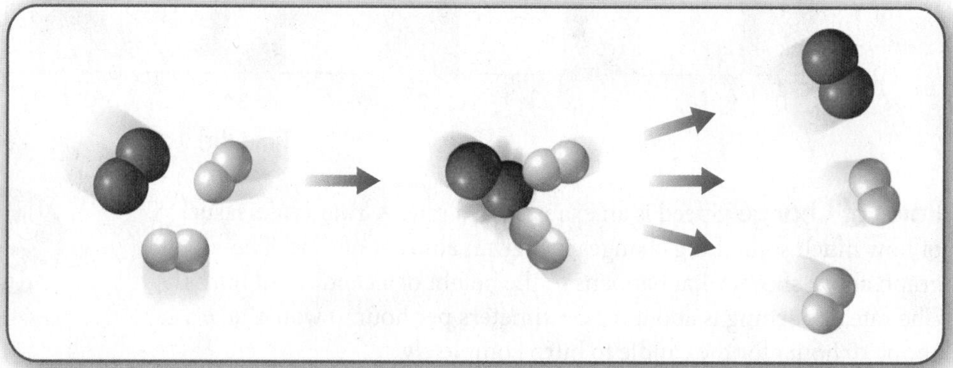

Collision Theory A model called *collision theory* is used to relate kinetic energy and reaction rates. According to **collision theory**, two things can happen when atoms, ions, or molecules collide. When the particles have enough kinetic energy, they can react and form products. When the particles do not have enough energy, they do not react. The figure above shows what can happen when hydrogen and oxygen molecules collide.

You can use two balls of soft clay to show how collision theory works. If you throw the balls of clay together gently, they do not stick together. This is like a collision between particles with low kinetic energy. If the same balls of clay are thrown together with great force, they stick tightly to each other. This is like a collision between particles with high kinetic energy.

Activation Energy The minimum energy that colliding particles must have in order to react is called the **activation energy**. You can think of the activation energy for a reaction as a barrier that reactants must cross before products can form. The net on a volleyball court is a barrier. To have a chance to score a point, a player must hit the ball over the net.

Look at the graphs on the next page. They compare energy changes during an exothermic reaction and an endothermic reaction. Find the activated complex at the highest point on each graph. An **activated complex** is a temporary and unstable arrangement of atoms. For an activated complex to form, the particles must have enough energy and be lined up correctly when they collide.

BUILD Vocabulary

VOCABULARY FLASHCARDS

collision theory reactants can form products if they collide with enough kinetic energy

activation energy the minimum energy that colliding particles need to react

activated complex an unstable arrangement of atoms that exists at the top of the activation-energy barrier

ROOT WORDS

The word *act* can mean "to do something." To activate means "to make able to act." Activation energy makes particles able to react when they collide.

Collision theory can explain why some reactions are very slow at room temperature. For example, a combustion reaction takes place between carbon and oxygen when charcoal burns. This reaction has a high activation energy because energy is needed to break the O-O and C-C bonds. At room temperature, oxygen and carbon do not have enough energy when they collide to break those bonds. So carbon and oxygen have a reaction rate of about zero at room temperature.

Key Question How is the rate of a chemical reaction expressed? **The rate of a chemical reaction is usually expressed as the change in the amount of reactant or product per unit of time.**

Energy Changes in Reactions The activation-energy barrier must be crossed before reactants are changed to products. The activation energy is higher than the energy of either the reactants or the products. *Go to your Chemistry Skills and Math Workbook to practice interpreting graphs.*

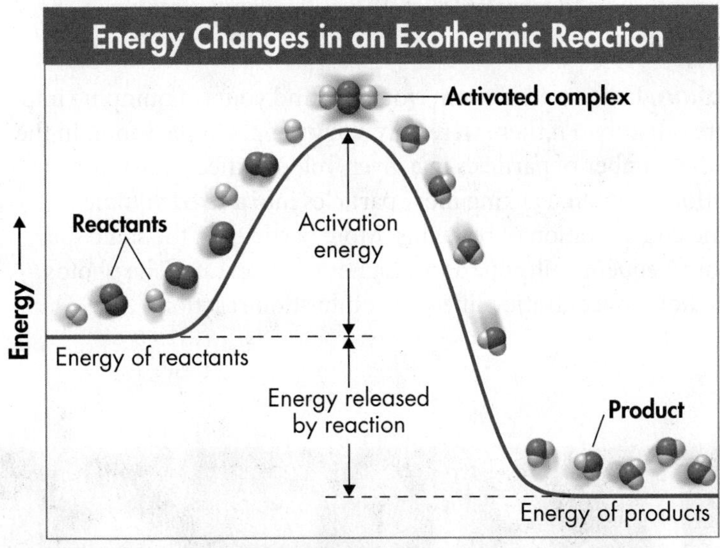

Exothermic In an exothermic reaction, heat is released from the system. The energy of the reactants is higher than the energy of the products. The formation of water is an exothermic reaction.

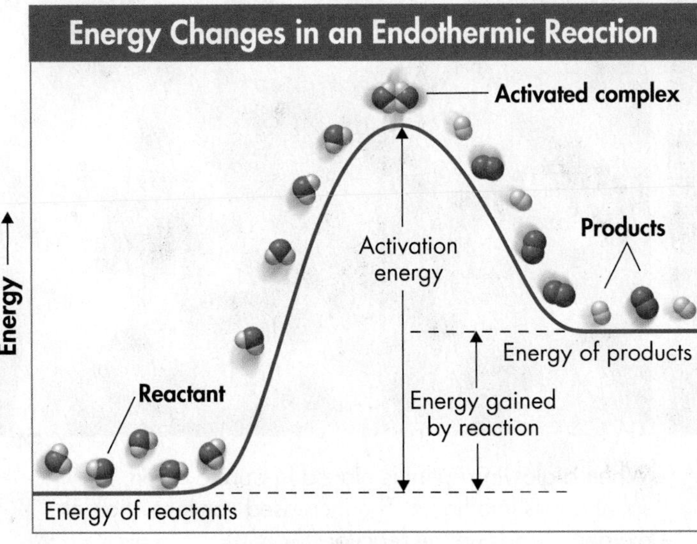

Endothermic In an endothermic reaction, heat is absorbed by the system. The energy of the reactants is lower than the energy of the products. The decomposition of water is an endothermic reaction.

Cause and Effect

Use a cause-and-effect organizer to summarize how temperature, concentration, particle size, and catalysts can affect the rate of a reaction.

Factors Affecting Reaction Rates

The rate of a chemical reaction can change. Factors that can affect the rate of a reaction are temperature, concentration, particle size, and the use of a catalyst. Collision theory helps explain why changing these factors may affect the rate of a chemical reaction.

Temperature Raising the temperature usually speeds up a reaction. Lowering the temperature usually slows down a reaction. At higher temperatures, particles move faster and collide more often. Also, more of the particles have enough kinetic energy to get over the activation-energy barrier. So an increase in temperature causes products to form faster.

Temperature has an effect on the burning of charcoal. The reactants are carbon and oxygen. The product is carbon dioxide. At room temperature, charcoal in contact with oxygen in air does not burn. However, when a flame touches the charcoal, collisions between carbon atoms and oxygen molecules take place more often and with higher energy. Some collisions have enough energy to form the product. The heat given off by the reaction allows more collisions to form product. When the flame is removed, the reaction continues.

Concentration In a crowded room, you may find yourself bumping into people more often than if there were only a few people in the room. In the same way, the number of particles in a given volume affects the rate at which reactions happen. Packing more particles into a fixed volume increases the concentration of reactants. More particles in the same space leads to more frequent collisions and a higher reaction rate. The photos below show how concentration affects a combustion reaction.

Effect of Concentration on Reaction Rate

In air, a lighted splint glows and soon goes out. Air is only 20 percent oxygen. This concentration of oxygen is not high enough to keep the reaction going.

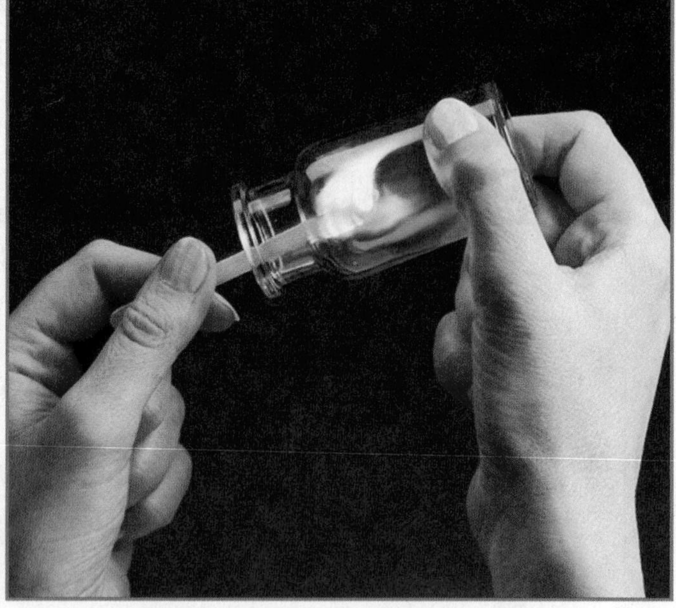

When a glowing splint is placed in pure oxygen, the splint bursts into flame. The increased concentration of oxygen speeds up the reaction.

Effect of Particle Size on Surface Area The large cube has the same volume as the 27 smaller cubes. But the total surface area of the smaller cubes is much larger.

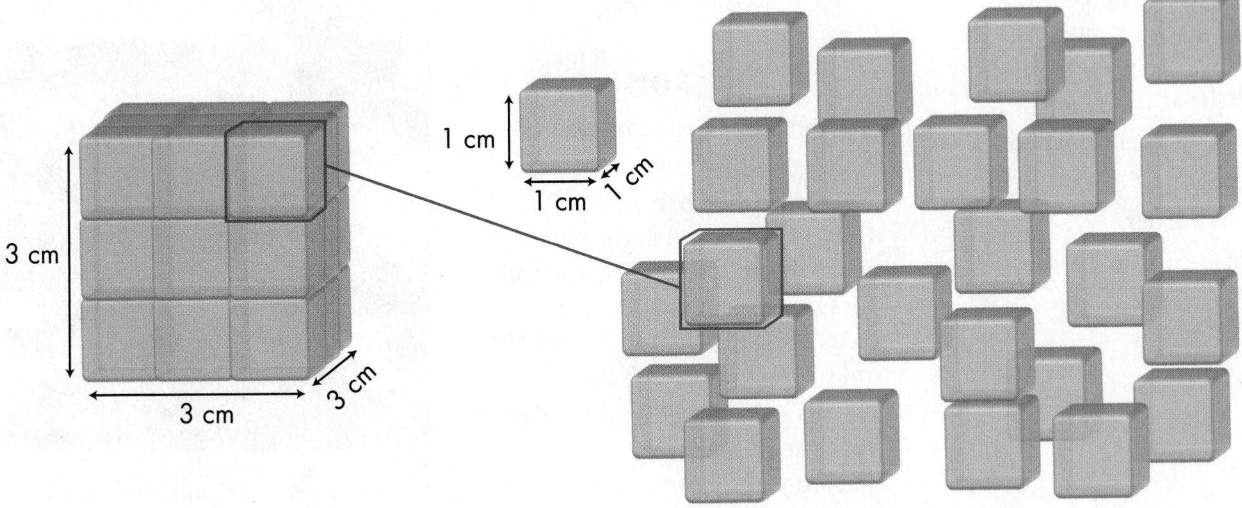

To find area, multiply length times width. For a cube, the length equals the width. The area of one side of the large cube is 3 cm $\times$ 3 cm = 9 cm^2. The total surface area of the large cube is the area of one side times the number of sides: 9 cm^2 $\times$ 6 = 54 cm^2.

The large cube is made up of 27 small cubes. The area of one side of a small cube is 1 cm^2. The total surface area of one small cube is 6 cm^2. The 27 small cubes have a total surface area of 27 $\times$ 6 cm^2 = 162 cm^2.

Particle Size Did you every wonder why water can sit in a pail for days before it completely evaporates? Yet the same amount of water spread out in a thin layer will evaporate much faster. Evaporation takes place only at the surface of a liquid. The surface area of the thin layer of water is much larger than the surface area of the water in the pail. Surface area has a similar effect on chemical reactions.

The total surface area of a solid or liquid reactant affects the rate of a reaction. The general rule is that the greater the surface area, the faster the reaction rate. This rule make sense because collisions take place at the surface of reactants.

▶ **Reducing Particle Size** One way to increase surface area is to cut a solid, such as a metal bar, into smaller pieces. The drawing at the top of this page uses a large cube and smaller cubes to show why this process works. The large cube and the 27 smaller cubes have the same total volume.

Grinding a solid into a fine powder also increases surface area—sometimes to the point of danger. Coal dust mixed with air can explode because of the large surface area of the coal particles. The same risk exists in flour mills, grain elevators, and sugar refineries like the one described on page 563.

▶ **Dissolving Reactants** Another way to increase the surface area of solids is to dissolve them. In a solution, particles are separated. More of them are able to collide with other reactants.

BUILD Connections

If you put a bundle of sticks on a fire, they burn quickly. A log with the same mass burns more slowly. The small pieces of wood have more surface area than the log. So the oxygen molecules can collide with more of the wood. In fact, small pieces of wood are used to start a log fire.

Quick Lab

Purpose To determine whether steel will burn

Materials

- #0000 steel wool pad
- tongs
- gas burner
- heat-resistant pad
- tweezers

Does Steel Burn?

Procedure

1. Roll a small piece of steel wool into a very tight, pea-sized ball.

2. Holding the ball with tongs, heat the steel wool in the blue-tip flame of the burner. Heat the ball for no longer than 10 seconds. **CAUTION:** Observe all safety rules for working with flames.

3. Place the heated steel wool on the heat-resistant pad to cool. Record your observations.

4. Gently roll a second small piece of steel wool into a loose ball. Repeat Steps 2 and 3.

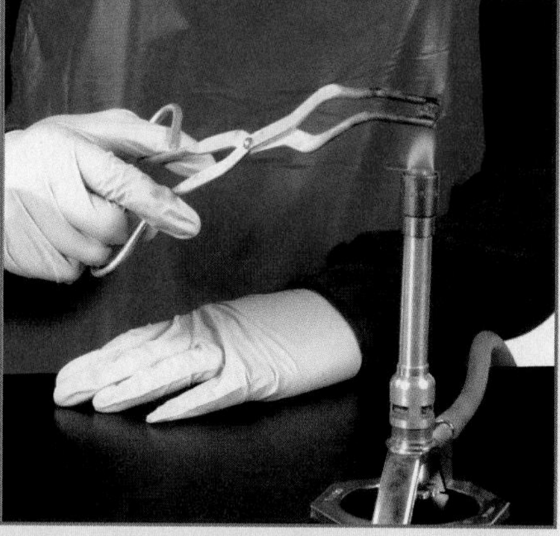

5. Use tweezers to pull a few single fibers of steel wool from the pad. Hold one end of the loose fibers with the tongs. Repeat Steps 2 and 3.

Analyze and Conclude

1. Observe What differences did you observe when the tight ball, the loose ball, and the loose fibers were heated in the flame?

2. Relate Cause and Effect Give a reason for any differences you observed.

3. Describe The steel wool is mainly iron (Fe). Write a balanced equation for a reaction between iron and oxygen.

4. Compare and Contrast How do your results differ from those observed when an auto body rusts?

5. Apply Concepts Explain why steel wool is a danger in shops where there are open flames or sparking motors.

Catalysts Increasing the temperature is not always the best way to increase the rate of a reaction. A catalyst is often better. Remember that a catalyst increases the rate of a reaction without being used up in the reaction. Catalysts allow reactions to happen along a lower energy path.

Look at the graph at the top of the next page. It shows that the activation energy is much lower when a catalyst is used. When the energy barrier is lower, more of the reactant particles have enough energy to form products. Consider the reaction of hydrogen and oxygen. At room temperature, the rate of the reaction is small. When a small amount of platinum (Pt) is used as a catalyst, the rate is fast.

$$2H_2(g) + O_2(g) \xrightarrow{Pt} 2H_2O(l)$$

A catalyst is not used up during a reaction. So it does not appear as a reactant in the chemical equation. Instead, the catalyst is often written above the yield arrow, as in the equation above.

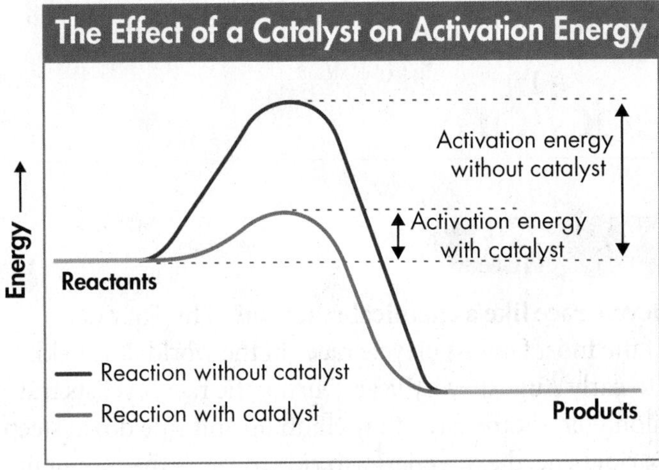

Effect of a Catalyst on Reaction Rates Reactant particles must have an energy equal to or greater than the activation energy to form products. A catalyst lowers the activation energy for a reaction. Now more particles have enough energy for a successful collision.

Go to your Chemistry Skills and Math Workbook to practice interpreting graphs.

Normal body temperature is only about 37°C. Your body needs to keep this temperature to avoid damage to cells. At 37°C, reactions in the body would be too slow without catalysts. The catalysts that work in the body are called enzymes. When you eat a meal containing protein, enzymes in your digestive tract help break down the protein molecules. This process takes a few hours. Without enzymes, this process would take years!

An **inhibitor** is a substance that blocks the action of a catalyst. Some inhibitors react with, or "poison," the catalyst itself. This action reduces the amount of catalyst available for a reaction. Reactions slow or even stop when a catalyst is poisoned.

inhibitor a substance that blocks the action of a catalyst

WORD ORIGINS

Inhibit comes from the Latin word *inhibère*, which means to hold back or contain.

Key Question What four factors influence the rate of a chemical reaction? **Factors that can affect the rate of a chemical reaction are temperature, concentration, particle size, and the use of a catalyst.**

18.1 LessonCheck

Key Concept Check

1. **Explain** How can you express the rate of a chemical reaction?
2. **Identify** List four factors that can affect the rate of a chemical reaction.

Vocabulary Check *Choose a highlighted word from the lesson to complete the sentence correctly.*

3. The energy that is required in order for colliding particles to react is the ________.

Think Critically

4. **Relate Cause and Effect** Food stored in a refrigerator can stay fresh for long periods. Why does the same food stored at room temperature quickly spoil?
5. **Summarize** Does every collision between reacting particles lead to products? Explain.

6. When water is added to the mixture in an MRE heater, the rate of rusting increases. Which factor that affects reaction rates is being used in this case? (Hint: See pages 568–570.)

BIGIDEA MATTER AND ENERGY

7. Make a Venn diagram with two circles. Label one Matter and the other Energy. Choose a location in the diagram for each factor that can affect the rate of a reaction. Write a paragraph explaining your choices.

18.2 The Progress of Chemical Reactions

CHEMISTRY & YOU

Q: How is a bicycle race like a chemical reaction? The Tour de France is one of the most famous bicycle races in the world. It is held from mid-July to early August every year. During the race, cyclists travel almost 4,000 kilometers. Some days, they climb up and ride down steep mountains. The riders need extra energy to ride through the mountains.

Key Questions

What is the relationship between the value of the specific rate constant (k) and the speed of a chemical reaction?

How do most reactions progress from start to finish?

BUILD Vocabulary

rate law an expression for the rate of a reaction in terms of the concentration of reactants

specific rate constant (k) a constant that relates the concentrations of reactants to the rate of the reaction

reaction mechanism the series of steps that take place during a complex reaction

ACADEMIC WORDS

There are different kinds of constants. Some constants, such as pi (π), always have the same value. Some can vary. The value of the specific rate constant depends on the reaction and the temperature.

Rate Laws

Remember that concentration is one factor that can affect the rate of a reaction. This equation represents a reaction with one reactant (A) and one product (B).

$$A \longrightarrow B$$

The rate at which A forms B can be expressed as a change in A over time.

$$\text{Rate} = \frac{\Delta A}{\Delta t} = k \times [A]$$

Δ means "change in." ΔA is the change in reactant A over time.

The symbol [A] is shorthand for the concentration of A.

The expression is a rate law. A **rate law** describes the rate of a reaction in terms of the concentration of reactants. The rate of the reaction changes as the concentration of A changes.

Most reactions have more than one reactant. This reaction has two reactants and two products.

$$aA + bB \longrightarrow cC + dD$$

So the rate law for this reaction must include both reactants A and B.

$$\text{Rate} = k[A]^x[B]^y$$

[A] and [B] are the concentrations of two reactants, A and B.

The exponents x and y show how many times each concentration is multiplied by itself.

Changes in Reaction Rate The rate at any point on this graph is the slope of the tangent to the curve at that point. Two tangents are shown in red. The slope is the change in concentration of A divided by the change in time.

Go to your Chemistry Skills and Math Workbook to practice interpreting graphs.

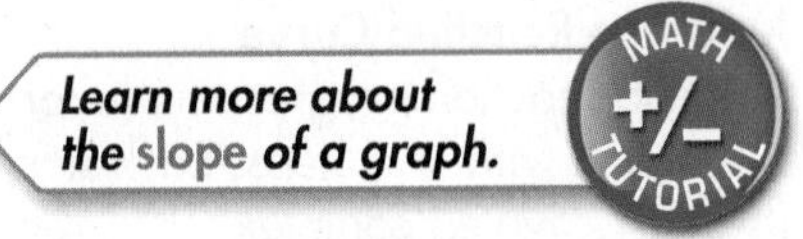

Learn more about the slope of a graph.
MATH
+/–
TUTORIAL

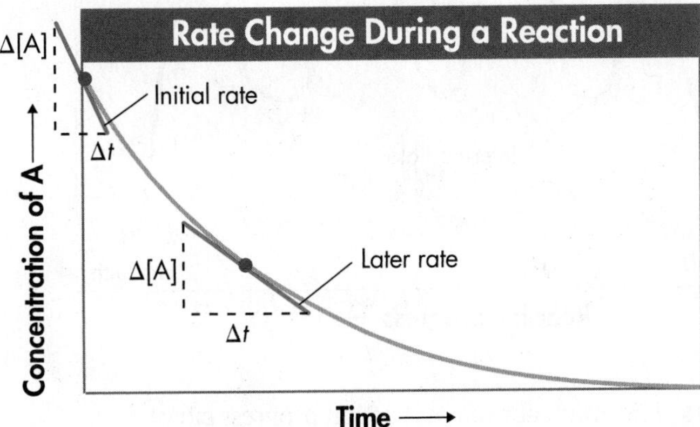

Specific Rate Constant In a rate law, the concentrations are multiplied by a constant, k. The **specific rate constant** (k) relates the concentrations of reactants to the rate of a reaction. The value of the specific rate constant depends on the reaction and on conditions such as temperature. Experiments are used to find the value. The value of k is large if the products form quickly. The value of k is small if the products form slowly.

Look at the graph above. It shows how the concentration of a single reactant changes over time. As reactant A forms a product, the amount of A decreases. The rate of the reaction also decreases. The initial rate is high because the concentration of A is high at the start of the reaction. When the concentration of A is cut in half, the rate will be half of the initial rate.

Key Question What is the relationship between the value of the specific rate constant (k) and the speed of a chemical reaction? **The value of the specific rate constant (k) in a rate law is large if the products form quickly. The value is small if the products form slowly.**

Reaction Mechanisms

Chemical equations tell you what reactants are present at the start of a reaction and what products are present at the end. What an equation does not tell you is the path of the reaction from start to finish. For example, plants capture and store light energy. The process can be summarized by stating that carbon dioxide reacts with water to yield simple sugars and oxygen. However, the process is not as simple as this summary implies. It is made up of many small steps. Most chemical reactions have two or more steps. The series of steps that take place during the course of a complex reaction is called a **reaction mechanism.**

One-Step Reactions If you had enough data, you could graph all the energy changes that take place as reactants are changed to products in a chemical reaction. This kind of graph is called a *reaction progress curve.* For a reaction that has only one step, you would get a graph like the one to the right. A reaction with one step has only one activated complex.

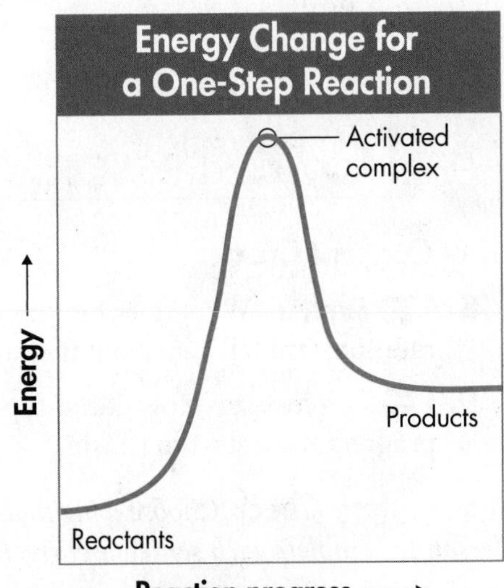

One-Step Reaction Curve
A one-step reaction has only one activation-energy peak.

Multistep Reaction Curve
This is a reaction progress curve for a reaction with four steps. Each step has its own activated complex. The products of the first three steps are intermediates.

Go to your Chemistry Skills and Math Workbook to practice interpreting graphs.

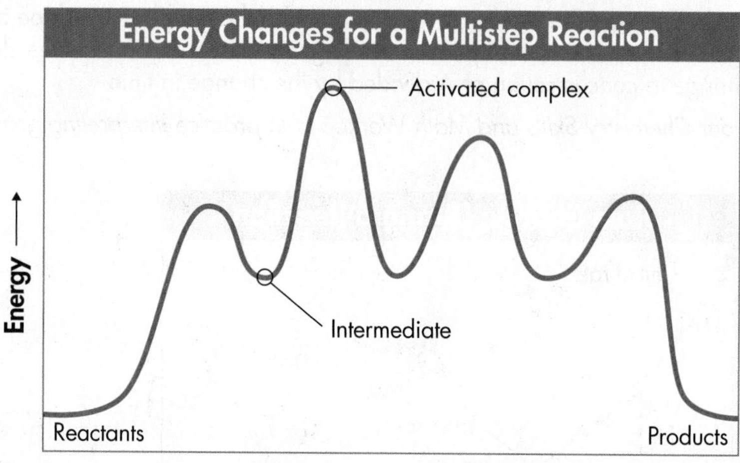

BUILD Vocabulary

intermediate a substance that is a product in one step of a reaction mechanism and a reactant in the next step

PREFIXES

The prefix *inter-* means "between." An intermission is a pause between acts in a play. In chemistry, intermediates are products that appear between the initial reactants and the final products of a reaction.

Multistep Reactions The graph above is a reaction progress curve for a complex chemical reaction. The graph has a peak for each activated complex and a valley for each intermediate. An **intermediate** is a product of one step in a reaction mechanism and a reactant in the next step. Intermediates do not appear in the overall equation for a reaction.

Rate-Determining Steps In a multistep chemical reaction, the steps do not all happen at the same rate. One step will be slower than the others. The rate of the overall reaction depends on the rate of the slowest step.

As an analogy, think about shopping in a supermarket. First, you collect the items you want to buy. Then, you go through the checkout line to pay for them. If you are buying many items, the first step is likely to take longer than the second. If you are buying only one or two items, getting through the checkout line may be the slower step. The slower step determines the rate of the entire trip to the grocery store.

Key Question How do most reactions progress from start to finish? **Most chemical reactions consist of two or more steps.**

18.2 LessonCheck

Key Concept Check

8. **Explain** What does the size of the specific rate constant tell you about the rate of a reaction?

9. **Summarize** How does a typical reaction progress from start to finish?

Vocabulary Check *Choose a highlighted word from the lesson to complete each sentence correctly.*

10. A(n) __________ describes the rate of a reaction in terms of the concentration of reactants.

11. The series of steps that take place in a complex reaction is called a(n) __________.

Think Critically

12. **Describe** How can you use a graph of reactant concentration versus time to figure out the rate of a chemical reaction?

13. **Classify** Is an intermediate a reactant or a product? Explain.

CHEMISTRY & YOU

14. Part of the Tour de France course has peaks and valleys. In terms of energy, compare the trip through the mountains to what happens during a multistep reaction? (Hint: See graph above.)

18.3 Reversible Reactions and Equilibrium

CHEMISTRY & YOU

Q: How did chemists help farmers grow more food? Fertilizers can increase the amount of a crop grown on an acre of land. Most fertilizers contain ammonia or nitrogen compounds made from ammonia. For years, scientists tried and failed to find a way to produce a high yield of ammonia from nitrogen and hydrogen. In the early 1900s, two German chemists, Fritz Haber and Karl Bosch, found the answer.

Key Questions

What happens at the molecular level in a chemical system at equilibrium?

What three stresses can cause a change in the equilibrium position of a chemical system?

What does the size of an equilibrium constant indicate about a system at equilibrium?

BUILD Vocabulary

reversible reaction a reaction in which reactants change to products and products change back to reactants at the same time

chemical equilibrium the state at which the rates of the forward reaction and reverse reaction are equal

USING PRIOR KNOWLEDGE

The reverse gear in a car changes the car's direction. It allows the car to back up. In a reverse reaction, products change back to reactants.

Reversible Reactions

Based on the chemical equations you have seen, you may think that chemical reactions always happen in one direction. This is not true. Some reactions are reversible. A **reversible reaction** is one in which reactants change to products and products change to reactants at the same time. Here is an example of a reversible reaction.

$$\text{Forward reaction: } 2SO_2(g) + O_2(g) \longrightarrow 2SO_3(g)$$

$$\text{Reverse reaction: } 2SO_2(g) + O_2(g) \longleftarrow 2SO_3(g)$$

The direction of the yield arrow tells you which way to read the equation. The first reaction is read from left to right and is called the *forward reaction*. In the first reaction, sulfur dioxide and oxygen produce sulfur trioxide. The second reaction is read from right to left and is called the *reverse reaction*. In the second reaction, sulfur trioxide decomposes into sulfur dioxide and oxygen.

The two equations can be combined into one by using a double arrow as shown below. The double arrow tells you that the reaction is reversible.

$$2SO_2(g) + O_2(g) \rightleftharpoons 2SO_3(g)$$

Establishing Equilibrium What happens when sulfur dioxide and oxygen are mixed in a sealed container? The forward reaction begins. The rate of the reverse reaction is zero at the start because no sulfur trioxide is present. Once some sulfur trioxide forms, the reverse reaction begins. The rate of the reverse reaction is slow at first.

As more sulfur trioxide forms, the reverse reaction speeds up. At the same time, the rate of the forward reaction is slowing down because sulfur dioxide and oxygen are being used up. At some point, the sulfur trioxide will decompose as quickly as it forms. When the rates of the forward and reverse reactions are equal, the reaction has reached a state of balance called **chemical equilibrium**.

Establishing Equilibrium The formation of SO_3 from SO_2 and O_2 happens at the same time that SO_3 breaks down into SO_2 and O_2. *Go to your Chemistry Skills and Math Workbook to practice interpreting graphs.*

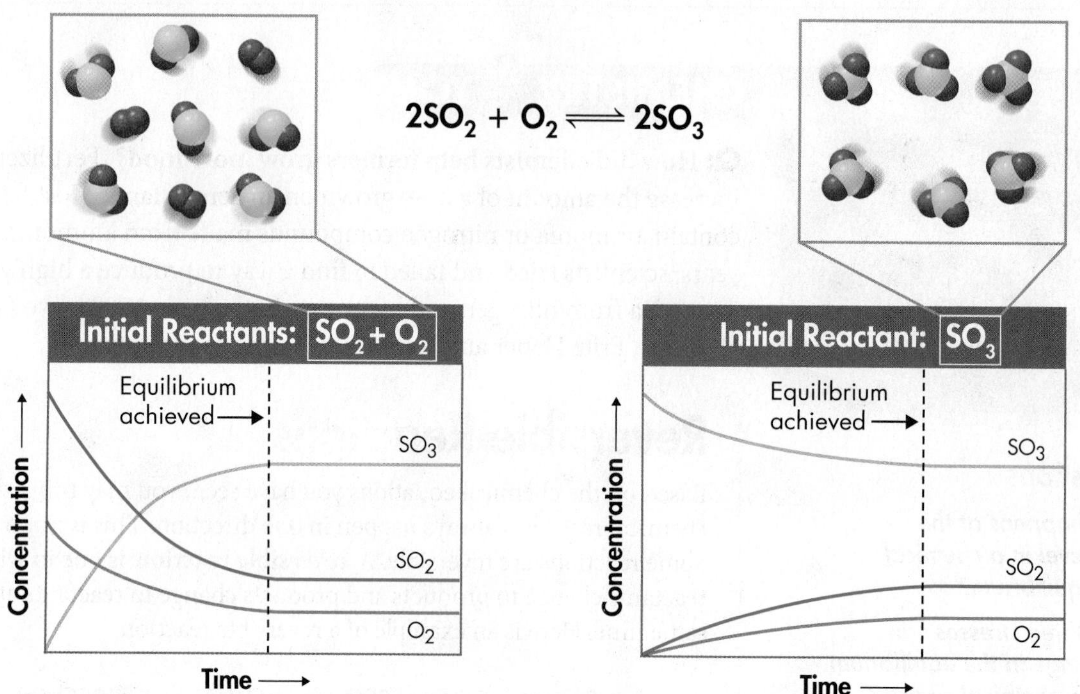

This graph shows what happens when the reaction starts with SO_2 and O_2. As SO_3 forms, the concentrations of SO_2 and O_2 go down and the concentration of SO_3 goes up.

This graph shows what happens when the reaction starts with SO_3. As SO_3 decomposes, the concentration of SO_3 goes down and the concentrations of SO_2 and O_2 go up.

Look at the graphs in the diagram. The graph on the left represents the forward reaction. The graph on the right represents the reverse reaction. Each graph shows the course of the reaction in terms of concentration. After the system reaches equilibrium, the concentrations do not change. Also, the concentrations of SO_2, O_2, and SO_3 at equilibrium are the same no matter which reaction you start with.

Conditions at Equilibrium The constant amounts of SO_2, O_2, and SO_3 in the reaction mixture at equilibrium might make you think that both reactions have stopped. This is not the case. A chemical equilibrium is dynamic, which means that the reactions continue to take place. The important fact is that the rates of the forward and reverse reactions are equal. These equal rates explain why the concentrations in the reaction mixture do not change.

Look at the drawings of the up and down escalators on the next page. They provide an analogy for how equilibrium is established and how it keeps going. The people are like particles in a reaction. The "forward reaction" starts when the store opens.

Equilibrium Analogy The up and down escalators in a store could represent a forward reaction and its reverse reaction.

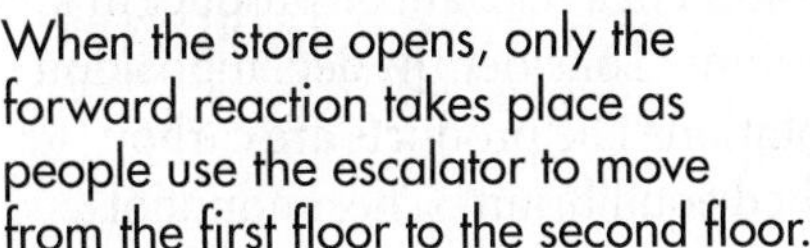

When the store opens, only the forward reaction takes place as people use the escalator to move from the first floor to the second floor.

At equilibrium, the rate at which people move to the second floor is equal to the rate at which they move from the second floor to the first.

Concentrations at Equilibrium The rates of the forward and reverse reactions are equal at equilibrium, but the concentrations of the components usually are not. The relative concentrations of the reactants and products at equilibrium are the **equilibrium position** of a reaction. This position tells you which reaction is more likely to happen. Suppose a single reactant (A) forms a single product (B). If the equilibrium mixture is 1 percent A and 99 percent B, then the formation of B is favored.

$$\underset{1\%}{\mathrm{A}} \rightleftharpoons \underset{99\%}{\mathrm{B}}$$

If the mixture has 99 percent A and 1 percent B at equilibrium, then the formation of A is favored.

$$\underset{99\%}{\mathrm{A}} \rightleftharpoons \underset{1\%}{\mathrm{B}}$$

Notice that the equilibrium arrows are not the same length. The longer of the two arrows shows which reaction is favored and whether reactants or products will be more common at equilibrium.

Almost all reactions are reversible to some extent under the right conditions. Often, one set of components is so favored at equilibrium that the other set cannot be measured. When no reactants can be measured, you can say that the reaction has gone to completion. When no products can be measured, you can say that no reaction has taken place.

Key Question What happens at the molecular level in a chemical system at equilibrium? **At chemical equilibrium, both the forward and reverse reactions continue. Because their rates are equal, no net change occurs in the concentrations of the reaction components.**

equilibrium position
the relative concentrations of reactants and products at equilibrium

PREFIXES

The prefix *equi-* means "equal." An equilateral triangle has three equal sides. A forward reaction and a reverse reaction have equal rates at equilibrium.

Le Châtelier's principle an equilibrium system will change in a way that reduces the stress on the system

SYNONYMS

In science, when you see the word *principle*, think of the word *law*. A scientific law summarizes the results of many observations and experiments.

BUILD Connections

Farmers can remove a product to increase the production of eggs. Hens lay eggs and then sit on the eggs until they hatch. If the eggs are removed right after they are laid, the hen will lay more eggs.

Factors Affecting Equilibrium: Le Châtelier's Principle

The balance in a system at equilibrium is delicate. Changing one or more conditions of the reactions can upset the balance. When this happens, the system adjusts to get back to equilibrium. A new equilibrium is reached. The new equilibrium has an equilibrium position that is different than the original equilibrium position. This change is called a *shift in equilibrium.*

The French chemist Henri Le Châtelier (1850–1936) studied these shifts. His explanation is called **Le Châtelier's principle.** It states that when a stress is applied to a system in equilibrium, the system changes in a way that relieves the stress. Conditions that can stress a system include changes in concentration, changes in temperature, and changes in pressure.

In the examples of stresses described in this lesson, a blue arrow is used to show the shift when something is added to or removed from the system. The blue arrow always points in the direction of the shift in the equilibrium position. So the blue arrow points toward the favored side of the reaction.

Concentration Changing the concentration of a reactant or product in a system at equilibrium upsets the equilibrium. Consider the decomposition of carbonic acid (H_2CO_3) in aqueous solution. The products are carbon dioxide and water. The system has reached equilibrium. The amount of carbonic acid is less than 1 percent.

$$\underset{<1\%}{H_2CO_3(aq)} \underset{\text{Remove } CO_2 \text{ / Direction of shift}\rightarrow}{\overset{\text{Add } CO_2 \text{ / }\leftarrow\text{Direction of shift}}{\rightleftharpoons}} \underset{>99\%}{CO_2(aq) + H_2O(l)}$$

▶ **Adding a Product** Suppose CO_2 is added to the system. Because CO_2 is used up in the reverse reaction, that reaction speeds up. As more H_2CO_3 forms, the forward reaction also speeds up. In time, the rates of the forward and reverse reactions become equal again.

Equilibrium is restored but with a different equilibrium position. The concentration of reactant (H_2CO_3) is higher and the concentrations of the products (CO_2 and H_2O) are lower. Adding a product to a system at equilibrium pushes a reversible reaction in the direction of the reactants.

▶ **Removing a Product** Now suppose CO_2 is removed from the system. This decrease in the concentration of CO_2 causes the reverse reaction to slow down. As less H_2CO_3 is formed, the forward reaction also slows down. In time, the rates of the forward and reverse reactions again become equal.

At the new equilibrium position, the concentration of reactant (H_2CO_3) is lower and the concentrations of the products (CO_2 and H_2O) are higher. Removing a product from a system at equilibrium pulls a reversible reaction in the direction of the products.

What happens if you keep removing a product from the reaction mixture? Equilibrium will not be restored. The system will continue to make product until the reaction goes to completion.

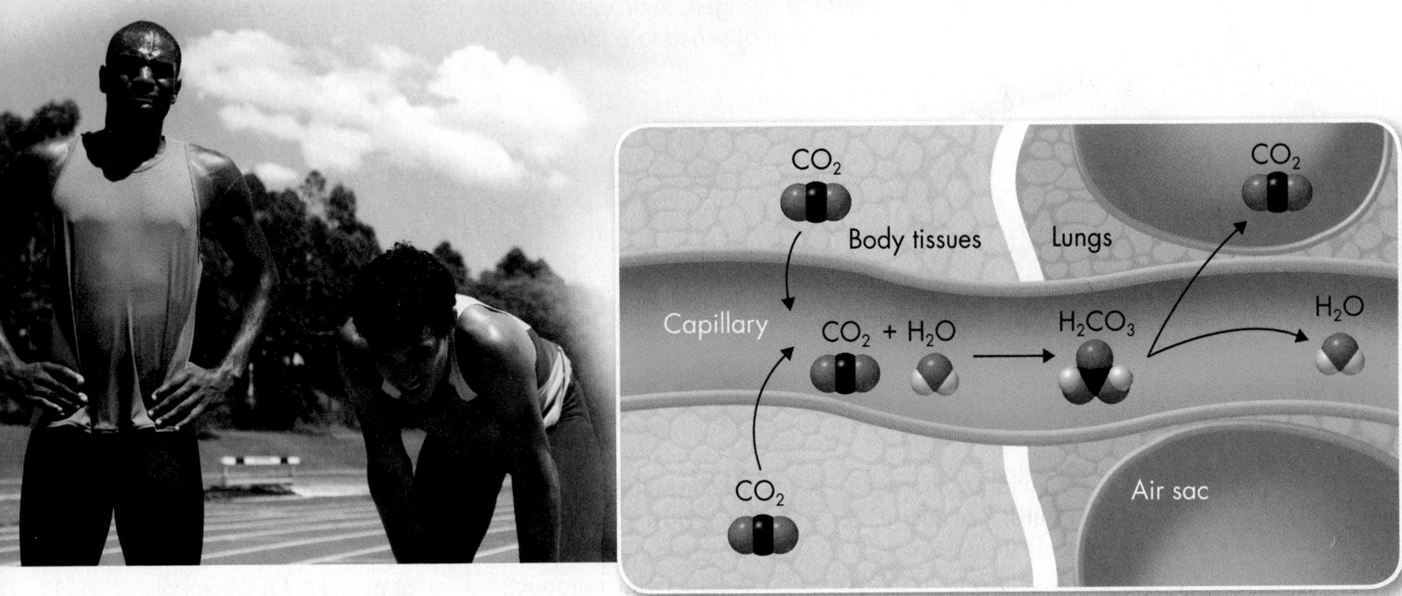

An Equilibrium System in Blood
Blood carries CO_2 from your cells to your lungs. Some CO_2 diffuses into the lungs and is exhaled into the air. These actions help control the amount of carbonic acid (H_2CO_3) in the blood.

▶ **Concentration in Action** Carbon dioxide is a product of reactions in your cells that give your body the energy it needs. An equilibrium exists between the carbon dioxide, water, and carbonic acid in your blood. Too much carbonic acid in the blood is not good for your health.

The young men shown above have just finished a race. When you run or do other exercise, your body needs more energy. As your cells produce this energy, the concentration of carbon dioxide in your blood rises. This increase in carbon dioxide shifts the equilibrium in the direction of carbonic acid.

Luckily, a rise in carbon dioxide causes your breathing rate to speed up. With more breaths per minute, more carbon dioxide moves through and out of the lungs. Removing carbon dioxide shifts the equilibrium back toward carbon dioxide. This shift lowers the amount of carbonic acid in the blood.

The rules for adding or removing products also work for reactants. When a reactant is added, the reaction shifts toward the products. When a reactant is removed, the reaction shifts toward the reactants.

Temperature N_2 and H_2 can react to form ammonia (NH_3) in a reversible reaction. The forward reaction produces heat. The reverse reaction absorbs heat. What happens if the temperature of the reaction mixture is raised? Removing heat will reduce this stress. The reverse reaction is favored because it absorbs heat. The equilibrium position shifts in the direction of the reactants. Less ammonia is produced.

$$N_2(g) + 3H_2(g) \underset{\substack{\text{Remove heat (cool)} \\ \text{Direction of shift} \rightarrow}}{\overset{\substack{\text{Add heat} \\ \leftarrow \text{Direction of shift}}}{\rightleftharpoons}} 2NH_3(g) + \text{heat}$$

What happens if the reaction mixture is cooled? Adding heat to the reaction mixture will reduce this stress. The forward reaction produces heat. So the forward reaction is favored. The equilibrium position moves in the direction of the product. More ammonia is produced.

Effect of Pressure on Equilibrium
Pressure affects a mixture of nitrogen, hydrogen, and ammonia. The three gases are in a cylinder with a piston attached to a plunger.

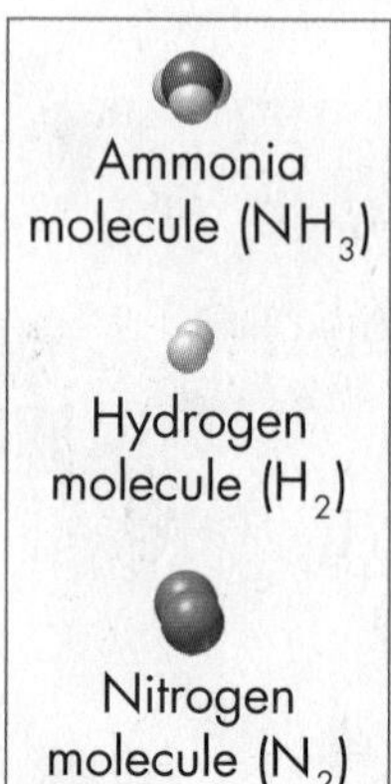

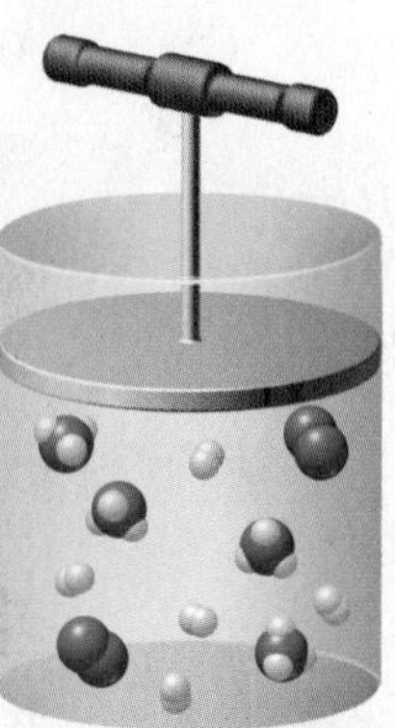

1 Initial equilibrium mixture: 7 molecules of reactant and 4 molecules of product, for a total of 11 molecules.

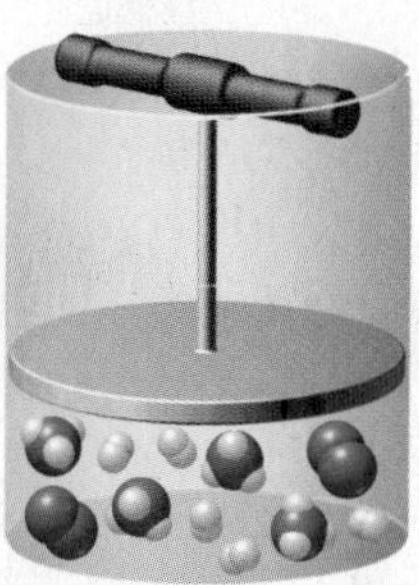

2 Pushing the plunger decreases the volume and increases the pressure. A shift toward products will help relieve this stress.

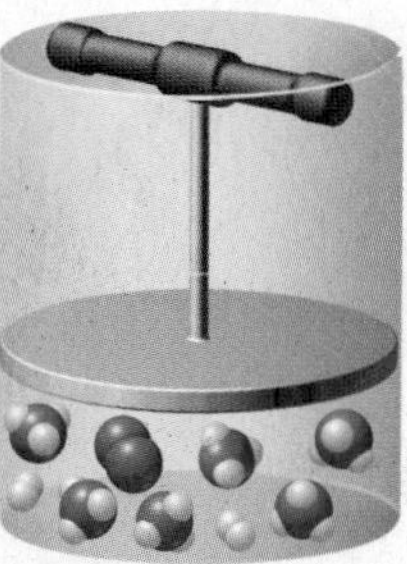

3 New equilibrium mixture: 3 molecules of reactant and 6 molecules of product, for a total of 9 molecules.

Pressure Equilibrium systems that have gases as reactants and products may be affected by a change in pressure. This happens only when the numbers of moles of gas on each side of the equation are not equal. Look again at the reaction in which ammonia forms. There are four moles of reactant gases and two moles of product gases. In other words, there are four molecules of reactant to every two molecules of product. The model above shows how a change in pressure affects the system.

$$N_2(g) + 3H_2(g) \underset{\text{Decrease pressure} \atop \leftarrow \text{Direction of shift}}{\overset{\text{Increase pressure} \atop \text{Direction of shift} \rightarrow}{\rightleftharpoons}} 2NH_3(g)$$

▶ **Increase in Pressure** An increase in pressure upsets the equilibrium. Pressure is directly related to the number of particles. The forward reaction can reduce the number of particles. So the reaction will shift toward products. There will be more product at the new equilibrium position.

▶ **Decrease in Pressure** If the plunger is pulled up, the pressure will decrease. The reverse reaction can increase the number of particles, which will increase the pressure. So the reaction will shift toward reactants.

Catalysts and Equilibrium Catalysts reduce the time needed to get to equilibrium. Catalysts do not affect the amounts of reactants and products at equilibrium. The energy path for a reverse reaction is the opposite of the energy path for the forward reaction. So adding a catalyst lowers the energy path by the same amount for both reactions.

Key Question What stresses can cause a change in the equilibrium position of a chemical system? **Stresses that upset the equilibrium of a chemical system include changes in the concentration of reactants or products, changes in temperature, and changes in pressure.**

Sample Problem 18.1

Applying Le Châtelier's Principle

What effect will each of the following changes have on the equilibrium position for this reversible reaction?

$$PCl_5(g) + \text{heat} \rightleftharpoons PCl_3(g) + Cl_2(g)$$

a. Cl_2 is added. **b.** Pressure is increased. **c.** Heat is removed.

1 Analyze Identify the relevant concepts. According to Le Châtelier's principle, the equilibrium position will shift in the direction that relieves the stress on the system.

2 Solve Apply the concepts to this problem.

Analyze the stress of adding Cl_2.

a. Cl_2 is a product. The reverse reaction lowers the concentration of a product. So the equilibrium shifts toward reactants.

Analyze the stress of an increase in pressure.

b. Compare the number of moles of gas on each side of the equation. There are two moles of product gases for each mole of reactant gas. A shift toward reactants reduces the number of gas particles and the pressure.

Increase pressure ← Direction of shift

1 mol | 1 mol | 1 mol

$$PCl_5(g) + \text{heat} \rightleftharpoons PCl_3(g) + Cl_2(g)$$

Analyze the stress of removing heat.

c. The reverse reaction adds heat to the system, which relieves the stress. So the equilibrium shifts toward reactants.

Practice Problems

15. How is the equilibrium position of this reaction affected by the following changes?

$$2SO_2(g) + O_2(g) \rightleftharpoons 2SO_3(g) + \text{heat}$$

a. lowering the temperature
b. decreasing the pressure

1 Analyze Identify the relevant concepts.

2 Solve Apply the concepts to this problem.

Hint: For a change in pressure, compare the number of gas molecules on each side of the equation.

16. Challenge How is the equilibrium position of this reaction affected by the following changes?

$$C(s) + H_2O(g) + \text{heat} \rightleftharpoons CO(g) + H_2(g)$$

a. lowering the temperature
b. increasing the pressure
c. removing hydrogen as it forms
d. adding water vapor

VOCABULARY FLASHCARDS
BUILD
Vocabulary

equilibrium constant (K_{eq}) ratio of product concentrations to reactant concentrations at equilibrium

RELATED SYMBOLS

In chemistry, many constants have the abbreviation *K*. You need to look at the subscript (*eq*) to identify the constant.

Equilibrium Constants

The equilibrium position is expressed as a number. This number relates the amount of products to the amount of reactants at equilibrium. Look at the general reaction below in which two reactants form two products. The coefficients *a*, *b*, *c*, and *d* stand for the number of moles.

$$aA + bB \rightleftharpoons cC + dD$$

The **equilibrium constant** (K_{eq}) is the ratio of the concentrations of products to the concentrations of reactants at equilibrium. Each concentration is raised to a power equal to the number of moles of that substance in the balanced equation. Here is the expression for the general reaction of A and B.

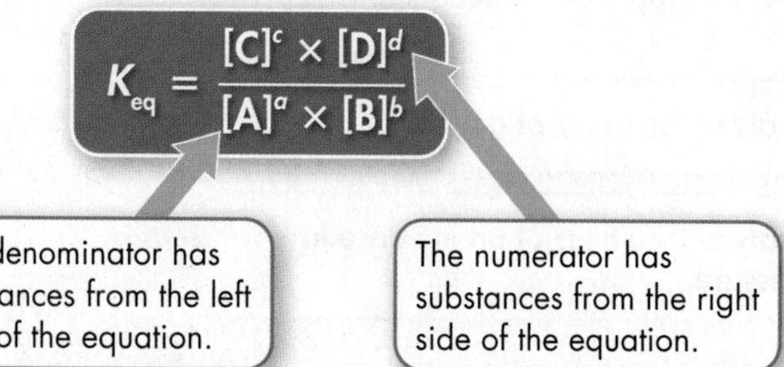
$K_{eq} = \frac{[C]^c \times [D]^d}{[A]^a \times [B]^b}$
The denominator has substances from the left side of the equation.
The numerator has substances from the right side of the equation.

Always place the concentrations of products in the numerator. Place the concentrations of reactants in the denominator. The unit of concentration is moles per liter (mol/L). The exponents in the expression are the coefficients in the balanced chemical equation.

▶ **Units for K_{eq}** When you calculate an equilibrium constant, you will need to cancel units of concentration. This process may lead to a unit for the constant or it may not. So chemists have agreed to report equilibrium constants without a unit.

▶ **Value of K_{eq}** From the size of the equilibrium constant, you can tell whether reactants or products are more common at equilibrium. When the value is large, such as 3.1×10^{11}, the equilibrium mixture will be mostly product. When the value is small, such as 3.1×10^{-11}, the equilibrium mixture will be mostly reactants. With a value such as 0.15 or 50, the equilibrium mixture will have significant amounts of both reactants and products.

▶ **Temperature and K_{eq}** The value of K_{eq} depends on temperature. If the temperature of a system changes, the value of K_{eq} changes too. The figure to the left shows the effect of temperature on an equilibrium between two gases.

Key Question What does the size of an equilibrium constant indicate about a system at equilibrium? **The size of the equilibrium constant indicates whether reactants or products are more common at equilibrium.**

Effect of Temperature Colorless dinitrogen tetroxide (N_2O_4) and brown nitrogen dioxide (NO_2) can exist in equilibrium.

$N_2O_4(g) + \text{heat} \rightleftharpoons 2NO_2(g)$

When the temperature rises, the equilibrium shifts toward NO_2 and the mixture is darker. The value of K_{eq} is higher in the hot water.

Ice Hot water

SampleProblem 18.2

Finding the Equilibrium Constant

One mole of colorless hydrogen gas and one mole of violet iodine vapor are sealed in a 1 L flask and allowed to react at 450°C. At equilibrium, 1.56 mol of colorless hydrogen iodide is present—together with some of the reactant gases. Calculate K_{eq} for this reaction.

$$H_2(g) + I_2(g) \rightleftharpoons 2HI(g)$$

1 Analyze List the knowns and the unknown. Find the concentrations of the reactants at equilibrium. Then, substitute these concentrations in the expression for the equilibrium constant for this reaction.

KNOWNS	UNKNOWN
$[H_2]$(initial) = 1.00 mol/L	$K_{eq} = ?$
$[I_2]$(initial) = 1.00 mol/L	
[HI](equilibrium) = 1.56 mol/L	

2 Calculate Solve for the unknown.

Use the equation to find conversion factors from moles of HI to moles of H_2 and I_2.

$1 \text{ mol } H_2 = 2 \text{ mol HI}$; the conversion factor is $\frac{1 \text{ mol } H_2}{2 \text{ mol HI}}$

$1 \text{ mol } I_2 = 2 \text{ mol HI}$; the conversion factor is $\frac{1 \text{ mol } I_2}{2 \text{ mol HI}}$

Calculate the number of moles of H_2 and I_2 used in the reaction.

$$1.56 \cancel{\text{mol HI}} \times \frac{1 \text{ mol } H_2}{2 \cancel{\text{mol HI}}} = 0.780 \text{ mol } H_2$$

$$1.56 \cancel{\text{mol HI}} \times \frac{1 \text{ mol } I_2}{2 \cancel{\text{mol HI}}} = 0.780 \text{ mol } I_2$$

Calculate how much H_2 and I_2 remain at equilibrium.

$$\text{mol } H_2 = (1.00 \text{ mol} - 0.780 \text{ mol}) = 0.22 \text{ mol}$$

$$\text{mol } I_2 = (1.00 \text{ mol} - 0.780 \text{ mol}) = 0.22 \text{ mol}$$

Write the expression for K_{eq}.

$$K_{eq} = \frac{[HI]^2}{[H_2] \times [I_2]}$$

Substitute the equilibrium concentrations of the reactants and products into the equation and then solve for K_{eq}.

$$K_{eq} = \frac{(1.56 \text{mol/L})^2}{0.22 \text{ mol/L} \times 0.22 \text{ mol/L}} = \frac{1.56 \cancel{\text{mol/L}} \times 1.56 \cancel{\text{mol/L}}}{0.22 \cancel{\text{mol/L}} \times 0.22 \cancel{\text{mol/L}}} = 5.0 \times 10^1$$

3 Evaluate Does the result make sense? Each concentration is raised to the correct power. The value of the constant reflects the presence of significant amounts of reactants and product in the equilibrium mixture.

Hint: Place substances from the left side of the equation in the denominator. Place substances from the right side of the equation in the numerator.

BUILD Math Skills

Properties of Exponents An exponent, or power, tells you how many times a number, known as the base, is a factor in a math operation.

The expression 8^2 is read as 8 to the second power or, more often, eight squared. The exponent 2 tells you that the base 8 appears twice in the multiplication. An exponent of 3 tells you that the 8 appears three times.

exponent
8^2
base

$8^2 = 8 \times 8 = 64$

$8^3 = 8 \times 8 \times 8 = 512$

The equation for the equilibrium constant uses exponents. Suppose the numerator of an equilibrium constant were $[C]^2 \times [D]^2$. The numerator could be rewritten as $[C] \times [C] \times [D] \times [D]$.

Practice Problems

17. Suppose the following system reaches equilibrium:

$$N_2(g) + O_2(g) \rightleftharpoons 2NO(g)$$

The equilibrium mixture is in a 1 L flask. The mixture contains 0.50 mol of N_2, 0.50 mol of O_2, and 0.020 mol of NO. Calculate K_{eq} for the reaction.

1 Analyze List the knowns and the unknown.

2 Calculate Solve for the unknown.

3 Evaluate Does the result make sense?

KNOWNS	UNKNOWN
$[N_2]$(equilibrium) = 0.50 mol/L	K_{eq} = ?
$[O_2]$(equilibrium) = 0.50 mol/L	
[NO](equilibrium) = 0.020 mol/L	

18. A mixture at equilibrium at 827°C contains 0.552 mol CO_2, 0.552 mol H_2, 0.448 mol CO, and 0.448 mol H_2O. Here is the balanced equation for the reaction.

$$CO_2(g) + H_2(g) \rightleftharpoons CO(g) + H_2O(g)$$

What is the value of K_{eq}?

KNOWNS	UNKNOWN
$[CO_2]$(equilibrium) = 0.552 mol/L	K_{eq} = ?
$[H_2]$(equilibrium) = 0.552 mol/L	
[CO](equilibrium) =	
$[H_2O]$(equilibrium) =	

19. Challenge At 750°C, the following reaction reaches equilibrium in a 1 L flask:

$$H_2(g) + CO_2(g) \rightleftharpoons H_2O(g) + CO(g)$$

The reaction starts with 0.100 mol H_2 and 0.100 mol CO_2. At equilibrium, there is 0.047 mol H_2O and 0.047 mol CO. Calculate K_{eq} for the reaction.

Hint: In Problem 19, you must first find the equilibrium concentrations of H_2 and CO_2.

Sample Problem 18.3

Finding Concentrations at Equilibrium

Bromine chloride (BrCl) decomposes to form bromine and chlorine.

$$2BrCl(g) \rightleftharpoons Br_2(g) + Cl_2(g)$$

At a certain temperature, the equilibrium constant for the reaction is 11.1. A sample of pure BrCl is placed in a 1 L container and allowed to decompose. At equilibrium, the reaction mixture contains 4.00 mol Cl_2. What are the equilibrium concentrations of Br_2 and BrCl?

1 Analyze List the knowns and the unknowns. Use the balanced equation, equilibrium constant, and equilibrium constant expression to find the unknown concentrations. According to the balanced equation, when BrCl decomposes, an equal number of moles of Br_2 and Cl_2 are formed.

KNOWNS	UNKNOWNS
$[Cl_2]$(equilibrium) = 4.00 mol/L	$[Br_2]$ (equilibrium) = ? mol/L
K_{eq} = 11.1	[BrCl](equilibrium) = ? mol/L

2 Calculate Solve for the unknowns.

Calculate $[Br_2]$ at equilibrium. The volume of the container is 1 L.

$$[Br_2] = \frac{4.00\text{ mol}}{1\text{ L}} = 4.00\text{ mol/L}$$

Write the equilibrium expression for the reaction.

$$K_{eq} = \frac{[Br_2] \times [Cl_2]}{[BrCl]^2}$$

Rearrange the equation to solve for $[BrCl]^2$. Multiply both sides of the equation by $[BrCl]^2$. Divide both sides of the equation by K_{eq}.

$$K_{eq} \times [BrCl]^2 = \frac{[Br_2] \times [Cl_2]}{\cancel{[BrCl]^2}} \times \cancel{[BrCl]^2}$$

$$\cancel{K_{eq}} \times \frac{[BrCl]^2}{\cancel{K_{eq}}} = \frac{[Br_2] \times [Cl_2]}{K_{eq}}$$

$$[BrCl]^2 = \frac{[Br_2] \times [Cl_2]}{K_{eq}}$$

Hint: Based on the reaction equation, $[Br_2] = [Cl_2]$.

Substitute the known values for K_{eq}, $[Br_2]$, and $[Cl_2]$.

$$[BrCl]^2 = \frac{[Br_2] \times [Cl_2]}{K_{eq}} = \frac{4.00\text{ mol/L} \times 4.00\text{ mol/L}}{11.1}$$

$$= 1.44\text{ mol}^2/\text{L}^2$$

Find [BrCl] by taking the square root of each side of the equation.

$$[BrCl] = \sqrt{1.44\text{ mol}^2/\text{L}^2} = 1.20\text{ mol/L}$$

Use your calculator to find the square root.

3 Evaluate Does the result make sense? It makes sense that both the reactant and the products are present in significant amounts at equilibrium because K_{eq} has an intermediate value.

BUILD Math Skills

Finding the Square Root Finding a square root is the inverse, or opposite, of finding the square of a number. For example, $\sqrt{64}$ is the opposite of 8^2.

The number 64 is called a perfect square because its square root is a whole number. The number 12 is not a perfect square. Say that you need to find $\sqrt{12}$. Find the two perfect squares on either side of 12 on an imaginary number line.

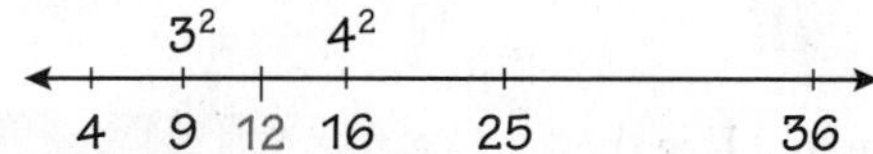

The $\sqrt{9}$ is 3, and the $\sqrt{16}$ is 4. So the $\sqrt{12}$ is between 3 and 4.

Divide 12 by one of the perfect square roots: $12 \div 3 = 4$. Add the answer to the square root: $4 + 3 = 7$. Divide 7 by 2 to get the average: $7 \div 2 = 3.5$.

To check your work, find the square of 3.5: $3.5^2 = 3.5 \times 3.5 = 12.25$. Because the answer is close to 12, the square root of 12 is about 3.5.

Go to your Chemistry Skills and Math Workbook for more practice.

Practice Problems

20. At a certain temperature, the equilibrium constant for the reaction in which nitrogen dioxide forms dinitrogen tetroxide is 5.6.

$$2NO_2(g) \rightleftharpoons N_2O_4(g)$$

In a 1 L container, the amount of N_2O_4 at equilibrium is 0.66 mol. What is the equilibrium concentration of NO_2?

1 Analyze **List the knowns and the unknown.**

2 Calculate **Solve for the unknown.**

3 Evaluate **Does the result make sense?**

KNOWNS	UNKNOWN
$[N_2O_4]$(equilibrium) = 0.66 mol/L	$[NO_2]$ (equilibrium) = ? mol/L
$K_{eq} = 5.6$	

21. Phosphorus pentachloride (PCl_5) decomposes when heated.

$$PCl_5(g) \rightleftharpoons PCl_3(g) + Cl_2(g)$$

In a 1 L container, the amount of PCl_3 at equilibrium is 0.15 mol at 170°C. What are the equilibrium concentrations of PCl_5 and Cl_2? ($K_{eq} = 0.022$)

22. Challenge Hydrogen iodide decomposes to form hydrogen and iodine.

$$2HI(g) \rightleftharpoons H_2(g) + I_2(g)$$

In a 1 L container at 450°C, the equilibrium mixture contains 0.50 mol of hydrogen. What are the equilibrium concentrations of hydrogen and hydrogen iodide? ($K_{eq} = 0.020$)

Hint: For Problems 21 and 22, start by making a Knowns and Unknowns box.

CHEMISTRY & YOU: CAREERS

Chemical Engineer

You may think that surfing is about as far away from chemistry as you can get. But you would be wrong! Surfboards, wetsuits, and even the waxes used to help keep your feet on the board are made from products developed by chemical engineers.

A major goal of chemical engineers is the large-scale manufacture of such products as plastics and medicines. Chemical engineers may design factories and evaluate their operation after they are built. These engineers may also design ways to extract substances from their ores.

Take It Further

1. Infer What are some reasons why chemical engineers might need a wide range of science and engineering knowledge in their work?

2. Identify What are some products you use every day that could have been developed by a chemical engineer?

18.3 LessonCheck

Key Concept Check

23. **Review** What happens to the amounts of reactants and products after a reaction has reached chemical equilibrium?

24. **List** What are three stresses that can upset the equilibrium of a chemical system?

25. **Explain** What does the value of the equilibrium constant tell you about the amounts of reactants and products present at equilibrium?

Vocabulary Check

Choose a highlighted word from the lesson to complete this sentence correctly.

26. The relative concentrations of reactants and products of a reaction that has reached equilibrium is called the ______.

Think Critically

27. **Describe** How can you use a balanced equation to write an equilibrium constant expression?

28. **Apply Concepts** Which of the equilibrium constants indicates a reaction in which the amount of product is much larger than the amount of reactant at equilibrium? Explain.

a. $K_{eq} = 1 \times 10^{8}$ **b.** $K_{eq} = 3 \times 10^{-6}$

CHEMISTRY & YOU

29. Fritz Haber and Karl Bosch found a way to increase the yield of ammonia when nitrogen and hydrogen react. Their success came from controlling the temperature and pressure. In which direction did they adjust each factor and why? (Hint: See pages 579 and 580.)

BIGIDEA REACTIONS

30. Review the definition of percent yield in Lesson 12.3. How can understanding Le Châtelier's principle help chemists increase the percent yield of a reversible chemical reaction?

18.4 Solubility Equilibrium

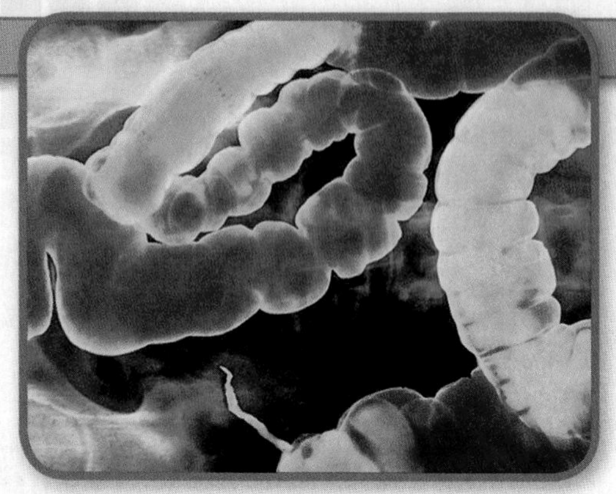

CHEMISTRY & YOU

Q: How is it possible to drink a poison without being harmed? A substance is needed to make organs other than bones visible on X-ray images. For one test, the patient drinks a thick liquid that contains barium sulfate. Because barium sulfate can absorb X-rays, tissues coated with the liquid will show up as light areas on an X-ray image. Barium sulfate is a poison. This lesson will help you understand how barium sulfate can be safely used for this test.

Key Questions

What is the relationship between the solubility product constant and the solubility of a compound?

How can you predict whether precipitation will occur when two solutions are mixed?

BUILD Vocabulary

solubility product constant (K_{sp}) an equilibrium constant that is based only on the concentration of dissolved ions in a solution

WORD ORIGINS

The word *solubility* comes from the Latin word *solvere,* which means "to loosen." When an ionic compound dissolves in water, the attraction of the water molecules causes the bonds between ions to "loosen" or break.

The Solubility Product Constant

A substance that can dissolve in water is defined as *soluble.* Most ionic compounds of alkali metals are soluble in water. For example, more than 35 g of sodium chloride can dissolve in only 100 g of water. A substance that does not dissolve in water is defined as *insoluble.* For example, compounds that contain phosphate or carbonate ions tend to be insoluble in water. The table below gives some general rules for the solubility of ionic compounds in water.

Solubility of Ionic Compounds in Water

Compounds	Solubility	Exceptions
Salts of Group 1A metals and ammonia	Soluble	Some lithium compounds
Ethanoates, nitrates, chlorates, and perchlorates	Soluble	Few exceptions
Sulfates	Soluble	Compounds of Pb, Ag, Hg, Ba, Sr, and Ca
Chlorides, bromides, and iodides	Soluble	Compounds of Ag and some compounds of Hg and Pb
Sulfides and hydroxides	Most are insoluble	Alkali metal sulfides and hydroxides are soluble. Compounds of Ba, Sr, and Ca are slightly soluble.
Carbonates, sulfites, and phosphates	Insoluble	Compounds of alkali metals and of ammonium ions

Solubility Product Constants (K_{sp}) at 25°C					
Ionic compound	K_{sp}	**Ionic compound**	K_{sp}	**Ionic compound**	K_{sp}
Halides		**Sulfates**		**Hydroxides**	
$AgCl$	1.8×10^{-10}	$PbSO_4$	6.3×10^{-7}	$Al(OH)_3$	3.0×10^{-34}
$AgBr$	5.0×10^{-13}	$BaSO_4$	1.1×10^{-10}	$Zn(OH)_2$	3.0×10^{-16}
AgI	8.3×10^{-17}	$CaSO_4$	2.4×10^{-5}	$Ca(OH)_2$	6.5×10^{-6}
$PbCl_2$	1.7×10^{-5}	**Sulfides**		$Mg(OH)_2$	7.1×10^{-12}
$PbBr_2$	2.1×10^{-6}	NiS	4.0×10^{-20}	$Fe(OH)_2$	7.9×10^{-16}
PbI_2	7.9×10^{-9}	CuS	8.0×10^{-37}	**Carbonates**	
PbF_2	3.6×10^{-8}	Ag_2S	8.0×10^{-51}	$CaCO_3$	4.5×10^{-9}
CaF_2	3.9×10^{-11}	ZnS	3.0×10^{-23}	$SrCO_3$	9.3×10^{-10}
Chromates		FeS	8.0×10^{-19}	$ZnCO_3$	1.0×10^{-10}
$PbCrO_4$	1.8×10^{-14}	CdS	1.0×10^{-27}	Ag_2CO_3	8.1×10^{-12}
Ag_2CrO_4	1.2×10^{-12}	PbS	3.0×10^{-28}	$BaCO_3$	5.0×10^{-9}

Describing Solubility Scientists use the constant K_{sp} to compare the solubilities of ionic compounds. The **solubility product constant** (K_{sp}) is an equilibrium constant based only on the concentrations of dissolved ions in a solution. You can use this equation to find a solubility product constant.

$$K_{sp} = [A]^a \times [B]^b$$

[A] and [B] are the concentrations of the dissolved ions.

The exponents a and b are the coefficients of A and B from the balanced equation.

The figure on the right shows that silver chloride is a compound that is only slightly soluble in water.

$$AgCl(s) \rightleftharpoons Ag^+(aq) + Cl^-(aq)$$

In the balanced equation, the coefficient for each ion is 1. So the K_{sp} expression for the dissociation is written as:

$$K_{sp} = [Ag^+] \times [Cl^-]$$

Value of Solubility Product Constant What does the size of the solubility product constant tell you about solubility? The smaller the value of the constant, the lower the solubility of a compound. Look at the table at the top of this page. It lists the K_{sp} values for some ionic compounds that are slightly soluble in water. Compare the K_{sp} values of silver chloride (AgCl) and silver bromide (AgBr). For AgCl, the K_{sp} value is 1.8×10^{-10}. For AgBr, the K_{sp} value is 5.0×10^{-13}. Because its K_{sp} value is larger, silver chloride is more soluble than silver bromide.

Key Question What is the relationship between the solubility product constant and the solubility of a compound? **The smaller the value of the solubility product constant, the lower the solubility of the compound.**

Silver Chloride When AgCl is added to water, a small amount of it dissolves. The rest of the AgCl remains a solid.

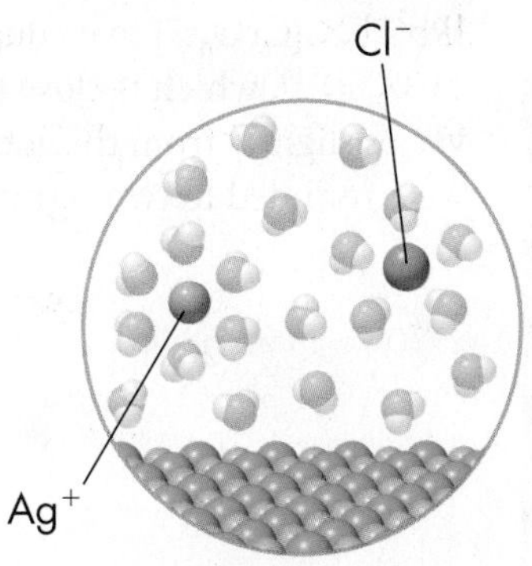

Sample Problem 18.4

Finding the Ion Concentrations in a Saturated Solution

What is the concentration of lead ions and chromate ions in a saturated solution of lead(II) chromate at 25°C? ($K_{sp} = 1.8 \times 10^{-14}$)

1 Analyze **List the knowns and the unknowns.** Write the expression for K_{sp}. Then, change it so there is a single unknown.

KNOWNS	UNKNOWNS
$K_{sp} = 1.8 \times 10^{-14}$	$[Pb^{2+}] = ?\ M$
$PbCrO_4(s) \rightleftharpoons Pb^{2+}(aq) + CrO_4^{2-}(aq)$	$[CrO_4^{2-}] = ?\ M$

2 Calculate **Solve for the unknowns.**

Start with the general expression for the solubility product constant.

$$K_{sp} = [A]^a \times [B]^b$$

Use the balanced chemical equation to write the correct expression for K_{sp} for the reaction.

$$K_{sp} = [Pb^{2+}] \times [CrO_4^{2-}] = 1.8 \times 10^{-14}$$

At equilibrium, $[Pb^{2+}] = [CrO_4^{2-}]$.

Substitute $[Pb^{2+}]$ for $[CrO_4^{2-}]$ in the expression to get an equation with one unknown.

$$K_{sp} = [Pb^{2+}] \times [Pb^{2+}] = [Pb^{2+}]^2 = 1.8 \times 10^{-14}$$

Solve for $[Pb^{2+}]$.

$$[Pb^{2+}] = \sqrt{1.8 \times 10^{-14}}$$

$$[Pb^{2+}] = [CrO_4^{2-}] = 1.3 \times 10^{-7} M$$

3 Evaluate **Does the result make sense?** Calculate $[Pb^{2+}] \times [CrO_4^{2-}]$ to evaluate the answer. The result is 1.7×10^{-14}, which is close to the value for K_{sp}. The result varies slightly from the actual value because the answers were rounded to two significant figures.

If a formula in the balanced equation does not have a coefficient, the coefficient is understood to be 1.

BUILD Math Skills

Negative Exponents Remember that an exponent is a value that tells you how many times a number is a factor in an operation. In 8^2, the exponent is positive. So the operation is multiplication: $8^2 = 8 \times 8 = 64$.

base → 8^2 ← positive exponent

A negative exponent tells you how many times to divide by the base number. Division is the opposite operation of multiplication.

base → 8^{-2} ← negative exponent

To do a calculation with a negative exponent, it helps to think of the negative sign in the exponent as a fraction bar. You can rewrite 8^{-2} as 8^2 and then make it the denominator of a fraction in which 1 is the numerator. This operation is called finding the reciprocal:

$$8^{-2} = \frac{1}{(8 \times 8)} = 0.015625$$

Practice Problems

31. Lead(II) sulfide (PbS) has a K_{sp} value of 3.0×10^{-28}. What is the concentration of lead(II) ions in a saturated solution of PbS at 25°C?

❶ **Analyze** **List the knowns and the unknown.**

❷ **Calculate** **Solve for the unknown.**

❸ **Evaluate** **Does the result make sense?**

KNOWNS	UNKNOWN
$K_{sp} = 3.0 \times 10^{-28}$	$[Pb^{2+}] = ?M$
$PbS(s) \rightleftharpoons Pb^{2+}(aq) + S^{2-}(aq)$	

32. Barium carbonate ($BaCO_3$) has a K_{sp} value of 5.0×10^{-9}. What is the concentration of barium ions in a saturated solution of $BaCO_3$ at 25°C?

KNOWNS	UNKNOWN
$K_{sp} = 5.0 \times 10^{-9}$	$[Ba^{2+}] = ?M$
$BaCO_3(s) \rightleftharpoons Ba^{2+}(aq) + CO_3^{2-}(aq)$	

33. What is the concentration of carbonate ions in a saturated solution of $SrCO_3$? ($K_{sp} = 9.3 \times 10^{-10}$)

34. **Challenge** What is the concentration of calcium ions in a saturated calcium carbonate solution at 25°C? Use the K_{sp} value for calcium carbonate from the table on page 589.

Hint: Start by writing the equation for the dissociation of the solid ionic compound.

common ion an ion that is found in more than one ionic compound in a solution

common ion effect the lowering of the solubility of an ionic compound due to the addition of a common ion

RELATED WORDS

To help keep the words *affect* and *effect* straight, try this: Affect comes from a word meaning "to act." Use *affect* to describe an action. Effect comes from a word meaning "to accomplish." Use *effect* to describe a result.

The Common Ion Effect

In a saturated solution of lead(II) chromate, an equilibrium is established between the solid lead(II) chromate and its ions in solution. Remember that a saturated solution is not able to dissolve any more solute. Look at the value of K_{sp} below. The value is low, which tells you that lead(II) chromate is only slightly soluble in water.

$$PbCrO_4(s) \rightleftharpoons Pb^{2+}(aq) + CrO_4^{2-}(aq) \quad K_{sp} = 1.8 \times 10^{-14}$$

The photographs below show what happens when some crystals of solid lead(II) nitrate, $Pb(NO_3)_2$, are added to a saturated solution of lead(II) chromate. Lead(II) nitrate is soluble in water. When the crystals dissolve, the concentration of lead ions in solution increases.

According to Le Châtelier's principle, the added lead ions are a stress on the system. Adding a product to a system at equilibrium causes a shift toward reactants. So adding lead ions increases the rate of the reverse reaction. The extra lead ions combine with chromate ions in the solution to form solid $PbCrO_4$. The ions continue to react until the product of their concentrations is once again 1.8×10^{-14}. At the new equilibrium position, the concentration of lead ions in solution is higher. The concentration of chromate ions is lower.

Common Ions in Solution In this example, the lead ion is a common ion. A **common ion** is an ion that is found in both ionic compounds in a solution. Adding a common ion does not change the K_{sp}. It can change the amount of solid in the equilibrium mixture. Look again at the photographs. There is more solid lead(II) chromate in the test tube after lead ions are added.

Adding lead ions lowered the solubility of lead(II) chromate. The lowering of the solubility of an ionic compound due to the addition of a common ion is called the **common ion effect**. For this effect to work, the added compound must be more soluble than the compound that is already in the solution.

Example of the Common Ion Effect

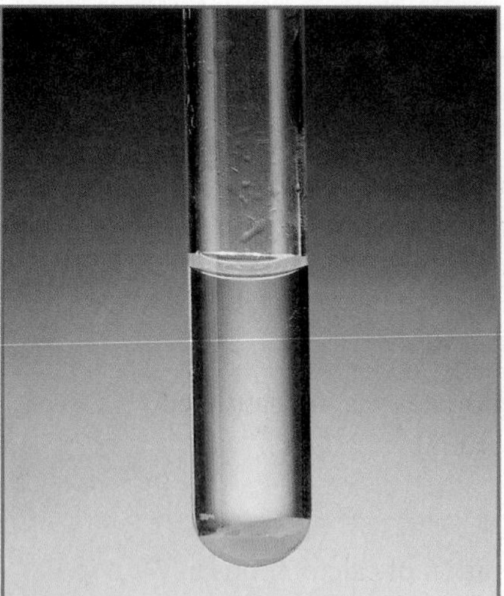

The yellow solid is $PbCrO_4$. The solid cannot dissolve because the solution is saturated with Pb^{2+} and CrO_4^{2-} ions.

When lead(II) nitrate, $Pb(NO_3)_2$, is added to the solution, $PbCrO_4$ precipitates from the solution.

SampleProblem 18.5

Finding Equilibrium Ion Concentrations in the Presence of a Common Ion

Small amounts of silver bromide can be added to the lenses used for eyeglasses. The silver bromide causes the lenses to darken in the presence of large amounts of UV light. The K_{sp} of silver bromide is 5.0×10^{-13}. What is the concentration of bromide ion when 0.020 mol of $AgNO_3$ is added to a 1.00 L saturated solution of AgBr?

❶ Analyze List the knowns and the unknown. Use one unknown to express both $[Ag^+]$ and $[Br^-]$. Let x be the equilibrium concentration of bromide ion and $x + 0.020$ be the equilibrium concentration of silver ion.

KNOWNS	UNKNOWN
$K_{sp} = 5.0 \times 10^{-13}$	$[Br^-] = ?\ M$
moles of $AgNO_3$ added = 0.020 mol $AgBr(s) \rightleftharpoons Ag^+(aq) + Br^-(aq)$	

❷ Calculate Solve for the unknown.

Write the expression for K_{sp}.

$$K_{sp} = [Ag^+] \times [Br^-]$$

Substitute x for $[Br^-]$ in the solubility product expression.

$$K_{sp} = [Ag^+] \times x$$

Rearrange the equation to solve for x.

$$x = \frac{K_{sp}}{[Ag^+]}$$

Based on the small value of K_{sp}, you can assume that x will be very small compared to 0.020. Thus, $[Ag^+] \approx 0.020M$.

Substitute the values for K_{sp} and $[Ag^+]$ in the expression and solve.

$$x = \frac{(5.0 \times 10^{-13})}{0.020}$$

$$[Br^-] = 2.5 \times 10^{-11}M$$

❸ Evaluate Does the result make sense? The concentration of Br^- in a saturated solution of AgBr is $7.1 \times 10^{-7}M$ (the square root of the K_{sp}). It makes sense that the addition of $AgNO_3$ would lower the concentration of Br^- because adding a common ion, Ag^+, causes AgBr to precipitate from the solution.

For a slightly soluble compound, assume that the amount of the compound that dissolves is small compared to the amount of the common ion that is added.

BUILD Math Skills

Ordering Numbers With Negative Exponents It is sometimes hard to order numbers that have negative exponents. A common mistake is to treat 10^{-2} like -2 and place it to the left of 0 on a number line. Numbers with negative exponents actually fall between 0 and 1. Consider 2^{-1} and 2^{-2}. You can rewrite these numbers as their reciprocals and then divide to find their values.

$$2^{-1} = \frac{1}{2^1} = \frac{1}{2} = 0.50$$

$$2^{-2} = \frac{1}{2^2} = \frac{1}{4} = 0.25$$

Placing the values on a number line makes it easy to see the order.

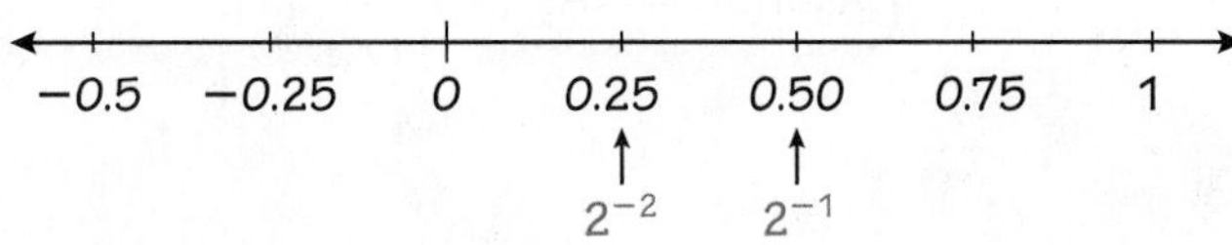

Practice Problems

35. What is the concentration of sulfide ion in a 1.0 L solution of iron(II) sulfide to which 0.04 mol of iron(II) nitrate is added? The K_{sp} of FeS is 8×10^{-19}.

❶ Analyze **List the knowns and the unknown.**

❷ Calculate **Solve for the unknown.**

❸ Evaluate **Does the result make sense?**

KNOWNS	UNKNOWN
$K_{sp} = 8 \times 10^{-19}$	$[S^{2-}] = ?\ M$
moles of $Fe(NO_3)_2$ added = 0.04 mol	
$FeS(s) \rightleftharpoons Fe^{2+}(aq) + S^{2-}(aq)$	

36. The K_{sp} value for barium sulfate is 1.1×10^{-10}. What is the sulfate-ion concentration of a 1.00 L saturated solution of $BaSO_4$ to which 0.015 mol of $Ba(NO_3)_2$ is added?

KNOWNS	UNKNOWN
$K_{sp} = 1.1 \times 10^{-10}$	$[SO_4^{2-}] = ?\ M$
moles of $Ba(NO_3)_2$ added = 0.015 mol	
$BaSO_4(s) \rightleftharpoons Ba^{2+}(aq) + SO_4^{2-}(aq)$	

37. What is the equilibrium concentration of barium ion in a 1.0 L saturated solution of barium carbonate to which 0.25 mol K_2CO_3 is added?

38. Challenge The K_{sp} of $SrSO_4$ is 3.2×10^{-7}. What is the equilibrium concentration of sulfate ion in a 1.0 L solution of strontium sulfate to which 0.10 mol of $Sr(CH_3CO_2)_2$ is added?

Predicting Precipitates You can use the solubility product constant to predict whether a precipitate will form when two solutions are mixed. Suppose you mix 0.50 L of 0.002*M* $Ba(NO_3)_2$ with 0.50 L of 0.008*M* Na_2SO_4. The volume of the mixture is 1.00 L. A compound that might form a precipitate is barium sulfate ($BaSO_4$). Barium sulfate has a K_{sp} of 1.1×10^{-10}. If the product of the concentrations of Ba^{2+} and SO_4^{2-} is greater than the K_{sp} value of barium sulfate, a precipitate will form. If the product is less than the K_{sp} value, no precipitate forms. This table summarizes the two possible outcomes.

Condition	Precipitate	Type of Solution
$[Ba^{2+}] \times [SO_4^{2-}] > K_{sp}$	Yes	Saturated
$[Ba^{2+}] \times [SO_4^{2-}] < K_{sp}$	No	Unsaturated

To predict the outcome, you need to know the concentrations of the ions after the solutions are mixed. For each ion in the solution, the final volume is twice the original volume. So the concentrations of both Ba^{2+} and SO_4^{2-} are half their original concentrations: $[Ba^{2+}] = 0.001M$ and $[SO_4^{2-}] = 0.004M$. Multiply the concentrations and then compare the result with the K_{sp} value.

$$[Ba^{2+}] \times [SO_4^{2-}] = (0.001M) \times (0.004M) = 4 \times 10^{-6}$$

The product of the ion concentrations is greater than 1.1×10^{-10}. So $BaSO_4$ precipitates as shown in the photo. The process goes on until the product of the concentrations of the ions in solution is once again 1.1×10^{-10}.

Formation of a Precipitate When these solutions of barium nitrate and sodium sulfate are mixed, a precipitate of $BaSO_4$ forms.

Key Question How can you predict whether precipitation will occur when two solutions are mixed? **A precipitate will form if the product of the concentrations of two ions in the mixture is greater than the K_{sp} value of the compound formed from the ions.**

18.4 LessonCheck

Key Concept Check

39. Summarize What does the solubility product constant tell about the solubility of a compound?

40. Identify What two values should you compare to predict whether a precipitate will form when two solutions are mixed?

Vocabulary Check

Choose a highlighted word from the lesson to complete the sentence correctly.

41. An ion found in two ionic compounds in a solution is called the ________.

Think Critically

42. Compare Which compound has the higher solubility: FeS ($K_{sp} = 8.0 \times 10^{-19}$) or CuS ($K_{sp} = 8.0 \times 10^{-37}$)?

43. Predict Will a precipitate form when 500 mL of a 0.02*M* solution of $AgNO_3$ is mixed with 500 mL of a 0.001*M* solution of NaCl? Explain.

CHEMISTRY & YOU

44. How can patients drink a mixture containing $BaSO_4$ without being harmed? (Hint: See pages 588 and 589.)

BIGIDEA REACTIONS

45. Explain how the common ion effect illustrates Le Châtelier's principle.

18.5 Free Energy and Entropy

Key Questions

What are two characteristics of spontaneous reactions?

What part does entropy play in a reaction?

What two factors determine whether a reaction is spontaneous?

How is the value of ΔG related to the spontaneity of a reaction?

CHEMISTRY & YOU

Q: How can a fire start on its own? Sometimes a fire can start without an external source of ignition, such as a match or an electrical spark. The fuel might be a pile of oily rags or a stack of hay that is not dry. *Spontaneous combustion* is the term used to describe these fires. In this lesson, you will study the conditions that can cause such a fire.

Free Energy and Spontaneous Reactions

Some of the energy released in a chemical reaction can be used to do work. The energy that is available to do work is called **free energy**. An important word in this definition is *available* because free energy is not always used to do work. For example, only about 30 percent of the free energy released when gasoline burns in an internal combustion engine is used to move the car. The other 70 percent is lost as friction and waste heat.

A process that uses only 30 percent of the free energy released is not very efficient. An *efficient* process uses the least amount of energy, time, or money to produce a desired result. For example, suppose you need to buy five items at the grocery store. Making five trips to the store to buy one item at a time is less efficient than making one trip to buy five items.

No process can be made 100 percent efficient. Living things are among the most efficient users of free energy. But even processes that take place in cells are seldom more than 70 percent efficient.

Spontaneous Versus Nonspontaneous Reactions Energy can be obtained from a reaction only if the reaction happens. Reactions can be divided into two broad groups based on whether they tend to occur. Some reactions, such as those used in fireworks displays, are spontaneous. A **spontaneous reaction** happens naturally and favors the formation of products at the stated conditions. These reactions release free energy.

A reaction that does not favor the formation of products at the stated conditions is a **nonspontaneous reaction**. An example would be the decomposition of carbon dioxide into carbon and oxygen. This type of reaction produces little, if any, product.

Reversible Reactions In nearly all reversible reactions, one reaction is favored over the other. Look at this equation for the decomposition of carbonic acid in water.

$$\underset{<1\%}{H_2CO_3(aq)} \rightleftharpoons \underset{>99\%}{CO_2(g) + H_2O(l)}$$

In the forward reaction, carbonic acid is the reactant. Suppose you could start with pure carbonic acid in water and let the system come to equilibrium. More than 99 percent of the reactant would be changed to carbon dioxide and water. These products are highly favored at equilibrium. The forward reaction is spontaneous because carbonic acid tends to decompose.

In the reverse reaction, carbon dioxide and water are the reactants. Suppose you let a solution of carbon dioxide in water come to equilibrium. Less than 1 percent of the reactants will combine to form carbonic acid. The products are not favored at equilibrium. So the reverse reaction is nonspontaneous.

The Rate of Spontaneous Reactions The words *spontaneous* and *nonspontaneous* do not describe the rate of a reaction. Some spontaneous reactions are so slow that they appear to be nonspontaneous. One example is the reaction of table sugar and oxygen.

$$C_{12}H_{22}O_{11} + 12O_2 \longrightarrow 12CO_2 + 11H_2O$$

At room temperature, the reaction is so slow that it would take thousands of years for the reaction to reach completion. If you supply energy in the form of heat, the same reaction happens quickly. With heat, it becomes clear that the formation of carbon dioxide and water is highly favored.

Changing the conditions of a chemical reaction can affect more than the reaction rate. It can also affect whether a reaction will take place. A reaction that is nonspontaneous in one set of conditions may be spontaneous in other conditions. Think about photosynthesis. The equation below summarizes this multistep reaction that takes place in plants. The process could not happen without energy from sunlight.

Key Question What are two characteristics of spontaneous reactions? **Spontaneous reactions produce large amounts of products and release free energy.**

BUILD Vocabulary

free energy the energy that is available to do work

spontaneous reaction a reaction that favors the formation of products at the stated conditions

nonspontaneous reaction a reaction that does not favor the formation of products at the stated conditions

ACADEMIC WORDS

The word *spontaneous* can mean natural or unplanned. You might use it to describe the applause after someone dunks a basketball or a person who suddenly jumps up on stage at a concert.

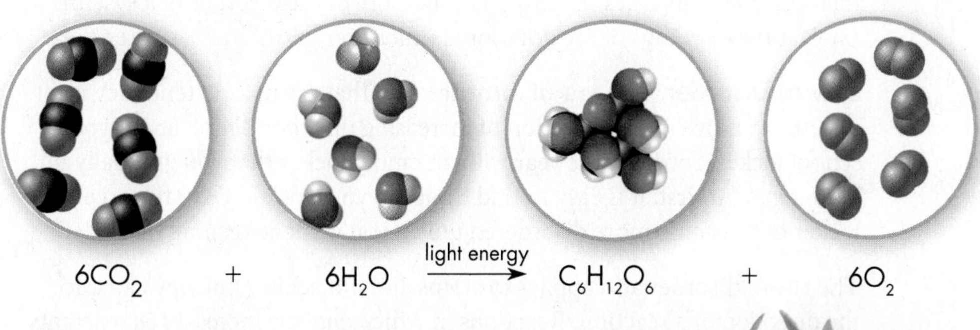

Photosynthesis Outside of plants, carbon dioxide and water do not tend to combine to produce glucose ($C_6H_{12}O_6$) and oxygen.

Comparison of Order and Disorder When the dog walker unleashes the dogs, the dogs are less ordered. Entropy increases.

All the dogs are on leashes and are strolling together along the path. This situation represents order.

Dogs that are no longer on leashes tend to run freely. This situation represents disorder.

entropy a measure of the disorder of a system

law of disorder the natural tendency is for systems to move in the direction of increasing disorder or randomness

PREFIXES

The prefix *dis-* means "not" or "opposite." To connect means to bring things together. To disconnect means to separate things. Connect and disconnect are opposites, as are order and disorder.

Entropy

Changes in the heat content, or enthalpy, of a system help determine whether a chemical or physical change is spontaneous. You might expect only systems that release energy to be spontaneous, but systems that absorb energy can be spontaneous too.

Think about what happens as ice melts. As ice changes to a liquid, it absorbs heat from its surroundings. The liquid water has a higher energy than the solid ice. Melting is both endothermic and spontaneous. So enthalpy change cannot be the only factor that determines whether a change is spontaneous.

Order and Disorder The other factor is disorder. A pile of marbles is relatively ordered because the marbles are in one place. If the marbles are scattered, they become disordered. The scattered marbles have higher entropy than the pile of marbles. **Entropy** is a measure of the disorder of a system. Look at the drawings of the dogs for another example of increasing entropy.

Law of Disorder The **law of disorder** says that the natural tendency is for systems to move in the direction of increasing disorder. Think about your school locker. You start the year with an empty locker that you gradually fill with items. At first, it is easy to find things in your locker. Over time, your locker can become more disordered unless you work at keeping the order.

The law of disorder also applies to atoms and molecules. Entropy can affect the direction of a reaction. Reactions in which entropy increases as reactants form products tend to be favored. The figure on the next page provides some general rules to help you predict the effect of entropy on a reaction.

Key Question What part does entropy play in a reaction? **Reactions in which entropy increases as reactants form products tend to be favored.**

Entropy Here are four examples of changes that can increase the entropy of a system.

States of Matter A gas has more entropy than a liquid or a solid because the particles in a gas move freely. A solid has less entropy than a liquid because the particles in a solid have fixed positions. So entropy increases when solid reactants form liquid or gaseous products. Entropy also increases when liquid reactants form gaseous products.

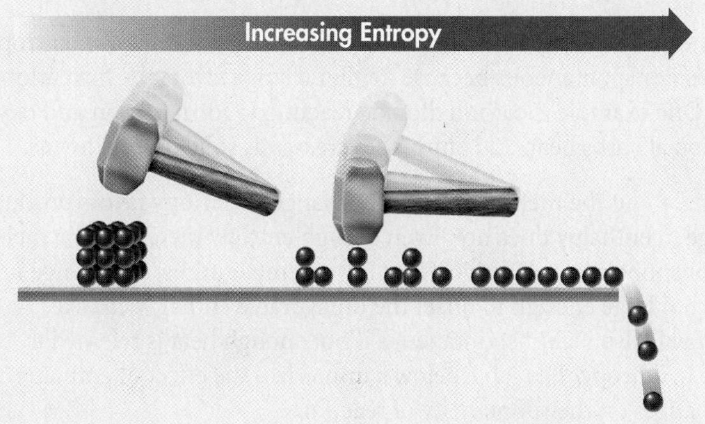

Parts of a Whole Entropy increases when a substance is divided into parts. For example, entropy increases when a hammer breaks an object into pieces. The many small pieces are less ordered than the single object. Entropy also increases when solids form solutions.

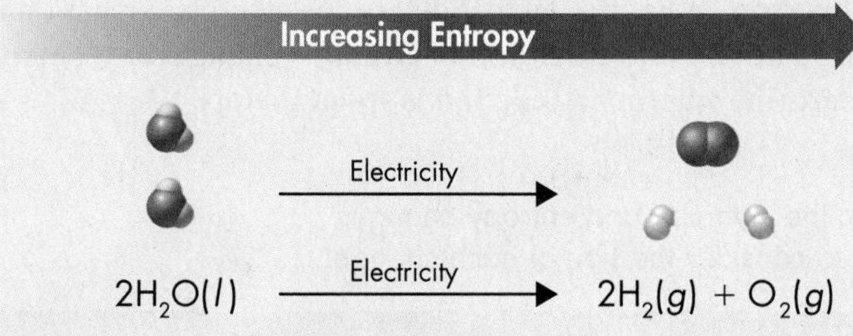

$$2H_2O(l) \xrightarrow{\text{Electricity}} 2H_2(g) + O_2(g)$$

Number of Molecules Entropy tends to increase in chemical reactions when the total number of product molecules is greater than the total number of reactant molecules.

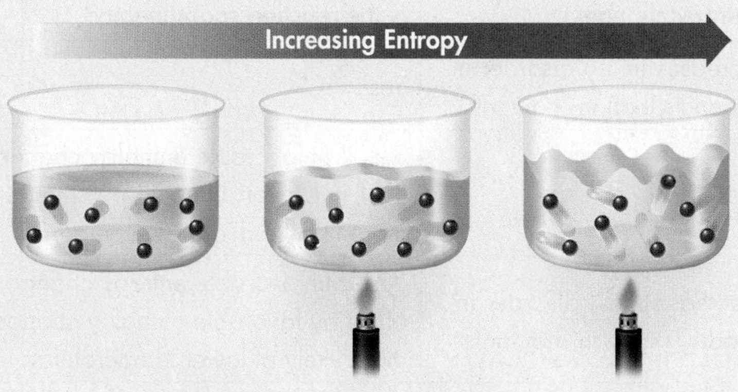

Temperature Effect As the temperature rises, particles gain kinetic energy and are able to move faster. More motion leads to more disorder. So entropy tends to increase at higher temperatures.

Enthalpy and Entropy

In every chemical reaction, heat is either released or absorbed. In every reaction, entropy either increases or decreases. The size and direction of changes in enthalpy and entropy affect whether a reaction is spontaneous.

Spontaneous Reactions An exothermic reaction in which entropy increases is always spontaneous because both changes favor the formation of products. The combustion of carbon is an example. The reaction is exothermic, and entropy increases as solid carbon forms carbon dioxide gas.

What happens when one change favors products and one change does not? Recall the example of ice melting. The change in enthalpy is not favorable because heat is absorbed. The change in entropy is favorable because a solid is changing to a liquid. Even though heat is absorbed, the melting of ice is spontaneous above 0°C. At higher temperatures, the change in entropy is large enough to offset the unfavorable enthalpy change. A reaction will also be spontaneous if a decrease in entropy is offset by a large release of heat.

Nonspontaneous Reactions An endothermic reaction in which entropy decreases is nonspontaneous because neither change favors the formation of products. One example is carbon dioxide reacting to form carbon and oxygen. The reaction absorbs heat, and entropy decreases as solid carbon forms.

Think again about the melting of ice. The change in entropy favors products. The change in enthalpy does not. Even though entropy increases, the melting of ice is nonspontaneous below 0°C. At lower temperatures, the change in entropy is not large enough to offset the unfavorable enthalpy change. A reaction will also be nonspontaneous if not enough heat is released to offset a decrease in entropy. The table below summarizes the effect of enthalpy and entropy changes on the spontaneity of reactions.

Key Question What two factors determine whether a reaction is spontaneous? **The size and direction of enthalpy changes and entropy changes determine whether a reaction is spontaneous.**

Determining Spontaneity When the enthalpy and entropy changes have opposite effects, you need to consider the size of each change.

How Changes in Enthalpy and Entropy Affect Reaction Spontaneity

Enthalpy change	Entropy change	Is the reaction spontaneous?
Decreases (exothermic)	Increases (more disorder in products than in reactants)	Yes
Increases (endothermic)	Increases	Yes, if unfavorable enthalpy change is offset by favorable entropy change; more likely at higher temperatures
Decreases (exothermic)	Decreases (less disorder in products than in reactants)	Yes, if unfavorable entropy change is offset by favorable enthalpy change; more likely at lower temperatures
Increases (endothermic)	Decreases	No

Free Energy Change

Free energy is often called Gibbs free energy. The term is named for Josiah Gibbs, the scientist who defined this property. The symbol for Gibbs free energy is G. Free energy can either be released or absorbed during a physical or chemical process. The equation below is used to calculate the change in Gibbs free energy (ΔG).

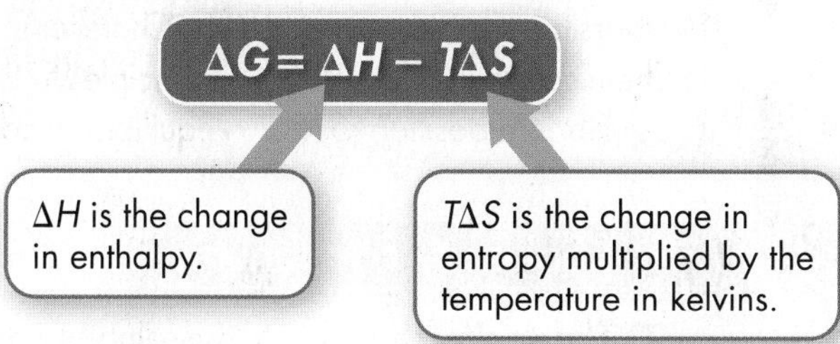

$\Delta G = \Delta H - T\Delta S$
ΔH is the change in enthalpy.
$T\Delta S$ is the change in entropy multiplied by the temperature in kelvins.

Recall that spontaneous processes release free energy, which decreases the amount of free energy in the system. When the amount of free energy in a system decreases, ΔG is negative. In contrast, work must be done for a nonspontaneous process to occur. So the amount of free energy in the system increases and ΔG is positive.

The equation helps explain how temperature can affect the spontaneity of a reaction. In the equation, ΔS is multiplied by T. So as the temperature rises, the effect of entropy is magnified. At higher temperatures, a favorable change in entropy is more likely to offset an unfavorable change in enthalpy.

Key Question How is the value of ΔG related to the spontaneity of a reaction? **When the value of ΔG is negative, a process is spontaneous. When the value is positive, a process is nonspontaneous.**

18.5 LessonCheck

Key Concept Check

46. Review What two characteristics do all spontaneous reactions share?

47. Explain How can you use entropy to determine whether a chemical reaction is more or less likely to be spontaneous?

48. Review What two factors determine the spontaneity of a chemical reaction?

49. Summarize When the Gibbs free energy change for a process is negative, what does this tell you about the process?

Vocabulary Check

Choose a highlighted word from the lesson to complete the sentence correctly.

50. A(n) ________ occurs naturally and favors the formation of products at the stated conditions.

Think Critically

51. Define What is free energy?

52. Draw Conclusions Suppose the products of a reaction are more ordered than the reactants. Is the entropy change favorable or unfavorable?

53. Explain How can a reaction be spontaneous at some conditions but nonspontaneous at other conditions?

CHEMISTRY & YOU

54. Decomposition reactions that occur inside a pile of oily rags release heat. If the heat cannot escape, the temperature within the pile will rise. How can an increase in temperature cause a fire to start on its own? Think about the reaction of table sugar and oxygen. (Hint: See page 597.)

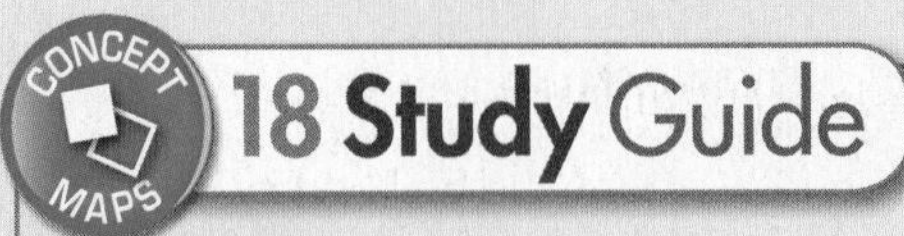

18 Study Guide

BIGIDEAS

REACTIONS; MATTER AND ENERGY

The rate of a chemical reaction can be controlled by adjusting temperature, concentration, or particle size. Adding a catalyst speeds up a reaction by lowering the activation energy. Energy is released in some reactions and absorbed in others. Changes in enthalpy and entropy can be used to explain why some reactions occur naturally and others do not.

18.1 Rates of Reaction

The rate of a chemical reaction, or reaction rate, is usually expressed as the change in the amount of reactant or product per unit time.

Factors that can affect the rate of a chemical reaction are temperature, concentration, particle size, and the use of a catalyst.

- rate (565)
- collision theory (566)
- activation energy (566)
- activated complex (566)
- inhibitor (571)

18.2 The Progress of Chemical Reactions

The value of the specific rate constant (*k*) in a rate law is large if the products form quickly. The value is small if the products form slowly.

Most chemical reactions have two or more steps.

- rate law (572)
- specific rate constant (573)
- reaction mechanism (573)
- intermediate (574)

18.3 Reversible Reactions and Equilibrium

At chemical equilibrium, both the forward and reverse reactions continue. Because their rates are equal, no net change occurs in the concentrations of the reaction components.

Changes in the concentration of reactants or products, changes in temperature, and changes in pressure are stresses that can upset the equilibrium of a chemical system.

The size of the equilibrium constant indicates whether reactants or products are more common at equilibrium.

- reversible reaction (575)
- chemical equilibrium (575)
- equilibrium position (577)
- Le Châtelier's principle (578)
- equilibrium constant (582)

18.4 Solubility Equilibrium

The smaller the value of the solubility product constant, the lower the solubility of the compound.

A precipitate will form if the product of the concentrations of two ions in the mixture is greater than the K_{sp} value of the compound formed from the ions.

- solubility product constant (589)
- common ion (592)
- common ion effect (592)

18.5 Free Energy and Entropy

Spontaneous reactions produce large amounts of products and release free energy.

Reactions in which entropy increases as reactants form products tend to be favored.

The size and direction of enthalpy and entropy changes determine whether a reaction is spontaneous.

When the value of ΔG is negative, a process is spontaneous. When the value is positive, a process is nonspontaneous.

- free energy (596)
- spontaneous reaction (596)
- nonspontaneous reaction (596)
- entropy (598)
- law of disorder (598)

Key Equations

$$\text{Rate} = \frac{\Delta A}{\Delta t} = k \times [A] \qquad \text{Rate} = k[A]^x[B]^y$$

$$K_{eq} = \frac{[C]^c \times [D]^d}{[A]^a \times [B]^b}$$

$$K_{sp} = [A]^a \times [B]^b$$

$$\Delta G = \Delta H - T\Delta S$$

Math Tune-Up: Equilibrium Problems

Problem	❶ Analyze	❷ Calculate	❸ Evaluate
Gaseous sulfur dioxide reacts with oxygen in a 1.0 L container at 600°C to form gaseous sulfur trioxide. $2SO_2(g) + O_2(g) \rightleftharpoons 2SO_3(g)$ At equilibrium, a mixture of these gases contains 1.5 mol SO_2, 1.2 mol O_2, and 3.4 mol SO_3. What is the equilibrium constant for this reaction?	Knowns: $[SO_2] = 1.5$ mol/L $[O_2] = 1.2$ mol/L $[SO_3] = 3.4$ mol/L Unknown: $K_{eq} = ?$ Use the expression for K_{eq}: $K_{eq} = \frac{[C]^c \times [D]^d}{[A]^a \times [B]^b}$	Write the expression for K_{eq} for this equation and then substitute the equilibrium concentrations in the expression. $K_{eq} = \frac{[SO_3]^2}{[SO_2]^2 \times [O_2]}$ $= \frac{(3.4 \text{ mol/L})^2}{(1.5 \text{ mol/L})^2 \times (1.2 \text{ mol/L})}$ $K_{eq} = 4.3$	Each concentration is raised to the correct power. The value for K_{eq} is appropriate for an equilibrium mixture that contains a larger number of moles of products than of reactants.
What is the concentration of silver ions and chloride ions in a saturated solution of silver chloride at 25°C? ($K_{sp} = 1.8 \times 10^{-10}$)	Knowns: $K_{sp} = 1.8 \times 10^{-10}$ $AgCl(s) \rightleftharpoons Ag^+(aq) + Cl^-(aq)$ Unknowns: $[Ag^+] = ?M$ $[Cl^-] = ?M$ Use the expression for K_{sp}: $K_{sp} = [A]^a \times [B]^b$	Write the expression for K_{sp}, modify it so there is a single unknown, and then solve for that unknown. $K_{sp} = [Ag^+] \times [Cl^-]$ $1.8 \times 10^{-10} = [Ag^+]^2$ $[Ag^+] = \sqrt{1.8 \times 10^{-10}}$ $[Ag^+] = 1.3 \times 10^{-5}M$ $[Cl^-] = 1.3 \times 10^{-5}M$	If you multiply $[Ag^+] \times [Cl^-]$, the result is 1.7×10^{-10}, which is close to the value of K_{sp}. The value is not exactly the same because the answers are rounded to two significant figures.
Predict whether a precipitate will form when 0.50 L of 0.001M $Ca(NO_3)_2$ is mixed with 0.50 L of 0.0008M Na_2CO_3 to form one liter of solution. The K_{sp} of $CaCO_3$ is 4.5×10^{-9}.	Knowns: 0.50 L of 0.001M $Ca(NO_3)_2$ 0.50 L of 0.0008M Na_2CO_3 K_{sp} of $CaCO_3 = 4.5 \times 10^{-9}$ Unknown: $[Ca^{2+}] \times [CO_3^{2-}] > K_{sp}$? Precipitation will occur if the product of the concentrations of the two ions exceeds the K_{sp} value of $CaCO_3$.	Divide the initial concentrations in half because the volume of the solution has doubled. Multiply the concentrations together as a trial product and then compare with K_{sp}. $[Ca^{2+}]$ (final) $= 0.0005M$ $[CO_3^{2-}]$ (final) $= 0.0004M$ $[Ca^{2+}] \times [CO_3^{2-}] = (0.0005M) \times (0.0004M) = 2 \times 10^{-7}$ $2 \times 10^{-7} > K_{sp}$, so a precipitate will form.	A precipitate will form in this case because 2×10^{-7} is greater than 4.5×10^{-9}.

Hint: At equilibrium, $[Ag^+] = [Cl^-]$.

Remember: Equilibrium constants are not reported with units.

18 Assessment

★ Solutions appear in Appendix D

Lesson by Lesson

18.1 Rates of Reaction

★**55.** According to collision theory, what are two things that can happen when molecules collide?

56. What is activation energy?

57. The gas to a burner must be lit by a flame before it burns. Explain this observation in terms of the effect of temperature on reaction rate.

★**58.** Explain how a catalyst is able to change the rate of a reaction.

18.2 The Progress of Chemical Reactions

59. What is a rate law?

60. Use this graph to answer the following questions about a reaction.

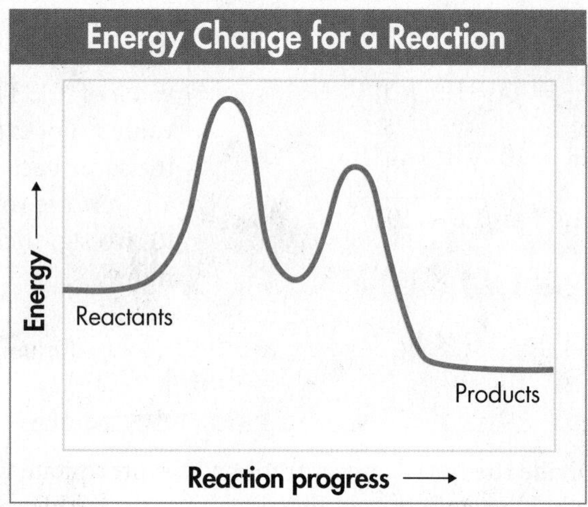

a. How many steps are in this reaction? Explain your answer.
b. Is the reaction endothermic or exothermic? How can you tell?

18.3 Reversible Reactions and Equilibrium

61. In your own words, define a reversible reaction.

62. Compare the rates of the forward and reverse reactions at equilibrium.

63. What is Le Châtelier's principle?

★**64.** Write the expression for the equilibrium constant for each reaction.

a. $4H_2(g) + CS_2(g) \rightleftharpoons CH_4(g) + 2H_2S(g)$
b. $PCl_5(g) \rightleftharpoons PCl_3(g) + Cl_2(g)$

18.4 Solubility Equilibrium

65. Write the expression for K_{sp} for each of the following compounds.

a. NiS
b. $BaCO_3$

★**66.** Use the table on page 589 to rank these compounds from most soluble to least soluble.

a. CuS
b. $BaSO_4$
c. $SrCO_3$
d. AgI

67. What happens when a common ion is added to a saturated solution of an ionic compound?

18.5 Free Energy and Entropy

68. Explain what it means to say that a process is 50 percent efficient.

69. State the law of disorder in your own words.

70. Compare the amount of product at equilibrium in a spontaneous reaction to the amount at equilibrium in a nonspontaneous reaction.

71. Which system in each example below has the lower entropy?

a. 50 mL of liquid water or 50 mL of ice
b. 10 g of sodium chloride crystals or a solution containing 10 g of sodium chloride

★**72.** Does entropy increase or decrease in each of the following reactions?

a. $CaCO_3(s) \longrightarrow CaO(s) + CO_2(g)$
b. $NH_3(g) + HCl(g) \longrightarrow NH_4Cl(s)$

73. Is it true that all spontaneous processes are exothermic? Explain your answer.

74. How is a change in Gibbs free energy used to predict whether a reaction will be spontaneous?

Understand Concepts

75. Consider this reversible reaction.

$$2NO_2(g) \rightleftharpoons N_2O_4(g)$$

What will happen to the reaction rate if the concentration of NO_2 is changed from 0.020 mol/L to 0.030 mol/L? What will happen to the equilibrium position?

★76. For the reaction $A + B \rightleftharpoons C$, the activation energy of the forward reaction is 5 kJ and the total energy change is −20 kJ. What is the activation energy of the reverse reaction?

77. For each reaction, decide whether products or reactants will be more common at equilibrium.

a. $H_2(g) + F_2(g) \rightleftharpoons 2HF(g)$; $K_{eq} = 1 \times 10^{13}$
b. $2H_2O(g) \rightleftharpoons 2H_2(g) + O_2(g)$; $K_{eq} = 6 \times 10^{-28}$

★78. What would be the effect on the equilibrium position if the volume is decreased in this reaction?

$$4HCl(g) + O_2(g) \rightleftharpoons 2Cl_2(g) + 2H_2O(g)$$

★79. What must be true about the concentrations of two ions if precipitation occurs when solutions of the two ions are mixed?

★80. Which of the following statements is always true for a reaction that is spontaneous?

a. The reaction is exothermic.
b. Entropy is increased in the reaction.
c. Free energy is released in the reaction.

★81. Suppose equilibrium is established for this reaction at 425 K.

$$Fe_3O_4(s) + 4H_2(g) \rightleftharpoons 3Fe(s) + 4H_2O(g)$$

How would the equilibrium concentration of H_2O be affected by these actions?

a. adding more H_2 to the mixture
b. increasing the pressure
c. removing $H_2(g)$
d. adding a catalyst

82. A student prepares a solution by combining 0.025 mol $CaCl_2$ and 0.015 mol $Pb(NO_3)_2$ and adding water to make 1.0 L of solution. Will a precipitate of $PbCl_2$ form in this solution?

Think Critically

83. Relate Cause and Effect An increase in temperature raises the energy of the collisions between reactant molecules. An increase in the concentration of reactants increases the number of collisions. What is the effect of a catalyst on the collisions between molecules?

84. Use Analogies A speed bump is a raised ridge that runs across the surface of a street or a parking lot. What is the purpose of a speed bump, and how is it similar to activation energy?

★85. Apply Concepts In the reversible reaction for the formation of ammonia, the enthalpy change favors the forward reaction, but the entropy change favors the reverse reaction.

$$N_2(g) + 3H_2(g) \rightleftharpoons 2NH_3(g) + \text{heat}$$

You are the chemical engineer in charge of the large-scale production of ammonia. What are three things you can do to increase the percent yield of your product?

FOUNDATIONS Wrap-Up

Changing But Constant

1. Draw Conclusions At the beginning of this chapter, you and a partner moved water between two containers. How is what you did similar to what happens at equilibrium?

Concept Check

Now that you have finished studying Chapter 18, answer these questions:

2. At the same temperature, which will cook faster—a large baking potato or a similar potato cut into chunks? Explain.

3. A catalytic converter uses metal catalysts to change harmful gases into less harmful gases. Using leaded gasoline would make the converter less effective. How could you describe lead's role in the process?

4. Fire laws limit the number of people that can be in a store at the same time. How could a store let more people shop without breaking the law? How is this situation like an equilibrium system in chemistry?

Write About Science

86. Explain Compost is a mixture that gardeners add to soil to improve the soil. Many gardeners make their own compost by recycling yard and kitchen waste. What types of reactions take place in a compost pile? Why is it important that the compost pile be turned regularly?

87. Connect to the BIGIDEA Sometimes, it is important to slow down a reaction, such as combustion. Use Le Châtelier's principle to explain why some of the methods that are used to fight fires work.

CHEMYSTERY

Explosive Sugar

The U.S. Chemical Safety Board (CSB) investigates chemical accidents in the workplace. In 2009, the CSB issued a report on the explosion at the sugar refinery in Georgia.

A year before the blast, a steel cover was added to the conveyor belt where the first explosion took place. The cover kept the sugar clean. But the cover also let high concentrations of sugar dust build up near the belt. The CSB suspected that a part of the belt overheated and ignited the dust.

Vibrations from the small explosion shook loose sugar dust from many surfaces in the warehouse. Suddenly, the air inside the warehouse was filled with tiny particles of sugar.

88. Relate Cause and Effect Explain how the first explosion made it more likely that a second, more violent explosion would happen.

89. Connect to the BIGIDEA The CSB uses what it learns to recommend ways to improve safety. What would you suggest to prevent similar fires in the future?

Cumulative Review

***90.** Why is it wrong to say that solid potassium chloride is composed of KCl molecules? (See Lesson 7.2 for help.)

91. Which atoms in the list below would you expect to form positive ions? Which would you expect to form negative ions? (See Lesson 9.1 for help.)

a. Cl **b.** Ca **c.** P **d.** Se **e.** Cu **f.** Sn **g.** K **h.** Fe

92. Find the mass in grams of each quantity. (See Lesson 10.2 for help.)

a. 4.50 mol Fe
b. 36.8 L CO (at STP)
c. 1 molecule of glucose ($C_6H_{12}O_6$)

***93.** When heated, potassium chlorate decomposes into potassium chloride and oxygen gas. (See Lessons 11.1 and 12.2 for help.)

a. Write the balanced equation for this chemical reaction.
b. How many grams of oxygen are formed when 4.88 g $KClO_3$ decompose?

94. Is the boiling point of a liquid substance a constant? Explain. (See Lesson 13.2 for help.)

95. What happens to the pressure of a contained gas in each instance? (See Lesson 14.1 for help.)

a. More gas particles are added.
b. The temperature of the gas is decreased.
c. The volume of the container is reduced.

96. A small amount of ethanol (C_2H_5OH) is dissolved in a large beaker of water. (See Lessons 16.1 and 16.3 for help.)

a. Identify the solute and the solvent.
b. Is the freezing point of the solution above or below 0°C?

97. How many liters of a stock solution of 6.00*M* HCl would you need to prepare 15.0 L of 0.500*M* HCl? (See Lesson 16.2 for help.)

***98.** When solid sodium hydroxide is dissolved in water, the temperature of the solution rises. Is this an exothermic or endothermic process? Explain your answer. (See Lesson 17.1 for help.)

Standardized Test Prep

For help with answering test questions, go to your Chemistry Skills and Math Workbook.

Select the choice that best answers each question or completes each statement.

1. Which reaction is represented by the following expression for an equilibrium constant?

$$K_{eq} = \frac{[CO]^2 \times [O_2]}{[CO_2]^2}$$

(A) $2CO_2 \rightleftharpoons O_2 + 2CO$
(B) $CO_2{}^2 \rightleftharpoons O_2 + 2CO^2$
(C) $O_2 + 2CO \rightleftharpoons 2CO_2$
(D) $O_2 + CO_2 \rightleftharpoons CO_2{}^2$

2. At 25°C, zinc sulfide has a K_{sp} of 3.0×10^{-23}, zinc carbonate has a K_{sp} of 1.0×10^{-10}, and silver iodide has a K_{sp} of 8.3×10^{-17}. Order these salts from most soluble to least soluble.
(A) zinc carbonate, zinc sulfide, silver iodide
(B) silver iodide, zinc carbonate, zinc sulfide
(C) zinc carbonate, silver iodide, zinc sulfide
(D) zinc sulfide, silver iodide, zinc carbonate

Tips for Success

Multiple Parts Sometimes, two phrases in a true/false question are connected with a word, such as *because, therefore,* or *so.* These words imply a cause-and-effect relationship between the two phrases. Be aware that the overall statement can be false even if each phrase is true on its own.

Use the table to answer Questions 3 and 4.

ΔS	ΔH	ΔG	Spontaneous?
+	–	(a)	Yes
+	(b)	+ or –	At high *T*
(c)	+	+	No
–	–	(d)	At low *T*

3. The value of ΔG depends on the enthalpy (ΔH) and entropy (ΔS) terms for a reaction. The value of ΔG also varies as a function of temperature. Use the data in the table to identify the missing entries (a), (b), (c), and (d).

4. Which of these reactions would you expect to be spontaneous at relatively low temperatures? At relatively high temperatures?
(A) $H_2O(l) \longrightarrow H_2O(g)$
(B) $H_2O(g) \longrightarrow H_2O(l)$
(C) $H_2O(s) \longrightarrow H_2O(l)$

5. The atomic windows below represent different degrees of entropy. Arrange the windows in order of increasing entropy.

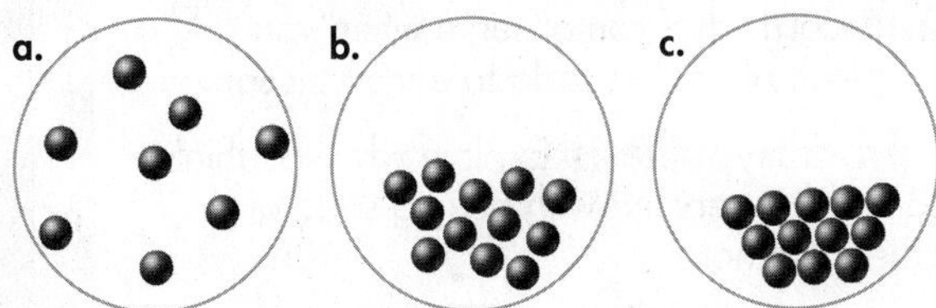

For each question below, there are two statements. Decide whether each statement is true or false. Then decide whether Statement II is a correct explanation for Statement I.

	Statement I		Statement II
6.	A catalyst lowers the activation energy for a chemical reaction.	BECAUSE	A catalyst makes a reaction more exothermic.
7.	The entropy of ice is greater than the entropy of steam.	BECAUSE	The density of ice is greater than the density of steam.
8.	The rate of a chemical reaction is affected by a change in temperature.	BECAUSE	The kinetic energy of particles is related to the temperature.
9.	A large value for an equilibrium constant indicates that products are favored at equilibrium.	BECAUSE	The ratio of products to reactants at equilibrium is always > 1.

If You Have Trouble With . . .

Question	1	2	3	4	5	6	7	8	9
See Lesson	18.3	18.4	18.5	18.5	18.5	18.1	18.5	18.1	18.3

19 Acids, Bases, and Salts

FOUNDATIONS for Learning

Which Fruits React with Baking Soda?

1. You will need a few small pieces of a lemon, a banana, an apple, and an orange.
2. Place the fruit pieces on a large paper plate. Make sure they are well separated from each other.
3. Record what you observe when you add a pinch of baking soda to each fruit sample.

Form a Hypothesis Explain why you think some fruits reacted with baking soda and others did not.

PearsonChem.com

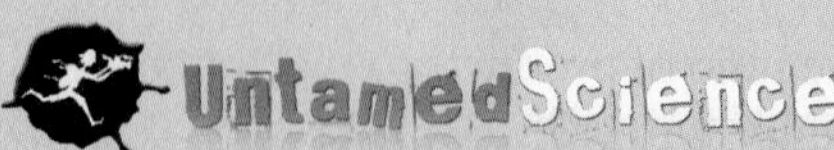

Tag along with the Untamed Science crew to learn how carbon dioxide in the atmosphere can affect the acidity of ocean waters.

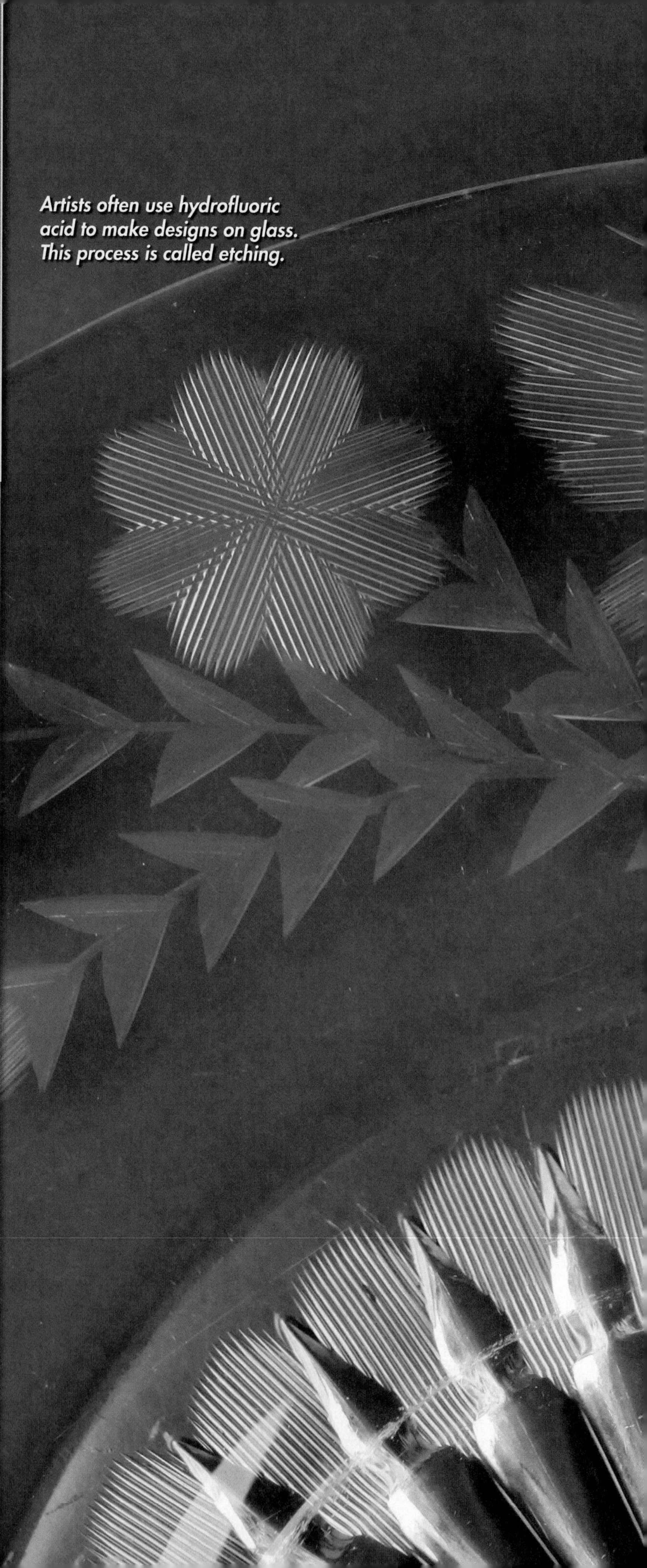

Artists often use hydrofluoric acid to make designs on glass. This process is called etching.

BIGIDEA

REACTIONS

Essential Questions:

1. *What are the different ways chemists define acids and bases?*
2. *What does the pH of a solution mean?*
3. *How do chemists use acid-base reactions?*

CHEMYSTERY

Paper Trail

The invention of the printing press in 1440 meant that more books could be printed. More books meant more paper was needed. At the time, paper was made out of cotton. Cotton is about 80 percent cellulose, an insoluble polymer. This type of paper is called rag-based paper. Books printed on rag-based paper can last for hundreds of years.

By 1880, the demand for paper was so great that many printers switched from rag-based paper to wood-based paper. Over time, wood-based paper can crack and become yellow. Very old wood-based paper can become so brittle that it even crumbles when touched.

Why did a change in the content of paper cause such a dramatic change in the properties of the paper?

▶ Connect to the BIGIDEA As you read about acids and bases, think about what could cause paper to crumble.

19.1 Acid-Base Theories

CHEMISTRY & YOU

Q: How can high levels of ammonia hurt you? Bracken Cave, near San Antonio, Texas, is home to millions of Mexican free-tailed bats. Nitrogen compounds in bat urine can break down and release ammonia into the air. Visitors to the cave must wear goggles and respirators. They need to do this because of what happens when ammonia reacts with water. Ammonia is an example of a base. In this lesson, you will learn about some of the properties of acids and bases.

Key Questions

How did Arrhenius define an acid and a base?

How do acids and bases differ in the Brønsted-Lowry theory?

How did Lewis define an acid and a base?

Arrhenius Acids and Bases

You may not know it, but acids and bases are common in your life. Look at the figure below. Citrus fruits, such as lemons, limes, and oranges, contain acids. The soap you use to clean your hands has the properties of a base.

Properties of Acids and Bases Acids and bases have distinctive properties. Certain acids give foods a sour taste. For example, lemons taste sour because they have citric acid in them. Aqueous solutions of acids are electrolytes, which can conduct electricity. The electrolyte in a car battery is an acid. Acids also cause certain chemical dyes, called indicators, to change color. Many metals, such as zinc and magnesium, react with aqueous solutions of acids to produce hydrogen gas.

Bases share some properties with acids. Like acids, bases cause indicators to change color. Bases also form aqueous solutions that are electrolytes. Bases generally taste bitter, but it is dangerous to test this property. If you have ever accidentally tasted soap, you know about this bitter taste. The slippery feel of soap is another property of bases.

Common Acids and Bases

Some items contain acids or bases or produce acids and bases when you dissolve them in water.

Citrus fruits contain citric acid ($HC_6H_7O_7$).

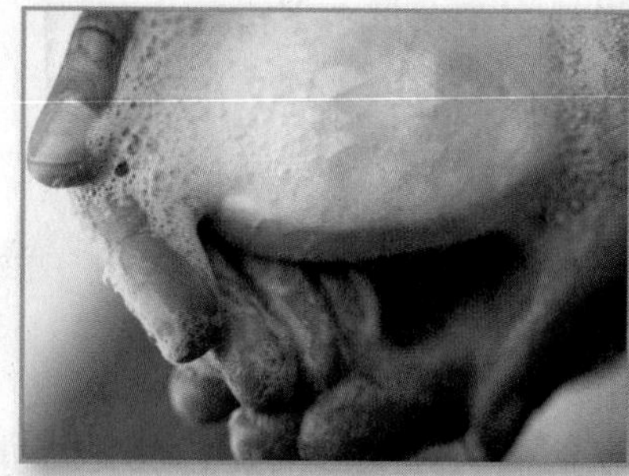

Some soap makers use the common base sodium hydroxide (NaOH).

Arrhenius Acids In 1887, the Swedish chemist Svante Arrhenius defined acids and bases in a new way. He defined acids as hydrogen-containing compounds that separate to yield hydrogen ions (H^+) in aqueous solution.

▶ **Arrhenius Acids with Highly Polar Bonds** The table to the right lists six common acids. Each of these acids has at least one hydrogen. However, not all compounds that contain hydrogen are acids. Also, some hydrogens in an acid may not form hydrogen ions. A hydrogen atom that can form a hydrogen ion is described as ionizable. To be ionizable, a hydrogen must be bonded to a very electronegative element. A bond between hydrogen and a very electronegative element is highly polar. When a compound with this type of bond dissolves in water, it may release a hydrogen ion. The equation below shows one example of this type of compound—hydrogen chloride. When dissolved in water, it yields a hydrogen ion and a chloride ion, and is called hydrochloric acid.

$$\overset{\delta+}{H}-\overset{\delta-}{Cl}(g) \xrightarrow{H_2O} H^+(aq) + Cl^-(aq)$$

Hydrogen chloride; Hydrogen ion; Chloride ion (hydrochloric acid)

Some Common Acids	
Name	**Formula**
Hydrochloric acid	HCl
Nitric acid	HNO_3
Sulfuric acid	H_2SO_4
Phosphoric acid	H_3PO_4
Ethanoic acid	CH_3COOH
Carbonic acid	H_2CO_3

Hydrogen ions are not found in aqueous solutions. Instead, the hydrogen ions join to water molecules to form hydronium ions. A **hydronium ion** (H_3O^+) is the ion that forms when a water molecule gains a hydrogen ion. Look at the equation below. When hydrogen chloride dissolves in water, it ionizes and forms an aqueous solution of hydronium ions and chloride ions. Hydrogen chloride is an acid because it forms hydronium ions in aqueous solution.

hydronium ion (H_3O^+) the ion that forms when a water molecule gains a hydrogen ion

PREFIXES

The prefix *hydro-* is from a Greek word meaning "water." Use this to help you remember that a hydronium ion is a water molecule with an extra H^+.

HCl + H_2O ⟶ H_3O^+ + Cl^-

Hydrogen chloride; Water; Hydronium ion; Chloride ion

▶ **Arrhenius Acids with Weakly Polar Bonds** Unlike the bond in hydrogen chloride, the bonds between carbon and hydrogen in methane (CH_4) are weakly polar. So methane has no ionizable hydrogens and is not an acid. Ethanoic acid (CH_3COOH), also called acetic acid, has both types of hydrogens—three that do not ionize and one that does ionize. To recognize which hydrogen can be ionized, you need to look at the structural formula. Look below at the structural formula for ethanoic acid.

```
     H  O
     |  ||
  H—C—C—O—H  ← Ionizable hydrogen
     |
     H
```

Ethanoic acid (CH_3COOH)

The three hydrogens attached to a carbon atom are in weakly polar bonds, just like in methane. These hydrogens do not ionize. Only the hydrogen bonded to the highly electronegative oxygen atom can be ionized.

Some Common Bases	
Name	**Formula**
Sodium hydroxide	$NaOH$
Potassium hydroxide	KOH
Calcium hydroxide	$Ca(OH)_2$
Magnesium hydroxide	$Mg(OH)_2$

Arrhenius Bases Arrhenius bases are compounds that ionize to yield hydroxide ions (OH^-) in aqueous solution. The table to the left lists four common bases. Each of these bases is an ionic solid that has at least one hydroxide ion.

▶ **Arrhenius Bases with High Solubility** You might be familiar with the base sodium hydroxide (NaOH). Sodium hydroxide is also known as lye. Sodium hydroxide is very soluble in water. In aqueous solution, it dissociates into sodium ions and hydroxide ions.

$$\underset{\text{Sodium hydroxide}}{NaOH(s)} \xrightarrow{H_2O} \underset{\text{Sodium ion}}{Na^+(aq)} + \underset{\text{Hydroxide ion}}{OH^-(aq)}$$

Potassium hydroxide (KOH) is another base that is very soluble in water. It dissociates to form potassium ions and hydroxide ions in aqueous solution.

$$\underset{\text{Potassium hydroxide}}{KOH(s)} \xrightarrow{H_2O} \underset{\text{Potassium ion}}{K^+(aq)} + \underset{\text{Hydroxide ion}}{OH^-(aq)}$$

Making concentrated aqueous solutions of sodium hydroxide and potassium hydroxide is easy. This is because both compounds are very soluble in water. The solutions made from these compounds would have a bitter taste and a slippery feel. But you should not test these properties. These solutions are extremely caustic. A caustic substance can burn or eat away materials that it touches. If these solutions touch your skin, they can cause painful wounds if they are not washed off right away.

Sodium hydroxide can be made by reacting sodium with water. Likewise, potassium hydroxide can be made by reacting potassium with water. Sodium and potassium are Group 1A elements. Elements in Group 1A are alkali metals. These elements react violently with water. The products of these reactions are aqueous solutions of a hydroxide and hydrogen gas. The equation below shows the reaction of sodium with water.

$$\underset{\text{Sodium metal}}{2Na(s)} + \underset{\text{Water}}{2H_2O(l)} \longrightarrow \underset{\text{Sodium hydroxide}}{2NaOH(aq)} + \underset{\text{Hydrogen}}{H_2(g)}$$

▶ **Arrhenius Bases with Low Solubility** Calcium hydroxide, $Ca(OH)_2$, and magnesium hydroxide, $Mg(OH)_2$, are compounds of Group 2A metals. These two compounds are not very soluble in water. Their solutions are always very dilute. The photo to the left shows a suspension of magnesium hydroxide in water. Most bases are too caustic to be swallowed. But, the low solubility of magnesium hydroxide makes this suspension safe to consume.

Milk of Magnesia
This product is a suspension of magnesium hydroxide in water. Some people use this as an antacid and a mild laxative.

Key Question How did Arrhenius define an acid and a base? **According to Arrhenius, acids are hydrogen-containing compounds that ionize to yield hydrogen ions (H^+) in aqueous solution. Bases are compounds that ionize to yield hydroxide ions (OH^-) in aqueous solution.**

Brønsted-Lowry Acids and Bases

The Arrhenius definition of acids and bases does not include some substances that have acidic or basic properties. For example, sodium carbonate (Na_2CO_3) and ammonia (NH_3) act as bases when they are in aqueous solutions. But neither of these compounds contains hydroxide, so neither compound is an Arrhenius base.

In 1923, two chemists working independently proposed the same definition of acids and bases. Johannes Brønsted lived in Denmark, and Thomas Lowry lived in England. They both proposed that an acid is a hydrogen-ion donor and a base is a hydrogen-ion acceptor. This definition is known as the Brønsted-Lowry theory. This theory is a little broader than the Arrhenius definition of acids and bases. It includes all the Arrhenius acids and bases plus some other compounds that Arrhenius did not classify as bases.

Identifying Brønsted-Lowry Acids and Bases You can use the Brønsted-Lowry theory to understand why ammonia is a base. Ammonia gas is very soluble in water. Follow along in the equation below to see what happens when ammonia dissolves in water.

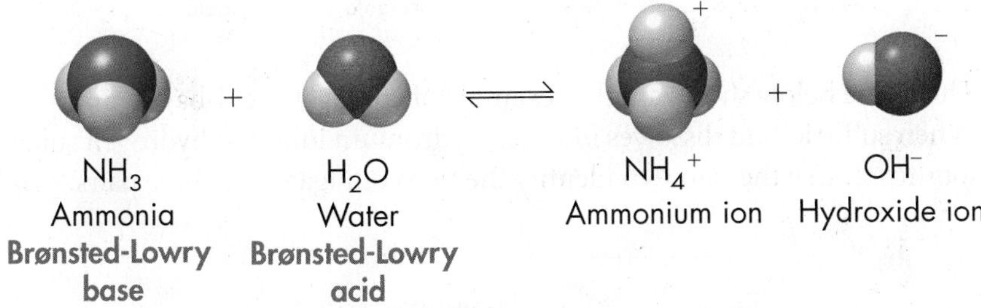

When ammonia and water react, water molecules donate hydrogen ions to ammonia molecules. Water is a Brønsted-Lowry acid because it donates hydrogen ions. Ammonia is a Brønsted-Lowry base because it accepts hydrogen ions.

Conjugate Acids and Bases The chemical reaction described in the equation above is reversible. In the reverse reaction, ammonium ions donate hydrogen ions to hydroxide ions. In this situation, NH_4^+ (the donor) acts as a Brønsted-Lowry acid, and OH^- (the acceptor) acts as a Brønsted-Lowry base. So the reversible reaction of ammonia and water has two acids and two bases. The two pairs of acids and bases are labeled in the equation below.

$$\underset{\text{Base}}{NH_3(aq)} + \underset{\text{Acid}}{H_2O(l)} \rightleftharpoons \underset{\text{Conjugate acid}}{NH_4^+(aq)} + \underset{\text{Conjugate base}}{OH^-(aq)}$$

To distinguish between the two pairs of acids and bases, chemists add the term *conjugate* to one acid and base from each pair. A **conjugate acid** is the ion or molecule formed when a base gains a hydrogen ion. It is an acid because it can donate the hydrogen ion in the reverse reaction. In the reaction above, NH_4^+ is the conjugate acid of the base NH_3. A **conjugate base** is the ion or molecule that remains after an acid loses a hydrogen ion. It is a base because it can accept a hydrogen ion in the reverse reaction. In the reaction above, OH^- is the conjugate base of the acid H_2O.

conjugate acid the ion or molecule formed when a base gains a hydrogen ion

conjugate base the ion or molecule formed when an acid loses a hydrogen ion

WORD ORIGINS

The adjective *conjugate* comes from the Latin word that means "coupled." An acid and its conjugate base differ only by a hydrogen ion. Together, they form a couple, or a pair.

Some Conjugate Acid-Base Pairs	
Acid	**Base**
HCl	Cl^-
H_2SO_4	HSO_4^-
H_3O^+	H_2O
HSO_4^-	SO_4^{2-}
CH_3COOH	CH_3COO^-
H_2CO_3	HCO_3^-
HCO_3^-	CO_3^{2-}
NH_4^+	NH_3
H_2O	OH^-

▶ **Conjugate Acid-Base Pairs** A conjugate acid is always paired with a base, and a conjugate base is always paired with an acid. A **conjugate acid-base pair** consists of two ions or molecules related by the loss or gain of one hydrogen ion. The table to the left shows some conjugate acid-base pairs. One of the pairs in the table is the ammonium ion and ammonia. Look at the equation below to see how these two substances are a conjugate acid-base pair. Notice that the water molecule and the hydroxide ion are also a conjugate acid-base pair.

$$\underset{\text{Base}}{NH_3(aq)} + \underset{\text{Acid}}{H_2O(l)} \rightleftharpoons \underset{\text{Conjugate acid}}{NH_4^+(aq)} + \underset{\text{Conjugate base}}{OH^-(aq)}$$

The dissociation of hydrogen chloride in water gives another example of conjugate acids and bases. Look at the equation below. Hydrogen chloride is the Brønsted-Lowry acid because it donates a hydrogen ion. Water is the Brønsted-Lowry base because it accepts a hydrogen ion. The chloride ion is the conjugate base of the acid HCl. The hydronium ion is the conjugate acid of the base water.

$$\underset{\text{Acid}}{HCl(g)} + \underset{\text{Base}}{H_2O(l)} \rightleftharpoons \underset{\text{Conjugate acid}}{H_3O^+(aq)} + \underset{\text{Conjugate base}}{Cl^-(aq)}$$

The figure below shows another example of conjugate acid-base pairs. When sulfuric acid dissolves in water, hydronium ions and hydrogen sulfate ions form. Use the figure to identify the two conjugate acid-base pairs.

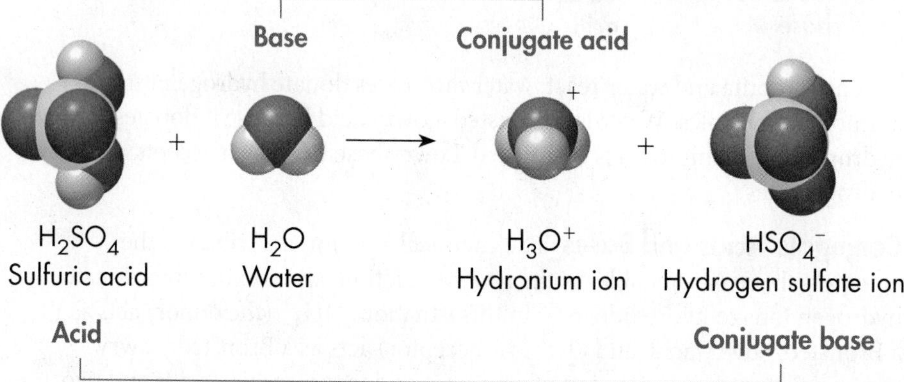

Conjugate Acid-Base Pairs
In this reaction, sulfuric acid and the hydrogen sulfate ion are a conjugate acid-base pair. Water and the hydronium ion are another conjugate acid-base pair.

▶ **Amphoteric Substances** Look again at the table above. Notice that water appears in both columns—as an acid and as a base. Water can accept a hydrogen ion. It can also donate a hydrogen ion. A substance that can act as either an acid or a base is described as **amphoteric.** Water is amphoteric. How water behaves depends on the other reactant. In the reaction with hydrogen chloride, water accepts a hydrogen ion, so it is a base. In the reaction with ammonia, water donates a hydrogen ion, so it is an acid. The table also lists two other substances that are amphoteric, HSO_4^- and HCO_3^-.

Key Question How do acids and bases differ in the Brønsted-Lowry theory? **According to the Brønsted-Lowry theory, an acid is a hydrogen-ion donor, and a base is a hydrogen-ion acceptor.**

Lewis Acids and Bases

Scientist Gilbert Lewis proposed yet another definition of acids and bases. According to Lewis, an acid accepts a pair of electrons during a reaction, and a base donates a pair of electrons during a reaction. A **Lewis acid** is a substance that can accept a pair of electrons to form a covalent bond. A **Lewis base** is a substance that can donate a pair of electrons to form a covalent bond.

The Lewis definition is broader than the definitions offered by Arrhenius or by Brønsted and Lowry. Lewis acids and bases include all the acids and bases defined by Brønsted-Lowry and Arrhenius.

Examples of Lewis Acids and Bases Look at the reaction below between a hydrogen ion (H^+) and a hydroxide ion (OH^-). The hydrogen ion donates itself to the hydroxide ion. So H^+ is a Brønsted-Lowry acid, and OH^- is a Brønsted-Lowry base. Now look at the reaction with the Lewis definitions in mind. The hydroxide ion can bond to the hydrogen ion by donating its unshared pair of electrons. This means OH^- is also a Lewis base. H^+ is a Lewis acid because it accepts the pair of electrons.

$$H^+ + {}^-{:}\ddot{O}{-}H \longrightarrow H_2\ddot{O}{:}$$

Lewis acid   Lewis base

A second example of a reaction between a Lewis acid and a Lewis base is what happens when ammonia dissolves in water. A hydrogen ion from the dissociation of water is the electron-pair acceptor, so it is a Lewis acid. Ammonia is the electron-pair donor, so it is a Lewis base.

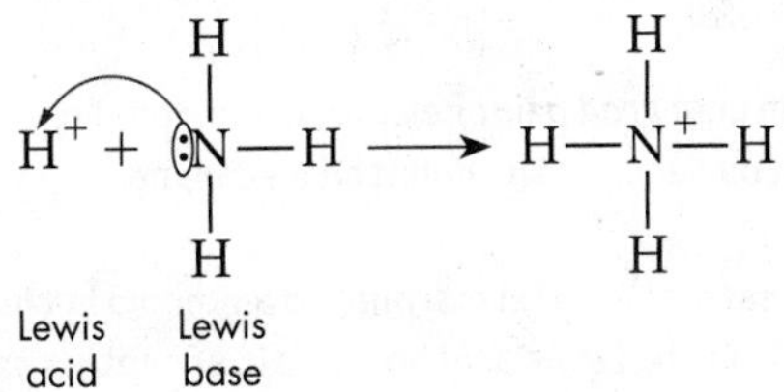

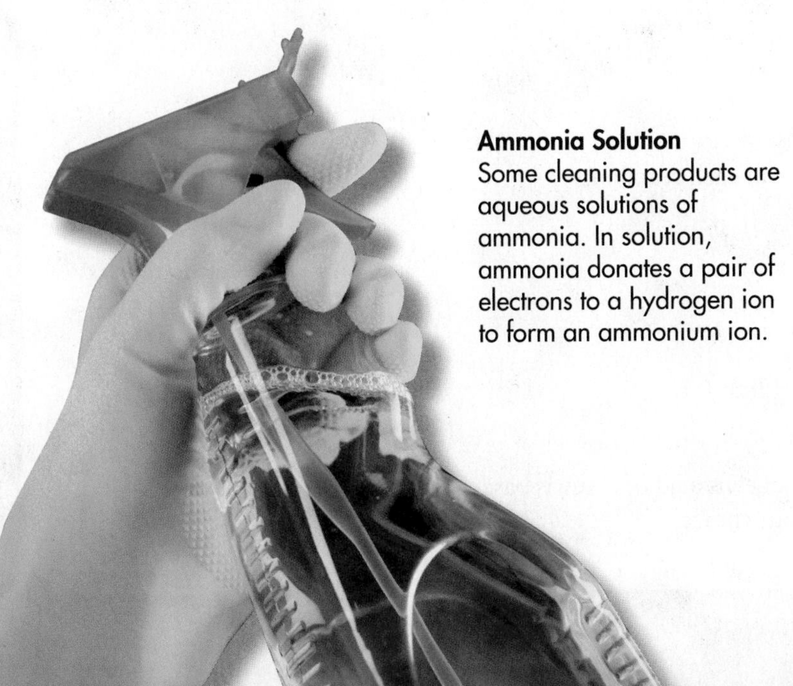

Ammonia Solution
Some cleaning products are aqueous solutions of ammonia. In solution, ammonia donates a pair of electrons to a hydrogen ion to form an ammonium ion.

BUILD Vocabulary

conjugate acid-base pair two substances that are related by the loss or gain of one hydrogen ion

amphoteric the property of being able to act as either an acid or a base

Lewis acid a substance that can accept a pair of electrons to form a covalent bond

Lewis base a substance that can donate a pair of electrons to form a covalent bond

PREFIXES

The prefix *amphi-* is from a Greek word meaning "on both sides." For example, an animal that can live both on land and in the water is an amphibian.

SampleProblem 19.1

Identifying Lewis Acids and Bases

Identify the Lewis acid and the Lewis base in this reaction between ammonia and boron trifluoride.

$$NH_3 + BF_3 \longrightarrow NH_3BF_3$$

In each electron dot structure, draw a pair of shared electrons as a bond.

❶ Analyze **Identify the relevant concepts.**
A Lewis base donates a pair of electrons. A Lewis acid accepts the donated pair of electrons.

❷ Solve **Apply the concepts to this problem.**

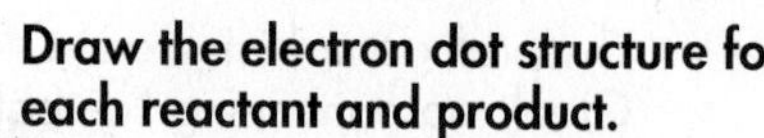

Draw the electron dot structure for each reactant and product.

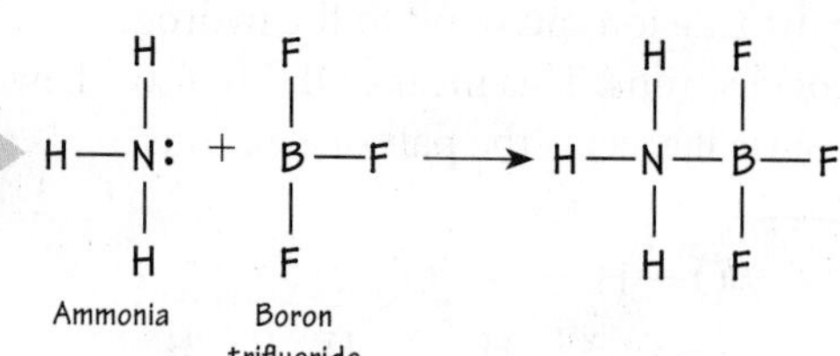

Identify the reactant with the unshared pair of electrons and the reactant that can accept the pair of electrons.

Ammonia

Boron trifluoride

Ammonia has an unshared pair of electrons to donate. The boron atom can accept the donated electrons.

Classify the reactants based on their behavior.

Lewis bases donate a pair of electrons, so **ammonia is the Lewis base. Boron trifluoride is the Lewis acid** because it accepts a pair of electrons.

Practice Problems

1. Identify the Lewis acid and the Lewis base in each reaction.

a. $H^+ + H_2O \longrightarrow H_3O^+$
b. $AlCl_3 + Cl^- \longrightarrow AlCl_4^-$

❶ Analyze **Identify the relevant concepts.**

❷ Solve **Apply the concepts to this problem.**

2. Challenge Do you think PCl_3 would be a Lewis acid or a Lewis base in a typical chemical reaction? Explain your choice.

Comparing Acid-Base Definitions		
Type	**Acid definition**	**Base definition**
Arrhenius	H^+ producer	OH^- producer
Brønsted-Lowry	H^+ donor	H^+ acceptor
Lewis	electron-pair acceptor	electron-pair donor

Comparing Acid-Base Definitions You have now studied three different definitions of acids and bases. The table above compares these three definitions. The Lewis definition is the broadest. It includes many acids and bases that the Brønsted-Lowry theory does not include. The Arrhenius definition is the most narrow. Many substances that are acids and bases according to the other two definitions are not Arrhenius acids and bases.

Key Question How did Lewis define an acid and a base? **According to Lewis, an acid accepts a pair of electrons, and a base donates a pair of electrons during a reaction.**

19.1 LessonCheck

Key Concept Check

3. **Review** What is the Arrhenius definition of an acid and a base?
4. **Describe** How are acids and bases defined by the Brønsted-Lowry theory?
5. **Explain** How did Lewis broaden the definition of acids and bases?

Vocabulary Check

Choose a highlighted word from the lesson to complete each sentence correctly.

6. The ion formed when a water molecule gains a hydrogen ion is called a(n) ________.
7. A substance that can accept a pair of electrons to form a covalent bond is a(n) ________.
8. A(n) ________ substance is able to act as either an acid or a base.
9. Two ions or molecules that are related by the loss or gain of one hydrogen ion are a(n) ________.

Think Critically

10. **Compare and Contrast** How are the properties of acids and bases similar? How are they different?
11. **Apply Concepts** Write a chemical equation for the ionization of HNO_3 in water. Identify the hydrogen-ion donor and the hydrogen-ion acceptor. Label each conjugate acid-base pair.

CHEMISTRY & YOU

12. Visitors to Bracken Cave wear protective gear to keep ammonia gas out of their eyes and respiratory tracts. Think about the properties of bases. Why are high levels of ammonia harmful? (Hint: See pages 612–613.)

BIGIDEA REACTIONS

13. Some household drain cleaners contain sodium hydroxide and small particles of aluminum or zinc. Research how adding these metals can increase the effectiveness of the product.

19.2 Hydrogen Ions and Acidity

CHEMISTRY & YOU

Q: What factors do you need to control in a fish's water to help the fish stay healthy? Goldfish can live for 20 years or more in an aquarium if the conditions are right. You need to keep the water in the aquarium clean. You must also control the temperature of the water. In this lesson, you will study another factor that affects a goldfish's ability to survive.

Key Questions

How are [H+] and [OH−] related in an aqueous solution?

How is pH used to classify a solution as neutral, acidic, or basic?

What are two methods that are used to measure pH?

BUILD Vocabulary

self-ionization the process in which two water molecules react to produce ions

neutral solution an aqueous solution that has equal concentrations of hydrogen ions and hydroxide ions

MULTIPLE MEANINGS
A solution that is neutral is neither acidic nor basic. In a political debate, being neutral means not taking sides.

Hydrogen Ions From Water

Water molecules are constantly moving and colliding with one another. Sometimes, the collisions between water molecules have enough energy for a reaction to occur. When this happens, a hydrogen ion moves from one water molecule to another, as shown below. A water molecule that gains a hydrogen ion becomes a hydronium ion (H_3O^+). A water molecule that loses a hydrogen ion becomes a hydroxide ion (OH^-).

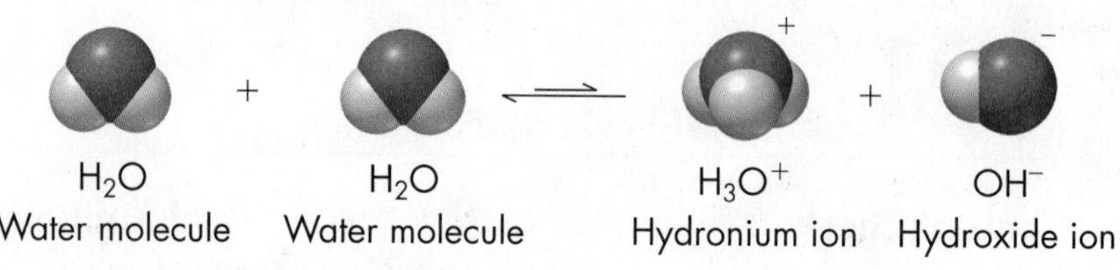

Self-Ionization of Water The reaction in which water molecules produce ions is called the **self-ionization** of water. You can write this reaction as a dissociation, like this:

$$H_2O(l) \rightleftharpoons \underset{\text{Hydrogen ion}}{H^+(aq)} + \underset{\text{Hydroxide ion}}{OH^-(aq)}$$

Remember, in water or in an aqueous solution, hydrogen ions are always joined to water molecules as hydronium ions. Chemists sometimes refer to hydronium ions as hydrogen ions or even protons. This textbook uses either H^+ or H_3O^+ to represent hydrogen ions in aqueous solution.

Look again at the equation above. Note that the reverse arrow is longer than the forward arrow. This uneven set of arrows means that the reverse reaction is favored at equilibrium. In other words, the reaction favors water molecules instead of ions. So the self-ionization of water occurs to a very small extent. In fact, the concentration of H^+ is only $1 \times 10^{-7}M$ in pure water at 25°C. The concentration of OH^- is also $1 \times 10^{-7}M$ because the numbers of H^+ and OH^- are equal in pure water. Any aqueous solution that has equal concentrations of hydrogen ions and hydroxide ions is a **neutral solution.**

Ion-Product Constant for Water The self-ionization of water is a reversible reaction. Le Châtelier's principle applies to reversible reactions. Look at the equation below. Adding either hydrogen ions or hydroxide ions to the system is a stress to the system. In response to this stress, the equilibrium will shift toward the formation of water. This shift will cause the concentration of the other ion to decrease.

$$H^+(aq) + OH^-(aq) \rightleftharpoons H_2O(l)$$

Remember that you can use brackets to mean concentration. For example, you can write "$[H^+]$" to mean "the concentration of H^+." In an aqueous solution, when $[H^+]$ increases, $[OH^-]$ decreases. Likewise, when $[OH^-]$ increases, $[H^+]$ decreases. In an aqueous solution, the product of the concentrations of H^+ and OH^- equals 1.0×10^{-14}. This relationship is shown below.

$$[H^+] \times [OH^-] = 1.0 \times 10^{-14}$$

This relationship is true for all dilute aqueous solutions at 25°C. The individual concentrations of H^+ and OH^- may change. But the product of $[H^+]$ and $[OH^-]$ does not change—it is always 1.0×10^{-14}. The product of the concentrations of hydrogen ions and hydroxide ions in water is called the **ion-product constant for water** (K_w).

$$K_w = [H^+] \times [OH^-] = 1.0 \times 10^{-14}$$

$[H^+]$ = hydrogen-ion concentration

$[OH^-]$ = hydroxide-ion concentration

▶ **Acidic Solutions** When some substances dissolve in water, they release hydrogen ions. One example is hydrogen chloride, as shown in the equation below. When it dissolves in water, it forms hydrochloric acid.

$$HCl(aq) \longrightarrow H^+(aq) + Cl^-(aq)$$

In hydrochloric acid, the hydrogen-ion concentration is greater than the hydroxide-ion concentration. (The hydroxide ions come from the self-ionization of water.) A solution in which $[H^+]$ is greater than $[OH^-]$ is an **acidic solution.** In acidic solutions, $[H^+]$ is greater than $1 \times 10^{-7}M$.

▶ **Basic Solutions** When sodium hydroxide dissolves in water, it forms hydroxide ions, as shown in the equation below.

$$NaOH(aq) \longrightarrow Na^+(aq) + OH^-(aq)$$

In the resulting solution, the hydrogen-ion concentration is less than the hydroxide-ion concentration. Remember, the hydrogen ions are present from the self-ionization of water. A **basic solution** is one in which $[H^+]$ is less than $[OH^-]$. In basic solutions, $[H^+]$ is less than $1 \times 10^{-7}M$. Basic solutions are also known as alkaline solutions.

Key Question How are $[H^+]$ and $[OH^-]$ related in an aqueous solution? **In an aqueous solution, the product of the hydrogen-ion concentration and the hydroxide-ion concentration equals 1.0×10^{-14}.**

BUILD Vocabulary

ion-product constant for water (K_w) the product of the concentrations of H^+ and OH^- in water

acidic solution an aqueous solution that has a higher concentration of H^+ than OH^-

basic solution an aqueous solution that has a higher concentration of OH^- than H^+

USING PRIOR KNOWLEDGE

Ion-product constant for water is a long term, but you can easily remember what it means. You already know that ions, such as H^+ and OH^-, are charged particles. You also know from math class that a product is the result of a multiplication operation. Now, put those two things together.

Sample Problem 19.2

Using the Ion-Product Constant for Water

If the $[H^+]$ in a solution is $1.0 \times 10^{-5}M$, is the solution acidic, basic, or neutral? What is the $[OH^-]$ of this solution?

1 Analyze **List the knowns and the unknowns.**

KNOWNS	UNKNOWNS
$[H^+] = 1.0 \times 10^{-5}M$	Is the solution acidic, basic, or neutral?
$K_w = 1.0 \times 10^{-14}$	$[OH^-] = ?M$

2 Calculate **Solve for the unknowns.** Use the expression for the ion-product constant for water to find the concentration of hydroxide ions.

Use $[H^+]$ to determine whether the solution is acidic, basic, or neutral.

$[H^+]$ is $1.0 \times 10^{-5}M$, which is greater than $1.0 \times 10^{-7}M$. So the solution is acidic.

Write the equation for the ion-product constant for water.

$$K_w = [H^+] \times [OH^-]$$

Rearrange the equation to isolate $[OH^-]$.

Isolate $[OH^-]$ by dividing both sides by $[H^+]$.

$$\frac{K_w}{[H^+]} = \frac{\cancel{[H^+]} \times [OH^-]}{\cancel{[H^+]}}$$

Rewrite the equation so that your unknown is on the left.

$$[OH^-] = \frac{K_w}{[H^+]}$$

Substitute the knowns into the equation. Then, solve for $[OH^-]$.

$$[OH^-] = \frac{1.0 \times 10^{-14}}{1.0 \times 10^{-5}}$$

$$= 1.0 \times 10^{-9}M$$

When comparing numbers written in scientific notation, just remember that the greater the value of the negative exponent, the smaller the number.

3 Evaluate **Do the results make sense?** If $[H^+]$ is greater than $1.0 \times 10^{-7}M$, then $[OH^-]$ must be less than $1.0 \times 10^{-7}M$. $1.0 \times 10^{-9}M$ is less than $1.0 \times 10^{-7}M$. To check your calculation, multiply the values for $[H^+]$ and $[OH^-]$. The result must equal 1.0×10^{-14}.

BUILD Math Skills

Dividing Numbers Written in Scientific Notation When you divide numbers written in scientific notation, you subtract the exponent in the denominator from the exponent in the numerator. Here's an example:

$$\frac{1 \times 10^5}{1 \times 10^3} = 1 \times 10^{5-3} = 1 \times 10^2$$

Concentrations of hydrogen and hydroxide ions usually have negative exponents. Remember that subtracting a negative number is the same as adding its opposite. Look at this example:

$$\frac{1 \times 10^{-14}}{1 \times 10^{-2}} = 1 \times 10^{-14-(-2)} = 1 \times 10^{-14+2} = 1 \times 10^{-12}$$

Practice Problems

14. Is a solution acidic, basic, or neutral if $[H^+] = 6.0 \times 10^{-10}M$? What is the $[OH^-]$ of this solution?

KNOWNS	UNKNOWNS
$[H^+] = 6.0 \times 10^{-10}M$	Is the solution acidic, basic, or neutral?
$K_w = 1.0 \times 10^{-14}$	$[OH^-] = ?M$

❶ **Analyze** **List the knowns and the unknowns.**

❷ **Calculate** **Solve for the unknowns.**

❸ **Evaluate** **Do the results make sense?**

15. A solution's hydroxide-ion concentration is $3.0 \times 10^{-2}M$. Classify the solution as acidic, basic, or neutral.

KNOWN	UNKNOWN
$[OH^-] =$	Is the solution acidic, basic, or neutral?

16. Classify each solution as acidic, basic, or neutral:

a. $[H^+] = 2.0 \times 10^{-7}M$

b. $[OH^-] = 1.0 \times 10^{-7}M$

17. Challenge If the hydroxide-ion concentration of an aqueous solution is $1.0 \times 10^{-3}M$, what is the hydrogen-ion concentration? Is the solution acidic, basic, or neutral?

Hint: For Problem 17, rearrange the equation for the ion-product constant to solve for $[H^+]$.

pH the negative logarithm of the hydrogen-ion concentration

WORD ORIGINS

In 1909, the Danish scientist Søren Sørensen proposed the term *pH*. It is short for ***p**ondus **H**ydrogenii*, meaning "potential of hydrogen" or "power of hydrogen."

The pH Concept

Referring to a hydrogen-ion concentration in molarity is not practical. It's too long and hard to read aloud. Another option—the pH scale—was proposed by a scientist named Søren Sørensen. The pH scale ranges from 0 to 14.

Hydrogen Ions and pH The **pH** of a solution is the negative logarithm of the hydrogen-ion concentration. You can calculate the pH of a solution using the following equation:

$$\text{pH} = -\log[\text{H}^+]$$

A pH value is an easy way to show how acidic or basic a substance is.

You take the negative logarithm of the concentration of hydrogen ions to find the pH.

In pure water or a neutral solution, $[\text{H}^+] = 1 \times 10^{-7}M$, and the pH is 7. If a solution's $[\text{H}^+]$ is greater than $1 \times 10^{-7}M$, the pH is less than 7. A solution with a pH less than 7 is acidic. If a solution's $[\text{H}^+]$ is less than $1 \times 10^{-7}M$, the pH is greater than 7. A solution with a pH greater than 7 is basic. A solution with a pH of 7 is neutral. The table below shows the relationships among $[\text{H}^+]$, $[\text{OH}^-]$, and pH. It also shows the pH values of some common aqueous systems, such as milk and blood.

Relationships Among $[\text{H}^+]$, $[\text{OH}^-]$, and pH

	$[\text{H}^+]$ (mol/L)	$[\text{OH}^-]$ (mol/L)	pH	
Increasing acidity ↑	1×10^{0}	1×10^{-14}	0.0	1*M* HCl
	1×10^{-1}	1×10^{-13}	1.0	0.1*M* HCl
	1×10^{-2}	1×10^{-12}	2.0	Gastric juice
	1×10^{-3}	1×10^{-11}	3.0	Lemon juice
	1×10^{-4}	1×10^{-10}	4.0	Tomato juice
	1×10^{-5}	1×10^{-9}	5.0	Black coffee
	1×10^{-6}	1×10^{-8}	6.0	Milk
Neutral	1×10^{-7}	1×10^{-7}	7.0	Pure water
	1×10^{-8}	1×10^{-6}	8.0	Blood Seawater
Increasing basicity ↓	1×10^{-9}	1×10^{-5}	9.0	
	1×10^{-10}	1×10^{-4}	10.0	Milk of magnesia
	1×10^{-11}	1×10^{-3}	11.0	Household ammonia
	1×10^{-12}	1×10^{-2}	12.0	
	1×10^{-13}	1×10^{-1}	13.0	0.1*M* NaOH
	1×10^{-14}	1×10^{0}	14.0	1*M* NaOH

Note: When $[\text{H}^+]$ is given in the format 1×10^{-n}, it is easy to find the pH. It's just the absolute value of the exponent *n*. Also, note that $[\text{H}^+] \times [\text{OH}^-]$ always equals 1×10^{-14}.

Calculating pH From [H^+] Writing [H^+] in scientific notation can make it easier to calculate pH. For example, you would rewrite 0.0010*M* as $1.0 \times 10^{-3}M$. The coefficient 1.0 has two significant figures. The pH for a solution with this concentration is 3.00. The two numbers to the right of the decimal point in 3.00 correspond to the two significant figures in the concentration ($1.0 \times 10^{-3}M$). Remember this rule for significant figures as you solve problems involving pH.

It is easy to find the pH for solutions when the coefficient is 1.0. The pH of the solution simply equals the exponent with the sign changed from minus to plus. Look at the examples below.

[H^+]	pH
$1.0 \times 10^{-2}M$	2.00
$1.0 \times 10^{-5}M$	5.00

When the coefficient is a number other than 1.0, finding the pH is not as simple. In these cases, you will need to use a calculator with a log function key.

Calculating [H^+] From pH You can calculate the hydrogen-ion concentration of a solution if you know the pH. If the pH is a whole number, it is easy to find the value of [H^+]. Study the examples below.

pH	[H^+]
9.00	$1.0 \times 10^{-9}M$
4.00	$1.0 \times 10^{-4}M$

Most pH values are not whole numbers. For example, the pH of milk of magnesia is about 10.50. The value 10.50 is between 10 and 11. So [H^+] must be less than $1 \times 10^{-10}M$ (pH 10) but greater than $1 \times 10^{-11}M$ (pH 11). The hydrogen-ion concentration of milk of magnesia is between these two values—it is $3.2 \times 10^{-11}M$. When the pH value is not a whole number, you will need a calculator with an antilog (10^x) function to get an accurate value for the hydrogen-ion concentration.

Calculating pH From [OH^-] What if you know the value for [OH^-] instead of the value of [H^+]? Remember that [H^+] × [OH^-] equals 1×10^{-14}. The ion-product constant for water defines this relationship. You can use the equation for the ion-product constant for water to find [H^+] for a known [OH^-]. Then, you can use [H^+] to calculate the pH.

There is another way to calculate pH from [OH^-]. The first step in this method is to find the pOH, a value that is analogous to pH. The pOH of a solution equals −log [OH^-]. Once you know the pOH, you can use the relationship pH + pOH = 14 to find the pH.

Key Question How is pH used to classify a solution as neutral, acidic, or basic? **A solution with a pH of 7.0 is neutral. A solution with a pH less than 7.0 is acidic. A solution with a pH greater than 7.0 is basic.**

BUILD Connections

Have you ever heard of heartburn? Heartburn occurs when gastric juices travel up the esophagus from the stomach. Gastric juices have a very low pH—less than 2. Your stomach uses these acidic juices to help break down food. Gastric juices do not burn your stomach, but they do burn the esophagus.

SampleProblem 19.3

Calculating pH From $[H^+]$

What is the pH of a solution that has a hydrogen-ion concentration of $4.2 \times 10^{-10} M$?

❶ Analyze List the known and the unknown.

KNOWN	UNKNOWN
$[H^+] = 4.2 \times 10^{-10} M$	pH = ?

❷ Calculate Solve for the unknown. To find the pH from the hydrogen-ion concentration, you use the equation $pH = -\log[H^+]$.

Start with the equation for finding pH from $[H^+]$.

$$pH = -\log[H^+]$$

Substitute the known $[H^+]$ into the equation. Then, use the log function on your calculator to find the pH.

$$pH = -\log(4.2 \times 10^{-10})$$
$$= -(-9.37675)$$
$$= 9.37675$$

Round the pH to two decimal places.

9.37675 rounded to two decimal places is 9.38.

❸ Evaluate Does the result make sense? The value of the hydrogen-ion concentration is between $1 \times 10^{-9} M$ and $1 \times 10^{-10} M$. So the calculated pH should be between 9 and 10, and it is.

You need to round the pH to two decimal places because the value for $[H^+]$ has two significant figures.

BUILD Math Skills

Logarithms The common logarithm (log) is the exponent that 10 must be raised to in order to get a certain number. So if $x = 10^y$, then the log of x is y. To find the log using your calculator, you'll need to use the [log] key. Grab your calculator and try to calculate the log of 3.45. Follow the steps below for your type of calculator.

Basic scientific calculator	Advanced scientific calculator
[3][.][4][5] [log] [=]	[log] [3][.][4][5] [=]

You should get the answer 0.5378191. This value must be rounded to three decimal places (0.538) to equal the number of significant figures in the original value (3.45).

Go to your Chemistry Skills and Math Workbook for more practice.

Practice Problems

18. Find the pH of a solution in which $[H^+] = 0.045M$.

KNOWN	UNKNOWN
$[H^+] = 0.045M$	pH = ?

1 Analyze **List the known and the unknown.**

2 Calculate **Solve for the unknown.**

3 Evaluate **Does the result make sense?**

19. Find the pH of a solution that has a hydrogen-ion concentration of $8.7 \times 10^{-6}M$.

KNOWN	UNKNOWN
$[H^+] =$	pH = ?

20. Find the pH of each solution.

a. $[H^+] = 0.0015M$
b. $[H^+] = 1.2 \times 10^{-3}M$

21. Challenge Calculate the pH values of the following solutions. Which solution is more acidic?

Solution A: $[H^+] = 1.0 \times 10^{-12}M$
Solution B: $[H^+] = 1 \times 10^{-4}M$

Sample Problem 19.4

Calculating $[H^+]$ From pH

The pH of an unknown solution is 6.35. What is the hydrogen-ion concentration of the solution?

1 Analyze List the known and the unknown.

KNOWN	UNKNOWN
pH = 6.35	$[H^+] = ?M$

2 Calculate Solve for the unknown. Use the antilog function on your calculator to find the concentration.

First, simply swap the sides of the equation for finding pH.

$$pH = -\log [H^+]$$
$$-\log [H^+] = pH$$

Change the signs on both sides of the equation. Then, solve for the unknown.

$$\log [H^+] = -pH$$
$$[H^+] = \text{antilog}(-pH)$$

Hint: To solve for $[H^+]$, take the antilog of each side of the equation.

Substitute the known pH into the equation.

$$[H^+] = \text{antilog}(-6.35)$$

Use the antilog (10^x) function on your calculator to find $[H^+]$.

$$[H^+] = 0.000000447$$

Write the answer in scientific notation, and make sure it is rounded to the correct number of significant figures.

$$[H^+] = 4.5 \times 10^{-7} M$$

On most calculators, use the [2nd] or the [INV] key followed by [log] to get the antilog.

3 Evaluate Does the result make sense? The pH is between 6 and 7. So the hydrogen-ion concentration must be between $1 \times 10^{-6} M$ and $1 \times 10^{-7} M$. The answer is rounded to two significant figures because the pH was measured to two decimal places.

BUILD Math Skills

Antilogarithms Finding the antilogarithm (antilog) is the reverse of finding the log. The antilog of the log of x is x itself, or antilog(log x) = x. To find the antilog using your calculator, you'll need to use the [10^x] key. Grab your calculator and try to calculate the antilog of 0.53. Follow the steps below for your type of calculator. If your calculator does not have a [10^x] key, you'll need to press the [2nd] or [INV] key first, then the [log] key.

Basic scientific calculator	Advanced scientific calculator
[.][5][3] [10^x] [=]	[10^x] [.][5][3] [=]

You should get the answer 3.38844. This value must be rounded to two significant figures (3.4) to equal the number of decimal places in the original value (0.53).

Go to your Chemistry Skills and Math Workbook for more practice.

Practice Problems

22. Calculate [H^+] for a solution that has a pH of 5.00.

1 Analyze **List the known and the unknown.**

2 Calculate **Solve for the unknown.**

3 Evaluate **Does the result make sense?**

KNOWN	UNKNOWN
pH = 5.00	[H^+] = ?M

23. Calculate the hydrogen-ion concentration for a solution that has a pH of 12.83.

KNOWN	UNKNOWN
pH =	[H^+] = ?M

24. What are the hydrogen-ion concentrations for solutions with the following pH values?

a. 4.00
b. 11.55

25. Challenge Three solutions have different pH values. Solution A has a pH of 8.50, Solution B has a pH of 1.00, and Solution C has a pH of 6.22. Order the solutions from the lowest concentration of hydrogen ions to the greatest concentration of hydrogen ions.

Measuring pH

In many situations, knowing the pH is useful. You might need to maintain the correct acid-base balance in a swimming pool. A gardener might want to know whether a certain plant will thrive in the garden. A doctor might be trying to diagnose a medical condition. The pH of a solution can be found using either an acid-base indicator or a pH meter.

Acid-Base Indicators Scientists often use indicators to find initial pH measurements or for samples with small volumes. An indicator is an acid or a base that dissociates in a certain pH range. Indicators work because their acid forms and base forms have different colors in solution. The following general equation shows the dissociation of an acid-base indicator.

$$\underset{\text{Acid form}}{HIn(aq)} \rightleftharpoons H^+(aq) + \underset{\text{Base form}}{In^-(aq)}$$

The acid form of the indicator (HIn) is one color. It is dominant at low pH values. The base form (In^-) is another color. It is dominant at high pH values. The change from the acid form to the base form occurs within a narrow range of pH units. Within this narrow range, the color of the solution is a mixture of the two colors of the acid and the base forms.

Indicators do not give precise pH measurements. If you know the pH range in which the indicator changes color, you can make a rough estimate of the pH of a solution. At all pH values below this range, you would see only the color of the acid form. At all pH values above this range, you would see only the color of the base form.

Different indicators change colors over different pH ranges. You would need many indicators to span the entire pH spectrum. The figure below shows the pH ranges of some common acid-base indicators.

Acid-Base Indicators Each indicator is useful for a specific range of pH values. Find methyl red on the graph. This indicator changes color at a pH of about 5. Its acid form is red, and its base form is yellow.

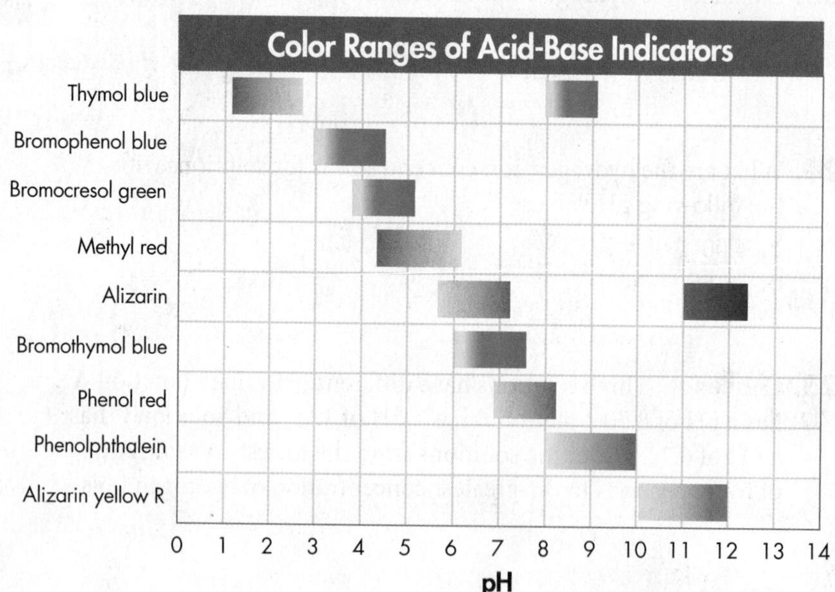

Effects of Soil pH

Acidic Soils Hydrangeas produce blue flowers in acidic soils.

Basic Soils Hydrangeas produce pink flowers in basic soils.

Limitations of Acid-Base Indicators Indicators have properties that limit their usefulness. First, the pH values of indicators are usually given for 25°C. At other temperatures, an indicator may change color at a different pH. Second, if the solution you are testing is not colorless, it may be difficult to judge the color of the indicator. Finally, dissolved salts in a solution may react with the indicator. This may change the indicator's ability to dissociate and change colors.

Using indicator strips can help overcome these problems. An indicator strip is a piece of paper or plastic that has been soaked in an indicator, and then dried. When a drop of solution is placed on the strip, it changes color. You can compare the color of the strip with a color chart to find the pH of the solution. Many landscapers use indicator strips to test the pH of soil before planting shrubs and flowers. The pH of the soil can affect how plants develop. Compare the two photos above if you find this hard to believe.

pH Meters You can also use a pH meter to measure pH. A pH meter can make fast, continuous measurements of pH. The measurements taken with a pH meter are more accurate than those obtained using an indicator. Measurements taken with a pH meter may be accurate to within 0.01 pH unit of the true pH.

Unlike indicators, pH meters are not affected by the color or cloudiness of a solution. A pH meter may also be easier to use than indicators. Look to the right at the photo of a pH meter. The pH reading is visible in a display window on the meter.

Key Question What are two methods that are used to measure pH? **Either acid-base indicators or pH meters can be used to measure pH.**

pH Meter A pH meter provides a quick and accurate way to measure the pH of a system.

Quick Lab

Purpose To measure the pH of household materials using a natural indicator

Materials

- red cabbage leaves
- measuring cup
- hot water
- 2 jars
- spoon
- cheesecloth
- 3 sheets of plain white paper
- transparent tape
- metric ruler
- pencil
- 10 small, clear plastic cups
- permanent marker
- white vinegar (CH_3COOH)
- baking soda ($NaHCO_3$)
- spatula
- household ammonia
- dropper
- assorted household materials

Indicators From Natural Sources

Procedure

1. Put one-half cup of finely chopped red cabbage leaves in a jar. Add one-half cup of hot water. Stir and crush the leaves with a spoon. Continue this process until the water has a distinct color.

2. Strain the mixture through a piece of clean cheesecloth into a clean jar. The liquid that collects in the jar is your indicator.

3. Tape three sheets of paper end to end. Draw a line along the center of the taped sheets. Label the line at 5 cm intervals with the numbers 1 to 14. This labeled line is your pH scale.

4. Use a permanent marker to label three cups "vinegar," "baking soda," and "ammonia." Pour the indicator into each cup to a depth of about 1 cm.

5. Add several drops of vinegar to the first cup. Use a spatula to add a pinch of baking soda to the second cup. Add several drops of ammonia to the third cup. The pH values for the solutions of vinegar, baking soda, and household ammonia are about 3, 9, and 11, respectively. Record the colors you observe at the correct locations on your pH scale.

6. Repeat the procedure for household items such as table salt, milk, lemon juice, laundry detergent, milk of magnesia, toothpaste, shampoo, and carbonated beverages.

Analyze and Conclude

1. Observe What color is the indicator in acidic, neutral, and basic solutions?

2. Relate Cause and Effect What caused the color of the indicator to change when a material was added to a cup?

3. Classify Divide the household materials you tested into three groups: acidic, basic, and neutral.

19.2 LessonCheck

Key Concept Check

26. Review How are $[H^+]$ and $[OH^-]$ related in an aqueous solution?

27. Identify What is the range of pH values in each type of solution:

a. basic **b.** acidic **c.** neutral

28. List What methods can you use to measure the pH of a solution?

Vocabulary Check *Choose a highlighted word from the lesson to complete the sentence correctly.*

29. A(n) __________ has equal concentrations of hydrogen ions and hydroxide ions.

Think Critically

30. Relate Cause and Effect What happens to the $[H^+]$ as the pH of a solution increases?

31. Compare How do basic solutions and acidic solutions differ in terms of ion concentrations?

CHEMISTRY & YOU

32. In an aquarium, the pH of water is important for fish to be able to survive. Some fish need a slightly acidic pH. Other fish need a slightly basic or neutral pH. If you had an aquarium, how would you measure the pH of the water? (Hint: See pages 628–629.)

19.3 Strengths of Acids and Bases

CHEMISTRY & YOU

Q: What makes one acid safer than another? Lemon juice contains citric acid and has a pH of about 2.3. Yet, you can drink lemon juice. When you cut a lemon, you probably don't wear gloves or goggles. But some acids do require these safety measures. This lesson will explain the difference between a "weak" acid such as citric acid and a "strong" acid such as sulfuric acid.

Key Question

How are acids and bases classified as either strong or weak?

BUILD Vocabulary

strong acid an acid that ionizes completely in aqueous solution

weak acid an acid that ionizes only slightly in aqueous solution

ACADEMIC WORDS

Think of the word *aqueous* as meaning "watery." An aqueous solution is a solution that is mostly water.

Strong and Weak Acids and Bases

The table below shows the strengths of some acids and bases. Acids and bases are classified as strong or weak depending upon how much they ionize in water. Recall that a compound ionizes when it dissociates into ions. In general, a **strong acid** ionizes completely in aqueous solution. Hydrochloric acid (HCl) is a strong acid, as the equation below shows.

$$HCl(g) + H_2O(l) \longrightarrow \underset{\text{100\% ionized}}{H_3O^+(aq) + Cl^-(aq)}$$

A **weak acid** ionizes only a little in aqueous solution. Ethanoic acid (CH_3COOH) is a weak acid. Less than 1 percent of ethanoic acid ionizes in solution, as shown below.

$$CH_3COOH(aq) + H_2O(l) \rightleftharpoons \underset{<1\%\text{ ionized}}{H_3O^+(aq) + CH_3COO^-(aq)}$$

Relative Strengths of Common Acids and Bases

Substance	Formula	
Hydrochloric acid	HCl	Strong acids
Nitric acid	HNO_3	
Sulfuric acid	H_2SO_4	
Phosphoric acid	H_3PO_4	Increasing strength of acid ↑
Ethanoic acid	CH_3COOH	
Carbonic acid	H_2CO_3	
Hypochlorous acid	$HClO$	
		Neutral solution
Ammonia	NH_3	Increasing strength of base ↓
Sodium silicate	Na_2SiO_3	
Calcium hydroxide	$Ca(OH)_2$	Strong bases
Sodium hydroxide	$NaOH$	
Potassium hydroxide	KOH	

Dissociations of Strong and Weak Acids *Go to your Chemistry Skills and Math Workbook to practice interpreting graphs.*

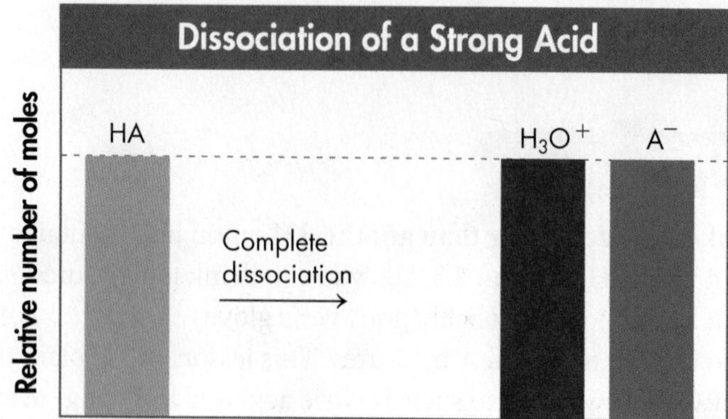

Strong Acid All three bars in this graph have the same height. This is because a strong acid dissociates completely in solution, as the equation below shows. If 1 mol of acid (HA) is added to water, it will ionize and form 1 mol H_3O^+ and 1 mol A^-. When a strong acid dissociates, [HA] equals zero, so there is not a bar for HA on the right side of the arrow.

$$HA(aq) + H_2O(l) \longrightarrow H_3O^+(aq) + A^-(aq)$$

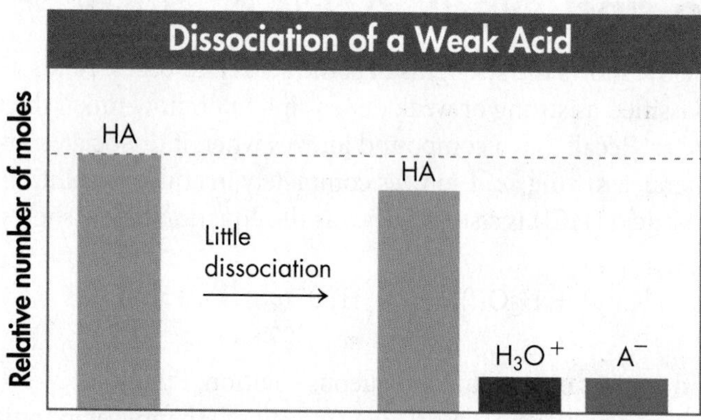

Weak Acid This graph's bars have different heights because a weak acid does not dissociate completely. Look at the equation below. Most of the acid (HA) remains undissociated. Notice the two green bars differ in height only slightly. A very small amount of the acid ionizes and forms H_3O^+ and A^-. Notice that the bars for H_3O^+ and A^- are very short.

$$HA(aq) + H_2O(l) \rightleftharpoons H_3O^+(aq) + A^-(aq)$$

acid dissociation constant

(K_a) ratio of the concentration of the dissociated form of an acid to the concentration of the undissociated form

RELATED WORDS

The word *dissociate* and the word *dissolve* are related. Both words mean "to break apart." If something is dissociated, it is broken apart. If something is undissociated, it is still together.

Acid Dissociation Constant The figure above compares the extent of dissociation of strong and weak acids. A strong acid completely dissociates in water. As a result, $[H_3O^+]$ is high in an aqueous solution of a strong acid.

Weak acids do not dissociate much at all. For example, in an aqueous solution of ethanoic acid, less than 1 percent of the molecules are ionized at any time. You can use the balanced equation for the reaction between ethanoic acid and water to write the equilibrium-constant expression (K_{eq}). This expression is shown below. Note that the concentrations of the products are in the numerator. The concentrations of the reactants are in the denominator.

$$K_{eq} = \frac{[H_3O^+] \times [CH_3COO^-]}{[CH_3COOH] \times [H_2O]}$$

For dilute aqueous solutions, the concentration of water is a constant. So $[H_2O]$ can be taken out of the expression to give an acid dissociation constant, as shown below. An **acid dissociation constant** (K_a) is the ratio of the concentration of the acid's dissociated form to the concentration of its undissociated form.

$$K_a = \frac{[H_3O^+] \times [CH_3COO^-]}{[CH_3COOH]}$$

Dissociation Constants of Some Weak Acids		
Acid	**Chemical equation for dissociation**	**K_a (25°C)**
Oxalic acid	$HOOCCOOH(aq) \rightleftharpoons H^+(aq) + HOOCCOO^-(aq)$	5.6×10^{-2}
	$HOOCCOO^-(aq) \rightleftharpoons H^+(aq) + OOCCOO^{2-}(aq)$	5.1×10^{-5}
Phosphoric acid	$H_3PO_4(aq) \rightleftharpoons H^+(aq) + H_2PO_4^-(aq)$	7.5×10^{-3}
	$H_2PO_4^-(aq) \rightleftharpoons H^+(aq) + HPO_4^{2-}(aq)$	6.2×10^{-8}
	$HPO_4^{2-}(aq) \rightleftharpoons H^+(aq) + PO_4^{3-}(aq)$	4.8×10^{-13}
Methanoic acid	$HCOOH(aq) \rightleftharpoons H^+(aq) + HCOO^-(aq)$	1.8×10^{-4}
Benzoic acid	$C_6H_5COOH(aq) \rightleftharpoons H^+(aq) + C_6H_5COO^-(aq)$	6.3×10^{-5}
Ethanoic acid	$CH_3COOH(aq) \rightleftharpoons H^+(aq) + CH_3COO^-(aq)$	1.8×10^{-5}
Carbonic acid	$H_2CO_3(aq) \rightleftharpoons H^+(aq) + HCO_3^-(aq)$	4.3×10^{-7}
	$HCO_3^-(aq) \rightleftharpoons H^+(aq) + CO_3^{2-}(aq)$	4.8×10^{-11}

Comparing Acid Dissociation Constants The acid dissociation constant (K_a) shows the fraction of an acid that ionizes. For this reason, dissociation constants are sometimes called ionization constants. Weak acids have small K_a values because only a small amount of the acid ionizes. The stronger an acid is, the larger its K_a value will be.

Find the K_a values for methanoic acid and ethanoic acid in the table above. Methanoic acid has a K_a of 1.8×10^{-4}. Ethanoic acid has a K_a of 1.8×10^{-5}. This means that methanoic acid is more ionized in solution than ethanoic acid. So methanoic acid is a stronger acid than ethanoic acid.

Some of the acids in the table above have more than one dissociation constant. This is because they have more than one ionizable hydrogen. Find oxalic acid in the table. Oxalic acid loses two hydrogen ions, one at a time. So it has two dissociation constants. Oxalic acid is found naturally in certain herbs and vegetables—including the chives shown to the right.

Calculating Acid Dissociation Constants You can use the equation below to calculate the K_a of a weak acid. You will need to substitute the equilibrium concentrations of each product and reactant into the equation.

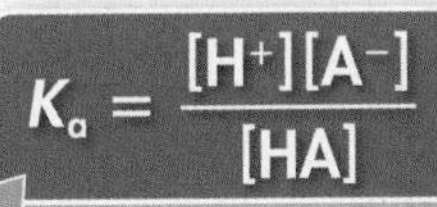

$$K_a = \frac{[H^+][A^-]}{[HA]}$$

K_a is the acid dissociation constant.

$[H^+]$ = equilibrium concentration of hydrogen ions

$[A^-]$ = equilibrium concentration of the anion from the acid dissociation

$[HA]$ = equilibrium concentration of the acid

Oxalic Acid Chives and other foods such as parsley contain oxalic acid.

CHEMISTRY TUTORIAL

Sample Problem 19.5

Calculating a Dissociation Constant

In a $0.1000M$ solution of ethanoic acid, $[H^+] = 1.34 \times 10^{-3}M$. Calculate K_a of this acid. The dissociation equation for this acid is shown below.

$$CH_3COOH(aq) \rightleftharpoons H^+(aq) + CH_3COO^-(aq)$$

1 Analyze **List the knowns and the unknown.**

KNOWNS	UNKNOWN
[ethanoic acid] = $0.1000M$	$K_a = ?$
$[H^+] = 1.34 \times 10^{-3}M$	

2 Calculate **Solve for the unknown.**

First, write the equation for K_a.

$$K_a = \frac{[H^+] \times [CH_3COO^-]}{[CH_3COOH]}$$

State the relationship between the equilibrium concentrations of the ions.

$$[H^+] = [CH_3COO^-] = 1.34 \times 10^{-3}M$$

Hint: Use the balanced equation above. Each molecule of CH_3COOH that ionizes gives a H^+ ion and a CH_3COO^- ion.

Find the equilibrium concentration of the undissociated acid. To do this, subtract the equilibrium concentration of H^+ from the initial concentration of the acid.

$$[HA]_{initial} - [H^+]_{equilibrium} = [HA]_{equilibrium}$$

$$0.1000M - 0.00134M = 0.0987M$$

Substitute the equilibrium concentrations into the equation for K_a.

$$K_a = \frac{(1.34 \times 10^{-3}) \times (1.34 \times 10^{-3})}{0.0987}$$

$$= 1.82 \times 10^{-5}$$

3 Evaluate **Does the result make sense?** The table on the previous page lists the K_a value for ethanoic acid as 1.8×10^{-5}. The calculated value matches that value.

BUILD Math Skills

Using a Table to Organize Data For certain types of problems, you may find it useful to use a table. A table can help you organize the numbers you will use to solve a problem. You can use a table like the one below as you work the problems on this page.

In the row labeled "Initial," write the starting concentrations of each component. Write the equilibrium concentrations of each component in the row labeled "Equilibrium." For Sample Problem 19.5, you could have organized the concentration data as follows:

Concentration	[HA]	$[H^+]$	$[A^-]$
Initial	0.1000*M*	0	0
Equilibrium	0.0987*M*	$1.34 \times 10^{-3}M$	$1.34 \times 10^{-3}M$

Practice Problems

33. In a 0.1000*M* solution of methanoic acid, $[H^+] = 4.2 \times 10^{-3}M$. Calculate the K_a of this acid.

1 Analyze List the knowns and the unknown.

2 Calculate Solve for the unknown.

3 Evaluate Does the result make sense?

KNOWNS	UNKNOWN
[methanoic acid] = 0.1000*M*	$K_a = ?$
$[H^+] = 4.2 \times 10^{-3}M$	

34. In a 0.2000*M* solution of a weak acid, the concentration of hydrogen ions is $9.86 \times 10^{-4}M$. What is the K_a for this acid?

KNOWNS	UNKNOWN
[HA] =	$K_a = ?$
$[H^+]$ =	

35. A 0.500*M* solution of a weak acid has a hydronium-ion concentration of $5.77 \times 10^{-6}M$. Calculate the K_a of this acid.

36. Challenge The sugar substitute saccharin is a weak acid that has one acidic hydrogen. A 1.000*M* aqueous solution of saccharin has a pH of 1.71. Calculate the K_a of saccharin.

Hint: For Problem 36 you'll need to use the pH to find $[H^+]$.

strong base a base that dissociates completely into metal ions and hydroxide ions in aqueous solution

weak base a base that reacts with water to form the conjugate acid of the base and hydroxide ions

base dissociation constant (K_b) the ratio of the concentration of the conjugate acid times the concentration of the hydroxide ion to the concentration of the base

ABBREVIATIONS

Constants usually have abbreviations. Dissociation constants are abbreviated as the letter *K* with a subscript. The subscript *b* is for *base.*

Base Dissociation Constant Just as there are strong acids and weak acids, there are strong bases and weak bases. A **strong base** dissociates completely into metal ions and hydroxide ions in aqueous solution. Some strong bases, such as calcium hydroxide and magnesium hydroxide, are not very soluble in water. The small amounts of these bases that dissolve in water dissociate completely.

A **weak base** reacts with water to form the conjugate acid of the base and hydroxide ions. For a weak base, the amount of dissociation is relatively small. Ammonia is a weak base. One use for an aqueous solution of ammonia is shown in the photo below.

Calculating Base Dissociation Constants The reaction between ammonia and water is shown below. When this reaction reaches equilibrium, only a small amount of the ammonia is present as NH_4^+. This ion is the conjugate acid of NH_3.

$$\underset{\text{Ammonia}}{NH_3(aq)} + \underset{\text{Water}}{H_2O(l)} \rightleftharpoons \underset{\text{Ammonium ion}}{NH_4^+(aq)} + \underset{\text{Hydroxide ion}}{OH^-(aq)}$$

You write the equilibrium-constant expression for the reaction as follows:

$$K_{eq} = \frac{[NH_4^+] \times [OH^-]}{[NH_3] \times [H_2O]}$$

Recall that the concentration of water is constant in dilute solutions. So $[H_2O]$ can be taken out of the expression to give a base dissociation constant (K_b) for ammonia as follows:

$$K_b = \frac{[NH_4^+] \times [OH^-]}{[NH_3]}$$

The **base dissociation constant** (K_b) is the ratio of the concentration of the conjugate acid times the concentration of the hydroxide ion to the concentration of the base. The general form of the equation for K_b is shown below. You can use this equation to calculate the K_b of a weak base.

$$K_b = \frac{[\text{conjugate acid}] \times [OH^-]}{[\text{base}]}$$

Use of Ammonia Window cleaners often use a solution of ammonia in water to clean glass.

Comparing Concentration and Strength of Acids

Acidic solution	Concentration		Strength
	Quantitative [or Molar]	Relative	
Hydrochloric acid	12*M* HCl	Concentrated	Strong
Gastric juice	0.08*M* HCl	Dilute	Strong
Ethanoic acid	17*M* CH_3COOH	Concentrated	Weak
Vinegar	0.2*M* CH_3COOH	Dilute	Weak

Concentration Versus Strength When thinking about acids and bases, don't confuse the concepts of concentration and strength. The words *concentrated* and *dilute* refer to the number of moles of the acid or base in a given volume. The words *strong* and *weak* refer to whether an acid or base ionizes completely or only slightly.

The table above shows four possible combinations of concentration and strength for acids. Hydrochloric acid, HCl(*aq*), is a strong acid. The gastric juice in your stomach is a dilute solution of HCl. Even when concentrated HCl is diluted with water, it is still a strong acid. Ethanoic acid is a weak acid. Vinegar is a dilute solution of ethanoic acid. Even at a high concentration, ethanoic acid is still a weak acid.

Key Question How are acids and bases classified as either strong or weak? **Acids and bases are classified as strong or weak based on the degree to which they ionize in water.**

BUILD Connections

You may use the words *strong* and *weak* to describe how concentrated your tea is. In chemistry class, remember that these two words are used differently. A strong acid is one that dissociates completely, and a weak acid is one that dissociates only a little.

19.3 LessonCheck

Key Concept Check

37. Review What factor determines whether an acid or base is strong or weak?

Vocabulary Check

Choose a highlighted word from the lesson to complete each sentence correctly.

38. A(n) __________ is an acid that dissociates completely in aqueous solution.

39. The __________ can be calculated using the equilibrium concentrations of the base, the conjugate acid of the base, and hydroxide ions.

Think Critically

40. Compare How do acid dissociation constants differ for strong acids and weak acids?

41. Describe How do you calculate the K_a of a weak acid?

42. Predict Acid HX has a very small K_a. How will the amount of H^+ compare to the amount of HX at equilibrium?

43. Describe Write a balanced chemical equation for the dissociation of each acid or base in water.
a. nitric acid **b.** magnesium hydroxide

CHEMISTRY & YOU

44. Citric acid, found in lemon juice, is a weak acid. Citric acid has three K_a values. What does this information tell you about citric acid? (Hint: See page 633.)

Stone Erosion

All around the world, famous stone structures are slowly being eroded by acid rain. The gargoyles on the facade of the Notre Dame Cathedral in Paris, France, are among them. Acid rain is rain with a pH of 5.0 or less. It forms when certain pollutants in the air combine with water vapor to produce acids.

Many of these famous buildings and statues are made of marble or limestone. Both of these materials consist of calcium carbonate, $CaCO_3$. The acids in acid rain react with the calcium carbonate in the stones to form calcium ions, water, and carbon dioxide. In this process, the intricate detail of the structure is lost. Find out for yourself how acids affect materials made of calcium carbonate by trying the activity below.

On Your Own

1. For this activity you will need **2 bowls, 2 same-size pieces of chalk made of calcium carbonate, white vinegar, tap water, masking tape, a permanent marker,** and **a paper towel.** Put vinegar in the first bowl. Label the bowl with a piece of tape and a marker. Put the same amount of water in the second bowl and label it. *Optional:* If you like, scratch a design (with a needle or a nail) into each piece of chalk before going to Step 2.

2. Place a piece of chalk in each bowl. Observe what happens to the chalk.

3. After about 5 minutes, remove the chalk pieces from the bowls. Place the pieces on a paper towel. Compare the pieces of chalk.

Think About It

1. Compare How do the effects of vinegar and of water on the chalk compare?

2. Infer What causes the bubbles you see when the chalk is placed in vinegar?

3. Describe Write a balanced equation to explain what happens to the chalk when it is placed in vinegar. (Hint: Let $H^+(aq)$ represent the acid.)

4. Draw Conclusions What would be the effect of acid rain on a statue over a long period of time?

19.4 Neutralization Reactions

CHEMISTRY & YOU

Q: What could cause a plant's leaves to turn yellow? You may have noticed leaves that were turning yellow for no apparent reason. The plant may have a condition called *chlorosis*. This means the plant lacks the green pigment called chlorophyll. To produce chlorophyll, plants must absorb iron from the soil. Sometimes the soil has plenty of iron, but the plant roots can't take it in. This can happen when the pH of the soil is too high.

Key Questions

What products form when an acid and a base react?

At what point in a titration does neutralization occur?

BUILD Vocabulary

neutralization reaction
reaction of an acid and a base to produce a salt and water

USING PRIOR KNOWLEDGE
A neutralization reaction is a double-replacement reaction. Recall from Chapter 11 that this type of reaction happens when both positive ions switch from one reactant to the other.

Learn more about acid-base reactions online.

Acid-Base Reactions

Suppose you mix a solution of a strong acid, such as HCl, with a solution of a strong base, such as NaOH. The products of this reaction are sodium chloride and water.

$$HCl(aq) + NaOH(aq) \longrightarrow NaCl(aq) + H_2O(l)$$

Most of the time, acids and bases react to produce a salt and water. The complete reaction of a strong acid and a strong base produces a neutral solution. So this type of reaction is called a **neutralization reaction.**

Salts When you hear the word *salt,* you may think of the stuff you use to flavor food. That's table salt (NaCl), and it is only one example of a salt. Salts are ionic compounds that have an anion from an acid and a cation from a base. Other examples of salts include potassium chloride (KCl), sodium sulfate (Na_2SO_4), and calcium chloride ($CaCl_2$).

Mole Ratios in Acid-Base Reactions Chemists often use the term neutralization to describe the point at which a neutralization reaction is complete. For the reaction to go to completion, the acid and base solutions must have equal numbers of hydrogen ions and hydroxide ions. Knowing the mole ratio for the reaction is useful in these situations. You can use the balanced equation to find the correct mole ratio of acid to base. For the reaction shown below, the mole ratio of HCl to NaOH is 1:1.

$$\underset{1\ \text{mol}}{HCl(aq)} + \underset{1\ \text{mol}}{NaOH(aq)} \longrightarrow \underset{1\ \text{mol}}{NaCl(aq)} + \underset{1\ \text{mol}}{H_2O(l)}$$

The mole ratio of reactants in acid-base reactions is not always 1:1. For sulfuric acid and sodium hydroxide, the mole ratio is 1:2. Two moles of NaOH are required to neutralize one mole of H_2SO_4.

$$\underset{1\ \text{mol}}{H_2SO_4(aq)} + \underset{2\ \text{mol}}{2NaOH(aq)} \longrightarrow \underset{1\ \text{mol}}{Na_2SO_4(aq)} + \underset{2\ \text{mol}}{2H_2O(l)}$$

Key Question What products form when an acid and a base react? **In general, acids and bases react to produce a salt and water.**

Sample Problem 19.6

Finding the Moles Needed for Neutralization

How many moles of sulfuric acid are required to neutralize 0.50 mol of sodium hydroxide? The equation for the reaction is shown below.

$$H_2SO_4(aq) + 2NaOH(aq) \longrightarrow Na_2SO_4(aq) + 2H_2O(l)$$

1 Analyze **List the known and the unknown.**

KNOWN	UNKNOWN
mol NaOH = 0.50 mol	mol H_2SO_4 = ? mol

2 Calculate **Solve for the unknown.**

Use the balanced equation to find the ratio of moles of acid to moles of base. → 1 mol H_2SO_4 to 2 mol NaOH

Use the mole ratio to write a conversion factor to convert moles of NaOH to moles of H_2SO_4. → $\frac{1 \text{ mol } H_2SO_4}{2 \text{ mol NaOH}}$

Use the conversion factor to find the moles of H_2SO_4 needed. → $0.50 \text{ mol NaOH} \times \frac{1 \text{ mol } H_2SO_4}{2 \text{ mol NaOH}} = 0.25 \text{ mol } H_2SO_4$

3 Evaluate **Does the result make sense?** The mole ratio of H_2SO_4 to NaOH is 1:2. This means the number of moles of H_2SO_4 should be half the number of moles of NaOH, and it is.

Practice Problems

Hint: Always start by writing the balanced equation.

45. How many moles of potassium hydroxide are needed to neutralize 1.56 mol of phosphoric acid (H_3PO_4)?

1 Analyze **List the known and the unknown.**

2 Calculate **Solve for the unknown.**

3 Evaluate **Does the result make sense?**

KNOWN	UNKNOWN
mol H_3PO_4 = 1.56 mol	mol KOH = ? mol

46. How many moles of sodium hydroxide are required to neutralize 0.20 mol of nitric acid (HNO_3)?

KNOWN	UNKNOWN
mol HNO_3 =	mol NaOH = ? mol

47. Challenge How many moles of hydrochloric acid are needed to neutralize 3.0×10^{-2} mol of potassium hydroxide?

Titration

You can use a neutralization reaction to find the concentration of an acid or base. To do this, you use a process called titration. In a **titration,** you add a measured volume of a solution of known concentration to a known volume of a solution of unknown concentration. A titration allows you to find the concentration of the solution.

Acid-Base Titration You can use the steps below for performing a titration to find the concentration of an acid solution of unknown concentration. Follow along in the figure below.

1. Measure a known volume of the acid solution of unknown concentration, and add it to a flask. Add several drops of an indicator. Gently swirl the flask to mix.
2. Add small volumes of a base of known concentration. Swirl the flask to mix after each addition.
3. When the indicator just barely changes color, stop the titration and record the volume of base that you added.

titration the process used to find the concentration of a solution, which involves adding a measured volume of a solution of known concentration to a known volume of a solution of unknown concentration

WORD ORIGINS

The word *titration* comes from the French word *titre* meaning "qualification." The goal of a titration is to find the concentration (a quality) of an unknown solution.

Acid-Base Titration The photographs show how to titrate an acid with a base using some phenolphthalein indicator.

Step 1 Fill a buret with a base of known concentration. Place the flask with the acid and indicator in it under the buret.

Step 2 Slowly add the base of known concentration from the buret to the acid. Gently swirl the flask to mix.

Step 3 Stop adding base when the color of the solution changes. The color change signals that neutralization has occurred.

Titration Curve The titration curve shows that the equivalence point is located at the midpoint of the vertical part of the curve (at 50 mL on the *x*-axis and pH 7 on the *y*-axis). The flask drawings show what color the solution would be if you used a phenolphthalein indicator.

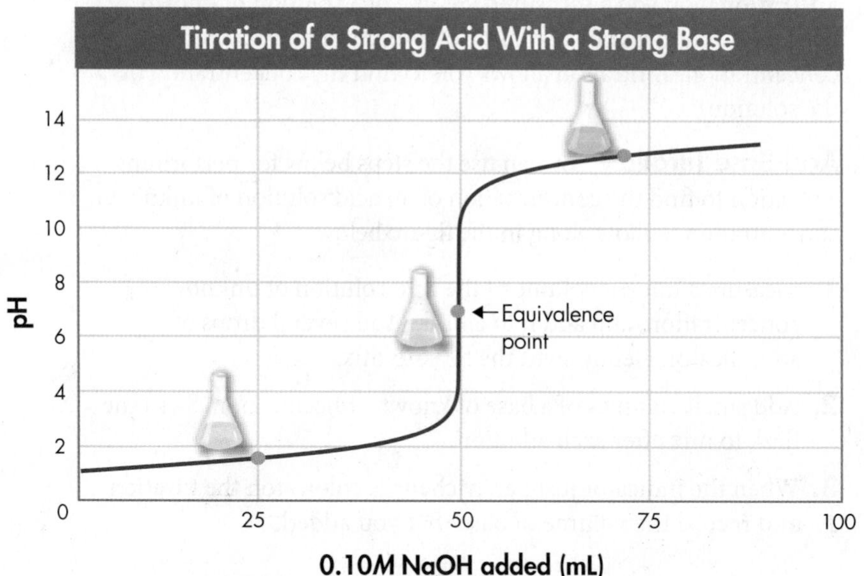

standard solution the solution with the known concentration in a titration

equivalence point the point in a titration when neutralization occurs

end point the point in a titration when the indicator changes color

WORD ORIGINS

The word *equivalent* is from the Latin word *aequivalens,* meaning "the same." At the equivalence point in a titration, the number of moles of H^+ and OH^- are the same.

Standard Solutions The solution of known concentration in a titration is called the **standard solution.** The standard solution in a titration can be either an acid or a base. If the unknown solution is a base, the standard solution will be an acid. If the unknown solution is an acid, the standard solution will be a base.

Equivalence Point Versus End Point Neutralization occurs when the number of moles of hydrogen ions is equal to the number of moles of hydroxide ions. Two things that are equal in value are said to be equivalent. So the point in a titration at which neutralization occurs is called the **equivalence point.**

You can tell about when the equivalence point of a titration is reached because the indicator will change color. You must choose an indicator that changes color at or near the pH of the equivalence point. The point in the titration when the indicator changes color is the **end point.** The equivalence point and the end point are not exactly the same. The end point is the visible change in indicator color that occurs near the equivalence point.

Titration Curves A titration curve shows how the pH of a solution changes during a titration. The figure above shows a titration curve of a strong acid (HCl) with a strong base (NaOH). The initial acid solution has a low pH. As NaOH is added, the pH increases because some of the acid reacts with the base. As the titration nears the equivalence point, the pH rises rapidly. Continuing the titration beyond the equivalence point causes a further increase of pH.

Key Question At what point in a titration does neutralization occur? **Neutralization occurs when the number of moles of hydrogen ions equals the number of moles of hydroxide ions.**

CHEMISTRY TUTORIAL

Sample Problem 19.7

Determining Concentration by Titration

A 25 mL solution of H_2SO_4 is neutralized by 18 mL of 1.0*M* NaOH. What is the concentration of the H_2SO_4 solution? The equation for the reaction is

$$H_2SO_4(aq) + 2NaOH(aq) \longrightarrow Na_2SO_4(aq) + 2H_2O(l)$$

1 Analyze **List the knowns and the unknown.**

KNOWNS	UNKNOWN
[NaOH] = 1.0*M*	$[H_2SO_4]$ = ?*M*
V_{NaOH} = 18 mL = 0.018 L	
$V_{H_2SO_4}$ = 25 mL = 0.025 L	

2 Calculate **Solve for the unknown.** The conversion steps are:
L NaOH ⟶ mol NaOH ⟶ mol H_2SO_4 ⟶ *M* H_2SO_4.

Write the molarity of NaOH as mol/L so you can use it as a conversion factor.

$$\frac{1.0 \text{ mol NaOH}}{1 \text{ L NaOH}}$$

Use the conversion factor to convert the volume of base to moles of base.

$$0.018 \text{ L NaOH} \times \frac{1.0 \text{ mol NaOH}}{1 \text{ L NaOH}} = 0.018 \text{ mol NaOH}$$

Use the mole ratio from the balanced equation to find the moles of acid.

$$0.018 \text{ mol NaOH} \times \frac{1 \text{ mol } H_2SO_4}{2 \text{ mol NaOH}} = 0.0090 \text{ mol } H_2SO_4$$

Calculate the molarity by dividing moles of acid by liters of solution.

$$\text{molarity} = \frac{\text{mol of solute}}{\text{L of solution}} = \frac{0.0090 \text{ mol}}{0.025 \text{ L}} = 0.36M\,H_2SO_4$$

3 Evaluate **Does the result make sense?**
If the acid had the same molarity as the base (1.0*M*), 50 mL of base would neutralize 25 mL of acid. Because the volume of base is about 2/5 of 50 mL, the molarity of the acid must be about 2/5 of 1.0*M*.

Practice Problems

48. How many milliliters of 0.45*M* HCl will neutralize 25.0 mL of 1.00*M* KOH?

1 Analyze **List the knowns and the unknown.**

2 Calculate **Solve for the unknown.**

3 Evaluate **Does the result make sense?**

KNOWNS	UNKNOWN
[KOH] = 1.00*M*	V_{HCl} = ?mL
[HCl] = 0.45*M*	
V_{KOH} = 25.0 mL	

49. What is the molarity of a solution of H_3PO_4 if 15.0 mL is neutralized by 38.5 mL of 0.150*M* NaOH?

KNOWNS	UNKNOWN
[NaOH] =	[H_3PO_4] = ?*M*
$V_{H_3PO_4}$ =	
V_{NaOH} =	

50. Challenge Suppose you slowly add 0.1*M* NaOH to 50.0 mL of 0.1*M* HCl. What volume of NaOH must you add before neutralization will occur? Explain your reasoning.

19.4 LessonCheck

Key Concept Check

51. Review What are the products of a reaction between an acid and a base?

52. Explain Why is the point in the titration when neutralization occurs called the equivalence point?

Vocabulary Check

Choose a highlighted word from the lesson to complete each sentence correctly.

53. The reaction between an acid and a base to form a salt and water is called a(n) __________.

54. The point at which neutralization happens during a titration is the __________.

55. In a titration, the solution of known concentration is called the __________.

56. The point at which the indicator changes color during a titration is called the __________.

Think Critically

57. Describe Write complete balanced equations for the following acid-base reactions:

a. $H_2SO_4(aq) + KOH(aq) \longrightarrow$

b. $H_3PO_4(aq) + Ca(OH)_2(aq) \longrightarrow$

CHEMISTRY & YOU

58. Iron compounds need to dissociate before iron in the soil can be taken in by plant roots. Iron compounds can't dissociate unless the pH is ideal. Most plants can get enough iron when the soil's pH is between 5.0 and 6.5. How could you change the pH of soil? (Hint: See page 642.)

BIGIDEA REACTIONS

59. Review the information on types of chemical reactions in Lesson 11.2. Which types of reactions are neutralization reactions? Explain.

19.5 Salts in Solution

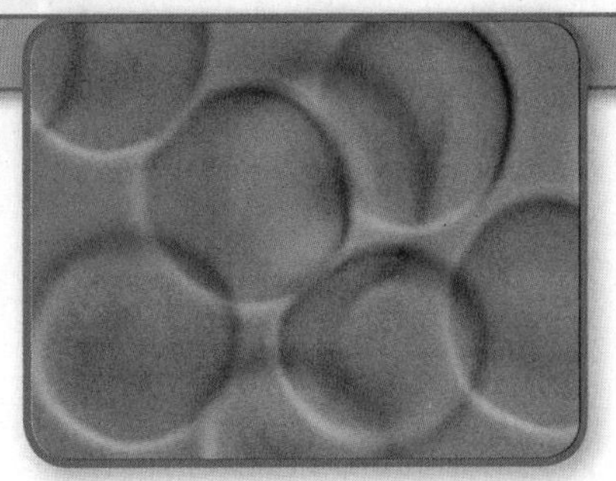

CHEMISTRY & YOU

Q: How is the pH of blood controlled in the human body? Chemical reactions in cells are sensitive to even slight changes in pH. For this reason, the pH of human blood needs to be kept close to 7.4. A person cannot live for more than a few minutes if the pH of blood drops below 6.8 or rises above 7.8. This lesson will explain the process that keeps the pH of blood within a safe range.

Key Questions

When is the solution of a salt acidic or basic?

What are the components of a buffer?

Salt Hydrolysis

Recall that a salt is one of the products of a neutralization reaction. A salt is made up of an anion from an acid and a cation from a base. The solutions of some salts are neutral. For example, a solution of sodium chloride is neutral.

Salt Solutions and pH It is important to remember that not all salt solutions are neutral. Some salts form acidic or basic solutions. The figure below shows three different salt solutions mixed with the same indicator. This indicator is called universal indicator because it can be used for a wide range of pH values.

The pH of Salt Solutions
You can use the indicator color to classify each solution as acidic, neutral, or basic.

A solution of ammonium chloride, NH_4Cl, is acidic. The pH of the solution is about 5.3.

A solution of sodium chloride, NaCl, is neutral. The pH of the solution is 7.

A solution of sodium ethanoate, CH_3COONa, is basic. The pH of the solution is about 8.7.

Comparing Titration Curves
The graphs compare the titration curves for two different titrations.
Go to your Chemistry Skills and Math Workbook to practice interpreting graphs.

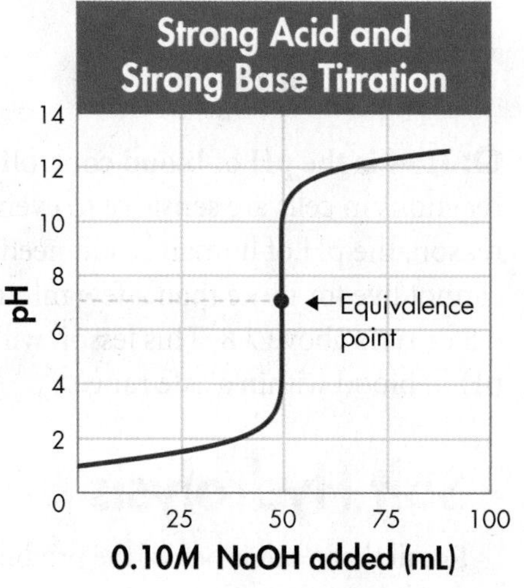

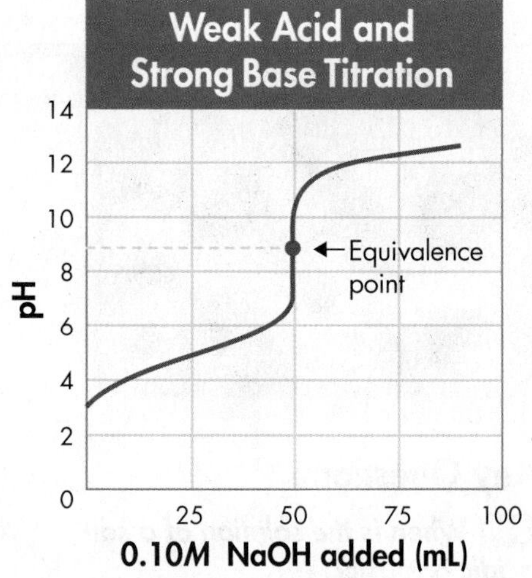

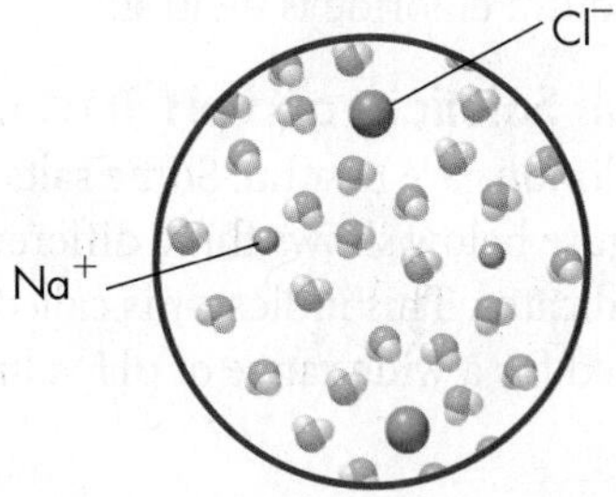

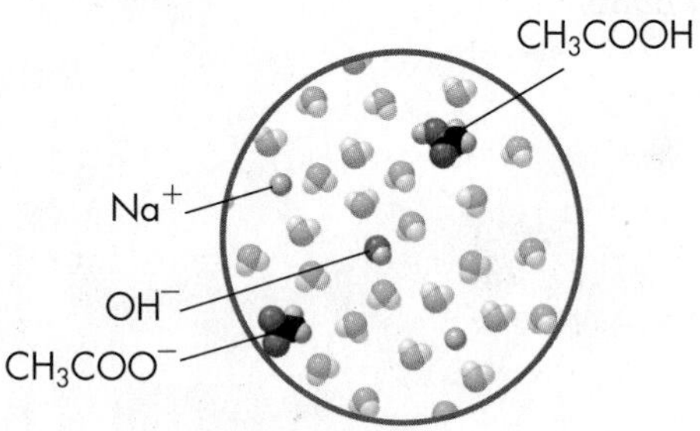

Strong Acid-Strong Base Titration
This titration curve shows how the pH changes as you titrate a strong acid (HCl) with a strong base (NaOH). Notice the pH at the equivalence point is neutral.

Weak Acid-Strong Base Titration
This titration curve shows how the pH changes as you titrate the weak acid ethanoic acid (CH_3COOH) with a strong base (NaOH). Notice the pH at the equivalence point is basic.

salt hydrolysis a reaction in which the cations or anions of a dissociated salt remove hydrogen ions from water or donate hydrogen ions to water

SUFFIXES
During *hydrolysis,* a hydrogen ion may be split off from a water molecule. The suffix *-lysis* comes from a Greek word meaning "to loosen."

What Is Salt Hydrolysis? The figure above shows two titration curves. The first curve is for the addition of a strong base to a strong acid. Note that the equivalence point for this titration is at a pH of 7, which is neutral. The second curve is for the addition of a strong base to a weak acid. Note that the equivalence point for this titration is at a pH of 9, which is basic.

The pH difference between the two solutions exists because of a process called hydrolysis. In **salt hydrolysis,** the cations or anions of a dissociated salt remove hydrogen ions from water or donate hydrogen ions to water.

Salt hydrolysis causes a solution to become either acidic or basic. If ions donate hydrogen ions to water, H_3O^+ ions form. The additional H_3O^+ ions cause the solution to be acidic. If ions remove hydrogen ions from water, OH^- ions form. The additional OH^- ions cause the solution to be basic.

▶ Hydrolysis of the Salt of a Weak Acid and Strong Base Sodium ethanoate (CH_3COONa) is the salt of the weak acid ethanoic acid (CH_3COOH) and the strong base sodium hydroxide. Sodium ethanoate ionizes completely in solution, as the equation below shows.

$$\underset{\text{Sodium ethanoate}}{CH_3COONa(aq)} \longrightarrow \underset{\text{Ethanoate ion}}{CH_3COO^-(aq)} + \underset{\text{Sodium ion}}{Na^+(aq)}$$

The ethanoate anion (CH_3COO^-) is a Brønsted-Lowry base. This means it can accept a hydrogen ion. Look at the equation below. The ethanoate ion reacts with water to form ethanoic acid and hydroxide ions. This is an example of salt hydrolysis. In this case, the solution becomes basic because the concentration of OH^- increases.

$$\underset{\substack{H^+ \text{ acceptor,} \\ \text{Brønsted-Lowry base}}}{CH_3COO^-(aq)} + \underset{\substack{H^+ \text{ donor,} \\ \text{Brønsted-Lowry acid}}}{H_2O(l)} \rightleftharpoons CH_3COOH(aq) + \underset{\substack{\text{(makes the} \\ \text{solution basic)}}}{OH^-(aq)}$$

▶ Hydrolysis of the Salt of a Strong Acid and Weak Base Ammonium chloride (NH_4Cl) is the salt of the strong acid hydrochloric acid and the weak base aqueous ammonia. Ammonium chloride ionizes completely in solution, as the equation below shows.

$$\underset{\text{Ammonium chloride}}{NH_4Cl(aq)} \longrightarrow \underset{\text{Ammonium ion}}{NH_4^+(aq)} + \underset{\text{Chloride ion}}{Cl^-(aq)}$$

The ammonium cation (NH_4^+) is a Brønsted-Lowry acid. In solution, it donates a hydrogen ion to a water molecule. The products of this reaction are ammonia molecules and hydronium ions. This is another example of salt hydrolysis. In this case, the solution becomes acidic because the concentration of H_3O^+ increases.

$$\underset{\substack{H^+ \text{ donor,} \\ \text{Brønsted-Lowry acid}}}{NH_4^+(aq)} + \underset{\substack{H^+ \text{ acceptor,} \\ \text{Brønsted-Lowry base}}}{H_2O(l)} \rightleftharpoons NH_3(aq) + \underset{\substack{\text{(makes the} \\ \text{solution acidic)}}}{H_3O^+(aq)}$$

▶ Rules for Salt Hydrolysis and pH Remember, if a salt has a cation that can donate hydrogen ions to water, its solution will be acidic. If a salt has an anion that can accept hydrogen ions from water, its solution will be basic. Use the rules below to predict whether a salt will form a solution that is acidic, basic, or neutral.

Strong acid + **Strong base** ⟶ Neutral solution

Strong acid + Weak base ⟶ **Acidic** solution

Weak acid + **Strong base** ⟶ **Basic** solution

Key Question When is the solution of a salt acidic or basic? **Salts that produce acidic solutions have positive ions that release hydrogen ions to water. Salts that produce basic solutions have negative ions that attract hydrogen ions from water.**

BUILD Understanding

Find Main Ideas Before you read the section called *What Is Salt Hydrolysis?*, create a list of the section's headings. Leave space under each heading for notes. As you read, identify the main ideas for each heading. Write them below the headings on your paper.

Effect of a Buffer

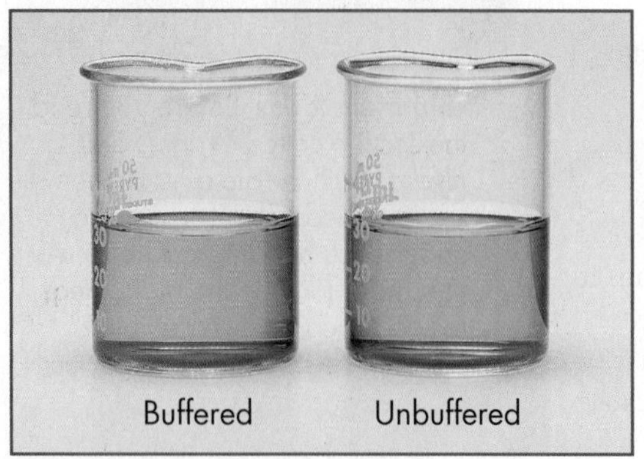

❶ The two beakers contain solutions of the same pH. One solution contains a buffer and the other does not. Both solutions have a pH of about 8.

HCl is added to each solution.

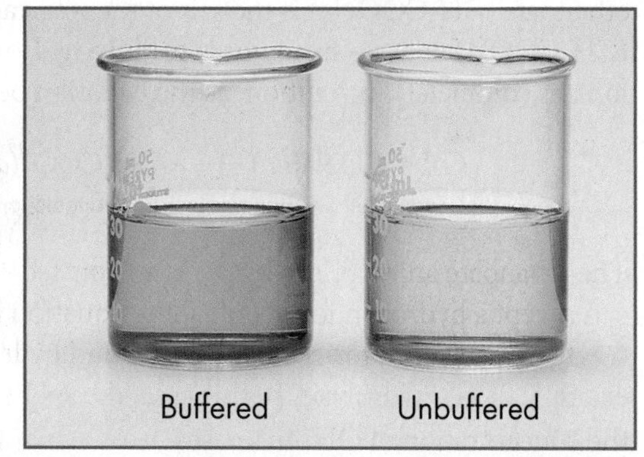

❷ The indicator shows no visible pH change in the buffered solution. The pH of the unbuffered solution changes from 8 to about 5.

BUILD Vocabulary

buffer a solution in which the pH remains fairly constant when small amounts of acid or base are added

buffer capacity the amount of acid or base that can be added to a buffer solution before a large change in pH happens

USING PRIOR KNOWLEDGE

The word *capacity* is similar to the word *limit.* If you reach your spending limit, you can't spend any more money. Similarly, a buffer stops working once it reaches its limit.

Buffers

A solution that contains a weak acid and one of its salts can resist pH changes. A solution of a weak base and one of its salts can also resist pH changes. Such solutions are called buffers. A **buffer** is a solution in which the pH remains fairly constant when small amounts of acid or base are added. The figure above compares what happens when you add acid to an unbuffered solution and to a buffered solution.

How Buffers Work A buffer solution can resist changes in pH better than water can. The reason is simple. One of the two components in a buffer solution can react with hydrogen ions. This component acts as a hydrogen-ion acceptor. The second component in a buffer solution can react with hydroxide ions. It acts as a hydrogen-ion donor. Together, these two components are able to act like a sponge and "mop up" hydrogen ions and hydroxide ions that are added to the solution. This is how the solution resists changes in pH.

Think about a buffer that contains the weak acid ethanoic acid and its salt sodium ethanoate. The equation below shows how this buffer keeps the pH fairly constant when you add acid (H^+). When you add H^+, the ethanoate ions, from the salt sodium ethanoate, react with the hydrogen ions. The product of this reaction is the weak acid ethanoic acid. Ethanoic acid ionizes only slightly in water. So the change in pH is very small.

$$\underset{\text{Ethanoate ion}}{CH_3COO^-(aq)} + \underset{\text{Hydrogen ion}}{H^+(aq)} \rightleftharpoons \underset{\text{Ethanoic acid}}{CH_3COOH(aq)}$$

The Capacity of a Buffer At some point, the hydrogen-ion acceptors or hydrogen-ion donors in the buffer become tied up. At that point, the buffer can no longer control the pH. Adding too much acid or base exceeds the solution's buffer capacity. The **buffer capacity** is the amount of acid or base that can be added to a buffer solution before a large change in pH occurs.

Key Question What are the components of a buffer? **A buffer is a solution of a weak acid and one of its salts or a solution of a weak base and one of its salts.**

Sample Problem 19.8

Describing Buffer Systems

A carbonic acid–hydrogen carbonate buffer can "mop up" added hydroxide ions and hydrogen ions. Write a balanced chemical equation to show what happens when hydroxide ions are added.

1 Analyze Identify the relevant concepts. A buffer contains a hydrogen-ion donor that can react with hydroxide ions.

2 Solve Apply the concepts to this problem.

Identify the hydrogen-ion donor.

H_2CO_3, a weak acid, can release hydrogen ions. HCO_3^- is the conjugate base, which can accept hydrogen ions.

Write the equation for the reaction that occurs when OH^- is added to the buffer.

When a base is added, the hydroxide ions react with H_2CO_3.

$$H_2CO_3(aq) + OH^-(aq) \rightleftharpoons HCO_3^-(aq) + H_2O(l)$$

Practice Problems

60. Write an equation to show what happens when you add an acid to a solution that contains HPO_4^{2-} ions.

1 Analyze Identify the relevant concepts.

2 Solve Apply the concepts to this problem.

61. Challenge A buffer consists of methanoic acid (HCOOH) and methanoate ion ($HCOO^-$). Write an equation to show what happens when an acid is added to this buffer.

19.5 LessonCheck

Key Concept Check

62. Review What type of salt produces an acidic solution? A basic solution?

63. Describe What types of substances can be combined to make a buffer solution?

Vocabulary Check *Choose a highlighted word from the lesson to complete the sentence correctly.*

64. When a solution is a(n) __________, small amounts of acid or base can be added without significantly changing the solution's pH.

Think Critically

65. Relate Cause and Effect Use Le Châtelier's principle to explain how a buffer system maintains the pH of a solution.

CHEMISTRY & YOU

66. The equilibrium between carbonic acid (H_2CO_3) and hydrogen carbonate ions (HCO_3^-) helps keep the pH of blood within a healthy range. If the pH rises, molecules of carbonic acid donate hydrogen ions. What can happen if the pH drops? (Hint: See page 648.)

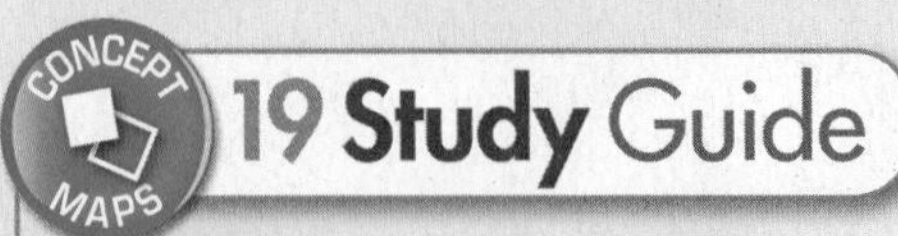

19 Study Guide

BIGIDEA REACTIONS

Chemists define acids and bases according to the ions they yield in aqueous solution. Chemists also define acids and bases based on whether they accept or donate hydrogen ions. Finally, chemists define acids and bases based on whether they are electron-pair donors or acceptors. The pH of a solution reflects the hydrogen-ion concentration. Chemists use acid-base reactions to determine the concentration of an acid or a base in solution.

19.1 Acid-Base Theories

According to Arrhenius, acids are hydrogen-containing compounds that ionize to yield hydrogen ions in aqueous solution. Bases are compounds that ionize to yield hydroxide ions in aqueous solution.

According to the Brønsted-Lowry theory, an acid is a hydrogen-ion donor, and a base is a hydrogen-ion acceptor.

According to Lewis, an acid accepts a pair of electrons, and a base donates a pair of electrons.

- hydronium ion (H_3O^+) (611)
- conjugate acid (613)
- conjugate base (613)
- conjugate acid-base pair (614)
- amphoteric (614)
- Lewis acid (615)
- Lewis base (615)

19.2 Hydrogen Ions and Acidity

In an aqueous solution, the product of the hydrogen-ion concentration and the hydroxide-ion concentration equals 1.0×10^{-14}.

A solution with a pH of 7.0 is neutral. A solution with a pH less than 7.0 is acidic. A solution with a pH greater than 7.0 is basic.

Either acid-base indicators or pH meters can be used to measure pH.

- self-ionization (618)
- neutral solution (618)
- ion-product constant for water (K_w) (619)
- acidic solution (619)
- basic solution (619)
- pH (622)

Key Equations

$$K_w = [H^+] \times [OH^-] = 1.0 \times 10^{-14}$$

$$pH = -\log[H^+]$$

19.3 Strengths of Acids and Bases

Acids and bases are classified as strong or weak based on the degree to which they ionize in water.

- strong acid (631)
- weak acid (631)
- acid dissociation constant (K_a) (632)
- strong base (636)
- weak base (636)
- base dissociation constant (K_b) (636)

Key Equation

$$K_a = \frac{[H^+][A^-]}{[HA]}$$

19.4 Neutralization Reactions

In general, acids and bases react to produce a salt and water.

Neutralization occurs when the number of moles of hydrogen ions equals the number of moles of hydroxide ions.

- neutralization reaction (639)
- titration (641)
- standard solution (642)
- equivalence point (642)
- end point (642)

19.5 Salts in Solution

Salts that produce acidic solutions have positive ions that release hydrogen ions to water. Salts that produce basic solutions have negative ions that attract hydrogen ions from water.

A buffer is a solution of a weak acid and one of its salts or a solution of a weak base and one of its salts.

- salt hydrolysis (646)
- buffer (648)
- buffer capacity (648)

Math Tune-Up: Acid-Base Problems

Problem	❶ Analyze	❷ Calculate	❸ Evaluate
The pH of an unknown solution is 3.70. What is the hydrogen-ion concentration?	Known: pH = 3.70 Unknown: $[H^+] = ?M$ Use the following equation: $pH = -\log[H^+]$	Rearrange the expression for pH and substitute the known pH value to solve for the unknown: $-\log[H^+] = pH$ $-\log[H^+] = 3.70$ $\log[H^+] = -3.70$ The antilog of −3.70 is 2.0×10^{-4}. Thus, $[H^+] = 2.0 \times 10^{-4}M$. Note: To determine the antilog, on most calculators, press the [2nd] or [INV] key, then the [log] key.	The pH is between 3 and 4. So, the hydrogen ion concentration must be between $1 \times 10^{-3}M$ and $1 \times 10^{-4}M$.
In a 0.500M solution of a weak acid (HA), the $[H^+]$ is $4.02 \times 10^{-3}M$ at equilibrium. Find the K_a for this acid. The acid dissociates as follows: $HA(aq) \rightleftharpoons H^+(aq) + A^-(aq)$	Knowns: $[HA] = 0.500M$ $[H^+] = 4.02 \times 10^{-3}M$ Unknown: $K_a = ?$ Use the general expression for K_a: $K_a = \frac{[H^+] \times [A^-]}{[HA]}$ Hint: Review Sample Problem 19.5 for help finding equilibrium concentrations.	At equilibrium, $[H^+]$ is equal to $[A^-]$: $[H^+] = [A^-] = 4.02 \times 10^{-3}M$ Calculate [HA] at equilibrium: $0.500M - 0.00402M = 0.496M$ Substitute the equilibrium concentrations into the equation for K_a and solve: $K_a = \frac{(4.02 \times 10^{-3}) \times (4.02 \times 10^{-3})}{0.496}$ $K_a = 3.26 \times 10^{-5}$	The value of K_a is consistent with that of a weak acid.
How many moles of KOH are needed to neutralize 0.25 mol of H_2SO_4? The equation for the reaction is $2KOH(aq) + H_2SO_4(aq) \longrightarrow K_2SO_4(aq) + 2H_2O(l)$	Known: mol H_2SO_4 = 0.25 mol Unknown: mol KOH = ? mol	Use the mole ratio of base to acid (2 mol KOH to 1 mol H_2SO_4) to determine the number of moles of base: $0.25 \text{ mol } H_2SO_4 \times \frac{2 \text{ mol KOH}}{1 \text{ mol } H_2SO_4}$ = 0.50 mol KOH	The mole ratio of KOH to H_2SO_4 is 2:1. So, the number of moles of KOH should be twice the number of moles of H_2SO_4.

19 Assessment

★ Solutions appear in Appendix D.

Lesson by Lesson

19.1 Acid-Base Theories

★**67.** How did Arrhenius describe acids and bases?

68. Write an equation for the dissociation of each compound in water.

a. KOH
b. $Mg(OH)_2$

★**69.** Write balanced equations for the reaction of each metal with water.

a. lithium
b. barium

70. Identify each reactant in the following equations as a hydrogen-ion donor (acid) or a hydrogen-ion acceptor (base). All the reactions take place in aqueous solution.

a. $HNO_3 + H_2O \longrightarrow H_3O^+ + NO_3^-$
b. $CH_3COOH + H_2O \rightleftharpoons H_3O^+ + CH_3COO^-$
c. $NH_3 + H_2O \rightleftharpoons NH_4^+ + OH^-$
d. $H_2O + CH_3COO^- \rightleftharpoons CH_3COOH + OH^-$

71. What is a Lewis acid? What is a Lewis base?

19.2 Hydrogen Ions and Acidity

72. Write an equation showing the self-ionization of water.

73. What are the concentrations of H^+ and OH^- in pure water at 25°C?

74. How is the pH of a solution calculated?

★**75.** Calculate the pH for the following solutions and indicate whether each solution is acidic or basic.

a. $[OH^-] = 1 \times 10^{-2}M$
b. $[H^+] = 1 \times 10^{-2}M$

76. Calculate the pH or $[H^+]$ for each solution.

a. $[H^+] = 2.4 \times 10^{-6}M$
b. pH = 13.20

19.3 Strengths of Acids and Bases

★**77.** Identify each compound as a strong or weak acid or base.

a. NaOH **b.** NH_3 **c.** H_2SO_4 **d.** HCl

78. Would a strong acid have a large or a small K_a? Explain your answer.

79. Write the expression for K_a for each acid. Assume only one hydrogen is ionized.

a. HF **b.** H_2CO_3

19.4 Neutralization Reactions

80. Write a general word equation for a neutralization reaction.

81. Identify the products and write balanced equations for each neutralization reaction.

a. $HNO_3(aq) + KOH(aq) \longrightarrow$
b. $HCl(aq) + Ca(OH)_2(aq) \longrightarrow$
c. $H_2SO_4(aq) + NaOH(aq) \longrightarrow$

82. How is it possible to recognize the end point of a titration?

★**83.** What is the molarity of sodium hydroxide if 20.0 mL of the solution is neutralized by each of the following 1.00*M* solutions?

a. 28.0 mL of HCl
b. 17.4 mL of H_3PO_4

19.5 Salts in Solution

★**84.** Write an equation showing why an aqueous solution of sodium hydrogen carbonate is basic.

85. Explain why solutions of salts that undergo hydrolysis in water do not have a pH of 7.

86. Predict whether an aqueous solution of each salt will be acidic, basic, or neutral.

a. $NaHCO_3$ **d.** Na_2CO_3
b. NH_4NO_3 **e.** Na_2SO_4
c. KCl **f.** NH_4Cl

Understand Concepts

*87. Write equations showing that the hydrogen phosphate ion (HPO_4^{2-}) is amphoteric.

88. How do $[H^+]$ and $[OH^-]$ compare in each type of solution?
   a. neutral solution
   b. basic solution
   c. acidic solution

*89. Write the formula and name of the conjugate acid of each Brønsted-Lowry base.
   a. ClO_2^-
   b. H_2O
   c. $H_2PO_4^-$
   d. NH_3

*90. Write an equation for the reaction of each antacid with hydrochloric acid.
   a. magnesium hydroxide
   b. calcium carbonate
   c. aluminum hydroxide

*91. Arrange the following solutions in order of decreasing acidity:
   a. $0.1M$ NaOH
   b. $0.1M$ HCl
   c. $0.1M$ NH_4Cl
   d. $0.1M$ CH_3COONa

92. Vapors of the strong acid HCl(*aq*) and the weak base NH_3(*aq*) combine to form a white salt.

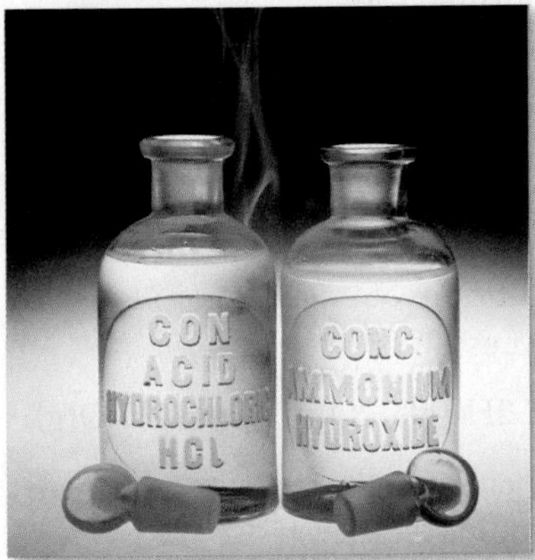

   a. What is the name and formula of the salt?
   b. What kind of solution will this salt form when it dissolves in water—acidic, basic, or neutral?

Think Critically

93. **Evaluate** Critique the accuracy of each of these statements.
   a. Indicators such as methyl red provide accurate and precise measurements of pH.
   b. According to the Arrhenius definition of acids and bases, ammonia qualifies as a base.
   c. The strength of an acid or base changes as its concentration changes.

*94. **Identify** Which quantity might correspond to the *y*-axis on this graph: $[H^+]$, pH, or $[OH^-]$? Explain your answer.

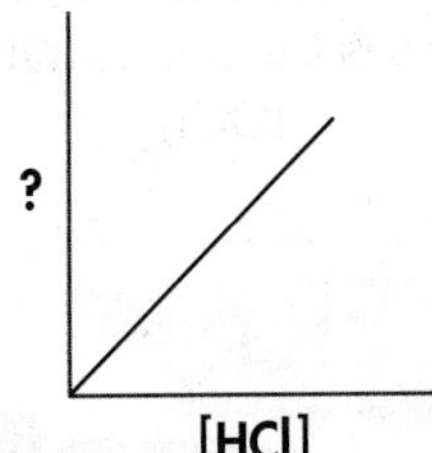

95. **Predict** Will the resulting solutions be neutral, acidic, or basic at the equivalence point for each of the following titrations? Explain.
   a. NaOH titrated with HCl
   b. NH_3 titrated with HCl
   c. CH_3COOH titrated with NaOH

FOUNDATIONS Wrap-Up

Which Fruits React with Baking Soda?

1. **Draw Conclusions** At the beginning of the chapter, you placed baking soda on different fruits. Explain why the foods reacted the way they did.

Concept Check

Now that you've finished studying Chapter 19, answer these questions.

2. Citrus fruits contain citric acid ($HC_6H_7O_7$). Which acid-base definitions explain why citric acid is an acid? Explain.
3. How could you measure the pH of apple juice?

Write About Science

96. Research The main cause of tooth decay is the weak acid lactic acid (C_2H_5OCOOH). Lactic acid forms when bacteria, such as *Streptococcus mutans*, feed on sugar. In the mouth, sugars are present in the sticky plaque on tooth surfaces. Research current efforts to fight tooth decay. Write a report summarizing your findings.

97. Connect to the BIGIDEA Hypochlorite salts are used to disinfect swimming pools. Conduct research to find out what happens when chlorine compounds are added to pool water. Use hydrolysis reactions to explain how the pH of the water affects the concentration of hypochlorous acid (HOCl).

CHEMYSTERY

Paper Trail

The wood pulp used to make paper is a suspension of cellulose fibers in water. Wood chips can be ground into a pulp. This is the process used to make newsprint. For higher-quality paper, the pulp is treated chemically to remove parts of the wood other than cellulose.

The paper is often coated with aluminum sulfate to keep it from absorbing too much ink. While the aluminum sulfate keeps the paper from absorbing too much ink, it also leaves a residue of sulfuric acid in the paper. Over time, this acid causes the cellulose fibers to decay.

98. Infer The process of treating the paper is called de-acidification. The first step in a popular de-acidification method is to dip the paper in a solution of calcium hydroxide. Write a chemical equation to describe what happens in this step.

***99. Connect to the BIGIDEA** What type of reaction is performed in the process of de-acidification? Would you expect the pH of the paper to be raised or lowered in the process of de-acidification?

Cumulative Review

100. Write the product of each of these combination reactions. (See Lesson 11.2 for help.)
- **a.** $K(s) + O_2(g) \longrightarrow$
- **b.** $F_2(g) + Al(s) \longrightarrow$

101. How many grams of oxygen are needed to completely burn 87.4 g of sulfur to form sulfur trioxide? (See Lesson 12.2 for help.)

$$S(s) + O_2(g) \longrightarrow SO_3(g)$$

***102.** Which state of matter is not part of the process of sublimation? (See Lesson 13.4 for help.)

103. Which of these laws describes an inverse relationship? (See Lesson 14.2 for help.)
- **a.** Charles's law
- **b.** Boyle's law
- **c.** Gay-Lussac's law

***104.** What type of bond is responsible for water's high surface tension? (See Lesson 15.1 for help.)

***105.** How many liters of 8.0*M* HCl are needed to prepare 1.50 L of 2.5*M* HCl? (See Lesson 16.2 for help.)

106. Which of these is an endothermic process? Provide an explanation. (See Lesson 17.1 for help.)
- **a.** burning wax
- **b.** evaporating water
- **c.** melting wax
- **d.** roasting a marshmallow

107. How would each change affect the position of equilibrium of this reaction? (See Lesson 18.3 for help.)

$$2H_2(g) + O_2(g) \rightleftharpoons 2H_2O(g) + \text{heat}$$

- **a.** increasing the pressure
- **b.** adding a catalyst
- **c.** increasing the concentration of $H_2(g)$
- **d.** cooling the reaction mixture
- **e.** removing water vapor from the container

***108.** In each pair, which has the higher entropy? (See Lesson 18.5 for help.)
- **a.** NaCl(*s*) or NaCl(*aq*)
- **b.** hot water or cold water

Standardized Test Prep

For help with answering test questions, go to your Chemistry Skills and Math Workbook.

Select the choice that best answers each question or completes each statement.

1. If an acid has a measured K_a of 3×10^{-6},
(A) the acid is a strong acid.
(B) an aqueous solution of the acid would have a pH < 7.
(C) the acid is a strong electrolyte.
(D) All of the above are correct.

2. The pH of a sample of orange juice is 3.5. A sample of tomato juice has a pH of 4.5. Compared to the $[H^+]$ of orange juice, the $[H^+]$ of tomato juice is:
(A) 100 times higher. (C) 10 times higher.
(B) 10 times lower. (D) 100 times lower.

Tips for Success

Eliminate Wrong Answers If you don't know which choice is correct, eliminate those you know are wrong. If you can rule out some choices, you'll increase your chances of choosing the correct answer.

3. Which ion or molecule is the conjugate base of the ammonium ion, NH_4^+?
(A) H_2O (B) OH^- (C) NH_3 (D) H_3O^+

4. How many moles of NaOH are required to neutralize 2.4 mol H_2SO_4?
(A) 1.2 mol (B) 2.4 mol (C) 3.6 mol (D) 4.8 mol

5. A solution with a hydrogen-ion concentration of $2.3 \times 10^{-8}M$ has a pH between:
(A) 2 and 3. (B) 3 and 4. (C) 7 and 8. (D) 8 and 9.

6. The net ionic equation for the neutralization reaction between solutions of potassium hydroxide and hydrochloric acid is:
(A) $H^+(aq) + OH^-(aq) \longrightarrow H_2O(l)$
(B) $KOH(aq) + HCl(aq) \longrightarrow H_2O(l) + KCl(aq)$
(C) $K^+(aq) + Cl^-(aq) \longrightarrow KCl(aq)$
(D) $K^+(aq) + OH^-(aq) + H^+(aq) + Cl^-(aq) \longrightarrow KCl(aq) + H_2O(l)$

7. Calculate the molarity of an HCl solution if 25.0 mL of the solution is neutralized by 15.5 mL of 0.800*M* NaOH.
(A) 0.248*M* (B) 0.496*M* (C) 1.29*M* (D) 0.645*M*

8. Which combination of compound and ion would not make a useful buffer solution?
(A) ammonium ion and ammonia
(B) hydrogen carbonate ion and carbonic acid
(C) sulfate ion and sulfuric acid
(D) ethanoate ion and ethanoic acid

The lettered choices below refer to Questions 9–11. In each formula, P is the cation, and Q is the anion.

(A) PQ (B) P_2Q_3 (C) PQ_3 (D) P_3Q

Which of the choices completes the general formula for the salt formed in each of the following neutralization reactions?

9. $H_3PO_4 + NaOH \longrightarrow$

10. $H_2SO_4 + Mg(OH)_2 \longrightarrow$

11. $HNO_3 + Al(OH)_3 \longrightarrow$

Use the drawings below to answer Questions 12 and 13. Water molecules have been omitted from the solution windows.

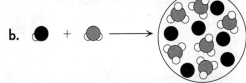

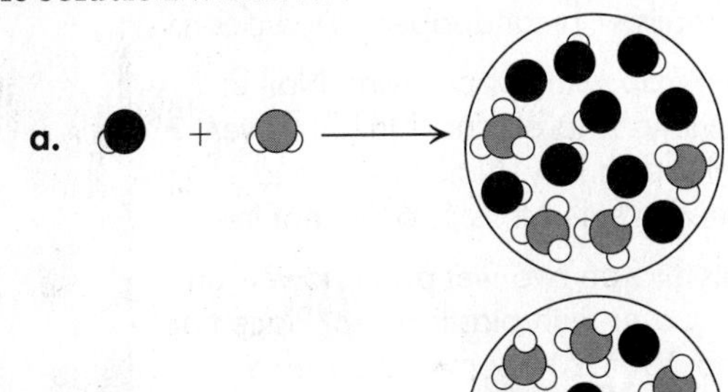

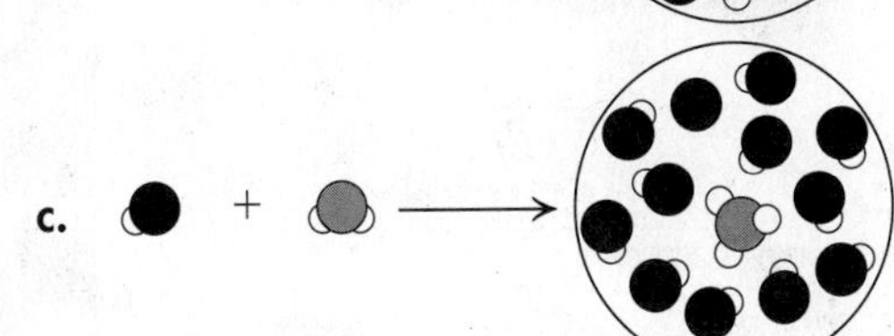

Undissociated acid

Water

Conjugate base

Hydronium ion

12. Rank the acids in order of increasing strength.

13. How many of the acids are strong acids?

If You Have Trouble With . . .

Question	1	2	3	4	5	6	7	8	9	10	11	12	13
See Lesson	19.3	19.2	19.1	19.4	19.2	19.4	19.4	19.5	19.4	19.4	19.4	19.3	19.3

20 Oxidation-Reduction Reactions

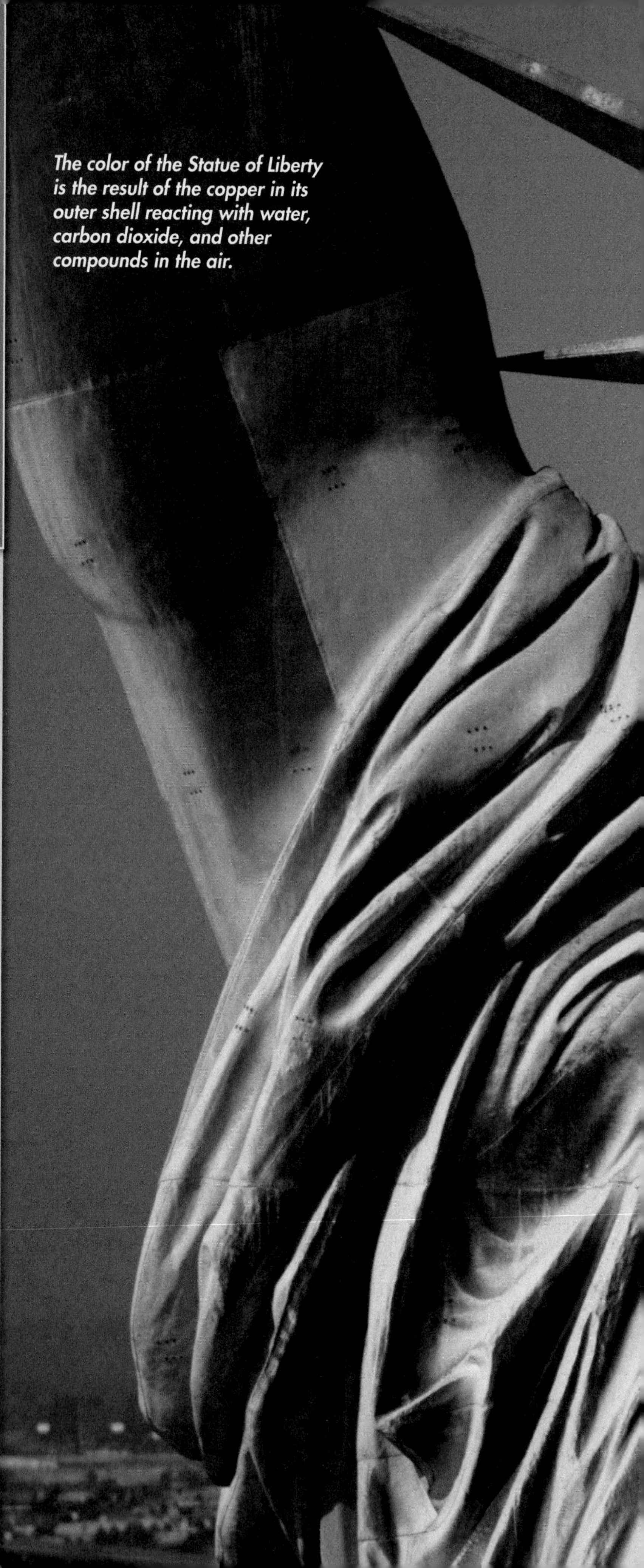

The color of the Statue of Liberty is the result of the copper in its outer shell reacting with water, carbon dioxide, and other compounds in the air.

FOUNDATIONS for Learning

Rusting

1. Rub six nails with sandpaper. Wipe clean.
2. Nail 1: Wrap with copper wire. Nail 2: Wrap with a strip of zinc. Nail 3: Cover with petroleum jelly. Nail 4: Wet and sprinkle with salt. Nails 5, 6: Do not treat.
3. Set nails 1–5 on two wet paper towels on a plate. Cover with plastic wrap. Place nail 6 on top. Wait 24 hours and observe.

Form a Hypothesis Explain why some nails rusted and others did not.

PearsonChem.com

UntamedScience™

Take a video field trip with the Untamed Science crew as they learn more about what can be done to prevent bridges from rusting.

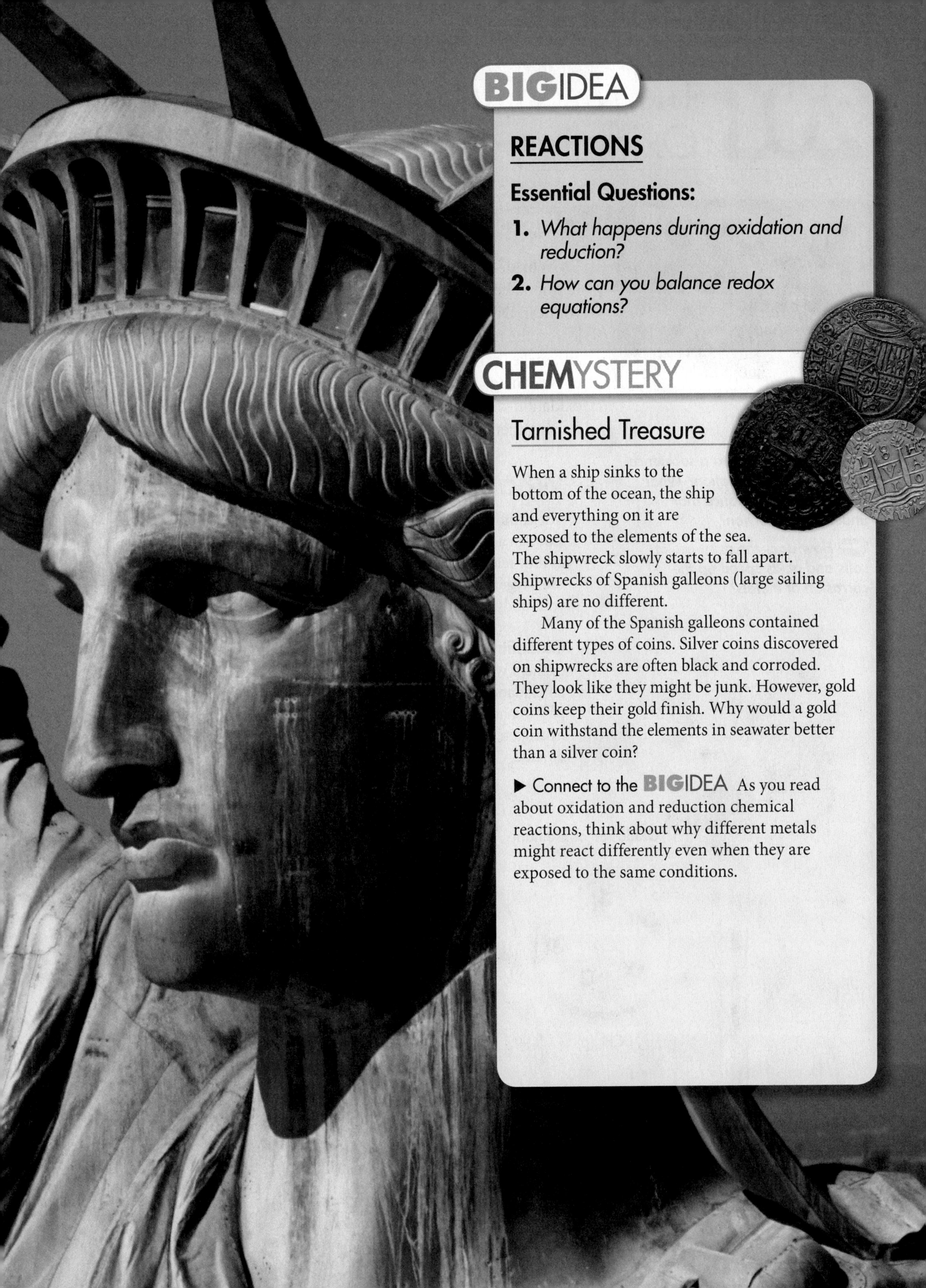

BIGIDEA

REACTIONS

Essential Questions:

1. *What happens during oxidation and reduction?*
2. *How can you balance redox equations?*

CHEMYSTERY

Tarnished Treasure

When a ship sinks to the bottom of the ocean, the ship and everything on it are exposed to the elements of the sea. The shipwreck slowly starts to fall apart. Shipwrecks of Spanish galleons (large sailing ships) are no different.

Many of the Spanish galleons contained different types of coins. Silver coins discovered on shipwrecks are often black and corroded. They look like they might be junk. However, gold coins keep their gold finish. Why would a gold coin withstand the elements in seawater better than a silver coin?

▶ Connect to the **BIGIDEA** As you read about oxidation and reduction chemical reactions, think about why different metals might react differently even when they are exposed to the same conditions.

20.1 The Meaning of Oxidation and Reduction

CHEMISTRY & YOU

Q: Why do you need to wash the bottom of your car? A clean car may look better than a dirty car, but looks aren't the only reason to wash your car. During winter in cold climates, salt is spread on roads. Salt lowers the freezing point of water. It prevents the buildup of slippery ice and makes driving safer. The salt also clings to your car. The salt can cause damage to the metal parts. In this lesson, you will learn about oxidation-reduction reactions, including those that damage salty cars by causing them to rust relatively quickly.

Key Questions

What happens to a substance that undergoes oxidation? What happens to a substance that undergoes reduction?

How does the presence of salts and acids speed up the corrosion of metals?

What Are Oxidation and Reduction?

The combustion of gasoline in an automobile engine and the burning of wood in a fireplace are chemical reactions. Both reactions require oxygen as they release energy. The reactions that break down food in your body use oxygen from the air you breathe. These reactions release energy for your body to use.

Oxidation Early chemists saw oxidation only as the combining of an element with oxygen to produce an oxide. The burning of a fuel is also an oxidation reaction that uses oxygen. When methane (CH_4), the main part of natural gas, burns in air, it oxidizes. It forms oxides of carbon and hydrogen, as shown in the figure below. One oxide formed is carbon dioxide, CO_2.

Oxidation of Methane

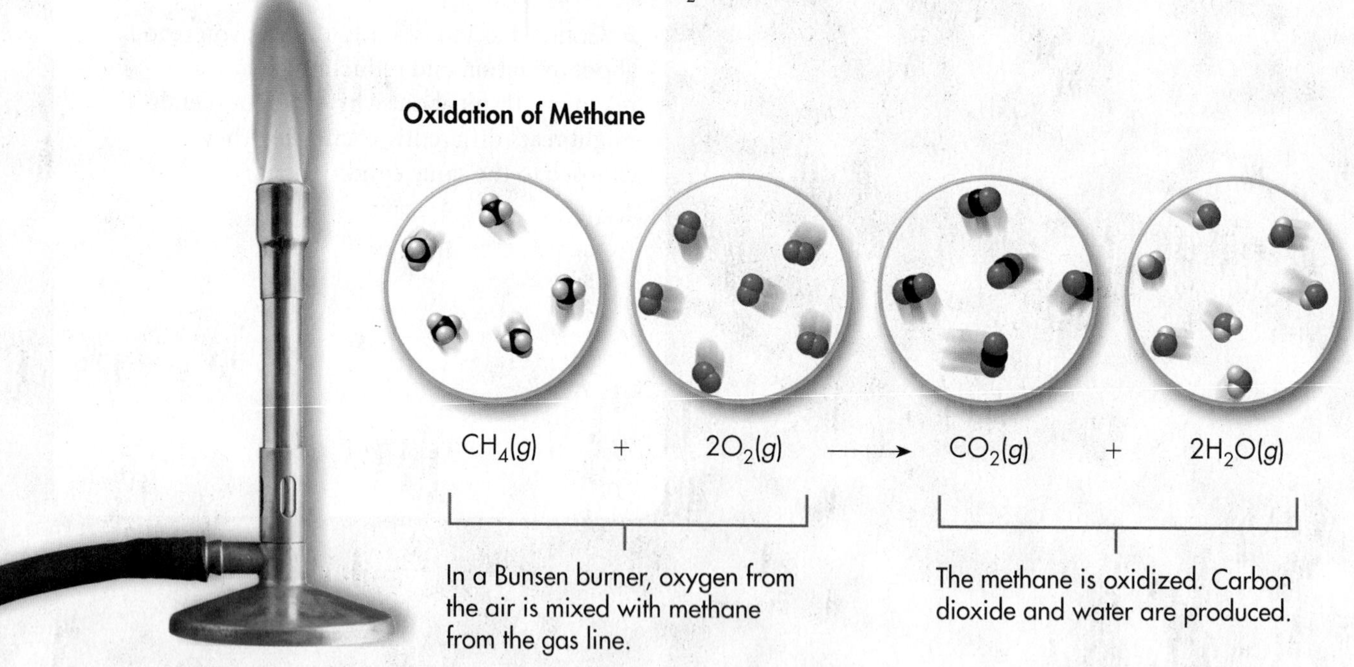

$CH_4(g)$ + $2O_2(g)$ ⟶ $CO_2(g)$ + $2H_2O(g)$
In a Bunsen burner, oxygen from the air is mixed with methane from the gas line.
The methane is oxidized. Carbon dioxide and water are produced.

Oxidation of Iron

4Fe(s) + 3O2(g) → 2Fe2O3(s)
Iron
Oxygen
Iron(III) oxide
When items made of iron are exposed to moist air, the iron reacts with oxygen in the air.
The iron is oxidized to compounds such as iron(III) oxide. This is commonly known as rusting.

Oxidation can also take place without burning. Iron turning to rust is undergoing oxidation, as shown in the figure above. Bleaching stains is another example. Common household bleach contains a substance that releases oxygen. The stain undergoes oxidation and is changed to a colorless form. Another example of oxidation without burning is when hydrogen peroxide (H_2O_2) decomposes. It acts as both a bleach and a substance that can kill bacteria by oxidizing them.

Reduction Reduction is the opposite of oxidation. In the past, reduction meant only the loss of oxygen from a compound. You will learn later that reduction does not always involve the loss of oxygen. In the reduction of iron ore, oxygen is removed from iron(III) oxide. Iron and carbon dioxide are formed. This reaction takes place when the ore is heated with carbon. The equation for the reduction of iron ore is shown below.

$$\underset{\text{Iron(III) oxide}}{2Fe_2O_3(s)} + \underset{\text{Carbon}}{3C(s)} \longrightarrow \underset{\text{Iron}}{4Fe(s)} + \underset{\text{Carbon dioxide}}{3CO_2(g)}$$

Oxidation and Reduction Oxidation and reduction always happen together. In the equation above, iron(III) oxide is reduced to iron by losing oxygen. At the same time, carbon oxidizes to carbon dioxide by gaining oxygen. A substance that undergoes oxidation gains oxygen. A substance that undergoes reduction loses oxygen. Oxidation doesn't happen without reduction, and reduction doesn't happen without oxidation. Reactions that involve oxidation and reduction are called *oxidation-reduction reactions.* Oxidation-reduction reactions are also known as *redox reactions.*

oxidation-reduction reaction a reaction that includes a transfer of electrons between reactants

oxidation complete or partial loss of electrons or gain of oxygen

reduction complete or partial gain of electrons or loss of oxygen

USING PRIOR KNOWLEDGE

The word *reduction* indicates a decrease in something. In chemistry, though, a substance that is reduced actually gains electrons. The gain of electrons makes the charge of the substance more negative.

Electron Shift in Redox Reactions Today's concepts of oxidation and reduction include many reactions that do not even involve oxygen. Recall from Chapter 6 that, with the exception of fluorine, oxygen is the most electronegative element. When oxygen bonds with an atom of a different element (other than fluorine), electrons from that atom shift toward oxygen. Today, **oxidation-reduction reactions** are defined as those reactions that include a transfer of electrons between reactants. **Oxidation** means complete or partial loss of electrons or gain of oxygen. **Reduction** means complete or partial gain of electrons or loss of oxygen.

Oxidation	Reduction
Loss of electrons	Gain of electrons
Gain of oxygen	Loss of oxygen

Redox Reactions That Form Ions During a reaction between a metal and a nonmetal, electrons are transferred from the metal to the nonmetal. As shown below, when magnesium metal is heated with the nonmetal sulfur, magnesium sulfide is produced.

Synthesis of an Ionic Compound

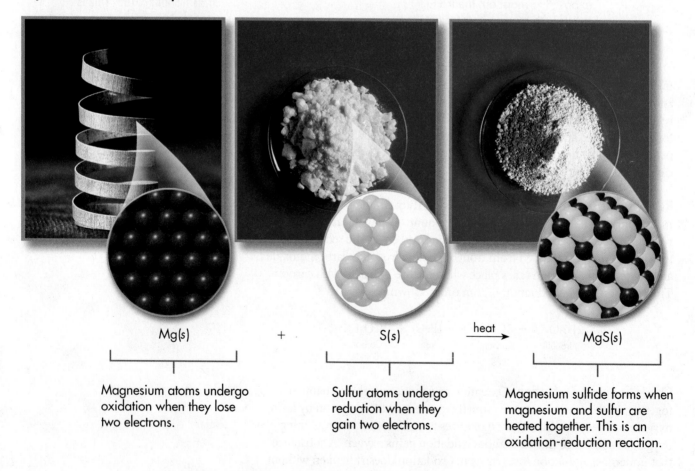

$Mg(s)$ + $S(s)$ $\xrightarrow{heat}$ $MgS(s)$

Magnesium atoms undergo oxidation when they lose two electrons.

Sulfur atoms undergo reduction when they gain two electrons.

Magnesium sulfide forms when magnesium and sulfur are heated together. This is an oxidation-reduction reaction.

In the reaction between magnesium and sulfur, two electrons are transferred from a magnesium atom to a sulfur atom. The magnesium atoms are made more stable by the loss of electrons. The sulfur atoms become more stable due to the gain of electrons.

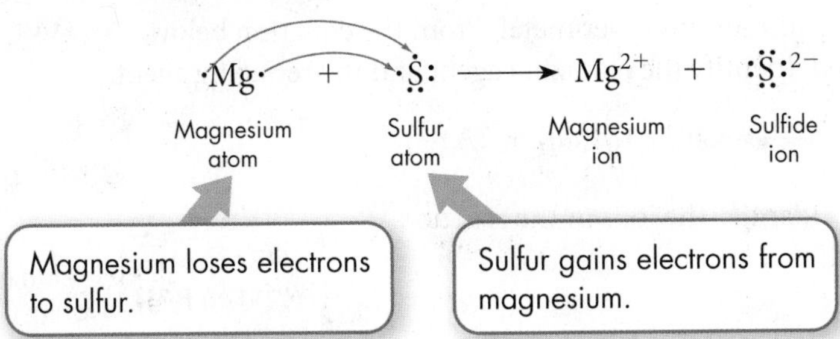

The magnesium atom loses electrons. So, it is said to be oxidized to a magnesium ion. At the same time, the sulfur atom gains two electrons. It is reduced to a sulfide ion. The overall process is represented as the two component processes below.

Oxidation: $\cdot Mg \cdot \longrightarrow Mg^{2+} + 2e^-$ (loss of electrons)

Reduction: $\cdot\ddot{S}: + 2e^- \longrightarrow :\ddot{S}:^{2-}$ (gain of electrons)

Oxidizing and Reducing Agents A substance that undergoes oxidation loses electrons. A substance that undergoes reduction gains electrons. The substance that loses electrons is the **reducing agent.** By losing electrons to sulfur, magnesium reduces the sulfur. Magnesium is the reducing agent. The substance that gains electrons is the **oxidizing agent.** By accepting electrons from magnesium, sulfur oxidizes the magnesium. Sulfur is the oxidizing agent. The equation below shows the relationship between the substance that is oxidized, the substance that is reduced, the oxidizing agent, and the reducing agent.

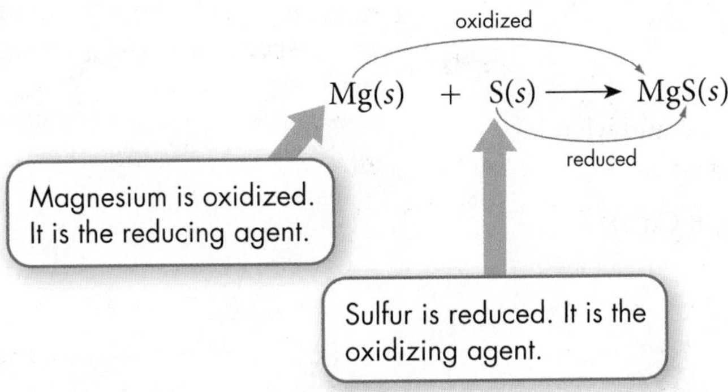

Another way to identify oxidizing and reducing agents is to remember that the substance reduced is the oxidizing agent. The substance that is oxidized is the reducing agent. Use the table below to compare oxidizing and reducing agents.

Comparing Oxidizing and Reducing Agents

Oxidizing Agent	Reducing Agent
Gains electrons	Loses electrons
Is reduced	Is oxidized

BUILD Understanding

Use Mnemonics To help you remember the definitions of *oxidation* and *reduction,* use the phrase "LEO the lion goes GER." LEO stands for Losing Electrons is Oxidation; GER stands for Gaining Electrons is Reduction.

BUILD Vocabulary

reducing agent substance that undergoes oxidation and loses electrons

oxidizing agent substance that undergoes reduction and gains electrons

USING PRIOR KNOWLEDGE

An *agent* is something that produces an effect, or causes something to happen.
A reducing agent causes reduction to happen.
An oxidizing agent causes oxidation to happen.

Go to your Chemistry Skills and Math Workbook to practice identifying oxidized and reduced reactants.

CHEMISTRY TUTORIAL

SampleProblem 20.1

Identifying Oxidized and Reduced Reactants

Silver nitrate reacts with copper to form copper nitrate and silver metal. From the equation below, determine what is oxidized and what is reduced. Identify the oxidizing agent and the reducing agent.

$$2AgNO_3(aq) + Cu(s) \longrightarrow Cu(NO_3)_2(aq) + 2Ag(s)$$

1 Analyze Identify the relevant concepts. Identify the ions in the reaction. Then trace how the electrons were transferred.

Hint: The positive ion is written first in ionic compounds. The negative ion is written second.

2 Solve Apply concepts to this situation.

Rewrite the equation in ionic form.	$2Ag^+ + 2NO_3^- + Cu \rightarrow Cu^{2+} + 2NO_3^- + 2Ag$
Identify which substance loses electrons.	In this reaction, the copper atom (Cu) loses two electrons. It becomes a Cu^{2+} ion.
Identify which substance gains electrons.	Two silver ions (Ag^+) gain the electrons lost by copper. They become neutral silver atoms (Ag).
Identify which substance is oxidized and which is reduced.	Oxidation: $Cu \rightarrow Cu^{2+} + 2e^-$ (loss of electrons) Reduction: $2Ag^+ + 2e^- \rightarrow 2Ag$ (gain of electrons)
Identify the oxidizing agent and the reducing agent.	Cu is the reducing agent. Ag^+ is the oxidizing agent.

Remember: The substance that is oxidized is the reducing agent. The substance that is reduced is the oxidizing agent.

Practice Problems

1. From the equation below, determine what is oxidized and what is reduced. Identify the oxidizing agent and reducing agent.

$$Cu(NO_3)_2(aq) + Mg(s) \longrightarrow Mg(NO_3)_2(aq) + Cu(s)$$

1 Analyze Identify the relevant concepts.

2 Solve Apply the concepts to the problem.

2. Determine what is oxidized and what is reduced in each reaction. Identify the oxidizing agent and reducing agent.

a. $2Na(s) + S(s) \longrightarrow Na_2S(s)$ **b.** $4Al(s) + 3O_2(g) \longrightarrow 2Al_2O_3(s)$

3. **Challenge** Identify these processes as either oxidation or reduction.

a. $Li \longrightarrow Li^+ + e^-$ **c.** $Zn^{2+} + 2e^- \longrightarrow Zn$

b. $2I^- \longrightarrow I_2 + 2e^-$ **d.** $Br_2 + 2e^- \longrightarrow 2Br^-$

Redox With Covalent Compounds When a metal and a nonmetal react and form ions, it is easy to identify complete transfers of electrons. However, some reactions involve covalent compounds. In these reactions, electrons do not transfer completely. Recall that electrons are shared by atoms of a covalent compound. Redox reactions that involve covalent compounds can release a lot of energy. For example, the figure on the right and the equation below show hydrogen reacting with oxygen to form water.

$$2H_2(g) + O_2(g) \longrightarrow 2H_2O(l)$$

▶ **Partial Loss of Electrons** What happens to the bonding electrons when a water molecule forms? In each hydrogen molecule, the two hydrogen atoms share electrons equally. In water, however, the electrons are pulled toward oxygen. This is because oxygen is much more electronegative than hydrogen. The bonding electrons shift away from hydrogen, but are not completely transferred. Hydrogen undergoes a partial loss of electrons and is oxidized.

▶ **Partial Gain of Electrons** In an oxygen molecule, the bonding electrons are shared equally between oxygen atoms. When oxygen bonds to hydrogen to form a water molecule, there is a shift of electrons toward oxygen. Oxygen undergoes a partial gain of electrons. Therefore, it is reduced. This is shown below.

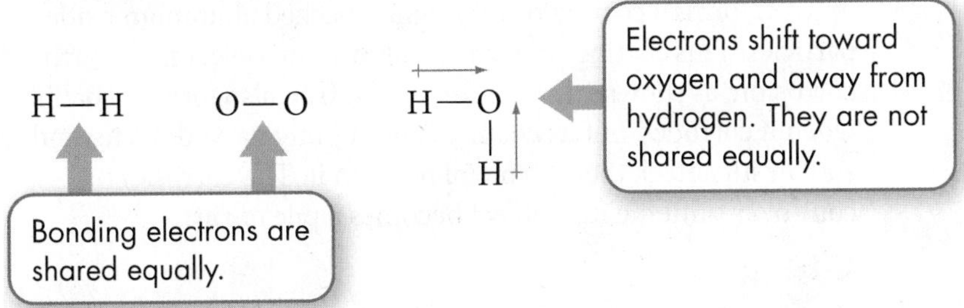
H—H
O—O
H—O
H
Electrons shift toward oxygen and away from hydrogen. They are not shared equally.
Bonding electrons are shared equally.

Welding This welder is using a torch to cut and weld steel. The torch is fueled with a mixture of H_2 and O_2 called *oxyhydrogen*. When hydrogen burns in oxygen, the redox reaction generates temperatures of about 2600°C.

The table below summarizes oxidation and reduction. The last entry in the table refers to oxidation numbers, which are introduced in Lesson 20.2.

Defining Oxidation and Reduction

Oxidation	**Reduction**
Complete loss of electrons in ionic reactions	Complete gain of electrons in ionic reactions
Shift of electrons away from an atom in a covalent bond	Shift of electrons toward an atom in a covalent bond
Gain of oxygen	Loss of oxygen
Loss of hydrogen by a covalent compound	Gain of hydrogen by a covalent compound
Increase in oxidation number	Decrease in oxidation number

Key Question What happens to a substance that undergoes oxidation? What happens to a substance that undergoes reduction? **A substance that undergoes oxidation loses electrons. A substance that undergoes reduction gains electrons.**

BUILD Connections

Why is that statue green? Oxidation of copper occurs when copper reacts with water vapor, carbon dioxide, and other substances in the air. The oxidation forms a patina on the copper's surface. This patina is a pale-green coating of basic copper(II) carbonate. Although many people like the patina color, others prefer to remove the patina to reveal the copper color again.

KINETIC ART See corrosion animated online.

Corrosion

Each year, billions of dollars are spent to prevent and to repair damage caused by the corrosion of metals. Iron, a metal found in steel, corrodes or rusts. Iron atoms are oxidized by oxygen to ions of iron. Water in the environment speeds up the rate of corrosion. Oxygen, the oxidizing agent, is reduced to oxide ions (in compounds such as Fe_2O_3) or to hydroxide ions. The following equations describe the corrosion of iron to iron hydroxides in moist conditions.

$$2Fe(s) + O_2(g) + 2H_2O(l) \longrightarrow 2Fe(OH)_2(s)$$
$$4Fe(OH)_2(s) + O_2(g) + 2H_2O(l) \longrightarrow 4Fe(OH)_3(s)$$

Corrosion happens faster when salts and acids are present. This is because salts and acids produce conductive solutions. These solutions make electron transfer easier. The corrosion of some metals can be desirable, as in the patina of copper.

Resistance to Corrosion Not all metals corrode easily. Gold and platinum are called *noble metals.* They are very resistant to losing their electrons by corrosion. Other metals lose electrons easily but form an oxide coating on their surfaces. The coating helps protect the metal from damage. For example, aluminum oxidizes quickly in air. It forms a coating of very tightly packed aluminum oxide particles. This coating protects the aluminum object from further corrosion, as shown in the figure below. Iron also forms a coating when it corrodes, but its coating is not tightly packed. Water and air can still attack the iron metal beneath it. The corrosion continues until the iron object becomes a pile of rust.

Comparing Oxides Oxidation causes more corrosion to some metals than to others.

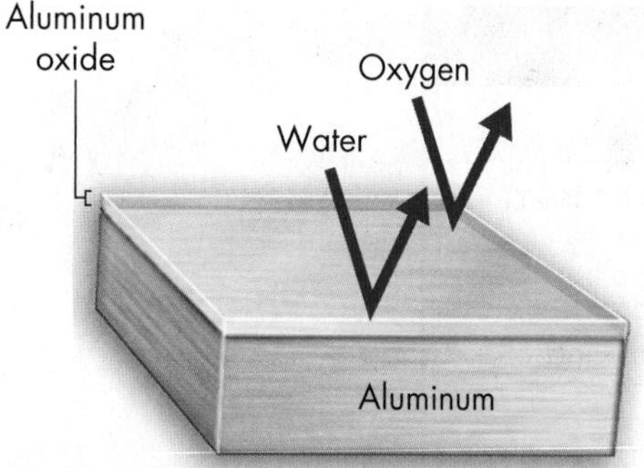

Aluminim reacts with water and oxygen to form aluminum oxide. Aluminum resists corrosion because the aluminum oxide forms a protective coating on the surface.

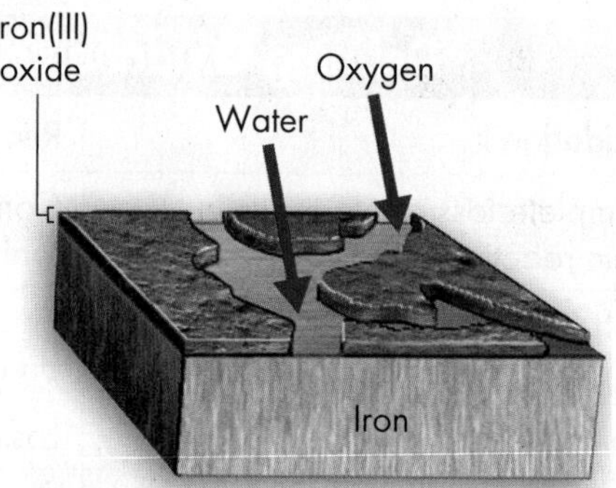

Iron reacts with water and oxygen to form iron(III) oxide, or rust. Water and oxygen can get under the layer of rust, which allows more of the iron metal to rust.

Corrosion Control

Coatings Chromium metal serves as a protective coating. It also gives an attractive, shiny finish. Like aluminum, chromium forms an oxide coating on its surface that resists corrosion.

Sacrificial Metals Zinc blocks are attached to the steel hull of this ship. The zinc blocks corrode instead of the iron in the steel. This prevents the ship from corroding.

Controlling Corrosion The corrosion of objects such as shovels or knives is a common problem. Luckily, it is not a serious one. In contrast, the corrosion of a bridge's steel support pillar or an oil tanker's steel hull is much more serious. Both can be dangerous and are expensive to fix. Two methods are used to prevent corrosion in these cases.

▶ **Coating the Surface** Often, metal is coated with oil, paint, plastic, or another metal. The coating protects the metal by keeping air and water away from the metal. This protection prevents corrosion. If the coating is scratched or worn away, however, the exposed metal will begin to corrode. The photograph above shows how chromium can be used as a protective coating.

▶ **Using Sacrificial Metals** In another method of corrosion control, one metal is "sacrificed." It is allowed to corrode in order to save another metal. Sacrificial magnesium or zinc blocks, shown in the photograph above on the right, are sometimes attached to ships to prevent damage from corrosion. The zinc or magnesium is placed in direct contact with the iron of the ship. When oxygen and water attack the iron, the iron atoms lose electrons. Iron begins to be oxidized. Zinc and magnesium, however, are better reducing agents than iron. Zinc and magnesium immediately transfer electrons to the iron atoms. This prevents the oxidation of iron.

Underground pipelines, storage tanks, and bridge supports may also be protected by sacrificial metals. It is easier and cheaper to replace a block of magnesium or zinc than to replace a bridge or a pipeline.

Key Question How does the presence of salts and acids speed up the corrosion of metals? **The presence of salts and acids accelerates corrosion by producing conductive solutions that make electron transfer easier.**

Quick Lab

Purpose To test the effect of oxidizing agents on stains and dyes

Materials

- spot plate
- dropper
- water

Oxidizing Agents

- liquid chlorine bleach (5% (m/v) sodium hypochlorite)
- powder bleach
- oxalic acid solution (1% (m/v))
- sodium thiosulfate solution (hypo) ($0.2M$ $Na_2S_2O_3$)
- hydrogen peroxide (3% (v/v) H_2O_2)

Samples

- iodine solution (1% I_2 in 2% (m/v) KI)
- potassium permanganate solution ($0.05M$ $KMnO_4$)
- grape juice
- rusty water
- piece of colored fabric
- colored flower petals
- grass stain on piece of white fabric

Bleach It! Oxidize the Color Away

Procedure

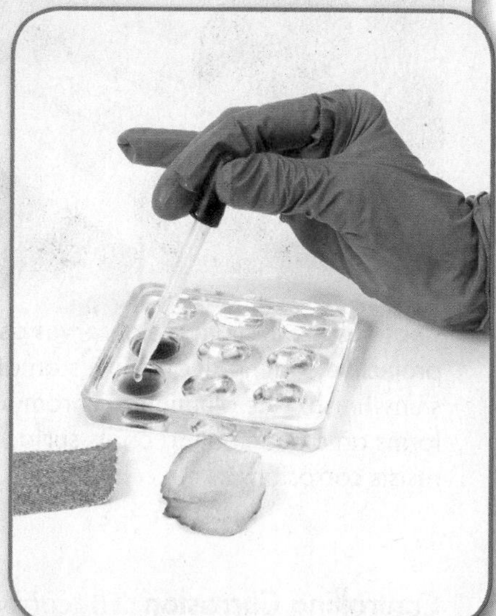

1. Place samples on a spot plate. Use 4 drops of each liquid or a small piece of each solid.
2. Describe the color and appearance of each sample in Step 1.
3. Add a few drops of the first oxidizing agent to each sample.
4. Describe any immediate change in appearance and any further change after 15 minutes.
5. Repeat Steps 1–4 with each oxidizing agent, using a new sample for each oxidizing agent.

Analyze and Conclude

1. **Organize Data** Make a grid and record your observations.
2. **Compare and Contrast** Compare the oxidizing power of the oxidizing agents.
3. **Explain** How do you know that chemical changes have occurred?

20.1 LessonCheck

Key Concept Check

4. **Define** Define oxidation and reduction in terms of the gain or loss of oxygen.
5. **Define** Define oxidation and reduction in terms of the gain or loss of electrons.
6. **Explain** How does the presence of salts and acids speed the corrosion of metals?

Vocabulary Check

Choose a highlighted word from the lesson to complete each sentence correctly.

7. A substance that loses electrons is the ________.
8. A substance that undergoes ________ gains oxygen or loses electrons.

Think Critically

9. **Explain** How do you identify the oxidizing agent and the reducing agent in a redox reaction?
10. **Apply Concepts** Use electron transfer or electron shift to identify what is oxidized and what is reduced in each reaction. Identify the reducing agent and the oxidizing agent. For item *c*, note that oxygen is more electronegative than nitrogen.
    a. $2Na(s) + Br_2(l) \longrightarrow 2NaBr(s)$
    b. $H_2(g) + Cl_2(g) \longrightarrow 2HCl(g)$
    c. $N_2(g) + 2O_2(g) \longrightarrow 2NO_2(g)$

CHEMISTRY & YOU

11. If your car is exposed to salt on the roads in the winter, why is it important to wash the salt off your car? (Hint: See page 664.)

CHEMISTRY & YOU: TECHNOLOGY

Fireworks

It's New Year's Eve! At the stroke of midnight, a dazzling array of fireworks begins bursting overhead. The sights and sounds of each explosion are caused by several oxidation-reduction reactions taking place within the firework as it goes up into the sky.

There are four basic components in any firework:

- Oxidizing agents such as chlorates and nitrates produce the oxygen needed to let the firework burn.
- Reducing agents, usually sulfur and carbon, combine with the oxygen to produce the heat energy for the explosion.
- Metal ions, such as lithium, calcium, and sodium, create the bright colors you see.
- Binders, such as starch, hold the materials together.

These four materials are formed into small lumps known as *stars*. The stars are placed in a cardboard or paper shell along with gunpowder and two charges. When the first charge is lit, the gunpowder propels the firework up into the air. Then, the second charge causes additional gunpowder to propel the stars out into the sky and light the oxidizers. The oxidizers react with the reducing agents, and the stars explode in brilliant flashes of color.

RED, WHITE, AND BLUE Different metal salts and compounds are used to create the different colors in fireworks. Lithium and strontium are used for red. Magnesium and aluminum are used for white. Copper is used for blue.

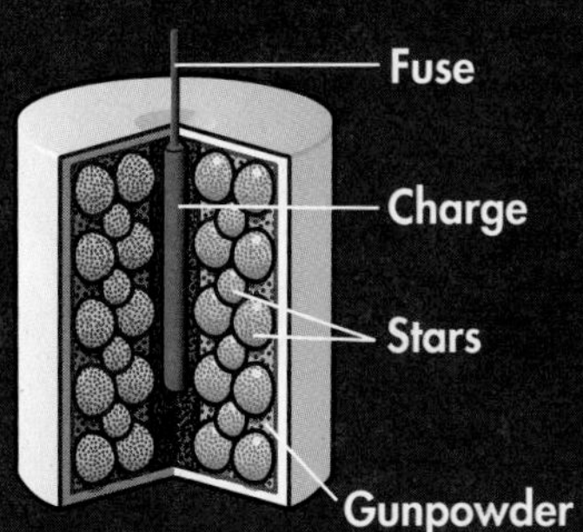

FIREWORK ANATOMY Aerial fireworks contain stars and gunpowder within a cardboard shell. The charge and fuse are used to ignite the firework. The arrangement of stars determines the shape of the burst. The size and shape of the stars determine the size and speed of the burst.

Take It Further

Identify Potassium nitrate (KNO_3) was originally used in fireworks and gunpowder.
The reaction for the production of KNO_3 is

$$4KCl + 4HNO_3 + O_2 \longrightarrow 4KNO_3 + 2Cl_2 + 2H_2O$$

Is this a redox reaction? If so, which substance is oxidized and which is reduced?

20.2 Oxidation Numbers

CHEMISTRY & YOU

Q: Why does a sparkler have such a bright light? If you have ever seen a sparkler, then you know that sparklers give off very bright light. They are like handheld fireworks. Sparklers contain powdered metals. As the sparklers burn, a chemical reaction changes the metals. In this lesson, you will learn about how oxidation and reduction in reactions like these are defined by a change in oxidation number.

Key Questions

What is the general rule for assigning oxidation numbers?

How can oxidation and reduction be defined by a change in oxidation number?

VOCABULARY FLASHCARDS
BUILD
Vocabulary

oxidation number a positive or negative number assigned to an atom to indicate its degree of oxidation or reduction

USING PRIOR KNOWLEDGE

Remember that *oxidation* means a complete or partial loss of electrons or a gain of oxygen. An atom or ion that is oxidized will show an increase in *oxidation number.*

Assigning Oxidation Numbers

An **oxidation number** is a positive or negative number assigned to an atom to indicate its degree of oxidation or reduction. The set of rules on the next page should help you determine oxidation numbers. As a general rule, however, a bonded atom's oxidation number is the charge that it would have if the electrons in the bond were assigned to the atom of the more electronegative element. In the next lesson, you will use oxidation numbers to balance equations of complex redox reactions.

Ionic Compounds In ionic compounds made up of two elements, such as NaCl and $CaCl_2$, the oxidation numbers of the atoms equal their ionic charges (Rule 1). Sodium chloride (NaCl) is made up of sodium ions (Na^{1+}) and chloride ions (Cl^{1-}). Thus the oxidation number of sodium is +1, and that of chlorine is −1. In $CaCl_2$, the oxidation number of calcium is +2, and that of chlorine is −1. Notice that the plus or minus sign is put before the oxidation number.

Molecular Compounds Molecular compounds, such as water, do not have ionic charges associated with their atoms. However, oxygen is reduced when hydrogen and oxygen form water. This is because oxygen is more electronegative than hydrogen. So, in water, the two shared electrons in the H—O bond are shifted toward oxygen and away from hydrogen. Picture the electrons from the two hydrogen atoms being completely transferred to the oxygen atom. The charges that would result are the oxidation numbers. Oxidation numbers are often written above the chemical symbols in a formula, as shown below.

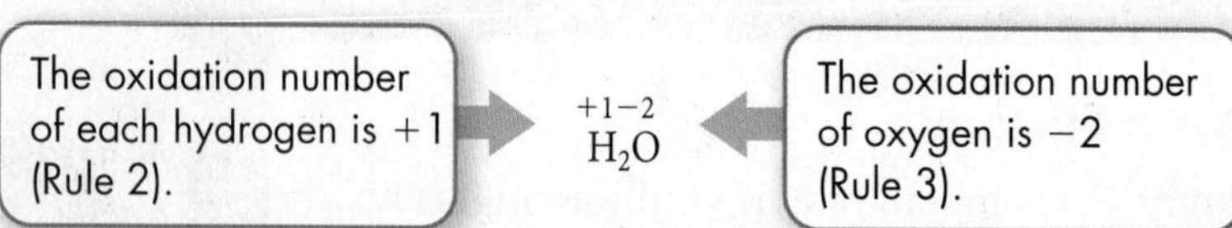

The oxidation number of each hydrogen is +1 (Rule 2).
+1 −2
H_2O
The oxidation number of oxygen is −2 (Rule 3).

Assigning Oxidation Numbers Many elements can have several different oxidation numbers. Use rules 5 and 6 to determine the oxidation number of atoms of these elements and other elements not covered in the first four rules. One example of an element that can have several oxidation numbers is chromium (Cr), shown on the next page.

Rules for Assigning Oxidation Numbers			
Substance	**Rule**	**Examples**	**Exceptions**
1. Monatomic Ions	The oxidation number of a monatomic ion is equal in size and sign to its ionic charge.	The oxidation number of the bromide ion (Br^{1-}) is −1; the oxidation number of the Fe^{3+} ion is +3.	No exceptions.
2. Hydrogen	The oxidation number of hydrogen in a compound is +1.	In CH_4, the oxidation number of each hydrogen is +1.	In metal hydrides, such as NaH, the oxidation number of hydrogen is −1.
3. Oxygen	The oxidation number of oxygen in a compound is −2.	In CO_2, the oxidation number of each oxygen atom is −2.	In peroxides, such as H_2O_2, the oxidation number of oxygen is −1. In compounds with the more electronegative fluorine, it is positive.
4. Elemental Atoms	The oxidation number of an elemental atom is 0.	The oxidation number of potassium atoms in potassium metal (K) is 0; in nitrogen gas (N_2), nitrogen's oxidation number is 0.	No exceptions.
5. Neutral Compounds	The sum of the oxidation numbers of the atoms in a neutral compound must equal 0.	In NaCl, the oxidation number of sodium (+1) plus that of chlorine (−1) equals 0. In CH_4 the oxidation number of carbon (−4) plus that of each hydrogen (+1) equals 0.	No exceptions.
6. Polyatomic Ions	The sum of the oxidation numbers must equal the ionic charge of a polyatomic ion.	The ammonium ion, NH_4^+, has an ionic charge of +1. The oxidation number of of nitrogen (−3) plus that of each hydrogen (+1) equals +1.	No exceptions.

Key Question What is the general rule for assigning oxidation numbers? **A bonded atom's oxidation number is the charge that it would have if the electrons in the bond were assigned to the atom of the more electronegative element.**

Oxidation Numbers of Chromium Some elements, like chromium, can have different oxidation numbers in the uncombined state and in different compounds.

Chromium (Cr)
Oxidation number of Cr = 0

Potassium dichromate ($K_2Cr_2O_7$)
Oxidation number of Cr = +6

Chromium(III) potassium sulfate dodecahydrate ($CrK(SO_4)_2 \cdot 12H_2O$)
Oxidation number of Cr = +3

CHEMISTRY TUTORIAL

Sample Problem 20.2

Assigning Oxidation Numbers to Atoms

What is the oxidation number of each kind of atom in the following ions and compounds?

a. SO_2 **b.** CO_3^{2-} **c.** Na_2SO_4

1 Analyze Identify the relevant concepts. An oxidation number is a positive or negative number assigned to an atom to indicate its degree of oxidation or reduction.

2 Solve Apply concepts to this situation. Use the set of rules you just learned to assign and calculate oxidation numbers.

Rule 3: The oxidation number of each oxygen is −2.

a. $\overset{?-2}{SO_2}$

Find the sum of the oxidation numbers for both oxygen atoms.

$2 \times (-2) = -4$

So, the sum of the oxidation numbers for the oxygen atoms is −4.

Rule 5: The sum of all the oxidation numbers in the compound must be 0. Solve for the oxidation number of sulfur.

$? + (-4) = 0$

$+4 + (-4) = 0$

So, the oxidation number of sulfur is +4.

$\overset{+4-2}{SO_2}$

Rule 3: The oxidation number of each oxygen is −2.

b. $\overset{?-2}{CO_3^{2-}}$

Find the sum of the oxidation numbers for all three oxygen atoms.

$3 \times (-2) = -6$

So, the sum of the oxidation numbers for the oxygen atoms is −6.

Rule 6: The sum of the oxidation numbers of all the carbon and oxygen atoms must equal the ionic charge, −2. Solve for the oxidation number of carbon.

$? + (-6) = -2$

$+4 + (-6) = -2$

So, the oxidation number of carbon is +4.

$\overset{+4-2}{CO_3^{2-}}$

Rule 3: The oxidation number of each oxygen is −2.
Rule 1: The oxidation number of each sodium ion, Na^+, is the same as its charge, +1.

c. $\overset{+1\ ?-2}{Na_2SO_4}$

Rule 5: The sum of the oxidation numbers must be 0. Solve for the oxidation number of sulfur.

$(2 \times (+1)) + (?) + (4 \times (-2)) = 0$

$(2 \times (+1)) + (+6) + (4 \times (-2)) = 0$

So, the oxidation number of sulfur is +6.

$\overset{+1\ +6-2}{Na_2SO_4}$

BUILD Math Skills

Solving Equations When you need to solve for the oxidation number of an atom or ion, it is sometimes helpful to write an equation. An x is often used to represent an unknown quantity. For example, in the problem below, x equals the oxidation of sulfur.

$$\overset{+1}{Na_2}\overset{?}{S}\overset{-2}{O_4}$$

$2(+1) + x + 4(-2) = 0$ Set up the equation so the sum of

$2 + x - 8 = 0$ the oxidation numbers equals 0.

$x - 6 = 0$

$x = 6$ The oxidation number of sulfur is +6.

Go to your Chemistry Skills and Math Workbook for more practice.

Practice Problems

12. Determine the oxidation number of each element in the following:

a. S_2O_3
b. Na_2O_2
c. P_2O_5
d. NO_3^-

Hint: Remember the rule for oxygen. Na_2O_2 is a peroxide.

❶ Analyze Identify the relevant concepts.

❷ Solve Apply concepts to this situation.

13. Determine the oxidation number of chlorine in each of the following substances:

a. $KClO_3$
b. Cl_2
c. $Ca(ClO_4)_2$
d. Cl_2O

14. Challenge What is the oxidation number for chromium in each of these compounds?

a. K_2CrO_4 **b.** Cr_2O_3

BUILD Connections

Do you know how gemstones get their color? Gemstones are cut and polished minerals that are used in jewelry. The mineral's color changes if it contains impurities such as iron, chromium, or copper. Oxidation number can also change the gem's color. For example, the presence of iron(III) ion causes the mineral beryl to be yellow. If the beryl is heated, the iron is reduced to iron(II) ion and the color changes to blue.

Oxidation-Number Changes in Chemical Reactions

In the first lesson, you learned how to find what is oxidized and what is reduced in a reaction. You look at the transfer of electrons. Oxidation is a loss of electrons, and reduction is a gain of electrons. Here, you will see how to identify what is oxidized and reduced by using a change in oxidation number.

The figure below shows what happens when copper wire is placed in a solution of silver nitrate. In this reaction, each silver ion (Ag^{1+}) gains an electron. It is reduced to silver metal (Ag^0). The oxidation number of silver decreases from $+1$ to 0. At the same time, each atom of copper metal (Cu^0) loses two electrons. It is oxidized to a copper(II) ion (Cu^{2+}). Copper's oxidation number increases from 0 to $+2$. Here is the equation for this reaction with oxidation numbers added:

$$\overset{+1+5-2}{2AgNO_3(aq)} + \overset{0}{Cu(s)} \longrightarrow \overset{+2\ +5-2}{Cu(NO_3)_2(aq)} + \overset{0}{2Ag(s)}$$

You can define oxidation and reduction in terms of a change in oxidation number. An increase in the oxidation number of an atom or ion indicates oxidation. A decrease in the oxidation number of an atom or ion indicates reduction.

Key Question How can oxidation and reduction be defined by a change in oxidation number? **An increase in the oxidation number of an atom or ion indicates oxidation. A decrease in the oxidation number of an atom or ion indicates reduction.**

Oxidation of Copper

A copper wire is placed in a silver nitrate solution.

Crystals of silver coat the wire. The solution slowly turns blue as copper(II) nitrate forms.

Sample Problem 20.3

Identifying Oxidized and Reduced Atoms

Use changes in oxidation number to identify which atoms are oxidized and which are reduced in the following reactions. Also identify the oxidizing agent and the reducing agent.

a. $Cl_2(g) + 2HBr(aq) \longrightarrow 2HCl(aq) + Br_2(l)$

b. $C(s) + O_2(g) \longrightarrow CO_2(g)$

1 Analyze **Identify the relevant concepts.** If an oxidation number increases, it indicates oxidation. If an oxidation number decreases, it indicates reduction. The substance that is oxidized in a redox reaction is the reducing agent. The substance that is reduced is the oxidizing agent.

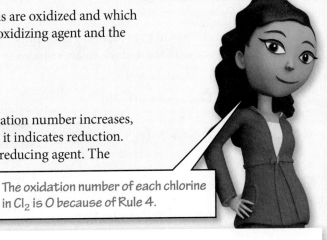

2 Solve **Apply concepts to this situation.**

The oxidation number of each chlorine in Cl_2 is 0 because of Rule 4.

Use the rules on page 669 to assign oxidation numbers to each atom in the equation.

a. $\overset{0}{Cl_2}(g) + 2\overset{+1\,-1}{HBr}(aq) \longrightarrow 2\overset{+1\,-1}{HCl}(aq) + \overset{0}{Br_2}(l)$

Identify the changes in oxidation numbers.

Chlorine: oxidation number decreases. (0 to −1)
Bromine: oxidation number increases. (−1 to 0)
Hydrogen: oxidation number stays the same. (0)

Identify which atoms are oxidized and which are reduced.

The element chlorine is reduced because its oxidation number decreases.
The bromide ion in HBr(*aq*) is oxidized because its oxidation number increases.

Identify the oxidizing agent and the reducing agent.

Cl_2 is the oxidizing agent. Since Cl_2 gained electrons, Cl_2 is the agent that causes bromide to be oxidized.
Br^- is the reducing agent. Since Br^- lost electrons, Br^- is the agent that causes chlorine to be reduced.

Use the rules on page 669 to assign oxidation numbers to each atom in the equation.

b. $\overset{0}{C}(s) + \overset{0}{O_2}(g) \longrightarrow \overset{+4\,-2}{CO_2}(g)$

Identify the changes in oxidation numbers.

Carbon: oxidation number increases. (0 to +4)
Oxygen: oxidation number decreases. (0 to −2)

Identify which atoms are oxidized and which are reduced.

The element carbon is oxidized because its oxidation number increases.
The element oxygen is reduced because its oxidation number decreases.

Identify the oxidizing and reducing agents.

C is the reducing agent. Since C lost electrons, it is the reducing agent that causes oxygen to be reduced.
O_2 is the oxidizing agent. Since O_2 gained electrons, it is the oxidizing agent that causes C to be oxidized.

Practice Problems

15. Use the changes in oxidation numbers to identify which atoms are oxidized and which are reduced in each reaction.

a. $2H_2(g) + O_2(g) \longrightarrow 2H_2O(l)$
b. $2KNO_3(s) \longrightarrow 2KNO_2(s) + O_2(g)$
c. $NH_4NO_2(s) \longrightarrow N_2(g) + 2H_2O(g)$

TO GET YOU STARTED...

Here are the oxidation numbers for the first reaction:

$$\overset{0}{2H_2}(g) + \overset{0}{O_2}(g) \longrightarrow \overset{+1\,-2}{2H_2O}(l)$$

❶ Analyze **Identify the relevant concepts.**

❷ Solve **Apply concepts to this situation.**

16. Identify the oxidizing agent and the reducing agent in each equation in Problem 15.

17. Challenge Identify which atoms are oxidized and which are reduced in each reaction. Also identify the oxidizing agent and the reducing agent in each reaction.

a. $Zn(s) + 2MnO_2(s) + 2NH_4Cl(aq) \longrightarrow$
$ZnCl_2(aq) + Mn_2O_3(s) + 2NH_3(g) + H_2O(l)$
b. $PbO_2(aq) + 4HI(aq) \longrightarrow I_2(aq) + PbI_2(s) + 2H_2O(l)$

20.2 LessonCheck

Key Concept Check

18. Explain What is the general rule for assigning oxidation numbers?

19. Explain How is a change in oxidation number related to the process of oxidation and reduction?

Think Critically

20. Identify Use the changes in oxidation numbers to identify which atoms are oxidized and which are reduced in each reaction.

a. $2Na(s) + Cl_2(g) \longrightarrow 2NaCl(s)$
b. $3H_2S(g) + 2HNO_3(aq) \longrightarrow 3S(s) + 2NO(g) + 4H_2O(l)$

21. Identify Identify the oxidizing agent and the reducing agent in each reaction in Problem 20.

22. Explain How is charge used to assign oxidation numbers to the elements in a polyatomic ion?

CHEMISTRY & YOU

23. What happens to the oxidation numbers of metals as they burn in a sparkler? (Hint: See page 672.)

20.3 Describing Redox Equations

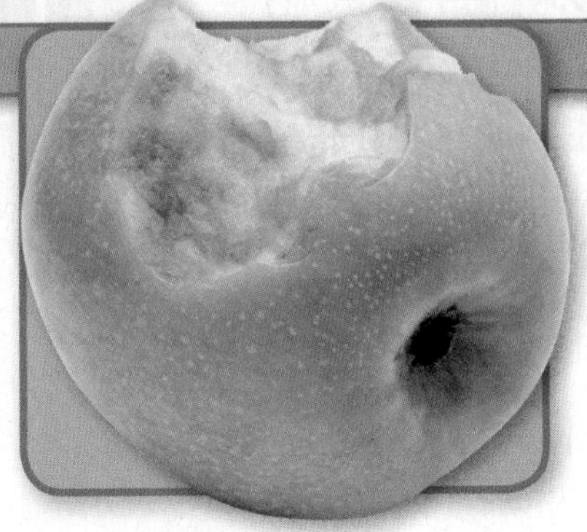

CHEMISTRY & YOU

Q: Why does cut fruit turn brown? You have probably noticed how the inside of an apple turns brown after you bite into it. The apple is still safe to eat; it just doesn't look as tasty. The browning is due to a chemical reaction. In this lesson, you will learn more about identifying types of chemical reactions. You will also learn how to write and balance chemical equations for redox reactions.

Key Questions

What are the two classes of chemical reactions?

What are two different methods for balancing a redox equation?

Identifying Redox Reactions

Recall from Chapter 11 that chemical reactions can be classified as combination, decomposition, single-replacement, double-replacement, or combustion reactions. There is also another way to classify reactions.

Classes of Chemical Reactions In general, all chemical reactions can be assigned to one of two classes. One class of chemical reactions is oxidation-reduction (redox) reactions. Electrons are transferred from one reacting species to another in redox reactions. Many single-replacement reactions, combination reactions, decomposition reactions, and combustion reactions are redox reactions. Two examples of redox reactions are shown in the pictures below.

The other class of reactions includes all other reactions in which no electron transfer takes place. Examples of reactions that are not redox reactions include double-replacement reactions and acid-base reactions.

Single-Replacement Redox Reactions

Potassium metal reacts violently with water to produce hydrogen gas (shown burning) and potassium hydroxide.

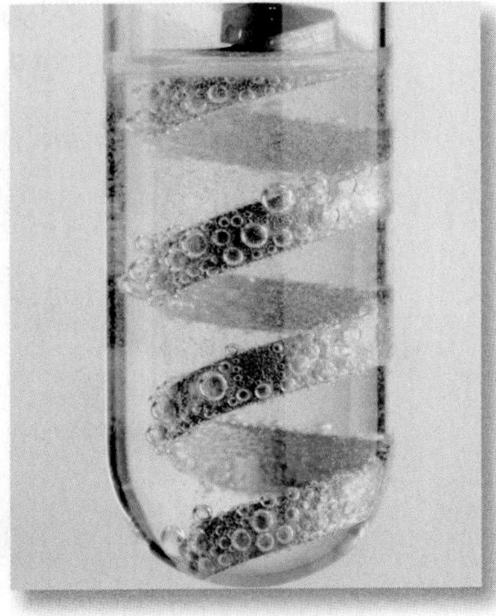

Zinc metal reacts with hydrochloric acid to produce hydrogen gas and zinc chloride.

Redox in Lightning
When lightning bolts heat the air, a redox reaction takes place.

Using Oxidation Numbers to Identify Redox Reactions

During a lightning storm, as shown above, oxygen molecules and nitrogen molecules in the air react to form nitrogen monoxide. The equation for the reaction is shown below.

$$\overset{0}{N_2}(g) + \overset{0}{O_2}(g) \longrightarrow 2\overset{+2}{N}\overset{-2}{O}(g)$$

How can you tell if this is a redox reaction? It is a redox reaction if the oxidation number of an element in a reactant changes. In this example, the oxidation number of nitrogen increases from 0 to +2. Nitrogen is oxidized. Also, the oxidation number of oxygen decreases from 0 to −2. Oxygen is reduced. Since oxidation and reduction take place, the reaction is a redox reaction. When an element in a reacting species undergoes oxidation or reduction, the reaction as a whole must be a redox reaction.

Many reactions with color changes are redox reactions. One example is the apple on the first page of this lesson. Another example is shown below. Written in ionic form, the unbalanced equation for this reaction is

$$\overset{+7}{Mn}\overset{-2}{O_4}{}^-(aq) + \overset{-1}{Br}{}^-(aq) \longrightarrow \overset{+2}{Mn}{}^{2+}(aq) + \overset{0}{Br_2}(aq)$$

Permanganate ion (purple)	Bromide ion (colorless)	Manganese(II) ion (colorless)	Bromine (brown)

Key Question What are the two classes of chemical reactions? **One class is oxidation-reduction (redox) reactions, in which electrons are transferred from one reacting species to another. The other class includes all other reactions, in which no electron transfer occurs.**

Color Clues Color change is a clue that a redox reaction is happening.

Permanganate ions are purple in color.

When colorless bromide ions are added, a color change takes place.

The purple color is replaced with the orange-brown color of bromine.

SampleProblem 20.4

Identifying Redox Reactions

Use oxidation numbers to decide whether each reaction is a redox reaction or not.

a. $Cl_2(g) + 2NaBr(aq) \longrightarrow 2NaCl(aq) + Br_2(aq)$

b. $2NaOH(aq) + H_2SO_4(aq) \longrightarrow Na_2SO_4(aq) + 2H_2O(l)$

See Lesson 20.2 to review the rules for assigning oxidation numbers.

1 Analyze **Identify the relevant concepts.** If changes in oxidation number happen, the reaction is a redox reaction. The element whose oxidation number increases is oxidized. The element whose oxidation number decreases is reduced.

2 Solve **Apply concepts to this situation.**

Assign oxidation numbers.

$$\text{a. } \overset{0}{Cl_2}(g) + 2\overset{+1}{Na}\overset{-1}{Br}(aq) \longrightarrow 2\overset{+1}{Na}\overset{-1}{Cl}(aq) + \overset{0}{Br_2}(aq)$$

Identify if there are changes in oxidation numbers.

Chlorine: oxidation number decreases. (0 to −1)
Bromine: oxidation number increases. (−1 to 0)

Determine whether the reaction is a redox reaction or not.

The element chlorines is reduced. The bromide ion is oxidized. This is a redox reaction.

Assign oxidation numbers.

$$\text{b. } 2\overset{+1}{Na}\overset{-2}{O}\overset{+1}{H}(aq) + \overset{+1}{H_2}\overset{+6}{S}\overset{-2}{O_4}(aq) \longrightarrow \overset{+1}{Na_2}\overset{+6}{S}\overset{-2}{O_4}(aq) + 2\overset{+1}{H_2}\overset{-2}{O}(l)$$

Identify if there are changes in oxidation numbers.

None of the elements are reduced or oxidized.

Determine whether the reaction is a redox reaction or not.

This is not a redox reaction.

This is an acid-base (neutralization) reaction.

Practice Problems

24. Identify whether these reactions are redox reactions or not. If a reaction is a redox reaction, name the element oxidized and the element reduced.

a. $Mg(s) + Br_2(l) \longrightarrow MgBr_2(s)$

b. $H_2CO_3(aq) \longrightarrow H_2O(l) + CO_2(g)$

1 Analyze **Identify the relevant concepts.**

2 Solve **Apply the concepts to this situation.**

Hint: An increase in the oxidation number of an atom or ion indicates oxidation. A decrease in the oxidation number of an atom or ion indicates reduction.

25. Challenge Identify if this reaction is a redox reaction. If it is a redox reaction, name the element oxidized and the element reduced.

$CaCO_3(s) + 2HCl(aq) \longrightarrow CaCl_2(aq) + H_2O(l) + CO_2(g)$

oxidation-number-change method a method of balancing a redox equation by comparing the changes in oxidation numbers

ACADEMIC WORDS
A *method* is a way of doing something. The *oxidation-number-change method* has five steps to follow to balance a redox equation.

Balancing Redox Equations

Many oxidation-reduction reactions are too complex to balance by trial and error. Fortunately, there are two methods you can use to help you. Both use the following fact: The number of electrons gained in reduction equals the number of electrons lost in oxidation.

Using Oxidation-Number Changes In the **oxidation-number-change method,** you balance a redox equation by comparing the changes in oxidation numbers. To use this method, start with the unbalanced skeleton equation for the redox reaction and use the five steps below. For example, the reaction below is used to obtain metallic iron from iron ore.

$$Fe_2O_3(s) + CO(g) \longrightarrow Fe(s) + CO_2(g) \text{ (unbalanced)}$$

Step 1 Assign oxidation numbers to all the atoms in the equation. Write the numbers above the atoms.

$$\overset{+3\ -2}{Fe_2O_3}(s) + \overset{+2-2}{CO}(g) \longrightarrow \overset{0}{Fe}(s) + \overset{+4-2}{CO_2}(g)$$

Step 2 Identify which atoms are oxidized and which are reduced. Iron's oxidation number changes from +3 to 0, a change of −3. Therefore, iron is reduced. Carbon's oxidation number changes from +2 to +4, a change of +2. So, carbon is oxidized.

Step 3 Use one bracketing line to connect the atoms that undergo oxidation. Use another bracketing line to connect those that undergo reduction. Remember that a change in oxidation number represents the number of electrons transferred. Write the oxidation number change at the midpoint of each line.

+2 (oxidation)

$$\overset{+3\ -2}{Fe_2O_3}(s) + \overset{+2-2}{CO}(g) \longrightarrow \overset{0}{Fe}(s) + \overset{+4-2}{CO_2}(g)$$

−3 (reduction)

Step 4 Use coefficients to make the total increase in oxidation number equal the total decrease in oxidation number. In this case, the oxidation-number increase is multiplied by 3 and the oxidation number decrease is multiplied by 2. This gives an increase of +6 and a decrease of –6.

Place the coefficient 3 in front of both CO and CO_2.

$3 \times (+2) = +6$

$$Fe_2O_3(s) + 3CO(g) \longrightarrow 2Fe(s) + 3CO_2(g)$$

$2 \times (-3) = -6$

Fe_2O_3 does not need a coefficient because the formula already has 2 Fe.

Place the coefficient 2 in front of Fe.

Step 5 Make sure the equation is balanced for both atoms and charge. If necessary, finish balancing the equation by inspection.

$$Fe_2O_3(s) + 3CO(g) \longrightarrow 2Fe(s) + 3CO_2(g)$$

Sample Problem 20.5

Balancing Redox Equations by Oxidation-Number Change

Balance this redox equation by using the oxidation-number-change method.

$$K_2Cr_2O_7(aq) + H_2O(l) + S(s) \longrightarrow KOH(aq) + Cr_2O_3(s) + SO_2(g)$$

1 Analyze **Identify the relevant concepts.** You can balance redox equations by finding changes in oxidation numbers and using the five steps.

2 Solve **Apply concepts to this situation.**

Step 1: Assign oxidation numbers to all the atoms in the equation.

$$\overset{+1\,+6\,-2}{K_2Cr_2O_7}(aq) + \overset{+1\,-2}{H_2O}(l) + \overset{0}{S}(s) \longrightarrow \overset{+1\,-2\,+1}{KOH}(aq) + \overset{+3\,-2}{Cr_2O_3}(s) + \overset{+4\,-2}{SO_2}(g)$$

Step 2: Identify the atoms that are oxidized and the atoms that are reduced.

Chromium: oxidation number decreases. (+6 to +3)

Sulfur: oxidation number increases. (0 to +4)

Step 3: Connect the atoms that change in oxidation number. Indicate the signs and magnitudes of the changes.

$$\overset{+6}{K_2Cr_2O_7}(aq) + H_2O(l) + \overset{0}{S}(s) \longrightarrow KOH(aq) + \overset{+3}{Cr_2O_3}(s) + \overset{+4}{SO_2}(g)$$

Cr: −3; S: +4

Step 4: Balance the increase and decrease in oxidation numbers.

$$\overset{+6}{K_2Cr_2O_7}(aq) + H_2O(l) + \overset{0}{S}(s) \longrightarrow KOH(aq) + \overset{+3}{Cr_2O_3}(s) + \overset{+4}{SO_2}(g)$$

Cr: $(4) \times (-3) = -12$; S: $(3)(+4) = +12$

$$2K_2Cr_2O_7(aq) + H_2O(l) + 3S(s) \longrightarrow KOH(aq) + 2Cr_2O_3(s) + 3SO_2(g)$$

Four chromium atoms must be reduced for every three sulfur atoms that are oxidized. So, put the coefficient 2 in front of $K_2Cr_2O_7$ and Cr_2O_3. Put the coefficient 3 in front of S and SO_2.

Step 5: Check the equation. Is it balanced? Finish by balancing by inspection.

$$2K_2Cr_2O_7(aq) + 2H_2O(l) + 3S(s) \longrightarrow 4KOH(aq) + 2Cr_2O_3(s) + 3SO_2(g)$$

The coefficient 4 in front of KOH balances potassium.
The coefficient 2 in front of H_2O balances hydrogen and oxygen.

BUILD Math Skills

Use a Table A table is a helpful way to organize what you know about a reaction. Use this example about the equation in Practice Problem 28 to help you make your own tables.

Element	Reactant oxidation number	Product oxidation number	Change in oxidation number	Oxidized or reduced?
Bi	+3	+3	no change	neither
S	−2	0	+2	oxidized
H	+1	+1	no change	neither
N	+5	+5, +2	−3	reduced
O	−2	−2	no change	neither

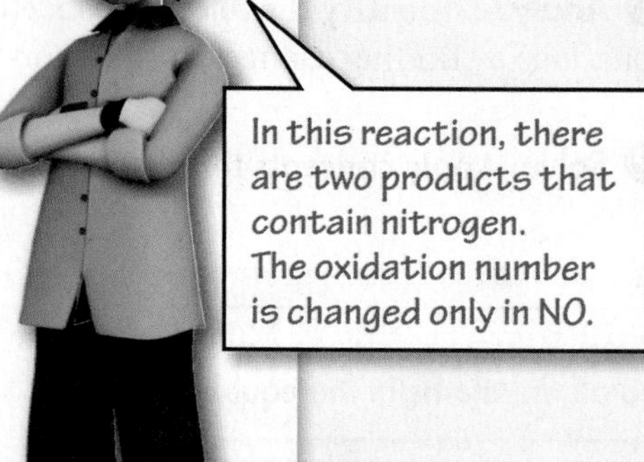

In this reaction, there are two products that contain nitrogen. The oxidation number is changed only in NO.

Go to your Chemistry Skills and Math Workbook for more practice.

Practice Problems

26. Balance each redox equation using the oxidation-number-change method.

a. $KClO_3(s) \longrightarrow KCl(s) + O_2(g)$

b. $HNO_2(aq) + HI(aq) \longrightarrow NO(g) + I_2(s) + H_2O(l)$

❶ Analyze Identify the relevant concepts.

❷ Solve Apply concepts to this situation.

27. Balance each redox equation using the oxidation-number-change method.

a. $HNO_3(aq) + H_2S(g) \longrightarrow S(s) + NO(g) + H_2O(l)$

b. $SbCl_5(aq) + KI(aq) \longrightarrow SbCl_3(aq) + KCl(aq) + I_2(s)$

28. Challenge Balance the redox equation using the oxidation-number-change method.

$Bi_2S_3(s) + HNO_3(aq) \longrightarrow Bi(NO_3)_3(aq) + NO(g) + S(s) + H_2O(l)$

Remember: Don't forget to balance by inspection.

Using Half-Reactions The second method for balancing redox equations uses half-reactions. A **half-reaction** is an equation that shows just the oxidation or just the reduction that takes place in a redox reaction. In the half-reaction method, you write and balance the oxidation half-reaction. Then, you write and balance the reduction half-reaction. For example, unbalanced half-reactions for the oxidation of sulfur by nitric acid are shown below.

$$S(s) + HNO_3(aq) \longrightarrow SO_2(g) + NO(g) + H_2O(l) \text{ (unbalanced)}$$

Oxidation half-reaction → $\overset{0}{S}(s) + \longrightarrow \overset{+4}{S}O_2(g)$

Reduction half-reaction → $\overset{+5}{N}O_3^-(aq) \longrightarrow \overset{+2}{N}O(g)$

For each half-reaction, the atoms must be balanced then the charges must be balanced so that electrons gained equals electrons lost. After each half-reaction is balanced, you combine them into a balanced redox equation. The half-reaction method is very useful in balancing equations for reactions that take place in acidic or basic solutions. The steps of the half-reaction method are different, but the outcome is the same as with the oxidation-number-change method.

Key Question What are two different methods for balancing a redox equation? **The two different methods for balancing a redox equation are the oxidation-number-change method and the half-reaction method.**

half-reaction an equation showing just the oxidation or just the reduction that takes place in a redox reaction

USING PRIOR KNOWLEDGE

Oxidation and reduction always happen together. Each is one half of a redox reaction, or a *half-reaction*.

20.3 LessonCheck

Key Concept Check

29. **Identify** What are the two classes of chemical reactions?

30. **Compare** What are two different methods for balancing a redox equation?

Vocabulary Check *Choose a highlighted word from the lesson to complete each sentence correctly.*

31. When you balance a redox equation by comparing the increases and decreases in oxidation numbers, you are following the ________.

32. The oxidation part of a redox reaction is a(n) ________.

Think Critically

33. **Identify** The equations for the production of sodium, bromine, and iodine are below. Identify the oxidizing agent and the reducing agent in each reaction.

a. $2NaCl(l) \longrightarrow 2Na(l) + Cl_2(g)$

b. $2NaBr(aq) + Cl_2(g) \longrightarrow 2NaCl(aq) + Br_2(l)$

c. $2NaIO_3(aq) + 5NaHSO_3(aq) \longrightarrow I_2(g) + 2Na_2SO_4(aq) + 3NaHSO_4(aq) + H_2O(l)$

34. **Calculate** Balance each redox equation, using the oxidation-number-change method.

a. $K(s) + H_2O(l) \longrightarrow KOH(aq) + H_2(g)$

b. $P_4(s) + O_2(g) \longrightarrow P_4O_{10}(s)$

CHEMISTRY & YOU

35. Some fruits, including apples, turn brown when you cut them. What do you think is happening on the surface of the fruit that causes it to turn brown? (Hint: See page 676.)

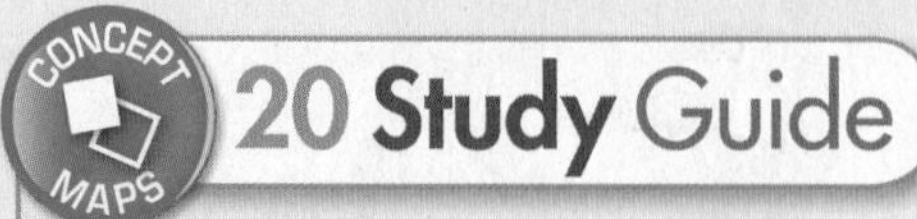

20 Study Guide

BIGIDEA REACTIONS

Oxidation-reduction reactions always occur simultaneously in redox reactions. Losing electrons is oxidation. Gaining electrons is reduction. If oxygen is involved in the reaction, then the substance gaining oxygen is oxidized, while the substance losing oxygen is reduced. The species that is reduced is the oxidizing agent, while the oxidized species is the reducing agent. Redox reactions are identified by changes in oxidation number. Redox equations can be balanced by two methods, the oxidation-number-change method and the half-reaction method.

20.1 The Meaning of Oxidation and Reduction

A substance that undergoes oxidation gains oxygen or loses electrons, while a substance that undergoes reduction loses oxygen or gains electrons.

The presence of salts and acids speeds up corrosion by producing conductive solutions that make electron transfer easier.

- oxidation-reduction reaction (660)
- oxidation (660)
- reduction (660)
- reducing agent (661)
- oxidizing agent (661)

20.2 Oxidation Numbers

As a general rule, a bonded atom's oxidation number is the charge that it would have if the electrons in the bond were assigned to the atom of the more electronegative element.

An increase in the oxidation number of an atom or ion indicates oxidation. A decrease in the oxidation number of an atom or ion indicates reduction.

- oxidation number (668)

20.3 Describing Redox Equations

One class is oxidation-reduction (redox) reactions, in which electrons are transferred. The other class includes all other reactions, in which no electron transfer occurs.

To balance a redox equation using the oxidation-number-change method, the total increase in oxidation number of the element oxidized must be balanced by the total decrease in the oxidation number of the element reduced.

To balance a redox reaction using half-reactions, write separate half-reactions for the oxidation and the reduction. After you balance atoms in each half-reaction, balance electrons gained in the reduction with electrons lost in the oxidation.

- oxidation-number-change method (678)
- half-reaction (681)

Skills Tune-Up: Redox Reactions

Problem	❶ Analyze	❷ Solve
Use the changes in oxidation number to identify which atoms are oxidized and which are reduced in each reaction. $2ZnS(s) + 3O_2(g) \longrightarrow 2ZnO(s) + 2SO_2(g)$	Assign an oxidation number to each atom on both sides of the equation. A decrease in oxidation number indicates reduction. An increase in oxidation number indicates oxidation.	Use the Rules for Assigning Oxidation Numbers to identify the oxidation number of each atom. $\overset{+2\,-2}{2ZnS(s)} + \overset{0}{3O_2(g)} \longrightarrow \overset{+2\,-2}{2ZnO(s)} + \overset{+4-2}{2SO_2(g)}$ The oxidation number of sulfur increases from −2 to +4, so sulfur is oxidized. The oxidation number of oxygen decreases from 0 to −2, so oxygen is reduced. *Remember: The sum of the oxidation numbers of the atoms in a neutral compound must equal zero.*
Use the oxidation-number-change method to write a balanced equation. $Ba(ClO_3)_2(s) \longrightarrow BaCl_2(s) + O_2(g)$	Follow the steps of the oxidation-number-change method to balance the equation.	**Step 1: Assign oxidation numbers.** $\overset{+2\ +5-2}{Ba(ClO_3)_2(s)} \longrightarrow \overset{+2-1}{BaCl_2(s)} + \overset{0}{O_2(g)}$ **Step 2: Identify the atoms that are oxidized and the atoms that are reduced.** Cl is reduced. O is oxidized. **Step 3: Connect the atoms that change in oxidation number.** −6 (Cl: +5 → −1) $\overset{+2\ +5-2}{Ba(ClO_3)_2(s)} \longrightarrow \overset{+2-1}{BaCl_2(s)} + \overset{0}{O_2(g)}$ +2 (O: −2 → 0) **Step 4: Balance the increase and decrease in oxidation numbers.** −6 $\overset{+2\ +5-2}{Ba(ClO_3)_2(s)} \longrightarrow \overset{+2-1}{BaCl_2(s)} + \overset{0}{3O_2(g)}$ (3) × (+2) = +6 **Step 5: Check the equation.** $Ba(ClO_3)_2(s) \longrightarrow BaCl_2(s) + 3O_2(g)$ *Remember: The total number of electrons gained in reduction must equal the total number of electrons lost in oxidation.*

20 Assessment

★ Solutions appear in Appendix D.

Lesson by Lesson

20.1 The Meaning of Oxidation and Reduction

36. What chemical process must always accompany a reduction process?

37. What happens to an oxidizing agent during a redox reaction?

★38. Balance each redox equation and identify whether the first substance in each equation was oxidized or reduced.

a. $Ba(s) + O_2(g) \longrightarrow BaO(s)$
b. $CuO(s) + H_2(g) \longrightarrow Cu(s) + H_2O(l)$
c. $C_2H_4(g) + O_2(g) \longrightarrow CO_2(g) + H_2O(l)$
d. $CaO(s) + Al(s) \longrightarrow Al_2O_3(s) + Ca(s)$

39. Identify each process as either oxidation or reduction.

a. $Al \longrightarrow Al^{3+} + 3e^-$
b. $2Cl^- \longrightarrow Cl_2 + 2e^-$
c. $S^{2-} \longrightarrow S + 2e^-$
d. $Sr \longrightarrow Sr^{2+} + 2e^-$

★40. Which of the following would most likely be oxidizing agents, and which would most likely be reducing agents? (Hint: Think in terms of tendencies to lose or gain electrons.)

a. Cl_2
b. K
c. Ag^+
d. Zn^{2+}

★41. Refer to the electronegativity values in Lesson 6.3 to determine which reactant is oxidized and which reactant is reduced in each reaction.

a. $H_2(g) + S(s) \longrightarrow H_2S(g)$
b. $N_2(g) + 3H_2(g) \longrightarrow 2NH_3(g)$
c. $S(s) + O_2(g) \longrightarrow SO_2(g)$
d. $2H_2(g) + O_2(g) \longrightarrow 2H_2O(l)$

42. Identify the oxidizing agent and the reducing agent for each of the reactions in Problem 41.

20.2 Oxidation Numbers

43. In your own words, what is an oxidation number?

44. Which of these statements is false?

a. The oxidation number of an uncombined element is zero.
b. The sum of the oxidation numbers of the atoms in a polyatomic ion must equal the charge of the ion.
c. Every element has a single oxidation number.
d. The oxidation number of oxygen in a compound or a polyatomic ion is almost always −2.

45. Determine the oxidation number of each metal atom.

a. Ca^{2+}
b. Al_2S_3
c. Na_2CrO_4
d. V_2O_5
e. MnO_4^-

★46. Assign oxidation numbers to the atoms in the following ions:

a. OH^-
b. PO_4^{3-}
c. IO_3^-
d. $H_2PO_4^-$
e. HSO_4^-

20.3 Describing Redox Equations

47. Use the changes in oxidation numbers to identify which atoms are oxidized and which are reduced in each reaction.

a. $4Al(s) + 3MnO_2(s) \longrightarrow 2Al_2O_3(s) + 3Mn(s)$
b. $2HgO(s) \longrightarrow 2Hg(l) + O_2(g)$

★48. Balance each redox equation.

a. $Al(s) + Cl_2(g) \longrightarrow AlCl_3(s)$
b. $Al(s) + Fe_2O_3(s) \longrightarrow Al_2O_3(s) + Fe(s)$
c. $Cl_2(g) + KOH(aq) \longrightarrow KClO_3(aq) + KCl(aq) + H_2O(l)$
d. $KIO_4(aq) + KI(aq) + HCl(aq) \longrightarrow KCl(aq) + I_2(s) + H_2O(l)$

★49. Identify which of these unbalanced equations represent redox reactions.

a. $Li(s) + H_2O(l) \longrightarrow LiOH(aq) + H_2(g)$
b. $K_2Cr_2O_7(aq) + HCl(aq) \longrightarrow KCl(aq) + CrCl_3(aq) + H_2O(l) + Cl_2(g)$
c. $Al(s) + HCl(aq) \longrightarrow AlCl_3(aq) + H_2(g)$
d. $Cl_2(g) + H_2O(l) \longrightarrow HCl(aq) + HClO(aq)$
e. $I_2O_5(s) + CO(g) \longrightarrow I_2(s) + CO_2(g)$
f. $H_2O(l) + SO_3(g) \longrightarrow H_2SO_4(aq)$

Understand Concepts

*50. Determine the oxidation number of phosphorus in each substance.

a. P_4O_8
b. PO_4^{3-}
c. P_2O_5
d. P_4O_6
e. $H_2PO_4^-$
f. PO_3^{3-}

51. Identify the element oxidized, the element reduced, the oxidizing agent, and the reducing agent in each unbalanced redox equation.

a. $MnO_2(s) + HCl(aq) \longrightarrow MnCl_2(aq) + Cl_2(g) + H_2O(l)$
b. $Cu(s) + HNO_3(aq) \longrightarrow Cu(NO_3)_2(aq) + NO_2(g) + H_2O(l)$
c. $P(s) + HNO_3(aq) + H_2O(l) \longrightarrow NO(g) + H_3PO_4(aq)$
d. $Bi(OH)_3(s) + Na_2SnO_2(aq) \longrightarrow Bi(s) + Na_2SnO_3(aq) + H_2O(l)$

52. Balance each redox equation in Problem 51 by using the oxidation-number-change method.

*53. An alcohol-content measuring device is used to test a person's breath for the alcohol ethanol, C_2H_5OH. In this test, ethanol reacts with a solution of orange dichromate ion to form green chromium(III) ion.

$$Cr_2O_7^{2-}(aq) + C_2H_5OH(aq) \longrightarrow Cr^{3+}(aq) + CO_2(g)$$

The greater the color change, the greater the amount of ethanol in the person's breath. Is dichromate ion an oxidizing agent or a reducing agent?

54. Silver tarnishes when it reacts with hydrogen sulfide in the air.

$$Ag(s) + H_2S(g) \longrightarrow Ag_2S(s) + H_2(g)$$

a. Is silver oxidized or reduced in this reaction?
b. Identify the oxidizing agent and the reducing agent.
c. Balance the equation.

Think Critically

*55. **Explain** The highest possible oxidation number that chlorine exhibits in any compound is +7, and its most negative oxidation number is −1. Write the electron configuration of chlorine, and explain why these are the limiting oxidation numbers for chlorine.

56. **Explain** Why must the number of electrons lost equal the number of electrons gained in every redox reaction?

*57. **Make Generalizations** Why must every redox reaction have a reducing agent and an oxidizing agent?

58. **Infer** Humankind began to make and use iron tools more than 3000 years ago, but few iron artifacts from ancient times have survived. Explain.

59. **Explain** Which of the following ions is most likely to be an oxidizing agent? Explain your choice.

a. MnO_4^-
b. MnO_4^{2-}
c. Mn^{+2}

FOUNDATIONS Wrap-Up

Rusting

1. **Draw Conclusions** At the beginning of the chapter, you observed rusting in iron nails. How does the reactivity of zinc compare to the reactivity of iron? How did their reactivities affect the rusting observed in the nails?

Concept Check

Now that you've finished studying Chapter 20, answer these questions.

2. What happens to iron when it is oxidized?
3. How do salts cause metals to corrode more quickly?
4. What is the oxidation number of iron in Fe_2O_3?
5. What are the two main classes of chemical reactions?

Write About Science

60. **Explain** Silver recovered from shipwrecks may have layers of black tarnish. Research and write a report on how the thick layers of tarnish are removed from the silver artifacts.

61. **Connect to the BIGIDEA** Write a paragraph about five different real-world examples of oxidation-reduction reactions.

CHEMYSTERY

Tarnished Treasure

Gold and silver coins were recovered from the same shipwrecked Spanish galleon. They were exposed to the same elements in the sea. However, silver coins corrode faster than gold coins. This is because silver is more easily oxidized than gold. Oxidation reactions cause silver coins to corrode. The surface of the coins becomes black and crumbly. Since gold is not as easily oxidized, the gold coins keep their gold color. They do not show as many signs of oxidation.

62. **Infer** Suppose two types of coins are exposed to the same conditions. One coin is made of magnesium and one is made of iron. Which coin would you expect to tarnish faster?

63. **Connect to the BIGIDEA** Why would it be helpful for shipbuilders to have a knowledge of redox reactions?

Cumulative Review

64. Name a change of state that does not involve a liquid. (See Lesson 13.4 for help.)

*65. A gas cylinder has a volume of 6.8 L and is filled with 13.8 g of N_2. Calculate the pressure of N_2 at 25°C. (See Lesson 14.3 for help.)

66. A particular paint must be stirred before using. Is the stirred paint a colloid, solution or a suspension? Explain. (See Lesson 15.3 for help.)

*67. How would you make 440 mL of 1.5*M* HCl solution from a stock solution of 6.0*M* HCl? (See Lesson 16.2 for help.)

68. One mole of LiF and of $Ca(NO_3)_2$ are each dissolved in 1.0 L of water. Which solution has the higher boiling point? Explain. (See Lesson 16.3 for help.)

*69. The K_{sp} of lead(II) bromide ($PbBr_2$) at 25°C is 2.1×10^{-6}. What is the solubility of $PbBr_2$ (in mol/L) at this temperature? (See Lesson 18.4 for help.)

70. Identify the conjugate acid-base pairs in each equation. (See Lesson 19.1 for help.)
   a. $NH_4^+(aq) + H_2O(l) \longrightarrow NH_3(aq) + H_3O^+(aq)$
   b. $H_2SO_3(aq) + NH_2^-(aq) \longrightarrow HSO_3^-(aq) + NH_3(aq)$
   c. $HNO_3(aq) + I^-(aq) \longrightarrow HI(aq) + NO_3^-(aq)$

*71. Calculate the pH of solutions with the following hydrogen-ion or hydroxide-ion concentrations. Classify each as acidic, basic, or neutral. (See Lesson 19.2 for help.)
   a. $[H^+] = 0.000\,010M$
   b. $[OH^-] = 1.0 \times 10^{-4}M$
   c. $[OH^-] = 1.0 \times 10^{-1}M$
   d. $[H^+] = 3.0 \times 10^{-7}M$

72. How many milliliters of a 4.00*M* KOH solution are needed to neutralize 45.0 mL of 2.50*M* H_2SO_4 solution? (See Lesson 19.4 for help.)

Standardized Test Prep

For help with answering test questions, go to your Chemistry Skills and Math Workbook.

Select the choice that best answers each question or completes each statement.

1. Which of these processes is not an oxidation?
(A) a decrease in oxidation number
(B) a complete loss of electrons
(C) a gain of oxygen
(D) a loss of hydrogen by a covalent molecule

2. In which of these pairs of nitrogen-containing ions and compounds is the oxidation number of nitrogen in the ion higher than in the nitrogen compound?

I. N_2H_4 and NH_4^+
II. NO_3^- and N_2O_4
III. N_2O and NO_2^-

(A) I only
(B) I and II only
(C) I and III only
(D) II and III only
(E) I, II, and III

3. Identify the elements oxidized and reduced in this reaction.

$$2ClO^- + H_2 + 2e^- \longrightarrow 2Cl^- + 2OH^-$$

(A) Cl is oxidized; H is reduced.
(B) H is oxidized; Cl is reduced.
(C) Cl is oxidized; O is reduced.
(D) O is oxidized; Cl is reduced.

4. Which of these half-reactions represents a reduction?

I. $Fe^{2+} \longrightarrow Fe^{3+}$
II. $Cr_2O_7^{2-} \longrightarrow Cr^{3+}$
III. $MnO_4^- \longrightarrow Mn^{2+}$

(A) I and II only
(B) II and III only
(C) I and III only
(D) I, II, and III

5. Which of these general types of reactions is not a redox reaction?
(A) single replacement
(B) double replacement
(C) combustion
(D) combination

6. What is the reducing agent in this reaction?

$$MnO_4^- + SO_2 \longrightarrow Mn^{2+} + SO_4^{2-}$$

(A) SO_2
(B) SO_4^{2-}
(C) Mn^{2+}
(D) MnO_4^-

Tips for Success

Interpreting Data Tables To interpret the content in a table, start by reading the title (if there is one). Then, read the headings. Try to figure out the relationships among the different columns and rows of information. Ask yourself: *What information is related in the table? How are the relationships represented?*

Use the table to answer Questions 7–9.

Metal	Metal ion
K (group 3)	K^+
Ca (group 3)	Ca^{2+}
Na (group 3)	Na^+
Mg (group 4)	Mg^{2+}
Fe (group 4)	Fe^{2+}
Sn (group 4)	Sn^{2+}
Pb (group 4)	Pb^{2+}
Cu (group 5)	Cu^{2+}
Ag (group 5)	Ag^+

(Arrow 1 points upward along the Metal column; arrow 2 points downward along the Metal ion column.)

7. Which arrow indicates increasing ease of oxidation? Of reduction?

8. Which numbered group of metals are the strongest reducing agents? Which numbered group of metals are the most difficult to oxidize?

9. Which is a stronger oxidizing agent, Na or Fe?

Use this diagram to answer Questions 10 and 11. It shows the formation of an ion from an atom.

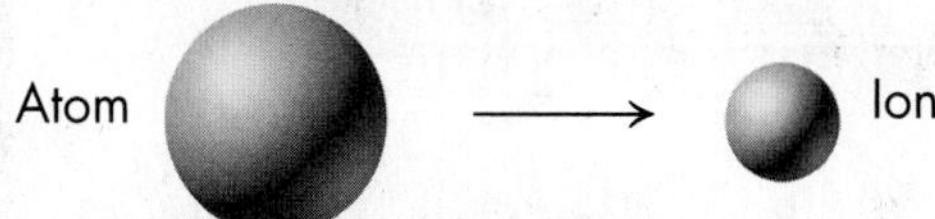

10. Does the diagram represent oxidation or reduction? Does the oxidation number increase or decrease when the ion forms?

11. Draw a diagram showing the formation of a sulfide ion from a sulfur atom. Make the relative sizes of the atom and ion realistic. Does your drawing represent an oxidation or a reduction?

If You Have Trouble With . . .

Question	1	2	3	4	5	6	7	8	9	10	11
See Lesson	20.1	20.2	20.2	20.2	20.3	20.2	20.2	20.2	20.2	20.2	20.1

21 Electrochemistry

FOUNDATIONS for Learning

A Lemon Battery

1. Polish and clean a 1 cm × 3 cm strip of copper and a 1 cm × 3 cm strip of zinc.
2. Push the strips halfway into a lemon about 1 cm apart.
3. Briefly touch both metal strips at the same time with your tongue. What happens?

Form a Hypothesis What do you think caused the sensation on your tongue?

PearsonChem.com

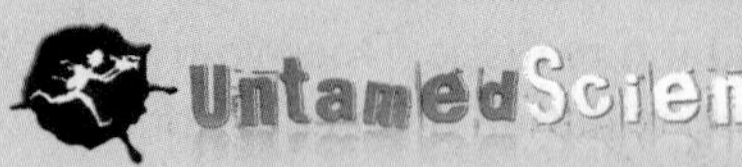

Take a video field trip with the Untamed Science crew as they visit a research lab and learn all about technologies that can make rechargeable batteries easier to use.

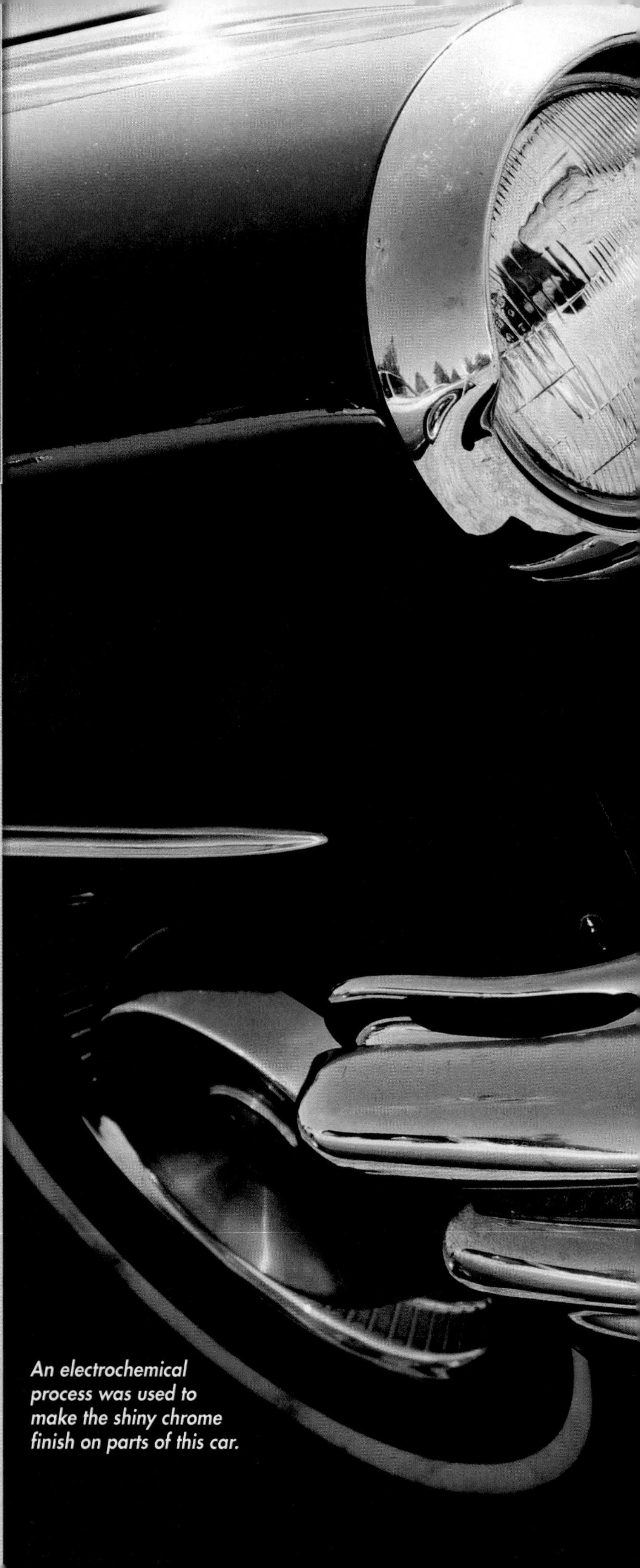

An electrochemical process was used to make the shiny chrome finish on parts of this car.

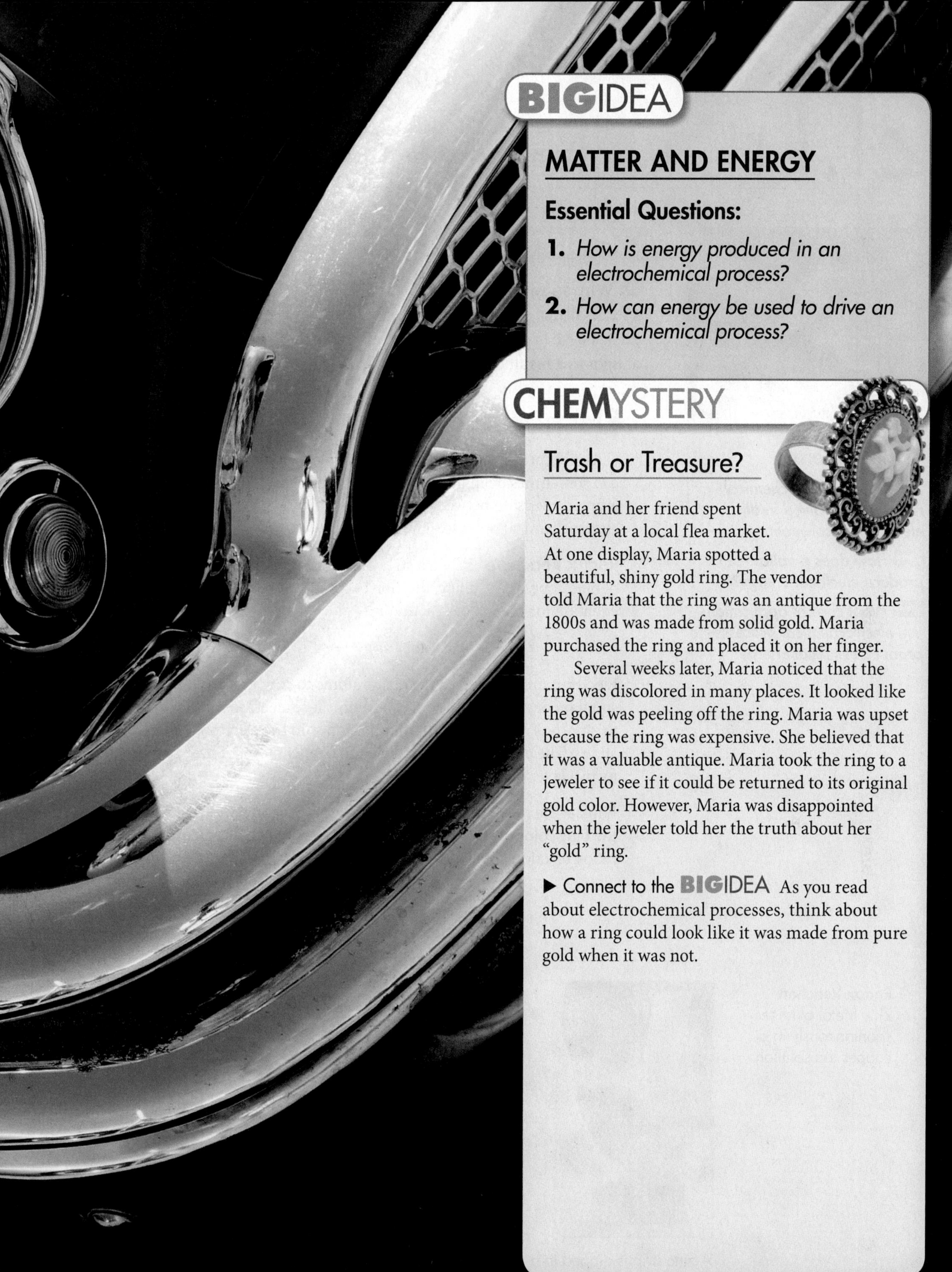

BIGIDEA

MATTER AND ENERGY

Essential Questions:

1. *How is energy produced in an electrochemical process?*
2. *How can energy be used to drive an electrochemical process?*

CHEMYSTERY

Trash or Treasure?

Maria and her friend spent Saturday at a local flea market. At one display, Maria spotted a beautiful, shiny gold ring. The vendor told Maria that the ring was an antique from the 1800s and was made from solid gold. Maria purchased the ring and placed it on her finger.

Several weeks later, Maria noticed that the ring was discolored in many places. It looked like the gold was peeling off the ring. Maria was upset because the ring was expensive. She believed that it was a valuable antique. Maria took the ring to a jeweler to see if it could be returned to its original gold color. However, Maria was disappointed when the jeweler told her the truth about her "gold" ring.

▶ Connect to the BIGIDEA As you read about electrochemical processes, think about how a ring could look like it was made from pure gold when it was not.

21.1 Electrochemical Cells

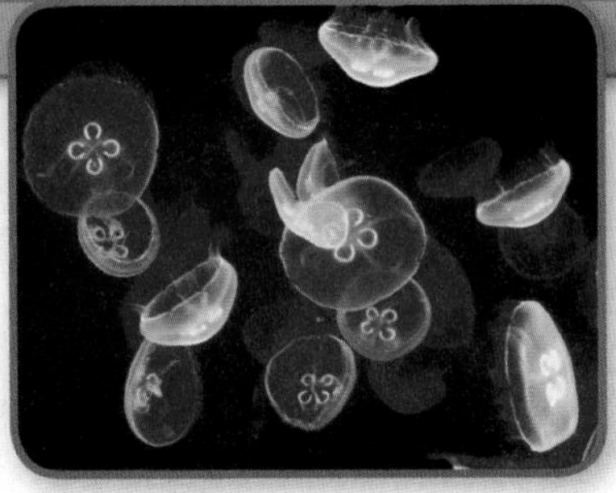

CHEMISTRY & YOU

Q: Why do some kinds of jellyfish glow? In the ocean, angelfish give off light to attract prey. Glowing shrimp, squid, jellyfish, and even bacteria also exist. These organisms, and others, are able to give off energy in the form of light as a result of redox reactions.

Key Questions

What type of chemical reaction is involved in all electrochemical processes?

How does a voltaic cell produce electrical energy?

What current applications use electrochemical processes to produce electrical energy?

Electrochemical Processes

Chemical processes can either release energy or absorb energy. The energy can sometimes be in the form of electricity. An **electrochemical process** is any conversion between chemical energy and electrical energy. All electrochemical processes involve redox reactions.

Redox Reactions When a strip of zinc is dipped into an aqueous solution of blue copper(II) sulfate, the zinc becomes copper-plated. The net ionic equation for this redox reaction is:

$$Zn(s) + Cu^{2+}(aq) \longrightarrow Zn^{2+}(aq) + Cu(s)$$

Electrons are transferred from zinc atoms to copper ions. This is a spontaneous redox reaction. Zinc atoms lose electrons as they are oxidized to zinc ions. Copper ions in the solution gain the electrons lost by the zinc atoms. The copper ions are reduced to copper atoms. These copper atoms form a layer on the zinc strip.

Look at the figures below. As zinc ions replace copper ions in the solution, the blue color of the solution fades. The balanced half-reactions for this redox reaction are:

$$\text{Oxidation: } Zn(s) \longrightarrow Zn^{2+}(aq) + 2e^-$$

$$\text{Reduction: } Cu^{2+}(aq) + 2e^- \longrightarrow Cu(s)$$

Redox Reaction
Zinc metal oxidizes spontaneously in a copper ion solution.

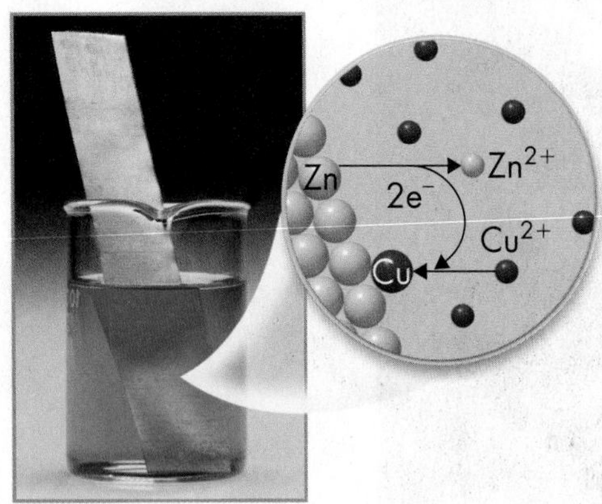

A zinc strip is dipped in a solution of copper(II) sulfate.

The copper begins to plate onto the zinc.

Activity Series of Metals		
	Element	**Oxidation half-reaction**
Most active and most easily oxidized	Lithium	$Li(s) \longrightarrow Li^{+}(aq) + e^{-}$
	Potassium	$K(s) \longrightarrow K^{+}(aq) + e^{-}$
	Barium	$Ba(s) \longrightarrow Ba^{2+}(aq) + 2e^{-}$
↓ Decreasing activity	Calcium	$Ca(s) \longrightarrow Ca^{2+}(aq) + 2e^{-}$
	Sodium	$Na(s) \longrightarrow Na^{+}(aq) + e^{-}$
	Magnesium	$Mg(s) \longrightarrow Mg^{2+}(aq) + 2e^{-}$
	Aluminum	$Al(s) \longrightarrow Al^{3+}(aq) + 3e^{-}$
	Zinc	$Zn(s) \longrightarrow Zn^{2+}(aq) + 2e^{-}$
	Iron	$Fe(s) \longrightarrow Fe^{2+}(aq) + 2e^{-}$
	Nickel	$Ni(s) \longrightarrow Ni^{2+}(aq) + 2e^{-}$
	Tin	$Sn(s) \longrightarrow Sn^{2+}(aq) + 2e^{-}$
	Lead	$Pb(s) \longrightarrow Pb^{2+}(aq) + 2e^{-}$
	Copper	$Cu(s) \longrightarrow Cu^{2+}(aq) + 2e^{-}$
	Silver	$Ag(s) \longrightarrow Ag^{+}(aq) + e^{-}$
Least active and least easily oxidized	Mercury	$Hg(s) \longrightarrow Hg^{2+}(aq) + 2e^{-}$
	Gold	$Au(s) \longrightarrow Au^{3+}(aq) + 3e^{-}$

Activity Series
The half-reaction for the oxidation of each metal is shown. The more active metal will be oxidized. The less active metal will be reduced.

Go to your Chemistry Skills and Math Workbook to practice interpreting data.

Look at the table above. For any two metals in an activity series, the more active metal is the more readily oxidized metal. Zinc is above copper on the list. Therefore, when zinc is dipped into a copper(II) sulfate solution, zinc is oxidized and copper is reduced. Zinc becomes plated with copper. When a copper strip is dipped into a solution of zinc sulfate, the copper does not become plated with zinc. This is because copper metal is not oxidized by zinc ions.

Electrochemical Cells The flow of electrons is an electric current. When the two half-reactions are separated, the redox reaction between zinc atoms and copper ions can be used to produce electrical energy. The electrons released by the zinc atoms must flow through an external circuit to reach the copper ions. In this situation, electrical energy is produced. The system is an electrochemical cell. An electric current can also be used to produce a chemical change. Such a system is also an electrochemical cell. Any device that converts chemical energy into electrical energy or electrical energy into chemical energy is an **electrochemical cell.** Redox reactions occur in all electrochemical cells.

Key Question What type of chemical reaction is involved in all electrochemical processes? **All electrochemical processes involve redox reactions.**

electrochemical process any conversion between chemical energy and electrical energy

electrochemical cell any device that converts chemical energy into electrical energy or electrical energy into chemical energy

WORD ORIGINS
The word *electron* and the prefix *electro-* come from the Greek word for amber. When you rub a piece of amber with wool cloth, it gains an electrical charge.

voltaic cell an electrochemical cell used to convert chemical energy into electrical energy

half-cell one part of a voltaic cell in which either oxidation or reduction occurs

salt bridge a tube containing a strong electrolyte that connects the two half-cells of an electrochemical cell

electrode a conductor in a circuit that carries electrons to or from a substance other than a metal

anode electrode at which oxidation occurs

cathode electrode at which reduction occurs

RELATED WORDS

An anode produces electrons, and a cathode consumes electrons. Compare the word *anode* to the word *anion.* Both words relate to negative charges. Likewise, the words *cathode* and *cation* relate to positive charges.

BUILD Connections

Voltaic cells provide power to electronics that you use every day. Cell phones, watches, mp3 players, and many calculators run on batteries. These batteries are voltaic cells.

Voltaic Cells

A **voltaic cell** is an electrochemical cell used to convert chemical energy into electrical energy. Electrical energy is produced in a voltaic cell by a spontaneous redox reaction within the cell.

Constructing a Voltaic Cell A voltaic cell consists of two half-cells. A **half-cell** is one part of a voltaic cell in which either oxidation or reduction occurs. A half-cell is often made of a piece of metal in a solution of its ions. The figure on the next page shows a voltaic cell that uses the zinc–copper reaction. One half-cell is a zinc strip in a solution of zinc sulfate. The other half-cell is a copper strip in a solution of copper(II) sulfate.

▶ **Salt Bridge** The two half-cells are connected by a **salt bridge,** which is a tube containing a strong electrolyte. An electrolyte often used in salt bridges is potassium sulfate (K_2SO_4).

The salt bridge lets ions pass from one half-cell to the other, but it keeps the solutions from mixing completely. A wire carries the electrons in the external circuit from the zinc strip to the copper strip. A lightbulb or voltmeter can be connected in the circuit. The driving force of the voltaic cell is the spontaneous redox reaction between zinc metal and copper ions in solution.

▶ **Electrodes** The zinc and copper strips in this voltaic cell are the electrodes. An **electrode** is a conductor in a circuit that carries electrons to or from a substance other than a metal. The electrode at which oxidation occurs is called the **anode.** Electrons are produced at the anode. Therefore, the anode is labeled the negative electrode in a voltaic cell. The electrode at which reduction occurs is called the **cathode.** Electrons are consumed at the cathode. Therefore, the cathode is labeled the positive electrode in a voltaic cell. Neither electrode is charged in a voltaic cell. All parts of the voltaic cell remain balanced in terms of charge at all times by the moving electrons.

How a Voltaic Cell Works The electrochemical process that occurs in a zinc–copper voltaic cell can be described in a number of steps. These steps occur at the same time. Look at the figure on the facing page as you read.

Step 1 Zinc is oxidized at the zinc strip, so the zinc strip is the anode, or negative electrode, in the voltaic cell. The half-reaction is:

$$Zn(s) \longrightarrow Zn^{2+}(aq) + 2e^-$$

Step 2 Electrons move from the zinc anode to the copper strip through the external circuit.

Step 3 Copper ions are reduced at the copper strip, so the copper strip is the cathode, or positive electrode. The half-reaction is:

$$Cu^{2+}(aq) + 2e^- \longrightarrow Cu(s)$$

Step 4 Positive and negative ions move through the aqueous solutions via the salt bridge. This movement completes the circuit.

Zinc–Copper Voltaic Cell

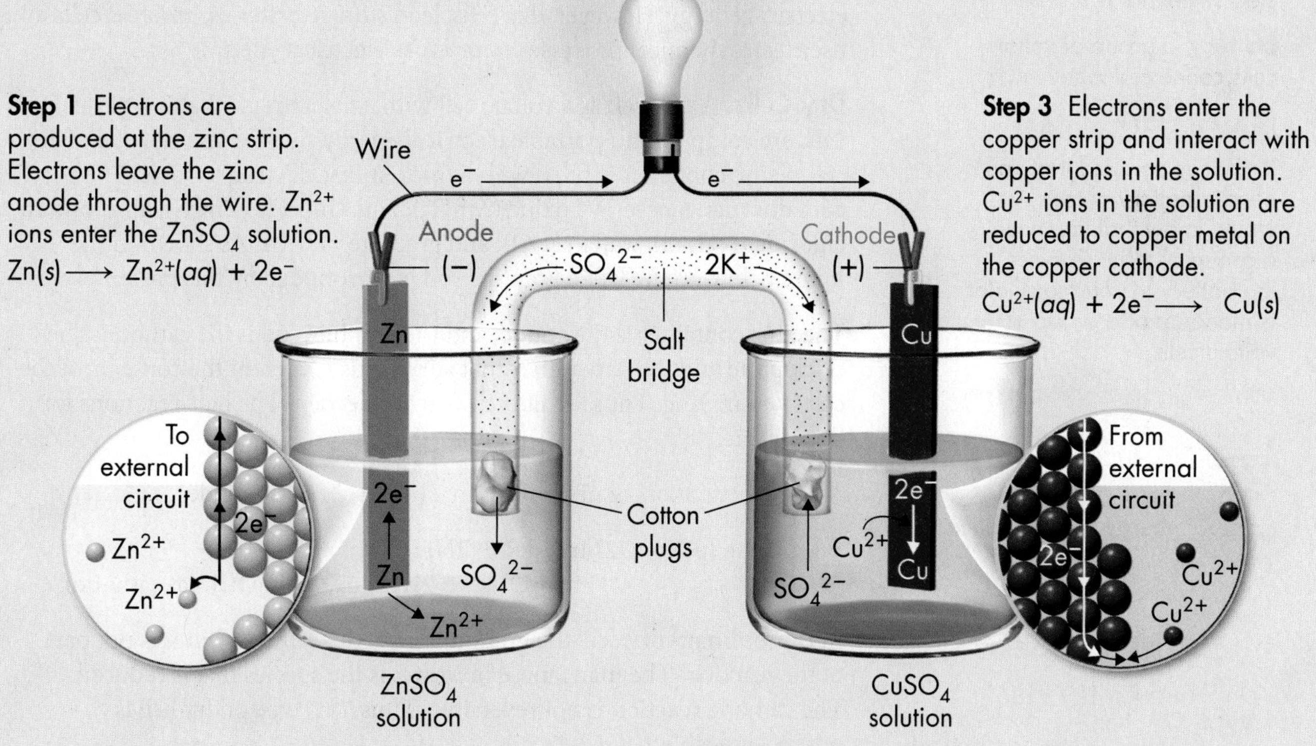

Step 2 The electrons pass through the external circuit. The electron flow causes the bulb to light.
Step 1 Electrons are produced at the zinc strip. Electrons leave the zinc anode through the wire. Zn2+ ions enter the ZnSO4 solution.
Zn(s) ⟶ Zn2+(aq) + 2e−
Step 3 Electrons enter the copper strip and interact with copper ions in the solution. Cu2+ ions in the solution are reduced to copper metal on the copper cathode.
Cu2+(aq) + 2e− ⟶ Cu(s)
Wire
e−
e−
Anode
(−)
SO42−
2K+
Cathode
(+)
Zn
Salt
bridge
Cu
To
external
circuit
2e−
Zn2+
Zn2+
2e−
Zn
SO42−
Zn2+
Cotton
plugs
Cu2+
2e−
Cu
SO42−
From
external
circuit
2e−
Cu2+
Cu2+
ZnSO4
solution
CuSO4
solution
Step 4 Positive and negative ions move through the aqueous solutions via the salt bridge. This movement completes the circuit.

The two half-reactions can be summed to show the overall cell reaction. Notice that the electrons cancel:

$$Zn(s) \longrightarrow Zn^{2+}(aq) + \cancel{2e^-} \text{ (at anode)}$$

$$Cu^{2+}(aq) + \cancel{2e^-} \longrightarrow Cu(s) \text{ (at cathode)}$$

$$Zn(s) + Cu^{2+}(aq) \longrightarrow Zn^{2+}(aq) + Cu(s)$$

See a voltaic cell animated online.
KINETIC
ART

Representing Electrochemical Cells You can use a shorthand notation to describe an electrochemical cell. For the zinc–copper cell, you would write:

$$Zn(s) \mid ZnSO_4(aq) \parallel CuSO_4(aq) \mid Cu(s)$$

The single vertical lines indicate boundaries of phases that are in contact. The zinc strip ($Zn(s)$) and the zinc sulfate solution ($ZnSO_4(aq)$) are separate phases that are in contact. The double vertical lines represent the salt bridge that separates the two half-cells. The anode (oxidation half-cell) is written to the left of the double vertical lines. The cathode (reduction half-cell) is written to the right of the double vertical lines.

Key Question How does a voltaic cell produce electrical energy? **Electrical energy is produced in a voltaic cell by a spontaneous redox reaction within the cell.**

dry cell a voltaic cell with an electrolyte that is a paste

battery a group of voltaic cells connected together

MULTIPLE MEANINGS

If your doctor said that you need a battery of tests, you would know that you need a group of tests. Likewise, the battery in your calculator is made up of a group of voltaic cells.

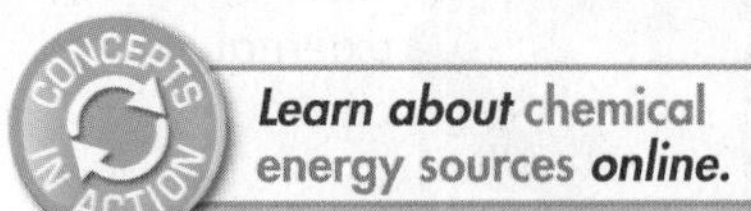

Using Voltaic Cells as Energy Sources

The zinc–copper voltaic cell is not used commercially as a source of electrical energy. However, dry cells, lead storage batteries, and fuel cells all use electrochemical processes to produce electrical energy.

Dry Cells A **dry cell** is a voltaic cell with an electrolyte that is a paste. Dry cells are compact and portable electrical energy sources. In one type of dry cell, a zinc container is filled with a thick, moist electrolyte paste. The paste contains manganese(IV) oxide (MnO_2), zinc chloride ($ZnCl_2$), ammonium chloride (NH_4Cl), water (H_2O), and graphite powder. As shown in the figure below on the left, a graphite rod is surrounded by this paste.

The zinc container is the anode, and the graphite rod is the cathode. The thick paste and the paper liner that surrounds it prevent the contents of the cell from mixing. Thus, a salt bridge is not needed. The half-reactions for this cell are:

$$\text{Oxidation: } Zn(s) \longrightarrow Zn^{2+}(aq) + 2e^- \text{ (at anode)}$$

$$\text{Reduction: } 2MnO_2(s) + 2NH_4^+(aq) + 2e^- \longrightarrow Mn_2O_3(s) + 2NH_3(aq) + H_2O(l) \text{ (at cathode)}$$

In this ordinary dry cell, the graphite rod is the cathode, but it is not part of the reaction. The manganese in MnO_2 is the species that is reduced. The cathode reaction is not reversible. Thus, this type of dry cell is not rechargeable.

The alkaline battery, shown below on the right, is an improved dry cell. In an alkaline battery, the reactions are similar to those in the typical dry cell, but the electrolyte is a basic potassium hydroxide (KOH) paste. The zinc electrode corrodes more slowly under basic, or alkaline, conditions.

Dry Cells

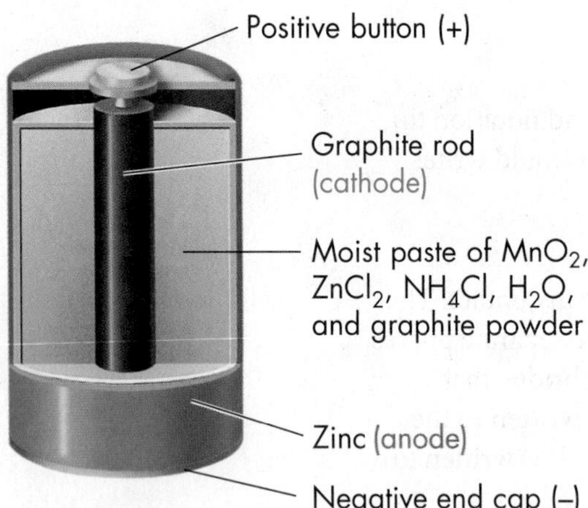

Typical Dry Cell The typical dry cell is inexpensive, but it has a short shelf life.

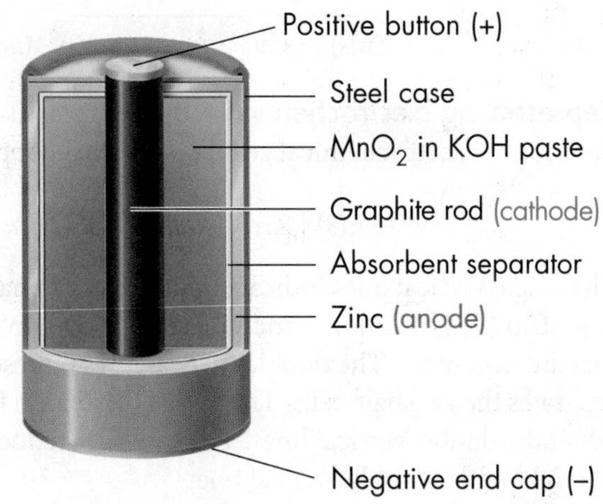

Alkaline Battery The alkaline battery has a longer shelf life than the typical dry cell.

Lead Storage Battery
Electric current is produced when lead at the anode and lead(IV) oxide at the cathode are converted to lead(II) sulfate. These processes decrease the sulfuric acid concentration in the battery. Reversing the reaction recharges the battery.

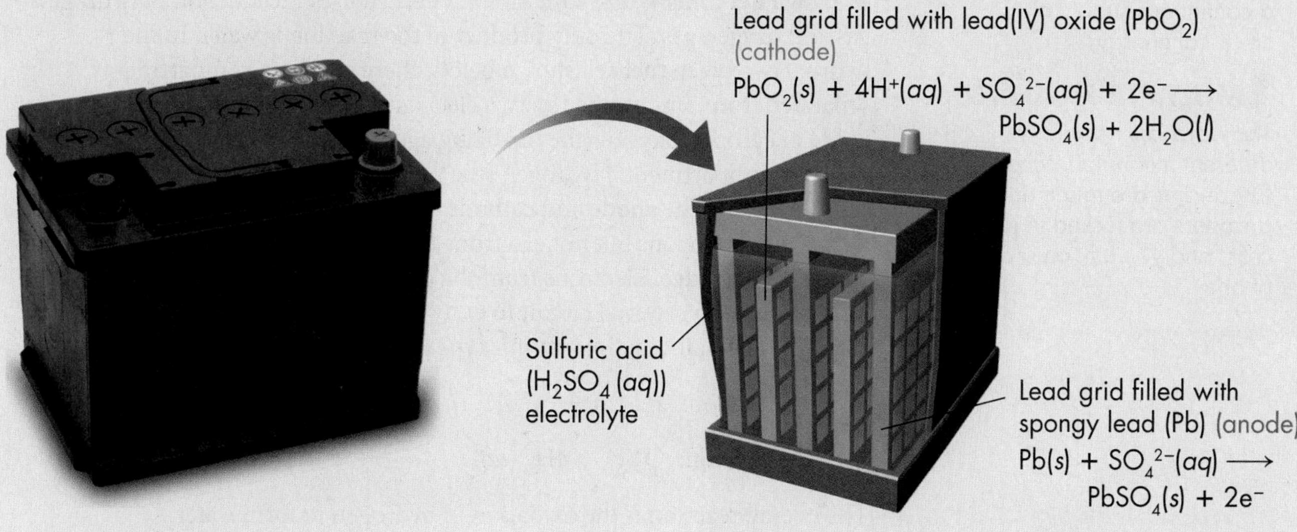

Lead Storage Batteries A **battery** is a group of voltaic cells connected together. People depend on lead storage batteries to start their cars. A 12 volt car battery consists of six voltaic cells connected together. Each cell is made up of lead grids, as shown above. One set of grids, the anode, is packed with spongy lead. The other set, the cathode, is packed with lead(IV) oxide (PbO_2).

The electrolyte for both half-cells is sulfuric acid. There is no salt bridge because both half-cells contain the same electrolyte. The half-reactions are:

$$\text{Oxidation: } Pb(s) + SO_4^{2-}(aq) \longrightarrow PbSO_4(s) + 2e^- \text{ (at anode)}$$

$$\text{Reduction: } PbO_2(s) + 4H^+(aq) + SO_4^{2-}(aq) + 2e^- \longrightarrow PbSO_4(s) + 2H_2O(l) \text{ (at cathode)}$$

When a lead storage battery discharges, it produces the electrical energy needed to start a car. The overall spontaneous redox reaction that occurs is written below. This equation shows that lead(II) sulfate ($PbSO_4$) forms during the reaction.

$$Pb(s) + PbO_2(s) + 2H_2SO_4(aq) \longrightarrow 2PbSO_4(s) + 2H_2O(l)$$

The reverse reaction occurs when a lead storage battery is recharged by a car's generator:

$$2PbSO_4(s) + 2H_2O(l) \longrightarrow Pb(s) + PbO_2(s) + 2H_2SO_4(aq)$$

In theory, a lead storage battery can be discharged and recharged over and over again. However, this is not the case. Small amounts of lead(II) sulfate fall from the electrodes and collect on the bottom of the cell. Over time, the electrodes lose too much lead(II) sulfate. The recharging process becomes no longer effective, and the battery must be replaced.

BUILD Understanding

Compare and Contrast The technical term *battery* refers to a group of cells connected together. You commonly hear dry cells, such as alkaline batteries, called batteries. However, they are not considered to be true batteries. How are dry cells and batteries alike? How are they different?

fuel cell a voltaic cell in which a fuel is oxidized to produce a continuous supply of electrical energy

MULTIPLE MEANINGS

The word *cell* has many different meaning in English. Organisms are made of cells; prisoners are locked in jail cells; and you talk on a cell phone.

Fuel Cells A **fuel cell** is a voltaic cell in which a fuel is oxidized to produce a continuous supply of electrical energy. Fuel cells do not have to be recharged. They can be designed so they do not give off any air pollutants. They can also be quieter and more cost effective than a conventional electrical generator.

▶ **How Fuel Cells Work** One simple fuel cell uses the reaction of hydrogen gas and oxygen gas. The only product of the reaction is water. In the hydrogen–oxygen fuel cell shown below, there are three compartments separated from one another by two electrodes. The electrodes are usually made of carbon. Oxygen (the oxidizing agent) from the air flows into the cathode compartment. Hydrogen (the fuel) flows into the anode compartment. The anode and cathode are separated by a thin membrane that allows hydrogen ions but not electrons to pass through. Thus, the membrane acts as a salt bridge. Electrons from the oxidation half-reaction at the anode pass through an external circuit to enter the reduction half-reaction at the cathode. The half-reactions in this type of fuel cell are:

$$\text{Oxidation: } 2H_2(g) \longrightarrow 4H^+(aq) + 4e^- \text{ (at anode)}$$

$$\text{Reduction: } O_2(g) + 4H^+(aq) + 4e^- \longrightarrow 2H_2O(g) \text{ (at cathode)}$$

The overall reaction is the oxidation of hydrogen to form water:

$$2H_2(g) + O_2(g) \longrightarrow 2H_2O(g)$$

▶ **Applications of Fuel Cells** Since the 1960s, astronauts have relied on fuel cells as an energy source aboard spacecraft. However, the use of fuel cells is no longer limited to space travel. Scientists and engineers have developed fuel cell cars. These vehicles run on electric motors powered by fuel cells. Fuel cell vehicles use pure hydrogen gas, which is stored in high-pressure tanks. Currently, fuel cells are expensive to make, and it is difficult to store hydrogen.

Key Question What current applications use electrochemical processes to produce electrical energy? **Current applications that use electrochemical processes to produce electrical energy include dry cells, lead storage batteries, and fuel cells.**

Hydrogen–Oxygen Fuel Cell
The hydrogen–oxygen fuel cell is a clean source of power for vehicles, such as the one shown here. The $H^+(aq)$ ions produced by the oxidation of $H_2(g)$ at the anode pass through the membrane to the cathode, where $H_2O(g)$ is formed.

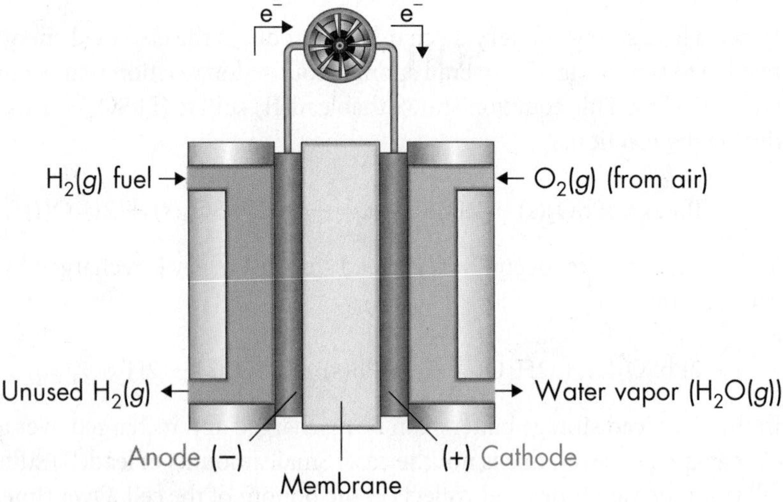

CHEMISTRY & YOU: HISTORY

Alessandro Volta

Italian physicist Alessandro Volta (1745–1827) discovered that you could produce electricity just by placing two different metals in contact with one another. In 1799, he built a pile of alternating zinc and copper discs that were separated by pasteboard soaked in saltwater. When he connected a wire to both ends of the pile, a steady current flowed. This device was called the "voltaic pile." The voltaic pile was the first battery.

Volta found that different types of metals could change the amount of current produced. He also found that he could increase the current by adding discs to the stack. Later, he improved on the pile by creating a "crown of cups," which were separate cups of salt solution linked by metal straps. In 1881, the unit of electrical potential was named the "volt" in Volta's honor.

THE BATTERY REINVENTED
Modern batteries look much different from Volta's alternating zinc and copper discs.

Take It Further

1. **Explain** What was the function of the pasteboard soaked in saltwater in Volta's battery?
2. **Infer** What is one possible reason why Volta's "crown of cups" would generate more current than a "voltaic pile"?

21.1 LessonCheck

Key Concept Check

1. **Identify** What type of reaction occurs during an electrochemical process?
2. **Describe** What is the source of electrical energy produced in a voltaic cell?
3. **List** Name three devices that use electrochemical processes to supply electrical energy.

Vocabulary Check

Choose a highlighted term from the lesson to complete the sentence correctly.

4. A(n) __________ is an electrochemical cell that can convert chemical energy into electrical energy.

Think Critically

5. **Compare** Which metal is more easily oxidized: lead or calcium?
6. **Predict** What happens when a strip of copper is dipped into a solution of iron(II) sulfate?

CHEMISTRY & YOU

7. Jellyfish and other creatures that glow contain compounds that undergo redox reactions. What do these reactions have in common with redox reactions that occur in electrochemical cells? (Hint: See page 691.)

21.2 Half-Cells and Cell Potentials

CHEMISTRY & YOU

Q: How can you calculate the electrical potential of a cell in a laptop battery? Batteries provide current to power many kinds of electronic devices, such as the laptop shown here. The electrical potential between the negative and positive terminals of a lithium laptop battery is 3.7 V. In this lesson, you learn how to calculate electrical potential.

Key Questions

What causes the electrical potential of an electrochemical cell?

How can you determine the standard reduction potential of a half-cell?

How can you determine if a redox reaction is spontaneous?

BUILD Vocabulary

electrical potential a measure of the ability of a voltaic cell to produce an electric current

reduction potential the tendency of a given half-reaction to occur as a reduction

cell potential the difference between the reduction potentials of the two half-cells in an electrochemical cell

Electrical Potential

In an electrochemical cell, the two half-cells compete for electrons. This results in electrical potential. The **electrical potential** of a voltaic cell is a measure of the cell's ability to produce an electric current. The SI unit for electrical potential is the volt (V). This unit was named after Italian physicist Alessandro Volta.

Cell Potential The potential of a single half-cell by itself cannot be measured. For example, you cannot measure the electrical potential of a zinc half-cell. Likewise, you cannot measure the electrical potential of a copper half-cell. However, when these two half-cells are connected to form a voltaic cell, the difference in potential can be measured.

In a voltaic cell, reduction occurs in the half-cell that has the greater tendency to acquire electrons. Oxidation occurs in the other half-cell. The tendency of a given half-reaction to occur as a reduction is called the **reduction potential.** The half-cell in which reduction occurs has a greater reduction potential than the half-cell in which oxidation occurs.

The difference between the reduction potentials of the two half-cells is the **cell potential.** The cell potential can be calculated as:

$$\text{cell potential} = \begin{pmatrix}\text{reduction potential}\\ \text{of half-cell in which}\\ \text{reduction occurs}\end{pmatrix} - \begin{pmatrix}\text{reduction potential}\\ \text{of half-cell in which}\\ \text{oxidation occurs}\end{pmatrix}$$

The symbol E_{cell} is used to represent cell potential. The symbol E_{red} is used to represent the reduction potential of the half-cell in which reduction occurs. The symbol E_{oxid} is used to represent the reduction potential of the half-cell in which oxidation occurs. Using these symbols, the equation can be written as:

$$E_{cell} = E_{red} - E_{oxid}$$

Standard Cell Potential The **standard cell potential** (E°_{cell}) is the measured cell potential under standard conditions. Under standard conditions, the ion concentrations in the half-cells are $1M$, any gases are at a pressure of 101 kPa, and the temperature is 25°C.

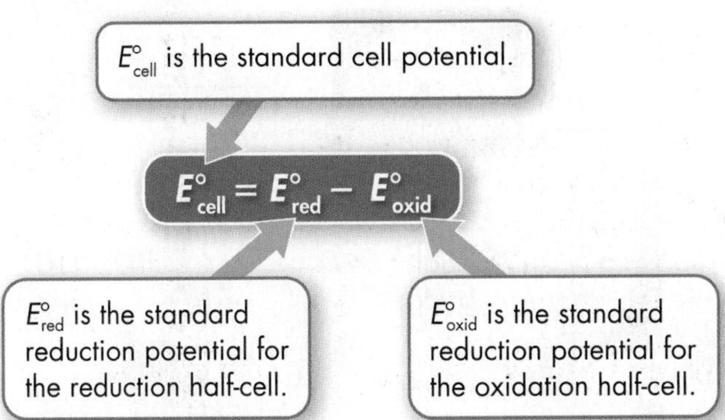

standard cell potential (E°_{cell}) cell potential measured when ion concentrations in the half-cells are $1M$, any gas pressures are 101 kPa, and the temperature is 25°C

standard hydrogen electrode the reference electrode used to measure the reduction potentials of other half-cells

ACADEMIC WORDS

The word *potential* refers to something that is possible but has not yet happened. The difference in the activities of the metal electrodes creates the potential for electrons to move from one electrode to the other.

Standard Hydrogen Electrode We cannot study a half-reaction by itself. Therefore, half-cell potentials cannot be measured directly. Half-cell potentials must be measured relative to another half-cell. Scientists have chosen an electrode to serve as a reference in order to determine half-cell potentials. The **standard hydrogen electrode** is a reference electrode used to measure the reduction potentials of other half-cells. The standard reduction potential of the hydrogen electrode has been assigned a value of 0.00 V.

The standard hydrogen electrode is shown below. The electrode consists of a small square of platinum foil. The foil is coated with finely divided platinum known as platinum black. The platinum electrode is in a solution containing a hydrogen-ion concentration of $1M$. The solution is at 25°C. Hydrogen gas at a pressure of 101 kPa is bubbled around the platinum electrode.

The half-cell reaction that occurs at the platinum black surface is written below. Notice the double arrows in the equation. They indicate that the reaction can occur in both directions.

$$2H^+(aq, 1M) + 2e^- \rightleftharpoons H_2(g, 101\text{ kPa}) \quad E^\circ_{H^+} = 0.00\text{ V}$$

The symbol $E^\circ_{H^+}$ represents the standard reduction potential of H^+. The standard reduction potential of H^+ is the tendency of H^+ ions to gain electrons and be reduced to H_2. The standard hydrogen electrode is usually connected to another half-cell. Whether the half-cell reaction above occurs as a reduction or as an oxidation is determined by the reduction potential of the other half-cell.

Key Question What causes the electrical potential of an electrochemical cell? **The electrical potential of a cell is caused by a competition for electrons between two half-cells.**

Standard Hydrogen Electrode
The standard hydrogen electrode has been assigned a standard reduction potential of 0.00 V.

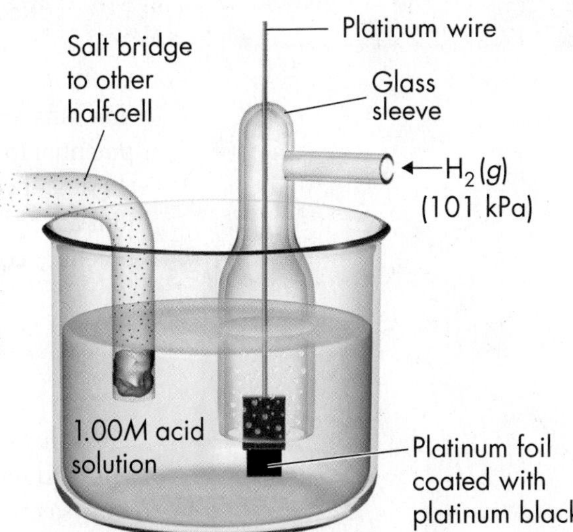

Zinc–Hydrogen Cell This voltaic cell consists of zinc and hydrogen half-cells. Electrons move from the zinc anode to the hydrogen cathode.

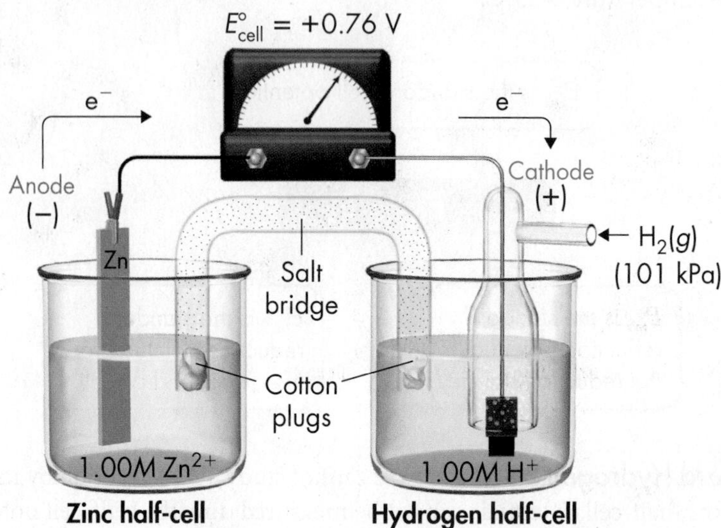

Standard Reduction Potentials

The standard hydrogen electrode allows scientists to measure the standard reduction potentials of half-cells. This is done by connecting a standard hydrogen half-cell to another half-cell.

Zinc–Hydrogen Cell A voltaic cell can be made by connecting a standard hydrogen half-cell to a standard zinc half-cell. An example of this is the zinc–hydrogen cell, which is shown above. The zinc half-cell is connected to the negative side of a voltmeter. The hydrogen half-cell is connected to the positive side. In this setup, the voltmeter gives a reading of +0.76 V. The zinc is oxidized. This means that the zinc strip is the anode. Hydrogen ions are reduced. This means that the hydrogen electrode is the cathode.

Now you can write the half-reactions and the overall cell reaction:

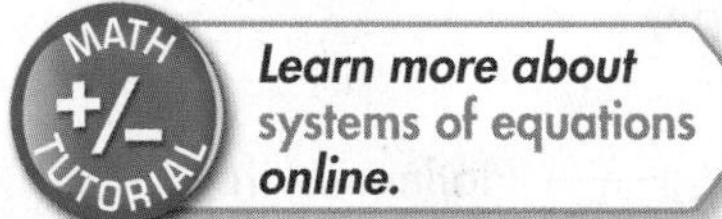

MATH TUTORIAL
Learn more about systems of equations online.

$$\begin{array}{ll} \text{Oxidation:} & Zn(s) \longrightarrow Zn^{2+}(aq) + 2e^- \ \text{(at anode)} \\ \text{Reduction:} & 2H^+(aq) + 2e^- \longrightarrow H_2(g) \ \text{(at cathode)} \\ \hline \text{Cell reaction:} & Zn(s) + 2H^+(aq) \longrightarrow Zn^{2+}(aq) + H_2(g) \end{array}$$

You can use a standard hydrogen electrode and the equation for standard cell potential to determine the standard reduction potential of the zinc half-cell. In the zinc–hydrogen cell, zinc is oxidized. Therefore, $E^\circ_{oxid} = E^\circ_{Zn^{2+}}$. Hydrogen ions are reduced, so $E^\circ_{red} = E^\circ_{H^+}$. Substitute these into the standard cell potential equation:

$$E^\circ_{cell} = E^\circ_{red} - E^\circ_{oxid}$$
$$E^\circ_{cell} = E^\circ_{H^+} - E^\circ_{Zn^{2+}}$$

The voltmeter reads +0.76 V. This is the standard cell potential (E°_{cell}). The standard reduction potential of the hydrogen half-cell ($E^\circ_{H^+}$), by definition, is always equal to 0.00 V.

Substitute the values for E°_{cell} and $E^\circ_{H^+}$ into the equation to solve for $E^\circ_{Zn^{2+}}$:

$$+0.76\text{ V} = 0.00\text{ V} - E^\circ_{Zn^{2+}}$$
$$E^\circ_{Zn^{2+}} = 0.00\text{ V} - (+0.76\text{ V})$$
$$E^\circ_{Zn^{2+}} = -0.76\text{ V}$$

The standard reduction potential for the zinc half-cell is -0.76 V. The value is negative because the tendency of zinc ions to be reduced to zinc metal is less than the tendency of hydrogen ions to be reduced to hydrogen gas.

You can connect a standard hydrogen half-cell to many different half-cells in a similar way. Then, you can determine the standard reduction potential of the other half-cell.

Hydrogen–Copper Cell Consider the hydrogen–copper cell shown below. The copper electrode is connected to the positive side of the voltmeter. The hydrogen electrode is connected to the negative side. Copper is the cathode, and copper ions are reduced to copper metal. The hydrogen half-cell is the anode, and hydrogen gas is oxidized to hydrogen ions. The measured cell potential is $+0.34$ V. You can calculate the standard reduction potential for the copper half-cell as:

$$E^\circ_{cell} = E^\circ_{red} - E^\circ_{oxid}$$
$$E^\circ_{cell} = E^\circ_{Cu^{2+}} - E^\circ_{H^+}$$
$$+0.34\text{ V} = E^\circ_{Cu^{2+}} - 0.00\text{ V}$$
$$E^\circ_{Cu^{2+}} = +0.34\text{ V} + 0.00\text{ V}$$
$$E^\circ_{Cu^{2+}} = +0.34\text{ V}$$

This value is positive because the tendency for copper ions to be reduced is greater than the tendency of hydrogen ions to be reduced.

Key Question How can you determine the standard reduction potential of a half-cell? **You can determine the standard reduction potential of a half-cell by using a standard hydrogen electrode and the equation for standard cell potential.**

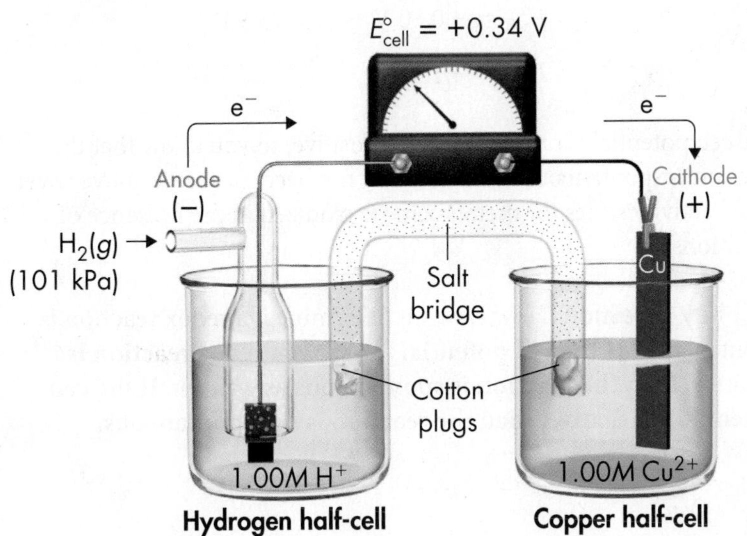

Hydrogen–Copper Cell
This voltaic cell consists of hydrogen and copper half-cells. Electrons move from the hydrogen anode to the copper cathode.
Go to your Chemistry Skills and Math Workbook to practice calculating standard cell potential.

BUILD Connections

Zinc is a common metal. You may handle zinc every day. Since 1982, the metal in U.S. pennies is 97.5% zinc and 2.5% copper.

Calculating Standard Cell Potentials

The standard reduction potentials for some half-cells are listed on the next page. The half-reactions are listed in order of their tendency to occur in the forward direction. Notice that these half-reactions are all reduction reactions. Therefore, the half-reactions at the top of the table have the least tendency to occur as reductions. The half-reactions at the bottom of the table have the greatest tendency to occur as reductions.

You can use the values in the table to predict the half-cells in which reduction and oxidation will occur. In a voltaic cell, reduction occurs in the half-cell with the more positive (or less negative) reduction potential. Oxidation occurs in the half-cell with the less positive (or more negative) reduction potential.

You can also use this table to find the standard cell potential of a given electrochemical cell without having to assemble the cell. If the cell potential for a given redox reaction is positive, then the reaction is spontaneous as written. If the cell potential is negative, then the reaction is nonspontaneous.

A nonspontaneous redox reaction will be spontaneous in the reverse direction. When you reverse the direction of a redox reaction, the cell potential will have the same numerical value but the opposite sign.

CHEMISTRY TUTORIAL
Practice writing the cell reaction *online.*

Consider this redox reaction between zinc metal and silver ions:

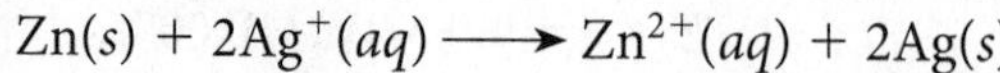

How can you determine if this reaction is spontaneous? In the equation, zinc metal is oxidized and silver ions are reduced. Therefore, $E^{\circ}_{red} = E^{\circ}_{Ag^{+}}$ and $E^{\circ}_{oxid} = E^{\circ}_{Zn^{2+}}$. From the table of reduction potentials, $E^{\circ}_{Ag^{+}} = +0.80$ V and $E^{\circ}_{Zn^{2+}} = -0.76$ V. Substitute these values into the standard cell potential equation to calculate E°_{cell}:

Look at the table on the facing page. Find the values of E°_{red} for the Ag^{+}/Ag and Zn^{2+}/Zn half-cells.

$$E^{\circ}_{cell} = E^{\circ}_{red} - E^{\circ}_{oxid}$$

$$E^{\circ}_{cell} = E^{\circ}_{Ag^{+}} - E^{\circ}_{Zn^{2+}}$$

$$E^{\circ}_{cell} = +0.80\text{ V} - (-0.76\text{ V})$$

$$E^{\circ}_{cell} = +1.56\text{ V}$$

The cell potential for this reaction is positive, so you know that this reaction is spontaneous. This makes sense because zinc is above silver in the activity series for metals. Zinc is oxidized in the presence of silver ions.

Key Question How can you determine if a redox reaction is spontaneous? **If the cell potential for a given redox reaction is positive, then the reaction is spontaneous as written. If the cell potential is negative, then the reaction is nonspontaneous.**

Reduction Potentials at 25°C With 1*M* Concentrations of Aqueous Species

	Electrode	Half-reaction	$E°$ (V)
Least tendency to occur as a reduction	Li^+/Li	$Li^+ + e^- \longrightarrow Li$	−3.05
	K^+/K	$K^+ + e^- \longrightarrow K$	−2.93
	Ba^{2+}/Ba	$Ba^{2+} + 2e^- \longrightarrow Ba$	−2.90
	Ca^{2+}/Ca	$Ca^{2+} + 2e^- \longrightarrow Ca$	−2.87
	Na^+/Na	$Na^+ + e^- \longrightarrow Na$	−2.71
	Mg^{2+}/Mg	$Mg^{2+} + 2e^- \longrightarrow Mg$	−2.37
Increasing tendency to occur as a reduction (stronger oxidizing agent) ↓	Al^{3+}/Al	$Al^{3+} + 3e^- \longrightarrow Al$	−1.66
	H_2O/H_2	$2H_2O + 2e^- \longrightarrow H_2 + 2OH^-$	−0.83
	Zn^{2+}/Zn	$Zn^{2+} + 2e^- \longrightarrow Zn$	−0.76
	Cr^{3+}/Cr	$Cr^{3+} + 3e^- \longrightarrow Cr$	−0.74
	Fe^{2+}/Fe	$Fe^{2+} + 2e^- \longrightarrow Fe$	−0.44
	H_2O/H_2 (pH 7)	$2H_2O + 2e^- \longrightarrow H_2 + 2OH^-$	−0.42
	Cd^{2+}/Cd	$Cd^{2+} + 2e^- \longrightarrow Cd$	−0.40
	$PbSO_4/Pb$	$PbSO_4 + 2e^- \longrightarrow Pb + SO_4^{2-}$	−0.36
	Co^{2+}/Co	$Co^{2+} + 2e^- \longrightarrow Co$	−0.28
	Ni^{2+}/Ni	$Ni^{2+} + 2e^- \longrightarrow Ni$	−0.25
	Sn^{2+}/Sn	$Sn^{2+} + 2e^- \longrightarrow Sn$	−0.14
	Pb^{2+}/Pb	$Pb^{2+} + 2e^- \longrightarrow Pb$	−0.13
	Fe^{3+}/Fe	$Fe^{3+} + 3e^- \longrightarrow Fe$	−0.036
	H^+/H_2	$2H^+ + 2e^- \longrightarrow H_2$	0.000
	$AgCl/Ag$	$AgCl + e^- \longrightarrow Ag + Cl^-$	+0.22
	Hg_2Cl_2/Hg	$Hg_2Cl_2 + 2e^- \longrightarrow 2Hg + 2Cl^-$	+0.27
	Cu^{2+}/Cu	$Cu^{2+} + 2e^- \longrightarrow Cu$	+0.34
	O_2/OH^-	$O_2 + 2H_2O + 4e^- \longrightarrow 4OH^-$	+0.40
	Cu^+/Cu	$Cu^+ + e^- \longrightarrow Cu$	+0.52
	I_2/I^-	$I_2 + 2e^- \longrightarrow 2I^-$	+0.54
	Fe^{3+}/Fe^{2+}	$Fe^{3+} + e^- \longrightarrow Fe^{2+}$	+0.77
	Hg_2^{2+}/Hg	$Hg_2^{2+} + 2e^- \longrightarrow 2Hg$	+0.79
	Ag^+/Ag	$Ag^+ + e^- \longrightarrow Ag$	+0.80
	O_2/H_2O (pH 7)	$O_2 + 4H^+ + 4e^- \longrightarrow 2H_2O$	+0.82
	Hg^{2+}/Hg	$Hg^{2+} + 2e^- \longrightarrow Hg$	+0.85
	Br_2/Br^-	$Br_2 + 2e^- \longrightarrow 2Br^-$	+1.07
	O_2/H_2O	$O_2 + 4H^+ + 4e^- \longrightarrow 2H_2O$	+1.23
	MnO_2/Mn^{2+}	$MnO_2 + 4H^+ + 2e^- \longrightarrow Mn^{2+} + 2H_2O$	+1.28
	$Cr_2O_7^{2-}/Cr^{3+}$	$Cr_2O_7^{2-} + 14H^+ + 6e^- \longrightarrow 2Cr^{3+} + 7H_2O$	+1.33
	Cl_2/Cl^-	$Cl_2 + 2e^- \longrightarrow 2Cl^-$	+1.36
	PbO_2/Pb^{2+}	$PbO_2 + 4H^+ + 2e^- \longrightarrow Pb^{2+} + 2H_2O$	+1.46
Greatest tendency to occur as a reduction	MnO_4^-/Mn^{2+}	$MnO_4^- + 8H^+ + 5e^- \longrightarrow Mn^{2+} + 4H_2O$	+1.51
	$PbO_2/PbSO_4$	$PbO_2 + 4H^+ + SO_4^{2-} + 2e^- \longrightarrow PbSO_4 + 2H_2O$	+1.69
	F_2/F^-	$F_2 + 2e^- \longrightarrow 2F^-$	+2.87

SampleProblem 21.1

Calculating the Standard Cell Potential

Determine the cell reaction for a voltaic cell composed of the following half-cells. Then, calculate the standard cell potential for the cell:

$$Fe^{3+}(aq) + e^- \longrightarrow Fe^{2+}(aq) \quad E^\circ_{Fe^{3+}} = +0.77\text{ V}$$

$$Ni^{2+}(aq) + 2e^- \longrightarrow Ni(s) \quad E^\circ_{Ni^{2+}} = -0.25\text{ V}$$

KNOWNS	UNKNOWNS
$E^O_{Fe^{3+}} = +0.77\text{ V}$	cell reaction = ?
$E^O_{Ni^{2+}} = -0.25\text{ V}$	$E^O_{cell} = ?\text{ V}$

❶ Analyze List the knowns and the unknowns.

❷ Calculate Solve for the unknowns. Determine which species is reduced and which species is oxidized. Use the equation $E^\circ_{cell} = E^\circ_{red} - E^\circ_{oxid}$ to calculate the standard cell potential.

First, identify the cathode and the anode in this cell.

The Fe^{3+} half-cell has the more positive reduction potential, so reduction occurs in this half-cell. The Ni^{2+} half-cell has the more negative reduction potential, so oxidation occurs in this half-cell. Ni is oxidized at the anode and Fe^{3+} is reduced at the cathode.

Write the half-cell reactions in the direction in which they actually occur.

Oxidation: $Ni(s) \longrightarrow Ni^{2+}(aq) + 2e^-$ (at anode)

Reduction: $Fe^{3+}(aq) + e^- \longrightarrow Fe^{2+}(aq)$ (at cathode)

If necessary, multiply the half-reactions by the appropriate factors so the electrons cancel when the half-reactions are added.

$$Ni(s) \longrightarrow Ni^{2+}(aq) + 2e^-$$

$$2[Fe^{3+}(aq) + e^- \longrightarrow Fe^{2+}(aq)]$$

Multiply the Fe^{3+} half-cell equation by 2 so the number of electrons are present in equal numbers on both sides of the equation.

Add the half-reactions to obtain the cell reaction.

$$Ni(s) \longrightarrow Ni^{2+}(aq) + \cancel{2e^-}$$

$$2Fe^{3+}(aq) + \cancel{2e^-} \longrightarrow 2Fe^{2+}(aq)$$

$$Ni(s) + 2Fe^{3+}(aq) \longrightarrow Ni^{2+}(aq) + 2Fe^{2+}(aq)$$

Now write the equation for the standard cell potential.

$$E^O_{cell} = E^O_{red} - E^O_{oxid} = E^O_{Fe^{3+}} - E^O_{Ni^{2+}}$$

Substitute the values for the standard reduction potentials and then solve the equation.

$$E^O_{cell} = +0.77\text{ V} - (-0.25\text{ V}) = +1.02\text{ V}$$

❸ Evaluate Does the result make sense? The reduction potential of the reduction is positive, and the reduction potential of the oxidation is negative. Therefore, E°_{cell} must be positive.

Note: When you multiply a half-reaction to balance the number of electrons for the cell, the reduction potential for the half-reaction does not change.

Practice Problems

8. A voltaic cell is constructed by using these half-reactions:

$$Ag^+(aq) + e^- \longrightarrow Ag(s) \quad E^\circ_{Ag^+} = +0.80\ V$$

$$Cu^{2+}(aq) + 2e^- \longrightarrow Cu(s) \quad E^\circ_{Cu^{2+}} = +0.34\ V$$

Determine the cell reaction and then calculate the standard cell potential.

1 Analyze **List the knowns and the unknowns.**

2 Calculate **Solve for the unknowns.**

3 Evaluate **Does the result make sense?**

KNOWNS	UNKNOWNS
$E^\circ_{Ag^+} = +0.80\ V$	cell reaction = ?
$E^\circ_{Cu^{2+}} = +0.34\ V$	$E^\circ_{cell} = ?\ V$

9. A voltaic cell is constructed by using these half-reactions:

$$Cu^{2+}(aq) + 2e^- \longrightarrow Cu(s) \quad E^\circ_{Cu^{2+}} = +0.34\ V$$

$$Al^{3+}(aq) + 3e^- \longrightarrow Al(s) \quad E^\circ_{Al^{3+}} = -1.66\ V$$

Determine the cell reaction and then calculate the standard cell potential.

KNOWNS	UNKNOWNS
$E^\circ_{Cu^{2+}} =$	cell reaction = ?
$E^\circ_{Al^{3+}} =$	$E^\circ_{cell} = ?\ V$

Remember: The half-cell with the more positive reduction potential is the cathode.

10. Challenge A voltaic cell is constructed with these half-reactions:

$$AgCl(s) + e^- \longrightarrow Ag(s) + Cl^-(aq)$$

$$Ni^{2+}(aq) + 2e^- \longrightarrow Ni(s)$$

Determine the cell reaction and then calculate the standard cell potential.

21.2 LessonCheck

Key Concept Check

11. Explain What causes the electrical potential of a cell?

12. Describe How can you find the standard reduction potential of a half-cell?

13. Review What cell potential values indicate a spontaneous reaction? What cell potential values indicate a nonspontaneous reaction?

Think Critically

CHEMISTRY & YOU

14. What do you need to know to calculate the electrical potential of a cell in a laptop battery? (Hint: See page 700.)

BIGIDEA MATTER AND ENERGY

15. Why does a lead-storage battery produce energy? Calculate the standard cell potential of one voltaic cell in a lead-acid battery.

21.3 Electrolytic Cells

CHEMISTRY & YOU

Q: How can an aluminum bottle be colored? Aluminum is a metal that is silver in color. How then can an aluminum object be colored? These aluminum bottles were anodized and then dyed. In the anodizing process, the aluminum object is the anode in an electrolytic cell. The electrolyte is a dilute acid. When an electric current flows through the cell, aluminum oxide forms on the surface of the aluminum object. In this lesson, you learn about electrochemical processes that require electrical energy.

Key Questions

How do voltaic and electrolytic cells differ?

What are some applications that use electrolytic cells?

BUILD Vocabulary

electrolysis process in which electrical energy is used to bring about a chemical change

electrolytic cell an electrochemical cell used to cause a chemical change through the application of electrical energy

SUFFIXES

The suffix *-lysis* means "to break down." In many common electrolysis reactions, a compound is broken down into its elements. Another example is the word *analysis,* which means to break down complex information to make it more understandable.

Electrolytic vs. Voltaic Cells

You have learned how a spontaneous chemical reaction can generate an electric current. Now you will learn how an electric current can make a nonspontaneous redox reaction occur.

The process in which electrical energy is used to bring about such a chemical change is called **electrolysis.** You may be familiar with some results of electrolysis. Gold-plated jewelry, chrome car parts, and the silver-plated serving set shown below obtained their shiny metal coatings using electrolysis.

Electrolysis is carried out in an electrolytic cell. An **electrolytic cell** is an electrochemical cell used to cause a chemical change through the application of electrical energy. An electrolytic cell uses electrical energy to make a nonspontaneous redox reaction occur.

Products of Electrolysis Pure silver can be plated onto steel by using electrolysis.

Comparing Electrolytic and Voltaic Cells

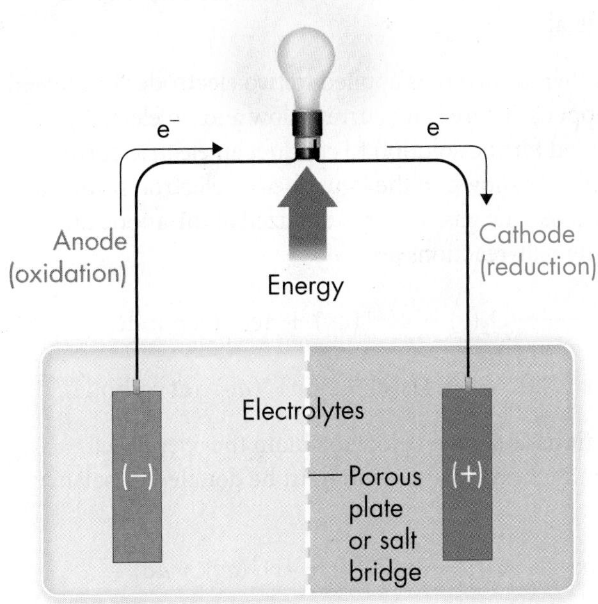

Voltaic Cell In a voltaic cell, energy is released from a spontaneous redox reaction. The system (cell) does work on the surroundings (lightbulb).

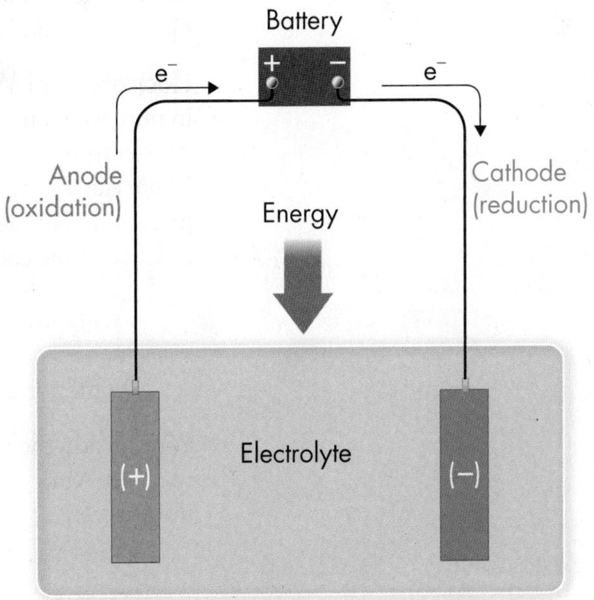

Electrolytic Cell In an electrolytic cell, energy is absorbed to drive a nonspontaneous reaction. The surroundings (battery) do work on the system (cell).

In voltaic and electrolytic cells, electrons flow from the anode to the cathode in the external circuit. The figure above on the left shows a voltaic cell. The figure above on the right shows an electrolytic cell. Notice that the electrode at which reduction occurs is always the cathode. The electrode at which oxidation occurs is always the anode.

There are major differences between a voltaic cell and an electrolytic cell. In a voltaic cell, electrons flow due to a spontaneous redox reaction. In an electrolytic cell, electrons are caused to flow by an outside power source, such as a battery. The redox process in the voltaic cell is spontaneous. In the electrolytic cell, the redox process is nonspontaneous.

The charges that are assigned to the anode and cathode are different in electrolytic and voltaic cells. In a voltaic cell, the anode is the negative electrode and the cathode is the positive electrode. In an electrolytic cell, the cathode is the negative electrode because it is connected to the negative electrode of the battery. The anode in the electrolytic cell is the positive electrode. The anode is connected to the positive electrode of the battery. It is important to remember how the charges are assigned in these two kinds of cells.

Key Question How do voltaic and electrolytic cells differ? **In a voltaic cell, electrons flow due to a spontaneous redox reaction. In an electrolytic cell, electrons flow from an outside power source, such as a battery.**

Driving Nonspontaneous Processes

Electrolysis can be used to separate elements from ionic compounds in solution or in the melted or molten state. Electrolytic cells are also used to plate, purify, and refine metals.

Electrolysis of Water When a current is applied to two electrodes immersed in pure water, nothing happens. There is no current flow and no electrolysis. An electrolyte must be added for the solution to conduct an electric current. Then, electrolysis can occur. As shown in the figure below, electrolysis of water produces hydrogen gas and oxygen gas. Water is oxidized at the anode and reduced at the cathode. The half-reactions are:

$$\text{Oxidation: } 2H_2O(l) \longrightarrow O_2(g) + 4H^+(aq) + 4e^- \text{ (at anode)}$$

$$\text{Reduction: } 2H_2O(l) + 2e^- \longrightarrow H_2(g) + 2OH^-(aq) \text{ (at cathode)}$$

You can add the half-reactions as shown below to obtain the overall cell reaction. Notice that the reduction half-reaction must be doubled to balance the electrons.

$$\text{Oxidation: } 2H_2O(l) \longrightarrow O_2(g) + 4H^+(aq) + \cancel{4e^-}$$

$$\text{Reduction: } 4H_2O(l) + \cancel{4e^-} \longrightarrow 2H_2(g) + 4OH^-(aq)$$

$$\text{Overall cell reaction: } 6H_2O(l) \longrightarrow 2H_2(g) + O_2(g) + 4H^+(aq) + 4OH^-(aq)$$

The ions produced tend to recombine to form water:

$$4H^+(aq) + 4OH^-(aq) \longrightarrow 4H_2O(l)$$

The net reaction can therefore be written as:

$$2H_2O(l) \longrightarrow 2H_2(g) + O_2(g)$$

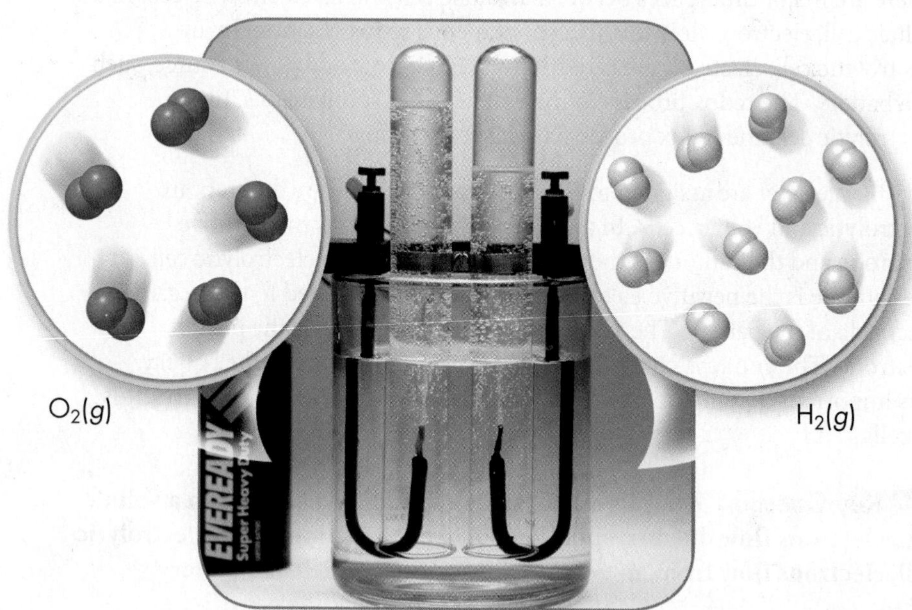

Electrolysis of Water
When an electric current passes through water, the water decomposes into oxygen gas and hydrogen gas.

Electrolysis of Brine Chlorine gas, hydrogen gas, and sodium hydroxide are produced when an electric current passes through an aqueous solution of sodium chloride.

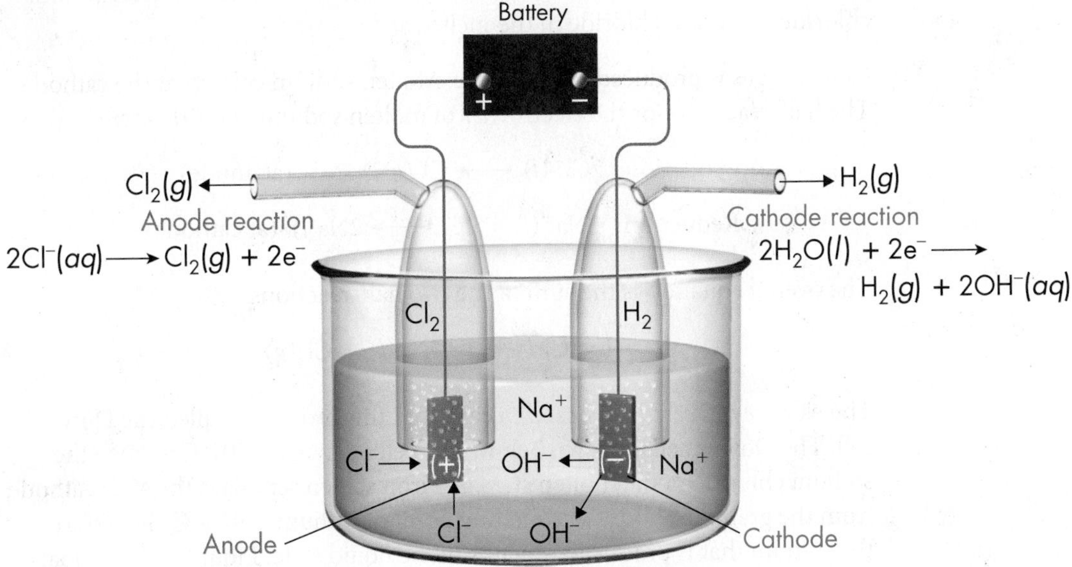

Electrolysis of Brine What happens if the electrolyte in an aqueous solution is more easily oxidized or reduced than water? The products of the electrolysis will be substances other than hydrogen and oxygen. An example of this is the electrolysis of brine. Brine is a concentrated solution of sodium chloride in water. The electrolysis of brine produces, at the same time, three important industrial chemicals: chlorine gas, hydrogen gas, and sodium hydroxide.

The electrolytic cell for the electrolysis of brine is shown above. Chloride ions are oxidized to produce chlorine gas at the anode. Water is reduced to produce hydrogen gas at the cathode. The reduction of water also produces hydroxide ions. Sodium ions are not reduced to sodium metal because water molecules are more easily reduced than are sodium ions. Sodium ions and hydroxide ions in solution become sodium hydroxide (NaOH). The half-reactions are:

$$\text{Oxidation: } 2Cl^-(aq) \longrightarrow Cl_2(g) + 2e^- \text{ (at anode)}$$

$$\text{Reduction: } 2H_2O(l) + 2e^- \longrightarrow H_2(g) + 2OH^-(aq) \text{ (at cathode)}$$

The overall ionic equation is the sum of the two half-reactions:

$$2Cl^-(aq) + 2H_2O(l) \longrightarrow Cl_2(g) + H_2(g) + 2OH^-(aq)$$

The sodium ion (Na^+) is a spectator ion. It can be included in the equation as part of NaCl and NaOH. This overall equation shows the formation of sodium hydroxide during the electrolytic process:

$$2NaCl(aq) + 2H_2O(l) \longrightarrow Cl_2(g) + H_2(g) + 2NaOH(aq)$$

When the sodium hydroxide concentration reaches about 10 percent (mass/volume), the solution is removed from the cell.

Electrolysis of Molten Sodium Chloride Sodium and chlorine are important chemicals. Sodium is used in sodium vapor lamps and as the coolant in some nuclear reactors. Chlorine is used to sterilize drinking water and is used in making certain plastics and pesticides. These elements are products of the electrolysis of pure molten sodium chloride. Molten sodium chloride is sodium chloride in the melted state.

Chlorine gas is produced at the anode. Molten sodium collects at the cathode. The half-reactions for the electrolysis of molten sodium chloride are:

$$\text{Oxidation: } 2Cl^-(l) \longrightarrow Cl_2(g) + 2e^- \text{ (at anode)}$$

$$\text{Reduction: } 2Na^+(l) + 2e^- \longrightarrow 2Na(l) \text{ (at cathode)}$$

The overall equation is the sum of the two half-reactions:

$$2NaCl(l) \longrightarrow 2Na(l) + Cl_2(g)$$

The electrolytic cell that is used to carry out this process is called the Downs cell. The Downs cell is shown below. The cell operates at 801°C to keep the sodium chloride in the molten state. An iron screen separates the steel cathode from the graphite anode. The melting point of sodium is 97.8°C. Therefore, the sodium that is produced remains in the liquid state. Liquid sodium floats on top of the molten sodium chloride, so it is easy to separate. The chlorine gas bubbles up and out through the top of the cell. The Downs cell is designed to keep the products separated so they do not react to reform sodium chloride.

Downs Cell
The Downs cell produces sodium metal and chlorine gas from the electrolysis of molten sodium chloride.

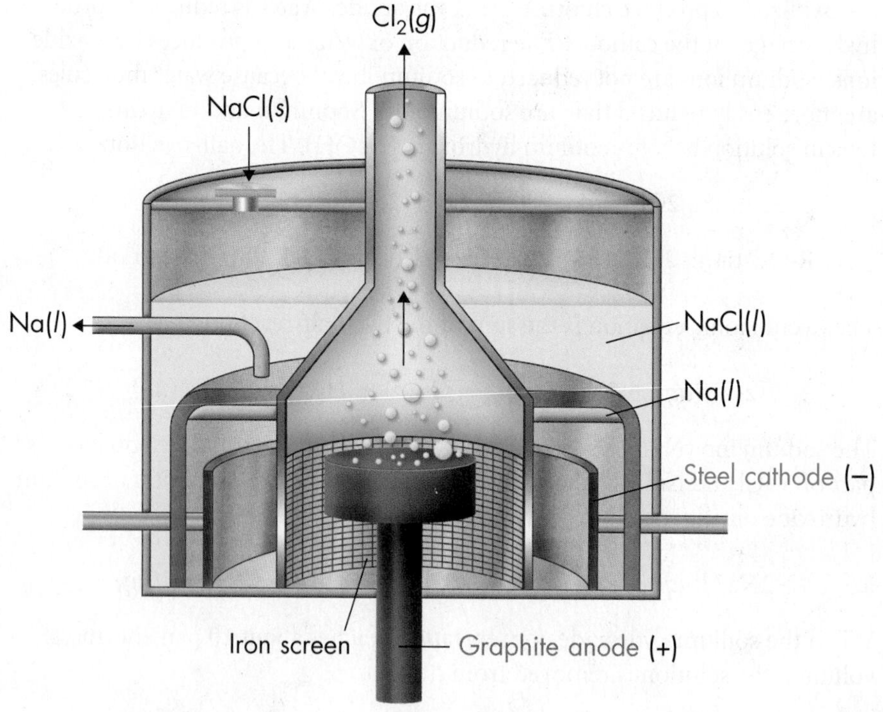

Using Electrolysis in Metal Processing Electrolysis has many important applications in the field of metallurgy. Electrolytic processes were used to make many of the metallic objects you see every day shiny.

▶ **Electroplating** When an object is electroplated, a thin layer of a metal is deposited on the object in an electrolytic cell. Sometimes, an object is electroplated to protect its metal surface from corrosion. Other times, objects are electroplated to make them more attractive. An object that is to be silver-plated is made the cathode in an electrolytic cell. The anode of the cell is the silver that will be plated onto the object. The electrolyte is a solution of a silver salt, such as silver cyanide. When a current is applied, silver ions move from the anode to the object at the cathode. The reduction half-reaction is:

$$\text{Reduction: } Ag^+(aq) + e^- \longrightarrow Ag(s) \text{ (at cathode)}$$

The overall result is that silver transfers from the anode to the object being plated. The photo on the right shows small statues that were electroplated with copper, nickel, and gold.

Electroplating Copper, nickel, and gold were electroplated onto pewter to produce these statues.

▶ **Electrowinning and Electrorefining** Electrowinning is a process that uses an electrolytic cell to purify metal. Cations are reduced at the cathode to yield very pure metals. A common use of electrowinning is in the extraction of aluminum from its ore, which is called bauxite.

Bauxite is impure alumina (Al_2O_3). Alumina is dissolved in molten cryolite (Na_3AlF_6) and heated to above 1000°C in a carbon-lined tank. The carbon lining becomes the cathode of the cell. The anodes are carbon rods that are dipped into the tank. At the cathode, Al^{3+} ions are reduced to aluminum. At the anodes, carbon is oxidized to form carbon dioxide gas. The overall reaction is:

$$2Al_2O_3(l) + 3C(s) \longrightarrow 4Al(l) + 3CO_2(g)$$

In the electrorefining process, a piece of impure metal becomes the anode of the cell. It is oxidized to the cation. The cation is then reduced to the pure metal at the cathode. This technique is used to obtain ultrapure silver, lead, and copper.

▶ **Other Processes** Other electrolytic processes are centered on the anode rather than the cathode. In electropolishing, the surface of a metal object at the anode is dissolved to give it a high polish. In electromachining, a piece of metal at the anode is partially dissolved until it is an exact copy of the object at the cathode.

Key Question What are some applications that use electrolytic cells? **Electrolysis can separate the elements from ionic compounds in solution or in the molten state. Electrolytic cells are also used to plate, purify, and refine metals.**

Quick Lab

Purpose To electrochemically oxidize metals and identify the products

Materials

- reaction surface
- aluminum foil
- filter paper
- micropipette or dropper
- sodium sulfate (Na_2SO_4) solution
- penny
- 9 volt battery
- nickel coin
- iron nail

Electrochemical Analysis of Metals

Procedure

1. Stack the following in order on a reaction surface: a 3 cm square of aluminum foil, a 2 cm square of filter paper, 1 drop of Na_2SO_4 solution, and a penny. The penny should be roughly centered on the filter paper, which should be roughly centered on the foil.

2. Apply the negative (−) terminal of the 9 volt battery to the aluminum foil and the positive (+) terminal to the penny for no more than 3 seconds.

3. Remove the penny and then observe the filter paper.

4. Repeat Steps 1–3, replacing the penny with the nickel coin.

5. Repeat Steps 1–3, replacing the penny with the iron nail.

Analyze and Conclude

1. Observe What colors formed on the filter paper for each object?

2. Describe For each metal object you tested, the battery oxidized the metal atoms to form metal cations with a 2+ charge. Write a half-reaction for each metal oxidation you observed. Did these reactions take place at the anode or the cathode?

3. Relate Cause and Effect Explain in your own words why the colors formed on the filter paper.

4. Describe The aluminum foil serves as the cathode, where the reduction of water takes place. Write the half-reaction for the reduction of water.

5. Describe Combine the half-reaction for the oxidation of copper with the half-reaction for the reduction of water to form the overall equation for the cell reaction.

21.3 LessonCheck

Key Concept Check

16. Describe What is the difference between an electrolytic cell and a voltaic cell?

17. List What are some applications of electrolytic cells?

Think Critically

18. Compare What is the charge on the anode of an electrolytic cell? What is the charge on the anode of a voltaic cell?

19. Apply Concepts Which process, oxidation or reduction, always occurs at the cathode of an electrolytic cell?

CHEMISTRY & YOU

20. In the process of anodizing aluminum, the aluminum object serves as the anode. To which electrode of the power source is the anode connected? (See pages 707 and 711.)

BIGIDEA MATTER AND ENERGY

21. Does the redox reaction in a voltaic cell release free energy? If no electrical energy is supplied, does the redox reaction in an electrolytic cell release free energy? Explain.

21 Study Guide

BIGIDEA MATTER AND ENERGY

The two types of electrochemical cells are voltaic cells and electrolytic cells. In a voltaic cell, electric current is produced by a spontaneous redox reaction. Voltaic cells are used in batteries and fuel cells. In an electrolytic cell, a nonspontaneous redox reaction is driven by the application of electrical energy. Electrolytic cells are used to produce commercially important chemicals and to plate, purify, and refine metals.

21.1 Electrochemical Cells

All electrochemical processes involve redox reactions.

Electrical energy is produced in a voltaic cell by a spontaneous redox reaction within the cell.

Current applications that use electrochemical processes to produce electrical energy include dry cells, lead storage batteries, and fuel cells.

- electrochemical process (690)
- electrochemical cell (691)
- voltaic cell (692)
- half-cell (692)
- salt bridge (692)
- electrode (692)
- anode (692)
- cathode (692)
- dry cell (694)
- battery (695)
- fuel cell (696)

21.2 Half-Cells and Cell Potentials

The electrical potential of a cell is caused by a competition for electrons between two half-cells.

You can determine the standard reduction potential of a half-cell by using a standard hydrogen electrode and the equation for standard cell potential.

If the cell potential for a given redox reaction is positive, then the reaction is spontaneous as written. If the cell potential is negative, then the reaction is nonspontaneous.

- electrical potential (698)
- reduction potential (698)
- cell potential (698)
- standard cell potential (699)
- standard hydrogen electrode (699)

Key Equation

$$E^{\circ}_{\text{cell}} = E^{\circ}_{\text{red}} - E^{\circ}_{\text{oxid}}$$

21.3 Electrolytic Cells

In a voltaic cell, electrons flow due to a spontaneous redox reaction. In an electrolytic cell, electrons flow from an outside power source, such as a battery.

Electrolysis can separate the elements of ionic compounds in solution or in the molten state. Electrolytic cells are also used to plate, purify, and refine metals.

- electrolysis (706)
- electrolytic cell (706)

21 Assessment

★ Solutions appear in Appendix D.

Lesson by Lesson

21.1 Electrochemical Cells

22. If the relative activities of two metals are known, which metal is more easily oxidized?

23. Write the half-reactions that occur when a strip of aluminum is dipped into a solution of copper(II) sulfate.

★**24.** For each pair of metals listed below, identify which metal is more readily oxidized.

a. Hg, Cu
b. Ca, Al
c. Ni, Mg
d. Sn, Ag
e. Pb, Zn
f. Cu, Al

25. What would you expect to happen when a strip of lead is placed in an aqueous solution of magnesium nitrate?

26. Explain the function of the salt bridge in a voltaic cell.

27. At which electrode in a voltaic cell does reduction always occur?

★**28.** Describe the structure of a typical dry cell. What substance is oxidized? What substance is reduced?

29. How are typical dry cells and alkaline batteries similar? How are they different?

★**30.** Use the shorthand method to represent the electrochemical reaction that occurs when a lead storage battery discharges.

31. List the advantages of a fuel cell over a lead storage battery.

21.2 Half-Cells and Cell Potentials

32. What is the electrical potential of a voltaic cell?

★**33.** What is the difference between standard cell potential and standard reduction potential?

34. What is the electrical potential of a standard hydrogen electrode? How was it determined?

35. Explain how to determine the standard reduction potential for the aluminum half-cell.

★**36.** Determine whether these redox reactions will occur spontaneously. Calculate the standard cell potential in each case.

a. $Cu(s) + 2H^+(aq) \longrightarrow Cu^{2+}(aq) + H_2(g)$
b. $2Ag(s) + Fe^{2+}(aq) \longrightarrow 2Ag^+(aq) + Fe(s)$

37. Use the information in the table on page 703 to calculate standard cell potentials for these voltaic cells.

a. $Zn \mid Zn^{2+} \parallel Cu^{2+} \mid Cu$
b. $Ni \mid Ni^{2+} \parallel Cl_2 \mid Cl^-$
c. $Sn \mid Sn^{2+} \parallel Ag^+ \mid Ag$

21.3 Electrolytic Cells

★**38.** Distinguish between voltaic cells and electrolytic cells.

Use this diagram to answer Problems 39 and 40.

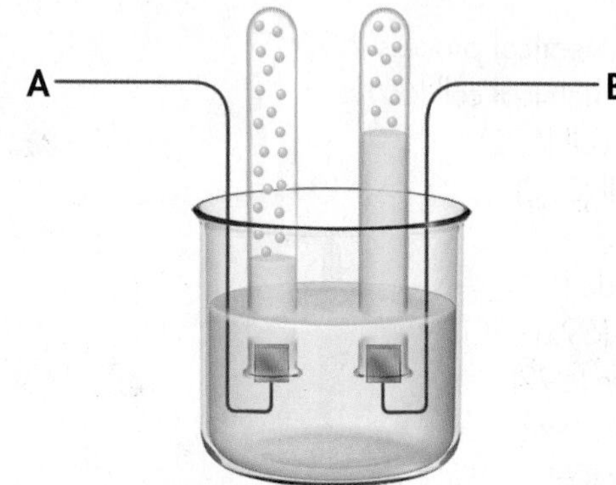

39. Write the equation for the decomposition of water by electrolysis.

40. At which electrode, A or B, is hydrogen produced?

★**41.** What chemical changes occur during the electrolysis of brine?

42. What are the products of the electrolysis of molten sodium chloride?

43. Describe briefly how you would electroplate a teaspoon with silver.

Understand Concepts

*44. Predict what will happen, if anything, when an iron nail is dipped into a solution of copper(II) sulfate. Write the oxidation and reduction half-reactions for this process and the balanced equation for the overall reaction.

45. The standard reduction potential for a cadmium half-cell is −0.40 V. What does this mean?

*46. Calculate E°_{cell} and then write the overall cell reaction for these cells.

a. $Sn \mid Sn^{2+} \parallel Pb^{2+} \mid Pb$

b. $H_2 \mid H^+ \parallel Br_2 \mid Br^-$

47. The reactions that take place in voltaic cells produce electric current, and the reactions in electrolytic cells can be made to take place when an electric current is applied. What common feature do these redox reactions share?

48. Use the information in the table on page 703 to determine which of the following cell reactions will proceed spontaneously.

a. $Zn + Pb^{2+} \longrightarrow ?$

b. $Cu + Fe^{2+} \longrightarrow ?$

c. $Ag + Cu^{2+} \longrightarrow ?$

d. $H_2 + Cu \longrightarrow ?$

e. $Fe + Pb^{2+} \longrightarrow ?$

f. $Na + Cl_2 \longrightarrow ?$

49. Why is it not possible to measure the potential of an isolated half-cell?

50. In certain cases, more than one reaction is possible at an electrode. How can you determine which reaction actually takes place?

51. Gold is not included in the table on page 703. Where in the table does gold belong?

52. Write the overall cell reactions and then calculate E°_{cell} for voltaic cells composed of the following sets of half-reactions.

a. $Ag^+(aq) + e^- \longrightarrow Ag(s)$
$Cr^{3+}(aq) + 3e^- \longrightarrow Cr(s)$

b. $Al^{3+}(aq) + 3e^- \longrightarrow Al(s)$
$Cd^{2+}(aq) + 2e^- \longrightarrow Cd(s)$

Think Critically

*53. **Relate Cause and Effect** Lead storage batteries can be recharged. Why are typical dry cells not rechargeable?

*54. **Interpret Diagrams** Describe the process that is occurring in this illustration.

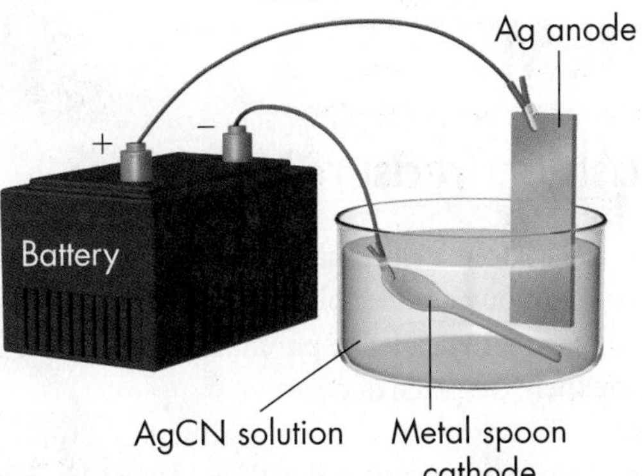

55. **Relate Cause and Effect** In most voltaic cells, the half-cells are connected by a salt bridge or a porous barrier instead of a piece of wire made of copper or some other metal. Why is a metal wire not suitable for connecting the half-cells of a voltaic cell? Explain your answer.

FOUNDATIONS Wrap-Up

A Lemon Battery

1. **Draw Conclusions** At the beginning of this chapter, you made a lemon battery and touched it to your tongue. Explain why the lemon battery caused a sensation on your tongue.

Concept Check

Now that you have finished studying Chapter 21, answer these questions. Use your own words.

2. What type of reaction, if any, will occur if a strip of copper is dipped into a solution of silver nitrate?

3. Is this redox reaction spontaneous as written?
$Co^{2+}(aq) + Fe(s) \longrightarrow Fe^{2+}(aq) + Co(s)$

4. How are voltaic cells and electrolytic cells similar? How are they different?

Write About Science

56. Explain Write a paragraph explaining how a zinc–copper voltaic cell works. Make sure to mention the half-reactions and the overall reaction in your explanation. (Hint: Use the illustration on page 693 as a reference.)

CHEMYSTERY

Trash or Treasure?

The jeweler told Maria that she did not buy a pure gold antique ring. Instead, she purchased an inexpensive piece of costume jewelry. The ring was made of stainless steel that was electroplated with gold. As Maria wore the ring, the thin layer of gold began to wear off. As the gold wore off, the stainless steel underneath began to show. The jeweler offered to replate the ring with more gold.

The process by which gold is plated onto another metal is similar to the process by which silver is plated onto an object. The object that is to be gold-plated is the cathode in the electrolytic cell. The anode is metallic gold, which supplies the gold to be deposited onto the object. The electrolyte is a solution of a gold compound. Electroplating of the object occurs when a current is applied.

57. Describe Draw the electrolytic cell that is used to plate gold onto an object. Label the anode and the cathode and then assign charges to the electrodes. Indicate the direction of electron flow and then write the half-reactions.

*** 58. Infer** How could you remove the gold from a gold-plated object by using an electrolytic cell?

59. Connect to the BIGIDEA Will the half-reactions in an electrochemical cell used to plate gold onto an object occur if no electric current is supplied to the cell? Explain.

Cumulative Review

***60.** A sample of oxygen gas has a volume of 425 mL at 30°C. What is the new volume of the gas if the temperature is raised to 60°C while the pressure is kept constant? (See Lesson 14.2 for help.)

***61.** Calculate the grams of solute required to make these solutions. (See Lesson 16.2 for help.)

a. 250 g of 0.90% NaCl (m/m)
b. 500 mL of 2.0M KNO_3

62. Convert the following. (See Lesson 17.1.)

a. 4.32×10^5 joules to kilojoules
b. 255 Calories to calories
c. 645 calories to joules

***63.** The combustion of natural gas, methane (CH_4), is an exothermic reaction.

$$CH_4(g) + 2O_2(g) \longrightarrow CO_2(g) + 2H_2O(l) \quad \Delta H = -890 \text{ kJ}$$

Calculate the amount of heat liberated when 4.80 g CH_4 reacts with an excess of oxygen. (See Lesson 17.2 for help.)

***64.** Four reactions have the following equilibrium constants. Identify in which of these reactions the reactants are favored over products. Why? (See Lesson 18.3 for help.)

a. $K_{eq} = 0.006$
b. $K_{eq} = 5.3$
c. $K_{eq} = 8 \times 10^{-4}$
d. $K_{eq} = 2 \times 10^3$

***65.** Determine the pH for each solution. (See Lesson 19.2 for help.)

a. $[H^+] = 1.0 \times 10^{-8}M$
b. $[H^+] = 0.000010M$

***66.** Determine the oxidation number of sulfur in each of the following substances. (See Lesson 20.2 for help.)

a. H_2SO_4
b. H_2S
c. SO_2
d. $Na_2S_2O_3$
e. S
f. SO_3^{2-}

***67.** Identify which of the following are oxidation-reduction reactions. If a reaction is a redox reaction, name the element oxidized and the element reduced. (See Lesson 20.3 for help.)

a. $CaCO_3(s) \longrightarrow CaO(s) + CO_2(g)$
b. $Ca(s) + Cl_2(g) \longrightarrow CaCl_2(s)$
c. $Ca(s) + 2H_2O(l) \longrightarrow Ca(OH)_2(aq) + H_2(g)$

Standardized Test Prep

For help with answering test questions, go to your Chemistry Skills and Math Workbook.

Select the choice that best answers each question or completes each statement.

Tips for Success

Eliminate Wrong Answers If you do not know which response is correct, start by eliminating those you know are wrong. If you can rule out some choices, you will have fewer left to consider and you will increase your chances of choosing the correct answer.

1. Which statement describes electrolysis?
(A) Reduction occurs at the anode.
(B) Energy is produced.
(C) Oxidation occurs at the cathode.
(D) Positive ions move to the cathode.

2. A voltaic cell is constructed by using these half-reactions:

$Cd^{2+}(aq) + 2e^- \longrightarrow Cd(s) \quad E^\circ_{Cd^{2+}} = -0.40\ V$
$Sn^{2+}(aq) + 2e^- \longrightarrow Sn(s) \quad E^\circ_{Sn^{2+}} = -0.14\ V$

What is the standard cell potential for this voltaic cell?
(A) −0.54 V
(B) −0.26 V
(C) +0.26 V
(D) +0.54 V

3. Which of the following is a product of the reaction that occurs in a hydrogen–oxygen fuel cell?
(A) $CO(g)$
(B) $CO_2(g)$
(C) $H_2O(g)$
(D) $H_2O_2(l)$

4. Magnesium metal is prepared by the electrolysis of molten $MgCl_2$. One half-reaction is:

$$Mg^{2+}(l) + 2e^- \longrightarrow Mg(l)$$

Which of the following statements is true?
(A) This half-reaction occurs at the cathode.
(B) Magnesium ions are oxidized.
(C) Chloride ions are reduced at the anode.
(D) Chloride ions gain electrons during this process.

5. If the cell potential for a redox reaction is positive,
(A) the redox reaction is spontaneous.
(B) the redox reaction is not spontaneous.
(C) the reaction only occurs during electrolysis.
(D) More than one statement is correct.

Use the data table to answer Questions 6–12. Hydrogen is included as a reference point for the metals.

Activity Series of Selected Metals

Element	Oxidation half-reaction
Lithium	$Li(s) \longrightarrow Li^+(aq) + e^-$
Potassium	$K(s) \longrightarrow K^+(aq) + e^-$
Sodium	$Na(s) \longrightarrow Na^+(aq) + e^-$
Aluminum	$Al(s) \longrightarrow Al^{3+}(aq) + 3e^-$
Zinc	$Zn(s) \longrightarrow Zn^{2+}(aq) + 2e^-$
Iron	$Fe(s) \longrightarrow Fe^{2+}(aq) + 2e^-$
Hydrogen	$H_2(g) \longrightarrow 2H^+(aq) + 2e^-$
Copper	$Cu(s) \longrightarrow Cu^{2+}(aq) + 2e^-$

6. Which metal will more easily lose an electron: sodium or potassium?

7. Which metal is more easily oxidized: copper or aluminum?

8. What is the relationship between ease of oxidation and the activity of a metal?

9. Describe what would happen if you placed a clean strip of aluminum in a solution of copper(II) sulfate. Explain your answer.

10. Would a copper strip placed in a solution containing zinc ions react spontaneously with the zinc ions? Explain your reasoning.

11. Based on the positions of zinc and iron in the table, explain how attaching zinc blocks to a steel ship hull protects the steel from corrosion.

12. Write the half-reaction for the reduction of aluminum ions.

13. An electrolytic cell is shown at the right. Draw this cell on a separate piece of paper and then label the anode, cathode, and direction of electron flow.

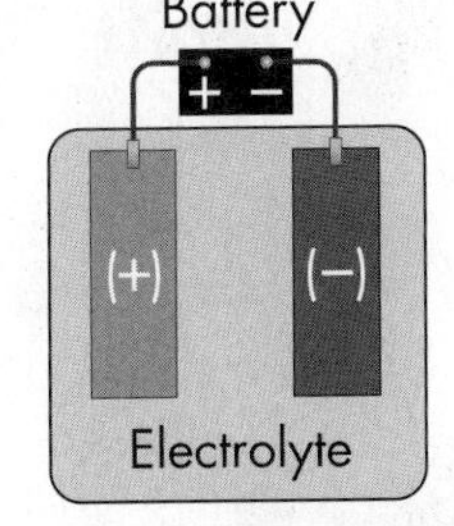

If You Have Trouble With . . .

Question	1	2	3	4	5	6	7	8	9	10	11	12	13
See Lesson	21.3	21.2	21.1	21.3	21.2	21.1	21.1	21.1	21.1	21.1	21.1	21.1	21.3

22 Hydrocarbon Compounds

FOUNDATIONS for Learning

What Dissolves What?

1. Place 3 pea-sized dots of petroleum jelly 10 cm apart on a glass plate.
2. Add 5 drops of rubbing alcohol to one dot. Add 5 drops of mineral oil to the second. Add 5 drops of water to the third.
3. Use a clean toothpick to mix each jelly dot and liquid very well. Observe whether the petroleum jelly appears to dissolve.
4. Repeat Steps 1–3 on a new glass plate. Use candle wax instead of petroleum jelly.

Predict Use your observations to describe the solubility of the materials you tested.

PearsonChem.com

UntamedScience™

Take a video field trip with the Untamed Science crew as they follow the processing journey of crude oil all the way to a car's gas tank.

Turkmenistan has some of the world's largest deposits of natural gas. This natural gas deposit in the city of Darvaza has been burning for over three decades!

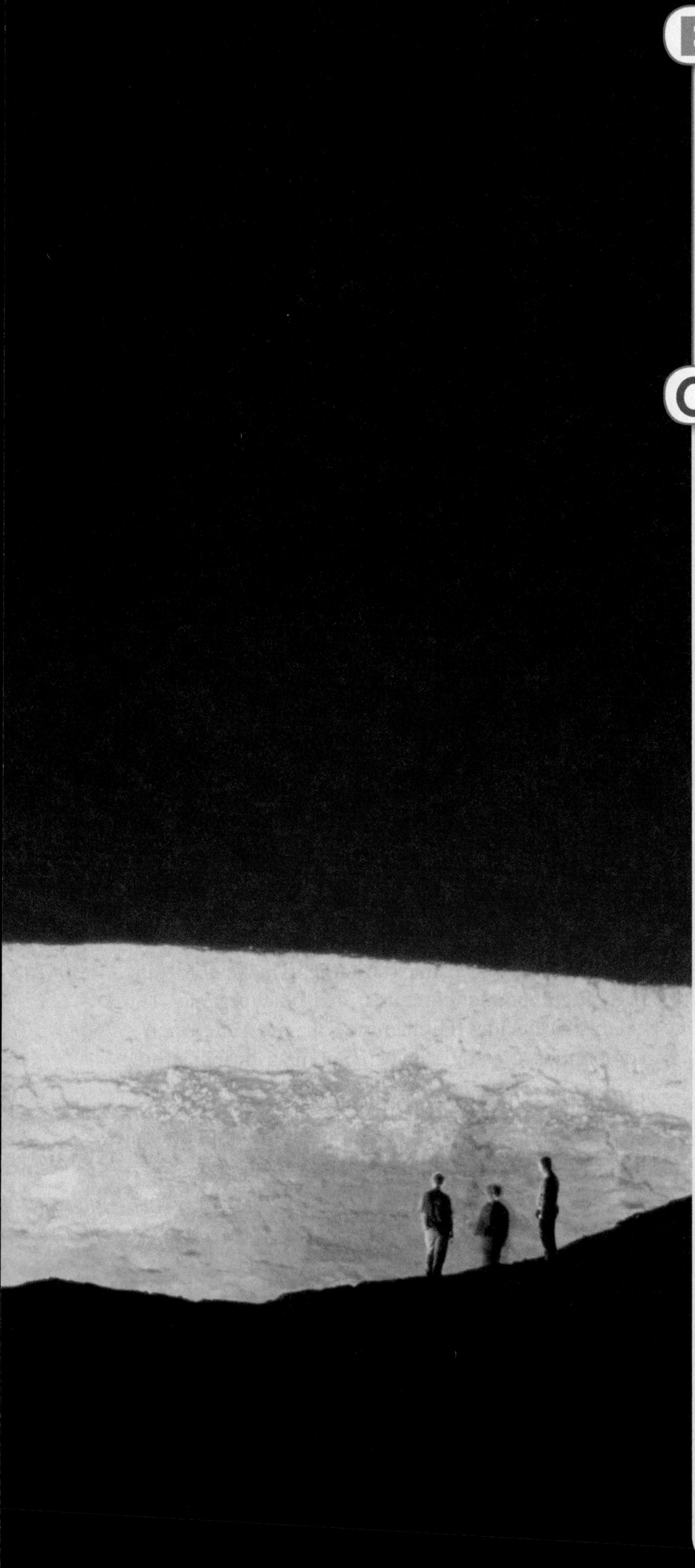

CARBON CHEMISTRY

Essential Questions:

1. *How are hydrocarbons named?*
2. *What are the general properties of hydrocarbons?*

CHEMYSTERY

Nose for Hire

Anthony spotted a poster asking for people to take part in a smell test. The poster offered each person $50 for less than an hour of time. So he decided to go for it.

Anthony signed up for the study. A researcher asked him to smell two chemical samples. The first one smelled like a freshly cut orange. The second one had an odor that reminded him of pine trees.

Anthony was curious. "What is that smell?" he asked. "Limonene," the researcher answered. "What about the second one?" Anthony asked. The researcher gave the same reply: "Limonene." Anthony was confused. How could two substances with the same name smell so different?

▶ Connect to the **BIG**IDEA As you read about hydrocarbons, think about why two compounds with the same name could have different properties.

22.1 Hydrocarbons

CHEMISTRY & YOU

Q: Why are some fossil fuels gases while others are liquids or solids? The gasoline used to fuel this motorcycle is a liquid at STP. Diesel fuel and kerosene are also liquids. Diesel fuel is used in some trucks and buses. Kerosene is used in some lanterns. Other fuels are gases or solids. For example, the fuel used in a furnace might be natural gas or a solid such as coal. All of these fuels contain mixtures of compounds called hydrocarbons. In this lesson, you will learn about the structure and properties of hydrocarbons.

Key Questions

Why does a carbon atom form four covalent bonds?

What are two possible arrangements of carbon atoms in an alkane?

BUILD Vocabulary

hydrocarbon an organic compound that contains only carbon and hydrogen

ROOT WORDS

The word *hydrocarbon* contains the root word *carbon*. This root word tells you that a hydrocarbon is a compound that must contain carbon atoms.

Organic Chemistry and Hydrocarbons

Scientists who lived about 200 years ago thought that only living organisms could make the carbon compounds found in living cells. Because the term *organic* means "related to or made by living things," these compounds were classified as organic compounds. The study of these compounds was known as organic chemistry. However, a German chemist, Friedrich Wöhler (1800–1882), changed the definition of organic chemistry. In 1828, Wöhler used an inorganic substance to make urea—an organic compound found in urine. Today, organic chemistry includes the chemistry of almost all carbon compounds, even ones that are not made by living things.

Introduction to Hydrocarbons There are many known organic compounds. In fact, new organic compounds are made every day. The simplest organic compounds are called hydrocarbons. By definition, a compound contains at least two kinds of elements. A **hydrocarbon** is an organic compound that contains only carbon and hydrogen. The two simplest hydrocarbons are methane (CH_4) and ethane (C_2H_6).

Natural gas is mostly methane. Methane is sometimes called marsh gas because it is found in swamps and other marshy places. Bacteria make methane as they break down dead plants. Livestock and termites also produce large quantities of methane as they digest food.

Carbon Bonds A carbon atom has four valence electrons. A hydrogen atom has only one valence electron. So one carbon atom can form a single covalent bond with four hydrogen atoms, as shown below.

$$\cdot\dot{\underset{\cdot}{C}}\cdot + 4H\cdot \longrightarrow H:\overset{H}{\underset{H}{\ddot{\underset{\cdot\cdot}{C}}}}:H$$

Carbon atom | Hydrogen atoms | Methane molecule

Because carbon has four valence electrons, a carbon atom always forms four covalent bonds. Remembering the number of valence electrons will help you to write correct structures for organic compounds.

Methane has only one carbon atom. But most other organic compounds have more than one carbon atom. In these cases, there is a bond between the carbon atoms. For example, there is a carbon-carbon bond in ethane. Two carbon atoms share a pair of electrons in an ethane molecule. The remaining six valence electrons form bonding pairs with the electrons from six hydrogen atoms, as shown below.

$$2\cdot\dot{\underset{\cdot}{C}}\cdot + 6H\cdot \longrightarrow \cdot\dot{\underset{\cdot}{C}}:\dot{\underset{\cdot}{C}}\cdot + 6H\cdot \longrightarrow H:\overset{H}{\underset{H}{\ddot{\underset{\cdot\cdot}{C}}}}:\overset{H}{\underset{H}{\ddot{\underset{\cdot\cdot}{C}}}}:H$$

Carbon atoms | Hydrogen atoms | Ethane molecule

Carbon's ability to form stable carbon-carbon bonds is one reason that carbon can form so many different compounds.

Representing Hydrocarbons The table below shows the structural formulas, ball-and-stick models, and space-filling models for methane and ethane. Structural formulas are an easy way to show how the atoms in a molecule are connected together. But they do not show how the atoms in a molecule are arranged in space. Three-dimensional molecular models represent the shapes of molecules more accurately. Hybrid orbital theory and VSEPR theory are used to predict the molecular shapes. In this chapter and the next chapter, organic molecules will be represented in the three ways shown in the table.

Different Ways of Representing Hydrocarbons

Name	Structural formula	Ball-and-stick model	Space-filling model
Methane	$\begin{array}{c}H\\ \mid\\ H—C—H\\ \mid\\ H\end{array}$		
Ethane	$\begin{array}{c}H\;\;H\\ \mid\;\;\;\mid\\ H—C—C—H\\ \mid\;\;\;\mid\\ H\;\;H\end{array}$		

BUILD Understanding

Cluster Diagram Make a cluster diagram to organize the different types of hydrocarbons as you read the chapter. Use a different color for each group.

alkane a hydrocarbon in which there are only single covalent bonds

straight-chain alkane an alkane in which the carbon atoms bond together to form a single chain

USING PRIOR KNOWLEDGE

According to VSEPR theory, a molecule's valence-electron pairs stay as far apart as possible. For this reason, straight-chain alkanes are not truly straight. You can see the zig-zag pattern of the carbon chains in the figures below.

Go online to learn more about hydrocarbon fuels.

Properties of Hydrocarbons The electron pair in a carbon-hydrogen bond is shared almost equally between the carbon and the hydrogen. This is also true in a carbon-carbon bond. Because the electrons are shared equally, hydrocarbons are nonpolar molecules. Nonpolar molecules are attracted to one another by weak van der Waals forces. So hydrocarbons that have low molar masses tend to be gases or liquids that boil at a low temperature.

Remember the general rule "like dissolves like." This rule means that two nonpolar compounds will form a solution. Two polar compounds will also form a solution. But a nonpolar compound and a polar compound will not form a solution. For example, oil floats on top of water. The nonpolar hydrocarbon molecules in oil do not mix with polar water molecules.

Key Question Why does a carbon atom form four covalent bonds? **A carbon atom always forms four covalent bonds because it has four valence electrons.**

Alkanes

Methane and ethane are examples of alkanes. An **alkane** is a hydrocarbon in which there are only single covalent bonds. All of the carbon-carbon bonds in alkanes are single covalent bonds. All other bonds in an alkane are carbon-hydrogen bonds. The carbon atoms in an alkane can be arranged in a straight chain or in a chain that has branches.

Straight-Chain Alkanes A **straight-chain alkane** is an alkane in which the carbon atoms bond together to form a single chain. Ethane is the simplest straight-chain alkane. The figure below shows models and uses of propane and butane. Propane (C_3H_8) has three carbon atoms bonded in a chain. Butane (C_4H_{10}) has a chain of four carbon atoms. The hydrogen atoms are attached to the carbon atoms that form the chain.

Hydrocarbon Fuels

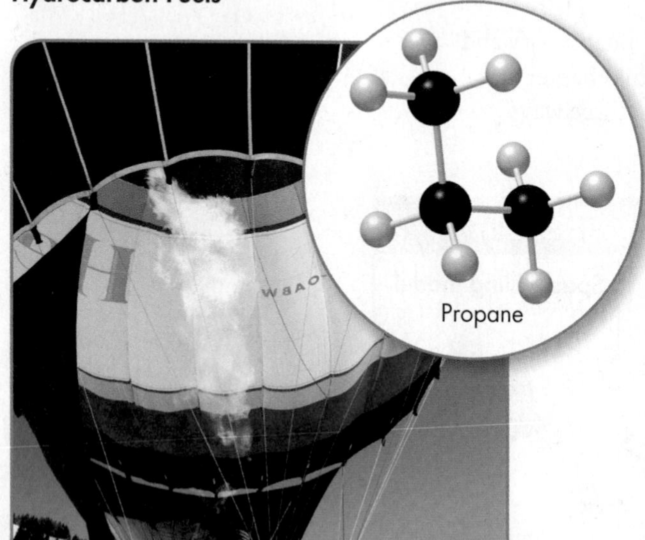

Propane is used to fuel the burners in hot-air balloons.

Butane gas is used as a fuel for camping stoves.

Properties of Straight-Chain Alkanes This graph shows how the melting and boiling points vary with the number of carbons in straight-chain alkanes.

Go to your Chemistry Skills and Math Workbook to practice interpreting graphs.

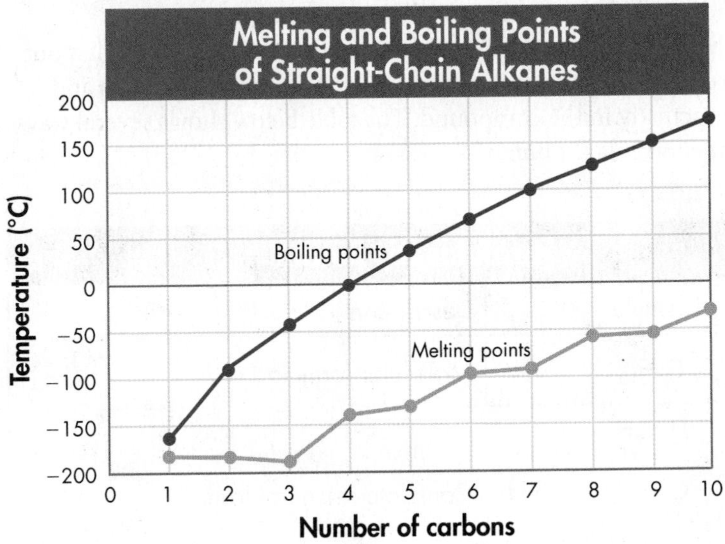

▶ **Properties of Straight-Chain Alkanes** Look at the graph above. It shows the relationship between the number of carbons in a straight-chain alkane and the melting and boiling points. As the number of carbons in the chain increases, the melting and boiling points increase. Room temperature is about 22°C. The boiling points of methane, ethane, propane, and butane are all below room temperature. So, these alkanes are gases at room temperature. The other alkanes included in the graph are liquids at room temperature.

▶ **Naming Straight-Chain Alkanes** The names of straight-chain alkanes follow the rules of the International Union of Pure and Applied Chemistry (IUPAC). Every alkane has a name that ends with the suffix *-ane.* The official names and the common names are the same for the straight-chain alkanes with one to four carbon atoms. They are methane, ethane, propane, and butane. A mixture of Latin and Greek prefixes are used to name the hydrocarbons that have straight chains longer than four carbon atoms. The prefixes are *pent-* for five, *hex-* for six, *hept-* for seven, and so on. Use the table below to review the names of the first ten straight-chain alkanes.

Straight-Chain Alkanes

Name	Formula	Name	Formula
Methane	CH_4	Hexane	C_6H_{14}
Ethane	C_2H_6	Heptane	C_7H_{16}
Propane	C_3H_8	Octane	C_8H_{18}
Butane	C_4H_{10}	Nonane	C_9H_{20}
Pentane	C_5H_{12}	Decane	$C_{10}H_{22}$

BUILD Connections

You have probably seen octane ratings on gasoline pumps. Regular gasoline has an octane rating of 87. But what does this rating mean? Knocking is the sound an engine makes when gasoline ignites too soon. Knocking reduces a vehicle's performance and can eventually lead to engine damage. Gasoline with an octane rating of 87 prevents knocking as much as a mixture that is 87 percent isooctane by volume.

condensed structural formula a structural formula with some bonds and/or atoms left out

ROOT WORDS

The word *condensed* contains the root word *dense*. *Dense* means "thick" or "crowded." You can think of a condensed structural formula as one that has been made denser by removing atoms or bonds from the formula.

In each condensed structural formula, certain features of the complete structural formula are left out.

▶ **Drawing Structural Formulas for Straight-Chain Alkanes** There are a few steps involved in drawing the structural formula for a straight-chain alkane. First, write a "C" for each carbon in the formula. Then complete the formula by writing an "H" for each hydrogen and adding lines to represent covalent bonds. A complete structural formula shows all the atoms and bonds in a molecule. Sometimes, however, a shorthand or condensed structural formula works just as well. In a **condensed structural formula,** some bonds and/or atoms are left out of the structural formula. It is understood that the missing bonds and atoms are actually in the compound. The table below shows several ways to write the formula for butane.

Formulas for Butane

Formula	Description
C_4H_{10}	Molecular formula
H—C(H)(H)—C(H)(H)—C(H)(H)—C(H)(H)—H	Complete structural formula
$CH_3—CH_2—CH_2—CH_3$	Condensed structural formula (C—H bonds understood)
$CH_3CH_2CH_2CH_3$	Condensed structural formula (C—H and C—C bonds understood)
$CH_3(CH_2)_2CH_3$	Condensed structural formula (all bonds understood)
(zigzag line)	Line-angle formula (carbons and hydrogens understood) Carbon atoms are located at each intersection and at the ends of lines.

Let's look more carefully at the condensed structural formula $CH_3(CH_2)_2CH_3$. The CH_2 unit in parentheses is called a methylene group. The subscript *2* to the right of the parentheses indicates that two methylene groups are linked together. This shorthand method for writing the formula for butane is shown below.

$$CH_3(CH_2)_2CH_3$$

Methylene unit — Subscript

For other straight-chain alkanes, the subscript after the parentheses in the condensed structural formula would be different. This subscript always indicates how many methylene groups are linked together.

Sample Problem 22.1

Drawing Structural Formulas for Alkanes

Draw complete structural formulas for the straight-chain alkanes that have:

a. three carbon atoms **b.** four carbon atoms

1 Analyze **Identify the relevant concepts.**
In an alkane, each carbon atom forms four covalent bonds to hydrogen or to other carbon atoms. The carbon atoms are in a straight line.

2 Solve **Apply the concepts to this problem.**

Draw the appropriate number of carbons connected in a straight line.

a. C—C—C **b.** C—C—C—C

Draw four bonds on each carbon.

Add the hydrogens to the bonds.

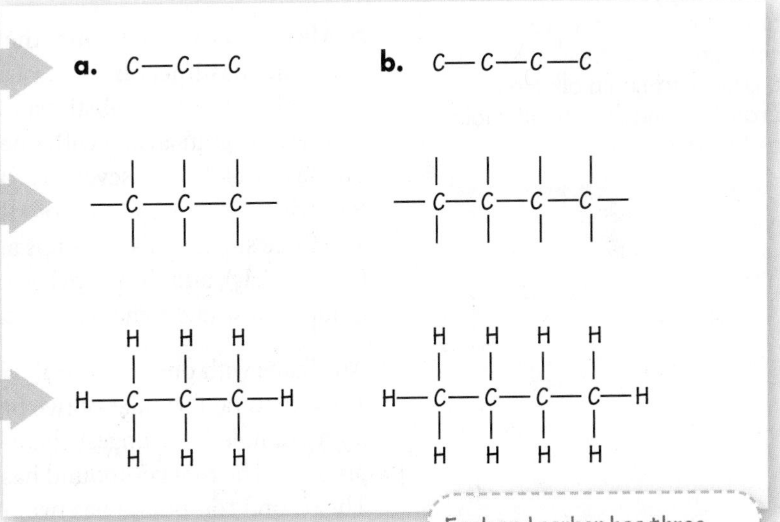

Each end carbon has three hydrogens. Each carbon within the chain has two hydrogens.

Practice Problems

1. Draw complete structural formulas for the straight-chain alkanes with five and six carbon atoms.

1 Analyze **Identify the relevant concepts.**

2 Solve **Apply the concepts to this problem.**

2. How many single bonds are there in a propane molecule?

3. Challenge Draw the structural formula for octane. How many hydrogen atoms are in an octane molecule?

Hint: Each carbon has four bonds.

substituent an atom or group of atoms that can take the place of a hydrogen atom on a parent hydrocarbon molecule

alkyl group a hydrocarbon substituent that is derived from an alkane

branched-chain alkane an alkane with one or more alkyl groups

USING PRIOR KNOWLEDGE

When you think of the word *branched,* you probably think of the branches in a tree. You can think of the alkyl groups in a branched-chain alkane as branches and the parent chain as the tree trunk.

Branched-Chain Alkanes Alkanes and other hydrocarbons do not always have carbon atoms bonded in straight chains. A carbon atom forms four covalent bonds that can bond to as many as four other carbons. When a carbon atom bonds with three or four other carbons, branched chains form. In organic chemistry, branches on a hydrocarbon chain are thought of as replacing a hydrogen atom on the chain. An atom or group of atoms that can take the place of a hydrogen atom on a parent hydrocarbon molecule is called a **substituent.** Look at the diagrams below. The longest continuous carbon chain of a branched-chain hydrocarbon is called the parent alkane. All other carbon atoms or groups of carbon atoms are substituents. In Chapter 23, you will study other substituents that can take the place of hydrogen.

Substituent: C attached to the middle carbon of C—C—C (Parent alkane (propane))

Substituents: three C atoms attached to carbons 2, 3 and 4 of C—C—C—C—C—C (Parent alkane (hexane))

▶ Alkyl Groups Sometimes the substituent is made from an alkane. In these cases, the substituent is a hydrocarbon with only single covalent bonds. This kind of hydrocarbon substituent is called an **alkyl group.** You can think of an alkyl group as an alkane with one of the hydrogens removed. An alkyl group can be one carbon or several carbons long. Alkyl groups are named by removing the *-ane* ending from the parent hydrocarbon name and adding *-yl.* The three smallest alkyl groups are the methyl group ($—CH_3$), the ethyl group ($—CH_2CH_3$), and the propyl group ($—CH_2CH_2CH_3$). A substituent alkyl group on a straight-chain hydrocarbon forms branches to the chain.

An alkane with one or more alkyl groups is called a **branched-chain alkane.** The structural formulas of two branched-chain alkanes are shown below. In both examples, the longest chain has three carbons. So the parent chains are propane. The first compound has one methyl group attached to the propane. The second compound has two methyl groups.

$$CH_3—CH(CH_3)—CH_3 \qquad CH_3—C(CH_3)_2—CH_3$$

▶ Naming and Drawing Structures The first compound is called 2-methylpropane. The root word (ending in *-ane*) tells you what the parent hydrocarbon is. The part of the word that ends in *-yl* tells you what the substituents are. The number written before the substituent group tells you where the substituent is attached.

The steps on the next page guide you in naming branched-chain alkanes. To draw the structural formula based on the name, start with the parent chain of carbons. Number the carbons. Attach the substituents to the parent chain at the correct location. Complete the structural formula by adding hydrogens so each carbon has four bonds.

Key Question What are two possible arrangements of carbon atoms in an alkane? **The carbon atoms in an alkane can be arranged in a straight chain or in a chain that has branches.**

Rules for Naming Branched-Chain Alkanes

The IUPAC rules for naming branched-chain alkanes are quite straightforward. The name of a branched-chain alkane is based on the name of the longest continuous carbon chain. Each substituent is named according to the length of its chain and numbered according to its position on the main chain. You can use the rules to name any compound, including the one shown at the right.

$$CH_3-CH_2-CH_2-\underset{\underset{CH_3}{|}{CH_2}}{\underset{|}{CH}}-\underset{\underset{|}{CH_3}}{CH}-\underset{\underset{|}{CH_3}}{CH}-CH_3$$

1. Find the longest continuous chain of carbons in the molecule. This chain is considered the parent hydrocarbon.

$$CH_3-CH_2-CH_2-\underset{\underset{CH_3}{|}{CH_2}}{\underset{|}{CH}}-\underset{\underset{|}{CH_3}}{CH}-\underset{\underset{|}{CH_3}}{CH}-CH_3$$

The longest chain is highlighted to the right. It contains seven carbon atoms. So, the parent hydrocarbon is heptane.

2. Number the carbons in the main chain in sequence. To do this, start at the end that will give the substituent groups attached to the chain the smallest numbers.

$$\overset{7}{CH_3}-\overset{6}{CH_2}-\overset{5}{CH_2}-\underset{\underset{CH_3}{|}{CH_2}}{\underset{|}{\overset{4}{CH}}}-\underset{\underset{|}{CH_3}}{\overset{3}{CH}}-\underset{\underset{|}{CH_3}}{\overset{2}{CH}}-\overset{1}{CH_3}$$

Numbering the chain from right to left gives the substituents the lowest numbers (2, 3, and 4). Numbering the chain the other way violates the rule.

3. Add numbers to the names of the substituent groups to identify their positions on the chain. These numbers become prefixes to the name of the substituent group.

The substituents and positions are 2-methyl, 3-methyl, and 4-ethyl.

4. Use prefixes to indicate when the same group appears more than once in the structural formula. Common prefixes are *di-* (twice), *tri-* (three times), and *tetra-* (four times).

The two methyl groups are combined as 2,3-dimethyl.

5. List the names of alkyl substituents in alphabetical order. When you alphabetize, ignore the prefixes *di-*, *tri-*, and so on.

The 4-ethyl group is listed first, followed by 2,3-dimethyl.

6. Combine all the parts and use the correct punctuation. Write the entire name without any spaces. Use commas to separate numbers. Use hyphens to separate numbers and words.

The correct name of the compound is 4-ethyl-2,3-dimethylheptane. It is incorrect to write the name as 4-ethyl-2,3-dimethyl heptane.

Sample Problem 22.2

Naming Branched-Chain Alkanes

Name this compound using the IUPAC system.
Notice that the longest chain is not written in a straight line.

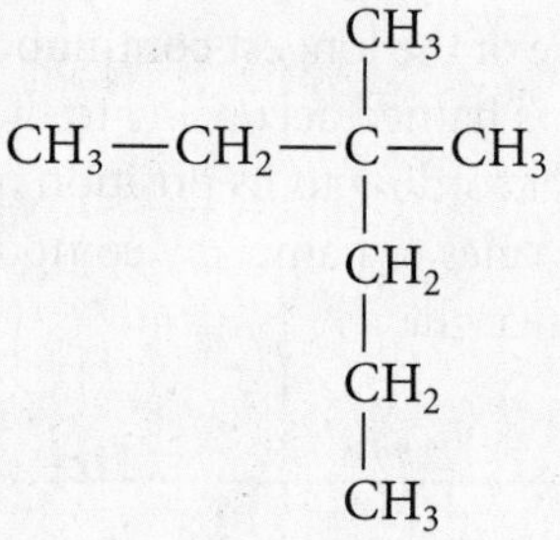

$$CH_3-CH_2-C(CH_3)(CH_3)-CH_2-CH_2-CH_3$$

(Structure: a CH$_3$ above and a CH$_2$–CH$_2$–CH$_3$ chain below the central C.)

1 Analyze Identify the relevant concepts. The longest chain of carbons is the parent chain. Number the carbons to give the first substituent the lowest number. List the substituents in alphabetical order with numbers separated by commas. Separate numbers and words with hyphens.

2 Solve Apply the concepts to this problem.

Identify the longest carbon chain in the molecule. Number the carbons in the chain.

The longest chain has six carbons, so the name ends with hexane.

Identify the substituents and their positions on the parent hydrocarbon. Write the prefix.

There are two methyl substituents on carbon 3. The prefix is 3,3-dimethyl.

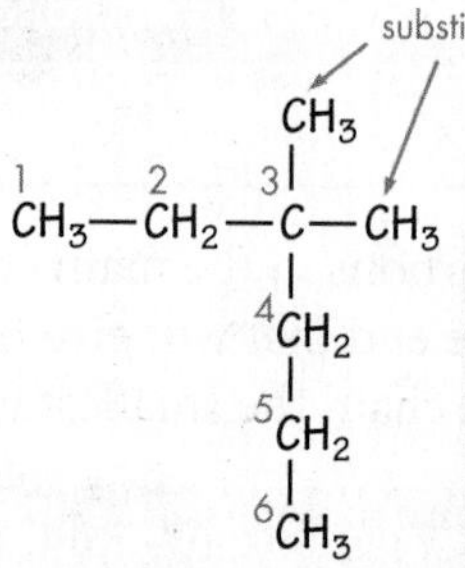

Structure with numbered carbons: 1 CH$_3$ — 2 CH$_2$ — 3 C(CH$_3$)(CH$_3$) — 4 CH$_2$ — 5 CH$_2$ — 6 CH$_3$ (substituents: the two CH$_3$ groups on carbon 3)

Remember to start numbering at the end that gives the substituents the smallest numbers!

Combine the prefix and the name of the longest chain.

The correct IUPAC name is **3,3-dimethylhexane.**

Practice Problems

4. Name the following compound according to the IUPAC system.

$$CH_2-CH_2-CH-CH_2-CH_3$$

(with CH$_3$ below the first CH$_2$, and CH$_2$–CH$_3$ below the CH)

1 Analyze Identify the relevant concepts.

2 Solve Apply the concepts to this problem.

Remember: The longest chain is not always written in a straight line.

5. Name the following compound according to the IUPAC system.

$$CH_3-CH_2-CH(CH_3)-CH_3$$

Sample Problem 22.3

Drawing Structural Formulas for Branched-Chain Alkanes

Draw the structural formula for 2,2,4-trimethylpentane, or isooctane.

1 Analyze Identify the relevant concepts. The part of the name that ends in *-ane* indicates the parent structure. Prefixes indicate the types of substituents, the number of times each appears, and their locations on the parent chain. Hydrogens are added as needed.

2 Solve Apply the concepts to this problem.

Identify the name of the parent chain and the prefix for the substituents.

2,2,4-trimethylpentane (prefix: 2,2,4-trimethyl; parent: pentane)

The parent structure is pentane.
The prefix is 2,2,4-trimethyl-.

Draw the carbons in the parent chain.

Pentane has five carbon atoms. C—C—C—C—C

Number the carbon atoms.

C—C—C—C—C
1 2 3 4 5

Identify the number and type of substituents.

The *trimethyl-* prefix indicates there are three methyl groups.

Attach the substituents to the carbons indicated in the prefix.

The numbers in the prefix *2,2,4-trimethyl-* indicate that there are two methyl groups on carbon 2 and one methyl group on carbon 4.

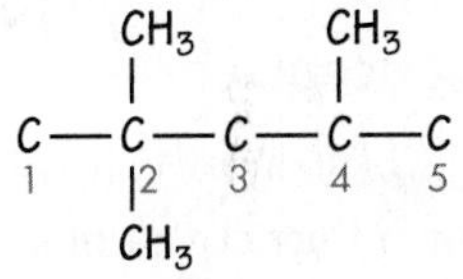

```
       CH3       CH3
        |         |
   C —— C —— C —— C —— C
   1    |2   3    4    5
       CH3
```

Finish by adding hydrogens so that each carbon has four bonds.

A total of nine hydrogens are needed to complete the structure.

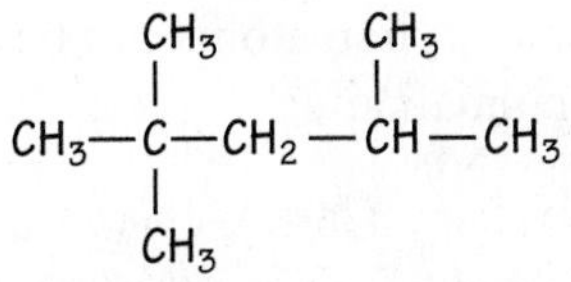

```
        CH3        CH3
         |          |
   CH3 — C — CH2 — CH — CH3
         |
        CH3
```

Be careful: Each carbon has four, and only four, bonds.

Practice Problems

6. Draw the structural formula for 2,3-dimethylhexane.

❶ Analyze **Identify the relevant concepts.**

❷ Solve **Apply the concepts to this problem.**

TO GET YOU STARTED...

Here is the carbon chain for the parent alkane:

Hexane

C—C—C—C—C—C

7. Write a condensed structural formula for 2,2-dimethylbutane.

8. Write a condensed structural formula for 3-methylhexane.

Hint: The prefix in the name of the parent alkane tells you how many carbon atoms they contain. The prefix *oct-* means eight.

9. Challenge Draw the structural formula for 4-ethyl-2,3,4-trimethyloctane.

22.1 LessonCheck

Key Concept Check

10. Review Why do carbon atoms form four covalent bonds?

11. Identify What are two ways that carbon atoms can be arranged in an alkane?

Vocabulary Check

Choose a highlighted term from the lesson to complete each sentence correctly.

12. A(n) __________ is an alkane that has attached alkyl groups.

13. A(n) __________ is a hydrocarbon with only single covalent bonds.

Think Critically

14. Infer Mineral oil is a mixture of hydrocarbons. Explain why it is not soluble in water.

15. Describe Draw the complete structural formula for 3-ethylhexane.

16. Identify Name the following alkanes using the IUPAC system.

a.

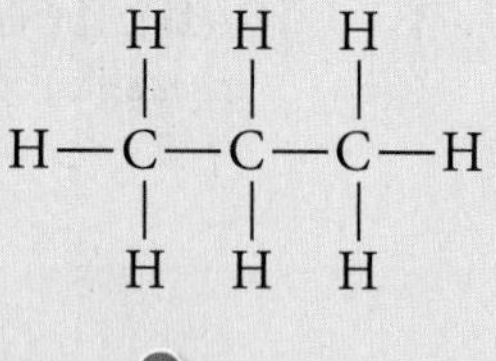

```
   H  H  H
   |  |  |
H—C—C—C—H
   |  |  |
   H  H  H
```

b.

```
CH3—CH—CH—CH2—CH3
     |    |
    CH3  CH3
```

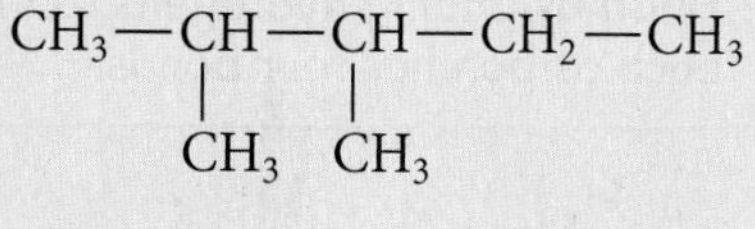

CHEMISTRY & YOU

17. Explain why some hydrocarbon fuels are gases and others are liquids. (Hint: See page 723.)

BIGIDEA CARBON CHEMISTRY

18. Describe the bond polarity of alkane molecules.

22.2 Unsaturated Hydrocarbons

CHEMISTRY & YOU

Q: What does it mean if a fat is unsaturated? You may have read nutrition labels that listed saturated and unsaturated fat content. For example, olives are high in unsaturated fat but low in saturated fat. On the other hand, butter is high in saturated fat. In this lesson, you'll find out what the terms saturated and unsaturated mean.

Key Questions

What are the structural characteristics of alkenes?

What are the structural characteristics of alkynes?

saturated compound an organic compound that contains only single carbon-carbon bonds

unsaturated compound an organic compound that contains double or triple carbon-carbon bonds

alkene a hydrocarbon that contains one or more carbon-carbon double covalent bonds

PREFIXES

The prefix *un-* means "not." So an unsaturated compound is not saturated, which means it does not have the maximum number of hydrogen atoms per carbon atom.

Alkenes

An organic compound that has only single covalent bonds is called a **saturated compound.** For example, alkanes are saturated compounds. Each carbon is bonded to as many hydrogen atoms as possible. An organic compound that contains double or triple carbon-carbon bonds is called an **unsaturated compound.** Unlike a saturated compound, an unsaturated compound does not contain the maximum number of hydrogen atoms.

Alkenes are a type of unsaturated compound. An **alkene** is a hydrocarbon that contains one or more carbon-carbon double covalent bonds. A carbon-carbon double bond is shown in structural formulas as two parallel lines. At least one carbon-carbon bond in an alkene is a double covalent bond. Other bonds may be single carbon-carbon bonds and carbon-hydrogen bonds.

Ethene (C_2H_4) is the simplest alkene. It is often called by the common name ethylene. The figure below shows the ball-and-stick model and condensed structural formula of ethene. Notice ethene contains two carbon atoms connected by a double bond. It has two fewer hydrogen atoms than ethane. The atoms in ethene cannot rotate freely around the double bond. For this reason, they lie in a single plane.

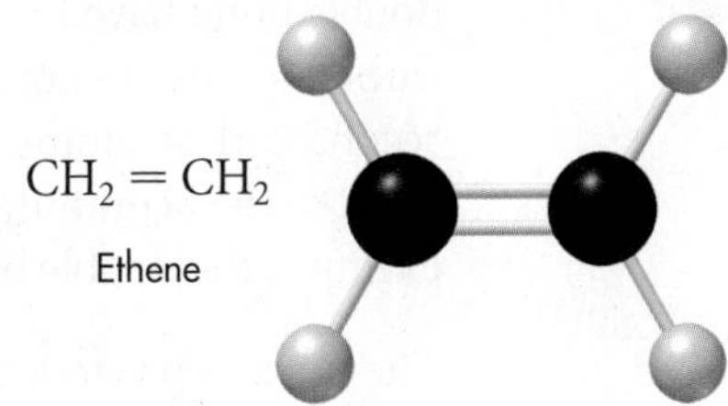

BUILD Understanding

Compare and Contrast Table Build a compare and contrast table to take notes about alkanes, alkenes, and alkynes. As you read this lesson, add details about each type of hydrocarbon.

Naming Alkenes The IUPAC system for naming alkenes is similar to the system for naming alkanes. However, the location of the double bond is important. Some examples of the structures and IUPAC names of simple alkenes are shown below.

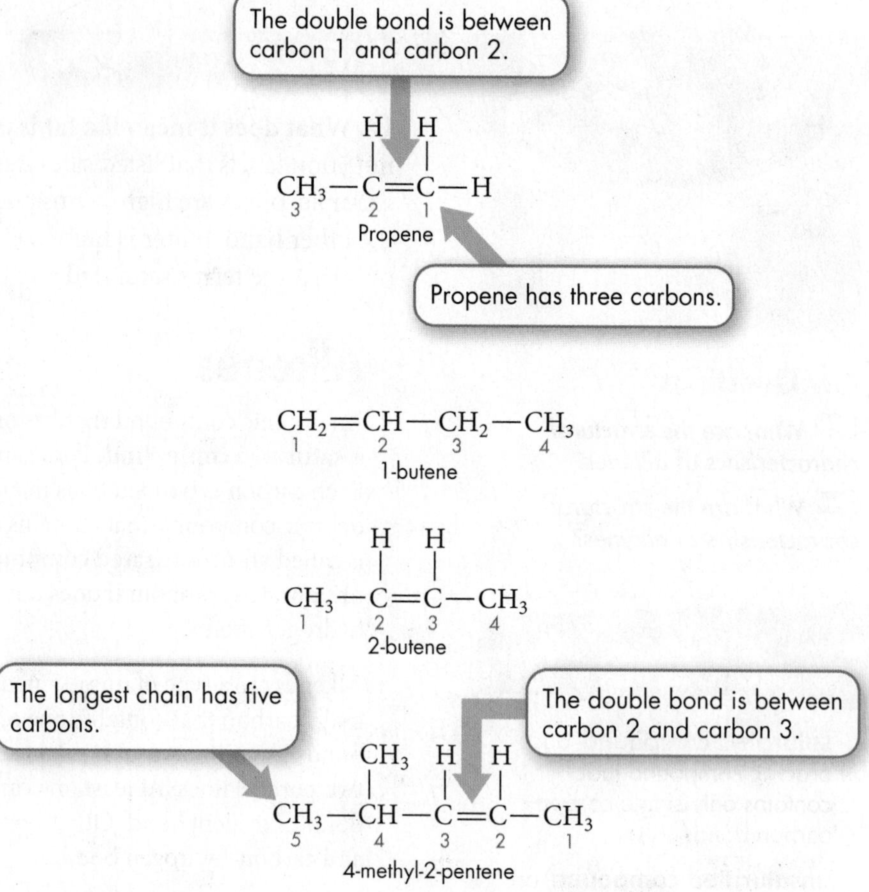

The double bond is between carbon 1 and carbon 2.
Propene
Propene has three carbons.
1-butene
2-butene
The longest chain has five carbons.
The double bond is between carbon 2 and carbon 3.
4-methyl-2-pentene

The first step to name an alkene is to find the longest chain in the molecule that contains the double bond. This chain is the parent alkene. It has the root name of the alkane with the same number of carbons plus the ending *-ene*. For example, both propene and propane contain three carbon atoms. You know propene contains a double bond because it ends in *-ene*.

The second step is to number the carbon chain so that the carbon atoms of the double bond have the lowest possible numbers. For example, in 1-butene, the carbon atoms are numbered so that the double bond is between the first and second carbon atoms. You add the number of the first carbon in the double bond to the beginning of the name of the parent alkene. In 2-butene, for example, the double bond is between the second and third carbon atoms.

The third step is to identify the substituent groups and their positions on the chain. Follow the same rules you used for alkanes to name and number substituents. Finally, use the correct punctuation when you combine the name of the parent alkene and the substituent groups.

Key Question What are the structural characteristics of alkenes? **At least one carbon-carbon bond in an alkene is a double covalent bond. Other bonds may be single carbon-carbon bonds and carbon-hydrogen bonds.**

Alkynes

A hydrocarbon that contains one or more carbon-carbon triple covalent bonds is called an **alkyne.** Other bonds in an alkyne may be single or double carbon-carbon bonds and carbon-hydrogen bonds. Like alkenes, alkynes are unsaturated compounds. The carbon-carbon triple bond in alkynes is shown in structural formulas as three parallel lines.

Alkynes are not common in nature. The simplest alkyne is ethyne (C_2H_2), which has the common name acetylene. Acetylene is the fuel burned in oxyacetylene torches used to weld metal. The figure below shows that ethyne is a linear molecule. This is because the single bonds in the carbon-carbon triple bond are separated by an angle of 180°. As for naming alkynes, you can follow the same rules as for naming alkenes.

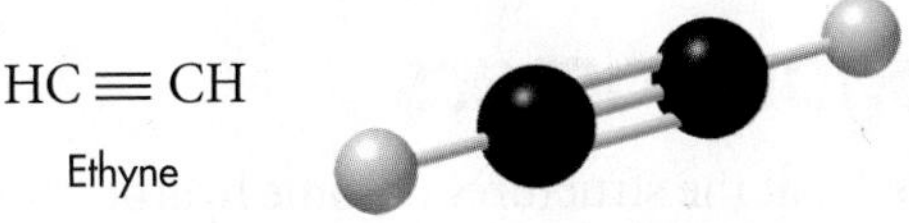

Like alkanes, the major attractions between alkenes and alkynes are weak van der Waals forces. As a result, a double or triple bond in a hydrocarbon does not have a big effect on physical properties. For example, the boiling points for alkanes, alkenes, and alkynes with the same number of carbon atoms are similar.

Key Question What are the structural characteristics of alkynes? **At least one carbon-carbon bond in an alkyne is a triple covalent bond. Other bonds may be single or double carbon-carbon bonds and carbon-hydrogen bonds.**

alkyne a hydrocarbon that contains one or more carbon-carbon triple covalent bonds

SUFFIXES

In chemistry, the suffixes *-ane*, *-ene*, and *-yne* are used to describe whether a hydrocarbon has a single, double, or triple bond. Knowing these suffixes will help you name and identify the structure of hydrocarbons. You should memorize that *-ane* means "single bond," *-ene* means "double bond," and *-yne* means "triple bond."

22.2 LessonCheck

Key Concept Check

19. Review Describe the bonding between atoms in an alkene.

20. Identify What types of bonds are present in an alkyne?

Vocabulary Check

Choose a highlighted term from the lesson to complete each sentence correctly.

21. A(n) __________ is a hydrocarbon that contains at least one double bond.

22. A(n) __________ is an organic compound that contains the maximum number of hydrogen atoms per carbon atom.

Think Critically

23. Explain How does the number of hydrogen atoms in propyne compare to the number of hydrogen atoms in propene? Explain.

24. Make Generalizations How do the boiling points of alkenes and alkynes compare to those of alkanes?

CHEMISTRY & YOU

25. Describe how the structure of saturated fats differs from the structure of unsaturated fats. (Hint: See page 731.)

22.3 Isomers

CHEMISTRY & YOU

Q: How do isomers help you see? Chemistry in your eyes helps you see. Light entering the eye causes a change in the structure of retinal molecules in your eye. Before the light strikes, the three-dimensional retinal molecules appear bent. Afterward, the molecules appear relatively straight. This structural change is part of the biological processes that help you see.

Key Questions

How do the properties of constitutional isomers differ?

What are two types of stereoisomers?

isomers compounds that have the same molecular formula but different molecular structures

constitutional isomers compounds that have the same molecular formula, but the atoms are joined together differently

stereoisomers molecules in which the atoms are joined in the same order, but the position of atoms in space is different

***cis-trans* isomers** molecules in which the spatial positions of the groups differ around a double bond even though the atoms are joined in the same order

PREFIXES

The prefix *iso-* means "equal." The chemical formulas of isomers are equal, even though their structures are different.

Constitutional Isomers

You may have noticed that the structures of some hydrocarbons differ only in the positions of substituents or the positions of multiple bonds. Look at the structural formulas and models of butane and 2-methylpropane below.

$CH_3—CH_2—CH_2—CH_3$

Butane (C_4H_{10})
(bp −0.5°C)

CH_3
|
$CH_3—CH—CH_3$

2-methylpropane (C_4H_{10})
(bp −11.7°C)

Both butane and 2-methylpropane have the molecular formula C_4H_{10}, but their atoms are arranged differently. They are different substances because their structures are different. Compounds that have the same molecular formula but different molecular structures are called **isomers.**

Butane and 2-methylpropane are constitutional isomers, or structural isomers. **Constitutional isomers** are compounds that have the same molecular formula, but the atoms are joined together differently. Constitutional isomers have different chemical properties and physical properties. For example, hydrocarbon isomers that are more branched tend to have lower boiling points than isomers that are less branched.

Key Question How do the properties of constitutional isomers differ? **Constitutional isomers differ in physical properties, such as boiling point and melting point, and in chemical properties.**

Quick Lab

Purpose To build ball-and-stick models and name the nine constitutional isomers of heptane (C_7H_{16})

Materials

- **ball-and-stick molecular model kit** (Colors used for the elements in the kit may differ from those used in this book.)
- **pencil and paper**

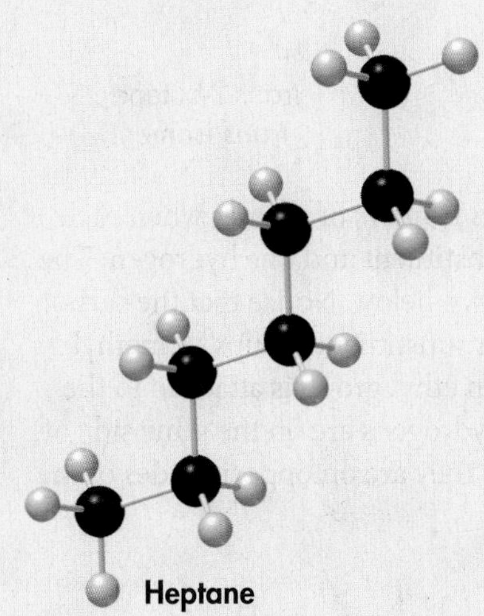
Heptane

Isomers of Heptane

Procedure

1. Build a model for the straight-chain isomer of C_7H_{16}. Draw the structural formula for this isomer.

2. Remove one carbon atom from the end of the chain and reattach it as a methyl substituent to form a branched-chain alkane. Draw the structural formula for this isomer.

3. Move the methyl group to a new position on the chain. Then draw this third isomer. Is there another position in which the methyl group can be placed on the chain of six carbons to form another isomer?

4. Make other constitutional isomers by shortening the longest straight chain and using the removed carbons as substituents. Draw the structural formulas for each isomer.

Analyze and Conclude

1. List What are the names of the nine constitutional isomers of C_7H_{16}?

2. Identify What is the shortest possible straight carbon chain in the group of heptane isomers?

3. Explain Why does each constitutional isomer have its own unique name?

Stereoisomers

Remember that molecules are three-dimensional structures. So molecules that have the same molecular formula may still be isomers even if their atoms are joined in exactly the same order. **Stereoisomers** are molecules in which the atoms are joined in the same order, but the positions of the atoms in space are different. Two types of stereoisomers are *cis-trans* isomers and enantiomers.

***Cis-Trans* Isomers** A double bond between two carbon atoms keeps other atoms in the molecule from rotating with respect to each other. Because of this, groups on either side of the double bond can have different positions in space. ***Cis-trans* isomers** have atoms joined in the same order, but the spatial positions of the groups differ. They are also called geometric isomers. *Cis-trans* isomers are most often molecules with double bonds. But these kinds of isomers are possible in other molecules. *Cis-trans* isomers have different physical and chemical properties.

enantiomers pairs of molecules that are mirror images and not superimposable

asymmetric carbon a carbon atom with four different atoms or groups attached

ROOT WORDS

In math, the word *symmetry* is used to describe shapes that are the same on both sides of a plane. The prefix *a-* means "not." Asymmetric carbons are carbon atoms that are not the same across any plane because they are attached to four different atoms or groups.

Look at the models of 2-butene below. As you can see, each molecule has four carbons and eight hydrogens. However, the methyl groups and hydrogen atoms have different positions with respect to the double bond. In the *cis* isomer, the methyl groups (CH_3) are on the same side of the double bond. In the *trans* isomer, the methyl groups are on opposite sides of the double bond.

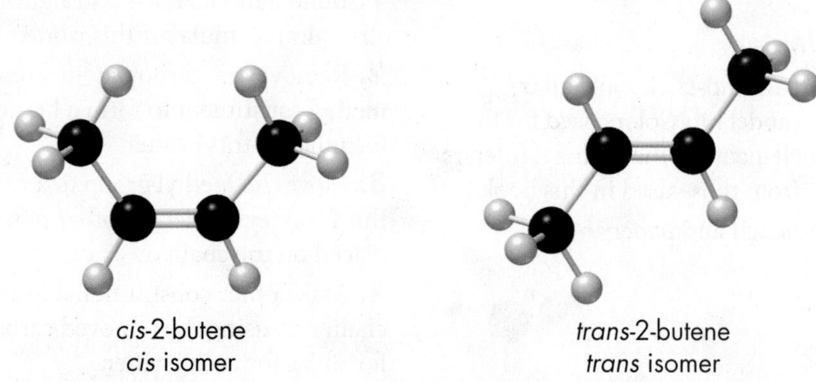

cis-2-butene
cis isomer

trans-2-butene
trans isomer

You should be able to identify *cis-trans* isomers of alkenes when each carbon of the double bond has one substituent and one hydrogen. The *cis-trans* isomers of 2-pentene are shown below. Notice that the carbon in the double bond may have different substituent groups. A methyl group is attached to one carbon and an ethyl group is attached to the other carbon. In the *cis-* isomer, the hydrogens are on the same side of the double bond. In the *trans-* isomer, they are on opposite sides of the double bond.

$$\begin{array}{ccc} CH_3 & & CH_2CH_3 \\ & C{=}C & \\ H & & H \end{array} \qquad \begin{array}{ccc} CH_3 & & H \\ & C{=}C & \\ H & & CH_2CH_3 \end{array}$$

cis-2-pentene

trans-2-pentene

Enantiomers Pairs of molecules that are mirror images and are not superimposable are called **enantiomers.** Enantiomers are also called optical isomers. They may be described as *right-handed* and *left-handed* because they are mirror images of each other. Enantiomers contain a central atom that has four different atoms or groups attached. A carbon atom with four different atoms or groups attached is an **asymmetric carbon.** For example, a carbon that is bonded to an H, an F, a Cl, and a Br atom is an asymmetric carbon. Unlike other isomers, enantiomers have identical physical properties such as boiling points and densities. Enantiomers interact differently with other molecules that have asymmetric carbons.

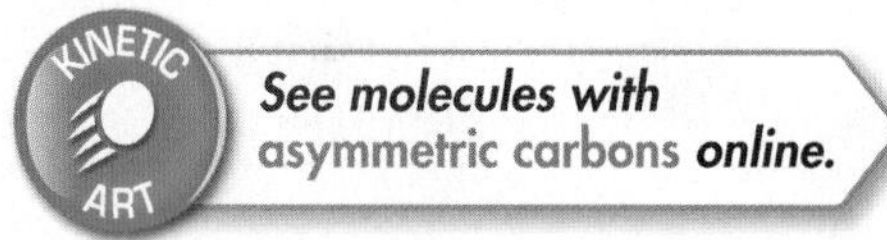

See molecules with asymmetric carbons ***online.***

Key Question What are two types of stereoisomers? **Two types of stereoisomers are *cis-trans* isomers and enantiomers.**

CHEMISTRY
TUTORIAL

Sample Problem 22.4

Identifying Asymmetric Carbon Atoms

Which compound has an asymmetric carbon?

a. CH_3CHCH_3 with OH attached to the central C

b. $CH_3CHCH_2CH_3$ with OH attached to the second C

Any carbon with two or more hydrogens attached cannot be asymmetric.

❶ Analyze **Identify the relevant concepts.**
An asymmetric carbon has four different substituents.

❷ Solve **Apply the concepts to this problem.**

Identify carbons that might be asymmetric.

Any carbon with two or more hydrogens attached cannot be asymmetric.

a. CH_3CHCH_3 with OH attached to the central C

b. $CH_3CHCH_2CH_3$ with OH attached to the second C

Draw all of the bonds around the carbon atom that might be asymmetric.

a. $CH_3—C—CH_3$ with H above and OH below the C

b. $CH_3—C—CH_2CH_3$ with H above and OH below the C

Compare the groups around the carbon atom.

a. There is one H, one OH, and two CH_3 groups.

b. There is one H, one OH, one CH_3, and one CH_2CH_3 group.

Decide whether the carbon is asymmetric.

a. Two groups are the same. This carbon is not asymmetric.

b. All of the groups are different. This carbon is asymmetric.

Compound *b* has an asymmetric carbon.

Practice Problems

26. Identify the asymmetric carbon, if any, in the following compound.

$$\underset{\displaystyle Cl}{CH_3\overset{}{C}HCHO}$$

❶ **Analyze Identify the relevant concepts.**

❷ **Solve Apply the concepts to this problem.**

27. Identify any asymmetric carbons in the following compound.

$$CH_3CH_2-\underset{\displaystyle F}{\overset{\displaystyle CH_3}{\overset{|}{\underset{|}{C}}}}-Br$$

28. Challenge Identify any asymmetric carbons in the compound dichloromethane, CH_2Cl_2.

Hint: All four groups attached to carbon must be different for the carbon to be asymmetric.

22.3 LessonCheck

Key Concept Check

29. Explain Why would you expect two constitutional isomers to have different properties such as boiling points?

30. Review Name two types of stereoisomers.

Vocabulary Check

Choose a highlighted term from the lesson to complete each sentence correctly.

31. *Cis-trans* isomers are __________.

32. Isomers in which atoms are connected in different ways are called __________.

Think Critically

33. Apply Concepts Draw structural formulas for the following alkenes. If a compound has *cis-trans* isomers, draw both the *cis* and *trans* forms.

a. 1-pentene　　**b.** 2-methyl-1-butene

34. Compare How are constitutional isomers and stereoisomers similar? How are they different?

35. Explain How can you identify an asymmetric carbon?

36. Summarize Draw a concept map to show how the following vocabulary words are related: isomers, constitutional isomers, stereoisomers, *cis-trans* isomers, and enantiomers.

CHEMISTRY & YOU

37. *Cis-trans* isomers aid in vision. Before light strikes, the retinal structure appears bent. After light strikes, the structure appears straight. Explain how the overall structure of a retinal molecule would appear relatively straight or bent depending on which *cis-trans* isomer it is. (Hint: See page 736.)

22.4 Hydrocarbon Rings

CHEMISTRY & YOU

Q: Does a compound have to smell nice to be classified as aromatic? You might think of perfume or flowers when you hear the word *aromatic.* But in organic chemistry, aromatic means something else.

Key Questions

What is the general structure of a cyclic hydrocarbon?

What is the most accurate description of bonding in benzene?

BUILD Vocabulary

cyclic hydrocarbon a compound that contains a hydrocarbon ring

cycloalkane a cyclic hydrocarbon that contains only single bonds

ROOT WORDS ___ The word parts *cycl-* or *cyclo-* mean "circle" or "ring." So, a cycloalkane is an alkane that forms a ring.

Cyclic Hydrocarbons

Not all hydrocarbons are straight chains or branched chains. The carbon chain in some hydrocarbon compounds is in the form of a ring. A compound that contains a hydrocarbon ring is called a **cyclic hydrocarbon.** Many molecules found in nature contain cyclic hydrocarbons. Rings made of five or six carbons are the most common.

Cyclic hydrocarbons can be either saturated or unsaturated. A cyclic hydrocarbon that contains only single bonds is called a **cycloalkane.** Determining the IUPAC name of cycloalkanes is similar to naming other alkanes. First, count the number of carbons in the ring. Then, use the alkane name that matches that number. Add the prefix *cyclo-* to the alkane name. Several examples of cycloalkanes are shown below.

Key Question What is the general structure of a cyclic hydrocarbon? **In cyclic hydrocarbon compounds, the carbon chain is in the form of a ring.**

Cycloalkanes
These compounds are all cycloalkanes.

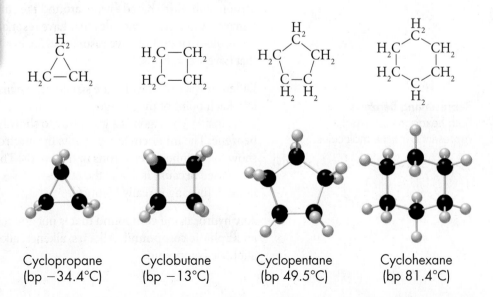

H_2C ring of 3 (CH_2)	H_2C ring of 4 (CH_2)	H_2C ring of 5 (CH_2)	H_2C ring of 6 (CH_2)
Cyclopropane (bp −34.4°C)	Cyclobutane (bp −13°C)	Cyclopentane (bp 49.5°C)	Cyclohexane (bp 81.4°C)

aromatic compound an organic compound that contains a benzene ring or other ring in which the bonding is like that of benzene

aliphatic compound any compound that is not an aromatic compound

ROOT WORDS

The word *aromatic* comes from the word *aroma,* which means "seasoning" or "spice." Aromatic compounds are often found in spices.

Aromatic Hydrocarbons

Could you use your nose to identify vanilla, cinnamon, and ginger? These compounds were originally called aromatic compounds because they have pleasant aromas. However, some aromatic compounds do not have any odor.

The Structure of Benzene Benzene is the simplest aromatic compound. An **aromatic compound** is an organic compound that contains a benzene ring or other ring in which the bonding is like that of benzene. Friedrich Kekulé (1829–1896) was the first person to describe the structure of a benzene molecule. Look at the models of benzene shown below. The benzene molecule is a six-membered carbon ring with one hydrogen atom attached to each carbon. One electron from each carbon is free to be in a double bond.

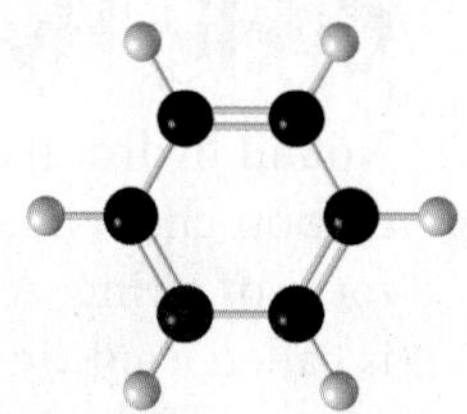

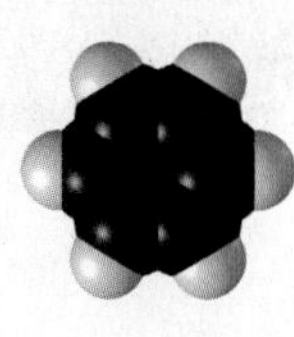

Two different structures with alternating double bonds can be written for benzene. These structural formulas are shown below. They show that neighboring carbons may be attached by a single bond or by a double bond.

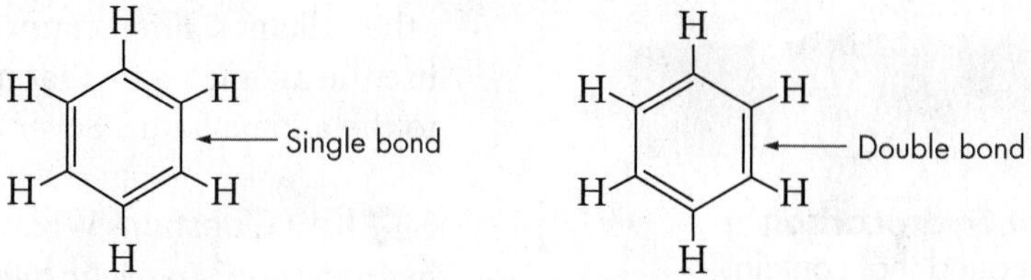

H H H H H H — Single bond

H H H H H H — Double bond

Remember that resonance occurs when two or more structures can be drawn for a molecule. The structural formulas above are two resonance structures of benzene. The bonding in a benzene ring doesn't really switch between resonance structures. Instead, all the bonds in the ring are the same. They are mixes, or hybrids, of single and double bonds. The bonding electrons between carbon atoms are shared evenly around the ring in a benzene molecule. Benzene and other molecules that have resonance are more stable than similar molecules that do not have resonance. So, benzene is not as reactive as alkenes that have six carbons.

Representing Benzene
Both hexagons are used to represent benzene molecules.

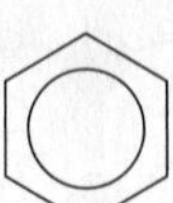

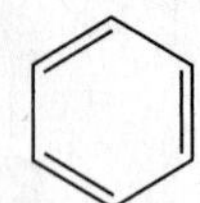

Different ways of drawing the structure of benzene molecules are shown to the left. Each point of the hexagon represents a carbon atom. Drawing a solid circle inside a hexagon is a good way to show how the electrons are shared in benzene. The inner circle represents the electron cloud. However, it does not show the number of electrons in the bonds. The other structure at the left is often used because it shows the number of electrons. Remember that each bond in the ring is really identical.

Any hydrocarbon compound that is not an aromatic compound is an **aliphatic compound.** Alkanes, alkenes, alkynes, and cycloalkanes are aliphatic compounds.

Substituted Aromatic Compounds The dye that makes your blue jeans blue is an aromatic compound. Many brightly colored dyes are substituted aromatic compounds. They have groups attached to a ring. Compounds that contain substituents attached to a benzene ring are named using benzene as the parent hydrocarbon. However, the C_6H_5 group is called a phenyl group when the benzene ring is a substituent.

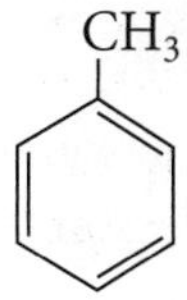
CH3

Methylbenzene (toluene)

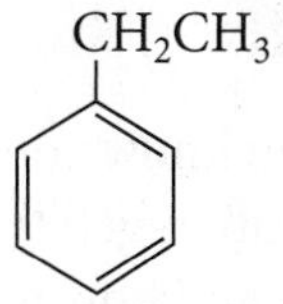
CH2CH3

Ethylbenzene

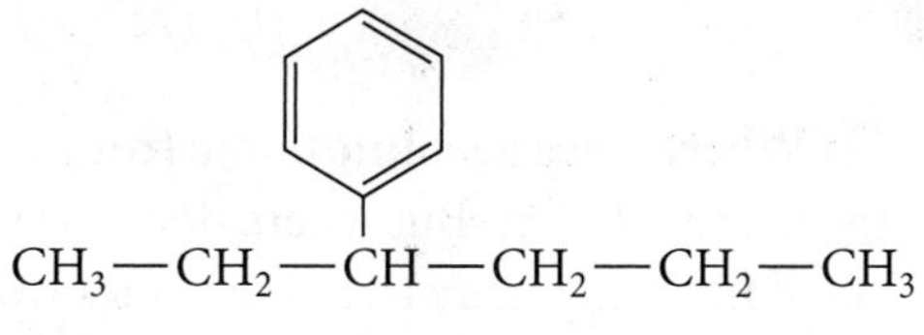
CH3—CH2—CH—CH2—CH2—CH3

3-phenylhexane

Some compounds contain a benzene ring and two substituents. These compounds have constitutional isomers. The three constitutional isomers for dimethylbenzene ($C_6H_4(CH_3)_2$) are shown below.

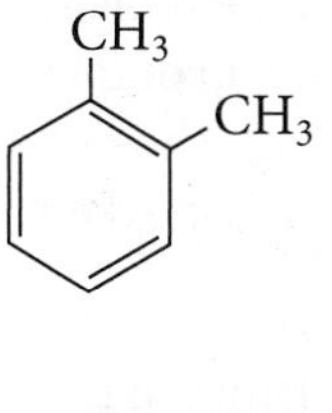
CH3
CH3

1,2-dimethylbenzene

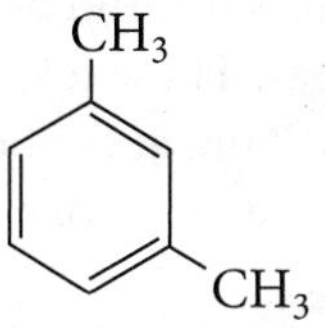
CH3
CH3

1,3-dimethylbenzene

CH3
CH3

1,4-dimethylbenzene

Key Question What is the most accurate description of bonding in benzene? **The bonding electrons between carbon atoms are shared evenly around the ring in a benzene molecule.**

Dyes
Many dye molecules have phenyl groups. The indigo dye that colors blue jeans has two phenyl groups.

22.4 LessonCheck

Key Concept Check

38. **Define** What is a cyclic hydrocarbon?

39. **Review** Describe the bonding between carbon atoms in benzene.

Vocabulary Check
Choose a highlighted term from the lesson to complete the sentence correctly.

40. Any compound that does not have a benzene-like ring is a(n) ________.

Think Critically

41. **Evaluate** Aromatic compounds are also called *arenes.* Do you think arene is a good option? Consider what the suffix *-ene* means when used with aliphatic compounds.

CHEMISTRY & YOU

42. Explain what it means for a compound to be aromatic. (Hint: See page 740.)

BIGIDEA CARBON CHEMISTRY

43. Hexane, 1-hexene, cyclohexane, and benzene each have six carbon atoms. What is the difference between these hydrocarbons? Use the words *aliphatic, aromatic, saturated,* and *unsaturated* to explain your answer.

22.5 Hydrocarbons From Earth's Crust

CHEMISTRY & YOU

Q: Where does gasoline come from? You know you can get gasoline from a gas station. But where does a gas station get it? In this lesson, you'll find out where gasoline comes from and how it is refined.

Key Questions

What hydrocarbons are in natural gas?

What is the first step in the refining of petroleum?

What characteristics are used to classify coal?

Natural Gas

Much of the world's energy is produced by the burning of fossil fuels. Fossil fuels come from living things that died millions of years ago. The remains of marine organisms settled on the ocean floor and were buried by ocean sediments. Heat, pressure, and bacteria changed the remains into petroleum and natural gas. These fossil fuels are made up of mostly aliphatic hydrocarbons. The figure at the bottom of this page shows how natural gas is often found on top of oil deposits or in separate pockets in rock.

Gaseous Fuels Natural gas is an important source of alkanes of low molar mass, such as methane, ethane, propane, and butane. It also contains a small amount of nitrogen, helium, and hydrocarbons of higher molar mass. In fact, natural gas is a major source of helium. Although natural gas has several components, it is mostly methane. Methane produces a hot, clean flame when it burns. The combustion equation for methane is shown below.

$$CH_4(g) + 2O_2(g) \longrightarrow CO_2(g) + 2H_2O(g) + \text{heat}$$

Propane and butane are heating fuels that are sold as liquid petroleum gas (LPG). They are condensed from gases to liquids and separated from the other gases in natural gas.

Combustion Oxygen is necessary for a hydrocarbon to burn completely. If there is not enough oxygen available, the combustion is incomplete. Complete combustion of a hydrocarbon produces a blue flame. Incomplete combustion produces a yellow flame. The yellow color is caused by small, glowing carbon particles that form during incomplete combustion. The particles are deposited as soot when they cool. Carbon monoxide, a toxic gas, also forms during incomplete combustion.

Key Question What hydrocarbons are in natural gas? **Natural gas is an important source of alkanes of low molar mass.**

Oil and Gas Wells
Wells are drilled to reach natural gas and petroleum deposits.

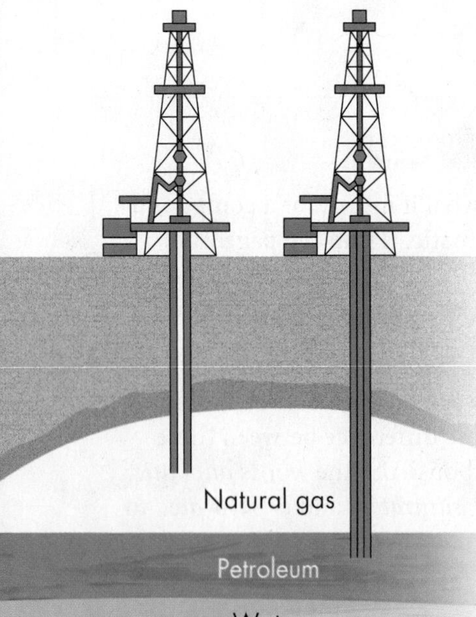

Petroleum

Petroleum is also called crude oil. It contains organic compounds that are more complex than those in natural gas. Most of the hydrocarbons in petroleum are straight-chain and branched-chain alkanes. Petroleum also contains small amounts of aromatic compounds and organic compounds that contain sulfur, oxygen, and nitrogen.

Ancient people found petroleum seeping from the ground in some areas. People didn't drill wells to reach petroleum until centuries later. In the late 1850s, a huge deposit of petroleum was discovered while drilling in Pennsylvania. More deposits were soon found around the world.

Distilling Crude Oil Crude oil is a mixture of hydrocarbons. Some of the hydrocarbons have more than 40 carbon atoms. To be useful, the complex mixture needs to be separated. This separation is called refining. Petroleum refining begins with the distillation of crude oil into fractions that have different boiling points. The diagram below shows a distillation tower. Notice that each distillation fraction contains several different hydrocarbons.

Cracking Hydrocarbons Gasoline makes up just 40 percent of the crude oil mixture. However, gasoline is the most commonly used petroleum product. To meet the demand, gasoline must be made from other fractions of petroleum. **Cracking** is a controlled process by which hydrocarbons are broken down or rearranged into smaller, more useful molecules. For example, fractions containing compounds of higher molar mass are "cracked" to make lower molar mass compounds of gasoline and kerosene. A catalyst and heat are used to crack hydrocarbons. Cracking also produces low-molar-mass alkanes that are used to manufacture paints and plastics.

Key Question What is the first step in the refining of petroleum? **Petroleum refining begins with the distillation of crude oil into fractions that have different boiling points.**

cracking a controlled process by which hydrocarbons are broken down or rearranged into smaller, more useful molecules

USING PRIOR KNOWLEDGE

What do you think of when you hear the word *cracking?* Maybe ice cracking. You know cracking usually means an object is breaking into pieces. You can use this knowledge to remember that cracking means that hydrocarbons are broken into smaller molecules.

See fractional distillation of crude oil *animated online.*

Fractional Distillation of Crude Oil
The crude oil is heated so that it vaporizes and rises through the column shown at the far right. Compounds with the highest boiling points condense near the bottom. Compounds with the lowest boiling points condense near the top.

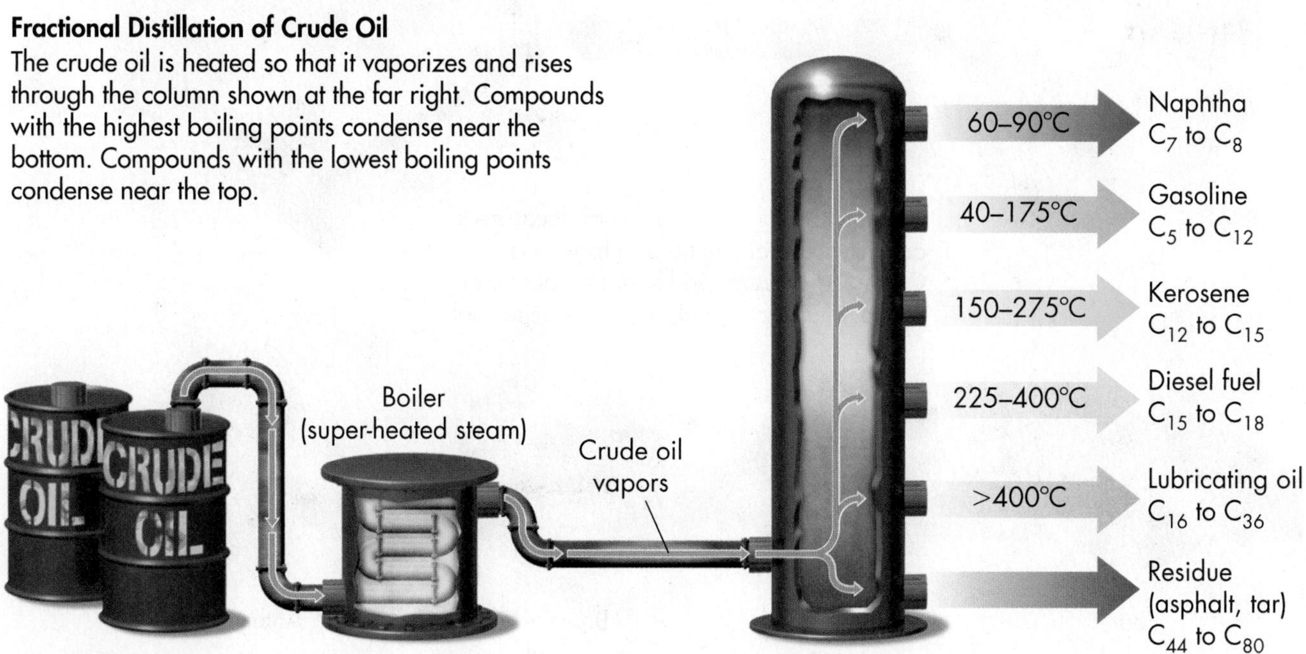

Coal

Geologists think that huge tree ferns and mosses grew in swampy tropical areas about 300 million years ago. When the plants died, they formed thick layers of decaying material. This material was eventually covered by layers and layers of soil and rock that caused intense pressure. This pressure and heat from inside Earth slowly turned the plant remains into coal.

Coal Formation The different types of coal are classified by hardness and carbon content. The figure below shows the stages in coal formation. Peat forms first. Peat is a brown, spongy, fibrous material found in bogs. It can be dug up and dried to make a low-cost fuel. But it makes a lot of smoke when it burns. If left in the ground, peat continues to change. After a long time, peat becomes lignite, or brown coal. Lignite is much harder than peat and has more carbon. Lignite contains a lot of water. Continued pressure and heat slowly change lignite into bituminous coal, or soft coal. Bituminous coal is harder than lignite. It also contains less water and more carbon than lignite. Soft coal changes into anthracite, or hard coal, in places where there is even greater pressure. Anthracite has a carbon content that is greater than 85 percent. So it is an excellent fuel source.

Coal is obtained from both underground and surface mines. In North America, coal mines are usually less than 100 meters underground. Because the coal is so close to the surface, it is strip mined. On the other hand, many coal mines in Europe and Asia are 1000 to 1500 meters below Earth's surface.

Coal Formation
The decomposing remains of tree ferns and mosses build up.

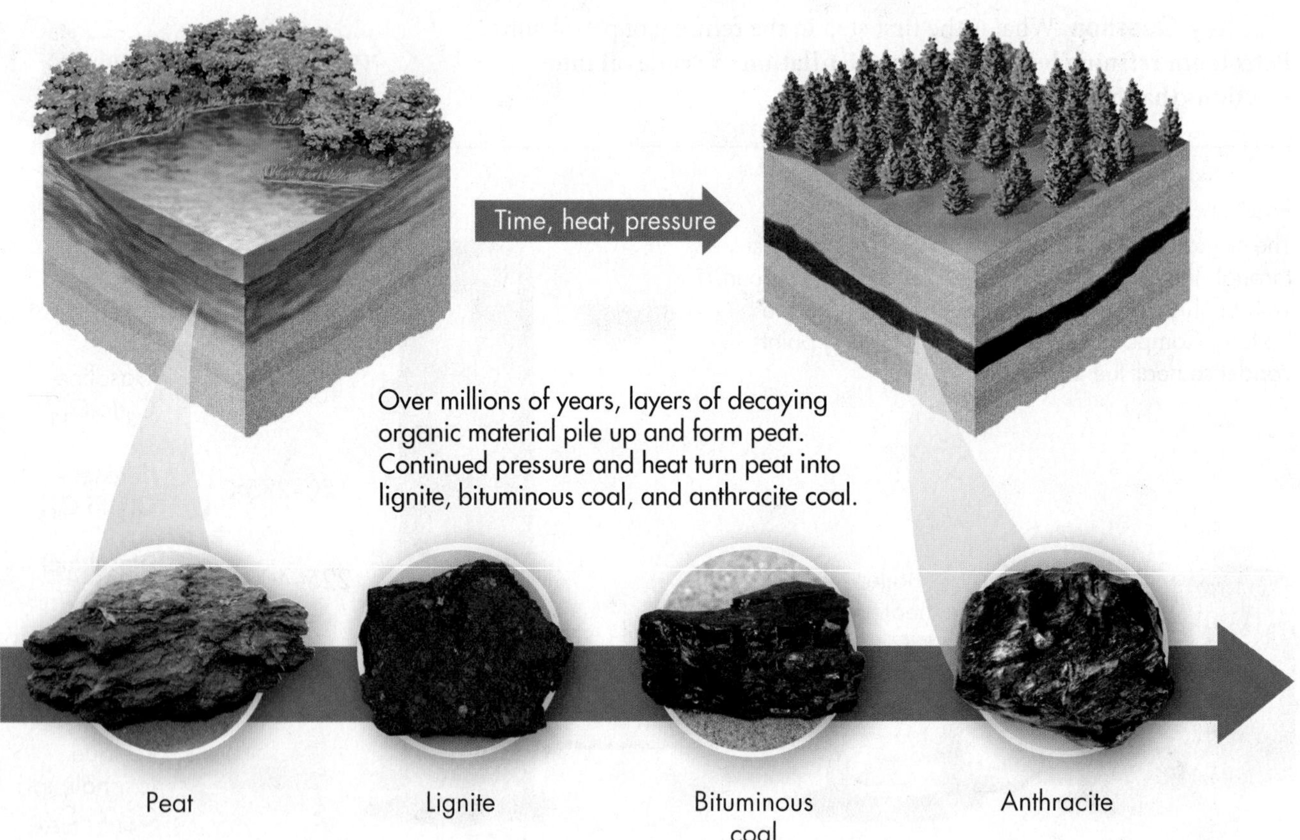
Time, heat, pressure
Over millions of years, layers of decaying organic material pile up and form peat. Continued pressure and heat turn peat into lignite, bituminous coal, and anthracite coal.
Peat
Lignite
Bituminous coal
Anthracite

Composition of Coal Coal consists of mostly aromatic compounds that have very high molar masses. The amount of carbon in these compounds is high compared to the amount of hydrogen. The aromatic compounds of coal produce more soot than petroleum fuels when they are burned. Coal also contains a small amount of sulfur. The sulfur forms SO_2 and SO_3 as coal burns. These compounds are major air pollutants that contribute to acid rain and the smog shown here. To reduce air pollution, most of the sulfur is removed from coal before it is burned. Sulfur oxides are also captured in the smokestacks of power plants after coal is burned.

Coal may be distilled to yield coke, coal gas, coal tar, and ammonia. Coke is the solid material left after coal distillation. Coke is almost pure carbon. It is used as a fuel in many industrial processes and is important in the smelting of iron ore. Coal gas is mainly hydrogen, methane, and carbon monoxide. Coal tar can be distilled even more to get benzene, toluene, naphthalene, phenol, and pitch. The ammonia from distilled coal is converted to ammonium sulfate that is used as a fertilizer.

Key Question What characteristics are used to classify coal? **Coal is classified by its hardness and carbon content.**

BUILD Connections

If you live near a large city, chances are you've seen a brown layer of smog in the sky on warm, sunny days. Most of the smog in the U.S. is caused by pollution from cars and trucks, not from burning coal. Burning gasoline in car engines releases nitrogen oxides and organic compounds that react to form smog in sunlight. Vehicles in many places get "smog tests" to make sure they are not producing too many pollutants that cause smog.

Smog in Beijing
Sulfur oxides from emissions of coal-fired plants in China often contribute to dense smog.

22.5 LessonCheck

Key Concept Check

44. **Describe** Which type of hydrocarbons can be found in natural gas?

45. **Review** Describe the first process used in the refining of petroleum.

46. **Identify** What are the two characteristics used to classify coal?

Think Critically

47. **List** What are some common products made from natural gas, petroleum, and coal?

48. **Compare** How do the chemical compositions of natural gas, petroleum, and coal differ?

49. Where does gasoline come from? Where does coal come from? (Hint: See pages 743–744.)

22 Study Guide

BIGIDEA CARBON CHEMISTRY

Hydrocarbons are named using the IUPAC system, although sometimes common names are used for certain familiar compounds. All hydrocarbons are nonpolar molecules. In general, the fewer carbon atoms in a hydrocarbon, the lower its melting and boiling points. Hydrocarbons with the same molecular formula but different molecular structures can have different properties.

22.1 Hydrocarbons

A carbon atom always forms four covalent bonds because it has four valence electrons.

The carbon atoms in an alkane can be arranged in a straight chain or in a chain that has branches.

- hydrocarbon (720)
- alkane (722)
- straight-chain alkane (722)
- condensed structural formula (724)
- substituent (726)
- alkyl group (726)
- branched-chain alkane (726)

22.2 Unsaturated Hydrocarbons

At least one carbon-carbon bond in an alkene is a double covalent bond. Other bonds may be single carbon-carbon bonds and carbon-hydrogen bonds.

At least one carbon-carbon bond in an alkyne is a triple covalent bond. Other bonds may be single or double carbon-carbon bonds and carbon-hydrogen bonds.

- saturated compound (731)
- unsaturated compound (731)
- alkene (731)
- alkyne (733)

22.3 Isomers

Constitutional isomers differ in physical properties, such as boiling point and melting point, and in chemical properties.

Two types of stereoisomers are *cis-trans* isomers and enantiomers.

- isomer (734)
- constitutional isomer (734)
- stereoisomer (735)
- *cis-trans* isomer (735)
- enantiomer (736)
- asymmetric carbon (736)

22.4 Hydrocarbon Rings

In cyclic hydrocarbon compounds, the carbon chain is in the form of a ring.

The bonding electrons between carbon atoms are shared evenly around the ring in a benzene molecule.

- cyclic hydrocarbon (739)
- cycloalkane (739)
- aromatic compound (740)
- aliphatic compound (740)

22.5 Hydrocarbons from Earth's Crust

Natural gas is an important source of alkanes of low molar mass.

Petroleum refining begins with the distillation of crude oil into fractions that have different boiling points.

Coal is classified by its hardness and carbon content.

- cracking (743)

Skills Tune-Up: Structural Formulas

Problem 1

Problem

Name this compound using the IUPAC system.

$$\begin{array}{l} CH_3 \\ | \\ CH_2 \\ | \\ CH_2 \\ | \\ CH_2 \\ | \\ CH—CH_2—CH_3 \\ | \\ CH—CH_3 \\ | \\ CH—CH_3 \\ | \\ CH_3 \end{array}$$

❶ Analyze

- The carbons on the parent hydrocarbon should be numbered to give the substituents the lowest possible numbers.
- The location numbers for the substituents are included in the prefix. If there are multiple substituents of the same type, include that information in the prefix. For example, use *di-* or *tri-* for two or three substituents, respectively.
- The names of the substituents should be listed in alphabetical order with correct punctuation.

Hint: Review Sample Problem 22.2 if you have trouble naming branched-chain alkanes.

❷ Solve

Parent hydrocarbon: eight carbon atoms (octane)

Substituents and their locations:

- methyl group on carbon 2
- methyl group on carbon 3
- ethyl group on carbon 4

$$\begin{array}{l} 8\ CH_3 \\ \quad | \\ 7\ CH_2 \\ \quad | \\ 6\ CH_2 \\ \quad | \\ 5\ CH_2 \\ \quad | \\ 4\ CH—\boxed{CH_2—CH_3} \\ \quad | \\ 3\ CH—\boxed{CH_3} \\ \quad | \\ 2\ CH—\boxed{CH_3} \\ \quad | \\ 1\ CH_3 \end{array}$$

Substituents

Prefix: 4-ethyl-2,3-dimethyl

The IUPAC name is 4-ethyl-2,3-dimethyloctane.

Problem 2

Problem

Draw a condensed structural formula for 4-ethyl-2-methylheptane.

Hint: Review Sample Problem 22.3 if you have trouble drawing structural formulas for branched-chain alkanes.

❶ Analyze

- The part of the name that ends in *-ane* identifies the parent hydrocarbon.
- Prefixes identify the substituents, how many times they appear, and the location of each on the parent hydrocarbon.
- Each carbon atom must have four covalent bonds. Hydrogens should be added to meet this need.

❷ Solve

Parent hydrocarbon: heptane (seven carbon atoms)

Substituents and their locations:

- ethyl group on carbon 4
- methyl group on carbon 2

The structural formula for 4-ethyl-2-methylheptane is

$$\begin{array}{l} CH_3 \\ | \\ CH—CH_3 \\ | \\ CH_2 \\ | \\ CH—CH_2—CH_3 \\ | \\ CH_2 \\ | \\ CH_2 \\ | \\ CH_3 \end{array}$$

22 Assessment

* Solutions appear in Appendix D

Lesson by Lesson

22.1 Hydrocarbons

*50. Draw condensed structural formulas for pentane and hexane. Assume that the C—H and C—C bonds are understood.

51. Name the alkanes that have the following molecular formulas.

a. $CH_3CH_2CH_3$
b. $CH_3(CH_2)_6CH_3$

52. Draw structures for the alkyl groups derived from methane, ethane, and propane.

*53. Give the IUPAC name for each compound.

a.
```
CH3—CH—CH2
    |   |
   CH3 CH3
```

b.
```
CH3—CH—CH—CH3
    |   |
   CH3 CH3
```

22.2 Unsaturated Hydrocarbons

54. Give the IUPAC name for these alkenes.

a. $CH_3CH{=}CH_2$

b.
```
CH3       H
   \     /
    C=C
   /     \
  H       CH2CH3
```

c.
```
CH3CHCH2CH=CH2
   |
   CH3
```

*55. Classify each of the following compounds as saturated or unsaturated. Explain.

a. $CH_3CH{=}CHCH_2CH_3$
b. $CH_3CH_2CH_3$

22.3 Isomers

56. Draw and name all the constitutional isomers with the molecular formula C_6H_{14}.

57. Draw one constitutional isomer of each compound.

a.
```
        CH3
        |
CH3—C—CH3
        |
        CH3
```

b.
```
        CH3
        |
CH3—CH—CH—CH3
            |
            CH2
            |
            CH3
```

58. Draw a structural formula for each of the following alkenes. If *cis* and *trans* forms are present, include both forms.

a. 2-pentene
b. 3-ethyl-2-pentene

59. Can you draw a constitutional isomer of hexane that has an asymmetric carbon? Explain.

*60. Do all molecules have enantiomers? Explain.

22.4 Hydrocarbon Rings

61. Give the IUPAC name for the following cyclic hydrocarbons.

a. 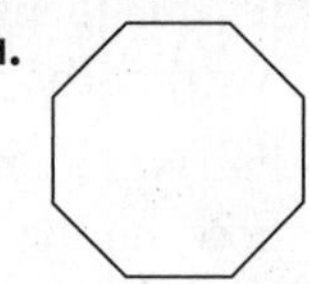

b. 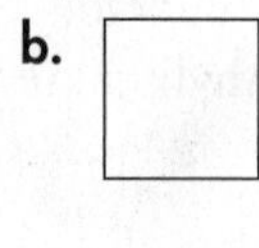

*62. Draw a structural formula for each compound.

a. 1,4-diethylbenzene
b. 2-methyl-3-phenylpentane

22.5 Hydrocarbons from Earth's Crust

63. Rank these materials in order of increasing carbon content: bituminous coal, peat, lignite, and anthracite coal.

64. How are catalysts used in petroleum refining?

*65. What happens to the sulfur when coal burns?

Understand Concepts

*66. For each hydrocarbon shown, identify the type of covalent bonds and name the compound.

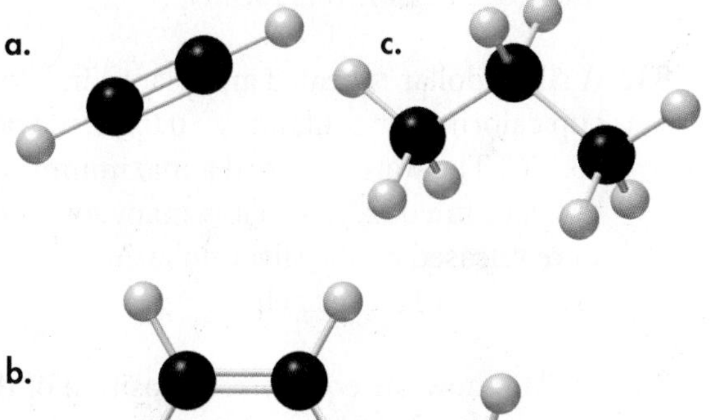

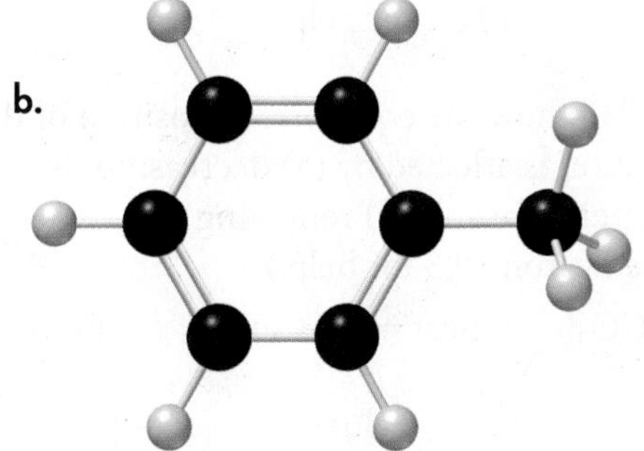

67. Write structural formulas for these compounds.

a. propyne
b. cyclohexane
c. 2-phenylpropane
d. 2,2,4-trimethylpentane

68. Draw electron dot structures for each compound.

a. propane
b. propene
c. propyne
d. cyclobutane

69. Compare *cis-trans* isomers and enantiomers.

*70. Compare these three molecular structures. Which would you expect to be most stable? Explain your answer.

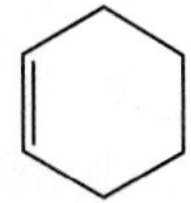
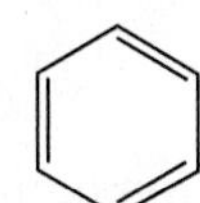

*71. Are these two structures *cis-trans* isomers? Explain your answer.

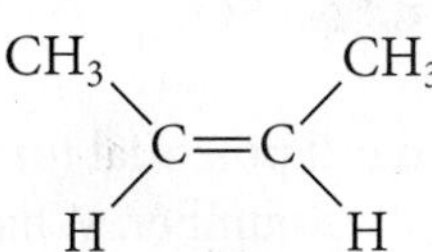

H H
C=C
CH$_3$ CH$_3$

Think Critically

72. **Apply Concepts** Alkadienes are hydrocarbons with two double bonds. Draw the structural formula of the alkadiene with the molecular formula C_3H_4.

73. **Compare** What structural feature is associated with each of these hydrocarbons: an alkane, an alkene, an aromatic hydrocarbon, and a cycloalkane?

*74. **Apply Concepts** Draw structural formulas for the following compounds:

a. 3,4-dimethyl-3-hexene
b. 1-ethyl-2-methylcyclopentane
c. 5,5-dipropyldecane

75. **Apply Concepts** The alkanes 2-methylbutane and pentane are readily isomerized in the presence of a catalyst.

a. Write a balanced chemical equation for the isomerization reaction.
b. What kind of isomers are 2-methylbutane and pentane?

FOUNDATIONS Wrap-Up

What Dissolves What?

1. **Draw Conclusions** At the beginning of this chapter, you tried to dissolve petroleum jelly and wax in different solvents. Explain why the petroleum jelly and wax did not dissolve in water.

Concept Check

Now that you've finished studying Chapter 22, answer these questions.

2. Why are there so many types of compounds that contain carbon?
3. How can two different compounds have the same molecular formula?
4. How is cyclohexane different from benzene?
5. How are coal, petroleum, and natural gas similar to and different from each other?

Write About Science

76. Research a Problem When fossil fuels burn in an internal combustion engine, the exhaust contains more than carbon dioxide gas and water vapor. Research how catalytic converters work. Then write a paragraph explaining what happens to pollutants in a catalytic converter.

77. Connect to the BIGIDEA You've probably seen the instruction "Shake well before using" on a salad dressing bottle. These instructions usually appear on dressings that contain olive oil and water as two of the main ingredients. The molecules in olive oil have long hydrocarbon tails. Explain why you need to shake these types of salad dressings before pouring them onto your salad.

CHEMYSTERY

Nose for Hire

After finishing up with the smell test, Anthony went home and jumped on the Internet to research limonene. He discovered that the two limonene compounds were enantiomers. The right-handed enantiomer smells like oranges, and the left-handed one smells like pine trees. He read more to learn that a nose, like all human tissue, is composed of molecules with asymmetric carbons. As a result, the molecules in your nose that are responsible for detecting smell react differently to the two enantiomers of limonene.

Compounds with asymmetric carbons often have different odors. Another example is the two enantiomers of the compound carvone. One enantiomer smells like spearmint and the other enantiomer smells like the spice caraway.

***78. Infer** Do physical properties such as color, density, and boiling point differ for the two enantiomers of limonene?

79. Connect to the BIGIDEA Many medications have asymmetric carbons. There are cases in which one enantiomer helps, while the other causes severe harm. How is this difference possible?

Cumulative Review

***80.** How many moles of solute are in 750 mL of 1.50*M* KNO_3? How many grams of KNO_3 is this? (See Lesson 16.2 for help.)

81. A silver dollar is heated and placed in a foam cup calorimeter containing 50.0 mL of water at 26.5°C. The water reached a maximum temperature of 27.3°C. How many joules of heat were released by the silver dollar? (See Lesson 17.2 for help.)

***82.** Explain how the equilibrium position of this reaction is affected by (a) decreasing the temperature and (b) removing CO_2. (See Lesson 18.3 for help.)

$CaCO_3(s) + \text{heat} \rightleftharpoons CaO(s) + CO_2(g)$

***83.** What are the pH values for aqueous solutions containing each of the following hydroxide ion concentrations? (See Lesson 19.2 for help.)

a. $1.0 \times 10^{-4}M$
b. $3.9 \times 10^{-7}M$
c. $0.010M$
d. $0.0050M$

84. A colorless solution of unknown pH turns blue when tested with the acid-base indicator bromothymol blue. It remains colorless when tested with phenolphthalein. (See Lesson 19.2 for help.)

a. What is the approximate pH of the solution?
b. How could you determine the pH more accurately?

85. Are these processes oxidation or reduction? (See Lesson 20.1 for help.)

a. $Fe^{3+} + e^- \rightarrow Fe^{2+}$
b. $Cl_2 + 2e^- \rightarrow 2Cl^-$
c. $Fe^{3+} + 3e^- \rightarrow Fe$
d. $Zn \rightarrow Zn^{2+} + 2e^-$

***86.** Give the oxidation number of each element in the following substances. (See Lesson 20.2 for help.)

a. $CaCO_3$
b. Cl_2
c. $LiIO_3$
d. Na_2SO_3

***87.** The calculated standard cell potential for a redox reaction is a negative number. What does a negative number tell you about the reaction? (See Lesson 21.2 for help.)

Standardized Test Prep

For help with answering test questions, go to your Chemistry Skills and Math Workbook.

Select the choice that best answers each question or completes each statement.

1. What is the name of the compound with the following structural formula?

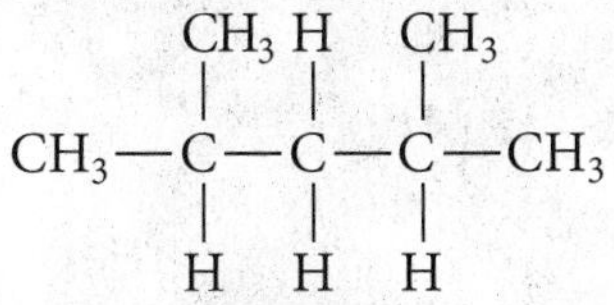

```
       CH3 H   CH3
        |  |    |
CH3—C—C—C—CH3
        |  |    |
        H  H    H
```

(A) 1,2,3,3-tetramethylpropane
(B) heptane
(C) 2,4-dimethylpentane
(D) 1,5-dimethylbutane

2. Which of these are characteristic of all alkenes?

I. unsaturated
II. carbon-carbon double bond
III. enantiomers

(A) I and II only
(B) II and III only
(C) I and III only
(D) I, II, and III

3. How many carbon atoms are in a molecule of 4,5-diethyloctane?

(A) 10 (C) 14
(B) 12 (D) 16

4. *Cis-trans* isomerism is possible in:

(A) 2-pentene. (C) propyne.
(B) 2-butane. (D) benzene.

Tips for Success

Eliminate Wrong Answers If you don't know which response to a question is correct, start by eliminating those you know are wrong. If you can rule out some choices, you'll have fewer choices left to consider, which will increase your chances of choosing the correct answer.

5. A constitutional isomer of heptane is:

(A) methylbenzene.
(B) 3,3-dimethylpentane.
(C) cycloheptane.
(D) 3-methylhexene.

6. Which molecule can have enantiomers?

(A) CH_4 (C) CFClBrI
(B) CF_2H_2 (D) CF_2ClH

7. Draw structural formulas for three constitutional isomers of pentane, C_5H_{12}. Name each isomer.

8. Write structural formulas for the four constitutional isomers of cyclopentane. Name each of the isomers.

The lettered choices below refer to Questions 9–12. A lettered choice may be used once, more than once, or not at all.

(A) alkene
(B) arene
(C) alkyne
(D) alkane

To which of the above classes of hydrocarbons does each of the following compounds belong?

9. C_7H_{16}
10. C_5H_8
11. C_6H_6
12. C_8H_{16}

Use the molecular structures below to answer Questions 13–16. A molecular structure may be used once, more than once, or not at all.

(A) 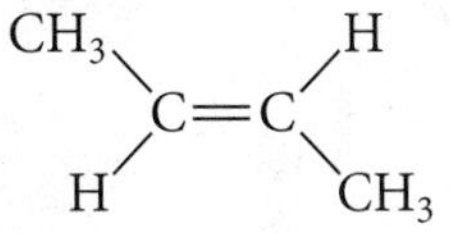
```
CH3       H
   \     /
    C=C
   /     \
  H       CH3
```

(C)
```
 H        H
   \     /
    C=C
   /     \
CH3       CH3
```

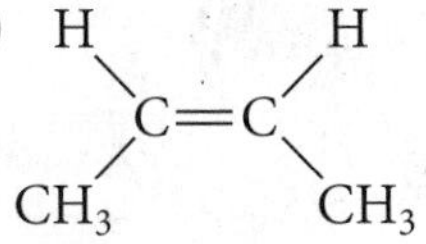

(B) $CH_3CH_2CH_2CH_3$

(D) 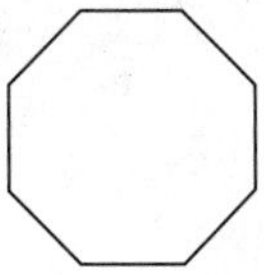 [octagon: cyclooctane]

13. Which structure is a cycloalkane?
14. Which structure is a saturated hydrocarbon?
15. Which structure is a *cis*-isomer?
16. Which structure is a *trans*-isomer?

If You Have Trouble With . . .

Question	1	2	3	4	5	6	7	8	9	10	11	12	13	14	15	16
See Lesson	22.1	22.2	22.1	22.3	22.3	22.3	22.3	22.3	22.1	22.2	22.4	22.2	22.4	22.2	22.3	22.3

23 Functional Groups

FOUNDATIONS for Learning

The Smell of Chemistry!

1. Work with a partner. Obtain a piece of a few different fruits such as apples, bananas, pears, pineapples, or strawberries.
2. Take turns closing your eyes and try to identify each fruit only by smell. Were you able to identify each fruit?

Form a Hypothesis What do you think gives each of these fruits its unique smell?

PearsonChem.com

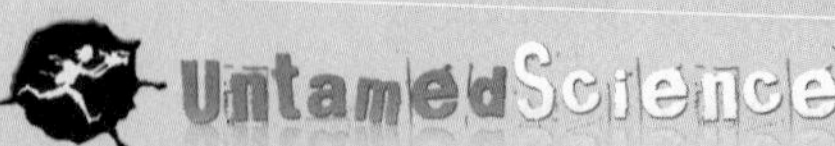

Take a video field trip with the Untamed Science crew as they learn the chemistry behind the specialized gear that helps protect firefighters.

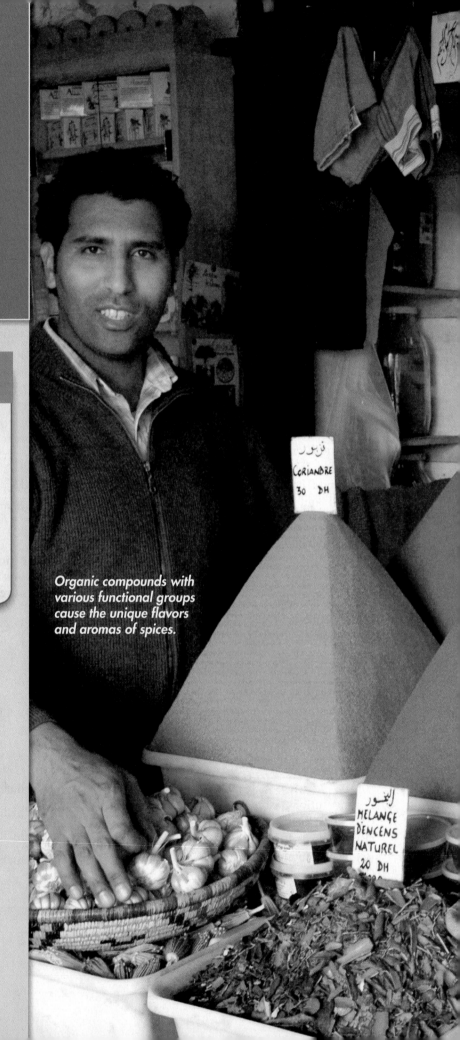

Organic compounds with various functional groups cause the unique flavors and aromas of spices.

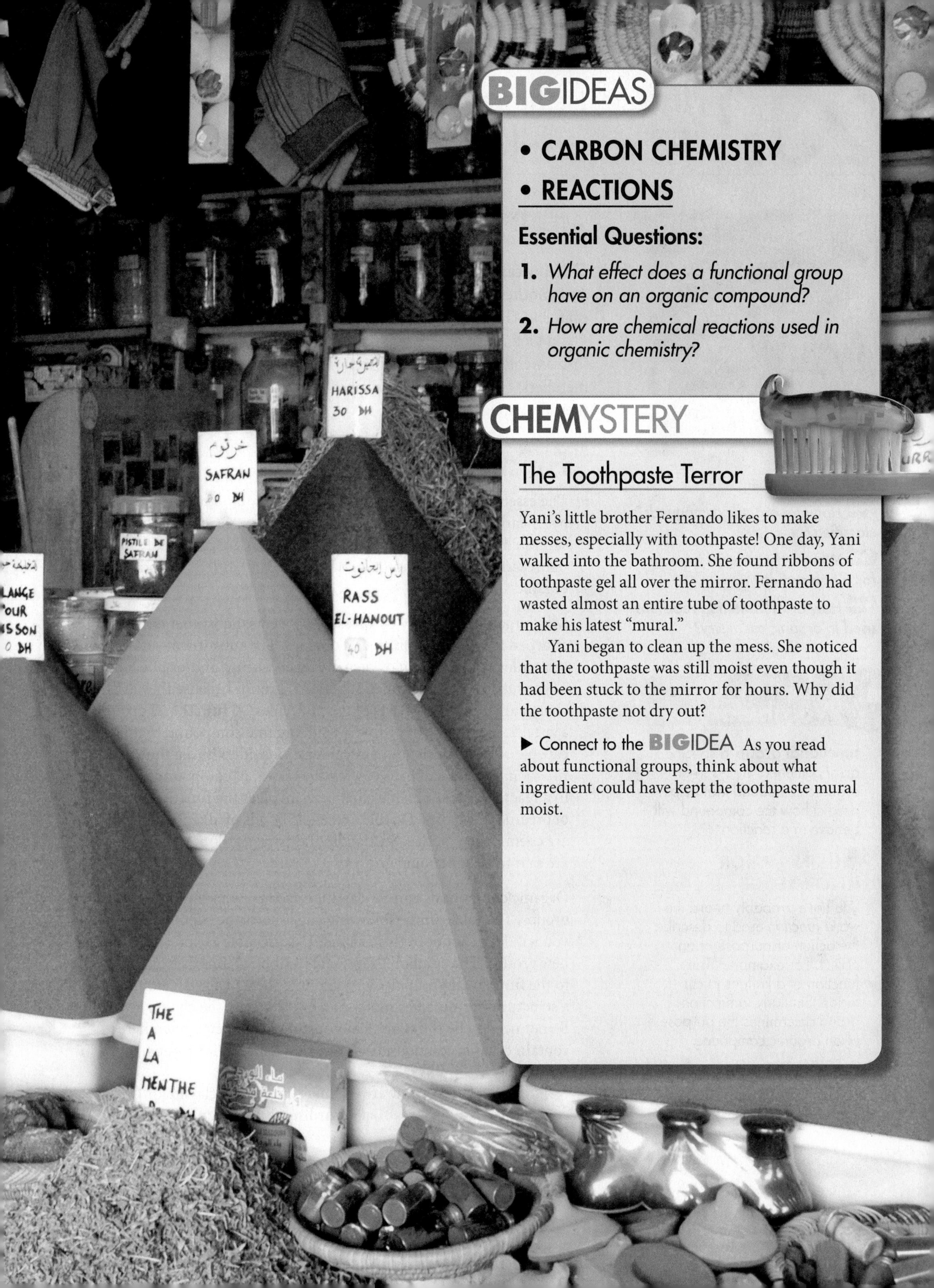

BIG IDEAS

- **CARBON CHEMISTRY**
- **REACTIONS**

Essential Questions:

1. *What effect does a functional group have on an organic compound?*
2. *How are chemical reactions used in organic chemistry?*

CHEMYSTERY

The Toothpaste Terror

Yani's little brother Fernando likes to make messes, especially with toothpaste! One day, Yani walked into the bathroom. She found ribbons of toothpaste gel all over the mirror. Fernando had wasted almost an entire tube of toothpaste to make his latest "mural."

Yani began to clean up the mess. She noticed that the toothpaste was still moist even though it had been stuck to the mirror for hours. Why did the toothpaste not dry out?

▶ Connect to the **BIG IDEA** As you read about functional groups, think about what ingredient could have kept the toothpaste mural moist.

23.1 Introduction to Functional Groups

CHEMISTRY & YOU

Q: How can you tell the difference between one organic compound and another? In a marching band, all the members wear the same uniform. This makes the musicians look the same from a distance. If you look more closely, you can distinguish differences in the instruments they hold. Hydrocarbons are similar to marching band members. Hydrocarbons look mostly alike until you look closely at their functional groups.

Key Questions

How are organic compounds classified?

What is the general formula for a halocarbon?

How are substitution reactions used in organic chemistry?

BUILD Vocabulary

functional group a specific arrangement of atoms in an organic compound that helps predict how the compound will behave in a reaction

USING PRIOR KNOWLEDGE

You have probably heard the word *function* used to describe the action or purpose of an object. For example, "The function of a knife is to cut food." Similarly, a functional group determines the purpose of an organic compound.

Functional Groups

The essential components in every organic compound are hydrocarbon chains and rings. In most organic reactions, the saturated hydrocarbon skeletons of molecules are chemically inert or nonreactive. So, how can there be hundreds of different kinds of organic reactions?

Most organic chemistry involves substituents. Substituents are groups attached to hydrocarbon chains or rings. The substituents of organic molecules often contain oxygen, nitrogen, sulfur, and/or phosphorus. These substituents are called functional groups because they are the chemically functional parts of the molecules. A **functional group** is a specific arrangement of atoms in an organic compound that is capable of characteristic chemical reactions. Identifying the functional group can help you predict how that compound would act in a reaction. Most organic chemistry involves the functional groups of organic molecules. Double and triple bonds of alkenes and alkynes are chemically reactive. So, double and triple carbon-carbon bonds are said to be functional groups.

Organic compounds can be classified according to their functional groups. The table on the following page shows the functional groups you will learn about in this chapter. Use the table as you learn about new groups. The symbol R represents carbon chains or rings attached to the functional group. R can sometimes be a hydrogen atom. When a structural formula has more than one R group, the chains or rings do not need to be the same. The consumer products shown here contain organic compounds with various functional groups.

Key Question How are organic compounds classified? **Organic compounds can be classified according to their functional groups.**

Go online to learn more about products containing organic compounds.

Organic Compounds Classified by Functional Group

Functional group	General structure	Compound type
Halogen	R—X (X = F, Cl, Br, or I)	Halocarbon
Hydroxy	R—OH	Alcohol
Ether	R—O—R	Ether
Amino	$R{-}NH_2$	Amine
Carbonyl	$R{-}C({=}O){-}H$	Aldehyde
	$R{-}C({=}O){-}R$	Ketone
Carboxyl	$R{-}C({=}O){-}OH$	Carboxylic acid
Ester	$R{-}C({=}O){-}O{-}R$	Ester
Amide	$R{-}C({=}O){-}N(R){-}R$	Amide

Consumer Products
The hydrocarbon backbones in these products are structurally similar. Functional groups give each product unique properties and uses.

Some Common Substituent Groups	
Name	Group structure
Isopropyl	$CH_3-\overset{\overset{CH_3}{\vert}}{\underset{\underset{H}{\vert}}{C}}-$
Isobutyl	$CH_3-\overset{\overset{CH_3}{\vert}}{CH}-CH_2-$
Vinyl	H₂C=CH– (H, H on one carbon; H on the other)
Phenyl	C_6H_5- (benzene ring)

Halocarbons

A **halocarbon** is an organic compound that contains at least one covalently bonded atom of fluorine, chlorine, bromine, or iodine. The general formula for a halocarbon is RX. The R stands for carbon chains or carbon rings, and the X stands for the halogen substituent.

Naming Halocarbons The IUPAC rules for naming halocarbons are based on the parent hydrocarbon. The halogen groups are named as substituents. The table below shows examples of IUPAC names for some simple halocarbons. The common names are in parentheses.

Common names of halocarbons have two parts. The first part names the hydrocarbon portion of the molecule as an alkyl group, such as *methyl-* or *ethyl-*. The second part names the halogen with an *-ide* ending. A halocarbon that has a halogen attached to a carbon of an aliphatic chain is called an alkyl halide. Recall that an aliphatic hydrocarbon is any straight-chain or branched alkane, alkene, or alkyne. A halocarbon that has a halogen attached to a benzene ring is called an aryl halide. The table on the left lists the names of some common substituent groups in halocarbons.

Properties of Halocarbons Attractions between halocarbon molecules are mostly due to weak van der Waals interactions. Generally, as more halogens are substituted, the attractions increase. So, compounds that are highly halogenated have higher boiling points.

Uses of Halocarbons Very few halocarbons are found in nature. They can be easily made, however, and have many uses. Halocarbons are used as solvents and as ingredients in stretchable polymers. Hydrofluorocarbons (HFCs) are used as refrigerants in automobile air-conditioning systems.

Key Question What is the general formula of a halocarbon? **The general formula of a halocarbon is RX, where X is a halogen substituent.**

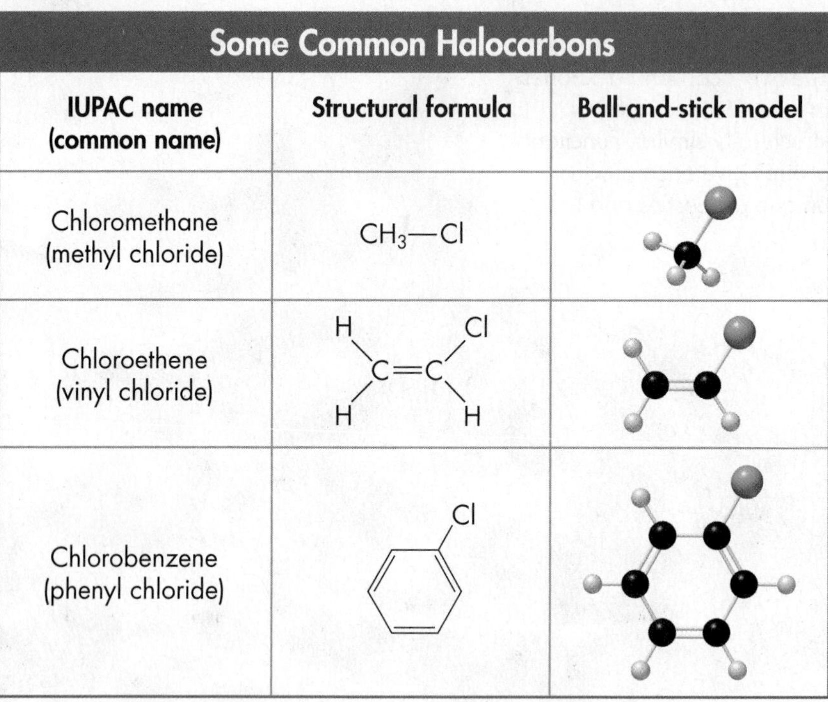

Some Common Halocarbons		
IUPAC name (common name)	Structural formula	Ball-and-stick model
Chloromethane (methyl chloride)	CH_3-Cl	
Chloroethene (vinyl chloride)	H₂C=CHCl (H, H on one carbon; Cl, H on the other)	
Chlorobenzene (phenyl chloride)	C_6H_5-Cl (benzene ring with Cl)	

The first structure has chlorine as a substituent group. In the IUPAC name the -ine is replaced with -o so the name begins with chloro-. The hydrocarbon portion of the molecule contains one carbon so the IUPAC name ends with -methane.

Substitution Reactions

Organic reactions commonly involve the breaking of relatively strong covalent bonds. So organic reactions often proceed more slowly than inorganic reactions. Organic reactions often require catalysts. Many organic reactions are complex. They usually give a mixture of products. The desired product must be separated by distillation, crystallization, or other means. A common type of organic reaction is a substitution reaction. In a **substitution reaction,** an atom or group of atoms replaces another atom or group of atoms.

Substitution reactions are an important method of introducing new functional groups to organic molecules. For example, a halogen atom can replace a hydrogen atom on an alkane to produce a halocarbon. The symbol X stands for a halogen in this generalized equation:

$$\underset{\text{Alkane}}{R{-}H} + \underset{\text{Halogen}}{X_2} \longrightarrow \underset{\text{Halocarbon}}{R{-}X} + \underset{\text{Hydrogen halide}}{HX}$$

You can use this general equation to write a specific one. For example, in this next equation, a chlorine atom replaces a hydrogen atom.

$$\underset{\text{Methane}}{CH_4} + \underset{\text{Chlorine}}{Cl_2} \xrightarrow{\text{UV light}} \underset{\text{Chloromethane}}{CH_3Cl} + \underset{\text{Hydrogen chloride}}{HCl}$$

This type of substitution reaction is also called a halogenation reaction. The reaction introduces a halogen atom into the molecule. Sunlight or another source of ultraviolet radiation is usually a catalyst.

Key Question How are substitution reactions used in organic chemistry? **Substitution reactions are an important method of introducing new functional groups to organic molecules.**

BUILD Vocabulary

halocarbon an organic compound that has at least one covalently bonded atom of fluorine, chlorine, bromine, or iodine

substitution reaction a reaction in which one atom or group of atoms replaces another

WORD PARTS

The prefix *halo-* means salt. The halogens are called "salt formers" because of their ability to form compounds that are called salts. The word *halocarbon* is made from the prefix *halo-* + the word *carbon.* Thus, a halocarbon is any compound that has one or more of the **halo**gens + **carbon.**

23.1 LessonCheck

Key Concept Check

1. **Review** How are organic compounds classified?
2. **Identify** What is the general formula of a halocarbon?
3. **Explain** Why are substitution reactions useful in organic chemistry?

Vocabulary Check *Choose a highlighted word from the lesson to complete each sentence correctly.*

4. An atom or group of atoms replaces another atom or group of atoms in a(n) ________.
5. A(n) ________ contains at least one covalently bonded atom of fluorine, chlorine, bromine, or iodine.

Think Critically

6. **Classify** Identify the functional group in each structure. Then, classify the compound according to its functional group. (Hint: See page 755.)
   a. $CH_3{-}OH$
   b. $CH_3{-}CH_2{-}NH_2$
   c. $CH_3{-}CH_2{-}CH_2{-}Br$
   d. $CH_3{-}CH_2{-}O{-}CH_2{-}CH_3$
   e. $CH_3{-}CH_2{-}I$

CHEMISTRY & YOU

7. Adding a halogen substituent to a hydrocarbon affects the physical properties of a compound. How can you tell the difference between hydrocarbons and halocarbons? Give your answer in terms of structures and properties. (Hint: See page 756.)

23.2 Alcohols, Ethers, and Amines

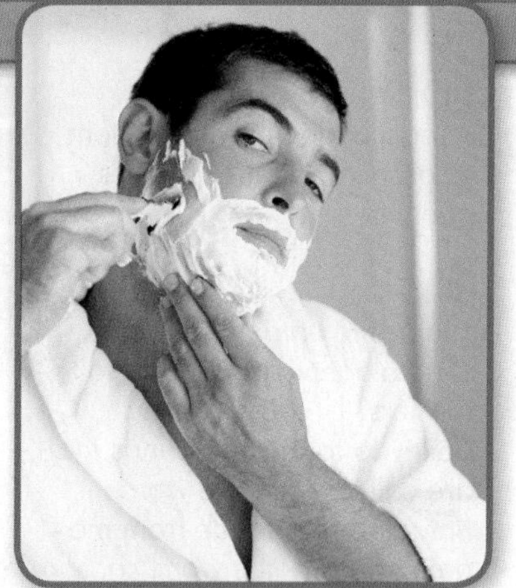

CHEMISTRY & YOU

Q: How can organic chemistry cool you down? Aftershave lotion contains an organic compound that imparts a cooling sensation on the skin. This same ingredient can be found in mint-flavored candy, cough drops, and muscle rubs. In this lesson, you learn about three different classes of organic compounds. The compounds have a wide variety of uses.

Key Questions

What is the general formula of an alcohol?

How are addition reactions used in organic chemistry?

What is the general formula of an ether?

What is the general formula of an amine?

BUILD Vocabulary

alcohol an organic compound with an —OH group

hydroxy group the —OH functional group in alcohols

ACADEMIC WORDS

The prefix *hydr-* can mean "water" or "the presence of hydrogen." A hydroxy group is an —OH group. An —OH group contains hydrogen and is also found in water.

Alcohols

What do mouthwash, perfume, and hair spray have in common? They all contain a type of alcohol. An **alcohol** is an organic compound with an —OH group. The general formula of an alcohol is ROH.

The —OH functional group in alcohols is called a **hydroxy group** or a hydroxyl group. The oxygen atom in the —OH group has two pairs of nonbonding electrons. These electrons make the R—O—H bond angle smaller. This causes an alcohol functional group to have a bent shape as shown here:

$$\mathrm{R{-}\ddot{\underset{..}{O}}{-}H}$$

Alcohol

Categories of Aliphatic Alcohols Aliphatic alcohols can be classified into structural categories. The categories are based on the number of carbons attached to the carbon with the hydroxy group. Sometimes, only one carbon (or no carbon) is attached to C—OH. In this case, the carbon bonded to the —OH group is considered a primary carbon. The alcohol is a primary alcohol. If two carbons are attached, the carbon is a secondary carbon. This results in a secondary alcohol. If there are three carbons, the result is a tertiary carbon and a tertiary alcohol. The structural categories of aliphatic alcohols are summarized below. Here, an R is used to represent carbon chains or rings.

Primary alcohol	$R{-}CH_2{-}OH$	Only one R group is attached to C—OH of a primary (abbreviated 1°) alcohol.
Secondary alcohol	$R{-}\overset{R}{\overset{\vert}{C}}H{-}OH$	Two R groups are attached to C—OH of a secondary (2°) alcohol.
Tertiary alcohol	$R{-}\underset{R}{\underset{\vert}{\overset{R}{\overset{\vert}{C}}}}{-}OH$	Three R groups are attached to C—OH of a tertiary (3°) alcohol.

Naming Alcohols IUPAC and common names are used in naming alcohols. To name aliphatic alcohols in the IUPAC system, drop the *-e* ending of the parent hydrocarbon name. Then, add the ending *-ol.* The parent hydrocarbon is the longest continuous chain of carbons that includes the carbon attached to the hydroxy group. When numbering the parent hydrocarbon, the position of the hydroxy group is given the lowest possible number.

Some alcohols have more than one hydroxy group. To name these alcohols, add the ending *-diol* to the parent hydrocarbon name if the alcohol has two hydroxy groups. If the alcohol has three hydroxy groups, add *-triol.*

Write the common names of aliphatic alcohols in the same way you write the names of halocarbons. The first part names the hydrocarbon portion of the molecule. The second part names the hydroxy group. For example, the word *alcohol* follows the alkyl group ethyl in ethyl alcohol. The common name for an alcohol with two hydroxy groups is glycol.

If the hydroxy group is attached directly to an aromatic ring, the compound is called a phenol. For the IUPAC name, use phenol as the parent hydrocarbon. A phenol with a methyl group attached is called a methylphenol. The table below shows the naming of some simple alcohols and phenols.

Some Common Alcohols and Phenols

IUPAC name (common name)	Structural formula	Ball-and-stick model
Ethanol (ethyl alcohol)	$CH_3—CH_2—OH$	
2-propanol (isopropyl alcohol)	$CH_3—CH(OH)—CH_3$	
1,2-ethanediol (ethylene glycol)	$CH_2(OH)—CH_2(OH)$	
1,2,3-propanetriol (glycerol)	$CH_2(OH)—CH(OH)—CH_2(OH)$	

BUILD Connections

You have probably used many products that contain alcohols. The alcohol 1,2,3-propanetriol is used as a base for perfumes, creams, lotions, and other cosmetics. Isopropyl alcohol is used as an antiseptic to clean your skin before doctors give you a shot.

Properties of Alcohols Alcohols are capable of intermolecular hydrogen bonding. This affects the physical properties of alcohols. Alcohols boil at higher temperatures than alkanes and halocarbons that contain a similar number of atoms.

Alcohols are similar to water (the hydroxy group is part of a water molecule). It is the hydroxy group of an alcohol that makes alcohols somewhat soluble in water. Alcohols with up to four carbons are completely soluble in water. Alcohols with more than four carbons in the chain have a much lower solubility. This is because alcohols have two parts: the carbon chain and the hydroxy group. The hydroxy group is polar. It is attracted to water through hydrogen bonding. The carbon chain is nonpolar. It is not attracted to water. As the number of carbon atoms increases, the nonpolarity of the carbon chain has a greater effect than the polarity of the hydroxy group.

Uses of Alcohols There are many common uses for alcohols. For example, 1,2,3-propanetriol has a tendency to absorb water from its surroundings. This makes 1,2,3-propanetriol a valuable moistening agent in cosmetics, foods, and medicines. Some antifreezes use 1,2-ethanediol as the main ingredient. This alcohol has a high boiling point and a low freezing point. The high boiling point of the alcohol helps prevent vehicle engines from overheating. The low freezing point makes it effective as an anti-icing agent.

Ethanol is an important industrial chemical. Most ethanol is produced by yeast fermentation of sugar. **Fermentation** is the production of ethanol from sugars by yeasts or bacteria. The enzymes of the yeasts or bacteria are catalysts for the fermentation reaction. Fermentation is also important in the food industry. Many baked breads rise because of fermentation. Sugar molecules in bread dough are broken down and release carbon dioxide. The carbon dioxide causes the dough to rise. The ethanol in alcoholic beverages is made by fermentation too. Ethanol is an intoxicating substance. It is a depressant that can be fatal if taken in large doses.

Key Question What is the general formula of an alcohol? **The general formula of an alcohol is ROH.**

Addition Reactions

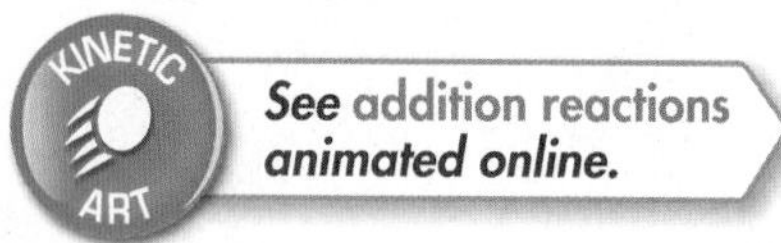

See addition reactions animated online.

The carbon-carbon single bonds in alkanes are not easy to break. In an alkene, one of the bonds in the double bond is somewhat weaker. So, it is sometimes possible for a compound of general structure X—Y to add to a double bond. In an **addition reaction**, a substance is added at the double or triple bond of an alkene or alkyne. Addition reactions are an important method of introducing new functional groups to organic molecules. They are also used to convert alkenes to alkanes. In the equation below, X and Y represent the two parts of the reagent that are added to the alkene.

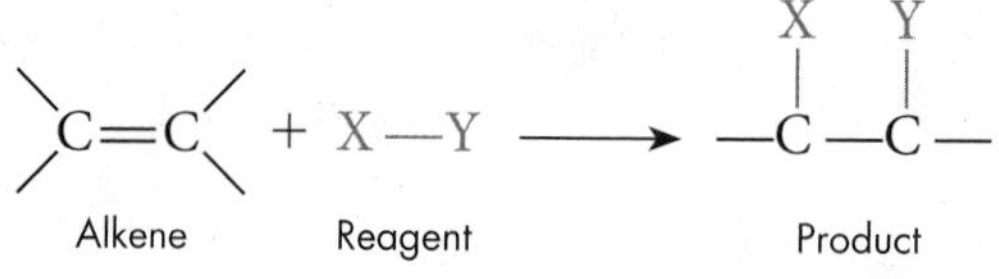

Hydration Reactions The addition of water to an alkene is called a **hydration reaction.** A hydration reaction forms an alcohol. An acid—usually hydrochloric acid or sulfuric acid—serves as a catalyst for the reaction. For example, the addition of water to ethene to form ethanol is a hydration reaction. The parts of ethanol that come from the water are shown in blue in this equation:

$$\underset{\text{Ethene}}{H_2C{=}CH_2} + \underset{\text{Water}}{H{-}OH} \xrightarrow[100^\circ C]{H^+} \underset{\text{Ethanol}}{H{-}\overset{H}{\underset{H}{C}}{-}\overset{OH}{\underset{H}{C}}{-}H}$$

Hydrogenation Reactions The addition of hydrogen to a carbon-carbon double bond to produce an alkane is called a **hydrogenation reaction.** You usually need a catalyst to make this reaction happen. A platinum (Pt) or palladium (Pd) catalyst is often used. The manufacture of margarine or spreads from oils like the ones below is a common use of hydrogenation.

$$\underset{\text{Ethene}}{H_2C{=}CH_2} + \underset{\text{Hydrogen}}{H{-}H} \xrightarrow{Pt} \underset{\text{Ethane}}{H{-}\overset{H}{\underset{H}{C}}{-}\overset{H}{\underset{H}{C}}{-}H}$$

Key Question How are addition reactions used in organic chemistry? **Addition reactions are an important method of introducing new functional groups to organic molecules. They are also used to convert alkenes to alkanes.**

fermentation the production of ethanol from sugars by the action of yeasts or bacteria

addition reaction the addition of a substance at the double bond of an alkene or at the triple bond of an alkyne

hydration reaction the addition of water to an alkene

hydrogenation reaction the addition of hydrogen to an alkene

RELATED WORDS

When you hydrate after exercising, you drink water or you add water to your body. In a hydration reaction, you add water to a reactant.

Hydrogenation

The fat molecules in cooking oils have double bonds. Oils are converted to solid spreads by adding hydrogen to the double bonds.

Carbon-carbon double bond
Each carbon in the double bond is bonded to one hydrogen.

Carbon-carbon single bond
Hydrogen has been added to the fat molecules. Each carbon is bonded to two hydrogens.

ether an organic compound in which oxygen is bonded to two carbon groups

amine an organic compound in which nitrogen is bonded to a carbon group

WORD ORIGINS

An amine is a chemical compound that contains nitrogen. Amines are derived from ammonia, which contains nitrogen. The name "amine" comes from the word *ammonia*.

Ethers

An **ether** is an organic compound in which oxygen is bonded to two carbon groups. The general formula of an ether is ROR. Like an alcohol, an ether molecule is bent. The repulsion between the unshared pairs of electrons on the oxygen atom bend the molecule.

$$R-\ddot{O}-R$$

Ether

Naming Ethers To name an ether using the IUPAC system, identify the two R groups. The smaller R group is treated as part of the substituent. Replace the *-ane* or *-ene* ending with *-oxy*. The larger R group is the parent hydrocarbon. In the common names of ethers, both R groups are treated as substituents. Replace the *-ane* or *-ene* endings with *-yl* for both R groups. To form the common name, list the names of the two R groups in alphabetical order. Follow them with the word *ether*. Two simple ethers are shown below, along with their IUPAC and common names.

$CH_3CH_2—O—CH_3$

Methoxyethane (ethyl methyl ether)

$CH_3—O—C_6H_5$

Methoxybenzene (methyl phenyl ether)

Ethyl methyl ether and methyl phenyl ether are nonsymmetric molecules. This is because the R groups attached to the oxygen atom are different. When both R groups are the same, the ether is symmetric. Use the same rules to name symmetric ethers with the IUPAC system. Use the prefix *di-* for the common names of symmetric ethers. Sometimes, you drop the prefix *di-*. Diethyl ether is simply called ethyl ether.

$CH_3CH_2—O—CH_2CH_3$

Ethoxyethane (diethyl ether)

$C_6H_5—O—C_6H_5$

Phenoxybenzene (diphenyl ether)

Properties of Ethers Ethers usually have lower boiling points than alcohols of comparable molar mass. Ethers have higher boiling points than comparable hydrocarbons and halocarbons. Ethers are not capable of forming hydrogen bonds with other ether molecules. However, ethers can form hydrogen bonds with water. So, ethers are more soluble in water than hydrocarbons and halocarbons. Ethers are less soluble in water than alcohols.

Key Question What is the general formula of an ether? **The general formula of an ether is ROR.**

Uses of Ethers
Isoflurane ($C_3H_2ClF_5O$) is an ether used as an inhaled anesthetic. This veterinarian is administering an inhaled anesthetic to a koala.

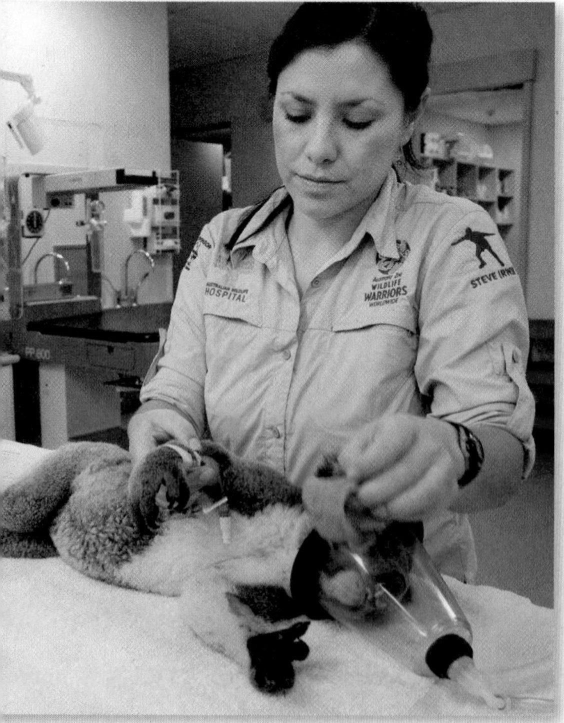

Amines

An **amine** is an organic compound in which nitrogen is bonded to a carbon group. Amines are similar to ammonia (NH_3). In an amine, carbon groups replace one, two, or three of the hydrogens in ammonia. You can classify amines according to the number of R groups attached to the nitrogen atom. The general formula of an amine is RNH_2, R_2NH, or R_3N. An amine with the general formula RNH_2 has one R group attached to the nitrogen atom. So it is a primary amine. Amines with two R groups attached to the nitrogen atom are secondary amines. Amines with three R groups attached to the nitrogen atom are tertiary amines.

Naming Amines Name primary amines similar to the way you name alcohols. Change the *-e* ending of the parent hydrocarbon to *-amine*. For example, CH_3NH_2 is named methanamine. The common names of primary amines are similar to the IUPAC names. Name the alkyl or aryl group and then follow it by *-amine*.

Properties of Amines Primary amines form intermolecular hydrogen bonds. Nitrogen is less electronegative than oxygen. So, the hydrogen bonds in amines are not as strong as those of alcohols. This causes primary amines to have lower boiling points than alcohols with a comparable number of carbons. Amines can also hydrogen-bond with water. So, smaller amines are soluble in water.

Key Question What is the general formula of an amine? **The general formula of an amine is RNH_2, R_2NH, or R_3N.**

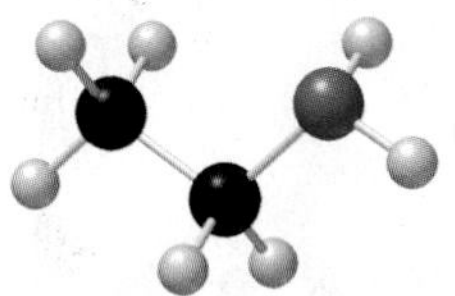

Ethanamine (ethylamine)

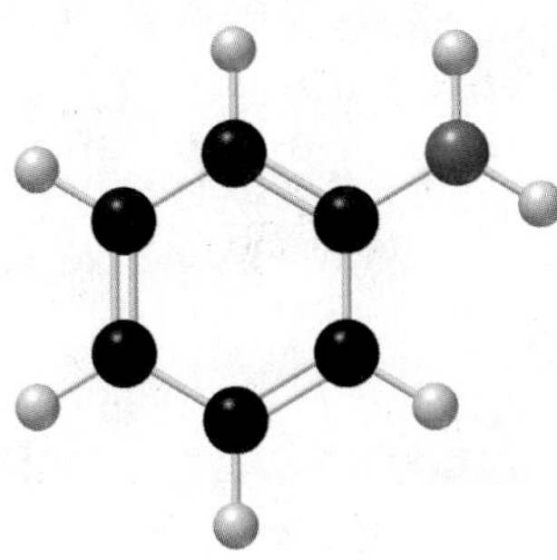

Benzenamine (phenylamine)

Uses of Amines The primary amine ethanamine is used to make plastics, pharmaceuticals, and pesticides. Benzenamine is used to make furniture foam. It is also used in some of the dyes that give clothing their colors.

23.2 LessonCheck

Key Concept Check

8. **Review** What is the general formula of an alcohol?

9. **Review** How do people use addition reactions in organic chemistry?

10. **Describe** Write the general formula of an ether.

11. **List** What are three possible general formulas of an amine?

Vocabulary Check

Choose a highlighted word from the lesson to complete each sentence correctly.

12. A(n) __________ is an organic compound in which oxygen is bonded to two carbon groups.

13. Water is added to an alkene in a(n) __________. In a(n) __________, hydrogen is added to a carbon-carbon double bond.

Think Critically

14. **Predict** Give the structure for the expected organic product from each of the following addition reactions.

a. $CH_3CH{=}CHCH_3 + H_2O \xrightarrow[100°C]{H^+}$

b. $CH_3CH{=}CHCH_3 + H_2 \xrightarrow{catalyst}$

CHEMISTRY & YOU

15. Menthol is the name of an organic compound used in products such as shaving cream. Menthol is a cyclohexanol with two alkyl substituents. Is menthol an alcohol or an ether? How can you tell? (Hint: See pages 759 and 762.)

BIGIDEA REACTIONS

16. Write a short paragraph in which you compare and contrast substitution reactions and addition reactions. Illustrate your examples with balanced equations.

23.3 Carbonyl Compounds

CHEMISTRY & YOU

Q: What gives a banana its special smell? A banana has a smell like no other fruit. Many organic molecules have good smells. These molecules provide the smells of food and flowers. You will learn about some of them later in this lesson.

Key Questions

What structural characteristic do an aldehyde and a ketone share?

What is the general formula of a carboxylic acid?

Why is dehydrogenation classified as an oxidation reaction?

What is the general formula of an ester?

carbonyl group a functional group with the general structure C=O

aldehyde an organic compound in which the carbon of the carbonyl group is joined to at least one hydrogen

ketone an organic compound in which the carbon of the carbonyl group is joined to two other carbons

WORD PARTS

A ketone and an aldehyde contain a carbonyl group. An aldehyde has at least one hydrogen joined to the carbonyl group. A ketone does not have hydrogen. To remember the difference, note that alde**hyd**e and **hyd**rogen contain *hyd*.

Aldehydes and Ketones

In an alcohol, an oxygen atom is bonded to a carbon group and a hydrogen atom. In an ether, an oxygen atom is bonded between two carbon groups. An oxygen atom can also be bonded to a single carbon atom by a double covalent bond. This arrangement is called a carbonyl group. A **carbonyl group** is a functional group with the general structure C=O.

The C=O functional group is present in aldehydes and ketones. An **aldehyde** is an organic compound in which the carbon of the carbonyl group is joined to at least one hydrogen. The general formula of an aldehyde is RCHO. A **ketone** is an organic compound in which the carbon of the carbonyl group is joined to two other carbons. The general formula of a ketone is RCOR. The structures of an aldehyde and a ketone are shown here:

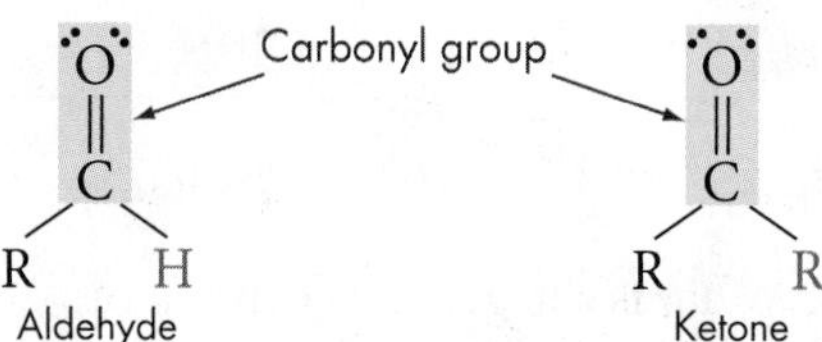

Naming of Aldehydes and Ketones To use the IUPAC system for naming either class of compounds, first identify the longest carbon chain that contains the carbonyl group. Replace the *-e* ending of the parent structure with *-al* for an aldehyde.

Ketones are named by changing the ending of the longest continuous carbon chain that contains the carbonyl group from *-e* to *-one.* Sometimes, a carbonyl group of a ketone could occur at more than one place on the chain. If so, then its position is designated by the lowest possible number. The table on the next page shows the naming of some common aldehydes and ketones.

Uses of Aldehydes and Ketones The simplest aldehyde is methanal (HCHO). It is also called formaldehyde. Methanal is very important in industry. Its greatest use is in the manufacture of synthetic resins. Many flavoring agents, like the cinnamon sticks on the next page contain aromatic aldehydes.

Some Common Aldehydes and Ketones

Compound type	IUPAC name (common name)	Structural formula	Ball-and-stick model
Aldehyde	Methanal (formaldehyde)	$H-\overset{\overset{\displaystyle O}{\|}}{C}-H$	
Aldehyde	Ethanal (acetaldehyde)	$CH_3-\overset{\overset{\displaystyle O}{\|}}{C}-H$	
Aldehyde	Benzaldehyde (benzaldehyde)	$C_6H_5-\overset{\overset{\displaystyle O}{\|}}{C}-H$	
Ketone	Propanone (acetone)	$CH_3-\overset{\overset{\displaystyle O}{\|}}{C}-CH_3$	
Ketone	Diphenylmethanone (benzophenone)	$C_6H_5-\overset{\overset{\displaystyle O}{\|}}{C}-C_6H_5$	

The most common industrial ketone is propanone. Another name for propanone is acetone. Propanone is a colorless, volatile liquid that boils at 56°C. Propanone is used in industry as a solvent for resins, plastics, and varnishes. Many nail polish removers contain propanone too.

Properties of Aldehydes and Ketones Aldehydes and ketones do not have —OH and —NH groups. That means that they cannot form hydrogen bonds with other molecules. They have lower boiling points than corresponding alcohols. Aldehydes and ketones can attract each other through polar-polar interactions of their carbonyl groups. As a result, their boiling points are higher than the corresponding alkanes. These attractive forces make nearly all aldehydes and ketones liquids or solids at room temperature. Some aldehydes and ketones can dissolve in water. They are all soluble in nonpolar solvents.

Cinnamaldehyde The cinnamon sticks in this drink contain an aldehyde. The common name of this aldehyde is cinnamaldehyde.

Go to your Chemistry Skills and Math Workbook to practice interpreting data.

Some Organic Compounds With Three Carbons

Compound	Structural formula	Boiling point (°C)	Primary intermolecular interactions
Propane	$CH_3—CH_2—CH_3$	–42	Dispersion forces
Propanal	$CH_3—CH_2—C(=O)—H$	49	Polar-polar interactions
Propanone	$CH_3—C(=O)—CH_3$	56	Polar-polar interactions
1-propanol	$CH_3—CH_2—CH_2—O—H$	97	Hydrogen bonding

The table above compares the boiling points of an alkane, an aldehyde, a ketone, and an alcohol with the same number of carbon atoms. You can see that intermolecular forces play a role in boiling point.

Key Question What structural characteristic do an aldehyde and a ketone share? **The C=O functional group is present in aldehydes and ketones.**

BUILD Vocabulary

carboxyl group a functional group made of a carbonyl group attached to a hydroxy group

carboxylic acid an organic compound with a carboxyl group

WORD ORIGINS

The word *carboxyl* comes from **carb**(on) + **ox**(ygen) + **yl**. A carboxyl group is made up of a carbon atom joined by covalent bonds to two oxygen atoms. One of the oxygen atoms is joined to a hydrogen atom.

Carboxylic Acids

A **carboxyl group** is a functional group made of a carbonyl group attached to a hydroxy group. It can be written as —COOH or —CO_2H. An organic compound with a carboxyl group is a **carboxylic acid**. The general formula of a carboxylic acid is RCOOH.

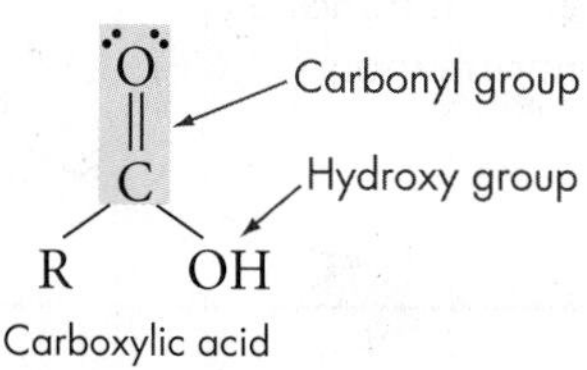

Carboxylic acid

Naming Carboxylic Acids In the IUPAC system, name a carboxylic acid by replacing the *-e* ending of the parent structure with the ending *-oic acid.* Remember, the parent hydrocarbon of a carboxylic acid is the longest continuous carbon chain containing the carboxyl group. So, for example, the carboxylic acid CH_3COOH is named ethanoic acid.

Properties of Carboxylic Acids Carboxylic acids are weak acids. They ionize weakly in solution. In water, they can lose a hydrogen ion and form a carboxylate ion. Like alcohols, carboxylic acids form intermolecular hydrogen bonds. So, carboxylic acids have higher boiling and melting points than other compounds of similar molar mass.

Citric Acid Citric acid is a common carboxylic acid. Citric acid gives lemons and limes their sour taste.

Uses of Carboxylic Acids Fruits like the ones shown on the left contain carboxylic acids. Household vinegar contains about 5% (v/v) ethanoic acid. Many carboxylic acids were first isolated from fats and are called fatty acids.

Key Question What is the general formula of a carboxylic acid? **The general formula of a carboxylic acid is RCOOH.**

Oxidation-Reduction Reactions

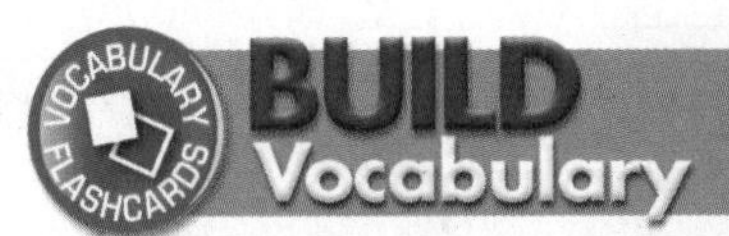

BUILD Vocabulary

dehydrogenation reaction
a reaction in which an organic molecule loses a hydrogen molecule

WORD PARTS
You can break the word *dehydrogenation* into parts. The prefix *de-* means "taking something away." The root word *hydrogen* refers to the element hydrogen. The suffix *-ation* means a process. So, a de + hydrogen + ation reaction is a process where hydrogen is taken away from a single or double bond.

Aldehydes, ketones, and carboxylic acids are related by oxidation and reduction reactions. Oxidation is the gain of oxygen, loss of hydrogen, or loss of electrons. Reduction is the loss of oxygen, gain of hydrogen, or gain of electrons. Recall from Chapter 20 that oxidation and reduction reactions always happen together.

In organic chemistry, the number of oxygen atoms and hydrogen atoms attached to carbon indicates the degree of oxidation of a compound. The less hydrogens in a carbon-carbon bond, the more oxidized the bond is. A triple bond is more oxidized than a double bond. A double bond is more oxidized than a single bond.

The loss of a molecule of hydrogen from an organic molecule is called a **dehydrogenation reaction.** It is the opposite of a hydrogenation reaction. Strong heating and a catalyst are usually needed to make dehydrogenation reactions occur. Dehydrogenation is an oxidation reaction. This is because the loss of each molecule of hydrogen involves the loss of two electrons from the organic molecule. The remaining carbon electrons pair to make a second or third bond, as shown in this equation:

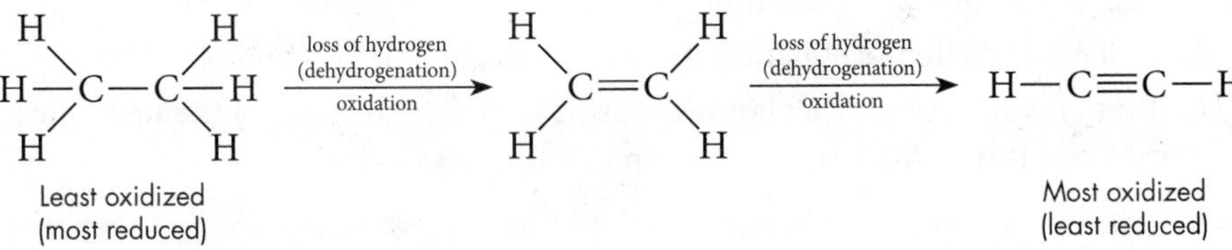

Oxidation in organic molecules also involves the number and degree of oxidation of oxygen atoms attached to a carbon atom. For example, methane is a saturated hydrocarbon. Methane can be oxidized in steps to form carbon dioxide. As shown below, methane alternately gains oxygen atoms and loses hydrogen atoms.

$$\underset{\substack{\text{Methane}\\\text{(most energetic molecule)}}}{\mathrm{H{-}\overset{H}{\underset{H}{C}}{-}H}} \xrightarrow[\text{oxidation}]{\text{gain of oxygen}} \underset{\text{Methanol}}{\mathrm{H{-}\overset{OH}{\underset{H}{C}}{-}H}} \xrightarrow[\text{oxidation}]{\text{loss of hydrogen}} \underset{\text{Methanal}}{\mathrm{H{-}\overset{O}{\overset{\|}{C}}{-}H}} \xrightarrow[\text{oxidation}]{\text{gain of oxygen}} \underset{\text{Methanoic acid}}{\mathrm{H{-}\overset{O}{\overset{\|}{C}}{-}OH}} \xrightarrow[\text{oxidation}]{\text{loss of hydrogen}} \underset{\substack{\text{Carbon dioxide}\\\text{(least energetic molecule)}}}{\mathrm{O{=}C{=}O}}$$

The more reduced a carbon compound is, the more energy it can release upon its complete oxidation to carbon dioxide. The oxidation of organic compounds releases thermal energy. The energy-releasing properties of oxidation reactions convert energy for use in living systems.

Key Question Why is dehydrogenation classified as an oxidation reaction? **Dehydrogenation is an oxidation reaction because the loss of each molecule of hydrogen involves the loss of two electrons from the organic molecule.**

Quick Lab

Purpose To distinguish an aldehyde from an alcohol or a ketone using Tollens's reagent

Materials

- **1*M* sodium hydroxide**
- **5 percent silver nitrate**
- **6*M* aqueous ammonia**
- **four small test tubes**
- **test tube rack**
- **plastic droppers**
- **glucose solution**
- **propanone**
- **ethanol**

Testing for an Aldehyde

Procedure

1. Add one drop of 1*M* sodium hydroxide to 2 mL of 5 percent silver nitrate in a test tube. Add 6*M* aqueous ammonia drop by drop. Gently mix the tube after each addition until the brownish precipitate dissolves. This will be your Tollens's reagent.

2. Place ten drops of Tollens's reagent in each of three clean, labeled test tubes.

3. To test tube 1, add two drops of glucose solution. To test tube 2, add two drops of propanone. To test tube 3, add two drops of ethanol. Gently agitate each test tube to mix the contents.

4. Observe the contents of the test tubes. Do not disturb the test tubes for at least five minutes.

Analyze and Conclude

1. Observe What evidence of a chemical reaction did you observe in test tube 1? In test tube 2? In test tube 3?

2. Describe Write the equation for any chemical reaction you observed.

3. Infer If you observed a chemical reaction in one or more of the test tubes, how do you think this type of reaction could be useful?

Esters
The characteristic aromas of many fruits are due to esters. Isopentyl acetate is an ester found in bananas. Strawberries contain the ester benzyl acetate. Benzyl acetate can be synthesized by esterification of acetic acid and benzyl alcohol.

Esters

Esters can smell delicious! Many esters have pleasant, fruity odors. Esters give blueberries, pineapples, apples, pears, bananas, and many other fruits like the ones shown below their wonderful smells. Esters also give many perfumes their fragrances. An **ester** is an organic compound in which the —OH of the carboxyl group has been replaced by an —OR from an alcohol. Esters contain a carbonyl group and an ether link to the carbonyl carbon. The general formula of an ester is RCOOR.

Ester

Properties of Esters The molecules in esters are polar, but they cannot form hydrogen bonds with one another. This is because esters do not contain hydrogen attached to oxygen or to nitrogen or fluorine. So, only weak polar-polar interactions hold ester molecules to one another. Esters have much lower boiling points than carboxylic acids. Esters with more than four or five carbons are not very soluble in water.

Esterification Esters may be prepared by a process is called esterification. The reactants are usually a carboxylic acid and an alcohol. They are heated with an acid as a catalyst. The synthesis of ethyl ethanoate from ethanoic acid and ethanol is an example of esterification. The equation for the synthesis of ethyl ethanoate is shown here:

$$\underset{\text{Ethanoic acid}}{CH_3-\overset{\overset{\displaystyle O}{\|}}{C}-OH} + \underset{\text{Ethanol}}{CH_3CH_2O-H} \overset{H^+}{\rightleftharpoons} \underset{\text{Ethyl ethanoate}}{CH_3-\overset{\overset{\displaystyle O}{\|}}{C}-OCH_2CH_3} + H_2O$$

Key Question What is the general formula of an ester?
The general formula of an ester is RCOOR.

BUILD Vocabulary

ester an organic compound in which the —OH of the carboxyl group has been replaced by an —OR group from an alcohol

WORD ORIGINS

The word ester comes from the word *vinegar* in German. Esters are a class of compounds produced by a reaction between a carboxylic acid and an alcohol. Vinegar is made up of about 5 percent ethanoic acid, a carboxylic acid.

23.3 LessonCheck

Key Concept Check

17. **Review** Describe the structure of the carbonyl groups that are characteristic of aldehydes and ketones.

18. **Identify** What is the general formula of a carboxylic acid?

19. **Explain** Why is dehydrogenation an oxidation reaction?

20. **Describe** What is the general formula of an ester?

Vocabulary Check *Choose a highlighted word from the lesson to complete each sentence correctly.*

21. The general formula of a(n) __________ is RCHO.

22. A(n) __________ is an organic compound in which the carbon of the carbonyl group is joined to two other carbons.

Think Critically

23. **Describe** Draw structural formulas for these organic compounds.

a. hexanoic acid

b. butanal

c. 2-pentanone

CHEMISTRY & YOU

24. The smell of strawberries is caused by benzyl acetate. The smell of almonds is caused by benzaldehyde. How are the general formulas of these compounds similar? How do you think they may be different?
(Hint: See page 764, 765, and 768.)

BIGIDEA CARBON CHEMISTRY

25. How can you describe the degree of oxidation of an organic compound?

Scratch and Sniff Stickers

Kids like scratch and sniff stickers. Some scratch and sniff stickers smell like fruit. Other scratch and sniff stickers smell like root beer or pickles. Others smell like pizza or even stinky sneakers! Where do those scents come from?

Esters give most scratch and sniff stickers their smells. The esters used in the stickers are volatile liquids. A volatile liquid evaporates easily. This explains why you are able to smell them. A single type of ester or a mixture of esters is contained in tiny brittle capsules. Then, the brittle capsules are glued onto the sticker paper. The capsules are so tiny that you can barely notice their rough texture on the sticker. When you scratch the sticker, some of the capsules break. This allows you to smell the esters.

SNIFF IT Esters leave the broken capsules. You can smell the esters when they are released.

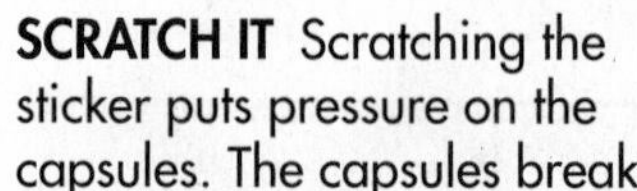

SCRATCH IT Scratching the sticker puts pressure on the capsules. The capsules break.

Take It Further

1. Explain If you scratch a sticker a lot, the smell gets fainter. Why does this happen?

2. Describe Methyl butanoate smells like pineapple. Write a structural formula for this ester.

3. Infer Ethyl heptanoate smells like grapes. You can make this substance from a carboxylic acid and an alcohol. Which carboxylic acid and alcohol would you use?

23.4 Polymers

CHEMISTRY & YOU

Q: How do organic molecules bond together to form long chains? The skydivers are linked together in a chain. Organic molecules bond together to form chains too. As more and more molecules bond together, the molecular chains grow longer and longer.

Key Questions

How does an addition polymer form?

How are condensation polymers formed?

BUILD Vocabulary

polymer a large molecule that forms from the covalent bonding of many smaller molecules

monomers the smaller molecules that combine to form a polymer

PREFIXES

The prefix *poly-* means "many." The prefix *mono-* means "one." A polymer is made of many monomers.

Addition Polymers

Some of the most important organic compounds are giant molecules called polymers. Each day, you see many different polymers. Plastics are an example of polymers. There are many kinds and uses of plastics

A **polymer** is a large molecule formed by the covalent bonding of repeating smaller molecules. The smaller molecules that combine to form a polymer are called **monomers**. Some polymers contain only one type of monomer. Other polymers contain two or more types of monomers. Polymerization is the reaction that joins monomers to form a polymer. Most polymerization reactions require a catalyst. Addition polymers and condensation polymers are two types of polymers.

An addition polymer forms when unsaturated monomers react to form a polymer. Ethene undergoes addition polymerization. The equation below describes the polymerization of ethene. The ethene molecules bond to one another to form the long-chain polymer polyethylene.

$$\underset{\text{Ethene (ethylene)}}{x\text{CH}_2{=}\text{CH}_2} \longrightarrow \underset{\text{Polyethylene}}{\text{H}(\text{CH}_2{-}\text{CH}_2)_x\text{H}}$$

The letter x on the reactant side of the equation is the number of monomers that combine to form the polymer. The x on the product side is the number of repeating units in the polymer. Parentheses identify the repeating unit. In this case, the repeating unit is $-\text{CH}_2-\text{CH}_2-$.

Polyethylene Polyethylene is resistant to chemicals and easy to clean. These properties make polyethylene an important product in industry. Polyethylene is used to make plastic bottles, containers, and even toys, such as the one shown below. Polyethylene with short chains is soft like paraffin wax. Polyethylene with long chains is harder and more rigid.

Uses of Polyethylene Many common items, such as this toy duck, are made of polyethylene.

Uses of Polystyrene
Protective helmets are often made of polystyrene foam.

Polypropylene Polypropylene is a stiffer polymer than polyethylene. Polypropylene is used in utensils and beverage containers. It is prepared by the polymerization of propene, as shown in the equation below.

$$x\text{CH}_2{=}\underset{\text{Propene (propylene)}}{\text{CH}(\text{CH}_3)} \longrightarrow \underset{\text{Polypropylene}}{+\!\!\left(\text{CH}_2{-}\text{CH}(\text{CH}_3)\right)_x}$$

Polystyrene Bike helmets like the one on the left are often made from polystyrene. Polystyrene does not conduct heat well. This makes it useful for insulating homes. Polystyrene is used to make molded items, such as coffee cups and picnic coolers. Polystyrene is prepared by the polymerization of styrene.

$$x\text{CH}_2{=}\text{CH}(\text{C}_6\text{H}_5) \longrightarrow \left(\text{CH}_2{-}\text{CH}(\text{C}_6\text{H}_5)\right)_x$$

Styrene (vinyl benzene) → Polystyrene

Polyvinyl Chloride Many halocarbon polymers, including polyvinyl chloride (PVC), have useful properties. Polyvinyl chloride is used in plumbing pipes, rainwear, and garden hoses. It is also produced in sheets. A fabric backing can be added to these sheets and used as a tough plastic upholstery covering. Vinyl chloride is the monomer of polyvinyl chloride.

$$x\text{CH}_2{=}\text{CH}(\text{Cl}) \longrightarrow \left(\text{CH}_2{-}\text{CH}(\text{Cl})\right)_x$$

Chloroethene (vinyl chloride) → Polyvinyl chloride (PVC)

Polytetrafluoroethene Polytetrafluoroethene (PTFE) is the product of the polymerization of tetrafluoroethene monomers. PTFE is very resistant to heat and to chemicals. This polymer functions as a coating on nonstick cookware. PTFE is also used to insulate wires and cables.

$$x\text{CF}_2{=}\text{CF}_2 \longrightarrow \left(\text{CF}_2{-}\text{CF}_2\right)_x$$

Tetraflouroethene → PTFE

Polyisoprene Polyisoprene is the polymer that constitutes natural rubber. The monomer of polyisoprene is isoprene. Isoprene is harvested from tropical plants, such as the rubber tree shown below.

$$x\mathrm{CH_2{=}C(CH_3)CH{=}CH_2} \longrightarrow \mathrm{{+}CH_2C(CH_3){=}C(H)CH_2{+}}_x$$

Isoprene → Polyisoprene

Key Question How does an addition polymer form? **An addition polymer forms when unsaturated monomers form a polymer.**

Uses of Polyisoprene

❶ Harvesters cut rubber trees. The sap contains isoprene. Harvesters collect the sap in bowl-like containers.

❷ The harvested rubber dries. The isoprene polymerizes and changes form. For higher-grade rubber, the polymerization of the isoprene happens under controlled conditions.

❸ The manufacturer processes and molds the polymer into the final product. Polyisoprene is used to make many common items, such as rubber bands, soles of athletic shoes, and tires.

BUILD Understanding

Venn Diagram Draw a Venn diagram to compare and contrast different types of polymers. How are they formed? What are they made of? Use the Venn diagram to record how they are the same and how they are different.

Condensation Polymers

The formation of a polyester is a common example of condensation polymerization. Condensation polymers are formed by the joining of monomers with the loss of a small molecule, such as water. Polyesters are polymers that consist of many repeating units of dicarboxylic acids and dihydroxy alcohols. The dicarboxylic acids and dihydroxy alcohols are joined by ester bonds.

You can use a block diagram to represent the formation of a polyester. This kind of diagram shows only the functional groups involved in the polymerization reaction. The squares and circles represent unreactive parts of the organic molecules. Condensation polymerization requires two functional groups on each monomer molecule.

$$x\mathrm{HO{-}\overset{\displaystyle O}{\overset{\|}{C}}{-}\square{-}\overset{\displaystyle O}{\overset{\|}{C}}{-}OH} + x\mathrm{HO{-}\bigcirc{-}OH} \longrightarrow$$

Dicarboxylic acid   Dihydroxy alcohol

$$\left(\mathrm{\overset{\displaystyle O}{\overset{\|}{C}}{-}\square{-}\overset{\displaystyle O}{\overset{\|}{C}}{-}O{-}\bigcirc{-}O}\right)_x + 2x\mathrm{H_2O}$$

Representative polymer unit of a polyester

PET PET is an abbreviation for the polyester polyethylene terephthalate. PET is formed from terephthalic acid and ethylene glycol, as shown below.

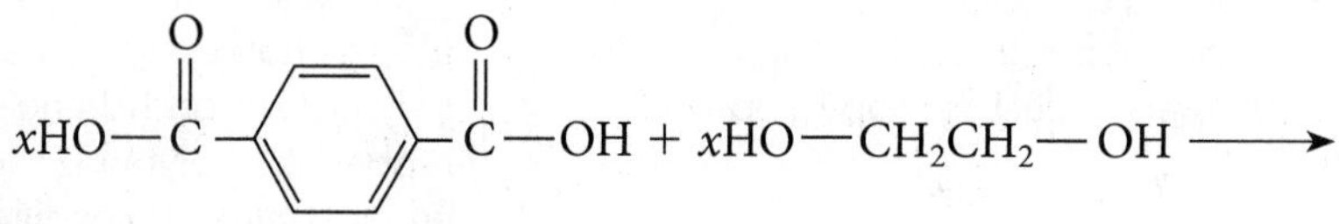

$$\left(\mathrm{\overset{\displaystyle O}{\overset{\|}{C}}{-}C_6H_4{-}\overset{\displaystyle O}{\overset{\|}{C}}{-}O{-}CH_2CH_2{-}O}\right)_x + 2x\mathrm{H_2O}$$

Representative polymer unit of PET

Today, you are sipping from plastic bottles made of PET. Tomorrow, someone else may be wearing them! It takes about a dozen large bottles that are made from PET to make one fleece jacket.

The fabric of this woman's jacket is made from recycled PET bottles. To form PET fibers, the compound is melted and forced through tiny holes in devices called spinnerettes. People use the fibers to make tire cord and clothing. PET fibers are often blended with cotton to make clothing. This blend is more comfortable to wear on hot days than 100 percent polyester. PET fiber tubing can also be used to replace major blood vessels.

Recycling PET Plastic bottles can be made into clothing, such as this fleece jacket.

Polyamides Many important polymers are formed by the reaction of carboxylic acids and amines. The amines used to make polymers generally contain the amino functional group (—NH_2). The condensation of a carboxylic acid and an amine produces an amide.

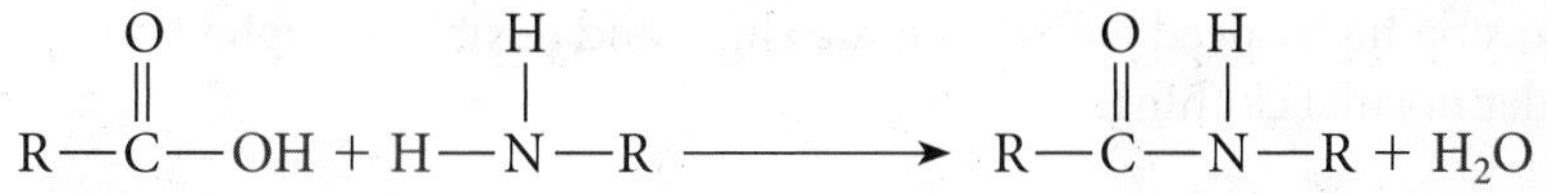

$$\underset{\text{Carboxylic acid}}{R-\overset{\overset{\displaystyle O}{\|}}{C}-OH} + \underset{\text{Amine}}{H-\overset{\overset{\displaystyle H}{|}}{N}-R} \longrightarrow \underset{\text{Amide}}{R-\overset{\overset{\displaystyle O}{\|}}{C}-\overset{\overset{\displaystyle H}{|}}{N}-R} + H_2O$$

Polyamides are polymers. In these polymers, the carboxylic acid and amine monomer units are linked by amide bonds.

▶ **Nylon** The many types of nylon are polyamides. The representative polymer unit of nylon is derived from 6-aminohexanoic acid. This compound contains carboxyl and amino functional groups. How is the long polymer chain formed? The carboxyl group of the monomer of one molecule attaches to the amino group of the next monomer by the formation of an amide bond.

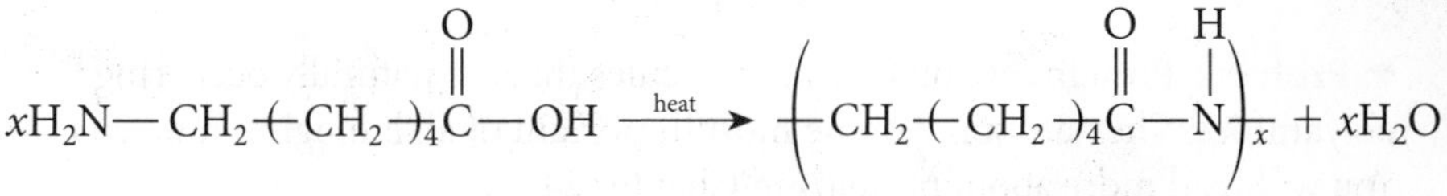

$$\underset{\text{6-Aminohexanoic acid}}{xH_2N-CH_2{(CH_2)}_4\overset{\overset{\displaystyle O}{\|}}{C}-OH} \xrightarrow{\text{heat}} \underset{\text{Representative polymer unit of nylon}}{\left(CH_2{(CH_2)}_4\overset{\overset{\displaystyle O}{\|}}{C}-\overset{\overset{\displaystyle H}{|}}{N}\right)_x} + xH_2O$$

The melted polymer can be spun into very fine but very strong fibers. Nylon fibers are used to make carpeting, tire cords, fishing lines, sheer hosiery, and textiles. Nylon is also molded into ropes, such as the ones used by the climber shown on the right.

Uses of Nylon
Many climbers use climbing ropes with cores that are made of nylon. Nylon makes these ropes very strong.

BUILD Connections

Would you like to increase your athletic performance? Kevlar is used in many different types of high-performance athletic equipment. Because Kevlar is light and tough, such equipment as bikes, helmets, and skis can be lightweight and more resistant to breakage.

▶ Kevlar Polyamides that contain aromatic rings are extremely tough. They are also resistant to fire. The aromatic rings make the resulting fiber stiffer and tougher. Kevlar™ is a polyamide with a carbon backbone consisting of aromatic rings. The aromatic rings are derived from terephthalic acid and *p*-phenylenediamine. A properly constructed vest made of Kevlar is strong enough to stop high-speed bullets. It is also light and flexible enough to be worn under normal clothing.

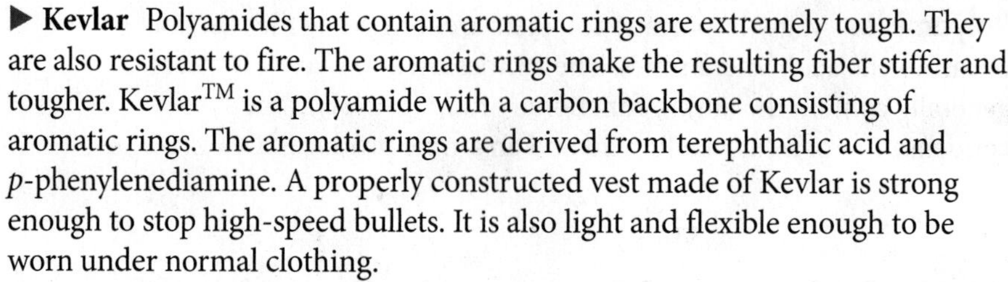

Representative unit of Kevlar

▶ Proteins Proteins are biological molecules that are naturally occurring polyamides. They are some of the most important of all biological molecules. You will read more about proteins in Chapter 24.

Key Question How are condensation polymers formed? **Condensation polymers are formed by the joining of monomers with the loss of a small molecule, such as water.**

23.4 LessonCheck

Key Concept Check

26. Review Describe how addition polymers form.

27. Review How do condensation polymers form?

Vocabulary Check

Choose a highlighted word from the lesson to complete each sentence correctly.

28. Small molecules that combine to form long chains are ___________.

29. A large molecule formed by the covalent bonding of repeating smaller molecules is a(n) ___________.

Think Critically

30. Describe What structure must a monomer have if it is to undergo addition polymerization?

31. Identify What is formed when a carboxylic acid and an amine combine? Give an example of the polymer formed in the reaction.

CHEMISTRY & YOU

32. Polymers make up most of the bottles, containers, and packing that you see around you. Try to identify the polymers in some of them. Are they addition polymers or condensation polymers? (Hint: See pages 771-776.)

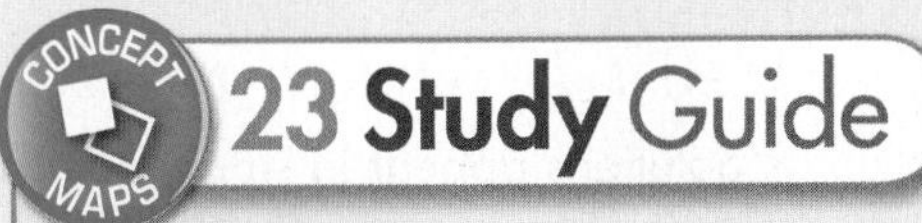

23 Study Guide

BIGIDEAS

CARBON CHEMISTRY; REACTIONS

Functional groups affect the physical and chemical properties of organic compounds. Chemical reactions can be used to change the structure of organic molecules. These reactions may introduce a new functional group. Organic chemists use substitution, addition, oxidation-reduction, and polymerization reactions.

23.1 Introduction to Functional Groups

Organic compounds can be classified according to their functional groups.

The general formula of a halocarbon is RX, where X is a halogen substituent.

Substitution reactions are an important method of introducing new functional groups to organic molecules.

- functional group (754)
- halocarbon (756)
- substitution reaction (757)

23.2 Alcohols, Ethers, and Amines

The general formula of an alcohol is ROH.

Addition reactions are an important method of introducing new functional groups to organic molecules. They are also used to convert alkenes to alkanes.

The general formula of an ether is ROR.

The general formula of an amine is RNH_2, R_2NH, or R_3N.

- alcohol (758)
- hydroxy group (758)
- fermentation (760)
- addition reaction (760)
- hydration reaction (761)
- hydrogenation reaction (761)
- ether (762)
- amine (763)

23.3 Carbonyl Compounds

The C=O functional group is present in aldehydes and ketones.

The general formula of a carboxylic acid is RCOOH.

Dehydrogenation is an oxidation reaction because the loss of each molecule of hydrogen involves the loss of two electrons from the organic molecule.

The general formula of an ester is RCOOR.

- carbonyl group (764)
- aldehyde (764)
- ketone (764)
- carboxyl group (766)
- carboxylic acid (766)
- dehydrogenation reaction (767)
- ester (768)

23.4 Polymers

An addition polymer forms when unsaturated monomers react to form a polymer.

Condensation polymers are formed by the joining of monomers with the loss of a small molecule, such as water.

- polymer (771)
- monomers (771)

23 Assessment

★ Solutions appear in Appendix D.

Lesson by Lesson

23.1 Introduction to Functional Groups

33. What does R in the formula RCH_2Cl represent?

★**34.** Write a structural formula for each compound.

a. 1,2,2-trichlorobutane
b. 1,3,5-tribromobenzene
c. 1,2-dichlorocyclohexane

35. Name the following halocarbons.

a. $CH_2{=}CHCH_2Cl$

b. $CH_3CH(CH_3)CH_2CH(Cl)CH_2Cl$

36. Write structural formulas and give IUPAC names for all the isomers of the following compounds.

a. $C_3H_6Cl_2$ **b.** C_4H_9Br

23.2 Alcohols, Ethers, and Amines

★**37.** Give the IUPAC names for these alcohols.

a. $CH_3{-}CH(OH){-}CH_3$

b. $CH_2(OH){-}CH(OH){-}CH_3$

c. $CH_3{-}C(CH_3)(OH){-}CH_3$

★**38.** Write structures and names of the products obtained upon addition of each of the following reagents to ethene.

a. HBr **b.** Cl_2 **c.** H_2O **d.** H_2 **e.** HCl

39. Give the IUPAC and common names for the following ethers.

a. $CH_3OCH_2CH_3$
b. $CH_2{=}CHOCH{=}CH_2$
c. $CH_3CH(CH_3)OCH(CH_3)CH_3$

40. Name the following amines.

a. $CH_3CH_2CH_2CH_2NH_2$
b. $CH_3CH_2NH_2$

23.3 Carbonyl Compounds

★**41.** Give the IUPAC names for the following carbonyl compounds.

a. CH_3CHO
b. $CH_3CH(CH_3)CH_2CHO$
c. $CH_3(CH_2)_3COOH$
d. $CH_3C({=}O)CH_3$
e. $CH_3CH_2C({=}O)CH_2CH_2CH_3$
f. 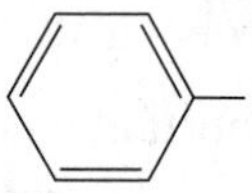 $C_6H_5{-}CH_2CHO$ (benzene ring bonded to CH_2CHO)

42. Identify the type of molecule that would contain the following functional groups.

a. $-CO_2H$
b. $C{=}O$

23.4 Polymers

43. Different samples of a polymer, such as polyethylene, can have different properties. Explain.

★**44.** Draw the structure of the repeating units in a polymer that has the following monomers.

a. 1-butene
b. 1,2-dichloroethene

Understand Concepts

45. Write a general formula for each type of compound.

a. halocarbon
b. ketone
c. aldehyde
d. ester
e. amide
f. ether

46. Write the structure and name of the expected products for the following reaction.

$$CH_3COOH + CH_3OH \xrightarrow{H^+}$$

★47. Classify each compound as an alcohol, a phenol, or an ether.

a. OH

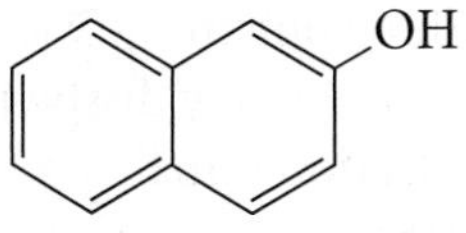

b. O

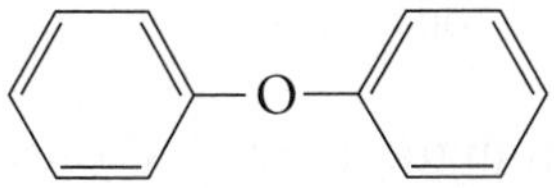

c. $-CH_2OH$

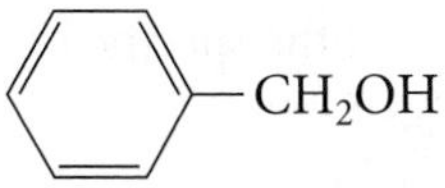

d. OH

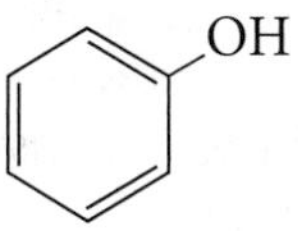

e. CH_3CH_2CHOH with CH_3 on the CHOH carbon

f. $CH_3CH_2OCH_3$

48. Write the structural formulas for the products of these reactions.

a. $CH_3CH_2CH{=}CH_2 + Cl_2 \longrightarrow$

b. $CH_3CH_2CH{=}CH_2 + Br_2 \longrightarrow$

49. Explain why a carbon-carbon double bond is nonpolar, but a carbon-oxygen double bond is very polar.

Think Critically

50. Evaluate Propane ($CH_3CH_2CH_3$) and acetaldehyde (CH_3CHO) have the same molar mass, but propane boils at $-42°C$ and acetaldehyde boils at 21°C. Explain this difference.

★51. Compare and Contrast How would you expect the water solubility of ethanoic and decanoic acids to compare?

52. Infer The processes used to synthesize many organic compounds often use compounds that contain double or triple bonds as reactants. Explain why using unsaturated reactants might be better than using saturated reactants.

53. Apply Concepts Write a chemical equation showing how to produce these compounds.

a.

b.

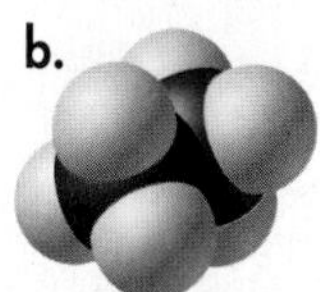

★54. Infer Tetrahydrofuran (THF) is an important industrial organic solvent. THF is a cyclic ether containing four carbon atoms in the ring. Draw a structural formula for this cyclic ether.

FOUNDATIONS Wrap-Up

The Smell of Chemistry!

1. Draw Conclusions At the beginning of this chapter, you tried to identify fruits by their smell. What type of organic compounds give fruits their unique smell?

Concept Check

Now that you have finished studying Chapter 23, answer these questions:

2. How are organic compounds classified?

3. What is the general formula for an alcohol, an ether, and an amine?

4. What kind of functional group would you find in aldehydes and ketones?

5. Why are polymers so useful?

Write About Science

55. Research a Problem Methyl tert-butyl ether (MTBE) is a commonly used gasoline additive. Recently, regulatory agencies have begun to limit its use. Explain the function of MTBE in gasoline and why its use is now limited.

56. Compare and Contrast Acetylsalicylic acid (aspirin) and ibuprofen are active ingredients of over-the-counter pain relievers. They work by preventing certain proteins from sending pain signals to the brain. Look up the structures of these two active ingredients. Compare their structures and functional groups.

57. Propose a Solution Hydrocarbons from petroleum are an important source of material for industry. How do you think you could create ethylene glycol using petrochemical ethene?

CHEMYSTERY

The Toothpaste Terror

Manufacturers include moistening agents in their formulas for toothpaste. The most common moistening agent in toothpaste is glycerol. Usually, glycerol is listed as glycerin on toothpaste ingredient labels. Glycerol is an alcohol with three hydroxy groups. The hydroxy groups help keep the toothpaste moist. They form hydrogen bonds with water molecules in the air. Glycerin has a sweet taste too. It sweetens the toothpaste.

***58. Compare** Counterfeiters have made cheap toothpaste by substituting ethylene glycol for glycerol. Like glycerol, ethylene glycol is a moistening agent. But it is also toxic. Compare the structures of ethylene glycol and glycerol.

59. Connect to the **BIGIDEA** Often, there is more than one moistening agent in toothpaste. Look at the ingredient list on your toothpaste container. Are there any other alcohols besides glycerol that may serve as moistening agents? Search the Internet to find the structures of each alcohol. Identify the number of hydroxy groups.

Cumulative Review

***60.** What is the maximum number of orbitals in the *p* sublevel of an atom? (See Lesson 5.1 for help.)

a. 1 **b.** 3 **c.** 5 **d.** 9

61. Using electron dot structures, illustrate the formation of F^- from a fluorine atom and OH^- from atoms of hydrogen and oxygen. (See Lesson 7.1 for help.)

62. Assume that water enters a power plant at 20°C and leaves at 30°C. Will the amount of dissolved oxygen in the water be greater entering or leaving the plant? (See Lesson 16.1 for help.)

63. In a saturated solution containing undissolved solute, the solute is continually dissolving, but the solution concentration remains constant. Explain this statement. (See Lesson 16.1 for help.)

***64.** A 500 g aluminum tray at 22°C is heated to 180°C in an oven. How many kJ of heat does the aluminum tray absorb if the specific heat of aluminum is 0.90 J/(g•°C)? (See Lesson 17.1 for help.)

65. Predict the direction of shift in the equilibrium position for each change in conditions. (See Lesson 18.3 for help.)

$$2NO_2(g) \rightleftharpoons 2NO(g) + O_2(g)$$

a. O_2 partial pressure decrease
b. total pressure increase
c. O_2 partial pressure increase
d. NO partial pressure increase

66. Assign an oxidation number to each atom in these compounds. (See Lesson 20.2 for help.)

a. $NaNO_2$
b. $CoSO_4$
c. SeO_2
d. $Zn(OH)_2$
e. K_2PtCl_4

67. What is the source of the electrical energy produced in a voltaic cell? (See Lesson 21.1 for help.)

***68.** Is petroleum or coal most likely to be a good source of aromatic compounds? (See Lesson 22.5 for help.)

Standardized Test Prep

For help with answering test questions, go to your Chemistry Skills and Math Workbook.

Select the choice that best answers each question or completes each statement.

1. The acid-catalyzed hydrolysis of an ester gives a carboxylic acid and
   (A) an amine. (C) an alcohol.
   (B) an ether. (D) an alkene.

2. Ethane, methanal, and methanol have similar molar masses. Which series lists the compounds in order of increasing boiling point?
   (A) ethane, methanal, methanol
   (B) methanal, methanol, ethane
   (C) methanol, methanal, ethane
   (D) ethane, methanol, methanal

3. A carbonyl group is characterized by a
   (A) carbon-carbon double bond.
   (B) carbon-oxygen double bond.
   (C) carbon-nitrogen single bond.
   (D) carbon-oxygen single bond.

The lettered choices below refer to Questions 4–7. A lettered choice may be used once, more than once, or not at all.

(A) alcohol (C) carboxylic acid
(B) ketone (D) ether

To which class of organic compounds does each of the following compounds belong?

4. CH_3CH_2COOH
5. $CH_3CH_2CH_2OH$
6. $CH_3CH_2OCH_3$
7. CH_3COCH_3

Use the following models with Question 8.

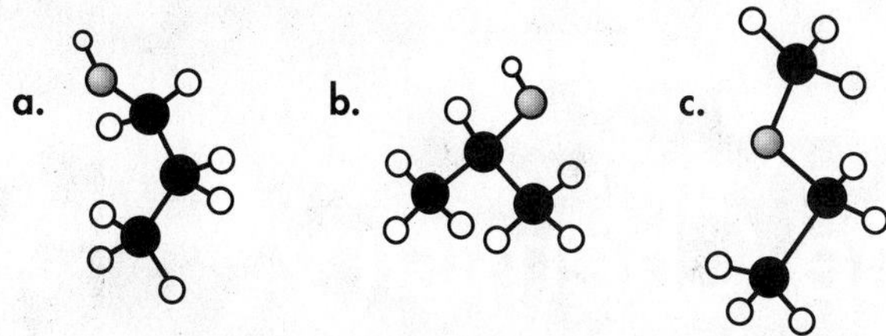

8. The molecular formula for each compound is C_3H_8O. Write the name for each compound.

9. There are two compounds with a carbonyl group that have the molecular formula C_3H_6O. Write a complete structural formula for each compound. Name each compound.

Tips for Success

Eliminate Wrong Answers If you do not know which choice is correct, eliminate those you know are wrong. If you can rule out some choices, you will increase your chances of choosing the correct answer.

Characterize the reactions in Questions 10–14 as an addition, esterification, oxidation, polymerization, or substitution reaction.

10. $CH_3CHO \xrightarrow[H_2SO_4]{K_2Cr_2O_7} CH_3COOH$

11. $CH_2{=}CH_2 + HCl \longrightarrow CH_3CH_2Cl$

12. $CH_3CO_2H + CH_3CH_2OH \xrightarrow{H^+} CH_3COOCH_2CH_3 + H_2O$

13. $xCH_2{=}CH_2 \longrightarrow H{+}CH_2{-}CH_2{+_x}H$

14. $C_6H_6 + Br_2 \xrightarrow{\text{catalyst}} C_6H_5Br + HBr$

For each question, there are two statements. Decide whether each statement is true or false. Then, decide whether Statement II is a correct explanation for Statement I.

	Statement I		Statement II
15.	The addition of hydrogen to an alkene is a reduction reaction.	BECAUSE	The addition of hydrogen to any molecule is a reduction reaction.
16.	Aldehydes are easily oxidized.	BECAUSE	Oxidation of aldehydes produces alcohols.
17.	Ethanol (CH_3CH_2OH) is immiscible in water in all proportions.	BECAUSE	Ethanol molecules can form hydrogen bonds with other ethanol molecules.

If You Have Trouble With . . .

Question	1	2	3	4	5	6	7	8	9	10	11	12	13	14	15	16	17
See Lesson	23.3	23.3	23.3	23.3	23.2	23.2	23.3	23.2	23.3	23.3	23.2	23.3	23.4	23.1	23.2	23.3	23.2

24 The Chemistry of Life

FOUNDATIONS for Learning

Feeding the Yeast

1. Put 50 mL of warm water and one package of dry yeast in a zippered sandwich bag. Close the bag and shake gently.
2. Note any changes after 15 minutes.
3. Open the bag and add 500 mg of sugar.
4. Close the bag and place it in a bowl of warm water.
5. Note any changes after 15 minutes.

Form a Hypothesis What is a possible explanation for any changes you observed?

PearsonChem.com

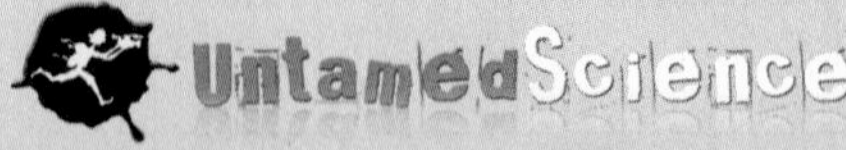

Take a video field trip with the Untamed Science crew as they go diving with dolphins to learn more about the chemistry behind oxygen storage in animals.

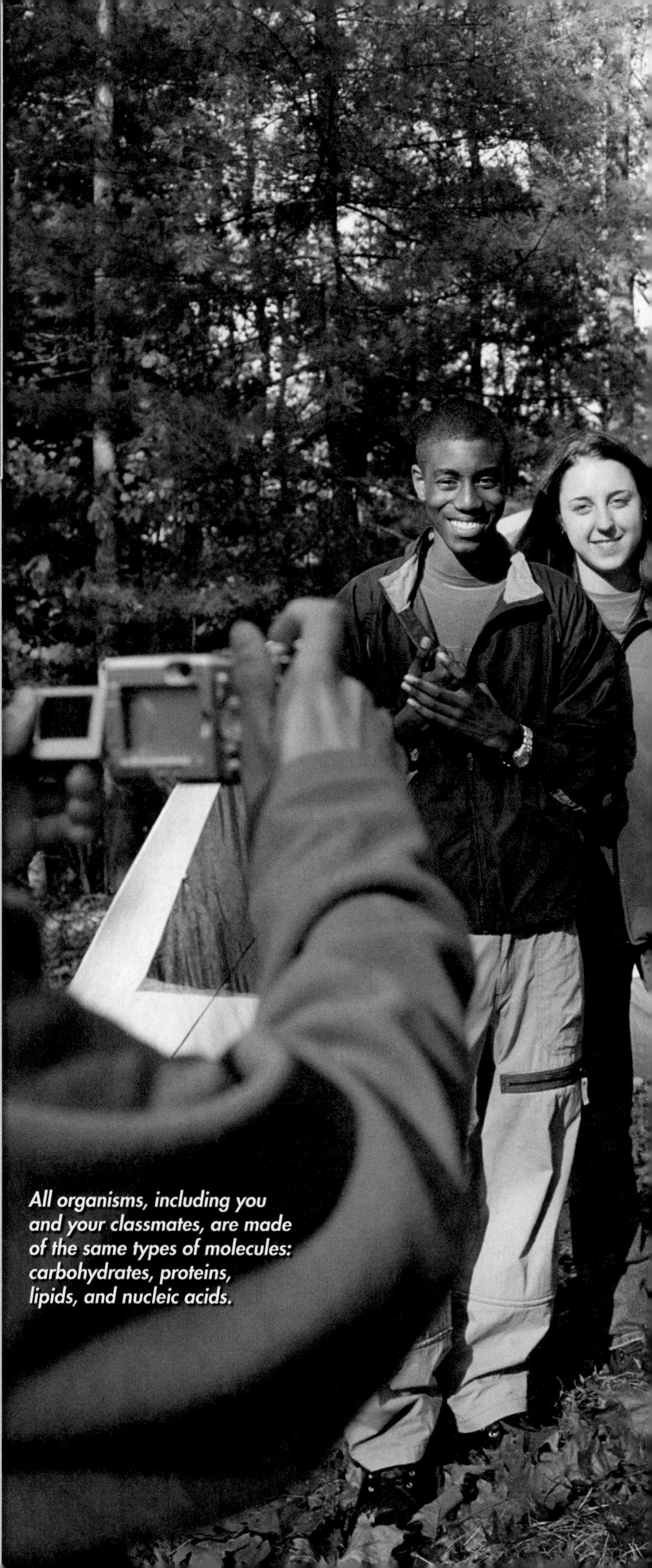

All organisms, including you and your classmates, are made of the same types of molecules: carbohydrates, proteins, lipids, and nucleic acids.

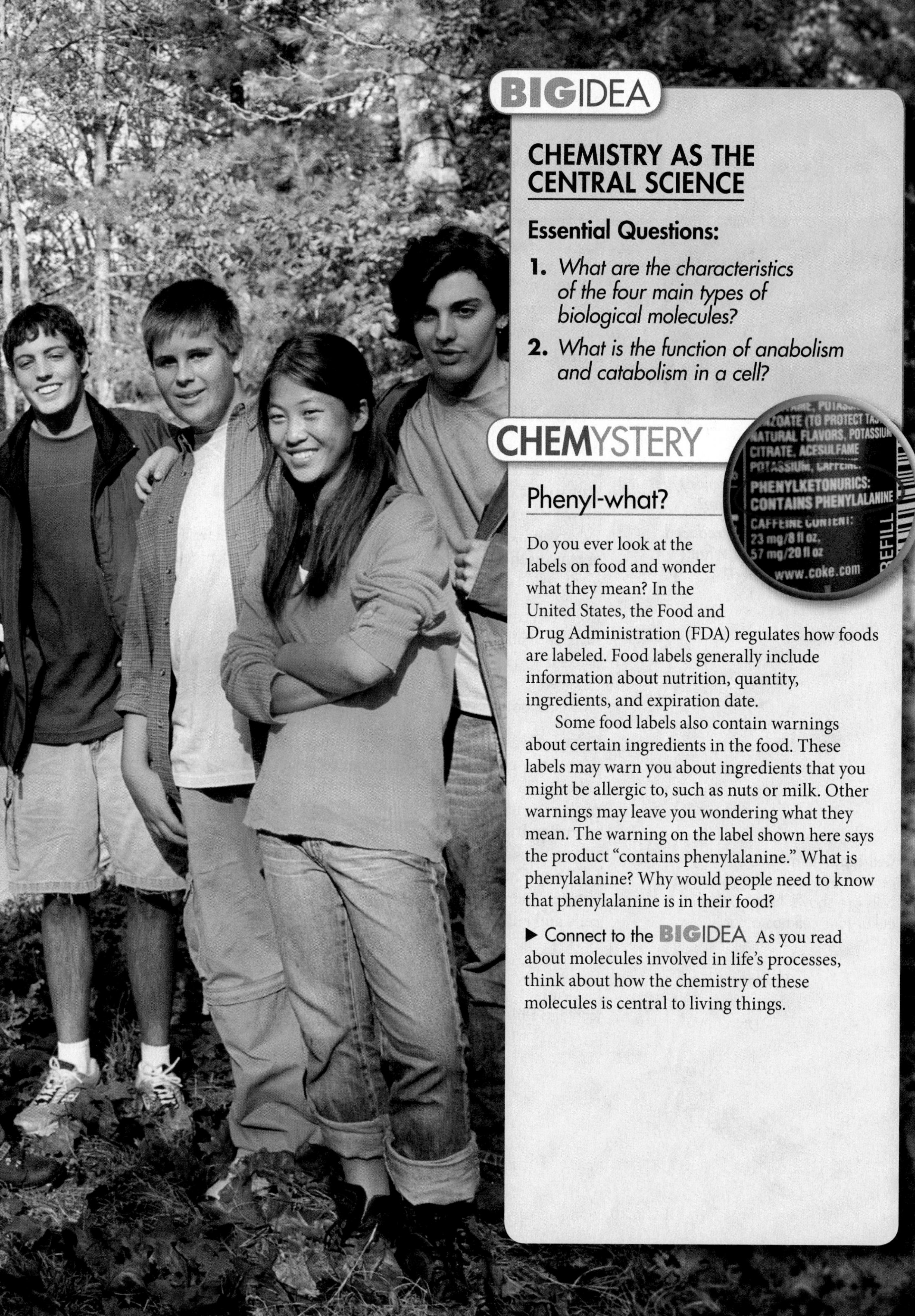

BIGIDEA

CHEMISTRY AS THE CENTRAL SCIENCE

Essential Questions:

1. *What are the characteristics of the four main types of biological molecules?*
2. *What is the function of anabolism and catabolism in a cell?*

CHEMYSTERY

Phenyl-what?

Do you ever look at the labels on food and wonder what they mean? In the United States, the Food and Drug Administration (FDA) regulates how foods are labeled. Food labels generally include information about nutrition, quantity, ingredients, and expiration date.

Some food labels also contain warnings about certain ingredients in the food. These labels may warn you about ingredients that you might be allergic to, such as nuts or milk. Other warnings may leave you wondering what they mean. The warning on the label shown here says the product "contains phenylalanine." What is phenylalanine? Why would people need to know that phenylalanine is in their food?

▶ Connect to the **BIG**IDEA As you read about molecules involved in life's processes, think about how the chemistry of these molecules is central to living things.

24.1 A Basis for Life

CHEMISTRY & YOU

Q: Where do fish get their oxygen? All animals need oxygen to survive. Fish obtain oxygen that is dissolved in water. We breathe in oxygen from the air around us. Where does all this oxygen come from? In this lesson, you will learn how oxygen in the air and water is produced.

Key Questions

What are the two major types of cells that occur in nature?

What compound is reduced during photosynthesis? What compounds are formed?

The Structure of Cells

Every organism is composed of one or more cells. Prokaryotic cells and eukaryotic cells are the two major cell types that occur in nature. Prokaryotic cells are more ancient than eukaryotic cells. Fossilized remains show that prokaryotic cells were present on Earth at least 3 billion years ago. Eukaryotic cells appeared about 1 billion years ago. Bacteria are single celled organisms that are each made of a prokaryotic cell. Plants and animals are many celled organisms that are made of eukaryotic cells.

Every cell contains all the chemicals necessary for life. A cell membrane surrounds all the parts inside the cell. This membrane holds everything in place. It also allows needed substances to pass into and out of the cell. Eukaryotic cells are much larger and more complex than prokaryotic cells. However, both types of cells carry out very similar chemical processes.

Eukaryotic cells contain organelles, which are small structures suspended in the interior cellular fluid. Organelles carry out many specific functions in the cell. The nucleus and mitochondrion are types of organelles. The nucleus contains the genetic information for each eukaryotic cell. The mitochondrion uses oxygen to provide energy to eukaryotic cells.

Key Question What are the two major types of cells that occur in nature? **The two major cell types that occur in nature are prokaryotic cells and eukaryotic cells.**

Cell Types Examples of prokaryotic and eukaryotic cells are shown here. Only the eukaryotic cell has a nucleus.

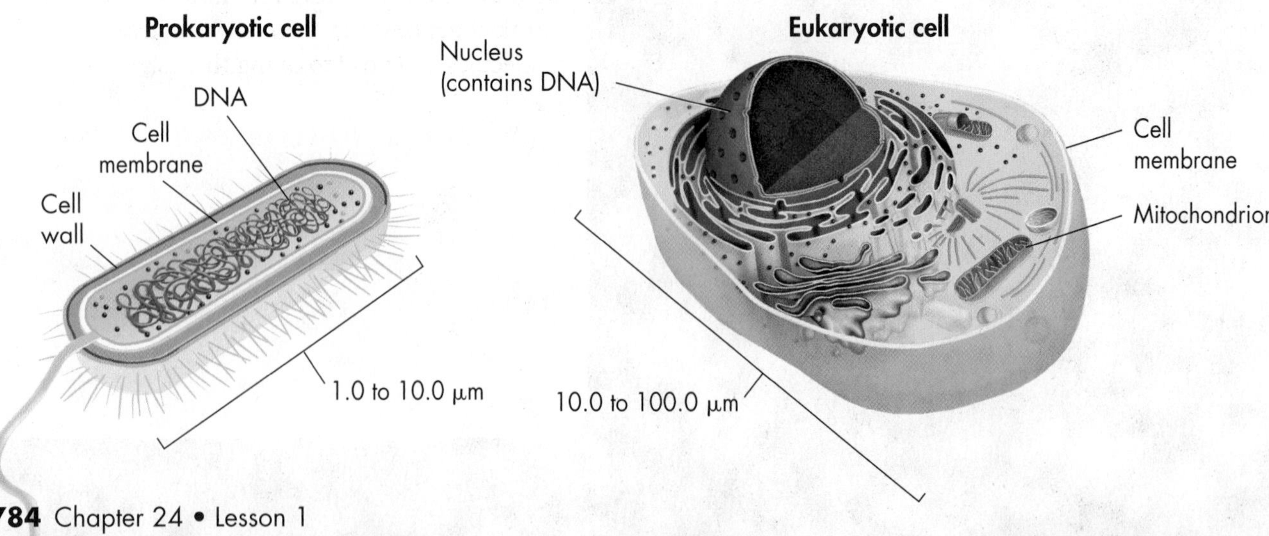

Energy and the Carbon Cycle

Every organism on Earth must have energy to survive. The primary source of energy for living things is the sun. The cells of green plants and certain algae contain organelles called chloroplasts. Chloroplasts absorb solar energy and use it to make food.

Energy Inside each chloroplast is a light capturing system of membranes, as shown in the picture below. These membranes convert light energy into chemical energy—a process called **photosynthesis.** The process of photosynthesis requires carbon dioxide, water, and sunlight. Photosynthesis uses the energy from sunlight to reduce carbon dioxide to compounds that contain C—H bonds. The products of photosynthesis are glucose ($C_6H_{12}O_6$) and oxygen. This equation shows the reactants and products of photosynthesis:

$$\underset{\text{Carbon dioxide}}{6CO_2} + \underset{\text{Water}}{6H_2O} + \underset{\text{(sunlight)}}{\text{Energy}} \longrightarrow \underset{\text{Glucose}}{C_6H_{12}O_6} + \underset{\text{Oxygen}}{6O_2}$$

Glucose is an important product of photosynthesis. The energy stored in the chemical bonds of glucose is used by plants. It is also used by animals that eat the plants. When this stored energy is used, it is oxidized back to carbon dioxide and water in the reaction that is shown in this equation:

$$\underset{\text{Glucose}}{C_6H_{12}O_6} + \underset{\text{Oxygen}}{6O_2} \longrightarrow \underset{\text{Carbon dioxide}}{6CO_2} + \underset{\text{Water}}{6H_2O} + \underset{\text{(chemical energy)}}{\text{Energy}}$$

Oxygen is also an important product of photosynthesis. The oxygen in Earth's atmosphere, oceans, and lakes was produced by photosynthetic organisms. Most organisms need oxygen to live. Oxygen is a key part of the reaction that releases energy from glucose.

photosynthesis the process that organisms use to convert light energy into chemical energy

ROOT WORDS

The word *photosynthesis* is built from the prefix *photo*, which means "light," and the word *synthesis*, which means "to put together." During photosynthesis, light provides the energy to put together molecules of food in the plant.

Learn more about* oxygen *online. CONCEPTS IN ACTION

Chloroplast Photosynthesis takes place on the inner membranes and in the spaces between membranes of a chloroplast. The pigments in chloroplasts give leaves their green color.

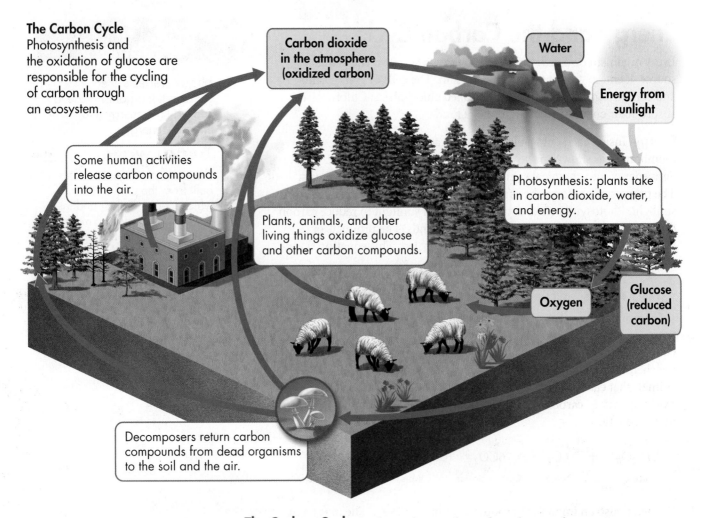

The Carbon Cycle
Photosynthesis and the oxidation of glucose are responsible for the cycling of carbon through an ecosystem.

Carbon dioxide in the atmosphere (oxidized carbon)

Water

Energy from sunlight

Some human activities release carbon compounds into the air.

Photosynthesis: plants take in carbon dioxide, water, and energy.

Plants, animals, and other living things oxidize glucose and other carbon compounds.

Oxygen

Glucose (reduced carbon)

Decomposers return carbon compounds from dead organisms to the soil and the air.

The Carbon Cycle In the carbon cycle, carbon changes form as it moves through plants, animals, soils, and the atmosphere. This illustration shows how the parts of the carbon cycle are connected.

Key Question What compound is reduced during photosynthesis? What compounds are formed? **Photosynthesis uses the energy from sunlight to reduce carbon dioxide to compounds that contain C—H bonds, mainly in the form of glucose ($C_6H_{12}O_6$).**

24.1 LessonCheck

Key Concept Check

1. **Identify** What two types of cells occur in nature?

2. **Review** What chemical changes occur during photosynthesis?

Vocabulary Check *Choose a highlighted word from the lesson to complete the sentence correctly.*

3. The process organisms use to convert light energy into chemical energy is ________.

Think Critically

4. **Describe** What is the function of chloroplasts in green plants and algae?

5. **Explain** Explain how carbon moves through the environment.

CHEMISTRY & YOU

6. Fish, like all animals, need oxygen to survive. What process produces oxygen? (Hint: See page 785.)

24.2 Carbohydrates

CHEMISTRY & YOU

Q: Why does a cow chew all day? Cows spend most of their day chewing their food. A cow's diet is rich in cellulose, which belongs to a class of organic molecules known as carbohydrates. In this lesson, you will learn about the structures and functions of carbohydrates.

Key Question

What is the general formula of carbohydrates?

BUILD Vocabulary

carbohydrate a monomer or polymer of sugar molecules

monosaccharide a simple sugar containing five or six carbon atoms

ROOT WORDS

The general formula for carbohydrates ($C_n(H_2O)_n$) makes them appear to be hydrates of carbon. Even though this is how they get their name, they are not true hydrates. The definition of hydrate is found on page 472.

Classifying Carbohydrates

Some long-distance runners prepare for a big race by eating a lot of bread and pasta. These foods are excellent sources of important food molecules called carbohydrates. **Carbohydrates** are monomers and polymers of sugars. Sugars are compounds made of carbon, hydrogen, and oxygen. Carbohydrates are the main source of energy for the body. They are found in most foods, including fruits, breads, pasta, and beans. The formula of most carbohydrates can be expressed as $C_n(H_2O)_n$.

Monosaccharides The simplest carbohydrates are called monosaccharides. **Monosaccharides** are simple sugars containing five or six carbon atoms. Glucose and fructose are examples of simple sugars. Glucose is the product of photosynthesis. It is the primary energy source for our bodies. Fructose occurs in honey and in a large number of fruits. Glucose and fructose each have the molecular formula $C_6H_{12}O_6$. These molecules are shown below. Both glucose and fructose have a ring structure. Each molecule of these compounds contains five hydroxy groups. The hydroxy groups are polar, so sugars are easy to dissolve in water. Because the two compounds have the same formula, they are constitutional isomers.

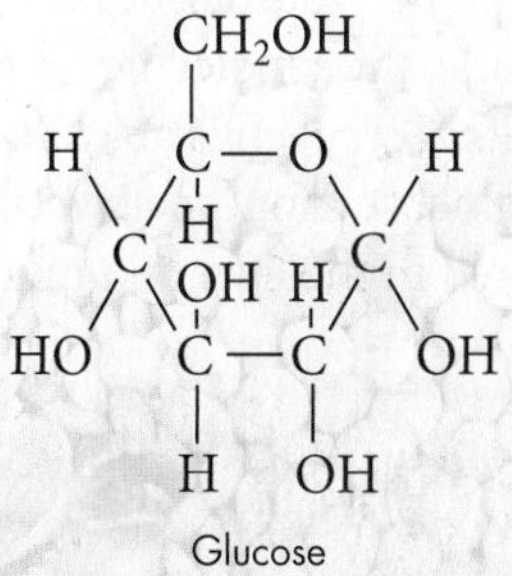

Glucose

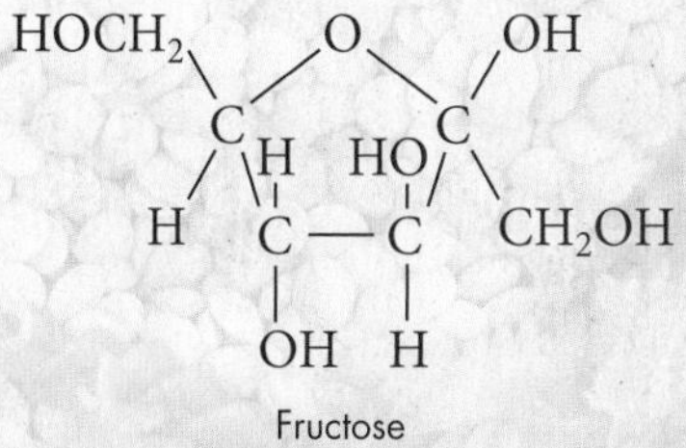

Fructose

disaccharide a sugar that forms from the condensation of two monosaccharide molecules

polysaccharide a polymer produced by the linkage of many monosaccharide monomers

PREFIXES

The word *saccharide* is from the Sanskrit word *sarkara*, which means "sugar." The prefixes *mono-*, *di-*, and *poly-* mean "one," "two," and "many," respectively.

Disaccharides Simple sugars form the building blocks of other carbohydrates. The cyclic forms of two simple sugars can join together in a condensation reaction. A condensation reaction also produces a small molecule such as water. A sugar that forms from the condensation of two monosaccharide molecules is known as a **disaccharide.** A disaccharide forms when a glucose molecule and a fructose molecule react with one another, as shown in the diagram below. The products are water and sucrose, which is common table sugar.

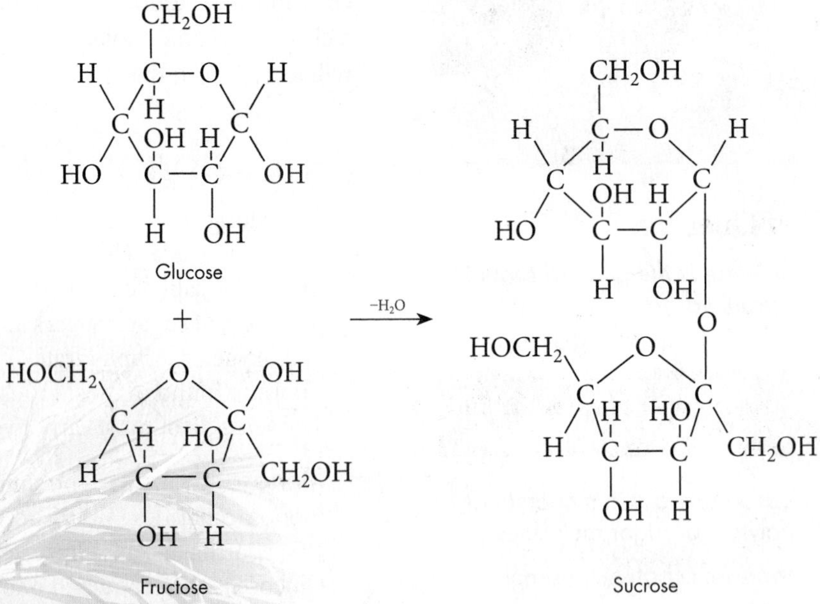

Glucose + Fructose $\xrightarrow{-H_2O}$ Sucrose

Polysaccharides Polymers produced by the condensation reactions of many monosaccharide monomers are called **polysaccharides.** Starches are the major storage form of glucose in plants. Starches are also polysaccharides. Starch molecules are very long chains of glucose units. A typical starch molecule contains hundreds of glucose monomers.

Some polysaccharides do not form long chains. Instead, they are made up of branched molecules. Each branch may consist of about a dozen glucose units. Glycogen is an example of a polysaccharide that consists of chains of glucose monomers with many branches. Glycogen is the energy source stored in the liver and muscle cells of animals.

Sugar Cane
Sucrose is obtained commercially mainly from the juice of sugar cane and sugar beets. Sugar cane, shown here, grows as a tall grass and is often harvested by hand.

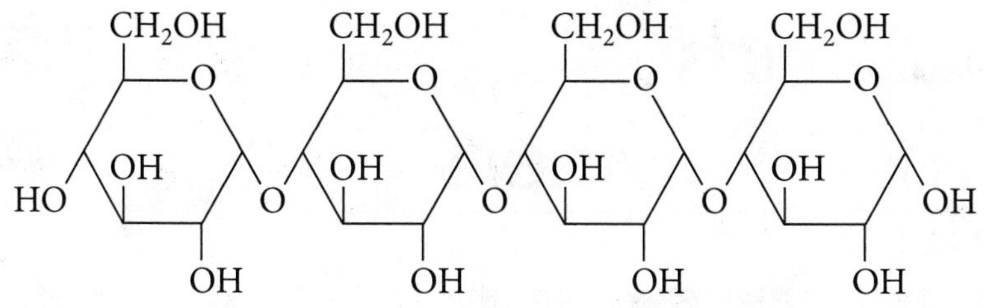

Starch

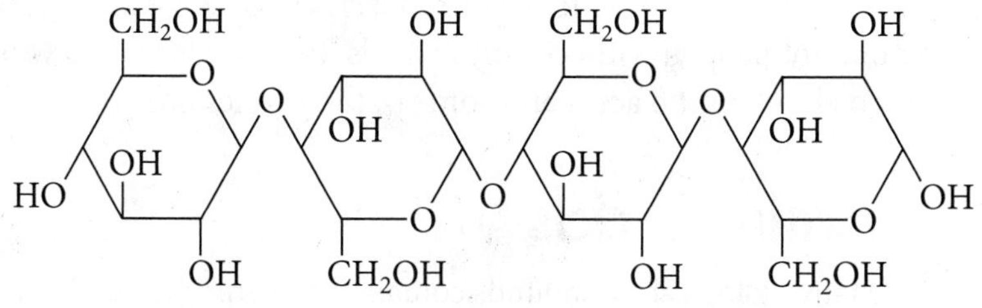

Cellulose

Polysaccharides Starch and cellulose are both polymers made up of hundreds of glucose monomers. This diagram only shows part of each polysaccharide. The position of the bonds between glucose units is different in each of these molecules. Because of this difference, starch is easily digested, but cellulose is not digestible by most organisms.

Cellulose is probably the most abundant biological molecule on Earth. It is a polysaccharide that provides rigidity to plant cell walls. As the diagram shows, cellulose is a glucose polymer like starch. However, the position of the bond that links the glucose monomers in each of these polymers is different. This difference causes starch and cellulose to have different properties. Starch can be digested by most organisms. It is also somewhat soluble in water. Cellulose is insoluble in water. Only a few microorganisms can digest cellulose. Some of these microorganisms live in the digestive tracts of cattle and termites.

Key Question What is the general formula of carbohydrates?
Most carbohydrates have the general formula $C_n(H_2O)_n$.

24.2 LessonCheck

Key Concept Check

7. **Review** What is the general formula for carbohydrates?

Vocabulary Check

Choose a highlighted word from the lesson to complete each sentence correctly.

8. To form a(n) __________, two monosaccharides combine in a condensation reaction.

9. The sugars glucose and fructose are two examples of __________.

Think Critically

10. **Identify** Where is glucose found in nature?

11. **Describe** What are the main characteristics of monosaccharides, disaccharides, and polysaccharides?

12. **Compare** Starch and cellulose have different properties, but both are composed of glucose units. Explain what makes them different.

CHEMISTRY & YOU

13. A cow's diet consists mostly of cellulose. A cow's stomach contains several parts. Food enters the first part of the stomach and is then regurgitated so the cow can chew it again. The regurgitated food then goes to a later part of the stomach where special bacteria live. Why is regurgitating and chewing necessary for a cow to digest cellulose? (Hint: See page 789.)

24.3 Amino Acids and Their Polymers

CHEMISTRY & YOU

Q: Why do your muscles need amino acids? Strength building exercises can cause some of your muscles to become larger. This could not happen without amino acids. In this lesson, you will learn about amino acids and some of their functions.

Key Questions

What is the general structure of an amino acid?

What determines the differences in the chemical and physiological properties of peptides and proteins?

How do enzymes affect the rates of reactions in living things?

BUILD Vocabulary

amino acid a compound that contains an amino group and a carboxyl group

peptide any combination of amino acids where the amino group of one amino acid is united with the carboxyl group of another amino acid

peptide bond a bond between the carboxyl group of one amino acid and the nitrogen of the next amino acid in the chain

protein a polypeptide with more than 100 amino acid units

WORD ORIGINS

Peptide comes from *pepsin*, a stomach enzyme that was one of the first proteins to be studied. Pepsin is a Greek word that means "to digest."

Amino Acids

Many biological compounds contain nitrogen. Some of the most important nitrogen containing molecules in organisms are amino acids. An **amino acid** is a compound that contains both an amino group (—NH_2) and a carboxyl group (—COOH). Chemists and biochemists generally only use the term amino acid to refer to any one of the 20 common amino acids that are made and used by living organisms. An amino acid consists of a carboxyl group, an amino group, a hydrogen, and an R group side chain that are all covalently bonded to a central carbon atom, as shown in this diagram.

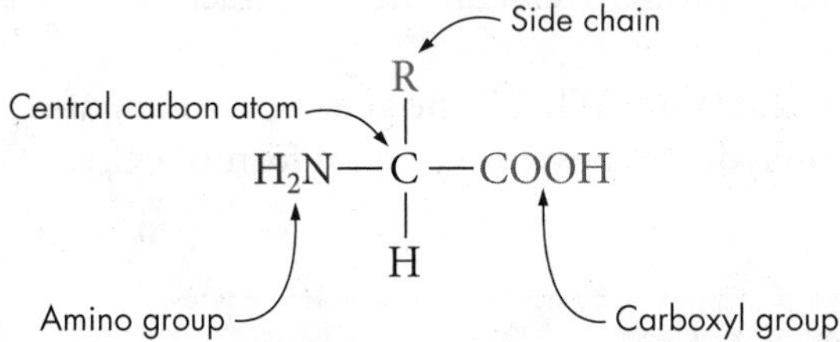

Each amino acid has different properties. The chemical nature of the side chain group accounts for the differences in properties of the 20 common amino acids. In some, the side chains are nonpolar hydrocarbons. In others, the side chains are neutral but polar. In a few, the side chains are acidic or basic.

The names of the 20 common amino acids and their symbols are shown in the table on the next page. The symbol for each amino acid is three letters long. These symbols are used to show which amino acids combine to form peptides.

Key Question What is the general structure of an amino acid? **An amino acid consists of a carboxyl group, an amino group, a hydrogen, and an R group side chain that are all covalently bonded to a central carbon atom.**

Common Amino Acids							
Name	**Symbol**	**Name**	**Symbol**	**Name**	**Symbol**	**Name**	**Symbol**
Alanine	Ala	Glutamine	Gln	Leucine	Leu	Serine	Ser
Arginine	Arg	Glutamic acid	Glu	Lysine	Lys	Threonine	Thr
Asparagine	Asn	Glycine	Gly	Methionine	Met	Tryptophan	Trp
Aspartic acid	Asp	Histidine	His	Phenylalanine	Phe	Tyrosine	Tyr
Cysteine	Cys	Isoleucine	Ile	Proline	Pro	Valine	Val

Peptides and Proteins

A **peptide** is any combination of amino acids where the amino group of one amino acid is united with the carboxyl group of another amino acid. The bond between the carboxyl group of one amino acid and the nitrogen of the next amino acid in the chain is a **peptide bond.** Peptide bonds always involve the central amino and central carboxyl groups. The side chains are not involved in the bonding. The equation below shows how amino acids combine to form a peptide:

$$H_2N-\underset{\underset{H}{|}}{\overset{\overset{R}{|}}{C}}-\overset{\overset{O}{\|}}{C}-OH + H-\underset{\underset{H}{|}}{N}-\underset{\underset{H}{|}}{\overset{\overset{R}{|}}{C}}-\overset{\overset{O}{\|}}{C}-OH \longrightarrow H_2N-\underset{\underset{H}{|}}{\overset{\overset{R}{|}}{C}}-\overset{\overset{O}{\|}}{C}-\underset{\underset{H}{|}}{N}-\underset{\underset{H}{|}}{\overset{\overset{R}{|}}{C}}-\overset{\overset{O}{\|}}{C}-OH + H_2O$$

Amino acid — Amino acid — Peptide (Peptide bond: the C—N bond between the two amino acid units)

Amino Acid Sequence The peptide formula is written so that a free amino group is at the left end of the molecule and a free carboxyl group is at the right end. More amino acids may be added to the right end to form long chains. Each addition involves a condensation reaction. The order in which the amino acids are linked is called the amino acid sequence of that molecule. The amino acid sequence of a peptide is expressed by using three-letter abbreviations for the amino acids. For example, Asp—Glu—Gly represents a peptide containing aspartic acid, glutamic acid, and glycine, respectively.

Proteins A peptide with more than 10 amino acids is a polypeptide. A polypeptide with more than about 100 amino acids is a **protein.** Proteins are an important class of biomolecules. Your skin, hair, nails, and muscles are all made of proteins. Almost all chemical reactions in the body use proteins.

Differences in the chemical and physiological properties of peptides and proteins result from differences in amino acid sequences. Twenty amino acids can be linked in an enormous number of ways in a protein molecule. There are 20^{100} different amino acid sequences possible for a protein of 100 amino acids containing a combination of the 20 different amino acids.

Peptide Structures Peptides form three dimensional shapes.

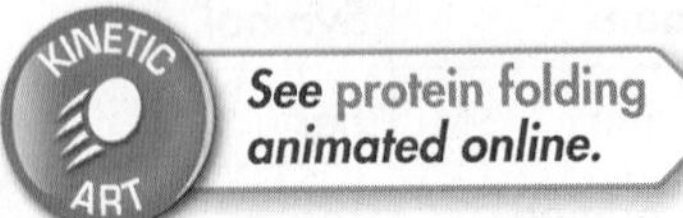

Each color represents a different amino acid in a protein.

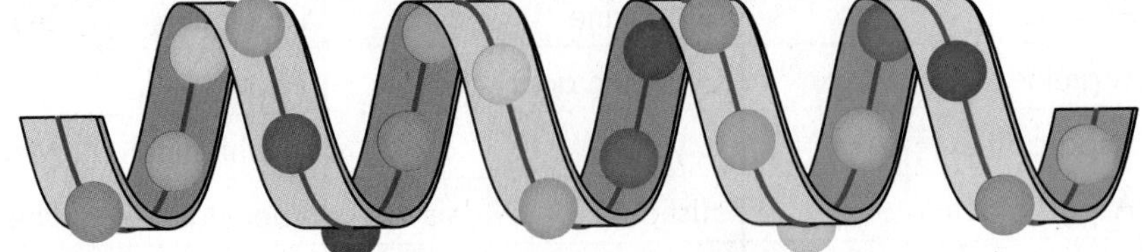

The chain can coil into a helix.

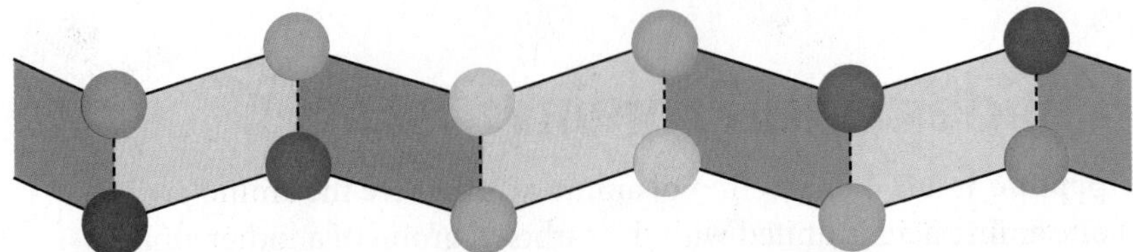

Two peptide chains can form a pleated, sheetlike structure.

3-D Protein Structure Interactions between amino acids in a polypeptide chain allow proteins to have complicated three dimensional shapes, as shown above. Hydrogen bonds form to hold together folded chains. Covalent bonds allow separate polypeptides to join together to form a single protein. The three dimensional structure is a very important part of protein function. If the shape is changed, the protein molecule may act very differently.

The illustration below shows the complicated folding of a protein molecule. Myoglobin is a protein that stores oxygen in muscle cells. The peptide chains of most of the myoglobin molecule are twisted into helixes. These helixes are folded to give a specific shape to the molecule. A nonprotein structure called heme is attached to the folded protein. Oxygen binds to the iron in heme.

Key Question What determines the differences in the chemical and physiological properties of peptides and proteins? **Differences in the chemical and physiological properties of peptides and proteins result from differences in the amino acid sequence.**

Myoglobin The three dimensional structure of myoglobin is shown here. Marine animals, such as this dolphin, have a large amount of myoglobin in their muscles. Oxygen stored in myoglobin allows them to make long dives.

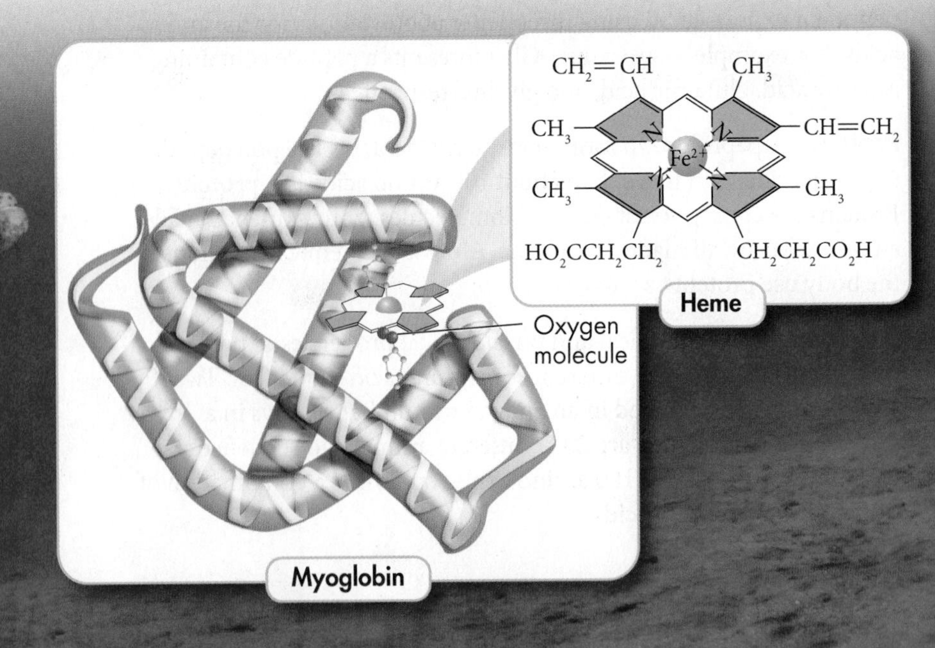

Enzymes

enzyme a protein that acts as a biological catalyst

substrate a molecule that reacts with the help of an enzyme

active site the place on an enzyme where the substrate binds

ACADEMIC WORDS

When something is *active,* it causes change. A change occurs at the *active site* of an enzyme.

Many biological reactions occur inside living cells. These reactions would normally occur very slowly at the temperatures that exist inside the cells. Cells use proteins called enzymes to speed up biological reactions. **Enzymes** are proteins that act as biological catalysts. Enzymes increase the rates of chemical reactions in living things.

In 1926, American chemist James B. Sumner was the first person to isolate and purify an enzyme. This enzyme, called urease, helps break down urea into ammonia and carbon dioxide. Urea is a compound in urine. Wet diapers can get a strong ammonia smell from the action of bacteria that contain urease. The equation for this reaction is:

$$\underset{\text{Urea}}{H_2N{-}\overset{\overset{\displaystyle O}{\|}}{C}{-}NH_2(aq)} + \underset{\text{Water}}{H_2O(l)} \xrightarrow{\text{urease}} \underset{\text{Ammonia}}{2NH_3(g)} + \underset{\text{Carbon dioxide}}{CO_2(g)}$$

Enzymes promote reactions. They also share two other properties with other catalysts. They are unchanged during chemical reactions, and they do not change the equilibrium position of the chemical system. The same amount of product forms with or without the enzyme. Reactions in cells do not tend to reach equilibrium. Products usually change rapidly to another substance in another reaction that is catalyzed by an enzyme. Removing the product pulls the reaction toward completion instead of toward equilibrium.

How Enzymes Work Most chemical reactions that occur in a cell involve enzymes. The molecules that react with the help of an enzyme are called **substrates.** A substrate molecule must bind to an enzyme molecule before the substrate can be changed. The place on an enzyme where a substrate binds is called the **active site.** An active site is usually a pocket formed by folds in the peptide chains of the enzyme protein. The peptide chain of an enzyme is folded in a way that matches the substrate at the active site. Some enzymes work as shown below. They hold a substrate in place and help break it apart at a certain chemical bond. Other enzymes bring two substrates together in just the right way to form a new chemical bond.

Enzyme and Substrate
A substrate fits into the active site on an enzyme. In this example, a bond is broken at the active site to form the reaction products.

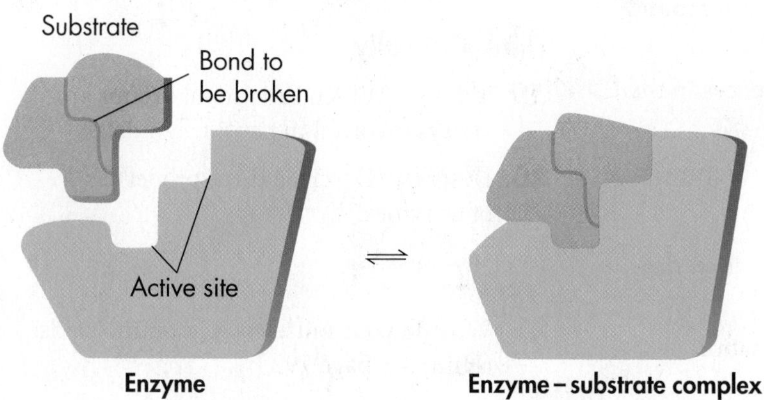

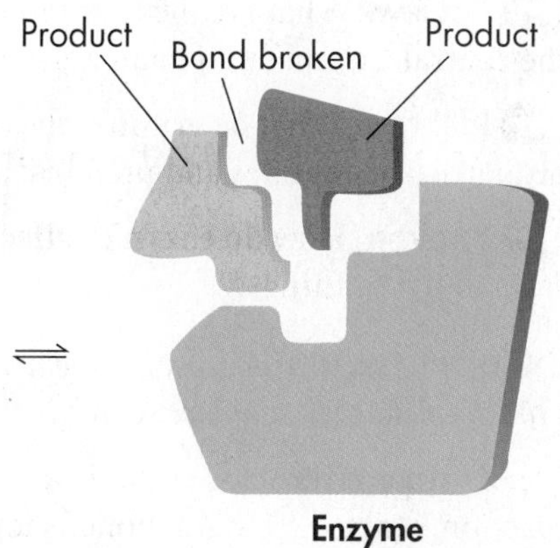

Formation of an Enzyme-Substrate Complex

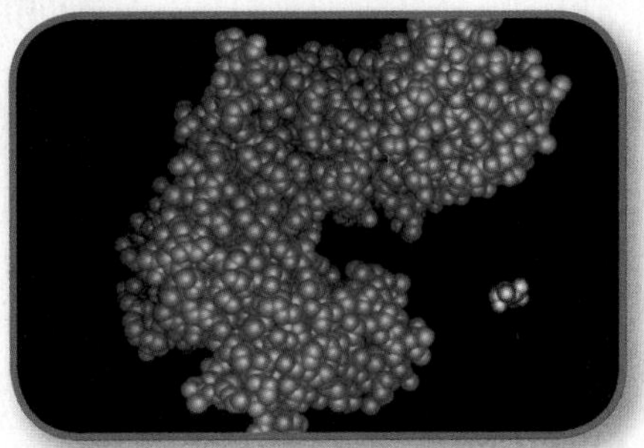
Carbonic anhydrase (blue) has only one substrate: carbonic acid (red). No other molecule will fit into the active site.

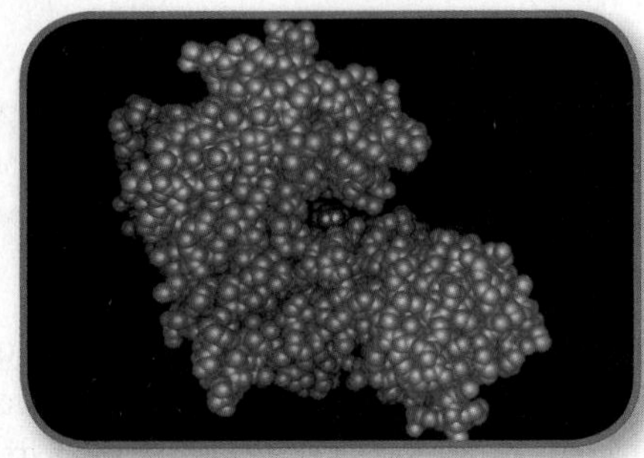
An enzyme-substrate complex forms when the substrate fits into the active site on the enzyme molecule.

The images above show how the carbonic acid substrate fits exactly into a carbonic anhydrase enzyme molecule to form an enzyme-substrate complex. Because the active site of every enzyme has a unique shape, only a specific substrate molecule can fit into the enzyme. That means that each enzyme can catalyze only one chemical reaction at a time.

The conversion of carbonic acid to carbon dioxide and water is a reversible reaction, as shown below.

$$\underset{\text{Carbonic acid}}{H_2CO_3(aq)} \xrightleftharpoons{\text{carbonic anhydrase}} \underset{\text{Carbon dioxide}}{CO_2(g)} + \underset{\text{Water}}{H_2O(l)}$$

Depending on conditions in the cell, the enzyme can help make carbonic acid or break it down. Enzymes are very efficient catalysts. One molecule of carbonic anhydrase can help break down 36 million molecules of carbonic acid in 1 minute!

Key Question How do enzymes affect the rates of reactions in living things? **Enzymes increase the rates of chemical reactions in living things.**

24.3 LessonCheck

Key Concept Check

14. **Review** What are the four groups that surround the central carbon atom in an amino acid?

15. **Identify** What determines the differences in the properties of peptides and proteins?

16. **Explain** How do enzymes affect the reaction rates in living things?

Vocabulary Check

Choose a highlighted word from the lesson to complete each sentence correctly.

17. When two amino acids undergo a condensation reaction, a(n) ________ bond is formed.

18. The active site of an enzyme fits exactly with a unique ________.

Think Critically

19. **Identify** Which functional groups are always involved in peptide bonds?

20. **Describe** Describe three properties of enzymes.

CHEMISTRY & YOU

21. Why do your muscles need amino acids? (Hint: See page 792.)

24.4 Lipids

CHEMISTRY & YOU

Q: Why is fat an important part of our diet? The media often portray fat as something that should be avoided because it is bad for you. You probably know that red meat can be high in fat. But you might not know that avocados, such as the one shown here, are also high in fat. In this lesson, you will learn why fats are actually necessary to our diet.

Key Question

What physical property distinguishes lipids from other classes of biological molecules?

BUILD Vocabulary

lipid a compound that is not soluble in water, such as fats and oils

triglyceride a lipid made of glycerol with three ester links to long chain fatty acids

ROOT WORDS

The word *lipid* is based on the Sanskrit word for "sticky," which became the Greek word *lipos*, meaning "greasy." Lipids feel sticky because they do not mix well with water.

Describing Lipids

Fats, oils, and other water insoluble compounds are called **lipids**. Unlike carbohydrates and proteins, lipids tend to dissolve easily in organic solvents, but not in water. Most fats are found in animal products, such as meat, butter, and cheese. Most oils are found in plant products, such as olive oil and canola oil.

You need some lipids in your diet to stay healthy. Lipids provide an efficient way for your body to store energy. They are also needed to keep your cell membranes healthy and flexible. However, too many lipids in your diet can lead to weight gain and other health issues.

Triglycerides Natural fats and oils exist as triglycerides. A **triglyceride** is a lipid made of a glycerol with three ester links to long chain fatty acids. Glycerol is a compound made of three carbon atoms, each of which has a hydroxy group attached. Fatty acids are long chain carboxylic acids that contain 12 to 24 carbon atoms. Triglycerides are important for the long term storage of energy in the human body.

The structural diagram and model below show the shape of the triglyceride molecule trimyristin. Trimyristin is formed from 1 molecule of glycerin and 3 molecules of myristic acid, a fatty acid with 14 carbon atoms. The long chains of carbon and hydrogen show that the molecule is nonpolar.

Trimyristin Trimyristin has long chains of carbon and hydrogen and no hydrogen-oxygen bonds. That means the molecule is nonpolar and that it will not dissolve in water.

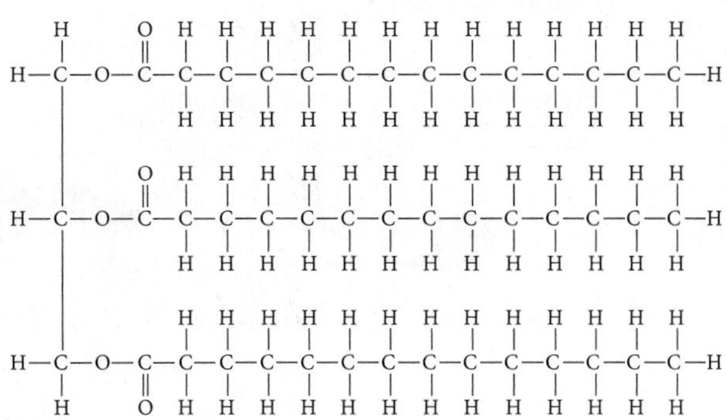

Fats in Foods Moderate levels of dietary fats and oils are essential to health.

Because fats and oils are triglycerides, they are very similar chemically. The main difference between fats and oils is their melting point. Fats are usually solid at room temperature, while oils are liquid at room temperature. The following equation shows the general reaction for the formation of triglycerides.

$$
\begin{array}{lclcll}
\mathrm{CH_2OH} & & \mathrm{HO-\overset{\displaystyle O}{\overset{\|}{C}}-R} & & \mathrm{CH_2-O-\overset{\displaystyle O}{\overset{\|}{C}}-R} & \\
| & & & & | & \\
\mathrm{CHOH} & + & \mathrm{HO-\overset{\displaystyle O}{\overset{\|}{C}}-R} & \longrightarrow & \mathrm{CH-O-\overset{\displaystyle O}{\overset{\|}{C}}-R} & + \ \mathrm{3H_2O} \\
| & & & & | & \\
\mathrm{CH_2OH} & & \mathrm{HO-\overset{\displaystyle O}{\overset{\|}{C}}-R} & & \mathrm{CH_2-O-\overset{\displaystyle O}{\overset{\|}{C}}-R} & \\
\text{Glycerol} & & \text{3 Fatty acid molecules} & & \text{Triglyceride (triester of glycerol)} & \text{Water}
\end{array}
$$

The long hydrocarbon chains combined with the ester groups make the molecule nonpolar. Unlike carbohydrates and proteins, triglycerides do not tend to dissolve in water. They dissolve easily in such nonpolar solvents as ether and chloroform.

Phospholipids Lipids that contain phosphate groups are called **phospholipids.** Phospholipids are abundant in cells. The picture below shows a typical phospholipid molecule called lecithin. The ionic head of the lecithin molecule is hydrophilic, or "water loving." This end of the molecule will dissolve in water. The tails of the molecule consist of long hydrocarbon chains that are hydrophobic, or "water fearing." This end of the molecule will dissolve in nonpolar solvents, but not in water.

Lecithin is partly hydrophobic and partly hydrophilic. That means it behaves like an insoluble hydrocarbon and a soluble ionic compound when it is in water. In water, the carbon chains of lecithin cluster together and exclude water. The head of each molecule interacts with the water. As a result, phospholipids form a spherical double layer called a lipid bilayer. In a lipid bilayer, the hydrophobic tails are sandwiched between two layers of hydrophilic heads.

Phospholipid This simplified diagram shows the hydrophilic head as a sphere and the hydrophobic tails as wavy lines. The space-filling model is the phospholipid lecithin.

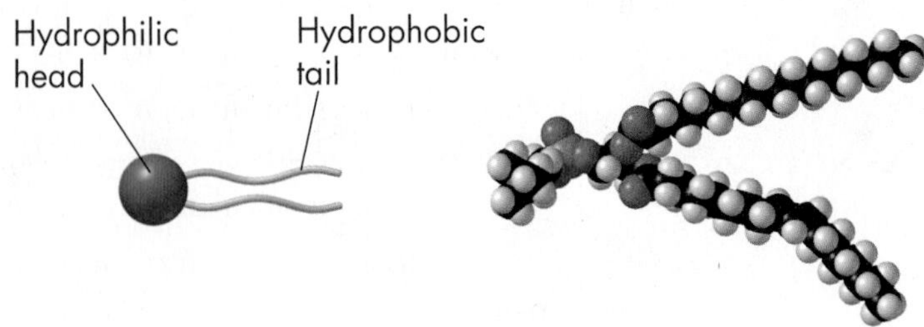

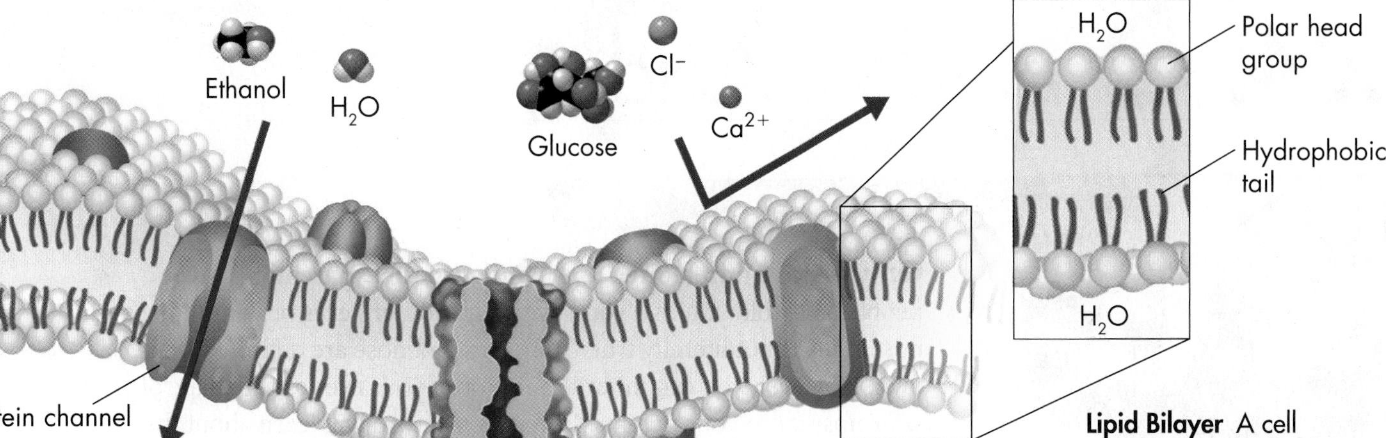

Lipid Bilayer A cell membrane is a lipid bilayer. The structure controls which types of molecules pass through the bilayer.

Cell membranes, such as the one above, are made of lipid bilayers. The lipid bilayer of a cell membrane acts as a barrier. It prevents molecules and ions from passing freely into and out of the cell. Cells do need to take in certain ions and molecules such as nutrients. Proteins form channels in the bilayer. These channels allow specific ions or molecules to enter the cell.

Waxes Waxes are another type of lipid. **Waxes** are esters of long chain fatty acids and long chain alcohols. Hydrocarbon chains of the acid and the alcohol usually contain 10 to 30 carbon atoms. Waxes are hydrophobic because both parts of the wax molecule are nonpolar. Waxes are stable solids. They coat the leaves of many plants and protect the plants from water loss and attack by microorganisms. Waxes coat the skin, hair, and feathers of animals and keep these structures flexible and waterproof.

Key Question What physical property distinguishes lipids from other classes of biological molecules? **Unlike carbohydrates and proteins, lipids do not tend to dissolve in water. Lipids dissolve easily in such nonpolar solvents as ether and chloroform.**

BUILD Vocabulary

phospholipid a lipid that contains a phosphate group

wax an ester of a long chain fatty acid and a long chain alcohol

WORD ORIGINS

The word *wax* comes from an old German word for "weave." Originally, wax referred to beeswax that bees "weave" into the shape of a honeycomb.

24.4 LessonCheck

Key Concept Check

22. **Compare** What physical property sets lipids apart from other biological substances?

Vocabulary Check *Choose a highlighted word from the lesson to complete each sentence correctly.*

23. A(n) __________ is a lipid that contains a phosphate group.

24. The condensation reaction of three fatty acids with a glycerol molecule makes a(n) __________.

Think Critically

25. **Compare** Compare the molecular structures of the three main types of lipids.

26. **Explain** What role do phospholipids and proteins play in cell membranes?

27. **Identify** What two classes of organic compounds combine to form a wax?

CHEMISTRY & YOU

28. Why is fat an important part of our diet? (Hint: See page 795.)

24.5 Nucleic Acids

CHEMISTRY & YOU

Q: Why do children often look similar to their parents? Maybe people have told you that you have your mother's eyes or your father's nose. This is not literally true. Your eyes and nose are definitely your own. However, you can inherit the color of your eyes or the shape of your nose from your parents. In this lesson, you will learn about the molecules involved in the inheritance of traits.

Key Questions

What are the functions of DNA and RNA?

How many bases of DNA are required to specify one amino acid in a peptide chain?

What are gene mutations?

What are two examples of DNA technologies used today?

nucleic acid a nitrogen containing polymer found primarily in the cell's nucleus

nucleotide the monomer that makes up DNA and RNA polymers

ACADEMIC WORDS

The words *nucleic* and *nucleotide* come from the word *nucleus*. The word *nucleus* has several meanings in science. In chemistry, it is the central part of an atom that contains protons and neutrons. In biology, it is the central organelle in a cell that contains genetic material.

DNA and RNA

More than 100 years ago, a Swiss biochemist discovered a class of nitrogen containing compounds in the nuclei of cells. The nuclei were first obtained from the white blood cells in the pus of infected wounds. This discovery led to a new understanding of how cells function and how organisms reproduce.

These nitrogen containing compounds, called **nucleic acids,** are polymers that are found primarily in a cell's nucleus. Nucleic acids are found in all living things. There are two kinds of nucleic acids in cells. The first kind is deoxyribonucleic acid, or DNA. DNA stores the information needed to make proteins. It also governs the reproduction and growth of cells and new organisms. The second kind of nucleic acid is ribonucleic acid, or RNA. RNA helps to transmit the information stored in DNA. RNA also takes part in the making of proteins.

Nucleotides The monomers that make up DNA and RNA polymers are called **nucleotides.** Each nucleotide consists of a phosphate group, a five carbon sugar, and a nitrogen containing unit called a nitrogen base.

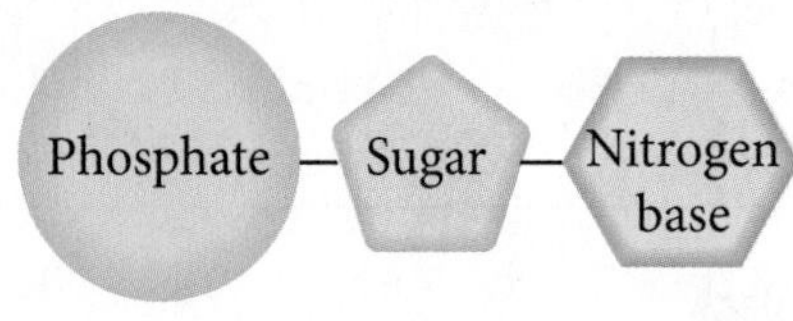

Nucleotide

The sugar in each nucleotide monomer of DNA is a five carbon monosaccharide known as deoxyribose. The sugar in each nucleotide monomer of RNA is a five carbon monosaccharide known as ribose. Ribose is different from deoxyribose because it has one more oxygen atom.

Nitrogen Bases There are four different nitrogen bases in DNA. These bases are adenine, guanine, thymine, and cytosine. They are abbreviated as A, G, T, and C. Two of the bases—A and G—have two rings in their structures. The other two bases—T and C—have only one ring.

DNA The nucleotide monomers of DNA are linked together through their sugar-phosphate groups. Two strands of DNA coil into a double helix. The two DNA strands are held together by many hydrogen bonds.

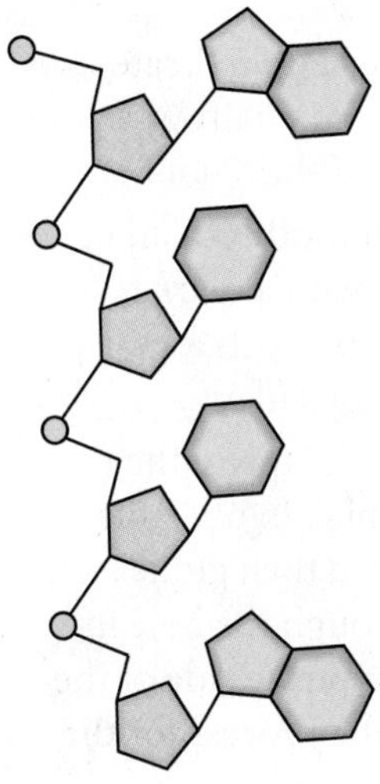

Sugar-phosphate backbone

Nitrogen base
Simple sugar
Phosphate group

DNA Strand

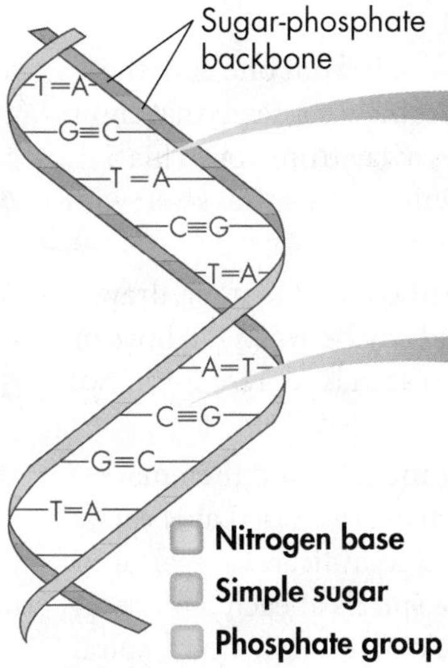

Two DNA strands in a double helix

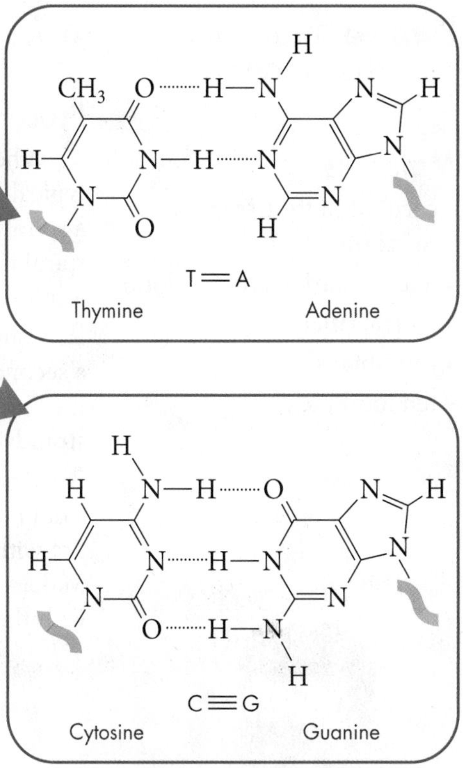

T=A
Thymine
Adenine

C≡G
Cytosine
Guanine

Hydrogen bonding in DNA

Chemists studying nucleic acids discovered that the amount of adenine in a sample of DNA was always equal to the amount of thymine. They also found that the amount of guanine was always equal to the amount of cytosine. The reason for this was not apparent until 1953, when James Watson and Francis Crick proposed that DNA consists of two polynucleotide chains wrapped into a spiral shape called a double helix.

Hydrogen Bonding and Base Pairing As shown in the diagram, hydrogen bonds form between bases on the DNA strands. Hydrogen bonds link the strands together and keep the double helix stable. For the nitrogen bases to fit into the double helix, a double ringed base on one strand must be paired with a single ringed base on the other strand. That means that A always has to pair with T and that C always has to pair with G. The maximum number of hydrogen bonds form when the base pairs are A—T and G—C.

RNA The chain structure of RNA is similar to that of DNA. However, there are two key differences. The structure of RNA is almost always a single polymer strand instead of a double strand. Also, the base thymine is replaced by uracil, which is abbreviated as U. Like thymine, uracil is a nitrogen base with a single ring structure.

Key Question What are the functions of DNA and RNA? **DNA stores the information needed to make proteins and governs the reproduction and growth of cells and new organisms. RNA has a key role in the transmission of the information stored in DNA and in the synthesis of proteins.**

Quick Lab

A Model of DNA

Purpose To construct a model of double stranded DNA

Materials

- cardboard tube from paper towel roll
- felt tip markers (two colors)
- metric ruler
- thumbtack
- ten toothpicks

Procedure 

1. When you look at it from one end, the typical cardboard tube has a seam that shows a spiral that moves away from you. This spiral is a helix. Outline the spiral seam with a colored marker.

2. Using a different colored marker, draw a second spiral midway between the lines of the first. These two spirals represent the two strands of double stranded DNA.

3. Measure along the tube and then mark a dot on each spiral every 5 cm. Label each dot with the letter *S* to indicate a sugar unit. Make a hole in the spirals at each *S* mark with the thumbtack. Move down each spiral to mark a letter *P* to indicate a phosphate group halfway between each of the *S* dots.

4. Color each toothpick along half its length with a marker. A toothpick represents a base pair in the DNA molecule.

5. Starting at the top of the tube, insert a toothpick in one hole at an *S* label and then guide it so it emerges through the hole in the *S* on the opposite side of the tube. Repeat the process for the other holes.

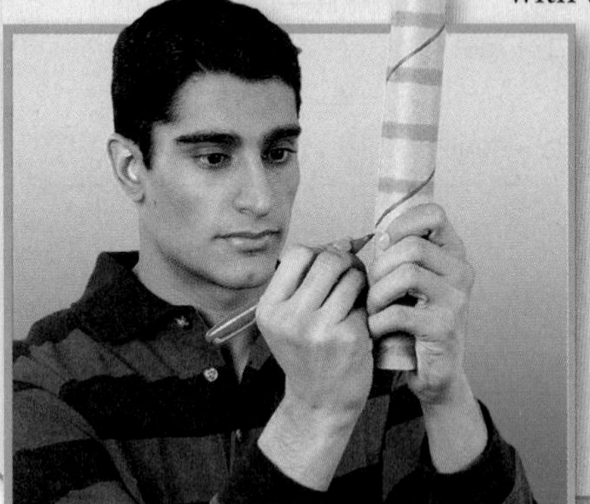

Analyze and Conclude

1. Use Models Are the bases on the interior or the exterior of the double helix? Are they randomly arranged or neatly stacked?

2. Analyze Data Are the phosphate groups on the interior or the exterior of the DNA structure?

3. Analyze Data Are the sugar groups on the interior or the exterior of the DNA molecule?

BUILD Vocabulary

gene a segment of DNA that carries the instructions for making one peptide chain

 **RELATED WORDS**

You might come across several words that are related to the word *gene*. Genealogy is the study of family history. Genetics is the study of heredity. Genome is the complete DNA of an organism.

The Genetic Code

The proteins in an earthworm are different from the proteins in a pine tree. The proteins in a pine tree are different from those in a human. In other words, an organism contains many proteins that are specific to that organism. How do cells in a given organism make the correct proteins for that organism? The cells use instructions contained in the organism's DNA. A **gene** is a segment of DNA that carries the instructions for making one peptide chain. The products of genes are the peptides and proteins found in an organism.

Think of DNA as a manual that stores the instructions for building proteins. The instructions are written by using four "letters": the bases A, T, G, and C. Each "word" in a DNA manual is exactly three letters in length. Each of these "words" is a three letter base sequence, or triplet, that codes for one of the 20 common amino acids. The code words, which are also called codons, are strung together to form "sentences." Each "sentence" is a gene that gives the order of amino acids in peptides or proteins.

Code Words and Peptides An example of a DNA code word is AAA (adenine-adenine-adenine), which specifies the amino acid phenylalanine. The DNA code word CGT specifies the amino acid alanine. A code word never matches more than one amino acid. A peptide chain of 300 amino acids in a specific sequence requires 900 DNA bases arranged in a specific sequence.

The code word TAC marks the beginning of a peptide. TAC is the initiation code word. Three code words (ATT, ATC, and ACT) can mark the end of a chain. These are termination code words. The translation of DNA bases in a gene into the amino acids of a peptide begins with the initiation code word. The termination code is like the period at the end of this sentence. Look at the diagram below to see how the code words in DNA are translated to make peptides.

Key Question How many bases of DNA are required to specify one amino acid in a peptide chain? **Three bases of DNA arranged in a specific sequence are required to specify one amino acid in a peptide or protein chain.**

BUILD Understanding

Concept Map As you read, construct a concept map describing the building of a protein from the codes in DNA.

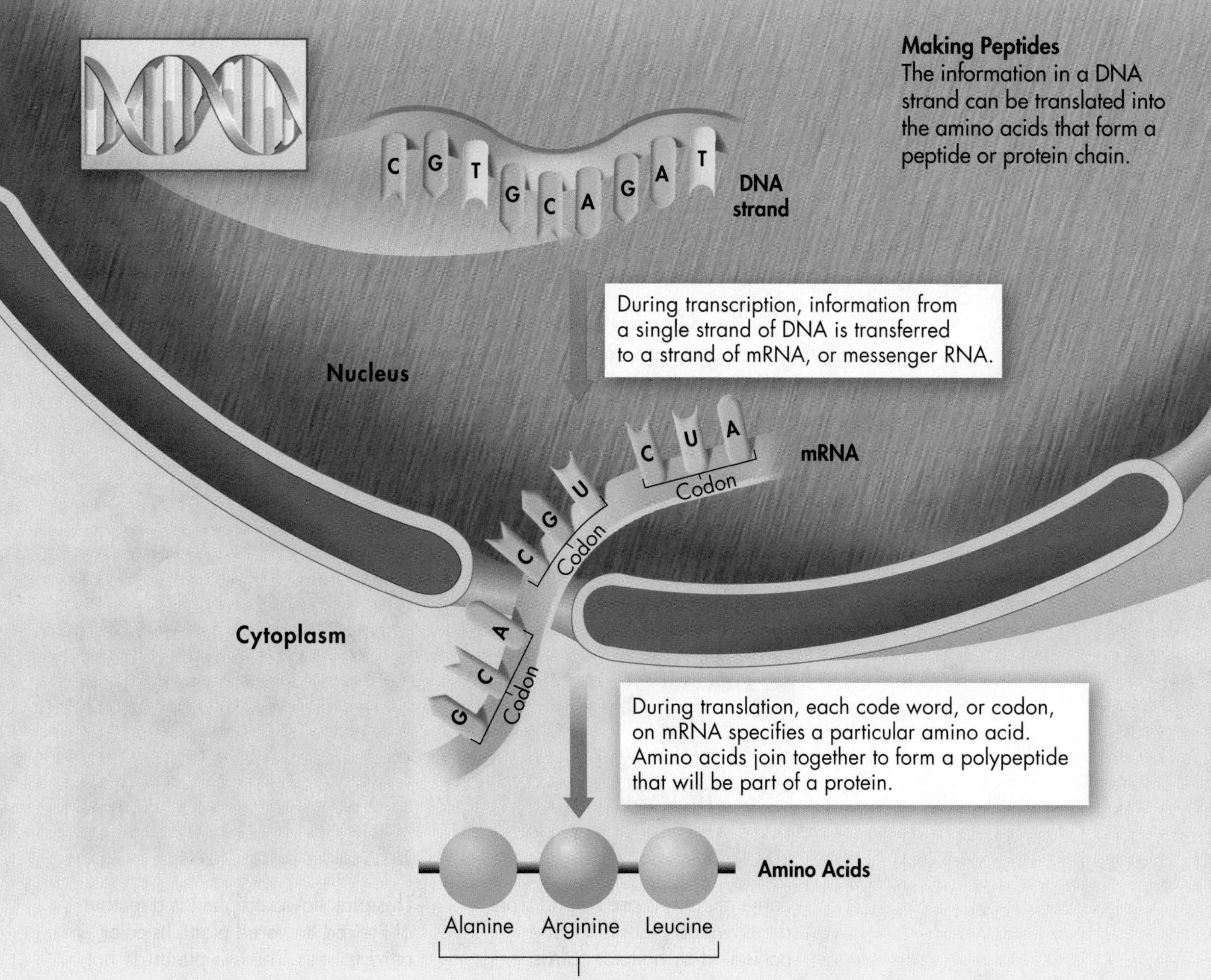
C G T G C A G A T
DNA strand
Nucleus
During transcription, information from a single strand of DNA is transferred to a strand of mRNA, or messenger RNA.
C U A
mRNA
Codon
U G C
Codon
A C G
Codon
Cytoplasm
During translation, each code word, or codon, on mRNA specifies a particular amino acid. Amino acids join together to form a polypeptide that will be part of a protein.
Amino Acids
Alanine
Arginine
Leucine
Portion of polypeptide

Making Peptides
The information in a DNA strand can be translated into the amino acids that form a peptide or protein chain.

BUILD Connections

Galactosemia is a genetic disorder that affects about 1 in 55,000 newborn babies. It is caused by a mutation in an enzyme that breaks down the sugar galactose. Without the normal enzyme, galactose can build up in the body and cause kidney failure and brain damage. The only way to treat galactosemia is to avoid foods that contain galactose, such as milk, cheese, and dried beans.

Gene Mutations

A mutation is a change that occurs in a DNA code word. Substitutions, additions, or deletions of one or more nucleotides in the DNA molecule are called gene mutations. The effect of the deletion of a single base from a gene can be illustrated by the following analogy. Suppose a string of three letter words goes as follows:

PAT THE RED CAT

This string of words makes sense. However, look what happens if you delete the first letter and then turn the string into three letter segments. The sequence loses it meaning:

ATT HER EDC AT

The deletion of a base in the DNA base sequence can turn the information into nonsense in the same way. A sequence that coded the amino acids in a necessary protein may be replaced. The new sequence could produce a useless or damaging peptide.

The same sort of harmful effect may be produced by mutations involving substitutions or additions of nucleotides. Mutations can cause the production of a faulty protein or of no protein at all. Diseases caused by gene mutations are called genetic disorders. Thousands of genetic disorders have been identified.

Not all gene mutations are harmful. Sometimes, a mutation can result in the synthesis of a protein that is more efficient than the previous version. Such a mutation could be beneficial to the survival of the affected organism.

Key Question What are gene mutations? **Substitutions, additions, or deletions of one or more nucleotides in the DNA molecule are called gene mutations.**

Beneficial Mutation

Some mutations are helpful. This red flowered plant is usually pollinated by hummingbirds.

This pink flowered plant is a mutant of the red flowered plant. Its color attracts bees. The two plants do not compete for pollinators.

DNA Technologies

You have learned how important DNA is to all living things. So, it might not surprise you to learn that DNA technology has had a significant impact on our society. In the following pages, you will learn about some of these technologies.

DNA Typing DNA sequences are similar among members of the same family. However, the base sequences of DNA are slightly different for different individuals. The only exception is identical twins, who have identical DNA. DNA typing uses the variation in the DNA of individuals as a basis for creating DNA profiles to identify a person. DNA sequences, like fingerprints, are unique for each individual. DNA typing has also been called DNA fingerprinting.

▶ **Sampling** To construct a DNA profile, a tiny sample is obtained. A sample can be anything that contains DNA. Samples can include teeth, fingernails, blood, hair, saliva, and skin cells. Items from crime scenes often contain DNA.

▶ **Typing** Samples can be typed in several different ways. The most common method used by the FBI is short tandem repeat, or STR, analysis. A short tandem repeat is a short segment of DNA that is repeated several times. To obtain a profile, the FBI looks at 13 different STR regions.

▶ **Identification** A DNA profile can be compared with a sample of DNA from a known individual. Labs around the country use FBI technology called the Combined DNA Indexing Systems, or CODIS, to share and search DNA profiles. The chance of two people who are not identical twins having the same DNA profile for the 13 STR regions is 1 in 1 billion.

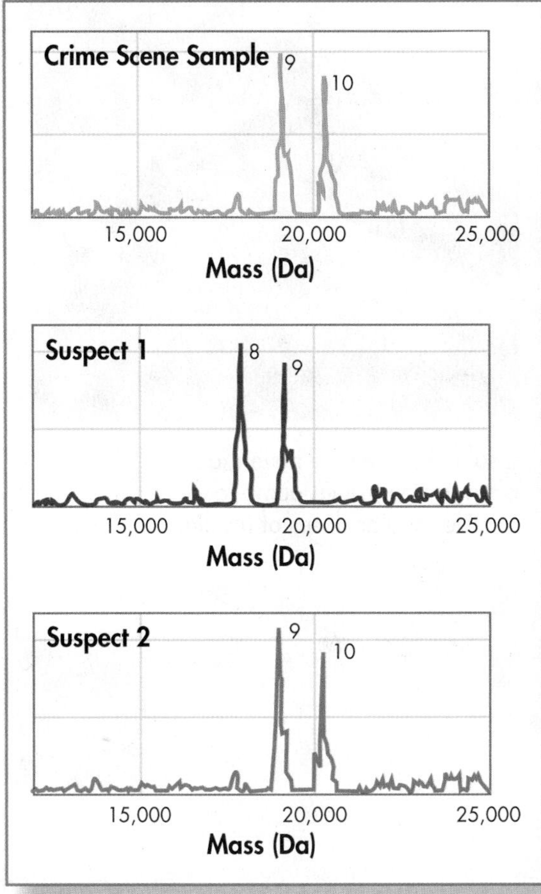

DNA Profile
This is an example of what a DNA profile for one STR region might look like. The DNA from the crime scene has a segment with 9 repeats and a segment with 10 repeats. Suspect 1 can be eliminated because the lengths of that person's segments do not match the crime scene sample.

Go to your Chemistry Skills and Math Workbook to practice interpreting graphs.

Crime Scene Evidence
These scientists are analyzing items taken from a crime scene. DNA may be isolated from blood on the items.

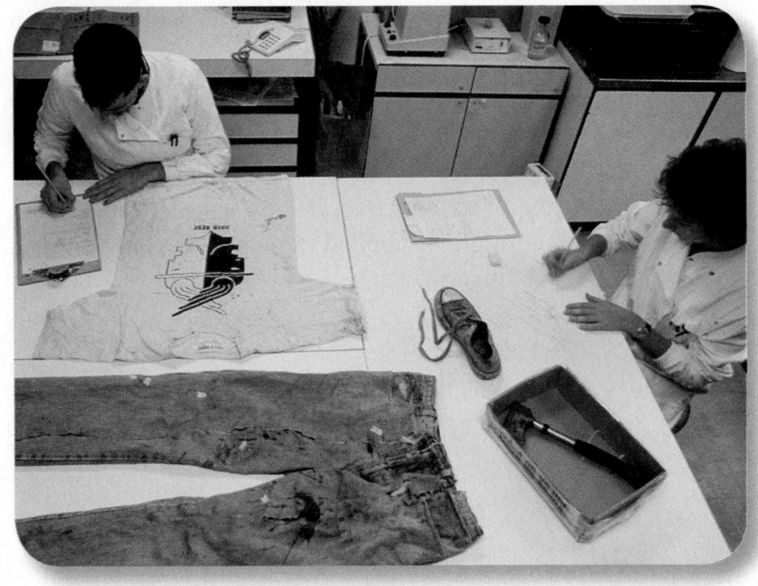

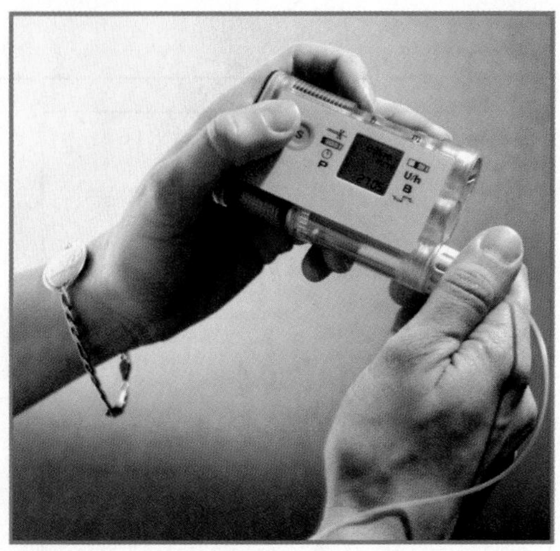

Insulin People who have diabetes often use an insulin pump to receive regular doses of insulin.

Recombinant DNA Technology Scientists have learned to manipulate genes by various methods. Recombinant DNA technology consists of methods for splitting a DNA chain and inserting a new piece of DNA into the gap. The altered DNA formed by this method is known as recombinant DNA.

▶ **Applications in Medicine** The first application of recombinant DNA technology inserted the gene for making human insulin into bacteria. Most people naturally make insulin, which is a polypeptide that controls levels of blood sugar. However, when a person's body does not make enough insulin, the person develops diabetes. The symptoms of diabetes can often be controlled by insulin injections. Today, diabetic patients use insulin produced by bacteria that have been altered by recombinant DNA technology. Other proteins produced by recombinant DNA technology are used as drugs to treat a variety of health problems.

▶ **Applications in Agriculture** Recombinant DNA techniques can make plants resistant to pests and weed killers. Recombinant DNA techniques can also produce fruits and vegetables that are easier to ship and store. The most common traits in genetically modified crops are herbicide resistance and insect resistance in corn, cotton, soybean, and canola. Crops have also been genetically modified to make drugs to treat or prevent such diseases as cancer and AIDS.

Key Question What are two examples of DNA technologies used today? **DNA typing uses the variation in the DNA of individuals to produce DNA profiles to identify a person. Recombinant DNA technology consists of methods for splitting a DNA chain and inserting a new piece of DNA into the gap.**

24.5 LessonCheck

Key Concept Check

29. **Review** What functions are performed by DNA and RNA?

30. **Review** What does a three letter base sequence of DNA specify?

31. **Identify** What are three types of gene mutations?

32. **Identify** What methods are used in recombinant DNA technology?

Vocabulary Check

Choose a highlighted word from the lesson to complete each sentence correctly.

33. The basic unit of a DNA or RNA molecule is called a(n) ________.

34. A(n) ________ carries the code for manufacturing one specific peptide chain.

Think Critically

35. **Explain** How can a language sentence be used as a model for a gene in DNA?

36. **Describe** Describe how scientific methods might be applied to the process of DNA fingerprinting.

CHEMISTRY & YOU

37. Why do children often look similar to their parents? (Hint: See page 800.)

DNA Testing

Would you want to know if you were predisposed to a treatable disease, such as diabetes or breast cancer? What about an incurable disease, such as Huntington's disease? The answers to these questions, and many more, are only a drop of saliva away.

In the past few years, researchers have learned how to test for hundreds of genetic disorders using genetic testing. Genetic testing involves analyzing a person's DNA to determine changes in genes that may indicate a specific disorder. The DNA used for the tests can be obtained from a sample of blood, urine, or even saliva. In fact, today you can mail a saliva sample to a lab, and then view your test results online!

Genetic testing can be valuable in determining a person's likelihood of developing a treatable disease. However, learning of a genetic predisposition for a disease that currently has no treatments or cures can cause anxiety or despair. In addition, there are many ethical concerns involved in genetic testing, including who gets access to the test results and how many actual tests are performed on the DNA. The information in DNA is much greater than just the specific disease a lab could test for. Because of these concerns, it is important to consider all the consequences of knowing your genetic information before getting tested.

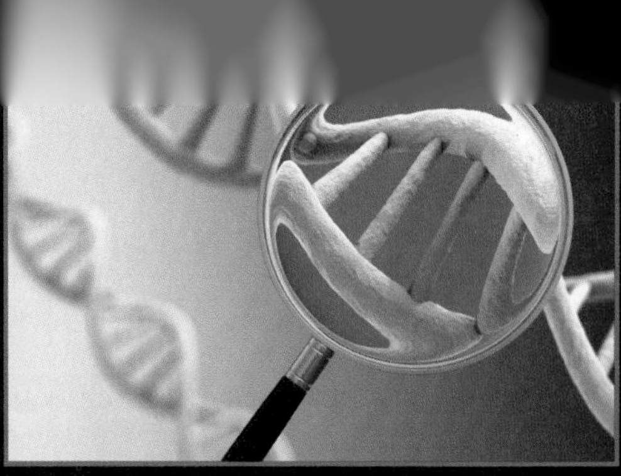

DNA MUTATIONS Alterations in the order of the bases in DNA cause gene mutations, which can lead to diseases.

TESTING FROM HOME At-home tests involve collecting saliva or blood samples. The sample is then sent to a lab, which analyzes the DNA for mutations known to correspond to different diseases and disorders.

Take It Further

1. Identify What are some of the possible benefits of genetic testing? What are some of the possible risks?

2. Form an Opinion Would you want to be tested for potential genetic disorders? Why or why not?

24.6 Metabolism

CHEMISTRY & YOU

Q: Why does a hummingbird eat so much? A hummingbird eats more than its weight in food each day. Hummingbirds have a high body temperature, fast heart rate, and a fast breathing rate. All these factors affect the hummingbird's metabolism. In this lesson, you will learn about the reactions that are part of an organism's metabolism.

Key Questions

What is the function of ATP in living cells?

What happens to biological molecules and energy during catabolism and anabolism?

How do nitrogen fixing bacteria provide plants with a usable form of nitrogen?

ATP

All living things need energy to perform life functions. The oxidation of glucose in a living cell is a spontaneous reaction that releases energy. **Adenosine triphosphate (ATP)** is a molecule that can store and then transmit this energy in the cells of living organisms. The structural formula for ATP is shown below. ATP is composed of an adenine, a ribose, and three phosphate groups. Inside cells, ATP is formed by the reaction between adenosine diphosphate (ADP) and an inorganic phosphate group.

ATP is the energy carrier between the reactions in a cell that release energy and the reactions that use energy. When the cell changes ADP to ATP, it makes a molecule that has an increased amount of energy in its chemical bonds. The ADP $\rightarrow$ ATP reaction is similar to charging a battery, because energy is added to the ADP molecule to form ATP. The ATP molecule can then move through the cell to make this stored energy available where it is needed. When the cell needs to use energy, the ATP molecule is changed back to ADP and energy is released. This is similar to what happens when you use a battery to power a cell phone or some other electronic device.

ATP ATP is made up of adenine, ribose, and three phosphate groups. ATP provides energy to muscles for moving the body.

NH_2 — Adenine; Adenosine; Ribose; OH OH; Triphosphate

$^{-}O-P(=O)(O^-)-O-P(=O)(O^-)-O-P(=O)(O^-)-O-CH_2$

$$\text{Adenosine}-\underset{\text{OH}}{\overset{\text{O}}{\text{P}}}-\text{O}-\underset{\text{OH}}{\overset{\text{O}}{\text{P}}}-\text{OH} + \text{HO}-\underset{\text{OH}}{\overset{\text{O}}{\text{P}}}-\text{OH} \longrightarrow \text{Adenosine}-\underset{\text{OH}}{\overset{\text{O}}{\text{P}}}-\text{O}-\underset{\text{OH}}{\overset{\text{O}}{\text{P}}}-\text{O}-\underset{\text{OH}}{\overset{\text{O}}{\text{P}}}-\text{OH} + H_2O$$

Adenosine diphosphate (ADP) | Inorganic phosphate (Pi) | Adenosine triphosphate (ATP) | Water

The reaction that changes ADP to ATP is shown above. During this reaction, ADP combines with an inorganic phosphate group to form ATP and water. This reaction is endothermic, which means that it absorbs energy. Every mole of ATP stores about 30.5 kJ of energy. The reaction that produces ADP from ATP is exothermic. That reaction releases about 30.5 kJ of energy. Cells use this energy to drive processes that would ordinarily not be spontaneous.

ATP plays an important role in the living cell. It allows the cell to use energy from oxidation reactions that cannot be directly captured by other chemical reactions within the cell. In addition, ATP allows the cell to store energy. This means that the reaction that uses energy does not have to occur at exactly the same time as the oxidation of food molecules. Like a battery, the ATP molecule allows energy to be stored and moved from one place to another.

Key Question What is the function of ATP in living cells? **In living cells, ATP is the energy carrier between the reactions that release energy and the reactions that use energy.**

Metabolism Reactions

Thousands of chemical reactions take place in the cells of a living organism. The entire set of chemical reactions carried out by an organism is known as the organism's **metabolism.** There are two types of metabolism reactions: catabolism and anabolism.

Catabolism Chemical compounds are broken down in cells into simpler compounds by chemical reactions. The compounds that are broken down can be molecules from food or cell parts that are being recycled. The group of reactions that break compounds down in the cell is called **catabolism.** Catabolic reactions break down many complex biological molecules. These molecules include carbohydrates, lipids, proteins, and nucleic acids. As catabolic reactions break down complex molecules, they provide the building blocks needed by the cell. The products of catabolic reactions usually have less chemical energy than the original molecules. That means catabolic reactions also provide energy to the cell.

The oxidation of glucose to carbon dioxide and water is one of the most important processes of catabolism. This process also releases most of the energy required by living cells.

adenosine triphosphate (ATP) a molecule that transmits energy in the cells of living organisms

metabolism all the chemical reactions carried out in an organism

catabolism reactions in a cell that break molecules down into simpler compounds

WORD ORIGINS

The word *metabolism* was coined in the late 1800s to describe recently discovered chemical reactions in cells. Metabolism was based on the Greek word for "changeable."

Animal Metabolism
Organisms, such as this mouse, use the energy stored in the chemical bonds of food molecules to power their body processes.

When 1 mol of glucose changes into 6 mol of carbon dioxide and 6 mol of water, the reaction produces 2.82×10^3 kJ of energy. Cells produce up to 38 mol of ATP by capturing the energy released by a single mole of glucose. Because it produces so much ATP, the oxidation of glucose shown in the equation below is the most common energy producing reaction in cells. The need for energy and chemical building blocks is the reason all organisms, such as the mouse at left, must have food.

$$\underset{\text{Glucose (carbon in more reduced state)}}{C_6H_{12}O_6} + \underset{\text{Oxygen}}{6O_2} \longrightarrow \underset{\text{Carbon dioxide (carbon in more oxidized state)}}{6CO_2} + \underset{\text{Water}}{6H_2O} + \text{Energy}$$

Anabolism Some of the simple compounds produced by catabolism are used to make more complex biological molecules that are necessary for health and growth. These biological molecules include carbohydrates, lipids, proteins, and nucleic acids. The group of synthesis reactions that makes these molecules is called **anabolism.**

The diagram below is an overview of the relationship between catabolism and anabolism. Nutrients and cell components that are no longer needed are broken down into simpler components by catabolic reactions. These reactions release energy that is stored as ATP or lost as heat. The products and stored energy produced by catabolism are used to make new compounds and cell parts through anabolism. Anabolic reactions obtain energy from ATP as it changes back to ADP and its stored energy is released.

Key Question What happens to biological molecules and energy during catabolism and anabolism? **In catabolism, biological molecules are broken down to provide energy and the building blocks for other compounds in the cell. In anabolism, the products and the energy of catabolism are used to make new compounds and cell parts needed for life and growth.**

Catabolism and Anabolism
This drawing shows that catabolism and anabolism work together to supply cells with the chemicals they need. Compounds shown in purple come from food or the recycling of materials the cell no longer needs. Compounds in red are used by cells as they grow and move. Intermediate carbon compounds are the building blocks that cells use to make other molecules.

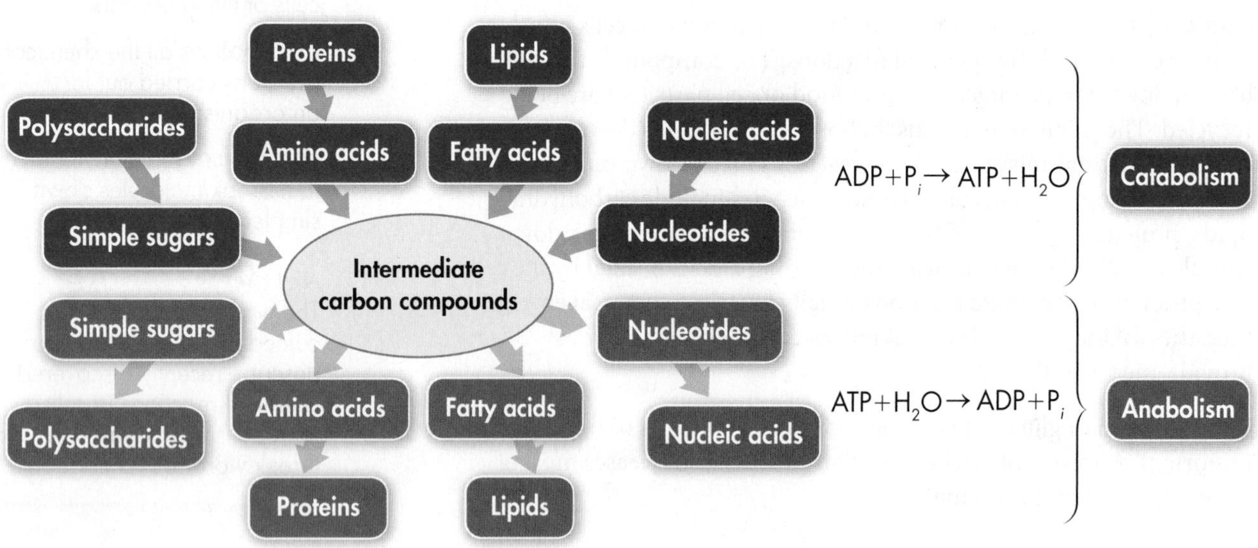

The Nitrogen Cycle

Biological molecules in food that are taken into an organism's body are broken down during catabolism. Food contains carbohydrates, proteins, lipids, nucleic acids, and vitamins and minerals. These nutrients are composed mainly of carbon, hydrogen, and oxygen atoms. Many biological compounds, like proteins, contain nitrogen as well. The atmosphere is 78 percent nitrogen gas. But most plants and all animals are unable to use nitrogen from the air to make nitrogen containing compounds. However, some bacteria can convert nitrogen gas into forms that plants can use. They do this using a process called nitrogen fixation.

Nitrogen fixing bacteria are part of the nitrogen cycle, which is shown below. These bacteria reduce nitrogen gas to ammonia. Ammonia is a water soluble nitrogen compound that can be used by plants. In soil and biological fluids, most ammonia is present as ammonium ions. Plants use ammonia to make such compounds as proteins, nucleic acids, and ATP. Animals get nitrogen by eating plants or by eating other animals that eat plants. Decaying plant and animal matter also returns nitrogen to the soil as ammonia, nitrite ions, and nitrate ions.

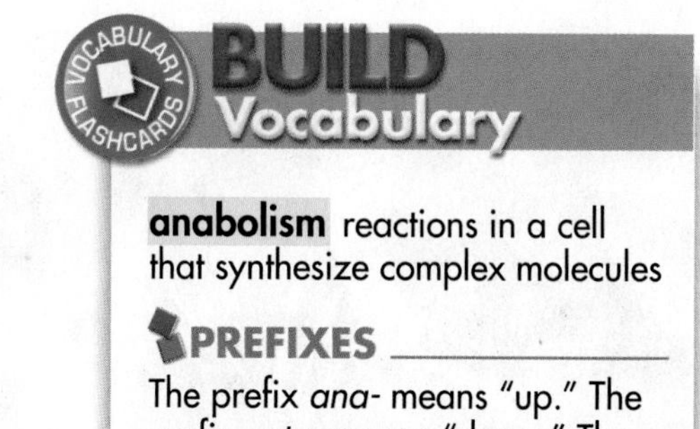

anabolism reactions in a cell that synthesize complex molecules

PREFIXES

The prefix *ana-* means "up." The prefix *cata-* means "down." The word *anabolism* means "to build up." The word *catabolism* means "to break down."

Nitrogen Cycle Nitrogen moves between the atmosphere and the biosphere in the nitrogen cycle.

See the* nitrogen cycle *animated online. KINETIC ART

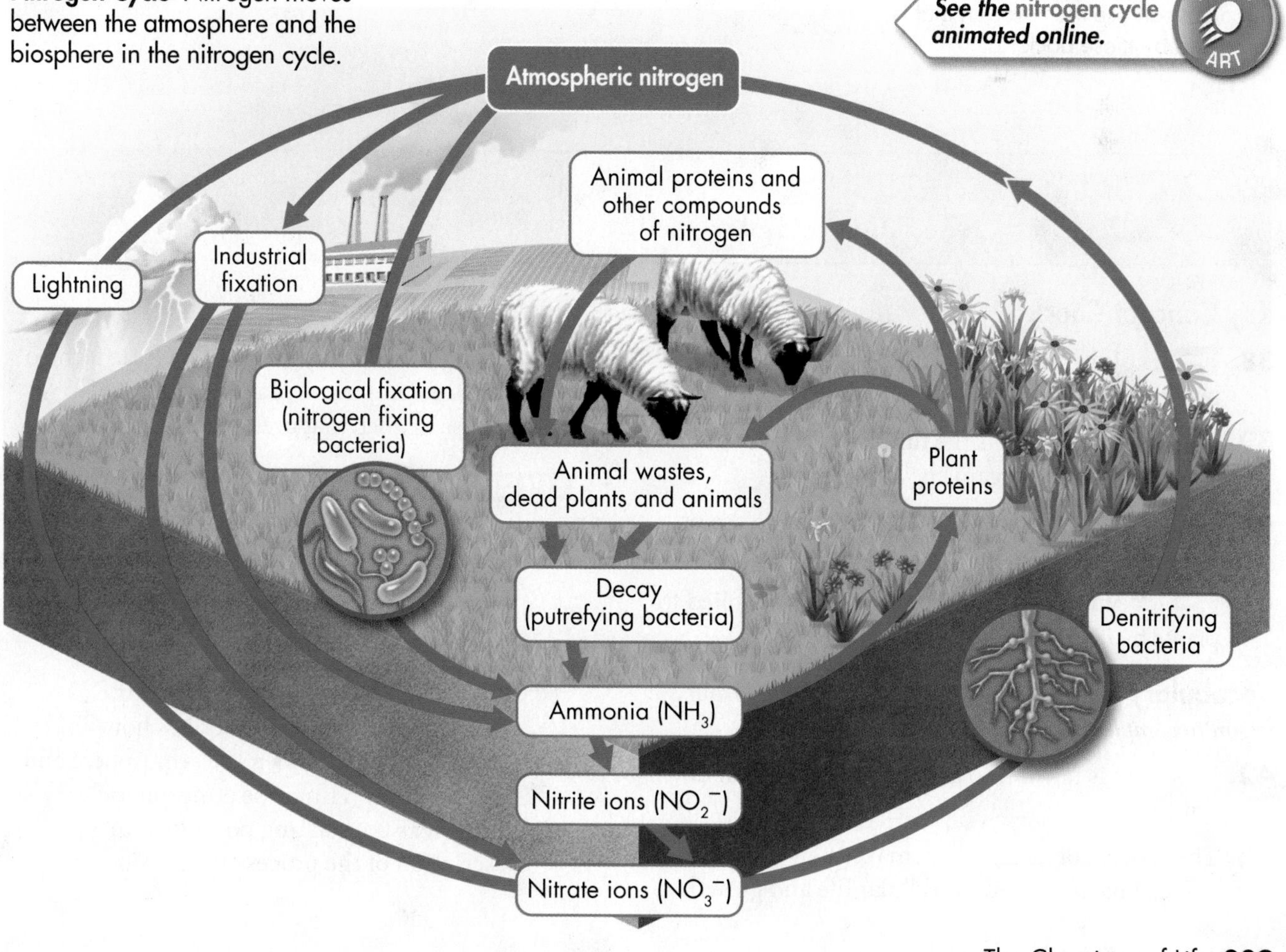

Atmospheric nitrogen
Animal proteins and other compounds of nitrogen
Lightning
Industrial fixation
Biological fixation (nitrogen fixing bacteria)
Animal wastes, dead plants and animals
Plant proteins
Decay (putrefying bacteria)
Denitrifying bacteria
Ammonia (NH_3)
Nitrite ions (NO_2^-)
Nitrate ions (NO_3^-)

Nitrogen Fixing Bacteria The bumps on these plant roots contain bacteria that fix nitrogen. The plant can use the nitrogen that is converted by these bacteria.

Biological Nitrogen Fixation There are two types of bacteria that fix nitrogen. Free living bacteria live independently in the soil. Symbiotic bacteria live in the root nodules of plants. The picture shows nodules on plant roots that contain symbiotic bacteria. The bacteria fix nitrogen that can be used by the plant. The plant produces sugars during photosynthesis that the bacteria can use. Legumes such as alfalfa, clover, peas, and beans have root nodules that contain symbiotic bacteria. Farmers plant legumes and then plow them into the soil instead of harvesting them to increase soil fertility.

Industrial Nitrogen Fixation Modern agriculture uses enormous amounts of nitrogen. Much of this nitrogen is made by industrial processes. These processes fix nitrogen from the air to produce nitrogen fertilizers. Nitrogen fertilizers enter the biosphere when they are taken up by plants.

Key Question How do nitrogen fixing bacteria provide plants with a usable form of nitrogen? **Nitrogen fixing bacteria reduce atmospheric nitrogen to ammonia. Ammonia is a water soluble nitrogen compound that can be used by plants.**

24.6 LessonCheck

Key Concept Check

38. **Explain** What is the role of ATP in energy production and energy use in living cells?

39. **Explain** What is the function of catabolism in the cells of living organisms?

40. **Describe** How does anabolism make use of the products of catabolism?

41. **Identify** What form of nitrogen is supplied to plants by nitrogen fixing bacteria?

Vocabulary Check

Choose a highlighted word from the lesson to complete each sentence correctly.

42. Food that is taken into an organism is broken down during ________.

43. The process of ________ makes new compounds and cell parts needed for cellular life and growth.

Think Critically

44. **Identify** How many moles of ATP are formed from the complete oxidation of 1 mol of glucose in a cell that uses oxygen?

CHEMISTRY & YOU

45. Why does a hummingbird eat so much? (Hint: See page 808.)

BIGIDEA
CHEMISTRY AS THE CENTRAL SCIENCE

46. Write a paragraph that describes how nitrogen moves between the atmosphere and the biosphere. (Hint: Use atmospheric nitrogen as the starting point in your description of the process.)

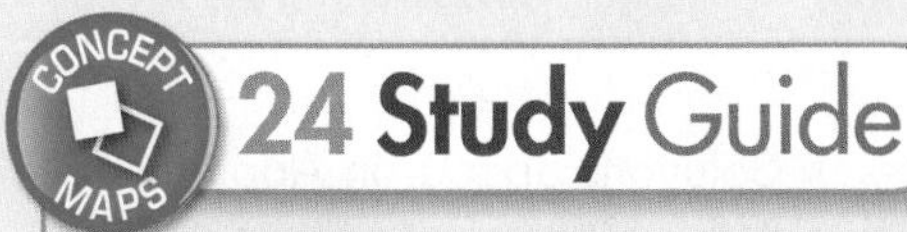

24 Study Guide

BIGIDEA

CHEMISTRY AS THE CENTRAL SCIENCE

There are four main types of biological molecules. Most carbohydrates are polymers that release energy when broken down. Proteins are polymers of amino acids and are needed for most chemical reactions in cells. Lipids are insoluble in water and can be used for long term energy storage. Nucleic acids are polymers of nucleotides. The nucleic acid DNA carries the instructions for a cell. Catabolic reactions break down biological molecules to provide energy and building blocks for the cell. Anabolic reactions build biological molecules to store energy and make new cell parts.

24.1 A Basis for Life

The two major types of cells that occur in nature are prokaryotic cells and eukaryotic cells.

Photosynthesis uses sunlight to reduce CO_2 to compounds that contain C—H bonds—mainly in the form of glucose.

- photosynthesis (785)

24.2 Carbohydrates

Most carbohydrates have the general formula $C_n(H_2O)_n$.

- carbohydrate (787)
- monosaccharide (787)
- disaccharide (788)
- polysaccharide (788)

24.3 Amino Acids and Their Polymers

An amino acid has a carboxyl group, an amino group, a hydrogen atom, and an R group bonded to a central carbon atom.

Differences in the amino acid sequence result in differences in the properties of peptides.

Enzymes increase reaction rates.

- amino acid (790)
- peptide (790)
- peptide bond (790)
- protein (790)
- enzyme (793)
- substrate (793)
- active site (793)

24.4 Lipids

Unlike carbohydrates and proteins, lipids do not tend to dissolve in water. Lipids dissolve easily in nonpolar solvents, such as ether and chloroform.

- lipid (795)
- triglyceride (795)
- phospholipid (796)
- wax (797)

24.5 Nucleic Acids

DNA stores information needed to make proteins and governs the reproduction of cells. RNA transmits information stored in DNA during protein synthesis.

A sequence of three bases of DNA is required to specify one amino acid in a peptide.

Gene mutations occur when one or more nucleotides in DNA are substituted, added, or deleted.

Examples of DNA technology include DNA typing, the production of bacteria that make human proteins, and genetically modifying foods and animals.

- nucleic acid (798)
- nucleotide (798)
- gene (800)

24.6 Metabolism

In living cells, ATP is the energy carrier between the reactions that release energy and the reactions that use energy.

In catabolism, biological molecules are broken down to provide energy and the building blocks for other compounds in the cell. In anabolism, the products and the energy of catabolism are used to make new compounds and cell parts needed for life and growth.

Nitrogen fixing bacteria reduce atmospheric nitrogen to ammonia. Ammonia is a water soluble nitrogen compound that can be used by plants.

- adenosine triphosphate (ATP) (806)
- metabolism (807)
- catabolism (807)
- anabolism (808)

24 Assessment

ONLINE PROBLEMS

★ Solutions appear in Appendix D.

Lesson by Lesson

24.1 A Basis for Life

47. What is the main difference between a prokaryotic cell and a eukaryotic cell?

★**48.** Explain what happens in photosynthesis.

49. Write a balanced equation for the complete oxidation of glucose.

24.2 Carbohydrates

50. Name two important monosaccharides.

51. Where in nature are glucose and fructose found?

52. Describe the general structure of a monosaccharide molecule.

53. Which monosaccharides combine to form the disaccharide sucrose?

54. What is the product of the complete breakdown of starch? Of glycogen?

55. What product is formed when cellulose is broken down?

24.3 Amino Acids and Their Polymers

56. What is the name given to the bond connecting two amino acids in a peptide chain?

57. How many peptide bonds does the tripeptide Ser—Gly—Phe have? Explain.

★**58.** Describe two common patterns found in the folding of protein chains.

59. Are the structures of the following two tripeptides the same? Explain.

a. Ala—Ser—Gly **b.** Gly—Ser—Ala

60. Describe the function of an enzyme.

61. What is an enzyme-substrate complex? How does it form?

24.4 Lipids

62. Distinguish between a fat and an oil.

63. What is a triglyceride?

64. Why are wax molecules hydrophobic?

65. Identify the molecules that react to form trimyristin.

66. Draw a simple representation of a lipid bilayer.

67. What two types of compounds combine to form a wax?

24.5 Nucleic Acids

68. What two types of nucleic acids do cells have?

★**69.** What are the components of a nucleotide?

70. What is the structural difference between the sugar unit in RNA and the sugar unit in DNA?

71. What type of bonding helps hold a DNA double helix together?

72. Which base pairs are found in a DNA molecule?

73. How many bases specify an amino acid in the genetic code?

★**74.** What is the basis for identifying an individual by DNA profiling?

24.6 Metabolism

75. Write an abbreviated, balanced equation for the hydrolysis of ATP to ADP.

★**76.** How are catabolism and anabolism related?

77. Describe the nitrogen cycle in your own words.

78. What is the source of raw materials used in anabolic reactions?

79. What is meant by industrial nitrogen fixation? What is produced during this process?

Understand Concepts

80. Why are the hydrophilic heads located on the outsides of the cell membrane?

81. Identify or classify each of the following biological molecules.

a.

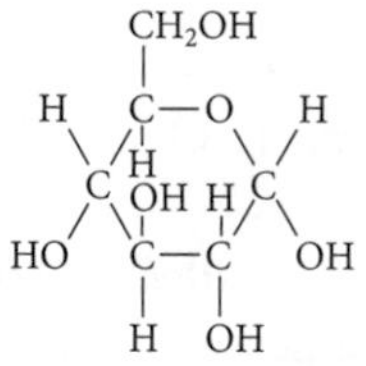

```
            CH2OH
            |
   H        C—O      H
     \     /H   \   /
      C   OH  H   C
     / \  |   |  / \
   HO    C——C      OH
         |   |
         H   OH
```

b.

```
          H3C    CH3
             \  /
              CH              R
              |               |
   H—N—C—C—N—C—C—OH
     |   |   ||  |   |   ||
     H   H   O   H   H   O
```

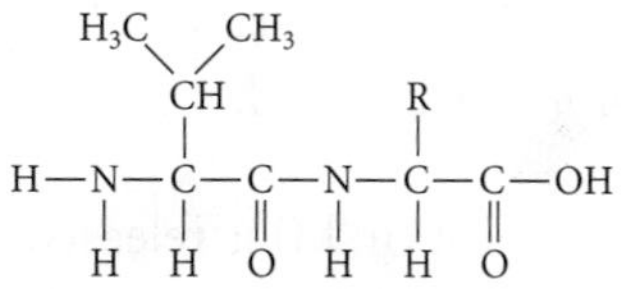

82. Which type of monomer produces each of the following polymers?

a. protein
b. polysaccharide
c. nucleic acid

83. What is one function of membrane proteins?

***84.** Does every code word in DNA specify an amino acid in protein synthesis? Explain.

85. Why can humans not digest cellulose, considering that it is made of the same monomers as starch?

86. How is an enzyme-substrate complex formed in the enzyme's active site?

87. What are the possible consequences of an error in DNA sequence?

88. Explain why photosynthesis might be considered the most important chemical process on Earth.

89. Describe how amino acids join to form a peptide bond.

***90.** What is base pairing? How does base pairing relate to the structure of DNA?

Think Critically

91. Explain Interpret this statement: "Carbon dioxide is an energy poor molecule, but glucose is an energy rich molecule."

92. Explain Which type of gene mutation do you think will do more damage to an organism: a substitution mutation in which one base is substituted for another base or an addition mutation in which a base is added to a sequence of bases? Explain.

93. Predict Suggest a reason why a bean plant might not grow well if planted in sterilized soil.

94. Identify What class of polymer is formed from each of the following monomers?
a. amino acids
b. monosaccharides
c. nucleotides

FOUNDATIONS Wrap-Up

Feed the Yeast

1. **Form a Hypothesis** At the beginning of this chapter, you placed yeast in water and in sugar solution. What is a possible explanation for any changes that you observed?

Concept Check

Now that you have finished studying Chapter 24, answer these questions.

2. Why do organisms need nutrients to grow and reproduce?
3. What kinds of nutrients do plants manufacture from nonliving materials?
4. What reaction do organisms use to obtain energy from glucose?
5. What metabolic process breaks nutrients down for the organism's use?

Write About Science

95. **Explain** Write a paragraph explaining how cells are able to selectively absorb certain ions and molecules while excluding other materials.

96. **Connect to the BIGIDEA** Choose one of the biological molecules discussed in this chapter. Write a paragraph describing how the elements and structure of the molecules relate to the function of the molecules.

CHEMYSTERY

Phenyl-what?

Phenylalanine is an amino acid—a monomer of proteins. So, how could phenylalanine be hazardous to your health? For most people, phenylalanine is not a health concern. But it is a concern for people who have the genetic disorder phenylketonuria, or PKU. Normally, phenylalanine is converted by the body to the amino acid tyrosine. People with PKU lack the enzyme that is required to convert phenylalanine to tyrosine. When this happens, phenylalanine accumulates to toxic levels in the body. PKU is treated by eating a diet low in phenylalanine. (The body still needs a small amount of phenylalanine.)

97. **Infer** Given that phenylalanine is an amino acid, which types of foods would you expect to be high in phenylalanine?

98. **Connect to the BIGIDEA** Why does a nutritionist need to understand chemistry?

Cumulative Review

99. Describe two factors that cause real gases to depart from the ideal gas law. (See Lesson 14.3 for help.)

100. Characterize these compounds as electrolytes or nonelectrolytes. (See Lesson 15.2 for help.)

a. NaCl **c.** CCl_4
b. $CuSO_4$ **d.** H_2O

*101. Calculate the boiling-point elevation for these aqueous solutions. (See Lesson 16.4 for help.)

a. 0.507*m* NaCl **c.** 0.155*m* $CaCl_2$
b. 0.204*m* NH_4Cl **d.** 0.222*m* $NaHSO_4$

*102. How much heat (in kJ) is released or absorbed when 0.265 mol of sodium bicarbonate are decomposed according to the reaction below? (See Lesson 17.2 for help.)

$$2NaHCO_3(s) \rightarrow Na_2CO_3(s) + H_2O(g) + CO_2(g)$$
$$\Delta H = 129 \text{ kJ}$$

103. What must be true at the equivalence point of an acid base titration? (See Lesson 19.4 for help.)

104. At which electrode in a voltaic cell does oxidation always occur? What is the charge on this electrode? (See Lesson 21.1 for help.)

105. What would you observe when a length of nickel wire is immersed in an aqueous solution of silver nitrate? (See Lesson 21.2 for help.)

106. Write a molecular formula for each compound. (See Lesson 23.3 for help.)

a. methyl acetate
b. 2-hydroxypropanoic acid

107. Capsaicin, shown below, is the major contributor to the heat of chili peppers. Circle and name the functional groups in capsaicin. (See Lessons 23.2 and 23.3 for help.)

CH_3O

HO— [benzene ring] —$CH_2NH\overset{O}{\overset{\|}{C}}(CH_2)_4CH{=}CHCH(CH_3)_2$

Standardized Test Prep

For help with answering test questions, go to your Chemistry Skills and Math Workbook.

Tips for Success

Anticipating the Answer You can sometimes figure out the answer to a question before you look at the answer choices. Try to answer the question in your mind before you look at the answer choices. Then, read the choices and choose the choice that agrees with the answer in your mind.

Select the choice that best answers each question or completes each statement.

1. What phrase best describes ATP?
   (A) energy producer
   (B) energy consumer
   (C) energy pump
   (D) energy transmitter

For Questions 2–5, match the category of organic compounds listed below that is most closely identified with each biological molecule.

I. monosaccharides
II. amino acids
III. fatty acids
IV. nucleotides

2. proteins
3. nucleic acids
4. lipids
5. carbohydrates

6. Which element is not found in amino acids?
   (A) phosphorus (C) oxygen
   (B) nitrogen (D) hydrogen

7. For any enzyme to function, the substrate must bind to the:
   (A) product. (C) active site.
   (B) cofactor. (D) peptide.

Use the paragraph to answer Questions 8–10.
Because an amino acid contains a carboxyl group and an amino group, it is amphoteric; that is, it can act as either an acid or a base. Crystalline amino acids have some properties—relatively high melting points and high water solubilities—that are more characteristic of ionic substances than of molecular substances.

8. Write an equation showing glycine acting as an acid in a reaction with water. (Glycine is the simplest amino acid. Its side chain is R = H.)
9. Write an equation showing glycine acting as a base in a reaction with water.
10. It is possible for glycine to undergo an internal Brønsted-Lowry acid-base neutralization reaction. Write the resulting structural formula. Explain how this reaction would account for the ionic properties of glycine.

For each question, there are two statements. Decide whether each statement is true or false. Then, decide whether Statement II is a correct explanation for Statement I.

	Statement I		Statement II
11.	Lipids tend to be insoluble in water.	BECAUSE	Lipids have mainly nonpolar bonds.
12.	Starch and cellulose are digestible by most organisms.	BECAUSE	Glucose is the monomer in starch and cellulose.
13.	Many of the reactions in catabolism are oxidation reactions.	BECAUSE	Oxidation reactions tend to be energy-producing reactions.
14.	The sequence of bases in DNA contains the code for making proteins.	BECAUSE	Each pair of bases in DNA codes for a specific amino acid.

If You Have Trouble With . . .

Question	1	2	3	4	5	6	7	8	9	10	11	12	13	14
See Lesson	24.6	24.3	24.5	24.4	24.2	24.3	24.3	24.3	24.3	24.3	24.4	24.2	24.6	24.5

25 Nuclear Chemistry

FOUNDATIONS for Learning

Simulating Radioactivity

1. Make a two-column table with the headings "Trial" and "Number of Heads."
2. Put 128 pennies into a container with a lid.
3. Pour the pennies onto a flat surface.
4. Record the number of pennies that land heads up. Move these pennies to the side.
5. Put the rest of the pennies in the container and put on the lid. Shake the container and repeat Steps 3 and 4. Do a total of 5 trials.

Analyze Data Make a graph with Trial on the *x*-axis and Number of Heads on the *y*-axis. Is the result a straight line or a curve?

PearsonChem.com

UntamedScience™

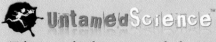

Take a trip back in time with the Untamed Science crew to "meet" Marie Curie and learn about her work.

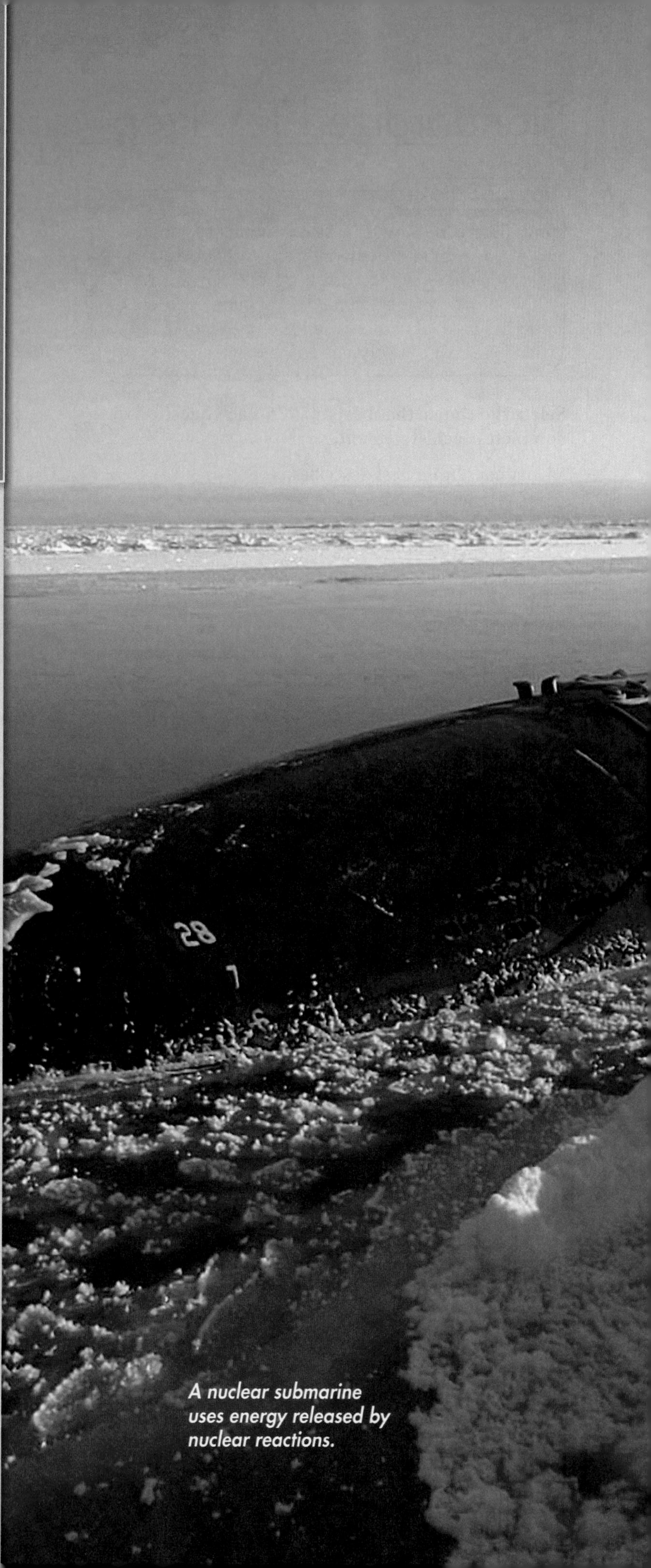

A nuclear submarine uses energy released by nuclear reactions.

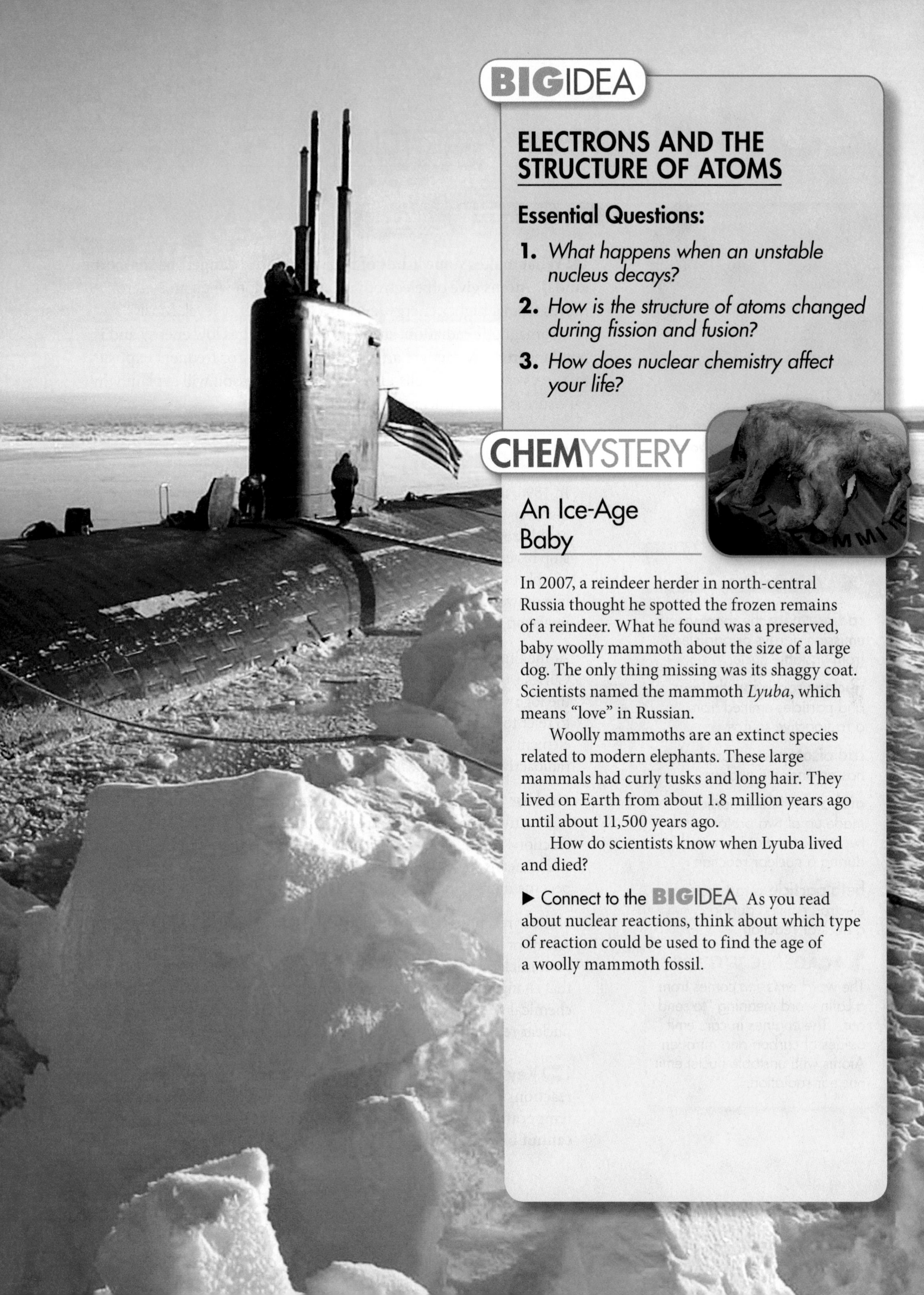

BIG IDEA

ELECTRONS AND THE STRUCTURE OF ATOMS

Essential Questions:

1. *What happens when an unstable nucleus decays?*
2. *How is the structure of atoms changed during fission and fusion?*
3. *How does nuclear chemistry affect your life?*

CHEMYSTERY

An Ice-Age Baby

In 2007, a reindeer herder in north-central Russia thought he spotted the frozen remains of a reindeer. What he found was a preserved, baby woolly mammoth about the size of a large dog. The only thing missing was its shaggy coat. Scientists named the mammoth *Lyuba*, which means "love" in Russian.

Woolly mammoths are an extinct species related to modern elephants. These large mammals had curly tusks and long hair. They lived on Earth from about 1.8 million years ago until about 11,500 years ago.

How do scientists know when Lyuba lived and died?

▶ Connect to the **BIGIDEA** As you read about nuclear reactions, think about which type of reaction could be used to find the age of a woolly mammoth fossil.

25.1 Nuclear Radiation

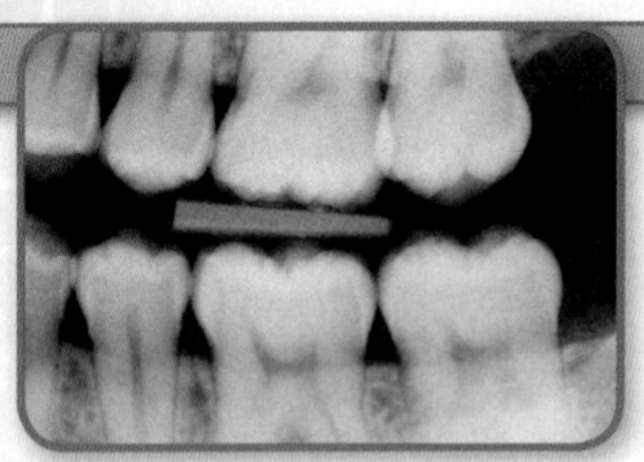

CHEMISTRY & YOU

Q: What makes some kinds of radiation more dangerous than other kinds? Atoms give off electromagnetic radiation when an electron moves from a higher energy level to a lower energy level. Most electromagnetic radiation, such as visible light, has low energy and is not dangerous. X-rays are an exception. Lengthy or frequent exposure to X-rays can damage cells in your body. This lesson will explain why exposure is also a concern with nuclear radiation.

Key Questions

How do nuclear reactions differ from chemical reactions?

What are three types of nuclear radiation?

BUILD Vocabulary

radioactivity the spontaneous emission of rays or particles from unstable nuclei

nuclear radiation the rays and particles emitted from a radioactive source

radioisotope an isotope that has an unstable nucleus

alpha particle a particle made up of two protons and two neutrons that is emitted during a nuclear reaction

beta particle a fast-moving electron emitted during a nuclear reaction

ACADEMIC WORDS

The word *emission* comes from a Latin word meaning "to send out." The engines in cars emit oxides of carbon and nitrogen. Atoms with unstable nuclei emit nuclear radiation.

Radioactivity

In 1896, the French chemist Antoine Henri Becquerel made an exciting discovery. He knew that uranium salts that had been exposed to sunlight could produce a foggy image on a photographic plate. Becquerel had to stop his experiment on a cloudy day because he could not expose the sample to sunlight. Instead, he put the sample and a photographic plate in a drawer. When he developed the plate days later, he found a foggy image on the plate. How had this happened?

At the time, Becquerel was working with Marie and Pierre Curie. The Curies were able to show that rays given off by uranium atoms caused the foggy image on the plate. Marie Curie used the term **radioactivity** to refer to the spontaneous emission of rays or particles from certain elements, such as uranium. The rays and particles emitted from a radioactive source are called **nuclear radiation.**

Nuclear Reactions vs. Chemical Reactions Radioactivity, or radioactive decay, is an example of a nuclear reaction. In both chemical reactions and nuclear reactions, atoms become more stable. The word *stable* means "not likely to change." In a chemical reaction, atoms become more stable by giving away, accepting, or sharing electrons.

Nuclear reactions begin with unstable isotopes, called **radioisotopes.** Atoms of these isotopes become more stable when changes happen in their nuclei. These changes release a large amount of energy. Remember that changes in pressure, temperature, and the use of catalysts can affect chemical reactions. These factors do not affect nuclear reactions. Also, nuclear reactions cannot be slowed down, speeded up, or stopped.

Key Question How do nuclear reactions differ from chemical reactions? **Nuclear reactions are not affected by changes in pressure, temperature, or the use of catalysts. The rate of a nuclear reaction cannot be changed.**

Types of Radiation

Radiation is emitted during radioactive decay. Three types of nuclear radiation are alpha radiation, beta radiation, and gamma radiation.

Alpha Radiation Some radioactive sources emit helium nuclei, which are also called alpha particles. An **alpha particle** has two protons and two neutrons. Because it has no electrons to balance the protons, it has a charge of 2+. The symbol for an alpha particle is ${}^{4}_{2}\text{He}$ or α. The superscript in ${}^{4}_{2}\text{He}$ is the mass number. The subscript is the atomic number.

The radioisotope uranium-238 emits alpha radiation and forms another radioisotope, thorium-234. When an atom loses an alpha particle, the atomic number of the product is lower by two and its mass number is lower by four. Here is the equation for the reaction of uranium-238.

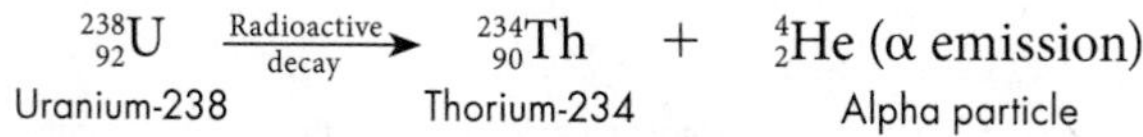

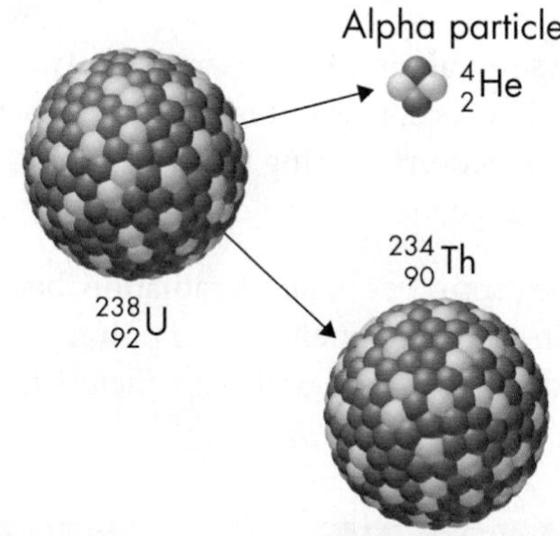

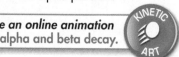

Alpha Decay Uranium-238 decays and forms thorium-234. The radiation emitted is an alpha particle.

See an online animation of alpha and beta decay.
KINETIC ART

In a balanced nuclear equation, the sum of the mass numbers on the right must equal the sum on the left. On the left side, the mass number is 238. On the right side, the sum is 234 + 4, or 238. The sum of the atomic numbers must be the same on both sides of the equation, too. On the left side, the atomic number is 92. On the right side, the sum is 90 + 2, or 92.

Beta Radiation In some nuclear reactions, one of the neutrons in the nucleus of an atom changes into a proton and a fast-moving electron. The fast-moving electron, or **beta particle,** is released from the atom.

$${}^{1}_{0}\text{n} \longrightarrow {}^{1}_{1}\text{p} + {}^{0}_{-1}\text{e}$$

Neutron — Proton — Electron (beta particle)

The symbol for a beta particle is β or ${}^{0}_{-1}\text{e}$. The -1 in ${}^{0}_{-1}\text{e}$ is the charge on the electron. The 0 stands for its mass, which is very small compared to a proton.

Carbon-14 emits a beta particle as it decays to form nitrogen-14. Look at the equation below and the model to the right. The nitrogen-14 atom has one more proton and one less neutron than the carbon-14 atom. So its atomic number is higher by one than carbon's but its mass number does not change.

$${}^{14}_{6}\text{C} \longrightarrow {}^{14}_{7}\text{N} + {}^{0}_{-1}\text{e}\ (\beta\ \text{emission})$$

Carbon-14 (radioactive) — Nitrogen-14 (stable) — Beta particle

Beta Decay When a carbon-14 atom decays, the products are nitrogen-14 and a beta particle.

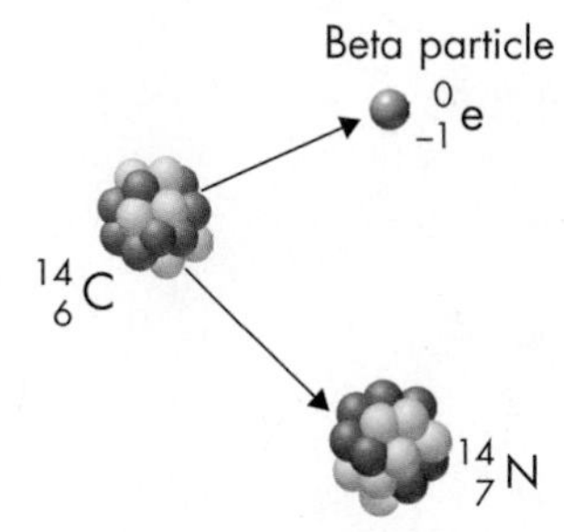

gamma ray a high-energy photon emitted by a radioisotope

WORD ORIGINS

The first letter of the Greek alphabet is alpha (α). The second letter is beta (β) and the third is gamma (γ). The letters were used to name types of nuclear radiation.

Gamma Radiation Recall that an electron moving from a higher energy level to a lower energy level emits a bundle of light energy called a photon. A high-energy photon emitted by a radioisotope is called a **gamma ray.** In the diagram of the electromagnetic spectrum in Chapter 5, gamma rays are on the far right. They have the shortest wavelength and the highest energy. The symbol for a gamma ray is γ.

Nuclei often emit gamma rays along with alpha or beta particles during radioactive decay. Gamma rays have no mass and no charge. So the emission of gamma radiation does not change the atomic number or mass number of an atom. Here are two examples of reactions that emit gamma rays.

$$^{230}_{90}\text{Th} \longrightarrow \, ^{226}_{88}\text{Ra} + \, ^{4}_{2}\text{He} + \gamma$$

Thorium-230, Radium-226, Alpha particle, Gamma ray

$$^{234}_{90}\text{Th} \longrightarrow \, ^{234}_{91}\text{Pa} + \, ^{0}_{-1}\text{e} + \gamma$$

Thorium-234, Protactinium-234, Beta particle, Gamma ray

The release of gamma rays reveals another difference between chemical and nuclear reactions. Mass is always conserved in chemical reactions. Mass is not conserved during nuclear reactions. During radioactive decay, an extremely small amount of mass is changed into energy.

This table summarizes the properties of alpha radiation, beta radiation, and gamma radiation. You can read about penetrating power on the next page. Lesson 25.4 will explain the importance of this characteristic for humans.

Characteristics of Some Types of Radiation

Type	Alpha radiation	Beta radiation	Gamma radiation
Consists of	Alpha particles (helium nuclei)	Beta particles (electrons)	High-energy photons
Symbol	α, $^{4}_{2}\text{He}$	β, $^{0}_{-1}\text{e}$	γ
Charge	2+	1−	0
Mass (amu)	4	1/1837	0
Common source	Radium-226	Carbon-14	Cobalt-60
Penetrating power	Low (0.05 mm body tissue)	Moderate (4 mm body tissue)	Very high (penetrates body easily)

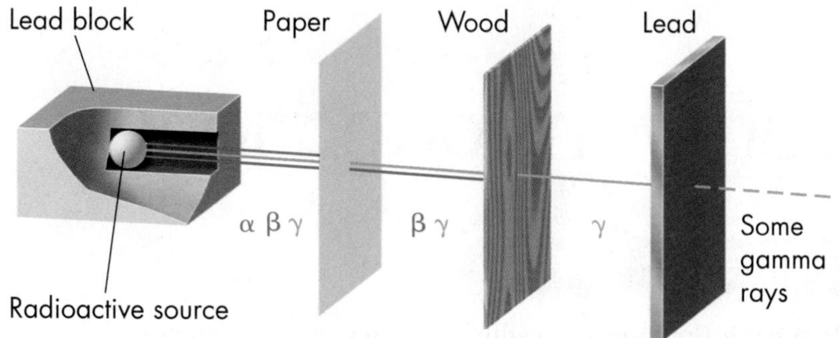

Penetrating Power of Nuclear Radiation One meaning of the word *penetrate* is "to pass through a barrier." The barriers in the diagram are paper, wood, and lead.

Penetrating Power The diagram compares the penetrating power of nuclear radiation. Alpha particles do not travel very far and are not very penetrating because of their large mass and charge. A sheet of paper or the surface of your skin can stop them. However, eating or breathing in a radioisotope that emits alpha particles can cause harm. Inside the body, the particles don't have to travel far to penetrate soft tissue.

A beta particle has less charge and much less mass than an alpha particle. So beta particles are more penetrating than alpha particles. Beta particles can pass through paper but are stopped by aluminum foil or thin pieces of wood.

Gamma rays are highly penetrating because they have no mass and no charge. They can be stopped, although not completely, by several meters of concrete or several centimeters of lead.

Key Question What are three types of nuclear radiation? **Three types of nuclear radiation are alpha radiation, beta radiation, and gamma radiation.**

25.1 LessonCheck

Key Concept Check

1. **Compare** What factors that affect chemical reactions do not affect nuclear reactions?
2. **Describe** Briefly describe the three main types of nuclear radiation.

Think Critically

3. **Identify** What part of an atom changes during radioactive decay?
4. **Compare and Contrast** How is the atomic number of a nucleus changed by alpha decay? How is it changed by beta decay? By gamma decay?
5. **Describe** What two items must be equal for a nuclear equation to be balanced?
6. **Relate Cause and Effect** How does alpha decay affect the mass number of a nucleus? How does beta decay affect the mass number?
7. **Compare** Alpha radiation and beta radiation have two properties that gamma radiation does not. What are those properties?
8. **Predict** When polonium-210 decays by alpha radiation, what isotope is formed?

9. Why are gamma rays and X-rays more dangerous than alpha radiation or beta radiation? (Hint: See discussion of penetrating power and see page 818.)

25.2 Nuclear Transformations

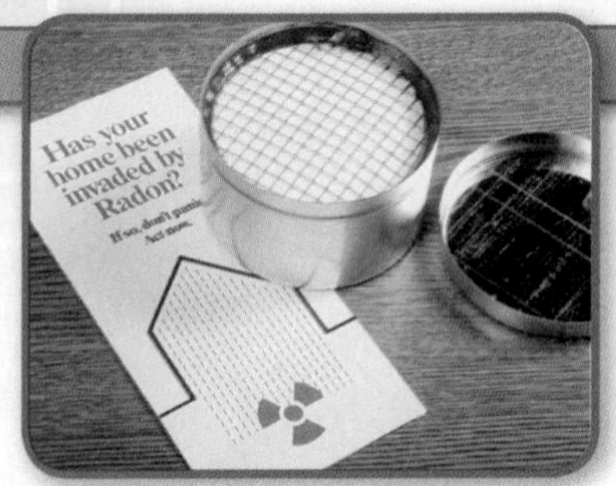

CHEMISTRY & YOU

Q: What is the source of radon in homes? All the isotopes of radon gas are unstable and give off radiation. Inhaled radon is the second leading cause of lung cancer in the United States. Radon may build up in a basement that is not well ventilated. Because radon is a colorless, odorless gas, people often don't know that they are breathing it. You can buy test kits to measure the levels of radon in a building. In this lesson, you will study the series of reactions that produce this hazardous gas.

Key Questions

What determines the type of decay a radioisotope undergoes?

How much of a radioactive sample remains after each half-life?

What are two ways in which transmutation can occur?

Nuclear Stability and Decay

All atomic nuclei, except those of hydrogen atoms, have neutrons and two or more protons. The positively-charged protons repel each other. They would fly apart without a force to hold them together. The **nuclear force** is an attractive force that acts between nuclear particles that are close together. At the short distances between protons and neutrons in a nucleus, the nuclear force is stronger than the force pushing the protons apart. The nuclear force holds the nucleus together.

Stable Nuclei More than 1,500 different nuclei are known. Only 264 of the known nuclei are stable. The rest are unstable and will change over time. The stability of a nucleus depends on the ratio of neutrons to protons. The graph below plots the number of neutrons versus the number of protons for all known stable nuclei. The region of the graph in which these points are located is called the **band of stability.** For elements with atomic numbers below 20, the ratio is about one neutron to one proton. For elements with atomic numbers above 20, stable nuclei have more neutrons than protons.

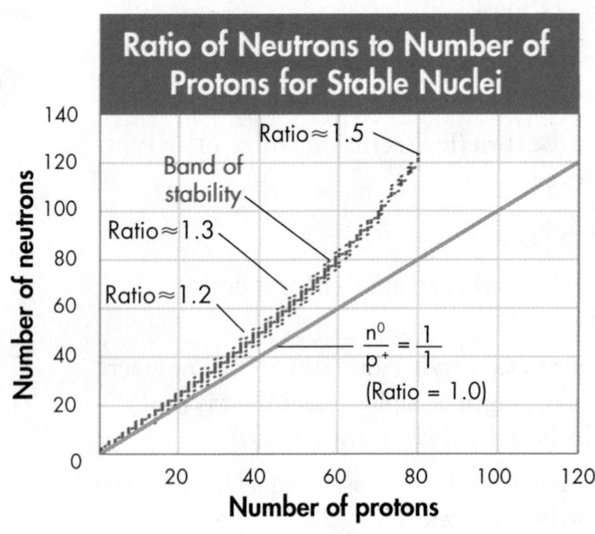

Comparing Stable Nuclei The band of stability is shown in purple. Each dot represents one of the 264 stable nuclei. The green line shows what the pattern would be if the ratio were one neutron for one proton in every stable nucleus. As the atomic number rises, the band of stability curves away from the green line.

Go to your Chemistry Skills and Math Workbook to practice interpreting graphs.

Unstable Nuclei Nuclei are unstable and undergo spontaneous decay for different reasons. The neutron-to-proton ratio in a radioisotope determines the type of decay that occurs.

▶ **Beta Emission** The nuclei in copper-66 and carbon-14 are unstable because they have too many neutrons compared to the number of protons. When these nuclei decay, a neutron emits a beta particle and becomes a proton. The atomic number increases by one.

$$^{66}_{29}\text{Cu} \longrightarrow {}^{66}_{30}\text{Zn} + {}^{0}_{-1}\text{e}$$

$$^{14}_{6}\text{C} \longrightarrow {}^{14}_{7}\text{N} + {}^{0}_{-1}\text{e}$$

▶ **Electron Capture** In nickel-59 and argon-37, the nuclei are unstable because there are too few neutrons compared to the number of protons. These nuclei become more stable by capturing an electron. In the process, a proton changes into a neutron. Electron capture is the opposite of beta emission.

$$^{59}_{28}\text{Ni} + {}^{0}_{-1}\text{e} \longrightarrow {}^{59}_{27}\text{Co}$$

$$^{37}_{18}\text{Ar} + {}^{0}_{-1}\text{e} \longrightarrow {}^{37}_{17}\text{Cl}$$

▶ **Positron Emission** Nuclei in boron-8 and oxygen-15 also have too few neutrons. They become more stable when a proton forms a neutron and a positron. A **positron** is a particle with the mass of an electron but a positive charge. Its symbol is ${}^{0}_{+1}\text{e}$. A nucleus gains a neutron and loses a proton in both positron emission and electron capture. The atomic number decreases by 1.

$$^{8}_{5}\text{B} \longrightarrow {}^{8}_{4}\text{Be} + {}^{0}_{+1}\text{e}$$

$$^{15}_{8}\text{O} \longrightarrow {}^{15}_{7}\text{N} + {}^{0}_{+1}\text{e}$$

▶ **Alpha Emission** All nuclei that have an atomic number greater than 83 are radioactive. These nuclei have both too many neutrons and too many protons to be stable. Most of them emit alpha particles. Remember that alpha emission removes two neutrons and two protons from a nucleus.

$$^{226}_{88}\text{Ra} \longrightarrow {}^{222}_{86}\text{Rn} + {}^{4}_{2}\text{He}$$

$$^{232}_{90}\text{Th} \longrightarrow {}^{228}_{88}\text{Ra} + {}^{4}_{2}\text{He}$$

The table below summarizes four ways a nucleus can decay spontaneously.

Type of Decay	Equation
Beta emission	${}^{1}_{0}\text{n} \longrightarrow {}^{1}_{1}\text{p} + {}^{0}_{-1}\text{e}$
Electron capture	${}^{1}_{1}\text{p} + {}^{0}_{-1}\text{e} \longrightarrow {}^{1}_{0}\text{n}$
Positron emission	${}^{1}_{1}\text{p} \longrightarrow {}^{0}_{+1}\text{e} + {}^{1}_{0}\text{n}$
Alpha emission	${}^{x}_{y}\text{L} \longrightarrow {}^{x-4}_{y-2}\text{M} + {}^{4}_{2}\text{He}$

Key Question What determines the type of decay a radioisotope undergoes? **The neutron-to-proton ratio in a radioisotope determines the type of decay that occurs.**

nuclear force an attractive force that acts among all nuclear particles

band of stability on a graph of neutrons versus protons, the region where stable nuclei appear

positron a particle with the mass of an electron and a positive charge

BLENDED WORDS

Some words are a blend of two words with a few letters left out. Smog blends *smoke* and *fog*. Brunch blends *breakfast* and *lunch*. Positron is a blend of *positive* and *electron*.

Radioactive Decay Curve In the circles, the purple dots stand for the reactant. The yellow dots stand for the product. During each half-life, half of the atoms in a radiactive sample decay into product.

Go to your Chemistry Skills and Math Workbook to practice interpreting graphs.

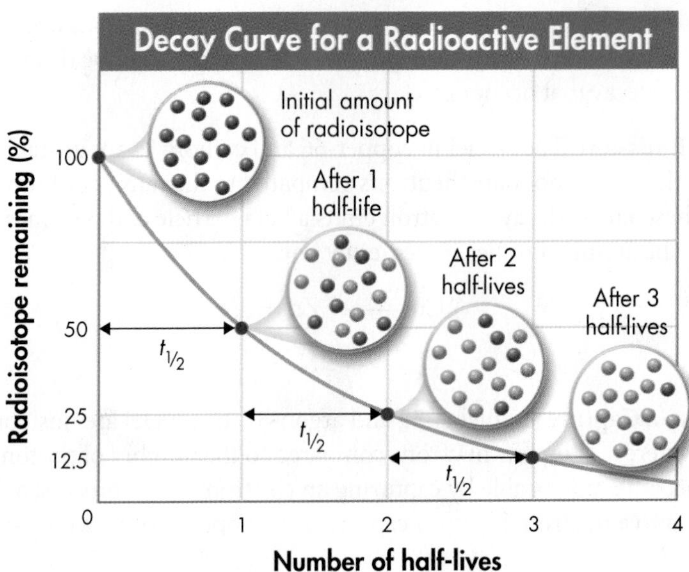

half-life ($t_{\frac{1}{2}}$) the time needed for half of the nuclei in a radioisotope sample to decay

USING PRIOR KNOWLEDGE

When the word is *half-life,* using what you know may be confusing. A half-hour is half an hour, but a half-life is not half the life of a radioisotope. After two half-lives the isotope will still be radioactive. It takes many half-lives for almost all of a sample to decay.

Half-Life

The rate of decay is a specific property of each radioisotope. This rate is given as a half-life. A **half-life** ($t_{\frac{1}{2}}$) is the time needed for half of the nuclei in a radioisotope sample to decay to products. During each half-life, half of the radioactive atoms in a sample decay.

The graph above shows how a sample changes during three half-lives. The initial sample is 100 percent reactant atoms. After one half-life, 50 percent of these atoms remain. After two half-lives, the amount of original atoms is cut in half again. Only 25 percent of the original atoms remain.

Comparing Half-Lives Half-lives can be less than one second or as long as billions of years. The table below shows the half-lives of some radioisotopes that occur in nature. Scientists can use radioisotopes with long half-lives to estimate the age of objects. Scientists can use radioisotopes with short half-lives to detect and treat some diseases. Lesson 25.4 will explain why the isotopes used in nuclear medicine must have short half-lives.

Half-Lives of Some Naturally Occurring Radioisotopes

Isotope	Half-life	Radiation emitted
Carbon-14	5.730×10^3 years	β
Potassium-40	1.25×10^9 years	β, γ
Radon-222	3.8 days	α
Radium-226	1.6×10^3 years	α, γ
Thorium-234	24.1 days	β, γ
Uranium-235	7.0×10^8 years	α, γ
Uranium-238	4.5×10^9 years	α

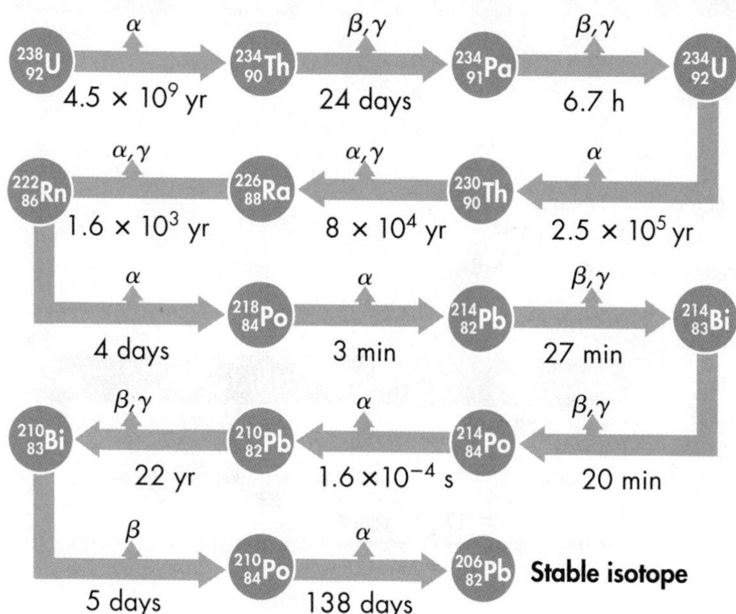

Decay Series of U-238 A decay series continues until a stable isotope is produced. The stable end product of this series is lead-206. Radon (Rn) gas is one of the unstable intermediates.

Dating Rocks One isotope that has a long half-life is uranium-238. It decays by alpha emission to thorium-234. But thorium-234 is also radioactive. It decays by beta emission to protactinium-234. The figure above shows that 14 different nuclear reactions take place before this decay series produces the stable isotope lead-206.

Scientists can estimate the age of minerals that contain uranium by measuring the ratio of uranium-238 to lead-206. This ratio tells them how many half-lives of uranium-238 have passed. Because the half-life of uranium-238 is 4.5×10^9 years, this method can be used to date rocks that are as old as the solar system.

Radiocarbon Dating Scientists use isotopes of carbon to date objects that were once part of living systems. The objects contain the stable isotopes carbon-12 and carbon-13. They also contain the radioisotope carbon-14, $^{14}_{6}C$. Carbon-14 has a half-life of 5730 years.

Carbon-14 forms when high energy cosmic rays strike nitrogen atoms in the atmosphere. This process keeps the ratio of $^{14}_{6}C$ to other carbon isotopes fairly constant in compounds such as carbon dioxide. Plants use carbon dioxide to produce carbon compounds such as glucose. In those compounds, the ratio of carbon isotopes is the same as in the air. The ratio is kept constant as animals eat plants and other animals.

The ratio of $^{14}_{6}C$ to other carbon isotopes does not change while an organism is alive. When an organism dies, it stops exchanging carbon with the environment. Its radioactive carbon-14 atoms decay without being replaced. So the ratio of $^{14}_{6}C$ to stable carbon in the remains of an organism decreases in a predictable way. Scientists can use carbon-14 data to estimate the age when an organism died.

Key Question How much of a radioactive sample remains after each half-life? **During each half-life, half of the remaining radioactive atoms decay into atoms of a new element.**

BUILD Connections

Scientists can use radiocarbon dating to estimate the age of an Egyptian mummy. They remove a small piece of cloth from the mummy to collect the data. The piece is burned, and the carbon dioxide that forms is analyzed. The process measures how much carbon-14 remains in the sample. Because people do not like to damage a mummy, scientists are looking for less destructive ways to collect the same data.

Using Half-lives in Calculations

Carbon-14 emits beta radiation. It has a half-life ($t_{\frac{1}{2}}$) of 5730 years. Assume that a sample of carbon-14 has an initial mass of 2.00×10^{-12} g and that the sample decays for a total of 17,190 years. How many grams of the isotope remain after 17,190 years?

1 Analyze **List the knowns and the unknowns.** First, calculate the number of half-lives. To find the mass of the radioisotope remaining, multiply the original mass by $\frac{1}{2}$ for each half-life that has passed.

KNOWNS	UNKNOWNS
$t_{\frac{1}{2}}$ = 5730 years	number of half-lives = ?
initial mass = 2.00×10^{-12} g	mass remaining = ? g
decay time = 17,190 years	

2 Calculate **Solve for the unknowns.**

Write an expression for calculating the number of half-lives. Divide the decay time in years by the half-life in years.

$$\text{Number of half-lives} = \frac{\text{number of years}}{\text{half-life}}$$

Substitute the known values into the expression and solve.

$$\text{Number of half-lives} = \frac{17{,}190\ \cancel{\text{years}}}{5730\ \cancel{\text{years}}}$$

$$\text{Number of half-lives} = 3$$

To find the remaining mass, multiply the initial mass by one half for each half-life.

$$\text{Remaining mass} = \text{initial mass} \times \frac{1}{2} \times \frac{1}{2} \times \frac{1}{2}$$

$$= 2.00 \times 10^{-12}\,\text{g} \times \frac{1}{8}$$

$$= 0.250 \times 10^{-12}\,\text{g}$$

Write the answer in scientific notation with the correct number of significant figures.

$$\text{Remaining mass} = 2.50 \times 10^{-13}\,\text{g}$$

Hint: Multiplying by $\frac{1}{8}$ is like multiplying by 1 and dividing by 8.

3 Evaluate **Do the results make sense?** The mass of carbon-14 after three half-lives should be one-eighth of the original mass. If you divide 2.50×10^{-13} g by 2.00×10^{-12} g, you will get 0.125, the decimal form of $\frac{1}{8}$.

BUILD Math Skills

Multiplying by a Fraction When you solve a problem that uses half-lives, you will almost always have to multiply by $\frac{1}{2}$ or a multiple of $\frac{1}{2}$.
When the numerator of a fraction is 1, as in $\frac{1}{2}$, the multiplication is actually a division.

$$4.8\,g \times \frac{1}{2} = \frac{4.8\,g \times 1}{2} = 2.4\,g$$

If the decay time equals two half-lives, you need to mupltiply by $\frac{1}{2}$ two times. Or you can multiply $\frac{1}{2}$ by $\frac{1}{2}$ first, and then complete the operation.

$$4.8\,g \times \frac{1}{2} = 2.4\,g \qquad \frac{1}{2} \times \frac{1}{2} = \frac{1}{4}$$

$$2.4\,g \times \frac{1}{2} = 1.2\,g \qquad 4.8\,g \times \frac{1}{4} = 1.2\,g$$

Go to your Chemistry Skills and Math Workbook for more practice.

Practice Problems

First, calculate the number of half-lives.

10. Manganese-56 is a beta emitter with a half-life of 2.6 h. What is the mass of manganese-56 in a 1.0-mg sample of the isotope at the end of 10.4 h?

❶ Analyze **List the knowns and the unknowns.**

❷ Calculate **Solve for the unknowns.**

❸ Evaluate **Do the results make sense?**

KNOWNS	UNKNOWNS
$t_{\frac{1}{2}}$ = 2.6 hours	Number of half-lives = ?
initial mass = 1.0 mg	mass remaining = ? g
decay time = 10.4 hours	

11. The radioisotope radium-226 has a half-life of 1.6×10^3 years. What is the mass of radium-226 in a 10.0-mg sample of the isotope at the end of 3.2×10^3 years?

KNOWNS	UNKNOWNS
$t_{\frac{1}{2}}$ =	number of half-lives = ?
initial mass =	mass remaining = ? g
decay time =	

12. Thorium-234 has a half-life of 24.1 days. Will all the thorium atoms in a sample decay in 48.2 days? Explain your answer.

13. Challenge A radioisotope has a half-life of 4 days. How much of a 20-gram sample of this radioisotope remains at the end of each time period?

a. 4 days **b.** 8 days

transmutation the change of an atom of one element into an atom of another element

transuranium element any element with an atomic number above 92

The prefix *trans-* can mean "to change." On the way to school, you may *trans*fer from a bus to a train. You may be asked to *trans*late a word from Spanish to English. During a *trans*mutation, atoms change from one element to another.

Transmutation Reactions

For thousands of years, alchemists tried to change lead into gold because gold was more valuable than lead. No matter how hard the alchemists tried, they did not succeed. What they wanted to achieve is **transmutation,** or the change of an atom of one element into an atom of another element. Transmutations happen during radioactive decay. They also take place when particles bombard, or strike, the nucleus of an atom. These particles can be protons, neutrons, alpha particles, or small atoms.

Transmutations are common in nature. One example is the change from nitrogen-14 to carbon-14 that takes place in the upper atmosphere. Another example is the series of reactions that occurs when uranium-238 decays.

Artificial Transmutations Transmutations that do not occur in nature can be forced to occur in a laboratory or in a nuclear reactor. Ernest Rutherford performed the first artificial transmutation in 1919. He used alpha particles to bombard nitrogen gas. When nitrogen atoms absorb alpha particles, they change into fluorine-18 atoms.

$$\underset{\text{Nitrogen-14}}{{}^{14}_{7}\text{N}} + \underset{\text{Alpha particle}}{{}^{4}_{2}\text{He}} \longrightarrow \underset{\text{Fluorine-18}}{{}^{18}_{9}\text{F}}$$

The unstable fluorine atoms quickly decay to form a stable isotope of oxygen and a proton.

$$\underset{\text{Fluorine-18}}{{}^{18}_{9}\text{F}} \longrightarrow \underset{\text{Oxygen-17}}{{}^{17}_{8}\text{O}} + \underset{\text{Proton}}{{}^{1}_{1}\text{p}}$$

The overall reaction looks like this.

The Transmutation of Nitrogen-14
In the first artificial transmutation, nitrogen-14 formed fluorine-18, which decayed to oxygen-17.

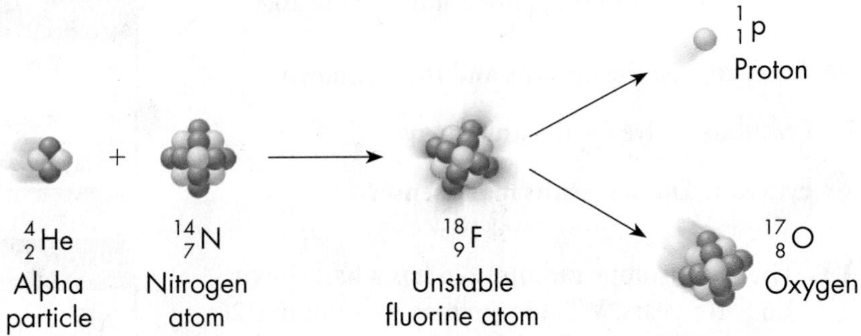

Rutherford's experiment led to the discovery of the proton. He and other scientists noticed a pattern as they did their transmutation experiments. In every case, hydrogen nuclei were emitted. Scientists realized that these hydrogen nuclei (protons) must have an important role in atomic structure. Transmutation also played a role in James Chadwick's discovery of the neutron in 1932. Neutrons were produced when beryllium-9 was bombarded with alpha particles. Here is the equation for the reaction.

$$\underset{\text{Beryllium-9}}{{}^{9}_{4}\text{Be}} + \underset{\text{Alpha particle}}{{}^{4}_{2}\text{He}} \longrightarrow \underset{\text{Carbon-12}}{{}^{12}_{6}\text{C}} + \underset{\text{Neutron}}{{}^{1}_{0}\text{n}}$$

Transmutations in Accelerators Elements with atomic numbers above 92, the atomic number of uranium, are called **transuranium elements.** Most of these elements do not occur in nature. All of them are radioactive.

Transuranium elements are made by artificial transmutation in nuclear reactors and nuclear accelerators. Reactors produce beams of low-energy particles. These particles are fed into accelerators, which increase the speed of the particles. The European Organization for Nuclear Research has many accelerators at its site on the border between France and Switzerland. The photograph to the right shows the largest accelerator at the site.

Particle Accelerator
This accelerator is the most powerful accelerator in the world. It has a circumference of about 27 km and is about 100 m underground.

When uranium-238 is bombarded with neutrons from a nuclear reactor, some uranium nuclei capture these neutrons. The product is uranium-239.

$$^{238}_{92}\text{U} + ^{1}_{0}\text{n} \longrightarrow ^{239}_{92}\text{U}$$

Uranium-239 is radioactive and emits a beta particle. Remember that beta emission increases the atomic number of an element. So the other product is an isotope of the element neptunium (atomic number 93).

$$^{239}_{92}\text{U} \longrightarrow ^{239}_{93}\text{Np} + ^{0}_{-1}\text{e}$$

Neptunium is unstable and also decays by beta emission. The other product is an isotope of the element plutonium (atomic number 94).

Plutonium and neptunium are both transuranium elements. Scientists in Berkeley, California, produced the first two artificial elements in 1940. Since that time, more than 20 other transuranium elements have been made.

Key Question What are two ways in which transmutation can occur? **Transmutation can occur by radioactive decay or when particles bombard the nucleus of an atom.**

25.2 LessonCheck

Key Concept Check

14. Identify What factor determines the type of decay that occurs in a radioisotope?

15. Predict How much of a sample of radioisotope remains after one half-life? After two half-lives?

16. Explain How can transmutation occur in a stable isotope?

Vocabulary Check *Choose a highlighted word from the lesson to complete the sentence correctly.*

17. A(n) __________ is the amount of time needed for half of the nuclei of a radioisotope to decay.

18. The change of an atom of one element into an atom of another element is called __________.

Think Critically

19. Apply Concepts Complete the following nuclear equations. Use what you know about balanced nuclear equations to identify the missing particles.

a. $^{27}_{13}\text{Al} + ^{4}_{2}\text{He} \longrightarrow ^{30}_{14}\text{Si} + ?$

b. $^{214}_{83}\text{Bi} \longrightarrow ^{4}_{2}\text{He} + ?$

CHEMISTRY & YOU

20. Uranium compounds are found in rocks and in the soils that form from these rocks. How can these uranium compounds lead to a build-up of radon in homes and other buildings? (Hint: See page 825.)

25.3 Fission and Fusion

CHEMISTRY & YOU

Q: Where does the sun's energy come from? The sun appears as a bright, fiery ball in the sky. It is so bright that you should never look at the sun directly without eye protection. The sun is about halfway through its life cycle. It has been producing energy for about 5 billion years. It is expected to produce energy for about 5 billion more. In this lesson, you will study the nuclear reaction that takes place in the sun.

Key Questions

What happens in a nuclear chain reaction?

How do fission reactions and fusion reactions differ?

BUILD Vocabulary

fission the splitting of a nucleus into smaller pieces

neutron moderation a process that slows down neutrons

neutron absorption a process that decreases the number of slow-moving neutrons

ROOT WORDS
The word *fissionable* is made from the words *fission* and *able*. An isotope is fissionable when its nuclei are able to go through the process of fission.

Nuclear Fission

When the nuclei of some isotopes are bombarded with neutrons, the nuclei split into smaller pieces. This process is called **fission.** The drawing below shows the fission of uranium-235. When an atom of uranium-235 is hit by a slow-moving neutron, it breaks into pieces of roughly the same size. Those pieces may be atoms of krypton-91 and barium-142. The other products of this reaction are energy and three neutrons. The neutrons can hit the nuclei of other uranium-235 atoms, which break apart and emit more neutrons. This process continues as long as enough fissionable atoms are present. The process is an example of a chain reaction.

Nuclear fission can release enormous amounts of energy. For example, fission of 1 kg of uranium-235 gives off the same amount of energy as the explosion of 20,000 tons of dynamite. In an uncontrolled nuclear chain reaction, all the energy is released in a fraction of a second. An atomic bomb is a device that can trigger an uncontrolled nuclear chain reaction.

Fission of Uranium When uranium-235 absorbs a slow-moving neutron, it forms uranium-236. This very unstable nucleus may split into krypton-91 and barium-142. The other products of this fission are three neutrons and energy.

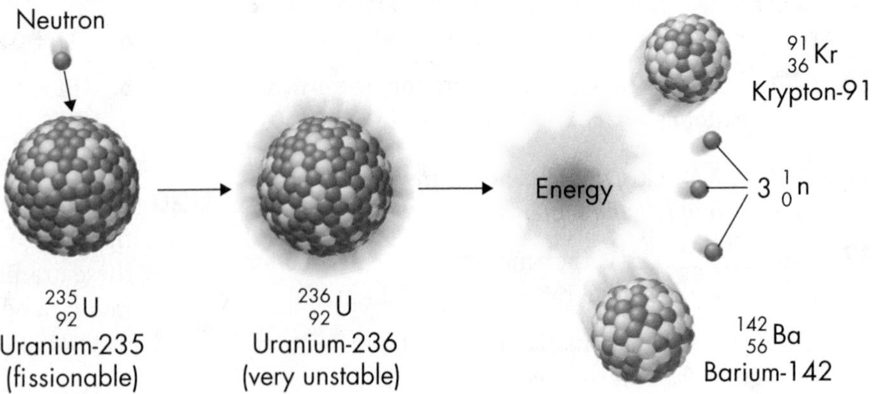

Controlling Fission Fission can be controlled so that energy is released slowly. Nuclear reactors, such as the one shown below, use controlled fission to produce useful energy. The reaction takes place in uranium-235 or plutonium-239 fuel rods. Much of the energy produced in this reaction is in the form of heat. A liquid, such as water or liquid sodium, removes heat from the *core*, or central part, of the reactor. So the liquid is called a *coolant*. The heated liquid is used to change water to steam. The steam drives a turbine that generates electricity. The control of fission in a nuclear reactor involves two steps—neutron moderation and neutron absorption.

▶ **Neutron Moderation** For a chain reaction to take place in a nuclear reactor, neutrons must be absorbed by the fuel. Most of the neutrons released by fission move so fast that they would pass right through a nucleus without being absorbed. **Neutron moderation** is a process that slows down neutrons. Water and carbon in the form of graphite are good moderators.

▶ **Neutron Absorption** To keep the chain reaction from going too fast, some of the slowed neutrons must be trapped before they hit fissionable atoms. **Neutron absorption** is the process that decreases the number of slow-moving neutrons. Control rods are used to absorb neutrons. When the control rods extend almost all the way into the reactor core, they absorb many neutrons, and fission takes place slowly. As the rods are pulled out, the control rods absorb fewer neutrons and the fission reaction speeds up.

Control rods allow a reactor to operate safely. If the chain reaction were too fast, heat would be produced faster than the coolant could remove it. The temperature in the core would rise, which could damage the core. In time, the shell could no longer contain the radioactive materials. They would escape into the atmosphere.

Nuclear Reactor A nuclear reactor is used to produce electricity. A coolant absorbs heat produced by the fission reaction. The heat is used to change liquid water to steam. The steam drives a turbine, which drives a generator that produces electricity.

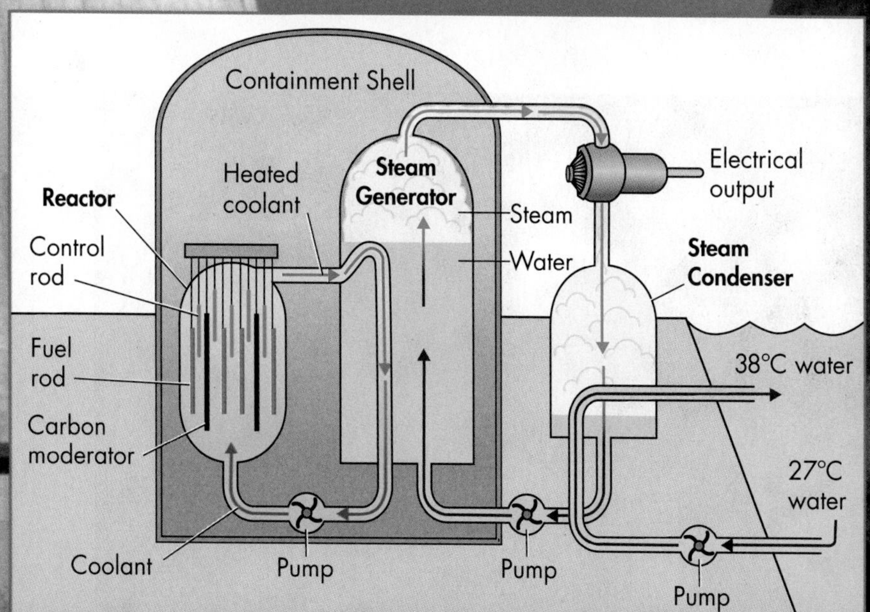

See a nuclear reactor *animated online.*

KINETIC ART

BUILD Understanding

Inference After you read this page, use inference to explain how the storage of nuclear wastes could affect the environment. You should base your inference on information in the text and any prior knowledge you may have. You can think of making an inference as "reading between the lines."

Nuclear Waste Fuel rods from nuclear power plants are one major source of nuclear waste. The fuel rods are made from uranium-235 or plutonium-239. The rods are long and narrow. In most reactors, 300 fuel rods are bundled together to form an assembly. Then, 100 assemblies are arranged to form the reactor core. Fission reduces the amount of fissionable isotope in each fuel rod. At some point, the amount of fuel left cannot keep up the supply of electricity from the power plant. When that happens, the fuel rods must be removed and replaced with new fuel rods.

▶ **Waste Storage** Depleted, or spent, fuel rods are classified as high-level nuclear waste. They contain a mixture of very radioactive isotopes. These include both fuel that was not used up and products made during fission. Some of the products have very short half-lives that are less than a second. Other products have half-lives of hundreds or thousands of years.

All nuclear power plants have holding tanks, or "swimming pools," for spent fuel rods. Water cools the spent rods, and also acts as a shield to reduce the level of radiation. In the pools, like the one shown below, the spent fuel rods are held in storage racks. The rods continue to produce heat for years after they are removed from the core.

▶ **Waste Disposal** At first, plant operators did not expect to store the rods for a long time. The plan was to recover the leftover fuel from the rods and use it to make new fuel rods. The problem with the plan was that it costs less to make new rods from uranium ore than it costs to recycle the old rods. Many large deposits of uranium ore are in the United States.

At some nuclear plants, the storage pool is full. In order to keep these plants open, the used rods must be moved to off-site storage facilities. Finding appropriate storage sites is difficult because dangerous waste may need to be stored for a long time. Plutonium-239, for example, will not decay to safe levels for 240,000 years. Often, people are concerned about having nuclear waste stored or shipped near their communities.

Key Question What happens in a nuclear chain reaction? **In a chain reaction, some of the emitted neutrons react with other fissionable atoms, which emit neutrons that can react with more fissionable atoms.**

Storage of Fuel Rods
A typical storage pool is 12 meters deep. Racks at the bottom of this pool contain spent fuel rods.

Nuclear Fusion

The sun is the source of most energy used on Earth. The energy from the sun is the result of nuclear fusion. **Fusion** takes place when small nuclei combine to make a nucleus of greater mass. In solar fusion, hydrogen nuclei (protons) fuse to make helium nuclei. This equation shows that the reaction also produces two positrons.

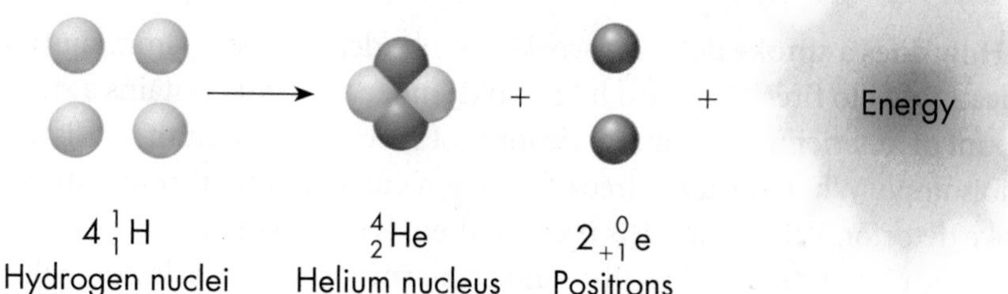

Fusion reactions release much more energy than fission reactions. So using controlled nuclear fusion as an energy source on Earth sounds like a great idea. The potential fuels are inexpensive and readily available. Some scientists are even studying a reaction in which a deuterium (hydrogen-2) nucleus and a tritium (hydrogen-3) nucleus combine to form a helium nucleus.

$$^{2}_{1}H + ^{3}_{1}H \longrightarrow ^{4}_{2}He + ^{1}_{0}n + \text{energy}$$

Fusion occurs only above 40,000,000°C. At this temperature, matter exists as a collection of charged particles. This high-energy state of matter is called plasma. The temperatures needed to start a fusion reaction can be reached by using a fission bomb. But once the reaction is started it cannot be controlled.

Key Question How do fission reactions and fusion reactions differ? **Fusion reactions, in which small nuclei combine, release much more energy than fission reactions, in which large nuclei split apart.**

BUILD Vocabulary

fusion the process of combining nuclei to make a nucleus of greater mass

MULTIPLE MEANINGS

The word *fusion* comes from a Latin word meaning "to melt." For example, the metals copper and zinc can be melted, or fused, to form the alloy brass. The connection between this meaning of *fusion* and nuclear fusion is the idea of combining two or more items to form a single item.

25.3 LessonCheck

Key Concept Check

21. **Relate Cause and Effect** Explain what happens in a nuclear chain reaction.

22. **Compare** How are fusion reactions different from fission reactions?

Vocabulary Check

Choose a highlighted word from the lesson to complete the sentence correctly.

23. A process that slows down neutrons in a nuclear reactor is called ________.

Think Critically

24. **Identify** What are two sources of the radioactive nuclei present in spent fuel rods?

25. **Interpret Diagrams** Review the diagram of the nuclear reactor on page 831. What role does water play in a nuclear reactor?

26. **Evaluate** Suppose it were possible to control a fusion reaction. What are two advantages to using fusion to produce electricity?

CHEMISTRY & YOU

27. The high temperatures needed to support fusion of hydrogen nuclei exist in the sun's core. Late in the sun's life cycle, other fusion reactions will occur. What element would form when two helium nuclei fuse? (Hint: How many protons are in two helium nuclei?)

25.4 Radiation in Your Life

CHEMISTRY & YOU

Q: How does a smoke detector work? Smoke detectors can limit injuries or deaths due to fires. A typical household smoke detector contains a small amount of americium, $^{241}_{95}Am$, in the form of AmO_2. Americium-241 is a radioisotope. When the air is free of smoke, a current flows through the smoke detector. When smoke is present, there is a drop in current. An electronic circuit detects this drop, and an alarm sounds. This lesson will help you understand the role of radiation in smoke detection.

Key Questions

What are three devices used to detect radiation?

What are some practical uses of radioisotopes?

BUILD Vocabulary

ionizing radiation radiation that has enough energy to knock electrons off atoms

SUFFIXES

The suffix *-ize* means "to make." So *ionize* means to make an atom into an ion. If you add *-ing* to *ionize*, you form *ionizing*. This word describes radiation that can cause an atom to ionize.

Detecting Radiation

The radiation emitted by radioisotopes has enough energy to knock some electrons off atoms that it hits. Because electrons have a negative charge, atoms that lose electrons become ions with a positive charge. That is why the radiation emitted by radioisotopes is called **ionizing radiation.**

It is not possible for humans to see, hear, smell, or feel ionizing radiation. So people must rely on detection devices to alert them to the presence of radiation and to measure its level. These devices work because of what happens when radiation strikes atoms or molecules in the detector.

Some devices use photographic film to detect radiation. When the film is developed, the darker areas show where radiation struck the film. A similar process produces X-ray images like the one below. Some devices rely on the current produced when atoms are ionized. Geiger counters, scintillation counters, and film badges are commonly used to detect radiation.

X-Rays Images produced by X-rays allow doctors to see inside the body without having to cut into the body. Color was added to highlight parts of the image.

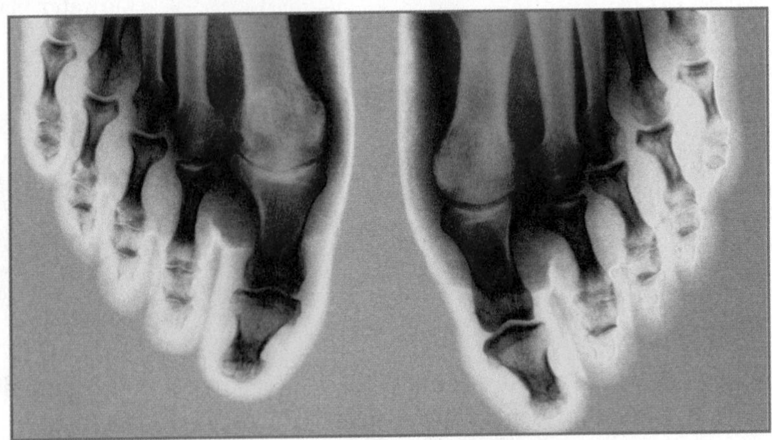

Geiger Counter A Geiger counter uses a gas-filled metal tube to detect radiation. A wire electrode that is connected to a power supply is inside the tube. When ionizing radiation penetrates a thin window at one end of the tube, the gas inside is ionized. The ions and free electrons that form can conduct electricity. Each time a Geiger tube is exposed to radiation, current flows. The bursts of current drive electronic counters or cause clicks that can be heard. Most Geiger counters can detect beta and gamma radiation.

Astronomers use Geiger counters to detect cosmic rays from outer space. Geologists use them to search for radioactive minerals, such as uranium ores. Geiger counters check for leaks in hospitals and other places that use radiation. The photo to the right shows one use for a Geiger counter.

Geiger Counters
This person is using a Geiger counter to check for pockets of radiation in dirt at a spill site.

Scintillation Counter Some counters have a surface coated with a phosphor to detect radiation. When ionizing radiation hits the surface, the phosphor produces bright flashes of light called scintillations. The number of flashes and their energies can be measured. Scintillation counters are more sensitive than Geiger counters. This means that they can detect some radiation that would not be detected by a Geiger counter. Scintillation counters are used to track the path of radioisotopes through the body. They are also used to watch for the movement of radioactive materials across national borders and through airports.

Film Badge The drawing below shows a film badge opened and laid flat. The badge contains layers of photographic film covered with black paper, which blocks visible light. The film is sealed in a plastic or metal holder. To reach the film, radiation may pass through a filter, which absorbs some radiation. Or it may pass through a transparent material that allows radiation to penetrate easily. People who work with or near ionizing radiation must wear a film badge to keep track of their exposures while they are at work.

At certain times, the film is removed and developed. New film is placed in the badge. The strength and type of radiation exposure are found by comparing the darkness of the film in all the exposed areas. Film badges do not protect a person from radiation. They do measure the amount of exposure. To protect themselves, workers must keep a safe distance from the radiation source. They often wear protective clothing.

Key Question What are three devices used to detect radiation? **Geiger counters, scintillation counters, and film badges are commonly used to detect radiation.**

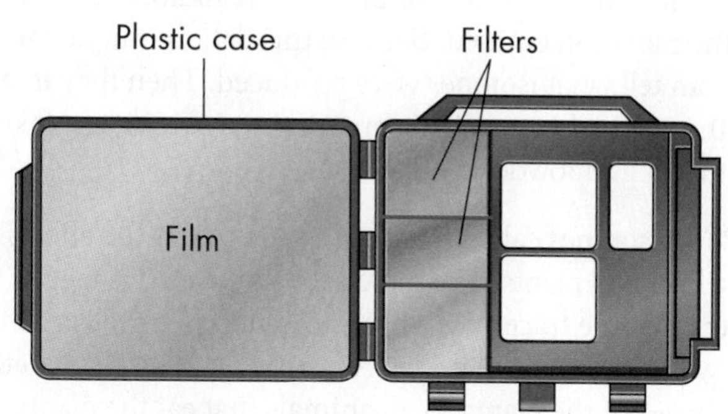

Film Badge In a film badge, radiation passes through one of several filters or through a transparent material before it strikes the film. Different amounts of radiation pass through each area.

Quick Lab

Purpose To demonstrate the relationship between radiation intensity and the distance from the radiation source

Materials

- flashlight
- strips of duct tape
- scissors
- poster board, white (50 cm × 50 cm)
- meter ruler or tape measure
- flat surface, long enough to hold the meter ruler
- graph paper

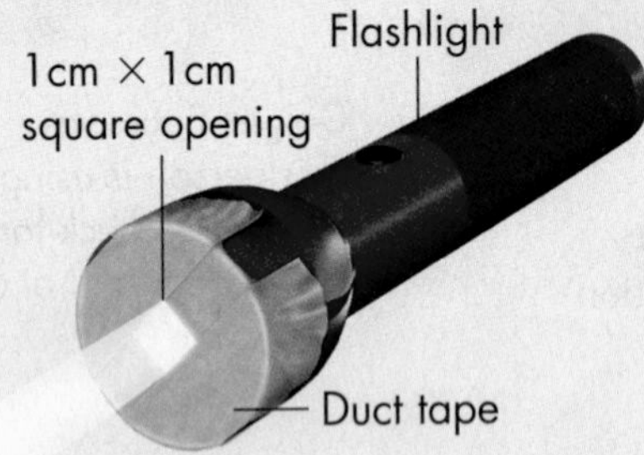

Inverse-Square Relationships

Procedure

1. Estimate and record the distance (A) from the bulb filament to the front surface of the flashlight.

2. Cover the end of the flashlight with strips of duct tape. Leave a square opening that is 1 cm × 1 cm in the center of the tape.

3. Place the flashlight on its side on a flat surface. Turn on the flashlight. Darken the room.

4. Mount a large piece of white poster board in front of the flashlight, perpendicular to the flat surface.

5. Use a short, repeated distance to gradually move the flashlight away from the board. At each position, record the distance (B) from the flashlight to the board and the length (L) of one side of the square image on the board.

6. On a sheet of graph paper, plot L on the y-axis versus $A + B$ on the x-axis. On another sheet, plot L^2 on the y-axis versus $A + B$ on the x-axis.

Analyze and Conclude

1. Make Generalizations As the flashlight is moved away from the board, what happens to the intensity of the light in the square image? Use your graphs to describe the relationship between intensity and distance.

2. Explain When the distance of the flashlight from the board (B) is doubled and tripled, what happens to the area of the square image and the intensity of the light?

Using Radiation

Although radiation can be harmful, it can be used safely, too. Radiation is used in analytical chemistry, in agriculture, and in medicine.

Analyzing Matter Scientists use radiation to identify traces of elements in matter. The process is called *neutron activation analysis.* When neutrons strike a sample of matter, some atoms in the sample become radioactive. A computer analyzes data on the radiation emitted. Because this data is unique for each isotope, scientists can tell what isotopes were produced. Then they infer what elements were in the original matter. This process is used to detect fake art. Crime labs use it to test gunpowder.

Using Tracers Radioisotopes called *tracers* are used to test the effects of pesticides and fertilizers on plants. The material being tested is tagged with a tracer. This means that the tracer becomes part of its chemical structure. Plants are treated with the tagged material. A device that detects radiation is used to locate the tracer in the plants, or in animals that eat the plants. The tracer may also be detected in water or soil.

Diagnosing Medical Problems Radioisotopes can be used to find problems with the thyroid gland. The thyroid uses iodide ions from the blood to make thyroxine. This hormone helps control the rate at which cells release energy from food. A person being tested for a thyroid problem is given a drink with a small amount of the radioisotope iodine-131. After a few hours, a scanner that can detect radiation measures the amount of iodide taken up by the thyroid. The photo at the right shows such a scan. Other radioisotopes are used to detect brain tumors, problems with the liver, and skin cancer.

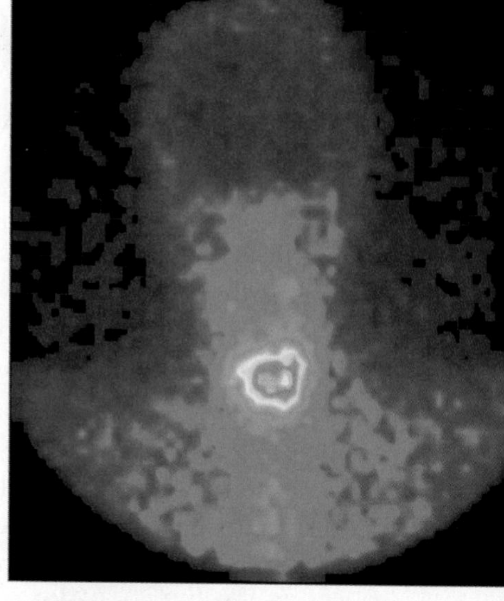

Radioactive Tracer The thyroid gland is located in the throat. This image shows where radioactive iodine-131 was absorbed by the gland. How much was absorbed provides clues to certain disorders.

Treating Diseases Radiation can be used to treat some cancers. Cancer cells are abnormal cells that grow and divide much faster than normal cells. A mass of cancer cells is called a *tumor*. Fast-growing cancer cells are more easily damaged by radiation than are healthy cells. So radiation can be used to kill cancer cells in a tumor. But some healthy cells are also killed. The benefits and risks must be carefully weighed before radiation treatment begins. There are three main kinds of radiation therapy.

▶ **External Beam Therapy** In the most common kind of radiation therapy, a narrow beam of X-rays is aimed at a specific region of the body. The source of the X-rays is usually a linear accelerator.

▶ **Seeding Therapy** Salts of radioisotopes can also be sealed in gold tubes and inserted into tumors. This method of treatment is called *seeding*. The salts emit beta and gamma rays that kill the surrounding cancer cells. Because the radioisotope is in a sealed container, it cannot travel to other parts of the body.

▶ **Drug Therapy** Sometimes prescribed drugs containing radioisotopes of gold, iodine, or phosphorus are used. For example, iodine-131 is used to treat thyroid disease. The dose used for therapy is larger than the dose used to detect the disease. Blood carries the iodine from the digestive system to the thyroid. The iodine that collects in the gland emits beta and gamma radiation.

Key Question What are some practical uses of radioisotopes? **Radioisotopes are used to analyze matter, study plant growth, diagnose medical problems, and treat diseases.**

25.4 LessonCheck

Key Concept Check

28. Compare In each detection device described in the lesson, what is used to detect the radiation?

29. Review What are two ways radioisotopes can be used in medicine?

Think Critically

30. Define Why is the radiation emitted by radioisotopes called *ionizing radiation*?

31. Compare Which radiation detector is most similar to a smoke detector? Explain.

32. Infer Why do airports use scintillation counters and not Geiger counters to search for radioactive materials?

33. Sequence Briefly describe the steps used to detect problems with a thyroid gland.

CHEMISTRY & YOU

34. Radiation emitted in a smoke detector ionizes the nitrogen and oxygen in air. The ions that form cause a current to flow. When smoke particles attach to the ions, the ions lose their charge. What happens next? (Hint: See page 834.)

25 Study Guide

BIGIDEA ELECTRONS AND THE STRUCTURE OF ATOMS

Unstable atomic nuclei decay by emitting alpha or beta particles. Often gamma rays are emitted, too. During fission and fusion, atoms change their chemical identity as the number of protons in their nuclei change. In fission, large nuclei split into two or more smaller nuclei. In fusion, smaller nuclei combine to form larger nuclei at an extremely high temperature and pressure. The ability to detect particles emitted when nuclei decay helps scientists study processes that take place in living organisms. This ability also allows scientists to determine the age of some objects.

25.1 Nuclear Radiation

Unlike chemical reactions, nuclear reactions are not affected by changes in pressure, temperature, or the use of catalysts. Also, the rate of nuclear reactions cannot be slowed down, speeded up, or stopped.

Three types of nuclear radiation are alpha radiation, beta radiation, and gamma radiation.

- radioactivity (818)
- nuclear radiation (818)
- radioisotope (818)
- alpha particle (819)
- beta particle (819)
- gamma ray (820)

25.2 Nuclear Transformations

The neutron-to-proton ratio in a radioisotope determines the type of decay that occurs.

During each half-life, half of the remaining radioactive atoms decay into atoms of a new element.

Transmutation can occur by radioactive decay or when particles bombard the nucleus of an atom.

- nuclear force (822)
- band of stability (822)
- positron (823)
- half-life (824)
- transmutation (828)
- transuranium elements (829)

25.3 Fission and Fusion

In a chain reaction, some of the emitted neutrons react with other fissionable atoms, which emit neutrons that react with more fissionable atoms.

Fusion reactions, in which small nuclei combine, release much more energy than fission reactions, in which large nuclei split apart.

- fission (830)
- neutron moderation (831)
- neutron absorption (831)
- fusion (833)

25.4 Radiation in Your Life

Geiger counters, scintillation counters, and film badges are commonly used to detect radiation.

Radioisotopes are used to analyze the composition of matter, study plant growth, diagnose medical problems, and treat diseases.

- ionizing radiation (834)

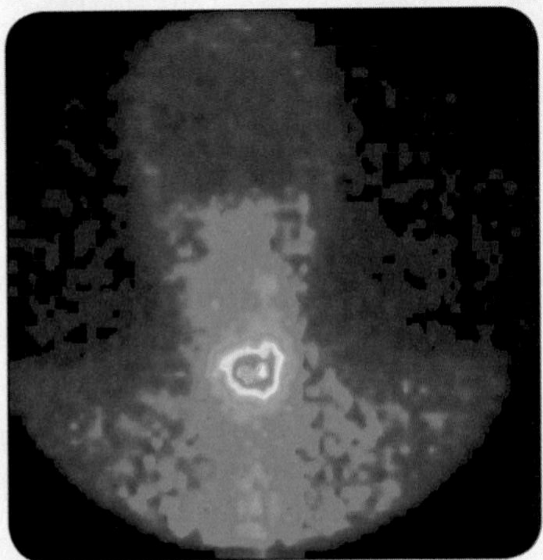

Math Tune-Up: Nuclear Reactions

Problem	❶ Analyze	❷ Calculate	❸ Evaluate
Plutonium-239 decays by emitting an alpha particle. What is the product of this reaction? $^{239}_{94}\text{Pu} \longrightarrow {}^{4}_{2}\text{He} + \text{X}$	Knowns: mass number of Pu = 239 mass number of α = 4 atomic number of Pu = 94 atomic number of α = 2 Unknowns: Mass number of X = ? Atomic number of X = ? Identity of X = ? In an equation for a nuclear reaction, mass numbers and atomic numbers must be balanced.	The mass number of *X* must equal the mass number of Pu minus the mass number of α. The atomic number of *X* must equal the atomic number of Pu minus the atomic number of α. $^{239}_{94}\text{Pu} \longrightarrow {}^{4}_{2}\text{He} + {}^{239-4}_{94-2}\text{X}$ $\longrightarrow {}^{4}_{2}\text{He} + {}^{235}_{92}\text{X}$ The element with atomic number 92 is uranium. $^{239}_{94}\text{Pu} \longrightarrow {}^{4}_{2}\text{He} + {}^{235}_{92}\text{U}$	The mass numbers total 239 on both sides of the equation. The atomic numbers total 94 on both sides of the equation. The isotope uranium-235 is a well-known radioisotope.
Thorium-234 has a half-life of 24.1 days. If a thorium-234 sample has a mass of 6.4×10^{-12} g, how much of the sample is left after 72.3 days?	Knowns: Original mass of Th = 6.4×10^{-12} g Decay time = 72.3 days $t_{\frac{1}{2}}$ = 24.1 days Unknowns: Mass of Th remaining = ? The mass of thorium-234 decreases by half with each half-life. Find the number of half-lives in 72.3 days and multiply the mass of thorium by $\frac{1}{2}$ for each half-life.	Divide the decay time by the half-life of thorium to find the number of half-lives. $\frac{72.3\ \cancel{\text{days}}}{24.1\ \cancel{\text{days}}/\text{half-life}} = 3$ half-lives Multiply the mass of thorium by $\frac{1}{2}$ three times. $6.4 \times 10^{-12}\text{ g} \times \frac{1}{2} \times \frac{1}{2} \times \frac{1}{2} = 8.0 \times 10^{-13}\text{ g}$	After three half-lives, the number of atoms of a radioisotope will decrease to $\frac{1}{8}$ of the original number.
Carbon-14 decays to nitrogen-14 through beta emission. The half-life for this process is 5730 years. In a sample from an ancient piece of pottery, only 25% of the carbon-14 atoms remains. How old is the pottery?	Knowns: $t_{\frac{1}{2}}$ = 5730 yr Ratio of C-14 to N-14 = 25% Unknown: Age of sample = ? The number of C-14 atoms decreases by half every 5730 years. Find the number of half-lives that reduce the number of C-14 atoms to $\frac{1}{4}$ (25%) and multiply by 5730.	Only $\frac{1}{4}$ of the original C-14 atoms remains. So C-14 has decayed for two half-lives. $\frac{1}{4} = \frac{1}{2} \times \frac{1}{2}$ Convert two half-lives to years. 5730 years × 2 = 11,460 years	The pottery sample is 11,460 years old, which is equal to two half-lives or the time required for 75 percent of the carbon-14 atoms to decay.

Hint: The product of $\frac{1}{2} \times \frac{1}{2} \times \frac{1}{2}$ is $\frac{1}{8}$. So you can also divide the original mass by 8.

25 Assessment

★ Solutions appear in Appendix D

Lesson by Lesson

25.1 Nuclear Radiation

35. Explain how radioisotopes are different from other isotopes.

★**36.** An isotope of the element lead (Pb) decays to an isotope of the element bismuth (Bi) by emission of a beta particle. Complete the equation for the reaction by supplying the missing atomic number and mass number.

$$^{210}_{?}\text{Pb} \longrightarrow {}^{?}_{83}\text{Bi} + {}^{0}_{-1}\text{e}$$

37. Write the symbol and charge for each item.

a. alpha particle
b. beta particle
c. gamma ray

★**38.** Alpha radiation is emitted during the decay of the following isotopes. Write balanced nuclear equations to describe each decay process. Name the element produced in each case.

a. uranium-238 ($^{238}_{92}\text{U}$)
b. thorium-230 ($^{230}_{90}\text{Th}$)
c. uranium-235 ($^{235}_{92}\text{U}$)
d. radon-222 ($^{222}_{86}\text{Rn}$)

39. The following radioisotopes are beta emitters. Write balanced nuclear equations to describe each decay process.

a. carbon-14 ($^{14}_{6}\text{C}$)
b. potassium-40 ($^{40}_{19}\text{K}$)

★**40.** How are the mass number and atomic number of a nucleus affected by the loss of the following?

a. beta particle
b. alpha particle
c. gamma ray

25.2 Nuclear Transformations

★**41.** What happens to an atom with a nucleus that falls outside the band of stability?

42. Identify the more stable isotope in each pair.

a. $^{14}_{6}\text{C}$, $^{13}_{6}\text{C}$
b. $^{3}_{1}\text{H}$, $^{1}_{1}\text{H}$
c. $^{15}_{8}\text{O}$, $^{16}_{8}\text{O}$
d. $^{13}_{7}\text{N}$, $^{14}_{7}\text{N}$

43. Define *half-life* in your own words.

44. How are a positron and an electron similar? How are they different?

45. What is the difference between natural and artificial transmutation?

25.3 Fission and Fusion

46. Describe the process of nuclear fission.

47. What do falling dominoes have in common with a nuclear chain reaction?

48. How are the nuclear reactions that take place in the sun different from the nuclear reactions that take place in a nuclear reactor?

49. Fusion reactions produce more energy than fission reactions. Why is fusion not used to produce electricity?

25.4 Radiation in Your Life

50. Why are X-rays and the radiation emitted by radioisotopes called *ionizing radiation*?

51. Why must people rely on devices such as Geiger counters to detect radiation?

52. Explain why people who work with or near ionizing radiation wear a film badge.

Understand Concepts

*53. Write balanced nuclear equations for these transmutations.

a. $^{30}_{15}P$ to $^{30}_{14}Si$
b. $^{13}_{6}C$ to $^{14}_{6}C$
c. $^{131}_{53}I$ to $^{131}_{54}Xe$

54. The graph shows the radioactive decay curve for thorium-234. Use the graph to answer the questions below.

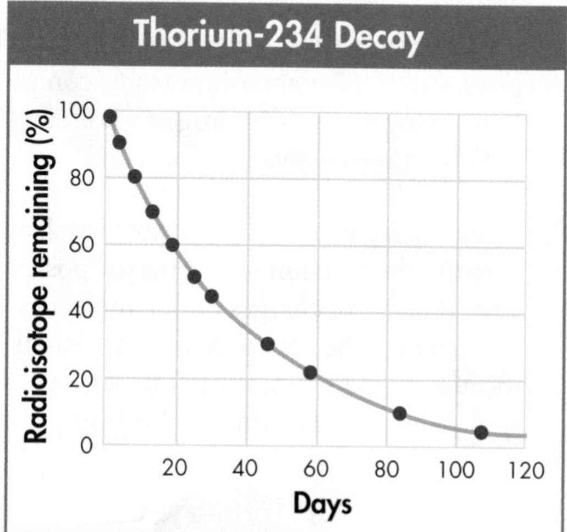

a. What percentage of the isotope remains after 60 days?
b. After 40 days have passed, how many grams of a 250-g sample of thorium-234 would remain?
c. How many days would it take for 44 g of thorium-234 to decay to 4.4 g of thorium-234?
d. What is the half-life of thorium-234?

*55. A sample of matter has 32 million radioactive atoms. How many of these atoms would be left after five half-lives?

*56. A patient is given 20 mg of iodine-131. The half-life of iodine-131 is 8 days. How much of the isotope will remain in the patient's body after 40 days?

57. Why is it important that radioactive isotopes used for the diagnosis or treatment of medical problems have relatively short half-lives?

Think Critically

58. **Interpret Graphs** Look again at the decay curve on page 824. Suppose the variable on the *x*-axis were time instead of number of half-lives. Could the same graph be used to represent all radioisotopes? Why or why not?

*59. **Predict** When neutrons strike magnesium-24 ($^{24}_{12}Mg$), a neutron is captured and photons are ejected. What new isotope is formed?

60. **Relate Cause and Effect** What effect did the discovery of radioactivity have on Dalton's model of the atom?

61. **Apply Concepts** Should a radioisotope with a half-life measured in days be used in a smoke detector? Why or why not?

*62. **Classify** Name the elements represented by the following symbols and indicate which of them would have no stable isotopes.

a. Pt b. Th c. Fr d. Ti
e. Xe f. Cf g. V h. Pd

FOUNDATIONS Wrap-Up

Simulating Radioactivity

1. **Compare** At the beginning of the chapter, you flipped coins and made a graph of your results. Identify the graph in the chapter that is similar to the graph you made.

Concept Check

Now that you've finished studying Chapter 25, answer these questions.

2. How was flipping coins a good analogy for radioactive decay? How was it not a good analogy?
3. Can you use half-life to predict whether a specific atom in a sample will decay during a half-life? Explain.
4. Isotope A has a half-life of 2 days. Isotope B has a half-life of 3 days. Both isotopes are radioactive. The samples decay for 6 days. Which sample will still have 25 percent of its original atoms? How do you know?

Write About Science

63. **Infer** Some nuclear waste is stored in caverns about 600 meters below the desert in New Mexico. The federal government owns the land above the storage site. Explain why you think this site was chosen.

64. **Summarize** Why are spent fuel rods removed from a reactor core? What do they contain? What happens to them after they are removed?

CHEMYSTERY

An Ice-Age Baby

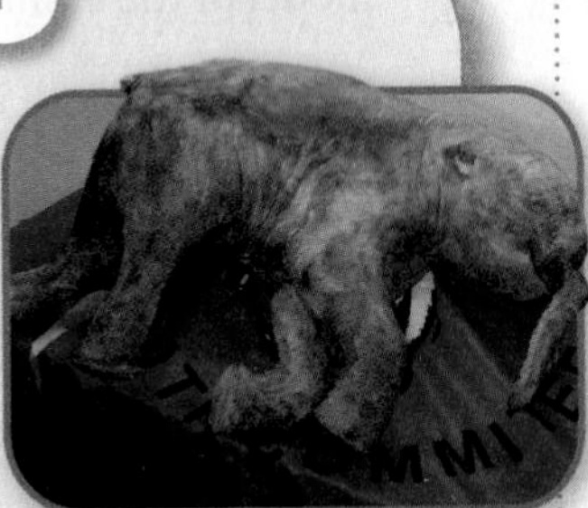

Scientists used carbon-14 dating to estimate the age of the baby mammoth. During Lyuba's short time on Earth, the ratio of carbon-14 to other carbon isotopes in her body was constant. After she died, carbon-14 atoms that decayed were no longer replaced. The ratio of carbon-14 atoms to other carbon atoms changed. Based on the ratio of carbon isotopes in the preserved sample, Lyuba lived and died about 40,000 years ago.

The same method is used to date artifacts left behind by ancient cultures. An artifact is an object made or shaped by humans. Examples of artifacts are tools, weapons, and ornaments.

65. **Calculate** About how many half-lives does 40,000 years represent? The half-life for carbon-14 is 5730 years.

66. **Apply Concepts** Scientists suspect that the site of an ancient culture is about 40,000 years old. They find a wooden bowl, a stone arrowhead, and a bone bead at the site. Which objects can they use to test their hypothesis? Explain.

67. **Connect to the BIGIDEA** Describe what happens to the structure of carbon-14 atoms as this isotope decays.

Cumulative Review

68. Balance the following equations. (See Lesson 12.1 for help.)
    - **a.** $Ca(OH)_2 + HCl \longrightarrow CaCl_2 + H_2O$
    - **b.** $Fe_2O_3 + H_2 \longrightarrow Fe + H_2O$
    - **c.** $NaHCO_3 + H_2SO_4 \longrightarrow Na_2SO_4 + CO_2 + H_2O$
    - **d.** $C_2H_6 + O_2 \longrightarrow CO_2 + H_2O$

*69. A piece of magnesium with a mass of 10.00 g is added to sulfuric acid. How many cubic centimeters of hydrogen gas (at STP) will be produced if the magnesium reacts completely? How many moles of hydrogen gas are in this volume? (See Lesson 12.2 for help.)

70. The drawing below shows a water molecule. Identify the location of any partial positive and partial negative charges on the molecule. Then explain how the partial charges and their locations produce an attraction between water molecules. (See Lesson 15.1 for help.)

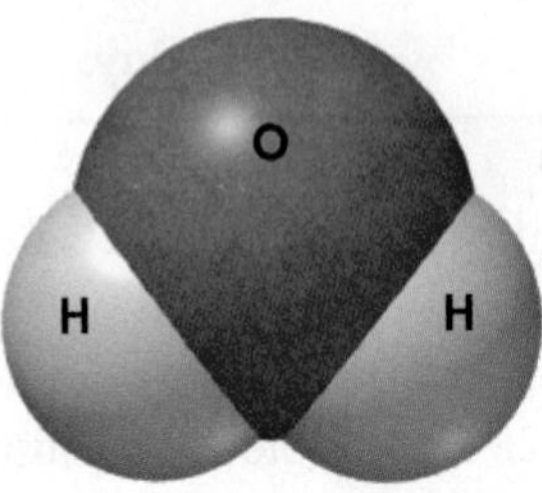

*71. You have a 0.30*M* solution of sodium sulfate. What volume (in mL) must be measured to give 0.0020 mol of sodium sulfate? (See Lesson 16.2 for help.)

72. Match a numbered item with each term. (See Lessons 24.2, 24.3, 24.4, and 24.5 for help.)

a. amino acid	**(1)** carbohydrate
b. fat	**(2)** nucleic acid
c. monosaccharide	**(3)** lipid
d. peptide bond	**(4)** protein
e. sugar	
f. DNA	
g. genetic code	
h. enzyme	
i. triglyceride	

Standardized Test Prep

For help with answering test questions, go to your Chemistry Skills and Math Workbook.

Tips for Success

Anticipate the Answer Use what you know to decide what you think the answer should be. Then see if your answer, or one similar to it, is given as a choice.

Select the choice that best answers each question.

1. If a radioisotope undergoes beta emission,
(A) the atomic number changes.
(B) the number of neutrons remains constant.
(C) the isotope loses a proton.
(D) the mass number changes.

2. The radioisotope radon-222 has a half-life of 3.8 days. How much of an initial 20.0-g sample of radon-222 would remain after 15.2 days?
(A) 5.00 g (C) 1.25 g
(B) 12.5 g (D) 2.50 g

3. Spent fuel rods from nuclear reactors
(A) are no longer radioactive.
(B) contain unused fuel and products of fission.
(C) contain only one isotope of uranium, ^{238}U.
(D) remain radioactive for less than 100 years.

4. What particle is needed to balance this equation?

$$^{27}_{13}Al + ^{4}_{2}He \longrightarrow ? + ^{30}_{15}P$$

For each nuclear equation in Questions 5–8, name the particle that is being emitted or captured.

5. $^{59}_{26}Fe \longrightarrow ^{59}_{27}Co + ^{0}_{-1}e$

6. $^{185}_{79}Au \longrightarrow ^{181}_{77}Ir + ^{4}_{2}He$

7. $^{59}_{27}Co + ^{1}_{0}n \longrightarrow ^{60}_{27}Co$

8. $^{118}_{54}Xe \longrightarrow ^{118}_{53}I + ^{0}_{+1}e$

Use the drawings of atomic nuclei to answer Questions 9 and 10.

9. Write the name and symbol for each isotope.

10. Which isotope is radioactive?

(A)
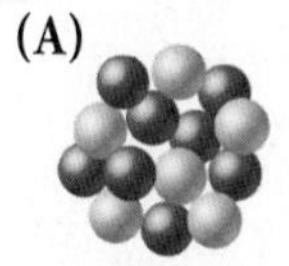
(B)
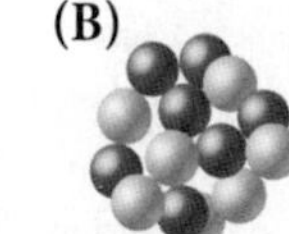
(C)
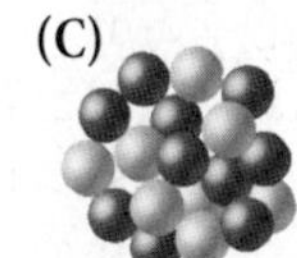

Proton Neutron

Use the graph to answer Questions 11–13.

Estimate the percent of the radioisotope that remains after the given number of half-lives.

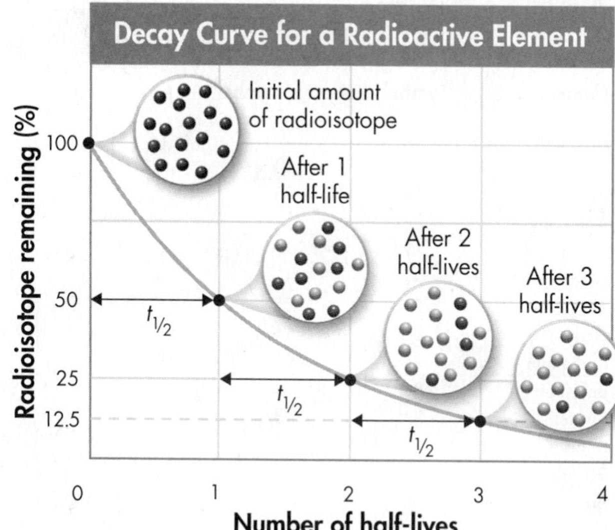

11. $0.5\ t_{1/2}$

12. $1.25\ t_{1/2}$

13. $3.75\ t_{1/2}$

The lettered choices below refer to Questions 14–17. A lettered choice may be used once, more than once, or not at all.

(A) film badge
(B) radioactive tracer
(C) radiation therapy
(D) neutron activation analysis
(E) Geiger counter

Which of the above items or processes is best described by each of the following applications?

14. treating some cancers

15. detecting ionizing radiation

16. monitoring exposure to radiation

17. diagnosing some diseases

If You Have Trouble With...

Question	1	2	3	4	5	6	7	8	9	10	11	12	13	14	15	16	17
See Lesson	25.1	25.2	25.3	25.3	25.1	25.1	25.3	25.2	25.1	25.2	25.2	25.2	25.2	25.4	25.4	25.4	25.4

Appendix A

Reference Tables

Table A.1

Some Properties of the Elements							
Element	**Symbol**	**Atomic number**	**Atomic mass**	**Melting point (°C)**	**Boiling point (°C)**	**Density (g/cm^3) (gases at STP)**	**Oxidation numbers**
Actinium	Ac	89	(227)	1050	3200	10.07	+3
Aluminum	Al	13	26.98154	660.37	2467	2.6989	+3
Americium	Am	95	243	994	2607	13.67	+3, +4, +5, +6
Antimony	Sb	51	121.75	630.74	1587	6.691	−3, +3, +5
Argon	Ar	18	39.948	−189.2	−185.7	0.0017837	
Arsenic	As	33	74.9216	817	613	5.73	−3, +3, +5
Astatine	At	85	(210)	302	337	—	
Barium	Ba	56	137.33	725	1640	3.5	+2
Berkelium	Bk	97	(247)	986	—	14.78	
Beryllium	Be	4	9.01218	1278	2970	1.848	+2
Bismuth	Bi	83	208.9804	271.3	1560	9.747	+3, +5
Bohrium	Bh	107	(264)	—	—	—	
Boron	B	5	10.81	2075	3675	2.34	+3
Bromine	Br	35	79.904	−7.2	58.78	3.12	−1, +1, +5
Cadmium	Cd	48	112.41	320.9	765	8.65	+2
Calcium	Ca	20	40.08	839	1484	1.55	+2
Californium	Cf	98	(251)	900	—	14	
Carbon	C	6	12.011	3550	4827	2.267	−4, +2, +4
Cerium	Ce	58	140.12	799	3426	6.657	+3, +4
Cesium	Cs	55	132.9054	28.40	669.3	1.873	+1
Chlorine	Cl	17	35.453	−100.98	−34.6	0.003214	−1, +1, +5, +7
Chromium	Cr	24	51.996	1907	2672	7.18	+2, +3, +6
Cobalt	Co	27	58.9332	1495	2870	8.9	+2, +3
Copernicium	Cn	112	(277)	—	—	—	
Copper	Cu	29	63.546	1083.4	2567	8.96	+1, +2
Curium	Cm	96	(247)	1340	—	13.51	+3
Darmstadtium	Ds	110	(269)	—	—	—	
Dubnium	Db	105	(262)	—	—	—	
Dysprosium	Dy	66	162.50	1412	2562	8.550	+3
Einsteinium	Es	99	(252)	—	—	—	
Erbium	Er	68	167.26	159	2863	9.066	+3
Europium	Eu	63	151.96	822	1597	5.243	+2, +3
Fermium	Fm	100	(257)	—	—	—	
Fluorine	F	9	18.998403	−219.62	−188.54	0.00181	−1
Francium	Fr	87	(223)	27	677	—	+1
Gadolinium	Gd	64	157.25	1313	3266	7.9004	+3
Gallium	Ga	31	69.72	29.78	2204	5.904	+3
Germanium	Ge	32	72.59	937.4	2830	5.323	+2, +4
Gold	Au	79	196.9665	1064.43	2856	19.3	+1, +3
Hafnium	Hf	72	178.49	2227	4602	13.31	+4
Hassium	Hs	108	(265)	—	—	—	
Helium	He	2	4.00260	−272.2	−268.934	0.001785	
Holmium	Ho	67	164.9304	1474	2695	8.795	+3
Hydrogen	H	1	1.00794	−259.14	−252.87	0.00008988	−1, +1
Indium	In	49	114.82	156.61	2080	7.31	+1, +3
Iodine	I	53	126.9045	113.5	184.35	4.93	−1, +1, +5, +7
Iridium	Ir	77	192.22	2410	4130	22.42	+3, +4
Iron	Fe	26	55.847	1535	2750	7.874	+2, +3
Krypton	Kr	36	83.80	−156.6	−152.30	0.003733	
Lanthanum	La	57	138.9055	921	3457	6.145	+3
Lawrencium	Lr	103	(262)	—	—	—	+3
Lead	Pb	82	207.2	327.502	1740	11.35	+2, +4

Table A.1

Some Properties of the Elements (cont.)

Element	Symbol	Atomic number	Atomic mass	Melting point (°C)	Boiling point (°C)	Density (g/cm³) (gases at STP)	Oxidation numbers
Lithium	Li	3	6.941	180.54	1342	0.534	+1
Lutetium	Lu	71	174.967	1663	3395	9.840	+3
Magnesium	Mg	12	24.305	648.8	1107	1.738	+2
Manganese	Mn	25	54.9380	1244	1962	7.32	+2, +3, +4, +7
Meitnerium	Mt	109	(268)	—	—	—	
Mendelevium	Md	101	257	—	—	—	+2, +3
Mercury	Hg	80	200.59	−38.842	356.58	13.55	+1, +2
Molybdenum	Mo	42	95.94	2617	4612	10.22	+6
Neodymium	Nd	60	144.24	1021	3068	6.90	+3
Neon	Ne	10	20.179	−248.67	−246.048	0.0008999	
Neptunium	Np	93	(237)	640	3902	20.25	+3, +4, +5, +6
Nickel	Ni	28	58.69	1453	2732	8.902	+2, +3
Niobium	Nb	41	92.9064	2468	4742	8.57	+3, +5
Nitrogen	N	7	14.0067	−209.86	−195.8	0.0012506	-3, +3, +5
Nobelium	No	102	(259)	—	—	—	+2, +3
Osmium	Os	76	190.2	3045	5027	22.57	+3, +4
Oxygen	O	8	15.9994	−218.4	−182.962	0.001429	-2
Palladium	Pd	46	106.42	1554	2970	12.02	+2, +4
Phosphorus	P	15	30.97376	44.1	280	1.82	-3, +3, +5
Platinum	Pt	78	195.08	1772	3627	21.45	+2, +4
Plutonium	Pu	94	(244)	641	3232	19.84	+3, +4, +5, +6
Polonium	Po	84	(209)	254	962	9.32	+2, +4
Potassium	K	19	39.0982	63.25	760	0.862	+1
Praseodymium	Pr	59	140.9077	931	3512	6.64	+3
Promethium	Pm	61	(145)	1168	2460	7.22	+3
Protactinium	Pa	91	231.0359	1560	4027	15.37	+4, +5
Radium	Ra	88	(226)	700	1140	5.5	+2
Radon	Rn	86	(222)	−71	−61.8	0.00973	
Rhenium	Re	75	186.207	3180	5627	21.02	+4, +6, +7
Rhodium	Rh	45	102.9055	1966	3727	12.41	+3
Roentgenium	Rg	111	(272)	—	—	—	
Rubidium	Rb	37	85.4678	38.89	686	1.532	+1
Ruthenium	Ru	44	101.07	2310	3900	12.41	+3
Rutherfordium	Rf	104	(261)	—	—	—	
Samarium	Sm	62	150.36	1077	1791	7.520	+2, +3
Scandium	Sc	21	44.9559	1541	2831	2.989	+3
Seaborgium	Sg	106	(263)	—	—	—	
Selenium	Se	34	78.96	217	684.9	4.79	-2, +4, +6
Silicon	Si	14	28.0855	1410	2355	2.33	-4, +2, +4
Silver	Ag	47	107.8682	961.93	2212	10.50	+1
Sodium	Na	11	22.98977	97.81	882.9	0.971	+1
Strontium	Sr	38	87.62	769	1381	2.63	+2
Sulfur	S	16	32.06	112.8	444.7	2.07	-2, +4, +6
Tantalum	Ta	73	180.9479	2996	5425	16.654	+5
Technetium	Tc	43	(98)	2172	4877	11.50	+4, +6, +7
Tellurium	Te	52	127.60	449.5	989.8	6.24	-2, +4, +6
Terbium	Tb	65	158.9254	1356	3123	8.229	+3
Thallium	Tl	81	204.383	303.5	1457	11.85	+1, +3
Thorium	Th	90	232.0381	1750	4790	11.72	+4
Thulium	Tm	69	168.9342	1545	1947	9.321	+3
Tin	Sn	50	118.69	231.968	2270	7.31	+2, +4
Titanium	Ti	22	47.88	1660	3287	4.54	+2, +3, +4
Tungsten	W	74	183.85	3410	5660	19.3	+6
Uranium	U	92	238.0289	1132.3	3818	18.95	+3, +4, +5, +6
Vanadium	V	23	50.9415	1890	3380	6.11	+2, +3, +4, +5
Xenon	Xe	54	131.29	−111.9	−107.1	0.005887	
Ytterbium	Yb	70	173.04	819	1194	6.965	+2, +3
Yttrium	Y	39	88.9059	1522	3338	4.469	+3
Zinc	Zn	30	65.38	419.58	907	7.133	+2
Zirconium	Zr	40	91.22	1852	4377	6.506	+4

Table A.2

Electron Configuration of the Elements

Element		Sublevels																		
		1s	2s	2p	3s	3p	3d	4s	4p	4d	4f	5s	5p	5d	5f	6s	6p	6d	7s	7p
1	Hydrogen	1																		
2	Helium	2																		
3	Lithium	2	1																	
4	Beryllium	2	2																	
5	Boron	2	2	1																
6	Carbon	2	2	2																
7	Nitrogen	2	2	3																
8	Oxygen	2	2	4																
9	Fluorine	2	2	5																
10	Neon	2	2	6																
11	Sodium	2	2	6	1															
12	Magnesium	2	2	6	2															
13	Aluminum	2	2	6	2	1														
14	Silicon	2	2	6	2	2														
15	Phosphorus	2	2	6	2	3														
16	Sulfur	2	2	6	2	4														
17	Chlorine	2	2	6	2	5														
18	Argon	2	2	6	2	6														
19	Potassium	2	2	6	2	6		1												
20	Calcium	2	2	6	2	6		2												
21	Scandium	2	2	6	2	6	1	2												
22	Titanium	2	2	6	2	6	2	2												
23	Vanadium	2	2	6	2	6	3	2												
24	Chromium	2	2	6	2	6	5	1												
25	Manganese	2	2	6	2	6	5	2												
26	Iron	2	2	6	2	6	6	2												
27	Cobalt	2	2	6	2	6	7	2												
28	Nickel	2	2	6	2	6	8	2												
29	Copper	2	2	6	2	6	10	1												
30	Zinc	2	2	6	2	6	10	2												
31	Gallium	2	2	6	2	6	10	2	1											
32	Germanium	2	2	6	2	6	10	2	2											
33	Arsenic	2	2	6	2	6	10	2	3											
34	Selenium	2	2	6	2	6	10	2	4											
35	Bromine	2	2	6	2	6	10	2	5											
36	Krypton	2	2	6	2	6	10	2	6											
37	Rubidium	2	2	6	2	6	10	2	6			1								
38	Strontium	2	2	6	2	6	10	2	6			2								
39	Yttrium	2	2	6	2	6	10	2	6	1		2								
40	Zirconium	2	2	6	2	6	10	2	6	2		2								
41	Niobium	2	2	6	2	6	10	2	6	4		1								
42	Molybdenum	2	2	6	2	6	10	2	6	5		1								
43	Technetium	2	2	6	2	6	10	2	6	6		1								
44	Ruthenium	2	2	6	2	6	10	2	6	7		1								
45	Rhodium	2	2	6	2	6	10	2	6	8		1								
46	Palladium	2	2	6	2	6	10	2	6	10										
47	Silver	2	2	6	2	6	10	2	6	10		1								
48	Cadmium	2	2	6	2	6	10	2	6	10		2								
49	Indium	2	2	6	2	6	10	2	6	10		2	1							
50	Tin	2	2	6	2	6	10	2	6	10		2	2							
51	Antimony	2	2	6	2	6	10	2	6	10		2	3							
52	Tellurium	2	2	6	2	6	10	2	6	10		2	4							
53	Iodine	2	2	6	2	6	10	2	6	10		2	5							
54	Xenon	2	2	6	2	6	10	2	6	10		2	6							
55	Cesium	2	2	6	2	6	10	2	6	10		2	6			1				
56	Barium	2	2	6	2	6	10	2	6	10		2	6			2				

Table A.2

Electron Configuration of the Elements (cont.)

Element		Sublevels																		
		1s	2s	2p	3s	3p	3d	4s	4p	4d	4f	5s	5p	5d	5f	6s	6p	6d	7s	7p
57	Lanthanum	2	2	6	2	6	10	2	6	10		2	6	1		2				
58	Cerium	2	2	6	2	6	10	2	6	10	2	2	6			2				
59	Praseodymium	2	2	6	2	6	10	2	6	10	3	2	6			2				
60	Neodymium	2	2	6	2	6	10	2	6	10	4	2	6			2				
61	Promethium	2	2	6	2	6	10	2	6	10	5	2	6			2				
62	Samarium	2	2	6	2	6	10	2	6	10	6	2	6			2				
63	Europium	2	2	6	2	6	10	2	6	10	7	2	6			2				
64	Gadolinium	2	2	6	2	6	10	2	6	10	7	2	6	1		2				
65	Terbium	2	2	6	2	6	10	2	6	10	9	2	6			2				
66	Dysprosium	2	2	6	2	6	10	2	6	10	10	2	6			2				
67	Holmium	2	2	6	2	6	10	2	6	10	11	2	6			2				
68	Erbium	2	2	6	2	6	10	2	6	10	12	2	6			2				
69	Thulium	2	2	6	2	6	10	2	6	10	13	2	6			2				
70	Ytterbium	2	2	6	2	6	10	2	6	10	14	2	6			2				
71	Lutetium	2	2	6	2	6	10	2	6	10	14	2	6	1		2				
72	Hafnium	2	2	6	2	6	10	2	6	10	14	2	6	2		2				
73	Tantalum	2	2	6	2	6	10	2	6	10	14	2	6	3		2				
74	Tungsten	2	2	6	2	6	10	2	6	10	14	2	6	4		2				
75	Rhenium	2	2	6	2	6	10	2	6	10	14	2	6	5		2				
76	Osmium	2	2	6	2	6	10	2	6	10	14	2	6	6		2				
77	Iridium	2	2	6	2	6	10	2	6	10	14	2	6	7		2				
78	Platinum	2	2	6	2	6	10	2	6	10	14	2	6	9		1				
79	Gold	2	2	6	2	6	10	2	6	10	14	2	6	10		1				
80	Mercury	2	2	6	2	6	10	2	6	10	14	2	6	10		2				
81	Thallium	2	2	6	2	6	10	2	6	10	14	2	6	10		2	1			
82	Lead	2	2	6	2	6	10	2	6	10	14	2	6	10		2	2			
83	Bismuth	2	2	6	2	6	10	2	6	10	14	2	6	10		2	3			
84	Polonium	2	2	6	2	6	10	2	6	10	14	2	6	10		2	4			
85	Astatine	2	2	6	2	6	10	2	6	10	14	2	6	10		2	5			
86	Radon	2	2	6	2	6	10	2	6	10	14	2	6	10		2	6			
87	Francium	2	2	6	2	6	10	2	6	10	14	2	6	10		2	6		1	
88	Radium	2	2	6	2	6	10	2	6	10	14	2	6	10		2	6		2	
89	Actinium	2	2	6	2	6	10	2	6	10	14	2	6	10		2	6	1	2	
90	Thorium	2	2	6	2	6	10	2	6	10	14	2	6	10		2	6	2	2	
91	Protactinium	2	2	6	2	6	10	2	6	10	14	2	6	10	2	2	6	1	2	
92	Uranium	2	2	6	2	6	10	2	6	10	14	2	6	10	3	2	6	1	2	
93	Neptunium	2	2	6	2	6	10	2	6	10	14	2	6	10	4	2	6	1	2	
94	Plutonium	2	2	6	2	6	10	2	6	10	14	2	6	10	6	2	6		2	
95	Americium	2	2	6	2	6	10	2	6	10	14	2	6	10	7	2	6		2	
96	Curium	2	2	6	2	6	10	2	6	10	14	2	6	10	7	2	6	1	2	
97	Berkelium	2	2	6	2	6	10	2	6	10	14	2	6	10	9	2	6		2	
98	Californium	2	2	6	2	6	10	2	6	10	14	2	6	10	10	2	6		2	
99	Einsteinium	2	2	6	2	6	10	2	6	10	14	2	6	10	11	2	6		2	
100	Fermium	2	2	6	2	6	10	2	6	10	14	2	6	10	12	2	6		2	
101	Mendelevium	2	2	6	2	6	10	2	6	10	14	2	6	10	13	2	6		2	
102	Nobelium	2	2	6	2	6	10	2	6	10	14	2	6	10	14	2	6		2	
103	Lawrencium	2	2	6	2	6	10	2	6	10	14	2	6	10	14	2	6	1	2	
104	Rutherfordium	2	2	6	2	6	10	2	6	10	14	2	6	10	14	2	6	2	2	
105	Dubnium	2	2	6	2	6	10	2	6	10	14	2	6	10	14	2	6	3	2	
106	Seaborgium	2	2	6	2	6	10	2	6	10	14	2	6	10	14	2	6	4	2	
107	Bohrium	2	2	6	2	6	10	2	6	10	14	2	6	10	14	2	6	5	2	
108	Hassium	2	2	6	2	6	10	2	6	10	14	2	6	10	14	2	6	6	2	
109	Meitnerium	2	2	6	2	6	10	2	6	10	14	2	6	10	14	2	6	7	2	
110	Darmstadium	2	2	6	2	6	10	2	6	10	14	2	6	10	14	2	6	9	1	
111	Roentgenium	2	2	6	2	6	10	2	6	10	14	2	6	10	14	2	6	10	1	
112	Copernicium	2	2	6	2	6	10	2	6	10	14	2	6	10	14	2	6	10	2	

Table A.3

Physical Constants

Atomic mass unit	1 amu = 1.6605×10^{-24} g
Avogadro's number	$N = 6.0221 \times 10^{23}$ particles/mol
Gas constant	$R = 8.31$ L·kPa/K·mol
Ideal gas molar volume	$V_m = 22.414$ L/mol
Masses of subatomic particles	
Electron (e^-)	$m_e = 0.0005486$ amu $= 9.1096 \times 10^{-28}$ g
Proton (p^+)	$m_p = 1.007277$ amu $= 1.67261 \times 10^{-24}$ g
Neutron (n^0)	$m_n = 1.008665$ amu $= 1.67492 \times 10^{-24}$ g
Speed of light (in vacuum)	$c = 2.997925 \times 10^8$ m/s

Table A.4

SI Units and Equivalents

Quantity	SI unit	Common equivalents
Length	meter (m)	1 meter = 1.0936 yards 1 centimeter = 0.39370 inch 1 inch = 2.54 centimeters 1 mile = 5280 feet = 1.6093 kilometers
Volume	cubic meter (m^3)	1 liter = 10^{-3} m^3 = 1.0567 quarts 1 gallon = 4 quarts = 8 pints = 3.7854 liters 1 quart = 32 fluid ounces = 0.94635 liter
Temperature	kelvin (K)	1 kelvin = 1 degree Celsius °C = $\frac{5}{9}$(F − 32) K = °C + 273.15
Mass	kilogram (kg)	1 kilogram = 1000 grams = mass weighing 2.2046 pounds 1 amu = 1.66057×10^{-27} kilograms
Time	second (s)	1 hour = 60 minutes 1 hour = 3600 seconds
Energy	joule (J)	1 joule = 1 kg·m^2/s^2 (exact) 1 joule = 0.23901 calorie 1 calorie = 4.184 joules
Pressure	pascal (Pa)	1 atmosphere = 101.3 kilopascals = 760 mm Hg (torr) = 14.70 pounds per square inch

Table A.5

Other Symbols and Abbreviations

α	alpha rays	ΔH_f	heat of formation	*m*	molality
β	beta rays	h	hour	mL	milliliter (*volume*)
γ	gamma rays	*h*	Planck's constant	mm	millimeter (*length*)
Δ	change in	Hz	hertz (*frequency*)	mol	mole (*amount*)
$\delta+$, $\delta-$	partial ionic charge	J	joule (*energy*)	mp	melting point
λ	wavelength	K	kelvin (*temperature*)	*N*	normality
π	pi bond	K_a	acid dissociation constant	n^0	neutron
σ	sigma bond	K_b	base dissociation constant	*n*	number of moles
ν	frequency	K_b	molal boiling point elevation constant	*n*	principal quantum number
amu	atomic mass unit			*P*	pressure
(*aq*)	aqueous solution	K_{eq}	equilibrium constant	p^+	proton
atm	atmosphere (*pressure*)	K_f	molal freezing point depression constant	Pa	pascal (*pressure*)
bp	boiling point			*R*	ideal gas constant
°C	degree Celsius (*temperature*)	K_w	ion product constant for water	*S*	entropy
c	speed of light in a vacuum			s	second
cm	centimeter (*length*)	K_{sp}	solubility product constant	(*s*)	solid
E	energy	kcal	kilocalorie (*energy*)	SI	International System of Units
e^-	electron	kg	kilogram (*mass*)		
fp	freezing point	kPa	kilopascal (*pressure*)	STP	standard temperature and pressure
G	Gibbs free energy	L	liter (*volume*)		
g	gram (*mass*)	(*l*)	liquid	*T*	temperature
(*g*)	gas	*M*	molarity	$t_{\frac{1}{2}}$	half-life
gfm	gram formula mass	m	meter (*length*)	*V*	volume
H	enthalpy	*m*	mass	v	velocity

Table A.6

Common Polyatomic Ions

Charge	Name	Formula	Charge	Name	Formula
1–	Chlorate	ClO_3^-	2–	Carbonate	CO_3^{2-}
	Chlorite	ClO_2^-		Chromate	CrO_4^{2-}
	Cyanide	CN^-		Dichromate	$Cr_2O_7^{2-}$
	Dihydrogen phosphate	$H_2PO_4^-$		Oxalate	$C_2O_4^{2-}$
	Ethanoate	CH_3COO^-		Peroxide	O_2^{2-}
	Hydroxide	OH^-		Silicate	SiO_3^{2-}
	Hydrogen carbonate	HCO_3^-		Sulfate	SO_4^{2-}
	Hydrogen sulfate	HSO_4^-		Sulfite	SO_3^{2-}
	Hydrogen sulfite	HSO_3^-		Thiosulfate	$S_2O_3^{2-}$
	Hypochlorite	ClO^-			
	Nitrate	NO_3^-	3–	Phosphate	PO_4^{3-}
	Nitrite	NO_2^-		Phosphite	PO_3^{3-}
	Perchlorate	ClO_4^-			
	Permanganate	MnO_4^-	1+	Ammonium	NH_4^+
	Thiocyanate	SCN^-			

Table A.7

Solubilities of Compounds at 25°C and 101.3 kPa

	ethanoate	bromide	carbonate	chlorate	chloride	hydroxide	iodide	nitrate	oxide	perchlorate	phosphate	sulfate	sulfide
aluminum	S	S	X	S	S	I	S	S	I	S	I	S	d
ammonium	S	S	S	S	S	X	S	S	X	S	S	S	S
barium	S	S	I	S	S	S	S	S	sS	S	I	I	d
calcium	S	S	I	S	S	S	S	S	sS	S	I	sS	I
copper(II)	S	S	X	S	S	I	S	S	I	S	I	S	I
iron(II)	S	S	I	S	S	I	S	S	I	S	I	S	I
iron(III)	S	S	X	S	S	I	S	S	I	S	I	sS	d
lithium	S	S	sS	S	S	S	S	S	S	S	sS	S	S
magnesium	S	S	I	S	S	I	S	S	I	S	I	S	d
potassium	S	S	S	S	S	S	S	S	S	S	S	S	S
silver	sS	I	I	S	I	X	I	S	I	S	I	sS	I
sodium	S	S	S	S	S	S	S	S	S	S	S	S	S
strontium	S	S	I	S	S	S	S	S	S	S	I	I	I
zinc	S	S	I	S	S	I	S	S	I	S	I	S	I

Key:
S = soluble
sS = slightly soluble
I = insoluble
d = decomposes in water
X = no such compound

Appendix B Safety in the Chemistry Lab

The experiments in this book have been carefully designed to minimize the risk of injury. However, safety is also your responsibility. The following rules are essential for keeping you safe in the laboratory. The rules address pre-lab preparation, proper laboratory practices, and post-lab procedures.

Pre-Lab Preparation

1. Read the entire procedure before you begin. Listen to all of your teacher's instructions. When in doubt about a procedure, ask your teacher.

2. Do only the assigned experiments. Do any experiment only when your teacher is present and has given you permission to work.

3. Know the location and operation of the following safety equipment: fire extinguisher, fire blanket, emergency shower, and eye wash station.

4. Know the location of emergency exits and escape routes. To make it easy to exit quickly, do not block walkways with furniture. Keep your work area orderly and free of personal belongings such as coats and backpacks.

5. Protect your clothing and hair from chemicals and sources of heat. Tie back long hair and roll up loose sleeves when working in the laboratory. Avoid wearing bulky or loose-fitting clothing. Remove dangling jewelry. Wear closed-toe shoes at all times in the laboratory.

Proper Laboratory Practices

6. Even with well-designed and tested laboratory procedures, an accident may occur while you are working in the lab. Report any accident, no matter how minor, to your teacher.

7. Wear chemical splash goggles at all times when working in the laboratory. These goggles are designed to protect your eyes from injury. While working in the lab, do not rub your eyes, because chemicals are easily transferred from your hands to your eyes.

⚠ If, despite these precautions, a chemical gets in your eye, remove any contact lenses and immediately wash your eye with a continuous stream of lukewarm water for at least 15 minutes.

8. To reduce danger, waste, and cleanup, always use the minimal amounts of chemicals specified for an experiment.

9. Never taste any chemical used in the laboratory, including food products that are the subject of an investigation. Treat all items as though they are contaminated with unknown chemicals that may be toxic. Keep all food and drink that is not part of an experiment out of the laboratory. Do not eat, drink, or chew gum in the laboratory.

⚠ If you accidentally ingest a substance, notify your teacher immediately.

10. Don't use chipped or cracked glassware. Don't handle broken glass. If glassware breaks, tell your teacher and nearby classmates. Discard broken glass as instructed by your teacher.

⚠ If, despite these precautions, you receive a minor cut, allow it to bleed for a short time. Wash the injured area under cold, running water and notify your teacher. More serious cuts or puncture wounds require immediate medical attention.

11. Do not handle hot glassware or equipment. You can prevent burns by being aware that hot and cold equipment can look exactly the same.

⚠ If you are burned, immediately run cold water over the burned area for several minutes until the pain is reduced. Cooling helps the burn heal. Ask a classmate to notify your teacher.

12. Recognize that the danger of an electrical shock is greater in the presence of water. Keep electrical appliances away from sinks and faucets to minimize the risk of electrical shock. Be careful not to spill water or other liquids in the vicinity of an electrical appliance.

⚠ If, despite these precautions, you spill water near an electrical appliance, stand back, notify your teacher, and warn other students in the area.

13. Report any chemical spills immediately to your teacher. Follow your teacher's instructions for cleaning up spills. Warn other students about the identity and location of spilled chemicals.

⚠ If, despite these precautions, a corrosive chemical gets on your skin or clothing, notify your teacher. Then wash the affected area with cold, running water for several minutes.

Post-Lab Procedures

14. Dispose of chemicals in a way that protects you, your classmates, and the environment. Always follow your teacher's directions for cleanup and disposal. Clean your small-scale reaction surface by draining the contents onto a paper towel. Then wipe the surface with a damp paper towel and dry the surface completely. Dispose of the paper towels in the waste bin.

15. Wash your hands thoroughly with soap and water before leaving the laboratory.

3 Flammability
1 Health
2 Reactivity
Specific Hazards

0 Low
1 Slight
2 Moderate
3 High
4 Extreme

A Materials Safety Data Sheet (MSDS) for a chemical describes any safety issues. A diagram summarizes risks related to flammability, health, and reactivity. A number scale indicates the level of risk.

Take appropriate precautions when any of the following safety symbols appears in an experiment.

Safety Symbols

Eye Safety Wear safety goggles.

Clothing Protection Wear a lab coat or apron when using corrosive chemicals or chemicals that can stain clothing.

Skin Protection Wear plastic gloves when using chemicals that can irritate or stain your skin.

Broken Glass Do not use chipped or cracked glassware. Do not heat the bottom of a test tube.

Open Flame Tie back hair and loose clothing. Never reach across a lit burner.

Flammable Substance Do not have a flame near flammable materials.

Corrosive Substance Wear safety goggles, an apron, and gloves when working with corrosive chemicals.

Poison Don't chew gum, drink, or eat in the laboratory. Never taste a chemical in the laboratory.

Fume Avoid inhaling substances that can irritate your respiratory system.

Thermal Burn Do not touch hot glassware or equipment.

Electrical Equipment Keep electrical equipment away from water or other liquids.

Sharp Object To avoid a puncture wound, use scissors or other sharp objects only as intended.

Disposal Dispose of chemicals only as directed.

Hand Washing Wash your hands thoroughly with soap and water.

Appendix C Problem Bank

Chapter 2

1. Are intensive or extensive properties most helpful in identifying a substance? Explain your choice.

2. Classify the following mixtures as homogeneous or heterogeneous.

a. a toaster

b. a calculator

c. the air on a clear day

d. a copper coin

3. Identify each of the following as a mixture or a substance.

a. tomato juice

b. a rusty, iron fence post

c. a drop of mercury

d. a milkshake

4. Classify each of the following as a physical change or a chemical change.

a. salad dressing separates into layers after standing

b. spilled acid burns a hole in cotton jeans

c. alcohol freezes

d. ice sublimes

5. Classify the following properties of an aluminum bar as either physical or chemical.

a. burns in pure oxygen

b. melts at 660°C

c. bends easily

d. is nonmagnetic

Chapter 3

6. How many significant figures are in each measurement?

a. 786.32 mg

b. 0.0004 s

c. 5.060 kg

d. 7006.0 g

e. 0.0500 s

f. 66.066 mg

g. 4000 m

h. 40.0×10^3 m

7. Write each of the measurements in Problem 6 in scientific notation.

8. What is the total mass of three gold bars that weigh 5543 mg, 23.45 mg, and 697.4 mg?

9. The normal daily high temperature on the planet Zork is −85°C. Express this temperature in kelvins.

10. Methane, a gas that contributes to global warming, has a density of 0.714 g/L. What is the mass, in grams, of 25.0 L of methane?

11. The density of zinc is 9.394 g/cm^3 at 20°C. What is the volume (in cubic centimeters) of a sphere of zinc metal that has a mass of 15.6 g?

12. Calculate the mass in kilograms of 964 mL of the element mercury. The density of mercury is 13.6 g/mL.

13. Make the following conversions:

a. 55 mg to grams

b. 5.76 dL to liters

c. 0.96 m to micrometers

d. 5.26 ns to seconds

e. 87 kg to milligrams

f. 846 mmol to centimoles

g. 3.4 nm to picometers

h. 6.66×10^3 kg to megagrams

i. 2.34×10^{-5} mL to microliters

14. When you donate a unit of blood to the Red Cross, you "give" about 0.55 L of blood. How many cubic centimeters (cm^3) of blood is this?

15. The recommended daily value (DV) of vitamin B_6 for adults is 0.2 cg. How many micrograms of vitamin B_6 should be consumed each day?

16. A person develops jaundice (characterized by yellowing of the skin) when the concentration of bilirubin in his or her blood is 18 mg bilirubin per liter of blood. Assuming a total blood volume of 5.2 L, what is the number of grams of bilirubin in the person's blood?

17. Mites are small eight-legged "bugs" in the same family as spiders. A particularly small mite has a mass of 0.0043 dg. What is the mass of this mite expressed in micrograms?

18. A runner covers a 3.00-mile course in 35.0 minutes. What is her average speed in kilometers/hour?

19. You are going to carry out a chemical reaction in which you need 16 g of oxygen for every 7.0 g of nitrogen that will be used. If you have 0.554 kg of oxygen, how many milligrams of nitrogen do you need?

20. If your heart beats at an average rate of 72 times per minute, how many times will your heart beat each year?

21. Four empty beakers weigh a total of 1.84 kg. Each beaker when full holds 0.75 kg of water. How much do two full beakers of water weigh?

22. How many days would it take you to count a million pennies if you could count one penny each second? Express the answer to 3 significant figures.

23. A soap bubble film is 8.0×10^2 nm thick. Express this thickness in the following units:

a. centimeters **c.** decimeters
b. micrometers **d.** millimeters

24. The pitcher's mound on a regulation baseball field is 60 feet 6 inches from home plate. How many seconds does it take a 96 mph fastball to reach home plate? (5280 ft = 1 mile)

25. Gemstones such as diamonds are measured in carats, where 1 carat = 2.00 dg. How many kilograms of diamonds were produced if 12.5 million carats of diamonds were mined in a recent year?

26. How many meters does a car moving at 95 km/hour travel in 1.0 second?

27. A milliliter of water is equal to 20 drops of water. If water is dripping from a faucet at the rate of 7 drops per minute, how many days will it take to completely fill a 2.00-L soda bottle?

28. A prescription for a certain drug calls for a dose of 0.200 mg/kg of body weight, four times a day. The drug is packaged in capsules of 5 mg. How many capsules per dose should be given to a patient who weighs 75 kg?

29. A certain low-tar cigarette contains 11.0 mg of tar per cigarette.

a. If all the tar gets into the lungs, how many packs of cigarettes (20 cigarettes per pack) would have to be smoked to produce 0.500 lb of tar? (454 g = 1 lb)

b. If a person smoked two packs per day, how many years would it take to accumulate 0.500 lb of tar?

30. A chemist needs 25.0 mL of a liquid compound.

a. What mass of the compound is necessary if the density is 0.718 g/cm^3?

b. If the compound costs \$1.75/gram, what is the cost of this amount of the compound?

31. What volume of sodium has the same mass as 22.0 cm^3 of silicon? The density of sodium is 0.97 g/cm^3; the density of silicon is 2.33 g/cm^3.

32. What is the mass, in kilograms, of a block of platinum that measures 23.0 cm by 78.4 cm by 122 cm? The density of platinum is 22.5 g/cm^3.

33. Sulfuric acid sold for laboratory use consists of 96.7% sulfuric acid, H_2SO_4, by mass. The density of the solution is 1.845 g/cm^3. Compute the number of kilograms of H_2SO_4 in a 2.20-L bottle of laboratory sulfuric acid.

34. How many kilograms of dry air are in a room that measures 15.0 ft by 18.0 ft by 8.00 ft? Use an average density of air of 1.168 g/L. There are 30.48 cm in one foot.

35. Calculate the number of cubic centimeters in each of the following:

a. 1 m^3 **c.** 5 nm^3
b. 1 dm^3 **d.** 2×10^{-3} km^3

Chapter 4

36. In which of these atom(s) is the number of protons equal to the number of neutrons?

a. germanium-72 **c.** silicon-28
b. calcium-40 **d.** hydrogen-1

37. Give the total number of subatomic particles (protons, electrons, and neutrons) in each atom.

a. vanadium-51 **c.** tin-120
b. aluminum-27 **d.** hafnium-178

38. Identify the element name and mass number of an atom with the given composition.

a. 42 protons, 56 neutrons, 42 electrons

b. 2 protons, 1 neutron, 2 electrons

c. 76 protons, 113 neutrons, 76 electrons

d. 31 protons, 40 neutrons, 31 electrons

39. Use the mass and percent abundance of the four isotopes of strontium to calculate the atomic mass of strontium.

Isotope	Mass (amu)	Abundance (%)
Strontium-84	83.193	0.560
Strontium-86	85.909	9.86
Strontium-87	86.908	7.00
Strontium-88	87.906	82.58

40. An atom of carbon and an atom of element Z together weigh 6 amu less than double the weight of an atom of oxygen. If an atom of oxygen weighs 16 amu and an atom of carbon weighs 12 amu, what does an atom of element Z weigh?

Chapter 5

41. What is the maximum number of electrons in each of the following?

a. the fourth energy level

b. the 5*p* energy sublevel

c. a single 4*f* orbital

d. the first three energy levels

42. Write the electron configuration of each atom.

a. nickel

b. sulfur

c. arsenic

d. rubidium

43. Identify the symbols of the elements with the following electron configurations:

a. $1s^2 2s^2 2p^6 3s^2 3p^6 3d^{10} 4s^1$

b. $1s^2 2s^2 2p^6 3s^2 3p^5$

c. $1s^2 2s^2 2p^6 3s^2 3p^6 3d^{10} 4s^2 4p^6 4d^2 5s^2$

d. $1s^2 2s^2 2p^6 3s^2 3p^6 3d^{10} 4s^2 4p^6$

44. How many electrons are in the

a. third energy level of an indium atom?

b. second energy level of an oxygen atom?

c. third energy level of a vanadium atom?

d. first energy level of a barium atom?

45. Calculate the wavelength (in meters) of each of these frequencies of electromagnetic radiation.

a. 9.82×10^{19}/s

b. 2.24×10^{14}/s

c. 5.31×10^{7}/s

d. 7.78×10^{10}/s

46. Order the wavelengths in Problem 45 from highest to lowest energy.

Chapter 6

47. Based on their relative positions on the periodic table, which atom in each pair has the smaller atomic radius?

a. Na, K

b. Cl, Br

c. K, Br

d. Ne, Na

48. Based on their relative positions on the periodic table, which atom in each pair has the greater electronegativity?

a. B, C

b. Na, Al

c. Li, Cs

d. As, F

49. Based on their relative positions on the periodic table, which atom in each pair has the highest first ionization energy?

a. F, Br

b. Li, F

c. Ca, Be

d. K, Ar

50. Here are the first, second, and third ionization energies (kJ/mol) respectively for the representative elements "X" and "Y."

Element	First ionization energy (kJ/mol)	Second ionization energy (kJ/mol)	Third ionization energy (kJ/mol)
X	738	1450	7732
Y	496	4565	6912

In what group on the periodic table would these elements most likely be found?

51. Would the ion formed from each element be larger or smaller than the atom from which it was formed?

a. calcium
b. aluminum
c. bromine
d. nitrogen

Chapter 7

52. In any group of representative elements on the periodic table, how does the number of valence electrons vary as the elements within the group increase in mass?

53. How many valence electrons are lost by the metallic element when forming each of these ionic compounds?

a. BaS
b. In_2Se_3
c. GaP
d. SrI_2

54. Write the formulas for two cations of representative elements that have the electron configuration $1s^2 2s^2 2p^6 3s^2 3p^6$.

55. How many electrons are in each ion?

a. Pb^{4+}
b. Cr^{3+}
c. Te^{2-}
d. C^{4-}

Chapter 8

56. Draw an electron dot structure for each substance.

a. H_2Te
b. AsH_3
c. $SiBr_4$
d. I_2

57. How many electrons are in the electron dot structure for each of these polyatomic ions?

a. cyanide, CN^-
b. bromate ion, BrO_3^-
c. phosphite ion, PO_3^{3-}
d. nitrite, NO_2^-

58. Use VSEPR theory to predict the shape of each molecule in Problem 56.

59. Classify each of the molecules in Problem 56 as polar or nonpolar.

Chapter 9

60. Classify each of these compounds as molecular or ionic.

a. CF_4
b. PtO_2
c. SrI_2
d. NH_4Br
e. K_2CO_3
f. NI_3
g. $C_5H_{10}O_5$
h. $Ba(OH)_2$

61. Name or write the formulas for these molecular compounds.

a. $SiCl_4$
b. phosphorus triiodide
c. Br_2O_7
d. iodine monofluoride
e. BrF_5
f. diarsenic trioxide
g. NCl_3
h. diphosphorus pentoxide

62. Write the formulas for these ionic compounds.

a. barium iodide
b. iron(III) acetate
c. potassium dichromate
d. ammonium bromide
e. cesium nitride
f. cobalt(III) nitrate
g. aluminum oxalate
h. mercurous chloride

63. Name these ionic compounds.

a. Rb_2S
b. LiI
c. $Pb(C_2H_3O_2)_2$
d. Mg_3N_2
e. $HgCl_2$
f. $CuClO_3$
g. NaCN
h. $Cr(ClO_4)_3$

64. Name these compounds.

a. Cs_2O
b. SnS_2
c. N_4S_4
d. B_2O_3
e. H_2CrO_4
f. CaC_2O_4
g. $(NH_4)_3PO_4$
h. As_4O_{10}

65. Write the formulas for these compounds.

a. calcium oxide

b. sulfurous acid

c. diboron tetrachloride

d. calcium hydrogen phosphate

e. tin(II) chromate

f. ferric hydroxide

g. manganese(II) chlorite

h. iodine monochloride

66. Explain why it is not fair to be asked to write a formula for each named "compound."

a. iron bromide

b. sulfur oxide

c. lead hypochlorite

d. phosphorus chloride

67. Iron forms two compounds with oxygen. One compound consists of 1.396 g of iron and 0.400 grams of oxygen. The other has 0.582 g iron and 0.250 g oxygen. Show by calculation whether this pair of compounds obeys the law of multiple proportions.

Chapter 10

68. How many of each kind of atom are in a formula unit of each compound?

a. $(NH_4)_2SO_3$

b. $AlPO_4$

c. $Ca(C_2H_3O_2)_2$

d. $Fe_2(SO_4)_3$

69. How many of each kind of atom are in a molecule of each compound?

a. $C_3H_7O_2$

b. $C_3H_5(OH)_3$

c. $C_2H_4(COOH)_2$

d. $C_7H_5(NO_3)_3$

70. Calculate the molar mass of each of these binary ionic compounds.

a. MgO

b. $AlCl_3$

c. Hg_2I_2

d. Sr_3N_2

71. Calculate the molar mass of each of these ionic compounds.

a. $(NH_4)_2C_2O_4$

b. $Ca(OH)_2$

c. Na_2HPO_4

d. $Mg(HSO_4)_2$

72. Calculate the molar mass of each of these molecular compounds.

a. N_2O_5

b. C_3H_7OH

c. SO_3

d. XeF_6

73. Calculate the molar mass of each of these compounds.

a. DEET, $C_{12}H_{17}ON$, an insect repellent

b. aspartame, $C_{14}H_{18}N_2O_5$, a sugar substitute

c. codeine, $C_{18}H_{21}NO_3$, an analgesic (painkiller)

d. sodium benzoate, $NaC_7H_5O_2$, a food preservative

74. What is the mass, in grams, of each of the following?

a. 5.000 mol Ar

b. 1.64 mol $NaNO_2$

c. 0.886 mol $(NH_4)_2SO_4$

d. 18.3 mol SiF_4

75. How many moles is each of the following?

a. 579 g Pt

b. 0.0426 g NO_2

c. 56.8 g H_2SO_3

d. 6.78×10^3 g CsH_2PO_4

76. Find the number of representative particles in each of the following:

a. 4.40 mol Pd

b. 0.284 mol NaI

c. 1.62 mol NH_3

d. 12.8 mol $Fe(C_2H_3O_2)_2$

77. How many moles is each of the following?

a. 7.26×10^{22} atoms Zr

b. 1.48×10^{24} molecules C_2H_6O

c. 4.00×10^{23} formula units $KClO_3$

d. 9.02×10^{24} molecules OF_2

78. Calculate the volume, in liters, of each of these gases at STP.

a. 3.64 mol H_2

b. 0.0648 mol C_2H_6

c. 8.44 mol SO_3

d. 1.26 mol Xe

79. How many moles is each of the following at STP?

a. 56.4 L He

b. 7.64 L N_2

c. 0.888 L CO

d. 126 L SO_2

80. Calculate the number of representative particles in each mass.

a. 14.6 g CO_2
b. 68.3 g Os
c. 0.847 g KCl
d. 174 g Au_2O_3

81. Calculate the mass of each of the following samples.

a. 7.00×10^9 molecules Br_2
b. 9.22×10^{22} formula units NaF
c. 4.8×10^{24} atoms Li
d. 2.66×10^{20} molecules H_2CO

82. Find the mass of each of the gases at STP.

a. 2.44 L O_2
b. 777 L CH_4
c. 78.0 L SO_3
d. 0.0642 L H_2

83. Calculate the volume of each of these gases at STP.

a. 0.469 g Cl_2
b. 44.8 g NO
c. 2.76 g N_2O_3
d. 93.2 g F_2

84. Calculate the number of representative particles in each volume.

a. 64.0 L H_2S
b. 3.36 L C_3H_8
c. 4.78×10^4 L HF
d. 6.88×10^{-2} L Kr

85. Find the volume at STP of the following:

a. 3.66×10^{21} molecules F_2
b. 6.11×10^{22} molecules PH_3
c. 1.16×10^{25} atoms Ne
d. 4.48×10^{24} molecules C_2H_2

86. Calculate the number of oxygen atoms in each of the following:

a. 7 molecules of the explosive nitroglycerine, $C_3H_5(NO_3)_3$
b. 3.00 mol of the antiseptic hydrogen peroxide, H_2O_2
c. a balloon filled with 2.00 L O_2
d. 8.04 g of the fertilizer, NH_4NO_3

87. Calculate the number of grams of hydrogen in each of the following.

a. a balloon filled with 7.06×10^{24} hydrogen molecules
b. a balloon filled with 14.0 L of methane, CH_4, at STP
c. a 2.00-L bottle of water (density of H_2O = 1.00 g/mL)
d. a 69.5-g ice cube (density of ice = 0.917 g/cm^3)

88. Calculate the percent composition of each compound.

a. PbO_2
b. $(CH_3)_2CO$
c. KIO_3
d. $Na_2S_2O_3$
e. IF_5
f. $HBrO_4$
g. P_4O_6
h. C_3H_7COOH

89. Use the answers from Problem 88 to calculate the number of grams of the indicated element in the compound.

a. lead in 63.8 g PbO_2
b. carbon in 1.664 g $(CH_3)_2CO$
c. oxygen in 36.8 g KIO_3
d. sulfur in 6.26 g $Na_2S_2O_3$
e. fluorine in 594 g IF_5
f. bromine in 82.7 g $HBrO_4$
g. phosphorus in 2.66 g P_4O_6
h. carbon in 55.0 g C_3H_7COOH

90. Which of these are empirical formulas?

a. $Al_2(SO_4)_3$
b. $C_6H_4Cl_2$
c. $C_2H_4(OH)_2$
d. $K_2Cr_2O_7$

91. What is the empirical formula of

a. $C_6H_{16}N_2$, a compound used to make nylon?
b. $C_6H_8N_2$, a component of chocolate?
c. C_8H_8, used to make polystyrene foam plastics?
d. C_3H_7OH, rubbing alcohol?

92. Determine the empirical formula for each compound from the percent composition data.

a. 85.71% C, 14.29% H
b. 60.94% Ba, 10.65% C, 28.41% O
c. 37.50% C, 12.50% H, 50.00% O
d. 27.87% P, 72.13% S
e. 67.61% U, 32.39% F
f. 74.19% Na, 25.79% O
g. 32.43% C, 5.41% H, 43.24% O, 18.92% N
h. 18.70% Li, 16.26% C, 65.04% O

93. Find the molecular formula from the given empirical formula and molar mass.

Empirical formula	Molar mass (g/mol)	Molecular formula
C_2H_3	54.0	a. ______
C_2H_2Cl	123.0	b. ______
$C_3H_4O_3$	176.0	c. ______

Chapter 11

94. What is the function of the element platinum in this reaction?

$$2H_2 + O_2 \xrightarrow{Pt} 2H_2O$$

95. Balance the following equations:

a. $Hg(NO_3)_2 + NH_4SCN \longrightarrow Hg(SCN)_2 + NH_4NO_3$

b. $CH_4O + O_2 \longrightarrow CO_2 + H_2O$

c. $Ca + Cl_2 \longrightarrow CaCl_2$

d. $Na_3PO_4 + CoCl_2 \longrightarrow Co_3(PO_4)_2 + NaCl$

e. $Fe + AgNO_3 \longrightarrow Fe(NO_3)_2 + Ag$

f. $N_2H_4 \longrightarrow NH_3 + N_2$

g. $C_{12}H_{26} + O_2 \longrightarrow CO_2 + H_2O$

h. $CuCl + Mg \longrightarrow Cu + MgCl_2$

96. Classify each of the equations in Problem 95 by type.

97. Write balanced equations for each of these reactions. Indicate states of matter in your equations.

a. Potassium metal reacts with water to form hydrogen gas and aqueous potassium hydroxide.

b. Nitrogen monoxide gas reacts with gaseous carbon monoxide to form carbon dioxide gas and nitrogen gas.

c. Hydrochloric acid reacts with oxygen gas to form liquid water and chlorine gas.

d. Aqueous calcium hydroxide reacts with acetic acid to form water and aqueous calcium acetate.

e. Oxygen gas reacts with solid lead(II) sulfide to form sulfur dioxide gas and lead(II) oxide.

f. Solid lithium oxide reacts with water to form aqueous lithium hydroxide.

g. Solid manganese dioxide reacts with oxalic acid to form solid manganese(II) oxide, water, and gaseous carbon dioxide.

h. Gaseous diboron hexahydride reacts with oxygen gas to form liquid water and solid diboron trioxide.

98. Complete and then balance each of these equations.

a. $HCl(aq) \xrightarrow{\text{electricity}}$

b. $Br_2(l) + AlI_3(aq) \longrightarrow$

c. $Na(s) + S(s) \longrightarrow$

d. $Ba(OH)_2(aq) + HNO_3(aq) \longrightarrow$

e. $C_7H_{14}O_2(l) + O_2(g) \longrightarrow$

f. $Ni(NO_3)_2(aq) + Na_2CO_3(aq) \longrightarrow$

99. Balance each of these equations.

a. $MnO_2 + HCl \longrightarrow MnCl_2 + Cl_2 + H_2O$

b. $PCl_5 + H_2O \longrightarrow H_3PO_4 + HCl$

c. $Ca_3P_2 + H_2O \longrightarrow PH_3 + Ca(OH)_2$

d. $Li_3N + H_2O \longrightarrow LiOH + NH_3$

e. $H_2O_2 + N_2H_4 \longrightarrow N_2 + H_2O$

f. $SiCl_4 + Mg \longrightarrow MgCl_2 + Si$

g. $V_2O_5 + H_2 \longrightarrow V_2O_3 + H_2O$

h. $HBr + KHSO_3 \longrightarrow KBr + H_2O + SO_2$

100. Use the solubility rules table in Lesson 11.3 to predict whether a precipitate will form when aqueous solutions of these pairs of salts are mixed. If a precipitate forms, write its formula.

a. ammonium sulfate and barium bromide

b. chromium(II) chloride and lithium carbonate

c. potassium nitrate and sodium chloride

d. sodium sulfide and mercury(II) nitrate

101. Write a balanced complete ionic equation for each of these double-replacement reactions. All the reactants are in aqueous solution.

a. nickel(II) chloride + potassium phosphate

b. ethanoic acid + calcium hydroxide

c. calcium iodide + sodium sulfate

d. sodium hydroxide + lead(II) nitrate

102. Identify the spectator ions in each of the reactions in Problem 101.

103. Write net ionic equations for each of the reactions in Problem 101.

Chapter 12

104. Interpret each equation in terms of interacting particles.

a. $H_2 + F_2 \longrightarrow 2HF$

b. $2K_3PO_4 + 3CoCl_2 \longrightarrow Co_3(PO_4)_2 + 6KCl$

c. $2PbS + 3O_2 \longrightarrow 2PbO + 2SO_2$

d. $Fe + S \longrightarrow FeS$

105. Write all possible mole ratios for these equations.

a. $2NO + Cl_2 \longrightarrow 2NOCl$

b. $2KClO_3 \longrightarrow 2KCl + 3O_2$

c. $3N_2H_4 \longrightarrow 4NH_3 + N_2$

d. $2Na + O_2 \longrightarrow Na_2O_2$

106. Show by calculation that the following equations obey the law of conservation of mass:

a. $3NO_2 + H_2O \longrightarrow 2HNO_3 + NO$

b. $4HCl + O_2 \longrightarrow 2H_2O + 2Cl_2$

c. $2Li + S \longrightarrow Li_2S$

d. $2CH_4O + 3O_2 \longrightarrow 2CO_2 + 4H_2O$

107. Nitric acid, HNO_3, is produced by a process that allows nitrogen dioxide to react with water.

$$3NO_2(g) + H_2O(l) \longrightarrow 2HNO_3(aq) + NO(g)$$

a. How many moles of nitrogen dioxide, NO_2, are required to produce 3.56 mol of nitric acid?

b. How many moles of water react with 0.946 mol of nitrogen dioxide?

108. Calcium hydroxide reacts with nitric acid to produce an aqueous solution of calcium nitrate.

$$Ca(OH)_2(aq) + 2HNO_3(aq) \longrightarrow 2H_2O(l) + Ca(NO_3)_2(aq)$$

a. How many moles of calcium hydroxide are needed to react with 5.88 mol of nitric acid?

b. How many moles of calcium nitrate are produced when 2.30 mol of water are made in this reaction?

109. Chromium combines with oxygen to form chromium(III) oxide.

$$4Cr(s) + 3O_2(g) \longrightarrow 2Cr_2O_3(s)$$

a. How many moles of chromium are needed to react with 45.6 g of oxygen?

b. How many moles of chromium(III) oxide are produced when 2.86 g of chromium react?

110. Sodium hydroxide is formed when sodium oxide reacts with water.

$$Na_2O(s) + H_2O(l) \longrightarrow 2NaOH(aq)$$

a. Calculate the grams of sodium hydroxide formed when 2.24 moles of sodium oxide react with water.

b. What mass of water (in centigrams) is needed to react with 0.126 mol of sodium oxide?

111. The reaction of nitrogen monoxide with carbon monoxide produces carbon dioxide and nitrogen.

$$2NO(g) + 2CO(g) \longrightarrow 2CO_2(g) + N_2(g)$$

a. How many liters of nitrogen monoxide at STP are needed to produce 3.40 mol of nitrogen gas?

b. When 2.18 moles of nitrogen are made in this reaction, how many liters of carbon dioxide at STP are produced?

112. Hydrogen fluoride gas is produced directly from its component elements.

$$H_2(g) + F_2(g) \longrightarrow 2HF(g)$$

a. When 40.0 L of fluorine at STP reacts with an excess of hydrogen, how many moles of hydrogen fluoride are made?

b. How many moles of fluorine are needed to make 8.04 L of hydrogen fluoride at STP?

113. Rust (iron(III) oxide) is formed by the reaction of oxygen with iron.

$$4Fe(s) + 3O_2(g) \longrightarrow 2Fe_2O_3(s)$$

a. Calculate the mass of oxygen required to react with 10.0 g of iron.

b. How many grams of rust form when 2.48 g of iron reacts with an excess of oxygen?

114. Silver chloride precipitates when aqueous solutions of calcium chloride and silver nitrate are mixed.

$$CaCl_2(aq) + 2AgNO_3(aq) \longrightarrow 2AgCl(s) + Ca(NO_3)_2(aq)$$

a. How many grams of calcium nitrate are formed when 0.500 g of calcium chloride reacts with an excess of silver nitrate?

b. How many grams of calcium chloride are required to react completely with 34.8 g of silver nitrate?

115. The complete combustion of octane, a component of gasoline, forms carbon dioxide and water.

$$2C_8H_{18}(l) + 25O_2(g) \longrightarrow 16CO_2(g) + 18H_2O(l)$$

a. How many grams of C_8H_{18} must be reacted to give 5.00 g of CO_2?

b. How many liters of oxygen gas at STP are required to burn 2.20 g C_8H_{18}?

116. A precipitate of nickel(II) carbonate forms when aqueous solutions of sodium carbonate and nickel(II) nitrate are mixed.

$$Ni(NO_3)_2(aq) + Na_2CO_3(aq) \longrightarrow NiCO_3(s) + 2NaNO_3(aq)$$

a. How many grams of each reactant must be used to form 67.2 g of the precipitate?

b. When 1.88 g of nickel(II) carbonate are formed, how many grams of sodium nitrate are produced?

117. One way to make ethanol is to react ethene with water at high pressure.

$$C_2H_4(g) + H_2O(g) \longrightarrow C_2H_6O(l)$$

a. How many grams of each reactant are needed to produce 8.84 g of ethanol?

b. How many liters of ethanol are produced when 1.00 kg of ethene is reacted with an excess of water? The density of ethanol is 0.789 g/mL.

118. Balance the equation for the formation of aluminum hydroxide, a common ingredient in some antacid tablets.

$$Al_2(SO_4)_3(aq) + NaOH(aq) \longrightarrow Al(OH)_3(s) + Na_2SO_4(aq)$$

a. How many grams of sodium hydroxide are required to react completely with 6.22 g of aluminum sulfate?

b. When 32.0 grams of sodium hydroxide reacts with an excess of aluminum sulfate, how many grams of aluminum hydroxide are formed?

119. One source of elemental oxygen in the laboratory is the decomposition of hydrogen peroxide.

$$2H_2O_2(l) \longrightarrow 2H_2O(l) + O_2(g)$$

a. How many grams of hydrogen peroxide are needed to produce 5.00 g of oxygen?

b. When 16.8 g of hydrogen peroxide are decomposed, how many liters (at STP) of oxygen are produced?

120. One source of acid rain is the production of nitric acid from nitrogen dioxide and water in the atmosphere.

$$3NO_2(g) + H_2O(l) \longrightarrow NO(g) + 2HNO_3(aq)$$

a. How many kilograms of nitric acid are produced when 5.60 kg of nitrogen dioxide reacts with an excess of water?

b. Calculate the mass in grams of nitrogen monoxide produced when 0.648 kg of nitric acid is formed by this reaction.

121. Steel rails for trains are welded together with the liquid (molten) iron formed by the immense heat generated by this reaction.

$$2Al(s) + Fe_2O_3(s) \longrightarrow Al_2O_3(s) + 2Fe(l)$$

a. How many grams of aluminum are needed to react completely with 0.500 kg of iron(III) oxide?

b. How many milliliters of molten iron are produced when 80.0 g of iron(III) oxide are reacted with an excess of aluminum? The density of iron is 7.87 g/cm^3. Assume the densities of molten iron and solid iron are the same.

122. Chlorine gas is made by reacting oxygen with hydrochloric acid.

$$4HCl(aq) + O_2(g) \longrightarrow 2Cl_2(g) + 2H_2O(l)$$

a. How many grams of each of the reactants are required to produce 44.0 g of chlorine?

b. At STP, how many liters of oxygen are needed to react completely with 125 g of hydrochloric acid?

123. Hydrogen fluoride is made by reacting sulfuric acid with calcium fluoride.

$$H_2SO_4(l) + CaF_2(s) \longrightarrow 2HF(g) + CaSO_4(s)$$

a. How many grams of hydrogen fluoride and calcium sulfate are produced when 2.86 g of calcium fluoride reacts with an excess of sulfuric acid?

b. Calculate the number of kilograms of calcium fluoride that must react with an excess of sulfuric acid to produce 1.00 kg of hydrogen fluoride.

124. When solid dinitrogen pentoxide is heated, it produces oxygen and nitrogen dioxide.

a. Write the balanced equation for this reaction.

b. How many grams of each product are formed when 4.00 g of dinitrogen pentoxide is completely decomposed?

125. Laundry bleach (NaClO) is made by reacting chlorine with sodium hydroxide.

$$Cl_2(g) + 2NaOH(aq) \longrightarrow NaClO(aq) + NaCl(aq) + H_2O(l)$$

a. How many grams of chlorine must react with an excess of sodium hydroxide to produce 2.50 kg of sodium hypochlorite?

b. At room temperature, chlorine gas has a density of 2.95 g/L. How many dL of chlorine gas are needed to react completely with 66.8 g of sodium hydroxide?

126. Bubbling oxygen gas through liquid acetaldehyde (C_2H_4O) forms a single product, acetic acid.

a. Write a balanced equation for this reaction.

b. How many grams of oxygen are needed to react completely with 542 g of acetaldehyde?

127. Water is decomposed into its elements by an electric current.

a. Write a balanced equation for the reaction.

b. What is the total volume (in liters at STP) of gases produced when 222 g of water are decomposed?

128. Oxygen is generated in a rebreathing gas mask by a reaction of water vapor with potassium superoxide, KO_2.

$$4KO_2(s) + 2H_2O(l) \longrightarrow 3O_2(g) + 4KOH(s)$$

a. How many liters of oxygen gas at STP are produced when 56.0 g of potassium superoxide react completely with water vapor?

b. How many grams of potassium hydroxide are produced when the 56.0 g of KO_2 react with an excess of water?

129. Find the limiting reagent for each set of reactants. Then calculate the number of moles of each reactant remaining and the amount of each product formed after the reaction.

$$4NH_3(g) + 3O_2(g) \longrightarrow 2N_2(g) + 6H_2O(l)$$

a. 4.00 mol NH_3 + 4.00 mol O_2

b. 2.00 mol NH_3 + 1.00 mol O_2

c. 7.00 mol NH_3 + 5.00 mol O_2

d. 3.25 mol NH_3 + 2.75 mol O_2

130. Diboron trioxide is formed by reacting 14.0 g of diboron hexahydride with 68.0 g of oxygen.

$$B_2H_6(g) + 3O_2(g) \longrightarrow 3H_2O(l) + B_2O_3(s)$$

a. Identify the limiting reagent.

b. Calculate the mass of diboron trioxide produced.

131. When hydrochloric acid is added to calcium carbonate, bubbles of carbon dioxide gas are produced.

$$CaCO_3(s) + 2HCl(aq) \longrightarrow CaCl_2(aq) + H_2O(l) + CO_2(g)$$

a. What is the limiting reagent when 1.68 g of HCl is added to 4.82 g $CaCO_3$?

b. In the reaction, how many milliliters of water are produced? (density = 1.00 g/cm^3)

c. What is the volume, in liters, of carbon dioxide produced? Assume STP.

132. The elements phosphorus and chlorine react to form phosphorus trichloride.

$$P_4(s) + 6Cl_2(g) \longrightarrow 4PCl_3(l)$$

a. What is the limiting reagent when 100.0 g of phosphorus reacts with 200.0 g of chlorine?

b. How many grams of phosphorus trichloride are formed?

133. Hydrogen gas is one of the products of the reaction of aluminum with hydrochloric acid.

$$2Al(s) + 6HCl(aq) \longrightarrow AlCl_3(aq) + 3H_2(g)$$

How many grams of H_2 are produced when 20.0 g of Al reacts with 60.0 g of HCl?

134. When copper(I) oxide, Cu_2O, is heated in oxygen, copper(II) oxide is formed.

$$2Cu_2O(s) + O_2(g) \longrightarrow 4CuO(s)$$

When 4.00 mol of copper(I) oxide reacts with 2.00 mol of oxygen, 7.44 mol of CuO is obtained. What is the percent yield of this reaction?

135. When 7.00 mol C reacts with 5.00 mol SO_2, 1.80 mol CS_2 is formed.

$$3C(s) + 2SO_2(g) \longrightarrow CS_2(l) + 2CO_2(g)$$

What is the percent yield of this reaction?

136. An excess of water is reacted with 25.0 g of calcium carbide. A mass of 7.20 g of C_2H_2 is obtained.

$$CaC_2(s) + 2H_2O(l) \longrightarrow C_2H_2(g) + Ca(OH)_2(aq)$$

What is the percent yield of C_2H_2?

137. An excess of sulfur dioxide was reacted with 0.150 g of oxygen gas. A mass of 0.725 g of sulfur trioxide was recovered.

$$2SO_2(g) + O_2(g) \longrightarrow 2SO_3(g)$$

What is the percent yield of sulfur trioxide?

138. When 30.0 g CH_4 reacts with 90.0 g O_2 and 30.0 g NH_3, 94.4 g H_2O is formed.

$$2CH_4(g) + 3O_2(g) + 2NH_3(g) \longrightarrow 2HCN(g) + 6H_2O(l)$$

What is the percent yield of this reaction?

Chapter 13

139. Make the following pressure conversions:

a. 364 kPa to atm

b. 815 mm Hg to kPa

c. 0.260 atm to mm Hg

d. 1555 mm Hg to atm

e. 85.8 kPa to mm Hg

f. 0.440 atm to kPa

140. Water evaporates much more slowly at room temperature than acetone. How does the relative strength of intermolecular forces compare in these two compounds?

141. In the same location, equal quantities of water are poured into a drinking glass and a glass pie pan. In which container will the water evaporate first? Explain your choice.

142. Equal masses of liquid and solid wax are placed in an oven maintained at a temperature exactly at the melting point of the wax. How would the relative amounts of liquid and solid wax change over time?

Chapter 14

143. A sample of gas at a pressure of 124 kPa has a volume of 3.00 L. If the gas is compressed to a volume of 1.26 L, what is its new pressure? (Assume constant temperature.)

144. A scuba tank has a volume of 11.0 L. What volume of gas in liters at 0.950 atm is required to completely fill the tank to a pressure of 45.0 atm, assuming no change in the temperature of the gas?

145. A syringe contains 2.60 mL of gas at 20.0°C. What is the volume of gas after the temperature is increased to 68.0°C?

146. A contained gas has a volume of 120.0 mL at −183°C. What volume does this gas occupy at 47.0°C?

147. To what temperature must a contained gas at a pressure of 464 mm Hg and a temperature of 40.0°C be raised to increase the pressure to 994 mm Hg?

148. The pressure of a gas in a cylinder at 27.0°C is 846 kPa. What is the pressure in the cylinder when the temperature is increased to 54.0°C?

149. Calculate the final pressure of a gas initially at 122 kPa pressure that is expanded from 4.50 L at 56°C to 18.0 L at 124°C.

150. A weather balloon has a volume of 3.5 kL at 1.01 atm and 18°C. What is the balloon's volume at a pressure of 0.420 atm and −18°C?

151. A cylinder contains 4.50 L of nitrogen at 35°C and a pressure of 644 kPa. How many moles of N_2 are in the cylinder?

152. A balloon containing 1.46 mol of neon gas has a volume of 36.2 L.

a. Under the same conditions, what is the volume of the balloon if an additional 0.34 mol of Ne is added to the balloon?

b. Would the answer change if 0.34 mol of He were added instead of neon?

153. What is the pressure (in kPa) in a 5.00-L tank containing 0.240 mol of oxygen gas at a temperature of 17°C?

154. Calculate the volume of 0.880 mol of fluorine gas at 26°C and 88.8 kPa.

155. A metal cylinder contains 0.440 mol of nitrogen gas at a pressure of 34.0 kPa. What is the pressure in the container after 0.128 mol of nitrogen are removed?

156. All the neon gas from a 10.0-L container at a pressure of 202 kPa is added to a 20.0-L container of argon at a pressure of 505 kPa. After the transfer, what are the partial pressures of neon and argon?

157. A child buys a balloon filled with 3.50 L of helium on a very hot day when it's 39.0°C outside. Assuming a constant pressure, what is the volume of the balloon when the child brings the balloon home to an air-conditioned house at 20.0°C?

158. Suppose you have a 0.500-L cylinder that contains 0.150 mol of oxygen gas, O_2, at 25°C.

a. What is the pressure inside the cylinder?

b. How would the pressure inside the cylinder change if you substituted 0.150 mol of sulfur dioxide gas, SO_2, for the 0.150 mol of oxygen gas?

c. How would the pressure inside the cylinder change if you added 0.150 mol of sulfur dioxide gas, SO_2, to the oxygen already in the cylinder?

159. In a typical automobile engine, the gas mixture in a cylinder is compressed and the pressure increases from 1.00 atm to 9.50 atm. If the uncompressed volume of the cylinder is 755 mL, what is the volume when fully compressed? (Assume constant temperature.)

160. What is the new pressure when an aerosol can with an initial pressure of 4.50 atm at 25°C is heated in a fire to 650°C?

161. How many moles of air are in the lungs of an average person with a total lung capacity of 3.8 L? Assume that the person is at sea level (1.00 atm) and has a normal body temperature of 37°C.

162. Two containers of equal size are filled with 4.0 g of He and 32.0 g of O_2, respectively. Assuming a constant temperature, would you expect the pressures of these two gases to be identical? Explain your answer.

163. Lithium nitride is formed from its elements.

$$6Li(s) + N_2(g) \longrightarrow 2Li_3N(s)$$

How many milliliters of nitrogen gas at STP are needed to react with 0.246 g of lithium?

164. Nitrogen and hydrogen react to form ammonia.

$$3H_2(g) + N_2(g) \longrightarrow 2NH_3(g)$$

How many liters of hydrogen gas measured at 86.4 kPa pressure and 245°C are needed to react completely with 6.44 g N_2?

165. Auto air bags are inflated by nitrogen gas formed through this decomposition reaction:

$$2NaN_3(s) \longrightarrow 2Na(s) + 3N_2(g)$$

How many grams of NaN_3 are needed to inflate an air bag to a volume of 10.6 L, assuming STP?

Chapter 15

166. Which of these molecules can form hydrogen bonds with water?

a. H_2 **c.** HCl

b. CH_3OH **d.** C_2H_6

167. Classify each substance as an electrolyte or a nonelectrolyte.

a. NH_4NO_3 **c.** $NaBr_2$

b. C_2H_6O **d.** Cl_2

168. Calculate the percent by mass of water in lithium perchlorate trihydrate.

169. An experiment requires making a solution that contains 34.6 g of $CaCl_2$. Your only source is the hydrate $CaCl_2{\cdot}2H_2O$. How many grams of the hydrate do you need to use to obtain the required mass of $CaCl_2$?

170. A 19.97-g sample of a hydrate contains 5.08 g Cu, 2.57 g S, 5.12 g O, and 7.20 g H_2O. What is the empirical formula of this hydrate?

Chapter 16

171. The solubility of carbon dioxide gas at 50°C and 1.00 atm pressure is 7.6×10^{-2} g/100 g H_2O. Assuming constant temperature, calculate the solubility of CO_2 when the pressure is increased to 2.50 atm.

172. Calculate the molarity of each of these solutions.

a. 4.24 mol NaCl in 2.00 L of solution

b. 0.164 mol of $C_5H_{10}O_5$ in 125 mL of solution

c. 0.0056 mol CsBr in 50.0 mL of solution

d. 2.84 mol C_2H_6O in 0.650 L of solution

173. What is the molarity of each of these solutions?

a. 3.34 g $CuNO_2$ in 0.150 L of solution

b. 0.0688 g CoF_2 in 20.0 mL of solution

c. 88.8 g KOH in 0.755 L of solution

d. 1.66 g $LiNO_3$ in 455 mL of solution

174. Find the moles of solute in the following solutions:

a. 650 mL of 0.28*M* $NaNO_3$

b. 1.4 L of 0.35*M* KI

c. 0.340 L of 2.22*M* $CaCl_2$

d. 148 mL of 0.0068*M* LiF

175. Calculate the mass of solute in each of these solutions.

a. 2.00 L of 0.440*M* MgF_2

b. 6.80 dL of 1.88*M* CH_4O

c. 65.0 mL of 0.0360*M* $NaNO_3$

d. 5.00 mL of 1.48*M* HCl

176. How many milliliters of a stock solution of 2.50*M* $SrCl_2$ solution are required to make each diluted solution?

a. 50.0 mL of 1.00*M* $SrCl_2$

b. 1.0 L of 0.40*M* $SrCl_2$

c. 750 mL of 0.25*M* $SrCl_2$

d. 65.0 dL of 0.146*M* $SrCl_2$

177. An aqueous solution is 65% (v/v) rubbing alcohol. How many milliliters of alcohol are in a 97-mL sample of this solution?

178. Calculate the percent by mass of each of these solutions.

a. 6.50 g CsI in 266 g H_2O

b. 246 g NaOH in 1.40 kg H_2O

c. 0.428 g K_2CO_3 in 8.58 g H_2O

d. 1.20 kg $NaNO_3$ in 2.00 kg H_2O

179. Calculate the mole fraction of each component of the following solutions:

a. 2.40 mol CH_4O and 5.36 mol C_2H_6O

b. 1.25 mol H_2O and 87.6 g HCl

c. 24.0 g C_2H_6O and 10.0 g H_2O

d. 0.464 g C_2H_6O and 2.36 g CH_4O

180. Potassium bromide is dissolved in water. Which statements are true when comparing the solution to pure water?

a. The boiling point of the solution is higher.

b. The vapor pressure of the solution is higher.

c. The freezing point of the solution is higher.

181. Calculate the molality of these solutions.

a. 0.246 mol KCl in 1.66 kg solvent

b. 0.116 mol $LiNO_3$ in 844 g solvent

c. 56.6 mmol CsI in 1.06 kg solvent

d. 6.66 mol $MgBr_2$ in 2.50 kg solvent

182. Calculate the freezing and boiling points of each of these aqueous solutions.

a. 2.34*m* NH_4Br

b. 1.17*m* $CaCl_2$

c. 24.4 g LiCl in 0.400 kg H_2O

d. 44.8 g $MgCl_2$ in 1.20 kg H_2O

Chapter 17

183. As the mass of a substance increases,

a. does its heat capacity increase, decrease, or remain constant?

b. does its specific heat increase, decrease, or remain constant?

184. The temperature of a 6.42-gram piece of glass is 15°C. How many calories would it take to increase the temperature of the glass to 96°C? The specific heat of glass is 0.12 cal/(g·°C).

185. Ethanol has a specific heat of 2.43 J/(g·°C). If 468 J of heat is added to 29.0 g of ethanol initially at 25.0°C, what is the final temperature of the liquid?

186. When 1564 J of energy is added to a sample of gold at 25.0°C, the temperature of the gold increases by 424.0°C. What is the mass of the gold? The specific heat of gold is 0.129 J/(g·°C).

187. Identical masses of aluminum and lead at the same temperature absorb identical amounts of heat energy. The specific heat of aluminum is 0.901 J/(g·°C); the specific heat of lead is 0.129 J/(g·°C). Which gets hotter, the aluminum or the lead?

188. Suppose your diet provides 2100 Cal (kcal) in a day, and your body weight is 68 kg. Start with an initial body temperature of a normal 37°C. Calculate the maximum temperature that your body would reach by absorbing all 2100 kcal at once. For purposes of this problem, assume that your body is 100% water. The specific heat of water is 1.00 cal/(g·°C).

189. Nitrogen monoxide is formed from its elements.

$$N_2(g) + O_2(g) \longrightarrow 2NO(g)$$
$$\Delta H = 181 \text{ kJ/mol}$$

a. Is this reaction exothermic or endothermic?

b. How many kilojoules of energy are needed to form 8.70 mol NO?

190. Carbon dioxide and water are produced by the complete combustion of propane, C_3H_8.

$$C_3H_8(g) + 5O_2(g) \longrightarrow 3CO_2(g) + 4H_2O(g) + 526 \text{ kcal}$$

a. Is this reaction exothermic or endothermic?

b. How many kcal of energy are produced when 14.4 g C_3H_8 burns in an excess of oxygen?

191. The following reaction was used to fuel the rockets in the Apollo mission landing module.

$$2N_2H_4(l) + N_2O_4(l) \longrightarrow 3N_2(g) + 4H_2O(g)$$
$$\Delta H = -1049 \text{ kJ}$$

a. Is this reaction endothermic or exothermic?

b. How many grams of N_2H_4 must be reacted with an excess of N_2O_4 to produce 645 kJ of energy?

c. How many kilojoules of energy are produced when 5.40 g N_2O_4 reacts with an excess of N_2H_4?

192. The heat of fusion of mercury is 2.30 kJ/mol. How much heat (in J) is released when 24.0 g Hg changes from the liquid state to the solid state at its freezing point?

193. How much heat energy is required to change 50.0 g of liquid water at 100°C to water vapor at 100°C? The molar heat of fusion is 6.01 kJ/mol, and the molar heat of vaporization is 40.7 kJ/mol.

194. There is a dramatic temperature change when solid ammonium nitrate is dissolved in water.

$$NH_4NO_3(s) \longrightarrow NH_4^+(aq) + NO_3^-(aq)$$
$$\Delta H_{soln} = 25.7 \text{kJ/mol}$$

a. Is there a temperature increase or decrease when ammonium nitrate dissolves in water?

b. Calculate the heat change when 55.0 g $NH_4NO_3(s)$ dissolves in water.

195. Use the data in the standard heats of formation table in Lesson 17.4 and the additional values for $\Delta H_f°$ given below to calculate the standard heat of reaction ($\Delta H°$) for each of these reactions.

Substance	$\Delta H_f°$ (kJ/mol)
$N_2H_4(l)$	50.63
$HNO_3(aq)$	-207.4

a. $2SO_2(g) + O_2(g) \longrightarrow 2SO_3(g)$

b. $3N_2H_4(l) \longrightarrow 4NH_3(g) + N_2(g)$

c. $3NO_2(g) + H_2O(g) \longrightarrow 2HNO_3(aq) + NO(g)$

d. $2NO(g) + 2CO(g) \longrightarrow 2CO_2(g) + N_2(g)$

196. Ethanol is manufactured by reacting water with ethane, C_2H_4.

$$C_2H_4(g) + H_2O(l) \longrightarrow C_2H_6O(l)$$

Use the following equations to calculate the $\Delta H°$ for this reaction.

$$C_2H_6O(l) + 3O_2(g) \longrightarrow 2CO_2(g) + 3H_2O(l)$$
$$\Delta H = -1367 \text{ kJ}$$

$$C_2H_4(g) + 3O_2(g) \longrightarrow 2CO_2(g) + 2H_2O(l)$$
$$\Delta H = -1411 \text{ kJ}$$

197. Use the following equations to calculate the standard heat of formation, in kJ/mol, of magnesium nitrate:

$$2MgO(s) \longrightarrow 2Mg(s) + O_2(g) \quad \Delta H = 1203 \text{ kJ}$$
$$Mg_3N_2(s) \longrightarrow 3Mg(s) + N_2(g) \quad \Delta H = 463 \text{ kJ}$$
$$Mg(NO_3)_2(s) + 8Mg(s) \longrightarrow 6MgO(s) + Mg_3N_2(s)$$
$$\Delta H = -3884 \text{ kJ}$$

198. The heat of sublimation of dry ice (solid CO_2) is 25.2 kJ/mol. How many grams of water at 0.0°C would be frozen by the complete sublimation of 48.0 g of dry ice that is dropped into the water? The heat of fusion of water is 6.01 kJ/mol.

Chapter 18

199. At equilibrium, are the reactants or the products favored for reactions that have the following equilibrium constants?

a. $K_{eq} = 5.6 \times 10^{-7}$ **c.** $K_{eq} = 5.6 \times 10^{-14}$

b. $K_{eq} = 5.6 \times 10^{21}$ **d.** $K_{eq} = 5.6 \times 10^{5}$

200. Write the expression for the equilibrium constant for each reaction.

a. $2PCl_3(g) + O_2(g) \rightleftharpoons 2POCl_3(g)$

b. $2HOCl(g) \rightleftharpoons Cl_2O(g) + H_2O(g)$

c. $Br_2(g) + 5F_2(g) \rightleftharpoons 2BrF_5(g)$

d. $N_2H_4(g) + 6H_2O_2(g) \rightleftharpoons 2NO_2(g) + 8H_2O(g)$

201. Using the equations in Problem 200, calculate the value of K_{eq} when the following amounts of reactants and products are present in a 1-L container at equilibrium.

a. 1.44 mol PCl_3, 1.44 mol O_2, and 2.60 mol $POCl_3$

b. 0.220 mol HOCl, 4.68 mol Cl_2O, and 6.82 mol H_2O

c. 0.0500 mol Br_2, 1.00 mol F_2, and 0.0465 mol BrF_5

d. 0.400 mol N_2H_4, 0.100 mol H_2O_2, 1.20 mol NO_2, and 1.00 mol H_2O

202. List three ways to cause a shift in this equilibrium to the right, forming more $CH_4O(g)$.

$$CO(g) + 2H_2(g) \rightleftharpoons CH_4O(g) + \text{heat}$$

203. A yellow gas (Y) reacts with a colorless gas (C) to produce a blue gas (B), according to this equation:

$$C(g) + 3Y(g) \rightleftharpoons 2B(g) + \text{heat}$$

The system is initially at equilibrium and has a green color. What happens to the color of the system if the following stresses are placed on the system? Note: Blue and yellow mix to form green.

a. A large amount of colorless C is removed from the reaction container.

b. The reaction container is heated.

204. Assume that the following chemical system is originally at equilibrium and the color of the liquid is purplish (a mixture of the colors pink and blue):

$$\text{heat} + \underset{\text{pink}}{[Co(H_2O)_6]^{2+}(aq)} + 4\,Cl^-(aq) \rightleftharpoons \underset{\text{blue}}{[CoCl_4]^{2-}(aq)} + 6\,H_2O(l)$$

a. How does the color change if chloride ion is added to the system?

b. How does the color change if the reaction mixture is cooled?

205. Use the table on page 588 to predict whether a precipitate will form when the following pairs of substances are mixed.

a. $K_2S(aq) + Cu(NO_3)_2(aq)$

b. $NH_4Cl(aq) + Pb(NO_3)_2(aq)$

c. $Na_2CO_3(aq) + ZnCl_2(aq)$

d. $KNO_3(aq) + BaCl_2(aq)$

206. Find the equilibrium concentrations of zinc and sulfide ions in a saturated solution of zinc sulfide with $K_{sp} = 3.0 \times 10^{-23}$.

207. For each change, does the entropy increase or decrease?

a. A gold nugget melts.

b. Liquid wax solidifies.

c. Liquid water forms from water vapor.

d. Liquid water forms from hydrogen and oxygen gas.

Chapter 19

208. Identify each of the species in each equation as a Brønsted-Lowry acid or a Brønsted-Lowry base.

a. $H_2O(aq) + CN^-(aq) \rightleftharpoons OH^-(aq) + HCN(aq)$

b. $HClO_3(aq) + H_2O(aq) \rightleftharpoons ClO_3^-(aq) + H_3O^+(aq)$

c. $C_5H_5NH^+(aq) + OH^-(aq) \rightleftharpoons C_5H_5N(aq) + H_2O(aq)$

d. $HSO_4^-(aq) + H_3O^+(aq) \rightleftharpoons H_2SO_4(aq) + H_2O(aq)$

209. Which of the following are conjugate acid-base pairs?

a. NH_4^+, NH_3 **c.** HSO_4^-, SO_4^{2-}

b. H_3PO_4, $H_2PO_4^-$ **d.** H_3O^+, OH^-

210. Ammonia can act as a Lewis base toward which of these compounds?

a. CH_4
b. BCl_3
c. NF_3
d. OF_2

211. Calculate the pH of each solution and classify it as acidic or basic.

a. $[H^+] = 4.6 \times 10^{-4}M$
b. $[H^+] = 1.2 \times 10^{-8}M$
c. $[OH^-] = 8.3 \times 10^{-4}M$
d. $[OH^-] = 2.8 \times 10^{-11}M$
e. $[H^+] = 3.9 \times 10^{-2}M$
f. $[OH^-] = 1.5 \times 10^{-9}M$

212. Calculate the $[H^+]$ and the $[OH^-]$ from the pH of each solution.

a. pH = 6.03
b. pH = 1.18
c. pH = 12.68
d. pH = 4.33
e. pH = 9.16
f. pH = 3.46

213. Rank these acids from strongest to weakest.

a. HX, $K_a = 1 \times 10^{-4}$
b. HY, $K_a = 1 \times 10^{-11}$
c. HP, $K_a = 1 \times 10^{-2}$
d. HQ, $K_a = 1 \times 10^{-9}$

214. Acetylsalicylic acid (aspirin) has a K_a of 3×10^{-4}. A 0.00056*M* solution of aspirin would be best described by which terms: weak, strong, dilute, concentrated?

215. A 0.10000*M* solution of an unknown acid, HX, has a hydrogen ion concentration of $3.65 \times 10^{-4}M$. Calculate the value of K_a for this acid.

216. Name and write the formula for the salt formed in each of the following acid-base neutralizations.

a. aluminum hydroxide with phosphoric acid
b. oxalic acid with magnesium hydroxide
c. sulfurous acid with lithium hydroxide
d. sodium hydroxide with carbonic acid

217. How many moles of sulfuric acid are required to neutralize 1.40 mol of potassium hydroxide?

$$2KOH(aq) + H_2SO_4(aq) \longrightarrow K_2SO_4(aq) + 2H_2O(l)$$

218. What is the molarity of a hydrochloric acid solution if 25.0 mL of the solution reacts completely with 1.66 g $NaHCO_3$?

$$HCl(aq) + NaHCO_3(s) \longrightarrow NaCl(aq) + H_2O(l) + CO_2(g)$$

219. In an acid base titration, how many mL of 0.180*M* HCl are required to neutralize 20.0 mL of 0.220*M* NaOH?

220. How many milliliters of 0.456*M* $Ca(OH)_2$ are needed to neutralize 25.0 mL of 0.300*M* HCl?

221. A buffer ($HBrO/BrO^-$) solution is made by mixing together equal quantities of hypobromous acid (HBrO) and sodium hypobromite (NaBrO).

a. Write an equation for the reaction that occurs when an acid is added to this buffer.
b. Write an equation for the reaction that occurs when a base is added to this buffer.

Chapter 20

222. What is the oxidation number of sulfur in each of these species?

a. SF_6
b. CaS_2O_3
c. K_2SO_3
d. SO_3
e. S
f. H_2SO_4

223. What is the oxidation number of bromine in each of the following?

a. CsBr
b. $NaBrO_3$
c. BrO_2^-
d. Br_2
e. BrCl
f. NaBrO

224. Consider the following reaction:

$$CuCl_2(aq) + Fe(s) \longrightarrow Cu(s) + FeCl_2(aq)$$

a. Which reactant lost electrons?
b. What is the oxidizing agent?
c. Which reactant was oxidized in this reaction?
d. What is the reducing agent?

225. In each of these reactions, is sulfur oxidized or reduced?

a. $HgS(s) \longrightarrow Hg(l) + S(s)$
b. $S(s) + O_2(g) \longrightarrow SO_3(g)$
c. $Al(s) + S(s) \longrightarrow Al_2S_3(s)$

226. Balance each of the equations in Problem 225.

227. Balance each of the following redox reactions and classify each as a combination, decomposition, or single-replacement reaction.

a. $Mg(s) + H_2O(l) \longrightarrow Mg(OH)_2 + H_2(g)$

b. $PF_3(g) + F_2(g) \longrightarrow PF_5(g)$

c. $C_2H_2(g) + H_2(g) \longrightarrow C_2H_6(g)$

d. $NaNO_3(s) \longrightarrow NaNO_2(s) + O_2(g)$

228. Iron(II) sulfite reacts with an acid solution of permanganate ion.

$$5FeSO_3 + 14H^+ + 3MnO_4^- \longrightarrow 3Mn^{2+} + 5Fe^{3+} + 5SO_4^{2-} + 7H_2O$$

a. What is the oxidation number of iron and of manganese in the reactants?

b. What is the oxidation number of sulfur and of oxygen in SO_4^{2-}?

c. Identify the oxidizing agent in this reaction.

d. What is reduced in this reaction?

229. Write a balanced chemical equation for each of these reactions, and identify the element oxidized and the element reduced.

a. Nitrogen monoxide reacts with hydrogen to form nitrogen and water.

b. Potassium permanganate, iron(II) sulfate, and sulfuric acid react, producing manganese(II) sulfate, iron(III) sulfate, potassium sulfate, and water.

c. Elemental phosphorus (P_4) and nitrogen monoxide react to form tetraphosphorus hexoxide and nitrogen.

d. Sulfur dioxide, nitric acid, and water react to produce sulfuric acid and nitrogen monoxide.

230. Balance each redox equation by the oxidation-number-change method. Identify the oxidizing agent and the reducing agent.

a. $KMnO_4(aq) + NaNO_2(aq) + H_2O(l) \longrightarrow MnO_2(s) + NaNO_3(aq) + KOH(aq)$

b. $I_2(s) + Na_2S_2O_3(aq) \longrightarrow Na_2S_4O_6(aq) + NaI(aq)$

c. $HCl(aq) + NH_4Cl(aq) + K_2Cr_2O_7(aq) \longrightarrow CrCl_3(aq) + KCl(aq) + N_2(g) + H_2O(l)$

d. $FeCl_2(aq) + H_2O_2(aq) + HCl(aq) \longrightarrow FeCl_3(aq) + H_2O(l)$

Chapter 21

231. What happens when a strip of zinc is dipped into a solution of aluminum chloride?

232. A strip of aluminum is dipped into a solution of nickel(II) sulfate. Explain the result.

233. A voltaic cell is constructed using the following half-reactions:

$Ag^+(aq) + e^- \longrightarrow Ag(s) \qquad E^\circ_{Ag^+} = +0.80\ V$

$Al^{3+}(aq) + 3e^- \longrightarrow Al(s) \qquad E^\circ_{Al^{3+}} = -1.66\ V$

Determine the cell reaction.

234. Calculate the standard cell potential for the voltaic cell described in Problem 233.

235. What process, reduction or oxidation, always occurs at the anode of an electrolytic cell?

Chapter 22

236. What bonding properties make carbon uniquely suited to make a very large number of organic compounds?

237. Draw structural formulas for these compounds.

a. 3-phenylpentane

b. 2-phenyl-1-butene

238. Describe the structural features of an alkene molecule that permits the existence of *cis-trans* isomers.

239. How is an asymmetric carbon produced in an organic molecule?

240. Which of these structures are *cis* isomers?

a. 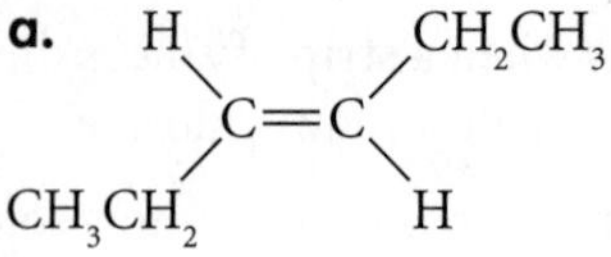
H $\quad$ CH_2CH_3
C=C
CH_3CH_2 $\quad$ H

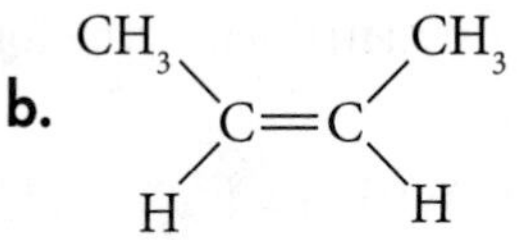

b.
CH_3 $\quad$ CH_3
C=C
H $\quad$ H

c.
H $\quad$ CH_3
C=C
H $\quad$ CH_3

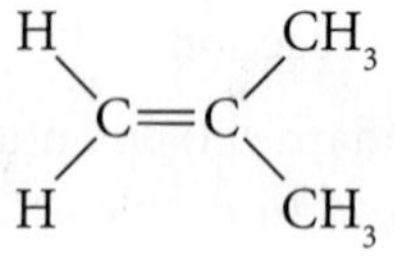

d. 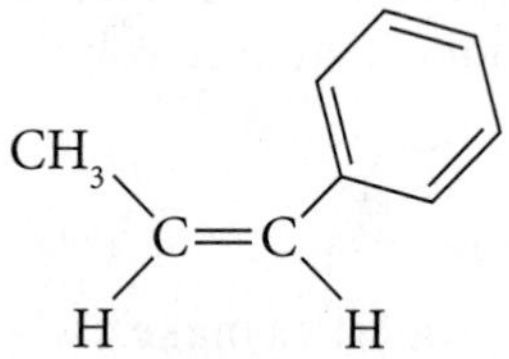
CH_3
C=C (phenyl)
H $\quad$ H

e. 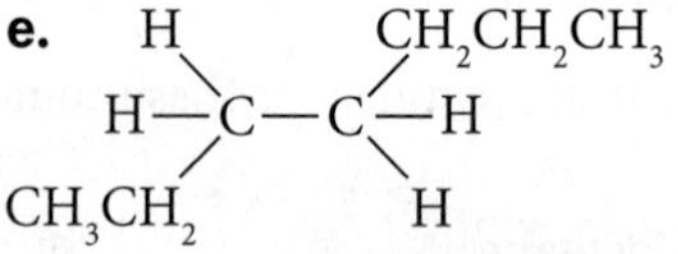
H $\quad$ $CH_2CH_2CH_3$
H—C—C—H
CH_3CH_2 $\quad$ H

241. Write the IUPAC names for these structures. Use *cis* and *trans* prefixes when appropriate.

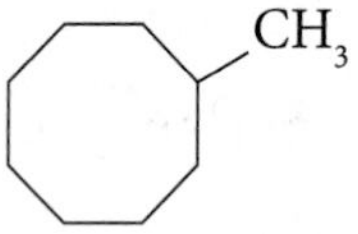

a. 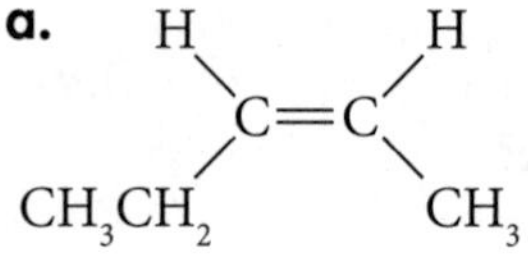
H $\quad$ H
C=C
CH_3CH_2 $\quad$ CH_3

b.
CH_3 (on cyclooctane ring)

c.
CH_3 $\quad$ CH_2CH_3
C=$CHCH_2CH_2CH_3$
CH_3

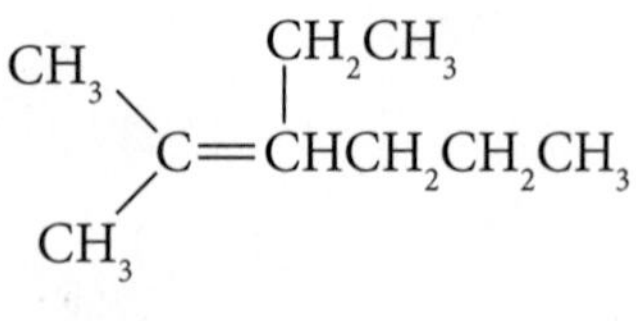

d. 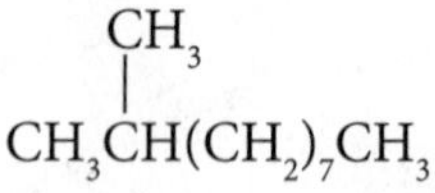
CH_3
$CH_3CH(CH_2)_7CH_3$

e. 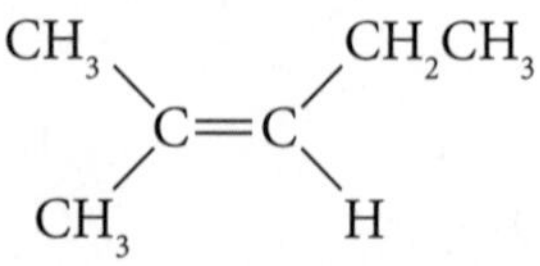
CH_3 $\quad$ CH_2CH_3
C=C
CH_3 $\quad$ H

242. What name is given to a benzene ring when it is a substituent in an organic molecule?

243. Are benzene rings more resistant or less resistant to chemical reactions than the carbon-carbon double bond in an alkane? Explain your answer.

244. Which structural feature(s) characterize alkanes?

a. carbon-hydrogen single bonds

b. carbon-carbon double bonds

c. carbon-carbon single bonds

d. may contain branched chains

e. may contain phenyl substituents

245. Draw structural formulas for these compounds.

a. 1,3-diethylbenzene

b. 1-ethyl-4-propylbenzene

c. 1,3,5-triethylbenzene

246. If you want to devise an industrial process to prepare methylbenzene, would you prefer petroleum or coal as your starting material? Explain your choice.

Chapter 23

247. Name the functional group in these molecular structures.

a. CH_3CH_2Br

b. 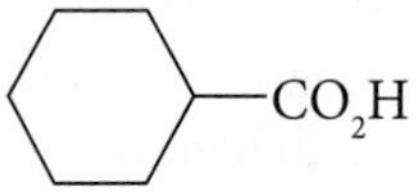 (cyclohexane ring)—CO_2H

c. 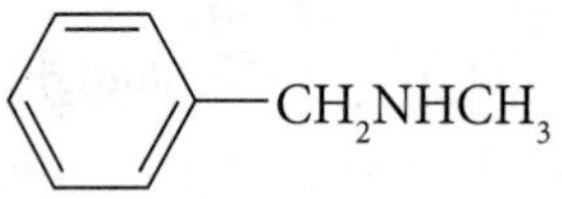 (benzene ring)—CH_2NHCH_3

d. 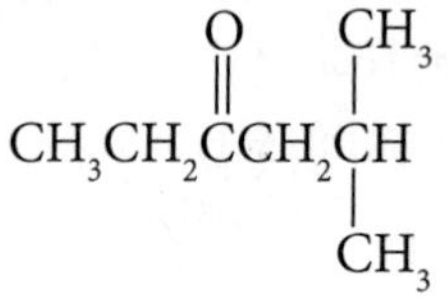
O $\quad$ CH_3
‖ $\quad$ |
$CH_3CH_2CCH_2CH$
|
CH_3

e. $CH_3CH_2CH_2OCH_3$

248. Which of these structures represent aryl halides?

a. 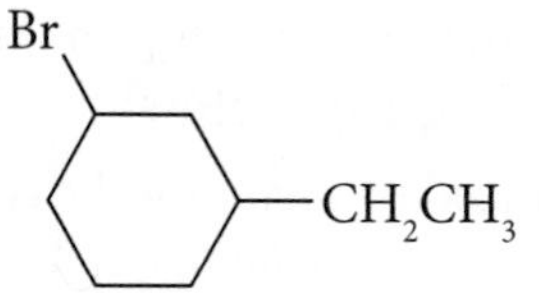 3-bromo-1-ethylcyclohexane (Br and $-CH_2CH_3$ on a cyclohexane ring)

b. 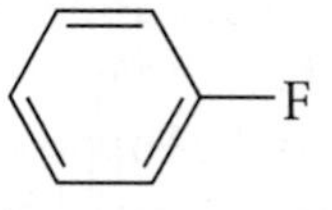 fluorobenzene (C_6H_5-F)

c. $C_6H_5-CH_2Cl$

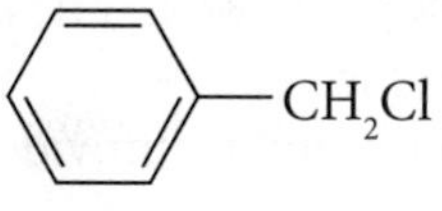

d. 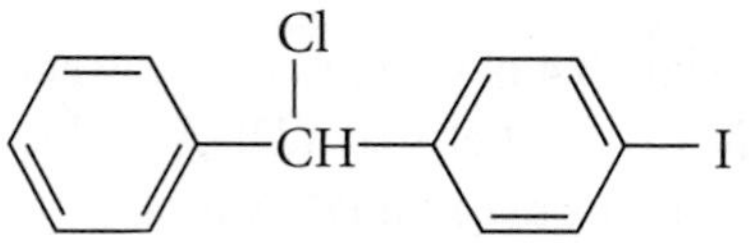 $C_6H_5-CH(Cl)-C_6H_4-I$

e. 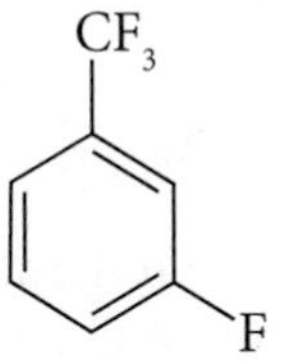 benzene ring with CF_3 and F (meta)

249. Write structural formulas for the organic product of these reactions.

a. $CH_2{=}CHCH_2CH_3 + Cl_2 \longrightarrow$

b. 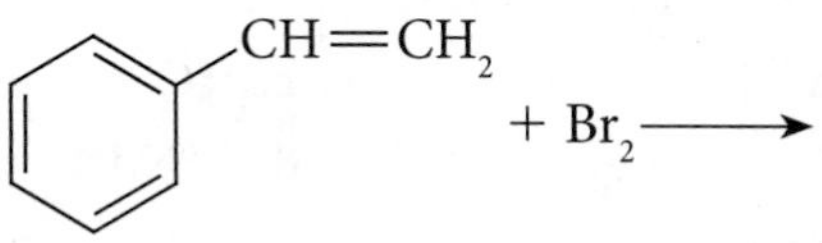 $C_6H_5-CH{=}CH_2 + Br_2 \longrightarrow$

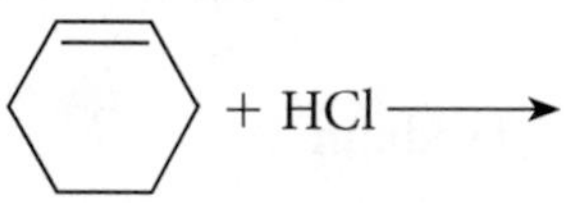

c. cyclohexene $+ HCl \longrightarrow$

d. 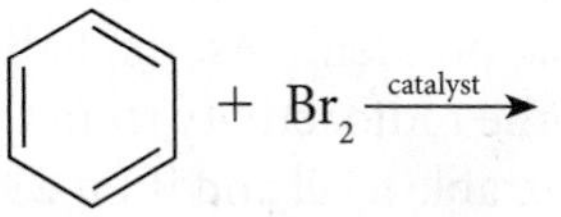 benzene $+ Br_2 \xrightarrow{\text{catalyst}}$

250. In each of these reactions, is the organic compound oxidized or reduced?

a. 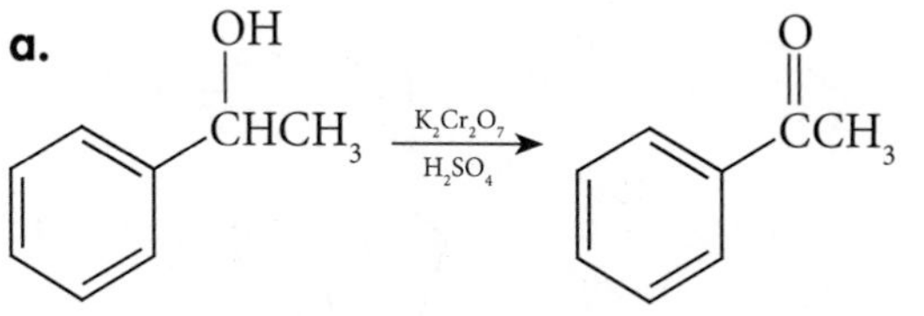 $C_6H_5-CH(OH)CH_3 \xrightarrow[H_2SO_4]{K_2Cr_2O_7} C_6H_5-C(=O)CH_3$

b. $CH_3CH_2CH_2CH_2CHO \xrightarrow{CuSO_4} CH_3CH_2CH_2CH_2CO_2H$

c. 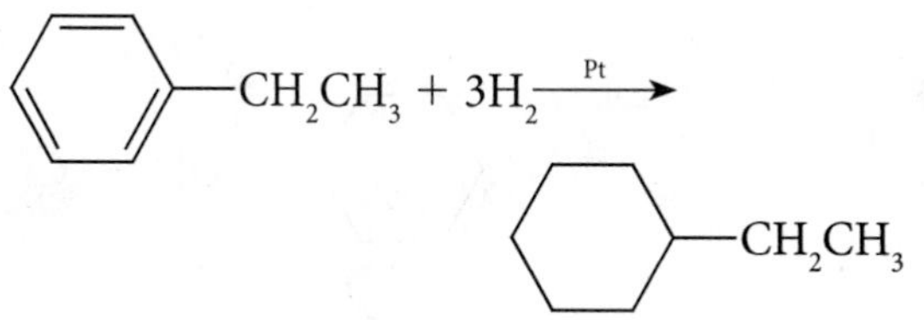 $C_6H_5-CH_2CH_3 + 3H_2 \xrightarrow{Pt} C_6H_{11}-CH_2CH_3$

d. $CH_4 + 2O_2 \longrightarrow CO_2 + 2H_2O$

251. How many liters of hydrogen gas at STP are required to saturate 0.150 mole of benzene?

252. Write complete equations for the following organic reactions. Be sure to include all reactants and catalysts required for the transformations.

a. 1-pentene to pentane

b. 2,3-dimethyl-2-butene to 2-chloro-2,3-dimethylbutane

c. ethane to chloroethane

253. A sample of benzaldehyde is oxidized to produce the crystalline white solid, benzoic acid. Write the structural formula of benzoic acid.

254. Classify each of these reactions as a hydration, hydrogenation, hydrolysis, or substitution.

a. $C_5H_9{-}CH_2Cl + KOH \xrightarrow[100°C]{H_2O} C_5H_9{-}CH_2OH + KCl$

b. $C_6H_{11}{-}\overset{O}{\overset{\|}{C}}OCH_3 + H_2O \xrightarrow{H^+} C_6H_{11}{-}\overset{O}{\overset{\|}{C}}OH + CH_3OH$

c. $C_6H_{10} + H_2O \xrightarrow[100°C]{H^+} C_6H_{11}{-}OH$

d. $C_6H_{11}{-}C{\equiv}CH + 2H_2 \xrightarrow{Pt} C_6H_{11}{-}CH_2CH_3$

Chapter 24

255. Saliva contains an enzyme called amylase, which catalyzes the breakdown of starch to its monomers. Suggest a reason why a piece of bread begins to taste sweet when it has been chewed for a short time.

256. Which of these statements apply to enzymes?

a. do not change position of equilibrium

b. catalyze biological reactions

c. bind substrates and sometimes cofactors at active sites

d. change position of equilibrium to favor products

e. are almost always nucleic acids

257. If one molecule of the enzyme catalase can break down 3.60×10^6 peroxide molecules in one minute, how many minutes would it take this enzyme molecule to break down 1 mole of peroxide? How many hours?

258. Sucrose, ordinary table sugar, has the molecular formula $C_{12}H_{22}O_{11}$.

a. What is the molar mass of sucrose?

b. What is the molarity of an aqueous solution containing 7.12 g/L of sucrose?

c. Write a balanced equation for the complete combustion of sucrose in air.

259. Walnuts, rich in fats and oils and with a chemical potential energy of 25.8 kJ/g, are a nutritious treat for many people. Suppose you eat 27.3 g of walnuts and then take a brisk walk. If you burn 3.76×10^2 kJ of kinetic energy for each kilometer you walk, how far will you need to walk to use up the energy provided by the walnuts?

260. There are 3.4 base pairs in every complete turn of the double helix in a DNA molecule. How many turns are in a DNA molecule that contains 5.0×10^8 base pairs?

Chapter 25

261. How do the mass number and the atomic number of radioactive atom A change if it first emits an alpha particle and the resulting atom then emits a beta particle to finally give atom C?

262. A radioactive atom undergoes beta decay to yield cesium-133. Write a balanced equation for this nuclear reaction.

263. Which nuclei would you predict to be stable? Explain your answer.

a. $^{9}_{3}Li$ **c.** $^{20}_{8}O$

b. $^{59}_{27}Co$ **d.** $^{146}_{60}Nd$

264. Write a balanced nuclear equation for the following:

a. beta decay of sodium-26

b. alpha decay of $^{234}_{92}U$

265. Plutonium-239 presents a serious nuclear waste disposal problem. If seven half-lives are required for the radioactivity from the waste to reach a tolerable level and if Pu-239 has a $t_{1/2} = 2.41 \times 10^4$ years, how long must the Pu-239 be stored?

Appendix D Selected Solutions

Chapter 1

23. $6\ \cancel{\text{blocks}} \times \frac{1\ \cancel{\text{mi}}}{10\ \cancel{\text{blocks}}} \times \frac{20\ \text{min}}{1\ \cancel{\text{mi}}} = 12\ \text{min}$

24. $48\ \cancel{\text{min}} \times \frac{1\ \cancel{\text{mi}}}{20\ \cancel{\text{min}}} \times \frac{10\ \text{blocks}}{1\ \cancel{\text{mi}}} = 24\ \text{blocks}$

32. Chemistry is concerned with the changes that matter undergoes.

34. A firefighter needs to know which chemicals to use to fight different types of fires; a knowledge of chemistry will help a reporter gather information during an interview with a chemist.

36. Scientists can study the composition of distant stars by analyzing the light they transmit to Earth.

37. The most powerful tool that any scientist can have is the scientific method.

39. c

41. Repeat the experiment. If you get the same result, you must propose a new hypothesis.

43. Good problem solvers do b, c, and d.

47. $1{,}000{,}000\ \cancel{\text{pennies}} \times \frac{1\ \cancel{\text{sec}}}{1\ \cancel{\text{penny}}} \times \frac{1\ \cancel{\text{min}}}{60\ \cancel{\text{sec}}} \times \frac{1\ \cancel{\text{h}}}{60\ \cancel{\text{min}}} \times \frac{1\ \text{day}}{24\ \cancel{\text{h}}} = 11.6\ \text{days (about 12 days)}$

48. Answers vary; possible answers: 1c, 2d, 3e, 4b, 5a

51. Method 1: Divide the weight of four beakers by 2; 2.0 lb/2 = 1.0 lb. Method 2: Multiply the weight of one beaker by 2; 0.5 lb × 2 = 1.0 lb. The answers are the same.

52. c; the 1 to 4 ratio of oxygen to nitrogen corresponds to the composition of air.

55. Possible answers are as follows: Factors: (1) PLA is made from natural resources; (2) producing PLA requires less energy than producing petroleum-based plastics; (3) compost facility availability. Factors (1) and (2) make PLA products a good choice, but factor (3) may make it difficult to choose PLA products.

Chapter 2

7. By lowering the temperature to below the boiling point of each gas, you could condense each substance and separate the gases.

14. Liquid A is probably a substance. Liquid B is a mixture because a solid remained after evaporation.

15. The liquid was not an element because a solid was left when the liquid evaporated. A physical process, such as evaporation, cannot be used to break down a compound. Therefore, the liquid was a mixture.

36. State; both are gases.

38. A vapor; the term *vapor* is used to refer to the gaseous state of a substance which normally exists as a liquid or solid at room temperature.

40. Sharpening a pencil is an irreversible change. Making ice cubes is a reversible change.

44. **a.** heterogeneous
b. homogeneous
c. depends on how well the batter is mixed
d. homogeneous
e. heterogeneous
f. homogeneous
g. heterogeneous

46. **a.** Sodium chloride (table salt) is a compound because it is made of two elements, sodium and chlorine.
b. Salt water is a mixture because it is made of two compounds, water (H_2O) and NaCl.
c. Sodium is an element because it is not combined with any other element.

49. The compound water contains two parts hydrogen to one part oxygen.

50. **a.** physical
b. chemical (color change)
c. physical

52. $40\ \text{g}\ NH_4NO_3 - 14\ \text{g N} - 8\ \text{g O} = 18\ \text{g}\ H_2O$

53. Mass is an extensive property, which depends only on the amount of matter in the sample, not on the composition of the sample.

55. The particles in solids are packed tightly together so it is difficult to compress them. The particles in a gas are spaced relatively far apart.

60. a. gas produced
b. formation of a precipitate
c. color and texture change
d. energy change, odor change
e. gas produced
f. color change, odor change

63. The wax appears to disappear because the products of the reaction—carbon dioxide and water vapor—are colorless gases.

66. Add sufficient water to dissolve all of the sugar. Separate the charcoal and sand from the sugar water by filtration. Large pieces of charcoal could be separated on the basis of color or size. Small pieces of charcoal could be burned.

69. Oxygen is most abundant element in the human body as well as in Earth's crust, oceans, and atmosphere. However, silicon, the second most abundant element in Earth's crust, is not abundant in the human body. Carbon, the second most abundant element in the human body, is not among the most abundant elements in Earth's crust.

Chapter 3

1. $\frac{8.4 \times 10^{-2}}{2.1 \times 10^{-6}} = \frac{8.4}{2.1} \times 10^{-2-(-6)} = 4.0 \times 10^{4}$

2. $(6.6 \times 10^{-8}) + (5.0 \times 10^{-9}) =$
$(6.6 \times 10^{-8}) + (0.5 \times 10^{-8}) =$
$(6.6 + 0.5) \times 10^{-8} = 7.1 \times 10^{-8}$

3. $(9.4 \times 10^{2}) - (2.1 \times 10^{2}) =$
$(9.4 - 2.1) \times 10^{2} = 7.3 \times 10^{2}$

4. Error = experimental value − accepted value = 2.04 m − 2.00 m = 0.04 m

$\%\ \text{error} = \frac{|\text{error}|}{\text{accepted value}} \times 100\% = \frac{|0.04\ \text{m}|}{2.00\ \text{m}} \times 100\%$
$= 2\%$

5. Error = experimental value − accepted value = 124.1°C − 125.7°C = −1.6°C

$\%\ \text{error} = \frac{|\text{error}|}{\text{accepted value}} \times 100\% = \frac{|-1.6°\text{C}|}{125.7°\text{C}} \times 100\%$
$= 1.3\%$

6. a. 4 b. 4

7. a. 2 b. 5

8. 4

9. a. 8.71×10^{1} m b. 4.36×10^{8} m

10. a. 1.6×10^{-2} m b. 9.0×10^{3} m

11. a. 9.44 m − 2.11 m = 7.33 m
b. 1.36 m + 10.17 m = 11.53 m

12. a. 61.2 m + 9.35 m + 8.6 m = 79.15 m = 79.2 m
b. 14.2 g + 8.73 g + 0.912 g = 23.842 g = 23.8 g

13. a. $8.3\ \text{m} \times 2.22\ \text{m} = 18.4\ \text{m}^2 = 18\ \text{m}^2 = 1.8 \times 10^{1}\ \text{m}^2$
b. $2.10\ \text{m} \times 0.70\ \text{m} = 1.47\ \text{m}^2 = 1.5\ \text{m}^2$
c. $0.365\ \text{m}^2 \div 0.0200\ \text{m} = 18.25\ \text{m} = 18.3\ \text{m}$

14. a. $8432\ \text{m}^2 \div 12.5\ \text{m} = 675\ \text{m} = 6.75 \times 10^{2}\ \text{m}$
b. $22.4\ \text{m} \times 11.3\ \text{m} \times 5.2\ \text{m} = 1316.2\ \text{m}^3$
$= 1.3 \times 10^{3}\ \text{m}^3$

22. mp: K = °C + 273 = 960.8 + 273 = 1234 K
bp: K = °C + 273 = 2212 + 273 = 2485 K

23. °C = K − 273 = 77.2 − 273 = −196°C

24. K = °C + 273 = −12 + 273 = 261 K
So, −12 °C is higher than 206 K.

25. $\text{Density} = \frac{\text{mass}}{\text{volume}} = \frac{68.0\ \text{g}}{6.48\ \text{cm}^3} = 10.5\ \text{g/cm}^3$

26. $\text{Density} = \frac{\text{mass}}{\text{volume}} = \frac{612\ \text{g}}{245\ \text{cm}^3} = 2.50\ \text{g/cm}^3$

No, because the density of aluminum is 2.70 g/cm^3

35. $570\ \cancel{\text{cm ribbon}} \times \frac{1\ \text{student}}{8.5\ \cancel{\text{cm ribbon}}} = 67\ \text{students}$

36. $5.00\ \cancel{\text{g Au}} \times \frac{1\ \text{atom Au}}{3.271 \times 10^{-22}\ \cancel{\text{g Au}}} = 1.53 \times 10^{22}\ \text{atoms Au}$

37. a. $15\ \cancel{\text{cm}^3} \times \frac{1\ \text{L}}{10^3\ \cancel{\text{cm}^3}} = 0.015\ \text{L} = 1.5 \times 10^{-2}\ \text{L}$

b. $7.38\ \cancel{\text{g}} \times \frac{1\ \text{kg}}{10^3\ \cancel{\text{g}}} = 7.38 \times 10^{-3}\ \text{kg}$

38. $7.3 \times 10^{-2}\ \cancel{\text{cm}} \times \frac{1\ \cancel{\text{m}}}{10^2\ \cancel{\text{cm}}} \times \frac{10^6\ \mu\text{m}}{1\ \cancel{\text{m}}}$
$= 7.3 \times 10^{-2-2+6}\ \mu\text{m} = 7.3 \times 10^{2}\ \mu\text{m}$

39. $14.8\ \cancel{\text{g B}} \times \frac{1\ \text{cm}^3}{2.34\ \cancel{\text{g B}}} = 6.32\ \text{cm}^3$

40. $4.62\ \cancel{\text{g Hg}} \times \frac{1\ \text{cm}^3}{13.5\ \cancel{\text{g Hg}}} = 0.342\ \text{cm}^3 = 3.42 \times 10^{-1}\ \text{cm}^3$

41. (39) $\text{Volume} = \frac{\text{mass}}{\text{density}} = \frac{14.8\ \cancel{\text{g B}}}{2.34\ \cancel{\text{g B}}/\text{cm}^3} = 6.32\ \text{cm}^3$

(40) $\text{Volume} = \frac{\text{mass}}{\text{density}} = \frac{4.62\ \cancel{\text{g Hg}}}{13.5\ \cancel{\text{g Hg}}/\text{cm}^3}$
$= 0.342\ \text{cm}^3 = 3.42 \times 10^{-1}\ \text{cm}^3$

50. a. 43 g c. 225.8 L
b. 7.3 cm^2 d. 92.0 m

53. nm, μm, mm, cm, dm, m, km;
$1\text{ nm} = 10^{-9}\text{ m}$, $1\ \mu\text{m} = 10^{-6}\text{ m}$, $1\text{ mm} = 10^{-3}\text{ m}$,
$1\text{ cm} = 10^{-2}\text{ m}$, $1\text{ dm} = 10^{-1}\text{ m}$, $1\text{ km} = 10^{3}\text{ m}$

56. $\text{Density} = \frac{\text{mass}}{\text{volume}} = \frac{57.3\text{ g}}{4.7\text{ cm}^3} = 12\text{ g/cm}^3$

No; the density of the metal bar is 12 g/cm^3, but the density of gold is 19 g/cm^3.

59. **a.** $157\text{ s} \times \frac{1\text{ min}}{60\text{ s}} = 2.62\text{ min}$

b. $42.7\text{ L} \times \frac{10^3\text{ mL}}{1\text{ L}} = 42{,}700\text{ mL} = 4.27 \times 10^4\text{ mL}$

c. $261\text{ nm} \times \frac{1\text{ m}}{10^9\text{ nm}} \times \frac{10^3\text{ mm}}{1\text{ m}} = 261 \times 10^{3-9}\text{ mm}$

$= 261 \times 10^{-6}\text{ mm} = 2.61 \times 10^{-4}\text{ mm}$

d. $0.065\text{ km} \times \frac{10^3\text{ m}}{1\text{ km}} \times \frac{10\text{ dm}}{1\text{ m}} = 650\text{ dm} =$

$6.5 \times 10^2\text{ dm}$

60. **a.** $\frac{0.44\text{ mL}}{1\text{min}} \times \frac{1\text{ L}}{10^3\text{ mL}} \times \frac{10^6\ \mu\text{L}}{1\text{ L}} \times \frac{1\text{ min}}{60\text{s}}$

$= (7.3 \times 10^{-3}) \times 10^3\ \mu\text{L/s} = 7.3\ \mu\text{L/s}$

b. $\frac{7.86\text{ g}}{1\text{ cm}^2} \times \frac{10^4\text{ cm}^2}{1\text{ m}^2} \times \frac{1\text{ m}^2}{10^6\text{ mm}^2} \times \frac{10^3\text{ mg}}{1\text{ g}}$

$= 7.86 \times 10^1\text{ mg/mm}^2 = 78.6\text{ mg/mm}^2$

c. $\frac{1.54\text{ kg}}{\text{L}} \times \frac{10^3\text{g}}{1\text{ kg}} \times \frac{1\text{ L}}{10^3\text{ mL}} \times \frac{1\text{ mL}}{1\text{ cm}^3} = 1.54\text{ g/cm}^3$

62. **a.** $28.3\text{ cg} \times \frac{1\text{ g}}{10^2\text{ cg}} \times \frac{10^3\text{ mg}}{\text{g}} = 283\text{ mg}$

b. $283\text{ mg} \times \frac{1\text{ g}}{10^3\text{ mg}} = 0.283\text{ g}$

c. $0.283\text{ g} \times \frac{1\text{ kg}}{10^3\text{ g}} = 0.000283\text{ kg}$

d. $6.6 \times 10^3\text{ mg} \times \frac{1\text{ g}}{10^3\text{ mg}} = 6.6\text{ g}$

e. $6.6\text{ g} \times \frac{10^2\text{ cg}}{1\text{ g}} = 660\text{ cg} = 6.6 \times 10^2\text{ cg}$

f. $6.6\text{ g} \times \frac{1\text{ kg}}{10^3\text{ g}} = 6.6 \times 10^{-3}\text{ kg}$

g. $2.8 \times 10^{-4}\text{ g} \times \frac{10^3\text{ mg}}{\text{g}} = 2.8 \times 10^{-1}\text{ mg}$

h. $2.8 \times 10^{-4}\text{ g} \times \frac{10^2\text{ cg}}{\text{g}} = 2.8 \times 10^{-2}\text{ cg}$

i. $2.8 \times 10^{-4}\text{ g} \times \frac{1\text{ kg}}{10^3\text{ g}} = 2.8 \times 10^{-7}\text{ kg}$

66. $125\text{ kg coal} \times \frac{1.30\text{ kg C}}{2.00\text{ kg coal}} = 81.25\text{ kg C} = 81.3\text{ kg C}$

67. $50.0\text{ g air} \times \frac{1\text{ cm}^3\text{ air}}{1.19 \times 10^{-3}\text{ g air}} = 42.0 \times 10^3\text{ cm}^3\text{ air}$

$= 4.20 \times 10^4\text{ cm}^3\text{ air}$

68. $\frac{0.15\text{ s}}{1\text{ min}} \times \frac{60\text{ min}}{1\text{h}} \times \frac{24\text{ h}}{1\text{ day}} \times \frac{1\text{ min}}{60\text{ s}}$

$= 0.15 \times 24\text{ min/day} = 3.6\text{ min/day lost}$

69. $1.5 \times 10^8\text{ km} \times \frac{10^3\text{ m}}{1\text{ km}} \times \frac{1\text{ s}}{3.0 \times 10^8\text{ m}} \times \frac{1\text{ min}}{60\text{ s}}$

$= 8.3\text{ min}$

70. $V = 28.6\text{ cm} \times (73.0 \times 10^{-1}\text{ cm}) \times (0.72 \times 10^2\text{ cm})$
$= 1.50 \times 10^4\text{ cm}^3$

$\text{Density} = \frac{\text{mass}}{\text{volume}} =$
$\frac{1.38 \times 10^4\text{ g}}{1.50 \times 10^4\text{ cm}^3} \times \frac{1\text{ kg}}{10^3\text{ g}} \times \frac{10^3\text{ cm}^3}{1\text{ L}} = 0.92\text{ kg/L}$

71. $\text{Mass}_{\text{amalgam}} = 26.0\text{ g} + 10.8\text{ g} + 2.4\text{ g} + 0.8\text{ g} = 40.0\text{ g}$

$25.0\text{ g amalgam} \times \frac{26.0\text{ g Ag}}{40.0\text{ g amalgam}} = 16.3\text{ g Ag}$

76. $\frac{112\text{ km}}{1\text{ hr}} \times \frac{10^3\text{ m}}{1\text{ km}} \times \frac{1\text{ hr}}{60\text{ min}} \times \frac{1\text{ min}}{60\text{ s}} =$

$0.0311 \times 10^3\text{ m/s} = 31.1\text{ m/s}$

Chapter 4

18. **a.** 9 protons and 9 electrons
b. 20 protons and 20 electrons
c. 13 protons and 13 electrons
d. 19 protons and 19 electrons

19. **a.** 35 **b.** 16 **c.** 16 **d.** 23
e. 23 **f.** B **g.** 5 **h.** 5

20. **a.** 35 protons and 35 electrons
number of neutrons = mass number − atomic number = 80 − 35 = 45 neutrons

b. 16 protons and 16 electrons
number of neutrons = mass number − atomic number = 32 − 16 = 16 neutrons

21. **a.** 47 electrons;
number of neutrons = mass number − atomic number = 108 − 47 = 61 neutrons

b. 82 electrons;
number of neutrons = mass number − atomic number = 207 − 82 = 125 neutrons

22. a. $^{12}_{6}C$ b. $^{11}_{5}B$ c. $^{9}_{4}Be$ d. $^{16}_{8}O$

23. $^{16}_{8}O$, $^{17}_{8}O$, $^{18}_{8}O$

24. $^{1}_{1}H$, $^{2}_{1}H$, $^{3}_{1}H$

25. number of neutrons = mass number − atomic number = 50 − 24 = 26; chromium-50 has 26 neutrons. Symbol: $^{50}_{24}Cr$.

number of neutrons = mass number − atomic number = 52 − 24 = 28; chromium-52 has 28 neutrons. Symbol: $^{52}_{24}Cr$.

number of neutrons = mass number − atomic number = 53 − 24 = 29; chromium-53 has 29 neutrons. Symbol: $^{53}_{24}Cr$.

26. for ^{63}Cu: 62.93 amu × 0.692 = 43.5 amu
for ^{65}Cu: 64.93 amu × 0.308 = 20.0 amu
atomic mass = 43.5 amu + 20.0 amu = 63.5 amu

27. for ^{79}Br: 78.92 amu × 0.5069 = 40.00 amu
for ^{81}Br: 80.92 amu × 0.4931 = 39.90 amu
atomic mass = 40.00 amu + 39.90 amu = 79.90 amu

28. Gallium's atomic mass (69.723 amu) is closer to 69 than it is to 71, so gallium-69 is more abundant than gallium-70.

42. repel (like charges repel each other)

46. He did not expect alpha particles to be deflected at a large angle.

53. a. 19 b. 9 c. 14 d. 29
e. 22 f. 22 g. 25 h. 30

55. for ^{6}Li: 6.015 amu × 0.075 = 0.45 amu
for ^{7}Li: 7.016 amu × 0.925 = 6.49 amu
atomic mass = 0.45 amu + 6.49 amu = 6.94 amu

56. because of the existence of isotopes

59. 5 protons and 6 neutrons in the nucleus; 5 electrons outside the nucleus

61. $[(82 + 122) \times 0.014] + [(82 + 124) \times 0.241] + [(82 + 125) \times 0.221] + [(82 + 126) \times 0.524] = 207$ amu

67. $6.941 = [6.015 \times (1 - A)] + (7.016 \times A)$
$6.941 = 6.015 - 6.015A + 7.016A$
$6.941 - 6.015 = 7.016A - 6.015A$

$$A = \frac{0.926}{1.001} = 0.925 = 92.5\%$$

75. 54 g H_2O − 6 g H_2 = 48 g O_2

76. $4.42\ \cancel{cm^3} \times \frac{22.5\text{ g Pt}}{1\ \cancel{cm^3}} = 99.5$ g Pt

Chapter 5

9. a. $1s^2 2s^2 2p^2$
b. $1s^2 2s^2 2p^1$

10. a. $1s^2 2s^2 2p^6 3s^2 3p^2$; 2 unpaired electrons
b. $1s^2 2s^2 2p^6 3s^2 3p^4$; 2 unpaired electrons

11. a. $1s^2 2s^2 2p^6 3s^2 3p^6$; 0 unpaired electrons
b. $1s^2 2s^2 2p^6 3s^2 3p^6 4s^2$; 0 unpaired electrons

12. $1s^2 2s^2 2p^6 3s^2 3p^6 3d^{10} 4s^2 4p^6$

20. $\lambda = \frac{c}{\nu} = \frac{2.998 \times 10^8\ \text{m}/\cancel{s}}{1.50 \times 10^{13}/\cancel{s}} = 2.00 \times 10^{-5}$m; longer wavelength than red light

21. $\nu = \frac{c}{\lambda} = \frac{2.998 \times 10^8\ \cancel{m}/\text{s}}{5.00 \times 10^{-8}\ \cancel{m}} = 6.00 \times 10^{15}$/s; ultraviolet

22. $E = h\nu = (6.626 \times 10^{-34}\ \text{J}\cdot\cancel{s}) \times (5.00 \times 10^{11}/\cancel{s}) = 3.31 \times 10^{-22}$ J

23. $\nu = \frac{c}{\lambda} = \frac{2.998 \times 10^8\ \cancel{m}/\text{s}}{260\ \cancel{nm}} \times \frac{10^9\ \cancel{nm}}{1\ \cancel{m}} = 1.15 \times 10^{15}/\text{s}$

$E = h\nu = (6.626 \times 10^{-34}\ \text{J}\cdot\cancel{s}) \times (1.15 \times 10^{15}/\cancel{s}) = 7.6 \times 10^{-19}$ J

39. The 2*p* sublevel contains three orbitals: $2p_x$, $2p_y$, $2p_z$.

40. a. 1 (1*s*) c. 3 (3*s*, 3*p*, 3*d*)
b. 2 (2*s*, 2*p*) d. 4 (4*s*, 4*p*, 4*d*, 4*f*)

41. Aufbau principle: Electrons occupy the lowest possible energy levels. Pauli Exclusion Principle: An atomic orbital can hold at most two electrons. Hund's Rule: One electron occupies each of a set of orbitals with equal energies before any pairing of electrons occurs.

42. 2*s*, 3*p*, 4*s*, 3*d*

43. a. valid b. invalid c. invalid d. valid

45. The *p* orbitals in the third quantum level have three electrons.

48. a. 2 b. 3 c. 1 d. 6

53. a. radio wave, microwave, infrared, visible, ultraviolet, X-ray
b. It is the reverse.

56. $1s^2 2s^2 2p^6 3s^2 3p^6 3d^{10} 4s^2 4p^3$; $n = 1$, 2 electrons; $n = 2$, 8 electrons; $n = 3$, 18 electrons; $n = 4$, 5 electrons; the fourth energy level ($n = 4$) is not filled.

57. a. Na, sodium (11 electrons)
b. N, nitrogen (7 electrons)
c. Ti, titanium (22 electrons)

59. a. ultraviolet

b. $\nu = \frac{c}{\lambda} = \frac{2.998 \times 10^8 \text{ m/s}}{4.36 \times 10^{-7} \text{ m}} = 6.88 \times 10^{14}/\text{s}$

61. According to the Bohr model, an orbit confines the electron to a fixed circular path around the nucleus. According to the quantum mechanical model, an orbital is a region around the nucleus in which electrons are likely to be found.

63. Two magnets would push each other apart. In the same way, electrons with the same spin would push apart and be unable to occupy the same orbital.

66. The light emitted from an incandescent bulb has wavelengths from about 400 nm to 700 nm, which corresponds to a frequency range of about $4 \times 10^{14}\ \text{s}^{-1}$ to $8 \times 10^{14}\ \text{s}^{-1}$:

$$\nu = \frac{c}{\lambda} = \frac{2.998 \times 10^8 \text{ m/s}}{700 \text{ nm}} \times \frac{10^9 \text{ nm}}{1 \text{ m}} = 4 \times 10^{14}\ \text{s}^{-1}$$

$$\nu = \frac{c}{\lambda} = \frac{2.998 \times 10^8 \text{ m/s}}{400 \text{ nm}} \times \frac{10^9 \text{ nm}}{1 \text{ m}} = 8 \times 10^{14}\ \text{s}^{-1}$$

This means that the energy absorbed by the photons is in the range of about 3×10^{-19} J to 5×10^{-19} J:

$E = h\nu = (6.626 \times 10^{-34}\ \text{J}\cdot\text{s}) \times (4 \times 10^{14}/\text{s})$
$= 3 \times 10^{-19}\ \text{J}$

$E = h\nu = (6.626 \times 10^{-34}\ \text{J}\cdot\text{s}) \times (8 \times 10^{14}/\text{s})$
$= 5 \times 10^{-19}\ \text{J}$

70. Volume of copper = 24.08 mL − 20.00 mL = 4.08 mL = 4.08 cm^3

$$\text{Density of copper} = \frac{\text{mass}}{\text{volume}} = \frac{36.4 \text{ g}}{4.08 \text{ cm}^3} = 8.92 \text{ g/cm}^3$$

71. $\text{mass of lead} = 28.0 \text{ cm}^3 \times \frac{11.3 \text{ g}}{1 \text{ cm}^3} = 316 \text{ g}$

$\text{mass of gold} = 16.0 \text{ cm}^3 \times \frac{19.3 \text{ g}}{1 \text{ cm}^3} = 309 \text{ g}$

The piece of lead has more mass.

Chapter 6

26. The close match between the predicted properties and the actual properties of gallium helped gain wider acceptance for Mendeleev's periodic table.

35. a. sodium c. germanium
b. strontium d. selenium

38. The ionic radius of a metal cation is smaller than the atomic radius of the metal atom.

40. a. O b. F c. O d. S

43. b; nitrogen and phosphorus are in the same group (Group 5A).

49. Zinc has a greater nuclear charge (more protons) than calcium.

58. a. physical change c. physical change
b. chemical change d. chemical change

64. a. none b. three c. one d. none

Chapter 7

10. In order to have a completely filled valence shell, the iodine atom must gain 1 electron. This electron comes from 1 potassium atom, which loses 1 electron. The formula is KI.

11. In order to have a completely filled valence shell, the fluorine atom must gain 1 electron. This electron comes from 1 lithium atom, which loses 1 electron. The formula is LiF.

12. A calcium atom loses 2 valence electrons to form a Ca^{2+} cation. A chlorine atom gains 1 electron to form a Cl^- anion. The formula of the compound that forms is $CaCl_2$.

13. Each oxygen atom needs 2 electrons to have an octet, but each aluminum atom loses 3 electrons, so 2 aluminum atoms are needed for every 3 oxygen atoms. The formula is Al_2O_3.

30. a. Group 5A; 5 valence electrons
b. Group 1A; 1 valence electron
c. Group 5A; 5 valence electrons
d. Group 2A; 2 valence electrons
e. Group 7A; 7 valence electrons
f. Group 4A; 4 valence electrons

33. a. 2; a calcium atom has 2 valence electrons, which it can lose.
b. 3; an aluminum atom has 3 valence electrons, which it can lose.
c. 1; a lithium atom has 1 valence electron, which it can lose.
d. 2; a barium atom has 2 valence electrons, which it can lose.

35. a. 3; a nitrogen atom has 5 valence electrons. It achieves an octet by gaining 3 electrons.
b. 2; a sulfur atom has 6 valence electrons. It achieves an octet by gaining 2 electrons.
c. 1; a chlorine atom has 7 valence electrons. It achieves an octet by gaining 1 electron.
d. 3; a phosphorus atom has 5 valence electrons. It achieves an octet by gaining 3 electrons.

36. **a.** A sulfur atom has 6 valence electrons and gains 2 electrons to attain a noble-gas configuration. The formula of the ion formed is S^{2-}.

b. A sodium atom has 1 valence electron and loses 1 electron to attain a noble-gas configuration. The formula of the ion formed is Na^{+}.

c. A fluorine atom has 7 valence electrons and gains 1 electron to attain a noble-gas configuration. The formula of the ion formed is F^{-}.

d. A phosphorus atom has 5 valence electrons and gains 3 electrons to attain a noble-gas configuration. The formula of the ion formed is P^{3-}.

39. a, c, e (ionic compounds form between atoms of metals and nonmetals)

41. **a.** Ca^{2+}, F^{-} **b.** Al^{3+}, Br^{-} **c.** Li^{+}, O^{2-} **d.** Al^{3+}, S^{2-} **e.** K^{+}, N^{3-}

45. Atoms in metals are arranged in a compact and orderly manner.

47. body-centered cubic: Na, K, Fe, Cr, or W; face-centered cubic: Cu, Ag, Au, Al, or Pb; hexagonal close-packed: Mg, Zn, or Cd

50. It has lost valence electrons.

52. **a.** sulfide ion (anion), S^{2-}

b. aluminum ion (cation), Al^{3+}

c. nitride ion (anion), N^{3-}

d. calcium ion (cation), Ca^{2+}

53. All have the noble-gas configuration of $1s^2 2s^2 2p^6 3s^2 3p^6$.

55. a, c, e, f (these substances are not composed of metals and nonmetals)

57. Each dot in the electron dot structure represents a valence electron in the electron configuration diagram.

59. Both metals and ionic compounds are composed of ions. Both are held together by electrostatic attractions. Metals always conduct an electric current, and ionic compounds conduct an electric current only when melted or dissolved in water. Ionic compounds are composed of cations and anions, but metals are composed of cations and free-floating valence electrons. Metals are ductile, but ionic compounds are brittle.

62. The charge on the copper cation is 2+. Its electron configuration is $1s^2 2s^2 2p^6 3s^2 3p^6 3d^9$.

65. **a.** liquid, vapor **b.** vapor **c.** liquid, vapor **d.** liquid, vapor

66. **a.** chemical **b.** chemical **c.** physical **d.** chemical

69. **a.** 1 **b.** 3 **c.** 1 **d.** 5

70. **a.** $500\ \cancel{nm} \times \frac{1\ m}{10^9\ \cancel{nm}} = 5 \times 10^{-7}\ m$ **b.** visible

71. **a.** K, $1s^2 2s^2 2p^6 3s^2 3p^6 4s^1$

b. Al, $1s^2 2s^2 2p^6 3s^2 3p^1$

c. S, $1s^2 2s^2 2p^6 3s^2 3p^4$

d. Ba, $1s^2 2s^2 2p^6 3s^2 3p^6 3d^{10} 4s^2 4p^6 4d^{10} 5s^2 5p^6 6s^2$

Chapter 8

9. $:\ddot{\underset{..}{Cl}}:\ddot{\underset{..}{Cl}}:$

10. $H:\ddot{\underset{..}{O}}:\ddot{\underset{..}{O}}:H$

11. $[H:\ddot{\underset{..}{O}}:]^{-}$

12. $\left[\begin{array}{c} :\ddot{O}: \\ :\ddot{\underset{..}{O}}:\ddot{S}:\ddot{\underset{..}{O}}: \\ :\underset{..}{O}: \end{array}\right]^{2-}$

29. **a.** 0.7; moderately polar covalent

b. 2.2; ionic

c. 1.0; moderately to very polar covalent

d. 1.0; moderately to very polar covalent

e. 2.5; ionic

f. 0; nonpolar covalent

30. c and d (tie at 0.4), b (0.7), a (0.9)

48. One atom contributes both electrons in a coordinate covalent bond, as in carbon monoxide (CO).

51. b and c; the P and S atoms each have 10 valence electrons.

54. **a.** $\begin{array}{c} H:\ddot{N}:H \\ H \end{array}$ **b.** $:\ddot{\underset{..}{Br}}:\ddot{\underset{..}{Cl}}:$ **c.** $H:\ddot{\underset{..}{O}}:\ddot{\underset{..}{O}}:H$ **d.** $\begin{array}{c} H \\ H:\underset{..}{\ddot{Si}}:H \\ H \end{array}$

55. **a.** linear **b.** tetrahedral **c.** trigonal planar **d.** bent **e.** linear **f.** bent

64. Ethyl alcohol can form intermolecular hydrogen bonds between its polar —OH groups, but dimethyl ether cannot form hydrogen bonds.

66. **a.** bent **b.** tetrahedral **c.** pyramidal

72. **a.** $66.5\ \cancel{mm} \times \frac{1\ \cancel{m}}{10^3\ \cancel{mm}} \times \frac{10^6\ \mu m}{1\ \cancel{m}} = 6.65 \times 10^4\ \mu m$

b. $4 \times 10^{-2}\ \cancel{g} \times \frac{100\ cg}{1\ \cancel{g}} = 4\ cg$

c. $\frac{5.62\ \cancel{mg}}{1\ \cancel{mL}} \times \frac{1\ \cancel{g}}{10^3\ \cancel{mg}} \times \frac{10\ dg}{1\ \cancel{g}} \times \frac{10^3\ \cancel{mL}}{1\ L} = 56.2\ dg/L$

d. $\frac{85\ \cancel{km}}{1\ \cancel{h}} \times \frac{1\ \cancel{h}}{60\ \cancel{min}} \times \frac{1\ \cancel{min}}{60\ s} \times \frac{10^3\ m}{1\ \cancel{km}} = 24\ m/s$

76. **a.** barium **b.** silicon **c.** sodium

78. All have the same number of electrons as a noble gas.

Chapter 9

1. **a.** selenide ion **b.** phosphide ion **c.** barium ion **d.** iodide ion

2. **a.** three electrons lost **b.** two electrons gained **c.** one electron lost **d.** two electrons lost

3. lead(IV) ion (or plumbic ion)

11. **a.** BaS **b.** Li_2O **c.** Ca_3N_2 **d.** CuI_2

12. **a.** NaI **b.** K_2S

13. **a.** $SnCl_2$ **b.** CaI_2

14. **a.** Incorrect; anion symbol should be listed second. The correct formula is Rb_3As.

b. Incorrect; charges are not balanced. The correct formula is $BeCl_2$.

15. **a.** zinc sulfide **b.** potassium chloride **c.** barium oxide **d.** aluminum fluoride

16. **a.** calcium oxide **b.** copper(I) selenide **c.** iron(II) sulfide **d.** copper(II) bromide

17. **a.** Na_2SO_3 **b.** $Ca_3(PO_4)_2$

18. **a.** $LiHSO_4$ **b.** $Cr(NO_2)_3$

19. The charges are not balanced. The correct formula is $MgSO_4$.

20. **a.** calcium oxalate

b. potassium hypochlorite

c. potassium permanganate

d. lithium sulfite

21. **a.** aluminum hydroxide **b.** sodium chlorate **c.** tin(II) phosphate **d.** sodium chromate

22. The ionic charge of lead must be given by a Roman numeral.

30. **a.** oxygen difluoride **b.** disulfur decafluoride **c.** sulfur trioxide **d.** sulfur hexafluoride

31. No; the prefix *mono-* should not be used with the first element in the formula. The correct name is silicon tetrachloride.

38. **a.** hydrofluoric acid

b. nitric acid

c. sulfurous acid

39. **a.** $HClO_4$ **b.** HI **c.** $HClO_2$

40. **a.** barium hydroxide

b. calcium hydroxide

c. iron(II) hydroxide

41. **a.** CsOH **b.** $Be(OH)_2$ **c.** $Mn(OH)_3$

56. **a.** 2+ **b.** 2+ **c.** 3+ **d.** 1+

60. Determine the charge of the anion, and then work the formula backward to find the charge of the transition metal cation needed to give a net charge of zero for the formula unit.

65. **a.** tri- **b.** mono- **c.** di- **d.** hexa- **e.** penta- **f.** tetra-

69. **a.** lead(II) hydroxide **b.** cobalt(II) hydroxide **c.** $Cu(OH)_2$ **d.** $Fe(OH)_2$

72. No, the ratio of nitrogen to oxygen is 42:26, which is not a 7:4 ratio.

77. binary molecular compound

78. $SnCl_4$

81. **a.** N_2O, dinitrogen monoxide

b. NO_2, nitrogen dioxide

c. NO, nitrogen monoxide

d. N_2O_4, dinitrogen tetroxide

82. **a.** The charges do not balance; CsCl.

b. Neon does not form compounds.

c. The charges do not balance; ZnO.

d. The subscripts are not the lowest whole-number ratio; BaS.

87. ionic; $Ca(OH)_2$

91. **a.** 2 **b.** protons **c.** electrons **d.** neutrons

92. **a.** neon **b.** carbon **c.** boron **d.** helium

93. **a.** 1 **b.** 6 **c.** 8 **d.** 2

95. b and c; molecular compounds formed by two nonmetals have covalent bonds.

Chapter 10

1. $$1.14\ \cancel{\text{mol } SO_3} \times \frac{6.02 \times 10^{23}\ \text{molecules } SO_3}{1\ \cancel{\text{mol } SO_3}} = 6.86 \times 10^{23}\ \text{molecules}$$

$$1.14\ \cancel{\text{mol } SO_3} \times \frac{6.02 \times 10^{23}\ \cancel{\text{molecules } SO_3}}{1\ \cancel{\text{mol } SO_3}} \times \frac{4\ \text{atoms}}{1\ \cancel{\text{molecule } SO_3}} = 2.75 \times 10^{24}\ \text{atoms}$$

2. $$2.80 \times 10^{24}\ \cancel{\text{atoms Si}} \times \frac{1\ \text{mol Si}}{6.02 \times 10^{23} \times \cancel{\text{atoms Si}}} = 4.65\ \text{mol Si}$$

3. $$2.17 \times 10^{23}\ \cancel{\text{molecules } Br_2} \times \frac{1\ \text{mol } Br_2}{6.02 \times 10^{23}\ \cancel{\text{molecules } Br_2}} = 0.360\ \text{mol } Br_2$$

4. $2.12\ \cancel{\text{mol } C_3H_8} \times \dfrac{6.02 \times 10^{23}\ \cancel{\text{molecules } C_3H_8}}{1\ \cancel{\text{mol } C_3H_8}} \times \dfrac{3\text{ C atoms}}{1\ \cancel{\text{molecule } C_3H_8}} = 3.83 \times 10^{24}\text{ C atoms}$

$2.12\ \cancel{\text{mol } C_3H_8} \times \dfrac{6.02 \times 10^{23}\ \cancel{\text{molecules } C_3H_8}}{1\ \cancel{\text{mol } C_3H_8}} \times \dfrac{8\text{ H atoms}}{1\ \cancel{\text{molecule } C_3H_8}} = 1.02 \times 10^{25}\text{ H atoms}$

5. $1\ \cancel{\text{mol P}} \times \dfrac{31.0\text{ g P}}{1\ \cancel{\text{mol P}}} = 31.0\text{ g P}$

$3\ \cancel{\text{mol Cl}} \times \dfrac{35.5\text{ g Cl}}{1\ \cancel{\text{mol Cl}}} = 106.5\text{ g Cl}$

mass of 1 mol PCl_3 = 31.0 g P + 106.5 g Cl = 137.5 g

molar mass of PCl_3 = 137.5 g/mol

6. $12\ \cancel{\text{mol C}} \times \dfrac{12.0\text{ g C}}{1\ \cancel{\text{mol C}}} = 144.0\text{ g C}$

$22\ \cancel{\text{mol H}} \times \dfrac{1.0\text{ g H}}{1\ \cancel{\text{mol H}}} = 22.0\text{ g H}$

$11\ \cancel{\text{mol O}} \times \dfrac{16.0\text{ g O}}{1\ \cancel{\text{mol O}}} = 176.0\text{ g O}$

mass of 1.00 mol $C_{12}H_{22}O_{11}$ = 144.0 g C + 22.0 g H + 176.0 g O = 342.0 g

7. $1\ \cancel{\text{mol Na}} \times \dfrac{23.0\text{ g Na}}{1\ \cancel{\text{mol Na}}} = 23.0\text{ g Na}$

$1\ \cancel{\text{mol H}} \times \dfrac{1.0\text{ g H}}{1\ \cancel{\text{mol H}}} = 1.0\text{ g H}$

$1\ \cancel{\text{mol C}} \times \dfrac{12.0\text{ g C}}{1\ \cancel{\text{mol C}}} = 12.0\text{ g C}$

$3\ \cancel{\text{mol O}} \times \dfrac{16.0\text{ g O}}{1\ \cancel{\text{mol O}}} = 48.0\text{ g O}$

mass of 1.00 mol $NaHCO_3$ = 23.0 g Na + 1.0 g H + 12.0 g C + 48.0 g O = 84.0 g

16. $1\ \cancel{\text{mol Fe}} \times \dfrac{55.8\text{ g Fe}}{1\ \cancel{\text{mol Fe}}} = 55.8\text{ g Fe}$

$2\ \cancel{\text{mol O}} \times \dfrac{16.0\text{ g O}}{1\ \cancel{\text{mol O}}} = 32.0\text{ g O}$

$2\ \cancel{\text{mol H}} \times \dfrac{1.0\text{ g H}}{1\ \cancel{\text{mol H}}} = 2.0\text{ g H}$

1 mol $Fe(OH)_2$ = 55.8 g Fe + 32.0 g O + 2.0 g H = 89.8 g $Fe(OH)_2$

$2.50\ \cancel{\text{mol } Fe(OH)_2} \times \dfrac{89.8\text{ g } Fe(OH)_2}{1\ \cancel{\text{mol } Fe(OH)_2}} = 225\text{ g } Fe(OH)_2$

17. $20\ \cancel{\text{mol C}} \times \dfrac{12.0\text{ g C}}{1\ \cancel{\text{mol C}}} = 240.0\text{ g C}$

$42\ \cancel{\text{mol H}} \times \dfrac{1.0\text{ g H}}{1\ \cancel{\text{mol H}}} = 42.0\text{ g H}$

1 mol $C_{20}H_{42}$ = 240.0 g C + 42.0 g H = 282.0 g $C_{20}H_{42}$

$4.52 \times 10^{-3}\ \cancel{\text{mol } C_{20}H_{42}} \times \dfrac{282.0\text{ g } C_{20}H_{42}}{1\ \cancel{\text{mol } C_{20}H_{42}}} = 1.27\text{ g } C_{20}H_{42}$

18. molar mass of $C_{12}H_{22}O_{11}$ = 342.0 g/mol (from Problem 6)

$3.75\ \cancel{\text{mol } C_{12}H_{22}O_{11}} \times \dfrac{342.0\text{ g } C_{12}H_{22}O_{11}}{1\ \cancel{\text{mol } C_{12}H_{22}O_{11}}} = 1.28 \times 10^3\text{ g } C_{12}H_{22}O_{11}$

19. $3.70 \times 10^{-1}\ \cancel{\text{g B}} \times \dfrac{1\text{ mol B}}{10.8\ \cancel{\text{g B}}} = 3.43 \times 10^{-2}\text{ mol B}$

20. $2\ \cancel{\text{mol H}} \times \dfrac{1.0\text{ g H}}{1\ \cancel{\text{mol H}}} = 2.0\text{ g H}$

$2\ \cancel{\text{mol O}} \times \dfrac{16.0\text{ g O}}{1\ \cancel{\text{mol O}}} = 32.0\text{ g O}$

1 mol H_2O_2 = 2.0 g H + 32.0 g O = 34.0 g H_2O_2

$26.7\ \cancel{\text{g } H_2O_2} \times \dfrac{1\text{ mol } H_2O_2}{34.0\ \cancel{\text{g } H_2O_2}} = 0.785\text{ mol } H_2O_2$

21. $2\ \cancel{\text{mol N}} \times \dfrac{14.0\text{ g N}}{1\ \cancel{\text{mol N}}} = 28.0\text{ g N}$

$3\ \cancel{\text{mol O}} \times \dfrac{16.0\text{ g O}}{1\ \cancel{\text{mol O}}} = 48.0\text{ g O}$

1 mol N_2O_3 = 28.0 g N + 48.0 g O = 76.0 g N_2O_3

$75.0\ \cancel{\text{g } N_2O_3} \times \dfrac{1\text{ mol } N_2O_3}{76.0\ \cancel{\text{g } N_2O_3}} = 0.987\text{ mol } N_2O_3$

22. $3.70\ \cancel{\text{mol } N_2} \times \dfrac{22.4\text{ L } N_2}{1\ \cancel{\text{mol } N_2}} = 82.9\text{ L } N_2$

23. $0.880\ \cancel{\text{L He}} \times \dfrac{1\text{ mol He}}{22.4\ \cancel{\text{L He}}} = 0.0393\text{ mol He}$

24. $3.20 \times 10^{-3}\ \cancel{\text{mol } CO_2} \times \dfrac{22.4\text{ L } CO_2}{1\ \cancel{\text{mol } CO_2}} = 7.17 \times 10^{-2}\text{ L } CO_2$

$0.960\ \cancel{\text{mol } CH_4} \times \dfrac{22.4\text{ L } CH_4}{1\ \cancel{\text{mol } CH_4}} = 21.5\text{ L } CH_4$

CH_4 has the larger volume.

33. mass of compound = 9.03 g + 3.48 g = 12.51 g

$\%\text{ Mg} = \dfrac{\text{mass of Mg}}{\text{mass of compound}} \times 100\% = \dfrac{9.03\ \cancel{\text{g}}}{12.51\ \cancel{\text{g}}} \times 100\% = 72.2\%\text{ Mg}$

$\%\text{ N} = \dfrac{\text{mass of N}}{\text{mass of compound}} \times 100\% = \dfrac{3.48\ \cancel{\text{g}}}{12.51\ \cancel{\text{g}}} \times 100\% = 27.8\%\text{ N}$

34. mass of oxygen = 14.2 g − 13.2 g = 1.0 g

$$\% \text{Hg} = \frac{\text{mass of Hg}}{\text{mass of compound}} \times 100\% = \frac{13.2 \cancel{g}}{14.2 \cancel{g}} \times 100\%$$

$$= 93.0\% \text{ Hg}$$

$$\% \text{O} = \frac{\text{mass of O}}{\text{mass of compound}} \times 100\% = \frac{1.0 \cancel{g}}{14.2 \cancel{g}} \times 100\%$$

$$= 7.0\% \text{ O}$$

35. mass of compound = 28.0 g + 6.0 g = 34.0 g

$$\% \text{N} = \frac{\text{mass of N}}{\text{mass of compound}} \times 100\% = \frac{28.0 \cancel{g}}{34.0 \cancel{g}} \times 100\%$$

$$= 82.4\% \text{ N}$$

$$\% \text{H} = \frac{\text{mass of H}}{\text{mass of compound}} \times 100\% = \frac{6.0 \cancel{g}}{34.0 \cancel{g}} \times 100\%$$

$$= 18\% \text{ H}$$

36. The elements C, H, and O are present in a 1:2:1 ratio in both CH_2O and $C_6H_{12}O_6$. Thus, the two compounds have the same percent composition.

37. mass of N in 1 mol NH_3 = 1 $\cancel{mol}$ × 14.0 g/$\cancel{mol}$ = 14.0 g

molar mass of NH_3 = 14.0 g + 3 × 1.0 g = 17.0 g

$$\% \text{N} = \frac{\text{mass of N in 1 mol NH}_3}{\text{molar mass of NH}_3} \times 100\% =$$

$$\frac{14.0 \cancel{g}}{17.0 \cancel{g}} \times 100\% = 82.4\% \text{ N}$$

38. mass of Na in 1 mol $NaHSO_4$ = 1 $\cancel{mol}$ × 23.0 g/$\cancel{mol}$ = 23.0 g

mass of H in 1 mol $NaHSO_4$ = 1 $\cancel{mol}$ × 1.0 g/$\cancel{mol}$ = 1.0 g

mass of S in 1 mol $NaHSO_4$ = 1 $\cancel{mol}$× 32.1 g/$\cancel{mol}$ = 32.1 g

mass of O in 1 mol $NaHSO_4$ = 4 $\cancel{mol}$ × 16.0 g/$\cancel{mol}$ = 64.0 g

molar mass of $NaHSO_4$ = 23.0 g + 1.0 g + 32.1 g + 64.0 g = 120.1 g

$$\% \text{Na} = \frac{\text{mass of Na in 1 mol NaHSO}_4}{\text{molar mass of NaHSO}_4} \times 100\%$$

$$= \frac{23.0 \text{ g}}{120.1 \text{ g}} \times 100\% = 19.2\% \text{ Na}$$

$$\% \text{H} = \frac{\text{mass of H in 1 mol NaHSO}_4}{\text{molar mass of NaHSO}_4} \times 100\%$$

$$= \frac{1.0 \text{ g}}{120.1 \text{ g}} \times 100\% = 0.83\% \text{ H}$$

$$\% \text{S} = \frac{\text{mass of S in 1 mol NaHSO}_4}{\text{molar mass of NaHSO}_4} \times 100\%$$

$$= \frac{32.1 \text{ g}}{120.1 \text{ g}} \times 100\% = 26.7\% \text{ S}$$

$$\% \text{O} = \frac{\text{mass of O in 1 mol NaHSO}_4}{\text{molar mass of NaHSO}_4} \times 100\%$$

$$= \frac{64.0 \text{ g}}{120.1 \text{ g}} \times 100\% = 53.3\% \text{ O}$$

39. Using percent composition data from Problem 37:

$$125 \text{ g } \cancel{NH_3} \times \frac{82.4 \text{ g N}}{100 \text{ g } \cancel{NH_3}} = 103 \text{ g N}$$

40. mass of C in 1 mol C_2H_6 = 2 $\cancel{mol}$ × 12.0 g/$\cancel{mol}$ = 24.0 g

mass of H in 1 mol C_2H_6 = 6 $\cancel{mol}$ × 1.0 g/$\cancel{mol}$ = 6.0 g

molar mass of C_2H_6 = 24.0 g + 6.0 g = 30.0 g

$$\% \text{H} = \frac{\text{mass of H in 1 mol C}_2\text{H}_6}{\text{molar mass of C}_2\text{H}_6} \times 100\%$$

$$= \frac{6.0 \cancel{g}}{30.0 \cancel{g}} \times 100\% = 2.0 \times 10^1\% \text{ H}$$

$$350 \text{ g } \cancel{C_2H_6} \times \frac{2.0 \times 10^1 \text{ g H}}{100 \text{ g } \cancel{C_2H_6}} = 7.0 \times 10^1 \text{ g H}$$

41. Using percent composition data from Problem 38:

$$20.2 \text{ g } \cancel{NaHSO_4} \times \frac{19.2 \text{ g Na}}{100 \text{ g } \cancel{NaHSO_4}} = 3.88 \text{ g Na}$$

$$20.2 \text{ g } \cancel{NaHSO_4} \times \frac{0.83 \text{ g H}}{100 \text{ g } \cancel{NaHSO_4}} = 0.17 \text{ g H}$$

$$20.2 \text{ g } \cancel{NaHSO_4} \times \frac{26.7 \text{ g S}}{100 \text{ g } \cancel{NaHSO_4}} = 5.39 \text{ g S}$$

$$20.2 \text{ g } \cancel{NaHSO_4} \times \frac{53.5 \text{ g O}}{100 \text{ g } \cancel{NaHSO_4}} = 10.8 \text{ g O}$$

42. $94.1 \text{ g } \cancel{O} \times \frac{1 \text{ mol O}}{16.0 \text{ g } \cancel{O}} = 5.88 \text{ mol O}$

$$5.9 \text{ g } \cancel{H} \times \frac{1 \text{ mol H}}{1.0 \text{ g } \cancel{H}} = 5.9 \text{ mol H}$$

The mole ratio of O to H is $O_{5.88}H_{5.9}$.

$$\frac{5.88 \text{ mol O}}{5.88} = 1 \text{ mol O}$$

$$\frac{5.9 \text{ mol H}}{5.88} = 1 \text{ mol H}$$

The mole ratio of O to H is OH.
The empirical formula is OH.

43. $67.6\ \cancel{g\ Hg} \times \frac{1\ mol\ Hg}{200.6\ \cancel{g\ Hg}} = 0.337\ mol\ Hg$

$10.8\ \cancel{g\ S} \times \frac{1\ mol\ S}{32.1\ \cancel{g\ S}} = 0.336\ mol\ S$

$21.6\ \cancel{g\ O} \times \frac{1\ mol\ O}{16.0\ \cancel{g\ O}} = 1.35\ mol\ O$

The mole ratio of Hg to S to O is $Hg_{0.337}S_{0.336}O_{1.35}$.

$\frac{0.337\ mol\ Hg}{0.336} = 1\ mol\ Hg$

$\frac{0.336\ mol\ S}{0.336} = 1\ mol\ S$

$\frac{1.35\ mol\ O}{0.336} = 4\ mol\ O$

The mole ratio of Hg to S to O is $HgSO_4$.
The empirical formula is $HgSO_4$.

44. $62.1\ \cancel{g\ C} \times \frac{1\ mol\ C}{12.0\ \cancel{g\ C}} = 5.18\ mol\ C$

$13.8\ \cancel{g\ H} \times \frac{1\ mol\ H}{1.0\ \cancel{g\ H}} = 13.8\ mol\ H$

$24.1\ \cancel{g\ N} \times \frac{1\ mol\ N}{14.0\ \cancel{g\ N}} = 1.72\ mol\ N$

$\frac{5.18\ mol\ C}{1.72} = 3\ mol\ C$

$\frac{13.8\ mol\ H}{1.72} = 8\ mol\ H$

$\frac{1.72\ mol\ N}{1.72} = 1\ mol\ N$

The empirical formula is C_3H_8N.

50. **a.** molecule
b. formula unit
c. molecule
d. atom

52. **a.** $2.41 \times 10^{24}\ \cancel{formula\ units\ NaCl} \times \frac{1\ mol\ NaCl}{6.02 \times 10^{23}\ \cancel{formula\ units\ NaCl}} = 4.00\ mol\ NaCl$

b. $9.03 \times 10^{24}\ \cancel{atoms\ Hg} \times \frac{1\ mol\ Hg}{6.02 \times 10^{23}\ \cancel{atoms\ Hg}} =$
$15.0\ mol\ Hg$

c. $4.65 \times 10^{24}\ \cancel{molecules\ NO_2} \times \frac{1\ mol\ NO_2}{6.02 \times 10^{23}\ \cancel{molecules\ NO_2}} = 7.72\ molecules\ NO_2$

53. **a.** $3.00\ \cancel{mol\ Sn} \times \frac{6.02 \times 10^{23}\ atoms\ Sn}{1\ \cancel{mol\ Sn}} =$
$1.81 \times 10^{24}\ atoms\ Sn$

b. $0.400\ \cancel{mol\ KCl} \times \frac{6.02 \times 10^{23}\ formula\ units\ KCl}{1\ \cancel{mol\ KCl}}$
$= 2.41 \times 10^{23}\ formula\ units\ KCl$

c. $7.50\ \cancel{mol\ SO_2} \times \frac{6.02 \times 10^{23}\ molecules\ SO_2}{1\ \cancel{mol\ SO_2}} =$
$4.52 \times 10^{24}\ molecules\ SO_2$

d. $4.80 \times 10^{-3}\ \cancel{mol\ NaI} \times$
$\frac{6.02 \times 10^{23}\ formula\ units\ NaI}{1\ \cancel{mol\ NaI}} =$
2.89×10^{21} formula units NaI.

56. **a.** $(3 \times 1.0\ g/mol) + (1 \times 31.0\ g/mol) + (4 \times 16.0\ g/mol) = 98.0\ g/mol$

b. $(2 \times 14.0\ g/mol) + (3 \times 16.0\ g/mol) = 76.0\ g/mol$

c. $2 \times [(1 \times 14.0\ g/mol) + (4 \times 1.0\ g/mol)] + (1 \times 32.1\ g/mol) + (4 \times 16.0\ g/mol) = 132.1\ g/mol$

d. $(4 \times 12.0\ g/mol) + (9 \times 1.0\ g/mol) + (2 \times 16.0\ g/mol) = 89.0\ g/mol$

61. **a.** $7.64\ \cancel{mol\ Ar} \times \frac{22.4\ L\ Ar}{1\ \cancel{mol\ Ar}} = 171\ L\ Ar$

b. $1.34\ \cancel{mol\ SO_2} \times \frac{22.4\ L\ SO_2}{1\ \cancel{mol\ SO_2}} = 30.0\ L\ SO_2$

c. $0.442\ \cancel{mol\ C_2H_6} \times \frac{22.4\ L\ C_2H_6}{1\ \cancel{mol\ C_2H_6}} = 9.90\ L\ C_2H_6$

d. $2.45 \times 10^{-3}\ \cancel{mol\ H_2S} \times \frac{22.4\ L\ H_2S}{1\ \cancel{mol\ H_2S}} =$
$5.49 \times 10^{-2}\ L\ H_2S$

63. Total mass = 13.3 g + 5.7 g = 19.0 g

$\%\ Fe = \frac{13.3\ \cancel{g}}{19.0\ \cancel{g}} \times 100\% = 70.0\%\ Fe$

$\%\ O = \frac{5.7\ \cancel{g}}{19.0\ \cancel{g}} \times 100\% = 3.0 \times 10^{1}\%\ O$

64. **a.** $\%\ H = \frac{2.0\ \cancel{g}}{34.1\ \cancel{g}} \times 100\% = 5.9\%\ H$

$\%\ S = \frac{32.1\ \cancel{g}}{34.1\ \cancel{g}} \times 100\% = 94.1\%\ S$

b. $\%\ N = \frac{28.0\ \cancel{g}}{124.0\ \cancel{g}} \times 100\% = 22.6\%\ N$

$\%\ H = \frac{8.0\ \cancel{g}}{124.0\ \cancel{g}} \times 100\% = 6.5\%\ H$

$\%\ C = \frac{24.0\ \cancel{g}}{124.0\ \cancel{g}} \times 100\% = 19.4\%\ C$

$\%\ O = \frac{64.0\ \cancel{g}}{124.0\ \cancel{g}} \times 100\% = 51.6\%\ O$

c. $\% \text{ Mg} = \frac{24.3 \text{ g}}{58.3 \text{ g}} \times 100\% = 41.7\% \text{ Mg}$

$\% \text{ O} = \frac{32.0 \text{ g}}{58.3 \text{ g}} \times 100\% = 54.9\% \text{ O}$

$\% \text{ H} = \frac{2.0 \text{ g}}{58.3 \text{ g}} \times 100\% = 3.4\% \text{ H}$

d. $\% \text{ Na} = \frac{69.0 \text{ g}}{164.0 \text{ g}} \times 100\% = 42.1\% \text{ Na}$

$\% \text{ P} = \frac{31.0 \text{ g}}{164.0 \text{ g}} \times 100\% = 18.9\% \text{ P}$

$\% \text{ O} = \frac{64.0 \text{ g}}{164.0 \text{ g}} \times 100\% = 39.0\% \text{ O}$

67. **a.** molecular **c.** molecular and empirical

b. molecular **d.** molecular and empirical

68. **a.** $1.00 \text{ mol } C_{12}H_{22}O_{11} \times$

$\frac{6.02 \times 10^{23} \text{ molecules } C_{12}H_{22}O_{11}}{1 \text{ mol } C_{12}H_{22}O_{11}} \times \frac{45 \text{ atoms}}{1 \text{ molecule } C_{12}H_{22}O_{11}} = 2.71 \times 10^{25} \text{ atoms}$

b. $2.00 \text{ mol } C_{12}H_{22}O_{11} \times$

$\frac{6.02 \times 10^{23} \text{ molecules } C_{12}H_{22}O_{11}}{1 \text{ mol } C_{12}H_{22}O_{11}} \times \frac{12 \text{ C atoms}}{1 \text{ molecule } C_{12}H_{22}O_{11}} = 1.44 \times 10^{25} \text{ C atoms}$

c. $2.00 \text{ mol } C_{12}H_{22}O_{11} \times$

$\frac{6.02 \times 10^{23} \text{ molecules } C_{12}H_{22}O_{11}}{1 \text{ mol } C_{12}H_{22}O_{11}} \times \frac{22 \text{ H atoms}}{1 \text{ molecule } C_{12}H_{22}O_{11}} = 2.65 \times 10^{25} \text{ H atoms}$

d. $3.65 \text{ mol } C_{12}H_{22}O_{11} \times$

$\frac{6.02 \times 10^{23} \text{ molecules } C_{12}H_{22}O_{11}}{1 \text{ mol } C_{12}H_{22}O_{11}} \times \frac{11 \text{ O atoms}}{1 \text{ molecule } C_{12}H_{22}O_{11}} = 2.42 \times 10^{25} \text{ O atoms}$

70. molar mass of $Cl_2O = 2 \times (35.5 \text{ g/mol}) + 16.0 \text{ g/mol} = 87.0 \text{ g/mol}$

$90.0 \text{ g } Cl_2O \times \frac{1 \text{ mol } Cl_2O}{87.0 \text{ g } Cl_2O} \times \frac{1 \text{ mol O}}{1 \text{ mol } Cl_2O} \times \frac{16.0 \text{ g O}}{1 \text{ mol O}} = 16.6 \text{ g O}$

72. **a.** Atomic mass of boron = 10.8 amu

$15 \text{ atoms B} \times \frac{10.8 \text{ amu}}{1 \text{ atom B}} = 162 \text{ amu}$

$\frac{162 \text{ amu}}{6} = 27.0 \text{ amu}$

b. aluminum

73. $5.50 \text{ L} \times \frac{1 \text{ mol He}}{22.4 \text{ L}} \times \frac{4.0 \text{ g He}}{1 \text{ mol He}} = 0.98 \text{ g He}$

77. Let the number of carbon atoms = x. Then, the empirical formula is $C_xH_{3x}O_{x/2}$. The smallest value of x that will give whole-number subscripts is 2. Therefore, the empirical formula is C_2H_6O.

83. $30.0 \text{ mg} \times \frac{1 \text{ g}}{1000 \text{ mg}} \times \frac{1 \text{ mol of compound}}{312 \text{ g}} = 9.62 \times 10^{-5} \text{ mol}$

$9.62 \times 10^{-5} \text{ mol} \times \frac{6.02 \times 10^{23} \text{ molecules}}{1 \text{ mol of compound}} = 5.79 \times 10^{19} \text{ molecules}$

85. **a.** physical change **d.** physical change

b. chemical change **e.** chemical change

c. chemical change

87. **a.** $4.72 \text{ g} \times \frac{1000 \text{ mg}}{1 \text{ g}} = 4.72 \times 10^3 \text{ mg}$

b. $\frac{2.7 \times 10^3 \text{ cm}}{\text{s}} \times \frac{1 \text{ m}}{100 \text{ cm}} \times \frac{1 \text{ km}}{1000 \text{ m}} \times \frac{60 \text{ s}}{1 \text{ min}} \times \frac{60 \text{ min}}{1 \text{ h}} = 97 \text{ km/h}$

88. **a.** 40 protons, 40 electrons, 50 neutrons

b. 46 protons, 46 electrons, 62 neutrons

c. 35 protons, 35 electrons, 46 neutrons

d. 51 protons, 51 electrons, 72 neutrons

89. **a.** $1s^2 2s^2 2p^5$

b. $1s^2 2s^1$

c. $1s^2 2s^2 2p^6 3s^2 3p^6 3d^{10} 4s^2 4p^6 5s^1$

94. **d.** CaS_2; charges do not balance

f. $Ba(OH)$; charges do not balance

Chapter 11

1. $CuS(s) + O_2(g) \longrightarrow Cu(s) + SO_2(g)$

2. $S(s) + O_2(g) \longrightarrow SO_2(g)$

3. When heated, sodium hydrogen carbonate reacts to form the products sodium carbonate, carbon dioxide, and water.

4. $2C(s) + O_2(g) \longrightarrow 2CO(g)$

5. $Mg(s) + 2AgNO_3(aq) \longrightarrow 2Ag(s) + Mg(NO_3)_2(aq)$

6. $3CO(g) + Fe_2O_3(s) \longrightarrow 2Fe(l) + 3CO_2(g)$

7. $FeCl_3 + 3NaOH \longrightarrow Fe(OH)_3 + 3NaCl$

8. $2Na + 2H_2O \longrightarrow 2NaOH + H_2$

16. $4Li(s) + O_2(g) \longrightarrow 2Li_2O(s)$

17. $H_2(g) + Br_2(g) \longrightarrow 2HBr(g)$

18. $P_4O_{10}(s) + 6H_2O(l) \longrightarrow 4H_3PO_4(aq)$

19. $3Mg(s) + N_2(g) \longrightarrow Mg_3N_2(s)$

20. $2HI \longrightarrow H_2 + I_2$

21. HBr

22. $2Al(OH)_3(s) \longrightarrow Al_2O_3(s) + 3H_2O(l)$

23. $Mg(s) + Pb(NO_3)_2(aq) \longrightarrow Mg(NO_3)_2(aq) + Pb(s)$

24. $Zn(s) + H_2SO_4(aq) \longrightarrow ZnSO_4(aq) + H_2(g)$

25. **a.** $Cl_2(aq) + 2NaI(aq) \longrightarrow 2NaCl(aq) + I_2(aq)$
b. $Ca(s) + 2H_2O(l) \longrightarrow Ca(OH)_2(aq) + H_2(g)$

26. $3NaOH(aq) + Fe(NO_3)_3(aq) \longrightarrow Fe(OH)_3(s) + 3NaNO_3(aq)$

27. $3KOH(aq) + H_3PO_4(aq) \longrightarrow K_3PO_4(aq) + 3H_2O(l)$

28. $3Ba(NO_3)_2(aq) + 2H_3PO_4(aq) \longrightarrow Ba_3(PO_4)_2(s) + 6HNO_3(aq)$

29. $CH_2O(g) + O_2(g) \longrightarrow CO_2(g) + H_2O(g)$

30. $C_7H_{16}(l) + 11O_2(g) \longrightarrow 7CO_2(g) + 8H_2O(g)$

31. $C_3H_6O(l) + 4O_2(g) \longrightarrow 3CO_2(g) + 3H_2O(g)$

37. $H^+(aq) + OH^-(aq) \longrightarrow H_2O(l)$

38. Complete ionic equation:
$3Ca^{2+}(aq) + 6OH^-(aq) + 6H^+(aq) + 2PO_4^{3-}(aq) \longrightarrow Ca_3(PO_4)_2(s) + 6H_2O(l)$
Net ionic equation: same as complete ionic equation

39. The precipitate formed is lead chloride.
$Pb^{2+}(aq) + 2Cl^-(aq) \longrightarrow PbCl_2(s)$

40. The precipitate formed is iron(III) phosphate.
$Fe^{3+}(aq) + PO_4^{3-}(aq) \longrightarrow FePO_4(s)$

41. $Co^{2+}(aq) + S^{2-}(aq) \longrightarrow CoS(s)$

42. Complete ionic equation:
$Fe^{3+}(aq) + NO_3^-(aq) + 3Na^+(aq) + 3OH^-(aq) \longrightarrow 3Na^+(aq) + NO_3^-(aq) + Fe(OH)_3(s)$
Net ionic equation:
$Fe^{3+}(aq) + 3OH^-(aq) \longrightarrow Fe(OH)_3(s)$

52. **a.** $2PbO_2(s) \longrightarrow 2PbO(s) + O_2(g)$
b. $2Fe(OH)_3(s) \longrightarrow Fe_2O_3(s) + 3H_2O(l)$
c. $(NH_4)_2CO_3(s) \longrightarrow 2NH_3(g) + H_2O(g) + CO_2(g)$
d. $CaCl_2(aq) + H_2SO_4(aq) \longrightarrow CaSO_4(s) + 2HCl(aq)$

53. **a.** $2Mg(s) + O_2(g) \longrightarrow 2MgO(s)$
b. $4P(s) + 5O_2(g) \longrightarrow 2P_2O_5(s)$
c. $Ca(s) + S(s) \longrightarrow CaS(s)$

61. **a.** $H^+(aq) + OH^-(aq) \longrightarrow H_2O(l)$
b. $Ag^+(aq) + Cl^-(aq) \longrightarrow AgCl(s)$

64. **a.** $Na_2O(s) + H_2O(l) \longrightarrow 2NaOH(aq)$
b. $Cl_2O_7(l) + H_2O(l) \longrightarrow 2HClO_4(aq)$

66. **a.** tube A
b. $2Na(s) + 2H_2O(l) \longrightarrow 2NaOH(aq) + H_2(g)$
single-replacement

69. **a.** $CdS(s)$
b. $Na^+(aq)$ and $NO_3^-(aq)$
c. $Cd^{2+}(aq) + S^{2-}(aq) \longrightarrow CdS(s)$

73. The reaction is a single-replacement reaction; the products are diatomic iodine and aqueous sodium chloride. The net ionic equation is:
$Cl_2(g) + 2I^-(aq) \longrightarrow I_2(aq) + 2Cl^-(aq)$

75. 22 protons, 28 neutrons, 22 electrons

76. **a.** K_2CrO_4 **c.** permanganic acid
b. $NaHSO_3$ **d.** potassium oxalate

Chapter 12

1. 2 molecules H_2 + 1 molecule $O_2 \longrightarrow$ 2 molecules H_2O

2 mol H_2 + 1 mol $O_2 \longrightarrow$ 2 mol H_2O

44.8 L H_2 + 22.4 L $O_2 \longrightarrow$ 44.8 L H_2O

2. 1 mol C_2H_5OH + 3 mol $O_2 \longrightarrow$ 2 mol CO_2 + 3 mol H_2O

$$\left(1\ \cancel{mol} \times \frac{46.0\ g}{\cancel{mol}}\right) + \left(3\ \cancel{mol} \times \frac{32.0\ g}{\cancel{mol}}\right) \longrightarrow \left(2\ \cancel{mol} \times \frac{44.0\ g}{\cancel{mol}}\right) + \left(3\ \cancel{mol} \times \frac{18.0\ g}{\cancel{mol}}\right)$$

46.0 g C_2H_5OH + 96.0 g $O_2 \longrightarrow$ 88.0 g CO_2 + 54.0 g H_2O

142.0 g = 142.0 g

3. $4(6.02 \times 10^{23} \text{ molecules } NH_3) + 5(6.02 \times 10^{23} \text{ molecules } O_2) \longrightarrow$
$4(6.02 \times 10^{23} \text{ molecules NO}) + 6(6.02 \times 10^{23} \text{ molecules } H_2O)$

$89.6 \text{ L } NH_3 + 112.0 \text{ L } O_2 \longrightarrow 89.6 \text{ L NO} + 134.4 \text{ L } H_2O$

4. $C_2H_4(g) + 3O_2 \longrightarrow 2CO_2(g) + 2H_2O(g);$

$1 \text{ mol } C_2H_4 + 3 \text{ mol } O_2 \longrightarrow 2 \text{ mol } CO_2 + 2 \text{ mol } H_2O;$

$22.4 \text{ L } C_2H_4 + 67.2 \text{ L } O_2 \longrightarrow 44.8 \text{ L } CO_2 + 44.8 \text{ L } H_2O;$

$$\left(1 \text{ mol} \times \frac{28.0 \text{ g}}{\text{mol}}\right) + \left(3 \text{ mol} \times \frac{32.0 \text{ g}}{\text{mol}}\right) \longrightarrow \left(2 \text{ mol} \times \frac{44.0 \text{ g}}{\text{mol}}\right) + \left(2 \text{ mol} \times \frac{18.0 \text{ g}}{\text{mol}}\right)$$

$28.0 \text{ g } C_2H_4 + 96.0 \text{ g } O_2 \longrightarrow 88.0 \text{ g } CO_2 + 36.0 \text{ g } H_2O$

$124.0 \text{ g} = 124.0 \text{ g}$

10. $3.7 \text{ mol } Al_2O_3 \times \frac{4 \text{ mol Al}}{2 \text{ mol } Al_2O_3} = 7.4 \text{ mol Al}$

11. $14.8 \text{ mol Al} \times \frac{3 \text{ mol } O_2}{4 \text{ mol Al}} = 11.1 \text{ mol } O_2$

12. $0.78 \text{ mol } O_2 \times \frac{2 \text{ mol } Al_2O_3}{3 \text{ mol } O_2} = 0.52 \text{ mol } Al_2O_3$

13. $5.00 \text{ g } CaC_2 \times \frac{1 \text{ mol } CaC_2}{64.1 \text{ g } CaC_2} \times \frac{1 \text{ mol } C_2H_2}{1 \text{ mol } CaC_2} \times \frac{26.0 \text{ g } C_2H_2}{1 \text{ mol } C_2H_2} = 2.03 \text{ g } C_2H_2$

14. $225 \text{ g } F_2 \times \frac{1 \text{ mol } F_2}{38.0 \text{ g } F_2} \times \frac{1 \text{ mol } N_2F_4}{5 \text{ mol } F_2} \times \frac{104.0 \text{ g } N_2F_4}{1 \text{ mol } N_2F_4} = 123 \text{ g } N_2F_4$

15. $4.65 \text{ g HF} \times \frac{1 \text{ mol HF}}{20.0 \text{ g HF}} \times \frac{2 \text{ mol } NH_3}{6 \text{ mol HF}} \times \frac{17.0 \text{ g } NH_3}{1 \text{ mol } NH_3} = 1.32 \text{ g } NH_3$

16. $6.54 \text{ g } KClO_3 \times \frac{1 \text{ mol } KClO_3}{122.6 \text{ g } KClO_3} \times \frac{3 \text{ mol } O_2}{2 \text{ mol } KClO_3} \times \frac{6.02 \times 10^{23} \text{ molecules } O_2}{1 \text{ mol } O_2} = 4.82 \times 10^{22} \text{ molecules } O_2$

17. $43.2 \text{ g } H_2O \times \frac{1 \text{ mol } H_2O}{18.0 \text{ g } H_2O} \times \frac{2 \text{ mol } HNO_3}{1 \text{ mol } H_2O} \times \frac{6.02 \times 10^{23} \text{ molecules } HNO_3}{1 \text{ mol } HNO_3} = 2.92 \times 10^{24} \text{ molecules } HNO_3$

18. $5.00 \times 10^{22} \text{ molecules NO} \times \frac{1 \text{ mol NO}}{6.02 \times 10^{23} \text{ molecules NO}} \times \frac{3 \text{ mol } NO_2}{1 \text{ mol NO}} \times \frac{46.0 \text{ g } NO_2}{1 \text{ mol } NO_2} = 11.5 \text{ g } NO_2$

19. $3.86 \text{ L CO} \times \frac{1 \text{ mol CO}}{22.4 \text{ L CO}} \times \frac{1 \text{ mol } O_2}{2 \text{ mol CO}} \times \frac{22.4 \text{ L } O_2}{1 \text{ mol } O_2} = 1.93 \text{ L } O_2$

20. $0.42 \text{ L } H_2 \times \frac{1 \text{ mol } H_2}{22.4 \text{ L } H_2} \times \frac{4 \text{ mol } PH_3}{6 \text{ mol } H_2} \times \frac{22.4 \text{ L } PH_3}{1 \text{ mol } PH_3} = 0.28 \text{ L } PH_3$

21. $11.20 \text{ L } PH_3 \times \frac{1 \text{ mol } PH_3}{22.4 \text{ L } PH_3} \times \frac{6 \text{ mol } H_2}{4 \text{ mol } PH_3} \times \frac{22.4 \text{ L } H_2}{1 \text{ mol } H_2} = 16.8 \text{ L } H_2$

22. $27.9 \text{ mL } O_2 \times \frac{2 \text{ mL } SO_2}{3 \text{ mL } O_2} = 18.6 \text{ mL } SO_2$

23. $42 \text{ L } SO_2 \times \frac{1 \text{ L } CO_2}{2 \text{ L } SO_2} = 21 \text{ L } CO_2$

24. $0.38 \text{ L } SO_2 \times \frac{1 \text{ L } CO_2}{2 \text{ L } SO_2} \times \frac{10 \text{ dL } CO_2}{1 \text{ L } CO_2} = 1.9 \text{ dL } CO_2$

31. $2.70 \text{ mol } C_2H_4 \times \frac{3 \text{ mol } O_2}{1 \text{ mol } C_2H_4} = 8.10 \text{ mol } O_2$

8.10 mol O_2 are needed to react with 2.70 mol C_2H_4, but there are only 6.30 mol O_2 given for the reaction. Therefore, O_2 is the limiting reagent.

32. $6.00 \text{ g HCl} \times \frac{1 \text{ mol HCl}}{36.5 \text{ g HCl}} = 0.160 \text{ mol HCl}$

$5.00 \text{ g Mg} \times \frac{1 \text{ mol Mg}}{24.3 \text{ g Mg}} = 0.210 \text{ mol Mg}$

$0.16 \text{ mol HCl} \times \frac{1 \text{ mol Mg}}{2 \text{ mol HCl}} = 0.080 \text{ mol Mg}$

0.080 mol Mg is needed to react with 0.160 mol HCl. 0.210 mol Mg $>$ 0.080 mol Mg, so Mg is in excess. HCl is the limiting reagent.

33. $1.75 \text{ mol } H_3PO_4 \times \frac{3 \text{ mol NaOH}}{1 \text{ mol } H_3PO_4} = 5.25 \text{ mol NaOH}$

5.25 mol NaOH are needed to react with 1.75 mol H_3PO_4, but there are only 5.00 mol NaOH given for the reaction. Therefore, NaOH is the limiting reagent.

34. **a.** $2.70 \text{ mol } C_2H_4 \times \frac{2 \text{ mol } O_2}{1 \text{ mol } C_2H_4} = 5.40 \text{ mol } O_2$

C_2H_4 is the limiting reagent.

b. $2.70 \text{ mol } C_2H_4 \times \frac{2 \text{ mol } H_2O}{1 \text{ mol } C_2H_4} = 5.40 \text{ mol } H_2O$

35. $2.40\ \text{mol C}_2\text{H}_2 \times \frac{5\ \text{mol O}_2}{2\ \text{mol C}_2\text{H}_2} = 6.00\ \text{mol O}_2$

C_2H_2 is the limiting reagent.

$$2.40\ \text{mol C}_2\text{H}_2 \times \frac{2\ \text{mol H}_2\text{O}}{2\ \text{mol C}_2\text{H}_2} \times \frac{18.0\ \text{g H}_2\text{O}}{1\ \text{mol H}_2\text{O}} = 43.2\ \text{g H}_2\text{O}$$

36. $50.0\ \text{g SiO}_2 \times \frac{1\ \text{mol SiO}_2}{60.1\ \text{g SiO}_2} \times \frac{3\ \text{mol C}}{1\ \text{mol SiO}_2} \times \frac{12.0\ \text{g C}}{1\ \text{mol C}} = 30.0\ \text{g C}$

SiO_2 is the limiting reagent.

$$50.0\ \text{g SiO}_2 \times \frac{1\ \text{mol SiO}_2}{60.1\ \text{g SiO}_2} \times \frac{2\ \text{mol CO}}{1\ \text{mol SiO}_2} \times \frac{28.0\ \text{g CO}}{1\ \text{mol CO}} = 46.6\ \text{g CO}$$

37. $84.8\ \text{g Fe}_2\text{O}_3 \times \frac{1\ \text{mol Fe}_2\text{O}_3}{159.9\ \text{g Fe}_2\text{O}_3} \times \frac{2\ \text{mol Fe}}{1\ \text{mol Fe}_2\text{O}_3} \times \frac{55.9\ \text{g Fe}}{1\ \text{mol Fe}} = 59.3\ \text{g Fe}$

38. $20.0\ \text{g Cu} \times \frac{1\ \text{mol Cu}}{63.5\ \text{g Cu}} \times \frac{1\ \text{mol Cu}_2\text{S}}{2\ \text{mol Cu}} \times \frac{95.6\ \text{g CuS}}{1\ \text{mol Cu}_2\text{S}} = 15.1\ \text{g Cu}_2\text{S}$

39. $73.1\ \text{g SiO}_2 \times \frac{1\ \text{mol SiO}_2}{60.1\ \text{g SiO}_2} \times \frac{3\ \text{mol C}}{1\ \text{mol SiO}_2} \times \frac{12.0\ \text{g C}}{1\ \text{mol C}} = 43.8\ \text{g C}$

C is the limiting reagent.

$$43.8\ \text{g C} \times \frac{1\ \text{mol C}}{12.0\ \text{g C}} \times \frac{1\ \text{mol SiC}}{3\ \text{mol C}} \times \frac{40.1\ \text{g SiC}}{1\ \text{mol SiC}} = 48.8\ \text{g SiC}$$

40. $\text{Cu}(s) + 2\text{AgNO}_3(aq) \longrightarrow 2\text{Ag}(s) + \text{Cu(NO}_3)_2(aq)$

$$5.00\ \text{g Cu} \times \frac{1\ \text{mol Cu}}{63.5\ \text{g Cu}} \times \frac{2\ \text{mol Ag}}{1\ \text{mol Cu}} \times \frac{107.9\ \text{g Ag}}{1\ \text{mol Ag}} = 17.0\ \text{g Ag}$$

41. $50.0\ \text{g SiO}_2 \times \frac{1\ \text{mol SiO}_2}{60.1\ \text{g SiO}_2} \times \frac{1\ \text{mol SiC}}{1\ \text{mol SiO}_2} \times \frac{40.1\ \text{g SiC}}{1\ \text{mol SiC}} = 33.4\ \text{g SiC}$

$$\%\ \text{yield} = \frac{27.9\ \text{g SiC}}{33.4\ \text{g SiC}} \times 100\% = 83.5\%$$

42. $\%\ \text{yield} = \frac{32.2\ \text{g SiC}}{33.4\ \text{g SiC}} \times 100\% = 96.4\%$

43. $202\ \text{g Fe}_2\text{O}_3 \times \frac{1\ \text{mol Fe}_2\text{O}_3}{159.6\ \text{g Fe}_2\text{O}_3} \times \frac{3\ \text{mol CO}}{1\ \text{mol Fe}_2\text{O}_3} \times \frac{28.0\ \text{g CO}}{1\ \text{mol CO}} = 106\ \text{g CO}$

Fe_2O_3 is the limiting reagent.

$$202\ \text{g Fe}_2\text{O}_3 \times \frac{1\ \text{mol Fe}_2\text{O}_3}{159.6\ \text{g Fe}_2\text{O}_3} \times \frac{2\ \text{mol Fe}}{1\ \text{mol Fe}_2\text{O}_3} \times \frac{55.8\ \text{g Fe}}{1\ \text{mol Fe}} = 141\ \text{g Fe}$$

$$\%\ \text{yield} = \frac{118\ \text{g Fe}}{141\ \text{g Fe}} \times 100\% = 83.7\%$$

44. $N_2 + 3H_2 \longrightarrow 2NH_3$

$$15.0\ \text{g N}_2 \times \frac{1\ \text{mol N}_2}{28.0\ \text{g N}_2} \times \frac{3\ \text{mol H}_2}{1\ \text{mol N}_2} \times \frac{2.0\ \text{g H}_2}{1\ \text{mol H}_2} = 3.2\ \text{g H}_2$$

N_2 is the limiting reagent, so use the given mass of nitrogen to find the theoretical yield of NH_3.

$$15.0\ \text{g N}_2 \times \frac{1\ \text{mol N}_2}{28.0\ \text{g N}_2} \times \frac{2\ \text{mol NH}_3}{1\ \text{mol N}_2} \times \frac{17.0\ \text{g NH}_3}{1\ \text{mol NH}_3} = 18.2\ \text{g NH}_3$$

$$\%\ \text{yield} = \frac{10.5\ \text{g NH}_3}{18.2\ \text{g NH}_3} \times 100\% = 57.7\%$$

58. **a.** $2.7\ \text{mol C} \times \frac{1\ \text{mol CS}_2}{5\ \text{mol C}} = 0.54\ \text{mol CS}_2$

b. $5.44\ \text{mol SO}_2 \times \frac{5\ \text{mol C}}{2\ \text{mol SO}_2} = 13.6\ \text{mol C}$

61. **a.** $32.9\ \text{g Li}_3\text{N} \times \frac{1\ \text{mol Li}_3\text{N}}{34.7\ \text{g Li}_3\text{N}} \times \frac{3\ \text{mol H}_2\text{O}}{1\ \text{mol Li}_3\text{N}} \times \frac{18.0\ \text{g H}_2\text{O}}{1\ \text{mol H}_2\text{O}} = 51.2\ \text{g H}_2\text{O}$

b. $32.9\ \text{g Li}_3\text{N} \times \frac{1\ \text{mol Li}_3\text{N}}{34.7\ \text{g Li}_3\text{N}} \times \frac{1\ \text{mol NH}_3}{1\ \text{mol Li}_3\text{N}} \times \frac{6.02 \times 10^{23}\ \text{molecules NH}_3}{1\ \text{mol NH}_3} = 5.71 \times 10^{23}\ \text{molecules NH}_3$

c. $15.0\ \text{L NH}_3 \times \frac{1\ \text{mol NH}_3}{22.4\ \text{L NH}_3} \times \frac{1\ \text{mol Li}_3\text{N}}{1\ \text{mol NH}_3} \times \frac{34.7\ \text{g Li}_3\text{N}}{1\ \text{mol Li}_3\text{N}} = 23.2\ \text{g Li}_3\text{N}$

64. a. $3.0 \text{ mol Al} \times \frac{3 \text{ mol } Cl_2}{2 \text{ mol Al}} = 4.5 \text{ mol } Cl_2$

Al is the limiting reagent.

b. $3.0 \text{ mol Al} \times \frac{2 \text{ mol } AlCl_3}{2 \text{ mol Al}} = 3.0 \text{ mol } AlCl_3$

c. $5.3 \text{ mol } Cl_2 - 4.5 \text{ mol } Cl_2 = 0.8 \text{ mol } Cl_2$

65. $15.0 \text{ g } Sb_2S_3 \times \frac{1 \text{ mol } Sb_2S_3}{339.9 \text{ g } Sb_2S_3} \times \frac{2 \text{ mol Sb}}{1 \text{ mol } Sb_2S_3} \times \frac{121.8 \text{ g Sb}}{1 \text{ mol Sb}} = 10.8 \text{ g Sb}$

$\% \text{ yield} = \frac{9.84 \text{ g Sb}}{10.8 \text{ g Sb}} \times 100\% = 91.1\%$

67. a. $1.0 \text{ kg } N_2H_4 \times \frac{10^3 \text{ g } N_2H_4}{1.0 \text{ kg } N_2H_4} \times \frac{1 \text{ mol } N_2H_4}{32.0 \text{ g } N_2H_4} \times \frac{1 \text{ mol } N_2}{1 \text{ mol } N_2H_4} \times \frac{22.4 \text{ L } N_2}{1 \text{ mol } N_2} = 7.0 \times 10^2 \text{ L } N_2$

$1.2 \text{ kg } O_2 \times \frac{10^3 \text{ g } O_2}{1 \text{ kg } O_2} \times \frac{1 \text{ mol } O_2}{32.0 \text{ g } O_2} \times \frac{1 \text{ mol } N_2}{1 \text{ mol } O_2} \times \frac{22.4 \text{ L } N_2}{1 \text{ mol } N_2} = 8.4 \times 10^2 \text{ L } N_2$

Since $7.0 \times 10^2 \text{ L } N_2 < 8.4 \times 10^2 \text{ L } N_2$, the limiting reagent is N_2H_4 and O_2 is in excess.

b. $1.0 \text{ kg } N_2H_4 \times \frac{10^3 \text{ g } N_2H_4}{1 \text{ kg } N_2H_4} \times \frac{1 \text{ mol } N_2H_4}{32.0 \text{ g } N_2H_4} \times \frac{1 \text{ mol } O_2}{1 \text{ mol } N_2H_4} \times \frac{32.0 \text{ g } O_2}{1 \text{ mol } O_2} = 1.0 \times 10^3 \text{ g } O_2 \text{ used}$

$1.0 \times 10^3 \text{ g } O_2 \times \frac{1 \text{ kg } O_2}{10^3 \text{ g } O_2} = 1.0 \text{ kg } O_2$

$1.2 \text{ kg } O_2 - 1.0 \text{ kg } O_2 = 0.2 \text{ kg } O_2$

The excess remaining reagent is 0.2 kg O_2.

69. $158 \text{ g } CH_4 \times \frac{1 \text{ mol } CH_4}{16.0 \text{ g } CH_4} \times \frac{3 \text{ mol } H_2}{1 \text{ mol } CH_4} \times \frac{6.02 \times 10^{23} \text{ molecules } H_2}{1 \text{ mol } H_2} = 1.78 \times 10^{25} \text{ molecules } H_2$

73. a. $SF_2(l) + 2F_2(g) \longrightarrow SF_6(g)$

b. $5.00 \text{ mg } SF_2 \times \frac{1 \text{ g } SF_2}{10^3 \text{ mg } SF_2} \times \frac{1 \text{ mol } SF_2}{70.1 \text{ g } SF_2} \times \frac{2 \text{ mol } F_2}{1 \text{ mol } SF_2} \times \frac{6.02 \times 10^{23} \text{ molecules } F_2}{1 \text{ mol } F_2} = 8.59 \times 10^{19} \text{ molecules}$

c. $6.66 \text{ g } SF_2 \times \frac{1 \text{ mol } SF_2}{70.1 \text{ g } SF_2} \times \frac{2 \text{ mol } F_2}{1 \text{ mol } SF_2} \times \frac{22.4 \text{ L } F_2}{1 \text{ mol } F_2} = 4.26 \text{ L } F_2$

86. $90 \text{ g} \times 0.267 = 24 \text{ g C}$

$24 \text{ g C} \times \frac{1 \text{ mol C}}{12.0 \text{ g C}} = 2.0 \text{ mol C}$

$90 \text{ g} \times 0.022 = 2.0 \text{ g H}$

$2.0 \text{ g H} \times \frac{1 \text{ mol H}}{1.0 \text{ g H}} = 2.0 \text{ mol H}$

$90 \text{ g} \times 0.711 = 64 \text{ g O}$

$64 \text{ g O} \times \frac{1 \text{ mol O}}{16.0 \text{ g O}} = 4.0 \text{ mol O}$

The empirical formula is CHO_2.

molar mass of $CHO_2 = 1(12.0 \text{ g/mol}) + 1(1.0 \text{ g/mol}) + 2(16 \text{ g/mol}) = 45 \text{ g/mol}$

The molar mass of oxalic acid is twice the molar mass of the empirical formula, so the molecular formula is $C_2H_2O_4$.

Chapter 13

1. $385 \text{ mm Hg} \times \frac{101.3 \text{ kPa}}{760 \text{ mm Hg}} = 51.3 \text{ kPa}$

$385 \text{ mm Hg} \times \frac{1 \text{ atm}}{760 \text{ mm Hg}} = 0.507 \text{ atm}$

2. $22.8 \text{ kPa} \times \frac{1 \text{ atm}}{101.3 \text{ kPa}} = 0.225 \text{ atm}$

$22.8 \text{ kPa} \times \frac{760 \text{ mm Hg}}{101.3 \text{ kPa}} = 171 \text{ mm Hg}$

3. $0.57 \text{ atm} \times \frac{101.3 \text{ kPa}}{1 \text{ atm}} = 58 \text{ kPa}$

$0.57 \text{ atm} \times \frac{760 \text{ mm Hg}}{1 \text{ atm}} = 4.3 \times 10^2 \text{ mm Hg}$

4. $33.7 \text{ kPa} \times \frac{1 \text{ atm}}{101.3 \text{ kPa}} = 0.33 \text{ atm} > 0.25 \text{ atm}$

37. $190 \text{ mm Hg} \times \frac{101.3 \text{ kPa}}{760 \text{ mm Hg}} = 25 \text{ kPa}$

$190 \text{ mm Hg} \times \frac{1 \text{ atm}}{760 \text{ mm Hg}} = 0.25 \text{ atm}$

45. Escaping molecules have more kinetic energy than the average. Thus, the average kinetic energy and temperature of the remaining molecules are lower.

48. The intermolecular attractions between molecules are weaker than the attractions between ions.

49. Water from the food sublimed and then condensed on the lid.

51. The average kinetic energy of the molecules is greater because, by definition, a fever is a state of increased body temperature.

54. Decrease; as the attractions become stronger, it becomes more difficult for molecules to overcome the attractions and vaporize.

57. The Kelvin temperature is directly proportional to the average kinetic energy. As the temperature rises, the air particles speed up and increase in kinetic energy, which causes the raft to expand. As the temperature drops, the air particles slow down, resulting in a decrease in kinetic energy, which causes the raft to not be fully inflated.

64. No; at 15 kPa, water would boil at a temperature of about 50°C, which is much higher than room temperature.

69. **a.** $1s^2 2s^2 2p^6 3s^2 3p^6$
b. $1s^2 2s^2 2p^6 3s^2 3p^6$

Chapter 14

6. $V_2 = \frac{P_1 \times V_1}{P_2} = \frac{105 \text{ kPa} \times 2.50 \text{ L}}{40.5 \text{ kPa}} = 6.48 \text{ L}$

7. $P_2 = \frac{P_1 \times V_1}{V_2} = \frac{205 \text{ kPa} \times 4.00 \text{ L}}{12.0 \text{ L}} = 68.3 \text{ kPa}$

8. $V_2 = \frac{P_1 \times V_1}{P_2} = \frac{90.0 \text{ kPa} \times 4.0 \text{ L}}{20.0 \text{ kPa}} = 18 \text{ L}$

9. $V_2 = \frac{P_1 \times V_1}{P_2} = \frac{355 \text{ kPa} \times 250 \text{ mL}}{157 \text{ kPa}} = 570 \text{ mL}$

$570 \text{ mL} \times \frac{1 \text{ L}}{10^3 \text{ mL}} = 0.57 \text{ L}$

10. $T_1 = 325°\text{C} + 273 = 598 \text{ K}$

$T_2 = 25°\text{C} + 273 = 298 \text{ K}$

$V_2 = \frac{V_1 \times T_2}{T_1} = \frac{6.80 \text{ L} \times 298 \text{ K}}{598 \text{ K}} = 3.39 \text{ L}$

11. $T_1 = -50.0°\text{C} + 273 = 223 \text{ K}$

$T_2 = 100.0°\text{C} + 273 = 373 \text{ K}$

$V_2 = \frac{V_1 \times T_2}{T_1} = \frac{5.00 \text{ L} \times 373 \text{ K}}{223 \text{ K}} = 8.36 \text{ L}$

12. It doubles because the temperature and the volume of a gas are directly proportional to one another.

13. $T_1 = 20°\text{C} + 273 = 293 \text{ K}$

$T_2 = \frac{T_1 \times V_2}{V_1} = \frac{293 \text{ K} \times 4.50 \text{ L}}{3.79 \text{ L}} = 348 \text{ K}$

14. $T_1 = 20°\text{C} + 273 = 293 \text{ K}$

$T_2 = 50°\text{C} + 273 = 323 \text{ K}$

$P_2 = \frac{P_1 \times T_2}{T_1} = \frac{1.00 \times 10^3 \text{ kPa} \times 323 \text{ K}}{293 \text{ K}}$

$= 1.10 \times 10^3 \text{ kPa}$

15. $T_1 = 41°\text{C} + 273 = 314 \text{ K}$

$T_2 = 22°\text{C} + 273 = 295 \text{ K}$

$P_2 = \frac{P_1 \times T_2}{T_1} = \frac{108 \text{ kPa} \times 295 \text{ K}}{314 \text{ K}} = 101 \text{ kPa}$

16. $T_1 = 27°\text{C} + 273 = 300 \text{ K}$

$T_2 = \frac{P_2 \times T_1}{P_1} = \frac{225 \text{ kPa} \times 300 \text{ K}}{198 \text{ kPa}} = 341 \text{ K} \ (68°\text{C})$

17. $T_1 = 266°\text{C} + 273 = 539 \text{ K}$

$T_2 = -62.0°\text{C} + 273 = 211 \text{ K}$

$P_2 = \frac{P_1 \times T_2}{T_1} = \frac{6580 \text{ Pa} \times 211 \text{ K}}{539 \text{ K}} = 2580 \text{ Pa}$

$2580 \text{ Pa} \times \frac{1 \text{ kPa}}{10^3 \text{ Pa}} = 2.58 \text{ kPa}$

18. $V_2 = \frac{P_1 \times V_1 \times T_2}{T_1 \times P_2} = \frac{101.3 \text{ kPa} \times 20.0 \text{ L} \times 75.0 \text{ K}}{273 \text{ K} \times 200.0 \text{ kPa}}$

$= 2.78 \text{ L}$

19. $T_1 = 25°\text{C} + 273 = 298 \text{ K}$

$T_2 = 125°\text{C} + 273 = 398 \text{ K}$

$V_2 = \frac{P_1 \times V_1 \times T_2}{T_1 \times P_2} = \frac{155 \text{ kPa} \times 1.00 \text{ L} \times 398 \text{ K}}{605 \text{ K} \times 298 \text{ kPa}}$

$= 0.342 \text{ L}$

20. $V_2 = \frac{P_1 \times V_1 \times T_2}{T_1 \times P_2} = \frac{1.00 \text{ atm} \times 57.9 \text{ L} \times 423 \text{ K}}{300.0 \text{ K} \times 2.00 \text{ atm}}$

$= 40.8 \text{ L}$

28. $n = \frac{P \times V}{R \times T} = \frac{1.89 \times 10^3 \text{ kPa} \times 685 \text{ L}}{8.31 \frac{\text{L} \cdot \text{kPa}}{\text{K} \cdot \text{mol}} \times 621 \text{ K}} = 251 \text{ mol He}$

29. $T = 25°\text{C} + 273 = 298 \text{ K}$

$P = \frac{n \times R \times T}{V}$

$P = \frac{0.450 \text{ mol} \times 8.31 \frac{\text{L} \cdot \text{kPa}}{\text{K} \cdot \text{mol}} \times 298 \text{ K}}{0.650 \text{ L}}$

$= 1.71 \times 10^3 \text{ kPa}$

30. $T = 27°C + 273 = 300\ K$

$$V = \frac{n \times R \times T}{P}$$

$$V = \frac{1.56\ \cancel{mol} \times 8.31\ \frac{L \cdot \cancel{kPa}}{\cancel{K} \cdot \cancel{mol}} \times 300\ \cancel{K}}{135\ \cancel{kPa}}$$

$$= 28.8\ L$$

31. $T = 35°C + 273 = 308\ K$

$$n = 4.50\ \cancel{g\ CH_4} \times \frac{1\ mol\ CH_4}{16.0\ \cancel{g\ CH_4}} = 0.281\ mol\ CH_4$$

$$P = \frac{n \times R \times T}{V}$$

$$P = \frac{0.281\ \cancel{mol} \times 8.31\ \frac{\cancel{L} \cdot kPa}{\cancel{K} \cdot \cancel{mol}} \times 308\ \cancel{K}}{2.00\ \cancel{L}}$$

$$= 360\ kPa = 3.60 \times 10^2\ kPa$$

32. $$n = \frac{P \times V}{R \times T} = \frac{99\ \cancel{kPa} \times 240\ \cancel{L}}{8.31\ \frac{\cancel{L} \cdot \cancel{kPa}}{\cancel{K} \cdot mol} \times 273\ \cancel{K}} = 10.5\ mol\ He$$

$$10.5\ \cancel{mol\ He} \times \frac{4.0\ g\ He}{1\ \cancel{mol\ He}} = 42\ g\ He$$

33. $T = 35°C + 273 = 308\ K$

$$n = \frac{P \times V}{R \times T} = \frac{360\ \cancel{kPa} \times 2.00\ \cancel{L}}{8.31\ \frac{\cancel{L} \cdot \cancel{kPa}}{\cancel{K} \cdot mol} \times 308\ \cancel{K}} = 0.28\ mol\ CH_4$$

$$0.28\ \cancel{mol\ CH_4} \times \frac{16.0\ g\ CH_4}{1\ \cancel{mol\ CH_4}} = 4.5\ g\ CH_4$$

34. $$n = 12.0\ \cancel{g\ O_2} \times \frac{1\ mol\ O_2}{32.0\ \cancel{g\ O_2}} = 0.375\ mol\ O_2$$

$$V = \frac{n \times R \times T}{P}$$

$$V = \frac{0.375\ \cancel{mol} \times 8.31\ \frac{L \cdot \cancel{kPa}}{\cancel{K} \cdot \cancel{mol}} \times 298\ \cancel{K}}{52.7\ \cancel{kPa}} = 17.6\ L$$

35. $T = 37°C + 273 = 310\ K$

$$n = \frac{P \times V}{R \times T} = \frac{102\ \cancel{kPa} \times 2.20\ \cancel{L}}{8.31\ \frac{\cancel{L} \cdot \cancel{kPa}}{\cancel{K} \cdot mol} \times 310\ \cancel{K}}$$

$$= 0.0871\ mol\ air$$

$$0.0871\ \cancel{mol\ air} \times \frac{29\ g\ air}{1\ \cancel{mol\ air}} = 2.5\ g\ air$$

43. $P_{total} = P_{O_2} + P_{N_2} + P_{CO_2}$

$$P_{CO_2} = P_{total} - P_{O_2} - P_{N_2}$$

$$P_{CO_2} = 32.9\ kPa - 6.6\ kPa - 23.0\ kPa$$

$$P_{CO_2} = 3.3\ kPa$$

44. $P_{total} = P_{O_2} + P_{N_2} + P_{He}$

$$P_{total} = 20.0\ kPa + 46.7\ kPa + 26.7\ kPa$$

$$P_{total} = 93.4\ kPa$$

45. $P_{total} = P_{O_2} + P_{Ar} + P_{CO_2}$

$$P_{Ar} = P_{total} - P_{O_2} - P_{CO_2}$$

$$P_{Ar} = 2.54\ atm - 1.52\ atm - 0.68\ atm$$

$$P_{Ar} = 0.34\ atm$$

46. $P_{He} = 0.20 \times 650.0\ kPa = 1.30 \times 10^2\ kPa$

$$P_{O_2} = 0.80 \times 650.0\ kPa = 5.20 \times 10^2\ kPa$$

59. $$P_2 = \frac{P_1 \times T_2}{T_1} = \frac{300\ kPa \times 101\ \cancel{K}}{303\ \cancel{K}} = 1.00 \times 10^2\ kPa$$

61. $T_1 = 150.0°C + 273 = 423\ K$

$$T_2 = \frac{T_1 \times V_2}{T_1} = \frac{423\ K \times 600\ \cancel{mL}}{300\ \cancel{mL}} = 846\ K\ \ (573°C)$$

63. $$P_2 = \frac{P_1 \times T_2}{T_1} = \frac{6.58\ kPa \times 211\ \cancel{K}}{539\ \cancel{K}} = 2.58\ kPa$$

64. $T_1 = 327.0°C + 273 = 600\ K$

$$T_2 = \frac{T_1 \times V_2}{T_1} = \frac{600\ K \times 5\ \cancel{L}}{15\ \cancel{L}} = 200\ K\ \ (-73°C)$$

67. $T = 35°C + 273 = 308\ K$

$$V = \frac{n \times R \times T}{P}$$

$$V = \frac{1.24\ \cancel{mol} \times 8.31\ \frac{L \cdot \cancel{kPa}}{\cancel{K} \cdot \cancel{mol}} \times 308\ \cancel{K}}{96.2\ \cancel{kPa}} = 33.0\ L$$

74. $T_1 = 20°C + 273 = 293\ K$

$$T_2 = \frac{T_1 \times P_2 \times V_2}{P_1 \times V_1}$$

$$T_2 = \frac{293\ K \times 56.7\ \cancel{kPa} \times 8.00\ \cancel{L}}{86.7\ \cancel{kPa} \times 3.50\ \cancel{L}} = 438\ K$$

$$T_2 = 438\ K - 273 = 165°C$$

77. **a.** The graph should form a straight line.

b. 700 mm Hg

c. directly proportional

d. The pressure rises 2.4 mm Hg for every 1°C.

$$\text{slope of line } (m) = \frac{750\text{ mm Hg} - 726\text{ mm Hg}}{20°\text{C} - 10°\text{C}} = \frac{24\text{ mm Hg}}{10°\text{C}} = 2.4\text{ mm Hg/°C}$$

e. Gay-Lussac's law; sample data points:
$(T_1, P_1) = (10°\text{C}, 726\text{ mm Hg})$
$(T_2, P_2) = (20°\text{C}, 750\text{ mm Hg})$

$T_1 = 10°\text{C} + 273 = 283\text{ K}$
$T_1 = 20°\text{C} + 273 = 293\text{ K}$

$$\frac{P_1}{T_1} = \frac{P_2}{T_2}$$

$$\frac{726\text{ mm Hg}}{283\text{ K}} = \frac{750\text{ mm Hg}}{293\text{ K}} = 2.6\text{ mm Hg/K}$$

84. **a.** tin(II) bromide

b. barium sulfate

c. magnesium hydroxide

d. iodine pentafluoride

85. **a.** molar mass of $Ca(CH_3CO_2)_2$ = (1 × 40.1 g/mol) + (4 × 12.0 g/mol) + (6 × 1.0 g/mol) + (4 × 16.0 g/mol) = 158.1 g/mol

b. molar mass of H_3PO_4 = (3 × 1.0 g/mol) + (1 × 31.0 g/mol) + (4 × 16.0 g/mol) = 98.0 g/mol

c. molar mass of $C_{12}H_{22}O_{11}$ = (12 × 12.0 g/mol) + (22 × 1.0 g/mol) + (11 × 16.0 g/mol) = 342.0 g/mol

d. molar mass of $Pb(NO_3)_2$ = (1 × 207.2 g/mol) + (2 × 14.0 g/mol) + (6 × 16.0 g/mol) = 331.2 g/mol

89. $$583\text{ g } Al_2O_3 \times \frac{1\text{ mol } Al_2O_3}{102\text{ g } Al_2O_3} = 5.72\text{ mol } Al_2O_3$$

$$5.72\text{ g } Al_2O_3 \times \frac{4\text{ mol Al}}{2\text{ mol } Al_2O_3} \times \frac{27.0\text{ g Al}}{1\text{ mol Al}} = 309\text{ g Al}$$

Chapter 15

11. mass of 5 mol H_2O = 5[(2 × 1.0 g) + 16.0 g] = 90.0 g

molar mass of $CuSO_4 \cdot 5H_2O$ = 63.5 g + 32.1 g + (4 × 16.0 g) + 90.0 g = 249.6 g

$$\%\text{ by mass } H_2O = \frac{\text{mass of water}}{\text{mass of hydrate}} \times 100\% = \frac{90.0\text{ g}}{249.6\text{ g}} \times 100\% = 36.1\%$$

12. mass of 7 mol H_2O = 7[(2 × 1.0 g) + 16.0 g] = 126.0 g

molar mass of $FeSO_4 \cdot 7H_2O$ = 55.8 g + 32.1 g + (4 × 16.0 g) + 126.0 g = 277.9 g

$$\%\text{ by mass } H_2O = \frac{\text{mass of water}}{\text{mass of hydrate}} \times 100\% = \frac{126.0\text{ g}}{277.9\text{ g}} \times 100\% = 45.3\%$$

13. $$5.00\text{ g } Na_2CO_3 \times \frac{100.0\text{ g } Na_2CO_3 \cdot 10\,H_2O}{37.06\text{ g } Na_2CO_3} = 13.5\text{ g } Na_2CO_3 \cdot 10H_2O$$

26. Surface molecules are attracted to the liquid molecules below but not to the air. Molecules inside the liquid are attracted in all directions.

28. A surfactant is a wetting agent such as soap or detergent. A surfactant interferes with hydrogen bonding between water molecules and reduces surface tension.

30. Water has low vapor pressure.

33. Bodies of water would freeze from the bottom up. This would kill many forms of aquatic life.

36. solvent: water; solute: sugar

37. No; the molecules and ions are smaller than the pores of the filter and would therefore pass through the filter.

38. Solvent molecules surround positively charged and negatively charged ions.

40. **a.** HCl (polar) dissolves.

b. K_2SO_4 (ionic) dissolves.

c. NaI (ionic) dissolves.

d. C_2H_6 (nonpolar) will not dissolve.

e. NH_3 (polar) dissolves.

f. $CaCO_3$ (strong ionic forces) will not dissolve.

42. Its ions are free to move toward positively and negatively charged electrodes.

44. **a.** $Na_2SO_4 \cdot 10H_2O$

b. $CaCl_2 \cdot 2H_2O$

c. $Ba(OH)_2 \cdot 8H_2O$

45. **a.** tin(IV) chloride pentahydrate

b. iron(II) sulfate heptahydrate

c. barium bromide tetrahydrate

d. iron(III) phosphate tetrahydrate

46. $MgSO_4 \cdot 7H_2O(s) \longrightarrow MgSO_4 \cdot H_2O(s) + 6H_2O(g)$

47. Hygroscopic substances absorb water vapor from the air and create a dry environment in a sealed container.

48. solutions, colloids, suspensions

49. Colloids and suspensions exhibit the Tyndall effect, but solutions do not. The particles in a suspension will settle out over time.

51. Brownian motion and repulsion between like-charged ions adsorbed on the surfaces of colloidal particles.

53. hexane, ethanol, water

54. **a.** 1.0000 g/mL

b. 4°C

c. No; there would be a break in the curve at 0°C as liquid water at 0°C changes to ice at 0°C.

55. **a.** Water expands when it freezes to ice.

b. Water is polar, and wax is nonpolar; water has a higher surface tension.

c. Water has a lower vapor pressure than alcohol.

56. **a.** No, both form clear, colorless solutions.

b. Evaporate the water to examine the crystals; test for electrical conductivity; do a flame test.

57. **a.** nonelectrolyte

b. weak electrolyte

c. strong electrolyte

58. The container would break because water expands as it freezes.

59. Most of the important chemical reactions of life take place in aqueous solutions inside cells.

62. The molecules in the dirt and grease dissolve in the water.

64. **a.** 5 **b.** 2 **c.** 2 **d.** 4

65. $H^+ + H\!:\!\ddot{\underset{\cdot\cdot}{O}}\!:\!H \longrightarrow \left[H\!:\!\ddot{\underset{\cdot\cdot}{O}}\!:\!H\right]^+$ (with a third H bonded below the O)

66. **a.** $6CO_2(g) + 6H_2O(l) \longrightarrow C_6H_{12}O_6(s) + 6O_2(g)$

b. $2Na(s) + 2H_2O(l) \longrightarrow$
$2Na^+(aq) + 2OH^-(aq) + H_2(g)$

67. $$2.00 \times 10^{-3}\,\cancel{\text{mol } H_2O_2} \times \frac{2\,\cancel{\text{mol } H_2O}}{2\,\cancel{\text{mol } H_2O_2}} \times \frac{18.0\text{ g } H_2O}{1\,\cancel{\text{mol } H_2O}} = 0.0360\text{ g } H_2O$$

$$2.00 \times 10^{-3}\,\cancel{\text{mol } H_2O_2} \times \frac{1\,\cancel{\text{mol } O_2}}{2\,\cancel{\text{mol } H_2O_2}} \times \frac{22.4\text{ L } O_2}{1\,\cancel{\text{mol } O_2}} = 0.0224\text{ L } O_2$$

68. **a.** $$40\,\cancel{\text{cm}^3} \times \frac{1\,\cancel{\text{mL}}}{1\,\cancel{\text{cm}^3}} \times \frac{1\,\cancel{\text{L}}}{1000\,\cancel{\text{mL}}} \times \frac{1\text{ mol } O_2}{22.4\,\cancel{\text{L}}} = 1.8 \times 10^{-3}\text{ mol } O_2$$

$$60\,\cancel{\text{cm}^3} \times \frac{1\,\cancel{\text{mL}}}{1\,\cancel{\text{cm}^3}} \times \frac{1\,\cancel{\text{L}}}{1000\,\cancel{\text{mL}}} \times \frac{1\text{ mol } H_2}{22.4\,\cancel{\text{L}}} = 2.7 \times 10^{-3}\text{ mol } H_2$$

$$1.8 \times 10^{-3}\,\cancel{\text{mol } O_2} \times \frac{2\text{ mol } H_2}{1\,\cancel{\text{mol } O_2}} = 3.6 \times 10^{-3}\text{ mol } H_2$$

Since 2.7×10^{-3} mol $H_2 < 3.6 \times 10^{-3}$ mol H_2, hydrogen is the limiting reagent.

b. $$2.7 \times 10^{-3}\,\cancel{\text{mol } H_2} \times \frac{2\,\cancel{\text{mol } H_2O}}{2\,\cancel{\text{mol } H_2}} \times \frac{18.0\text{ g } H_2O}{1\,\cancel{\text{mol } H_2O}} = 0.049\text{ g } H_2O$$

c. oxygen

d. $$2.7 \times 10^{-3}\,\cancel{\text{mol } H_2} \times \frac{1\text{ mol } O_2}{2\,\cancel{\text{mol } H_2}} = 1.4 \times 10^{-3}\text{ mol } O_2$$

Excess $O_2 = (1.8 \times 10^{-3} - 1.4 \times 10^{-3})$ mol $O_2 = 0.4 \times 10^{-3}$ mol O_2

$$0.4 \times 10^{-3}\,\cancel{\text{mol } O_2} \times \frac{22.4\text{ L}}{1\,\cancel{\text{mol } O_2}} = 9 \times 10^{-3}\text{ L}$$

70. $T_1 = 100°\text{C} + 273\text{ K} = 373\text{ K}$

$T_2 = 200°\text{C} + 273\text{ K} = 473\text{ K}$

$$P_2 = \frac{P_1 \times T_2}{T_1} = \frac{1.00\text{ atm} \times 473\,\cancel{\text{K}}}{373\,\cancel{\text{K}}} = 1.27\text{ atm}$$

Chapter 16

1. $S_2 = \dfrac{S_1 \times P_2}{P_1} = \dfrac{0.16\ \text{g/L} \times 288\ \text{kPa}}{104\ \text{kPa}} = 0.44\ \text{g/L}$

2. $P_2 = \dfrac{P_1 \times S_2}{S_1} = \dfrac{1.0\ \text{atm} \times 9.5\ \text{g/L}}{3.6\ \text{g/L}} = 2.6\ \text{atm}$

3. $S_2 = \dfrac{S_1 \times P_2}{P_1} = \dfrac{0.58\ \text{g/L} \times 250\ \text{kPa}}{104\ \text{kPa}} = 1.4\ \text{g/L}$

4. $S_2 = \dfrac{S_1 \times P_2}{P_1} = \dfrac{5.28\ \text{g/L} \times 2.5\ \text{atm}}{4.0\ \text{atm}} = 3.3\ \text{g/L}$

$S_1 - S_2 = 5.28\ \text{g/L} - 3.3\ \text{g/L} = 2.0\ \text{g/L}$

12. $\dfrac{36.0\ \text{g}\ C_6H_{12}O_6}{2.0\ \text{L}} \times \dfrac{1\ \text{mol}\ C_6H_{12}O_6}{180\ \text{g}\ C_6H_{12}O_6} = 0.10\ \text{mol/L}$

$= 0.10M$

13. $\dfrac{0.70\ \text{mol NaCl}}{250\ \text{mL}} \times \dfrac{10^3\ \text{mL}}{1\ \text{L}} = 2.8\ \text{mol/L} = 2.8M$

14. $\dfrac{0.50\ \text{g NaCl}}{100\ \text{mL}} \times \dfrac{1\ \text{mol NaCl}}{58.5\ \text{g NaCl}} \times \dfrac{10^3\ \text{mL}}{1\ \text{L}} =$

$0.085\ \text{mol/L} = 0.085M$

15. $\dfrac{400\ \text{g}\ CuSO_4}{4.00\ \text{L}} \times \dfrac{1\ \text{mol}\ CuSO_4}{159.6\ \text{g}\ CuSO_4} = 0.627\ \text{mol/L} =$

$0.627M$

16. $1.2\ \text{L} \times \dfrac{0.75\ \text{mol NaCl}}{1\ \text{L}} = 0.90\ \text{mol NaCl}$

17. $335\ \text{mL} \times \dfrac{1\ \text{L}}{10^3\ \text{mL}} \times \dfrac{0.425\ \text{mol}\ NH_4NO_3}{1\ \text{L}} =$

$0.142\ \text{mol}\ NH_4NO_3$

18. $250\ \text{mL} \times \dfrac{1\ \text{L}}{10^3\ \text{mL}} \times \dfrac{2.0\ \text{mol}\ CaCl_2}{1\ \text{L}} = 0.50\ \text{mol}\ CaCl_2$

$0.50\ \text{mol}\ CaCl_2 \times \dfrac{111.1\ \text{g}\ CaCl_2}{1\ \text{mol}\ CaCl_2} = 56\ \text{g}\ CaCl_2$

19. $V_1 = \dfrac{M_2 \times V_2}{M_1} = \dfrac{0.760M \times 250\ \text{mL}}{4.00M} = 47.5\ \text{mL}$

20. $M_2 = \dfrac{M_1 \times V_1}{V_2} = \dfrac{1.50M \times 35.0\ \text{mL}}{100.0\ \text{mL}} = 0.525M$

21. $\dfrac{10\ \text{mL propanone}}{200\ \text{mL}} \times 100\% = 5.0\%$ propanone (v/v)

22. $\dfrac{50\ \text{mL diethyl ether}}{2500\ \text{mL}} \times 100\% =$

2.0% diethyl ether (v/v)

23. $3.0\%\ \text{(v/v)} = \dfrac{V_{H_2O_2}}{V_{\text{soln}}} \times 100\%$

$V_{H_2O_2} = \dfrac{3.0\%}{100\%} \times 400.0\ \text{mL} = 12\ \text{mL}$

37. $750\ \text{g}\ H_2O \times \dfrac{0.400\ \text{mol NaF}}{10^3\ \text{g}\ H_2O} \times \dfrac{42.0\ \text{g NaF}}{1\ \text{mol NaF}} =$

$12.6\ \text{g NaF}$

38. $400.0\ \text{g}\ H_2O \times \dfrac{0.500\ \text{mol NaBr}}{10^3\ \text{g}\ H_2O} \times \dfrac{102.9\ \text{g NaBr}}{1\ \text{mol NaBr}} =$

$20.6\ \text{g NaBr}$

39. $\dfrac{10.0\ \text{g NaCl}}{600\ \text{g}\ H_2O} \times \dfrac{1\ \text{mol NaCl}}{58.5\ \text{g NaCl}} \times \dfrac{10^3\ \text{g}\ H_2O}{1\ \text{kg}\ H_2O} =$

$0.285m$ NaCl

40. $\dfrac{60.0\ \text{g}\ C_6H_{12}O_6}{2.0\ \text{L}\ H_2O} \times \dfrac{1\ \text{mol}\ C_6H_{12}O_6}{180.0\ \text{g}\ C_6H_{12}O_6} \times \dfrac{1\ \text{L}\ H_2O}{1\ \text{kg}\ H_2O}$

$= 0.17m\ C_6H_{12}O_6$

41. $10.0\ \text{g}\ C_6H_{12}O_6 \times \dfrac{1\ \text{mol}\ C_6H_{12}O_6}{180.0\ \text{g}\ C_6H_{12}O_6} =$

$0.0556\ \text{mol}\ C_6H_{12}O_6$

$m = \dfrac{0.0556\ \text{mol}\ C_6H_{12}O_6}{50.0\ \text{g}\ H_2O \times \dfrac{1\ \text{kg}\ H_2O}{10^3\ \text{g}\ H_2O}} = 1.11m\ C_6H_{12}O_6$

$\Delta T_f = K_f \times m = 1.86°\text{C}/m \times 1.11m = 2.07°\text{C}$

42. $12.0\ \text{g}\ C_{10}H_8 \times \dfrac{1\ \text{mol}\ C_{10}H_8}{128.0\ \text{g}\ C_{10}H_8} = 0.0938\ \text{mol}\ C_{10}H_8$

$m = \dfrac{0.0938\ \text{mol}\ C_{10}H_8}{50.0\ \text{g}\ C_6H_6 \times \dfrac{1\ \text{kg}\ C_6H_6}{1000\ \text{g}\ C_6H_6}} = 1.88m\ C_{10}H_8$

$\Delta T_f = K_f \times m = 5.12°\text{C}/m \times 1.88m = 9.60°\text{C}$

43. $200\ \text{g}\ C_3H_6O \times \dfrac{1\ \text{mol}\ C_3H_6O}{58.0\ \text{g}\ C_3H_6O} = 3.45\ \text{mol}\ C_3H_6O$

$m = \dfrac{3.45\ \text{mol}\ C_3H_6O}{400\ \text{g benzene} \times \dfrac{1\ \text{kg benzene}}{10^3\ \text{g benzene}}} = 8.62m\ C_3H_6O$

$\Delta T_f = K_f \times m = 5.12°\text{C}/m \times 8.62m = 44.1°\text{C}$

44. $50.0\ \text{g}\ C_2H_6O_2 \times \dfrac{1\ \text{mol}\ C_2H_6O_2}{62.0\ \text{g}\ C_2H_6O_2} = 0.806\ \text{mol}\ C_2H_6O_2$

$50.0\ \text{g}\ C_6H_{12}O_6 \times \dfrac{1\ \text{mol}\ C_6H_{12}O_6}{180.0\ \text{g}\ C_6H_{12}O_6} =$

$0.278\ \text{mol}\ C_3H_6O$

total moles in solution = 0.806 mol + 0.278 mol = 1.084 mol

$m = \dfrac{1.084\ \text{mol}}{200.0\ \text{g}\ H_2O \times \dfrac{1\ \text{kg}\ H_2O}{10^3\ \text{g}\ H_2O}} = 5.42m$

$\Delta T_f = K_f \times m = 1.86°\text{C}/m \times 5.42m = 10.1°\text{C}$

$T_f = 0.0°\text{C} - 10.1°\text{C} = -10.1°\text{C}$

45. $m = \dfrac{1.25 \text{ mol CaCl}_2}{1400 \text{ g H}_2\text{O} \times \dfrac{1 \text{ kg H}_2\text{O}}{10^3 \text{ g H}_2\text{O}}} = 0.893m \text{ CaCl}_2$

Each formula unit of $CaCl_2$ disassociates into 3 particles, so molality of total particles is:

$3 \times 0.893m = 2.68m$

$\Delta T_b = K_b \times m = 0.512°\text{C}/m \times 2.68m = 1.37°\text{C}$

$T_b = 100°\text{C} + 1.37°\text{C} = 101.37°\text{C}$

46. $m = \dfrac{2.00 \text{ mol NaCl}}{750 \text{ g H}_2\text{O} \times \dfrac{1 \text{ kg H}_2\text{O}}{10^3 \text{ g H}_2\text{O}}} = 2.67m \text{ NaCl}$

Each formula unit of NaCl disassociates into 2 particles, so molality of total particles is:

$2 \times 2.67m = 5.33m$

$\Delta T_b = K_b \times m = 0.512°\text{C}/m \times 5.33m = 2.73°\text{C}$

$T_b = 100°\text{C} + 2.73°\text{C} = 102.73°\text{C}$

47. $12.0 \text{ g C}_{10}\text{H}_8 \times \dfrac{1 \text{ mol C}_{10}\text{H}_8}{128.0 \text{ g C}_{10}\text{H}_8} = 0.0938 \text{ mol C}_{10}\text{H}_8$

$m = \dfrac{0.0938 \text{ mol C}_{10}\text{H}_8}{50.0 \text{ g C}_6\text{H}_6 \times \dfrac{1 \text{ kg C}_6\text{H}_6}{1000 \text{ g C}_6\text{H}_6}} = 1.88m \text{ C}_{10}\text{H}_8$

$\Delta T_b = K_b \times m = 2.53°\text{C}/m \times 1.88m = 4.76°\text{C}$

48. $m = \dfrac{\Delta T_b}{K_b} = \dfrac{2.00°\text{C}}{0.512°\text{C}/m} = 3.906m$

(molality of total particles)

Each formula unit of NaCl disassociates into 2 particles, so the solution concentration is:

$3.906m/2 = 1.953m$

Mass of NaCl needed per 1 kg of H_2O is:

$1.953 \text{ mol NaCl} \times \dfrac{58.5 \text{ g NaCl}}{1 \text{ mol NaCl}} = 114 \text{ g NaCl}$

60. a. $S_2 = \dfrac{S_1 \times P_2}{P_1} = \dfrac{0.026 \text{ g/L} \times 0.60 \text{ atm}}{1.00 \text{ atm}} = 0.016 \text{ g/L}$

b. $S_2 = \dfrac{S_1 \times P_2}{P_1} = \dfrac{0.026 \text{ g/L} \times 1.80 \text{ atm}}{1.00 \text{ atm}} = 0.047 \text{ g/L}$

63. $V_1 = \dfrac{M_2 \times V_2}{M_1} = \dfrac{0.100M \times 100.0 \text{ mL}}{0.500M} = 20.0 \text{ mL}$

64. $\dfrac{0.50 \text{ g NaCl}}{100 \text{ mL}} \times \dfrac{1 \text{ mol NaCl}}{58.5 \text{ g NaCl}} \times \dfrac{10^3 \text{ mL}}{1 \text{ L}} = 0.085M$

66. a. $2500 \text{ g solution} \times \dfrac{0.90 \text{ g NaCl}}{100 \text{ g solution}} = 23 \text{ g NaCl}$

b. $0.050 \text{ kg solution} \times \dfrac{1000 \text{ g solution}}{1 \text{ kg solution}} \times \dfrac{4.0 \text{ g MgCl}_2}{100 \text{ g solution}}$

$= 2.0 \text{ g MgCl}_2$

68. a. $\dfrac{25 \text{ mL ethanol}}{150 \text{ mL}} \times 100\% = 17\% \text{ (v/v) ethanol}$

b. $\dfrac{175 \text{ mL isopropyl alcohol}}{275 \text{ mL}} \times 100\% =$

63.6% (v/v) isopropyl alcohol

74. a. Molality of $Na_2SO_4 = \dfrac{1.40 \text{ mol Na}_2\text{SO}_4}{1750 \text{ g H}_2\text{O} \times \dfrac{1 \text{ kg H}_2\text{O}}{10^3 \text{ g H}_2\text{O}}}$

$= 0.800m \text{ Na}_2\text{SO}_4$

Each mol of Na_2SO_4 that dissolves yields 3 mol of particles.

Molality of total particles $= 3 \times 0.800m = 2.40m$

$\Delta T_f = K_f \times m = 1.86°\text{C}/m \times 2.40m = 4.46°\text{C}$

$T_f = 0°\text{C} - 4.46°\text{C} = -4.46°\text{C}$

b. Molality of $MgSO_4 = \dfrac{0.060 \text{ mol MgSO}_4}{100 \text{ g H}_2\text{O} \times \dfrac{1 \text{ kg H}_2\text{O}}{10^3 \text{ g H}_2\text{O}}}$

$= 0.60m \text{ MgSO}_4$

Each mol of $MgSO_4$ that dissolves yields 2 mol of particles.

Molality of total particles $= 2 \times 0.60m = 1.2m$

$\Delta T_f = K_f \times m = 1.86°\text{C}/m \times 1.2m = 2.2°\text{C}$

$T_f = 0°\text{C} - 22°\text{C} = -2.2°\text{C}$

83. $S = \dfrac{36.0 \text{ g NaCl}}{100 \text{ g H}_2\text{O}} \times \dfrac{0.750}{0.750} = \dfrac{27.0 \text{ g NaCl}}{75.0 \text{ g H}_2\text{O}}$

The solution contains 26.5 g NaCl/75.0 g H_2O and is therefore unsaturated.

87. $V_1 = \dfrac{M_2 \times V_2}{M_1} = \dfrac{0.50M \times 100 \text{ mL}}{2.0M} = 25 \text{ mL}$

Step 1: Start with a stock solution that is 2.0*M* KCl.

Step 2: Transfer 25 mL of 2.0*M* KCl to a 100-mL volumetric flask.

Step 3: Add distilled water up to the 100-mL mark.

92. Atomic mass of Rb = (0.72165)(84.912 amu) + (0.27835)(86.909 amu) = 61.277 amu + 24.191 amu = 85.468 amu

96. $1500 \text{ g H}_2 \times \dfrac{1 \text{ mol H}_2}{2.0 \text{ g H}_2} \times \dfrac{22.4 \text{ L H}_2}{1 \text{ mol H}_2} = 1.7 \times 10^4 \text{ L H}_2$

98. $T_1 = 25°\text{C} + 273 = 298 \text{ K}$

$T_1 = 45°\text{C} + 273 = 318 \text{ K}$

$P_2 = \dfrac{P_1 \times T_2}{T_1} = \dfrac{101.3 \text{ kPa} \times 318 \text{ K}}{298 \text{ K}} = 108 \text{ kPa}$

Chapter 17

1. The melted wax (the system) is at a higher temperature than the air (the surroundings). Heat flows from the liquid wax to the air, so the process is exothermic.

2. The potato (the system) is at a lower temperature than the air in the oven (the surroundings). Heat flows from the air to the potato, so the process is endothermic.

3. The reactants are the system. The beaker and the air that surrounds it are the surroundings. During the reaction, the system absorbs heat from the surroudings, so the reaction is endothermic.

4. $\Delta T = 85°C - 21°C = 64°C$

$$C_{\text{olive oil}} = \frac{q}{m \times \Delta T} = \frac{435\ J}{3.4\ g \times 64°C} = 2.0\ J/(g \cdot °C)$$

5. $C_{Ag} = \frac{q}{m \times \Delta T} = \frac{q/\Delta T}{m} = \frac{42.8\ J/°C}{181\ g} = 0.236\ J/(g \cdot °C)$

6. $C_{\text{stainless steel}} = \frac{q}{m \times \Delta T} = \frac{141\ J}{1.55\ g \times 178°C} = 0.511\ J/(g \cdot °C)$

7. $q = C_{Hg} \times m \times \Delta T = (0.14\ J/(\cancel{g} \cdot \cancel{°C}))(250.0\ \cancel{g})(52\cancel{°C}) = 1800\ J = 1.8\ kJ$

15. $V_{water} = 50.0\ mL + 50.0\ mL = 100.0\ mL$

$m_{water} = 100.0\ \cancel{mL} \times \frac{1.00\ g}{1\ \cancel{mL}} = 100.0\ g$

$\Delta T = 26.0°C - 22.5°C = 3.5°C$

$\Delta H = -q_{surr} = -m_{water} \times C_{water} \times \Delta T = -(100.0\ \cancel{g}) \times (4.18\ J/(\cancel{g} \cdot \cancel{°C}))(3.5\cancel{°C}) = -1500\ J = -1.5\ kJ$

(1.5 kJ of heat are released)

16. $\Delta T = 25.5°C - 21.7°C = 3.8°C$

$$m = \frac{-\Delta H}{C \times \Delta T} = \frac{-(-5.0 \times 10^3\ \cancel{J})}{(4.18\ \cancel{J}/g \cdot \cancel{°C}))(3.8\cancel{°C})} = 310\ g$$

17. $\Delta T = 26.4°C - 25.0°C = 1.4°C$

$\Delta H = -q_{surr} = -m_{water} \times C_{water} \times \Delta T = -(25.0\ \cancel{g}) \times (4.18\ J/(\cancel{g} \cdot \cancel{°C}))(1.4\cancel{°C}) = -150\ J$

(150 J of heat is released by the pebble)

18. $\Delta H = 3.40\ \cancel{mol\ Fe_2O_3(s)} \times \frac{26.3\ kJ}{1\ \cancel{mol\ Fe_2O_3(s)}} = 89.4\ kJ$

19. $\Delta H = 114\ \cancel{mol\ H_2O(l)} \times \frac{285.8\ kJ}{1\ \cancel{mol\ H_2O(l)}} = 3.26 \times 10^4\ kJ$

20. $\Delta H = 5.66\ \cancel{g\ CS_2(l)} \times \frac{1\ \cancel{mol\ CS_2(l)}}{76.2\ \cancel{g\ CS_2(l)}} \times \frac{89.3\ kJ}{1\ \cancel{mol\ CS_2(l)}} = 6.63\ kJ$

27. $m_{H_2O(s)} = 0.400\ \cancel{kJ} \times \frac{1\ \cancel{mol\ H_2O(s)}}{6.01\ \cancel{kJ}} \times \frac{18.0\ g\ H_2O(s)}{1\ \cancel{mol\ H_2O(s)}} = 1.20\ g\ H_2O(s)$

28. $\Delta H = 3.5\ \cancel{mol\ H_2O(s)} \times \frac{6.01\ kJ}{1\ \cancel{mol\ H_2O(s)}} = 21\ kJ$

29. $m_{H_2O(s)} = 12.0\ g - 8.50\ g = 3.5\ g$

$\Delta H = 3.5\ \cancel{g\ H_2O(s)} \times \frac{1\ \cancel{mol\ H_2O(s)}}{18.0\ \cancel{g\ H_2O(s)}} \times \frac{6.01\ kJ}{1\ \cancel{mol\ H_2O(s)}} = 1.2\ kJ$

30. $\Delta H = 50.0\ \cancel{g\ H_2O(l)} \times \frac{1\ \cancel{mol\ H_2O(l)}}{18.0\ \cancel{g\ H_2O(l)}} \times \frac{6.01\ kJ}{1\ \cancel{mol\ H_2O(l)}} = 16.7\ kJ$

31. $\Delta H = 63.7\ \cancel{g\ H_2O(l)} \times \frac{1\ \cancel{mol\ H_2O(l)}}{18.0\ \cancel{g\ H_2O(l)}} \times \frac{40.7\ kJ}{1\ \cancel{mol\ H_2O(l)}} = 144\ kJ$

32. $\Delta H = 50.0\ \cancel{g\ C_2H_6O(l)} \times \frac{1\ \cancel{mol\ C_2H_6O(l)}}{46.0\ \cancel{g\ C_2H_6O(l)}} \times \frac{38.6\ kJ}{1\ \cancel{mol\ C_2H_6O(l)}} = 42.0\ kJ$

33. $\Delta H = 0.800\ \cancel{mol\ NH_3(g)} \times \frac{-23.3\ kJ}{1\ \cancel{mol\ NH_3(g)}} = -18.6\ kJ$

34. $\Delta H = 0.46\ \cancel{g\ C_2H_5Cl(l)} \times \frac{1\ \cancel{mol\ C_2H_5Cl(l)}}{64.5\ \cancel{g\ C_2H_5Cl(l)}} \times \frac{24.7\ kJ}{1\ \cancel{mol\ C_2H_5Cl(l)}} = 0.18\ kJ$

42. $\Delta H_f°(\text{reactants}) = 1\ \cancel{mol\ Br_2(g)} \times \frac{30.91\ kJ}{1\ \cancel{mol\ Br_2(g)}} = 30.91\ kJ$

$\Delta H_f°(\text{products}) = 1\ \cancel{mol\ Br_2(l)} \times \frac{0\ kJ}{1\ \cancel{mol\ Br_2(l)}} = 0\ kJ$

$\Delta H° = \Delta H_f°(\text{products}) - \Delta H_f°(\text{reactants}) = 0\ kJ - 30.91\ kJ = -30.91\ kJ$

43. $\Delta H_f°(\text{reactants}) = 2\ \cancel{mol\ H_2O_2(l)} \times \frac{-187.8\ kJ}{1\ \cancel{mol\ H_2O_2(l)}} = -375.6\ kJ$

$\Delta H_f°(\text{products}) = 2\ \cancel{mol\ H_2O(l)} \times \frac{-285.8\ kJ}{1\ \cancel{mol\ H_2O(l)}} + 1\ \cancel{mol\ O_2(g)} \times \frac{0\ kJ}{1\ \cancel{mol\ O_2(g)}} = -571.6\ kJ$

$\Delta H° = \Delta H_f°(\text{products}) - \Delta H_f°(\text{reactants}) = -571.6\ kJ - (-375.6\ kJ) = -196.0\ kJ$

44. $\Delta H_f^\circ(\text{reactants}) = 2\ \text{mol C}(s,\text{graphite}) \times \dfrac{0\ \text{kJ}}{1\ \text{mol C}(s,\text{graphite})} + 1\ \text{mol O}_2(g) \times \dfrac{0\ \text{kJ}}{1\ \text{mol O}_2(g)} = 0\ \text{kJ}$

$\Delta H_f^\circ(\text{products}) = 2\ \text{mol CO}(g) \times \dfrac{-110.5\ \text{kJ}}{1\ \text{mol CO}(g)} = -221.0\ \text{kJ}$

$\Delta H^\circ = \Delta H_f^\circ(\text{products}) - \Delta H_f^\circ(\text{reactants})$
$= -221.0\ \text{kJ} - 0\ \text{kJ} = -221.0\ \text{kJ}$

45. $2\text{NO}(g) + \text{O}_2(g) \longrightarrow 2\text{NO}_2(g)$

$\Delta H_f^\circ(\text{reactants}) = 2\ \text{mol NO}(g) \times \dfrac{90.37\ \text{kJ}}{1\ \text{mol NO}(g)} + 1\ \text{mol O}_2(g) \times \dfrac{0\ \text{kJ}}{1\ \text{mol O}_2(g)} = 180.74\ \text{kJ}$

$\Delta H_f^\circ(\text{products}) = 2\ \text{mol NO}_2(g) \times \dfrac{33.85\ \text{kJ}}{1\ \text{mol NO}_2(g)} = 67.70\ \text{kJ}$

$\Delta H^\circ = \Delta H_f^\circ(\text{products}) - \Delta H_f^\circ(\text{reactants})$
$= 67.70\ \text{kJ} - 180.74\ \text{kJ} = -113.04\ \text{kJ}$

54. **a.** exothermic

b. The immediate surroundings are the glass beaker and the air. If one or more of the substances is in water, the water is also considered part of the surroundings.

55. **a.** exothermic **b.** endothermic **c.** exothermic

58. **a.** $8.50 \times 10^2\ \text{cal} \times \dfrac{1\ \text{Cal}}{1000\ \text{cal}} = 0.850\ \text{Cal}$

b. $444\ \text{cal} \times \dfrac{4.18\ \text{J}}{1\ \text{cal}} = 1.86 \times 10^3\ \text{J}$

c. $1.8\ \text{kJ} \times \dfrac{1000\ \text{J}}{1\ \text{kJ}} = 1.8 \times 10^3\ \text{J}$

d. $4.5 \times 10^{-1}\ \text{kJ} \times \dfrac{1000\ \text{J}}{1\ \text{kJ}} \times \dfrac{1\ \text{cal}}{4.18\ \text{J}} = 1.1 \times 10^2\ \text{cal}$

60. $q = C \times m \times \Delta T = (0.24\ \text{J/(g}\cdot{}^\circ\text{C)})(400.0\ \text{g})(45^\circ\text{C})$
$= 4.3 \times 10^3\ \text{J}$

64. $\Delta H = 0.75\ \text{mol Mg} \times \dfrac{-1204\ \text{kJ}}{2\ \text{mol Mg}} = -4.5 \times 10^2\ \text{kJ}$

66. **a.** $\Delta H = 0.44\ \text{mol H}_2\text{O}(g) \times \dfrac{-40.7\ \text{kJ}}{1\ \text{mol H}_2\text{O}(g)} = -18\ \text{kJ}$

b. $\Delta H = 1.25\ \text{mol NaOH}(s) \times \dfrac{-44.5\ \text{kJ}}{1\ \text{mol NaOH}(s)} = -55.6\ \text{kJ}$

68. **a.** $\Delta H = 1\ \text{mol Al}_2\text{O}_3(s) \times \dfrac{3352\ \text{kJ}}{2\ \text{mol Al}_2\text{O}_3(s)} = -1676\ \text{kJ}$

b. ΔH is positive, so the reaction is endothermic.

69. Reverse the second equation and change the sign of ΔH. Then, add the equations and the values of ΔH.

$\text{Pb}(s) + 2\text{Cl}_2(g) \longrightarrow \text{PbCl}_4(l) \qquad \Delta H = -329.2\ \text{kJ}$
$\text{PbCl}_2(s) \longrightarrow \text{Pb}(s) + \text{Cl}_2(g) \qquad \Delta H = 359.4\ \text{kJ}$

$\text{PbCl}_2(s) + \text{Cl}_2(g) \longrightarrow \text{PbCl}_4(l) \quad \Delta H = 30.2\ \text{kJ}$

70. Substance B; for equal masses, the substance with the greater specific heat undergoes the smaller temperature change.

71. **a.** $\Delta H_f^\circ(\text{reactants}) = 1\ \text{mol CH}_4(g) \times \dfrac{-74.86\ \text{kJ}}{1\ \text{mol CH}_4(g)} + \dfrac{3}{2}\ \text{mol O}_2(g) \times \dfrac{0\ \text{kJ}}{1\ \text{mol O}_2(g)} = -74.86\ \text{kJ}$

$\Delta H_f^\circ(\text{products}) = 1\ \text{mol CO}(g) \times \dfrac{-110.5\ \text{kJ}}{1\ \text{mol CO}(g)} + 2\ \text{mol H}_2\text{O}(l) \times \dfrac{-285.8\ \text{kJ}}{1\ \text{mol H}_2\text{O}(l)} = -682.1\ \text{kJ}$

$\Delta H^\circ = \Delta H_f^\circ(\text{products}) - \Delta H_f^\circ(\text{reactants})$
$= (-682.1\ \text{kJ}) - (-74.86\ \text{kJ}) = -607.2\ \text{kJ}$

b. $\Delta H_f^\circ(\text{reactants}) = 2\ \text{mol CO}(g) \times \dfrac{-110.5\ \text{kJ}}{1\ \text{mol CO}(g)} + 1\ \text{mol O}_2(g) \times \dfrac{0\ \text{kJ}}{1\ \text{mol O}_2(g)} = -221.0\ \text{kJ}$

$\Delta H_f^\circ(\text{products}) = 2\ \text{mol CO}_2(g) \times \dfrac{-393.5\ \text{kJ}}{1\ \text{mol CO}_2(g)} = -787.0\ \text{kJ}$

$\Delta H^\circ = \Delta H_f^\circ(\text{products}) - \Delta H_f^\circ(\text{reactants})$
$= (-787.0\ \text{kJ}) - (-221.0\ \text{kJ}) = -566.0\ \text{kJ}$

73. Multiply the first equation by 2, reverse it, and change the sign of ΔH.

$2\text{PCl}_3(g) + 2\text{Cl}_2(g) \longrightarrow 2\text{PCl}_5(s) \quad \Delta H = (2)(-156.5\ \text{kJ})$
$2\text{P}(s) + 3\text{Cl}_2(g) \longrightarrow 2\text{PCl}_3(g) \qquad \Delta H = -574\ \text{kJ}$

$2\text{P}(s) + 5\text{Cl}_2(g) \longrightarrow 2\text{PCl}_5(s) \qquad \Delta H = -887\ \text{kJ}$

75. **a.** Calculate the heat absorbed by the melting ice:

$40.0\ \text{g H}_2\text{O}(l) \times \dfrac{1\ \text{mol H}_2\text{O}(s)}{18.0\ \text{g H}_2\text{O}(s)} \times \dfrac{6.01\ \text{kJ}}{1\ \text{mol H}_2\text{O}(l)} \times \dfrac{1000\ \text{J}}{1\ \text{kJ}} = 1.34 \times 10^4\ \text{J}$

Convert to calories:

$1.34 \times 10^4\ \text{J} \times \dfrac{1\ \text{cal}}{4.18\ \text{J}} = 3.21 \times 10^3\ \text{cal}$

Convert to kilocalories:

$3.21 \times 10^3\ \text{cal} \times \dfrac{1\ \text{kcal}}{1000\ \text{cal}} = 3.21\ \text{kcal}$

b. $m_{\text{water}} = \dfrac{q}{C_{\text{water}} \times \Delta T} = \dfrac{1.34 \times 10^4\ \text{J}}{4.18\ \text{J/(g}\cdot{}^\circ\text{C)} \times (25.0^\circ\text{C})} = 128\ \text{g}$

77. $\Delta H_f°(\text{reactants}) = 1\ \cancel{\text{mol } C_6H_{12}O_6(s)} \times \frac{-1260\ \text{kJ}}{1\ \cancel{\text{mol } C_6H_{12}O_6(s)}} + 6\ \cancel{\text{mol } O_2(g)} \times \frac{0\ \text{kJ}}{1\ \cancel{\text{mol } O_2(g)}} = -1260\ \text{kJ}$

$\Delta H_f°(\text{products}) = 6\ \cancel{\text{mol } CO_2(g)} \times \frac{-393.5\ \text{kJ}}{1\ \cancel{\text{mol } CO_2(g)}} + 6\ \cancel{\text{mol } H_2O(l)} \times \frac{-285.8\ \text{kJ}}{1\ \cancel{\text{mol } H_2O(l)}} = -4075.8\ \text{kJ}$

$\Delta H° = \Delta H_f°(\text{products}) - \Delta H_f°(\text{reactants}) = (-4075.8\ \text{kJ}) - (-1260\ \text{kJ}) = -2820\ \text{kJ}$

83. **a.** $6.99\ m^2$ **b.** 10.68 g **c.** 3.6×10^2 m/s

84. $N_2(g) + O_2(g) \longrightarrow 2NO(g)$

$2NO(g) + O_2(g) \longrightarrow 2NO_2(g)$

85. $V_2 = \frac{V_1 \times T_2}{T_1} = \frac{8.57\ \text{L} \times 355\ \cancel{\text{K}}}{273\ \cancel{\text{K}}} = 11.1\ \text{L}$

Chapter 18

15. **a.** favors products **b.** favors reactants

16. **a.** favors reactants **b.** favors reactants **c.** favors products **d.** favors products

17. $K_{eq} = \frac{[NO]^2}{[N_2][O_2]} = \frac{(0.02M)^2}{0.50M \times 0.50M} = 1.6 \times 10^{-3}$

18. $K_{eq} = \frac{[CO] \times [H_2O]}{[CO_2] \times [H_2]} = \frac{0.448 \times 0.448}{0.552 \times 0.552} = 6.59 \times 10^{-1}$

19. $0.047\ \cancel{\text{mol } H_2O} \times \frac{1\ \text{mol } H_2}{1\ \cancel{\text{mol } H_2O}} = 0.047\ \text{mol } H_2$

$0.10 - 0.047 = 0.053$ mol H_2 at equilibrium (mol H_2 = mol CO_2)

$K_{eq} = \frac{[H_2O][CO]}{[H_2][CO_2]} = \frac{(0.047\cancel{M}) \times (0.047\cancel{M})}{(0.053\cancel{M}) \times (0.053\cancel{M})} = 0.79$

20. $K_{eq} = \frac{[N_2O_4]}{[NO_2]^2}$

$5.6 = \frac{0.66M}{[NO_2]^2}$

$[NO_2]^2 = \frac{0.66M}{5.6}$

$[NO_2] = \sqrt{\frac{0.66M}{5.6}} = 0.34M$

21. $[PCl_3] = [Cl_2] = 0.15M$

$K_{eq} = \frac{[PCl_3][Cl_2]}{[PCl_5]}$

$0.022 = \frac{0.15 \times 0.15}{[PCl_5]}$

$[PCl_5] = \frac{0.15 \times 0.15}{0.022} = \frac{0.0225}{0.022} = 1.0M$

22. $[H_2] = [I_2] = 0.50M;$

$K_{eq} = \frac{[H_2][I_2]}{[HI]^2}$

$0.020 = \frac{0.50M \times 0.50M}{[HI]^2}$

$[HI]^2 = \frac{0.50M \times 0.50M}{0.020} = \frac{0.25M^2}{0.020} = 12.5M^2$

$[HI] = \sqrt{12.5M^2} = 3.5M$

31. $K_{sp} = [Pb^{2+}] \times [S^{2-}]$

$3.0 \times 10^{-28} = [Pb^{2+}]^2$

$[Pb^{2+}] = \sqrt{3.0 \times 10^{-28}M^2} = 2 \times 10^{-14}M$

32. $K_{sp} = [Ba^{2+}] \times [CO_3^{2-}]$

$5.0 \times 10^{-9} = [Ba^{2+}]^2$

$[Ba^{2+}] = \sqrt{5.0 \times 10^{-9}M^2} = 7.1 \times 10^{-5}M$

33. $K_{sp} = [Sr^{2+}] \times [CO_3^{2-}]$

$9.3 \times 10^{-10} = [CO_3^{2-}]^2$

$[CO_3^{2-}] = \sqrt{9.3 \times 10^{-10}M^2} = 3.0 \times 10^{-5}M$

34. $K_{sp} = [Ca^{2+}] \times [CO_3^{2-}]$

$4.5 \times 10^{-9} = [Ca^{2+}]^2$

$[Ca^{2+}] = \sqrt{4.5 \times 10^{-9}M^2} = 6.7 \times 10^{-5}M$

35. $K_{sp} = [Pb^{2+}] \times [S^{2-}]$

$[S^{2-}] = \frac{K_{sp}}{[Pb^{2+}]} = \frac{(8 \times 10^{-19})}{0.04} = 2 \times 10^{-17}M$

36. $K_{sp} = [Ba^{2+}] \times [SO_4^{2-}]$

$[SO_4^{2-}] = \frac{K_{sp}}{[Ba^{2+}]} = \frac{(1.1 \times 10^{-10})}{0.015} = 7.3 \times 10^{-9}M$

37. $K_{sp} = [Ba^{2+}] \times [CO_3^{2-}]$

$[CO_3^{2-}] = \frac{K_{sp}}{[Ba^{2+}]} = \frac{(5.0 \times 10^{-9})}{0.25} = 2.0 \times 10^{-8}M$

38. $K_{sp} = [Sr^{2+}] \times [SO_4^{2-}]$

$[SO_4^{2-}] = \frac{K_{sp}}{[Sr^{2+}]} = \frac{(3.2 \times 10^{-7})}{0.10} = 3.2 \times 10^{-6}M$

55. Atoms, ions, or molecules can react to form products, or they can bounce apart unchanged.

58. A catalyst increases the rate of reactions by lowering the activation energy.

64. a. $K_{eq} = \dfrac{[CH_4] \times [H_2S]^2}{[H_2]^4 \times [CS_2]}$

b. $K_{eq} = \dfrac{[PCl_3] \times [Cl_2]}{[PCl_5]}$

66. c, b, d, a

72. a. Entropy increases. b. Entropy decreases.

76. For the reverse reaction, the total energy change is 20 kJ. The reaction progress curve for the reverse reaction is as follows:

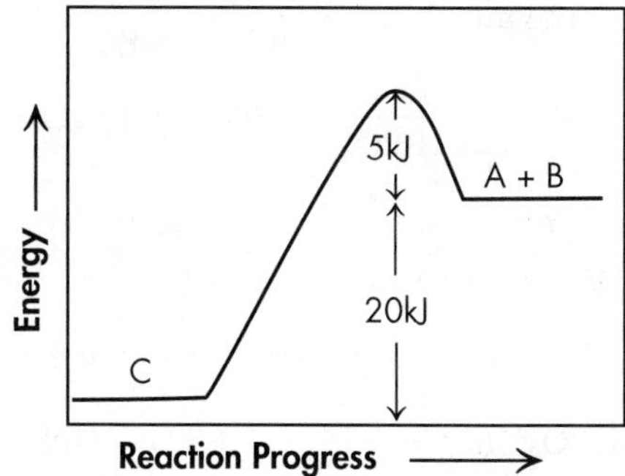

The activation energy of the reverse reaction is the total height of the peak (20 kJ + 5 kJ = 25 kJ).

78. increase in products

79. The product of the concentrations of the ions must be greater than the ion-product constant (K_{sp}).

80. c

81. a. favors products c. favors reactants

b. no effect d. no effect

85. Increase pressure, cool the reaction mixture, and remove NH_3

90. Potassium chloride is an ionic compound, not a molecular compound.

93. a. $2KClO_3(s) + \text{heat} \longrightarrow 2KCl(s) + 3O_2(g)$

b. molar mass = 39.1 + 35.5 + (3 × 16.0) = 122.6 g

$$4.88\ \text{g}\ \cancel{KClO_3} \times \frac{1\ \cancel{\text{mol}\ KClO_3}}{122.6\ \cancel{\text{g}\ KClO_3}} \times \frac{3\ \cancel{\text{mol}\ O_2}}{2\ \cancel{\text{mol}\ KClO_3}} \times \frac{32\ \text{g}\ O_2}{1\ \cancel{\text{mol}\ O_2}} = 1.91\ \text{g}\ O_2$$

98. The process is exothermic because heat is released.

Chapter 19

1. a. H^+ is the Lewis acid; H_2O is the Lewis base.

b. $AlCl_3$ is the Lewis acid; Cl^- is the Lewis base.

2. Lewis base; it has a nonbonding pair of electrons that it can donate.

14. basic;

$[OH^-] = \dfrac{K_w}{[H^+]} = \dfrac{1.0 \times 10^{-14}}{6.0 \times 10^{-10}M} = 1.7 \times 10^{-5}M$

15. basic

16. a. acidic b. neutral

17. $[H^+] = \dfrac{K_w}{[OH^-]} = \dfrac{1.0 \times 10^{-14}}{1.0 \times 10^{-3}M} = 1.0 \times 10^{-11}M$; basic

18. $pH = -\log[H^+] = -\log(0.045M) = 1.35$

19. $pH = -\log[H^+] = -\log(8.7 \times 10^{-6}M) = 5.06$

20. a. $pH = -\log[H^+] = -\log(0.0015M) = 2.82$

b. $pH = -\log[H^+] = -\log(1.2 \times 10^{-3}M) = 2.92$

21. Solution A:

$pH = -\log[H^+] = -\log(1.0 \times 10^{-12}M) = 12$

Solution B:

$pH = -\log[H^+] = -\log(1 \times 10^{-4}M) = 4$

Solution B is more acidic.

22. $pH = -\log[H^+]$

$5.00 = -\log[H^+]$

$-5.00 = \log[H^+]$

$[H^+] = 10^{-5.00} = 1.00 \times 10^{-5}M$

23. $pH = -\log[H^+]$

$12.83 = -\log[H^+]$

$-12.83 = \log[H^+]$

$[H^+] = 10^{-12.83} = 1.48 \times 10^{-13}M$

24. a. $pH = -\log[H^+]$

$4.00 = -\log[H^+]$

$-4.00 = \log[H^+]$

$[H^+] = 10^{-4.00} = 1.00 \times 10^{-4}M$

b. $pH = -\log[H^+]$

$11.55 = -\log[H^+]$

$-11.55 = \log[H^+]$

$[H^+] = 10^{-11.55} = 2.82 \times 10^{-12}M$

25. Solution A: $[H^+] = 10^{-8.50} = 3.16 \times 10^{-9}M$

Solution B: $[H^+] = 10^{-1.00} = 1.00 \times 10^{-1}M$

Solution C: $[H^+] = 10^{-6.22} = 6.03 \times 10^{-7}M$

Lowest concentration to greatest concentration: Solution A, Solution C, Solution B

33. $0.1000M - 4.2 \times 10^{-3}M = 0.0958M$

$K_a = \dfrac{(4.2 \times 10^{-3}) \times (4.2 \times 10^{-3})}{(0.0958)} = 1.8 \times 10^{-4}$

34. $0.2000M - 9.86 \times 10^{-4}M = 0.199M$

$K_a = \dfrac{(9.86 \times 10^{-4}) \times (9.86 \times 10^{-4})}{(0.199)} = 4.89 \times 10^{-6}$

35. $0.500M - 5.77 \times 10^{-6}M = 0.500M$

$K_a = \dfrac{(5.77 \times 10^{-6}) \times (5.77 \times 10^{-6})}{(0.500)} = 6.66 \times 10^{-11}$

36. $[H^+] = 10^{-1.71} = 1.95 \times 10^{-2}M$
$1.000M - 1.95 \times 10^{-2}M = 0.981M$
$$K_a = \frac{(1.95 \times 10^{-2}) \times (1.95 \times 10^{-2})}{(0.981)} = 3.88 \times 10^{-4}$$

45. $H_3PO_4(aq) + 3KOH(aq) \longrightarrow K_3PO_4(aq) + 3H_2O(l)$
$$1.56 \text{ mol } H_3PO_4 \times \frac{3 \text{ mol KOH}}{1 \text{ mol } H_3PO_4} = 4.68 \text{ mol KOH}$$

46. $HNO_3(aq) + NaOH(aq) \longrightarrow NaNO_3(aq) + H_2O(l)$
$$0.20 \text{ mol } HNO_3 \times \frac{1 \text{ mol NaOH}}{1 \text{ mol } HNO_3} = 0.20 \text{ mol NaOH}$$

47. $HCl(aq) + KOH(aq) \longrightarrow KCl(aq) + H_2O(l)$
$$3.0 \times 10^{-2} \text{ mol KOH} \times \frac{1 \text{ mol HCl}}{1 \text{ mol KOH}}$$
$$= 3.0 \times 10^{-2} \text{ mol HCl}$$

48. $$25.0 \text{ mL KOH} \times \frac{1.00 \text{ mol KOH}}{1000 \text{ mL KOH}} \times \frac{1 \text{ mol HCl}}{1 \text{ mol KOH}}$$
$$\times \frac{1000 \text{ mL HCl}}{0.45 \text{ mol HCl}} = 56 \text{ mL HCl}$$

49. $$38.5 \text{ mL NaOH} \times \frac{0.150 \text{ mol NaOH}}{1000 \text{ mL NaOH}} \times \frac{1 \text{ mol } H_3PO_4}{3 \text{ mol NaOH}}$$
$$= 0.001925 \text{ mol } H_3PO_4$$
$$\frac{0.001925 \text{ mol } H_3PO_4}{0.0150 \text{ L } H_3PO_4} = 0.128M \; H_3PO_4$$

50. 50 mL NaOH; the pH = 7 when $[H^+] = [OH^-]$. HCl is a strong acid and NaOH is a strong base. The mole ratio of acid to base is 1:1. Because the molarity is the same for each solution, equal volumes of the solutions would neutralize one another.

60. $HPO_4^{2-}(aq) + H^+(aq) \longrightarrow H_2PO_4^-(aq)$

61. $HCOO^-(aq) + H^+(aq) \longrightarrow HCOOH(aq)$

67. Acids ionize to give hydrogen ions in aqueous solution. Bases ionize to give hydroxide ions in aqueous solution.

69. **a.** $2Li(s) + 2H_2O(l) \longrightarrow 2LiOH(aq) + H_2(g)$
b. $Ba(s) + 2H_2O(l) \longrightarrow Ba(OH)_2(s) + H_2(g)$

75. **a.** $$pH = -\log[H^+] = -\log\left(\frac{K_w}{[OH^-]}\right)$$
$$= -\log\left(\frac{1 \times 10^{-14}}{1 \times 10^{-2}M}\right) = 12; \text{ basic}$$
b. $pH = -\log[H^+] = -\log(1 \times 10^{-2}M) = 2$; acidic

77. **a.** strong base
b. weak base
c. strong acid
d. strong acid

83. **a.** $NaOH(aq) + HCl(aq) \longrightarrow NaCl(aq) + H_2O(l)$
$$28.0 \text{ mL HCl} \times \frac{1 \text{ L HCl}}{10^3 \text{ mL HCl}} \times \frac{1 \text{ mol HCl}}{1 \text{ L HCl}}$$
$$\times \frac{1 \text{ mol NaOH}}{1 \text{ mol HCl}} = 0.028 \text{ mol NaOH}$$
$$\frac{0.028 \text{ mol NaOH}}{20.0 \text{ mL}} \times \frac{10^3 \text{ mL}}{1 \text{ L}} = 1.40M$$
b. $3NaOH(aq) + H_3PO_4(aq) \longrightarrow Na_3PO_4(aq) + 3H_2O(l)$
$$17.4 \text{ mL } H_3PO_4 \times \frac{1 \text{ L } H_3PO_4}{10^3 \text{ mL } H_3PO_4} \times \frac{1 \text{ mol } H_3PO_4}{1 \text{ L } H_3PO_4}$$
$$\times \frac{3 \text{ mol NaOH}}{1 \text{ mol } H_3PO_4} = 0.0522 \text{ mol NaOH}$$
$$\frac{0.0522 \text{ mol NaOH}}{20.0 \text{ mL}} \times \frac{10^3 \text{ mL}}{1 \text{ L}} = 2.61M$$

84. $HCO_3^-(aq) + H_2O(l) \longrightarrow H_2CO_3(aq) + OH^-(aq)$

87. $HPO_4^{2-}(aq) \longrightarrow H^+(aq) + PO_4^{3-}(aq)$
(acting as an acid)
$HPO_4^{2-}(aq) + H^+(aq) \longrightarrow H_2PO_4^-(aq)$
(acting as a base)

89. **a.** $HClO_2$, chlorous acid
b. H_3O^+, hydronium ion
c. H_3PO_4, phosphoric acid
d. NH_4^+, ammonium ion

90. **a.** $2HCl(aq) + Mg(OH)_2(aq) \longrightarrow MgCl_2(aq) + 2H_2O(l)$
b. $2HCl(aq) + CaCO_3(aq) \longrightarrow H_2O(l) + CO_2(g) + CaCl_2(aq)$
c. $3HCl(aq) + Al(OH)_3(aq) \longrightarrow AlCl_3(aq) + 3H_2O(l)$

91. b, c, d, a

94. The straight line on the graph represents a directly proportional relationship. The *y*-axis might correspond to $[H^+]$ because HCl is a strong acid. $[H^+]$ is directly proportional to [HCl] because HCl ionizes completely to form H^+ and Cl^- ions.

99. neutralization; raised

102. liquid

104. hydrogen bond

105. $$V_1 = \frac{M_2 \times V_2}{M_1} = \frac{2.5M \times 1.50 \text{ L}}{8.0M} = 0.47 \text{ L}$$

108. **a.** $NaCl(aq)$ **b.** hot water

Chapter 20

1. Mg: oxidized, loses electrons (reducing agent); Cu^{2+}: reduced, gains electrons (oxidizing agent)

2. **a.** Na: oxidized, loses electrons (reducing agent); S: reduced, gains electrons (oxidizing agent)

b. Al: oxidized, loses electrons (reducing agent); O_2: reduced, gains electrons (oxidizing agent)

3. **a.** oxidation (loss of 1 electron)

b. oxidation (loss of 2 electrons)

c. reduction (gain of 2 electrons)

d. reduction (gain of 2 electrons)

12. **a.** S, +3; O, −2 **c.** P, +5; O, −2

b. Na, +1; O, −1 **d.** N, +5; O, −2

13. **a.** $\overset{+1+5-2}{KClO_3}$; +5 **c.** $\overset{+2\ +7\ -2}{Ca(ClO_4)_2}$; +7

b. 0 **d.** $\overset{+1\ -2}{Cl_2O}$; +1

14. **a.** +6 **b.** +3

15. **a.** H_2 is oxidized (0 to +1); O_2 is reduced (0 to −2).

b. N is reduced (+5 to +3); O is oxidized (−2 to 0).

c. N in NH_4^+ is oxidized (−3 to 0); N in NO_2^- is reduced (+3 to 0) .

16. **a.** H_2 is the reducing agent; O_2 is the oxidizing agent.

b. N is the oxidizing agent; O is the reducing agent.

c. N in NH_4^+ is the reducing agent; N in NO_2^- is the oxidizing agent.

17. **a.** Zinc is oxidized (0 to +2); Mn^{4+} is reduced (+4 to +3). Zinc is the reducing agent; Mn^{4+} is the oxidizing agent.

b. Pb^{4+} is reduced (+4 to +2); I^- is oxidized (−1 in HI to 0 in I_2). Pb^{4+} is the oxidizing agent; I^- is the reducing agent.

24. **a.** redox reaction: Mg is oxidized (0 to +2); Br_2 is reduced (0 to −1)

b. not a redox reaction

25. not a redox reaction

26. **a.**

(1)(−6) = −6

$\overset{+1+5-2}{KClO_3(s)} \longrightarrow \overset{+1\ -1}{KCl(s)} + \overset{0}{O_2(g)}$

(3)(+2) = +6

One K atom must be reduced for every 3 oxygen atoms oxidized.

$KClO_3(s) \longrightarrow KCl(s) + O_2(g)$

Balance by inspection; put the coefficient 3 in front of O_2, and the coefficient 2 in front of $KClO_3$ and KCl:

$2KClO_3(s) \longrightarrow 2KCl(s) + 3O_2(g)$

b. $2HNO_2(aq) + 2HI(aq) \longrightarrow 2NO(g) + I_2(s) + 2H_2O(l)$

27. **a.** $2HNO_3(aq) + 3H_2S(g) \longrightarrow 3S(s) + 2NO(g) + 4H_2O(l)$

b. $SbCl_5(aq) + 2KI(aq) \longrightarrow SbCl_3(aq) + 2KCl(aq) + I_2(s)$

(2)(−3) = −6

28. $\overset{+3\ -2}{Bi_2S_3(s)} + \overset{+1+5-2}{HNO_3(aq)} \longrightarrow \overset{+3\ +5-2}{Bi(NO_3)_3(aq)} + \overset{+2\ -2}{NO(g)} + \overset{0}{S(s)} + \overset{+1\ -2}{H_2O(l)}$

(3)(+2) = +6

2 N atoms must be reduced for every 3 sulfur atoms oxidized.

$Bi_2S_3(s) + 2HNO_3(aq) \longrightarrow Bi(NO_3)_3(aq) + 2NO(g) + 3S(s) + H_2O(l)$

Balance by inspection; put the coefficient 2 in front of $Bi(NO_3)_3$, the coefficient 8 in front of HNO_3, and the coefficient 4 in front of H_2O:

$Bi_2S_3(s) + 8HNO_3(aq) \longrightarrow 2Bi(NO_3)_3(aq) + 2NO(g) + 3S(s) + 4H_2O(l)$

38. **a.** $2Ba(s) + O_2(g) \longrightarrow 2BaO(s)$; barium is oxidized

b. $CuO(s) + H_2(g) \longrightarrow Cu(s) + H_2O(l)$; copper is reduced

c. $C_2H_4(g) + 3O_2(g) \longrightarrow 2CO_2(g) + 2H_2O(l)$; carbon is oxidized

d. $3CaO(s) + 2Al(s) \longrightarrow Al_2O_3(s) + 3Ca(s)$; calcium is reduced

40. **a.** oxidizing agent **c.** oxidizing agent

b. reducing agent **d.** oxidizing agent

41. **a.** H_2 is oxidized; S is reduced.

b. N_2 is reduced; H_2 is oxidized.

c. S is oxidized; O_2 is reduced.

d. H_2 is oxidized; O_2 is reduced.

46. **a.** O, −2; H, +1 **d.** H, +1; P, +5; O, −2

b. P, +5; O, −2 **e.** H, +1; S, +6; O, −2

c. I, +5; O, −2

48. **a.** $2Al(s) + 3Cl_2(g) \longrightarrow 2AlCl_3(s)$

b. $2Al(s) + Fe_2O_3(s) \longrightarrow Al_2O_3(s) + 2Fe(s)$

c. $3Cl_2(g) + 6KOH(aq) \longrightarrow KClO_3(aq) + 5KCl(aq) + 3H_2O(l)$

d. $KIO_4(aq) + 7KI(aq) + 8HCl(aq) \longrightarrow 8KCl(aq) + 4I_2(s) + 4H_2O(l)$

49. **a.** Lithium changes from 0 in Li(*s*) to +1 in LiOH(*aq*), and hydrogen changes from +1 in $H_2O(l)$ to 0 in $H_2(g)$. This is a redox reaction.

b. Chromium changes from +8 in $K_2Cr_2O_7(aq)$ to +3 in $CrCl_3(aq)$, and chlorine changes from −1 in HCl(*aq*) to 0 in $Cl_2(g)$. This is a redox reaction.

c. Aluminum changes from 0 in Al(*s*) to +3 in $AlCl_3(aq)$, and hydrogen changes from +1 in HCl(*aq*) to 0 in $H_2(g)$. This is a redox reaction.

d. One chlorine in $Cl_2(g)$ changes from 0 to −1 in HCl(*aq*), and the other chlorine in $Cl_2(g)$ changes from 0 to +1 in HClO(*aq*). This is a redox reaction.

e. Iodine changes from +5 in $I_2O_5(s)$ to 0 in $I_2(s)$, and carbon changes from +2 in CO(*g*) to +4 in $CO_2(g)$. This is a redox reaction.

f. This is not a redox reaction.

50. **a.** $\overset{+4-2}{P_4O_8}$; +4 **b.** $\overset{+5-2}{PO_4^{3-}}$; +5 **c.** $\overset{+5-2}{P_2O_5}$; +5
d. $\overset{+3-2}{P_4O_6}$; +3 **e.** $\overset{+1\,+5-2}{H_2PO_4^{-}}$; +5 **f.** $\overset{+3-2}{PO_3^{3-}}$; +3

53. oxidizing agent because the oxidation number of chromium changes from +6 in $Cr_2O_7^{2-}$ to +3 in Cr^{3+}

55. $1s^22s^22p^63s^23p^5$; a chlorine atom can "lose" its 7 valence electrons or it can gain 1 electron to fill the last 3*p* orbital.

57. In every redox reaction one species loses one or more electrons and is a reducing agent. Another substance must gain one or more electrons and be an oxidizing agent.

65. $T = 25°C + 273 = 298\ K$

$$P = \frac{n \times R \times T}{V}$$

$$= \frac{\left(13.8\,\cancel{g\ N_2} \times \frac{1\ mol\ N_2}{28.0\,\cancel{g\ N_2}}\right) \times 8.31\left(\frac{\cancel{L}\cdot kPa}{\cancel{K}\cdot mol}\right) \times 298\,\cancel{K}}{6.8\,\cancel{L}}$$

$= 1.8 \times 10^2\ kPa$

67. $V_2 = \frac{M_1 \times V_1}{M_2} = \frac{1.5\cancel{M\ HCl} \times 440\ mL\ HCl}{6.0\cancel{M\ HCl}}$

$= 110\ mL\ 6.0M\ HCl$

Dilute 110 mL of 6.0*M* HCl to 440 mL total volume.

69. $PbBr_2(s) \longrightarrow Pb^{2+} + 2Br^-$

$K_{sp} = [Pb^{2+}][Br^-] = 2.1 \times 10^{-6}$

Let $x = [Pb^{2+}]$. Then, $2x = [Br^-]$.

$(x)(2x)^2 = 2.1 \times 10^{-6}$

$4x^3 = 2.1 \times 10^{-6}$

$x = [Pb^{2+}] = 8.1 \times 10^{-3}$

The solubility of $PbBr_2$ is $8.1 \times 10^{-3}M$.

71. **a.** $pH = -\log[H^+] = -\log(10^{-5}) = 5.00$ (acidic)

b. $[H^+] = \frac{K_w}{[OH^-]} = \frac{1.0 \times 10^{-14}M^2}{1 \times 10^{-4}M} = 1.0 \times 10^{-10}M$

$pH = -\log[H^+] = -\log(1.0 \times 10^{-10}M)$
$= 10.00$ (basic)

c. $[H^+] = \frac{K_w}{[OH^-]} = \frac{1.0 \times 10^{-14}M^2}{1 \times 10^{-1}M} = 1.0 \times 10^{-13}M$

$pH = -\log[H^+] = -\log(1.0 \times 10^{-13}M)$
$= 13.00$ (basic)

d. $pH = -\log[H^+] = -\log(3.0 \times 10^{-7})$
$= 6.50$ (acidic)

Chapter 21

8. Ag^+ is reduced, and Cu is oxidized.

Oxidation: $Cu(s) \longrightarrow Cu^{2+}(aq) + 2e^-$

Reduction: $Ag^+(aq) + e^- \longrightarrow Ag(s)$

$Cu(s) \longrightarrow Cu^{2+}(aq) + 2e^-$

$2[Ag^+(aq) + e^- \longrightarrow Ag(s)]$

$Cu(s) \longrightarrow Cu^{2+}(aq) + \cancel{2e^-}$

$2Ag^{2+}(aq) + \cancel{2e^-} \longrightarrow 2Ag(s)$

$Cu(s) + 2Ag^{2+}(aq) \longrightarrow Cu^{2+}(aq) + 2Ag(s)$

$E°_{cell} = E°_{red} - E°_{oxid} = E°_{Ag^+} - E°_{Cu^{2+}}$
$= +0.80\ V - (+0.34\ V) = +0.46\ V$

9. Cu^{2+} is reduced, and Al is oxidized.

Oxidation: $Al(s) \longrightarrow Al^{3+}(aq) + 3e^-$

Reduction: $Cu^{2+}(aq) + 2e^- \longrightarrow Cu(s)$

$2[Al(s) \longrightarrow Al^{3+}(aq) + 3e^-]$

$3[Cu^{2+}(aq) + 2e^- \longrightarrow Cu(s)]$

$2Al(s) \longrightarrow 2Al^{3+}(aq) + \cancel{6e^-}$

$3Cu^{2+}(aq) + \cancel{6e^-} \longrightarrow 3Cu(s)$

$2Al(s) + 3Cu^{2+}(aq) \longrightarrow 2Al^{3+}(aq) + 3Cu(s)$

$E°_{cell} = E°_{red} - E°_{oxid} = E°_{Cu^{2+}} - E°_{Al^{3+}}$
$= +0.34\ V - (-1.66\ V) = +2.00\ V$

10. The standard reduction potential for AgCl (+0.22 V) is more positive than the standard reduction potential for Ni^{2+} (−0.25 V), so AgCl is reduced and Ni is oxidized.

Oxidation: $Ni(s) \longrightarrow Ni^{2+}(aq) + 2e^-$

Reduction: $2[AgCl(s) + e^- \longrightarrow Ag(s) + Cl^-(aq)]$

Overall cell reaction:
$Ni(s) + 2AgCl(s) \longrightarrow 2Ag(s) + NiCl_2(aq)$

$E°_{cell} = E°_{red} - E°_{oxid} = E°_{AgCl} - E°_{Ni^{2+}}$
$= +0.22\ V - (-0.25\ V) = +0.47\ V$

24. Using the Activity Series table on page 691, the more active element is the most readily oxidized.

a. Cu **b.** Ca **c.** Mg **d.** Sn **e.** Zn **f.** Al

28. A zinc container (anode) filled with electrolyte paste; the cathode is a graphite rod embedded in the paste; Zn is oxidized; MnO_2 is reduced.

30. $Pb(s) \mid PbSO_4(s) \parallel PbO_2(s) \mid PbSO_4(s)$

33. The standard reduction potential of a half-cell is a measure of the tendency of a given half-reaction to occur as a reduction under standard conditions. The difference between the standard reduction potentials of the two half-cells is called the standard cell potential.

36. a. Cu is oxidized, and H^+ is reduced.
Writing both half-reactions as reductions:

$Cu^{2+}(aq) + 2e^- \longrightarrow Cu(s)$ $E^\circ_{Cu^{2+}} = +0.34\ V$

$2H^+(aq) + 2e^- \longrightarrow H_2(g)$ $E^\circ_{H^+} = 0.000\ V$

$E^\circ_{cell} = E^\circ_{red} - E^\circ_{oxid} = E^\circ_{H^+} - E^\circ_{Cu^{2+}}$
$= 0.000\ V - (+0.34\ V) = -0.34\ V$

$E^\circ_{cell} < 0$, so the reaction will not occur spontaneously.

b. Ag is oxidized, and Fe^{2+} is reduced.
Writing both half-reactions as reductions:

$Ag^+(aq) + e^- \longrightarrow Ag(s)$ $E^\circ_{Ag^+} = +0.80\ V$

$Fe^{2+}(aq) + 2e^- \longrightarrow Fe(s)$ $E^\circ_{Fe^{2+}} = -0.44\ V$

$E^\circ_{cell} = E^\circ_{red} - E^\circ_{oxid} = E^\circ_{Fe^{2+}} - E^\circ_{Ag^+}$
$= -0.44\ V - (+0.80\ V) = -1.24\ V$

$E^\circ_{cell} < 0$, so the reaction will not occur spontaneously.

38. Voltaic cells convert chemical energy into electrical energy. Electrolytic cells use electrical energy to cause a chemical reaction.

41. Chloride ions are oxidized to produce chlorine gas, and water is reduced to produce hydrogen gas.

44. The iron nail will become copper-plated as Fe is oxidized to Fe^{2+} and Cu^{2+} is reduced to Cu.

Oxidation: $Fe(s) \longrightarrow Fe^{2+}(aq) + \cancel{2e^-}$

Reduction: $Cu^{2+}(aq) + \cancel{2e^-} \longrightarrow Cu(s)$

Overall cell reaction:
$Fe(s) + Cu^{2+}(aq) \longrightarrow Fe^{2+}(aq) + Cu(s)$

46. a. Oxidation: $Sn(s) \longrightarrow Sn^{2+}(aq) + \cancel{2e^-}$

Reduction: $Pb^{2+}(aq) + \cancel{2e^-} \longrightarrow Pb(s)$

Overall cell reaction:
$Sn(s) + Pb^{2+}(aq) \longrightarrow Sn^{2+}(aq) + Pb(s)$

$E^\circ_{cell} = E^\circ_{red} - E^\circ_{oxid} = E^\circ_{Pb^{2+}} - E^\circ_{Sn^{2+}}$
$= -0.13\ V - (-0.14\ V) = +0.01\ V$

b. Oxidation: $H_2(g) \longrightarrow 2H^+(aq) + \cancel{2e^-}$

Reduction: $Br_2(l) + \cancel{2e^-} \longrightarrow 2Br^-(aq)$

Overall cell reaction:
$H_2(g) + Br_2(l) \longrightarrow 2H^+(aq) + 2Br^-(aq)$

$E^\circ_{cell} = E^\circ_{red} - E^\circ_{oxid} = E^\circ_{Br^-} - E^\circ_{H^+}$
$= +1.07\ V - 0.00\ V = +1.07\ V$

53. The cathode reaction in a dry cell is not reversible, so dry cells are not rechargeable. The anode and cathode reactions in a lead storage battery are reversible. Therefore, lead storage batteries are rechargeable when electrical energy is applied.

54. The spoon is being electroplated with silver in an electrolytic cell. The spoon serves as the cathode, and the anode is metallic silver. The electrolyte is a solution of silver cyanide. When a direct current is applied, silver ions move from the anode to the spoon, where they are reduced to silver metal.

58. Connect the positive electrode of the power source to the gold object, and connect the negative electrode to another metal. The gold object will then serve as the anode, and the gold will be oxidized.

60. $T_1 = 30°C + 273 = 303\ K$

$T_2 = 60°C + 273 = 333\ K$

$$V_2 = \frac{V_1 \times T_2}{T_1} = \frac{425\ mL \times 333\ \cancel{K}}{303\ \cancel{K}} = 467\ mL$$

61. a. $250\ \cancel{g} \times \dfrac{0.90\ g\ NaCl}{100\ \cancel{g}} = 2.3\ g\ NaCl$

b. $500\ \cancel{mL} \times \dfrac{1\ \cancel{L}}{1000\ \cancel{mL}} \times \dfrac{2\ \cancel{mol\ KNO_3}}{1\ \cancel{L}} \times \dfrac{101.1\ g\ KNO_3}{1\ \cancel{mol\ KNO_3}} = 101\ g\ KNO_3$

63. $4.80\ \cancel{g\ CH_4} \times \dfrac{1\ \cancel{mol\ CH_4}}{16.0\ \cancel{g\ CH_4}} \times \dfrac{-890\ kJ}{1\ \cancel{mol\ CH_4}} = -267\ kJ$

64. a and c; $K_{eq} < 1$

65. a. $pH = -\log[H^+] = -\log(1.0 \times 10^{-8}M) = 8.00$

b. $pH = -\log[H^+] = -\log(0.000010M) = 5.00$

66. a. +6 **b.** −2 **c.** +4 **d.** +2 **e.** 0 **f.** +4

67. b; Ca is oxidized to Ca^{2+}, and Cl_2 is reduced to Cl^-.
c; Ca is oxidized to Ca^{2+}, and H^+ is reduced to H_2.

Chapter 22

1.

$$\begin{array}{ccccccccccc} & & H & & H & & H & & H & & H \\ & & | & & | & & | & & | & & | \\ H & - & C & - & C & - & C & - & C & - & C & - & H \\ & & | & & | & & | & & | & & | \\ & & H & & H & & H & & H & & H \end{array}$$

$$\begin{array}{ccccccccccccc} & & H & & H & & H & & H & & H & & H \\ & & | & & | & & | & & | & & | & & | \\ H & - & C & - & C & - & C & - & C & - & C & - & C & - & H \\ & & | & & | & & | & & | & & | & & | \\ & & H & & H & & H & & H & & H & & H \end{array}$$

2. 10 single bonds

3. 18 hydrogen atoms

4. 3-ethylhexane

5. 2-methylbutane

6.

$$\begin{array}{l} \quad\quad CH_3 \\ \quad\quad | \\ CH_3CHCHCH_2CH_2CH_3 \\ \quad\quad\quad | \\ \quad\quad\quad CH_3 \end{array}$$

9.

$$\begin{array}{ccccccccccccccc} & & CH_3 & & CH_3 & & CH_3 & & & & & & & & \\ & & | & & | & & | & & & & & & & & \\ CH_3 & - & CH & - & CH & - & C & - & CH_2 & - & CH_2 & - & CH_2 & - & CH_3 \\ & & & & & & | & & & & & & & & \\ & & & & & & CH_2 & & & & & & & & \\ & & & & & & | & & & & & & & & \\ & & & & & & CH_3 & & & & & & & & \end{array}$$

26.

$$\begin{array}{ccccc} & & H & & \\ & & | & & \\ CH_3 & - & (C) & - & CHO \\ & & | & & \\ & & Cl & & \end{array}$$

27.

$$\begin{array}{ccccc} & & CH_3 & & \\ & & | & & \\ CH_3CH_2 & - & (C) & - & Br \\ & & | & & \\ & & F & & \end{array}$$

28. no asymmetric carbon

50. pentane: $CH_3CH_2CH_2CH_2CH_3$
hexane: $CH_3CH_2CH_2CH_2CH_2CH_3$

53. a. 2-methylbutane
b. 2,3-dimethylbutane

55. a. unsaturated; there is a double carbon-carbon bond
b. saturated; the compound contains the maximum number of hydrogen atoms per carbon atom

60. No, only molecules with at least one asymmetric carbon can have enantiomers.

62. a. CH_2CH_3 (benzene ring) CH_2CH_3 — benzene ring with CH_2CH_3 above and CH_2CH_3 below (para positions)

b.

$$\begin{array}{ccccccccc} & & CH_3 & & & & & & \\ & & | & & & & & & \\ CH_3 & - & CH & - & CH & - & CH_2 & - & CH_3 \\ & & & & | & & & & \\ & & & & C_6H_5 & & & & \end{array}$$

65. The combustion of sulfur in coal produces the air pollutants SO_2 and SO_3.

66. a. Ethyne (acetylene) has one triple carbon-carbon bond and two single carbon-hydrogen bonds.
b. In methylbenzene, there are hybrid bonds within the ring. All other bonds are single bonds.
c. All the bonds in propane are single bonds.

70. The middle structure is most stable due to resonance within the ring.

71. No, the structures are identical; one has been flipped over.

72. $CH_2{=}C{=}CH_2$

74. a.

$$\begin{array}{ccccccccccc} CH_3 & - & CH_2 & - & C & = & C & - & CH_2 & - & CH_3 \\ & & & & | & & | & & & & \\ & & & & CH_3 & & CH_3 & & & & \end{array}$$

b. cyclopentane ring with CH_2CH_3 and CH_3 on adjacent carbons

c.

$$\begin{array}{ccccccccc} & & & & CH_3 & & & & \\ & & & & | & & & & \\ CH_3 & & & & CH_2 & & & & \\ | & & & & | & & & & \\ CH_2 & & & & CH_2 & & & & \\ | & & & & | & & & & \\ CH_2 & - & CH_2 & - & C & - & CH_2 & - & CH_2 \\ & & & & | & & & & | \\ & & & & CH_2 & & & & CH_2 \\ & & & & | & & & & | \\ & & & & CH_2 & & & & CH_2 \\ & & & & | & & & & | \\ & & & & CH_3 & & & & CH_3 \end{array}$$

75. a.

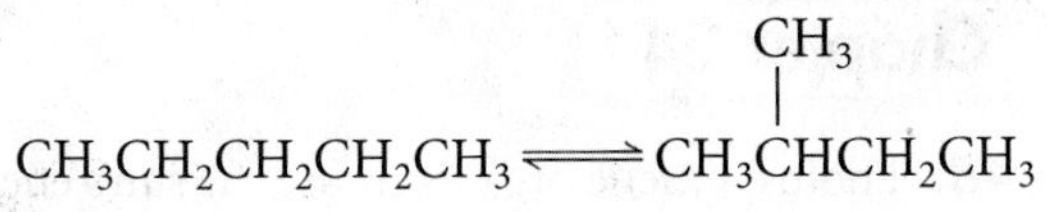

$$CH_3CH_2CH_2CH_2CH_3 \rightleftharpoons CH_3\underset{}{\overset{CH_3}{\overset{|}{C}}}HCH_2CH_3$$

b. constitutional

78. No, enantiomers have identical physical properties.

80. $750 \text{ mL } KNO_3 \times \frac{1 \text{ L } KNO_3}{1000 \text{ mL } KNO_3} \times \frac{1.50 \text{ mol } KNO_3}{1 \text{ L } KNO_3}$

$= 1.13 \text{ mol } KNO_3$;

$1.13 \text{ mol } KNO_3 \times \frac{101.1 \text{ g } KNO_3}{1.000 \text{ mol } KNO_3} = 114 \text{ g } KNO_3$

82. a. favors reactants b. favors products

83. a. $[H^+] = \frac{1.0 \times 10^{-14}}{[OH^-]} = \frac{1.0 \times 10^{-14}}{1.0 \times 10^{-4}} = 1.0 \times 10^{-10}M$

$pH = -\log[H^+] = -\log(1.0 \times 10^{-10}) = 10.00$

b. $[H^+] = \frac{1.0 \times 10^{-14}}{[OH^-]} = \frac{1.0 \times 10^{-14}}{3.9 \times 10^{-7}} = 2.6 \times 10^{-8}M$

$pH = -\log[H^+] = -\log(2.6 \times 10^{-8}) = 7.59$

c. $[H^+] = \frac{1.0 \times 10^{-14}}{[OH^-]} = \frac{1.0 \times 10^{-14}}{0.010} = 1.0 \times 10^{-12}M$

$pH = -\log[H^+] = -\log(1.0 \times 10^{-12}) = 12.00$

d. $[H^+] = \frac{1.0 \times 10^{-14}}{[OH^-]} = \frac{1.0 \times 10^{-14}}{5.0 \times 10^{-3}} = 2.0 \times 10^{-12}M$

$pH = -\log[H^+] = -\log(2.0 \times 10^{-12}) = 11.70$

86. a. $2 + C + 3(-2) = 0$

$-4 + C = 0$

$C = +4$

Ca, +2; C, +4 ; O, −2

b. Cl, 0

c. $1 + I + 3(-2) = 0$

$I - 5 = 0$

$I = +5$

Li, +1; I, +5; O, −2

d. $2(+1) + S + 3(-2) = 0$

$S - 4 = 0$

$S = +4$

Na, +1; S, +4; O, −2

87. The reaction is nonspontaneous.

Chapter 23

34. a. $ClCH_2CCl_2CH_2CH_3$ (ClCH₂CCH₂CH₃ with Cl above and below the central C)

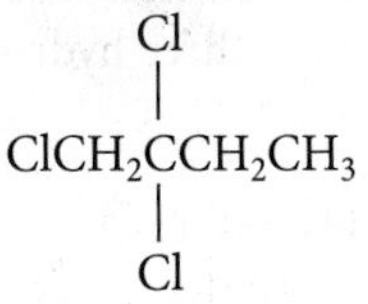

b. 1,3,5-tribromobenzene ring: Br, Br, Br

c. cyclohexane ring with Cl, Cl on adjacent carbons

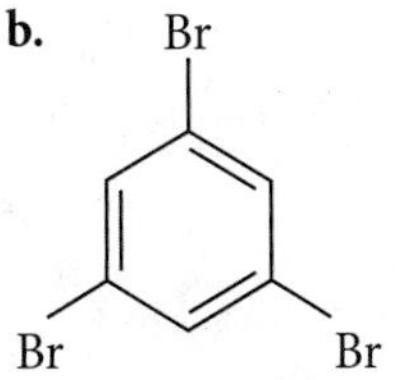

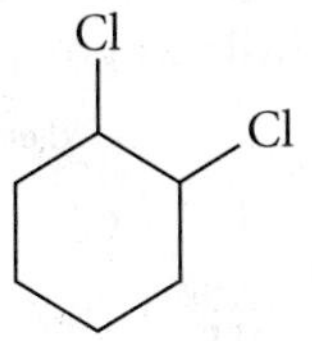

37. a. 2-propanol

b. 1,2-propanediol

c. 2-methyl-2-propanol

38. a. $\overset{H}{\overset{|}{CH_2}}-\overset{Br}{\overset{|}{CH_2}}$

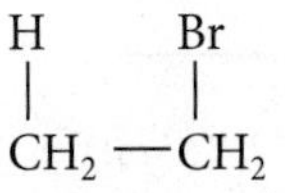

bromoethane

b. $\overset{Cl}{\overset{|}{CH_2}}-\overset{Cl}{\overset{|}{CH_2}}$

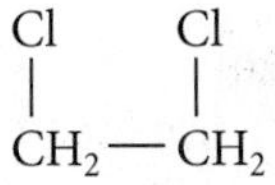

1,2-dichloroethane

c. $\overset{H}{\overset{|}{CH_2}}-\overset{OH}{\overset{|}{CH_2}}$

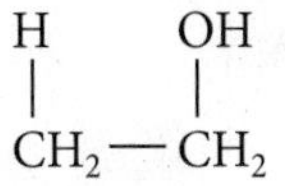

ethanol

d. $\overset{H}{\overset{|}{CH_2}}-\overset{H}{\overset{|}{CH_2}}$

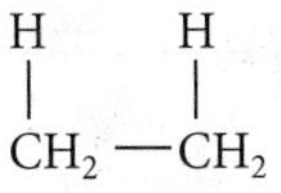

ethane

e. $\overset{H}{\overset{|}{CH_2}}-\overset{Cl}{\overset{|}{CH_2}}$

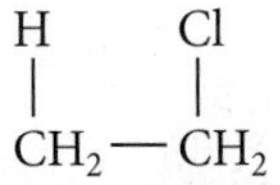

chloroethane

41. a. ethanal

b. 2-methylbutanal

c. pentanoic acid

d. propanone

e. 3-hexanone

f. 2-phenylethanal

44. a. $-CH_2-\underset{\underset{\underset{CH_3}{|}}{\underset{CH_2}{|}}}{CH}-$

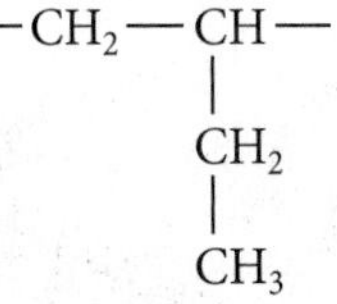

b. $-\underset{Cl}{\underset{|}{CH}}-\underset{Cl}{\underset{|}{CH}}-$

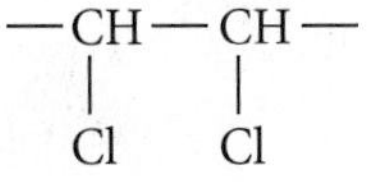

47. a. phenol

b. ether

c. alcohol

d. phenol

e. alcohol

f. ether

51. Ethanoic acid (two carbons long) is more soluble in water than decanoic acid (ten carbons long).

54. (five-membered ring containing O)

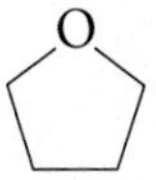

58. The two molecules are similar in size. Diethylene glycol has four carbons, and glycerol has three carbons. Diethylene glycol is an ether with two hydroxy groups. Glycerol has three hydroxy groups.

diethylene glycol

$$\underset{\displaystyle \text{OH}}{\overset{}{CH_2}}—CH_2—O—CH_2—\underset{\displaystyle \text{OH}}{\overset{}{CH_2}}$$

glycerol

$$\underset{\displaystyle \text{OH}}{CH_2}—\underset{\displaystyle \text{OH}}{CH}—\underset{\displaystyle \text{OH}}{CH_2}$$

60. b, 3

64. $\Delta T = 180°C - 22°C = 158°C$

$q = C_{Al} \times m \times \Delta T$

$$q = \frac{0.90\,\cancel{J} \times \dfrac{1\text{ kJ}}{10^3\,\cancel{J}} \times 500\,\cancel{g} \times 158\cancel{°C}}{(\cancel{g}\cdot\cancel{°C})} = 71\text{ kJ}$$

68. coal

Chapter 24

48. Photosynthetic organisms use the sun's energy to synthesize carbon compounds, such as glucose, from CO_2 and H_2O.

58. Peptide chains fold into helixes or into pleated sheets in which peptide chains lie side by side.

69. phosphate group, sugar unit, nitrogen base

74. Each individual's DNA is unique.

76. In catabolism, biological molecules are broken down and energy is released. In anabolism, energy and the products of catabolism are used to make biological molecules.

84. No; certain code words specify the initiation or termination of a peptide chain.

90. Base pairing describes the hydrogen bonding that occurs between thymine (T) and adenine (A) and between cytosine (C) and guanine (G) in DNA. Base pairing helps hold together the two DNA strands in a double helix.

101. a. Each formula unit of NaCl disassociates into 2 particles, so $0.507m \times 2 = 1.014m$.

$$\Delta T_b = K_b \times m = \frac{0.512°C}{\cancel{m}} \times 1.014\cancel{m} = 0.519°C$$

b. Each formula unit of NH_4Cl disassociates into 2 particles, so $0.204m \times 2 = 0.408m$.

$$\Delta T_b = K_b \times m = \frac{0.512°C}{\cancel{m}} \times 0.408\cancel{m} = 0.209°C$$

c. Each formula unit of $CaCl_2$ disassociates into 3 particles, so $0.155m \times 3 = 0.465m$.

$$\Delta T_b = K_b \times m = \frac{0.512°C}{\cancel{m}} \times 0.465\cancel{m} = 0.238°C$$

d. Each formula unit of $NaHSO_4$ disassociates into 2 particles, so $0.222m \times 2 = 0.444m$.

$$\Delta T_b = K_b \times m = \frac{0.512°C}{\cancel{m}} \times 0.444\cancel{m} = 0.227°C$$

102. $\Delta H = 0.265\ \cancel{\text{mol NaHCO}_3} \times \dfrac{129\text{ kJ}}{2\ \cancel{\text{mol NaHCO}_3}}$

$= 17.1$ kJ heat absorbed

Chapter 25

10. $10.4\ \cancel{h} \div 2.6\ \cancel{h}/\text{half-life} = 4$ half-lives

$1.0\ \text{mg} \times \frac{1}{2} \times \frac{1}{2} \times \frac{1}{2} \times \frac{1}{2} = 0.063$ mg Mn-56

11. $3.2 \times 10^3\ \cancel{\text{years}} \div 1.6 \times 10^3\ \cancel{\text{years}}/\text{half-life}$
$= 2$ half-lives

$10.0\ \text{mg} \times \frac{1}{2} \times \frac{1}{2} = 2.50$ mg Ra-226

12. No; after 48.2 days, or 2 half-lives, $\frac{1}{4}$ of the original sample will be left.

13. **a.** $4\ \cancel{\text{days}} \div 4\ \cancel{\text{days}}/\text{half-life} = 1$ half-life
$20\ \text{g} \times \frac{1}{2} = 10\ \text{g}$
b. $8\ \cancel{\text{days}} \div 4\ \cancel{\text{days}}/\text{half-life} = 2$ half-lives
$20\ \text{g} \times \frac{1}{2} \times \frac{1}{2} = 5\ \text{g}$

36. ${}^{210}_{82}\text{Pb} \longrightarrow {}^{210}_{83}\text{Bi} + {}^{0}_{-1}\text{e}$

38. **a.** ${}^{238}_{92}\text{U} \longrightarrow {}^{234}_{90}\text{Th} + {}^{4}_{2}\text{He}$; thorium-234
b. ${}^{230}_{90}\text{Th} \longrightarrow {}^{226}_{88}\text{Ra} + {}^{4}_{2}\text{He}$; radium-226
c. ${}^{235}_{92}\text{U} \longrightarrow {}^{231}_{90}\text{Th} + {}^{4}_{2}\text{He}$; thorium-231
d. ${}^{222}_{86}\text{Rn} \longrightarrow {}^{218}_{84}\text{Po} + {}^{4}_{2}\text{He}$; polonium-218

40. **a.** mass number is unchanged; atomic number increases by 1
b. mass number decreases by 4; atomic number decreases by 2
c. Mass number and atomic number are both unchanged.

41. The atom undergoes radioactive decay.

53. **a.** ${}^{30}_{15}\text{P} + {}^{0}_{-1}\text{e} \longrightarrow {}^{30}_{14}\text{Si}$
b. ${}^{13}_{6}\text{C} + {}^{1}_{0}\text{n} \longrightarrow {}^{14}_{6}\text{C}$
c. ${}^{131}_{53}\text{I} \longrightarrow {}^{131}_{54}\text{Xe} + {}^{0}_{-1}\text{e}$

55. $3.2 \times 10^7\ \text{atoms} \times \frac{1}{2} \times \frac{1}{2} \times \frac{1}{2} \times \frac{1}{2} \times \frac{1}{2}$
$= 1 \times 10^6$ atoms

56. $40\ \cancel{\text{days}} \div 8\ \cancel{\text{days}}/\text{half-life} = 5$ half-lives
$20\ \text{mg} \times \frac{1}{2} \times \frac{1}{2} \times \frac{1}{2} \times \frac{1}{2} \times \frac{1}{2} = 0.625$ mg I-131

62. **a.** platinum **d.** titanium **g.** vanadium
b. thorium **e.** xenon **h.** palladium
c. francium **f.** californium
Thorium (b), francium (c), and californium (f) have no stable isotopes.

59. ${}^{25}_{12}\text{Mg}$

69. $10.00\ \cancel{\text{g Mg}} \times \frac{1\ \cancel{\text{mol Mg}}}{24.3\ \cancel{\text{g Mg}}} \times \frac{1\ \text{mol H}_2}{1\ \cancel{\text{mol Mg}}} = 0.412\ \text{mol H}_2$

$0.412\ \cancel{\text{mol H}_2} \times \frac{22.4\ \cancel{\text{L H}_2}}{1\ \cancel{\text{mol H}_2}} \times \frac{1000\ \cancel{\text{mL H}_2}}{1\ \cancel{\text{L H}_2}} \times \frac{1\ \text{cm}^3\ \text{H}_2}{1\ \cancel{\text{mL H}_2}}$
$= 9.22 \times 10^3\ \text{cm}^3\ \text{H}_2$

71. $\text{volume} = \frac{\text{moles}}{\text{molarity}} = \frac{0.0020\ \cancel{\text{mol Na}_2\text{SO}_4}}{\frac{0.30\ \cancel{\text{mol Na}_2\text{SO}_4}}{1\ \cancel{\text{L}}} \times \frac{1\ \cancel{\text{L}}}{1000\ \text{mL}}}$
$= 6.7$ mL

Glossary

A

absolute zero: the zero point on the Kelvin temperature scale, equivalent to −273.15°C *(72)*

cero absoluto: punto cero en la escala de temperatura Kelvin; equivale a −273.15°C

accepted value: a quantity used by general agreement of the scientific community *(58)*

valor aceptado: cantidad que se usa por acuerdo general de la comunidad científica

accuracy: the closeness of a measurement to the true value of what is being measured *(57)*

exactitud: qué tan cerca está una medición del valor real de lo que se mide

acid: a compound that produces hydrogen ions in solution; see also hydrogen-ion donor, Lewis acid *(260)*

ácido: compuesto que, en solución, produce iones hidrógeno; ver también donante iones hidrógeno, ácido de Lewis

acid dissociation constant (K_a): the ratio of the concentration of the dissociated form of an acid to the undissociated form; stronger acids have larger K_a values than weaker acids *(632)*

constante de disociación ácida (K_a): razón de la concentración de la forma disociada de un ácido a la concentración de la forma no disociada; los ácidos fuertes tienen valores K_a más altos que los ácidos débiles

acidic solution: any solution in which the hydrogen-ion concentration is greater than the hydroxide-ion concentration *(619)*

solución ácida: cualquier solución en la que la concentración de iones hidrógeno es mayor que la de iones hidróxido

activated complex: an unstable arrangement of atoms that exists momentarily at the peak of the activation-energy barrier *(566)*

complejo activado: acomodo inestable de átomos que existe momentáneamente en el punto más alto de la barrera de energía de activación

activation energy: the minimum energy colliding particles must have in order to react *(566)*

energía de activación: energía mínima que deben tener las partículas para que, al chocar, reaccionen

active site: a groove or pocket in an enzyme molecule into which the substrate (reactant molecule) fits; where the substrate is converted to products *(793)*

sitio activo: hendidura o bolsa en una molécula de enzima, en la que embona el sustrato (molécula que reacciona); donde el sustrato se convierte en productos

activity series: a list of elements in order of decreasing activity; the activity series of halogens is Fl, Cl, Br, I *(332)*

serie de actividad: lista de elementos en orden de actividad decreciente; la serie de actividad de los halógenos es F, Cl, Br, I

actual yield: the amount of product that forms when a reaction is carried out in the laboratory *(381)*

rendimiento real: cantidad de producto que se forma cuando se lleva a cabo una reacción en el laboratorio

addition reaction: a reaction in which a substance is added at the double bond of an alkene or at the triple bond of an alkyne *(760)*

reacción de adición: reacción en la que una sustancia se añade al doble enlace de un alqueno o al triple enlace de un alquino

adenosine triphosphate (ATP): a molecule that transmits the energy needed by cells of all living things *(807)*

trifosfato de adenosina (ATP): molécula que transmite la energía que necesitan las células de todos los seres vivos

alcohol: an organic compound having an —OH (hydroxy) group; the general structure is R—OH *(758)*

alcohol: compuesto orgánico que posee un grupo —OH (hidroxilo); su estructura general es R—OH

aldehyde: an organic compound in which the carbon of the carbonyl group is joined to at least one hydrogen; the general formula is RCHO *(764)*

aldehído: compuesto orgánico en el que el carbono del grupo carbonilo está unido a por lo menos un hidrógeno; su fórmula general es RCHO

aliphatic compound: any organic compound that is not classified as an aromatic compound *(740)*

compuesto alifático: cualquier compuesto orgánico que no está clasificado como un compuesto aromático

alkali metal: any metal in Group 1A of the periodic table *(155)*

metal alcalino: cualquier metal del grupo 1A de la tabla periódica

alkaline earth metal: any metal in Group 2A of the periodic table *(155)*

metal alcalinotérreo: cualquier metal del grupo 2A de la tabla periódica

alkane: a hydrocarbon containing only single covalent bonds; alkanes are saturated hydrocarbons *(722)*

alcano: hidrocarburo que sólo contiene enlaces covalentes sencillos; los alcanos son hidrocarburos saturados

alkene: a hydrocarbon containing one or more carbon–carbon double bonds; alkenes are unsaturated hydrocarbons *(731)*

alqueno: hidrocarburo que contiene uno o más enlaces dobles carbono–carbono; los alquenos son hidrocarburos insaturados

alkyl group: a hydrocarbon substituent that is derived from an alkane; the methyl group (—CH_3) is an alkyl group *(726)*

grupo alquilo: un hidrocarburo sustituto derivado de un alcano; el grupo metilo (—CH_3) es un grupo alquilo

alkyne: a hydrocarbon containing a carbon–carbon triple bond; alkynes are unsaturated hydrocarbons *(733)*

alquino: hidrocarburo que contiene un triple enlace carbono–carbono; los alquinos son hidrocarburos insaturados

allotrope: one of two or more different molecular forms of an element in the same physical state; oxygen (O_2) and ozone (O_3) are allotropes of the element oxygen *(409)*

alótropo: una de dos o más formas moleculares distintas de un elemento en el mismo estado físico; el oxígeno (O_2) y el ozono (O_3) son alótropos del elemento oxígeno

alloy: a mixture composed of two or more elements, at least one of which is a metal *(195)*

aleación: mezcla formada por dos o más elementos, donde al menos uno de ellos es un metal

alpha particle: a positively charged particle emitted from certain radioactive nuclei; it consists of two protons and two neutrons and is identical to the nucleus of a helium atom *(818)*

partícula alfa: partícula con carga positiva emitida por ciertos núcleos radiactivos; consta de dos protones y dos neutrones, y es idéntica al núcleo de un átomo de helio

amine: an organic compound in which nitrogen is bonded to a carbon group *(763)*

amina: compuesto orgánico en el cual el nitrógeno se enlaza a un grupo de carbonos

amino acid: an organic compound having amino (—NH_2) and carboxyl (—COOH) groups in the same molecule; proteins are made from the 20 naturally occurring amino acids *(790)*

aminoácido: compuesto orgánico que posee grupos amino (—NH_2) y carboxilo (—COOH) en la misma molécula; las proteínas se forman a partir de los 20 aminoácidos naturales

amorphous solid: describes a solid that lacks an ordered internal structure; denotes a random arrangement of atoms *(410)*

sólido amorfo: describe un sólido que carece de una estructura interna ordenada; denota un acomodo aleatorio de átomos

amphoteric: a substance that can act as both an acid and a base *(615)*

anfótero: una sustancia que puede actuar como ácido y también como base

amplitude: the height of a wave's crest *(129)*

amplitud: altura de la cresta de una onda

anabolism: synthesis processes in the metabolism of cells; these processes usually require the expenditure of energy *(809)*

anabolismo: procesos de síntesis dentro del metabolismo de las células; por lo regular, esos procesos requieren gasto de energía

analytical chemistry: the area of chemistry that focuses on the composition of matter *(5)*

química analítica: rama de la química que estudia la composición de la materia

anhydrous: describes a substance that does not contain water *(472)*

anhidro: se refiere a una sustancia que no contiene agua

anion: any atom or group of atoms with a negative charge *(165)*

anión: cualquier átomo o grupo de átomos que posee carga negativa

anode: the electrode at which oxidation occurs *(692)*

ánodo: electrodo en el que hay oxidación

aqueous solution: water that contains dissolved substances *(468)*

solución acuosa: agua que contiene sustancias disueltas

aromatic compound: an organic compound that contains a benzene ring or other ring in which the bonding is like that of benzene; aromatic compounds are also known as arenes *(740)*

compuesto aromático: compuesto orgánico que contiene un anillo bencénico u otro anillo con enlaces similares a los del benceno; los compuestos aromáticos también se conocen como arenos

asymmetric carbon: a carbon atom that has four different atoms or groups attached *(736)*

carbono asimétrico: átomo de carbono unido a cuatro átomos o grupos distintos

atmospheric pressure: the pressure exerted by atoms and molecules in the atmosphere surrounding Earth, resulting from collisions of these particles with objects *(397)*

presión atmosférica: presión ejercida por átomos y moléculas de la atmósfera que rodea a la Tierra y que resulta de los choques de dichas partículas con los objetos

atom: the smallest particle of an element that retains its identity in a chemical reaction *(100)*

átomo: partícula más pequeña de un elemento que conserva su identidad en una reacción química

atomic emission spectrum: the pattern formed when light passes through a prism or diffraction grating to separate it into the different frequencies of light it contains *(132)*

espectro de emisión atómica: patrón que se forma cuando la luz atraviesa un prisma o una rejilla de difracción que la separa en las dife-rentes frecuencias de luz que contiene

atomic mass: the weighted average of the masses of the isotopes of an element *(115)*

masa atómica: promedio ponderado de las masas de los isótopos de un elemento

atomic mass unit (amu): a unit of mass equal to one-twelfth the mass of a carbon-12 atom *(114)*

unidad de masa atómica (uma): unidad de masa igual a un doceavo de la masa de un átomo de carbono 12

atomic number: the number of protons in the nucleus of an atom of an element *(108)*

número atómico: número de protones que hay en el núcleo del átomo de un elemento

atomic orbital: a mathematical expression describing the probability of finding an electron at various locations; usually represented by the region of space around the nucleus where there is a high probability of finding an electron *(122)*

orbital atómico: expresión matemática que describe la probabilidad de hallar un electrón en diversos lugares; se suele representar como la región del espacio en torno al núcleo donde hay una probabilidad elevada de hallar un electrón

atomic radius: one-half the distance between the nuclei of two atoms of the same element when the atoms are joined *(162)*

radio atómico: mitad de la distancia entre los núcleos de dos átomos del mismo elemento cuando dichos átomos están unidos

aufbau principle: the rule that electrons occupy the orbitals of lowest energy first *(124)*

principio de aufbau: regla según la cual los electrones primero ocupan los orbitales de energía más baja

Avogadro's hypothesis: equal volumes of gases at the same temperature and pressure contain equal numbers of particles *(292)*

hipótesis de Avogadro: volúmenes iguales de gases a la misma temperatura y presión contienen el mismo número de partículas

Avogadro's number: the number of representative particles contained in one mole of a substance; equal to 6.02×10^{23} particles *(279)*

número de Avogadro: número de partículas representativas contenidas en un mol de una sustancia; es igual a 6.02×10^{23} partículas

B

balanced equation: a chemical equation in which mass is conserved; each side of the equation has the same number of atoms of each element *(320)*

ecuación balanceada: ecuación química en la que se conserva la masa; cada lado de la ecuación tiene el mismo número de átomos de cada elemento

band of stability: the location of stable nuclei on a neutron-vs.-proton plot *(823)*

banda de estabilidad: región ocupada por los núcleos estables en un diagrama neutrones-protones

base: a compound that produces hydroxide ions in solution; see also hydrogen-ion acceptor, Lewis base *(261)*

base: compuesto que, en solución, produce iones hidróxido, ver también receptor de iones hidrógeno, base de Lewis

base dissociation constant (K_b): the ratio of the concentration of the conjugate acid times the concentration of the hydroxide ion to the concentration of the base *(636)*

constante de disociación básica (K_b): razón de la concentración del ácido combinado multiplicada por la concentración del ion hidróxido, a la concentración de la base

basic solution: any solution in which the hydroxide-ion concentration is greater than the hydrogen-ion concentration *(619)*

solución básica: cualquier solución en la que la concentración de ion hidróxido es mayor que la concentración de ion hidrógeno

battery: a group of voltaic cells that are connected to one another *(695)*

batería: grupo de celdas voltaicas conectadas entre sí

beta particle: an electron resulting from the breaking apart of neutrons in an atom *(818)*

partícula beta: electrón que se produce al descomponerse los neutrones de un átomo

binary compound: a compound composed of two elements; NaCl and Al_2O_3 are binary compounds *(244)*

compuesto binario: compuesto integrado por dos elementos; NaCl y Al_2O_3 son compuestos binarios

biochemistry: the area of chemistry that focuses on processes that take place in organisms *(5)*

bioquímica: rama de la química que se concentra en los procesos que se dan en los organismos

boiling point (bp): the temperature at which the vapor pressure of a liquid is just equal to the external pressure on the liquid *(405)*

punto de ebullición (p. eb.): temperatura en la que la presión de vapor de un líquido es apenas igual a la presión externa sobre el líquido

boiling point elevation: the difference in temperature between the boiling point of a solution and the boiling point of the pure solvent *(508)*

incremento del punto de ebullición: diferencia de temperatura entre el punto de ebullición de una solución y el punto de ebullición del disolvente puro

bond dissociation energy: the energy required to break the bond between two covalently bonded atoms; this value is usually expressed in kJ per mol of substance *(217)*

energía de disociación de enlaces: energía requerida para romper el enlace entre dos átomos unidos de forma covalente; este valor suele expresarse en kJ por mol de sustancia

bonding orbital: a molecular orbital that can be occupied by two electrons of a covalent bond *(220)*

orbital de enlace: orbital molecular que puede ser ocupado por los dos electrones de un enlace covalente

Boyle's law: for a given mass of gas at constant temperature, the volume of the gas varies inversely with pressure *(427)*

ley de Boyle: para una masa dada de gas a temperatura constante, el volumen del gas varía en proporción inversa con la presión

branched-chain alkane: an alkane with one or more alkyl groups attached to the parent structure *(726)*

alcano de cadena ramificada: alcano con uno o más grupos alquilo unidos a la estructura madre

Brownian motion: the chaotic movement of colloidal particles, caused by collision with particles of the solvent in which they are dispersed *(479)*

movimiento browniano: movimiento caótico de partículas coloidales, debido a los choques con las partículas del disolvente en el que están dispersas

buffer: a solution in which the pH remains relatively constant when small amounts of acid or base are added; a buffer can be either a solution of a weak acid and the salt of a weak acid or a solution of a weak base with the salt of a weak base *(648)*

solución amortiguadora: solución cuyo pH permanece relativamente constante si se le añaden pequeñas cantidades de ácido o base; una solución amortiguadora puede ser una solución de un ácido débil y la sal de un ácido débil o una solución de una base débil y la sal de una base débil

buffer capacity: a measure of the amount of acid or base that may be added to a buffer solution before a significant change in pH occurs *(648)*

capacidad amortiguadora: medida de la cantidad de ácido o base que se puede añadir a una solución amortiguadora sin que haya un cambio importante del pH

C

calorie (cal): the quantity of heat needed to raise the temperature of 1 g of pure water 1°C *(71)*

caloría (cal): cantidad de calor necesaria para elevar 1°C la temperatura de 1 g de agua pura

calorimeter: an insulated device used to measure the absorption or release of heat in chemical or physical processes *(534)*

calorímetro: aparato con material aislante que sirve para medir la absorción o desprendimiento de calor durante procesos químicos o físicos

calorimetry: the precise measurement of heat flow out of a system for chemical and physical processes *(533)*

calorimetría: medición precisa del cambio del calor durante procesos químicos y físicos

carbohydrate: the name given to monomers and polymers of aldehydes and ketones that have numerous hydroxyl groups; sugars and starches are carbohydrates *(787)*

carbohidrato: nombre dado a monómeros y polímeros de aldehídos y cetonas que tienen muchos grupos hidroxilo; los azúcares y almidones son carbohidratos

carbonyl group: a functional group having a carbon atom and an oxygen atom joined by a double bond; it is found in aldehydes, ketones, esters, and amides *(764)*

grupo carbonilo: grupo funcional que consiste en un átomo de carbono y uno de oxígeno unidos por un doble enlace; se le encuentra en aldehídos, cetonas, ésteres y amidas

carboxyl group: a functional group consisting of a carbonyl group attached to a hydroxyl group; it is found in carboxylic acids *(766)*

grupo carboxilo: grupo funcional que consiste en un grupo carbonilo unido a un grupo hidroxilo; se le encuentra en los ácidos carboxílicos

carboxylic acid: an organic acid containing a carboxyl group; the general formula is RCOOH *(766)*

ácido carboxílico: ácido orgánico que contiene un grupo carboxilo; su fórmula general es RCOOH

catabolism: the reactions in living cells in which substances are broken down and energy is produced *(807)*

catabolismo: reacción, dentro de las células vivas, por la que diversas sustancias se descomponen y producen energía

catalyst: a substance that increases the rate of reaction by lowering the activation-energy barrier; the catalyst is not used up in the reaction *(318)*

catalizador: sustancia que aumenta la velocidad de reacción disminuyendo la barrera de energía de activación; el catalizador no se consume en la reacción

cathode: the electrode at which reduction occurs *(692)*

cátodo: electrodo en el que hay reducción

cathode ray: a stream of electrons produced at the negative electrode (cathode) of a tube containing a gas at low pressure *(103)*

rayo catódico: haz de electrones producido en el electrodo negativo (cátodo) de un tubo que contiene un gas a baja presión

cation: any atom or group of atoms with a positive charge *(165)*

catión: cualquier átomo o grupo de átomos que posee carga positiva

cell potential: the difference between the reduction potentials of two half-cells *(698)*

potencial de celda: diferencia entre los potenciales de reducción de dos medias celdas

Celsius scale: the temperature scale on which the freezing point of water is 0°C and the boiling point is 100°C *(72)*

escala Celsius: escala de temperatura en la que el punto de congelación del agua es 0°C y el punto de ebullición del agua es 100°C

Charles's law: the volume of a fixed mass of gas is directly proportional to its Kelvin temperature if the pressure is kept constant *(431)*

ley de Charles: el volumen de una masa fija de gas es directamente proporcional a su temperatura Kelvin si la presión se mantiene constante

chemical change: a change that produces matter with a different composition than the original matter *(36)*

cambio químico: cambio que produce materia con una composición diferente que la de la materia original

chemical equation: an expression representing a chemical reaction; the formulas of the reactants (on the left) are connected by an arrow with the formulas for the products (on the right) *(318)*

ecuación química: expresión que representa una reacción química; las fórmulas de los reactantes (a la izquierda) se unen mediante una flecha a las fórmulas de los productos (a la derecha)

chemical equilibrium: a state of balance in which the rates of the forward and reverse reactions are equal; no net change in the amount of reactants and products occurs in the chemical system *(575)*

equilibrio químico: estado de equilibrio en el que las velocidades de la reacción de evolución y la reacción inversa son iguales; no hay un cambio total en la cantidad de reactantes y productos en el sistema químico

chemical formula: an expression that indicates the number and type of atoms present in the smallest representative unit of a substance *(187)*

fórmula química: expresión que indica el número y tipo de átomos que están presentes en la unidad más pequeña representativa de una sustancia

chemical potential energy: energy stored in chemical bonds *(527)*

energía potencial química: energía almacenada en los enlaces químicos

chemical property: the ability of a substance to undergo a specific chemical change *(43)*

propiedad química: capacidad de una sustancia para sufrir un cambio químico específico

chemical reaction: a change in which one or more reactants change into one or more products; characterized by the breaking of bonds in reactants and the formation of bonds in products *(44)*

reacción química: cambio en el que uno o más reactantes se convierten en uno o más productos; se caracteriza por la ruptura de enlaces en los reactantes y la formación de enlaces en los productos

chemical symbol: a one- or two-letter representation of an element *(40)*

símbolo químico: representación de un elemento que emplea una o dos letras

chemistry: the study of the composition of matter and the changes that matter undergoes *(4)*

química: estudio de la composición de la materia y los cambios que ésta sufre

***cis-trans* isomers:** compounds that have atoms in the same order, but differ in the orientation of groups around a double bond *(735)*

isómeros *cis-trans*: compuestos cuyos átomos tienen el mismo orden, pero difieren con respecto a la orientación de los grupos alrededor de un enlace doble

coefficient: a small whole number that appears in front of a formula in a balanced chemical equation *(320)*

coeficiente: número entero pequeño que aparece antepuesto a una fórmula en una ecuación química balanceada

colligative property: a property of a solution that depends only upon the number of solute particles, and not upon their identities; boiling point elevation, freezing point depression, and vapor pressure lowering are colligative properties *(505)*

propiedad coligativa: propiedad de una solución que depende únicamente del número de partículas de soluto, y no del tipo de soluto; el incremento del punto de ebullición, la disminución del punto de congelación y el descenso de la presión de vapor son propiedades coligativas

collision theory: atoms, ions, and molecules can react to form products when they collide, provided that the particles have enough kinetic energy *(566)*

teoría de choques: los átomos, iones y moléculas pueden reaccionar para formar productos cuando chocan, siempre que las partículas tengan suficiente energía cinética

colloid: a mixture whose particles are intermediate in size between those of a suspension and a solution *(478)*

coloide: mezcla cuyas partículas tienen un tamaño intermedio entre las de una suspensión y una solución

combination reaction: a chemical change in which two or more substances react to form a single new substance; also called a synthesis reaction *(326)*
reacción de combinación: cambio químico en el que dos o más sustancias reaccionan para formar una sola sustancia nueva; también llamado reacción de síntesis

combined gas law: the law that describes the relationship among the pressure, temperature, and volume of an enclosed gas *(437)*
ley combinada de los gases: ley que describe las relaciones entre la presión, la temperatura y el volumen de un gas encerrado

combustion reaction: a chemical change in which an element or a compound reacts with oxygen, often producing energy in the form of heat and light *(336)*
reacción de combustión: cambio químico en el que un elemento o un compuesto reacciona con oxígeno y por lo regular produce energía en forma de luz y calor

common ion: an ion that is common to both salts in a solution; in a solution of silver nitrate and silver chloride, Ag^+ would be a common ion *(592)*
ion común: ion que es común a dos sales disueltas en una solución; en una solución de nitrato de plata y cloruro de plata, Ag^+ sería un ion común

common ion effect: a decrease in the solubility of an ionic compound caused by the addition of a common ion *(592)*
efecto de ion común: disminución en la solubilidad de un compuesto iónico debida a la adición de un ion común

complete ionic equation: an equation that shows dissolved ionic compounds as dissociated free ions *(341)*
ecuación iónica completa: ecuación que muestra los compuestos iónicos disueltos en forma de iones disociados libres

compound: a substance that contains two or more elements chemically combined in a fixed proportion *(36)*
compuesto: sustancia que contiene dos o más elementos combinados químicamente en una proporción fija

compressibility: a measure of how much the volume of matter decreases under pressure *(422)*
compresibilidad: medida de cuánto disminuye el volumen de la materia cuando se le aplica presión

concentrated solution: a solution containing a large amount of solute *(495)*
solución concentrada: solución que contiene una gran cantidad de soluto

concentration: a measurement of the amount of solute that is dissolved in a given quantity of solvent; usually expressed as mol/L *(495)*
concentración: medida de la cantidad de soluto que está disuelto en una cantidad específica de disolvente; suele expresarse en mol/L

condensed structural formula: a structural formula that leaves out some bonds and/or atoms; the presence of these atoms or bonds is understood *(724)*
fórmula estructural condensada: fórmula estructural que no muestra algunos enlaces o átomos; se sobreentiende la presencia de estos enlaces o átomos

conjugate acid: the particle formed when a base gains a hydrogen ion; NH_4^+ is the conjugate acid of the base NH_3 *(613)*
ácido conjugado: partícula que se forma cuando una base gana un ion hidrógeno; NH_4^+ es el ácido conjugado de la base NH_3

conjugate acid-base pair: two substances that are related by the loss or gain of a single hydrogen ion; ammonia (NH_3) and the ammonium ion (NH_4^+) are a conjugate acid-base pair *(615)*
par conjugado ácido-base: dos sustancias relacionadas entre sí por la pérdida o ganancia de un solo ion hidrógeno; el amoníaco (NH_3) y el ion amonio (NH_4^+) son un par conjugado ácido-base

conjugate base: the particle that remains when an acid has donated a hydrogen ion; OH^- is the conjugate base of the acid water *(613)*
base conjugada: partícula que queda cuando un ácido transfiere un ion hidrógeno; OH^- es la base conjugada del ácido agua

constitutional isomers: compounds that have the same molecular formula, but whose atoms are bonded in a different order *(734)*
isómeros constitucionales: compuestos que tienen la misma fórmula molecular, pero cuyos átomos están enlazados en distinto orden

conversion factor: a ratio of equivalent measurements used to convert a quantity from one unit to another *(78)*
factor de conversión: razón de medidas equivalentes usadas para convertir una cantidad de una unidad a otra

coordinate covalent bond: a covalent bond in which one atom contributes both bonding electrons *(213)*
enlace covalente coordinado: enlace covalente en el que un átomo aporta dos electrones de enlace

covalent bond: a bond formed by the sharing of electrons between atoms *(205)*
enlace covalente: enlace que se forma cuando dos átomos comparten electrones

cracking: the controlled process by which hydrocarbons are broken down or rearranged into smaller, more useful molecules *(743)*
pirólisis: proceso controlado por el cual los hidrocarburos se descomponen o reacomodan para obtener moléculas más pequeñas y útiles

crystal: a solid in which the atoms, ions, or molecules are arranged in an orderly, repeating, three-dimensional pattern *(408)*
cristal: sólido en el que los átomos, iones o moléculas están dispuestos en un patrón tridimensional ordenado y repetitivo

cycloalkane: cyclic hydrocarbon that contains only single bonds *(739)*
cicloalcano: hidrocarburo cíclico que solamente contiene enlaces simples

cyclic hydrocarbon: an organic compound that contains a hydrocarbon ring *(739)*
hidrocarburo cíclico: compuesto orgánico que contiene un anillo de hidrocarburo

D

Dalton's atomic theory: the first theory to relate chemical changes to events at the atomic level *(101)*
teoría atómica de Dalton: primera teoría en relacionar los cambios químicos con sucesos a nivel atómico

Dalton's law of partial pressures: at constant volume and temperature, the total pressure exerted by a mixture of gases is equal to the sum of the partial pressures of the component gases *(448)*
teoría de Dalton de las presiones parciales: a volumen y temperatura constantes, la presión total ejercida por una mezcla de gases es igual a la suma de las presiones parciales de los gases componentes

decomposition reaction: a chemical change in which a single compound is broken down into two or more simpler products *(330)*
reacción de descomposición: cambio químico en el que un solo compuesto se descompone en dos o más productos más simples

dehydrogenation reaction: a reaction in which hydrogen is lost *(767)*
reacción de deshidrogenación: reacción en la que se pierde hidrógeno

deliquescent: describes a substance that removes sufficient water from the air to form a solution; the solution formed has a lower vapor pressure than that of the water in the air *(476)*
delicuescente: término que describe una sustancia que absorbe suficiente humedad del aire como para formar una solución; la solución formada tiene una presión de vapor más baja que la de la humedad del aire

density: the ratio of the mass of an object to its volume *(74)*
densidad: razón de la masa de un objeto a su volumen

dependent variable: the variable that is observed during an experiment; also called responding variable *(13)*
variable dependiente: variable que se observa durante un experimento; también llamada variable de repuesta

desiccant: a hygroscopic substance used as a drying agent *(473)*
desecante: sustancia higroscópica empleada como agente secante

diatomic molecule: a molecule consisting of two atoms *(205)*
molécula diatómica: molécula que cons-ta de dos átomos

diffusion: the tendency of molecules to move toward areas of lower concentration until the concentration is uniform throughout *(452)*
difusión: tendencia de las moléculas a moverse hacia áreas de baja concentración hasta que la concentración es uniforme en todo el medio

dilute solution: a solution that contains a small amount of solute *(495)*
solución diluida: solución que contiene muy poco soluto

dimensional analysis: a technique of problem solving that uses the units that are part of a measurement to help solve the problem *(79)*
análisis dimensional: técnica para resolver problemas que se apoya en las unidades de las mediciones para resolver el problema

dipole: a molecule that has two poles, or regions, with opposite charges *(225)*
dipolo: molécula que tiene dos polos o regiones de carga opuesta

dipole interactions: intermolecular forces resulting from the attraction of oppositely charged regions of polar molecules *(228)*
interacción dipolar: fuerzas intermoleculares que resultan de la atracción de regiones de moléculas polares que tienen cargas opuestas

disaccharide: a carbohydrate formed from two monosaccharide units; common table sugar (sucrose) is a disaccharide *(788)*
disacárido: carbohidrato formado por dos unidades de monosacárido; el azúcar de mesa común (sacarosa) es un disacárido

dispersion forces: attractions between molecules caused by the electron motion on one molecule affecting the electron motion on the other through electrical forces; these are the weakest interactions between molecules *(228)*
fuerzas de dispersión: atracciones entre moléculas que se dan cuando el movimiento de los electrones de una molécula afecta el movimiento de los electrones de la otra mediante fuerzas eléctricas; se trata de las interacciones más débiles entre moléculas

displacement reaction: see single-replacement reaction
reacción de desplazamiento: véase reacción de sustitución sencilla

distillation: a process used to separate components of a mixture using differences in boiling points *(34)*
destilación: proceso que se emplea para separar las sustancias de una mezcla por medio de diferentes puntos de ebullición

double covalent bond: a bond in which two atoms share two pairs of electrons *(212)*
enlace covalente doble: enlace en el que dos átomos comparten dos pares de electrones

double-replacement reaction: a chemical change that involves an exchange of positive ions between two compounds *(334)*
reacción de sustitución doble: cambio químico que implica un intercambio de iones positivos entre dos compuestos

dry cell: a commercial voltaic cell in which the electrolyte is a moist paste; despite their name, the compact, portable batteries used in flashlights are dry cells *(694)*
pila seca: celda voltaica comercial en la que, a pesar del nombre, el electrolito es una pasta húmeda; las baterías compactas y portátiles que se usan en las linternas son pilas secas

E

effloresce: to lose water of hydration; the process occurs when the hydrate has a vapor pressure higher than that of water vapor in the air *(473)*
eflorecerse: perder agua de hidratación; el proceso se presenta cuando la presión de vapor del hidrato es más alta que la del vapor de agua en el aire

effusion: the process that occurs when a gas escapes through a tiny hole in its container *(452)*
efusión: proceso en el cual un gas escapa por un agujero diminuto en su recipiente

electrical potential: the ability of a voltaic cell to produce an electric current *(698)*
potencial eléctrico: capacidad de una celda voltaica para producir corriente eléctrica

electrochemical cell: any device that converts chemical energy into electrical energy or electrical energy into chemical energy *(691)*
celda electroquímica: cualquier dispositivo que convierte energía química en energía eléctrica o energía eléctrica en energía química

electrochemical process: the conversion of chemical energy into electrical energy or electrical energy into chemical energy; all electrochemical processes involve redox reactions *(690)*
proceso electroquímico: conversión de energía química en energía eléctrica o energía eléctrica en energía química; en todos los procesos electroquímicos intervienen reacciones redox

electrode: a conductor in a circuit that carries electrons to or from a substance other than a metal *(692)*
electrodo: en un circuito, un conductor que transporta electrones hacia o desde una sustancia que no es un metal

electrolysis: a process in which electrical energy is used to bring about a chemical change; the electrolysis of water produces hydrogen and oxygen *(706)*
electrolisis: proceso en el que se usa energía eléctrica para realizar un cambio químico; la electrolisis del agua produce hidrógeno y oxígeno

electrolyte: a compound that conducts an electric current when it is in an aqueous solution or in the molten state; all ionic compounds are electrolytes, but most covalent compounds are not *(470)*
electrolito: compuesto que conduce una corriente eléctrica cuando está en solución acuosa o está derretido; todos los compuestos iónicos son electrolitos, pero muy pocos compuestos covalentes lo son

electrolytic cell: an electrochemical cell used to cause a chemical change through the application of electrical energy *(706)*
celda electrolítica: celda electroquímica que se usa para efectuar un cambio químico mediante la aplicación de energía eléctrica

electromagnetic radiation: energy waves that travel in a vacuum at a speed of 2.998×10^8 m/s; includes radio waves, microwaves, infrared waves, visible light, ultraviolet waves, X-rays, and gamma rays *(131)*
radiación electromagnética: ondas de energía que viajan en el vacío a una velocidad de 2.998×10^8 m/s; incluye las ondas de radio, microondas, ondas infrarrojas, luz visible, ondas ultravioleta, rayos X y rayos gamma

electron: a negatively charged subatomic particle *(103)*
electrón: partícula subátomica con carga negativa

electron configuration: the arrangement of electrons of an atom in its ground state into various orbitals around the nuclei of atoms *(124)*
configuración electrónica: distribución de los electrones de un átomo en su estado basal, en diversos orbitales alrededor del núcleo del átomo

electron dot structure: a notation that depicts valence electrons as dots around the atomic symbol of the element; the symbol represents the inner electrons and atomic nucleus; also called Lewis dot structure *(181)*
estructura de punto electrón: notación que muestra los electrones de valencia como puntos alrededor del símbolo atómico del elemento; el símbolo representa los electrones internos y el núcleo atómico; también se conoce como estructura de puntos de Lewis

electronegativity: the ability of an atom to attract electrons when the atom is in a compound *(170)*

electronegatividad: capacidad de un átomo para atraer electrones cuando el átomo está en un compuesto

element: the simplest form of matter that has a unique set of properties; an element cannot be broken down into simpler substances by chemical means *(36)*

elemento: forma más simple de materia que posee un conjunto único de propiedades; un elemento no puede descomponerse en sustancias más simples usando métodos químicos

empirical formula: a formula with the lowest whole-number ratio of elements in a compound; the empirical formula of hydrogen peroxide (H_2O_2) is HO *(302)*

fórmula empírica: fórmula que muestra las proporciones de los elementos en un compuesto con los números enteros más pequeños posibles; la fórmula empírica del peróxido de hidrógeno (H_2O_2) es HO

emulsion: the colloidal dispersion of one liquid in another *(480)*

emulsión: dispersión coloidal de un líquido en otro

enantiomers: molecules that differ from one another in the way that four different groups are arranged around a carbon atom *(736)*

enantiómero: moléculas que se diferencian entre sí por la forma en que cuatro grupos diferentes están dispuestos alrededor de un átomo de carbono

endothermic process: a process that absorbs heat from the surroundings *(527)*

proceso endotérmico: proceso en el que se absorbe calor del entorno

end point: the point in a titration at which the indicator changes color *(642)*

punto final: punto de una valoración química en cual el indicador cambia de color

energy: the capacity for doing work or producing heat *(71)*

energía: capacidad para efectuar trabajo o producir calor

energy level: the specific energies an electron in an atom or other system can have *(119)*

nivel energético: las energías específicas que puede tener un electrón en un átomo u otro sistema

enthalpy (*H*): the heat content of a system at constant pressure *(533)*

entalpía (*H*): cantidad de calor en un sistema a presión constante

entropy (*S*): a measure of the disorder of a system *(598)*

entropía (*S*): medida del desorden de un sistema

enzyme: a protein that acts as a biological catalyst *(793)*

enzima: proteína que actúa como catalizador biológico

equilibrium constant (K_{eq}): the ratio of product concentrations to reactant concentrations at equilibrium, with each concentration raised to a power equal to the number of moles of that substance in the balanced chemical equation *(582)*

constante de equilibrio (K_{eq}): razón de las concentraciones de los productos a las concentraciones de los reactantes en el equilibrio, con cada concentración elevada a una potencia igual al número de moles de esa sustancia en la ecuación química balanceada

equilibrium position: the relative concentrations of reactants and products of a reaction that has reached equilibrium; indicates whether the reactants or products are favored in the reversible reaction *(577)*

posición de equilibrio: las concentraciones relativas de reactantes y productos de una reacción que ha alcanzado el equilibrio; indica si se favorecen los reactantes o productos en la reacción reversible

equivalence point: the point in a titration where the number of moles of hydrogen ions equals the number of moles of hydroxide ions *(642)*

punto de equivalencia: punto de una valoración química en la que el número de moles de iones hidrógeno es igual al número de moles de iones hidróxido

error: the difference between the accepted value and the experimental value *(58)*

error: diferencia entre el valor aceptado y el valor experimental

ester: a derivative of a carboxylic acid in which the —OH of the carboxyl group has been replaced by the —OR from an alcohol; the general formula is RCOOR *(768)*

éster: derivado de un ácido carboxílico en el que el —OH del grupo carboxilo ha sido sustituido por el —OR de un alcohol; la fórmula general es RCOOR

ether: an organic compound in which oxygen is bonded to two carbon groups; the general formula is R—O—R *(762)*

éter: compuesto orgánico en el que el oxígeno está unido a dos grupos carbono; la fórmula general es R—O—R

evaporation: vaporization that occurs at the surface of a liquid that is not boiling *(402)*

evaporación: vaporización que se da en la superficie de un líquido que no está en ebullición

excess reagent: a reagent present in a quantity that is more than sufficient to react with a limiting reagent; any reactant that remains after the limiting reagent is used up in a chemical reaction *(375)*

reactivo excesivo: reactivo que está presente en una cantidad más que suficiente para reaccionar con un reactivo limitante; cualquier reactante que queda después de que se ha usado todo el reactivo limitante en una reacción química

exothermic process: a process that releases heat to its surroundings *(527)*
proceso exotérmico: proceso en el que se desprende calor hacia el entorno

experiment: a repeatable procedure that is used to test a hypothesis *(3)*
experimento: procedimiento repetido que sirve para probar una hipótesis

experimental value: a quantitative value measured during an experiment *(58)*
valor experimental: valor cuantitativo que se mide durante un experimento

extensive property: a property that depends on the amount of matter in a sample *(28)*
propiedad extensiva: propiedad que depende de la cantidad de materia en una muestra

F

fermentation: the production of ethanol from sugars by the action of yeast or bacteria *(760)*
fermentación: producción de etanol a partir de azúcares por la acción de levaduras o bacterias

filtration: a process that separates a solid from the liquid in a heterogeneous mixture *(34)*
filtración: proceso para separar un sólido de un líquido en una mezcla heterogénea

fission: the splitting of a nucleus into smaller fragments, accompanied by the release of neutrons and a large amount of energy *(830)*
fisión: división de un núcleo en fragmentos más pequeños, acompañada por desprendimiento de neutrones y una gran cantidad de energía

formula unit: the lowest whole-number ratio of ions in an ionic compound; in magnesium chloride, the ratio of magnesium ions to chloride ions is 1:2 and the formula unit is $MgCl_2$ *(187)*
unidad de fórmula: razón más baja, expresada en números enteros, de los iones de un compuesto iónico; en el cloruro de magnesio, la razón de iones magnesio a iones cloruro es de 1:2, así que la unidad de fórmula es $MgCl_2$

free energy: the energy available to do work *(596)*
energía libre: energía que está disponible para realizar trabajo

freezing point: the temperature at which a liquid changes to a solid *(408)*
punto de congelación: temperatura a la cual un líquido se convierte en un sólido

freezing-point depression: the difference in temperature between the freezing point of a solution and the freezing point of the pure solvent *(507)*
disminución del punto de congelación: diferencia de temperatura entre el punto de congelación de una solución y el del disolvente puro

frequency (ν): the number of wave cycles that pass a given point per unit of time; frequency and wavelength are inversely proportional to each other *(129)*
frecuencia (ν): número de ciclos de onda que pasan por un punto específico en la unidad de tiempo; la frecuencia y la longitud de onda son inversamente proporcionales

fuel cell: a voltaic cell that does not need to be recharged; the fuel is oxidized to produce a continuous supply of electrical energy *(696)*
celda de combustible: celda voltaica que no necesita recargarse; el combustible se oxida para producir un suministro continuo de energía eléctrica

functional group: a specific arrangement of atoms in an organic compound that is capable of characteristic chemical reactions; the chemistry of an organic compound is determined by its functional groups *(754)*
grupo funcional: distribución específica de átomos en un compuesto orgánico que puede participar en reacciones químicas características; la química de un compuesto orgánico está determinada por sus grupos funcionales

fusion: the process of combining nuclei to produce a nucleus of greater mass *(833)*
fusión: proceso en el que se combinan núcleos para producir un núcleo con mayor masa

gamma ray: a high-energy photon emitted by a radioisotope *(820)*
rayo gamma: fotón de alta energía emitido por un radioisótopo

gas: a form of matter that takes the shape and volume of its container; a gas has no definite shape or volume *(30)*
gas: estado de la materia que adopta la forma y el volumen del recipiente que la contiene; los gases no tienen forma ni volumen definidos

gas pressure: the force exerted by a gas on an object *(397)*
presión de gas: fuerza que ejerce un gas sobre un objeto

Gay-Lussac's law: the pressure of a gas is directly proportional to the Kelvin temperature if the volume is constant *(434)*
ley de Gay-Lussac: la presión de un gas es directamente proporcional a su temperatura Kelvin si se mantiene constante el volumen

gene: a segment of DNA that codes for a single peptide chain *(800)*

gen: segmento de ADN que contiene el código para una sola cadena péptida

glass: a product made of substances that cooled without crystallizing *(410)*

vidrio: producto formado por sustancias que se han enfriado sin cristalizarse

gram (g): a metric mass unit equal to the mass of 1 cm^3 of water at 4°C *(71)*

gramo (g): unidad métrica de masa equivalente a la masa de 1 cm^3 de agua a 4°C

ground state: the lowest possible energy of an atom described by quantum mechanics *(137)*

estado fundamental: energía más baja que puede tener un átomo descrito por la mecánica cuántica

group: a vertical column of elements in the periodic table; the constituent elements of a group have similar chemical and physical properties *(42)*

grupo: columna vertical de elementos en la tabla periódica; los elementos de un grupo tienen propiedades físicas y químicas similares

H

half-cell: the part of a voltaic cell in which either oxidation or reduction occurs; it consists of a single electrode immersed in a solution of its ions *(692)*

semicelda: parte de una celda voltaica en la que se lleva a cabo la oxidación o reducción; consta de un solo electrodo sumergido en una solución de sus iones

half-life ($t_{½}$): the time required for one-half of the nuclei of a radioisotope sample to decay to products *(824)*

semivida ($t_{½}$): tiempo que tarda en desintegrarse la mitad de los núcleos de una muestra de un radioisótopo

half-reaction: an equation showing either the oxidation or the reduction that takes place in a redox reaction *(681)*

semirreacción: ecuación que muestra la oxidación o bien la reducción que se da en una reacción redox

halide ion: a negative ion formed when a halogen atom gains an electron *(185)*

ion haluro: ion negativo que se forma cuando un átomo de halógeno gana un electrón

halocarbon: any member of a class of organic compounds containing covalently bonded fluorine, chlorine, bromine, or iodine *(756)*

compuesto halocarbonado: cualquier miembro de una clase de compuestos orgánicos que contienen flúor, cloro, bromo o yodo unidos mediante enlaces covalentes

halogen: a nonmetal in Group 7A of the periodic table *(155)*

halógeno: no metal del grupo 7A de la tabla periódica

heat (*q*): energy that transfers from one object to another because of a temperature difference between the objects *(527)*

calor (*q*): energía que fluye de un objeto a otro debido a la diferencia de temperatura entre los objetos

heat capacity: the amount of heat needed to increase the temperature of an object exactly 1°C *(529)*

capacidad calorífica: cantidad de calor necesaria para elevar exactamente 1°C la temperatura de un objeto

heat of combustion: the heat of reaction for the complete burning of one mole of a substance *(538)*

calor de combustión: calor de reacción al quemarse totalmente un mol de una sustancia

heat of reaction: the enthalpy change for a chemical equation exactly as it is written *(537)*

calor de reacción: cambio de entalpía correspondiente a una ecuación química en la forma exacta en que está escrita

Heisenberg uncertainty principle: it is impossible to know exactly both the velocity and the position of a particle at the same time *(139)*

principio de incertidumbre de Heisenberg: es imposible conocer con exactitud la velocidad y la posición de una partícula al mismo tiempo

Henry's law: at a given temperature the solubility of a gas in a liquid is directly proportional to the pressure of the gas above the liquid *(492)*

ley de Henry: a una temperatura determinada, la solubilidad de un gas en un líquido es directamente proporcional a la presión del gas sobre el líquido

hertz (Hz): the unit of frequency, equal to one cycle per second *(129)*

hertz (Hz): unidad de frecuencia, equivalente a un ciclo por segundo

Hess's law of heat summation: if you add two or more thermochemical equations to give a final equation, then you also add the heats of reaction to give the final heat of reaction *(550)*

ley de Hess de la suma de los calores: ley según la cual, si se suman dos o más ecuaciones termoquímicas para obtener una ecuación final, también se suman los calores de reacción para obtener el calor de reacción final

heterogeneous mixture: a mixture that is not uniform in composition; components are not evenly distributed throughout the mixture *(32)*

mezcla heterogénea: mezcla cuya composición no es uniforme; sus componentes no están distribuidos de forma equitativa en toda la mezcla

homogeneous mixture: a mixture that is uniform in composition; components are evenly distributed and not easily distinguished *(33)*

mezcla homogénea: mezcla cuya composición es uniforme; sus componentes están distribuidos de forma equitativa y no es fácil distinguirlos

Hund's rule: electrons occupy orbitals of the same energy in a way that makes the number or electrons with the same spin direction as large as possible *(125)*

regla de Hund: los electrones ocupan orbitales de la misma energía haciendo que el número de electrones cuyo espín tiene la misma dirección sea lo más grande posible

hybridization: the mixing of several atomic orbitals to form the same total number of equivalent hybrid orbitals *(223)*

hibridización: combinación de varios orbitales atómicos para formar el mismo número total de orbitales híbridos equivalentes

hydrate: a compound that has a specific number of water molecules bound to each formula unit *(472)*

hidrato: compuesto que tiene un número específico de moléculas de agua unidas a cada unidad de fórmula

hydration reaction: a reaction in which water is added to an alkene *(761)*

reacción de hidratación: reacción en la que se añade agua a un alqueno

hydrocarbon: an organic compound that contains only carbon and hydrogen *(720)*

hidrocarburo: compuesto orgánico que contiene sólo carbono e hidrógeno

hydrogenation reaction: a reaction in which hydrogen is added to a carbon–carbon double bond to give an alkane *(761)*

reacción de hidrogenación: reacción en la que se añade hidrógeno a un doble enlace carbono–carbono para obtener un alcano

hydrogen bonds: attractive forces in which a hydrogen covalently bonded to a very electronegative atom is also weakly bonded to an unshared electron pair of another electronegative atom *(229)*

enlaces de hidrógeno: fuerzas de atracción en las que un átomo de hidrógeno, unido por un enlace covalente a un átomo muy electronegativo, también se une débilmente a un par no compartido de electrones de otro átomo electronegativo

hydronium ion (H_3O^+): the positive ion formed when a water molecule gains a hydrogen ion *(611)*

ion hidronio (H_3O^+): ion positivo que se forma cuando una molécula de agua gana un ion hidrógeno

hydroxy group: the —OH functional group in alcohols *(758)*

grupo hidroxilo: el grupo funcional —OH de los alcoholes

hygroscopic: a term describing salts and other compounds that remove moisture from the air *(473)*

higroscópico: se llama así a las sales y otros compuestos que absorben humedad del aire

hypothesis: a proposed explanation for an observation *(13)*

hipótesis: explicación propuesta para una observación

I

ideal gas constant: the constant in the ideal gas law with the symbol R and the value 8.31 (L·kPa)/(K·mol) *(441)*

constante del gas ideal: constante de la ley del gas ideal; se representa con el símbolo R y tiene un valor de 8.31 (L·kPa)/(K·mol)

ideal gas law: the relationship $PV = nRT$, which describes the behavior of an ideal gas *(441)*

ley del gas ideal: relación $PV = nRT$, que describe el comportamiento del gas ideal

immiscible: describes liquids that are insoluble in one another; oil and water are immiscible *(490)*

inmiscible: se dice de los líquidos que son insolubles uno en el otro; el aceite y el agua son inmiscibles

independent variable: the variable that is changed during an experiment; also called manipulated variable *(13)*

variable independiente: variable que cambia durante un experimento; también se llama variable manipulada

inhibitor: a substance that interferes with the action of a catalyst *(571)*

inhibidor: sustancia que interfiere la acción de un catalizador

inner transition metal: an element in the lanthanide or actinide series; the highest occupied *s* sublevel and nearby *f* sublevel of its atoms generally contain electrons; also called inner transition element *(160)*

metal de transición interna: elemento de las series de los lantánidos o los actínidos; el subnivel *s* más alto ocupado y el subnivel *f* cercano de sus átomos contienen electrones; también se llama elemento de transición interna

inorganic chemistry: the study of substances that, in general, do not contain carbon *(5)*

química inorgánica: estudio de sustancias que, en general, no contienen carbono

intensive property: a property that depends on the type of matter in a sample, not the amount of matter *(28)*

propiedad intensiva: propiedad que depende del tipo de materia de una muestra, no de la cantidad de materia

intermediate: a product of one of the steps in a reaction mechanism; it becomes a reactant in the next step *(574)*

intermediario: producto de uno de los pasos de un mecanismo de reacción; se convierte en reactante en el siguiente paso

International System of Units (SI): the revised version of the metric system, adopted by international agreement in 1960 *(68)*

Sistema Internacional de Unidades (SI): versión modificada del sistema métrico, adoptada por acuerdo internacional en 1960

ion: an atom or group of atoms that has a positive or negative charge *(165)*

ion: átomo o grupo de átomos que tiene carga positiva o negativa

ionic bond: the electrostatic attraction that binds oppositely charged ions together *(186)*

enlace iónico: atracción electrostática que une a iones con carga opuesta

ionic compound: a compound composed of positive and negative ions *(186)*

compuesto iónico: compuesto formado por iones positivos y negativos

ionization energy: the energy required to remove an electron from an atom in its gaseous state *(166)*

energía de ionización: energía necesaria para sacar un electrón de un átomo en su estado gaseoso

ionizing radiation: radiation with enough energy to knock electrons off some atoms of a bombarded substance to produce ions *(834)*

radiación ionizante: radiación que tiene la energía suficiente para desprender electrones de algunos átomos de una sustancia bombardeada, produciendo así iones

ion-product constant for water (K_w): the product of the concentrations of hydrogen ions and hydroxide ions in water; it is 1×10^{-14} at 25°C *(619)*

constante de producto iónico del agua (K_w): producto de las concentraciones de iones hidrógeno y de iones hidróxido del agua; es 1×10^{-14} a 25°C

isomers: compounds that have the same molecular formula but different molecular structures *(734)*

isómeros: compuestos que tienen la misma fórmula molecular, pero diferentes estructuras moleculares

isotopes: atoms of the same element that have the same atomic number but different atomic masses due to a different number of neutrons *(112)*

isótopos: átomos del mismo elemento que tienen el mismo número atómico pero diferentes masas atómicas porque tienen un distinto número de neutrones

J

joule (J): the SI unit of energy; 4.184 J equal one calorie *(71)*

julio (J): unidad de energía en el SI; 4.184 J equivalen a una caloría

K

Kelvin scale: the temperature scale in which the freezing point of water is 273 K and the boiling point is 373 K; 0 K is absolute zero *(72)*

escala Kelvin: escala de temperatura en la que el punto de congelación del agua es 273 K, y el de ebullición, 373 K; 0 K es el cero absoluto

ketone: an organic compound in which the carbon of the carbonyl group is joined to two other carbons; the general formula is RCOR *(764)*

cetona: compuesto orgánico en el que el carbono del grupo carbonilo está unido a otros dos carbonos: la fórmula general es RCOR

kilogram (kg): the mass of 1 L of water at 4°C; it is the base unit of mass in SI *(71)*

kilogramo (kg): masa de 1 L de agua a 4°C; es la unidad base de masa en el SI

kinetic energy: the energy an object has because of its motion *(396)*

energía cinética: energía que tienen los objetos de acuerdo con su movimiento

kinetic theory: a theory explaining the states of matter, based on the concept that all matter consists of tiny particles that are in constant motion *(396)*

teoría cinética: teoría que explica los estados de la materia basándose en el concepto de que toda la materia está formada por pequeñas partículas que están en constante movimiento

L

law of conservation of energy: in any chemical or physical process, energy is neither created nor destroyed *(526)*

ley de conservación de la energía: ley según la cual en ningún proceso químico o físico se crea ni se destruye energía

law of conservation of mass: in any physical change or chemical reaction, mass is conserved; mass can be neither created nor destroyed *(46)*

ley de conservación de la masa: en cualquier cambio físico o reacción química, la masa se conserva; la masa no puede crearse ni destruirse

law of definite proportions: in samples of any chemical compound, the masses of the elements are always in the same proportion *(264)*

ley de las proporciones definidas: en muestras de cualquier compuesto químico, las masas de los elementos siempre están en la misma proporción

law of disorder: the natural tendency for systems to move in a direction of increasing disorder *(598)*

ley del desorden: tendencia natural de los sistemas a desplazarse hacia un desorden cada vez mayor

law of multiple proportions: whenever two elements form more than one compound, the different masses of one element that combine with the same mass of the other element are in the ratio of small whole numbers *(265)*

ley de las proporciones múltiples: siempre que dos elementos forman más de un compuesto, las diferentes masas de un elemento que se combinan con la misma masa del otro elemento están en razón de números enteros pequeños

Le Châtelier's principle: when a stress is applied to a system in dynamic equilibrium, the system changes in a way that relieves the stress *(578)*

principio de Le Châtelier: cuando se aplica una tensión a un sistema que está en equilibrio dinámico, el sistema cambia a modo de aliviar dicha tensión

Lewis acid: any substance that can accept a pair of electrons to form a covalent bond *(615)*

ácido de Lewis: cualquier sustancia capaz de aceptar un par de electrones para formar un enlace covalente

Lewis base: any substance that can donate a pair of electrons to form a covalent bond *(615)*

base de Lewis: cualquier sustancia capaz de ceder un par de electrones para formar un enlace covalente

limiting reagent: any reactant that is used up first in a chemical reaction; it determines the amount of product that can be formed in the reaction *(375)*

reactivo limitante: cualquier reactante que se haya consumido primero en una reacción química; determina la cantidad de producto que se puede formar en la reacción

lipid: a member of a large class of relatively water-insoluble organic compounds; fats, oils, and waxes are lipids *(795)*

lípido: miembro de una clase amplia de compuestos orgánicos relativamente insolubles en agua; las grasas, aceites y ceras son lípidos

liquid: a form of matter that flows, has a fixed volume, and an indefinite shape *(30)*

líquido: forma de materia que fluye; tiene volumen fijo pero forma indefinida

liter (L): the volume of a cube measuring 10 centimeters on each edge (1000 cm^3); it is the common unprefixed unit of volume in the metric system *(70)*

litro (L): volumen de un cubo cuyas aristas miden 10 centímetros cada una (1000 cm^3); es la unidad común de volumen en el sistema métrico

M

manipulated variable: *see* independent variable

variable manipulada: *véase* variable independiente

mass: a measure of the amount of matter that an object contains; the SI base unit of mass is the kilogram *(28)*

masa: medida de la cantidad de materia contenida en un objeto; la unidad base de masa en el SI es el kilogramo

mass number: the total number of protons and neutrons in the nucleus of an atom *(110)*

número de masa: número total de protones y neutrones que contiene el núcleo de un átomo

matter: anything that has mass and occupies space *(4)*

materia: todo lo que tiene masa y ocupa espacio

measurement: a quantitative description that includes both a number and a unit *(54)*

medición: descripción cuantitativa que incluye tanto números como unidades

melting point (mp): the temperature at which a substance changes from a solid to a liquid; the melting point of water is 0°C *(408)*

punto de fusión (p.f.): temperatura a la que una sustancia cambia del estado sólido al líquido; el punto de fusión del agua es 0°C

metabolism: all the chemical reactions carried out by an organism; includes energy-producing (catabolism) reactions and energy-absorbing (anabolism) reactions *(807)*

metabolismo: todas las reacciones químicas llevadas a cabo por los organismos; incluyen reacciones que producen energía (catabolismo) y reacciones que consumen energía (anabolismo)

metal: one of a class of elements that are good conductors of heat and electric current; metals tend to be ductile, malleable, and shiny *(152)*

metal: miembro de una clase de elementos que son buenos conductores del calor y la electricidad; los metales suelen ser dúctiles, maleables y brillantes

metallic bond: the force of attraction that holds metals together; it consists of the attraction of free-floating valence electrons for positively charged metal ions *(193)*

enlace metálico: fuerza de atracción que mantiene unidos los átomos de un metal; se debe a la atracción entre los electrones de valencia, que flotan libremente, y los iones metálicos de carga positiva

metalloid: an element that tends to have properties that are similar to those of metals and nonmetals *(153)*

metaloide: elemento cuyas propiedades son similares a las de los metales y de los no metales

meter (m): the base unit of length in SI *(69)*

metro (m): unidad base de longitud en el SI

miscible: describes liquids that dissolve in one another in all proportions *(490)*

miscible: se les llama así a los líquidos que se disuelven uno en el otro en todas las proporciones

mixture: a physical blend of two or more substances that are not chemically combined *(32)*

mezcla: incorporación física de dos o más sustancias que no se combinan químicamente

model: a representation of an object or event *(13)*

modelo: representación de un objeto o evento

molal boiling-point elevation constant (K_b): the change in boiling point for a 1-molal solution of a nonvolatile molecular solute *(513)*

constante molal de la elevación del punto de ebullición (K_b): cambio en el punto de ebullición de una solución 1-molal de un soluto molecular no volátil

molal freezing-point depression constant (K_f): the change in freezing point for a 1-molal solution of a nonvolatile molecular solute *(513)*

constante molal de la disminución del punto de congelación (K_f): cambio en el punto de congelación de una solución 1-molal de un soluto molecular no volátil

molality (m): the concentration of solute in a solution expressed as the number of moles of solute dissolved in 1 kilogram (1000 g) of solvent *(509)*

molalidad (m): concentración de soluto en una solución expresada como el número de moles de soluto disueltos en 1 kilogramo (1000 g) de disolvente

molar heat of condensation (ΔH_{cond}): the amount of heat released by one mole of a vapor as it condenses to a liquid at a constant temperature *(545)*

calor molar de condensación (ΔH_{cond}): cantidad de calor que un mol de vapor desprende al condensarse, convirtiéndose en líquido, a temperatura constante

molar heat of fusion (ΔH_{fus}): the amount of heat absorbed by one mole of a solid substance as it melts to a liquid at a constant temperature *(541)*

calor molar de fusión (ΔH_{fus}): cantidad de calor que un mol de una sustancia sólida absorbe al fundirse, convirtiéndose en líquido, a temperatura constante

molar heat of solidification (ΔH_{solid}): the amount of heat lost by one mole of a liquid as it solidifies at a constant temperature *(544)*

calor molar de solidificación (ΔH_{solid}): cantidad de calor que un mol de un líquido pierde al solidificarse a temperatura constante

molar heat of solution (ΔH_{soln}): the enthalpy change caused by the dissolution of one mole of a substance *(549)*

calor molar de disolución (ΔH_{soln}): cambio de calor debido a la disolución de un mol de una sustancia

molar heat of vaporization (ΔH_{vap}): the amount of heat absorbed by one mole of a liquid as it vaporizes at a constant temperature *(545)*

calor molar de vaporización (ΔH_{vap}): cantidad de calor absorbida por un mol de un líquido al evaporarse a temperatura constante

molarity (M): the concentration of solute in a solution expressed as the number of moles of solute dissolved in 1 liter of solution *(495)*

molaridad (M): concentración de soluto en una solución expresada como el número de moles de soluto disueltos en 1 litro de solución

molar mass: a term used to refer to the mass of a mole of any substance *(282)*

masa molar: término empleado para referirse a la masa de un mol de cualquier sustancia

molar volume: the volume occupied by 1 mole of a gas at standard temperature and pressure (STP); 22.4 L *(292)*

volumen molar: volumen ocupado por 1 mol de un gas a temperatura y presión estándar (TPE); 22.4 L

mole (mol): the amount of a substance that contains 6.02×10^{23} representative particles of that substance *(279)*

mol: cantidad de una sustancia que contiene 6.02×10^{23} partículas representativas de esa sustancia

molecular compound: a compound that is composed of molecules *(205)*

compuesto molecular: compuesto formado por moléculas

molecular formula: a chemical formula of a molecular compound that shows the kinds and numbers of atoms present in a molecule of a compound *(205)*

fórmula molecular: fórmula química de un compuesto molecular que indica los tipos y números de átomos presentes en una molécula de un compuesto

molecular orbital: an orbital that applies to the entire molecule *(220)*

orbital molecular: orbital que abarca toda la molécula

molecule: a neutral group of atoms joined together by covalent bonds *(205)*

molécula: grupo neutro de átomos unidos por enlaces covalentes

mole fraction: the ratio of the moles of solute in solution to the total number of moles of both solvent and solute *(510)*

fracción molar: razón de los moles de soluto en solución al número total de moles de disolvente y soluto

mole ratio: a conversion factor derived from the coefficients of a balanced chemical equation interpreted in terms of moles *(360)*

razón molar: factor de conversión derivado de los coeficientes de una ecuación química equilibrada interpretada en términos de moles

monatomic ion: a single atom with a positive or negative charge resulting from the loss or gain of one or more valence electrons *(238)*

ion monoatómico: un solo átomo con carga positiva o negativa debido a la pérdida o ganancia de uno o más electrones de valencia

monomer: a simple molecule that repeatedly combines to form a polymer *(771)*

monómero: molécula sencilla que se combina repetidamente para formar un polímero

monosaccharide: a carbohydrate consisting of one sugar unit; also called a simple sugar *(787)*

monosacárido: carbohidrato que consta de una sola unidad de azúcar; también llamado azúcar simple

N

net ionic equation: an equation for a reaction in solution showing only those particles that are directly involved in the chemical change *(341)*

ecuación iónica neta: ecuación de una reacción en solución que sólo muestra las partículas que intervienen directamente en el cambio químico

network solid: a solid in which all of the atoms are covalently bonded to each other *(230)*

sólido en cadena: sólido en el que todos los átomos están unidos entre sí por enlaces covalentes

neutralization reaction: a reaction in which an acid and a base react in an aqueous solution to produce a salt and water *(639)*

reacción de neutralización: reacción en la que un ácido y una base reaccionan en una solución acuosa para producir una sal y agua

neutral solution: an aqueous solution in which the concentrations of hydrogen and hydroxide ions are equal; it has a pH of 7.0 *(618)*

solución neutral: solución acuosa en la que las concentraciones de iones hidrógeno e iones hidróxido son iguales; tiene un pH de 7.0

neutron: a subatomic particle with no charge and a mass of 1 amu; found in the nucleus of an atom *(105)*

neutrón: partícula subatómica sin carga que tiene una masa de 1 uma; se le encuentra en el núcleo de los átomos

neutron absorption: a process that decreases the number of slow-moving neutrons in a nuclear reactor; this is accomplished by using control rods made of a material such as cadmium, which absorbs neutrons *(830)*

absorción de neutrones: proceso que reduce el número de neutrones lentos en un reactor nuclear; esto se logra mediante el uso de varillas de control hechas con un material como el cadmio, que absorbe neutrones

neutron moderation: a process used in nuclear reactors to slow down neutrons so the reactor fuel captures them to continue the chain reaction *(830)*

moderación de neutrones: proceso empleado en reactores nucleares para frenar los neutrones de modo que el combustible del reactor los capture para continuar la reacción en cadena

noble gas: an element in Group 8A of the periodic table; the *s* and *p* sublevels of the highest occupied energy level are filled *(158)*

gas noble: elemento del grupo 8A de la tabla periódica; los subniveles *s* y *p* del nivel energético ocupado más alto están totalmente llenos

nonelectrolyte: a compound that does not conduct an electric current in aqueous solution or in the molten state *(470)*

no electrolito: compuesto que no conduce una corriente eléctrica en solución acuosa ni en estado fundido

nonmetal: an element that tends to be a poor conductor of heat and electric current; nonmetals generally have properties opposite to those of metals *(152)*

no metal: elemento que suele ser mal conductor del calor y la electricidad; las propiedades de los no metales generalmente son opuestas a las de los metales

nonpolar covalent bond: a covalent bond in which the electrons are shared equally by the two atoms *(224)*

enlace covalente no polar: enlace covalente en el que los dos átomos comparten equitativamente los electrones

nonspontaneous reaction: a reaction that does not favor the formation of products at the specified conditions *(596)*

reacción no espontánea: reacción que no favorece la formación de productos en las condiciones especificadas

normal boiling point: the boiling point of a liquid at a pressure of 101.3 kPa or 1 atm *(406)*

punto normal de ebullición: el punto de ebullición de un líquido a una presión de 101.3 kPa o 1 atm

nuclear force: an attractive force that acts between all nuclear particles that are extremely close together, such as protons and neutrons in a nucleus *(823)*

fuerza nuclear: fuerza de atracción que actúa entre todas las partículas nucleares que están extremadamente cerca unas de otras, como los protones y los neutrones en un núcleo

nuclear radiation: the rays and particles emitted by a radioactive source *(818)*

radiación nuclear: rayos y partículas que una fuente radiactiva emite

nucleic acid: a polymer of ribonucleotides (RNA) or deoxyribonucleotides (DNA) found primarily in cell nuclei; nucleic acids play an important role in the transmission of hereditary characteristics, protein synthesis, and the control of cell activities *(798)*

ácido nucleico: polímero de ribonucleótidos (ARN) o desoxirribonucleótidos (ADN) que se encuentra primordialmente en el núcleo de las células; los ácidos nucleicos desempeñan un papel importante en la transmisión de las características hereditarias, en la síntesis de proteínas y en el control de las actividades celulares

nucleotide: one of the monomers that make up DNA and RNA; it consists of a nitrogen-containing base (a purine or pyrimidine), a sugar (ribose or deoxyribose), and a phosphate group *(798)*

nucleótido: uno de los monómeros que constituyen el ADN y el ARN; consiste en una base nitrogenada (una purina o una pirimidina), un azúcar (ribosa o desoxirribosa) y un grupo fosfato

nucleus: the tiny, dense central portion of an atom, composed of protons and neutrons *(106)*

núcleo: la diminuta porción central densa de un átomo; se compone de protones y neutrones

O

observation: information obtained through the senses; observation in science often involves a measurement *(12)*

observación: información obtenida a través de los sentidos; en la ciencia, la observación suele implicar la medición

octet rule: atoms react by gaining or losing electrons so as to acquire the stable electron structure of a noble gas, usually eight valence electrons *(181)*

regla del octeto: los átomos reaccionan ganando o perdiendo electrones a modo de adquirir la estructura electrónica estable de un gas noble, que por lo regular consta de ocho electrones de valencia

organic chemistry: the study of compounds containing carbon *(5)*

química orgánica: estudio de los compuestos que contienen carbono

oxidation: a process that involves complete or partial loss of electrons or a gain of oxygen; it results in an increase in the oxidation number of an atom *(660)*

oxidación: proceso que implica la pérdida total o parcial de electrones o la ganancia de oxígeno; conduce a un aumento en el número de oxidación de un átomo

oxidation number: a positive or negative number assigned to an atom to indicate its degree of oxidation or reduction; the oxidation number of an uncombined element is zero *(668)*

número de oxidación: número positivo o negativo que se asigna a un átomo para indicar su grado de oxidación o reducción; el número de oxidación de un elemento no combinado es cero

oxidation-number-change method: a method of balancing a redox equation by comparing the increases and decreases in oxidation numbers *(678)*

método de cambio del número de oxidación: método para balancear una ecuación redox comparando los incrementos y reducciones de los números de oxidación

oxidation-reduction reaction: a reaction that involves the transfer of electrons between reactants *(660)*

reacción de oxidación–reducción: reacción en la que hay transferencia de electrones entre los reactantes

oxidizing agent: the substance in a redox reaction that accepts electrons; in the reaction, the oxidizing agent is reduced *(661)*

agente oxidante: en una reacción redox, la sustancia que acepta electrones; en la reacción, el agente oxidante se reduce

P

partial pressure: the contribution each gas in a mixture of gases makes to the total pressure *(448)*

presión parcial: contribución de cada gas de una mezcla de gases a la presión total

pascal (Pa): the SI unit of pressure *(397)*

pascal (Pa): unidad de presión en el SI

Pauli exclusion principle: an atomic orbital may describe at most two electrons, each with opposite spin direction *(125)*

principio de exclusión de Pauli: orbital atómico puede describir como máximo a dos electrones, los cuales deben tener espín opuesto

peptide: an organic compound formed by a combination of amino acids in which the amino group of one acid is united with the carboxyl group of another through an amide bond *(790)*

péptido: compuesto orgánico formado por la combinación de aminoácidos de modo que el grupo amino de un ácido se une al grupo carboxilo de otro creando un enlace amida

peptide bond: the bond between the carbonyl group of one amino acid and the nitrogen of the next amino acid in the peptide chain; the structure is *(790)*

$$-\overset{\overset{\displaystyle O}{\|}}{C}-\overset{\overset{\displaystyle H}{|}}{N}-$$

enlace péptido: enlace que hay entre el grupo carbonilo de un aminoácido y el nitrógeno del siguiente aminoácido de la cadena péptida; la estructura es

$$-\overset{\overset{\displaystyle O}{\|}}{C}-\overset{\overset{\displaystyle H}{|}}{N}-$$

percent composition: the percent by mass of each element in a compound *(296)*

composición porcentual: porcentaje en masa de cada elemento de un compuesto

percent error: the percent that a measured value differs from the accepted value *(58)*

error porcentual: porcentaje en que un valor medido difiere del valor aceptado

percent yield: the ratio of the actual yield to the theoretical yield for a chemical reaction expressed as a percentage; a measure of the efficiency of a reaction *(381)*
rendimiento porcentual: razón del rendimiento real al rendimiento teórico de una reacción química, expresado como porcentaje; es una medida de la eficiencia de la reacción

period: a horizontal row of elements in the periodic table *(42)*
periodo: fila horizontal de elementos en la tabla periódica

periodic law: when the elements are arranged in order of increasing atomic number, there is a periodic repetition of their physical and chemical properties *(150)*
ley periódica: si los elementos se acomodan en orden de menor a mayor número atómico, se observa una repetición periódica de sus propiedades físicas y químicas

periodic table: an arrangement of elements in which the elements are separated into groups based on a set of repeating properties *(41)*
tabla periódica: distribución de los elementos divi-diéndolos en grupos según un conjunto de propiedades repetidas

pH: a number used to denote the hydrogen-ion concentration, or acidity, of a solution; it is the negative logarithm of the hydrogen-ion concentration of a solution *(622)*
pH: número empleado para denotar la concentración de ion hidrógeno (acidez) de una solución; es el logaritmo negativo de la concentración de ion hidrógeno en una solución

phase: any part of a sample with uniform composition and properties *(33)*
fase: cualquier parte de una muestra que tiene composición y propiedades uniformes

phase diagram: a graph showing the conditions at which a substance exists as a solid, liquid, or vapor *(413)*
diagrama de fases: gráfica que muestra las condiciones en las que una sustancia existe como sólido, líquido o vapor

phospholipid: a lipid that contains a phosphate group; because phospholipids have hydrophilic heads and hydrophobic tails, they form the lipid bilayers found in cell membranes *(797)*
fosfolípido: lípido que contiene un grupo fosfato; como los fosfolípidos tienen una cabeza hidrofílica y una cola hidrofóbica, pueden formar las bicapas lípidas de las membranas celulares

photoelectric effect: the ejection of electrons by certain metals when they absorb light with a frequency above a threshold frequency *(136)*
efecto fotoeléctrico: liberación de electrones por algunos metales cuando absorben la luz con una frecuencia superior a un umbral (o frecuencia mínima)

photon: a quantum of light; a discrete bundle of electromagnetic energy that interacts with matter similarly to particles *(136)*
fotón: cuanto de luz; paquete discreto de energía electromagnética que interactúa con la materia de forma similar a como lo hacen las partículas

photosynthesis: the process by which green plants and algae use radiant energy from the sun to synthesize glucose from carbon dioxide and water *(784)*
fotosíntesis: proceso por el cual las plantas y algas verdes aprovechan la energía radiante del Sol para sintetizar glucosa a partir de dióxido de carbono y agua

physical change: a change during which some properties of a material change, but the composition of the material does not change *(31)*
cambio físico: cambio durante el cual se alteran algunas propiedades de un material, pero sin que se altere la composición del material

physical chemistry: the area of chemistry that deals with the mechanism, the rate, and the energy transfer that occurs when matter undergoes a change *(5)*
fisicoquímica: área de la química que se relaciona con el mecanismo, la velocidad y la transferencia de energía que ocurre cuando la materia sufre un cambio

physical property: a quality or condition of a substance that can be observed or measured without changing the substance's composition *(29)*
propiedad física: cualidad o condición de una sustancia que se puede observar o medir sin alterar la composición de la sustancia

Planck's constant (*h*): a number used to calculate the radiant energy *(E)* absorbed or emitted by a body based on the frequency of radiation *(134)*
constante de Planck (*h*): número que se usa para calcular la energía radiante (*E*) que un cuerpo absorbe o emite basándose en la frecuencia de radiación

polar bond: a covalent bond between atoms in which the electrons are shared unequally *(224)*
enlace polar: enlace covalente entre átomos que no comparten equitativamente sus electrones

polar molecule: a molecule in which one side of the molecule is slightly negative and the opposite side is slightly positive *(225)*
molécula polar: molécula que tiene un lado ligeramente negativo y el otro ligeramente positivo

polyatomic ion: a tightly bound group of atoms that behaves as a unit and has a positive or negative charge *(214)*
ion poliatómico: grupo fuertemente enlazado de átomos, que se comporta como una unidad y tiene carga positiva o negativa

polymer: a very large molecule formed by the covalent bonding of repeating small molecules, known as monomers *(771)*

polímero: molécula muy grande formada por la unión, mediante enlaces covalentes, de moléculas pequeñas repetidas, llamadas monómeros

polysaccharide: a complex carbohydrate polymer formed by the linkage of many monosaccharide monomers; starch, glycogen, and cellulose are polysaccharides *(788)*

polisacárido: carbohidrato complejo formado por el encadenamiento de muchos monómeros monosacáridos; el almidón, el glucógeno y la celulosa son polisacáridos

positron: a particle with the mass of an electron but a positive charge *(823)*

positrón: partícula con la misma masa que un electrón pero con carga positiva

precipitate: a solid that forms and settles out of a liquid mixture *(45)*

precipitado: sólido que se forma a partir de una mezcla líquida y se asienta

precision: describes the closeness, or reproducibility, of a set of measurements taken under the same conditions *(57)*

precisión: cifra que describe la variabilidad de una serie de mediciones efectuadas en las mismas condiciones

product: a substance produced in a chemical reaction *(44)*

producto: sustancia que se obtiene en una reacción química

protein: any peptide with more than 100 amino acids *(790)*

proteína: cualquier péptido que tiene más de 100 aminoácidos

proton: a positively charged subatomic particle found in the nucleus of an atom *(105)*

protón: partícula subatómica con carga positiva que se encuentra en el núcleo de los átomos

Q

quantum: the amount of energy needed to move an electron from one energy level to another *(119)*

cuanto: cantidad de energía necesaria para desplazar un electrón de un nivel energético a otro

quantum mechanical model: the modern description, primarily mathematical, of the behavior of electrons in atoms *(120)*

modelo según la mecánica cuántica: descripción moderna, primordialmente matemática, del comportamiento de los electrones en los átomos

R

radioactivity: the spontaneous emission of rays and particles from unstable nuclei *(818)*

radiactividad: emisión espontánea de rayos y partículas generada por núcleos atómicos inestables

radioisotope: an isotope that has an unstable nucleus and undergoes radioactive decay *(818)*

radioisótopo: isótopo cuyo núcleo es inestable y sufre desintegración radiactiva

rate: describes the speed of change over an interval of time *(565)*

velocidad (de reacción): cifra que describe la velocidad de cambio a lo largo de un intervalo de tiempo

rate law: an expression relating the rate of a reaction to the concentration of the reactants *(572)*

ley de velocidad de reacción: expresión que relaciona la velocidad de una reacción con la concentración de los reactantes

reactant: a substance present at the start of a reaction *(44)*

reactante: sustancia presente al principio de una reacción

reaction mechanism: a series of elementary reactions that take place during the course of a complex reaction *(573)*

mecanismo de reacción: serie de reacciones básicas que se dan durante el curso de una reacción compleja

reducing agent: the substance in a redox reaction that donates electrons; in the reaction, the reducing agent is oxidized *(661)*

agente reductor: en una reacción redox, la sustancia que cede electrones; en la reacción, el agente reductor se oxida

reduction: a process that involves a complete or partial gain of electrons or the loss of oxygen; it results in a decrease in the oxidation number of an atom *(660)*

reducción: proceso que implica una ganancia total o parcial de electrones o pérdida de oxígeno; provoca una disminución en el número de oxidación de un átomo

reduction potential: a measure of the tendency of a given half-reaction to occur as a reduction (gain of electrons) in an electrochemical cell *(698)*

potencial de reducción: medida de la tendencia que tiene una semirreacción específica de efectuarse como reducción (con ganancia de electrones) en una celda electroquímica

representative element: an element in Groups 1A through 7A in the periodic table; as a group these elements display a wide range of physical and chemical properties. In their atoms, the *s* and *p* sublevels in the highest occupied energy level are partially filled *(159)*

elemento representativo: elemento de los Grupos 1A a 7A de la tabla periódica; en conjunto, estos elementos exhiben una amplia gama de propiedades físicas y químicas. En sus átomos, los subniveles *s* y *p* del nivel energético ocupado más alto están parcialmente llenos

representative particle: the smallest unit into which a substance can be broken down without a change in composition, usually atoms, molecules, or ions *(279)*

partícula representativa: unidad más pequeña en que puede dividirse una sustancia sin que cambie su composición; por lo regular es un átomo, molécula o ion

resonance structure: one of the two or more equally valid electron dot structures of a molecule or polyatomic ion *(218)*

estructura de resonancia: una de las dos o más estructuras electrón-punto igualmente válidas de una molécula o ion poliatómico

responding variable: *see* dependent variable

variable de respuesta: *véase* variable dependiente

reversible reaction: a reaction in which the conversion of reactants into products and the conversion of products into reactants occur simultaneously *(575)*

reacción reversible: reacción en la que se da en forma simultánea la conversión de reactantes en productos y la conversión de productos en reactantes

S

salt bridge: a tube containing a strong electrolyte used to separate the half-cells in a voltaic cell; it allows the passage of ions from one half-cell to the other, but prevents the solutions from mixing completely *(692)*

puente salino: tubo que contiene un electrolito fuerte y se usa para separar las semiceldas de una celda voltaica; permite el paso de iones de una semicelda a la otra, pero impide que las soluciones se mezclen totalmente

salt hydrolysis: a process in which the cations or anions of a dissociated salt accept hydrogen ions from water or donate hydrogen ions to water *(646)*

hidrólisis de sales: proceso por el cual los cationes o aniones de una sal disociada aceptan iones hidrógeno del agua o ceden iones hidrógeno al agua

saturated compound: an organic compound in which all carbon atoms are joined by single covalent bonds; it contains the maximum number of hydrogen atoms per carbon atom *(731)*

compuesto saturado: compuesto orgánico en el que todos los átomos de carbono están unidos unos a otros por enlaces covalentes sencillos; contiene el número máximo de átomos de hidrógeno por átomo de carbono

saturated solution: a solution containing the maximum amount of solute for a given amount of solvent at a constant temperature and pressure; an equilibrium exists between undissolved solute and ions in solution *(490)*

solución saturada: solución que contiene la cantidad máxima de soluto para una cantidad dada de disolvente a temperatura y presión constantes; existe equilibrio entre el soluto no disuelto y los iones en solución

scientific law: a concise statement that summarizes the results of many observations and experiments *(14)*

ley científica: expresión concisa que resume los resultados de muchas observaciones y experimentos

scientific methodology: a general style of investigation with a logical, systematic approach to the solution of a scientific problem; steps usually include making observations, testing hypotheses, and developing theories *(12)*

metodología científica: estilo general de investigación con un enfoque lógico y sistemático para resolver un problema científico; los pasos generalmente incluyen hacer observaciones, probar hipótesis y desarrollar teorías

scientific notation: an expression of numbers in the form $m \times 10^n$, where m is equal to or greater than 1 and less than 10, and n is an integer *(54)*

notación científica: convención por la cual los números se expresan en la forma $m \times 10^n$, donde m es un número mayor o igual que 1 y menor que 10, y n es un entero

self-ionization: a term describing the reaction in which two water molecules react to produce ions *(618)*

autoionización: reacción en la que dos moléculas de agua reaccionan para producir iones

significant figures: all the digits that can be known precisely in a measurement, plus a last estimated digit *(60)*

dígitos significativos: todos los dígitos de una medición que se pueden conocer con precisión, más un último dígito estimado

single covalent bond: a bond formed when two atoms share a pair of electrons *(209)*

enlace covalente sencillo: enlace que se forma cuando dos átomos comparten un par de electrones

single-replacement reaction: a chemical change in which one element replaces a second element in a compound; also called a displacement reaction *(332)*

reacción de sustitución sencilla: cambio químico en el que un elemento reemplaza a un segundo elemento en un compuesto; también llamado reacción de desplazamiento

skeleton equation: a chemical equation that does not indicate the relative amounts of reactants and products *(318)*

ecuación esqueleto: ecuación química que no indica las cantidades relativas de los reactantes y productos

solid: a form of matter that has a definite shape and volume *(30)*

sólido: estado de la materia que tiene forma y volumen definidos

solubility: the amount of a substance that dissolves in a given quantity of solvent at specified conditions of temperature and pressure to produce a saturated solution *(490)*

solubilidad: cantidad de una sustancia que se disuelve en una cantidad dada de disolvente, bajo condiciones específicas de temperatura y presión, para producir una solución saturada

solubility product constant (K_{sp}): an equilibrium constant that is based only on the concentration of dissolved ions in solution *(589)*
constante del producto de solubilidad (K_{sp}): constante de equilibrio que se basa únicamente en la concentración de los iones disueltos en una solución

solute: dissolved particles in a solution *(468)*
soluto: partículas disueltas en una solución

solution: a homogeneous mixture; consists of solutes dissolved in a solvent *(33)*
solución: mezcla homogénea que consiste en solutos disueltos en un disolvente

solvation: a process that occurs when an ionic solute dissolves; in solution, solvent molecules surround the positive and negative ions *(468)*
solvatación: proceso que tiene lugar cuando se disuelve un soluto iónico; en solución, las moléculas de disolvente rodean a los iones positivos y negativos

solvent: the dissolving medium in a solution *(468)*
disolvente: medio dispersor en una solución

specific heat: the amount of heat needed to increase the temperature of 1 g of a substance by 1°C; also called specific heat capacity *(530)*
calor específico: cantidad de calor requerida para elevar 1°C la temperatura de 1 g de una sustancia

specific rate constant: a constant relating the concentrations of reactants to the rate of the reaction *(573)*
constante específica de velocidad de reacción: constante que relaciona las concentraciones de los reactantes con la velocidad de la reacción

spectator ion: an ion that is not directly involved in a chemical reaction; an ion that does not change oxidation number or composition during a reaction *(341)*
ion espectador: ion que no interviene directamente en una reacción química; ion que no cambia de número de oxidación ni de composición durante una reacción

spectrum: wavelengths of visible light that are separated when a beam of light passes through a prism; range of wavelengths of electromagnetic radiation *(131)*
espectro: longitudes de onda de la luz visible que se separan cuando un haz de luz atraviesa un prisma; gama de longitudes de onda de radiación electromagnética

spin: a quantum mechanical property of electrons that may be thought of as clockwise or counterclockwise *(125)*
espín: propiedad de los electrones según la mecánica cuántica en la cual la rotación se considera en sentido de las agujas del reloj o en sentido contrario a las agujas del reloj

spontaneous reaction: a reaction that favors the formation of products at the specified conditions; spontaneity depends on enthalpy and entropy changes *(596)*
reacción espontánea: reacción que favorece la formación de productos, bajo las condiciones especificadas; la espontaneidad depende de los cambios de entalpía y de entropía

standard cell potential (E°_{cell}): the measured cell potential when the ion concentration in the half-cells are 1.00*M* at 1 atm of pressure and 25°C *(699)*
potencial estándar de celda (E°_{cell}): potencial de celda que se mide cuando las concentraciones de los iones en las semiceldas son 1.00*M* a 1 atm de presión y 25°C

standard heat of formation (ΔH_f°): the change in enthalpy that accompanies the formation of one mole of a compound from its elements with all substances in their standard states at 25°C *(552)*
calor estándar de formación (ΔH_f°): cambio de entalpía que acompaña a la formación de un mol de un compuesto a partir de sus elementos, estando todas las sustancias en su estado estándar a 25°C

standard hydrogen electrode: an arbitrary reference electrode (half-cell) used with another electrode (half-cell) to measure the standard reduction potential of that cell; the standard reduction potential of the hydrogen electrode is assigned a value of 0.00 V *(699)*
electrodo estándar de hidrógeno: electrodo (semicelda) arbitrario de referencia que se usa junto con otro electrodo (semicelda) para medir el potencial estándar de reducción de esa celda; se asigna al potencial estándar de reducción del electrodo de hidrógeno el valor de 0.00 V

standard solution: a solution of known concentration used in carrying out a titration *(642)*
solución estándar: solución cuya concentración se conoce; se usa para efectuar valoraciones químicas

standard temperature and pressure (STP): the conditions under which the volume of a gas is usually measured; standard temperature is 0°C, and standard pressure is 101.3 kPa, or 1 atmosphere (atm) *(292)*
temperatura y presión estándar (TPE): las condiciones en las que normalmente se mide el volumen de un gas; la temperatura estándar es 0°C y la presión estándar es 101.3 kPa, o sea, 1 atmósfera (atm)

stereoisomers: molecules that have atoms in the same order, but which differ in the arrangement of the atoms in space *(735)*
estereoisómeros: moléculas cuyos átomos están en el mismo orden, pero que difieren en la distribución de los átomos en el espacio

stoichiometry: that portion of chemistry dealing with numerical relationships in chemical reactions; the calculation of quantities of substances involved in chemical equations *(354)*

estequiometría: rama de la química que se ocupa de las relaciones numéricas en las ecuaciones químicas; el cálculo de las cantidades de sustancias presentes en las ecuaciones químicas

straight-chain alkane: a hydrocarbon that contains any number of carbon atoms arranged one after the other in a chain *(722)*

alcano de cadena lineal: hidrocarburo que contiene cualquier número de átomos de carbono distribuidos uno tras otro en una cadena

strong acid: an acid that is completely (or almost completely) ionized in aqueous solution *(631)*

ácido fuerte: ácido que se ioniza casi totalmente en solución acuosa

strong base: a base that completely dissociates into metal ions and hydroxide ions in aqueous solution *(636)*

base fuerte: base que se disocia totalmente en una solución acuosa para dar iones metálicos y iones hidróxido

strong electrolyte: a solution in which a large portion of the solute exists as ions *(470)*

electrolito fuerte: solución en la que una porción considerable del soluto existe en forma de iones

structural formula: a chemical formula that shows the arrangement of atoms in a molecule or a polyatomic ion; each dash between a pair of atoms indicates a pair of shared electrons *(209)*

fórmula estructural: fórmula química que indica la distribución de los átomos en una molécula o ion poliatómico; cada raya entre un par de átomos indica un par de electrones compartidos

sublimation: the process in which a solid changes to a gas or vapor without passing through the liquid state *(411)*

sublimación: proceso por el cual un sólido cambia a gas o vapor sin pasar por el estado líquido

substance: matter that has a uniform and definite composition; either an element or a compound; also called pure substance *(29)*

sustancia: materia que tiene una composición uniforme y definida; puede ser un elemento o un compuesto; también llamada sustancia pura

substituent: an atom or group of atoms that can take the place of a hydrogen atom on a parent hydrocarbon molecule *(726)*

sustituto: átomo o grupo de átomos que puede ocupar el lugar de un átomo de hidrógeno en una molécula precursora de hidrocarburo

substitution reaction: a common type of organic reaction; involves the replacement of an atom or group of atoms by another atom or group of atoms *(757)*

reacción de sustitución: tipo común de reacción orgánica; implica el reemplazo de un átomo o grupo de átomos por otro átomo o grupo de átomos

substrate: a molecule on which an enzyme acts *(793)*

sustrato: molécula sobre la que actúa una enzima

supersaturated solution: a solution that contains more solute than it can theoretically hold at a given temperature; excess solute precipitates if a seed crystal is added *(490)*

solución sobresaturada: solución que contiene más soluto del que en teoría puede contener a una temperatura específica; el soluto en exceso se precipita si se añade un cristal que actúa como semilla

surface tension: an inward force that tends to minimize the surface area of a liquid; it causes the surface to behave as if it were a thin skin *(464)*

tensión superficial: fuerza que tiende a reducir al mínimo la superficie total de un líquido y actúa hacia el seno de éste; hace que la superficie se comporte como si fuera una membrana elástica

surfactant: any substance that interferes with the hydrogen bonding between water molecules and thereby reduces surface tension; soaps are surfactants *(464)*

tensoactivo: cualquier sustancia que perturba la formación de enlaces de hidrógeno entre las moléculas de agua y así reduce la tensión superficial; los jabones y detergentes son tensoactivos

surroundings: everything in the universe outside of the system *(526)*

entorno: todo lo que no forma parte del sistema, es decir, el resto del universo

suspension: a mixture from which some of the particles settle out slowly upon standing *(477)*

suspensión: mezcla de la que se separan lentamente algunas partículas por asentamiento cuando no se agita

synthesis reaction: *see* combination reaction

reacción de síntesis: *véase* reacción de combinación

system: a part of the universe on which you focus your attention *(526)*

sistema: parte del universo en la que centramos nuestra atención

T

technology: the means by which a society provides its members with those things needed and desired *(9)*

tecnología: los medios por los cuales una sociedad proporciona a sus miembros las cosas que necesitan y desean

temperature: a measure of the average kinetic energy of particles in matter; temperature determines the direction of heat transfer *(72)*

temperatura: medida de la energía cinética promedio de las partículas de la materia; la temperatura determina la dirección de la transferencia de calor

tetrahedral angle: a bond angle of 109.5° that results when a central atom forms four bonds directed toward the center of a regular tetrahedron *(222)*

ángulo tetraédrico: ángulo de enlace de 109.5° que se forma cuando un átomo central forma cuatro enlaces dirigidos hacia el centro de un tetraedro regular

theoretical yield: the amount of product that could form during a reaction calculated from a balanced chemical equation; it represents the maximum amount of product that could be formed from a given amount of reactant *(381)*

rendimiento teórico: cantidad de producto que podría formarse durante una reacción, calculada a partir de una ecuación química balanceada; representa la cantidad máxima de producto que podría formarse a partir de una cantidad determinada de reactantes

theory: a well-tested explanation for a broad set of observations *(14)*

teoría: explicación, probada exhaustivamente, de un conjunto amplio de observaciones

thermochemical equation: a chemical equation that includes the enthalpy change *(537)*

ecuación termoquímica: ecuación química que incluye el cambio de calor

thermochemistry: the study of energy changes that occur during chemical reactions and changes in state *(526)*

termoquímica: estudio de los cambios de calor que acompañan a las reacciones químicas y a los cambios de estado físico

titration: process used to determine the concentration of a solution (often an acid or base) in which a solution of known concentration (the standard) is added to a measured amount of the solution of unknown concentration until an indicator signals the end point *(641)*

valoración química: proceso empleado para determinar la concentración de una solución (a menudo un ácido o base) por el cual una solución de concentración conocida (solución estándar) se añade a una cantidad medida de una solución cuya concentración se desconoce, hasta que un indicador marca el punto final

transition metal: one of the Group B elements in which the highest occupied *s* sublevel and a nearby *d* sublevel generally contain electrons *(160)*

metal de transición: uno de los elementos del grupo B en el que el subnivel *s* ocupado más alto y un subnivel *d* cercano generalmente contienen electrones

transmutation: the conversion of an atom of one element to an atom of another element *(828)*

transmutación: conversión de un átomo de un elemento en un átomo de otro elemento

transuranium element: any element in the periodic table with atomic number above 92, the atomic number of uranium *(828)*

elemento transuránico: cualquier elemento de la tabla periódica cuyo número atómico es mayor que 92, el número atómico del uranio

triglyceride: an ester in which all three hydroxyl groups on a glycerol molecule have been replaced by long-chain fatty acids; fats are triglycerides *(795)*

triglicérido: éster en el que los tres grupos hidroxilo de una molécula de glicerol han sido sustituidos por ácidos grasos de cadena larga; las grasas son triglicéridos

triple covalent bond: a covalent bond in which three pairs of electrons are shared by two atoms *(212)*

enlace covalente triple: enlace covalente en el que dos átomos comparten tres pares de electrones

triple point: the point on a phase diagram that represents the only set of conditions at which all three phases exist in equilibrium with one another *(413)*

punto triple: punto de un diagrama de fases que representa el único conjunto de condiciones en el que las tres fases existen en equilibrio

Tyndall effect: scattering of light by particles in a colloid or suspension, which causes a beam of light to become visible *(479)*

efecto Tyndall: dispersión de la luz por las partículas de un coloide o una suspensión, que hace que un haz de luz se vuelva visible

U

unit cell: the smallest group of particles within a crystal that retains the geometric shape of the crystal *(408)*

celda unitaria: grupo más pequeño de partículas dentro de un cristal que conserva la forma geométrica del cristal

unsaturated solution: a solution that contains less solute than a saturated solution at a given temperature and pressure *(490)*

solución insaturada: se dice de una solución que contiene menos soluto que una solución saturada a una temperatura y presión específicas

unsaturated compound: an organic compound with one or more double or triple carbon–carbon bonds *(731)*

compuesto insaturado: compuesto orgánico que tiene uno o más dobles o triples enlaces carbono–carbono

unshared pair: a pair of valence electrons that is not shared between atoms *(209)*

par no compartido: par de electrones de valencia que no es compartido por dos átomos

V

vacuum: a space where no particles of matter exist *(397)*

vacío: espacio en el que no existen partículas de materia

valence electron: an electron in the highest occupied energy level of an atom *(180)*

electrón de valencia: electrón que está en el nivel energético ocupado más alto de un átomo

van der Waals forces: the two weakest intermolecular attractions—dispersion interactions and dipole forces *(228)*

fuerzas de van der Waals: las dos atracciones intermoleculares más débiles—interacciones de dispersión y fuerzas dipolares

vapor: describes the gaseous state of a substance that is generally a liquid or solid at room temperature *(30)*

vapor: estado gaseoso de una sustancia que suele ser líquida o sólida a temperatura ambiente

vaporization: the conversion of a liquid to a gas or a vapor *(402)*

vaporización: conversión de un líquido en gas o vapor

vapor pressure: a measure of the force exerted by a gas above a liquid in a sealed container; a dynamic equilibrium exists between the vapor and the liquid *(403)*

presión de vapor: medida de la fuerza que ejerce un gas sobre un líquido en un contenedor sellado; equilibrio dinámico que existe entre el vapor y el líquido

voltaic cell: an electrochemical cell used to convert chemical energy into electrical energy; the energy is produced by a spontaneous redox reaction *(692)*

celda voltaica: celda electroquímica empleada para convertir energía química en energía eléctrica; la energía se produce por una reacción redox espontánea

volume: a measure of the space occupied by a sample of matter *(28)*

volumen: medida del espacio ocupado por una muestra de materia

VSEPR theory: valence-shell electron-pair repulsion theory; because electron pairs repel, molecules adjust their shapes so that valence electron pairs are as far apart as possible *(221)*

teoría RPENV: teoría de repulsión de pares de electrones del nivel de valencia; como los pares de electrones se repelen, las moléculas ajustan su forma de modo que los pares de electrones de valencia estén lo más alejados posible entre sí

W

water of hydration: water molecules that are an integral part of a crystal structure *(472)*

agua de hidratación: moléculas de agua que forman parte integral de una estructura cristalina

wavelength (λ): the distance between adjacent crests of a wave *(129)*

longitud de onda (λ): distancia entre crestas adyacentes de una onda

wax: an ester of a long-chain fatty acid and a long-chain alcohol *(797)*

cera: éster de un ácido graso de cadena larga y un alcohol de cadena larga

weak acid: an acid that is only slightly ionized in aqueous solution *(631)*

ácido débil: ácido que se ioniza poco en solución acuosa

weak base: a base that reacts with water to form the hydroxide ion and the conjugate acid of the base *(636)*

base débil: base que reacciona con agua para formar el ion hidróxido y el ácido combinado de la base

weak electrolyte: a solution that conducts electricity poorly because only a fraction of the solute exists as ions *(470)*

electrolito débil: solución que apenas conduce la electricidad porque sólo una fracción del soluto existe en forma de iones

weight: a force that measures the pull of gravity on a given mass *(71)*

peso: fuerza que mide la atracción de la gravedad sobre una masa específica

Index

The page on which a term is defined is indicated in **boldface** type.

A

D

E

I

J

K

L

M

T

U

V

W

Z

Credits

Staff Credits
Neil Benjamin, Diane Braff, Ken Chang, Lori-Anne Cohen, Jody Dogra, Kimberly Fekany Lee, Kathryn Fobert, Meredith Glassman, Ellen Granter, Kathy Immel, Courtenay Kelley, Beth Kun, Kathy Martin, Rich McMahon, Laura Morgenthau, Debbie Munson, Ken Myett, Deborah Nicholls, Kim Ortell, Maria Reyes, Michelle Reyes, Laurel Smith, Lisa Smith-Ruvalcaba, Ted Smykal, Emily Soltanoff, Heidi Wilson, Heather Wright

Additional Credits
James Ackroyd, Joan Archer-Scott, Jessica Beauchemin, Mark Breerwood, Vanessa Castleberry, Abhishek Dogra, Ellen Glisan, Jim Glynn, Ilene Goldman, Christine Griffith, Mark Hughes, Jemima Ingle, Beth Kelly, Margy Kuntz, Michael Mazza, Steve Miller, Sharon Munisamy, Heather Myler, Kathleen Naughton, Cathy Podeszwa, Laura Prescott, Kelly Rizk, Karen Rowan, Hugh Rutledge, Cecelia Schneider, Kay Sorg, Cheryl Steinecker, Jennifer Weinstein

Illustrations
Courtenay Kelley, Rich McMahon, Precision Graphics, Laurel Smith, Ted Smykal

Photographs
Every effort has been made to secure permission and provide appropriate credit for photographic material. The publisher deeply regrets any omission and pledges to correct errors called to its attention in subsequent editions.

Unless otherwise acknowledged, all photographs are the property of Pearson Education, Inc.

Photo locators denoted as follows: Top (T), Center (C), Bottom (B), Left (L), Right (R), Background (Bkgd)

Cover: (TL) James Steidl/Shutterstock, (TC) Elnur/Shutterstock, (TR) Gina Callaway/Shutterstock, (BR) Subbotina Anna/Shutterstock, (CL) Tom Nance/Shutterstock, (CC) Lana Langlois/Shutterstock, (CR) Andrey Armyagov/Shutterstock, (BL) Gunnar Pippel/Shutterstock, (BC) Peter Kirillov/Shutterstock.

Spine: hundreddays/iStockphoto.

Back Cover: (L) JGI/Jamie Grill/Blend Images/Getty Images, (R) Melanie DeFazio/Shutterstock.

Text:
x (T) Claudio Bertoloni/Shutterstock, Fundamental Photographs, (B) Murat Boylu/Shutterstock; **xi** (BL) Harry Taylor/Courtesy of the Natural History Museum, London/©DK Images, (BR) Steve Mason/Getty Images, (T) Traveler1116/iStockphoto; **xii** (T) Don Johnston/Stone/Getty Images, (B) ©DK Images; **xiii** Unarmed/Shutterstock; **xiv** Fundamental Photographs; **xv** linhof/Shutterstock;

2 (C) Alexander Raths/Shutterstock; **4** (T) Eric Isselée/Shutterstock, (B) Mitchell Funk/Getty Images; **5** (Inset) Andraz Cerar/Shutterstock; **6** (B) Mitchell Funk/Getty Images; **7** Steve Mason/Getty Images; **8** (TL) M. Kornmesser (ESA/Hubble)/NASA Image Exchange, (BL) Traveler1116/iStockphoto; **9** (Inset, T) Cathleen Clapper/Shutterstock, (Bkgrd) Paul Clarke/Shutterstock, (B) Sheila Terry/Photo Researchers, Inc.; **10** (T) NASA Image Exchange; **11** (TL) Photo Researchers, Inc., (B) Valentin Agapov/Shutterstock; **12** (B) Alexander Raths/Shutterstock, (T) The Metropolitan Museum of Art/Art Resource, NY/Art Resource, NY; **13** D.Richardson/NewsCom; **15** (TL) Bruce Ely/©AP Images; **16** Image Source/Christopher Robbins/Zuma Press, Inc.; **17** (TL) Ashley Whitworth/Shutterstock, (BR) Jupiter Images/Jupiter Images; **21** (Inset, B) blackpixel/Shutterstock, (Bkgrd) cla78/Shutterstock, (Inset, T) Karin Lau/Shutterstock; **22** Alexander Raths/Shutterstock; **26** Foodcollection/Getty Images; **27** (R) thumb/Shutterstock; **28** (BL) bunhill/iStockphoto, (BR) Leifr/Shutterstock, (T) tororo reaction/Shutterstock; **31** (L, C,) Geoffrey Nilsen Photography; **32** (T) Getty/Jupiter Images; **33** (R, L, C) Ken O'Donoghue; **36** (T) Dana Bartekoske/Shutterstock, (BR) David Lawrence, (BL) David lawrence, (B) Geoffrey Nilsen Photography; **37** (L) Alamy, (C) Getty Images; **38** (L) ©Andraz Cerar/Shutterstock, (CR) 300dpi/Shutterstock, (BR) DK Images; **40** Theodore Clutter/Photo Researchers, Inc.; **42** (TL) Dana Bartekoske/Shutterstock, (BR) David Lawrence; **43** (BL) Alamy, (T) devi/Shutterstock, (BR) elena moiseeva/Shutterstock; **44** (BL) ©Andraz Cerar/Shutterstock, (BR) DK Images, (B) Olga Utlyakova/Shutterstock, (T) Richard Megna/Fundamental Photographs, NYC; **45** (L) Andrew Lambert Photography/Photo Researchers, Inc., (R) Gusto Productions/Photo Researchers, Inc., (C) Stefano Scata/Foodcollection/Getty Images; **46** (R, L) Richard Megna/Fundamental Photographs; **47** tororo reaction/Shutterstock; **48** (TL) devi/Shutterstock; **49** (R, L) Fundamental Photographs, Wendy Kaveney Photography/Shutterstock; **50** thumb/Shutterstock; **52** (CC) Gordon Wiltsie/Getty Images; **53** (Inset) David Toase/Getty Images; **54** Technotr/iStockphoto; **55** Steve Gschmeissner/Photo Researchers, Inc.; **58** photodisc/AGE Fotostock; **60** (T) Gjermund Alsos/Shutterstock, (B) Hemera Technologies/Thinkstock; **74** (T) Lijuan Guo/Shutterstock; **75** Jupiter Images/Jupiter Images; **77** (Inset) JPerez/Shutterstock, (Bkgrd) White/Photolibrary Group, Inc.; **78** cheyennezj/Shutterstock; **87** (R) NASA; **88** (L) David Toase/Getty Images; **90** IBM Research/Almaden Center/IBM Almaden Research Center; **91** (Inset) ©The Trustees of The British Museum; **93** Harry Taylor/Courtesy of the Natural History Museum, London/©DK Images; **94** Image originally created by IBM Corporation; **95** Claudio Bertoloni/Shutterstock; **96** Richard Megna/Fundamental Photographs; **100** motorolka/Shutterstock, PK-Photos/iStockphoto; **108** Murat Boylu/Shutterstock; **111** rubberball/Getty Images; **114** (T) ©The Trustees of The British Museum, (BR) Alex Staroseltsev/Shutterstock, (BC) Ken O'Donoghue, (BL) Natural History Museum, London/Alamy Images; **116** Alexey Stiop/Shutterstock; **118** (B) Adrian Sherratt/Alamy Images, (T) Philippe Plailly/Photo Researchers, Inc.; **120** Chris Curtis/Shutterstock; **121** (T) Mary Evans/Photo Researchers, Inc.; (B) Prisma VWPics/SuperStock; **124** AYAKOVLEVdotCOM/Shutterstock; **126** Leifr/Shutterstock; **129** Karin Lau/Shutterstock; **131** Photos to Go/Photolibrary; **132** (L) H. Mark Weidman Photography/Alamy Images, (R) scoutingstock/Shutterstock; **134** Richard Megna/Fundamental Photographs; **138** Susumu Nishinaga/Photo Researchers, Inc.; **140** H. Mark Weidman Photography/Alamy Images; **143** scoutingstock/Shutterstock; **144** (R) Colin Keates/©DK Images; **146** artpartner-images/Alamy Images; **148** (B) ©sciencephotos/Alamy Images, (T) Tatiana Popova/Shutterstock; **149** (L) ©The Granger Collection, NY, (R) IgorGolovniov/Shutterstock; **152** (TR) ©DK Images, (BR) Ken Davies/Masterfile Corporation, (CR) slavchovr/Shutterstock, (L) Thomas Barrat/Shutterstock; **153** (R) Ilan Rosen/Alamy Images, (L) Volker Steger/Siemens/Photo Researchers, Inc.; **158** (R) Michael Ledray/Shutterstock, (L) Vibrant Image Studio/Shutterstock; **159** (B) Igumnova Irina/Shutterstock, (T) Vaughan Ryall/Alamy; **172** (R) Philip Dowell/©DK Images, (L) Photo Researchers, Inc., (T) Sebastian Kaulilzki/Shutterstock; **173** Vaughan Ryall/Alamy; **178** ©Carsten Peter/Speleoresearch & Films/National Geographic Image Collection; **179** (Inset) Hakimata Photography/Shutterstock; **180** (BR) Phillip Hayson/Photo Researchers, Inc., (BL) Yurchyks/Shutterstock; **182** A.T. Willett/Alamy Images; **185** Carlos Caetano/Shutterstock; **186** T.W. van Urk/Shutterstock; **187** Charles Falco/Photo Researchers, Inc.; **190** (BR) DK Images; **192** Ken O'Donoghue/Prentice Hall; **193** Christina Richards/Shutterstock; **195** (R) Aaron Amat/Shutterstock, (L) Tyler Olson/Shutterstock; **197** (L) Yurchyks/Shutterstock; **200** Hakimata Photography/Shutterstock; **202** Vera Volkova/Shutterstock; **203** (Inset) Danny E Hooks/Shutterstock; **204** (T) Ivonne Wierink/Shutterstock, (BL) Jupiter Images/Jupiter Images, (BR) Michael Newman/PhotoEdit,

Inc.; **206** (R) Christopher Elwell/Shutterstock, (L) Jupiterimages/Thinkstock; **208** NASA Image Exchange; **210** Jupiterimages/Jupiter Images; **212** Jupiterimages/Jupiter Images; **214** Arco Images GmbH/Alamy Images; **216** Jhaz Photography/Shutterstock; **218** Deborah Davis/Getty Images; **220** U.S. Geological Survey; **224** (B) ©Nivek Neslo/Getty Images, (T) Yaroslav/Shutterstock; **227** (B) magicinfoto/Shutterstock, (T) Mark Sykes/Alamy Images; **231** ©Nivek Neslo/Getty Images; **234** Danny E Hooks/Shutterstock; **236** Mitshu/Shutterstock; **237** (Inset) Thinstock Images/Thinkstock; **238** Santje/Shutterstock; **240** Richard Megna/Fundamental Photographs; **244** (T) Elena Schweitzer/Shutterstock, (B) Gary Ombler/©DK Images; **245** Geoffrey Kuchera/Shutterstock; **248** (R) Photos to Go/Photolibrary; **250** Erhan Dayi/Shutterstock; **252** (T) Beth Van Trees/Fotolia, (T) Mark Herreid/Fotolia; **255** (Inset, B) blickwinkel/Alamy Images, (Bkgrd) NewsCom, (Inset, T) Suzanne Long/The Image Works, Inc.; **256** Brand X/Getty Images; **257** Olegusk/Shutterstock; **260** Denis Tabler/Shutterstock; **261** Workbook Stock/Getty Images; **264** Westend61/SuperStock; **265** Fundamental Photographs; **266** Steve Bower/Shutterstock; **269** Christian Kover/PhotoLibrary Group, Inc.; **274** Thinkstock/Getty Images; **276** Robert Stone/Dreamstime LLC; **277** (Inset) Nicholas Monu/iStockphoto; **278** Eldad Yitzhak/Shutterstock; **287** Kinetic Imagery/Shutterstock; **296** GIPhotoStock/Photo Researchers, Inc.; **303** (L) Lisa F. Young/Shutterstock, (R) Sebastian Crocker/Shutterstock; **307** The Star-Ledger/Polaris Images; **308** Getty Images; **312** Nicholas Monu/iStockphoto; **314** Michael Gunther/PhotoLibrary Group, Inc.; **315** (Inset) Image Source/Getty Images; **316** (T) Alamy Images, (B) Stefano Tiraboschi/Shutterstock; **317** (L) LAimages/Shutterstock, (R) Custom Medical Stock Photo/Newscom; **325** Ken O'Donoghue; **326** Jupiter Images; **327** (R) Fundamental Photographs; **330** (R, L, C) Ken Karp/Addison Wesley; **332** (R, L, C) David Lawrence/Addison Wesley; **334** (R, L) Richard Megna/Fundamental Photographs; **336** Richard Megna/Fundamental Photographs; **338** (BR, BL, BC) David Lawrence/Addison Wesley, (TR) Fundamental Photographs, (CR, CL, CC) Ken Karp/Addison Wesley; **339** (TR, TL, B) Richard Megna/Fundamental Photographs; **340** (T) M. Wisshak/AGE Fotostock, (B) Richard Megna/Fundamental Photographs; **343** David Lawrence/Addison Wesley; **346** Stefano Tiraboschi/Shutterstock; **349** (TR) David Lawrence/Addison Wesley, (TL, BR, BL) Richard Megna/Fundamental Photographs; **350** Image Source/Getty Images; **352** Shutterstock; **353** (Inset) Alistair Scott/Shutterstock; **354** Maxim Petrichuk/Shutterstock; **355** B.S.Karan/Shutterstock; **356** Erich Karkoschka/NASA; **360** Andy Sotiriou/Getty Images; **366** ©Charles D. Winters/Photo Researchers, Inc.; **374** (T) Aleksi Markku/Shutterstock; **381** PeteMuller/iStockphoto; **385** (Inset, B) Alan C. Heison/Shutterstock, (Bkgrd) Joel Shawn/Shutterstock, (Inset, T) Maksud/Shutterstock; **388** PeteMuller/iStockphoto; **392** Alistair Scott/Shutterstock; **394** TechWizard/Shutterstock; **395** SilviaJansen/iStockphoto; **397** Richard Megna/Fundamental Photographs; **401** (L, BR) Richard Megna/Fundamental Photographs, (T) Volodymyr Krasyuk/Shutterstock; **402** Wendy Hope/Thinkstock; **403** (T) Ivan Demyanov/Shutterstock, (B) James King-Holmes/Photo Researchers, Inc.; **408** (TL) ©Colin Keates/Courtesy of the Natural History Museum, London/DK Images, (BL) ©dmitriyd/Shutterstock, (TR) Colin Keates/©DK Images, (TC) Harry Taylor/©DK Images, (BR) Jiri Slama/Shutterstock, (BC) Joel Arem/Photo Researchers, Inc., **410** Getty Images/Thinkstock; **411** bierchen/Shutterstock; **413** (T) Photodisc/Thinkstock, (L) Photos to Go/Photolibrary, (R) Steven Coling/Shutterstock; **418** SilviaJansen/iStockphoto; **420** John Ninomiya; **421** (Inset) ©Wolfgang Amri/iStockphoto; **422** Bob Daemmrich/PhotoEdit, Inc.; **423** Robert Llewellyn/PhotoLibrary Group, Inc.; **424** Magna Carta/Shutterstock; **427** ©Carlos Caetano/Shutterstock; **437** George Shelton/NASA; **440** (Inset, T) NOAA Earth System Research Laboratory, Chemical Sciences Division, (Inset, B) steinphoto/iStockphoto, (Bkgrd) Thomas Prior/Getty Images; **441** ©Kelly Redinger/AGE Fotostock; **446** (B) Ken O'Donoghue/Prentice Hall, (T) Simon Fraser/Newcastle General Hospital/Photo Researchers, Inc.; **448** maxstockphoto/Shutterstock; **452** (R, L) ©DK Images; **453** (C) ©DK Images, ©Larry Lee/Larry Lee Photography/Corbis; **454** ©Wolfgang Amri/iStockphoto, Simon Fraser/Newcastle General Hospital/Photo Researchers, Inc.; **457** (T) Charles D. Winters/Photo Researchers, Inc., (B) maxstockphoto/Shutterstock; **460** (Inset) Pascal Rondeau/Getty Images, Serg64/Shutterstock; **462** (B) ©DK Images, (T) NASA Image Exchange; **464** Denis Vrublevski/Shutterstock; **466** Ted Kinsman/Photo Researchers, Inc.; **467** Oxford Scientific/PhotoLibrary Group, Inc.; **472** (R) Richard Megna/Fundamental Photographs, (L) Richard Megna/Fundamental Photographs; **477** (T) MikeE/Shutterstock; **478** justin maresch/Shutterstock; **481** Ted Kinsman/Photo Researchers, Inc.; **484** Pascal Rondeau/Getty Images; **486** Robert Glusic/Corbis/Photolibrary Group, Inc.; **487** (Inset) ©Getty Images; **488** (BR, BL, BC) Ken Karp/Addison-Wesley, Photo Researchers, Inc.; **489** Charles D. Winters/Photo Researchers, Inc.; **491** (R, L) Charles D. Winters/Photo Researchers, Inc.; **495** J. Herlgason/Shutterstock; **496** (L) Ken Karp/Addison Wesley, (R, C) Ken Karp/Addison-Wesley; **500** (R, L) Ken Karp/Addison-Wesley; **505** Suzanne Kischnick/Alamy Images; **506** (R, C, BL) Ken Karp/Addison-Wesley; **507** Thomas Cooper/Getty Images; **508** jane/iStockphoto; **509** MIXA/Getty Images; **522** ©Getty Images; **524** Alamy Images, (Inset) Tony Ranze/Getty Images; **525** (BC) Ken Karp/Addison-Wesley; **526** Corbis/SuperStock; **527** (R) AGE Fotostock, (L) BananaStock/AGE Fotostock; **529** Unarmed/Shutterstock; **533** Roman Sigaev/Shutterstock; **537** tinabelle/iStockphoto; **538** Alamy; **541** Blend Images/Patrik Giardino/Getty Images; **544** JanPietruszka/iStockphoto; **550** James Steidl/Shutterstock; **552** (L) ©sciencephotos/Alamy Images, (R) Harry Taylor/©DK Images; **560** (R) pakowacz/Shutterstock, (L) Tony Ranze/Getty Images; **562** Lex Van Lieshout/AGE Fotostock; **563** (BC) Stepen Morton/©AP Images; **564** (B) Juice Images169/Alamy, (T) zumawirewestphotos/NewsCom; **568** (R) Ken Kalp\Addison Wesley, (L) Ken Karp/Addison Wesley; **570** Ken O'Donoghue; **572** CHRISTOPHE ENA/©AP Images; **575** David Frazier/Corbis; **579** Steve Baccon/Getty Images; **582** Geoffrey Nilson/Addison/Wesley; **587** (Bkgrd) Epic Stock/Shutterstock, (Inset) Science Source/Photo Researchers, Inc.; **588** CNRI/Photo Researchers, Inc.; **592** (R, L) Ken Karp/Addison Wesley; **595** Pyastolova Nadya/Shutterstock; **596** Pyastolova Nadya/Shutterstock; **597** Photos to Go/Photolibrary; **606** Stepen Morton/©AP Images; **608** Susan Van Etten/PhotoEdit, Inc.; **609** (Inset) Chet Gordon/The Image Works, Inc.; **610** (BR) Iconica/Getty Images, (BL) Igor Dutina/Shutterstock, (T) Rolf Nussbaumer/Nature Picture Library; **612** Fundamental Photographs; **615** Boris Franz/Shutterstock; **618** Sarah Holmlund/Shutterstock; **629** (TL) Kojiro/Shutterstock, (B) Michael Howes/AGE Fotostock, (TR) UVimages/Photolibrary Group, Inc.; **631** FOODCOLLECTION/AGE Fotostock; **633** Dhoxax/Shutterstock; **638** (Inset) Serg64/Shutterstock, (Bkgrd) Sylvain Sonnet/Getty Images; **639** Geoff Kidd/AGE Fotostock; **641** (R, L, C) Richard Megna/Fundamental Photographs; **645** (C, BR, BL) Ken Karp/Addison-Wesley, (T) London Scientific Films/PhotoLibrary Group, Inc.; **648** (R, L) Ken Karp/Addison-Wesley; **653** Richard Megna/Fundamental Photographs; **654** Chet Gordon/The Image Works, Inc.; **656** Henryk T. Kaiser/AGE Fotostock; **657** (Inset) ©DK Images; **658** (T) Julija Sapic/Shutterstock, (B) Richard Megna/Fundamental Photographs; **659** (L) Bluefly/Alamy, (R) Gregory Davies/Alamy; **660** (R, C) Ken Karp/Addison-Wesley, (L) Paul Silverman/Fundamental Photographs; **663** Blair Seitz/Shutterstock; **665** (L) Jose Gil/Shutterstock, (R) Shenval/

Alamy; **667** (Inset) Alexey Stiop/Shutterstock, (Bkgrd) MaxFX/Shutterstock; **668** LWA/AGE Fotostock; **672** (R, L) Ken Karp/Addison-Wesley; **675** (T) Kokhanchikov/Shutterstock, (BL) Richard Megna/Fundamental Photographs, (BR) Richard Megnal/Fundamental Photographs; **676** (T) 2009fotofriends/Shutterstock; **682** Blair Seitz/Shutterstock; **685** Kai Schwabe/AGE Fotostock; **686** ©DK Images; **688** Andreas Gradin/Shutterstock; **689** (Inset) linhof/Shutterstock; **690** (T) oktobernight/iStockphoto, (BR, BL) Richard Megna/Fundamental Photographs; **695** futureimage/iStockphoto; **696** Jim West/AGE Fotostock; **697** (L) ©ifong/Shutterstock, Mary Evans Picture Library/The Image Works, Inc.; **698** ©ifong/Shutterstock; **706** (B) Drozdowski/Shutterstock, (T) Peter Gudella/Shutterstock; **708** Charles D. Winters/Photo Researchers, Inc.; **711** John Gress/Reuters Media; **713** ©ifong/Shutterstock; **716** linhof/Shutterstock; **718** Christopher Herwig/Getty Images; **719** (Inset) Alex Staroseltsev/Shutterstock; **720** Imago/Zuma Press, Inc.; **722** (L) Photos to Go/Photolibrary, (R) Thinkstock; **731** Juanmonino/iStockphoto; **739** Tomtsya/Shutterstock; **741** Bedolaga/Shutterstock; **742** Stephen Bay/Alamy; **744** (L, CL) Andrew J. Martinez/Photo Researchers, Inc., (R) Martin Shields/Photo Researchers, Inc., (CL) Ted Kinsman/Photo Researchers, Inc.; **745** Oded Balilty/©AP Images; **750** Alex Staroseltsev/Shutterstock; **752** foodfolio/Alamy Images; **753** (Inset) Aleksandr Stennikov/Shutterstock; **754** (Bkgrd, B) Luxe/Shutterstock, (T) Thinkstock; **755** (CR, Bkgrd, R) Thinkstock, (C, BL) Yasonya/Shutterstock; **758** Yuri Arcurs/Shutterstock; **761** (R) Diane Diederich/iStockphoto, (L) Maram/Shutterstock; **762** Lisa Maree Williams/Getty Images; **764** Picsfive/Shutterstock; **765** Olga Lyubkina/Shutterstock; **766** Tom Robbrecht/Shutterstock; **769** Pixelbliss/Shutterstock; **771** (T) Darryl Leniuk/Getty Images, (B) KariDesign/Shutterstock; **772** Garry Wade/Getty Images; **773** (TL) Getty Images, (B) Getty Images/Staff/Getty Images, (TR) Jordi Cami/AGE Fotostock; **774** Danny Warren/Shutterstock; **775** Danny Warren/Shutterstock; **777** Garry Wade/Getty Images; **780** Aleksandr Stennikov/Shutterstock; **782** Yellow Dog Productions/Shutterstock; **784** Levent Konuk/Shutterstock; **785** Serp/Shutterstock; **787** (B) Geoffrey Lawrence/Shutterstock, (T) Kojat/Shutterstock; **788** Hywit Dimyadi/Shutterstock; **790** Jules Studio/Shutterstock; **792** tubuceo/Shutterstock; **794** (L) Thomas A. Steitz/Yale University; **795** Shutterstock; **796** Mark Stout Photography/Shutterstock; **798** Dorgie Productions/Getty Images; **800** Ken O'Donoghue/Prentice Hall; **802** (R) ©DK Images, (L) Roger Smith/©DK Images; **803** Peter Menzel/Photo Researchers, Inc.; **804** Thinkstock; **805** (B) Alberto Ruggieri/Getty Images, (T) Mark Evans/iStockphoto, (B) Peter Dazeley/Getty Images; **806** Kenmcgrath/Dreamstime LLC; **808** John Shaw/Photo Researchers, Inc.; **810** U.S. Department of Agriculture; **816** U.S. Navy/AGE Fotostock; **817** (Inset) RIA Novosti/Topham/The Image Works, Inc.; **818** d michel/iStockphoto; **822** Blair Seitz/Photo Researchers, Inc.; **829** Thomas Pflaum/The Image Works, Inc.; **830** SOHO Extreme Ultraviolet Imaging Telescope/NASA; **831** Joe Sohm/Photo Researchers, Inc.; **832** Richard Dickin/Tri-City Herald/MCT/Newscom; **834** (T) S. Wanke/PhotoLink/Getty Images; **835** SuperStock; **837** Oullette/Theroux/Publiphoto/Photo Researchers, Inc.; **842** RIA Novosti/Topham/The Image Works, Inc.

Periodic Table of the Elements

Representative Elements: Alkali metals; Alkaline earth metals; Other metals; Metalloids; Nonmetals; Noble gases

Transition Elements: Transition metals; Inner transition metals

C Solid; Br Liquid; He Gas; Tc Not found in nature

Key: 13 — Atomic number; 2 8 3 — Electrons in each energy level; Al — Element symbol; Aluminum — Element name; 26.982 — Atomic mass†

†The atomic masses in parentheses are the mass numbers of the longest-lived isotope of elements for which a standard atomic mass cannot be defined.

Period	1 1A	2 2A	3 3B	4 4B	5 5B	6 6B	7 7B	8 8B	9 8B	10 8B	11 1B	12 2B	13 3A	14 4A	15 5A	16 6A	17 7A	18 8A
1	1 H Hydrogen 1.0079 (1)																	2 He Helium 4.0026 (2)
2	3 Li Lithium 6.941 (2 1)	4 Be Beryllium 9.0122 (2 2)											5 B Boron 10.81 (2 3)	6 C Carbon 12.011 (2 4)	7 N Nitrogen 14.007 (2 5)	8 O Oxygen 15.999 (2 6)	9 F Fluorine 18.998 (2 7)	10 Ne Neon 20.179 (2 8)
3	11 Na Sodium 22.990 (2 8 1)	12 Mg Magnesium 24.305 (2 8 2)											13 Al Aluminum 26.982 (2 8 3)	14 Si Silicon 28.086 (2 8 4)	15 P Phosphorus 30.974 (2 8 5)	16 S Sulfur 32.06 (2 8 6)	17 Cl Chlorine 35.453 (2 8 7)	18 Ar Argon 39.948 (2 8 8)
4	19 K Potassium 39.098 (2 8 8 1)	20 Ca Calcium 40.08 (2 8 8 2)	21 Sc Scandium 44.956 (2 8 9 2)	22 Ti Titanium 47.90 (2 8 10 2)	23 V Vanadium 50.941 (2 8 11 2)	24 Cr Chromium 51.996 (2 8 13 1)	25 Mn Manganese 54.938 (2 8 13 2)	26 Fe Iron 55.847 (2 8 14 2)	27 Co Cobalt 58.933 (2 8 15 2)	28 Ni Nickel 58.71 (2 8 16 2)	29 Cu Copper 63.546 (2 8 18 1)	30 Zn Zinc 65.38 (2 8 18 2)	31 Ga Gallium 69.72 (2 8 18 3)	32 Ge Germanium 72.59 (2 8 18 4)	33 As Arsenic 74.922 (2 8 18 5)	34 Se Selenium 78.96 (2 8 18 6)	35 Br Bromine 79.904 (2 8 18 7)	36 Kr Krypton 83.80 (2 8 18 8)
5	37 Rb Rubidium 85.468 (2 8 18 8 1)	38 Sr Strontium 87.62 (2 8 18 8 2)	39 Y Yttrium 88.906 (2 8 18 9 2)	40 Zr Zirconium 91.22 (2 8 18 10 2)	41 Nb Niobium 92.906 (2 8 18 12 1)	42 Mo Molybdenum 95.94 (2 8 18 13 1)	43 Tc Technetium (98) (2 8 18 14 1)	44 Ru Ruthenium 101.07 (2 8 18 15 1)	45 Rh Rhodium 102.91 (2 8 18 16 1)	46 Pd Palladium 106.4 (2 8 18 18)	47 Ag Silver 107.87 (2 8 18 18 1)	48 Cd Cadmium 112.41 (2 8 18 18 2)	49 In Indium 114.82 (2 8 18 18 3)	50 Sn Tin 118.69 (2 8 18 18 4)	51 Sb Antimony 121.75 (2 8 18 18 5)	52 Te Tellurium 127.60 (2 8 18 18 6)	53 I Iodine 126.90 (2 8 18 18 7)	54 Xe Xenon 131.30 (2 8 18 18 8)
6	55 Cs Cesium 132.91 (2 8 18 18 8 1)	56 Ba Barium 137.33 (2 8 18 18 8 2)	71 Lu Lutetium 174.97 (2 8 18 32 9 2)	72 Hf Hafnium 178.49 (2 8 18 32 10 2)	73 Ta Tantalum 180.95 (2 8 18 32 11 2)	74 W Tungsten 183.85 (2 8 18 32 12 2)	75 Re Rhenium 186.21 (2 8 18 32 13 2)	76 Os Osmium 190.2 (2 8 18 32 14 2)	77 Ir Iridium 192.22 (2 8 18 32 15 2)	78 Pt Platinum 195.09 (2 8 18 32 17 1)	79 Au Gold 196.97 (2 8 18 32 18 1)	80 Hg Mercury 200.59 (2 8 18 32 18 2)	81 Tl Thallium 204.37 (2 8 18 32 18 3)	82 Pb Lead 207.2 (2 8 18 32 18 4)	83 Bi Bismuth 208.98 (2 8 18 32 18 5)	84 Po Polonium (209) (2 8 18 32 18 6)	85 At Astatine (210) (2 8 18 32 18 7)	86 Rn Radon (222) (2 8 18 32 18 8)
7	87 Fr Francium (223) (2 8 18 32 18 8 1)	88 Ra Radium (226) (2 8 18 32 18 8 2)	103 Lr Lawrencium (262) (2 8 18 32 32 9 2)	104 Rf Rutherfordium (261) (2 8 18 32 32 10 2)	105 Db Dubnium (262) (2 8 18 32 32 11 2)	106 Sg Seaborgium (263) (2 8 18 32 32 12 2)	107 Bh Bohrium (264) (2 8 18 32 32 13 2)	108 Hs Hassium (265) (2 8 18 32 32 14 2)	109 Mt Meitnerium (268) (2 8 18 32 32 15 2)	110 Ds Darmstadtium (269) (2 8 18 32 32 17 1)	111 Rg Roentgenium (272) (2 8 18 32 32 18 1)	112 Cn Copernicium (277) (2 8 18 32 32 18 2)	113 *Uut Ununtrium (284) (2 8 18 32 32 18 3)	114 Fl Flerovium (289) (2 8 18 32 32 18 4)	115 *Uup Ununpentium (288) (2 8 18 32 32 18 5)	116 Lv Livermorium (293) (2 8 18 32 32 18 6)	117 *Uus Ununseptium (294) (2 8 18 32 32 18 7)	118 *Uuo Ununoctium (299) (2 8 18 32 32 18 8)

Elements 104–118 are the transactinide elements.

*Discovery reported but not verified

Lanthanide Series

57	58	59	60	61	62	63	64	65	66	67	68	69	70
La Lanthanum 138.91 (2 8 18 18 9 2)	Ce Cerium 140.12 (2 8 18 20 8 2)	Pr Praseodymium 140.91 (2 8 18 21 8 2)	Nd Neodymium 144.24 (2 8 18 22 8 2)	Pm Promethium (145) (2 8 18 23 8 2)	Sm Samarium 150.4 (2 8 18 24 8 2)	Eu Europium 151.96 (2 8 18 25 8 2)	Gd Gadolinium 157.25 (2 8 18 25 9 2)	Tb Terbium 158.93 (2 8 18 27 8 2)	Dy Dysprosium 162.50 (2 8 18 28 8 2)	Ho Holmium 164.93 (2 8 18 29 8 2)	Er Erbium 167.26 (2 8 18 30 8 2)	Tm Thulium 168.93 (2 8 18 31 8 2)	Yb Ytterbium 173.04 (2 8 18 32 8 2)

Actinide Series

89	90	91	92	93	94	95	96	97	98	99	100	101	102
Ac Actinium (227) (2 8 18 32 18 9 2)	Th Thorium 232.04 (2 8 18 32 18 10 2)	Pa Protactinium 231.04 (2 8 18 32 20 9 2)	U Uranium 238.03 (2 8 18 32 21 9 2)	Np Neptunium (237) (2 8 18 32 22 9 2)	Pu Plutonium (244) (2 8 18 32 24 8 2)	Am Americium (243) (2 8 18 32 25 8 2)	Cm Curium (247) (2 8 18 32 25 9 2)	Bk Berkelium (247) (2 8 18 32 27 8 2)	Cf Californium (251) (2 8 18 32 28 8 2)	Es Einsteinium (252) (2 8 18 32 29 8 2)	Fm Fermium (257) (2 8 18 32 30 8 2)	Md Mendelevium (258) (2 8 18 32 31 8 2)	No Nobelium (259) (2 8 18 32 32 8 2)